ANTIQUES AND COLLECTIBLES:

A Bibliography of Works in English,
16th Century to 1976

by

Linda Campbell Franklin

with

linocuts by the author

The Scarecrow Press, Inc.
Metuchen, N.J. & London
1978

Library of Congress Cataloging in Publication Data

Franklin, Linda Campbell.
    Antiques and collectibles.

    Includes indexes.
    1. Antiques--Bibliography. 2. Collectors and collecting--
Bibliography. I. Title.
Z5956.A68F7   1978   [NK1125]   016.7451   77-25026
ISBN 0-8108-1092-1

To

Mummy,

Daddy

and

Robbie

TABLE OF CONTENTS

PREFACE

This book was planned, accumulated, sorted, added to, and indexed in order to provide the researcher, the serious collector and the librarian with a comprehensive listing of English language books and exhibition catalogues dealing with objects now considered "antiques or "collectibles." It is understood, of course, that quite a number of the titles will be generally unavailable to any but the most dedicated searcher. Collectors and libraries alike will have to depend on interlibrary loans, bookshop luck, or visits to the libraries whose catalogues have been used in this compilation. I would like very much to hand you a book which you could use in several ways--not the least important of which would be serendipitous use. One of the great pleasures of browsing in library catalogues and open shelves of libraries and bookshops is the happenstance of finding yourself face to spine with a book which you did not suspect existed! And so, if you wish to open this book and browse in it, you will find many such surprises.

This is more than a bibliography of antiques. It is a record of what people thought about the practical and decorative arts while they were being made, after they were a few bare decades old, and finally, after they could be looked back on as venerable antiques from an historical point of view. When I began compiling, I made an early decision to cover a broad range of subjects. I began with the question, "Out of what can man make things?" and came up with copper, iron, brass, tin, wood, clay, fibers, paper, steel, wire, gold, silver, glass, paint, leather, plaster, stone and plastic. What does he do to these materials? They are wrought, refined, cast, molded, carved, tooled, woven, blown, fired, cut, pressed, hammered, brushed, drawn, beaten, baked, sewn, fitted, pegged, pulled, painted, etched, spun and turned--all by hand or by machine.

For the purposes of this bibliography, I am going to assume that no longer can what is called fine art be kept free of honorable associations with applied arts, decorative arts, industrial arts, and even science. For that reason, I have included many books which might have been considered inappropriate by another bibliographer, or in another time. According to the Oxford English Dictionary, the fine arts "are concerned with the beautiful," or they "appeal to the faculty of taste." The histories and practical treatises in this bibliography are all concerned with the arts of design, and many deal with objects which will appeal to the faculty of taste.

People have asked me how I went about collecting titles. The amazing truth is that the bibliography grew geometrically, and that all I needed were the first two or three hundred titles (collected the first week) in order to find the more than 10,000 titles included here. The chief sources are listed following this preface. Each book found led to an author, a subject, a library or book-sale catalogue, a publisher's list or an advertisement, and each of these led to books. Study of the bibliographies included in many books helped me to discover scores of titles not already included. The hardest thing in the world was to stop looking for titles. After a year, there came a point of exceedingly diminished returns for hours spent. At that point, though my appetite was still sharp, I decided it was time to finish up. The index cards for each author and title were checked in the National Union Catalog of the Library of Congress, the General Catalogue of Printed Books of the British Museum, the card catalog on the third floor of the New York Public Library at 42nd Street, and then I went home to start typing.

SCOPE

Time. The publishing period encompassed in this book is from the late 16th century to 1976. Two of the earliest books are on the instruments of war, and the implements of fishing, both from 1590.

Form. This bibliography includes books, pamphlets, exhibition catalogues, and a very few English trade catalogues. It also
includes reprinted catalogues, off-prints, masters' theses, doctoral
dissertations, and periodicals.

Language. Only works in the English language are included.
These were published in the United States, Canada, the British Isles,
India, Australia, New Zealand, and, in a relatively few cases, in
Japan, Hungary, Russia, Sweden, Norway and other non-English-
speaking countries. In many subject areas, a misleading paucity of
titles exists only because of my imposed language restriction. Natu-
rally there will be many more works on German porcelains in German than in English, or on Japanese textiles in Japanese than in
English.

Comprehensiveness. This bibliography includes the holdings
of the Library of Congress in Washington, the New York Public Library, the Winterthur Library in Delaware, many municipal and private libraries across the country, the British Museum in London,
and many works not necessarily included in any of those holdings.

ENTRIES

This bibliography is arranged by subject matter, and alphabetically by author within each subject area. Where there is no author, the title is used. I have used full author names, or pseudo-
nyms. Different authors with the same name are distinguished by
their dates and/or by professional or academic designators.

Although I have used many sources for my information, I
have made each entry conform to a uniform style. Where there is
more than one work by an author, these works are listed alphabetically by title, except in two or three cases where I felt a chronological listing would be more useful (e.g., The First Book of...;
The Second Book of...; etc.). Where there are several works by
an author, including one or more with joint authorship, I have first
listed those works by the author alone, and then alphabetically by
joint author. I have sparingly used two types of cross references:
see and see also.

In most entries, all editions (including facsimile reprints)
are entered together. In some cases, where the number of editions
exceeded a reasonable number, or where the in-print life of the
book extended over a period of fifty years or more, I have left out
some of the middle editions. These omissions are noted with ellip-
sis dots. In order to make this bibliography more valuable for re-
searchers and librarians on both sides of the ocean, I have included
American and British editions of individual titles.

Each entry gives fairly detailed bibliographical information,
but does not include descriptions of the book's size (quarto, folio,
etc.), its binding, or other points which might be desired by the
book collector. I have compiled this book, not as a scholarly bibliography, but as a research tool for people who want the information contained within the books themselves. Although I became interested in book collecting halfway through (yes, so suddenly) the
compilation, it is a minor chagrin to me that I am unable to offer
here a perfect bibliographer's delight. I have included the number
of pages, the number of illustrations and color plates, and have
listed some important features such as "bibliography" or "glossary."

Finally, for many of the books before 1925 I have included
a location guide. I used the symbol system used in the Union Catalog, with the addition of a few such as BM for British Museum. In
many cases the National Union Catalog gave as many as 20 or 30
location symbols; but I selected two or three from those which would
be geographically widespread. A list of the symbols will follow this
preface.

ILLUSTRATIONS

The illustrations interspersed throughout this work are lino-
leum cuts, based for the most part on typical or imaginery scenes.
A few are based on engravings appearing in such works as Knight's
Mechanical Dictionary. The illustration for the section entitled
"Shoes" is drawn from a hooked rug design and made by my mother,
Mary Mac Franklin. It is reproduced here by permission from her and
from Saturday Review where it was published January 22, 1977, p. 38.

ACKNOWLEDGEMENTS

I am grateful for the pleasure and privilege of using the reference facilities of the grand New York Public Library and the Avery Library of Columbia University, and for the gracious comfort of the Alderman Library of the University of Virginia in Charlottesville. I also appreciate the help given me--through the mail--by the Grand Rapids Public Library; the British Library, Department of Printed Books; Dawson's of Pall Mall in London; and the Ceramic Book Company in Newport, Monmouth, England. Finally, I would not have finished without the patience shown me by my dear friends, and my wonderful librarian parents, who turned over many previously-tidy table and desk tops to me so that I could spread out literally thousands and thousands of p-slips and manuscript pages.

Linda Campbell Franklin
New York City
March 1978

LIBRARY LOCATION ABBREVIATIONS

Chiefly as they appear in the <u>National Union Catalog,</u>
Library of Congress

BM	British Museum, London
CaT	University of Toronto, Canada
CSmH	Henry Huntington Library, San Marino, California
CtY	Yale University, New Haven, Connecticut
CU	University of California, Berkeley
DAS	United States Department of Environmental Sciences, Atmospheric Science Library, Silver Springs, Maryland
DeGE	Eleutherian Mills Historical Library, Greenville, Delaware
DeWint	Winterthur Museum Library, Delaware
DFo	Folger Shakespeare Library, Washington, D.C.
DLC	Library of Congress, Washington, D.C.
DP	Patent Library, Washington, D.C.
ICJ	John Crerar Library, Chicago
ICN	Newbury Library, Chicago
ICRL	Center for Research Libraries, Chicago
InU	University of Indiana, Bloomington
IU	University of Illinois, Urbana
MB	Boston Public Library, Massachusetts
MdBE	Enoch Pratt Free Library, Baltimore, Maryland
MdPP	Peabody Institute, Baltimore, Maryland
MH	Harvard University, Cambridge, Massachusetts
MH-FA	Harvard, Fine Arts Library
MH-BA	Harvard, Graduate School of Business Library
MiD	Detroit Public Library
MiDA	Detroit Institute of Art
MiGr	Grand Rapids Public Library, Michigan
MiU	University of Michigan, Ann Arbor
MiU-C	University of Michigan, William L. Clements Library
MSaE	Essex Institute, Salem, Massachusetts
NB	Brooklyn Public Library, New York
NCorniC	Corning Museum of Glass Library, New York
NcRS	North Carolina State University, Raleigh
NjP	Princeton University Library, New Jersey
NN	New York Public Library, New York
NNAve	Avery Library, Columbia University, New York
NNC	Columbia University, New York
OC	Cincinnati Public Library, Ohio

OCl	Cleveland Public Library, Ohio
OClMA	Cleveland Museum of Art, Ohio
PBL	Lehigh University, Bethlehem, Pennsylvania
PPF	Franklin Institute, Philadelphia, Pennsylvania
PPL	Library Company of Philadelphia, Pennsylvania
PPLT	Lutheran Theological Seminary Library, Philadelphia, Pennsylvania
PPPM	Philadelphia Museum of Art, Pennsylvania
PPULC	Union Library Catalog of Pennsylvania, Philadelphia
PPWa	Wagner Free Institute of Science, Philadelphia
RPB	Brown University, Providence, Rhode Island
RPD	Rhode Island School of Design, Providence
SKM	South Kensington Museum (later Victoria and Albert Museum), London
TU	University of Tennessee, Knoxville
TxU	University of Texas, Austin
V & A	Victoria and Albert Museum, London
ViU	University of Virginia, Charlottesville
WaS	Seattle Public Library

OTHER ABBREVIATIONS

ECB	English Catalogue of Books
GPO	Government Printing Office, United States
HMSO	Her (or His) Majesty's Stationery Office, Britain
LoMag	London Magazine, 1732-1766
n. d.	no date
n. p.	no place of publication
n. t. p.	no title page
O. E. D.	Oxford English Dictionary
RNB	Register of National Bibliography, London, 1905
SIB-1, 2, 3	
SIB-3	Subject Index of Books Published up to 1880, London
SPCK	Society for the Promotion of Christian Knowledge, London
u. p.	unpaginated
U. Pr.	University Press (used with name, as in Oxford U. Pr.)
USGPO	see: GPO
v. p.	various paging

GLOSSARY

ANCIENT. Belonging to time past. According to the O. E. D. it is "specifically applied to the period before the fall of the Western Roman Empire."

ANTIQUE. Although you will find in the O. E. D. that this word was used by Goldsmith in the Vicar of Wakefield, 1766, in the line "his own business ... was to collect pictures, medals, intaglios and antiques of all kinds," this was not meant to be understood to mean what it means now. According to the magazine Antiques the modern use of "antique" dates to a book by William Sharp Ogden, Sketches of Antique Furniture (no. 2573), 1888. It is probable that scattered, earlier uses could be found. Many dealers and collectors use the United States Customs Regulation, adopted by Congress in 1930, for their definition. This, however, can be understood two ways.
    71 Congress. Session II. Ch. 497. 1930.
    Title II--Free List.
    Para. 1809. Works of Art, Collections in Illustration of the Progress of the Arts, Sciences, Agriculture, or Manufactures, Photographs, Works in Terra Cotta, Parian, Pottery, or Porcelain, Antiquities and Artistic Copies thereof in metal or other material, Imported in good faith for Exhibition at a fixed place....
    Para. 1811. Works of art (except rugs and carpets made after the year 1700), collections in illustration of the progress of the arts, works in bronze, marble, terra cotta, parian, pottery, or porcelain, artistic antiquities, and objects of art of ornamental character or educational value which shall have been produced prior to the year 1830, but the free importation of such objects shall be subject to such regulations as to proof of antiquity as the Secretary of the Treasury may prescribe. Violins, violas, violin cellos, and double basses, of all sizes, made in the year 1800 or prior year.
    United States Statutes at Large. 71st Congress 1929-1931.
    Volume 46, Part 1, Public Laws. Washington: USGPO, 1931. (Pp. 672-685)
This has been interpreted as meaning 1) only those objects made before 1830 are really antiques; or 2) anything which is a hundred years old is an antique.

ANTIQUITY. The period before the Middle Ages, more specifically the time of ancient Greece and Rome.

APPLIED ART. Art put to practical use. "Practical as distinguished from abstract or theoretical." O.E.D.

ART. The first meaning given in the O.E.D. is "I. Skill; its
display or application. 1. Skill in doing anything as the result
of knowledge or practice. 2. Human skill as an agent, human
workmanship. Opposed to nature." According to Longfellow,
art is a "revelation of man." More specifically, art can be
decorative or useful, but it is always the product of ability.

ART MANUFACTURES. A term invented by Henry Cole (1808-1882)
which means "fine arts or beauty applied to mechanical production."

ARTIFICER. A person who makes something with art or skill--
especially in the industrial arts. Artifice is either the skill he
uses, or the work he produces.

ARTISAN. A person employed in the industrial arts.

ARTIST. "One skilled in the 'liberal' or learned arts." O.E.D.

ARTS AND CRAFTS. This described a movement, spurred by exhibitions, which began in England about 1888, in Paris about
1896, and a year later in Boston. William Morris spearheaded
the movement in England, and was especially famous for his
printing and his wallpaper designs. The Boston Society of Arts
and Crafts included in its statement of purpose "to make the
artist more of a craftsman, the craftsman more of an artist;
... (to) uphold art handicraft of all kinds." It was partly based
on an erroneous idea that handwork is intrinsically more valuable than machine work.

CRAFT. For hundreds of years "art" and "craft" were used inter-
changeably to mean a skill. Then it came to be associated with
skills of the hands, and was supposed to occupy a lower place
than did art, which was to be "directed towards the gratifica-
tion of taste or production of what is beautiful." O.E.D.

DECORATIVE. "Having the function of decorating [adorning, embel-
lishing, beautifying, etc.]; tending to, pertaining to, or of the
nature of decoration." O.E.D. H. W. Kent wrote, in Charles
Russell Richards' Art in Industry (N.Y.: 1922), "the museum
of today groups its objects of art in two classes, those called
'fine,' and those called 'decorative.' Thus it follows a division
which came into use in France in the 18th century, when painting, sculpture, and architecture, as being concerned with the
mind and, particularly, the imagination, were elevated in a
phrase to a higher plane than those works of men's hands in
which usefulness was a primary concern.... The terms 'mechanical,' 'industrial,' and 'useful' have been used ... to distinguish
the lesser arts from the 'fine,' with the consequent belittlement
which has attached itself to them, much of it merited, though

none of it necessary. ... The museum of today, by its adoption
of the word 'decorative' to describe these arts instead of 'mechanical,' 'industrial,' or 'useful,' has recognized the element
in them which before has been overlooked, or, at least, unhinted
at in these words, namely, the art of design, which enters into
them, and which ... is often as truly fine as much painting and
sculpture, and represents just as surely, just as vividly ...,
the minds and the hearts of great nations ancient and modern,
and of great periods, like the Middle Ages and the Renaissance."
pp. 435-436.

DESIGN. "A plan or scheme conceived in the mind and intended for
subsequent execution; ... To fashion with artistic skill or decorative device; to furnish or adorn with a design." O.E.D.

FINE ARTS. Those areas which are "concerned with 'the beautiful,'
or which appeal to the faculty of taste. An art ... requiring
refined and subtle skill." So says the O.E.D. Although much
of what is considered fine art and industrial art has deteriorated
so as to repel the faculty of taste, there is less of a snobbish
distinction between the fine arts and the so-called useful arts.

HANDICRAFT. The word "handcraft" dates back to the 10th century.
This is a later form, and handicraft refers to skilled work of
the hands.

HANDMADE. Made by hand, and distinguished from that which is
made by machinery. It used to be considered artificial and
therefore opposite to what is a work of nature.

INDUSTRIAL ARTS. Since industry is defined in the O.E.D. as
"habitual employment in some useful work, now especially in
the productive arts or manufacture" so industrial arts are the
skills or products of such habitual employment.

LIBERAL ARTS. Used in the Middle Ages to refer to a course of
seven sciences introduced in the 6th century--the trivium and
the quadrivium--or Grammar, Logic, and Rhetoric; and Arith-
metic, Geometry, Music and Astronomy. These were pursuits
worthy of a free man.

MACHINE. "An apparatus for applying mechanical power, consisting
of a number of interrelated parts, each having a definite function." O.E.D. It does not necessarily require any strength or
motive power on the part of its user.

PHILOSOPHICAL. "Pertaining to, or used in the study of, natural
philosophy, or some branch of physical science." O.E.D. Found
in this bibliography with "instrument" as "philosophical instrument"--microscope, etc.

PRACTICAL. Used, as opposed to being theoretical or abstract.

TREATISE.   "A book or writing which treats of some particular sub-
     ject; commonly one containing a formal or methodical discussion
     or exposition of the principles of the subject." O.E.D.   It is
     often used with "practical" in the titles of books in this bibli-
     ography.   The works in this bibliography are basically either
     practical treatises, or histories.

BIBLIOGRAPHIES†

GENERAL

1 *Besterman, Theodore. A World Bibliography of Bibliographies
Catalogues, Calendars, Abstracts, Digests, Indexes, and the
Like. London: Author, U. Pr, Oxford, 1939- ; 2nd ed. 3
vol. 1947-49; rev. enl. ed. 3 vol. 1950; 3rd ed. rev. & enl.
4 vol. in 2. New York: Scarecrow Pr, 1956.

2 Evans, Charles. American Bibliography. A chronological dictionary of books, pamphlets and periodical publications printed
in the United States of America from 1639 to 1820. 14 vol.
Chicago: Blakely Pr., for Author, 1903-1959; reprint. New
York: P. Smith, 1941-59.

3 Library Bibliographies and Indexes. A subject guide to resource material available from libraries, information centers,
library schools and library associations in the United States
and Canada. Paul Wasserman and Esther Herman, editors.
Detroit: Gale, 1975. 301pp

4 Porter, G. W. Handlist of Bibliographies, Classified Catalogues
in Reading Room at British Museum. 1881; 2nd rev. ed. by
G. K. Fortescue. 1889.

---

†Obviously there should be at least several score bibliographies of
works on antiques, decorative arts, etc. There are. They have
been listed with their subject listings. Check the index under Bibliographies for a full listing.
*The asterisk has been employed to indicate the most complete or
worthwhile books throughout this work.

INDUSTRY

GENERAL WORKS ON MECHANICAL AND INDUSTRIAL ARTS

5   Abbott, R. D. Folk Museum, Gloucester; a guide to the collections. Gloucester, Eng: 1963. 23pp, ill (An industrial museum)

6   Adler, Irving. Tools in Your Life. New York: Day, 1956; London: Dobson, 1957. 144pp, ill

7   Aikin, Arthur, 1773-1854. Arts and Manufactures Illustrated; with historical and literary details, in lectures at the Society of Arts, Manufactures, and Commerce, also address, illustrations, appendix. London: the Society, 1831-1845. ill DLC, NN

8   _____. Illustrations of Arts and Manufactures. Being a selection from a series of papers, read before Society for Encouragement of Arts, Manufactures and Commerce. London: John Van Voorst, 1841. 376pp, ill BM, DLC

9   Allen, Henry B. The Useful Companion and Artificer's Assistant. A Complete Encyclopedia of Valuable Information. New York: Author, 1879. 701pp, ill

10 American Cabinet and Boston Athenaeum. A family journal of useful and entertaining literature, art, science, education, mechanical inventions, manufactures, agriculture, news. Boston: 184-?-1851. ill

11 American Machinist/Metalworking Manufacturing. New York: 1877-date.

12 Amman, Jost, and Hans Sachs. The Book of Trades (Standebuch). Frankfurt: 1568; reprint with introd. by Benjamin A. Fifkin. English paraphrases of verses. New York: Dover, 1973. 127pp, ill, index

13 Anderson, Sir John, 1814-1886. Tools. The address delivered at the opening of the exhibition of Appliances for the Economy

of Labour. Society for the Promotion of Scientific Industry.
May 14, 1875. Manchester, Eng: J. Heywood, 1875? 32pp
DLC

14 *Appleton's Cyclopedia of Applied Mechanics; a dictionary of
mechanical engineering and the mechanical arts. Ed. by
Park Benjamin. 2 vol. New York: D. Appleton, 1880;
1881; 1882; 1883; 1884 1 vol. 1885; 1 vol. with nearly 5000
engravings. 1886; 2 vol. 1886; with Vol. III. Modern Mechanism, exhibiting the latest progress in machines, motors, and
the transmission of power. 1886-1892; 1893; 2 vol. rev. ed.
1895; 3 vol. New York: N. W. Henley, 1904. ill, pls
(1885- 959pp, ill, pls)

15 *Appleton's Dictionary of Machines, Mechanics, Engine-work,
and Engineering with Appendix. Ed. by Oliver Byrne. 2 vol.
New York: Appleton, 1850-1851; 1852; 1855; 1857; 1861;
1867-73; new ed. 1869; 1873; new ed. 1884; etc. (Many other editions not listed.) 4000 wood-engravings

16 The Architect and the Industrial Arts; an exhibition of contemporary American design, February-March 1929. New York:
Metropolitan Museum, 1929. 83pp, ill, pls

17 The Architectural Magazine, and journal of improvement in
architecture, building, and furnishing, and in the various
arts and trades connected therewith. Periodical. 5 vol.
London: Longman, Rees, 1834-1838. ill

18 Architectural Record. Quarterly. New York: F. W. Dodge,
1891-1902; monthly. 1902-

19 Archives of Useful Knowledge, a work devoted to commerce,
manufactures, rural and domestic economy, agriculture, and
the useful arts. Quarterly. 3 vol. Philadelphia: D. Ho-
gan, 1810-1813. ill DeWint

20 Arnold, Roy, and Philip Walker. Illustrated Trade List of
Prices of Sheffield Goods, 1889 edition. Facsimile reprint.
London: Arnold & Walker, 1974. 31pp, ill

21 Art and the Industrial Revolution. Exhibition. May-July 1968.
Manchester, Eng: City Art Gallery, 1968. 100pp, pls

22 Art in Trades Club Yearbook. New York: 1926. DLC

23 The Art Worker. A journal of design devoted to art-industry.
Periodical. New York: J. O'Kane, 1878. (No more published) 94 pls

24 The Art Workers' Quarterly; a portfolio of practical designs for
decoration and applied art. London: Chapman & Hall, 1902-
06. pls

25 The Art Workman, a monthly journal for the artist, artificer,
     etc.   London: 1873-1877?; London: A. Fischer, 1883;
     London: The Art Decorator Office, 1890-91?

26 The Artist and Amateur's Magazine; a work devoted to the in-
     terests of the arts of design and the cultivation of taste.
     Monthly. London: Longman, Brown, 1843-1844.

27 Art's Masterpiece; or, A companion for the ingenious of either
     sex. In two parts. I. The art of limning and painting in
     oil.... II. The Art of Making Glass of Chrystal....   By
     C. K. 5th ed. London: G. Conyers, 1710? 124pp
     DeWint

28 *Asher and Adams' Pictorial Album of American Industry (1876),
     with illustrations and descriptions of mercantile and manu-
     facturing establishments, works of art, mechanism, trade-
     marks, etc. New York: Asher & Adams, 1874; 1876; re-
     print. New York: Rutledge Books, 1976. 192pp, hundreds
     of ill

29 Ashton, T(homas) S(outhcliff). Tools. n.p., 1939.

30 Audel, Theo, and Co. Guides and Libraries covering many sub-
     jects: i.e. carpentry, electricity, machinery, plumbing,
     engineering, sheet metal work, etc. New York, etc.: T.
     Audel, 190-?-present.

31 Audsley, William James, and G. A. Audsley. Popular Dic-
     tionary of Architecture and the Allied Arts. 3 vol. Liver-
     pool: 1878; 2nd ed. rev. London: H. Sotheran, 1879; 3
     vol. London: 1880-82; 3rd ed. New York: Putnam's,
     1881-82; no more published. ill (Vol. I. A-Aqueduct; II.
     Aquila to Babtisterium; III. Bar to Buttery)

32 Baker, Thomas, civil engineer. Elements of Mechanism:
     elucidating the scientific principles of the practical construc-
     tion of machines. London: John Weale, 1852; 2nd ed. cor-
     rected & enl. with Remarks on Tools and Machines by James
     Nasmyth. London: James Weale, 1858-59; 3rd ed. as Ele-
     ments of Practical Mechanism and Machine Tools ... with
     remarks.... London: Virtue, 1867. 225pp, ill; 243pp, ill;
     240pp, ill

33 Barber, Edwin Atlee. General Guide to the Collections of the
     Pennsylvania Museum and School of Industrial Art. Phila-
     delphia: the Museum, 1907.

34 Barlow, Peter, 1776-1862. Manufactures and Machinery in
     Britain. London: Encyclopedia Metropolitan, 1836.

35 Barnard, Charles. Tools and Machines. New York; Boston:
     Silver, Burdett, 1903.

36 Barrow, John, fl. 1735. Dictionarium Polygraphicum: or, the
    whole body of arts regularly digested containing the arts of
    drawing, painting, washing, japanning, carving, cutting in
    stone, historical account of painters, productions, refining,
    transmutation ... of all metals and minerals, art of making
    all sorts of glass and marble ... buying of all sorts of ma-
    terial, linen, woollen, silk, art of tapestry weaving, des-
    cription of colours. 2 vol. London: C. Hitch & C. Davis,
    1735; 2nd corrected ed. 1758. 56 pls DLC, NN, DeWint

37 _____, comp. A New and Universal Dictionary of Arts and
    Sciences, with an introductory preface, tracing the progress
    of literature. The whole being a complete body of arts and
    sciences, as they are at present cultivated. Extracted from
    the best authors. London: printed for the proprietors, and
    sold by J. Hinton, 1751; supplement. 1754. 1039pp, ill,
    62 pls (part color); 708pp, 44 (11 color) pls V & A, CU

38 Battison, Edwin A. Screw-thread Cutting by the Master-Screw
    Method Since 1480. Washington, D.C.: Smithsonian, 1964.
    119pp, ill

39 Bealer, Alex. The Tools That Built America. New York:
    Barre Books, C. N. Potter, 1976. 200 ill

40 Beitz, Lester V. Treasury of Frontier Relics; a collector's
    guide. New York: Edwin House, dist. by Crown, 1966.
    246pp, ill

41a Belknap, Henry Wyckoff. Trades and Tradesmen of Essex
    County, Massachusetts, Chiefly of the 17th Century. Salem,
    Mass: Essex Institute, 1929. 96pp, pls DeWint

41b Bemiss, Elijah. The Dyers' Companion in Two Parts: part
    first containing upward of 100 receipts for colouring woolen,
    cotton or silk cloths ... second part containing directions
    for ... varnishing leather; to make oilcloth, lacker brass,
    and tin-ware. New London, Conn: Cady & Eels, printers,
    1806; 2nd ed. New York: Evert Duyckinck, 1815. 75pp;
    307pp DeWint

42 Besterman, Theodore. Technology, Including Patents. A bib-
    liography of bibliographies. 2 vol. n.p., 1939; 1947; 1965;
    Totowa, NJ: Rowman & Littlefield, 1971. 681pp

43 *Bevan, George Phillips, ed. British Manufacturing Industries.
    15 vol. London: Edward Stanford, 1876, 1877, 1878. BM,
    PPULC, DLC, ViU
        I. Iron and Steel, by W. Mattieu Williams. Copper
    Smelting, by J. Arthur Phillips. Brass Founding, Tin Plate
    and Zinc Working, by Walter Graham. 1876. 181pp, ill, pls
        II. Metallic Mining and Collieries, by Warrington W.
    Smyth. Coal, by A. Galletly. Building Stones, by Professor

Hull.   Explosive Compounds, by W. Mattieu Williams.   1876.
211pp, ill, pls
    III.   Guns, nails, locks, wood screws, railway bolts and
spikes, buttons, pins, needles, saddlery, and electroplate, by
W. C. Aitken.   Pens and Papier Mache, by G. Lindsey.
1876.   180pp, ill, pls
    IV.   Acids, alkalies, soda, ammonia, and soap, by
Professor Church.   Oils and Candles, by W. M. Williams.
Gas and Lighting, by R. H. Patterson.   1876.   197pp, ill,
pls
    V.   Wool and Its Applications, by Professor Archer.
Flax and Linen, by W. T. Charley.   Cotton, by I. Watts.
Silk, by B. F. Cobb.   182pp, ill, pls
    VI.   Hosiery and Lace, by W. Felkin.   Carpets, by
Christopher Dresser.   Dyeing and Bleaching, by T. Sims.
1876.   189pp, ill, pls
    VII.   Pottery, by L. Arnoux.   Glass and Silicates, by
Professor Barff.   Furniture and Woodwork, by J. H. Pollen.
1876.   172pp, ill, pls
    VIII.   Paper, by Professor Archer.   Printing and Book-
binding, by J. Hatton.   Engraving, by S. Davenport.   Pho-
tography, by P. L. Foster.   Toys, by G. C. T. Bartley.
1877.   222pp, ill, pls
    IX.   Tobacco, by J. Dunning.   Hides and Leather, by
J. Collins.   Guttapercha and Indiarubber, by J. Collins.
Fibres and Cordage, by P. L. Simmons.   1876.   185pp,
ill, pls
    X.   Ship-building, by Bedford Pim; Telegraphs, by R.
Sabine.   Agricultural Machinery, by Professor Wrightson.
Railways and Tramways, by D. Kinnear Clark.   1876.   218pp,
ill, pls
    XI.   Jewellery, by George Wallis.   Gold Working, by
Reverend Charles Boutell.   Watches and Clocks, by F. J.
Britten.   Musical Instruments, by E. F. Rimbault.   Cutlery,
by F. Callis.   1876.   187pp, ill, pls
    XII.   Salt, preservation of food, bread and biscuits,
by J. J. Manley.   Sugar Refining, by C. H. Hill.   Butter
and Cheese, by M. Evans.   Brewing, distilling, by T. A.
Pooley.   1876.   222pp, ill, pls
    XIII, XIV.   The Industrial Classes and Industrial
Statistics, by G. Phillips Bevan.   2 vol.   1876, 1877.   ill,
maps
    XV.   Horticulture, by F. W. Burbidge.   ill, pls

44   .   A Handbook to the Industries of the British Isles
    and the United States.   London: David Bogue, 1882.   220pp

45   Bezold, Wilhelm von, 1837-1907.   The Theory of Color in Its
    Relation to Art and Art-Industry.   Tr. from German by S.
    R. Koehler.   Introd. by Edward C. Pickering.   Rev. & Enl.
    ed.   Boston: L. Prang, 1876.   274pp, ill, 13 color pls

46   Bigelow, David.   History of Prominent Mercantile and

Manufacturing Firms in the United States, with a collection
of truthful illustrations, representing mercantile buildings,
manufacturing establishments, and articles manufactured.
? vol. Boston: 1857- . text, pls DeWint (Vol. 6)

47 Bigelow, Jacob. Elements of Technology, taken chiefly from a
course of lectures delivered at Cambridge, on the application of the sciences to the useful arts. 2nd ed. Boston:
Hilliard, Gray, Little & Wilkins, 1831; 2 vol. Boston:
Marsh, Capen, 1840. 521pp, 22 pls DeWint

48 _____. The Useful Arts, considered in connection with the
application of science. 2 vol. Boston: Thomas H. Webb,
1840. ill DeWint

49 *Bishop, John Leander, 1820-1868. A History of American
Manufactures from 1608 to 1860 ... Comprising annals of the
industry of the United States in machinery, manufactures and
useful arts, with a notice of important inventions, tariffs,
and the result of each decennial census ... with an appendix,
containing statistics of the principal manufacturing centres,
and descriptions of remarkable manufactories at the present
time. Vol. I. Philadelphia: 1861; 3 vol. Philadelphia:
Edward Young; London: S. Low, 1866. ill DeWint

50 Blandford, Percy William. Country Craft Tools. Newton Abbot:
David & Charles, 1974. 240pp, ill, bib

51 Boehret, Paul C. The Ax and Its Variations, Military and
Civil. Easton, Pa: Hobson Printing, 1966. 79pp, ill

52 Boggs, Winthrop Smillie. Early American Perforation Machines
and Perforations, 1857-1867. New York: Collectors Club,
1954. ill (Postage stamp perforators)

53 Bolton, Henry Carrington. A Catalog of Scientific and Technical
Periodicals. Washington, D.C.: Smithsonian, 1885; 2nd ed.
1897. 1247pp (All countries)

54 The Book of English Trades, and Library of Useful Arts. new
ed. London: G. Sidney for R. Phillips, 1818; new ed.
London: F. C. & J. Rivington, 1821; new enl. 11th ed.
London: R. Phillips, 1823; 12th ed. London: G. B. Wit-
taker, 1825; new ed. London: Rivington, 1835. 442pp, 73
pls; 374pp, ill, pls; 454pp, ill, pls DLC, PPULC, CtY

55 The Book of Trades: or, circle of the useful arts. Glasgow:
R. Griffin, 1835; 3rd ed. 1836; 8th ed. 1846; 13th ed.
London: Bohn, 1861. 356pp, ill, 14 pls NN, MH

56 The Book of Trades; or, library of the useful arts. 3 vol.
New ed. London: B. & R. Crosby, 1805. color pls
DeWint

57   The Book of Trades. Showing the mechanical movements in
      each trade. London: Darton, 1859. 16pp, ill

58   Bowden, Witt. Industrial Society in England Towards the End
      of the 18th Century. New York: Macmillan, 1925; New
      York: Barnes & Noble, 1965. 343pp, bib

59   The Boys' Book of Trades and the Tools Used in Them, com-
      prising brickmaker, mason, bricklayer, plasterer, etc. Lon-
      don; New York: Routledge, 1873? 316pp, ill

60   Bradley, Ian. A History of Machine Tools. Hemel Hempstead,
      Eng: Model & Allied Publications, 1972. 224pp, ill, bib

61   British Industries Fair, 1915--. Catalogues. London: Birming-
      ham, 1915- . NN, DLC

62   Brooks, Henry Mason, 1822-1898, comp. The Olden Time
      Series: gleanings chiefly from old newspapers of Boston and
      Salem, Massachusetts. 6 vol. Boston: Ticknor, 1886. ill
      DeWint

63   Brown, Robert, ed. Science for All. 5 vol. London; New
      York: Cassell, 1877-82; 1890?-1895?; 1897. ill, pls (part
      color) (Juvenile literature)

64   Brush and Pencil; an illustrated magazine of the arts of today.
      Monthly. Chicago: Phillips, 1898-1907. ill

65   Buchanan, Robertson. Practical Essays on Millwork and Other
      Machinery, Mechanical and Descriptive. Edinburgh: J.
      Taylor, 1814; 3rd ed. rev. with additions by George Rennie.
      London: John Weale, 1841. 171pp, 15 pls; 479pp, pls
      (See also George B. Rennie)

66   Buchanan, W. W. A Technological Dictionary: explaining the
      terms of the arts, sciences, literature, professions, and
      trades. London: for T. Tegg, 1846; 1856; 4th ed. 1861;
      as The Dictionary of Scientific Terms. 1868; 5th ed. 1869;
      ed. by James A. Smith. London: G. Bell, 1884. 755pp,
      ill; 1884: 819pp, ill MH, NN, PP

66a   Burges, William, 1827-1881. Art Applied to Industry: lectures.
      Oxford; London: John Henry & James Parker, 1865. 120pp,
      ill

67   Burn, Robert Scott. The Colonists' and Emigrants' Hand Book
      of the Mechanical Arts. Edinburgh; London: W. Blackwood,
      1854. 130pp

68   _____. The Steam Engine, Its History and Mechanism; being
      descriptions and illustrations of the stationary, locomotive
      and marine engine, for the use of schools and students.

London: 1854; 2nd corrected ed. London: Ward, Lock, 1857; 1868; 6th ed. 1876; 7th ed. New York: Ward, Lock, 1893;... 189pp, ill; 142pp, ill;... NN, MiD

69 [No entry.]

70 Burris-Meyer, Elizabeth. Historical Color Guide, Primitive to Modern Times. New York: W. Helburn, 1938. 4pp, 30 color pls

71 Butterworth, Benjamin, comp. The Growth of Industrial Art. 2 vol. Washington, D.C.: GPO, 1884; 1 vol. 1888; 1892; reprint with new introd. by Mark Kramer. New York: Knopf, 1972. each vol. 3pp plus 100 pls of primitive methods and modern patents

72 Byrne, Oliver. The Handbook for the Artisan, Mechanic, and Engineer. Philadelphia: J. K. Collins, Jr., 1853. 183pp, ill, folding pls (Grinding and sharpening cutting tools; lapidary work; gem and glass engraving; varnishing and lackering) DeWint

73 Calder, Ritchie. The Evolution of the Machine. New York: American Heritage, and the Smithsonian Institution, dist. by Van Nostrand, 1968. 160pp, ill (some color), bib

74 Cameron, K. Cameron's Plasterer's Manual. Containing accurate descriptions of all tools and materials used in plastering; description of the appearance and action of every variety of lime and cement.... New York: Bicknell & Comstock, 1879. 58pp, ill DeWint

75 Castieau, William. The Modern Dictionary of Arts and Sciences;... (Literature, etc., by Percival Proctor). The Astronomical, Mechanical and Every Other Branch of the Mathematics, by W. Castieau.... 4 vol. London: the Authors, 1774. BM

76 Catalogue of an Exhibition of Antique Tools at the University of Maryland from the Collection of Herbert T. Shannon. College Park, Md: U of Maryland, Glenn L. Martin College of Engineering and Aeronautical Science, 1953. 23pp, ill

77 Catalogue of Exhibits, Palace of History. Scottish Exhibition of National History, Art and Industry. 2 vol. Glasgow: 1911. ill (Fine Art Section catalog--153pp; Industrial Section--214pp)

78 Catalogue of the Collection Illustrating Construction and Building Material in the South Kensington Museum. London: HMSO, 1859; 2nd ed. ed. by H. Sandham. London: Eyre & Spottiswoode, for HMSO, 1860; another 2nd ed. 1861; 3rd ed. 1862. 3rd ed: 241pp, ill DLC

79   A Catalogue of the Machines, Models, and Other Articles, in
     the Repository of the Society Instituted for the Encouragement
     of Arts, Manufactures, and Commerce.   London: Royal
     Society, R. Wilks, printer, 1814.   24pp

80   Catalogue of the Mechanical Engineering Collection in the Science
     Division of the Victoria and Albert.   3rd rev. ed.   London:
     HMSO, 1901; 4th ed. with supplement of illustrations.   Lon-
     don: 1907.   4th ed.:   419pp, 12 pls   (Steam engines, me-
     chanical measuring appliances, pumps, electrical fittings,
     etc.)

81   Chambers, Ephraim, 1680-1740.   Cyclopaedia: or, An universal
     dictionary of arts and sciences; containing an explication of
     terms, and an account of the things signified thereby, in the
     several arts both liberal and mechanical.   2 vol. 2nd ed.
     London: Midwinter, Bettesworth, Hitch, Senex, Gosling,
     1738; 7th ed. London: Innys, Knapton, Birt, 1751-52; Sup-
     plement, by George Lewis Scott, and John Hill.   2 vol.
     London: Innys, Richardson, etc., 1753; 4 vol. rev. ed. by
     Abraham Rees.   London: Rivington, Hamilton, 1799.   pls
     DeWint

82   *Cheney, Sheldon, and Martha C. Cheney.   Art and the Machine;
     an account of industrial design in 20th Century America.
     New York; London: Whittlesey House, McGraw-Hill, 1936.
     307pp, ill, bib   TxU, DLC, NN

83   Childe, Vere Gordon.   The Story of Tools.   London: Cobbett,
     1944.   44pp, pls   DLC

84   *Clark, Victor Selden.   History of Manufactures in the United
     States.   Introd. by Henry W. Farnam.   2 vol.   Washington,
     D.C.:   Carnegie Institution of Washington, 1916-1928; Vol. 3.
     1929; rev. ed. 1929; 3 vol. reprint.   New York: Peter
     Smith, 1949.   text, 17 pls, bib   (I. 1607-1860; II. 1860-
     1914; III. 1914-1929)   ViU, MH, CU, DLC

85   Clarke, Cuthbert.   A Philosophical Investigation of the Origin,
     Vicissitude, and Power of Steam Employed in a Fire Engine.
     With a candid and familiar explanation of the parts, powers,
     and true construction of that ingenious machine.   Newcastle,
     Eng: T. Slack, 1773.   24pp   BM

86   Clarke, Hewson, 1787-1832, and John Dougall, 1760-1822.   The
     Cabinet of Arts, or, general instructor in arts, sciences,
     trade, practical machinery, the means of preserving human
     life, and political economy.   London: T. Kinnersley, 1817;
     London: J. M'Gowan, 1825?   859pp, pls   ("The chapters on
     architecture, painting and engraving are for the most part
     the same as books 2 to 4 of T. Hodson's 1805 Cabinet of
     the Arts...."   Library Congress)   DeWint, DLC

87 Cleark, C. F. The Mechanics' Book of Reference; or, cabinet
    makers, carpenters, masons and bricklayers, smiths, coach
    makers, painters, watch makers, and machine makers as-
    sistant. n.p., ca.1845. 32pp

88 Cole, George, comp. The Contractors Book of Working Draw-
    ings of Tools and Machines, used in constructing canals,
    rail roads and other works. Buffalo, NY: Compton, Gibson,
    1855. 15 pls DeWint

89 Collector's Guide to Axes and Other 19th Century Swinging Tools.
    Gas City, Ind: L-W Promotions, 1973. 56pp, ill (1870-
    1900)

90 Collins Company Catalog, 1821. Reprint. Levittown, NY:
    Early Trades and Crafts Society, 197-?

91 The Collins Company, Collinsville, Connecticut. The Axe; its
    manufacture, choice and care. Collinsville: 1939; reprint.
    Canton, Conn: Antique Tools and Trades in Connecticut,
    and the Canton Historical Society, 1972. 15pp, ill

92 Common Tools of the 19th Century. Gas City, Ind: L-W Pro-
    motions, 197-? 80pp, ill (Old catalog reprints. Carpentry,
    blacksmithing, coopering, harness making, wagonwrighting,
    etc.)

93 Cook, Clarence Westgate. Steel Ship-builder's Handbook; an
    encyclopedia of the names of parts, tools, operations, trades,
    abbreviations, etc., used in the building of steel ships. New
    York: Longmans, Green, 1918. 123pp MH

94 Cripps, Ann. The Countryman Rescuing the Past. Newton
    Abbot: David & Charles, 1973. 206pp, ill (Reprints from
    column on old tools and crafts in The Countryman)

95 Croker, Temple Henry, Thomas Williams, and Samuel Clark.
    The Complete Dictionary of Arts and Sciences; in which the
    whole circle of human learning is explained, and the diffi-
    culties attending the acquisition of every art, whether liberal
    or mechanical, are removed.... 3 vol. London: Authors,
    1764-1766. 146 pls of machinery, engines, bridges, scien-
    tific apparatus, weapons, anatomy, architecture, etc. DeWint

96 *Cutbush, James. The American Artists Manual, or dictionary
    of practical knowledge in the application of philosophy to the
    arts and manufactures. Selected from most complete Euro-
    pean systems, with original improvements and appropriate
    engravings. Adapted to the use of manufacturers of the
    United States. 2 vol. Philadelphia: Johnson & Warner,
    and R. Risher, W. Brown, 1814. ill

97 Davis, Marvin, and Helen Davis. Relics of the Whiteman;

pictures and prices of hundreds of relics. Ashland, Ore:
Winema Publications, 1973. 63pp, ill (Implements, utensils, etc.)

98 Davison, Thomas Raffles, ed. The Arts Connected with
    Building: lectures on craftsmanship and design delivered
    at Carpenters Hall, London Wall, for the Worshipful
    Company of Carpenters. London: Batsford; New York:
    Scribner, 1909. 223pp, 98 ill (Includes essay by A. Rom-
    ney Green, "The Influence of Tools on Design." Old and
    modern work, architecture, plasterwork, furniture, iron-
    work, etc.) PP, MB, NNC-Ave, DLC

99 Dempsey, George Drysdale, d. 1859. The Machinery of the
    19th Century. Illustrated from original drawings, and in-
    cluding the best examples ... at the Exhibition of the
    Works of Industry of All Nations, 1851. Issued in parts?
    London: Atchley & Co, 1852. 72pp, ill, 30 pls MdBP,
    NN

100 Derry, Thomas Kingston, and Trevor I. Williams. A Short
    History of Technology from the Earliest Times to A.D.
    1900. Oxford: Clarendon Pr, 1960; New York: Oxford
    U Pr, 1961. 782pp, ill, bib

101 Design in Industry. Monthly. Newark, NJ: Public Library
    and Newark Museum, 1930-1932. (Presented latest book,
    magazine and pamphlet articles on design) NN

102 Dickinson, Henry Winram. A Short History of the Steam
    Engine. Cambridge, Eng: U Pr, for Babcock & Wilcox,
    1938; 1939; New York: Macmillan, 1939. 255pp, ill, pls

103 _____. Stationary Engines. Catalogue of the collections
    in the Science Museum, South Kensington. London: HMSO,
    1925. 188pp, 11 pls DLC, NN

    Dictionary of Arts and Sciences. 1757. See: A New and
    Complete Dictionary of Arts and Sciences...

104 *Diderot, Denis, 1713-1784. Encyclopedie, ou dictionnaire
    raisonné des sciences, des arts, et des metiers. 17 vol
    (11 vol of plates). Paris: Briasson, 1751-1765; Supple-
    ment. 4 vol. 1776-1777; as A Diderot Pictorial Encyclo-
    pedia of Trades and Industry. Selections from the original,
    ed. by Charles C. Gillespie. 2 vol. New York: Dover,
    1959; as Selections (from Encyclopédie of Denis Diderot
    and Jean Le R. D'Alembert.) Tr. by Nelly S. Hoyt, and
    Thomas Cassirer. New York: Bobbs Merrill, 1965; fac-
    simile ed. of the complete plates. 5 vol. New York:
    Tudor, 1966; reprint from original. 5 vol. New York:
    Readex Microprint, 1969; abbreviated ed, tr. by Stephen
    Gendzier, as Encyclopedia. New York: Harper, Row, 1969.

105　A Directory of Sheffield, containing the names and residences
　　of the merchants, manufacturers, tradesmen, and principal
　　inhabitants; an historical sketch and description of the town
　　and neighbourhood; the marks struck by the manufacturers,
　　and every other necessary information respecting the trade
　　and the place.　Sheffield:　James Montgomery, printer, for
　　John Robinson, 1797.　180pp

106　A Directory of Sheffield, including the manufacture of the ad-
　　jacent villages, with the several marks of the cutlers,
　　scissor and file-smiths, edge tool and sickle-makers.
　　Sheffield:　Gales & Martin, 1787; Sheffield:　John Robinson,
　　1797; reprint of 1787 ed.　New York:　Da Capo Pr, 1969.
　　85pp

107　A Directory of Sheffield, Published by Gales and Martin in
　　1787.　Reprinted in facsimile, with an introduction by
　　Sidney Oldall Addy.　Sheffield:　Pawson & Brailsford, 1889.
　　100pp, ill CU

108　Doblin, Jay.　100 Great Product Designs.　New York; London:
　　Van Nostrand-Reinhold, 1970.　128pp, ill (1742-1965)

109　Dodd, George, 1808-1881.　The Curiosities of Industry.　Lon-
　　don:　Routledge, 1852, 1853.　(Glass, calculating and
　　registering machines, india rubber and gutta percha, gold,
　　paper, fire and light--contrivances for their production,
　　wool, silk, etc.) BM

110　_____.　Days at the Factories, or, the manufacturing indus-
　　tries of Great Britain described, and illustrated by en-
　　gravings of machines and processes.　(His chapters 1-17
　　from Charles Knight's Encyclopedia.)　London:　1843; re-
　　print.　Wakefield:　E. P. Publishing, 1975.　408pp, ill, pls

111　_____.　Dictionary of Manufactures, mining, machinery, and
　　the industrial arts.　London:　1871.　BM

112　_____.　Manufactures.　London:　Charles Knight, 1844.
　　248pp, ill

113　_____.　Where Do We Get It, and How Is It Made?　A
　　familiar account of the modes of supplying our every-day
　　wants, comforts, and luxuries.　London:　1862.　ill BM

114　*Dossie, Robert.　The Handmaid to the Arts.... 2 vol.
　　London:　for J. Nourse, 1758; 2nd ed ... teaching, I. A
　　perfect knowledge of the materia pictoria.　II. The several
　　devices employed for the easily and accurately making de-
　　signs from nature, or depicted representations.　III. The
　　various manners of gilding, silvering, and bronzing ... the
　　art of japanning ... (Vol. I.).　... The preparation of inks,
　　cement and sealing-wax; art of engraving; nature and

preparation of glass and counterfeiting of gems; manner of
preparing papier mache; The nature and composition of porcelain, as well according to the methods practised in
China....; Preparation of transparent and coloured glazings
for stone or earthen-ware ... (Vol. II.). 2nd ed. with con-
siderable additions and improvements. London: for J.
Nourse, 1764; new ed. London: A. Millar, W. Law, and
R. Cater, 1796. NNC-Ave

115 *Dowling, Henry George. A Survey of British Industrial Arts.
Benfleet, Eng: F. Lewis, 1935. 57pp, ill, 100 pls DLC,
NN

116 Draper, John William, 1893- . 18th Century English Aesthetics;
a bibliography. Heidelberg: C. Winter, 1931. 140pp ViU,
DLC, DeWint

117 *Drepperd, Carl W. Pioneer America--its first three centuries.
Garden City, NY: Doubleday, 1949; New York: Cooper
Square Publishers, 1972. 311pp, ill (Social life and cus-
toms, implements, utensils, art industries, etc.)

118 Dresser, Christopher. General Principles of Art, Decorative
and Pictorial. With hints on color, its harmonies and
contrasts. Philadelphia: Pennsylvania Museum and School
of Industrial Art, 18- . 4pp NN, PPL

119 Drexler, Arthur, and Greta Daniel. Introduction to 20th
Century Design, from the Collection of the Museum of
Modern Art, N.Y. Garden City, NY: Doubleday, dist.,
1959. 94pp, ill

120 *Dunlap, William. A History of the Rise and Progress of the
Arts of Design in the United States. 2 vol. New York:
George P. Scott, 1834; 3 vol. rev. ed. with additions by
Frank W. Bayley, and Charles Goodspeed. Boston: Good-
speed, 1918; reprint with introd. by William P. Campbell,
ed. by Alexander Wyckoff. 3 vol. New York: B. Blom,
1965; reprint with new introd. by James Thomas Flexner.
Ed. by Rita Weiss. 2 vol. New York: Dover; London:
Constable, 1969. I. 435pp, ill, 119 pls; II. Part 1. 275pp,
ill, 123 pls; Part 2. 238pp, ill, 120 pls, bib (1700-1830)
NN, MdBP, DeWint, TxU

121 Earle, Alice Morse. Stage Coach and Tavern Days. New
York; London: Macmillan, 1900; 1905; 1915; 1935; etc.
449pp, 155 ill, pls (Anecdotal history with illustrations of
inn signs, glasses, phillpots, trunks, sleighs, carriages,
etc.)

122 Earle, Thomas, and Charles T. Congdon, ed. Annals of the
General Society of Mechanics and Tradesmen of the City of

New York, from 1785 to 1880. New York: the Society,
1882. 420pp, ill

123 *Early American Industries Association. The Chronicle. Quarterly. Northampton, Mass, etc.: 1933-date. ill (Tools
and processes of crafts and industries)

124 _____. Shavings. Bi-monthly newsletter. Ambridge, Pa:
197-?-date.

125 Ellacott, Samuel Ernest. A History of Everyday Things in
England, Vol. 5, 1914-1968. New York: Putnam, 1969.
ill (Juvenile literature)

126 Encyclopaedia Americana; a dictionary of arts, sciences, and
general literature and companion to Encyclopaedia Britannica (9th edition) and to all other encyclopaedias. 4 vol.
New York: J. M. Stoddart, etc., 1883-1889. ill, pls

127 Encyclopaedia Americana; a popular dictionary of arts, sciences,
literature, history, politics and biography. Ed. by Francis
Lieber. 13 vol. Philadelphia: Carey, Lea & Carey, 1829-
33; Supplementary Volume 14. 1846; etc.

128 Encyclopedia Americana; a universal reference library ... issued under the editorial supervision of the Scientific American. 16 vol. New York: 1903-06. ill, pls

129 *Encyclopaedia Britannica; or, A dictionary of Arts and Sciences
... in which the different sciences and arts are digested
into distinct treatises or systems; and the various technical
terms, etc., are explained as they occur in the order of the
alphabet. 3 vol. Edinburgh: for A. Bell & C. MacFarquhar, 1768-1771; 2nd ed. enl. 10 vol. Edinburgh: J.
Balfour, 1778-1783; 3rd ed. 18 vol. Edinburgh: A. Bell
& C. MacFarquhar, 1797; Supplement. 2 vol. 1801; 4th ed.
22 vol. 1810; 5th ed. 26 vol. (including 6 vol. supplement),
1815-1824; 6th ed. 20 vol. 1823; 6 vol. supplement 1824;
7th ed. 21 vol. 1842; 8th ed. 22 vol. 1853-1860; 9th ed.
24 vol. 1875-1888; 10th ed. Supplementary 11 volumes and
9th ed. 1902-03; 11th ed. 29 vol. Cambridge, Eng; New
York: U Pr, 1910-11; 32 vol. in 16. New York: Encyclopedia Britannica Co, 1910-1922; etc. Reprints: 1st ed.
facsimile reprint in 3 vol. Chicago: Encyclopedia Britannica, 1967; also New York: Praeger, 1968; 9th ed. many
reprints, some in 25, 29, 30 volumes, to 1907. 1st: 160
pls; 2nd: 200 pls; 3rd: 542 pls; supplement. 50 pls; 4th:
582 pls (part color)

130 *Engineering Heritage; highlights from the history of mechanical
engineering. Vol. I. London: Heinemann, for the Institution of Mechanical Engineers, London, 1963; Vol. II. ed.

by E. G Semler. London: Heinemann, 1966; New York:
Dover, 1967. 180pp, ill, bib; 170pp, ill, bib

131 English Mechanics and The World of Science. Weekly. London: 1865-1926.

132 Ewbank, Thomas, 1792-1870. A Descriptive and Historical
Account of Hydraulic and Other Machines for Raising Water,
ancient and modern, including the progressive development
of the steam engine. London: Tilt & Bogue; New York:
Appleton, 1842; 2nd rev. ed. 1846; with supplement. New
York: Greeley & McElrath, 1847; 1849; ...; New York:
Scribner, 1876. 582pp, ill; 582pp, 31pp of ill; 608pp, ill;
1876: 612pp, ill CtY, NN

133 Farnham, Alexander, comp. Tool Collectors Handbook of
Prices Paid at Auction for Early American Tools. Stockton,
NJ: Author, 1970; 2nd ed. 1972; 3rd ed. 1975. 39pp, ill;
67pp, ill; 72pp, ill (200 tools ill. Household, woodworking)

134 Ferebee, Ann. A History of Design from the Victorian Era to
the Present; a survey of the modern style in architecture,
interior design, industrial design, graphic design, and photography. New York; London: Van Nostrand Reinhold, 1970.
128pp, ill (1837-1969)

135 *Ferguson, Eugene S. Bibliography of the History of Technology. Cambridge, Mass: M.I.T. Pr, Society for the
History of Technology, 1968. 347pp

136 Ferguson, James, 1710-1776. The Description and Use of a
New Machine, called the mechanical paradox; invented by
J. Ferguson. London: Author, 1764. 16pp, 1 folding pl

137 _____. Lectures on Select Subjects in Mechanics, hydro-
statics, pneumatics, and optics. With the use of globes,
the art of dialing, and the calculation of the mean times of
new and full moons and eclipses. London: for A. Millar,
1760; 1764; with supplement. London: for W. Strahan,
1770; 4th ed. 1772; 2 vol. Edinburgh: Bell & Bradfute, J.
Fairbairn, 1806; 2 vol. Philadelphia: M. Carey, 1806;
etc. 417pp, ill; pls; 1772: 396pp, 23 folding pls DLC,
NN, ViU

138 _____. A Supplement to ... Lectures on Mechanics ...
containing 13 copper-plates, with descriptions of the machinery which he has added to his apparatus, since that
book was printed. London: for A. Millar, 1767. 40pp of
folding pls PPL

139 Fisher, George (pseud.?). The Instructor; or, Young man's
best companion. London: for E. Midwinter, at the Looking
Glass on London Bridge, 1727; 10th ed. as The American

Instructor.... Philadelphia: B. Franklin and D. Hall,
1753; 14th ed. New York: H. Gaine, 1770; Philadelphia:
Joseph Cruikshank, printer, 1787; etc. 424pp, ill, pls;
other editions 372-384pp, ill MiU, MH, ViU

140 Flanders, Ralph Edward. Gear-Cutting Machinery, comprising
a complete review of American and European practice. New
York: J. Wiley, 1909. 319pp, ill DLC, NN

141 Forbes, Robert James. Man the Maker; a history of technology
and Engineering. London: Constable; London; New York:
Abelard-Schuman, 1958. 365pp, ill, bib

142 _____, and Eduard J. Dijksterhuis. A History of Science
and Technology. 2 vol. Harmondsworth, Eng; Baltimore:
Penguin, 1963. ill, bib (Ancient times on)

143 Francis, George William, 1800-1865. The Dictionary of the
Arts, Sciences, and Manufactures. London: W. Brittain,
1842; 1846; new improved ed. London: D. Francis, 1853.
470pp, 1100 ill DLC, TxU

144 Franklin Institute. Annual Report. Philadelphia: 1824/25- .

145 _____. Bulletin. Philadelphia: 1889-1892.

146 _____. Journal ... Devoted to Science and the Mechanical
Arts. (Title varies.) Monthly. Philadelphia: 1826- .

147 *Franklin Institute Library Catalogue of Books. Philadelphia:
R. W. Barnard, 1851; Philadelphia: Franklin Institute,
1876. 117, 68pp; 472pp

148 Freedley, Edwin Troxell. Philadelphia and Its Manufactures:
a handbook exhibiting the development, variety and statistics
of the manufacturing industry of Philadelphia in 1857. Together with sketches of remarkable manufactories; and a
list of articles now made in Philadelphia. Philadelphia: E.
Young, 1860. 504pp BM

149 From Lenape Territory to Royal Province, New Jersey 1600-
1750. Exhibition. April-September 1971. Trenton, NJ:
State Museum, 1971. 88pp, ill, bib (Early American
trades and industries)

150 Gault, Phil. Collectors Guide to Early American Tools: an
illustrated price guide. Gas City, Ind: L-W Promotions,
1974. ill

151 *Giedion, Siegfried. Mechanization Takes Command, a contribution to anonymous history. New York: Oxford U Pr,
1948; 1955. 743pp, many ill, bib

152 Gilbert, Keith Reginald. The Machine Tool Collection; cata-
     logue of exhibitions with historical introduction. Science
     Museum. New ed. London: HMSO, 1966. 111pp, 32 pls,
     bib

153 Glass, Frederick James. The Industrial Arts: their history,
     development, and practice as educational factors, etc.
     London: U of London Pr, 1927. 311pp, ill

154 Gloag, John (Edwards). Artifex; or, the future of craftsman-
     ship. London: K. Paul, Trench, Trubner; New York:
     Dutton, 1926, 1927. 96pp MiU, DLC, NN

155 _____. Design in Everyday Life and Things. London:
     1927?

156 _____, ed. Design in Modern Life. With contributions by
     Robert Atkinson, Elizabeth Denby, E. Maxwell Fry, F.
     Pick, J. Laver, G. Russell, etc. London: G. Allen &
     Unwin, 1934. 138pp, pls NN, DLC

157 _____. Georgian Grace, a social history of design from
     1660 to 1830. New York: Macmillan; London: A. & C.
     Black, 1956; new ed. London: Spring Books, 1967. 426pp,
     ill, 48 pls, bib (One of trilogy)

158 _____. Industrial Art Explained. London: G. Allen &
     Unwin, 1934; 1946. 192pp, ill, 16 pls, bib; 248pp, ill, bib

159 Gompertz, Maurice. The Master Craftsmen, the story of the
     evolution of implements. London; New York: T. Nelson,
     1933. 268pp, ill, pls, bib DLC

160 *Goodholme, Todd S., ed. A Domestic Encyclopedia of Practical
     Information for Popular Use. New York: Holt, 1877; Hart-
     ford: S. S. Scranton, 1880; new rev. ed. New York:
     Scribner's, 1889. 652pp, ill PPL, DLC, MH, NN

161 Green, Constance M. Eli Whitney and the Birth of American
     Technology. Boston: Little, Brown, 1956. 215 pp

162 Greenough, Horatio, 1805-1852. Form and Function: remarks
     on art, design and architecture. Ed. by Harold A. Small.
     Introd. by Earle Loran. Berkeley, Cal: U Pr; London;
     Cambridge U Pr, 1947; 1957. 148pp, bib

163 Gregory, George, 1754-1808. A New and Complete Dictionary
     of Arts and Sciences, including the latest improvement and
     discovery and the present state of every branch of human
     knowledge. 3 vol. London: 1810; Charleston, Philadelphia,
     etc: Pierce, 1815-16; 4 vol. Philadelphia: T. Pierce,
     1816; 3 vol. New York: Collins, 1819; New York: William
     T. Robinson, 1821. text, ill, pls DeWint

164 Grey, Michael. Man the Toolmaker. London: Priory Pr,
     1973. 128pp, ill, bib

165 Griffin, Richard. The Book of Trades, or, circle of the use-
     ful arts. Glasgow: R. Griffin & Co, 1835; 3rd ed. 1837;
     London: J. J. Griffin, 1852. 356pp, pls; 388pp, pls
     DeWint

166 A Guide to the Machinery Hall of the Royal Scottish Museum.
     Edinburgh: 1928. 30pp, pls

167 A Guide to the Works of Art and Science, collected by ... the
     Duke of Edinburgh ... lent for exhibition 1872. London:
     South Kensington Museum, 1872. 74pp, ill BM

168 Hall, William Henry, d.1807. The New Royal Encyclopedia;
     or, complete modern universal dictionary of arts and
     sciences, on a new and improved plan. 3 vol. London:
     C. Cooke, 1788?; 1791; 3rd ed. rev. & enl. 1797? 150 pls
     DeWint, CtY, MB

169 Hamilton, Alexander. Report of the Secretary of the Treasury
     of the United States on the Subject of Manufactures, pre-
     sented to the House of Representatives. Washington, D.C.:
     December 5, 1791. NN

170 Handbook for Settlers in the United States. Frankfurt a. Main:
     1848. (Tools needed, etc.)

171 Hardware Age. Weekly. New York: David Williams, 1913- .

172a Hardware and Housewares. Toronto: Wrigley, 1909-1952.

172b Hardware and Implement Trade, and western industrial record.
     Weekly. Chicago: 1876- .

173 Hardware Catalogues. A miscellaneous collection. 11 vol.
     Milwaukee: 1851-1923. ill (Tools, cutlery, fences,
     building hardware, household utensils, lanterns, etc.) NN

174 The Hardware Journal. Monthly. Melbourne, Australia:
     Trade Pr, 1886- .

175 Hardware Trade Journal. Weekly. London: Benn Brothers,
     1873?- .

176 Harris, John, 1667?-1719. Lexicon Technicum: or, an uni-
     versal English dictionary of arts and sciences, explaining
     not only the terms of art, but the arts themselves. 1
     and 2 vol. London: D. Brown, 1704; ...; 1723; reprint.
     2 vol. New York: Johnson, 1966. 926pp, ill, pls. MH,
     CtY, NN, TxU

177   Harrison, Molly, and Anne A. M. Wells, and others. Picture
      Source Book for Social History. 7 vol. London: Allen &
      Unwin, 1953-1967. 1. 16th Century. 1951. 112pp, ill,
      bib; 2. 17th Century. 1953. 128pp, ill, bib; 3. 18th
      Century. 1955. 144pp, ill, bib; 4. Early 19th Century.
      1957. 151pp, ill, bib; 5. The Conquest to the Wars of the
      Roses. 1958. 130pp, ill, bib; 6. Late 19th Century.
      1961. 139pp, ill; 7. 20th Century. 1967. 164pp, ill

178   Hart, Ivor Blashka. The Mechanical Investigations of Leonardo
      da Vinci. London: Chapman & Hall, 1925; 2nd ed. Berke-
      ley, Cal: U of Cal. Pr, 1963. 240pp, ill, pls (Da Vinci,
      1452-1519)

179   Harvey, John. Mediaeval Craftsmen. New York: Drake,
      1975. 231pp, ill, bib (Stone, clay, timber, paint, metal
      workers)

180   Hasluck, Paul Nooncree, ed. Builders' Hoisting Machinery:
      simple lifting tackle, winches, crabs, cranes, travellers,
      motive power for lifting machinery. London: Cassell,
      1904; 1910. 96pp, ill NN, MiD

181   _____, ed. Cassell's Cyclopedia of Mechanics; containing
      receipts, processes, and memoranda for workshop use,
      based on personal experience and expert knowledge. 2nd
      series. London: New York: Cassell, 1902. 1250 ill,
      9250 entries.

182   _____, ed. The Metal Turner's Handbook, a practical
      manual for workers at the foot-lathe. London: C. Lock-
      wood, 1882; 2nd ed. rev. 1887; 1893; London: Technical
      Pr, 1920. 152pp, ill; 1920: 144pp, ill MiD, MB, ViU

183   _____, comp. Metalworking. A book of tools, materials,
      and processes for the handyman. London; New York:
      Dassell, 1904; Philadelphia: McKay, 1907; 1910; 1913.
      760pp, ill

184   _____. The Pattern Makers' Handybook. A practical manual
      on patterns for founders: embracing information on the tools,
      materials and appliances employed in their construction.
      London: Lockwood, 1887; 3rd ed. 1894; 7th ed. 1912. 144pp,
      ill, diagrams NN, MiU

185   _____, ed. Work; a weekly journal for amateur mechanics.
      London, etc: Cassell, 1889-1924. ill (The preceding works,
      edited by Hasluck, originally appeared as articles by various
      craftsmen in this weekly)

186   Hathaway, Esse Virginia, 1871-1939. Partners in Progress.
      Freeport, NY: 1968. 303pp (Machines in history)

187   Hazen, Edward. The Panorama of Professions and Trades.
      Philadelphia: Hunt, 1836; 1837; 1839; also as Popular
      Technology: or, professions and trades.   New York:
      Harper, 1839; Philadelphia: 184-; 1845; 2 vol. New York:
      1846; 1850;... 320pp, 82 ill MB, ViU, DLC, DeWint

188   Heck, Johann Georg, ed. Iconographic Encyclopedia of Science,
      literature, and art.   Tr. from German by S. F. Baird.
      4 vol. New York: R. Garrigue, 1851-52.   500 ill (From
      Bilder Atlas zum Conversations Lexicon, Leipzig, 185-?)

189   Hepburn, William Murray. A Manual of the William Freeman
      Myrick Goss Library of the History of Engineering and as-
      sociated collections.   Lafayette, Ind: Purdue U Pr, 1947.
      218pp, ill

190   Herbert, William, 1771-1851. Concise Account of the Wor-
      shipful Company of Haberdashers.   (... Salters, Ironmongers,
      Vintners, and Clothworkers.) 1 vol. London: Author,
      1838.

191   _____. The History of the 12 Great Livery Companies of
      London. 2 vol. London: Author, 1834-36; 1837. ill ViU,
      TxU, PP

192   Hiscox, Gardner D. Mechanical Movements, Devices and Ap-
      pliances. New York: Norman W. Henley, 190? ill

193   Historic Books on Machines. Exhibition. Science Museum.
      London: HMSO, 1953. 28pp NN, MH

194   Historic Preservation. Quarterly. Washington, D.C.: Na-
      tional Trust for Historic Preservation, 1949-date.

195   History News. Bi-monthly (then monthly). Chapel Hill, NC,
      etc. (Now Nashville, Tennessee): American Association
      for State and Local History, 1941-date. ill

196   Hobson, Arthur H. G. The Amateur Mechanic's Practical
      Handbook, describing the different tools required in the
      workshop, the uses of them, and how to use them, also
      examples of different kinds of work, etc. London: Long-
      mans; Philadelphia: Claxton, Remsen & Haffelfinger, 1877.
      114pp, ill, diagrams SKM, MB, ViU

197   Hollingshead, John, 1827-1904. The Illustrated Catalogue of
      the Industrial Department. Vol. I. A Concise History of
      the International Exhibition of 1862. London: 1862; 2nd ed.
      1871; 3rd ed. by S. Whitney. London: 1862. 183pp, ill,
      2 pls; 168pp, ill; 432pp, ill BM

198   *Holme, Geoffrey. Industrial Design and the Future. London:
      The Studio, 1934. 160pp, ill, pls NN, DLC

199 Holme, Randle, 1627-1699. The Academy of Armory, or, A
     storehouse of armory and blazon. Containing the several
     variety of created beings and how born in coats of arms,
     both foreign and domestick. With the instruments used in
     all trades and sciences, together with their terms of art,
     also the etymologies, definitions, and historical observa-
     tions.... 3 parts, 1 vol. Chester, Eng: Author, 1688;
     3 vol. London: Booksellers of London and Westminster,
     1701; reprint. 1 vol. Menston, Eng: Scolar Pr, 1872;
     1 vol. ed. by I. H. Jeayes. London: Roxburghe Club,
     1905. 1701: 107, 488, and 501pp, ill; 1872: 543pp, ill,
     pls BM, DLC, PP

200 Hopkins, Albert Allis, 1869-1939, ed. The Book of Progress.
     3 vol. New York: Cricks, 1915; vol. II. as The Scien-
     tific American War Book. New York: Munn, 1916. ill
     (Vol. II. 338pp, 572 ill) (I. Man the Creator; II. Man the
     Destroyer, the mechanism and technique of warfare; III.
     Man and Nature) (Compiled from files of Scientific Ameri-
     can) NN, MB

201 Houghton, John, 1640-1705, ed. Husbandry and Trade Im-
     proved: being a collection of many valuable materials re-
     lating to corn, cattle, coals, hops, wool, etc;... full and
     exact histories of trades, as malting, brewing, etc...; of
     weights and measures.... First published in weekly folios,
     1692-1703. 3 vol. rev. ed. with pref. and indexes by
     Richard Bradley. London: for Woodman & Lyon, 1727.
     NN

202 Houston, George. The Farmers' Mechanics' and Sportsmans'
     Magazine. Vol. I. 1826-27. New York: Vanderpool &
     Cole, printers, 1827. 472pp, ill, pl DLC, CtY

203 Howe, Henry, 1816-1893. Memoirs of the Most Eminent
     American Mechanics: also lives of distinguished European
     mechanics; together with a collection of anecdotes, descrip-
     tions, etc., relating to the mechanic arts. New York: W.
     F. Peckham, 1840; New York: Harper, 1847;...; New
     York: Derby & Jackson, 1858;...; New York: Peckham,
     1890. 482pp, 50 ill, pls NjP, PPL, NN, DLC

204 Hulton, Karl Gunnar Pontus. The Machine, as seen at the
     end of the mechanical age. Exhibition. New York:
     Museum of Modern Art, dist. by N.Y. Graphic Society,
     Greenwich, Conn, 1968. 216pp, ill, bib

205 Hunt, Robert, 1807-1887. Companion to the Official Catalogue
     of the Great Exhibition of the Works of Industry of All
     Nations of 1851. Synopsis of Contents. 2 vol. London:
     Official Catalogue Office, 1851; 2nd ed. London: Spicer
     Brothers, 1851. 95pp NN, PPF, BM

206 _____ . Companion to the Official Catalogue. Synopsis of
the Contents of the International Exhibition of 1862. London: 1862. 96pp InU, BM

Hunt, Robert, ed. 7th ed. Ure's Dictionary of Arts....
See: Andrew Ure.

207 Hutton, Frederick Remsen, 1853-1918. "Report on Machine
Tools and Woodworking Machinery" in Report on Power and
Machinery, United States 10th Census, 1880. Washington,
D.C.: GPO, 1883; 1885; 1888; 1892. 294pp, ill NN, PPFr

208 _____ . "Report on Steam-Pumps, and Pumping Engines,"
in United States Census Office, 10th Census, 1880. Washington, D.C.: GPO, 188-? 64pp, ill, pls NN

209 Iconographic Encyclopedia of the Arts and Sciences. Vol. I.
Anthropology and Ethnology, ethnography; II. Prehistoric
Archaeology, history of culture; III. Sculpture and painting,
ancient art; early Christian and medieval art; IV. Architecture; V. Constructive Arts, building and engineering;
VI. Applied Mechanics; VII. Geology. Tr. from the German
of the Bilder-Atlas, rev. and enl. by eminent American
specialists. 7 vol. Philadelphia: Iconographic Publishing
Co, 1886-90. ill NN

210 The Inventive Age, and Industrial Review. Monthly. Washington, D.C.: 1891-1897. ill, pls MB

211 Industrial Revolution: design. 4 vol. Shannon: Irish U Pr,
1968-71. 554pp; 622pp; 978pp; 646pp (From British
Parliamentary Papers)

212 Iron. A monthly review of metallurgy, mechanics, hardware,
machinery, and tools. Philadelphia: Iron Publishing, 18-?
ill DLC

213 Jackson, Giles B., and W. Webster Davis. The Industrial
History of the Negro Race of the United States. (Including
description of the Negro exhibits at the Jamestown Exposition, 1907.) Richmond, Va: Virginia Pr, 1908; Richmond:
Negro Educational Association, 1911. 400pp, ill, pls; 369pp,
ill, pls ViU, DLC, NN

214 Jamieson, Alexander. A Dictionary of Mechanical Science,
Arts, Manufactures, and Miscellaneous Knowledge. 2 vol.
London: Fisher, 1827; 7th ed. 1 or 2 vol. London:
1830;.... 1066pp, ill, 62 pls DLC, MiU, DeWint

215 Jenkins, Rhys. Links in the History of Engineering and Technology from Tudor Times; the collected papers of R. Jenkins
... comprising articles in the professional and technical

press, mainly prior to 1920. Cambridge, Eng: U Pr, for Newcomen Society, 1936. 246pp, ill, 7 pls DLC

216 Jewell, Andrew, comp. Crafts, Trades and Industries; a book list for local historians. London: National Council of Social Service, 1968. 24pp DeWint

217 Johnson, Philip (Cortelyou). Machine Art. Fore. by Alfred H. Barr, Jr. Exhibition. March-April 1934. New York: Museum of Modern Art, W. W. Norton, 1934. 112pp, ill, pls, bib

218 Johnson, William, 1823-1864. The Imperial Cyclopedia of Machinery, being a series of plans, sections, and elevations of stationary, marine and locomotive engines; spinning machinery, grinding mills, tools, etc. ... including some of the most useful and important machines from the Great Exhibition ... and a history of the railways of Great Britain. 2 vol. Glasgow: 1851; 1 vol. Glasgow; Edinburgh; London: William Mackensie, 1852-1856. text, pls; 16, 12, 67 and 34pp, ill, pls NN

219 Jolliffe, Anne. Man the Maker: a first history of tools and machines. London: Ward Lock, 1967. 32pp, ill (Juvenile literature)

220 *Josephson, Aksel G. S. A List of Books on the History of Industry and the Industrial Arts. January 1915. Chicago: John Crerar Library, 1915; reprint. Detroit: Gale Research, 1966. 486pp

221 [No entry.]

222 Journal of Design and Manufactures. Monthly. 6 vol. London: Chapman & Hall, 1849-1852. pls and mounted samples

223 The Journal of Science, and annals of astronomy, biology, geology, industrial arts, manufactures, and technology. London: J. Churchill, 1864-1885. ill

224 Journal of the London and Middlesex Archaeological Society. London: 18-?

225 Journal of the Royal Society of Antiquaries of Ireland. Dublin: Hodges, Figgis, 18-?

226 Journal of the Society of Arts. Periodical. London: the Society, 1849-1907.

227 Kaempffert, Waldemar B. From Cave Man to Engineer; the Museum of Science and Industry founded by Julius Rosenwald, and institution to reveal the technical ascent of man.

Chicago: R. R. Donnelley, 1933. 128pp, pls (Includes catalog of exhibits) DLC

228 *Kahn, Ely Jacques, 1884- . Design in Art and Industry. New York: Scribner's, 1935. 204pp, ill NN, DLC

229 *Kauffman, Henry J. American Axes; a survey of their development and their makers. Brattlesboro, Vt: S. Greene Pr, 1972. 151pp, ill, bib

230 Keller, A. G. A Theatre of Machines. Norwich, Eng: Jarrold, 1964; New York: Macmillan, 1965. 115pp, 52 pls (Anthology of plates, with some text, from earliest printed books on mechanical inventions, 1570-1630)

231 Kepes, Gyorgy. The Man-Made Object. New York: Braziller, 1966. 230pp, ill, bib

232 Kirby, Richard S., 1874- , and others. Engineering in History. New York: McGraw-Hill, 1956. 530pp, ill, bib

233 *Klemm, Friedrich. A History of Western Technology. Tr. from German by Dorothea W. Singer. New York: Scribner, 1959. 401pp, ill, bib

234 Klingender, Francis Donald. Art and the Industrial Revolution. Bradford-on-Avon, Wilts: Adams & Dart, 1968. 314pp, ill (8 color)

235 Knight, Charles, 1791-1873. Cyclopedia of the Industry of All Nations, 1851. Ed. by George Dodd. London: Author, 1851; New York: Putnam, 1851. 1806pp, 36 pls ViU, DeWint, SKM, DLC

236 _____. The English Cyclopedia. 8 vol. London: Bradbury & Evans, 1854-1872. ill

237 _____. The Pictorial Gallery of Arts. 2 vol. London: Author, C. Cox, 1847; 2 vol. in 1. London; New York: London Printing, 1852; 1858. ill, pls, color frontis (I. Useful Arts; II. Fine Arts) ViU, DeWint, NN, DLC

238 *Knight, Edward Henry, 1824-1883. (Knight's) American Mechanical Dictionary: being a description of tools, instruments, machines, processes and engineering; history of inventions; general technological vocabulary, and digest of mechanical appliances in science and the arts. 3 vol. New York: J. B. Ford, 1872-76; 1874-77; 1874-84; New York: Hurd & Houghton, 1876; New York: Hurd & Houghton; Cambridge, Mass: Riverside Pr, 1877; Boston: Houghton, Mifflin, 188-; 1880-81; Boston: 1882; 1884; as Practical Dictionary of Mechanics.... London: Cassell, Petter & Galpin;

Cambridge, Mass: Houghton, 187-?; Supplement. London:
Cassell; Boston: Houghton-Mifflin, 1884. 5000 ill DeWint,
NN

239 Koehler, Sylvester Ross. Architecture, Sculpture and the
     Industrial Arts Among the Nations of Antiquity. Boston:
     L. Prang, 1879. 246 pls DeWint

240 Langdon, William Chauncy, 1871- . Everyday Things in
     American Life. 2 vol. New York; London: Scribner's,
     1937, 1941; 1943. 353pp, 398pp, ill, pls, bib (I. 1607-
     1776; II. 1776-1876) MiU, ViU

241 *Lardner, Reverend Dionysius, 1793-1859. Cabinet Cyclopaedia
     of Useful Arts.... 133 parts or 7 vol. London: Longmans,
     1830-1849; London: Carey & Lee, 1830-1850; Philadelphia:
     1832. ill (Vol II. Useful and Fine Arts) (Porcelain, glass,
     metalwork, etc) MiU, DLC, NN

242 _____ . Common Things Explained ... containing air, earth,
     fire, water, time, the almanack, clocks and watches, spec-
     tacles, colour, kaleidoscope, pumps, from "The Museum of
     Science and Art." London: Walton & Maberly, 1855.
     192pp, 114 ill DLC

243 _____ , ed. The Museum of Science and Art. 12 vol (in
     12, 6, 4). London: Walton & Maberly, 1854-1856. ill
     ViU, MB

244 _____ . 1000 and 10 Things Worth Knowing. A book clearly
     explaining how to do rightly almost everything that can be
     necessary in the kitchen, the parlor, and dressing-room.
     And disclosing all the most valuable information, receipts,
     and instructions, in the useful and domestic arts.... Phila-
     delphia: T. B. Peterson, 18-? 143pp, ill

245 _____ . The Steam Engine Familiarly Explained and Illus-
     trated; with an account of its invention and progressive im-
     provement, and its application to navigation and railways.
     (Title changes and varies.) 1st American ed. Philadelphia:
     E. L. Carey & A. Hart, 1836. 535pp, ill, pls

246 Lethaby, William Richard, 1857-1931. Form in Civilization:
     collected papers on art and labour. Fore. by Lewis Mum-
     ford. London: Oxford U Pr, 1922; 1927; reprint. London:
     1938: 1957. 196pp, ill

247 *Lilley, Samuel. Men, Machines and History: the story of
     tools and machines in relation to social progress. London:
     Cobbett Pr, 1948; rev. enl. ed. London: Laurence &
     Wishart, 1965. 240pp, ill, bib; 352pp, ill, 48 pls

248 Lister, Raymond. Great Works of Craftsmanship. London:

Bell, 1967; South Brunswick, NJ: A. S. Barnes, 1968.
206pp, ill, 16 pls

249 List(s) of Books on ... in the South Kensington Museum,
London. National Art Library. 3 vol. London: HMSO,
1883-89. NNC-Ave
    I. Coins and Medals, Construction, engineering
and machinery.
    II. Drawing, furniture, gems, glass, gold and silver-
smiths work, jewellery, metalwork.
    III. Painting, sculpture, seals, textiles, fabrics,
lace and needlework.

250 Living Age. Periodical. New York: 1844-1941.

251 Lukin, James, 1828- . Amongst Machines; a description of
various mechanical appliances used in the manufacture of
wood, metal, and other substances. A book for boys.
New York: Putnam's, 1876. 335pp, ill (Juvenile literature) MH, NN

252 MacCarthy, Fiona. All Things Bright and Beautiful; design in
Britain, 1830 to today. London: Allen & Unwin, 1972.
327pp, ill, bib

253 Machine Tools. Illustrated catalogue of the collections in the
Science Museum, South Kensington. London: HMSO, 1920.
61pp, 3 pls NN, DLC

254 MacKensie's 5000 Recipes in All the Useful and Domestic
Arts. Philadelphia: James Kay, Jr., 1831. text, 26
wood engravings (Bleaching, brewing, calico printing,
confectionery, distillation, dyeing, oil colors, painting,
silk, silvering, varnishing, etc.)

255 Mallet, Robert, 1810-1881, ed. The Scientific Record of the
International Exhibition, 1862; being a synopsis of the chief
productions shown, relating to commerce, arts and manufactures. Glasgow: W. Mackensie; London: Longman,
1862. 592pp, ill, pls MiD

256 Manchester, Herbert (H.). The Evolution of the Screw. New
York: Parker-Kalon, 1928. 22pp, ill NN

257 Manning, Maxwell. Illustrated Catalogue of Railway and Machinists' Tools and Supplies. New York: 1894. 1071pp,
ill NNC-Ave

258 Mantoux, Paul, 1877-1956. The Industrial Revolution in the
18th Century; an outline of the beginnings of the modern
factory system in England. Tr. from French by Marjorie
Vernon. Pref. by T. S. Ashton. New York: Macmillan;

London: Cape, 1961; New York: Harper, 1965. 528pp,
ill, bib

259 Marmont, Paul, and George Rolstad. Tools from the Pacific
Northwest Collections: group 1, 1973. Seattle: Early
American Industries Association West, 1973. 49pp, ill

260 Marshall, Percival. Metal Working Tools and Their Uses.
London: P. Marshall, 1901; rev. enl. ed. 1939. 73pp,
86ill; 83pp, ill NN, DLC

261 Martin, Samuel, ed. The Useful Arts: their birth and development. Edited for Young Men's Christian Association.
London: Nisbet, 1851. BM

262 Martin, Thomas. Circle of the Mechanical Arts: containing
practical treatises on the various manual arts, trades and
manufactures. London: for R. Rees, 1813; 2nd ed. 1815.
616pp, ill, 39 pls NNC-Ave, PPL, MH

263 Martini, Herbert E., ed. Applied Art, a collection of designs
showing the tendencies of American industrial art. New
York: F. K. Ferenz, 1919. ill, pls (part color) NNC-
Ave, PP

264 Maskell, William. The Industrial Arts. Historical sketches
with numerous illustrations. South Kensington Museum.
London: Chapman; New York: Scribner, 1876; new ed.
London: 1885. 276pp, ill, pls NN, MB

265 Mason, George Champlin, 1820-1894. Application of Art to
Manufactures. New York: Putnam, 1858. 344pp, 150 ill,
pls SKM

266 The Masterpieces of the Centennial International Exhibition.
Profusely illustrated with woodcuts and steel engravings.
Vol. I. Fine Art; Vol. II. Industrial Art, by Prof. Walter
Smith; Vol. III. History, mechanics and science, by Joseph
M. Wilson. 3 vol. Philadelphia: Gebbie & Barrie, 1876-
78. ill, pls

267 Medieval Catalogue. London Museum. London: HMSO, 1954;
3rd imprint. 1967. 319pp, ill, 99 pls (Medieval arts and
industries)

268 *Mercer, Henry Chapman, comp. Tools of the Nation Maker.
A descriptive catalogue of objects in the Museum of the
Historical Society of Bucks County, Pa. Doylestown: 1897.
87pp DLC, NN

269 [No entry.]

Midland Counties Exhibition. Preliminary catalogue of works

of art and industrial products. 1870. See: A. Wallis,
and W. Bemrose, The Pottery and Porcelain of Derbyshire, no.

270 Millar, William, d. 1904. Plastering: plain and decorative.
Including full descriptions of the various tools, materials,
processes and appliances employed, together with an account of plastering in England, Scotland and Ireland, with
a chapter ... "A Glimpse of Its History," by G. T. Robinson. London: Batsford, 1897; 3rd ed. rev. London: Batsford; New York: John Lane, 1905. 604pp, 231 ill, 52 pls
NN, ViU

271 *Miller, Lewis, 1795-1882. The Virginia Journey of Lewis
Miller (1856-1857). 12 pages from his sketch book.
Facsimile reprint. New York: F. A. R. Gallery, 1951;
as Sketches and Chronicles; the reflections of a 19th
century Pennsylvania German folk artist. York, Pa: Historical Society of York County, 1966. 183pp, ill, bib
(Color illustrations by Miller of the tools and processes of
scores of trades and crafts)

272 Mitchell, Cyril Maynard. Applied Science and Technology Before the Industrial Revolution. London: Museums Association, 1961. 69pp, 4 pls

273 Morison, Elting Elmore. From Know-how to Nowhere; the
development of American Technology. New York: Basic
Books, 1975. 199pp, bib

274 _____. Men, Machines and Modern Times. Cambridge,
Mass: M.I.T. Pr, 1966. 235pp

275 Moxon, Joseph, 1627-1700. Mechanik Exercises; or, the doc-
trine of handy-works applied to the arts of smithing, joinery,
carpentry, turning, brick-laying. 2 vol. in 1. London:
Author, 1677-83; 3rd ed. London: Daniel Midwinter &
Thomas Leigh, 1703;...; facsimile reprint. London: Blades,
East & Blades, 1901; reprint of 3rd ed. with introd., table
of contents, and captions by Benno M. Forman; Charles F.
Montgomery, ed. New York; London: Praeger, 1970.
234pp, ill, 18 pls

276 Mumford, Lewis, 1895- . Art and Technics. Lectures. London: Oxford U Pr; New York: Columbia U Pr, 1952. 162pp

277 _____. Technics and Civilization. New York: Harcourt,
Brace; London: G. Routledge, 1934; 1945; 1955; etc.
495pp, pls, bib

278 *Mumford, Lewis. The Myth of the Machine: Technics and
Human Development. New York: Harcourt, Brace &
World, 1966. 342pp, ill, bib

279 A New and Complete Dictionary of the Arts and Sciences;
     comprehending all the branches of useful knowledge ...
     illustrated with above 300 copper-plates, curiously engraved
     by Mr. Jefferys. By a Society of Gentlemen. 4 vol. Lon-
     don: W. Owen, 1754; 2nd ed. with additions and improve-
     ments. London: 1763. 3538pp, 302 pls; 3506pp, 302 pls
     BM

280 The New Complete Dictionary of Arts and Sciences; or, an uni-
     versal system of useful knowledge ... the medicinal, chemi-
     cal, and anatomical (branches) by William Turnbull ... the
     gardening and botanical, by Thomas Ellis ... the mathe-
     matical, etc. by John Davison.... London: Authors, 1778.
     80 pls

281 A New Royal and Universal Dictionary of Arts and Sciences:
     or, complete system of human knowledge ... embellished
     with upwards of 100 copper-plates ... The anatomical,
     chemical and medicinal parts by M. Hinde, M.D.   The
     Mathematical parts by W. Squire ... Gardening and Botany
     by J. Marshall.... 2 vol. London: J. Cooke, 1771-72.
     100 pls   BM

282 New York History. Cooperstown, NY: 19-?

283 New York School of Applied Design for Women. Library Cata-
     logue. New York: 1896. 31pp

284 Newark Museum. Art, Science, Technology History. Irregular
     periodical. Newark, NJ: 1910-1913.

285 Newcomen Society for the Study of the History of Engineering
     and Technology. Transactions. London: 1922-   .

286 Nicholson, Peter, 1765-1844. Mechanical Exercises; or, the
     elements and practice of carpentry, joinery, bricklaying,
     masonry, slating, plastering, painting, smithing, and turning.
     Containing a full description of the tools belonging to each
     branch of business; and copious directions for their use.
     London: J. Taylor, 1812. 396pp, ill, 39 pls   DLC, NNC-
     Ave

287 *   . The Mechanic's Companion. Or the elements and
     practice of carpentry, joinery, bricklaying, masonry, slating,
     plastering, painting, smithing and turning. Containing a full
     description of the tools belonging to each branch of business.
     (First published 1824?); Philadelphia: Locken, 1832; Phila-
     delphia: Bell, 1863. 1863: 362pp, 40 pls   DLC

288 Noel-Hume, Ivor. A Guide to the Artifacts of Colonial America.
     New York: Knopf, 1969. 323pp, ill, bib

289 Noyce, Elisha. The Boy's Book of Industrial Information.

London: Ward & Lock, 1863. 334pp, 370 ill (Juvenile literature) DLC

290 Okill, John. Internal Combustion Engines. A Review of the development and construction of various types. London: Pitman, 1922. 126pp, ill BM

291 Oklahoma, University of. Library. The E. De Golyer Collection in the History of Science and Technology; a check-list of the books and other materials. 2nd ed. Norman, Okla: 1953.

292 Oliver, John William, 1886- . History of American Technology. New York: Ronald Pr, 1956. 676pp

293 *Pannell, John Percival Masterman. An Illustrated History of Civil Engineering. London: Thames & Hudson, 1964. 376pp, ill, pls, bib

294 Papers on Manufactures, published by the Society of Arts, Manufactures, and Commerce. London: Royal Society, 1811-1825. 406pp, ill, pls

295 Perrigo, Charles Oscar Eugene, 1848- . Change Gear Devices, showing the development of the screw and cutting lathe and the methods of obtaining various pitches of threads. New York: Locomotive Publishing, 1903. 81pp, ill NN

296 *Pevsner, Nikolaus. An Enquiry into Industrial Art in England. Cambridge, Eng: U Pr, 1937. 234pp, ill NN

297 _____ . The Sources of Modern Architecture and Design. London: Thames & Hudson; New York: Praeger, 1968. 216pp, ill

298 _____ . Studies in Art, Architecture and Design. Vol. I. From Mannerism to Romanticism. Vol. II. Victorian and After. 2 vol. London: Thames & Hudson, 1968. 256pp, 267 ill; 288pp, 519, ill (1520-1968)

299 Phillipps, Lisle March. Art and Environment. New York: Holt, 1911; 1914; as The Works of Man. Introd. by Herbert Read. London: Duckworth, 1932; 3rd ed. 1950. 343pp, 26 ill, pls, bib (Chiefly architecture)

300 Pictorial Album of American Industry. Philadelphia: Asher & Adams, 1876.

301 Pilkington, James, fl. 1841. The Artist's and Mechanic's Repository, and working men's informant; embracing chemestry, abstracts of electricity, galvanism, magnetism, pneumatics, optics, and astronomy. Also, mechanical

exercises in iron, steel, lead, zinc, copper and tin, sol-
dering, with a description of the slide rule ... and a
variety of useful receipts. Philadelphia: Author, 1839;
2nd ed. New York: A. V. Blake, 1841; Portland, Ore:
Sanborn & Carter, 1853. 379pp; 490pp; 490pp; ill DLC

302 Plat (or Platt), Sir Hugh, 1552-1611? The Jewel House of
Art and Nature: containing divers rare and profitable inventions, together with sundry new experiments in the art
of husbandry, distillation, and moulding. 3 vol. in 1.
London: P. Short, printer, 1594; new ed. with "A Rare
and Excellent Discourse of Minerals, stones, gums, and
resins..." by D. B., gent. London: Bernard Alsop,
1653. 1653: 232pp, ill DLC, BM

303 Popular Mechanics. Monthly. Chicago: 1902-date.

304 Posselt, Emanuel Anthony, 1858- . Iconographic Encyclopedia of the Arts and Sciences. Philadelphia: Posselt;
London: Low, Marston, 18- .

305 Quennell, Marjorie, and Charles Henry Bourne Quennell. A
History of Everyday Things in England. 4 vol. London:
Batsford, 1918-1942; as A History of Everyday Things in
England Covering the Years 1066 to 1968. 5 vol. London:
1965-68. ill, pls

306 Quimby, Ian M. G., and Polly Anne Earl, ed. Technological
Innovations and the Decorative Arts. 1973 Winterthur
Conference Report. Charlottesville, Va: U Pr of Va,
1973. 373pp, ill, bib (Includes: "Reflections on Technology and the Decorative Arts in the 19th Century," by
Cyril Stanley Smith; "Agent of Change in Style and Form
of Domestic Iron Castings;" "Stylistic Change in Printed
Textiles;" "Craftsmen and Machines: the 19th Century
furniture industry;" etc.)

307 Rawson, Marion Nicholl. Candle Days. The story of early
American arts and implements. New York; London:
Century, 1927. 307pp, ill, pls (Tools, implements for
making furniture, rugs, glass) DLC

308 _____ . When Antiques Were Young; a story of early
American social customs. New York: Dutton, 1931. 271pp,
pls

309 *Read, Sir Herbert Edward, 1893- . Art and Industry: the
principles of industrial design. London: Faber, 1934;
1944; 3rd rev. ed. 1953; 4th ed. rev. 1956; 5th ed. 1966.
143pp; 188pp; 205pp; 212pp; all ill NN, DLC

310 Redmayne, Paul B. The Changing Shape of Things. London:

Murray, 1945; new ed. 1960.   48pp, ill; 56pp, ill   (Industrial art)

311 *Rees, Abraham.   The Cyclopedia; or, universal dictionary of
arts, sciences and literature.   5 vol.   London: Longmans,
1819; as (The Cyclopedia.)   Rees's Manufacturing Industry,
1819-1820:   a selection from 'The Cyclopedia; or, Universal
Dictionary of Arts...'.   Ed. by Neil Cossons.   Facsimile
reprint of extracts from 1st ed.   Newton Abbott: David &
Charles, 1972.   Vol. I.   457pp, inc. 12pp ill; II. 421pp,
inc. 26pp ill; III.   526pp, inc. 66pp ill; IV.   507pp, inc. 13pp
ill; V.   519pp, inc. 24pp ill.

312 Reeve, Joseph Rebekoff.   The Craftsman and the Machine:
from Stone Age to Machine Age.   London: U of London Pr,
1951.   192pp, ill

313 _____.   History Through Familiar Things.   London: U of
London Pr, 1935.   270pp, 118 ill, 8 color pls   (Juvenile
literature.   Part 1.   Food and Tools; 2.   Shelter and Society)

314 Rennie, George Banks, 1791-1866, ed.   Practical Examples of
Modern Tools and Machines, by Messrs. Maclea and March,
of Leeds; Messrs. Whitworth and Co., of Manchester, and
Messrs. Carmichael, of Dundee.   Being supplementary to
the edition of Buchanan on millwork and other machinery,
now just published.   London: J. Weale, 1842-52.   27pp,
atlas of 18 pls   BM, DLC

315 The Repertory of Arts and Manufactures Consisting of Original
Communications, specifications of patent inventions, and
selections of useful practical papers from the transactions
of the Philosophical Societies of all nations.   6 vol.   London:
Wilkie, Robinson, Elmsly, Debrett & Bell, 1794-97.   141
engraved pls

316 *The Repository of the Arts, literature, commerce, manufactures,
fashions and politics... (Title varies slightly).   Periodical.
40 vol.   London: Rudolph Ackermann, 1809-1828; Supplement.   1815.   ill, color pls, textile specimens   NNC-Ave

317 Richards, Charles Russell, 1865-1936.   Art in Industry, being
the report of an industrial art survey conducted under the
auspices of the National Society for Vocational Education,
and the Department of Education, of the State of New York.
New York: Macmillan, 1922; 1929.   499pp, ill, 13 color
pls (Textile design, metalwork, lighting, wallpaper, printing,
furniture, etc.   Includes: "The Museum and Industrial Art,"
by Henry W. Kent; "The Arts and Crafts Movement in the
United States," by C. Howard Walker; "The Relation of
Beauty to Fashion," by Frank Alvah Parsons; etc.)

318 Richards, Charles Russell. The Industrial Museum. New
       York: Macmillan, 1925. 117pp, pls

319 *Richardson, Albert Edward, 1880- . Georgian England; a
       survey of social life, trades, industries and art from 1700
       to 1820. London: Batsford, 1931; facsim, reprint. Free-
       port, NY: Books for Libraries, 1967. 202pp, ill

320 Ritchie-Calder, Peter Ritchie. The Evolution of the Machine.
       New York: American Heritage; Toronto: McClelland &
       Stewart, 1968. 160pp, ill

321 Roe, Joseph Wickham. English and American Tool Builders.
       New Haven: Yale U Pr, 1916; New York; London: Mc-
       Graw-Hill, 1926. 315pp, ill, pls, bib (Machine tools)

322 Rolt, Lionel Thomas Caswell. A Short History of Machine
       Tools. Cambridge, Mass: M.I.T. Pr, 1965; as Tools
       for the Job: a short history of machine tools. London:
       Batsford, 1965. 256pp, 103 ill

322a*Romaine, Laurence B. A Guide to American Trade Catalogs,
       1744-1900. Fore. by A. Hyatt Mayor. New York: R. R.
       Bowker, 1960. 422pp, bib (Covers many subjects from
       agricultural implements to weathervanes. By no means
       complete, but author hopes that many new titles will turn
       up)

323 Rosenthal, Rudolph, and Helena L. Ratzka. The Story of
       Modern Applied Art. New York: Harper, 1948. 208pp,
       ill, bib

324 Royal Society of Arts. Journal. London: 18- .

325 _____. Transactions. London: 1783-1845.

326 Royal Society of Edinburgh. Transactions. Edinburgh: 1811-

327 *Ruskin, John, 1819-1900. The Two Paths: being lectures on
       art, and its application to decoration and manufacture, de-
       livered in 1858-59. London: Smith, Elder; New York: J.
       Wiley, 1859; New York: 1866; 1876; new ed. Sunnyside,
       Kent, Eng: G. Allen, 1878;... 271pp; 217pp, ill, pls;...;
       232pp DeWint

328 Salaman, Raphael A. Tools of the Shipwright, 1650-1925. In
       Folk Life, Vol. 19. St. Fagan's Castle: 1967. 33pp, ill,
       4 pls, bib

329 Sargent Tools Company. 1925 catalog. Facsimile reprint.
       Lancaster, Pa: Roger Smith, 1975. 56pp

330 Scammell, Henry B., comp. Scammell's Universal Treasure-

House of Useful Knowledge. An encyclopedia of valuable receipts in the principal arts of life, including complete treatises on practical chemistry; ... disease; household and culinary art; agriculture and stock-raising; the mechanical arts.... n.p. (St. Louis, Mo?): Buckland Publishing, 1891. 1616pp, 3000 ill

331 *Schaefer, Herwin. The Roots of Modern Design: functional tradition in the 19th century. London: Studio Vista, 1970; as 19th Century Modern; the functional tradition in Victorian Design. New York: Praeger, 1970. 211pp, 289 ill, bib (1750-1900)

332 (H. U.) Schurhoff Company. Catalog ca.1842. Reprint. Newcastle, Del: Carpenters Tool Chest, 1972. 15 pls (German export catalog, no text. Tools--agricultural, hand)

333 Scientific American, the advocate of industry, and enterprise and journal of mechanical and other improvements. Weekly. New York: Munn & Co, 1845-1919; monthly. 1920-date. ill

334 Scientific American Supplement. Monthly. New York: Munn, 1876-1919.

335 Shelley, Charles Percy Bysshe, 1827-1890. Workshop Appliances Including Descriptions of the Gauging and Measuring Instruments, the hand cutting tools, lathes, drilling, planing, and other machine-tools used by engineers. London: Longmans, Green, 1873; 7th ed. rev. & enl. 1885; 11th ed. with chapter on milling by R. R. Lister. New York; London: Longmans, Green, 1912. 312pp, ill; 355pp, ill; 377pp, ill DLC, SKM

336 Simmonds, Peter Lund. A Dictionary of Trade Products, commercial, manufacturing, and technical terms,.... London: 1858. BM

337 *Singer, Charles Joseph, ed. A History of Technology. I. Early Times to Fall of Ancient Empires; II. The Mediterranean Civilizations and the Middle Ages, ca.700 B.C. to ca.1500 A.D.; III. Renaissance to Industrial Revolution, ca.1500 to ca.1750; IV. The Industrial Revolution, ca.1750 to ca.1850; V. The Late 19th Century, ca.1850 to ca.1900. 5 vol. Oxford, Eng: Clarendon Pr, 1954-58; reprint. 1965. ill, bib

338 Sloane, Eric. ABC of Early Americana; a sketchbook of antiquities and American firsts. Garden City, NY: Doubleday, 1963. 61pp, ill (Implements)

339 _____. A Museum of Early American Tools. New York: Funk, 1964. 108pp, 100 sketches

340   Smith, Elmer Lewis, and Melvin Horst. Early Tools and
      Equipment. Lebanon, Pa: Applied Arts, 1973. 32pp,
      chiefly ill

341   Smith, George, comp.   The Laboratory; or School of Arts:
      containing a large collection of valuable secrets, experi-
      ments, and manual operations in arts and manufactures,
      highly useful to gilders, jewellers, enamellers, goldsmiths,
      dyers, cutlers, pewterers, joiners, japanners, bookbinders....
      3rd ed. London: J. Hodges, 1750; 4th ed. 1755; 6th ed.
      2 vol. London: C. Whittingham, printer, 1799. 352pp,
      16 pls (Includes silversmithing, fireworks, etc.) DLC

342   Smith, James. The Mechanic; or, Compendium of Practical
      Inventions; containing 213 articles, selected and original ...
      I. Manufactures and trade, II. Philosophical apparatus and
      the fine arts, III. Rural and domestic economy, and mis-
      cellaneous.... (The Marquis of Worcester's 'Scantling of
      Inventions,' first published in 1655.) 2 vol. Liverpool:
      H. Fisher at Caxton Pr, 1816. pls DLC, BM

343   _____. The Panorama of Science and Art; embracing the
      sciences of aerostation, agriculture and gardening, archi-
      tecture, astronomy, chemistry ... the arts of building,
      brewing, bleaching ... the methods of working in wood and
      metal ... and a miscellaneous selection of interesting and
      useful processes and experiments. 2 vol. Liverpool:
      Nuttall, Fisher & Dixon, at Caxton Pr, 1815?; 9th ed.
      London: H. Fisher, 1823. pls BM, DLC

344   Smith, Joseph. Explanation, or Key, to the Various Manu-
      factories of Sheffield with Engravings of Each Article, de-
      signed for the utility of merchants, wholesale ironmongers,
      and travellers. Sheffield: H. A. Bacon, printer, 1816;
      reprint. South Burlington, Vt: Early American Industries
      Association, 1975. 1975: 162pp, 1000 ill on 130 pls
      (Part 1. Tools for carpenters, joiners, coopers, curriers,
      farmers; 2. Cutlery trade; III. Surgical and dental instru-
      ments) DeWint

345   Smith, Robert Henry. Cutting Tools Worked by Hand and
      Machine. London: Cassell, 1882. 224pp, pls

346   Smith, Robert Henry Soden. A List of Books and Pamphlets
      in the National Art Library ... on construction, engineering,
      and machinery. South Kensington Museum. London: HMSO,
      1889. 68pp

347   Smith, Susan. Made in America. New York: Knopf, 1929;
      reprint. Detroit: Singing Tree Pr, 1971. 91pp, ill

348   _____. Made in England. New York: T. Nelson, 1932.
      88pp, ill, pls

349 _____. Made in France. New York: Knopf, 1931. 80pp,
      ill, pls

350 _____. Made in Germany and Austria. New York: Minton,
      Balch, 1933. 75pp, ill, pls

351 _____. Made in Mexico. New York: Knopf, 1930. 81pp,
      ill, pls

352 _____. Made in Sweden. New York: Minton, Balch, 1934.
      74pp, ill, pls

353 Smithsonian Institution. Annual Report. Washington, D.C.:
      1847-date. ill

354 Soulard, Robert. A History of the Machine. Adapted from
      French. New York: Hawthorn, 1963. 105pp, ill (part
      color)

355 The Steam Engine Familiarly Described, with a brief account
      of its history and uses. London: 1839? BM

356 Steeds, William. A History of Machine Tools, 1700-1910.
      Oxford, Eng: Clarendon Pr, 1969. 181pp, 51 ill, 153 pls

357 Sturgis, Russell. The Interdependence of the Arts of Design;
      a series of six lectures delivered at the Art Institute of
      Chicago. I., II. Modern judged by ancient art ... III. The
      industrial arts in which form predominates, IV. The indus-
      trial arts in which color predominates, V., VI. Sculpture,
      painting in architecture. Chicago: A. C. McClurg, 1905.
      227pp, 100 pls

358 Subject List of Works on Art and Art Industries. London:
      Patent Office, 1903. 374pp

359 Surrey, Dane E. Peter Stubs and the Lancashire Hand Tool
      Industry. Altrincham, Eng: John Sherratt, 1973. 291pp,
      21 ill (18th and 19th century English tools)

360 Taylor, Alfred, 1831-1899. A Set of Tools. New York:
      Phillips & Hunt; Cincinnati: Walden & Stowe, 1883. 12pp

361 Taylor, Frank A. Catalogue of the Mechanical Collections of
      the Division of Engineering, United States National Museum
      (Smithsonian). Washington, D.C.: GPO, 1939. 203pp,
      pls, bib

362 Taylor, Frank Sherwood. The Century of Science. London:
      Heinemann, 1941; 3rd ed. 1952; 1956. 277pp, ill, 12 pls
      (Industrial arts)

363 Technologist. A monthly record of science applied to art,
      manufacture, and culture. London: 1860-1867.

364 *Technology and Culture. Monthly. Chicago: U of Chicago
      Pr, 1959-date. ill

365 *Tomlinson, Charles, 1808-1897, ed. Cyclopedia of Useful
      Arts, mechanical and chemical, manufactures, mining, and
      engineering ... with an introductory essay on the Great
      Exhibition of the Works of Industry of All Nations, 1851.
      2 vol. London; New York: G. Virtue, 1854. ill, pls

366 _____ . Illustrations of the Useful Arts. 4 parts. London:
      A. & J. Myers, 1855-1864. BM

367 *   . Illustrations of Trades. London: S.P.C.K.,
      1860; 1867; reprint of 1st ed. Ambridge, Pa: Early Ameri-
      can Industries Association, 1975. 106pp, 48pp of ill with
      500 separate figures (Descriptions of 36 trades, divided
      into categories--food production; shelter [bricklayer, car-
      penter, slater, paper hanger]; clothing; furniture [cabinet
      maker, upholsterer, goldsmith, tinsmith]; locomotion; edu-
      cation; cooper; and soap boiler. Many tools.)

368 _____ . Illustrations of Useful Arts and Manufactures. ? vol.
      London: G. Virtue, 1859. hundreds of pls

369 _____ . The Useful Arts and Manufactures of Great Britain.
      1st and 2nd series. London: Christian Knowledge Society,
      1861. BM

369a Tool Collector's Picture Book Series. 8 vol. Levittown, NY:
      Early Trades and Crafts Society, 197-? - .

370 The Tool Collector's Picture Book. Levittown: 197-?

371 The Second Tool Collector's Picture Book. Levittown: 197-?

372 The Third Tool Collector's Picture Book: hammer king of
      tools. Levittown: 1974. 15pp, ill

373 Axes: fourth tool collector's picture book. Levittown: 1974.
      16pp, ill

374 The Fifth Tool Collector's Picture Book. Levittown: 1974.
      19pp, ill

375 The Sixth Tool Collector's Picture Book. Levittown: 1974.
      17pp, ill

376 The Seventh Tool Collector's Picture Book. Levittown: 1975.
      16pp of ill

377 Eighth Tool Collector's Book. Levittown: 1975. ill (Logging,
      coppersmithing, blacksmithing)

378 Tools, Their Use and Abuse. Periodical. London: 1914- .

379 Train, Arthur Kissam, Jr. The Story of Everyday Things.
      New York; London: Harper, 1941. 428pp, ill, pls, bib
      NNC-Ave

380 Transactions of the Society Instituted at London for the En-
      couragement of Arts, Manufactures, and Commerce.
      Periodical. London: 18-?- .

381 Tunis, Edwin. Colonial Craftsmen; and the beginnings of
      American industry. Cleveland, O: World, 1965. 159pp,
      ill, 450 drawings

382 United States Bureau of the Census. Census of Manufactures:....
      Washington, D.C.: GPO, 1905; 1914; 1921; 1923; 1925;
      1927; 1931; etc. (Every subject imaginable)

383 United States Library of Congress. Division of Bibliography.
      List of References on Art Industries and Trade. Select
      list no. 552. Washington, D.C.: 1921. 9pp typescript
      NN

384 United States National Museum. Annual Report. Washington,
      D.C.: 1883-1926. (Smithsonian Institution)

385 _____. Bulletin. 1875- .

386 _____. Proceedings. 1879- .

387 Urbino, Levina Buoncuore (Mrs. S. R.), and Henry Day. Art
      Recreations: being a complete guide to pencil drawing, oil
      paintings ... moss work, papier mache ... waxwork, shell
      work ... enamel painting, etc. With valuable receipts for
      preparing materials. Splendidly illustrated. Boston: J. E.
      Tilton, 1860; ed. by Marion Kemble. 1884. 331pp, ill;
      442pp, ill, 4 color pls

388 *Ure, Andrew, 1778-1857. Dictionary of the Arts, Manufactures
      and Mines: containing a clear exposition of their principles
      and practice. London: Longman, Orme, Brown, etc.,
      1839; from 2nd London ed. New York: D. Appleton, 1842;
      11th American from last London ed. "to which is appended,
      a supplement of recent improvements to the present time."
      New York; Philadelphia: Appleton, 1848; 4th ed. corrected
      & enl. 2 vol. London: Longman, 1853; 5th ed. ed. by
      Robert Hunt. 3 vol. London: 1860;... 1334pp, 1240 ill;
      ...; 1346pp, 304pp, 1500 ill;...

389 Wagoner, Harless D. The United States Machine Tool Industry

from 1900-1950. Cambridge, Mass: M.I.T. Pr, 1968.
421pp, ill

390 Wallance, Don. Shaping America's Products. New York:
Reinhold, 1956. 193pp, ill, bib

391 Wallis, Whitworth, and Arthur Bensley Chamberlain, comp.
Illustrated Handbook to the Permanent Collections of Industrial Art Objects. Birmingham Museum and Art Gallery.
Birmingham, Eng: 1895. 244pp, ill, bib (Stonework,
decorative ironwork, jewellery, Della Robbia Ware, glass,
lacquerwork, arms and armor, etc.)

392 Ward, Henry Snowden, ed. Useful Arts and Handicrafts.
4 vol. London: Dawbarn & Ward, 1900, 1901. ill BM

393 Ward, James. The World in Its Workshops; a practical ex-
amination of British and Foreign processes of manufacture,
with a critical comparison of the fabrics, machinery, and
works of art contained in the Great Exhibition. London:
W. S. Orr, 1851. 284pp

394 Webster, Thomas. Encyclopedia of Domestic Economy. London: 1844; New York: 1845. BM

395 Weiss, Harry Bischoff, and Grace M. Weiss. Forgotten Mills
of Early New Jersey: oil, plaster, bark, indigo, fanning,
tilt, rolling and slitting mills, nail and screw making.
Trenton: New Jersey Agriculture Society, 1960. 94pp, ill

396 _____, and _____. Trades and Tradesmen of Colonial
New Jersey. Trenton: Past Times Pr, 1965. 143pp, ill,
bib

397 Westcott, Gerald Francis. Handbook of the Collections Illustrating Pumping Machinery. Science Museum. Part 1.
London: HMSO, 1932- . pls NN, DLC

398 White, John, a lover of artificial conclusions, d.1671. Arts
Treasury of Rarities and Curious Inventions ... Part I.
Containing the mystery of dyeing cloth, silk, stuffs ... to
prepare and colour skins of leather ... to dye bristles,
hair ... The art of drawing, limning, painting in oil ...
Part II. Containing the generation of metals ... To cleanse
and perfume gloves ... with divers other curiosities. 5th
ed. London: for C. Conyers, 16-? 84pp DLC

399 _____. Art's Treasury; or a profitable ... invitation to the
lovers of ingenuity; contained in many extraordinary experiments, rarities and curious inventions. London: 1688;
6th ed. 1773. BM

400 _____. A Rich Cabinet, with Variety of Inventions: unlock'd

and open'd, for the recreation of ingenious spirits ... being
receipts and conceits of several natures ... As also variety
of recreative fireworks ... Whereunto is added divers experiments in drawing, painting, arithmetick, ... likewise directions for ringing the most usual peals....   5th ed.
London: for W. Whitwood, 1677. 190, 41pp, ill DLC

401   Whittock, Nathaniel, J. Bennett, and others. The Complete
Book of Trades, or the parents' guide and youths' instructor;
forming a popular encyclopedia of trades, manufactures, and
commerce, as at present pursued in England. London: J.
Bennett, 1837. 495pp, ill, pls

402   Williams, Archibald. The Romance of Modern Mechanism;
with interesting descriptions ... of wonderful machinery
and mechanical devices and marvelously delicate scientific
instruments, etc. Philadelphia: Lippincott, 1906; reprint
of 1st eight chapters as The Wonders of Mechanical Ingenuity. Philadelphia: Lippincott; London: Seeley, 1910.
355pp, 30 ill, 24 pls; 160pp, 8 pls DLC

403 *Willich, Anthony Florian Madinger. The Domestic Encyclopedia, or, a dictionary of facts and useful knowledge, comprehending a concise view of the latest discoveries, inventions, and improvements chiefly applicable to rural and
domestic economy. 5 vol. Philadelphia: W. Y. Brick,
and A. Small, 1803-1804; 3 vol. with additions by Dr.
Thomas Cooper. Philadelphia: A. Small, 1821. ill, pls

404   Willms, Auguste. Industrial Art. Birmingham, Eng: Cornish
Brothers, 1890. 16pp

405   Wilson, Aubrey. London's Industrial Heritage. Newton Abbot: David & Charles, 1967; New York: A. M. Kelley,
1968. 160pp, ill, bib

406   Wolf, Abraham, 1876- , and others. A History of Science,
technology and philosophy in the 18th century. London:
Allen & Unwin; New York: Macmillan, 1939; 2 vol. New
York: Harper & Row, 1961. 814pp, 345 ill, pls, bib

407 *_____, and others. A History of Science, technology, and
philosophy in the 16th and 17th centuries. London: G.
Allen & Unwin, 1935; 2nd ed. rev. by Douglas McKie.
London: 1950; 2 vol. New York: Harper, 1959. 692pp,
ill, pls, bib; 814pp, ill, pls, bib

408   Wood, Sir Henry. Trueman Wright, 1845-1929. A history
of the Royal Society of Arts. Pref. by Lord Sanderson.
London: J. Murray, 1913; abridged and updated, by G.
K. Menzies. London: 1935. 558pp, ill, pls; 81pp, ill,
pls

409 Woodbury, Robert S. History of the Gear-Cutting Machine.
     A historical study in geometry and machines. Cambridge,
     Mass: The Technology Press, M.I.T. 1958; 1964. 135pp,
     pls, bib

410 _____. History of the Grinding Machine; a historical study
     in tools and precision production. Cambridge, Mass:
     M.I.T., 1959; 1964. 191pp, ill, bib

411 _____. History of the Lathe to 1850. Cambridge, Mass:
     M.I.T., 1961.

412 _____. History of the Milling Machine; a study in technical
     development. Cambridge, Mass: M.I.T., 1960; 1964.
     107pp, ill, bib

413 *_____. Studies in the History of Machine Tools. 4 parts
     in 1 vol. Cambridge, Mass; London: M.I.T. Pr, 1972.
     588pp, ill, bib (See preceding titles, nos. 409-12)

414 Woodworth, Joseph Vincent. American Tool Making and Inter-
     changeable Manufacturing. London; New York: E. & F.
     N. Spon, 1905; London: Page, 1921. 535pp, 600 ill

415 Work; a weekly journal for amateur mechanics. 67 vol. Lon-
     don: Cassell, 1889-1924. (See P. N. Hasluck)

416 The Workshop; a monthly journal devoted to the progress of
     the useful arts. New York: E. Steiger, 1869-1884. ill
     (American edition of German Die Gewerbehalle)

417 Wullweber, Marvin. Northern Plains Antique Wrenches and
     Tools: collectors guide with pictures and prices. Virgil,
     South Dakota: Author, 1975. 88pp, ill

418 Wyatt, Sir Matthew Digby, 1820-1877. Fine Art: a sketch of
     its history, theory, practice, and application to industry;...
     a course of lectures ... at Cambridge. London; New York:
     Macmillan, 1870; 1877. 375pp

INTERNATIONAL EXHIBITIONS OF
THE APPLIED AND USEFUL ARTS

419 Alcock, Sir Rutherford. International Exhibition, 1862. Cata-
     logue of Works of Industry and Art, sent from Japan....
     London: W. Clowes, 1862. 12pp DLC

420 The Art Journal Catalogue of the International Exhibition.
     London, 1871. London: 1871; 2nd division. London: 1872.
     88pp; 64pp

421 The Art Journal. Contributions to the International Exhibition

at Philadelphia, 1876.   Reprinted from "The Art Journal."
London: Virtue, 1876.   54pp, 126 engravings, color frontis

422 _____.   The Exhibition of Art-Industry in Dublin.   London:
Virtue, 1853.   64pp, ill

423 _____.   The Exhibition of Art-Industry in Paris, 1855.
London: Virtue, 1855.   46pp, ill

424 *The Art Journal Illustrated Catalogue of the Industry of All
Nations, 1851: a catalogue of the Great Exhibition.   Special
Issue.   London: George Virtue, 1851; reprint.   New York:
Dover; New York: Bounty, Crown, 1970.   328, 62pp, 1500
ill   (Crystal Palace.   Sometimes bound with many pages of
special essays on textiles, ornamental art, etc.)

425 The Art Journal Illustrated Catalogue of the International Exhibition, 1862.   London; New York: J. S. Virtue, 1862.
324pp, hundreds of wood-engravings

426 The Art Journal Illustrated Catalogue of the Paris International
Exhibition, 1878.   London: Virtue, 1878.   212pp, ill

427 The Art Journal Illustrated Catalogue of the Universal Exhibition of 1867 (Paris).   Ed. by S. C. Hall.   London; New
York: Virtue, 1868.   331pp, ill with hundreds of wood-
engravings   (Furniture; glass; textiles, goldsmiths' work;
porcelain; lace (by Mrs. Bury Palliser), etc.)

428 Blake, William Phipps, ed.   Reports of the United States Com-
missioners to the Paris Universal Exposition, 1867.   6 vol.
Washington, D.C.:   GPO, 1870.   ill, pls, plans, etc.
(Fine arts; fine arts applied to useful arts; weights, measures; iron and steel; precious metals; machinery and processes of industrial arts; scientific apparatus; telegraphy;
building materials; preparation of food; photography; munitions of war; medical and surgical instruments; musical
instruments; textiles; clothing; etc.)   DeWint, BM

429 Braund, John.   Illustrations of Furniture, Candelabra, Musical Instruments, etc., from the great exhibitions of London
and Paris, with examples of similar articles from royal
palaces and noble mansions.   London: J. Braund, 1858.
(6)pp, ill, 48 pls   MiGr, DLC, NNC-Ave

430 Breuer, Robert.   German Arts and Crafts at the Brussels
Exhibition, 1910.   Stuttgart: Julius Hoffman, 1910.   4pp,
140 pls (some color)   (Chiefly interiors and furniture)

431 Catalogue of the Spanish Productions Sent to the Great Exhibition of the Works of Industry of All Nations of 1851.
London: 1851.   BM

432 Chitty, Edward. Descriptive Catalogue of Articles Exhibited
     by the Royal Society of Arts, Jamaica ... at the Interna-
     tional Exhibition, 1862. London: 1862. 18pp

433 The Crystal Palace and Its Contents. An Encyclopedia of the
     Great Exhibition of Works of Industry ... 1851. First is-
     sued in weekly parts, October 4, 1851-March 27, 1852.
     London: W. M. Clark, 1852. 134pp, over 500 engravings
     IU, TxU, BM

434 Crystal Palace Exhibition; complete illustrated catalogue.
     London: Art Journal, 1851; reprint, with new introd. by
     John Gloag. New York: Dover, 1970. 328pp, 62 pls,
     1500 specimens ill'd

435 Dowleans, A. M., comp. Official, classified, and descriptive
     catalogue of the contributions from India to the London Ex-
     hibition of 1862. Calcutta: Savielle & Cranenburgh, 1862.
     ix, 170, 6, 87, 31pp DLC

436 Elliott, Maud Howe, 1854-1948, ed. Art and Handicraft in the
     Woman's Building of the World's Columbian Exposition,
     Chicago, 1893. Paris; New York: Boussod, Valadon, 1893;
     Chicago; New York: Rand, McNally, 1894. 287pp, ill;
     320pp, ill DLC

437 Ellis, Robert, ed. Great Exhibitions of the Works of Industry
     of All Nations of 1851. Official Descriptive and illustrated
     catalogue. Introd. by Sir H. Cole. 3 vol. plus supple-
     mentary vol. London: 1851; new ed. in 5 vol. 1851; 4th
     corrected ed. by G. W. Yapp. London: 1851. ill BM

438 Ferris, George Titus. Gems of the Centennial Exhibition:
     consisting of illustrated descriptions of objects of an artistic
     character, in the exhibits of the United States, Great Britain,
     France, Spain, Italy, Germany, Belgium, Norway, Sweden,
     Denmark, Hungary, Russia, Japan, China, Egypt, Turkey,
     India, etc., etc., at the Philadelphia International Exhibition
     of 1876. New York: D. Appleton, 1877. 164pp, ill NN,
     DeWint

439 Ffrench, Yvonne. The Great Exhibition, 1851. London: Har-
     vill, 1950. 297pp, ill, bib

440 Frank Leslie's Illustrated Historical Register of the Centennial
     Exposition, 1876. New York: Frank Leslie's Newspaper,
     1876. 320pp of woodcut ill, color title (See also: Norton,
     F. H. no. 448)

441 Gibbs-Smith, Charles Harward. The Great Exhibition of 1851:
     a commemorative album. V & A Museum. London: HMSO,
     1950. 143pp, ill, bib

442 Greeley, Horace, 1811-1872, ed. Art and Industry as Repre-
      sented in the Exhibition at the Crystal Palace, N.Y. --
      1853-4; showing the progress and state of the various use-
      ful and esthetic pursuits. From the New York Tribune.
      New York: Redfield, 1853. 386pp DLC, PPL

443 Handy-book to the International Exhibition, 1862: its history,
      structure, and statistics. A guide to the objects most
      worthy of notice, etc. London: J. S. Hodson, 1862. 61pp

444 Hollingshead, John. The Official Illustrated Guide, to the
      Crystal Palace, and Park, containing a full description of
      all the art, industrial, natural and scientific exhibitions.
      London: R. K. Burt, 1866. 96pp, ill NN

445 Illustrated Record of the Industry of All Nations. New York
      Exhibition, 1853. New York: Putnam, 1853. ill

446 Jones, Owen, 1809-1874. Gleanings from the Great Exhibition
      of 1851: on the distribution of form and colour developed
      in the articles exhibited in the Indian, Egyptian, Turkish,
      and Tunisian departments. Reprint from "Journal of Design,"
      June 1851. London: Strangeways & Walden, 1863. 15pp
      DLC

447 Maass, John. The Glorious Enterprise. The Centennial Exhi-
      bition of 1876 in Philadelphia. Watkins Glen: Century
      House, American Life Foundation and Study Institute, 1973.
      ill

448 Norton, Frank Henry, 1836-1921. Illustrated Historical Regis-
      ter of the Centennial Exhibition, Philadelphia, 1876, and of
      the Exposition Universelle, Paris, 1878. New York:
      American News Company, 1879. 396pp, 800 wood-engravings,
      25 color lithographs (Printed without plates as Frank Leslie's
      Historical Register ...) DLC

449 Pevsner, Nikolaus. High Victorian Design: a study of the
      Exhibits of 1851. London: Architectural Pr, 1951. 162pp,
      ill

450 Smith, Walter, 1836-1886. Examples of Household Taste.
      The Industrial Art of the International Exhibition, 1876.
      New York: R. Worthington, 1880. 521pp, ill

451 * _____. Masterpieces of the Centennial International Exhibi-
      tion (1876): Vol. 2. Industrial Art. Philadelphia: Gobbie
      & Barrie, 1876. ill

452 Tallis, John, 1815 or 16-1876. Tallis's History and Descrip-
      tion of the Crystal Palace, and the Exhibition of the World's
      Industry in 1851; illustrated by 143 beautiful steel engravings

from original drawings and daguerreotypes, by Beard, Mayall, etc. 6 vol. London; New York: J. Tallis, (1852).
640pp, 143 pls

453 Timbs, John, 1801-1875. The Industry, Science and Art of
the Age: or, The International Exhibition of 1862 popularly
described from its origin to its close; including details of
the principal objects and articles exhibited. London: Lockwood, 1863. 354pp, 1 pl

454 Trailokyanatha Mukhopadhyaya. Art-Manufactures of India.
Compiled for the Glasgow International Exhibition, 1888.
Calcutta: Superintendent of Government Printing, 1888.
451pp DLC

455 United States Commission to the Paris Exposition, 1878. Reports. Washington, D.C.: GPO, 1880. (Includes "clocks
and watches," and "agricultural implements," by E. H.
Knight.)

456 *Waring, John Burley. Masterpieces of Industrial Art and
Sculpture at the International Exhibition, 1862. In English
and French. 3 vol. London: Day & Son, 1863. 301
chromolithographic pls from photos by Stephen Thompson.
("Ambitious Victorian color plate publication. A landmark
in the depiction of the decorative, ornamental, and industrial arts." Swann Gallery, N.Y.) MiGr

457 Whitworth, Sir Joseph, 1803-1887. The Industry of the
United States in Machinery, Manufactures, and Useful and
Ornamental Arts. Compiled from the official reports of
Messrs. Whitworth and (George) Wallis. London; New
York: Routledge, 1854. 172pp (N.Y. Industrial Exhibition
of the Industry of All Nations, 1853-54)

458 *Wyatt, Sir Matthew Digby. The Industrial Arts of the 19th
Century. A series of illustrations of the choicest speci-
mens produced by every nation at the Great Exhibition of
Works of Industry, 1851. 2 vol. in 3. London: Day &
Son, 1851-53. 158 pls (part color)

459 _____. On the Arts of Decoration at the International Exhibition at Paris, A.D. 1867. 4 parts. London: 1868.

INDUSTRIAL ARCHAEOLOGY

460 Ashmore, Owen. The Industrial Archaeology of Lancashire.
Newton Abbot: David & Charles, 1969. 352pp, ill, bib

461 Booker, Frank. The Industrial Archaeology of the Tamar
Valley. Newton Abbot: David & Charles, 1967. 303pp,
ill, bib

462 Bracegirdle, Brian, and others. The Archaeology of the Indus-
     trial Revolution. London: Heinemann; Rutherford, NJ:
     Fairleigh Dickinson U Pr, 1973. 207pp, ill, 48 pls, bib
     (British)

463 Buchanan, Robert Angus, and Neil Cossons. The Industrial
     Archaeology of the Bristol Region. Newton Abbot: David
     & Charles, 1969. 335pp, ill, bib

464 Harris, Helen. The Industrial Archaeology of Dartmoor.
     Newton Abbot: David & Charles, 1968. 239pp, ill, bib

465 Hudson, Kenneth. Guide to the Industrial Archaeology of
     Europe. Bath, Eng: Adams & Dart, 1971. 186pp, pls

466 *   . Handbook for Industrial Archaeologists: a guide to
     fieldwork and research. London: Baker, 1967. 84pp,
     ill, 4 pls, bib

467 *   . Industrial Archaeology: an introduction. London:
     Baker, 1963; Philadelphia: Dufour, 1964; 2nd ed. rev.
     London: Methuen, 1966. 184pp, 32 pls, bib

468   . The Industrial Archaeology of Southern England;
     Hampshire, Wiltshire, Dorset, Somerset, and Gloucester-
     shire East of the Severn. Dawlish: David & Charles,
     1965. 218pp, ill

469 *   , and Neil Cossons, ed. Industrial Archaeologists'
     Guide. Periodical. Newton Abbot: David & Charles,
     1969/70- .

470 Industrial Archaeology. Quarterly. Newton Abbot: David &
     Charles, 1964-1966; Annual. 1966- .

471 Marshall, John Duncan, and Michael Davies-Shiel. The Indus-
     trial Archaeology of the Lake Counties. Newton Abbot:
     David & Charles, 1969. 287pp, ill, bib

472 Minchinton, Walter E. Industrial Archaeology in Devon.
     Exeter, Eng: Devon County Council, 1968? 32pp, ill

473 Nixon, Frank. The Industrial Archaeology of Derbyshire.
     Newton Abbot: David & Charles, 1969. 307pp, ill, bib

474 Noel-Hume, Ivor. Historical Archaeology. New York: Knopf,
     1969. ill

475 Rix, Michael. Industrial Archaeology. London: Historical
     Association, 1967. 25pp, ill, 4 pls, bib

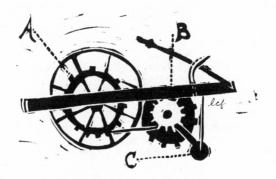

INVENTIONS AND PATENTS

476   An account of the Destruction by Fire of the North and West
      Halls of the Model Room in the United States Patent Office
      Building, on the 24th of September, 1877.   Together with a
      history of the Patent Office from 1790-1877.   Washington,
      D.C.:   1877.   38pp, ill, pls

477   Bakewell, Frederick Collier. Great Facts. A popular history
      and description of the most remarkable inventions during
      the present century. London: Houlston & Wright, 1859.
      304pp

478   Bartlett, Wallace A. Digest of Trademarks (registered in the
      United States for machinery, metals, jewelry, and the hard-
      ware and allied trades).... Washington, D.C.: Gibson
      Brothers, printer, 1893. 176pp, ill DeWint

479 *Beckmann, Johann, 1739-1811. Concise History of Ancient In-
      stitutions, Inventions and Discoveries in Science and Me-
      chanic Art. (Title varies.) Tr. from German (1783-1805)
      by William Johnston. 3 vol. London: J. Bell, 1797; 2nd
      ed., corrected and enl. with 4th vol. London: for J.
      Walker, 1814; 3rd corrected and enl. ed. London: for
      Longman, Hurst, Rees, Orme, and Brown, 1817; abridged
      in 2 vol. London: G. & W. B. Whittaker, 1823; 4th ed.
      enl. by William Francis and J. W. Griffith. 2 vol. Lon-
      don: H. G. Bohn, 1846; reprint. 2 vol. London: G. Bell,
      1877; 1883; 1884; 1892. I- 488pp; II- 443pp; III- 491pp;
      IV- 682pp; 1846 ed.: I. 518pp; II. 548pp ill DeWint,
      ViU, CtY, NN, MH

480 *Besterman, Theodore. Technology, including patents. A
      bibliography of bibliographies. 2 vol. 1939; 1947; 1965;
      Totowa, NJ: Rowman & Littlefield, 1971. 681pp

481   Brown, J. J. Ideas in Exile: a history of Canadian

Invention. Toronto: McClelland & Stewart, 1967. 372pp,
ill, bib

482 Butterworth, Benjamin, comp. The Growth of Industrial Art.
2 vol. Washington, D.C.: GPO, 1884; 1 vol. 1888; reproduced. 1 vol. 1892; reprint with new introd. by Mark
Kramer. New York: Knopf, 1972. each vol has 3pp plus
100 pls of primitive methods and modern patents. (Butterworth was Commissioner of Patents)

483 Carter, Ernest Frank. Dictionary of Inventions and Discoveries.
London: F. Muller, 1966; rev. ed. 1969. 193pp; 204pp
(20,000 references earliest times to present)

484 Catalogue of the Machines, Models, etc. in the Patent Museum,
South Kensington. London: HMSO, 1863. SIB-3

485 *Cochrane, Robert, comp. Romance of Industry and Invention.
London; Edinburgh: W. & R. Chambers; Philadelphia:
Lippincott, 1896; London; Philadelphia: 1897. 295pp, ill
DLC, NN, PPULC

486 Cowper, Edward Alfred. Catalogue of Machinery, Models,
etc., in the South Kensington Museum. London: Eyre &
Spottiswood, 1890; 2 parts. London: 1894-97; Part 1.,
2nd ed. London: 1896; 3rd rev. ed. as Catalogue of the
Mechanical Engineering Collection in the Science Division
of the Victoria and Albert, with descriptive and historical
notes. London: 1901- ; 4th ed. with supplement containing illustrations. 2 parts. London: 1907, 1908.
1890: 214pp; 1896: 203pp

487 Daumas, Maurice, ed. A History of Technology and Invention.
Tr. by Eileen B. Hennessy. Vol. I. The Origins of Technological Civilization; Vol. II. The First Stages of Mechanization. 2 vol, 4 planned. New York: Crown, 1969, 1970.
596pp, ill; 694pp, ill

488 De Bono, Edward, ed. Eureka! An illustrated history of inventions from the wheel to the computer. New York: Holt,
Rinehart, Winston, 1974. 248pp, ill (Transportation, communication, energy, food, medicine, work, warfare)

489 Dodd, George. Novelties, Inventions, and Curiosities in Arts
and Manufactures. 6th ed. London: Routledge, Warne &
Routledge, 1860. 267pp BM

490 Eco, Umberto, and G. B. Zorzoli. A Pictorial History of
Inventions. New York: Macmillan, 1963. ill

491 Ferguson, John, 1837-1916. Bibliographical Notes on the
Histories of Inventions and Books of Secrets. 2 vol.

Glasgow: U Pr, 1883; with supplement. Glasgow: 1895;
1916; reprint. London: Holland Pr, 1959; West Orange,
NJ: Saifer, 19-? 62pp;...; 79pp, ill NN

492 Fuller, Edmund M. Tinkers and Genius, the story of the
Yankee inventors. New York: Hastings House, 1955.
308pp, ill, bib

493 Glover, Alan Gordon, ed. The Story of Discovery and Invention; how the wonders of the modern world came into being.
London: Modern World Pr, 1935. 568pp, ill, pls

494 Grant, George. A Historical Account of Useful Inventions
and Scientific Discoveries: being a manual of instructions
and entertainment. Dublin: J. M'Glashan, 1849; London:
Partridge & Oakey, 1852. 320pp, frontis; 215pp, frontis
ViU, NB

495 Great Britain. Patent Office. Patents for Inventions.
Abridgements of Specifications relating to ... Artists' Instruments and Materials. 1855/66, -1897/1900. London:
HMSO, 1893-1905; Coin-freed Apparatus.... 1855/56, -
1897/1900. London: 1893-1905; Cooling and Ice-Making....
1855/66, -1905/1908. London: 1905-11; Lace-Making,
knitting, netting, braiding, and plaiting, 1877-83. London:
1893; Sewing and Embroidering. 1855-1866. London:
1905; Books, portfolios, cardcases, etc. 1768-1866. London: 1870; Lamps, candlesticks, chandeliers, and other
illuminating apparatus; excluding ... gas or electricity.
1637-1866. London: 1871; Optical, mathematical, and
other philosophical instruments.... 1636-1866. London:
1875; Toys, games, and exercises. 1672-1866. London:
1871; Pottery. London: 1863; Furniture and Upholstery,
A.D. 1620-1866. London: 1869; Weaving. London: 1861;
etc. (Small-arms; glass; railway signals; electricity, musical instruments; photography; printing; wearing apparel;
etc.) BM

496 Hanson, John Wesley, 1828-1901. Wonders of the 19th Century;
a panoramic review of the inventions and discoveries of the
past 100 years. Chicago: W. B. Conkey, 1900. 641pp,
ill, pl DeWint

497a Hill, Henry Chase, comp., ed. The Wonder Book of Knowledge; the marvels of modern industry and invention, the
interesting stories of common things, the mysterious processes of nature simply explained. By Experts. Philadelphia: J. C. Winston; New York: American Industries
Bureau, 1917; 1919; 1926; ed. and rev. by Will H. Johnston,
as The New Wonder Book.... Philadelphia; Chicago, etc:
J. C. Winston, 1929; 1944. 608pp, 780 ill, color frontis;
1944: 600pp, 700 ill, color frontis ViU, NN

497b Hooper, Meredith. Everyday Inventions. New York: Tap-
       linger, 1976. ill (Juvenile literature. Zippers, safety
       razors, locks and keys, vacuum cleaners, etc.)

498   Hugo, E. Harold, and Thompson R. Harlow. Abel Buell, a
       Jack of All Trades, and Genius Extraordinary: his life and
       trials. Illustrated by some of his works. Meridan, Conn:
       The Columbiad Club, 1953. 7pp, pls

499   Hylander, C. J. American Inventors. New York: Macmillan,
       1934; 22nd printing. 1967. 216pp, ill, pls

500   Invention and Industry. Vol. II of Our Wonderful World.
       Chicago: Shuman, 1914; 2nd ed. 1936. 398pp, ill, pls
       (some color) MB

501   The Inventor. Monthly. New York: Low, Haskell, 1855-57.

502   Johnson, Walter Rogers, 1794-1852. A Lecture on the Me-
       chanical Industry and the Inventive Genius of America.
       Delivered ... Maryland Institute for Promoting the Mechanic
       Arts, Baltimore. Baltimore: Sands & Mills, 1849. 23pp
       DLC

503   Kaempffert, Waldemar Bernhard. A Popular History of
       American Invention. 2 vol. New York; London: Scrib-
       ner's, 1924. 500 ill, pls (I. Transportation, communica-
       tion, power; II. Material and Labor-saving Machines)

504   Kirby, Richard Shelton, ed. Inventors and Engineers of Old
       New Haven; a series of six lectures. New Haven, Conn:
       Colony Historical Society, 1939. 111pp, 1 ill, pls (Eli
       Whitney, Yale inventors and engineers, etc.)

505   Larson, Egon (pseud. for Egon Lehrburger). A History of
       Inventions with 70 Photographs and 117 Line Illustrations.
       Rev. ed. London: Dent; New York: Roy, 1969. 382pp,
       ill, 33 pls

506   List of Patents for Inventions and Designs Issued by the
       United States from 1790-1847. Washington, D.C.: Gideon,
       1847.

507   McCloy, Shelby Thomas, 1848- . French Invention of the
       18th Century. Lexington, Ky: U of Kentucky Pr, 1952.
       212pp, ill, bib

508   McNeil, I. Joseph Bramah, a Century of Invention. Newton
       Abbot: David & Charles, 1968. ill (English inventor and
       locksmith, 1748-1814)

509   Nagler, Bernard, comp. Patent Pending. Los Angeles:

Price, Stern, Sloan, 1968.   46pp, ill of 22 humorous inventions   (Turn of century, American)

510   Newton's London Journal of Arts and Sciences; being a record of the progress of invention as applied to the arts.   London: 1820-1866.

511   Official Catalogue.   International Inventions Exhibition of 1885.   London: W. Clowes & Sons, 1885.   365pp

512   Pearsall, Ronald.   Collecting Mechanical Antiques.   Newton Abbot: David & Charles; New York: Arco, 1973.   197pp, ill, bib   (1830-1880)

513   *Ray, William, and Marlys Ray.   The Art of Invention; patent models and their makers.   Fore. by Peter Goldmark.   Princeton, NJ: Pyne Pr, 1974.   176pp, 190 (40 color) ill, bib   (1836-1860.   Objects mainly from the O. Rundle Gilbert Collection, part of 3500 cases of models bought at 1941 auction of Sir Henry Wellcome's collection, bought from Patent Office in 1925.   Both sales represent a tragic loss to the Nation of a true national treasure)

514   Ries, Estelle H.   Mother Wit.   New York; London: Century, 1930; 2nd enl. ed. as The Ingenuity of Man.   New York: Exposition Pr, 1962.   301pp, ill, pls; 333pp, ill

515   Roe, Joseph Wickham, 1871- .   Connecticut Inventors.   New Haven: Yale U Pr, for Tercentenary Commission, 1934.   30pp, bib

516   Routledge, Robert.   Discoveries and Inventions of the 19th Century.   London: C. Routledge, 1886; 9th ed. with additions.   1891; 1903.   594pp, ill; 681pp, ill, 8 pls   NN

517   Rowland, K. T.   18th Century Inventions.   Newton Abbot: David & Charles; New York: Barnes & Noble, 1974.   160pp, ill, bib

518   The Scientific American, the advocate of industry and enterprise and journal of mechanical and other improvements.   Weekly.   New York: Munn, 1845-1919; Monthly.   1920-date.   ill

519   The Scientific Artisan, a journal of patents, science, art, discovery, invention, etc.   Weekly.   Cincinnati: American Patent Co, 1859-1861.   (Merged into The Cincinnatus and Journal of the American Patent Company)

520   Smiles, Samuel.   Men of Invention and Industry.   London: J. Murray, 1884.   390pp, ill   DP

521   Szeeman, Harald, ed.   The Bachelor Machines.   English and

Italian text. New York: Rizzoli International Publications, 1976. 236pp, 200 ill (Bizarre inventions to present day)

522 Thomas, Holland. The Age of Invention; a chronicle of mechanical conquest. New Haven: Yale U Pr, 1921. 267pp, pls, bib

523 Timbs, John. Stories of Inventors and Discoveries in Science and the Useful Arts. New York: Harper, 1860. 473pp, ill, pls

524 Tissandier, Gaston. Marvels of Invention and Scientific Puzzles. Being a popular account of many useful and interesting inventions and discoveries. Tr. by Henry Frith. London; New York: Ward, Lock, 1890. 113pp, ill

525 United States. Department of Commerce. The Story of the United States Patent Office. Washington, D.C.: GPO, 1972.

526 _____ . Patent Office. Annual Report of the Commissioner of Patents. Washington, D.C.: 1840- . ill

527 _____ . _____ . A List of Patents Granted by the United States from April 10, 1790, to December 31, 1836.... Washington, D.C.: printed by American Photo-Lithographic Co, NY, 1872. 805pp, facsims of original documents

528 * _____ . _____ . Official Gazette of the United States Patent Office. Weekly. Washington, D.C.: GPO, 1872- date. General Index. 1872-1875. Index embodied in the Annual Report of the Commissioner. 1876- . ill

529 Usher, Abbott Payson. A History of Mechanical Inventions. New York: McGraw Hill, 1929; rev. ed. Cambridge, Mass: Harvard U Pr; London: Oxford U Pr, 1954. 401pp, ill, bib; 450pp, ill, bib

530 Welsh, Peter C. United States Patents, 1790-1870: new uses for old ideas. Washington, D.C.: Smithsonian Institution, GPO, 1965. 42pp (pp110-151), ill, bib

531 White, James, fl. 1822. A New Century of Inventions: being designs and descriptions of 100 machines relating to arts, manufacturers and domestic life. With 50 full-page engraved plates illustrating machines and mechanical inventions. Manchester, Eng: Leech & Cheetham, for Author, 1822; reprint. New York: Burt Franklin, 1966? 394pp, 50 pls

532 Williams, Archibald. The Romance of Modern Invention, containing interesting descriptions in non-technical language of

wireless telegraphy, liquid air, modern artillery, subma-
rines, dirigible torpedoes, solar motors, airships, etc.
Philadelphia: Lippincott; London: Pearson, 1903. 345pp,
ill, pls

533   Williams, John S. Consecrated Ingenuity. The Shakers and
      Their Inventions. Old Chatham, NY: Shaker Museum
      Foundation, 1957. 10pp, 13 pls

534   Wilson, Mitchell A. American Science and Invention, a pic-
      torial history; the fabulous story of how American dreamers,
      wizards, and inspired tinkerers converted a wilderness into
      the wonder of the world. New York: Simon & Schuster,
      1954. 437pp, ill, pls, bib

STORES AND PEDDLERS

535   Bigelow, David. History of Prominent Mercantile and Manu-
      facturing Firms in the United States, with a collection of
      truthful illustrations, representing mercantile buildings,
      manufacturing establishments, and articles manufactured.
      6(?) vol. Boston: 1857- . text, pls DeWint (Vol. 6)

536   Carson, Gerald. Country Stores in Early New England.
      Sturbridge, Mass: Old Sturbridge Village, 1955. 15pp, ill

537   _____ . The Old Country Store. New York: Oxford U Pr,
      1954. 330pp, ill, bib

538   Country Store Collectibles Price Guide. Des Moines: Wallace-
      Homestead, 1972. 90pp, ill

539   Dolan, F. R. The Yankee Peddlers of Early America. New
      York: Potter, 1964. ill

540   Freeman, Graydon La Verne. The Country Store. Early
      American Occupation. Watkins Glen, NY: Century House,
      1955. 51pp, ill, catalog facisms

541   *Goodwin, Mary R. M. The Colonial Store. 2 vol. Williams-
      burg, Va: Colonial Williamsburg, 1966. pls

542   Grossholz, Roselyn N. (Lyn). Country Store Collectibles.
      Des Moines, Io: Wallace-Homestead, 1974. 90pp ill
      (Includes early advertising items, tin containers, etc)

543   _____ . The Collectible Classics from Commerce. Erie,
      Pa: Author, 1975. ill (Thread & dye cabinets, fountain
      dispensers, advertising items)

544   *Johnson, Laurence A. Over the Counter and On the Shelf;

country storekeeping in America, 1620-1920.   Rutland, Vt:
Tuttle, 1961.   140pp, ill

545 Kauffman, Calvin Henry.   The Dictionary of Merchandise,
and Nomenclature in All Languages; for the use of counting-
houses: containing, the history, places of growth, culture,
use, and marks of excellency, of such natural productions,
as form articles of commerce; with their names in all
European languages.   London: Author, 1803; Philadelphia:
printed & sold by James Humphreys, 1805; 2nd ed. London:
printed for T. Boosey, 1805; enl. 3rd ed. London: Boosey,
1814; 4th ed., "considerably enlarged and improved by an
alphabetical arrangement of all European foreign names of
merchandize, with their translation into the English language,
by the Editor of the Commercial Dictionary, and Foreign
Prices Current of Europe (i. e. Joshua Montefiore).   London:
18-?   380pp; 9, 368pp; 380pp; 396pp MB, DLC, DeWint

546 Kresge's Catalog: 5 and 10 merchandise.   1913 catalog reprint. New York: Random House, 1975.   ill

547 Lord, Francis Alfred.   Civil War Sutlers and Their Wares.
New York: T. Yoseloff, 1969.   162pp, ill, bib (Sup-
pliers of necessities--food, tobacco, etc.)

548 Montgomery Ward and Company.   Catalog No. 57, 1895.   Un-
abridged facsimile reprint.   New York: Dover, 1969.   624pp

549 _____.   1901 Catalog.   Glass, china, toys, clocks, lamps,
canes, umbrellas.   Reprint.   Chattanooga, Tenn: J & S
Company, n. d.   48pp, ill

550a Rawson, Marion Nicholl.   Handwrought Ancestors.   The Story
of Early American Shops and Those Who Worked Therein.
New York: Dutton, 1936.   366pp, ill

550b Schreiber, G. R.   A Concise History of Vending in the U.S.A.
Chicago: Vend, the Magazine of the Vending Industry, 1961.
46pp, ill (Chiefly a reprint of material from earlier book,
Automatic Seller.   New York: Wiley, 1954)

551 Sears, Roebuck and Company.   1900 catalog.   Reprint. Little-
ton, Colo: The Country Store, 1974.   388pp, 4000 ill

552 _____.   1902 catalog.   Abridged facsimile reprint.   Fore.
by Cleveland Amory.   New York: Crown, 1969.   70pp, ill

553 _____.   1908 catalog.   Reprint.   East Tawas, Mich: J. W.
Holst, 1974.   736pp, ill

554 *Wright, Richardson Little, 1887- .   Hawkers and Walkers in
Early America; strolling peddlers, preachers, lawyers,

doctors, players, and others, from the beginning to the
Civil War. Philadelphia: Lippincott, 1927; New York:
F. Unger, 1965. 317pp, ill, pls, bib; 273pp, ill, bib

CONFECTIONERY, BREWING, BARBERING, AND BRUSHMAKING

555 Abbott, Henry George (pseud.). Historical Sketch of the Con-
     fectionery Trade of Chicago; compiled from various authen-
     tic sources of information. Chicago: Jobbing Confectioners'
     Association, 1905. 208pp, ill, frontis

556 Anderson, Will. The Beer Book, an illustrated guide to
     American Breweriana. Princeton, NJ: Pyne, 1973.
     224pp, 300 ill, 27 color pls (150 years of collectible
     bottles, trays, cans, signs, openers, steins, jugs, etc.)

557 Andrews, William, 1848-1909. At the Sign of the Barber's
     Pole; studies in hirsute history. Cottingham, Yorkshire:
     J. R. Tutin, 1904; reprint. Detroit: Singing Tree Pr,
     1969. 121pp, ill

558 Doyle, Bernard W., comp., and Perry Walton, ed. Comb
     Making in America. An Account of the origin and develop-
     ment of the industry for which Leominster has become
     famous. To which are added pictures of many of the early
     comb makers and views of the old time comb shops ... in
     commemoration of the 150th anniversary of the founding of
     the comb industry in Leominster, Massachusetts, 1925.
     Boston: priv. printed, 1925. many ill (Combs, shops,
     machines, tools, etc.)

559 Gill, J. Thompson. The Complete Practical Ornamenter for
     Confectioners and Bakers. Chicago: Confectionery &
     Baker Publishing, 1882; 5th ed. 1890; Chicago: Caterer
     Publishing, 1891. v.p. (17, 45, 38, 51pp), ill, pls (In-
     cludes utensils) NN, DeWint

560 Girtin, Thomas. In Love and Unity; a book about brushmaking.
     London: Hutchinson, 1961. 112pp, 8 pls, bib

561 Kiddier, William. The Brushmaker, and the Secrets of His
     Craft. London: Pitman, 1922; 2nd ed. enl. 1929. 142pp,
     ill; 152pp, ill

562 _____ . The Old Trade Unions from Unprinted Records of
     the Brushmakers. London: Allen & Unwin, 1930; 2nd ed.
     1931. 245pp, pls BM

563 Moler Barber Supply House. Catalogue of barber supplies
     and furnishings of the early 1900s. Reprint. Chattanooga,
     Tenn: J & S Company, 1968. 28pp, ill

564 Procter, Richard Wright, 1816-1881. The Barber's Shop.
     London: 1856; rev. enl. ed. with introd. by William E.
     A. Axon. Manchester, Eng: A. Heywood, 1883; reprint.
     Detroit: Singing Tree Pr, 1971. 244pp, ill

ORNAMENTAL DESIGNS

DECORATIVE MOTIFS, HERALDRY, COLOR AND AESTHETICS

565 *Ackermann, Rudolph. A Selection of Ornaments for the Use
of Sculptors, Painters, Carvers, Modellers, etc. 2 vol.
in 1. London: Repository of Arts, 1818-1819; 3 vol. in 1.
1817-1819. 120 pls (Includes ornamental details from
furniture)

566 Adam, Robert, 1728-1792. Designs for Vases and Foliage,
Composed from the Antique. London: Priestley & Weale,
1821. 13 pls DeWint

567 Adams, Edward. The Polychromatic Ornament of Italy. London: Nickisson; New York: Wiley & Putnam, 1846? 16pp,
11 pls DeWint

568 *Audsley, William James, and George A. Audsley. Outlines of
Ornament in the Leading Styles. Selected from executed
ancient and modern works. A book of reference for the
architect, sculptor, decorative artist, and practical painter.
London: Sampson Low, 1881; New York: Scribner & Wel-
ford, 1882; reprint with new list of plates as Designs and
Patterns from Historic Ornament. New York: Dover;
London: Constable, 1968. 14pp, ill, 60 pls

569 Baldwin, Muriel F., comp. Plant Forms in Ornament: a
selective list of references in the New York Public Library
and other libraries of N.Y.C. Reprint from its Bulletin,
June-August 1933. New York: the Library, 1933. 59pp

570 Ball, Katherine M. Decorative Motives of Oriental Art. San
Francisco: 1918; London: John Lane; New York: Dodd,
Mead, 1927; New York: Hacker, 1969. ...; 286pp, 673
ill, bib (Cherry Blossom, plum blossom, bamboo, pine,
maple, willow, peach ...) NN

571 Ballantine, James, 1808-1877. Essay on Ornamental Art, as
Applicable to Trade and Manufacturers. (The tradesmans'

book of ornamental designs.) London: G. Virtue, 1847.
36pp, ill, 40 pls NN, CtY, DeWint

572 Baretti, P. A New Book of Ornaments ... very useful for
cabinet-makers, carvers, etc. London: 1762. ill BM

573 Beunat, Joseph. Empire Style Designs and Ornament. Sarre-
bourg, France: 1813; reprint. New York: Dover, 1974.
ill, 95 pls

574 Bielefeld and Haselden, London. A Collection of Designs for
the Use of Upholsterers, Decorators, Gilders, etc., consisting of outlines from the original ornaments manufactured
by Bielefeld and Haselden, in the new papier mache. 2nd
ed. London: 1831. 2pp, 28 pls DeWint

575 *Binstead, Herbert Ernest. Useful Details in Several Styles (of
furniture and decorations). London: A. H. Botwright, 1906;
New York: Land, 1907; London: 1912. 152pp, ill (Gothic,
Moorish, Francis 1, Henri 2, Henri 4, Modern French,
Louis 14, 15, 16, Regency, Empire, English Renaissance,
Elizabethan, Jacobean, Chippendale, Sheraton, Hepplewhite,
Adam) DLC, NN, MiGr

576 A Book of Old English Designs: 47 plates of historical English
ornament. New York: Jacobson, 1921. 3pp, pls ViU

577 Booth, Lorenza. New Book of Ornamental Designs, intended
for the use of upholsterers, carvers, gilders. London:
William Robinson, 1861. ill BM

578 *Bossert, Helmuth Theodor. Decorative Art of Asia and Egypt;
400 decorative motifs in color, forming a survey of the
applied art of Egypt, China, Japan, Siam, Tibet, of the
Lapps and Siberian and Islamic peoples. New York: Praeger; London: Zwemmer, 1956; New York: 1964. 13pp,
40 color pls

579 _____ . An Encyclopedia of Colour Decoration from the
Earliest Times to the Middle of the 19th Century. Berlin:
Ernst Wasmuth; London: V. Gollancz; New York: E. Weyhe,
1928. 34pp, color ill, 120 color pls CtY, NN, BM

580 _____ . Ornament. 2000 Decorative motifs in colour, forming a survey of the applied art of all ages and all countries.
Tr. from German by L. Hamilton. London: E. Benn,
1924; as Ornament in Applied Art. New York: E. Weyhe,
1924; Berlin: Wasmuth, 1924; as Encyclopedia of Ornament;
a collection of applied decorative forms from all nations
and all ages. London: Simpkin Marshall, 1937. 48pp,
120 pls (80 in color facsimile) NN, BM

581 Bowles, Thomas. A Compleat Book of Ornaments Consisting

of a Variety of Compartments, shields, masks, prizework, moresk-work, etc., being very useful for painters, carvers, watch-makers, gravers, etc., invented and drawn by some of the best artists. (Somer, Berain, Moeldar, Durant.) London: The Bowles, 174-? 37 pls DeWint

582   Boyce, Allen P. Boyce's Fresco and Decorative Designs. Boston: Cupples, Upham, 1883. 3pp, 16 pls DeWint

583   Brøndsted, Johannes Balthasar. Early English Ornament; the sources, development and relation to foreign styles of pre-Norman ornamental art in England. Tr. from Danish by Albany F. Major. Pref. by Reginald A. Smith. London: Hachette Ltd; Copenhagen: Levin & Munksgaard, 1924. 352pp, ill DLC, NNC-Ave

584   Brook, Robert. Elements of Style in Furniture and Woodwork. Being a series of details of the Italian, German Renaissance, Elizabethan, Louis 14th, 15th, 16th, Sheraton, Adams, Empire, Chinese, Japanese, and Moresque styles, drawn from the best examples for the use of architects, furniture designers, cabinet makers, and others. London: Author, 1889. 36pp, 50 pls DeWint, NN, MB

585 *Burke, John, and Sir John Bernard Burke. Encyclopedia of Heraldry, or General Armory of England, Scotland, and Ireland. London: Edward Churton, 1842; 3rd ed. London: H. G. Bohn, 1844; 3rd ed. 1847; 1851; etc. 1109pp, ill BM, DLC

586   _____, and _____. Heraldic Illustrations, comprising the armorial bearings of the principal families of the Empire. 3 vol. London: E. Churton, 1844-46; reissued. 3 vol in 1. 1853. 51pp, ill, 16 color pls DLC, BM

587   Burn, Robert Scott, comp. The Ornamental Draughtsman and Designer; being a series of practical instructions and examples of freehand drawing in outline and from the round ... (also) practical papers on form and colour, as applied to industrial decoration and arts manufacture. London; New York: Ward, Lock, 1892; 1894. 142pp, 19 folding pls; 174pp, 300 ill (First published in another form in 1857) PPULC, MB

588   Burris-Meyer, Elizabeth. Color and Design in the Decorative Arts. New York: Prentice-Hall, 1935; 1937. 572pp, ill, color pls, bib

589   Busby, Charles Augustus, 1788-1834. A Collection of Designs for Modern Embellishments Suitable to Parlours, dining and drawing rooms, folding doors, chimney pieces, verandas, frizes, etc. London: J. Taylor, 1808? 25 pls (part color) DeWint

590 Butterfield, Lindsay P. Floral Forms in Historic Design, mainly from objects in the Victoria and Albert Museum, but including examples from designs by William Morris and C. F. A. Voysey. Pref. and notes by W. G. Paulson Townsend. London: Batsford, 1922. 18 pls in portfolio DLC, NN

591 Chapman, Suzanne E. Early American Design Motifs. New York: Dover, 1952; rev. and expanded. 1974. 191pp, ill; 138pp, ill, color pls, bib

592 Chippendale's 1133 Designs of Interior Decorations in the Old French and Antique Styles, for carvers, cabinet makers, ornamental painters, brass workers, chasers, silversmiths, general designers and architects. London: John Weale, 1834. 49 pls ("Most spuriously ascribed to Chippendale, and in fact by Thomas Johnson," Library of Congress) ViU

593 Christie, Archibald H. Traditional Methods of Pattern Designing; an introduction to the study of the decorative art. Oxford: Clarendon Pr, 1910; 2nd ed. 1929; reprint as Pattern Design. New York: Dover, 1969. 327pp, ill, 31 pls; 313pp, ill, 60 pls DLC, NN

594 Cole, Herbert. Heraldry and Floral Forms as Used in Decoration. London; Toronto: J. M. Dent; New York: Dutton, 1922. 243pp, ill DLC, NN

595 A Collection of Ornamental Designs, applicable to furniture, frames, and the decoration of rooms, in the style of Louis 14th, chiefly after Thomas Chippendale. London?: ca.1840? 23 pls ("Chippendale had little or no hand in these plates, most of them being after Matthew Lock. They include reprints (restrikes?) of his Six Tables (1746) and A New Book of Ornaments for Looking Glass Frames (ca.1768)," B. Quaritch, catalogue #906.) MiD, ICJ

596 Cottingham, Lewis Nockalls, 1787-1847. A Collection of Architectural Ornaments and Decorations. Selected from the best authorities for the use of architects, sculptors, ornamental painters, masons, carvers, modellers in plaster, casters in metal, paper stainers, and every business connected with the arts of design. London: Priestley & Weale, 1824. no text, 23 pls MB

597 Cutler, Thomas William. A Grammar of Japanese Ornament and Design, with introductory, descriptive and analytical text. London: Batsford, 1880. ill, 58 (i.e. 65) pls, several in color DLC, MB, NNC-Ave

598 Darly, Matthew, fl.1778. A New Book of Chinese Designs, calculated to improve the present taste, consisting of figures, buildings, and furniture, landskips, birds, beasts,

flowers and ornaments, etc.   London: Edwards & Darly, 1754.   120 pls   DLC

599   Day, Lewis Foreman, 1845-1910.   The Anatomy of Pattern. London: Batsford, 1887; 1889; 2nd rev. ed. 1889; 3rd ed. rev. 1892; 4th ed. rev. 1895; etc.   53pp, 35 pls; 1895: 56pp, 41 pls   DLC, MB

600   _____.   The Application of Ornament.   Textbook of ornamental design.   London: Batsford, 1888; rev. 2nd ed. 1891; 4th ed. rev. 1896.   73pp, ill, 42 pls; 1896:   76pp, 7 ill, 48 pls   DLC

601   _____.   Instances of Accessory Art; original designs and suggestive examples of ornament, with practical and critical notes.   London: Batsford, 1880.   32 leaves, ill, 29 pls MB, NNC-Ave

602   _____.   Nature and Ornament: nature the raw material of design, ornament its finished product.   2 vol.   London: Batsford, 1908-09; New York: Scribner's, 1909-10; 2 vol in 1.   1909.   284pp, ill, pls   NNC-Ave

603   _____.   Nature in Ornament, an inquiry into the natural element in ornamental design and a survey of the ornamental treatment of natural forms ... design and treatment in ornament, old and new.   London: Batsford, 1892; 2nd ed. 1894; 1896.   247pp, 192 ill, 123 pls   MiD, NNC-Ave

604   Dolmetsch, Heinrich.   The Historic Styles of Ornament.   Tr. from German.   London: Batsford, 1898; 2nd ed. rev. 1912.   100 pls (75 gold and color) of 1500 examples   NN

605   _____.   Ornamental Treasure; a collection of designs of all styles and periods, for architects, sculptors, modelers, gold and silversmiths, designers, porcelain and glass painters, glass stainers, engravers, lithographers, decorative painters, academies, schools of industry, etc.   New York: Hessling & Spielmeyer, n.d., 188-?; 1895?; 1898? 4pp, 85 pls

606   _____.   Ornamental Treasures; a collection of designs from India, China, Japan, Italy, Germany, France, etc., of all styles and times.   Stuttgart: J. Hoffmann, 1912; New York: P. Wenzel, n.d.   100 pls   NN

607   Dresser, Christopher.   Development of Ornamental Art in the International Exhibition: being a concise statement of the laws which govern the production and application of ornament.   London: 1862.   BM

608   _____.   Modern Ornamentation; being a series of original designs for the patterns of textile fabrics, for the

ornamentation of manufacturers in wood, metal, pottery, etc.; also for the decoration of walls and ceilings and other flat surfaces. London: Batsford, 1886. 8pp, 50 pls BM, MiD, NB

609 _____. Principles of Decorative Design. London; Paris; New York: Cassell, Petter & Galpin, 1870?; 1873; 1881; 4th ed. 1882;... 167pp, ill, color pls NN, CtY

610 _____. Studies in Design. London: Cassell, Petter & Galpin, 1876; 1877. 42pp, 60 pls (some color)

611 Dulberberg, Fritz Helmut von. Collectors Guide to German Decorations. Aberdeen, Scotland: New Order Publications, 1973. 20pp, 200 ill

612 Edmunds, William H., 1852- . Pointers and Clues to the Subjects of Chinese and Japanese Art as Shewn in Drawings, prints, carvings and the decoration of porcelain and lacquer. With brief notes on related subjects. London: Low, Marston, 1934; 1938? 706pp

613 Edwards, E(dward?), 1738-1806, and Matthew Darly, fl. 1778. A New Book of Chinese Designs Calculated to Improve the Present Taste, consisting of figures, buildings, and furniture, landskips, birds, beasts, flowrs and ornaments, etc. London: Authors, 1754. 2pp, 123 pls NNC-Ave, DLC

614 Evans, Joan. Nature in Design; a study of naturalism in decorative art from the Bronze Age to the Renaissance. London: Oxford U Pr, 1933. 117pp, ill, pls

615 _____. Pattern; a study of ornament in Western Europe from 1180-1900. 2 vol. Oxford: Clarendon, 1931; reprint. New York: Hacker, 1974. ill, pls, bib

616 _____. Style in Ornament. London; New York: Oxford U Pr, 1950. 63pp, ill

617 Exhibition of British Design for Surface Decoration. London: British Industries Fair, 1915. 47pp BM

618 *Fairbairn, James, comp. The Book of Crests of the Families of Great Britain and Ireland. (Title varies.) 2 vol. Edinburgh: T. C. Jack; London: Hamilton, Adams, 1860; 4th ed. enl. 2 vol. London: Jack, 1905; reprint, rev. & enl. 2 vol in 1. Baltimore: Heraldic Book Co, 1968; reprint. Rutland, Vt: C. E. Tuttle, 1968. 1905: 611 and 148pp, 314 pls; Tuttle: 644pp, 144 pls

618a Flat Ornament. A pattern book of designs of textiles, embroidery, wall papers, inlays, etc. Stuttgart: J. Engelhorn, n.d. 150 pls NN

619   Foley, Daniel J., and Priscilla Sawyer Lord. The Eagle,
      Emblem of Freedom in History and Art. Princeton, NJ:
      Pyne Pr, 1975. 256pp, ill (Indian, European and Ameri-
      can decorative arts)

620   Forms and Fantasies. Monthly. Chicago: 1898-99.

621   Fox-Davies, Arthur Charles, 1871-1928. Armorial Families.
      A directory of gentlemen of coat armour. Edinburgh: T.
      C. & E. C. Jack, 1895; 4th ed. 2 vol. 1902; 6th ed. 1910;
      7th ed. 1929; reprint. 1970. 1086pp, ill, 112 pls; 1136pp,
      ill, pls; 1803pp, ill

622   _____. The Art of Heraldry: an encyclopedia of armory.
      London: T. C. & E. C. Jack; New York: Brentano's,
      1904; reprint. New York: B. Blom, 1968. 503pp, ill,
      153 pls

623   [No entry.]

624   Gibbs, John, architect. Designs for Gothic Ornaments and
      Furniture, after the ancient manner, for ecclesiastical and
      domestic purposes for the use of architects, and workers
      in metal, stone, wood, etc. London: G. Bell, 1853; 1854.
      14pp, 48 pls SKM, DeWint

625   _____. English Gothic Architecture; or, suggestions rela-
      tive to the designing of domestic buildings, ornaments,
      church-yard memorials, chimney pieces, and alphabets.
      Manchester, Eng: Author, 1855. 13pp, 20 pls MB

626   Gillon, Edmund Vincent. Victorian Stencils for Design and
      Decoration. New York: Dover, 1968. 64pp, ill

627   Glazier, Richard. Historical Notes of Ornament. Manchester,
      Eng: 1887; as A Manual of Historic Ornament, treating upon
      the evolution, tradition, and development of architecture and
      the applied arts, prepared for the use of students and crafts-
      men. London: Batsford, 1899; 2nd ed. 1906; 4th ed. 1926;
      6th ed. rev. & enl. London; New York: Batsford, 1948;
      6th ed. New York; Dover, 1948. 136pp, 470 ill; 168pp,
      600 ill; 184pp, 670 ill, bib; Dover: 184pp, 700 ill, bib
      NN, NNC-Ave, DLC

628   Gorham Manufacturing Company. An Elementary Manual of
      Heraldry, with some account of its history and a simple
      explanation of its principal symbols; also, something about
      hall-marks and book-plates. New York: Gorham, 1905.
      120pp, ill, bib NN

629   Habermann, Franz Xavier. Louis 15; a collection of ornaments
      of the 18th century in correct rococo style, for architects,

decorative painters, stone and wood sculptors, frame-
manufacturers, gilders, plasterers, glass stainers and
glass painters, designers for textile-fabrics, modelers,
etc. New York: Hessling & Spielmeyer, n.d. (ca.189-?).
36 pls MiD

630 Hamlin, Alfred Dwight Foster. A History of Ornament; ancient
and medieval; Renaissance and modern. 2 vol. New York:
Century, 1916, 1923. 406pp, ill, pls (some color), bib
NN, DeWint

631 Handbook of Designs and Motifs; nearly 7000 designs, motifs,
forms and symbols based on Japanese family crests....
Introd. by P. K. Thomajan. New York: Tudor, 1950.
ill

632 Hasluck, Paul Nooncree, ed. Decorative Designs of All Ages
for All Purposes. London; New York: Cassell, 1899;
1903; Philadelphia: McKay, 1905; 1907; 1909. 160pp, ill
DLC, NNC-Ave

633 Hatton, Richard George, 1864-1926. Design; an exposition of
the principles and practice of the making of patterns.
London: Chapman & Hall, 1902; 1914; 1925. 182pp, 177
ill MiU, DLC

634 _____. Principles of Decoration. London: Chapman &
Hall, 1925. 224pp, ill, 4 pls NN, DLC

635 Hawley, Willis Meeker, 1896- . Chinese Folk Design, a
collection of cut-paper designs used for embroidery, together with 160 Chinese art symbols and their meanings.
Hollywood, Cal: 1949; New York: Dover, 1971. 16pp,
ill, 300 pls (part color)

636 Hessling, Bruno, firm. New Ideas for Surface Decoration,
suitable for wall papers, cretonnes, silks, etc. New York:
Gerbel, 1915?; New York: Hessling, 1916?; 1918. 1pp,
30 pls of 214 designs NN

637 Holme, Charles, 1848-1923. The Influence of Japanese Art
on English Design. Warrington, Eng: for the Literary
and Philosophical Society, by The Guardian, 1890. 32pp

638 Honour, Hugh. Chinoiserie--the vision of Cathay. London:
J. Murray, 1961; 1974. 294pp, pls

639 _____, and Nelly Schargo Hoyt. An Exhibition of Chinoi-
serie. Northampton, Mass: Smith College Museum of
Art, 1965. 65pp, pls

640 Hornung, Clarence Pearson. Handbook of Designs and
Devices; geometric elements. New York; London: Harper,

1932; 2nd rev. ed. New York: Dover, 1946. 204 pls of
1836 examples, bib; 218pp, ill, bib

641 Hulme, Frederick Edward, 1841-1909. Birth and Development
     of Ornament. London: Sonnenschein; New York: Mac-
     millan, 1893; London: 1894. 340pp, ill MH, CU

642 _____ . The History, principles and practice of heraldry.
     London: Sonnenschein; New York: Macmillan, 1892.
     281pp, ill

643 _____ . Principles of Ornamental Art. London; New York:
     Cassell, Petter & Galpin, 1875. 137pp, 32 pls BM, NN,
     MB

644 Humbert, Claude. Ornamental Design: Europe, Africa, Asia,
     the Americas, Oceania: a source book with 1000 illustra-
     tions. English, French and German text. London: Thames
     & Hudson; New York: Viking, 1970. 236pp, 1000 ill

645 Jackson, Frank G. Lessons on Decorative Design. London:
     Chapman, 1888; 1908. 173pp, ill, 34 pls

646 _____ . Theory and Practice of Design, an advanced text-
     book on decorative art. London: Chapman, 1894; new ed.
     1903;... 216pp, 700 ill DLC, TU

647 Johnson, Thomas, carver. A Book of Ornaments. London:
     John Weale, 1834. 8 pls NNC-Ave

648 _____ . Designs for Picture Frames, candelabra, ceilings,
     chimney-pieces, brackets, clockcases, gerandoles, metal-
     work, etc. Westminster, Eng: 1758. 10pp, ill, 52 pls
     NNC-Ave

649 _____ . 150 New Designs ... cielings (sic), chimney pieces,
     slab, glass and picture frames, stands for china, etc.,
     clock and watch cases, girondoles, brackets, grates, lan-
     thorns, etc. The whole well adapted for decorating all
     kinds of ornamental furniture, in the present taste. London:
     R. Sayer, 1761. no text, 56 pls (These plates were after-
     ward issued under the name of Chippendale) NNC-Ave,
     DLC

650 Jones, Owen, 1809-1874. Chinese Ornament. Philadelphia:
     Perleberg, n.d. 30 pls in portfolio

651 * _____ . Examples of Chinese Ornament Selected from Ob-
     jects in the South Kensington Museum and Other Collections.
     London: S. & T. Gilbert, 1867; 1868. 100 color pls
     (Patterns from porcelains and cloisonne) TxU, NN

652 * _____ . The Grammar of Ornament. Illustrated by examples

from various styles of ornament. With contributions by
J. B. Waring, J. O. Westwood, and M. D. Wyatt. London:
Day & Son, 1856; 1865; London: B. Quaritch, 1910; facism.
reprint of 1865 ed. New York; London: Van Nostrand-Rein-
hold, 1972. 157pp, ill, 112 color pls, bib ViU, TxU,
MdBP, BM

653 _____. The Gentlemen's or Builder's Companion, containing variety of useful designs for doors, gateways, peers,
pavilions, temples, chimney-pieces, slab tables, pier
glasses, or tabernacle frames.... London: Author, 1739.
7pp, ill, 56 pls, 4 folding pls DLC, NNC-Ave, DeWint

654 Jores, J. A New Book of Iron Work; containing a great
variety of designs (useful for painters, cabinet-makers,
carvers, smiths, fillegre-piercers, etc.) with gates of
various sorts, pilasters, fence for beaufets, tables, rails,
staircases, galleries, balconies, sign and lamp irons, door
lights, gratings, brackets, pedestals, weather-clocks,
spindles, etc. London: Robert Sayer, 1759? 20 pls
NNC-Ave

655 Kimball, Sidney Fiske, 1888-1955. The Creation of the Rococo. Philadelphia: Museum of Art; New York: W. W.
Norton, 1943. 242pp, pls, bib

656 _____. The Creation of the Style Louis 15. Reprint from
Art Bulletin. New York: 1941. 15pp, pls

657 * _____, and Edna Donnell. The Creators of the Chippendale
Style. 2 vol. New York: Metropolitan Museum, 1927;
1929. ill MiGr

658 King, Thomas. Designs for Carving and Gilding, used as interior decoration and furniture. With original patterns
for toilette glasses. London: The Architectural and Scientific Library, 185-? 1pp, 37 pls (part color) DeWint

659 Knight, Frederick. Knight's Cyclopedia of Ornaments Designed
for the Use of Architects, builders, silversmiths, chasers,
modellers, die sinkers, engravers, founders, carvers, and
all ornamental manufacturers. 2 vol. London: 183-?;
Edinburgh: T. C. Jack, 187-?; Edinburgh: 1881;... 123
pls NN

660 _____. Knight's Scroll Ornaments, designed for the use of
silversmiths, chasers, die-sinkers, modellers, etc. London: T. Griffiths, 1825-30; London: J. Williams, 1833?
50 pls NNC-Ave

661 * _____. Unique Fancy Ornaments. 5 parts, separate or
bound together. London: J. Williams, 1834. 30 pls
DeWint, NN

662 _____. Vases and Ornaments, designed for the use of
architects, silversmiths, jewellers, modellers, chasers,
die sinkers, founders, carvers, and all ornamental manufacturers. London: J. Williams, 1830; 1833. 7pp, 59
pls PPL, NN, DeWint

663 Knotts, Benjamin. Pennsylvania German Designs, a portfolio
of silk screen prints. The Index of American Design ...
Pennsylvania W.P.A. Art Project. New York: Metropolitan
Museum, 1943. 8pp, 20 color pls DeWint, DLC

664 *The Ladies Amusement; or, whole art of japanning made easy.
Illustrated in upwards of 1500 different designs drawn by
Pillement and other masters. 2nd ed. London: printed
for R. Sayer, 1762; reprint. Newport, Monm.: Ceramic
Book Co, 1959. 6pp, 200 pls with over 2000 designs and
borderings DeWint, DLC

665 Ladies' Manual of Art; or, profit and pastime, a self-teacher
in all branches of decorative art, embracing every variety
of painting and drawing on china, glass, velvet, canvas,
paper and wood. Philadelphia: American Mutual Library
Association, 1887. 294pp, ill

666 Landi, Gaetano. Architectural Decorations; a periodical work
of original designs invented from the Egyptian, the Greek,
the Roman, the Etruscan, the Attic, the Gothic, etc., for
exterior and interior decoration in whatever relates to
furniture, etc. London: 1810. color pls DeWint, SKM

667 Lee, Sherman E. Japanese Decorative Style. Cleveland:
Museum of Art, 1961; reprint. New York: Harper & Row,
1972. 161pp, ill, bib

668 Lichten, Frances. Folk Art Motifs of Pennsylvania. New
York: Hastings, 1954. 96pp, ill (some color)

669 Lipman, Jean. American Folk Decoration, with practical instruction by Eve Meulendyke. New York: Oxford U Pr,
1951; New York: Dover, 1972. 163pp, 226 ill, bib

670 Lock, Matthew (or Matthias). A Book of Ornaments, drawn
and engraved by M. Lock, principally adapted for carvers,
but generally usefull for various decorations in the present
taste. London: J. Weale, 1834. 5 pls NNC-Ave

671 _____. A Collection of Ornamental Designs, applicable to
furniture, frames and the decoration of rooms, in the style
of Louis 14th. London: M. Taylor, 1841. 24 pls DSI

672 _____. A New Drawing Book of Ornaments, shields, compartments, masks, etc. London: R. Sayer, n.d. (ca.1768).
6 pls

673 _____, and H. Copeland. A New Book of Ornaments, consisting of tables, sconces, spandles, clock cases, etc.
London: 1768. pls SKM

674 Loeb, Marcia. Art Deco Designs and Motifs. Over 100 examples. New York: Dover; London: Constable, 1972.
75pp, ill, bib (From architecture, fabrics, jewelry, etc.)

675 Lyon, J. T. Creative and Imitative Art; decoration and ornamentation. Brussels: M. Weissenbruch, 1873. 138pp,
ill DLC

676 Macmurdo, Arthur Heygate, 1851-1942, ed. Plain Handicrafts;
being essays by artists setting forth the principles of designs. Pref. by G. F. Watts. London: Percival, 1892.
63pp (Arts and Crafts Movement) BM

677 Mayeux, Henri. A Manual of Decorative Composition for
Designers, decorators, architects, and industrial artists.
Tr. from French. New York: Appleton, 1888; London:
D. Virtue, 1889. 310pp, 300 engravings PP

678 Meyer, Franz Sales. A Handbook of Ornament; a grammar
of art industrial and architecture designing in all its
branches. Tr. from 4th rev. German ed. London: Batsford, 1893; 2nd English ed. rev. by Hugh Stannus. London:
1894; New York: Architectural Book Co, 1894; Chicago:
Wilcox & Follett, 1945. 548pp, 300 pls with 3000 ill
(First published 1888, Germany) NNC-Ave, BM

679 Mookerjee, Ajitcoomar. 5000 Indian Designs and Motifs.
Calcutta: 1958; 1965. 11pp, 200 pp of ill

680 Morison, Stanley. Splendors of Ornament: specimens selected
from the 'Essempio di Recammi', the first Italian manual
of decoration, Venice 1524, by Giovanni Antonio Tagliente.
Pref. by Berthod Wolpe. London: Lion & Unicorn Pr,
1968. 72pp, ill

681 Morris, William. Some Hints on Pattern-Designing. A lecture ... Working Men's College, 1881. London: Longmans,
1899. 45pp, ill NN

682 Newbery, Robert. Gleanings from Ornamental Art of Every
Style: drawn from examples in the British Museum, South
Kensington, Indian, Crystal Palace, and other museums,
the Exhibitions of 1851 and 1862, and the best English and
foreign works. London: E. & F. N. Spon, 1863. 33pp,
ill, 100 pls

683 Oakeshott, George John. Detail and Ornament of the Italian
Renaissance. London: Batsford, 1888. 5pp, ill, 40 pls
(Chiefly architecture) DLC, NNC-Ave

684 O'Kane, James. Modern Romanesque; a collection of executed
     examples of carving and sculpture as applied to architecture
     and the accessory arts. New York: Author, 1892. 20 pls

685 Pattern Book of Ornaments and Fittings for Furniture. Lon-
     don?: ca. 1790. MiGr

686 Pergolesi, Michele Angelo. Designs on Various Ornaments.
     London: 1777-1784; reprint as Classical Ornament of 18th
     Century. Ed. by Edward A. Maser. New York: Dover,
     1970. NN has 41 pls, BM has 70 pls of original; 1970:
     99 pp (Designs for walls, doors, windows)

687 Perleberg, Hans Carl, comp. The Ornamental Motifs of the
     Period of the First Empire in France, epoque neo-classic.
     Philadelphia: Author, 193-? 32 pls in portfolio

688 Pether, Thomas. A Book of Ornaments. London?: 1834.
     SIB-3

689 Piggott, Sir Francis Taylor. Studies in the Decorative Art
     of Japan. London: Batsford, 1910. 130pp, many ill, 32
     pls (some color) DLC

690 Pillement, Jean Nicolas, 1719-1808. "The Fantastic Original
     Designs and Chinoseries, ca. 1755." Paris: 1769; reprint
     folio. Newport, Wales: Ceramic Book Co, 1959. 40 pls
     with 175 designs (See also Ladies Amusement....)

691 Polley, George H., comp. 18th Century Architectural Orna-
     mentation, furniture and decoration, by M. A. Pergolesi,
     and other eminent artists. Boston; New York: G. H.
     Polley, 1885? 58 pls MiGr

692 _____. Gothic Architecture, furniture and ornament of
     England from the 11th to the 16th century; comprising
     photographic and measured drawings of exteriors, interiors
     and details. Boston: G. H. Polley, 1908. 95 pls in port-
     folio NNC-Ave

693 Racinet, Albert Charles Auguste, 1825-1893. Polychromatic
     Ornament; 100 plates in gold, silver and colours ... various
     styles of ancient, Oriental and medieval and including the
     Renaissance and 17th and 18th centuries. Tr. from French.
     London: H. Sotheran, 1873; 1877. 58pp, 100 color pls
     NNC-Ave

694 Redgrave, Gilbert Richard, 1844- . Outlines of Historic
     Ornament. Tr. from German. New York: Scribner &
     Welford, 1884. 170pp, ill

695 Richardson, George. A Collection of Ornaments in the Antique
     Style, comprised in 37 plates. London: 1816. 37 pls

(Designs for friezes, panels, pilasters, chimney pieces, etc., by an assistant of the Adam brothers) DLC

696 _____. A New Collection of Chimney Pieces Ornamented in the Style of the Etruscan, Greek and Roman Architecture. London: 1781. 36 pls BM

697 _____, and Son. New Designs of Vases and Tripods Decorated in the Antique Taste. London: 1793. BM

698 Rostovtsev, Mikhail Ivanovich. The Animal Style in Southern Russia and China. New York: Hacker Art Books, 1973. 112pp, ill, 33 pls, bib

699 Sabine, Ellen S. American Antique Decoration. Princeton, NJ: Van Nostrand, 1956. 132pp, ill

700 _____. Early American Decorative Patterns and How to Paint Them. Princeton, NJ: Van Nostrand, 1962. 199pp, ill

701 Salandri, Enrico. Architectural and Decorative Designs, for use of those engaged in architecture, sculpture, working in metals, cabinet work, and other fine art productions. London: Atchley, 1869. ill, "incorporated with which are the plates of Page's Decorator" NNC-Ave

702 Scott, William Bell, 1811-1890. Ornamental Designs for Brass, Iron, and Glass Work, Earthenware, etc. London: n. d. SKM

703 _____. Ornamental Designs for Furniture and House Decoration, being a series of designs in lithography, selected from the works of the best French and German Ornamentalists, and an introductory essay on ornamental art. Edinburgh: A Fullarton, 1845. 21pp, ill, pls ViU, DLC, MiGr

704 _____. Ornamental Designs for Silver and Gold Work, Diesinkers, Enamellers, Modellers, Engravers, etc. ... with an introductory essay on ornamental art. Edinburgh; London: A. Fullarton, ca.1850. 21pp, 60 pls DeWint, SKM

705 Seddon, John Pollard. Progress in Art and Architecture, with Precedents for Ornament. London: D. Bogue, 1852. 60pp, ill, 12 pls DLC

706 *Shaw, Henry. Encyclopedia of Ornament. Issued in parts. London: Pickering, printed at Chiswick Pr, 1836- ; bound edition. 1842; reprint of 1842 ed. Edinburgh: J. Grant, 1898; reprint. New York: St. Martin's Pr, 1974. 2pp, 59 hand-colored wood-block pls, color title page; reprint: 60 (6 color) pls (Classical Greek to mid-19th century) MB, DM

707   Smith, Elmer Lewis, and Mel Horst. Hex Signs and Other
        Barn Decorations. Witmer, Pa: Applied Arts, 1965. 42pp,
        ill

708   Smith, George. A Collection of Ornamental Designs, after the
        manner of the antique, composed for the use of architects,
        ornamental painters, statuaries, carvers, casters in metal,
        paper makers, carpet, silk and printed calico manufacturers,
        and every trade dependent on the fine arts. London: J.
        Taylor, 1812. 43 pls

709   Smith, Robert Henry Soden. A List of Works on Ornament.
        South Kensington Museum, Science and Art Department.
        London: HMSO, 1882; 2nd ed. 1883. 101pp

710   Speltz, Alexander. The Coloured Ornament of All Historical
        Styles. 5 parts in 3 vol. Leipzig: K. F. Koehlers Anti-
        quarium, 1914-15. 183 color pls, bib (Antiquity to modern
        times)

711 * _____. Styles of Ornament, exhibited in designs, and ar-
        ranged in historical order, with descriptive text. Handbook
        for architects, designers, painters, sculptors, wood-carvers,
        chasers, modellers, cabinet-makers, and artistic locksmiths.
        Tr. from 2nd German ed. by David O'Connor. Berlin; New
        York: B. Hessling, 1906; rev. & enl. by R. Phene Spiers
        as The Styles of Ornament from Prehistoric Times to the
        Middle of the 19th Century. New York; Berlin; Paris:
        1910; London: Batsford, 1910; reprint of 1906 ed. New
        York: Grossett & Dunlap, 1936; reprint. New York: Dover,
        1959; reissue. 197-? 656pp; 647pp; 647pp; 3765 ill, 400
        full-page pls; 1959: 600pp, 3765 ill, bib

712   Spofford, Harriet Elizabeth (Prescott), 1835-1921. Art Deco-
        ration Applied to Furniture. New York: Harper, 1878.
        237pp, ill, pls

713   Stafford, Maureen, and Dora Ware. An Illustrated Dictionary
        of Ornament. Introd. by John Gloag. New York: St.
        Martin's Pr, 1975. 246pp, 2500 ill, bib

714   Stoudt, John Joseph. Consider the Lilies How They Grow; an
        interpretation of the symbolism of Pennsylvania German
        art. Allentown, Pa: Schlecter's, 1937; rev. ed. as Penn-
        sylvania Folk-Art; an interpretation.... Allentown: 1948.
        333pp, ill, bib; 402pp, ill, bib (First published as 2nd
        annual volume of the Pennsylvania German Folklore Society)

715   Talbert, Bruce James. Gothic Forms Applied to Furniture,
        Metal Work, and Decoration for Domestic Purposes.
        Birmingham, Eng: S. Birbeck, 1867; Boston: J. R. Os-
        good, 1873. 8pp, ill, 30 pls MB, NNC-Ave, MiGr

716 Thompson, Francis Benjamin, ed. The Universal Decorator.
     Illustrated by William Gibbs. 5 vol. London: G. Vickers,
     etc., 1858-60. ill, pls (Vol 4 & 5 ed. by John Wilson
     Ross) DLC

717 _____. The Universal Decorator; a complete guide to orna-
     mental design, including designs for cabinet-makers, wood
     carvers, metal workers, Birmingham, Sheffield, and the
     potteries, scrolls, panels, and general ornament, alphabets,
     initials, and monograms. Illustrations by William Gibbs.
     London: Houlston, 186-? 512pp, ill NNC-Ave

718 Tredwell, Winifred Reed. Chinese Art Motives Interpreted.
     New York: Putnam's, 1915. 110pp, 23 pls, bib

719 Vacher, Sydney. 15th Century Italian Ornament, chiefly taken
     from brocades and stuffs found in pictures in the National
     Gallery, London. London: B. Quaritch, 1886. 8pp, ill,
     30 color pls NNC-Ave

720 Voysey, Charles Francis Annesley, 1857-1941. Reason as a
     Basis of Art. London: Elkin Matthews, 1906. 29pp (Arts
     and Crafts Movement) BM

721 *Ward, James, 1851-1924. Historic Ornament: treatise on
     decorative art and architectural ornament. I. Prehistoric
     art; ancient art and architecture; eastern, early Christian,
     Byzantine, Saracenci, Romanesque, Gothic, and Renaissance
     architecture and ornament; II. Pottery; enamels; ivories;
     metal-work; furniture; textile fabrics; mosaics; glass; book
     decorations. 2 vol. London: Chapman & Hall, 1897.
     409pp, ill

722 Waring, John Burley. Illustrations of Architecture and Orna-
     ment. London: Blackie, 1871. 48pp, 70 pls (Sketches
     from France, Italy, Spain, Holland, Germany, and Belgium)

723 Warren, Garnet, and Horace B. Cheney. The Romance of
     Design. Garden City, NY: Doubleday, Page, 1926. 237pp,
     ill NNC-Ave

724 Weale, John, comp. Old English and French Ornament: for
     the interior embellishment of houses, for carvers and deco-
     rators; with designs for doors, windows, fire-places and
     chimney glasses, ornamental furniture, etc. By Chippen-
     dale, Inigo Jones, Lock and Pether. London: J. Weale,
     1846; republished. 1858-59. 100 pls with 220 designs
     BM, SKM, DLC

725 Wheeler, Monroe, ed. Textiles and Ornaments of India, a
     selection of designs. New York: Museum of Modern Art,
     1956. 93pp, ill, bib

726   Whitaker, Henry.   Materials for a New Style of Ornamentation,
       consisting of botanical subjects and compositions drawn from
       nature.   London: J. Weale, 1849.   8pp, 50 pls   BM

727 *Wornum, Ralph Nicholson.   Analysis of Ornament.   The Charac-
       teristics of Styles: an introduction to the study of the history
       of ornamental art.   2nd ed.   London: Chapman & Hall,
       1860; 4th ed. 1873; 9th ed. 1884;...   112pp; 138pp, 190pp;
       all with bib   NNC-Ave

ANTIQUES, COLLECTIBLES AND INTERIOR DESIGN

GENERAL WORKS

728 Adams, Maurice Spencer Rowe. Modern Decorative Art, a
series of 200 examples of interior decoration, furniture,
lighting, fittings and other ornamental features. London:
Batsford; Philadelphia: Lippincott, 1930. 249pp, ill, pls
MiGr

729 Addison, Julia DeWolf. Arts and Crafts in the Middle Ages;
a Description of Medieval Workmanship in several of the
departments of applied art, together with some account of
special artisans in the early Renaissance. Boston: L. C.
Page; London: G. Bell, 1908; Boston: 1914; 1921; 1933.
378pp, ill, plates (some color), bib DLC, NNC-Ave

730 _____. The Boston Museum of Fine Arts; Giving a descriptive and critical account of its treasures which represent the arts and crafts from remote antiquity to the
present time. Boston: L. C. Page, 1910; rev. ed. 1924.
454pp, plates; 493pp, plates, col. frontis

731 American and European Decorative Arts; furniture, ceramics,
metalwork, textiles from the collections of the Antiquarian
Society, Art Institute of Chicago, 1878-1951. Chicago:
1951. u.p., ill, pls

732 *American Art Association, New York. Auction catalogs.
After September 1929, American Art Association, Anderson Galleries. (These, like other auction catalogs, are
invaluable.)

733 The American Art Journal. Bi-annual. New York: The
Kennedy Galleries, 1969- . ill

734 American Art Journal. New York: 1864-1905.

735 The American Collector; magazine of art and antiques.

Bi-weekly, then monthly. New York: Collector's Publishing, 1933- .

736 *An American Museum of Decorative Art and Design: designs
      from the Cooper-Hewitt Collection, New York. Exhibition
      mounted by Arts Council of Great Britain, at V & A, June-
      August 1973. London: V & A, 1973. 118pp, chiefly ill

737 Angus, S. F. Ian. Collecting Antiques. London: Ward Lock,
      1972. 128pp, ill (1660-1900)

738 Antique Arts Weekly; the collector's newspaper. Forest Hills,
      NY: J. W. Haverty, 1930- .

739 The Antique Collector. Bi-monthly. London: 19- .

740 The Antique Collector: a weekly journal for dealers and col-
      lectors. London: 1930-32; monthly. 1932- .

741 The Antique Collectors' Club Year Book. Woodbridge, Suffolk:
      the Club, 1966/67- .

742 The Antique Dealers' Weekly and Collectors' Guide. London:
      1938-1946; as The Antique Dealer and Collectors' Guide.
      Monthly. London: Patina Pr, 1946- .

743 Antique Finder, incorporating 'Fine Art Finder.' Monthly.
      London: 1962- .

744 *Antique Monthly. Tuscaloosa, Ala: 196-?-date.

745 Antique News. Weekly. New York: Antique News Publishing,
      1930- .

746 Antique Talk. Bi-monthly. Utica, NY: Smith Publishing,
      1966- .

747 Antique Trader. Periodical. Dubuque, Iowa: Babka Pub-
      lishing, 19- .

748 Antiques. London: Library Association, 1963. 30pp (A
      bibliography)

749 *Antiques; a magazine for collectors. (Also, The Magazine
      Antiques.) Monthly. New York, etc.: Editorial Publica-
      tions, etc. (now Straight Enterprises), 1922-date. ill,
      color pls (Excellent) (See also no. 982)

750 Antiques and Investing. Monthly. Ross-on-Wye, Hereford-
      shire: R. V. S. Enterprises, 1969- .

751 *The Antiques Book. Ed. by Alice Winchester and staff of

Antiques Magazine. New York: Wyn, 1950. 319pp, ill
(Articles from the magazine, January 1922-December 1949)

752 The Antiques Catalogue. Monthly. Coventry, Eng: R. L.
Publications, 1970- .

753 The Antiques Dealer. Monthly. New York: Rosenthal &
Smythe, July 1949- .

754 The Antiques Journal. Monthly. Mount Vernon, Ohio: Guide
Publishing, January 1946- .

755 Antiques Review; the guide for connoisseurs and collectors.
Quarterly. London: Seven Oaks Pr, 1948- .

756 Antiques Today. Quarterly. Kermit, Tx: Collector's Weekly,
197- .

757 Antiques Treasury; a collection of information about antiques
and collectors' items. 8 vol. Uniontown, Pa: E. G.
Warman, 1967- . ill

758 *Antiques Treasury of Furniture and Other Decorative Arts at
Winterthur, Colonial Williamsburg, Old Sturbridge Village,
Old Deerfield, Ford Museum and Greenfield Village,...
Cooperstown, N.Y.: Shelburne. Ed. by Alice Winchester
and the Antiques Magazine staff. New York: Dutton, 1959.
ill

759 Antiques World: the international antiques trade monthly.
Aylesbury, Eng: Antique and General Advertising, 1969- .

760 Antiques Yearbook; encyclopedia and directory. London:
Tantivy Pr, etc., 1949/50- .

761 *Apollo. A journal of the arts. Monthly. London: 1925-date.

762 "Archaeologia: or, miscellaneous tracts relating to antiquity.
Periodical. London: J. Nichols, etc., 1773-18-?

763 Archaeological Journal. Quarterly. London: 1844-1926;
annual. 1927- . (Includes the Middle Ages)

764 Arnau, Frank (pseud. for Heinrich Schmitt). 3000 Years of
Deception in Art and Antiques. Tr. from German by J.
Maxwell Brownjohn. London: Cape, 1961. 349pp, 48 pls,
bib

765 Arrowsmith, H. W., and A. Arrowsmith. The House Decorator and Painter's Guide; containing a series of designs
for decorating apartments, suited to the various styles of
architecture. London: Thomas Kelly, 1840. 120pp, 61
pls (part color) DeWint

766 Art and Antiques Weekly. London: Morland, 1971- .

767 Art and Decoration. Monthly. New York: Art and Decoration
       Co., 1885-1886.

768 *Art at Auction. Annual. New York: Viking Pr, 1962/63- .
       many ill (some color) (Review of Sotheby Park Bernet's
       auctions. Paintings, furniture, prints, silver, porcelain,
       objects, etc. Also articles by experts. Same as Ivory
       Hammer)

769 *The Art Journal. Monthly. London: Virtue, 1839-1912. ill,
       pls

770 The Art of Furnishing on Rational and Aesthetic Principles.
       By C. H. J. London: H. S. King, 1876. 116pp DLC

771 L'Art pour Tous; Encyclopédie de l'art industriel et decoratif.
       Paris: A. Morel, 1861-1906. (Many plates of different
       subjects were reprinted)

772 Ashbee, Charles Robert. Table(s) of Arts and Crafts of the
       Renaissance. 3 parts in 1. London: Guild & School of
       Handicraft, 1892-95. (15th to 18th century)

773 Aslin, Elizabeth. The Aesthetic Movement: prelude to Art
       Nouveau. New York: Praeger, 1969. 189pp, 121 ill,
       pls, bib (Arts and Crafts movement)

774 Balfour, Henry. Evolution of Decorative Art, and essay upon
       its origin and development as illustrated by the art of
       modern races of mankind. London: Percival, 1893.
       131pp, ill, bib BM

775 Bankart, George Percy. The Art of the Plasterer: an ac-
       count of the decorative development of the craft, chiefly in
       England, from the 16th to the 18th century, with chapters
       on the stucco of the classic period and of the Italian Renais-
       sance, also on sgraffito, pargetting, Scottish, Irish and
       modern plasterwork. London: Batsford; New York:
       Scribner's, 1908. 350pp, ill, 2 pls (1 color) V & A

776 Barber, Anne Viccaro. Curios for Young Collectors. London:
       Bles, 1967. 128pp, ill (Juvenile literature)

777 Barker, Lady Mary Anne. The Bedroom and Boudoir. Lon-
       don: Macmillan, 1878. 116pp, ill SKM

778 *Batsford, Herbert. Reference Books on Architecture and
       Decoration; with hints on the formation of an architecture
       library. London: priv. printed, 1895; as Some suggestions
       on the Formation of a Small Reference Library of Books on

Ornament and the Decorative Arts. Paper read before
meeting of Library Association, London, October 1897.
London: Batsford, for priv. distribution, 1897. 24pp;
19pp plus 8pp of catalog NNC-Ave, CtY, DLC

779 Battersby, Martin. The Decorative Twenties. New York:
Walker; London: Studio Vista, 1969. 211pp, ill, bib

780 Batty, Joseph H., d.1906. Practical Taxidermy, and home
decoration; together with general information for sportsmen.
New York: Orange Judd, 1880. 203pp, ill, pls BM,
DeWint

781 Beard, Geoffrey William. Collecting Antiques on a Small Income. London: Hutchinson, 1957. 126pp, ill, bib

782 Bedford, John. The Collecting Man. New York: D. McKay;
London: Macdonald, 1968. 256pp, ill, bib

783 _____. Looking in Junk Shops. London: M. Parrish,
1961; New York: McKay, 1964; London: Macdonald, 1972.
254pp, ill, bib

784 _____. More Looking in Junk Shops. London: M. Parrish;
Chester Springs, Pa: Dufour Editions, 1962; New York:
McKay, 1965; 2nd ed. London: Macdonald, 1972. 248pp,
ill, bib; 252pp, ill, bib

785 _____. Still Looking for Junk. London: Macdonald, 1969;
New York: McKay, 1970. 228pp, ill, bib

786 Bennett, Ian, comp. The Sotheby Parke Bernet Guide to
Pricing Antiques from 25 to 2500 dollars. New York:
Studio Viking, 1975. 240pp, hundreds of ill

787 Bennett, Raymond. Collecting for Pleasure: a practical guide
to small antiques. London: Bodley Head, 1969. 120pp,
ill

788 Bernasconi, John Robert. The Collectors' Glossary of Antiques and Fine Arts. London: Estates Gazette, 1959;
rev. ed. 1963; 3rd ed. 1971. 559pp, 100 ill, 587pp, ill;
595pp, ill

789 Berrall, Julia S. A History of Flower Arrangement. London:
Thames & Hudson; London; New York: Studio/Crowell,
1953; rev. ed. New York: Viking, 1968. 176pp, chiefly
ill, bib; 159pp, ill, bib

790 Birren, Faber. Color for Interiors, historical and modern;
an essential reference work covering the major period
styles of history and including modern palettes for the

authentic decoration of homes, institutional and commercial
interiors. New York: Whitney Library of Design, 1963.
210pp, ill

791 Bjerkoe, Ethel Hall. Antiques for Your Home. Garden City,
NY: Doubleday, 1966. 72pp, ill

792 _____. Decorating for and with Antiques. Garden City,
NY: Doubleday, 1950. 250pp, ill, bib

793 Black, Charles Christopher. Catalogue of the Collection of
Paintings, Porcelain, Bronzes, Decorated Furniture, and
Other Works of Art, lent for exhibition in the Bethnal
Green Branch of the South Kensington Museum, by Sir
Richard Wallace. June 1872. London: 1872; rev. eds.
2nd-6th, 1872. 104pp

794 Black, Howard R. Fell's Collector's Guide to Valuable Antiques. New York: F. Fell, 1963. 328pp, ill, bib

795 Boger, Louise Ade. House and Garden's Antiques: questions
and answers. New York: Simon & Schuster, 1973. 429pp,
ill, bib (Selections from author's monthly column)

796 _____, and H. Batterson Boger, eds. The Dictionary of
Antiques and the Decorative Arts; a book of reference for
glass, furniture, ceramics, silver, periods, styles, technical terms, etc. New York: Scribner, 1957; enl. ed.
New York: Scribner, 1969; London: Black, 1969. 566pp,
ill, bib; 662pp, 816 ill, 37 (5 color) pls, bib

797 Bond, Harold Lewis. An Encyclopedia of Antiques. Boston:
Hale, Cushman & Flint, 1937; New York: Tudor, 1946;
1947. 389pp, ill, pls, bib, biogs MiGr

798 The Book of Antiques. Periodical. London: Arts & Crafts,
Ltd., 1928- .

799 Books on Architecture, Decoration, and Furniture in the Library of the Peabody Institute. Baltimore, Md: 1920.
23pp NNC-Ave

800 Bos, Evelyn F. Know About Antiques. New Augusta, Ind:
Editors & Engineers, 1966. 96pp, ill

801 Bossaglia, Rossana. Art Nouveau: revolution in interior
design. Tr. from Italian (1971). London: Orbis, 1973.
64pp, ill

802 Bowers, Kenneth William Macleod. Period Furnishing: pottery, porcelain, silver, glass, pictures, clocks, furniture,
textiles, floors, mixed styles, etc. Pref. by H. T. Sut-
cliffe. Tadworth: Elliot, 1971. 157pp, ill, bib (To 1860)

803 *Bowles, Ella Shannon. About Antiques. Philadelphia; London:
Lippincott, 1929; reprint. Detroit: Gale-Tower, 1971.
262pp, 75 ill, pls, bib

804 Boyce, Allen P. Modern Ornamenter and Interior Decorator.
A complete and practical illustration of the art of scroll,
arabesque, and ornamental painting. Boston: A. Williams,
1874; rev. ed. as A Collection of Scrolls and Ornaments....
Boston: 1878; rev. ed. Boston: Author, 1884. 3pp, ill,
20 plates; 2pp, 17 plates MB, PPULC, DLC

805 Bracegirdle, Cyril. A First Book of Antiques. London:
Heinemann, 1970. 144pp, ill, 4 pls, bib

806 Bradford, Ernle Dusgate Selby. Antique Collecting. London:
English Universities Pr, 1963. 214pp, ill, bib

807 _____. Dictionary of Antiques. London: English Universities Pr, 1963. 151pp, ill

808 Breck, Joseph, 1885- . The Cloisters, a Brief Guide. New
York: Metropolitan Museum, 1926; rev. 1927; rev. 1929;
rev. 1931. 58pp, ill (Medieval)

809 _____, and Meyric R. Rogers. The Pierpont Morgan Wing;
a handbook. New York: Metropolitan Museum, 1925; 2nd
ed. 1929. 395pp, ill

810 Brener, Carol. The Underground Collector; the neighborhood
guide to 500 offbeat, inexpensive shops in New York selling
antiques, vintage clothes and unusual items for the home.
New York: Simon & Schuster, 1970. 319pp, ill

811 Bricker, William Paul. The Complete Book of Collecting
Hobbies. New York: Sheridan House, 1951. 316pp

812 Bridgeman, Harriet. Erotic Antiques. Galashiel, Scotland:
Lyle Publications, 1974. 128pp, ill

813 Brooke, Iris. Four Walls Adorned; interior decoration, 1485-
1820. London: Methuen, 1952. 120pp, ill TxU, BM

814 Brown, Ivor, and others. About Antiques. Toronto: Burns
& MacEachern, 1973. 148pp, ill, bib (Releases from
syndicated column)

815 Brown, William Norman. A History of Decorative Art. London: Greenwood, 1900. 98pp

816 Bruce, Marjory. The Book of Craftsmen; the story of man's
handiwork through the ages. London: Harrap; New York:
Dodd, Meade, 1936; 1937; 1939; Reprint: New York: Dodd,
Mead; Detroit: Gale Research, 1974. 282pp, ill, plates,
color frontis

817   Brunner, Arnold William, and Thomas Tryon.   Interior Deco-
      ration.   New York: W. T. Comstock, 1887; 2nd ed. 1891.
      5pp, 65 ill, 16 pls   NN, MB

818   Buckley, Leo John.   Antiques and Their History.   Binghamton,
      NY: Author, 1927; 2nd ed. 1928.   320pp, 74 pls, bib
      (1600-1850.   French, English, American)   PPULC, NN

819   Burgess, Frederick William.   Chats on Household Curios.
      London: T. Fisher Unwin; New York: F. A. Stokes,
      1914.   360pp, 94 ill, 47 pls   PP, BM

820 *Burlington Magazine for Connoisseurs.   Monthly.   London:
      Saville Publishing; New York: S. Buckley, 1903- .

821   Burty, Philippe.   Chefs d'oeuvre of the Industrial Arts: Pot-
      tery and Porcelain, Glass, Enamel, Metal, Goldsmiths'
      Work, Jewellery, and Tapestry.   Ed. by William Chaffers.
      Tr. from French (1866).   London: Cassell, Potter, Galpin,
      1869; London: Chapman & Hall; New York: Appleton,
      1869.   391pp, ill, plates   MH, PPULC, NN

822   Cameron, Ian, and Elizabeth Kingsley-Rowe, eds.   Collins
      Encyclopedia of Antiques.   Introd. by Sir John Pope-Hen-
      nessy.   London: Collins, 1973; as The Random House
      Encyclopedia of Antiques.   New York: Random House,
      1973.   400pp, ill, bib

823   Candee, Helen Churchill.   Decorative Styles and Periods in
      the Home.   New York: F. A. Stokes, 1906; New York:
      Willy Book Co., 1938.   298pp, 177 ill, pls   (Earliest times
      to art nouveau)   NN, DLC, MiGr

824   Carmichael, Bill.   Incredible Collectors, Weird Antiques, and
      Odd Hobbies.   Englewood Cliffs, NJ: Prentice-Hall, 1971.
      282pp, ill, pls   (Tramp art, typewriters, beds, clothing,
      death masks, barbed wire, marbles, bawdy house tokens,
      etc.)

825   Catalog of the Avery Architectural Library, a Memorial Li-
      brary of Architecture and Decorative Art.   New York:
      Columbia College, 1895.   1139pp

826   Catalog of Books Relating to Architecture, Construction and
      Decoration in the Public Library of the City of Boston.
      November 1894.   With an Appendix.   Boston: the Library,
      1894; 2nd ed. 1914.   150pp; 535pp   NN-Ave

827   Chamberlain, Samuel.   The Chamberlain Calendar of Antiques,
      1976.   New York: Hastings House, 1975.   54 photographs.

828 *Christie Auctioneering Firm, of London; then Christie, Man-
      son and Woods, Ltd.   Sale Catalogues.   London: 177?-

present. (Hundreds of illustrated and non-illustrated catalogues of sales of art, tapestry, enamels, books, furniture,
metalwork, porcelain, etc. Note: often catalogued in libraries under name of the property owner)

829 Christie's Review of the Year. London: 19?- . (Reference
     guide to prices obtained at auction)

830 Chronicle of the Museum for the Arts of Decoration of Cooper
     Union for the Advancement of Science and Art, New York.
     Annual. New York: Cooper Union, 1934- . ill, bib

831 Classified List of Photographs of Works of Decorative Art ...
     in the South Kensington Museum and Other Collections.
     London: Eyre & Spottiswoode, 1887; Appendix. 1891;
     4 parts. London: Wyman for HMSO, 1898-1901. 308pp;
     49pp

832 Clement, Arthur Wilfred. The Gentle Art of Collecting; how
     to tell the facts from the fancies. New York: priv. printed,
     Court Pr, 1948. 34pp

833 Clifford, Chandler Robbins. The Decorative Periods. New
     York: Clifford & Lawton, 1906. 310pp, ill, bib (4000 B.C.
     to end of 19th century) NN, DLC, MiGr

834 _____. The Junk Snupper; the adventures of an antique col-
     lector. New York: Macmillan, 1927. 277pp, ill, pls DLC,
     NN

835 _____. Period Decoration. New York: Clifford & Lawton,
     1901. 261pp, ill, pls

836 Cohen, Hal L. Antiques and Collectibles. 4th ed. New
     York: House of Collectibles, 1971. ill, prices

837 _____. Official Guide to Popular Antiques, Curios; the
     prices to buy and sell. 2nd ed. New York: HC (House
     of Collectibles), 1970; 3rd ed. 1971; 4th ed. as Antiques,
     Curios; the price to buy and sell. 1973. 392pp, ill;
     415pp, ill; 222pp, ill

838 Coke, Desmond. Confessions of an Incurable Collector. Lon-
     don: Chapman & Hall, 1928. 254pp, 56 pls, color frontis.
     DLC

839 Cole, Ann Kilborn (pseud. for Claire Wallis Callahan). An-
     tiques: how to identify, buy, sell, refinish, and care for
     them. New York: McKay, 1957; new ed. New York:
     Collier, 1962. 246pp, ill, bib; 287pp, ill, bib

840 _____. The Beginning Antique Collector's Handbook and
     Guide to 1000 Items to Collect. New York: McKay, 1959.
     232pp, ill

841 _____ . Hitting the Antiques Trail. New York: D. McKay,
        1961. 211pp, ill

842 _____ . How to Collect the New Antiques; what they are,
        how to evaluate them. New York: McKay, 1966. 244pp,
        ill, bib (20th-century things)

843 _____ . Old Things for Young People; a guide to antiques.
        New York: McKay, 1963. 174pp, ill, bib (Juvenile
        literature)

844 Cole, Henry, 1808-1882. 50 Years of Public Work, of Sir
        Henry Cole, accounted for in his deeds, speeches and
        writing. Ed. and compiled by Alan S. Cole, and Henrietta
        Cole. 2 vol. London: G. Bell, 1884. ill (Cole was a
        remarkable man who founded the South Kensington Museum;
        invented the term "art manufactures;" and worked all his
        life to encourage the good design of useful objects) NN

845 * _____ , ed. Journal of Design. (Ed. by Felix Summerly,
        pseud.) 6 vol. London: Society for the Encouragement of
        Arts, Manufactures and Commerce, 1849-1852. ill (Covers
        every aspect of applied art) ill

846 _____ . Universal Art Inventory, consisting of brief notes of
        works of fine and ornamental art executed before A.D. 1800,
        chiefly to be found in Europe, especially in connexion with
        architecture, and for the most part existing in ecclesiasti-
        cal buildings. 4 parts. London: Privy Council, Committee
        for Education, 1870-79. BM

847 The Collector and Art Critic. Periodical. New York: D. C.
        Preyer, 1899-1907.

848 The Collectors' Annual. A guide to connoisseurs ... of the
        latest prices realized at auction of pictures ... furniture
        ... plate ... etc. sold during the last season in London
        Sale rooms. Comp. by G. E. East. London: E. Stock,
        1904-1906.

849 The Collector's Guide. Periodical. Cincinnati: W. Mercer,
        1881- .

850 The Collector's Guide. A Canadian amateur journal. Periodi-
        cal. Coleshill: 1942- .

851 *Collectors Weekly. Kermit, Tx: 1969- .

852 Collectors Weekly: the antiques and art newspaper. London:
        City Magazines, 1970- .

853 The Connoisseur. Bailey, Banks and Biddle's illustrated
        quarterly of art and decoration. Philadelphia: 1886-1889.

854 *The Connoisseur. A journal for art and curio collectors. 8
     times yearly. London: National Magazine Co, 1901-date.
     ill, pls

855 The Connoisseur Year Book. London: 1950-date.

856 Cook, Olive, and Edwin Smith. Collectors' Items from the
     "Saturday Book." London: Hutchinson, 1955. 128pp,
     267 ill

857 Cooper, G., architect. Designs for the Decoration of Rooms
     in the Various Styles of Modern Embellishment, with
     pilasters and friezes at large. London: J. Taylor, 1807.
     20 large pls DeWint

858 Cooper Union Museum for the Arts of Decoration. Chronicle.
     Annual; irregular. New York: 1934-date.

859   . An Illustrated Survey of the Collections. New
     York: 1957. 46pp, ill

860 Cowie, Donald P. Antiques: how to identify and collect them.
     South Brunswick, NJ: A. S. Barnes; London: Yoseloff,
     1970. 201pp, ill, 4 pls

861   , and Keith Henshaw. Antique Collectors' Dictionary.
     London: Arco; 1962; New York; London: Arco, 1963.
     208pp, ill, 12 pls, marks (1600 items arranged alpha-
     betically)

662 Coysh, Arthur Wilfred. The Antique Buyers' Dictionary of
     Names. New York: Praeger; Newton Abbot: David &
     Charles, 1970; rev. ed. London: Pan Books, 1972. 278pp,
     ill, 16 pls, bib (1700 names of designers and craftsmen)

863 Crane, Walter, 1845-1915. The Claims of Decorative Art.
     London: Lawrence & Bullen, 1892. 191pp, ill

864   . Ideals in Art: papers--theoretical--practical--
     critical. London: G. Bell, 1905. Includes house deco-
     ration, temporary street decorations, gilding, etc.

865 Crouch, Joseph, and Edmund Butler. The Apartments of the
     House. Their arrangement, furnishing and decoration.
     London: At the Sign of the Unicorn, 1900. 197pp, ill,
     pls MB

866 Curtis, Richard Anthony (Tony). The Antique Dealers Pocket-
     book. Galashiels, Scotland: Lyle Publications; New York:
     Scribner's, 1972- . 158pp, 2000 ill

867   , ed. The Lyle Book of Antiques and Their Value.
     Worthing, Eng: Lyle Publications, 1971. 138pp, ill (1600-
     1910)

868 _____. The Lyle Official Antiques Review. Worthing, Eng:
         Lyle Publications, 1972- . 500pp each, 5000 ill

869 _____, comp. More Popular Antiques and Their Values.
         Worthing, Eng: Lyle, 1973- . 127pp, over 1000 ill

870 _____, and M. J. Miller, comp. and ed. Popular Antiques
         and Their Values. Worthing, Eng: Lyle, 1971; 2nd ed.
         1973; 1974. 124pp, 1000 ill

871 Daubeny, Ulric, and H. Beresford Stevens. How to Choose
         Antiques: with a section on Chinese armorial porcelain by
         Sir Algernon Tudor-Craig. London: E. J. Burrow, 1924.
         106pp, ill, pls NN

872 Dauterman, Carl Christian, James Parker, and Edith Appleton
         Standen. Decorative Art from the Samuel H. Kress Collec-
         tion at the Metropolitan Museum: the tapestry room from
         Croome Court, furniture, textiles, Sevres porcelain and
         other objects. London: Phaidon Pr, for the Kress Founda-
         tion, 1964. 305pp, ill, 8 pls, bib

873 Day, Lewis Foreman. Every-day Art: short essays on the
         arts not fine. London: Batsford, 1882. 283pp, many ill
         NN-Ave, DLC

874 Deane, Ethel. Byways of Collecting. London: Cassell, 1908.
         192pp, 73 ill, pls DLC, NN

875 Decorative Art. The Studio Year Book. London: 1906- .

876 Decorative Arts. Periodical. New York: 1934- .

877 *The Delaware Antiques Show. Catalogues. Wilmington: Dela-
         ware Hospital, 19- . ill, pls, articles by experts

878 Dewing, Maria Richards (Mrs. T. W.), 1855-1927. Beauty in
         the Household. New York: Harper, 1882. 183pp, ill, pls
         DeWint, PPL, DLC

879 Dexter, George Blake. The Lure of Amateur Collecting.
         Boston: Little, Brown, 1923; London: Hutchinson, 1924.
         189pp, pls NN, MiGr

880 Dictionary Catalogue of the Art and Architecture Division, New
         York Public Library. Boston: G. K. Hall, 1975. (photo-
         reproduction of catalog)

881 Discovering Antiques: the story of world antiques. Issued in
         weekly parts, with binder. London: Purnell, 1970-1972;
         20 vol. New York: Greystone, 1972. (2523)pp, ill, bib,
         gloss (Renaissance to 20th century)

882 Doane, Ethel Mary. Antiques Dictionary. Brockton, Mass:
     Anthoesen Pr, 1949. 290pp, bib

883 Donahue, Kenneth. A Decade of Collecting, 1965-1975. Exhi-
     bition. April 1975. Los Angeles: County Museum of Art,
     1975. 248pp, 144 (124 color) pls

884 Dorn, Sylvia O'Neill. The Insider's Guide to Antiques, Art
     and Collectibles. Garden City, NY: Doubleday, 1974.
     334pp, bib

885 Douglas, Jane. Collectible Things. London: Longacre, 1961.
     63pp, ill, bib

886 _____ . How to Collect: silver, furniture, glass, china,
     things. First published in 5 parts. 5 vol. in 1. London:
     Newnes, 1966. 319pp, ill, bib

887 Doussy, Michel. Antiques: professional secrets for the ama-
     teur. Tr. from French (1971) by Patrick Dennis. London:
     Souvenir Pr, 1973. 373pp, ill

888 Dowling, Henry George. Painters' and Decorators' Work.
     London: Routledge, 1916. 151pp, ill, 33 (4 color) pls of
     400 figures, bib

889 Drepperd, Carl William. First Reader for Antique Collectors.
     Garden City, NY: Doubleday, 1946; 1948. 274pp, ill, bib
     DLC, MiGr

890 _____ . Treasures in Truck and Trash, by Morgan Towne
     (pseud.). Garden City, NY: Doubleday, 1950.

891 _____ , and Marjorie Matthews Smith. Handbook of Tomor-
     row's Antiques. New York: Crowell, 1953. 212pp, well-
     ill (Includes agricultural tools, gaming devices, kitchen
     utensils, signs, etc.)

892 DuCann, Charles Garfield Lott. Adventures in Antiques.
     London: F. Muller, 1965. 204pp, ill, 12 pls

893 _____ . Antiques for Amateurs. London: F. Muller, 1962;
     1968; New York: Barnes & Noble, 1968. 176pp, ill

894 Durant, Mary B. The American Heritage Guide to Antiques.
     New York: American Heritage Pr, 1970. u.p., ill, bib

895 Durdik, Jan, and others. The Pictorial Encyclopedia of An-
     tiques. Tr. from German ms. Feltham: Hamlyn, 1970.
     496pp, ill, 64 pls, bib

896 Duthie, Arthur Louis. Stencils and Stencilling for All Purposes:

artistic and decorative. London: Trade Papers; New York: Painters' Magazine, 1914. 159pp, ill NN, DLC

897   Eberlein, Harold Donaldson. Making and Furnishing Outdoor Rooms and Porches. New York: McBride, Nast, 1913. 61pp, ill, pls DLC

898   _____, Abbot McClure, and Edward Stratton Holloway. The Practical Book of Interior Decoration. Philadelphia; London: Lippincott, 1919; new ed. with supplement on modern decoration. 1937. 450pp, 290 ill, 7 color pls (English, Italian, Spanish and French) MiGr

899   Eccles, Lord David. On Collecting. London: Longmans, 1968. 136pp, ill, 8 pls, bib

900   Elliott, Huger. Fashions in Art. New York; London: Appleton-Century, 1937. 338pp, ill, pls, bib

901   Emmons, Verna. Briefs on Antiques: know your antiques before you buy or sell. New York: Vantage Pr, 1953. 57pp

902   European Decorative Arts. Exhibition. Indianapolis: Museum of Art, 1975. 50pp, ill (English, Continental and Russian)

903   European Decorative Arts in the 18th Century. Exhibition. Detroit: Institute of Arts, 1961. 52pp, ill, pls

904   Evolution of the Home. Exhibition of Sears, Roebuck and Company, at Museum of Science and Industry, Chicago 1941. Souvenir pamphlet and photographs bound by the New York Public Library. NN

905   Falke, Jakob von. Art in the House. Historical, critical, and aesthetical studies on the decoration and furnishing of the dwelling. Tr. from the 3rd German ed. Ed. by Charles C. Perkins. Boston: L. Prang, 1879. 356pp, ill, 60 pls (many color) MB, NNC-Ave

906   Farwell, William Henry, and George Farwell. What Is It Worth? Advice on buying and selling antiques. Rutland, Vt: Tuttle, 1973. 135pp

907   Field, June. The Ordinary Man's Guide to Collecting Antiques. London: Gifford, 1971. 126pp, ill, bib

908   The Fine Arts. Monthly. New York: 1923-1933.

909   Fine Arts Catalogue. Books in the Library on gardening and town planning, architecture, sculpture, carving, numismatics, pottery, art metal work, drawing and decoration, painting,

engraving, photography. Newcastle-upon-Tyne: Public Libraries, 1934. 226pp

910 Firth, Catherine Beatrice, ed. Museum Bookshelf, 3: modern centuries 1600 to 1960 A.D. 7 vol. London: Ginn, 1964. Vol. I-VI: 32pp each, ill; Vol. VII: 16pp (Dress; furniture; glass; houses; pottery and porcelain; silver; teacher's booklet. Juvenile literature)

911 Flayderman, E. Norman, and Edna Lagerwall. Collecting Tomorrow's Antiques Today. Garden City, NY: Doubleday, 1972. 222pp, ill, bib

912 Frankl, Paul Theodore. Form and Re-form; a practical handbook of modern interiors. New York: Harper, 1930. 203pp, ill, bib

913. Freeman, Graydon La Verne. How to Price Antiques. Watkins Glen, NY: Century, 1948; 1964. u.p., ill

914 _____. How to Restore Antiques. Watkins Glen, NY: Century, 1960. 96pp, ill

915 _____. One Collector's Luck. Watkins Glen, NY: Century, 1946. 98pp, ill

916 French, Lillie Hamilton. Homes and Their Decoration. New York: Dodd, Mead, 1903. 430pp, ill, 31 pls NN, DLC

917 _____. The House Dignified; its design, its arrangement and its decoration. New York; London: Putnam, 1908. 157pp, 45 pls PPL, DLC

918 Fry, Plantagenet Somerset (pseud.). Collecting Inexpensive Antiques. London: Hamlyn, 1973. 159pp, ill, bib (1850-1939)

919 _____. The World of Antiques. Introd. by Ralph and Terry Kovel. London; New York: Hamlyn, 1970. 141pp, ill

920 The Furnisher and Decorator. Periodical. London: 1889- .

921 Gabhart, Ann. Treasures and Rarities; Renaissance, mannerist, and baroque. Baltimore: Walters Art Gallery, 1971. 39pp, ill

922 Gade, Felix. Collecting Antiques for Pleasure and Profit; the narrative of 25 years search for antique furniture, prints, china, paintings, and other works of art.... London: Werner Laurie, 1921; New York: Putnam's, 1922. 222pp, ill, pls, price guide PP, MiGr

923 The Gallery: antiques, art, interior design. Bi-monthly.
     Lafayette, Cal: Alan Holmes, 1970- .

924 Gardner, Eugene Clarence, 1836-1915. Home Interiors.
     Boston: J. R. Osgood, 1878. 268pp, ill, pls NN, DeWint

925 _____. Homes and All About Them. Boston: J. R. Os-
     good, 1885. 710pp, ill, pls MB, MH

926 Gardner, Franklin B. Everybody's Paint Book. A complete
     guide to the art of outdoor and indoor painting. Designed
     for the special use of those who wish to do their own work,
     and consisting of practical lessons in plain painting, var-
     nishing, polishing, staining, paper-hanging, kalsomining,
     etc. New York: M. T. Richardson, 1881; 1884; 1886;
     1892. 188pp, ill NN, DLC, DeWint

927 Garrett, Rhoda, and Agnes Garrett. Suggestions for House
     Decoration in Painting, Woodwork, and Furniture. London:
     Macmillan, 1876; 3rd ed. London: Macmillan; Philadelphia:
     Porter & Coates, 1877; London: 1896. 90pp, ill, pls NN,
     MB, MiGr

928 Gaupp, Polly, and Charles Gaupp. My Grandmother Had One
     Like It: a picture book of antiques. East Sandwich, Mass:
     The House of the Clipper Ship Pr, 1970. u.p., ill

929 General Guide to the Art Collections. 12 parts. Dublin:
     Science & Art Museum, 1899-1935. 1. Greek and Roman
     Antiquities; 2. Medieval and Renaissance Sculpture and
     Decoration, by G. T. Plunkett, 1909. 48pp; 3. Egyptian
     Antiquities; 4. Lace and Embroidery, by Alan S. Cole,
     1899; 5. Enamels, by Plunkett; 6. Metal Work, Plunkett and
     M. S. D. Westropp, 1903-04; 1908-1914; 7. Pottery and
     Porcelain: chapter 1. British Pottery, by Aubrey J. Top-
     pin, 1904, 64pp; 2. British Porcelain, by Toppin, 1905,
     45pp; 3. French Pottery, by J. J. Buckley, 1910, 32pp,
     12 pls; 4. French Porcelain, by Westropp, 1905; 1915;
     37pp, 47pp; 5. Spanish Pottery and Porcelain, by Westropp,
     1906; 31pp; 6. Dutch Pottery and Porcelain, by J. Day,
     1905, 16pp; 7. Flemish and German Stoneware, by Day,
     1906, 16pp; 8. Porcelain, Northern, Central and Eastern
     Europe, by Day, 1906, 26pp; 9. Italian Pottery and Porce-
     lain, by Westropp, 1907, 40pp; 10. Chinese Porcelain, by
     Day, 1905, 42pp; 11 (or 12). Japanese Pottery and Porcelain,
     by Westropp, 1907, 44pp; Part 8. Furniture, by Plunkett,
     1905-1911; 9. Glass, by Day, 1906, 38pp; 9. English and
     Foreign Glass, Westropp, 1920, Irish Glass, Westropp,
     1913, 1918, 1920; 10. Japanese Art, chapter 1. Lacquer,
     by E. Alabaster, 1905, 24pp; 10. Arms and Armour--
     European, by Westropp, 2 parts. 1906, 29pp and 46pp;
     11. Coins and Medals; 12. Water-colour and Oil Paintings;
     15. Ivories, by E. P. Alabaster, 1910, 54pp; English

Pottery Figures, 1911, 39pp, 14 pls; Metal Work--Gold and Silver, by Westropp, 5th ed. 1934, 75pp, 22 pls; Pottery and Porcelain. Irish, by Westropp, 1935, 43pp, 13 pls.

930 Gilbert, Anne. Antique Hunting: a guide for freaks and fanciers. New York: Grossett & Dunlap, 1975. ill

931 *Gilman, Roger. Great Styles of Interior Architecture, with Their Decoration and Furniture. New York; London: Harper, 1924. 265pp, ill, 125 pls, bib NNC-Ave, MiGr

932 Glencross, June. The Story of Antiques. London: Ward Lock, 1973. 144pp, ill (To 1910)

933 Gohm, Douglas Charles. Small Antiques for the Collector. London: Gifford, 1968; New York: Arco, 1970. 223pp, ill, 8 color pls, bib

934 Goldstein, Harriet Irene, and Vetta Goldstein. Art in Everyday Life. New York: Macmillan, 1925; 1926; 1928; 1930; 4th ed. 1954. 465pp, ill, pls (part color); 1954: 515pp, ill, pls (Interior decoration, clothing, etc.)

935 Good Housekeeping. Monthly. New York: etc.: 1885-1919.

936 Goodwin, Michael. (The Country Life) Pocket Dictionary of Collectors' Terms. London: Country Life; New York: Philosophical Library, 1967. 317pp, ill, bib

937 Gordon, Hampden. Antiques; the amateur's questions. London: J. Murray, 1951; reprint. 1962. 174pp, ill, bib

938 _____. Antiques in Their Periods, 1600-1830. London: J. Murray, 1952; reprint. 1964. 167pp, ill, bib

939 Grant, Ian, ed. Great Interiors. Pref. by Cecil Beaton. London: Weidenfeld & Nicolson, 1967. 288pp, ill, color pls (1650-1960)

940 Great Britain Patent Office. Library. Subject List of Works on ... electricity (1904); enamelling, art metalwork, furniture, costume and hairdressing (1914); textile industries (1902); etc. London: HMSO. DLC

941 Griffith, Corinne. Antiques I Have Known. New York: F. Fell, 1961. 275pp, ill

942 Gross, Leslie. Housewives' Guide to Antiques; how to get the most for your money when furnishing your home with antiques. New York: Exposition Pr, 1959. 180pp, ill

943 Grotz, George. Antiques You Can Decorate With; a practical guide to what they are, where to find them, and how much

to pay for them. Rev. ed. with current price guide.
Garden City, NY: Doubleday, 1971. 322pp, ill

944   Guest, Edith E. Haden. Your Hearth and Home Through the
      Centuries. London: Allen & Unwin, 1949; 1954. 44pp,
      ill, bib

945 *Guppy, Henry, and Guthrie Vine, eds. A Classified Catalogue
      of the Works on Architecture and the Allied Arts in the
      Principal Libraries of Manchester and Salford. Manchester,
      Eng: U Pr, 1909. 310pp (Modified Dewey classification)
      MG, NN, DLC, DeWint

946   Hammond, Dorothy. Confusing Collectibles. Leon, Iowa:
      Mid-America Book, 1969. 221pp, pls

947 *Hand-List of the Books on the Decorative Arts in the Reference
      Department. Liverpool: Free Public Library, 1899; sup-
      plement. 1902. 113pp; 17pp

948   Harper, George W., ed. Antique Collector's Guide and Ref-
      erence Handbook. New York: G. W. Harper, 1939. 87pp,
      ill, bib (Contains: "The American Wing," by J. Down;
      "Why and How to Collect," by T. H. Ormsbee; Bibliography
      by Alice Winchester; Glossary by G. W. Harper) MiGr

949   Harrison, Constance Cary, 1843-1920, ed. Household Art.
      New York: Harper, 1893. 204pp (Interior decoration,
      wall-papers, ceilings and dados, furniture, decorative arts,
      etc.) DeWint

950   _____ . Woman's Handiwork in Modern Homes. New York:
      Scribner's, 1881; 1882. 242pp, pls (some color) (Em-
      broidery, painting, interior decoration) DeWint, PPL, DLC

951   Hasluck, Paul Nooncree, ed. Cassells's House Decoration; a
      practical guide to painters' and decorators' work. London;
      New York: Cassell, 1908; 1910. 568pp, 835 ill, 12 (9
      color) pls MB

952   Haweis, Mary Eliza, 1852-1898. The Art of Decoration. Lon-
      don: Chatto & Windus, 1881; new ed. 1889. 407pp, ill,
      pls MiGr, DeWint, NNC-Ave

953 *Hayden, Arthur, 1868-1946. Bye-paths in Curio Collecting.
      London: Fisher Unwin, 1919; 1920. 462pp, ill, 72 pls
      (Boxes, fans, toys, tobacco things, pomanders, watch
      stands, papier-mache trays, keys, door knockers, etc.)
      NN

954   Hayward, Helena, ed. The Connoisseur's Handbook of Antique
      Collecting; a dictionary of furniture, silver, ceramics,

glass, fine art, etc. Introd. by L. G. G. Ramsey. London: The Connoisseur; New York: Hawthorn, 1960. 320pp, ill

955 Heaton, John Aldam, 1830-1897. Beauty and Art. New York: Appleton, 1897. 208pp (House decoration, furniture, fabrics; 18th century) NN

956 Hensley, Martha L. Bibliography on Home Improvement; (or Bibliography on Home Furnishing). Washington, D.C.: Department of Agriculture, 1952. 26pp

957 Herrmann, Frank. The English as Collectors: a documentary chrestomathy, selected, introduced and annotated. London: Chatto & Windus, 1972. 461pp, ill, 48 pls, bib (Readings from contemporary sources 1750-1963)

958 Herts, Benjamin Russell. The Decoration and Furnishing of Apartments; the artistic treatment of apartments ranging from the small two-room suite to the elaborate duplex and triplex. New York; London: Putnam's, 1915. 190pp, ill, 40 color pls NNC-Ave, ViU

959 Hertz, Louis Heilbroner. Antique Collecting for Men. New York: Hawthorn, 1969. 416pp, ill (Typewriters, machines, tools, toys, clocks, weapons, etc., all equally suitable for women to collect)

960 Higgins, W. Mullingar. The House Painter, or Decorators' Companion, being a complete treatise on ... the manufacture of pigments, oils and varnishes, and the art of house painting, graining and marbling.... London: T. Kelly, 1841. 233pp, ill, 30 color facsimile pls

961 Higgs, Percy Jackson, comp. The Collectors Reference Book of Dates (from the antique to the 18th century). New York: The Lent & Graff Co, 1927. 48pp, ill, pls DLC

962 Hipkiss, Edwin James. Handbook of the Department of Decorative Arts of Europe and America. Boston: Museum of Fine Arts, 1928; 2nd ed. 1929. 110pp, ill

963 *History of the House. Ed. by Ettore Camesasca. Fore. by Sir Robert Matthew. Tr. from Italian (1968) by Isabel Quigly. New York: Putnam's, 1971. 432pp, ill (some color) (Furniture, interiors, paintings showing interiors, architecture)

964 Hobbies Magazine. Camden, NJ: 1918-1919. (Merged into Collectors Journal, Milford, Conn.)

965 *Hobbies. The magazine for collectors. Periodical. Chicago: Lightner, 1931-date. (Antiques and collectibles)

966 Hodes, Scott. The Law of Art and Antiques; a primer for
     artists and collectors. Dobbs Ferry, NY: Oceana Publica-
     tions, 1966. 112pp, forms

967 Hodgson, Mrs. (A.) Willoughby. The Quest of the Antique.
     London: Jenkins; New York: Dodd, Mead, 1924. 255pp,
     63 pls, color frontis MiGr, MB

968 Horn, Jeanne. Hidden Treasure; how and where to find it.
     New York: Arco, 1962. 234pp, ill

969 Hotchkiss, John F. Limited Edition Collectibles. Rochester,
     NY: Hotchkiss House, 1974. 192pp, ill (Old and new
     porcelain, pottery, paper, metal, etc.)

970 House and Garden. Monthly. Greenwich, Conn: 1901- .

971 House Beautiful. Monthly. New York, etc.: Hearst, 1896- .

972 The House Beautiful and the Home; an illustrated journal for
     those who design, beautify, furnish and inhabit houses.
     Monthly. London: 1897-1903; as The House Beautiful and
     Home. 1904-05.

973 The House Furnisher, and decorators, upholsterers and cabinet
     makers' monthly journal. London: 1871-1873.

974 Hughes, George Bernard. The Antique Collectors Pocket Book.
     New York: Hawthorn, 1963; 1965; as The 'Country Life'
     Collector's Pocket Book. London: Country Life, 1963;
     1965. 351pp, ill

975 _____. More About Collecting Antiques. London: Country
     Life; New York: Scribner, 1952. 272pp, ill, bib (China,
     toys, paste jewellery, shell-cameos, posy-holders, warming
     pans, Valentines, etc.)

976 Hughes, Therle. Antiques: an illustrated A to Z. London:
     Macgibbon & Kee, 1971. 175pp, 523 ill (To 1901)

977 * _____. More Small Decorative Antiques. London: Lutter-
     worth, 1962; New York: Macmillan, 1963. 216pp, ill, 51
     (4 color) pls

978 _____. Small Antiques for the Collector. London: Lutter-
     worth, 1964; New York: Macmillan, 1965. 222pp, ill,
     48 pls

979 _____. Small Decorative Antiques. London: Lutterworth,
     1959; New York: Macmillan, 1960. 223pp, ill, pls

980 *Husband, Timothy B. The Secular Spirit: life and art at the
     end of the middle ages. Exhibition at the Cloisters,

Metropolitan Museum of Art. April-June 1975. New York: Dutton, 1975. 279 objects ill (Whistles, falcon tags, boar spears, knives and swords, weapons, hunting horns, precious metal objects, ecclesiastical objects, etc.)

981 Hutchinson, Elsie Lillian. The Housefurnishings Department-- department store merchandise manual. New York: N.Y. University, Ronald Pr, 1918; 1922.

982 *Index to The Magazine Antiques. New York: Antiques, 1922- 1951; 1952-1956; 1957-1961; 1962-1966; 1967-1971.

983 *Interior Architecture and Decoration; a selected list of references compiled under the direction of the Committee on Education of the American Institute of Decorators. New York: N.Y. Public Library, 1938. 37pp

984 Interior Design. Monthly. New York: Anderson, 1932- .

985 Interiors. Monthly. New York: Whitney, 1888- .

986 International Antiques Yearbook. Compiled by Marcelle d'Argy Smith and Elizabeth Dick. Annual. London: Antiques Yearbook, 1949-date.

987 The International Studio. Monthly. New York: John Lane, 1897-1931. (From March 1897 to October 1921 it formed the American part of the London-printed Studio)

988 *The Ivory Hammer: the year at Sotheby's. Periodical. London: Longmans, 63-date. (See: Art at Auction, no. 768)

989 Jekyll, Gertrude, 1843-1932. Flower Decoration in the House. London: Country Life, 1907. 98pp, ill, pls MB

990 Jenkins, Dorothy Helen. A Fortune in the Junk Pile; a guide to valuable antiques. New York: Crown, 1963. 440pp, 300 photographs

991 Jennings, Arthur Seymour. The Decoration and Renovation of the Home. A practical handbook for house owners and tenants, architects, decorators and others. Includes chapter "Period Furniture from a Decorative Point of View," by Herbert E. Binstead. New York: Spon & Chamberlain; London: W. R. Howell, 1923. 220pp, ill, 14 color pls, bib NN, MB

992 _____, and Guy Cadogan Rothery. The Modern Painter and Decorator. A practical treatise on house, church, theatre, and public buildings painting and decorating. 3 vol. London: Caxton, 1922; 4th ed. London: 1944. text, ill, pls (some color), bib

993 Jerningham, Charles Edward W. The Art and Curio Collec-
     tor's Guide: being a guide to the dealers in art, old
     furniture, old plate.... London: Cassell, 1899; 1910.
     48pp, ill MiGr

994 _____, and Lewis Bettany. The Bargain Book. London:
     Chatto & Windus; New York: Warne, 1911. 339pp, ill,
     pls

995 Johns, Geoffrey (pseud. for Geoffrey John George Warner).
     Enjoy Collecting Antiques. London: Gollancz, 1963.
     125pp, ill

996 Johnson, Stowers. Collectors' Luck. London: Phoenix
     House, 1968. 211pp, 47 ill, 24 pls

997 Jones, Barbara, and Bill Howell. Popular Arts of the First
     World War. New York: McGraw-Hill, 1972. 175pp, ill
     (Handmade objects from shell cases; model airplanes;
     toys, etc.)

998 Kaduck, John M. Sleepers That Have a Future: small col-
     lectors items. Des Moines: Wallace-Homestead, 1970.
     21 color pls (Watch fobs, knives, pocket watches, button
     hooks, etc.)

999 Kelley, Austin P., and staff of Sotheby Parke Bernet. The
     Anatomy of Antiques: a collectors guide. New York:
     Studio-Viking, 1974. 189pp, ill, 19 color pls

1000 Kellogg, Alice Maude, 1862-1911. Home Furnishing, Prac-
      tical and Artistic. New York: F. A. Stokes, 1905;
      rev. by Amy L. Barrington. 1924. 265pp, 55 ill, 30
      pls; 271pp, ill, 43 pls ViU, DeWint, MB

1001 Kinard, Epsie. The Care and Keeping of Antiques. Fore.
      by Marvin D. Schwartz. New York: Hawthorn, 1971.
      160pp, ill, bib

1002 King, John, and Paul Smith. "Going for a Song": questions
      and answers (about antiques). London: British Broad-
      casting Co, 1971. 108pp, 153 ill

1003 Klamkin, Marian. Flower Arranging for Period Decoration.
      New York: Funk & Wagnalls, 1969. 213pp, ill, bib

1004 Kovel, Ralph, and Terry Kovel. The Complete Antique
      Price List; a guide to the 1969 (etc.) market for pro-
      fessionals, dealers and collectors. New York: Crown,
      1968; 1969;... rev. 7th ed. 1975. 436pp, ill; 720pp,
      500 ill, etc.

1005 * _____, and _____. Know Your Antiques. How to

recognize and evaluate any antique, large or small, like an expert. New York: Crown, 1967; rev. ed. 1973. 327pp, ill, bib, list of collector's groups in several fields

1006 Labarte, Jules, 1797-1880. Handbook of the Arts of the Middle Ages and Renaissance, as applied to the decoration of furniture, arms, jewels, etc. Tr. from French by Fanny Palliser. London: J. Murray, 1855. 443pp, many ill NN, DLC, NNC-Ave

1007 Lackschewitz, Gertrud, comp. Interior Design and Decoration; a bibliography; compiled for the American Institute of Interior Designers. New York: N.Y. Public Library, 1961. 86pp NNC-Ave

1008 Leeming, Joseph. Fun for Young Collectors; an introduction to 32 collection projects with information on sources for finds and on making cases for effective display. Philadelphia: Lippincott, 1953. 88pp, ill, bib (Juvenile literature)

1009 Lewer, Henry William, and MacIver Percival. The Bric-a-Brac Collector. London: Jenkins; New York: Dodd Mead, 1923. 256pp

1010 Library Association. County Libraries Section. Readers' Guide to Books on House and Home. London: 1948; 2nd ed. London: Chaucer House, 1959. 31pp (pp. 23-27 on antiques)

1011 List of Books on Decoration in Edinburgh Museum Library. Edinburgh: 1902.

1012 A List of Complete Periodical Holdings in the Art and Design Library. Manchester, Eng: Polytechnic Library, 1972. 28pp

1013 List of Works in the New York Public Library Relating to Furniture and Interior Decoration. Reprint from Bulletin, September 1908. New York: the Library, 1908. 32pp

1014 Litchfield, Frederick, 1850-1930. Antiques, Genuine and Spurious; an art expert's recollections and cautions.... New York: Harcourt, Brace & Howe; London: G. Bell, 1921; London: 1924. 277pp, pls, color frontis (Porcelain, furniture, enamels, bronzes) MiGr

1015 Loan Exhibition of Heirlooms and Many Other Old-Fashioned Things from the Homes on Nantucket Island, at the Charles G. Coffin Mansion. August 1935. Nantucket, Mass: Cottage Hospital, 1935. 79pp, ill, pls

1016 Lockwood, Sarah M. Decoration: past, present and future.

       Garden City, NY: Doubleday, Doran, 1934.   198pp, ill,
       bib MB, BM

1017 Loftie, Mrs. Martha Jane. The Dining Room. London:
       Macmillan, 1878. 128pp, ill

1018 Loftie, William John. A Plea for Art in the House, with
       special reference to the economy of collecting works of
       art, and the importance of taste in education and morals.
       London: Macmillan; Philadelphia: Porter & Coates, 1876.
       100pp, ill, 2 pls

1019 Looking at the Past. 11 vol. London: Ginn, 1959-1971.
       (Stone, by Elsa Nunn; Silver, by Erica O'Donnell; Every-
       day Metals, by E. Nunn; Gold, Silver and Precious Stones;
       Houses; Dress; Furniture; Glass; Pottery and Porcelain, by
       O'Donnell; Leather, by John William Waterer; Threads, by
       several authors. Juvenile literature)

1020 Lucas, Alfred, 1867-1945. Antiques: their restoration and
       preservation. 2nd ed. London: Arnold, 1924; 2nd rev.
       ed. 1932; reprint. Bath: Chivers, 1974. 240pp, bib

1021 The Lyle Official Antiques Review. Periodical. Selkirshire,
       Scotland: 19- .

1022 [No entry.]

1023 McClinton, Katharine Morrison. Antique Cats for Collectors.
       New York: Scribner's, 1973. 180pp, ill, 1 pl, bib
       (Porcelain, pottery, metal, chalkware, squeak-toy, needle-
       work, etc.)

1024 _____ . Antique Collecting for Everyone. New York:
       McGraw-Hill, 1951; abridged as Antique Collecting. Green-
       wich, Conn: Fawcett, 1952. 252pp, 200 ill, bib; 144pp,
       ill

1025 * _____ . Antiques Past and Present. New York: Potter,
       1970. 288pp, 285 ill (19th century)

1026 _____ . The Complete Book of Small Antiques Collecting.
       New York: Coward-McCann, 1965. 255pp, 100 ill (Fans,
       pudding molds, paperweights, hinges, souvenir spoons, etc.)

1027 _____ . A Handbook of Popular Antiques. Fore. by Alice
       Winchester. New York: Random House, 1946. 244pp,
       230 ill, bib

1027a Maccoun, Bill. The Antique Finder's Guide; or, the gentle
       art of acquiring antiques. Benicia?, Cal: 1966. 71pp,
       ill

1028   McDonald, John Wilson. In Search of Antiques. Liverpool:
       Gallery Pr, 1967. 115pp, ill

1029   *Macdonald-Taylor, Margaret Stephens, ed. A Dictionary of
       Marks: metalwork, furniture, ceramics. Introd. by L.
       G. G. Ramsey. London: Connoisseur, 1962; 1966; rev.
       ed. 1969; rev. ed. 1973. 318pp, ill, bib, marks (ca. 1500-
       ca. 1900. Includes tapestry marks)

1030   McGrath, Lee Parr. Housekeeping with Antiques. New York:
       Dodd, Mead, 1971. 175pp

1031   Mackay, James Alexander. Antiques of the Future: a guide
       for collectors and investors. London: Studio Vista, 1970.
       208pp, ill, bib

1032   _____. An Introduction to Small Antiques. London:
       Garnstone, 1970. 268pp, ill, 16 pls, bib

1033   _____. Turn-of-the-Century Antiques: an encyclopedia.
       New York: Dutton, 1975; as Dictionary of Turn-of-the-
       Century Antiques. London: 1975. 320pp, ill, color pls,
       350 entries (1890-1910)

1034   McVeigh, Patrick. Antiques: a guide to sensible buying.
       Edinburgh: John Donald Publishers, 1974. 136pp, ill

1035   Magazine of Art. Periodical. 27 vol. London; New York:
       Cassell, 1878-1904.

1036   The Magazine of Art. Monthly. 46 vol. Washington, D.C.;
       American Federation of Arts, 1909-1953.

1037   Marcus, Margaret Fairbanks. Period Flower Arrangement.
       Modern adaptations selected or arranged by Mrs. Anson
       H. Smith. New York: M. Barrows, 1952. 256pp, ill,
       bib (Includes history)

1038   Mayer, Joseph, 1803-1886. Catalogue of Medieval and Later
       Antiquities Contained in the Mayer Museum. (Free Public
       Library Museum.) Liverpool: 1883.

1039   Mebane, John. Collecting Nostalgia: the first guide to the
       antiques of the 30s and 40s. New Rochelle, NY: Arling-
       ton House, 1972. 367pp, ill, bib (370 items)

1040   _____. The Coming Collection Boom. South Brunswick,
       NJ: A. S. Barnes; London: Yoseloff, 1968. 320pp, ill,
       bib

1041 * _____. New Horizons in Collecting: Cinderella antiques.
       South Brunswick, NJ: A. S. Barnes, 1966. 280pp, well-
       ill (Advertising cards, political items, tin containers, etc.)

1042 _____ . The Poor Man's Guide to Antique Collecting.
          Garden City, NY: Doubleday, 1969. 209pp, ill with old
          catalog cuts (Law-enforcement collectibles, trinkets,
          knife rests, cake plates, pin cushions, etc.)

1043 * _____ . Treasures at Home. New York: A. S. Barnes,
          1964. 266pp, ill (Carnival glass, canes, music boxes,
          etc.)

1044 _____ . What's New That's Old; offbeat collectibles. South
          Brunswick, NJ: A. S. Barnes, 1969. 337pp, ill

1045 Menzies, William Gladstone. Collecting Antiques.... New
          York: Dodd, Mead, 1926; London: Lane, 1928. 231pp,
          ill, 65 pls, bib

1046 Metropolitan Museum of Art. Bulletin. Monthly. New York:
          1905-date. (Indexed)

1047 _____ . A Guide to the Collections. New York: 1919;
          1927; 1931; 1934; 1936; 1937; World's Fair edition.
          1939; ...

1048 Michael, George. Antiquing with George Michael. Brattle-
          boro, Vt: Stephen Greene Pr, 1967. 136pp, ill, bib, pls

1049 _____ . The Basic Book of Antiques. New York: Arco,
          1975. 293pp, ill, bib, gloss

1050 Miller, Fred. Interior Decoration. A practical treatise on
          surface decoration. With notes on colour, stencilling, and
          panel painting. London: Wyman, 1885; 2nd ed. 1892.
          145pp, ill, pls

1051 Mills, John FitzMaurice. The Care of Antiques. Pref. by
          A. E. Werner; Fore. by Norman Brommelle. London:
          Arlington Books; New York: Hastings House, 1964. 126pp,
          ill, 27 pls

1052 _____ . Collecting and Looking After Antiques. Feltham:
          Hamlyn, 1973. 159pp, ill, bib

1053 _____ . How to Detect Fake Antiques. London: Arlington
          Books, 1972. 88pp, ill, 28 pls

1054 Molinier, Emile. The Wallace Collection (Objets d'Art) at
          Hertford House. Introd. by Lady Dilke. 2 vol. London:
          Goupil & Co.; Paris: Manzi, Joyant, 1903. ill BM

1055 Moore, Hannah (N.) Hudson. The Collector's Handbooks.
          2 vol. London; Binghamton, NY: Hodder & Stoughton,
          1909. BM

1056 * _____ . The Collector's Manual. New York: F. A.
Stokes, 1906; London; Cambridge, Mass: Chapman & Hall,
1907; ...; New York: Tudor, 1935. 329pp, ill BM

1057 *Museum News. Irregular periodical. Toledo, O: Museum of
Art, 1907- .

1058 National Antiques Review. Monthly. Portland, Me: 1969.

1059 Noel-Hume, Ivor. All the Best Rubbish. New York: Harper
& Row, 1974. 320pp, ill, bib

1060 Noll, Bosco Cass. Upstairs and Downstairs with Antiques.
Garden City, NY: Doubleday, 1970. 80pp, ill

1061 Nystrom, Paul Henry. A Bibliography on Fashion, Costume,
Domestic Architecture and Home Furnishings. New York:
Columbia University, School of Business, 1937. 144pp
NNC-Ave

1062 Ormsbee, Thomas Hamilton. Care and Repair of Antiques.
New York: Medill McBride, 1949. 168pp, ill

1063 _____ . Know Your Heirlooms. New York: McBride,
1956. 128pp, ill

1064 _____ . Prime Antiques and Their Current Prices. New
York: McBride, 1947.

1065 _____ . A Storehouse of Antiques. New York: McBride,
1947. 155pp MiGr

1066 Ormston, Frank Dayton. Antiques for Profit; the art of buying
and selling antiques, near antiques and other old things.
New York: Greenburg, 1953. 172pp

1067 Orrinsmith, Mrs. Lucy. The Drawing-Room; its decorations
and furniture. London: Macmillan, 1877. 145pp, ill,
pls DLC, MiGr

1068 Osborne, Harold Philip. An Outline of the Home Furnishing
Periods; an open door to a better understanding of the
furniture periods. Ontario, Cal: Author, 1939; 3rd rev.
augmented ed. Long Beach, Cal: Outline Publishing Co,
1941. 168pp, ill, bib NNC-Ave

1069 Palmer, Merwyn. Face to Face with Antiques. Dunedin:
John McIndoe, 1971. 78pp, ill, bib

1070 *Parsons, Frank Alvah. The Art of Home Furnishing and
Decoration. Lancaster, Pa: Armstrong Cork Co, Linoleum
Department, 1918. 40pp, 12 (10 color) pls

1071 *_____. Interior Decoration; its principles and practice.
       Garden City, NY: Doubleday, Page, 1915. 284pp, ill,
       pls MiGr

1072 Patterson, Jerry E. The Collectors' Guide to Relics and
       Memorabilia. New York: Crown, 1974. 178pp, ill, bib
       (American Presidency, transportation, literature, music,
       royalty, religion, etc.)

1073 Pearsall, Ronald. Collecting Mechanical Antiques. Newton
       Abbot: David & Charles; New York: Arco, 1973. 197pp,
       ill, bib (1830-1880) (Includes household appliances, ma-
       chinery, inventions of various kinds)

1074 Peek, David T. The Book of Antiques for Boys and Girls.
       Indianapolis: Brand Printing and Photo-Litho, 1960. ill
       (Juvenile literature)

1075 *Phillips, Phoebe, ed. The Collectors' Encyclopedia of An-
       tiques. London: Connoisseur; New York: Crown, 1973.
       704pp, 2000 ill

1076 Phillips, S. A. Chats in Search of the Antique. London:
       Simpkin, Marshall, 1919. 35pp

1077 Philp, Peter. Antiques: a popular guide to antiques for
       everyone. London: Octopus, 1973. 144pp, ill

1078 _____. Antiques Today. London: J. Garnet Miller,
       1960. 157pp, ill, pls

1079 Pischel, Gina. The Golden History of Art: painting, sculp-
       ture, architecture, decorative arts. Tr. from Italian.
       New York: Golden Pr, 1968; Feltham: Hamlyn, 1971.
       718pp, ill

1080 Pollen, John Hungerford. Universal Catalogue of Books on
       Art, Comprehending: painting, sculpture, architecture,
       decoration, coins, antiquities, etc. 3 vol. London:
       Chapman & Hall, 1869-1877. 2212pp, ill

1081 Pope-Hennessy, John. The Random House Encyclopedia of
       Antiques. New York: Random House, 1973. 400pp, ill,
       bib

1082 Praz, Mario. An Illustrated History of Furnishing, from the
       Renaissance to the 20th century. (Also as An Illustrated
       History of Interior Decoration.) Tr. from Italian (1945)
       by William Weaver. New York: G. Braziller; London:
       Thames & Hudson, 1964. 396pp, 400 ill

1083 Price, Christine. Made in the Middle Ages. New York:

Dutton, 1961; London: 1962; new ed. London: Bodley Head, 1973. 118pp, ill; 120pp, ill (Juvenile literature. Crafts)

1084 _____. Made in the Renaissance. Arts and crafts of the Age of Exploration. New York: Dutton, 1963; London: Bodley Head, 1973. 120pp, ill (Juvenile literature)

1085 *Ramsey, L. G. G., ed. The Complete Encyclopedia of Antiques. Compiled by The Connoisseur, London. New York: Hawthorn, 1962. 1472pp, many ill, 512 pls, bib (Compiled from the 5 Volume Concise Encyclopedia of Antiques, and 2 Volume The Concise Encyclopedia of American Antiques)

1086 * _____. The Concise Encyclopedia of Antiques. 1 vol. London; New York: Connoisseur, 1954; 2 vol. 1955-56; 5 vol. New York: Hawthorn, 1955-1961. 288pp, ill, bib

1087 Rawson, Marion Nicholl. The Antiquer's Picture Book. New York: Dutton, 1940. 96pp, ill

1088 Reif, Rita. The Antique Collector's Guide to Styles and Prices. New York: Hawthorn, 1970. 276pp, ill (Gothic to 20th century)

1089 Renaissance Exhibition; tapestries, Italian paintings, Limoges enamels, majolica, bronzes, armor, and other objects of the 15th to 17th centuries. November-December 1926. Baltimore: Museum of Art, 1926. 63pp, ill

1090 Revi, Albert Christian, ed. Spinning Wheel's Antiques for Men. Hanover, Pa: Spinning Wheel, 1974. 160pp, ill (Another with antiques for men and women)

1091 _____, ed. Spinning Wheel's Antiques for Women. Hanover, Pa: Spinning Wheel, 1974. 160pp, ill (The same for this)

1092 _____, ed. The Spinning Wheel's Complete Book of Antiques. New York: Grosset & Dunlap, 1972; Hanover, Pa: Spinning Wheel, 1973. 600pp, ill (318 articles from back issues)

1093 Reynolds, Ernest Randolph. The Plain Man's Guide to Antique Collecting. London: M. Joseph, 1963; as Guide to European Antiques. New York: Barnes, 1964. 185pp, ill, 16 pls

1094 Rheims, Maurice. The Strange Life of Objects; 35 centuries of art collecting and collectors. Tr. from French by David Pryce-Jones. New York: Atheneum, 1961 274pp ill

1095   Roberts, Kenneth Lewis, 1885-1957, ed. Antiquamania; the
       collected papers of Professor Milton Kilgallen (pseud.),
       F.R.S. of Ugsworth College, elucidating the difficulties
       in the path of the antique dealer and collector, and pre-
       senting various methods of meeting and overcoming them.
       With further illustrations, elucidations and wood-cuts
       done on feather-edged boards, by Booth Tarkington.
       Garden City, NY: Doubleday, 1928. 260pp, pls (Face-
       tiae, satire)

1096   Roberts, William, 1862- . John Starkie Gardner Collection
       of Drawings, etchings, rubbings, photographs, woodcuts,
       prints, manuscript notes, etc., on the history of decora-
       tive art from earliest to modern times. London: Brom-
       head, Cutts & Co, 1923. BM

1097   Robie, Virginia Huntington. By-paths in Collecting; being aids
       in the quest of rare and unique things which have passed
       the century mark, such as old china, furniture, pewter,
       copper, brass, samplers, and sun dials, with comments
       on their age, decoration and value. New York: Century,
       1912. 568pp, ill, color frontis

1098   _____ . The Quest of the Quaint. Boston: Little, Brown,
       1916; new rev. ed. 1927. 287pp, ill; 302pp, ill, pls

1099   Robinson, John Charles. Inventory of the Objects Forming
       the Collections of the Museum of Ornamental Art at
       Marlborough House, Pall Mall. London: South Kensing-
       ton, 1856; 3rd ed. London: Chapman & Hall, 1856; 1859;
       1860; 1863. 1859: 118pp; 1863: 178pp NNC-Ave, BM

1100   _____ . The Treasury of Ornamental Art. Illustrations of
       objects of art and vertu. South Kensington Museum.
       London: HMSO, 1857. ill, 71 pls SKM

1101   Roe, Frederic Gordon. Home Furnishing with Antiques.
       London: J. Baker; New York: Hastings House, 1965.
       211pp, ill, pls, bib

1102   Rogers, John Charles. Furniture and Furnishing. London:
       Oxford U Pr, 1932. 110pp, ill, bib

1103   Rohan, Thomas. In Search of the Antique. London: Mills
       & Boon, 1927; New York: Lincoln MacVeagh, Dial Pr,
       1932. 213pp, 17 ill

1104   _____ . Old Beautiful. London: Mills & Boon, 1926;
       New York: Dial, 1932. 215pp, 23 ill

1105   Roith, Cynthia. Bygones--a gentleman's life. London:
       Corgi, 1972. 94pp, ill (Antiques, 1700-1900)

1106   Rollins, Alice R. Antiques for the Home. New York; Lon-
       don: Harper, 1946. 232pp, ill

1107   Rorimer, James J. The Cloisters, the Building and the Col-
       lection of Medieval Art, in Fort Tryon Park. New York:
       George Grady Pr, for Metropolitan Museum, 1938; 5th ed.
       1941. 118pp, ill

1108   Rothery, Guy Cadogan, 1863- . Ceilings and Their Decora-
       tion; art and archaeology. London: T. W. Laurie, 1911.
       281pp, ill, bib

1109   Rothschild, Alfred de. A Description of the Works of Art
       Forming the Collection of A. de Rothschild. Vol. I.
       Pictures; Vol. II. Sevres China, furniture, metal work,
       and objects de vitrine. 2 vol. London: priv. printed,
       1884. over 200 photographs

1110   Rowed, Charles. Collecting As a Pastime. London; New
       York: Cassell, 1920. 147pp, ill, 45 pls

1111   Runes, Dagobert D., and Harry G. Schrickel, eds. Encyclo-
       pedia of the Arts. New York: Philosophical Library,
       1946. 1064pp (Fine and applied arts)

1112   Salter, Stefan. Joys of Hunting Antiques. New York: Hart,
       1971. 255pp, ill

1113   The Saturday Book. Ed. by John Hadfield. Yearly. London:
       Hutchinson, 1941-date; New York: C. N. Potter, 19- .
       ill (Includes some antiques)

1114   Savage, George. The Antique Collector's Handbook. London:
       Barrie & Rockliff, 1959; new rev. ed. Feltham: Spring
       Books, 1968. 304pp, ill, 16 pls, bib

1115   _____ . The Art and Antique Restorer's Handbook; a dic-
       tionary of materials and processes used in the restoration
       and preservation of all kinds of works of arts. London:
       Barrie & Rockliff; New York: Philosophical Library,
       1954; rev. ed. London: 1967; New York: Praeger, 1967.
       140pp; 142pp, bib

1116   _____ . A Concise History of Interior Decoration. London:
       Thames & Hudson, 1966; New York: Grosset & Dunlap,
       1967. 285pp, 201, ill, bib

1117   _____ . Dictionary of Antiques. London: Barrie & Jenkins;
       New York: Praeger, 1970. 534pp, 695 (45 color) ill, 24
       pls, bib, marks (1500 entries)

1118   _____ . Forgeries, Fakes and Reproductions: a handbook for the collector. London: Barrie & Rockliff, 1963; New York: Praeger, 1964. 312pp, 29 pls, bib

1119   Saylor, Henry Hodgman, ed. Collecting Antiques for the Home.... New York: McBride, 1938. 416pp, ill   MiGr

1120   Scarisbrick, Diana. Baroque: the age of exuberance. London: Orbis, 1973. 64pp, chiefly ill, bib (Decoration and ornament)

1121   Schreiber, Lady Charlotte. Lady C. Schreiber's Journals: confidences of a collector of ceramics and antiques throughout Britain, France, Holland, Belgium, Spain, Portugal, Turkey, Austria and Germany from the year 1869 to 1885. Ed. by her son M. J. Guest. 2 vol. London; New York: John Lane, 1911. 114 (8 color) pls (Montague John Guest)

1122   Schwartz, Marvin D., ed. Antique Collectors Calendar, 1975. Princeton, NJ: Pyne Pr, 1974. 52 ill

1123 * _____, and Betsy Wade. The New York Times Book of Antiques. New York: Quadrangle Books, 1972; 1974. 344pp, over 230 ill (most from Metropolitan Museum), bib

1124   Schwenke, Friedrich. Designs for Decorative Furniture and Modern Chamber-Arrangement; including a practical guide to upholstery, exhibiting the latest improvements in this branch of industrial art.... London: H. Sotheran, 1882. ill, 72 pls   NN, MB

1125   Scott, Amoret, and Christopher Scott. The A to Z of Antique Collecting. London: M. Parrish, 1963. 143pp, ill

1126   _____, and _____. Antiques as an Investment. London: Oldbourne, 1967. 124pp, ill, 8 pls, bib

1127   _____, and _____. Collecting. London: Joseph, 1968. 127pp, ill, bib

1128   _____, and _____. Collecting Bygones. London: Parrish, 1964; New York: D. McKay, 1965. 142pp, ill, 8 pls

1129   _____, and _____. Treasures in Your Attic. London: Kaye & Ward, 1971. 144pp, ill, 16 pls

1130   Scott, William Bell. Half-hour Lectures on the History and Practice of the Fine and Ornamental Arts. London: Longman, Green, 1861; 3rd rev. ed. London: Longmans, 1874; New York: Scribner, Welford & Armstrong, 1875. 363pp, 50 ill; 370pp, ill NN, DeWint, DLC

1131 Shackleton, Robert, and Elizabeth Shackleton. Adventures in
      Homemaking. New York: Lane, 1910. 350pp, pls

1132 _____, and _____. The Book of Antiques. Reissue
      with many changes, of their Charm of the Antique. Phila-
      delphia: Penn Publishing; New York: Tudor, 1938; New
      York: 1943. 284pp, pls MiGr

1133 _____, and _____. The Charm of the Antique. New
      York: Hearst's International Library, 1914. 307pp, ill,
      pls (Furniture) MiGr

1134 Shapland, Henry Percival, and H. Pringuer Benn. Style
      Schemes in Antique Furnishing; interiors and their treat-
      ment. London: Simpkin, Marshall, Hamilton, Kent,
      1909. MiGr

1135 Shepard, Louise. The Antique Shop. New York: Rosenthal
      & Smythe, 1952. 160pp, ill

1136 Shoolman, Regina Lenore, and Charles E. Slatkin. The En-
      joyment of Art in America, a survey of the permanent
      collections of painting, sculpture, ceramics and decorative
      arts in American and Canadian museums; being an intro-
      duction to the masterpieces of art from prehistoric to
      modern times. Philadelphia; New York: Lippincott, 1942.
      792pp, pls

1137 Singleton, Esther. The Collecting of Antiques. New York:
      Macmillan, 1926; 1937. 338pp, ill

1138 Small, Tunstall, and Christopher Woodbridge. Architectural
      Turned Woodwork of the 16th, 17th, and 18th centuries.
      London: Architectural Pr; New York: Helburn, 1930.
      20 pls

1139 Smith, Donald. Woodwork. An introductory historical survey.
      London: Batsford, 1937; 2nd. as Old Furniture and Wood-
      work; an introductory historical survey. London: Bats-
      ford, 1947; 3rd ed. New York; London: 1949. 88pp, ill;
      68pp, ill MiGr

1140 Smith, Georgiana Reynolds. Table Decoration Yesterday, to-
      day and tomorrow. Rutland, Vt: Tuttle, 1968. 288pp,
      ill

1141 Smith, John Moyr. Ornamental Interiors, ancient and modern.
      London: S. Low, 1887. 236pp, ill, 32 pls

1142 Smithells, Roger, and St. John Woods. The Modern Home;
      its decoration, furnishing and equipment. Benfleet, Eng:
      F. Lewis, 1936. 180pp, pls (part color) color frontis

1143 *Spinning Wheel; antique magazine for the collector, dealer,
        hobbyist, homeowner. Monthly. Hanover, Pa: Every-
        bodys Pr, 1945-date. ill

1144 Stoutenburgh, John Leeds, ed. Dictionary of Arts and Crafts.
        New York: Philosophical Library, 1956; London: Owen,
        1957. 259pp, ill

1145 Stratton, Deborah. The 'Sunday Telegraph' Guide to Antiques
        Collecting. London: Sunday Telegraph, 1972. 39pp, ill

1146 Stuart, Sheila (pseud. for Mary Gladys Steel Baker). Antiques
        for the Modern Home. Edinburgh; London: Chambers,
        1962. 147pp, ill, bib

1147 _____. Antiques on a Modest Income. London; Edinburgh:
        W. & R. Chambers, 1939. 254pp, 16 ill BM

1148 _____. A Dictionary of Antiques. London; Edinburgh:
        Chambers, 1953. 263pp, ill

1149 _____. Small Antiques for the Home. South Brunswick,
        NJ: A. S. Barnes, 1969. 139pp, ill

1150 Sturgis, Russell, 1836-1909. Annotated Bibliography of Fine
        Arts, Painting, Sculpture, Architecture, Arts of Decora-
        tion and Illustration. Music by Henry Edward Krebheil.
        Boston: American Library Association, 1897. 89pp

1151 *Talbert, Bruce James, 1838-1881. Examples of Ancient and
        Modern Furniture, metal work, tapestries, decorations,
        etc. Part 2. of Gothic Forms.... Birmingham, Eng:
        S. Birbeck; London: Batsford, 1876; Boston: J. R. Os-
        good, 1877. 6pp, ill, 21 pls CtY, NNC-Ave, MiGr, DLC

1152 * _____. Gothic Forms, applied to furniture, metalwork,
        and decoration for domestic purposes. London: Batsford,
        1867; Boston: J. R. Osgood, 1873. 30 pls

1153 Tarkington, Booth, Kenneth Lewis Roberts, and Hugh Mac-
        Nair Kahler. The Collector's Whatnot; a compendium,
        manual and syllabus of information and advice on all sub-
        jects appertaining to the collection of antiques, both an-
        cient and not so ancient. Compiled by Cornelius Oben-
        chain Van Loot, Milton Kilgallen, and Murgatroyd Elphin-
        stone. Boston; New York: Houghton-Mifflin, 1923; re-
        print. Watkins Glen, NY: American Life Foundation,
        1969. 147pp, ill, pls; 112pp, ill (Facetiae, satire)

1154 Tatlock, Robert Rattray, Roger Fry, R. L. Hobson, and
        Percy Macquoid. A Record of the Collection in the Lady
        Lever Art Gallery, Port Sunlight, Cheshire, formed by

the first Viscount Leverhulme. 3 vol. London: Batsford, 1928.

1155 Taussig, Charles William, and Theodore Arthur Meyer. The
Book of Hobbies; or, A guide to happiness. New York:
Minton, Balch, 1924. 318pp, ill, pls, bib (Prints, phi-
lately, books, china, furniture, angling, playing cards,
photography)

1156 Taylor, Talbot Jones. The Talbot J. Taylor Collection:
furniture, woodcarving, and other branches of the decorative arts. New York; London: Putnam's, 1906. 139pp,
ill, pls MiGr

1157 *Teall, Gardner Callahan. The Pleasures of Collecting; being
sundry delectable excursions in the realm of antiques and
curios, American, European, and Oriental. New York:
Century, 1920. 328pp, ill, bib MiGr

1158 Thomas, Dennis, ed. "The Connoisseur's" Concise Encyclopedia of Antiques. Abridged in 2 vol. London: Sphere,
1969. Vol. I. 246pp, ill, 48 pls; Vol. II. 254pp, ill,
48 pls

1159 Thomas, Gilbert. Antiques for the Small Collector. London:
Barker, 1961. 160pp, ill

1160 Throop, Lucy Abbot. Furnishing the Home of Good Taste; a
brief sketch of the period styles in interior decoration....
New York: McBride, Nast, 1912; new rev. ed. 1920.
220pp, ill, pls, bib; 251pp NNC-Ave

1161 Toller, Jane. Living with Antiques. London: Ward Lock,
1968. 143pp, ill

1162 _____. Searching for Antiques. London: Ward Lock,
1970; 1973. 159pp, ill, 17 pls, bib

1163 Tomson, Rosamund Marriott (afterwards Watson). The Art
of the House. London: G. Bell, 1897. 185pp, 32 ill,
8 pls

1164 Treadwell, Prentice. Textile Fabrics: fictile ware: metal
work: furniture: printing: and painting: with glossary.
Handbook published for use in the loan exhibition, Albany,
March 1879. Albany: C. W. Van Benthuysen, printer,
1879. 85pp, 9 pls

1165 Treasures from the Cooper Union Museum. Washington, D.C.:
Smithsonian, 1967. 48pp, ill

1166 Triggs, Oscar Lovell, 1865- . Chapters in the History of

the Arts and Crafts Movement. Chicago: Bohemia Guild
of the Industrial Art League, 1902. 198pp, frontis NN

1167 Truman, Nevil. Historic Furnishing. London: Pitman,
       1950. 204pp, ill

1168 United States Library of Congress. Division of Bibliography.
       Collectors and Collecting: a list of books. No. 1198.
       Washington, D.C.: 1931; supplement. No. 1400. 1936.
       65 books; 63 books NN

1169 Universal Guide to Decorative Art, Embroidery, Church Work,
       etc. Kent: 1882. 60pp, ill

1170 Usher, James Ward. The Collection of Objects of Art Formed
       by J. W. Usher of London. Part the first: portrait minia-
       tures, gold boxes, antique gold watches, and rings. Lon-
       don: Waterlow & Sons, 1900. ill

1171 Vancouver Collects Decorative Art of the 18th Century. Exhi-
       bition. Vancouver, B.C.: Art Gallery, 1965. 32pp, ill

1172 Veronesi, Giulia. Into the Twenties: style and design 1909-
       1929. Tr. from Italian (1966) by Diana Barram. London:
       Thames & Hudson, 1968; as Style and Design, 1909-1929.
       New York: Braziller, 1968. 372pp, ill, 256 (10 color)
       pls

1173 Victoria and Albert Museum Bulletin. Quarterly. London:
       18- .

1174 Vivian, Margaret Collins. Antique Collecting. London: Pit-
       man, 1937. 234pp, ill, pls

1175 Vors, Frederic. Bibelots and Curios; a manual for collectors,
       with a glossary of technical terms. New York: Appleton,
       1879. 116pp

1176 *Walpole, Horace, 1717-1797. Description of the Villa at
       Strawberry Hill, with an inventory of the furniture, pic-
       tures, curiosities, etc. Strawberry Hill: Thomas Kir-
       gate, printers, 1774; with additions. 1784.

1177 Walpole Society, London, Annual. Oxford: 1912- .

1178 Wardell-Yerburgh, J. C. The Pleasure of Antiques. London:
       Octopus, 1974. 96pp 135 color pls (Middle Ages to
       early 19th century)

1179 Waring, John Burley, 1823-1875. A Handbook to the Museum
       of Ornamental Art. Manchester, Eng: n.d.

1180 Warman, Edwin G. Antiques and Their Current Prices; a check list and price guide for antiques dealers and collectors. Periodically revised and corrected. Uniontown, Pa: Warman Publishing, 1950- . 1975 ed.: 493pp, ill

1181   . Antiques--oddities and curiosities. Uniontown, Pa: Warman, 1969. 114pp, ill with drawings (Clocks, patch boxes, pomanders, etc.)

1182 Wenham, Edward. Antiques from A to Z. A pocket handbook ... with sections on weapons and armour by "Segalas." London: G. Bell, 1954; New York: Crowell, 1955. 159pp, ill, bib

1183 West Coast Peddler. Bi-weekly. Downey, Cal: 197-?

1184 Western Collector. Periodical. ?-1972.

1185 *Wharton, Edith, and Ogden Codman. The Decoration of Houses. London: Batsford; New York: Scribner's, 1897; New York: Scribner's, 1902. 204pp, ill, 56 pls, bib MiGr

1186 Wheeler, Candace Thurber, ed. Household Art. New York: Harper, 1893. 204pp

1187 Whiton, Sherrill. Elements of Interior Design and Decoration. Chicago; London: Lippincott, 1951. 829pp, ill, bib (Includes history)

1188 Whittington, Peter. Undiscovered Antiques. London: Garnstone Pr, 1972; New York: Scribner, 1973. 135pp, ill

1189 Williams, Guy Richard. Instructions to Young Collectors. London: Museum Pr, 1959. 126pp, ill (Juvenile literature)

1190 Williams, Henry Lionel, and Ottalie K. Williams. Antiques in Interior Decoration. New York: Barnes; London: Yoseloff, 1966. 387pp, 445 ill, 10 pls

1191 Williamson, George Charles. Everybody's Book on Collecting. London: Herbert Jenkins, 1924. 324pp, ill BM

1192 Wills, Geoffrey. Antiques. London: Arco, 1961; as Practical Guide to Antique Collecting. New York: Arco, 1963. 161pp, ill, 8 pls, bib

1193   . A Concise Encyclopedia of Antiques. New York: Van Nostrand Reinhold, 1976. ill

1194 Wilson, Doris C. Parlez-vous Antiques? The when, where, and how of buying antiques in Europe. South Brunswick, NJ: A. S. Barnes, 1969. 154pp, ill

1195 *Winchester, Alice, ed. The Antiques Treasury of Furniture
       and Other Decorative Arts. New York: Dutton, 1959.
       ill

1196 _____, and others, ed. Collectors and Collections; the
       Antiques anniversary book. New York: Antiques Maga-
       zine, 1961. 165pp, ill

1197 Witthaus, F. E., ed. Selected Examples of Decorative Art
       from South Kensington Museum. London: Longmans,
       1899. 72 pls BM

1198 Woodhouse, Charles Platten. Investment in Antiques and
       Art: what, where and how to buy. London: Bell, 1969.
       200pp, 47 ill, 24 pls

1199 Woman's Day. Monthly. Greenwich, Conn, etc.: 1927-
       date.

1200 Woman's Day Dictionaries of Antiques. Reprints from the
       magazine on American Painted Tinware; American Glass;
       Sandwich Glass; Victorian Art Glass; Paperweights;
       Carnival Glass; Art Glass Baskets.

1201 World of Antiques: 'Collection Guide' classic edition. Bi-
       annual. Worcester: Collectors Guide, 1970- .

1202 Yapp, George Wagstaffe, 1811-1880, ed. Art Industry:
       furniture, upholstery, and house decoration illustrative
       of the arts of the carpenter, joiner, cabinet-maker,
       painter, decorator and upholsterer. London: J. S. Vir-
       tue, 1879. 76pp, 320 pls (European and English) NNC-
       Ave, MiGr

1203 Yates, Raymond Francis, comp. The Antique Collectors
       Manual: a price guide and data book. New York: Harper,
       1952. 303pp, ill

1204 _____. Antique Fakes and Their Detection. New York:
       Harper; London: H. Hamilton, 1950. 229pp, ill (In-
       cludes hardware and construction)

1205 _____. How to Restore Antiques. New York: Harper,
       1948. 228pp, ill

1206 _____. How to Restore China, Bric-a-brac, and Small
       Antiques. New York: Harper, 1953. 210pp, ill

1207 Young, Francis Chilton, ed. Decorative Work for House and
       Home. 3 parts. London: Ward & Lock, 1893. ill
       (House Painting and Papering, by G. Edwinson; Stencilled
       Decoration for Walls, by L. L. Stokes; Floor Staining and
       Decorating, by M. Mallet)

1208 Yoxall, Sir James Henry, 1857- . The ABC about Collecting.
      London: S. Paul, 1910; 4th ed. New York: Dutton, 1923.
      382pp, ill, pls

1209 _____. More About Collecting. London: Stanley Paul,
      1913. 339pp, ill, pl

AMERICAN ANTIQUES AND INTERIOR DECORATION

1210 Adams, James Truslow, 1878-1949, ed. Album of American
      History. Vol. I. Colonial; II. 1783-1853; III. 1853-1893;
      IV. End of an Era; V. Index; VI. 1917-1953. 6 vol. New
      York: Scribner, 1944-49. ill, pls (History through con-
      temporary pictures)

1211 Adams, Ruth Constance. Pennsylvania Dutch Art. Cleveland:
      World Publishing, 1950. 64pp, ill, color pls

1212 American Antiques Collector. Monthly. Scranton, Pa: S.
      Laidacker, 1939- .

1213 *American Heritage. Bimonthly. New York: 1947-date.

1214 American Heritage; an exhibition of paintings and crafts.
      March-April 1948. Denver: Art Museum, 1948. 28pp,
      ill

      *The American Heritage History of American Antiques. See:
      Marshall B. Davidson, ed.

1215 The American Home. Monthly. Garden City, NY: Double-
      day, Doran, 1928- .

1216 American Homes. Monthly. Boston: 1872- .

1217 American Homes. A journal devoted to planning, building
      and beautifying the home. Knoxville, Tenn: American
      Homes, 18-?-1901; New York: Hite-Smith, 1902-04.
      ill, pls

1218 American Homes and Gardens. Monthly. New York: Munn,
      1905-1915. (Merged into House and Garden)

1219 American Painter and Decorator; a practical journal. New
      York: Charles Palm, 1876- .

1220 The American Wing. Introd. by Joseph Downs. New York:
      Metropolitan Museum, 1933; reprint. 1938. 3pp, 20 pls
      MiGr

1221 *Americana. Bi-monthly. New York: American Heritage
      Co, 1972-date.

1222 *America's Arts and Skills. By the editors of Life. Introd.
      by Charles F. Montgomery. New York: Dutton, 1957;
      rev. ed. New York: Time-Life, 1968. 172pp, ill (First
      appeared in Life, 1955-56)

1223 Antiques at Williamsburg. By the editors of Antiques Maga-
      zine. New York: Hastings House, 1953. 68pp, ill

1224 Artistic Homes (or Houses): a series of interior views of a
      number of the most beautiful and celebrated homes in the
      United States, with a description of the art treasures con-
      tained therein. 4 vol. New York: Appleton, 1883-84.
      ill (Includes homes of Tiffany, A. T. Stewart, J. P.
      Morgan, Hunnewell, Marquand, Ruppert, Vanderbilt, Vil-
      lard, etc.)

1225 Arts and Crafts. Philadelphia: Art Workers' Guild, 1893- .

1226 Arts and Decoration. Monthly. New York: Artspur, 1910-
      1942.

1227 Ayres, James. American Antiques. London: Orbis, 1973.
      113pp, ill, bib (ca.1670-1920)

1228 Banyas, Frank Augustine. The Moravians of Colonial Penn-
      sylvania: their arts, crafts, and industries. Columbus:
      Ohio State U, PhD Dissertation, 1940. DeWint

1229 Beasley, Ellen, and others. Made in Tennessee; an exhibit
      of early arts and crafts. Cheekwood, Fine Arts Center,
      Nashville. September-October 1971. Nashville?: Wil-
      liams Printing, 1971. 67pp, ill, plates

1230 Beck's Journal of Decorative Art. An international journal.
      New York: 1886-88.

1231 Belknap, Henry Wyckoff. Artists and Craftsmen of Essex
      County, Mass. Salem, Mass: Essex Institute, 1927.
      127pp, ill, plates, bib

1232 Belote, Theodore Thomas. Descriptive Catalogue of the
      (George) Washington Relics in the United States National
      Museum. Washington, D.C.: GPO, 1915; 1916. 24pp,
      27 pls

1233 Bennett, Ian. Book of American Antiques. The American
      tradition from early Colonial crafts to the furniture,
      ceramics, silver, glass, toys of the 18th and 19th century.
      Feltham; New York: Hamlyn, 1973. 96pp, 100 (40 color)
      ill, bib

1234 Better Homes and Gardens. Monthly. Des Moines: Meredith,
      1922-date.

1235 Biddle, James. American Art from American Collections;
      decorative arts, paintings, and prints of the Colonial and
      Federal periods, from private collections. Exhibition.
      March-April 1963. New York: Metropolitan Museum,
      1963. 114pp, ill

1236 Brazer, Esther Stevens. Early American Decoration. A
      comprehensive treatise revealing the technique involved in
      the art of early American decoration of furniture, walls,
      tinware, etc.... Springfield, Mass: Pond-Ekburg, 1940;
      2nd ed. 1947; 1950. 273pp, ill, plates; 265pp, ill, plates
      DLC, ViU, MH

1237 *Bridenbaugh, Carl. The Colonial Craftsman. New York:
      NYU Pr; London: Oxford U Pr, 1950; Chicago; London:
      Chicago U Pr, 1961. 214pp, ill, bib

1238 Brooklyn Institute News. Monthly. Brooklyn, NY: 1905-1913.

1239 Brooklyn Museum Bulletin. Monthly. Brooklyn: 1939-date.

1240 Browne, W. R. Century Library of American Antiques. New
      York: Century, 1926.

1241 Buffalo Historical Society. Museum Notes. Irregular. Buf-
      falo, NY: 1930-1945.

1242 Burroughs, Paul H. Southern Antiques. Introd. by Elizabeth
      Hatcher Sadler. Richmond, Va: Garrett & Massie, 1931.
      191pp, ill, pls DLC, MiGr

1243 Butler, Joseph Thomas. American Antiques, 1800-1900; a
      collector's history and guide. New York: Odyssey, 1965.
      203pp, ill, bib

1244 _____ . Wheatland, 1848-1868, the home of James Buchanan.
      Thesis. 1957. 127pp, pls DeWint

1245 *Carpenter, Ralph E. The Arts and Crafts of Newport, Rhode
      Island, 1640-1820. Newport, RI: The Preservation So-
      ciety of Newport County, 1954. 211pp, ill, bib (A loan
      exhibition 1953 at Nichols-Wanton-Hunter House)

1246 _____ . The 50 Best Historic American Houses, Colonial
      and Federal, now furnished and open to the public. New
      York: Dutton, 1955. 112pp, ill

1247 *Chamberlain, Samuel. Beyond New England Thresholds. New
      York: Hastings; Brattleboro, Vt: 1937. 96pp, chiefly ill
      ViU, PPULC, DLC

1248 *_____ . Salem Interiors. Two centuries of New England

taste and decoration. New York: Hastings House, 1950.
176pp, chiefly ill

1249 *   , and Narcissa Chamberlain. Chamberlain Selection
of New England Rooms, 1693-1863. New York: Hastings
House, 1972. 192pp, ill (Detail study of 56 interiors)

1250   , and   . Southern Interiors of Charleston,
South Carolina. New York: Hastings House, 1956.
172pp, chiefly ill

1251   , and Henry N. Flynt. Frontier of Freedom; the
soul and substance of America portrayed in one extraordinary village. New York: Hastings House, 1952; rev.
enl. ed. as Historic Deerfield: houses and interiors.
New York: Hastings House, 1965. 154pp; 170pp; 182pp;
all ill (Massachusetts)

1252 Charles Carroll of Carrollton (1737-1832) and His Family.
An Exhibition of portraits, furniture, silver and manu-
scripts. September-October 1937. Museum of Art.
Baltimore: Lord Baltimore Pr, 1937. 54pp, ill

1253 Christensen, Erwin Ottomar. American Crafts and Folk Arts.
Washington, D.C.: R. B. Luce, 1964; Bombay: Vora,
1970. 90pp, ill, bib

1254   . Arts and Crafts, a bibliography for craftsmen by
National Gallery of Art, Index of American Design, in
collaboration with the Federal Security Agency, Office of
Education. Washington, D.C.: National Gallery, 1949.

1255 Clark, Maryjane. An Illustrated Glossary of Decorated
Antiques from the Late 17th to Early 19th Century. Rut-
land, Vt: Tuttle, for the Historical Society of Early
American Decoration, 1972. 400pp, ill, bib

1256 Clark, Robert Judson, ed. The Arts and Crafts Movement in
America, 1876-1916. Exhibition. Princeton Art Museum,
Art Institute of Chicago, Renwick Gallery. Princeton, NJ:
U Pr, 1972. 190pp, ill, bib

1257 Clarke County (Virginia) Historical Collection: a list of por-
traits, furniture, silver and family heirlooms from early
Colonial days up to the present time. Exhibition. July.
Berryville, Va: Clarke Courier Pr, 1936. 28pp ViU

1258 Cole, Ann Kilborn. The Golden Guide to American Antiques.
New York: Golden Pr, 1967. 160pp, ill

1259 The Collection of Samuel Dale Stevens (1859-1922). Arranged
and presented by the North Andover Historical Society.

North Andover, Mass: Advance Reproductions, 1971.
66pp, ill

1260 Colonial Architecture and Other Early American Arts. (A
       Bibliography.) Pittsburgh: Carnegie Library, 1926.
       28pp.

1261 [No entry.]

1262 *Comstock, Helen, ed. The Concise Encyclopedia of American
       Antiques. 2 vol. London: The Connoisseur; New York:
       Hawthorne, 1958; 1 vol. New York: 1965. 543pp, pls,
       bib; 848pp, including 352 pls, bib

1263 _____. 100 Most Beautiful Rooms in America. New York:
       Studio, 1958; New York: Viking, 1959; rev. ed. 1965.
       210pp, ill

1264 Connecticut Magazine. Quarterly. Hartford: 1895-1908.

1265 *Cousins, Frank. Colonial Architecture of the United States,
       photographs bound in 14 volumes, 1911-1913. 1058 photo-
       graphs (Vol. I-XI. Various states and cities; Vol. XII.
       Doorways and windows; Vol. XIII. Fireplaces, stairways,
       furniture, interiors; Vol. XIV. Ironwork, tombstones, etc.)
       NNC-Ave

1266 Craig, James Hicklin. The Arts and Crafts in North Carolina,
       1699-1840. Winston-Salem, NC: Museum of Early Southern
       Decorative Arts, Old Salem, Inc., 1965. 480pp, ill, bib
       (Compiled from newspaper advertisements, etc.)

1267 Cramer, Edith. Handbook of Early American Decoration.
       Boston: Branford, 1951; London: Bailey & Swinfen, 1952.
       96pp, ill

1268 Creekmore, Betsey Beeler. Traditional American Crafts.
       New York: Hearthside, 1968. 191pp, ill, bib

1269 Creer, Doris. "The Influence of the War of 1812 on Ameri-
       can Decorative Arts, as seen through the collection at
       Winterthur." Museum Course Paper. 1957. 8pp type-
       script DeWint

1270 Cunningham, Anna K. Schuyler Mansion, a critical catalogue
       of the furnishings and decorations. Albany, NY: State
       Education Department, 1955. 141pp, ill (Philip John
       Schuyler, 1733-1804) NN, DLC

1271 Cunningham, Charles Crehore, pref. Art in New England.
       The arts and crafts of New England and a survey of the
       taste of its people. 7 parts in 1 vol. (Reissue of cata-
       logues of 7 exhibits.) Cambridge, Mass: Harvard U Pr,

1939. pls, facsims, bib (Includes, with painting catalogues, Masterpieces of New England Silver, 1650-1800.
Exhibition at Yale, 1939)

1272 Darmstadt, Jo, comp. Craftsmen and Artists of Norwich:
furniture, paintings, clocks, silver, pewter, pottery.
Exhibition. Society of the Founders of Norwich, Connecticut. Stonington: Pequot Pr, 1965. 67pp, ill

1273 *Davidson, Marshall B., general ed. and author, and others.
The American Heritage History of American Antiques.
Vol. I. ... Colonial Antiques; Vol. II. ... From the
Revolution to the Civil War; Vol. III. ... From the Civil
War to World War I. 3 vol. New York: American Heri-
tage, 1967, 1968, 1969. 384pp, ill, pls; 416pp, 652 (91
color) ill, bib, gloss; 415pp, ill, pls

1274 Davis, Alexander Jackson, 1803-1892. Rural Residences,
etc., consisting of designs, original and selected, for
cottages, farm-houses, villas, and village churches. 5
parts in 1 vol. New York: The Architect, 1837. color
pls NN

1275 Decorative Arts of New Hampshire, 1725-1825. Exhibition.
Summer 1964. Manchester, NH: Currier Gallery of Art,
1964. 73pp, ill

1276 Decorative Furnisher. Monthly. New York: T. A. Cawthra,
1918- .

1277 The Decorator. Journal of the Historical Society of Early
American Decoration, and the Esther Stevens Brazer Guild.
Semi-annual. Noroton Heights, Conn: 1946- .

1278 The Decorator and Furnisher. Monthly. New York: 1882-
1898.

1279 *de-Jonge, Eric, ed. Country Things, from the pages of
Antiques. Princeton, NJ: Pyne Pr; New York: Scribner's,
1973. 224pp, 1000 ill (Articles from early issues of
Antiques by Alice Winchester, Frank O. Spinney, Nina
Fletcher Little, Edward D. and Faith Andrews, etc.)

1280 Dempsey, Bruce. Beauty Fixed in Many Mediums; an exhibition of the works of Louis Comfort Tiffany from the Collection of Hugh and Jeannette McKean. Florida State University Art Gallery. Tallahassee?: 1972. 36pp, ill, bib

1281 Denver Art Museum. Quarterly. Denver, Colo: 1949- .

1282 *Dow, George Francis, 1868-1936. The Arts and Crafts of
New England, 1704-1775; Gleanings from Boston newspapers
relating to painting, engravings, silversmiths, pewterers,

clockmakers, furniture, pottery, old houses, costume, trades and occupations. Topsfield, Mass: Wayside P, 1927; reprint. New York: Da Capo. 1967. 326pp, ill, plates

1283 * _____. Domestic Life in New England in the 17th Century-- a discourse delivered in the Metropolitan Museum of New York to open the American Wing. Topsfield, Mass: Perkins Pr, 1925.

1284 _____. An Inventory of the Contents of the Shop and House of Captain George Corwin of Salem, Massachusetts Bay, who died January 3, 1684-5. Salem: City Hall Alley Pr, for Author, 1910. 19pp DeWint

1285 *Downing, Andrew Jackson, 1815-1852. The Architecture of Country Houses; including designs for cottages, farmhouses, and villas, with remarks on interiors, furniture, and the best modes of warming and ventilating. New York: Appleton, 1850; 1851; 1852; ... 1866; reprints of 1850 ed. With introd. by George B. Tatum. New York: Da Capo Pr, 1968; with introd. by J. Stewart Johnson. New York: Dover, 1969. 484pp, 320 ill, pls DeWint, MiGr

1286 * _____. Cottage Residences, Rural Architecture and Landscape Gardening. New York; London: Wiley & Putnam, 1842; 4th rev. ed. New York: Wiley, 1853; new ed. by George Harney. New York: 1873; reprint with new introd. by Michael Hugo-Brunt. Watkins Glen, NY: Library of Victorian Culture, 1967. 187pp, pls; 215pp, 11 pls; 261pp, ill, pls; 200pp, ill, bib

1287 Downs, Joseph. A Handbook of the Pennsylvania German Galleries in the American Wing. New York: Metropolitan Museum, 1934. 22pp, ill, pls (Collection gift of Emily (Mrs. Robert W.) de Forest)

1288 _____. The House of the Miller at Millbach, (Pa.); the architecture, arts and crafts of the Pennsylvania Germans. Philadelphia: Franklin printing, 1929. 31pp, ill, pls (First half of 18th century)

1289 _____. Pennsylvania German Arts and Crafts, a picture book. New York: Metropolitan Museum, 1942; 1943; 1946; 1949. 28pp, ill, 30 pls

1290 _____, and John Marshall Phillips. The (Mrs. Edmund A.) Prentis Collection of Colonial New England Furnishings. New York: Historical Society, 1951. 32pp, pls (part color)

1291 _____, and Alice Winchester. A Selection of American Interiors 1640-1840 in the Henry Francis Du Pont

Winterthur Museum, Delaware. New York: Antiques
Magazine, 1951. 47pp, ill, pls (part color) DeWint,
TxU

1292   Drepperd, Carl William. A Dictionary of American Antiques.
       Garden City, NY: Doubleday, 1952. 404pp, chiefly ill,
       bib

1293 *   . The Primer of American Antiques. Garden City,
       NY: Doubleday, Doran, 1944; 1945. 271pp, ill, bib

1294   , and Lurelle Van Arsdale Guild. New Geography
       of American Antiques. Garden City, NY: Doubleday,
       1948. 254pp, ill MiGr

1295   Duprey, Kenneth. Old Houses on Nantucket. New York:
       Architectural Book Co, 1959. 242pp, ill, bib

1296 *Dyer, Walter A. Early American Craftsmen ... being a
       series of sketches of the lives of the more important
       personalities in the early development of the industrial
       arts in America, together with sundry facts and photo-
       graphs of interest and value to the collector of Americana.
       New York: Century, 1915; 1920; New York: Burt Franklin,
       1971. 387pp, ill, pls, bib (Samuel McIntire; Duncan
       Phyfe; Windsor chairs; Connecticut clockmakers; The Wil-
       lards and their clocks; Baron Stiegel's glassware; Paul
       Revere; other silversmiths, pewterers and brasiers; Ben-
       nington pottery, etc.)

1297 *   . The Lure of the Antique. Being a book of ready
       reference for collectors of old furniture, china, mirrors,
       candlesticks, silverware, pewter, glassware, copper uten-
       sils, clocks, and other household furnishings of our Ameri-
       can forefathers, and a handy guide for the determination of
       age, style, maker, genuineness and value. New York: Cen-
       tury, 1910. 499pp, ill, 159 photographs DLC, NNC-Ave

1298   Early American Arts and Crafts from the Earliest Times to
       1810. Exhibit catalog and bibliography.... Little Gallery
       School of Architecture and Allied Arts, April 1949. Eu-
       gene, Ore: University of O, 1949.

1299   Early Arts in the Genesee Valley, 18th and 19th Centuries.
       Exhibition. Genesee, NY: Genesee Valley Council on the
       Arts, 1974. 158pp, 83 (1 color) ill, bib

1300   Early Arts of New Jersey; furniture, pewter, samplers, 1695-
       1840. Exhibition. April-June 1953. Trenton, NJ: State
       Museum, 1953. 18pp

1301   Eaton, Allen Hendershott. Handicrafts of New England. New
       York: Harper, 1949. 374pp, ill

1302 _____ . Handicrafts of the Southern Highlands, with an
account of the rural handicraft movement in the United
States. New York: Russell Sage Foundation, 1937; reprint. 1946; 2nd ed. with new pref. by Ralph Rinzler,
and new introd. by Rayna Green. New York: Dover;
London: Constable, 1973. 370pp, 58 ill, 111 pls, bib

1303 _____ , and Lucinda Crile. Rural Handicrafts in the United
States. Introd. by M. L. Wilson. Washington, D.C.:
GPO, 1946. 40pp, ill

1304 *Eberlein, Harold Donaldson, and Cortlandt Van Dyke Hubbard.
Colonial Interiors, Federal and Greek Revival. 3rd
Series. New York: W. Helburn, 1938. 7pp, 153pp of
pls (Pennsylvania, New Hampshire, New Jersey and
Maryland.) (See Also: Leigh French, no. 1312; Edith
D. T. Sale, no. 1437)

1305 _____ , and Abbott McClure. The Practical Book of Early
American Arts and Crafts. Philadelphia; London: Lippincott, 1914; rev. ed. as The Practical Book of American
Antiques, exclusive of furniture, revised with a new supplement. The chapter on early lace by Mabel Foster Bainbridge; on Sandwich glass by Lenore Wheeler Williams.
1916; Philadelphia: 1927; 1936. 330pp, 232 ill, pls, bib;
390pp, 257 ill, bib

1306 Elliott, Charles Wyllys, 1817-1883. (Household Art.) The
Book of American Interiors. Prepared from existing
houses, with preliminary essays. Boston: J. R. Osgood,
1876. 135pp, ill, 31 pls

1307 Elwell, Newton W., comp. The Architecture, Furniture, and
Interiors of Maryland and Virginia During the 18th Century.
Boston: G. H. Polley, 1897. 6pp, ill, 63 pls NNC-Ave,
MiGr

1308 _____ . Colonial Furniture and Interiors. Boston: G. H.
Polley, 1896. 3pp, ill, 66 pls DLC, NNC-Ave, MiGr

1309 Fashionable, Neat and Good: the Williamsburg Collection of
antique furnishings. New York: Holt, Rinehart & Winston,
1973. 123pp, over 2000 items ill

1310 Fisher, Louise Bang. An 18th-Century Garland; the flower
and fruit arrangements of Colonial Williamsburg. Williamsburg, Va: 1951. 91pp, ill, pls, bib

1311 Freeman, Graydon La Verne. Nursery Americana. Watkins
Glen: Century, 1947; 1948. u.p., ill

1312 *French, Leigh, Jr. Colonial Interiors; photographs and
measured drawings of the Colonial and Early Federal

periods. 2nd Series. Introd. by Charles O. Cornelius.
New York: W. Helburn, 1923. text, 125 pls (See also:
E. D. Sale, no. 1437; H. D. Eberlein, no. 1304)

1313   . 12 Colonial Interiors, 17th century. Paris:
        Charles Huard, 1925? 12 pls

1313a From Colony to Nation; an exhibit of American painting,
        silver, and architecture from 1650 to War of 1812. April-
        June 1949. Chicago: Art Institute, 1949. 140pp, ill

1314 Furnishing Plan for the Bishop White House. By the staff,
        Independence National Historical Park. 2 vol. Philadel-
        phia: 1961. ill (Vol. II. Inventory of the Philadelphia
        contents of the library of Bishop White)

1315 Furnishings for Diplomatic Rooms. Washington, D.C.: De-
        partment of State, 1963. 17pp, pls

1316 Garrett, Wendell Douglas. The Newport Rhode Island In-
        terior, 1780-1800. Thesis. 1957. 172pp, pls DeWint

1317 Glubock, Shirley. The Art of Colonial America. New York:
        Macmillan, 1970. 48pp, ill

1318 Gores, Stan. 1876 Centennial Collectibles and Price Guide.
        Fond du Lac, Wisc: Author, 1975. 163pp, ill

1319 *Gottesman, Rita Susswein, comp. The Arts and Crafts in
        New York; advertisements and news items from New York
        City newspapers. Vol. I. 1726-1776; II. 1777-1799; III.
        1800-1804. 3 vol. New York: N.Y. Historical Society,
        1938, 1954, 1965; 3 vol. in 1. New York: Da Capo Pr,
        1970. 1970: 450pp, ill TxU, PP

1320 *Gould, Mary Earle. The Early American House; household
        life in America, 1620-1850. New York: McBride, 1949;
        rev. ed. as The Early American House; household life
        in America with special chapters on the construction and
        evaluation of old American homes, fireplaces and iron
        utensils, and hearthside and barnyard activities. Rutland,
        Vt: Tuttle, 1965. 143pp, ill; 152pp, ill, bib

1321 *Graham, John Meredith, II. Popular Art in America; wood-
        carvings and lawn sculpture, decorative pictures, weather
        vanes, toys, firebacks and stoves, ceramics and chalk-
        wares, Valentines, advertisements, prints. Brooklyn In-
        stitute of Arts and Sciences, Department of American
        rooms. Brooklyn, NY: Museum Pr, 1939. 39pp, ill
        TxU

1322 Greene, Richard Lawrence, and Kenneth Edward Wheeling.

A Pictorial History of the Shelburne Museum. Shelburne, Vt: 1972. 127pp, ill

1323 Greenfield Village and the Henry Ford Museum. Combined edition of "Greenfield Village" and "The Henry Ford Museum." New York: Crown, 1972. 247pp, ill

1324 Greiff, Constance M., ed. Great Houses From the Pages of The Magazine Antiques. Princeton, NJ: Pyne Pr, 1973. v.p., ill

1325 Guide to the Collections: the American Wing. New York: Metropolitan Museum, 1961. 49pp, ill

1326 Guild, Lurelle Van Arsdale. The Geography of American Antiques. Garden City, NY: Doubleday; London: Heinemann, 1927; Garden City: 1931. 283pp, many ill, color frontis, bib PPL, DLC, MiGr

1327 Guillet, Edwin Clarence. Pioneer Arts and Crafts. Toronto: U of T Pr, 1968. 97pp, ill

1328 Hall, Peg. Decorating Designs: some early American, some modern. 4 vol. Scituate, Mass: Peg Hall Studios, 1952-55. ill

1329 _____. Early American Decorating Patterns. New York: M. Barrows, 1951. 150pp, ill with drawings

1330 *Halsey, Richard Townley Haines, and Charles Over Cornelius. A Handbook of the American Wing Opening Exhibition. Metropolitan Museum. New York: 1924; 3rd ed. with corrections. New York: 1926; 4th ed. 1928; 5th ed. 1932; 6th ed. 1938; 7th ed. Halsey, Cornelius and Joseph Downs. 1942. 283pp, ill; 1928: 295pp, ill; 1938: 312pp, ill MiGr, NN

1331 _____, and Elizabeth Tower. Homes of Our Ancestors as Shown in the American Wing of the Metropolitan Museum of New York, from the beginnings of New England through the early days of the Republic, exhibiting the development of the arts of interior architecture and household decoration, the arts of cabinet making, silversmithing, etc. Garden City, NY: Doubleday, Page, 1925; 1929; 1934; 1935; 1937; ... 302pp, 217 ill, 20 color pls PP, DLC, MiGr

1332 Hammond, Dorothy. Price Guide to Country Antiques and American Primitives. New York: Funk & Wagnalls, 1975. 280pp, ill, gloss

1333 Handicraft; representing the arts and crafts movement. Monthly. Boston: 1902-04; Montague, Mass: 1910-1912.

1334   Hands That Built New Hampshire. The story of Granite State
       craftsmen past and present. New Hampshire Works Pro-
       gress Administration. Writers' Program. Brattleboro,
       Vt: Stephen Daye Pr, 1940. 288pp, ill, pls, bib

1335   Hanson, Frederick Banfield. The Interior Architecture and
       Household Furnishings of Bergen County, New Jersey,
       1800-1810. Thesis. 1959. 195pp, pls DeWint

1336   Harris, Marleine Reader. Virginia Antiques, a History and
       Handbook for Collectors. New York: Exposition Pr,
       1953. 183pp, ill

1337   Harvard Tercentenary Exhibition. Catalogue of furniture,
       silver, pewter, glass, ceramics, paintings, prints, to-
       gether with allied arts and crafts of the period 1636-1836.
       School of Architecture. July-September 1936. Cambridge,
       Mass: Harvard U Pr, 1936. 114pp, ill NNC-Ave

1338   Haynes, Elizabeth. A Guide to the American Rooms of the
       Brooklyn Museum. Brooklyn: 1930?; 1936. 13pp, ill,
       pls; 46pp, ill

1339   Hayward, Samuel, architect. Four Interiors. Boston: 187-?
       4 pls MB

1340   Hendrick, Robert E. P., John D. Davis, and Ruth Y. Cox.
       The Glen-Sanders Collection from Scotia, New York. Ex-
       hibition. January-February 1966. Williamsburg, Va:
       Williamsburg Antiques Forum, Colonial Williamsburg, 1966.
       47pp, ill (Furniture, by Hendrick; Silver and Gold, by
       Davis; and Textiles, by Cox)

1341   Hill, Ralph Nading, and Lilian Baker Carlisle. The Story
       of the Shelburne Museum. Shelburne, Vt: the Museum,
       1955; 2nd ed. 1960. 55pp, pls; 113pp, ill

1342   *Hipkiss, Edwin James. 18th Century American Arts. The
       M(axim) and M(artha) Karolik Collection of Paintings,
       drawings, engravings, furniture, silver, needlework and
       incidental objects gathered to illustrate the achievements
       of American artists and craftsmen of the period from
       1720-1820. With notes by Maxim Karolik. Cambridge,
       Mass: Harvard U Pr, for the Boston Museum of Fine
       Arts, 1941. 366pp, ill, pls, bib NNC-Ave

1343   _____. Interior Woodwork in New England During the 17th
       and 18th Centuries. New York: R. F. Whitehead, 1925.
       18pp, ill, pls

1344   _____. Three McIntire Rooms from Peabody, Massa-
       chusetts. Boston: Museum of Fine Arts, 1931. 93pp,
       ill, pls, bib MiGr, NNC-Ave

1345   Holloway, Edward Stratton, 1859?-1939.   American Furniture
       and Decoration, Colonial and Federal.   Philadelphia; Lon-
       don: Lippincott, 1928; new rev. ed. as The Practical
       Book of American Furniture and Decoration....   1937.
       191pp, ill, 140 pls   NN, DLC

1346   Holly, Henry Hudson, 1834-1892.   Modern Dwellings in Town
       and Country, adapted to American wants and climate with
       a treatise on furniture and decoration ... Cottages, villas
       and mansions.   New York: Harper, 1878.   219pp, 100 ill
       TxU, DeWint

1347   Home Furnishings Daily.   Chicago: National Housewares
       Manufacturing Association, 1934-date.

1348   Hornung, Clarence Pearson, comp.   An Old-fashioned Christ-
       mas in Illustration and Decoration.   New York: Dover,
       1970.   121pp, chiefly ill

1349   .   Treasury of American Design.   A pictorial survey
       of popular folk arts based upon watercolor renderings in
       the Index of Design, Washington.   Fore. by J. Carter
       Brown; Introd. by Holger Cahill.   2 vol.   New York: H.
       N. Abrams, 1973.   875pp, ill (some color)   (Based on
       2900 renderings)

1350   Howe, Lois Lilley, and Constance Fuller.   Details from Old
       New England Houses, measured and drawn.   New York:
       Architectural Book Publishing, 1913.   50 pls in portfolio
       (Details of a number of furniture pieces included)   NN,
       MiGr

1351   Hudson, Norman, ed.   Antiques at Auction.   Cranbury, NJ:
       A. S. Barnes; London: Yoseloff, 1972.   403pp, 160 ill
       (Over 1600 New England pieces, auctioned from 1964 to
       1970)

1352   *Hummel, Charles F.   With Hammer in Hand; the Dominy
       craftsmen of East Hampton, New York.   Charlottesville,
       Va: U Pr of Va, for Winterthur Museum, 1968; rev.
       enl. ed. 1974.   424pp, 300 ill   (18th and 19th centuries)

1353   Hunter, George Leland.   Home Furnishing; facts and figures
       about furniture, carpets and rugs, lamps and lighting
       fixtures, wall papers, window shades and draperies,
       tapestries, etc.   New York: John Lane, 1913.   231pp,
       107 ill, pls   MB, MiU

1354   .   Inside the House That Jack Built, the story, told
       in conversation, of how two homes were furnished.   New
       York: John Lane, 1914.   208pp, ill, pls   NN

1355   I Remember That.   An exhibition of interiors of a generation

ago.   Fore. by Benjamin Knotts.   New York: WPA,
Federal Art Project, 1942.   24pp of ill   (Illustrated from
Index of American Design)

1356   Index of American Design Exhibition, Fogg Museum of Art,
       Harvard University.   Washington, DC: WPA, Federal Art
       Project, 1937.   28pp

1357   Isham, Norman Morrison, and Albert F. Brown.   Early Con-
       necticut Houses.   Providence, RI: Preston & Rounds,
       1900; reprint. New York: Dover, 1965.   303pp, 188 ill,
       bib   (29 Colonial dwellings)

1358   Johnson, Elba, comp.   Handbook of Arts and Crafts, Milwau-
       kee Biennial, Public Library and Museum Building, June
       1900.   Milwaukee: King-Cramer, 1900.   182pp, ill DLC

1359   Johnson, Theodore Elliot.   Hands to Work and Hearts to God;
       the Shaker tradition in Maine.   Exhibition.   Brunswick,
       Me: Bowdoin College Museum of Art, 1969.   72pp, 46 ill,
       bib   (Mostly of Maine manufacture, now at Sabbathday
       Lake)

1360   Johnson, William Mertin.   Inside of 100 Homes.   Philadelphia:
       Curtis (Ladies Home Journal); New York: Doubleday, Mc-
       Clure, 1898; New York: Doubleday, Page, 1904.   139pp,
       ill (See also: William L. Price, no. 1422) NN, DLC

1361   Jones, Alvin Lincoln.   Under Colonial Roofs.   Boston:
       Charles B. Webster, 1894.   237pp, 40 pls ViU, MB

1362   Journal of Early Southern Decorative Arts.   Bi-annual.
       Winston-Salem, NC: Museum of Early Southern Decora-
       tive Arts, 1975- .

1363   Kelley, Lilla Elizabeth.   300 Things a Bright Girl Can Do.
       Boston: D. Estes, 1903; Boston: Page, 1908.   630pp,
       ill MB, DLC

1364   Kemble, Marion, ed.   Art Recreations; a guide to decorative
       art.   Boston: S. W. Tilton, 1884.   443pp, ill

1365   *Kent, Henry Watson, Florence Nightingale Levy, and W. R.
       Valentiner.   The Hudson-Fulton Celebration.   Catalog of
       an exhibition held in the Metropolitan Museum of Art com-
       memorative of the tercentenary of the discovery of the
       Hudson River by Henry Hudson in 1609, and the centenary
       of the first use of steam in navigation of said river by
       Robert Fulton in 1807.   September-November 1909.   Vol.
       I. Dutch Master Paintings; Vol. II. American Paintings,
       furniture, silver, objects of art from 1625-1825.   2 vol.
       New York: Metropolitan Museum, 1909.   223pp, ill
       ("... an exhibition staged in part to test the question of

whether or not American decorative arts deserved a place in an art museum." Berry B. Tracy, Bulletin, Metropolitan Museum, Winter 1975/1976)

1366 *Kettell, Russell Hawes, ed. Early American Rooms: a consideration of the changes in style between the arrival of the 'Mayflower' and the Civil War in the regions originally settled by the English and the Dutch. Articles by Frederick Lewis Allen and others. Portland, Me: Southworth-Athoensen Pr, 1936; reprint as Early American Rooms, 1650-1858. New York: Dover; London: Constable, 1967. 200pp, 84 (13 color) ill (12 rooms, each representing a different period or place) NN

1367 Kimball, Marie (Goebel). The Furnishings of Monticello. Philadelphia?: 1940; Charlottesville, Va: Thomas Jefferson Memorial Foundation, 1946. 32pp, ill (Jefferson, 1743-1826) ViU, DeWint

1368 Kirk, John. The Impecunious Collector's Guide to American Antiques. Knopf, 1975. 178pp, ill

1369 Klamkin, Marian. Hands to Work: Shaker folk art and industries. New York: Dodd, Mead, 1972. 212pp, ill, bib

1370 Lavine, Sigmund A. Handmade in America; the heritage of Colonial craftsmen. New York: Dodd, Mead, 1966. 148pp, ill, bib

1371 Leed, Gretel, and L. M. Goodman, ed. New York Crafts, 1700-1875; an historical survey. Ithaca College, Museum of Art. Ithaca, NY: Cayuga Pr, 1967; Watkins Glen, NY: Century, 1972. 56pp, ill

1372 Lehman, John. Old Things from Country Auctions. Bainbridge, Pa: Katydid Pr, 1959. 24pp, ill

1373 Leland, E. H. Farm Homes In-doors and Out-doors. New York: Orange Judd, 1881; 1882. 204pp, ill, pls PBL, DLC, NN

1374 Lerch, Lila. Pennsylvania German Antiques. Allentown: Schlecter's, 1970. 157pp, ill, pls

1375 Little, Nina Fletcher. Country Arts in Early American Homes. Fore. by Wendell Garrett. New York: Dutton, 1975. 221pp, 210 (20 color) ill, pl (New England, to mid-19th century)

1376 Lockwood, Sarah M. Antiques, with special reference to early American furniture. Garden City, NY: Doubleday,

Page; London: Heinemann, 1925; New York: 1926; 1930;
1936. 161pp, ill, bib (ca.1620-ca.1850) ViU, MiGr

1377 [No entry.]

1378 *McClelland, Nancy Vincent. Furnishing the Colonial and
Federal House; with 202 illustrations from photographs.
Philadelphia; London: Lippincott, 1936; rev. ed. 1947.
164pp, ill; 173pp, 202 ill NNC-Ave, MiGr

1379 McClinton, Katharine Morris. Antiques of American Child-
hood. New York: C. N. Potter, 1970. 351pp, ill, bib

1380 _____. The Complete Book of American Country Antiques.
New York: Coward-McCann, 1967. 224pp, ill, bib

1380a Mackson, I. American Architecture, interiors and furniture,
during the latter part of the 19th century. Boston: G.
H. Polley, 1900. 3pp, 59 pls PP, DLC

1381 Madden, Betty. Art, Crafts, and Architecture in Early
Illinois. Chicago: U of Illinois Pr, 1974. 297pp, ill,
color pls, bib (From prehistoric Indians to ca.1860)

1382 Marsh, Moreton. Easy Expert in Collecting and Restoring
American Antiques. Philadelphia: Lippincott, 1960.
176pp, ill

1383 Martin, Shirley Ann. Craftsmen of Bucks County, Pennsylvania, 1750-1800. Thesis. 1956. 207pp, pls DeWint

1384 *Masonic Symbols in American Decorative Arts. Exhibition.
Lexington, Mass: Museum of Our National Heritage,
Scottish Rite-Masonic Museum, 1976. 110pp, 90 ill, bib
(18th century to 1900)

1385 Maxon, John. Edward B. Aldreich, collector. An Exhibition of Furniture, Ceramics, and Glass from His Collection. Museum of Art, Rhode Island School of Design.
Providence, RI: 1958. ill

1386 Measured Drawings of Woodwork Displayed in the American
Wing. Drawings by H. W. Waldron Faulkner. Metropolitan Museum. New York: 1925. 4pp, 40 pls

1387 Michael, George. Treasury of Federal Antiques 1770-1830.
New York: Hawthorn, 1972. 235pp, ill, bib

1388 _____. The Treasury of New England Antiques. New York:
Hawthorn, 1969. 210pp, ill

1389 Miller, Lillian B. The Dye Is Now Cast: the road to
American independence, 1774-1776. Exhibition, 2nd of

three Bicentennial exhibitions. Washington, D.C.: National Portrait Gallery, 1975. 320pp, 170 ill (16 period room settings, decorative arts, paintings)

1390 Miller, Robert William. American Primitives. Des Moines: Wallace-Homestead, 1972. 109pp, ill (Butter molds, churns, coffee grinders, etc. from the Museum of Appalachia, Norris, Tennessee, collection)

1391 _____, comp. Wallace-Homestead Price Guide to Antiques. Des Moines: Wallace-Homestead, 1975. 370pp, 1000 photographs, 12 color pls

1392 Mitchell, Edwin Valentine. The Romance of New England Antiques. New York: Current Books, 1950. 265pp, ill

1393 Morningstar, Connie. Flapper Furniture and Interiors of the 1920s. Des Moines: Wallace-Homestead, 1971. 123pp, chiefly ill

1394 New England Magazine. Monthly. 61 vol. Boston: J. N. McClintock, 1884-1917.

1395 Newark Art Museum. The Museum. Periodical. Newark, NJ: 1917- .

1396 19th Century America: furniture and other decorative arts; an exhibition in celebration of the 100th anniversary of the Metropolitan Museum of Art, April-September 1970. Introd. by Berry B. Tracy; furniture texts by Marilynn Johnson; other decorative texts by Marvin D. Schwartz and Suzanne Boorsch. New York: N.Y. Graphic, 1970. u.p., ill (some color)

1397 Noel-Hume, Ivor. James Geddy and Sons: Colonial craftsmen. Williamsburg, Va: Colonial Williamsburg, 1970. ill

1398 _____. Wells of Williamsburg: Colonial time capsules. Williamsburg, Va: Colonial Williamsburg, 1969. ill

1399 *Northend, Mary Harrod. Colonial Homes and Their Furnishings. Boston: Little, Brown, 1912. 252pp, 117 pls (Chiefly New England homes)

1400 _____. Photographs of Colonial Interiors. Salem, Mass: Author, 1916. 25 mounted pls NN

1401 Nutting, Wallace. Connecticut Beautiful. Framingham, Mass: Old America Co, 1923. 294pp, 304 ill

1402 _____. Maine Beautiful. Framingham, Mass: Old America Co, 1924; Garden City, NY: 1935. 296pp, 304 ill

1403 _____ . Massachusetts Beautiful. Framingham, Mass:
       Old America Co, 1924; Garden City, NY: Doubleday,
       1935. 254pp, 304 ill

1404 _____ . New Hampshire Beautiful. Framingham, Mass:
       Old America Co, 1923. 302pp, 304 ill

1405 _____ . New York Beautiful. Framingham, Mass: Old
       America Co, 1927. 305pp, 304 ill, color frontis

1406 _____ . Pennsylvania Beautiful (Eastern). Framingham,
       Mass: Old America Co, 1924. 304pp, 304 ill

1407 _____ . Vermont Beautiful. Framingham, Mass: Old
       America Co, 1922. 304pp, 304 ill

1408 _____ . Virginia Beautiful. Garden City, NY: Garden
       City Publishing, 1935. 262pp, 304 ill

1409 Ormsbee, Thomas Hamilton. Collecting Antiques in America.
       New York: McBride, 1940; 3rd ed. New York: Deerfield
       Books, dist. by Hearthside Pr, 1962. 321pp, ill, 62 pls

1410 Page, John F. The Decorative Arts of New Hampshire; a
       sesquicentennial exhibition. Hanover, NH: U Pr of New
       England, 1973. ill

1411 Pennsylvania German Arts and Crafts. New York: Metropoli-
       tan Museum, 1942.

1412 Pennsylvania German Folklore Society. Periodical. Allen-
       town, Pa: 1936- .

1413 Pennsylvania Magazine of History and Biography. Quarterly.
       Philadelphia: Historical Society of Pa, 1877- .

1414 Pennsylvania Museum Bulletin. Philadelphia: 19- .

1415 Peterson, Harold Leslie. Americans at Home: from the
       Colonists to the late Victorians; a pictorial source book of
       American domestic interiors, with an appendix on inns and
       taverns. New York: Scribner, 1971. (18)pp, 205 pls

1416 *Philadelphia: three centuries of American art. Exhibition.
       Philadelphia: Museum of Art, 1976. 720pp, 600 ill of
       546 pieces, bib

1417 *Philadelphia: three centuries of American art. (Picture
       book.) Philadelphia: Museum of Art, 1976. 160pp, ill
       (Abbreviated version of preceding title)

1418 *Phipps, Frances. Collector's Complete Dictionary of American
       Antiques. Garden City, NY: Doubleday, 1974. 640pp, 1000

ill (Thousands of words as they were used to describe applied and decorative arts between 1640 and 1840)

1419   Polley, George Henry.   The Architecture, Interiors and Furniture of the American Colonies During the 18th Century. Boston: Polley, 1914.   2pp, 90 pls

1420   *Pratt, Richard.   Second Treasury of Early American Homes. New York: Hawthorn; London: Bailey & Swinfen, 1954; New rev. ed. with Dorothy Pratt.   New York; London: 1959.   144pp, 200 color ill   (1607-1845)

1421   *_____.   The Treasury of Early American Homes.   New York: Hawthorn, 1949; New rev. ed. with Dorothy Pratt. New York: Hawthorn; London: Prentice Hall, 1959. 144pp, 200 color ill

1422   Price, William L., and W. M. Johnson.   Home Building and Furnishing; being a combined new edition of "Model Houses for Little Money," by Price, and "Inside of 100 Homes," by Johnson.   New York: Doubleday, Page, 1903.   193pp, 139pp, pls

1423   *Prime, Alfred Coxe, comp.   The Arts and Crafts in Philadelphia, Maryland and South Carolina, 1721-1785.   Boston: Walpole Society, 1929; Series Two, 1786-1800.   1932; reprint in 2 vol.   New York: Da Capo Pr, 1969.   323pp

1424   Quimby, Ian M. G., ed.   Arts of the Anglo-American Commerce in the 17th Century.   Winterthur Conference Report 1974.   Charlottesville, Va: U Pr of Va, 1975.   229pp, ill

1425   Ramsey, Natalie Allen, ed.   The Decorator Digest; chapters in the history of early American decoration and its European background, selected from The Decorator.   Rutland, Vt: Tuttle, 1965.   372pp, ill

1426   Raycraft, Donald R.   Early American Folk and Country Antiques.   Fore. by Mary Earle Gould.   Rutland, Vt: Tuttle, 1971.   148pp, ill, 24 color pls. bib (18th and 19th centuries)

1427   Reader's Digest Pocket Guide to American Antiques.   By the editors of American Heritage.   New York: American Heritage, 1974.   ill

1428   Reif, Rita.   Treasure Rooms of America's Mansions, manors and houses.   New York: Coward-McCann, 1970.   297pp, ill

1429   *Reinert, Guy F.   Yearbook of the Pennsylvania German Folklore Society.   Allentown, Pa: 1948.

1430   Reutlinger, Dagmar E.   Arts of the Colonial Period.

Exhibition. Worcester, Mass: Art Museum, 1975. 160pp,
103 ill, 1 color pl

1431   Robacker, Earl Francis. Old Stuff in Up-Country Pennsyl-
       vania. New York: A. S. Barnes, 1973. 283pp, ill, bib

1432   _____. Pennsylvania Dutch Stuff, a guide to country an-
       tiques. Philadelphia: U of Pa Pr, 1944. 163pp, ill,
       bib

1433   _____. Touch of the Dutchland. New York: A. S. Barnes,
       1965; Witmer, Pa: Applied Arts, 1966. 240pp, ill

1434   Rockmore, Cynthia, and Julian Rockmore. The Country Auc-
       tion Antiques Book. New York: Hawthorn, 1974. 160pp,
       ill with paintings

1435   _____, and _____. The Room-by-Room Book of Ameri-
       can Antiques. New York: Galahad, 1970. 240pp, 800 ill

1436   Rogers, Meyric Reynold. American Interior Design, the tra-
       ditions and development of domestic design from Colonial
       times to the present. New York: Norton, 1947; reprint.
       New York: 1963. 309pp, ill, bib DeWint, NNC-Ave,
       MiGr

1437   Sale, Mrs. Edith Dabney Tunis. Colonial Interiors. 2nd
       Series. Introd. by J. Frederick Kelly. Richmond, Va:
       Byrd Pr, 1927; New York: Helburn, 1930. 15pp, 159
       pls, color frontis (See also: Leigh French, no. 1312;
       H. D. Eberlein, no. 1304) (Virginia, Maryland, and
       North Carolina--Monticello, Carlyle House, York Hall,
       etc.) NNC-Ave

1438   _____. Interiors of Virginia Houses of Colonial Times,
       from the beginnings of Virginia to the Revolution. Rich-
       mond, Va? 1927. 503pp, 371 pls

1439   Schiffer, Margaret Berwind. Chester County, Pennsylvania,
       Inventories, 1684-1850. Exton, Pa: Schiffer, 1975.

1440   Schwartz, Marvin D. American Interiors, 1675-1885; a
       guide to the American period rooms in the Brooklyn
       Museum. Brooklyn, NY: Institute of Arts and Sciences,
       1968. 114pp, ill

1441   Seale, William. The Tasteful Interlude: American interiors,
       through the camera's eye, 1860-1917. New York: Prae-
       ger, 1975. 256pp, ill

1442   Shackleton, Robert, and Elizabeth Fleming (Shackleton). The
       Quest of the Colonial. New York: Century, 1907; reprint.
       Detroit: Gale/Singing Tree Pr, 1970. 425pp, ill, 44 pls

1443 Shaker Handicrafts. Exhibition. New York: Whitney Museum, 1935.

1444 Shaker Museum Foundation Publications. 6 vol. in 1. Chatham, NY: 1956-60.

1445 The Shakers: their arts and crafts. Exhibition. Philadelphia: Museum of Art, 1962. 112pp, ill

1446 Shelley, Donald A. Popular Antiques at the Henry Ford Museum. Dearborn, Mich: 1959. ill

1447 Sherman, Frederic Fairchild. Early Connecticut Artists and Craftsmen. New York: priv. printed, 1925. 78pp, pls, bib

1448 Skiff, Frederick Woodward. Adventures in Americana; recollections of 40 years collecting books, furniture, china, guns and glass. Portland, Ore: Metropolitan Pr, 1935. 366pp, ill

1449 Smith, Elmer Lewis. Antiques in Pennsylvania Dutchland. Witmer, Pa: Applied Arts, 1963. 42pp, ill

1450 _____, comp. Arts and Crafts of the Shenandoah Valley; a pictorial presentation. Witmer, Pa: Applied Arts, for Shenandoah Valley Folklore Society, 1968. 43pp, ill

1451 Snead, Jane Wanger. Pennsylvania Dutch Designs. Chicago: J. Snead, 1950. 50pp, chiefly ill

1452 A Souvenir of Romanticism in America; or, an elegant exposition of taste and fashion from 1812 to 1865 including, handsome canvases, distinguished and renowned sculptural works, superb examples of the arts of engraving, etching and lithography ... an array of snuffboxes, fans, valentines, music and knickknacks of various descriptions.... May-June 1940. Baltimore: Museum of Art, 1940. 71pp, ill

1453 Sprackling, Helen. Customs on the Table Top; how New England housewives set out their tables. Sturbridge, Mass: Old Sturbridge Village, 1958. 22pp, ill

1454 Sprigg, June. By Shaker Hands. Their Art and Their World. New York: Knopf, 1975. 250 drawings of furniture and objects

1455 Stephen, Walker Lewis, comp. Pennsylvania German and Huguenot Antiques; a list of articles giving Pennsylvania "Dutch" and English names and uses as employed by ancestors of many living folk. Compiled as a reference for antiquarians and collectors of elaborate and crude antiques. 2nd rev. ed. Reading, Pa: Reading Eagle Pr, 1925. 32pp, ill MiGr

1456 Stillinger, Elizabeth. The Antique Guide to Decorative Arts in America, 1600-1875. Introd. by Alice Winchester. New York: Dutton, 1972. 463pp, 416 ill, bib (No index)

1457 Stone, Sarah. Art and Artifacts of the 18th Century; objects in the Leverian Museum as painted by S. Stone. Text by Roland W. Force and Maryanne Force. Honolulu, Hawaii: Bishop Museum Pr, 1968. 232pp, ill

1458 *Stoudt, John Joseph. Early Pennsylvania Arts and Crafts. Fore. by S. K. Stevens. New York: A. S. Barnes; London: Yoseloff, 1964. 364pp, 344 ill, 16 pls (1700-1860)

1459 Strahan, Edward. Mr. Vanderbilt's House and Collection. 8 parts in 4 vol. Boston: George Barrie, 1883-84. 162 pls NN, MiGr

1460 Sweeney, John A. H. Great Winterthur Rooms. Winterthur, Del: Winterthur Museum, 1964. 43pp, ill

1461 _____. The Treasure House of Early American Rooms. (Also as Winterthur Illustrated.) Introd. by Henry Francis du Pont. New York: Viking Pr, 1963. 179pp, ill

1462 Technological Innovation and the Decorative Arts. Exhibition. Charlottesville, Va: U Pr of Va, for Hagley-Winterthur, 197-? 80pp, ill

1463 Thorne, Narcissa (Mrs. James Ward). American Rooms in Miniature. Exhibition. December 1940-June 1941. (Then circulated.) Chicago: Art Institute, 1940; 3rd ed. with more pls. 1941; 4th ed. 1944. 78pp, ill; 87pp, ill; 78pp, ill

1464 Townsend, Reginald T., ed. The Country Life Book of Building and Decorating. Garden City, NY: Doubleday, Page, 1922. 100pp, ill, color frontis (Contains "Early American Industries That Have Added Greatly to the Charm and Character of Our Country Houses To-day," by Charles Over Cornelius) MB

1465 Tracy, Berry B., and William H. Gerdts. Classical America 1815-1845. Exhibition. Newark, NJ: Museum Association, 1963.

1466 *_____, Marilynn Johnson, Marvin D. Schwartz, and Suzanne Boorsch. 19th Century America: furniture and other decorative arts. An exhibition in celebration of the

100th anniversary of the Metropolitan Museum.   New
York: 1970.   256pp, 297 (67 color) ill

1467 Turner, Thomas Edward.   Old Timey Stuff; a compilation
of historical facts, illustrations, and classifications of
iron, wire, guns, and glass, etc. from the American
West.   Mesquite, Tx: 1968.   176pp, ill

1468 Vanity Fair.   Weekly.   New York: 1860-63; monthly.   New
York: Standard Pr, etc., 1896-1936.

1469 Varney, Almon Clother, 1849- .   Our Homes and Their
Adornments; or, How to build, finish, and adorn a home,
containing practical instruction for the building of homes,
interior decoration, wood carving, scroll sawing, house
painting, window hangings, screens, curtains, window
gardening, incidental decorations, decorative-art needlework, and economic landscape gardening; to which is
added ... household ... recipes.   Detroit: J. C. Chilton,
1883; rev. ed. 1884; 1885.   498pp, ill, pls DLC

1470 Wallis, Frank Edwin.   American Architecture, Decoration and
Furniture of the 18th Century ... measured drawings and
sketches.   New York: P. Wenzel, 1896.   ill, 52 pls
NNC-Ave

1471 Wardlaw, Mrs. Georgia Dickinson.   The Old and Quaint in
Virginia.   Richmond: Dietz Pr, 1939.   328pp, ill, pls

1472 *Waring, Janet.   Early American Stencils on Walls and Furni-
ture.   New York: W. R. Scott, 1937; reprint as Early
American Stencil Decorations.   New York: Dover; London:
Constable, 1968; Watkins Glen, NY: Century, 1968; New
York: Peter Smith, 1975.   147pp, ill, 129 pls, bib
(Century reprint 112pp, ill) (To 1900)

1473 *Warren, David B.   Bayou Bend--American furniture, paintings
and silver from the Bayou Bend Collection.   Fore. by
Ima Hogg.   Houston, Tx: New York Graphic Society, for
Museum of Fine Arts, 1974.   200pp, 355 photographs, 22
color pls (1650-1870. Furniture collection in former
home of Miss Ima Hogg)

1474 Wharton, Anne Hollingsworth, 1845-1928.   Through Colonial
Doorways.   Philadelphia: Lippincott, 1893.   237pp, ill

1475 White, Margaret E.   The Decorative Arts of Early New
Jersey.   Princeton, NJ: Van Nostrand, 1964.   137pp,
ill, bib

1476 The White House Collection; preliminary catalogue: furniture,
furnishings, fine arts, documents acquired 1961-November
1964.   Washington, D.C.: GPO, 1964.   u.p.

1477 Wilde, Oscar Fingall O'Flahertie Wills, 1854-1900. Decora-
        tive Art in America: a lecture by Oscar Wilde, together
        with letters, reviews and interviews. Ed. with Introd. by
        Richard Butler Glaenzer. New York: Brentano's, 1906.
        294pp

1478 Williams, Henry Lionel, and Ottalie K. Williams. How to
        Furnish Old American Houses. New York: Pelligrini &
        Cudahy, 1949. 250pp, 150 ill, bib, gloss

1479 The Williamsburg Collection of Antique Furnishings. Williams-
        burg, Va: Colonial Williamsburg, dist. by Holt, Rinehart
        & Winston, NY, 1973. 120pp, ill

1480 Williamson, Scott Graham. The American Craftsman. New
        York: Crown, 1940; reprint as Early American Antiques:
        the American craftsman. 19-? 239pp, 343 ill, bib,
        checklists

1481 Wilson, Everett Broomall. Vanishing Americana. New York:
        Barnes, 1961; 1966. 187pp, ill (Social life and customs
        and implements, utensils, etc.)

1482 *Winchester, Alice. How to Know American Antiques. New
        York: New American Library; New York: Dodd, Mead,
        1951; New York: New American Library; London: New
        English Library, 1965. 191pp, ill (To 1840)

1483 _____, and staff of Antiques, ed. Living with Antiques;
        a treasury of private Homes in America. New York:
        Dutton, 1963. 288pp, ill

1484 *Winterthur Portfolio. Ed. by Ian Quimby. Periodical.
        Charlottesville, Va: U Pr of Va, 1967-date.

BRITISH ANTIQUES AND INTERIOR DECORATION

1485 Aitken, William Costen. Official Guide to Aston Hall and
        Park, and its exhibition of fine arts and art manufactures.
        Birmingham, Eng: 1858. 65pp BM

1486 Andre, James Lewis. Chests, Chairs, Cabinets and Old
        English Woodwork, etc. Horsham, Eng: S. Price, 1879.
        8pp, 12 pls BM

1487 Art Decorator. Monthly magazine of designs in colour for
        art workers and amateurs. London: H. Grevel, 1890- .
        color pls

1488 The Art Record; a monthly illustrated review of the arts and
        crafts. London: 1901-1902. ill

1489 The Artist and Journal of Home Culture. Monthly. London:
      to 1880; as The Artist, photographer and decorator. Lon-
      don: 1880-1895.

1490 The Artist. Monthly record of arts, crafts and industries.
      London: 1880-1902; American ed. New York: Truslove,
      1890-1902.

1491 Arts and Crafts. Monthly. London: 1903-29.

1492 *Arts and Crafts Essays. Pref. by William Morris. London:
      Rivington, Percifal; New York: Scribner, 1893; London;
      Bombay: Longmans, Green, 1899; 1903. 420pp, ill
      (Partial contents by members of the Arts and Crafts Exhi-
      bition Society: On the Revival of Design and Handicraft;
      textiles; wall papers; fictiles; metalwork; table glass; cast
      iron; embroidery; lace; furniture; decorated furniture)

1493 Arts and Crafts Exhibition Society Catalogue of the Exhibitions.
      London: Chiswick Pr, 1888- .

1494 Audsley, George Ashdown. Influence of Decorative Art and
      Art-workmanship in Household Details. A paper read be-
      fore the Art Section of the Social Science Congress at
      Liverpool, 17th October. Liverpool: 1876. DLC, CtY

1495 _____, and Maurice Ashdown Audsley. The Practical
      Decorator and Ornamentist. For use of architects, painters,
      decorators, and designers. London; Glasgow: Blackie,
      1892; 6 vol. Glasgow: 1892; 7 vol. 1892. 102 (100 gold
      and color) pls NNC-Ave

1496 Barfoot, Audrey. Homes in Britain, from the Earliest Times
      to 1900. London: Batsford, 1963. 96pp, ill, bib

1497 Barley, Maurice Willmore. The House and Home; a review
      of 900 years of house planning and furnishing in Britain.
      London: 1963; Greenwich, Conn: N.Y. Graphic Society,
      1971. 208pp, ill, bib

1498 The Bazaar, Exchange and Mart. Periodical. London: 18?-
      1936.

1499 Beard, Geoffrey William. Georgian Craftsmen and Their
      Work. London: Country Life, 1966; South Brunswick,
      NJ: A. S. Barnes, 1967. 206pp, 124 ill, bib (1700 to
      1800)

1500 Boynton, Lindsay, ed. The Hardwick Hall (Derbyshire) Inven-
      tories of 1601. Commentary by Peter Thornton. V & A.
      London: Furniture History Society, 1971. 47pp, ill,
      16 pls

1501   The British Antique Trades and Collectors Director. London:
          Woodhouse, 1949? - .

1502   Byrns, John H.   Where the Antiques Are in Britain and Ire-
          land; the complete guide to hundreds of antique shops and
          markets in more than 65 towns and villages.   East Meadow,
          NY: R. P. Long, 1972.   128pp, ill

1503   The Cabinet Maker and Complete House Furnisher.   Monthly.
          London: J. W. Benn, 1880-1919.

1504   Caldicott, John William.   Values of Antiques; the values of
          old English silver, Sheffield plate, pewter, china, furni-
          ture, clocks, etc., from the 15th century.   2nd ed.   Bath,
          Eng: J. M. Caldicott, 1929.   735pp, 500 ill, bib

1505   Carrick, Alice Van Leer.   Collector's Luck in England.
          Boston: Little, Brown, 1926.   229pp, ill, pls MB, DLC

1506   Cary, Elisabeth Luther.   William Morris, Poet, Craftsman,
          Socialist.   New York; London: Putnam, 1902.   286pp,
          ill, plates, bib

1507   Catalogue of a Loan Exhibition of Scottish Art and Antiquities.
          London: H. J. Hall, 1931.   BM

1508   Catalogue of an Exhibition of Late Elizabethan Art.   London:
          Burlington Fine Arts Club, 1926.   100pp, 50 pls

1509   Catalogue of Articles of Irish Manufacture, Produce, and In-
          vention, exhibited at the Society's House, 1847.   Dublin:
          Royal Dublin Society, 1847.   BM

1510   A Catalogue of the Antiquities and Works of Art, exhibited at
          Ironmongers' Hall, London, May 1861.   Compiled by a
          committee of the Council of the London and Middlesex
          Archaeological Society.   2 vol.   London: 1869.   ill, 10
          pls, facsims

1511   A Catalogue of the Furniture, marbles, bronzes, clocks,
          candelabra, majolica, porcelain, jewellery, and objects
          of art generally, in the Wallace Collection, Hertford
          House, London.   London: 1902; 2nd ed. London: HMSO,
          1904; 3rd ed. 1905; ...   303pp, ill

1512   Catalogue of the Hamilton Palace Collection of the Pictures,
          works of art and decorative objects.   London: 1882.
          234pp

1513   Chappelow, Archibald Cecil.   The Old Home in England,
          A.D. 1100 to 1830; a running commentary on the life of
          the times, the home and its furniture.   London: 1953.
          156pp, ill, bib NNC-Ave, DLC, NN

1514 Charles, C. J. (pseud. for Charles Joel Duveen). Eliza-
        bethan Interiors. London: Newnes; New York: F. Green-
        field, 1911; 2nd ed. 1916; 3rd ed. as Old English Interiors.
        New York: John Lane, 1919; reprint. 1926? 40pp, 32
        pls; 45pp, 38 pls DLC, MiGr

1515 *Chippendale's Ornaments and Interior Decoration, in the old
        French style. Consisting of hall, glass and picture
        frames, chimney pieces, stands for china, clock and
        watch cases, girandoles, brackets, grates, lanterns, orna-
        mental furniture, and various ornaments for carvers,
        modellers, etc., etc. London: sold by John Weale, 183-?
        30 pls (including 9 of fire-places) NN

1516 Choice Examples of Art Workmanship Selected from the Exhi-
        bition of Ancient and Medieval Art at the Society of Arts.
        London: Cundall & Addey, Royal Society of Arts, 1851.
        14pp, 59 pls

1517 *Church, Sir Arthur Herbert, William Younger Fletcher, John
        Starkie Gardner, Albert Hartshore, and Sir Charles Her-
        cules Read. Some Minor Arts as Practiced in England.
        London: Seeley, 1894. 82pp, 16 pls ("English Work in
        Impressed Horn," Read; "English Effigies in Wood,"
        Hartshorne; "Old English Fruit Trenchers" and "Old
        English Pottery," Church; "English Bookbindings," Flet-
        cher; "English Enamels," Gardner)

1518 Clinch, George. Handbook of English Antiquities for the Col-
        lector and the Student. London: L. U. Gill; New York:
        Scribner's, 1905. 351pp, ill, gloss

1519 Cole, Herbert. An Introduction to the Period Styles of Eng-
        land and France, with a chapter on the Dutch Renaissance.
        Introd. by W. G. Sutherland. Manchester, Eng: Suther-
        land Publishing, 1927; 1936. 73pp, ill MiGr

1520 Comparative Chart of Decorative Styles and Periods in France
        and Great Britain. London: Bishopgate Pr, 1909. BM

        The Connoisseur Period Guides. 6 vol. New York: Reynal,
        1956-58. See: Edwards, R.

1521 Cornforth, John, and John Fowler. English Decoration in the
        18th Century. Princeton, NJ: Pyne, 1974. 288pp, ill,
        40 color pls, bib

1522 Country Life. Weekly. London: 1897-date.

1523 Country Life Annual. London: issued each November.

1524 Coysh, Arthur Wilfred, and J. King. Buying Antiques: how
        old? how good? how much? Newton Abbot, Eng: David &

Charles, 1967; as Buying Antiques: a beginner's guide to English antiques. New York: Praeger, 1967; extended version of first half of original. Newton Abbot: 1968. 224pp, ill, bib; ...; 180pp, ill

1525 * _____, and _____. The Buying Antiques Reference Book, for buyers of English antiques. Newton Abbott; North Pomfret, Vt: David & Charles; New York: Praeger, 1968- . 232pp, ill (Contains: museums and collections, books and periodicals; auction room prices; clubs and societies)

1526 Crane, Walter, 1845-1915. William Morris to Whistler; papers and addresses on art and craft and the Commonweal. London: G. Bell, 1911; reprint. Folcroft, Pa: Folcroft Library Editions, 1973. 277pp, ill, pls (Embroidery, animals in art, English revival in decorative arts, etc.)

1527 Creative Art. Magazine of fine and applied art. Monthly. New York: A. & C. Boni, 1927-1933.

1528 Crow, Gerald H. William Morris, designer. London: special issue of The Studio, 1934. 120pp, ill, 4 color pls, bib DLC, MH, CtY

1529 Curran, C. P. Dublin Decorative Plasterwork of the 17th and 18th Centuries. London: Tiranti, 1967. 124pp, 177 ill on pls

1530 Curtis, Dewey Lee. The Decorative Arts of Ireland. Exhibition. Morrisville, Pa: Pennsbury Manor, 1971. 24pp, ill

1531 Dainton, Courtney. Clock Jacks and Bee Holes; a dictionary of country sights. London: Phoenix House, 1957. 128pp, pls

1532 Dalton, Ormonde Maddock, and Alec Bain Tonnochy. A Guide to Mediaeval Antiquities and Objects of Later Date in the Department of British and Mediaeval Antiquities. London: British Museum, 1924. 322pp, 217 ill, 17 pls

1533 Day, Lewis Foreman. Decorative Art of William Morris and His Work. London: Virtue, 1899. 32pp, ill, 4 color pls (Morris, 1834-1896)

1534 The Decorator. An illustrated magazine for the furnishing trades. Periodical. London: 1864- .

1535 The Decorator's Assistant. Weekly. London: Gibbs, 1847-1849.

1536 A Descriptive Catalogue of the Arts and Crafts Museum.
      Manchester, Eng: Municipal School of Technology, for
      the School of Art, 1913. 64pp, pls PPPM

1537 Dresser, Christopher, 1834-1904. Pottery, Glass, Metal-
      work: an exhibition. October 1972. London: Fine Art
      Society, 1972. 37pp, chiefly ill (His work)

1538 Dutton, Ralph. The English Interior, 1500-1900. London;
      New York: Batsford, 1948. 192pp, ill

1539 *Dyer, Walter Alden. Creators of Decorative Styles; being a
      survey of the decorative periods in England from 1600 to
      1800, with specific reference to the masters of applied
      art who developed the dominant styles. Garden City, NY:
      Doubleday, Page, 1917. 177pp, ill, 64 pls (I. Jones,
      Daniel Marot, Wren, G. Gibbons, Jean Tijou, Chippen-
      dale, Adam, Wedgwood, Hepplewhite, Sheraton) MiGr

1540 Edwards, Ralph, and L. G. G. Ramsey, ed. The Connois-
      seur Guides to the Houses, Decoration, Furnishing, and
      Chattels of the Classic Periods. The Tudor Period (1500-
      1603); The Stuart Period (1603-1714); The Early Georgian
      Period (1714-1760); The Late Georgian Period (1760-1810);
      and The Early Victorian Period or Regency Period (1810-
      1830). 6 vol. London; New York: Reynal, 1956-1958;
      1 vol. London: Connoisseur, 1968. 180pp each, 96 pls,
      bib; 1536pp, ill

1541 English Doorways and Architectural Woodwork of the 18th
      Century, in the Collection of the Art Institute of Chicago.
      Chicago: 1940. 15pp, ill

1542 English Panelled Rooms of the Classical Period, Bowes Mu-
      seum. Barnard Castle, County Durham: Bowes Museum,
      1972. 14pp, ill (1675-1749)

1543 Examples of the Works of Art in the Museum, and of deco-
      rations of the building, with brief descriptions. British
      Museum. 2 vol. London: Sampson Low, 1880, 1881.

1544 Farleigh, John. The Creative Craftsman. London: Bell,
      1950. 268pp, ill (Historical survey and modern methods)

1545 Fedden, Robin, and Rosemary Joekes, comp. The National
      Trust Guide to England, Wales and Northern Ireland.
      New York: A. Knopf, 1974. ill (Architecture and in-
      teriors with decoration)

1546 50 Masterpieces of Woodwork. V & A. London: HMSO,
      1955. 103pp, ill

1547 Finlay, Ian. Scottish Crafts. London: G. Harrap, 1948.
      127pp, ill, color pls

1548 *Foley, Edwin. The Book of Decorative Furniture, its form,
      colour, and history...; Correlated charts of British wood-
      work styles and contemporaries; decorative furnishing ac-
      cessories; principal trees, etc. 2 vol. London: Edin-
      burgh: T. C. & E. C. Jack, 1910-11; New York: Put-
      nam's, 1911-1912. 1000 ill, 100 color pls, bib, gloss
      (All countries, earliest times to 1815. Also fixed wood-
      work--panelling, chimney-pieces, etc.) ViU, CU, MB,
      MiGr

1549 Fry, Roger Eliot, J. B. Manson, Geoffrey Webb, Bernard
      Rackham, W. W. Watts, Oliver Brackett, A. F. Kenricks,
      Louise Gordon-Stables. Georgian Art (1760-1820). An
      introductory review of English Painting, architecture,
      sculpture, ceramics, glass, metalwork, furniture, tex-
      tiles and other arts during the reign of George III. Lon-
      don: Burlington Magazine, 1929. 68pp, 70 pls, color
      fronits DeWint

1550 Geerlings, Gerald Kenneth. Color Schemes of Adam Ceilings.
      New York: Scribner's, 1928. BM

1551 Geffrye Museum, London. Handbook. London: 1931; 1948;
      1951; 1964.

1552 _____. 16th Century English Homes. London: London
      County Council, 1958.

1553 _____. 17th Century English Homes. London: London
      County Council, 1958. 16 pls

1554 _____. 18th Century English Homes. London: London
      County Council, 1959; 1968. 4pp, 16 pls

1555 Gentleman's Magazine. Monthly. 320 vol. London: 1731-
      1907.

1556 The Georgian Society Records of 18th Century Domestic
      Architecture and Decoration in Dublin. 5 vol. Dublin:
      (Irish) Georgian Society, 1909-13. pls (See: Thomas
      U. Sadleir, and P. L. Dickinson) BM

1557 Gillespie, James. Details of Scottish Domestic Architecture;
      a series of selected examples from the 16th and 17th
      centuries, of stonework, woodwork, furniture, plaster-
      work, and metalwork. Edinburgh: G. Waterston, 1922.
      34pp, 130 pls DeWint, NNC-Ave, NN

1558 Gilliatt, Mary. English Style. London; Sydney: Bodley

Head, 1967; as English Style in Interior Decoration. New
York: Viking, 1967. 144pp, ill

1559 Glenister, Sydney Haywood. Stories of Great Craftsmen.
London: G. Harrap, 1939. 234pp, ill (Gutenberg; Caxton; Wren; Gibbons, Wedgwood; Watt; etc., chiefly British)

1560 Gloag, John (Edwards). Colour and Comfort ... original
designs by Palmer-Jones. London: Duckworth; New York:
F. A. Stokes, 1924; London: 1925. 186pp, ill, color
frontis

1561 Gordon, Hampden. The Lure of Antiques; looking and learning
today. New York: Macmillan; London: Murray, 1961.
130pp, ill, 24 pls, bib

1562 *Gotch, John Alfred. The English Home from Charles 1 to
George 4th: its architecture, decoration, and garden design. London: Batsford; New York: Scribner's, 1918;
1919. 410pp, 300 ill

1563 *_____. Old English Houses. London: Methuen; New York:
Dutton, 1925. 215pp, ill, pls, bib

1564 A Guide to Irish Antiques and Antique Dealers. Cork: Mercier Pr, 1968- .

1565 Guide to Woburn Abbey. Woburn Abbey, Bedfordshire: 19-?
ill (Room by room description)

1566 Guinness, Desmond. The Georgian Society Records of 18th
Century Domestic Architecture and Decoration in Dublin.
5 vol. Shannon: Irish U Pr, 1969. ill

1567 Halfpenny, William, fl.1750. New Designs for Chinese
Temples, triumphal arches, garden seats, palings, Chinese bridges, temples, obelisks, terminis, doors, windows, pilasters, green houses, etc. Gates, palisades,
stair-cases, chimney pieces, ceilings, chairs, etc. 4
parts in 1 vol. London: for R. Sayer, 1750-1752; 3rd
ed. as Rural Architecture in the Chinese Taste. London:
1755; reprint. New York: B. Blom, 1968. 44 pls; ...;
64 pls MiU, NNC-Ave, DeWint

1568 Halliwell-Phillipps, James Orchard, 1820-1889, ed. Ancient
Inventories of Furniture, Pictures, Tapestry, Plate, etc.
Illustrative of the domestic manners of the English in the
16th and 17th centuries, selected from unedited manuscripts. London: Adlard, 1854. 160pp

1569 Hampson Simpson, John Frederick Norman. The English at
Table. London: W. Collins, 1944; 1946. 47pp, 25 ill,
8 color pls

1570   Handicrafts and Reconstruction; notes by members of the Arts
       and Crafts Exhibition Society.   London: J. Hogg, 1919.
       138pp

1571   Harding, Arthur.   Collecting English Antiques.   London: W.
       & G. Foyle, 1963.   92pp, ill   (1300-1840)

1572   Harris, John.   A Catalogue of British Drawings for Archi-
       tecture, decoration, sculpture and landscape gardening,
       1550-1900, in American collections.   Introd. by Henry
       Russell Hitchcock.   Upper Saddle River, NJ: Gregg Pr,
       1971.   355pp, ill

1573   Havinden, Michael Ashley, ed.   Household and Farm Inven-
       tories in Oxfordshire, 1550-1590.   London: HMSO, 1965.
       365pp

1574   Hayward, Charles Harold.   English Rooms and Their Deco-
       ration at a Glance; a simple review in pictures of English
       rooms and their decoration from the 11th to 18th centuries,
       1066-1800.   London: Architectural Pr, 1925; New York;
       London: Pitman, 1926.   289pp, ill NjP, DLC

1575   Heal and Son, London.   Furnishings for the Middle Class.
       Heal's Catalogues, 1853-1934.   Reprint.   Newton Abbot:
       David & Charles; New York: St. Martin's Pr, 1972.
       u. p. , ill

1576   Heaton, John Aldam.   A Record of Work: being illustrations
       of printing, stencilling and painting, stained glass, cabinet-
       work and marquetry, embroidery, woven fabrics and other
       decorative works designed and executed by J. A. Heaton.
       London: Author, 1887; 1893; London: Simpkin & Marshall,
       1894.   8pp, 63 pls; 8pp, 92 pls   PPL, BM

1577   Helburn, William.   Historic English Interiors from the Eliza-
       bethan and All Other Renaissance Periods.   2 vol. in 1.
       New York: W. Helburn, 189-?

1578   Helm, William Henry.   Homes of the Past, a sketch of do-
       mestic buildings and life in England from the Norman to
       the Georgian Age, with a proposal for preserving certain
       typical houses, each to be furnished as an example of its
       own time.   New York; London: John Lane, 1921.   155pp,
       59 ill, pls, bib   MiGr

1579   Henderson, Philip.   William Morris; his life, work, and
       friends.   Fore. by Allan Temko.   New York: McGraw-
       Hill, 1967.   388pp, 90 (8 color) ill, bib

1580   Hennell, Thomas.   British Craftsmen.   London: Collins;
       New York: Hastings, 1943.   48pp, ill, 8 color pls

1581 Hessling, Bruno. Historic English Interiors; 40 plates repro-
      duced from watercolours by W. W. Quatremain, C. Essen-
      high Corke, etc. New York: B. Hessling, 1916?; New
      York: W. Helburn, 192-? 40 color pls NN

1582 Holme, Charles, 1848-1923, ed. Modern British Domestic
      Architecture and Decoration. London; New York: The
      Studio, 1901. 212pp, ill, pls (part color) NjP

1583 Hope, Thomas, 1770?-1831. Household Furniture and Inte-
      rior Decoration Executed from Designs by Thomas Hope.
      London: T. Bensley for Longman, Hurst, etc., 1807;
      reprint. London: Tiranti, 1937; 1946; reprint with pref.
      by Clifford Musgrave. London: 1970; facsimile reprint
      of 1807 ed. with new introd. by David Watkin. New York:
      Dover; London: Constable, 1971. 53pp, 60 pls, (bib in
      reprints) MB, NNC-Ave, MiGr

1584 Howarth, Thomas. Charles Rennie Mackintosh and the Mod-
      ern Movement. London: Routledge & K. Paul, 1952.
      329pp, 96 pls (Arts and Crafts Movement)

1585 Hughes, George Bernard. Collecting Antiques. London:
      Country Life; New York: Scribner, 1949; 2nd enl. ed.
      London: Country Life, 1960; New York: Macmillan,
      1961. 351pp, ill, bib; 391pp, ill, bib (Battersea and
      Bilston enamels, pewter, Sheffield plate, samplers, lace,
      Toby jugs, Tunbridge wares, fans, etc.)

1586 *_____. Horse Brasses and Other Small Items for the Col-
      lector. London: Country Life, 1956; 1963. 104pp, ill,
      16 pls (Also sugar tongs, snuffboxes, music boxes, por-
      celain, all English)

1587 _____, and Therle Hughes. After the Regency; a guide to
      late Georgian and early Victorian collecting, 1820-1860.
      London: Lutterworth Pr, 1952; New York: Macmillan,
      1954. 231pp, ill

1588 Hughes, Therle. Cottage Antiques. London: Lutterworth;
      New York: Praeger, 1967. 219pp, 48 pls

1589 *Hussey, Christopher. English Country Houses. Vol. I.
      Early Georgian, 1715-1760; Vol. II. Mid Georgian, 1760-
      1800; Vol. III. Late Georgian, 1800-1840. 3 vol. Lon-
      don: Country life, 1955; 1956; 1958; rev. ed. 1965.
      I: 256pp, ill; II: 255pp, ill; III: 255pp, ill, pls

1590 In the Days of Queen Charlotte. An exhibition of furniture
      and works of art used in English homes in the 2nd half
      of the 18th century. Luton, England: Public Museum,
      1939.

1591   Jeans, Herbert. The Periods in Interior Decoration; a prac-
          tical guide. (With a chapter on paperhanging in England,
          by Metford Warner.) London: The Trade Papers; New
          York: The Painters' Magazine, 1921. 118pp, pls (Late
          Tudor to William Morris) MiGr, DLC

1592   Jekyll, Gertrude. Old English Household Life. Some account
          of cottage objects and country folk. London: Batsford;
          New York: Putnam, 1925; 1933; rev. 2nd ed. with addi-
          tions of suggestions by Herbert Batsford on village crafts-
          manship, and observations and drawings by Sydney R.
          Jones. London: Batsford; New York: Scribner's, 1939;
          London: 1945. 222pp, many ill, pls; 120pp, ill, pls (1
          color) ViU, NN, PPL

1593   Jenkins, John Geraint. Traditional Country Craftsmen. Lon-
          don: Routledge & K. Paul, 1965. 236pp, ill, bib

1594   Jones, Inigo, and William Kent, 1684-1748. Some Designs of
          Mr. Inigo Jones and Mr. William Kent. London?: J.
          Vardy, 1744. 3pp, 53 pls (House decoration, architec-
          tural details) DLC

1595   *Jourdain, Margaret. English Decoration and Furniture of the
          Early Renaissance (1500-1650), an account of its develop-
          ment and characteristic forms. London: Batsford; New
          York: Scribner, 1924. 305pp, 400 ill, 8 pls NjP, NN,
          DeWint, MiGr

1596   *_____. English Decoration and Furniture of the Later 18th
          Century (1760-1820); an account of its development, and
          characteristic forms. 2 vol in 1. New York: Scribner's;
          London: Batsford, 1922. 269pp, ill, pls, bib NNC-Ave,
          MiGr, DLC

1597   _____. English Decorative Plasterwork of the Renaissance.
          London: Batsford; New York: Scribner, 1926; London:
          1933. 258pp, ill, pls MB

1598   *_____. English Interior Decoration, 1500 to 1830; a study
          in the development of design. London; New York: Bats-
          ford, 1950; 1953. 84pp, ill, pls (Based on Batsford's
          Library of Decorative Art, 4 vol.)

1599   *_____. English Interiors in Smaller Houses, from the
          Restoration to the Regency, 1660-1830. London: Bats-
          ford; New York: Scribner's, 1923; 1933. 202pp, ill, pls
          ViU, DLC

1600   Journal of Decorative Art. Manchester, Eng: 1881- .

1601   Keogh, Brian, and Melvyn Gill. British Domestic Design

Through the Ages. Ed. by Robert Patterson. London: Barker, 1970. 126pp, chiefly ill

1602 Laking, Guy Francis. An Illustrated Guide to Osborne. The Royal House, incorporating the Durbar Room and the various other places of interest, with a catalogue of the pictures, porcelain and furniture in the state apartments. Also notes on the Swiss Cottage and Swiss Cottage Museum. London: HMSO, 1919; 1922; rev. by H. A. Russell. London: 1928; 1933; 1937; 16th ed. 1947. 88pp, 11 pls

1603 *Latham, Charles. In English Homes: the internal character, furniture, and adornments of some of the most notable houses of England. 3 vol. London: Country Life, 1904-1909; 2nd ed. London: Country Life, G. Newnes; New York: Scribner's, 1907-1909. 421pp, hundreds of ill NN

1604 Lavine, Sigmund A. Handmade in England; the tradition of British craftsmen. New York: Dodd, Mead, 1968. 148pp, ill

1605 *Lenygon, Francis Henry, 1877-1943. The Decoration and Furniture of English Mansions During the 17th and 18th Centuries. London: T. W. Laurie; New York: Scribner, 1909. 215pp, ill, pls, bib ("Actual writing of this work has been attributed to Margaret Jourdain." Library of Congress) MiGr, ViU

1606 *_____. Decoration in England from 1660 to 1770. London: Batsford; New York: Scribner, 1914; London: 1915; 2nd rev. ed. as Decoration in England from 1640 to 1760: English decoration and furniture of the 16th to 19th centuries. New York: Scribner's; London: Batsford, 1927. 296pp, 350 ill, 4 pls; 276pp, 323 ill, bib ("The actual writing of this work has been attributed to Margaret Jourdain," Library of Congress. A standard work) NNC-Ave

1607 Lesley, Everett Parker, and William Osmun. The Prince Regent's Style: decorative arts in England, 1800-1830. Exhibition. New York: Cooper Union, 1953. 24pp, 8 pls, bib

1608 Lethaby, William Richard. Home and Country Arts. London: Home and Country, 1923; 2nd ed. 1924; 3rd ed. enl. 1930. 118pp, ill; ...; 143pp, ill

1609 Lievre, Edouard. Works of Art in the Collections of England. Drawn by E. Lievre and engraved. London: Holloway, 1871? 50 etched pls of 60 objects (Arms, pottery, miniatures, watches, fans, ivories, bronzes, cutlery, hunting cups, etc.) CtY, NN

1610   A List of the Wedding Presents Accepted by Their Royal
       Highnesses the Prince and Princess of Wales, and exhi-
       bited by their Royal Highness's permission at the South
       Kensington Museum. April 1863. London: 1863.

1611   Lister, Raymond. Great Craftsmen. London: Bell, 1962.
       191pp, ill

1612   Looking at Antiques. Introd. by Jane Probyn. Based on
       Thames T.V. series. London: S. Paul, 1971. 128pp,
       ill (1500-1900)

1613   Mainstone, Madeleine, and Arete Swartz. Looking at the
       Tudor Period. V & A. London: HMSO, 1974. ill

1614   Megson, Barbara. English Homes and Housekeeping, 1700-
       1960. London: Routledge & K. Paul, 1968. 119pp, ill,
       bib

1615   Miller, Fred. The Training of a Craftsman. New York:
       Truslove & Comba, 1898; London: H. Virtue, 1901.
       249pp, ill MH, MB, DeWint

1616   Morris, William, 1834-1896. Art and Its Producers, and
       the arts and crafts of to-day: two addresses ... before
       the National Association for the Advancement of Art.
       London: Longmans, 1901. 47pp MB

1617   _____ . The Decorative Arts: their relation to modern
       life and progress. London: Ellis & White; Boston:
       Roberts Brothers, 1878. 32pp; 50 pp NN

1618   William Morris. Exhibition. V & A. London: HMSO,
       1958. 5pp, 27 pls

1619   William Morris. V & A. London: HMSO, 1974. 28 pls

1620   *Mulliner, Herbert Hall. The Decorative Arts in England,
       1660-1780. Introduction by J. Starkie Gardner. London:
       Batsford, 1923; 1924. (343)pp, many ill (Mulliner's col-
       lection of furniture, silver, needlework, etc.) MiGr

1621   Nash, Joseph. The Mansions of England in the Olden Time.
       4 vol in 2. London: T. M'Lean, 1838-1849; ... 5 vol.
       London: Sotherna, 1869; ... 1 vol. as Mansions of Eng-
       land ... Facades and interiors in English gothic and
       Renaissance. New York: B. Hessling, 1900. 104 color
       pls; ...; 14pp, 104 pls (Companion to Richardson's
       Studies from Old English Mansions)

1622   _____ . Views of the Interior and Exterior of Windsor
       Castle. London: T. M'Lean, 1848. 4pp, 25 color pls
       TxU, MB

1623   Naylor, Gillian. The Arts and Crafts Movement: a study of
its sources, ideals and influence on design theory. London: Studio Vista, 1971. 208pp, ill, bib (1836-1950)

1624   Negus, Sir Victor Ewings. Artistic Possessions at the Royal
College of Surgeons of England. Fore. by Lord Brock.
Edinburgh; London: E. & S. Livingstone, 1967. 212pp,
ill

1625   Newby, Donald. Donald Newby's Guide to East Anglian Arts,
Crafts and Antiques. Periodical. Halesworth, Suffolk:
Norfolk & Suffolk Publicity Services, 196 -1971; London:
Picton Pr, 1972- .

1626   A 19th Century Miscellany. Exhibition. Preston, Lanc:
Harris Museum, 1952. 35pp, ill

1627   Objects of Art. Illustrations of 450 examples of sculpture,
furniture, metal-work, etc..... in the Hertford House,
London. London: 1924. 202pp, ill BM

1628   Our English Home; its early history and progress with notes
on the introduction of domestic inventions. Oxford; London: 1860. BM

1629   Parkes, Judith. Antique Collecting with B.P. (British
Petroleum.) 2 vol. 2nd ed. Havant: Kenneth Mason,
for the B.P. Retail Market Division of Shell-Mex and
B.P. Ltd., 1969. 160pp, ill, bib; 162pp, ill, bib

1630   Peate, Iorwerth C. Guide to the Collection of Welsh Bygones,
a descriptive account of old-fashioned life in Wales, together with a catalogue of the objects exhibited. Cardiff:
National Museum of Wales, 1929. 148pp, ill, 52 pls, bib
DLC, NN

1631   _____. Guide to the Collection Illustrating Welsh Folk
Crafts and Industries; in two parts: I: a descriptive
account; II: a catalogue of the collection. Cardiff: National Museum of Wales, Press Board of the U of Wales,
1935; 2nd ed. 1945. 75pp, ill, 16 pls, bib DLC

1632   *Polley, George Henry. Domestic Architecture, Furniture
and Ornament of England from the 14th to the 18th Century; comprising photographic and measured drawings of
exteriors, interiors and details. Boston: G. H. Polley
& Co., 1912. 76 pls (Companion to his Gothic Architecture) NNC-Ave, MiGr

1633   *_____. Gothic Architecture, furniture and ornament of
England from the 11th to the 16th century; comprising
photographic and measured drawings of exteriors, interiors,
and details. Boston: Polley, 1908. 4pp, 95 pls

1634 Portfolio. Irregular. London: Seeley, 1870-1907.

1635 Potter, Margaret, and Alexander Potter. Interiors; a record
      of some of the changes in interior design and furniture of
      the English home from mediaeval times to the present day.
      London: J. Murray, 1957. 48pp, ill

1636 The Prince Regent's Style: decorative arts in England, 1800-
      1830. Introd. by Everett P. Lesley, Jr., and William
      Osmun. Exhibition. New York: Cooper Union Museum,
      1953. 24pp, 8 pls, bib

1637 Pugin, Augustus Wilby N. Ornaments of the 15th and 16th
      Centuries. Ancient timber houses..., Gothic furniture of
      the 15th century, designs for gold and silver ornaments,
      and designs for iron and brass-work in the style of the
      15th and 16th centuries. 4 parts in 1 vol. London: M.
      A. Nattali, n.d. (ca.1835); as 15th and 16th Century Orna-
      ments. I. Gold and silver ornament designs; II. Iron and
      brass work designs; III. Gothic furniture; IV. Details of
      ancient timber roofs. 4 parts in 1. Edinburgh: J. Grant,
      1904. 98 pls, 4 color frontis

1638 Pyne, W. H. The History of the Royal Residences of Windsor
      Castle, St. James Palace, Carlton House, Kensington Pal-
      ace, Hampton Court, Buckingham House and Frogmore.
      3 vol. London: A. Dry, 1819. 100 hand-colored aqua-
      tints of (chiefly) interiors

1639 Read, Sir Charles Hercules. A Guide to the Medieval Room
      and to the Specimens of Medieval and Later Times in the
      Gold Ornament Room, British Museum. Oxford: Horace
      Hart, 1907. 276pp, ill BM

1640 Reade, Brian. Regency Antiques. London: Batsford, 1953.
      270pp, ill, bib

1641 Records of 18th Century Domestic Architecture and Decora-
      tion in Dublin. 5 vol. Dublin: Ponsonby & Gibbs at the
      Dublin U Pr, for the Georgian Society, 1909-1913. ill,
      pls

1642 Reveirs-Hopkins, Alfred Edward. The Sheraton Period; post-
      Chippendale designers, 1760-1820. New York: F. A.
      Stokes; London: W. Heinemann, 1912. 135pp, 32 pls,
      color frontis, bib MiGr

1643 *Riccardi, Saro John, comp. Bibliography of English Regency
      Furniture, interiors and architecture, 1795-1830; an anno-
      tated and selected list of references exemplifying the taste
      of the Prince Regent, later George 4th. Reprint from
      Bulletin. New York: N.Y. Public Library, 1940. 8pp
      NN

1644 Ricci, Seymour de. Louis 14th and Regency Furniture and
      Decoration. Tr. by Dr. W. E. Walz. New York: W.
      Helburn; London: Batsford, 1929. 215pp, 414 ill NNC-
      Ave

1645 Richardson, Charles James, 1806-1871. Fragments and
      Details of Architecture, decoration and furniture of the
      Elizabethan Period; 92 plates selected from "Studies from
      Old English Mansions." New York: Helburn, 191-?
      NNC-Ave

1646 *   . Studies from Old English Mansions: their furniture,
      gold and silver plate, etc. 4 vol. London: T. McLean,
      1841-48. 137 pls (part color) (Companion to Nash's Man-
      sions) MiGr

1647   . Workman's Guide to the Study of Old English
      Architectural Sketches of Carved Woodwork, furniture,
      etc., of the reigns of Elizabeth and James 1. London:
      1845. ill SKM

1648 Richardson, George, 1736?-1817?. A Book of Ceilings, com-
      posed in the style of the antique grotesque. French and
      English text. Londrs: L'auteur, 1776. 11pp, 48 pls

1649 Roberson, Charles L. Historical Rooms from the Manor
      Houses of England. 3 vol. London: Robersons, The
      Knightsbridge Halls, 1920? pls NN

1650 *Roberts, Henry David. A History of the Royal Pavilion,
      Brighton, with an account of its original furniture and deco-
      ration. London: Country Life, 1939. 224pp, ill, pls

1651 Rouquet, J. B. The Present State of the Arts in England.
      Dublin: for G. & A. Ewing, 1756. 124pp

1652 The Royal Pavilion Souvenir Catalogue of the Regency Exhibi-
      tion. July-October 1966. Brighton, Eng: Royal Pavilion,
      Museums and Libraries Commission, 1966. 31pp, ill

1653 Sadleir, Thomas Ulick, and Page L. Dickinson. Georgian
      Mansions in Ireland, with some account of the evolution of
      Georgian architecture and decoration. Dublin: U Pr,
      1915. 103pp, 80 pls (Continuation of Georgian Society
      Records of 18th Century Domestic Architecture ...) MiGr,
      BM

1654 St. Fagans Castle; a folk museum for the Welsh nation.
      Cardiff: National Museum of Wales, 1946. 8pp, ill NN,
      TxU

1655 Schreiber, Lady Charlotte, ed. Schreiber Collection Catalogue
      of English Porcelain, earthenware, enamels, etc., collected

by C. Schreiber and Lady C. E. Schreiber, and presented
to the South Kensington Museum in 1884. London: 1885.
241pp (See Bernard Rackham, nos. 3466-3468, for later
catalogues)

1656 Scott, William Bell (1811-1890). Antiquarian Gleanings in the
North of England, being examples of antique furniture,
plate, church decorations, objects of historical interest,
etc. Drawn and etched. London: G. Bell, 1849; 1851.
12pp, ill, 20 hand-color pls; 18pp, ill, 38 hand-color pls
V & A, ViU, DLC

1657 Shaw, Henry, 1800-1873. The Decorative Arts, Ecclesiastical
and Civil, of the Middle Ages. London: W. Pickering,
1851. 90pp, ill, 41 pls (part color) DLC, BM, NNC-Ave

1658 Sitwell, Sir Sacheverell. British Architects and Craftsmen,
a Survey of Taste, Design, and Style During Three Centuries, 1600-1830. London: Batsford, 1945; 2nd ed.
New York: Scribner; London: Batsford, 1946; rev. ed.
London: Pan Books, 1960; rev. and reprinted. London:
1973. 196pp, ill, pls; ...; 284pp, ill, bib

1659 *Small, John William. Scottish Woodwork of the 16th and 17th
Centuries, measured and drawn for the stone. Edinburgh:
David Douglas; London: Stirling, 1878; Boston: Polley,
1892? 100 pls MiGr

1660 Smith, George, Upholder Extraordinary to His Royal Highness
the Prince of Wales. Cabinet-Maker and Upholsterer's
Guide; being a complete drawing book, in which will be
comprised treatises on geometry and perspective, as applicable to the above branches of mechanics ... to which
is added a complete series of new and original designs
for household furniture and interior decoration. London:
Jones & Co, 1826. 219pp, 150 pls (many in color) MiGr

1661 _____ . A Collection of Designs for Household Furniture
and Interior Decoration, in the most approved and elegant
taste, viz. curtains, draperies ... with various designs
for rooms, geometrical and in perspective, showing the
decorations, adjustment of the furniture. London: J.
Taylor, 1808; facsimile reprint with new index to the
plates. Ed. by Charles F. Montgomery and Benno M.
Forman. Introd. by Constance V. Hershey. New York;
London: Praeger, 1970. 33pp, 158 (159) pls (sometimes
hand-colored) MiGr

1662 *Smith, Harold Clifford. Buckingham Palace. Its furniture,
decorations and history with introductory chapters on the
building and site by Christopher Hussey. London: Country Life; New York: Scribner's, 1931. 299pp, ill, 205
pls, bib

1663 _____ . Catalogue of English Furniture and Woodwork. Gothic and early Tudor; late Tudor and early Stuart. Vol. I, II of 4. 2 vol. London: V & A, 1929, 1930. ill

1664 _____ . A Catalogue Raisonne of the Principal Articles of Furniture and Other Objects of Artistic and Historical Importance at the Mansion House, London. Including the clocks, barometers, cut crystal-glass chandeliers, busts, statuary, and Royal Windsor tapestries. Together with descriptions of surviving examples of the ancient fittings and equipment of the Great Kitchen. London; Corporation of London for General Purposes Committee, 1954. 37pp typescript BM

1665 _____ . The Haynes Grange Room. V & A. London: 1935. 27pp, ill, 13 pls, bib (Woodwork and furniture)

1666 _____ , and Oliver Brackett. The Panelled Rooms. I. The Bromley Room, by Smith; II. The Clifford's Inn Room, by Brackett. 2 vol. London: HMSO, for V & A, 1914; rev. ed. 1922. ill, pls

1667 Speck, Gerald Eugene, and Euan Sutherland, comp. English Antiques. London: Ward Lock, 1969: 1970. 191pp, ill, 4 color pls, bib

1668 Stacpoole, George, ed. A Guide to Irish Antiques and Antique Dealers. Cork: Mercier, 1967. 104pp

1669 Steegman, John. The Rule of Taste from George 1 to George 4. London: Macmillan, 1936. 202pp, ill, pls, bib

1670 Stillman, Damie. The Decorative Work of Robert Adam. London: Tiranti; New York: St. Martin's Pr, 1966. 119pp, 180 ill, pls, bib

1671 *Strange, Thomas Arthur. A Guide to Collectors. English furniture, decoration, woodwork and allied arts during the last half of the 17th century, and the whole of the 18th century, and the earlier part of the 19th. Enl. ed. London: Simpkin, Marshall, 1900; new ed. London: McCorquodale; New York: Scribner, 1903; London: 1950. 368pp, 3000 ill; 1903: 3500 ill MiGr

1672 Stratton, Arthur. The English Interior: a review of the decoration of English homes from Tudor times to the 19th century. London: Batsford, 1920. 82 ill, 115 (6 color) pls MiGr

1673 The Studio. An illustrated magazine of fine and applied art. Monthly. London: 1893- .

1674 Swan, Abraham. Some 18th Century Designs for Interior
        Decoration, with Details Selected from Published Works of
        Abraham Swan. London: Tiranti, 1923; as Interior Deco-
        ration of the 18th Century (Woodwork, wall-treatments,
        staircases, chimneypieces and other details.) From the
        Designs of A. Swan, selected by Arthur Stratton. London:
        1928. 76 pls; 64 pls

1675 Swarbrick, John. Robert Adam and His Brothers; their lives,
        work, and influence on English architecture, decoration
        and furniture. London: Batsford; New York: Scribner's,
        1915. 316pp, ill, pls NN

1676 Tanner, Henry, Jr. English Interior Woodwork of the 16th,
        17th, and 18th centuries. Examples of chimney-pieces,
        panelling, staircases, doors, screens, etc. London:
        Batsford, 1902. 10pp, ill, 50 pls NN, MB

1677 *Tatlock, Robert Rattray, ed. Georgian Art; an introductory
        review of English painting, architecture, sculpture, ce-
        ramics, glass, metalwork, furniture, textiles and other
        arts during the reign of George III. London: Batsford,
        1929. 68pp, ill RICC

1678 Taylor, John, upholsterer. Taylor's Original and Novel
        Designs for Decorative Household Furniture, more par-
        ticularly for the department connected with upholstery ...
        Drapery for embellishment of saloons, drawing and dining
        rooms ... ornamental bed hangings, choice assemblage
        of sofas, couches, and chairs, elegantly and richly carved.
        London: John Taylor, Bedford Court, Covent Garden,
        1824. 30 color pls NNC-Ave

1679 Thomas, Gertrude Z. Richer than Spices; how a royal bride's
        dowry introduced cane, lacquer, cottons, tea, and porce-
        lain to England, and so revolutionized taste, manners,
        craftsmanship, and history in both England and America.
        New York: Knopf, 1965. 223pp, ill, bib

1680 Thomas, Gilbert. Antiques in Your Home; a book for the
        small collector of English antiques. London: Barker,
        1957; rev. ed. New York: Sterling, 1959; rev. ed.
        London: 1964. 174pp, ill; 221pp, ill, bib

1681 *Tipping, Henry Avray, ed. English Homes. I. Norman and
        Plantagenet, 1066-1485; II. Early Tudor, 1485-1558; III.
        Late Tudor and Early Stuart, 1558-1649; IV. Late Stuart,
        1649-1714; V. Early Georgian, 1714-1760; VI. Late
        Georgian, 1760-1820. 6 vol. London: Country Life,
        1920-1926. many ill, pls

1682 _____, ed. English Homes of the Early Renaissance;
        Elizabethan and Jacobean houses and gardens. London:

Country Life; New York: Scribner's, 1912. 423pp, ill,
pls

1683 _____. Grinling Gibbons and the Woodwork of His Age.
(1648-1720.) London: Country Life, 1914. 259pp, ill,
pls (Chiefly architecture, but including interiors) MiGr

1684 Turner, Walter James, ed. British Craftsmanship. Introd.
by W. B. Honey. London: Collins, 1948. 322pp, ill

1685 Twopeny, William. Specimens of Ancient Wood-work. London: priv. printed, 1859. ill

1686 Vallance, Aymar. The Art of William Morris ... with reproductions from designs and fabrics.... London: G.
Bell, 1897. 167pp, ill, bib NN

1687 *Vallois, Grace. Antiques and Curios in Our Homes. London:
T. W. Laurie; New York: F. A. Stokes, 1912; 2nd ed.
London: 1922; 5th ed. 1938. 323pp, 31 pls (17th, 18th
and early 19th century, chiefly English)

1688 * _____. First Steps in Collecting. Furniture, glass, china.
London: T. W. Laurie, 1913; Philadelphia: Lippincott,
1914; New York: Dodd Mead, 1926; New York: McBride,
1950. 324pp, ill, 36 (4 color) pls, bib (Interesting
chapter called "The Flotsam and Jetsam of Old Lumber
Rooms")

1689 Vernay, Arthur Stannard. Decorations and English Interiors.
New York: W. Helburn, 1927. 6pp, 53 pls NNC-Ave

1690 Walthamstow, England. William Morris Gallery and Brangwyn
Gift. (Catalogue.) Walthamstow: 1951. 32pp

1691 Ward, John. Handbook to the Collection of Welsh Antiquities.
June-October 1913. Cardiff: National Museum of Wales,
1913. 59pp, pls DLC

1692 Warrack, John. Domestic Life in Scotland, 1488-1688; a
sketch of the development of furniture and household usage.
New York: Dutton; London: Methuen, 1920. 213pp, ill,
16 pls (Rhind Lectures in Archaeology, 1919-1920) MiGr

1693 Watkin, David. Thomas Hope 1769-1831, and the Neo-classi-
cal idea. London: Murray, 1968. 316pp, ill, 60 pls,
bib

1694 Watkinson, Ray. William Morris as Designer. London:
Studio Vista, 1967. 84pp, ill, 64 pls, bib

1695 Weaver, Sir Lawrence, ed. The House and Its Equipment.

London: Country Life; New York: Scribner's, 1912.
212pp, ill

1696 Whitaker, Henry. The Practical Furnishing, decorating and
      embellishing assistant. Original designs ... of cabinet
      and upholstery work. Parts 1-18. London: P. Jacson,
      1847-48. ill BM

1697 Whiteman, G. W. Halls and Treasures of the City Companies.
      London: Ward Lock, with the Antique Collector, 1970.
      160pp, many ill (Mercers', Grocers', Drapers', Fish-
      mongers', Goldsmiths', Skinners', Merchant Taylors',
      Ironmongers', Vintners', Clothworkers', Armourers',
      Saddlers , Stationers , Apothecaries)

      William Morris. See: Morris, William, nos. 1618-1619.

1698 Wintersgill, Donald. English Antiques. The Age of Elegance,
      1700-1830. New York: William Morrow, 1975. 200 ill,
      16 color pls

1699 Wood, Henry, furniture designer. A Series of Designs of
      Furniture and Decoration in the Styles of Louis 14th,
      Francis 1st, Elizabeth, and Gothic. Designed and drawn
      by H. Wood. London: W. Pickering, 1845. 2pp, ill,
      24 color pls NNC-Ave, DLC

1700 Woodhouse, Charles Platten, ed. The British Antique Trade
      and Collector's Directory. London; Luton: Woodhouse,
      1949. 108pp, ill

1701 Wright, W(illiam) H(enry) K(earley). Exhibition of Armada
      and Elizabethan Relics, 1888. Plymouth, Eng: 1888.
      74pp (16th century) BM

1702 Wymer, Norman. English Country Crafts: a survey of their
      development from early times to present day. London:
      Batsford, 1946. 116pp, ill

1703 _____ . English Town Crafts, a survey of their develop-
      ment from early times to the present day. London; New
      York: Batsford, 1949. 128pp, pls, bib

ANTIQUES OF EUROPE, NORTH AMERICA AND
MISCELLANEOUS COUNTRIES

1704 Anthony, Edgar Waterman. Early Florentine Architecture and
      Decoration. Cambridge, Mass: Harvard U Pr, 1927.
      108pp, ill, 82 pls, bib

1705 Bayer, Herbert, Walter Gropius, and Ise Groupius, ed.
      Bauhaus, Weimer, 1919-1925; Dessau, 1925-1928. New

York: Metropolitan Museum, 1938; London: Allen & Unwin, 1939; Boston: Branford; London: Bailey & Swinfen, 1952. 223pp, ill, pls, bib of Bauhaus publications

1706 Bochnak, Adam, and I. Buczkowski. Decorative Art in Poland. Tr. from Polish by Paul Crossley and Marek Latynski. Warsaw: Arkady, 1972. 331pp, pls

1707 Boutell, Charles, 1812-1877. The Arts and the Artistic Manufactures of Denmark. London: J. Mitchell, 1874. 156pp, ill (For the opening of the Royal Danish Gallery, London) BM

1708 Breuer, Robert. German Arts and Crafts at the Brussels Exhibition, 1910. Stuttgart: Julius Hoffman, 1910. 4pp, 140 pls (some color) (Chiefly furniture and interiors) DLC, MiGr

1709 Bromberg, Paul. Decorative Arts in the Netherlands. New York: Netherland Information Bureau, 1944. 62pp, ill, bib

1710 Brunner, Herbert, comp. The Treasury in the Residenz Munich. Tr. by M. D. Senft-Howie. Munich: Bayerische Verwaltung d. Staatlichen Schlosser, 1967. 65pp, 12 ill

1711 *Bunt, Cyril George Edward. Russian Art. From scyths to Soviets. London; New York: Studio, 1949. 272pp, ill

1712 Butler, Ellis Parker, and Brittain B. Wilson. The French Decorative Styles from the Earliest Times to the present day: a handbook for ready reference. New York: T. A. Cawthra, 1904. 102pp, ill (476-1900) ViU, DLC, MiGr

1713 Byne, Arthur, and Mildred Stapley. Decorated Wood Ceilings in Spain. New York; London: Putnam's, for Hispanic Society of America, 1920. 112pp, pls DLC, TxU

1714 _____, and _____. Decorated Wooden Ceilings in Spain. A collection of photographs and measured drawings with descriptive text. New York; London: Putnam's, 1920. 222pp, ill, 56 pls in portfolio ViU, DLC, BM

1715 The Canadiana Guidebook: collecting antiques in Ontario. Toronto: Greey de Pencier, 1974.

1716 Carrick, Alice Van Leer. Collectors' Luck in France. Boston: Atlantic Monthly Pr, 1924. 207pp, ill, pls DLC, NN

1717 _____. Collectors' Luck in Spain. Boston: Little, Brown, 1930. 202pp, ill, pls

1718   Catalogue of the Spanish Productions Sent to the Great Exhi-
        bition of the Works of Industry of All Nations of 1851.
        London: 1851. BM

1719   Chirkov, D., comp. Daghestan Decorative Art. Moscow:
        Sovietsky Khudozhnik, 1971. 277pp, pls

1720   *A Classified Collection of Kunstgewerbe; arranged by the
        Deutsches Museum fur Kunst in Handel un Gewerbe, Hagen,
        i. W., and the Oesterreischen Museum fur Kunst und In-
        dustrie in Vienna, for exhibition in the American Art Mu-
        seums. Newark: Museum Association; St. Louis: City
        Art Museum; Chicago: Art Institute; Indianapolis: John
        Herron Art Institute; Cincinnati: Museum Association;
        Pittsburgh: Carnegie Institute, 1912-1913. 113pp, ill,
        1 pl (Show assembled by Karl Ernst Osthaus of the
        Deutsches Museum. John Cotton Dana, 1856-1929, of the
        Newark Museum, had the inspiration for the exhibition.
        He was early to recognize the artistic worth of industrial
        art. The show included 1300 pieces and photographs) NN

1721   Cole, Arthur Harrison, and George B. Watts. The Handi-
        crafts of France as Recorded in the "Descriptions des Arts
        et Metiers" 1761-1788. Boston: Baker Library, Harvard
        Graduate School of Business Administration, 1952. 43pp,
        pls

1722   Cole, Herbert. An Introduction to the Period Styles of Eng-
        land and France, with a chapter on the Dutch Renaissance.
        Introd. by W. G. Sutherland. Manchester: Sutherland
        Publishing, 1927; 1936? 73pp, ill MiGr

1723   Comparative Chart of Decorative Styles and Periods in France
        and Great Britain. London: Bishopgate Pr, 1909. BM

1724   Costantino, Ruth Teschner. How to Know French Antiques.
        New York: C. N. Potter; New York: New American Li-
        brary, 1961; London: Owen, 1963. 240pp, ill, 210 pls,
        bib (1380-1850) NN

1725   Daalder, Truus. Hunting Antiques in New Zealand. Dunedin,
        NZ: J. McIndoe, 1969. 187pp, ill

1726   Danish Art Treasures Through the Ages. Illustrated catalogue.
        Exhibition arranged by the Danish government and the
        V & A Museum. October 1948-January 1949. London:
        HMSO, 1948.

1727   Decorative Arts of the Italian Renaissance, 1400-1600. Exhi-
        bition. November 1958-January 1959. Detroit: Institute
        of Arts, 1958. 179pp, ill

1728   Decorative Arts; plates from l'Art Pour Tous. (1861-1879)

French, German, English text. 2 vol. Paris: A. Rorel, 1879? mounted pls (part color) NN, DLC

1729 Dulberberg, Fritz Helmut von. Collectors Guide to German Decorations. Aberdeen, Scotland: New Order Publications, 1973. 20pp, 200 ill

1730 Dutch Interiors from the 15th to the 18th Century. New York: Architectural Book Co, 191-? 1pp, 48 pls in portfolio CU

1731 Eberlein, Harold Donaldson. Interiors, fireplaces, and furniture of the Italian Renaissance. New York: Architectural Book Publishing, 1916; 1927. ill, 82 pls ViU, NNC-Ave, MiGr

1732 _____. Spanish Interiors, furniture and details, from the 14th to the 17th century. New York: Architectural Book Publishing, 1925. 450 photographs on 136 pls MiGr

1733 Eriksen, Svend. Early Neo-Classicism in France: the creation of Louis 16 style in architectural decoration, furniture and ormolu, gold and silver, and Sevres porcelain in the mid-18th century. Tr. from Danish and ed. by Peter Thornton. London: Faber, 1974; text ed. Atlantic Highlands, NJ: Humanities Pr, 1974. 432pp, 285pp of pls (ca. 1740-ca. 1770)

1734 Exhibition of Danish Art Treasures Through the Ages. (A brief guide.) V & A. London: 1948. 6pp BM

1735 Feulner, Adolf. Historic Interiors in Color; 80 colored views from castles and private house. Tr. by William E. Walz. New York: Helburn, 1929. 10pp, 80 color pls ViU, DLC, DeWint

1736 Godfrey, Denis. Antiques and Bygones: notes for South African Collectors. Cape Town: Timmins, 1967. 23pp, ill

1737 Gonzalez-Palacios, Alvar. The Age of Louis 15. Tr. from Italian by Henry Vidon. London; New York: Hamlyn, 1969. 156pp, 69 color ill

1738 _____. The Age of Louis 16. Tr. from Italian by M. H. L. Jones. London; New York: Hamlyn, 1969. 158pp, 63 color ill

1739 _____. The French Empire Style. Tr. from Italian by Raymond Rudorff. Feltham, Eng: Hamlyn, 1970. 157pp, color ill

1740 Habitations of Man; a merchants' house of the Middle Ages.

Exhibition.   Newark, NJ: Museum Association, 1916?
6pp, ill   (House in Strassburg, Germany)   NN

1741   Helburn, William.   Interiors of Old Belgium.   New York:
Helburn, n.d.   no text, 48 pls

1742 *   .   Italian Renaissance Interiors and Furniture.   New
York: Helburn, 1875; as Interiors of the Italian Renaissance.   1916.   50 mounted pls   MiGr

1743   Hirschfeld-Mack, Ludwig.   The Bauhaus: an introductory
survey.   Fore. by Walter Gropius; introd. by Joseph
Burke; epilogue by Sir Herbert Read.   London: Longmans, 1963.   54pp, ill, bib

1744   Hopstock, Carsten H.   Norwegian Design: from Viking Age
to Industrial Revolution.   Oslo: Dreyer, 19-?   210pp,
ill

1745 *Hunter, George Leland.   Italian Furniture and Interiors.   10
parts in 1 vol.   New York: Helburn, 1917-1918; 2 vol.
New York: 1918; 2nd ed. New York: Architectural Book
Publishing, 1920.   200 pls   PPPM, MiGr

1746   Husa, Vaclav, Joseph Petran, and Alena Subrtova.   Tradi-
tional Crafts and Skills: life and work in medieval and
Renaissance times.   Tr. from Czechoslovakian by Iris
Urwin.   London: Hamlyn, 1968.   228pp, chiefly ill, bib

1747   Lessard, Michel, and Huguette Marquis.   Complete Guide to
French-Canadian Antiques.   Tr. from French by Elisabeth Abbott.   New York: Hart, 1974.   255pp, ill, bib,
gloss   (Late-18th to 20th century)

1748   Loan Exhibition of the Arts of the Italian Renaissance.   May-
September.   New York: Metropolitan Museum, 1923.   38pp,
pls

1749   McClinton, Katharine Morrison (Kahle).   Modern French Decoration.   New York: Putnam's, 1930.   219pp, 27 pls

1750 *Maillard, Elisa.   Old French Furniture and Its Surroundings,
1610-1815.   Tr. by MacIver Percival.   New York: Scribner's; London: Heinemann, 1925.   128pp, ill, pls, bib
MiGr, NN

1751 *Martinell, Cesar.   Gaudi: his life, his theories, his work.
Tr. from Spanish by Judith Rohrer.   Ed. by George R.
Collins.   Cambridge, Mass: MIT Pr, 1976.   555 photo-
graphs, 60 color pls   (Includes interiors and furniture)

1752 *Maskell, Alfred.   Russian Art and Art Objects in Russia.
A handbook to the reproduction of goldsmiths' work and

other art treasures from that country in the South Kensington Museum. London: Chapman & Hall, 1884. 278pp,
24 pls NN

1753   Mayer, August Liebmann. Architecture and Applied Arts in
       Old Spain. New York: Brentano's, 1921. 176pp of ill
       NNC-Ave, MB

1754   [No entry.]

1755   Minhinnick, Jeanne. At Home in Upper Canada. Toronto:
       Clarke, Irwin, 1970. 228pp, ill, pls, bib

1756   Modern French Decorative Art. A collection of examples of
       modern French decoration. Introd. by Leon Deshairs.
       2 vol. London: Architectural Pr, 1926-30. ill

1757   *Molinier, Emile. Royal Interiors and Decorations of the 17th
       and 18th Centuries; their history and description. 5 vol.
       London; New York; Paris: Goupil & Co, 1902. ill, pls
       (French) NN

1758   Morassi, Antonio. Art Treasures of the Medici: jewel-
       lery, silverware, hard-stone. Tr. from Italian by
       Paul Colacicchi. London: Oldbourne, 1964. 45pp, 63
       pls, bib

1759   Naylor, Gillian. The Bauhaus. London: Studio Vista, 1968.
       159pp, chiefly ill (1919-1928)

1760   Oglesby, Catharine. French Provincial Decorative Art. Lon-
       don; New York: Scribner, 1951. 214pp, 301 ill, bib

1761   Perleberg, Hans Carl. Spanish Plastic Decorative Details
       and Historical Styles. New York: Perleberg, 1927?
       ill NN

1762   Pignati, Terisio. The Age of Rococo. Tr. from Italian by
       Lorna Andrade. London; New York: Hamlyn, 1969.
       157pp, 69 color ill (First half 18th century)

1763   Plath, Iona. The Decorative Arts of Sweden. New York:
       Dover, 1966. 218pp, ill

1764   Polley, George H. and Co., comp. Spanish Architecture
       and Ornament. Boston; New York: Polley, 1889. 50
       pls

1765   Riano, Juan Facundo, 1829-1901. Classified and Descrip-
       tive Catalogue of the Art Objects of Spanish Produc-
       tion in the South Kensington Museum. London: 1872.
       75pp, ill

1766   Ricci, Seymour de. Catalogue of a Collection of Germanic
       Antiquities Belonging to J. Pierpont Morgan. Paris: C.
       Berger, 1910. 86pp, 32 pls

1767   _____ . Louis 14 and Regency Furniture and Decoration.
       Tr. by Dr. W. E. Walz. New York: Helburn; London:
       Batsford, 1929. 215pp, 414 ill NNC-Ave

1768   Robinson, John Charles, 1824-1913. Catalogue of the Special
       Loan Exhibition of Spanish and Portuguese Ornamental Art,
       South Kensington Museum, 1881. London: Chapman &
       Hall, 1881. 211pp

1769   Rybakov, Boris Aleksandrovich. Russian applied art of the
       10th to 13th centuries. Leningrad: 1971. 125pp, 161 ill

1770   _____ . Treasures in the Kremlin. London: Hamlyn,
       1962; rev. ed. 1964. 127pp, chiefly ill

1771   Salvatore, Camillo, comp. Italian Architecture, furniture
       and interiors during the 14th, 15th and 16th century.
       Boston: G. H. Polley, 1904. 2pp, ill, 66 pls MiGr

1772   Savage, George. French Decorative Art, 1638-1793. London:
       Allen Lane, Penguin Pr; New York: Praeger, 1969.
       188pp, ill, 73 pls, bib

1773   Scheidig, Walther. Crafts of the Weimar Bauhaus, 1919-
       1924: an early experiment in industrial design. Tr.
       from German by Ruth Michaelis-Jena. London: Studio
       Vista; New York: Reinhold, 1967. 150pp, 81 ill, bib

1774   *Schottmuller, Frida. Furniture and Interior Decoration of the
       Italian Renaissance. New York: Brentano's, 1921; 2nd
       rev. ed. Stuttgart: Hoffmann, 1928. 246pp, ill, bib;
       250pp NNC-Ave

1775   Shipway, Verna Cook, and Warren Shipway. Decorative De-
       sign in Mexican Homes. New York: Architectural Book
       Co, 1966. 249pp, ill

1776   Smith, Jean, and Elizabeth Smith. Collecting Canada's Past.
       Scarborough, Ontario: Prentice-Hall, 1974. 220pp, ill,
       gloss (Authors' collection)

1777   Smith, Robert Chester. The Art of Portugal, 1500-1800.
       New York: Meredith, 1968. 320pp, ill (part color), bib

1778   Spendlove, Francis St. George. Collectors' Luck. Introd.
       by L. G. G. Ramsey. Scarborough, Ont: McGraw-Hill
       Ryerson, 1960. 208pp, ill, bib (Canadian antiques)

1779   Steingraber, Erich, ed. Royal Treasures. Tr. from German

(1968) by Stefan de Haan. London: Weidenfeld & Nicolson; New York: Macmillan, 1968. 101pp, ill, 170 pls

1780 Stevens, Gerald F. The Canadian Collector. Glass, pottery, furniture, firearms of the 19th century, etc. Introd. by F. St. George Spendlove. Toronto, Ont: Ryerson Pr, 1957; Rexdale, Ont: Coles, 1974. 100pp, ill, bib

1781 _____. In a Canadian Attic. Toronto: Ryerson Pr, 1963; 1965. 260pp, ill, bib

1782 *Strange, Thomas Arthur. Historical Guide to French Interiors, furniture, decoration, woodwork, and allied arts, during the last half of the 17th century, the whole of the 18th century, and the earlier part of the 19th. London: Author, 1903; New York: Scribner's, 1903?; London: McCorquodale, 1907?; reprint. New York: 1968. 400pp of 1200 ill

1783 Sully, Anthony. European Interior Design Through the Ages. London: Barker, 1970. 127pp, chiefly ill

1784 Tatlock, Robert Rattray, and others. Spanish Art. An introductory review of architecture, painting, sculpture, textiles, ceramics, woodwork, metalwork. London: Burlington Magazine Monograph, 1927. 121pp, 128 (8 color) pls, bib (Contributors include G. Webb; A. F. Kendrick; B. Rackham; B. Bevan; P. M. de Artinano)

1785 Thorne, Narcissa (Mrs. James Ward). Handbook to the European Rooms in Miniature. Fore. and text by Meyric Rogers. Chicago: Art Institute, 1943; 3rd ed. 1948. 63pp, ill

1786 Tombor, Ilona R. Old Hungarian Painted Woodwork, 15th to 19th century. Tr. by Lili Halapy. Budapest: Corvina Pr, 1967. 61pp, 51 pls

1787 Unitt, Doris Joyce. Collect in the Kawarthas. Peterborough, Ont: Clock House Publications, 1967. 83pp, ill (Kawartha Lakes, Canada)

1788 Unitt, Peter, and Doris Unitt. Unitt's Canadian Price Guide to Antiques and Collectibles. Peterborough: The Clock House, 1968. Guide. 1969. 200pp, ill; 240pp, ill

1789 Verdier, Philippe. Russian Art: icons and decorative arts from the origin to the 20th century. A selection of objects from an exhibition. November 1959-January 1960. Baltimore: Walters Art Gallery, 1959. 86pp, ill

1790 Verlet, Pierre. The 18th Century in France; society, decoration, furniture. Tr. from French by George Savage.

Rutland, Vt: Tuttle, 1967, as French Furniture and Interior Decoration of the 18th Century. London: Barrie & Rockliff, 1967. 291pp, ill, 24 color pls

1791 Wark, Robert R. French Decorative Art in the Huntington Collection. San Marino, Cal: Henry E. Huntington Library and Art Gallery, 1961; 2nd ed. 1968. 123pp, ill; 128pp, ill

1792 Weale, John, comp. Ornaments and Interior Decoration in the Old French Style. London: ca.1850. 33 pls (Selections from 18th century pattern books)

1793 *Webster, Donald Blake, ed. The Book of Canadian Antiques. New York: McGraw Hill, 1974. 352pp, 400 ill, color pls, bib

1794 Williams, Leonard. The Arts and Crafts of Older Spain. Vol. I. Gold, silver, and jewel work, ironwork, bronzes, arms; II. Furniture, ivories, pottery, glass; III. Textile Fabrics. 3 vol. London: Foulis, 1907. 172 pls, bib DLC

1795 *Wingler, Hans Marie. Bauhaus: Weimar, Dessau, Berlin, Chicago. Tr. from German (1962) by Wolfgang Jabs and Basil Gilbert. Cambridge, Mass; London: MIT Pr, 1969. 653pp, ill, 24 pls, bib (Adaptation with extensive supplementary material)

VICTORIAN ANTIQUES AND INTERIORS

1796 Barnard, Julian. The Decorative Tradition. Princeton, NJ: Pyne Pr, dist. by Scribner, 1974. 144pp, 350 ill, bib (Great Britain machine-produced ornament)

1797 Bøe, Alf. From Gothic Revival to Functional Form; a study of Victorian theories of design. Oslo: U Pr; New York: Humanities Pr; Oxford: Basil Blackwell, 1957. 183pp, ill, 16 pls, bib

1798 Brand, Alison, comp. Antiques: Victoriana, boxes, fans, Chinese bronze, jade and ceramics, samplers, pipes and tobacco jars, porcelain, clocks and watches. London: Octopus, 1974. 128pp, ill (Articles by Frank Davis, Walter de Sager, etc.)

1799 Bridgeman, Harriet, and Elizabeth Drury, ed. The Encyclopedia of Victoriana. New York: Macmillan, 1975. 368pp, 421 ill, 32 color pls

1800 Design, 1860-1960. 6th Conference Report. London: Victorian Society, 1970. 29pp, ill

1801 D'Imperio, Dan. ABCs of Victorian Antiques. New York:
      Dodd, Mead, 1973. 100 ill, 700 entries

1802 Drepperd, Carl William. Victorian, the Cinderella of An-
      tiques. Garden City, NY: Doubleday, 1950. 260pp, ill,
      bib

1803 Durant, Stuart. Victorian Ornamental Design. London:
      Academy Editions; New York: St. Martin's Pr, 1972.
      103pp, chiefly ill, bib

1804 Dutton, Ralph. The Victorian Home, Some Aspects of 19th
      Century Taste and Manners. London: Batsford, 1954.
      206pp, ill

1805 Field, June. Collecting Georgian and Victorian Crafts.
      London: Heinemann; New York: Scribners, 1973. 162pp,
      238 ill, 13 color pls, bib (1700-1900) (Patchwork, sand
      pictures, painting on velvet, ribbon and glass, embroidery,
      cut-paper, feathers, wax, shells, etc.)

1806 Freeman, John Crosby, comp. Late Victorian Decoration
      from Eastlake's Gothic to Cook's House Beautiful. Ed.
      by Hugh Guthrie. Watkins Glen, NY: American Life
      Foundation, 1968. 223pp, ill (Charles Eastlake, Clarence
      Cook, and others)

1807 Gabriel, Juri. Victoriana. Feltham: Hamlyn, 1969; as
      Victorian Furniture and Furnishings. New York: Grosset
      & Dunlap, 1971. 159pp, color ill, bib

1808 *Gloag, John Edwards. Victorian Comfort: a social history of
      design from 1830-1900. London: Black; New York: Mac-
      millan, 1961; 2nd ed. New York: St. Martin's Pr, 1973.
      252pp, 300 ill, bib (Companion to Georgian Grace, and
      Victorian Taste)

1809 *_____. Victorian Taste; some social aspects of architec-
      ture and industrial design, from 1820-1900. London: A.
      & C. Black; New York: Macmillan, 1962; Newton Abbot:
      David & Charles, 1972. 175pp, ill, bib

1810 Grotz, George. The New Antiques: knowing and buying Vic-
      torian furniture. (An illustrated guide to identification,
      appraisal....) Garden City, NY: Doubleday, 1964; rev.
      ed. with current price guide. 1970. 224pp, ill; 290pp,
      ill

1811 Hansen, Hans Jurgen. Late 19th Century Art; the art, archi-
      tecture, and applied art of the "Pompous Age." With
      contributions by Hanna Theodor Flemming, and others.
      Tr. by Marcus Bulloch. New York: McGraw-Hill, 1972.
      264pp, ill, bib

1812 Harrod's, Ltd. Catalogue 1895. Reprint as Victorian Shop-
        ping; Harrod's Catalogue, 1895. A facsimile of the Har-
        rod's Stores 1895 issue of the Price List. Introd. by
        Alison Adburgham. New York: St. Martin's Pr, 1972.
        1510pp, ill

1813 Hornung, Clarence Pearson, comp. A Source Book of An-
        tiques and Jewelry Designs, containing over 3800 en-
        gravings of Victorian Americana, including jewelry, silver-
        ware, clocks, cutlery, glassware, musical instruments,
        etc., etc., etc. New York: G. Braziller, 1968. 244pp,
        chiefly ill

1814 Howe, Bea. Antiques from the Victorian Home. London:
        Batsford; New York: Scribners, 1973. 232pp, 437 ill,
        bib

1815 Jervis, Simon. Victorian and Edwardian Decorative Art:
        Handley-Read Collection. London: Royal Academy of
        Arts, 1972. 138pp, 148 ill, bib

1816 Jones, Mrs. C. S., and Henry T. Williams. Household Ele-
        gancies: suggestions in household art and tasteful home
        decoration. New York: H. T. Williams, 1875; 5th ed.
        1877; reprint as Household Elegancies: how to make and
        restore Victorian art objects.... Watkins Glen, NY:
        Century, 1967. 300pp, ill, 5 pls MB, DLC

1817 _____, and _____. Ladies' Fancy Work. Hints and
        helps to home taste and recreations. New York: H. T.
        Williams, 1876. 300pp, ill ViU, DLC, DeWint

1818 Latham, Jean. Victoriana. London: Muller; New York:
        Stein & Day, 1971. 159pp, ill, 24 pls, bib

1819 Laver, James. Victoriana. London: Ward Lock, 1966; rev.
        ed. 1973; Princeton, NJ: Pyne Pr, 1975. 256pp, ill,
        bib; 192pp, 200 ill, bib

1820 *Lichten, Frances. Decorative Art of Victoria's Era. London;
        New York: Scribner, 1950. 274pp, many ill (many color),
        bib

1821 Maass, John. Gingerbread Age. A view of Victorian America.
        New York: Rinehart, 1957. 212pp, chiefly ill, bib

1822 _____. The Victorian Home in America. New York: Haw-
        thorn, 1972. 235pp, ill, bib

1823 *McClinton, Katharine Morrison. Collecting American Victorian
        Antiques. New York: Scribner, 1966. 288pp, ill

1824 *Mackay, James Alexander. Turn of the Century Antiques, an

<u>Encyclopedia.</u> New York: Dutton, 1974. 350 ill, 32
color pls

1825   <u>19th Century.</u> Quarterly. Philadelphia: Victorian Society
       in America, 1975- .

1826   Norbury, James. <u>The World of Victoriana: illustrating the</u>
       <u>progress of furniture and the decorative arts in Britain</u>
       <u>and America from 1837 to 1901.</u> Feltham; New York:
       Hamlyn, 1972. 128pp, ill (some color)

1827   Peter, Mary. <u>Collecting Victoriana.</u> London: Arco, 1965;
       New York: Praeger, 1968. 189pp, 65 ill, pls

1828   Pevsner, Nikolaus. <u>High Victorian Design: a study of the</u>
       <u>exhibits of 1851.</u> London: Architectural Pr, 1951.
       162pp, ill

1829   <u>Random House Collectors Encyclopedia: Victoriana to Art</u>
       <u>Deco.</u> Introd. by Roy Strong. New York: Random House,
       1974. 303pp, ill

1830   Roe, Frederick Gordon. <u>Victorian Corners: the style and</u>
       <u>taste of an era.</u> London: Allen & Unwin, 1968; New
       York: Praeger, 1969. 116pp, ill, 18 pls

1831   Shull, Thelma. <u>Victorian Antiques.</u> Rutland, Vt: Tuttle,
       1963; London: Prentice-Hall, 1964. 421pp, ill, bib

1832   Steegman, John. <u>Consort of Taste.</u> London: Sidgwick &
       Jackson, 1950; as <u>Victorian Taste: a study of the arts</u>
       <u>and architecture from 1830 to 1870.</u> Fore. by Nikolaus
       Pevsner. London: Nelson, 1970. 33pp, ill, 25 pls

1833   Swinney, H. J., and Mary-Ellen Earl Perry. <u>A Scene of</u>
       <u>Adornment, decoration in the Victorian home.</u> Exhibition.
       Rochester, NY: Margaret Woodbury Strong Museum, 1975.
       109pp, ill, color pls, bib

1834   <u>Victorian and Edwardian Decorative Arts.</u> Exhibition. V &
       A. London: HMSO, 1952. 149pp, 34 ill, bib

1835   <u>Victorian Exhibition for St. Bartholemew's Hospital, 1931.</u>
       <u>Victorian Crafts.</u> London: Committee of the Exhibition,
       1931. 45pp, ill, 26 pls (Contributors include Rackham,
       Hodgson, F. L. Carter, Mrs. N. Jackson, R. W. Sy-
       monds, Lady J. J. Smith, W. Lawrence, etc.) CtY

1836   <u>The Victorian Exhibition, illustrating 50 years of Her Majesty's</u>
       <u>reign, 1837-1887.</u> London: New Gallery, 1891. 291pp,
       ill BM

1837   <u>Victoriana.</u> An exhibition of the arts of the Victorian era in

America. April-June 1960. Brooklyn, NY: Museum,
1960. ill

1838 Wellman, Rita. Victoria Royal: the flowering of a style.
      New York; London: Scribner's, 1939; rev. ed. by
      Serry Wood (pseud.). Watkins Glen: Century, 1970.
      334pp, ill, bib; 192pp, ill (1851 Crystal Palace Exposi-
      tion to the 1876 Centennial Exposition)

1839 Williams, Guy Richard. Collecting Victoriana. London:
      Corgi, 1970. 127pp, ill, bib

1840 Wood, Violet. Victoriana, a collector's guide. London: G.
      Bell, 1960; New York: Macmillan, 1961. 175pp, ill,
      30 pls, bib

1841 Woodhouse, Charles Platten. The Victoriana Collector's
      Handbook. London: Bell; New York: St. Martin's Pr,
      1970; London: 1972. 239pp, ill

1842 Yates, Raymond F., and Marguerite W. Yates. A Guide to
      Victorian Antiques, with notes on the early 19th century.
      New York: Harper, 1949. 246pp, drawings and photo-
      graphs

ART NOUVEAU COLLECTIBLES AND DESIGN

1843 Abbate, Francesco, ed. Art Nouveau; the Style of the 1890s.
      Tr. from Italian by Elizabeth Evans. London; New York:
      Octopus, 1972. 158pp, 92 ill, bib

1844 *Amaya, Mario. Art Nouveau. London: Studio Vista, 1966.
      168pp, ill, plates (some color)

1845 *Art Nouveau. Exhib. April-June 1969. Assembled by Paul
      Magriel. Introd. by Alden Murray. New York: Finch
      College Museum of Art, 1969. u.p., ill

1846 Art Nouveau; a Loan Exhibition at the Virginia Museum,
      November-December 1971. Richmond, Va: 1971. 39pp,
      ill

1847 Art Nouveau. Jugendstil. Nieuwe Kunst. Exhib. April-
      July 1972. Rijks Museum, Amsterdam. 's-Gravenhage,
      Holland: Staatsuitgeverij, 1972. 72pp, ill

1848 Art Nouveau Sampler; exhibition. December 1952-January
      1963. Ann Arbor, Michigan: University of Michigan,
      1962. u.p., ill

1849 Aslin, Elizabeth. The Aesthetic Movement: Prelude to Art

Nouveau. New York: Praeger, 1969. 189pp, 121 ill, plates, bib (The Arts & Crafts movement.)

1850 Barilli, Renato. Art Nouveau. Tr. from Italian (Il Liberty. Milan, 1966) by Raymond Rudorff. London; New York: Hamlyn, 1969. 157pp, 67 color ill

1851 *Battersby, Martin. Art Nouveau. Feltham: Hamlyn, 1969. 40pp, 48 plates, ill (1889-1903.)

1852 *_____. The World of Art Nouveau. London: Arlington, 1968; New York: Funk & Wagnalls, 1969. 183pp, ill, 40 pls (1896-1900--Paris)

1853 Bossaglia, Rossana. Art Nouveau: Revolution in Interior Design. Tr. from Italian (1971). London: Orbis, 1973. 64pp, ill

1854 British Sources of Art Nouveau; an Exhibit of 19th and 20th century British textiles and wallpapers. Whitworth Art Gallery, March-May 1969. Manchester, Eng: Victoria University, 1969. 64pp, ill

1855 Cirici Pellicer, Alejandro. 1900 in Barcelona: Modern style, Art Nouveau, modernismo, jugendstil. New York: Wittenborn, 1967. 55pp, ill, 88 pls

1856 Gillon, Edmund Vincent. Art Nouveau. An Anthology of Designs and Illustrations from The Studio. New York: Dover, 1969. 91pp, 199 ill

1857 Hutter, Heribert. Art Nouveau. Tr. from German by J. R. Foster. London: Methuen; New York: Crown, 1967. 56pp of ill, bib (1880-1914)

1858 Julian, Phillipe. The Triumph of Art Nouveau, Paris Exhibition 1900. New York: Larousse, 1974. 216pp, ill

1859 Klamkin, Marian. The Collector's Book of Art Nouveau. Newton Abbot: David & Charles; New York: Dodd, Mead, 1971. 112pp, ill, bib (French, German, English, American)

1860 Lenning, Henry F. The Art Nouveau. The Hague: M. Nijhoff, 1951. 142pp, ill, bib

1861 Madsen, Stephen Tschudi. Art Nouveau. Tr. from Norwegian by Ragnar I. Christopherson. London: Weidenfeld & Nicolson; New York: McGraw-Hill, 1967. 256pp, ill, bib

1862 _____. Sources of Art Nouveau. Tr. from Norwegian by R. I. Christopherson. New York: Wittenborn, 1955; Oslo: H. Aschehong, 1956. 488pp, 264 ill, bib

1863   Mebane, John. The Complete Book of Collecting Art Nouveau.
       New York: Coward-McCann, 1970. 256pp, ill (Tiffany,
       Lalique, Guimard, commercial)

1864   Melvin, Andrew. Art Nouveau: Posters and Designs. Lon-
       don: Academy Editions, 1971. 105pp, chiefly ill

1865   Mourey, Gabriel, and Aymer Vallance, et al. Modern Design
       in Jewellery and Fans. London: 1902; reprint as Euro-
       pean (Art Nouveau) Jewelry. Watkins Glen, NY: Century,
       1969; as Art Nouveau Jewellery and Fans. London: Con-
       stable; New York: Dover, 1973; New York: Dover, 1975.
       149pp, chiefly ill, 8 pls; 200pp, ill (French, British,
       Austrian, German, Belgian, and Danish)

1866   Mucha, Alphonse, Maurice Verneuil, and Georges Aurio.
       Art Nouveau Designs in Color. Republication of the port-
       folio Combinaisons Ornementales se Multipliant a' l'infini
       a l'aide du Miroir. Paris: 1900. Original French fore-
       ward summarized in English. New York: Dover, 1975.
       60 color pls

1867   Pevsner, Nikolaus. Art Nouveau in Britain. Exhibit. Lon-
       don: Arts Council of Great Britain, 1965. 24pp, ill

1868   Reade, Brian. Art Nouveau and Alphonse Mucha. V & A.
       Museum. London: HMSO, 1963; 2nd ed. 1967. 34pp,
       36 ill, 32 pls (Alphonse Marie Mucha, 1860-   .)

1869   Rheims, Maurice. The Age of Art Nouveau. Tr. from
       French (L'art 1900. Paris: 1965) by Patrick Evans.
       London: Thames & Hudson, 1966; as The Flowering of
       Art Nouveau. New York: Abrams, 1966. 450pp, 595
       ill, 12 pls

1870   Richards, J. M., and Nikolaus Pevsner, ed. The Anti-
       Rationalists. London: Architectural Pr; Toronto: U of
       Toronto Pr, 1973. 210pp, ill, bib

1871   Schmutzler, Robert. Art Nouveau. Tr. from German by
       Edouard Roditi. New York: Abrams, 1962; London:
       Thames & Hudson, 1964. 322pp, 439 ill, 12 color pls, bib

1872   Selz, Peter Howard, and Mildred Constantine, ed. Art
       Nouveau; art and design at the turn of the century. Ex-
       hibit. New York: Museum of Modern Art; distrib. by
       Doubleday, 1959; reprint. New York: Arno Pr for
       MOMA, 1972. 192pp, ill, bib

1873   Warren, Geoffrey. All Color Book of Art Nouveau. London:
       Octopus, 1972; New York: Crown, 1974. 92pp, 105 color
       pls (Tiffany, Lalique, Mucha; furniture, posters, objects;
       includes collection of Lillian Nassau, NYC)

ART DECO COLLECTIBLES AND DESIGN

1874   Adams, Maurice Spencer Rowe. Modern Decorative Art, a
       Series of 200 Examples of interior decoration, furniture,
       lighting, fittings and other ornamental features. London:
       Batsford; Philadelphia: Lippincott, 1930. 249pp, ill,
       plates MiGr

1875   The Architect and the Industrial Arts; an Exhibition of Con-
       temporary American design, February-March 1929. New
       York: Metropolitan Museum, 1929. 83pp, ill, pls

1876   *Battersby, Martin. The Decorative Thirties. London:
       Studio Vista; New York: Walker, 1971. 208pp, ill, bib

1877   Bruenhammer, Yvonne. The 1920s Style. Tr. from Italian
       by Raymond Rudorff. London; New York: Hamlyn, 1969.
       159pp, ill, 70 color pls

1878   Exhibition of Swedish Contemporary Decorative Arts, under
       the auspices of H. R. H. the Crown Prince of Sweden.
       January-February 1927. New York: Metropolitan Museum,
       1927. 48pp, plates

1879   Frankl, Paul Theodore. New Dimensions; the decorative arts
       of today in words and pictures. New York: Payson &
       Clarke & Brewer & Warren, 1928. 88pp, 122pp of ill

1880   *Hillier, Bevis. Art Deco of the 20s and 30s. London:
       Studio Vista, 1968. 168pp, chiefly ill (Jewelry, ceram-
       ics, glass)

1881   *_____. The World of Art Deco: exhibit organized by the
       Minneapolis Institute of Arts, July-August 1971. Minne-
       apolis: the Institute; London: Studio Vista; New York:
       Dutton, 1971. 224pp, ill, bib

1882   Klein, Dan. All Color Book of Art Deco. London: Octo-
       pus, 1974. 72pp, 100 color pls

1883   Loeb, Marcia. Art Deco Designs and Motifs. Over 100
       examples. New York: Dover; London: Constable, 1972.
       75pp, ill, bib (Drawn from photos of architecture, jew-
       elry, fabrics, etc.)

1884   McClinton, Katharine Morrison. Art Deco: A guide for
       collectors. New York: Clarkson N. Potter, 1972.
       288pp, 275 ill, 69 color pls, bib (French, German,
       English, and American silver, glass and furniture, etc.)

1885   _____. Modern French Decoration. New York: Putnam's,
       1930. 219pp, 27 pls

1886 *Menten, Theodore, ed. The Art Deco Style: in household
      objects, architecture, sculpture, graphics, jewelry. 468
      authentic examples. New York: Dover; London: Con-
      stable, 1972. 183pp, 435 photos (Also gardens, furniture,
      interiors)

1887 Sembach, Klaus-Jurgen. Into the 30s. Style and Design,
      1927-1934. Tr. from German (1971) by Judith Filson.
      London: Thames & Hudson; as Style 1930. New York:
      Universe, 1972. 175pp, ill.

1888 Walters, Thomas. Art Deco. London: Academy Editions,
      1973. 87pp of ill

GENERAL AND MISCELLANEOUS
ORIENTAL APPLIED ARTS (See
also "Oriental" sub-headings under
specific sections, e.g. CERAMICS;
TEXTILES)

1889 Art of India, China and Japan;
      picture book. Detroit:
      Institute of Arts, 1946.
      28pp, ill

1890 *Audsley, George Ashdown,
          ed. Catalogue Raisonne
      of the Oriental Exhibition
      of the Liverpool Art Club.
      Liverpool: 1872. 163pp,
      ill BM

1891 Chu, Arthur, and Grace Chu.
      Oriental Antiques and
      Collectibles, a guide.
      New York: Crown, 1973.
      248pp, 250 ill, 8 color
      pls

1892 *Dimand, Maurice Sven. A Handbook of Mohammedan Deco-
      rative Arts. New York: Metropolitan Museum, 1930;
      2nd ed. rev. & enl. New York: 1944. 287pp, ill, 4
      color pls

1893 Eastern Art Objects. Catalogue of a Collection Lent by Lord
      Curzon of Kedleston. V & A. London: 1907; 1908;
      1910; 3rd ed. 1915. 57pp; 60pp; 60pp; 66pp

1894 Eckhardt, Andreas. A History of Korean Art. Tr. by J.
      M. Kindersley. London: E. Goldston, 1929. 506 ill
      on 172 pls (4 color); 8 inset-plates, bib

1895   Gunsaulus, Helen Cowen. Handbook of the Department of
       Oriental Art, Art Institute of Chicago. Chicago: Lake-
       side Pr, 1933.

1896   [No entry.]

1897   Hansford, Sidney Howard. The Seligman Collection of Oriental
       Art. Vol. I of 2. London: Arts Council of Great Bri-
       tain, by Lund Humphries, 1957. 135pp, ill, 80 pls (Vol.
       I. Chinese, Central Asian & Luristan Bronzes, and Chinese
       Jades and Sculptures. Vol. II. See: Ayers, John, no. 3983.

1898   Kelley, Charles Fabens. Handbook of the Department of Ori-
       ental Art, Art Institute of Chicago. Chicago: Lakeside
       Pr, 1933. 62pp, ill (Prints & minor arts)

1899   Kim, Chewon, and Won-Yong Kim. The Arts of Korea: ce-
       ramics, sculpture, gold, bronze and lacquer. Ed. by
       Katherine Watson. London: Thames & Hudson, 1966; as
       Treasures of Korean Art; 2000 Years of Ceramics, Sculp-
       ture, and Jeweled Arts. New York: Abrams, 1966. 284
       pp, ill, bib

1900   Koechlin, Raymond, and G. Migeon. Oriental Art: Ceramics,
       fabrics, carpets. Tr. by Florence Heywood. In English,
       French & German. New York: Macmillan, 1928; London:
       Benn, n. d. 20pp, 100 color pls

1901   Kohnell, Ernst. The Minor Arts of Islam. Tr. from German
       by Katherine Watson. Ithaca, NY: 1971. 242pp, 209
       photos, 15 color pls, bib

1902   *La Plante, J. Asian Art. Dubuque, Io: William C. Brown,
       1968.

1903   *Lee, Sherman E. A History of Far Eastern Art. Englewood
       Cliffs, NJ: Prentice-Hall, 1964. 527pp, ill (part color),
       bib

1904   Lockwood, Isabell Ingersoll. Oriental Brasses and Other Ob-
       jects for Temple and Household Use. Glendale, Cal:
       Author, 1935. 339pp, ill, 75 pls, bib (From the Lock-
       wood Collection) MB

1905   McCune, Evelyn. The Arts of Korea: an illustrated history.
       Rutland, Vt; Tuttle; London: Prentice-Hall, 1962. 452pp,
       314 ill, bib

1906   Miller, Robert William. Oriental Primer. Des Moines, Io:
       Wallace-Homestead, 1974. 135pp, ill

1907   Oriental Art, the Denver Museum Collection. Denver: Art
       Museum Winter Quarterly, 1952. 102pp, ill

1908 Pope, Arthur Upham. An Introduction to Persian Art Since
      the Seventh Century. New York: Scribner's, 1931.
      256pp, pls, bib

1909 *_____, and Phyllis Ackerman, ed. A Survey of Persian
      Art. 15 vol. London: Oxford U Pr, 1938-39. ill, pls

1910 Ridley, Michael J. Far Eastern Antiquities. Chicago: H.
      Regnery; London: Gifford, 1972. 144pp, ill, bib (300
      B.C. to 19th century)

1911a Smith, Robert Murdoch. Guide to the Persian Collection.
      Edinburgh: Museum of Science & Art, 1896. 16pp, ill

1911b _____. Persian Art. South Kensington Museum. London:
      Chapman & Hall, 1876; New York: Scribner, 1877. 60pp,
      ill, pls

1912 *Swann, Peter C. The Art of China, Korea and Japan. Lon-
      don: Thames & Hudson, 1963. 285pp, ill (part color),
      bib

1913 Woodward, C. S. Oriental Antiques at the Cape of Good
      Hope. Rotterdam, Netherlands: A. A. Balkema, 1974.
      228pp, ill, color pls, bib

CHINESE APPLIED AND DECORATIVE ARTS

1914 Alabaster, Chaloner. Catalogue of Chinese Objects in the
      South Kensington Museum. London: 1872. 80pp

1915 Ardenne de Tizac, Jean Henri d'. Animals in Chinese Art;
      a collection of examples. Pref. by Roger Fry. London:
      Benn, 1923. 6pp, 50 pls (part color)

1916 *Ashton, Sir Arthur Leigh B., and Basil Gray. Chinese Art.
      London: Faber, 1935; 1936; Boston; New York: Hale,
      Cushman & Flint, 1937; London: Faber, 1945; 1947;
      1951; 1953; New York: Beechhurst Pr, 1953. 397pp, ill,
      pls, bib; 1945: 366pp, ill, pls, bib

1917 Bertin, Henri L. J. B. de la Martiniere. China: its cos-
      tume, arts, manufactures, etc. Edited from the origi-
      nals in the cabinet of the late M. Bertin. Tr. from
      French. 4 vol. 2nd ed. London: Stockdale, 1812; 4 vol.
      in 2. 5th ed. London: Stockdale, 1812; 4 vol. 3rd ed.
      1813; 4 vol. London: Howlett & Brimmer, 1824. text,
      ill, 74 pls (Also found under: Breton de La M., J. B.
      J.) BM, DeWint

1918 Beurdeley, Michel. The Chinese Collector Through the

Centuries, from the Han to the 20th century. Tr. by
Diane Imber. Rutland, Vt: Tuttle, 1966. 286pp, ill, bib

1919 Brinkley, Frank. China; its history, arts and literature. 4
vol. Boston; Tokyo: J. B. Millet, 1902; Edinburgh; London: T. C. & E. C. Jack, 1904. pls (some color), text

1920 Bushell, Stephen Wootton, 1844-1908. Chinese Art. South
Kensington Museum. London: Wyman & Sons, for HMSO,
1904; 1906; 1906-07; 1908; 2nd ed. rev. London: 1909;
1910; 1914; 1919; 1921; 1924. ill, pls NN, PPULC, DLC

1921 Catalogue of a Collection of Objects of Chinese Art. London:
Burlington Fine Arts Club, 1915. 54 pls

1922 Catalogue of an Exhibition of Chinese Applied Art; bronzes,
pottery, porcelain, jades, embroideries, carpets, enamels,
lacquers, etc. Arranged by William Burton. Manchester,
Eng: G. Falkner for the Art Gallery, 1913. 104pp, 17
(1 color) pls NN

1923 Chambers, Sir William, 1726-1796. Designs of Chinese
Buildings, Furniture, Dresses, Machines, and Utensils,
to which is annexed, a description of their temples,
houses, gardens, etc. London: Author, 1757; reprint
of English text. New York: B. Blom, 1968. 19pp, 21
pls DeWint, DLC, MB

1924 China, Its Ancient Arts and Modern Life. Exhibition. October-November 1924. Baltimore, Md: Museum of Art,
1924. 23pp, ill

1925 Chinese Art. The Eumorfopoulos Collection. A Guide.
V & A. London: HMSO, 1936. 23pp, 6 pls

1926 The Chinese Exhibition: a commemorative catalogue of the
International Exhibition of Chinese Art in 1935-36. London: Royal Academy of Arts, 1936. 264pp, ill, 288 pls

1927 Chow, Fong. Animals and Birds in Chinese Art. New York:
China House, 1968.

1928 Collectable Chinese Art and Antiques, Classic and Common.
Uniontown, Pa: E. G. Warman, 197-? ill

1929 Crossman, Carl L. The China Trade: export paintings,
furniture, silver and other objects. Princeton, NJ:
Pyne Pr, 1972. 288pp, 290 (40 color) ill, bib (1780s
to 1850s)

1930 An Explanatory Book of the Chinese Exhibition, 94 Pall Mall.
London: 1825? BM

1931 *Feddersen, Martin. Chinese Decorative Art; a handbook for
       collectors and connoisseurs. Tr. from German by Arthur
       Lane. London: Faber; New York: T. Yoseloff, 1961.
       286pp, ill, bib

1932 *Fenollosa, Ernest Francisco. Epochs of Chinese and Japanese
       Art. An outline history of East Asiatic design. 2 vol.
       New York: F. A. Stokes, 1911; London: Heinemann,
       1912; 1913; 1917; rev. 2nd ed. with notes by Raphael
       Petrucci. New York: Stokes; London: Heinemann, 1921.
       ill, color frontis, pls (some color)

1933 Ferguson, John Calvin. Survey of Chinese Art. Shanghai,
       China: The Commercial Pr, 1939; 1940. 153pp, pls
       DLC

1934 Forman, Werner. A Book of Chinese Art: 4000 years of
       sculpture, painting, bronze, jade, lacquer and porcelain.
       Text by Lubor Hajek. Tr. from Czeck by Arnost Jappel.
       London: Spring Books, 1966. 74pp, 212 pls, bib

1935 Fry, Roger Eliot, Lawrence Binyon, Osvald Siren, Bernhard
       Rackham, A. F. Kendrick, and W. W. Winkworth.
       Chinese Art: An introductory handbook to painting, sculp-
       ture, ceramics, textiles, bronzes and minor arts. Introd.
       by Madame Quo Tai-Chi. London: Burlington Magazine
       monograph, 1925; reprint. London: Batsford, 1935;
       1945-46; 1949; 1952. 86pp, ill, 81 (23 color) pls, marks,
       bib

1936 *Gyllensvard, Bo. Chinese Gold, Silver, and Porcelain: the
       Kempe Collection. New York: 1953; New York: Asia
       Society, dist. by N.Y. Graphic, 1971; London: Asia
       House Gallery, 1974. 135pp, 118 ill

1937a Hansford, Sidney Howard. Chinese, Central Asian and Luris-
       tan Bronzes and Chinese Jades and Sculptures. (Seligman
       Collection of Oriental Art, Vol. I.) London: Lund-
       Humphries, 1957.

1937b _____ . A Glossary of Chinese Art and Archaeology. Lon-
       don: China Society, 1954; 1961. 104pp, ill, gloss

1938 Hartman, Alan S. Arts of the T'ang Dynasty; an exhibition
       organized by the Indianapolis Museum of Art and Rare Art,
       Inc. Introd. by Paul A. J. Spheeris. Indianapolis, Octo-
       ber-November 1973; New York, November-December 1973.
       Indianapolis: Speedway Pr, printer, 1973. 62pp, ill
       (618-960 A.D.)

1939 Hobson, Robert Lockhart, comp. Chinese Art: 100 plates
       in colour reproducing pottery and porcelain of all periods;
       jades, paintings, lacquer, bronzes and furniture; introduced

by an out-line sketch of Chinese art. London: E. Benn;
New York: Macmillan, 1927; 2nd ed. rev. by Soame
Jenyns. London: Benn, 1952; New York: 1954; rev.
London: Spring, 1964. 21pp, 121 ill, 100 color pls,
bib

1940 _____, ed. The Romance of Chinese Art. Garden City,
NY: Doubleday, 1936. 187pp, ill (Articles by 12 authorities)

1941 Jayne, Horace Howard F. The Chinese Collections of the
University Museum; a handbook of the principal objects.
Philadelphia: University Museum, U. of Penna, 1941.
62pp, ill

1942 *Jenyns, R. Soame, and William Watson. Chinese Art; the
minor arts: Vol. I: Gold, silver, bronze, cloisonne,
Cantonese enamel, lacquer, furniture, wood; Vol. II:
Glass vessels, mirror paintings, snuff bottles, ivory
carvings, semi-precious stones, textiles and carpets.
2 vol. New York: Universe, 1963-64. Vol. I. 462pp,
143 ill, 68 pls; Vol. II. text, ill, pls, bib

1943 *Jourdain, Margaret, and Roger Soame Jenyns. Chinese Export Art in the 18th Century. London: Country Life;
New York: Scribner, 1950; London: Spring, 1967. 152pp,
71pp of ill, color frontis, bib

1944 Karlgren, Bernhard. A Catalogue of the Chinese Bronzes in
the Alfred F. Pillsbury Collection. Minneapolis: Museum,
1952.

1945 Koop, Albert James. Early Chinese Bronzes. London:
Benn, 1924. 84pp, 110 pls, bib

1946 Langdon, William B. , comp. "10,000 Chinese Things;" descriptive catalogue of the Chinese collection ... with condensed accounts of the genius, government, history, literature, agriculture, arts, trade, manners, customs and
social life of the people of the Celestial Empire ... owned
by Nathan Dunn in Philadelphia. Philadelphia: 1839;
London: 1842; 1843; 1844; 1851; 1855; 1877; etc. 163pp
to 265pp, ill, pls (Dunn, 1782-1844. Collection deposited
in Philadelphia Museum, whence it was removed to London
in 1842, exhibited at Celestial Palace, Hyde Park) De-
Wint, NN, BM

1947 _____. 10,000 Things Relating to China and the Chinese;
an epitome of the genius, government, history of the
Celestial Empire, together with a sinopsis of the Chinese
Collection. "To be had only at the exhibit." London:
1842. 273pp

178   Antiques and Collectibles

1948 Lee, Sherman E., and Wai-Kam Ho. Chinese Art under the
      Mongols: the Yuan Dynasty (1279-1368). Cleveland: Mu-
      seum of Art, 1969. 403pp, ill, catalog of exhibit, bib

1949 Leth, Andre. Chinese Art; a selection of the exhibits shown
      at the Museum of Decorative Arts, Copenhagen, 1950.
      Copenhagen: Nyt Nordisk Forlag, 1953. 129pp, ill

1950 *Lion-Goldschmidt, Daisy, and Jean-Claude Moreau-Gobard.
      Chinese Art: Bronze, jade, sculpture, ceramics. Tr.
      from French (Arts de la Chine, Paris: 1937) by Diana
      Imber. Fore. by George Savage. London: Studio Uni-
      verse, 1961. 427pp, 133 ill, 65 pls, bib

1951 Masterpieces of Chinese Ju-i Scepters in the National Palace
      Museum. Taipei, Taiwan: 1974. 107pp, ill, 50 color
      pls (Ch'ing)

1952 Masterpieces of Chinese Seals in the National Palace Museum.
      Taipei, Taiwan: 1974. 111pp, 100 color pls, seal im-
      pressions (Early Warring States to early Ch'ing)

1953 Maust, Don, ed. Collectable Chinese Art and Antiques, a
      collection of information on classic and common Chinese
      art objects that will teach one to recognize good Chinese
      art and antique collectables. Uniontown, Pa: E. G.
      Warman, 1973. 159pp, ill

1954 Medley, Margaret. A Handbook of Chinese Art: for col-
      lectors and students. London: Bell, 1964. 140pp, ill,
      bib

1955 Palmgren, Nils. Selected Chinese Antiquities from the Col-
      lection of Gustav Adolf, Crown Prince of Sweden. Stock-
      holm: Generalstabens Litografiska anstalts forlag, 1948.
      (Bronzes, earthenware, sculpture, ivories, jades, lacquers,
      fabric, silver)

1956 Prodan, Mario. Chinese Art. London: Hutchinson; New
      York: Pantheon, 1958; new ed. London: Spring, 1966.
      220pp, ill, bib; 220pp, 71 (7 color) pls, bib

1957a Sullivan, Michael. Chinese Art, Recent Discoveries. London;
      New York: Thames & Hudson, 1973. 63,64pp, ill (some
      color)

1957b _____. Chinese Ceramics, Bronzes and Jades in the Col-
      lection of Sir Alan and Lady Barlow. London: Faber,
      1963. 173pp, 160 pls, bib (Ashmolean Museum, Oxford)

1958 _____. Introduction to Chinese Art. Berkeley: U of
      California Pr, 1961; rev. ed. as A Short History of

Chinese Art. 1967; completely revised ed. as The Arts of China. 1973. 1973: 256pp, 238 ill (some color), bib

1959 Swann, Peter Charles. Art of China, Korea and Japan. London: Thames & Hudson; New York: Praeger, 1963. 285pp, 259 ill, 51 color pls, bib

1960 Ting, Hsing-wu, ed. Treasures of China. Rev. by Wu Chia Ching. Tr. by Wu Ping Chung. Chinese & English. 2 vol. Taipei: International Culture Pr, 1970. chiefly ill

1961 Willetts, William. Foundations of Chinese Art: from Neolithic pottery to modern architecture. Harmondsworth: Penguin, 1958; new & rev. ed. London: Thames & Hudson, 1965. 465pp, ill, bib

1962 Yetts, Walter Percival. The George Eumorfopoulos Collection; catalogue of the Chinese and Corean bronzes, sculpture, jade, jewellery and miscellaneous objects. London: Benn, 1929-32. ill, pls, bib

JAPANESE APPLIED & DECORATIVE ARTS†

1963 Alcock, Sir Rutherford. Art and Art Industries in Japan. London: Virtue, 1878. 292pp, ill, color frontis DLC

1964   . International Exhibition, 1862. Catalogue of Works of Industry and Art, sent from Japan.... London: W. Clowes & Sons, 1862. 12pp DLC

1965 Audsley, George Ashdown. Gems of Japanese Art and Handicraft. London: Sampson Low, Marston, 1913. 60pp, ill, 72 pls (some color)

1966   . Notes on Japanese Art; paper read before the Architectural Association, London 1872. Illustrated by specimens of Japanese art from the collection of J. L. Bowes. London: priv. printed, 1872; Liverpool: priv. printed, 1874. 31pp, pls DLC

1967   . The Ornamental Arts of Japan. Vol. I. Part 1. Drawing, painting, engraving, printing, embroideries; part 2. Textile fabrics, lacquer; Vol. II. Part 1. Incrusted work, metal work; part 2. Cloisonné enamel, modelling and carving, heraldry. 2 vol, issued in 4

---

†Perhaps the most comprehensive pictorial coverage of this subject is the 30-volume The Arts of Japan in Color (Tokyo: Shogakukan Publishing). Unfortunately the text is in Japanese. There are 30,000 color plates of the major and minor arts.

parts. London: Sampson Low, Marston, etc. 1882-85;
2 and 4 vol. ed. New York: Scribner's, 1883-1884; 2
vol. London: Low, 1892; London: Low, 1932. text, ill,
101 pls (some color) BM

1968   Bing, Samuel, 1838-1905. Artistic Japan: illustrations and
       essays. 6 vol. in 3. London: S. Low, Marston, 1888-
       1891. ill, pls

1969   Blacker, James F. The ABC of Japanese Art. Boston:
       Cornhill; London: S. Paul; Philadelphia: G. W. Jacobs,
       1911; London: 1912; 2nd ed. London: 1922; 1928. 460pp,
       ill, 48 pls DLC, NN

1970   Boger, H. Batterson. The Traditional Arts of Japan. Lon-
       don: W. H. Allen; Garden City, NY: Doubleday, 1964.
       351pp, ill, bib

1971   Bowes, James Lord. Handbook to the Bowes Museum of
       Japanese Art Work, Liverpool. Liverpool: E. Howell,
       1890; Liverpool: D. Marples, 1893; 3rd ed. 1894; 1897.
       48pp, ill NN, DLC

1972 * _____. Japanese Marks and Seals. London: H. Sotheran,
       1862. 378pp, ill, color frontis, over 700 marks on pot-
       tery, porcelain, wood, ivory, lacquer, enamels, metals,
       netsuke, manuscripts, books CU, MiD

1973   Brinkley, Frank. The Art of Japan. Vol. I. Pictorial Art;
       Vol. II. Applied Art. 2 vol. Boston: J. B. Millet,
       1901. ill, some color DLC

1974   _____. Japan; its history, arts and literature. 9 vol.
       Boston; Tokyo: J. Millet, 1901. ill

1975   Crossman, Carl L. Japanese and Indian Export Art. Exhi-
       bition. March 1975. Springfield, Mass: Museum, 1975.
       ill (From Peabody Museum and private Boston collection,
       18th and 19th centuries)

1976   Dick, Stewart. Arts and Crafts of Old Japan. Chicago:
       McClurg, 1904; 1905; 1906; Edinburgh; London: T. N.
       Foulis, 1906; 1908; Chicago: 1909; 4th ed. 1912; London:
       Foulis, 1914; 1923. 152pp, 28 pls CU, NN

1977   Dillon, Edward. The Arts of Japan. London: Methuen,
       1906; 2nd ed. 1909; 3rd ed. 1911; Chicago: McClurg,
       1914; 4th ed. London: 1922. 212pp, 41 pls, bib

1978   Dresser, Christopher. Japan: its architecture, art and art
       manufactures. London: Longmans, Green, 1882. 467pp,
       ill BM, DLC

1979   Explanation of the Japanese Lady's Boudoir, with the articles
        therein, exhibited in the Woman's Building of the World's
        Columbian Exposition, Chicago 1893. Chicago: priv.
        printed by A. S. McClurg, 1893. 16pp, ill

1980   Feddersen, Martin. Japanese Decorative Art: Handbook for
        collectors and connoisseurs. Tr. from German by Kathe-
        rine Watson. London: Faber, 1962. 296pp, ill, bib

1981   *Fenollosa, Ernest Francisco.   Epochs of Chinese and Japanese
        Art. An outline history of East Asiatic Design. 2 vol.
        New York: F. A. Stokes, 1911; London: Heinemann,
        1912; 1913; 1917; rev. 2nd ed. with notes by Raphael Pe-
        trucci. New York: Stokes; London: Heinemann, 1921.
        ill, color frontis, pls (some color)

1982   Gonse, Louis. Japanese Art. Tr. by M. P. Nickerson.
        Chicago: Belford-Clarke, 1891. 269pp, ill MH

1983   Gunsaulus, Helen Cowen. Japanese Collections (Frank
        Wakeley Gunsaulus Hall). Chicago: Field Museum, 1922.
        19pp, pls

1984   Huish, Marcus Bourne. Japan and Its Art. London: Fine
        Art Society, 1889; ...; 3rd ed. rev. & enl. London:
        Batsford, 1912. 254pp, ill; ...; 373pp, ill, 6 pls PP,
        NN

1985   Japanese Works of Art; armour, weapons, sword-fittings,
        lacquer, pictures, textiles, colour-prints, selected from
        the Nosle collection. (Ed. by Alexander George Nosle ?)
        2 vol. Leipzig: 1914. 204 (4 color) pls

1986   Joly, Henri L. Legend in Japanese Art. A Description of
        historical episodes, legendary characters, folk-lore,
        myths, religious symbolism, illustrated in the arts of
        old Japan. London; New York: J. Lane, 1908. 453pp,
        700 ill, 111 (16 color) pls, bib DLC, NN

1987   _____, and Kumasaku Tomita. Japanese Art and Handi-
        craft. Exhibition. London: Yamanaka, 1916. 213pp,
        170 pls (part color) DLC

1988   Lee, Sherman E. Japanese Decorative Style. Cleveland:
        Cleveland Museum, dist. by Abrams, N.Y., 1961; reprint.
        1971. 161pp, ill (part color), bib (By-product of exhi-
        bition)

1989   Minamoto, (Hoshu) Toyomune. An Illustrated History of
        Japanese Art. Tr. by Harold G. Henderson. Kyoto:
        K. Koshino, 1935. 264pp, 218 pls DLC

1990   Morse, Edward Sylvester, 1838-1925. Japanese Homes and

Their Surroundings. New York: Harper, 1885; Boston: Tichnor; London: Low, Marston, 1886. 372pp, 307 ill

1991 Munsterberg, Hugo. The Arts of Japan, an illustrated history. Tokyo; Rutland, Vt.: Tuttle, 1956; London: Thames & Hudson, 1957; London: Prentice-Hall, 1964. 201pp, ill, bib

1992 Newman, Alexander R., and Egerton Ryerson. Japanese Art: a collector's guide. London: Bell, 1964. 271pp, ill, 32 pls, bib

1993 Noma, Seiroku. The Arts of Japan: (Vol. I) ancient and medieval; (Vol. II) Late medieval to modern. Tr. from Japanese by Glenn Webb, and adapted by John Rosenfield. Tokyo: Kodansha International; London: Ward Lock, 1965-67. 236pp, 198 ill, bib; 229pp, chiefly ill, bib

1994 _____, and Jiro Harada. Sculpture and Art Crafts. Tokyo: Bunka Koryu Kurabu, 1948.

1995 Okakura, Kakuyo. The Ideals of the East: with special reference to the art of Japan. London: J. Murray, 1903; facsim. reprint. Rutland, Vt.: Tuttle; Hemel Hempstead: Prentice-Hall, 1970. 244pp, ill

1996 Okomoto, Toyo. Shoji: the screens of Japan. 1961. 150pp, 105 pls

1997 Piggott, Sir Francis Taylor. Studies in the Decorative Art of Japan. London: Batsford, 1910. 130pp, many ill (some color), 32 pls (Art of the temples, decoration, lattice work, cloud forms, motifs, etc.) DLC

1998 Salmon, Patricia. A Guide to Japanese Antiques. New York: Van Nostrand Reinhold, 1975. 256pp, ill, bib, gloss

1999 Shirasu, F. An Exhibition of Japanese Paintings and Metal Work. Lent by Mr. F. Shirasu, of Tokio, Japan. Boston: A. Mudge, for the Museum of Fine Arts, 1894. 38pp

2000a Sullivan, Michael. Chinese and Japanese Art. (Vol. IX of Great Art and Artists of the World.) New York: F. Watts, 1966. 302pp, ill (part color), bib

2000b Swann, Peter Charles. Art of China, Korea and Japan. London: Thames & Hudson; New York: Praeger, 1963. 285pp, 259 ill, 51 color pls, bib

2001 _____. An Introduction to the Arts of Japan. Oxford: Cassirer; New York: Praeger, 1958. 220pp, ill, bib

2002 Tomkinson, Michael. A Japanese Collection made by M.

Tomkinson. 2 vol. London: G. Allen, 1898. ill, 160 (7 color) pls

2003 Tsuda, Noritake. Handbook of Japanese Art. Tokyo: San-seido, 1935; London: 1937. 525pp, 345 ill, 10 color pls

2004 Turk, Frank Archibald. Japanese Objects d'Art (A Breviary of the Arts of Japan). London; New York: Arco, 1962; rev. by Judith Cohen. New York: Sterling, 1963. 176pp, ill, 8 pls, bib; 156pp, ill, bib

2005 Yamada, Chisaburoh F., ed., and others. Decorative Arts of Japan. Tr. by Toshizo Imai and Yuko Kobayashi. Tokyo: Japan Publications, 1963; Tokyo: Kodansha International; London: Ward, Lock, 1965. 262pp, ill, 110 pls (Editors: Ceramics, Jujio Koyama; Metal Work, Osamu Kurata; Lacquer Ware, Yuzuru Okada; Textiles, Tomoyuki Yamaobe.)

2006 Yanagi, Soetsu. Folk-Crafts in Japan. Tr. by Shigeyoshi Sakabe. Tokyo: Society for International Cultural Relations, 1936. 55pp, ill, 19 pls (part color) NNC-Ave

2007 Yashiro, Yukio, ed. Art Treasures of Japan. 2 vol. Tokyo: Society for International Cultural Relations, 1960. ill, pls

2008 _____. 2000 Years of Japanese Art. Ed. by Peter C. Swann. New York: Abrams; London: Thames & Hudson, 1958. 268pp, ill, 177 (42 color) pls

APPLIED ARTS OF INDIA, CEYLON,
PAKISTAN, NEPAL AND TIBET

2009 Birdwood, George Christopher Molesworth, 1832-1917. The Industrial Arts of India. 2 vol. London: Chapman & Hall for South Kensington Museum, 1880; new ed. London: 1884; Facsim. reprint in 1 vol. London: Reprint Pr, 1971. 344pp, ill, 91 pls SKM, DLC

2010 Blacker, James F. The ABC of Indian Art. Boston: Cornhill; London: S. Paul, 1922. 302pp, ill, pls, color frontis (Hindu art objects) NN, DLC

2011 Coomaraswamy, Ananda Kentish. The Arts and Crafts of India and Ceylon. London; Edinburgh: T. N. Foulis, 1913. 255pp, 225 ill, color pls, bib MiU, NN

2012 _____. Catalogue of the Indian Collections in the Museum of Fine Arts. Boston: 1923- . pls

2013 _____. Domestic Handicraft and Culture; a lecture.

Broad Campden, Gloucestershire: Essex House Pr, 1910.
35pp NN

2014 _____ . The Indian Craftsman. Fore. by C. R. Ashbee.
Appendices by Sir George Birdwood, William Morris, E.
B. Havell, Lafcadio Hearn. London: Probsthain & Co,
1909. 130pp, bib DLC

2015 Craft Museum. Calcutta: Gossain, for Indian Institute of
Art in Industry, 1959. 127pp

2016 Dowleans, A. M., comp. Official, Classified, and Descriptive Catalogue of the Contributions from India to the London Exhibition of 1862. Calcutta: Savielle & Cranenburgh,
printers, 1862. ix, 170, 6, 87, 31pp DLC

2017 Griggs, William, 1832-1911. Indian Art at Marlborough
House and Sandringham. Introd. by Sir George C. M.
Birdwood. London: W. Griggs, 1892. 11pp, 28 pls
(part color) DLC

2018 Hendley, Thomas Holbein, comp. Catalogue of the Collections in the Jeypore Museum. 1. Art, 2. Industrial and
Educational. 2 vol. Delhi: Imperial Medical Hall Pr,
1896. text only DLC

2019 _____ . Handbook to the Jeypore Museum. Calcutta:
Calcutta Central Pr, 1895. 126pp, pls (part color) DLC

2020 _____ . Memorials of the Jeypore Exhibition, 1883. Vol.
I-III. Industrial Art, Vol. IV. The Razm Namah (an illuminated poem). 4 vol. London: W. Griggs, 1883. text,
pls (part color), bib DLC

2021 Jones, Owen, 1809-1874. Gleanings from the Great Exhibi-
tion of 1851: on the distribution of form and colour de-
veloped in the articles exhibited in the Indian, Egyptian,
Turkish, and Tunisian Departments. Reprint from
"Journal of Design," June 1851. London: Strangeways
& Walden, 1863. 15pp DLC

2022 Journal of Indian Arts. Quarterly. London: W. Griggs,
18- .

2023 Ridley, Michael J. Oriental Art of India, Nepal and Tibet.
New York: Arco; London: Gifford, 1970. 195pp, ill

2024 Rivett-Carnac, John Henry, 1839-1923. On Some Specimens
of Indian Metal Work. London: Blackwood?, 1901. ill

2025 [No entry.]

2026 Srinivasan, K. S.   A Short Guide to the Industrial Section
       Galleries of the Indian Museum.   Calcutta: Indian Mu-
       seum, 1953.   11pp, ill

2027 Swarup, Shanti.   5000 Years of Arts and Crafts in India and
       Pakistan: sculpture, architecture, painting, dance, music,
       handicrafts, ritual decorations from earliest times to
       present day.   Bombay: Taraporevala, 1968.   271pp, 251
       ill, 101 (5 color) pls

2028 Trailokyanatha Mukhopadhyaya.   Art Manufactures of India.
       Compiled for the Glasgow International Exhibition, 1888.
       Calcutta: Superintendent of Government Printing, 1888.
       451pp DLC

2029 Varadachariyar.   Indian Arts.   Madras: Srinivasa & Co,
       1894.   24pp BM

SECTION V

FURNITURE

GENERAL WORKS

2030 Andrews, John. The Price Guide to Antique Furniture.
      Periodical. Woodbridge, Suffolk: Antique Collectors
      Club, Baron Publishing, 1969- . 356pp, chiefly ill

2031 Antique Furniture. Chicago: Smith & Packard, n.d. 28
      pls in portfolio MiGr, DLC

2032 Antique Furniture Handbook. Part 1. Victorian Furniture,
      by Ruth and Larry Freeman; Part 2. Primitive Pine
      Furniture, by J. Lazeare. 2 parts. Watkins Glen, NY:
      Century, 1950. ill

2033 Antique Furniture in Carved Oak and Mahogany. Grand
      Rapids, Mich: Berkey & Gay Furniture Co, n.d. (ca.1910).
      ill MiGr

2034 Antique Oriental Rugs and Period Furniture. Exhibition.

March 1915.   Detroit: Museum of Art, 1915.   75pp,
ill

2035 *Aronson, Joseph. The Book of Furniture and Decoration:
period and modern. New York: Crown, 1936; London:
Putnam, 1937; as The Encyclopedia of Furniture; covering
every period and development to the present, the designers, and makers, woods and other materials, architecture and decoration. New York: Crown, 1938; rev.
ed. 1941; new rev. and augmented ed. 1952; 3rd rev. ed.
1965. London: Batsford, 1966; as The New Encyclopedia
of Furniture. New York: 1967. 347pp, ill, bib; 1948:
202pp, 1115 ill, bib; . .; 1967: 484pp, 2000 ill

2036 Artistic Furniture and Architectural Interiors, Decorations,
etc., During the Last Two and a Half Centuries. n. p.:
1892. MiD

2037 Bertram, (C.) Anthony G. The House: a Machine for Living
In; a summary of the art and science of homemaking con-
sidered functionally. London: A. & C. Black, 1935; 2nd
ed. as The House: a Summary of the Art and Science of
Domestic Architecture. London: 1945. 115pp, ill, bib
(Furniture, architecture, appliances) DLC, NNC-Ave

2038 Bibliography of Furniture and Decoration. Furniture Gazette,
Vol. 6. London: 1876. MB

2039 Binstead, Herbert Ernest, (1869-). Furniture. London;
New York: I. Pitman, 1900?; 1918; 1921. 132pp, ill
MiGr

2040 _____. Useful Details in Several Styles. London: A. H.
Botwright, 1906. ill (Furniture, Gothic to Adam. English and French) MiGr

2041 _____, Gustav Stickley, and J. Newton Nind. The Furniture Styles, with chapters on modern Mission and Craftsman furniture. Chicago: Trade Periodical Co, 1901; 2nd
ed. London: Botwright, 1904; Chicago: 1909; new rev.
ed. London; New York: I. Pitman, 1929. 192pp, many
ill BM, MiGr

2042 Bles, Arthur de. Genuine Antique Furniture. Garden City,
NY: Garden City Publishing; New York: Crowell, 1929.
376pp, 200 ill, pls, bib NNC-Ave

2043 Boger, Louise Ade. Complete Guide to Furniture Styles.
New York: Scribner's, 1959; London: Allen & Unwin,
1961; enl. ed. New York: Scribner, 1969. 438pp, ill,
pls, bib; 500pp, ill, pls, bib (European and American)

2044 _____. Furniture Past and Present; a complete illustrated

guide to furniture styles from ancient to modern.   Garden
City, NY: Doubleday, 1966.   520pp, ill, bib

2045   Bowers, Kenneth William Macleod.   Antique Furniture Ex-
       plained and Illustrated.   (1500-1901).   Tadworth: Elliot,
       1971.   157pp, ill

2046   Bradford, Ernle Dusgate Selby.   Antique Furniture.   London:
       English Universities Pr, 1970.   248pp, ill, 8 pls   (To
       1900)

2047 *Burgess, Frederick William.   Antique Furniture.   London:
       G. Routledge; New York: Putnam's, 1915; 1921.   499pp,
       ill, pls   (16th, 17th and 18th century; French, American
       and chiefly English) NN, DLC, MiGr

2048   Cabinet-Maker's Assistant: a series of original designs for
       modern furniture, with descriptions and details of con-
       struction....   Glasgow; London; New York: Blackie, 1853;
       1863; reprint as The Victorian Cabinet-Maker's Assistant;
       418 original designs with descriptions ... etc.   Introd. by
       John Gloag.   New York: Dover, 1970.   60pp, 63pp of
       ill, 103 pls; 217pp, ill ViU, MiGr, NN

2049   Carrick, Alice Van Leer.   Collector's Luck; or, A repository
       of pleasant and profitable discourses descriptive of the
       household furniture and ornaments of olden time....   Boston:
       The Atlantic Monthly Pr, 1919; 1923; Boston: Little Brown,
       1926; deluxe ed. Garden City, NY: Garden City Publishing,
       1937.   text, ill ViU, NN

2050   _____. The Next to Nothing House. Boston: Atlantic
       Monthly, 1922; 1923; Boston: Little Brown, 1927.   252pp,
       ill, pls (Collecting furniture) NNC-Ave, MH

2051   Ye Catalogue of Ye Furniture Trades Exhibition, held in 1883.
       London: C. Messent, 1883.   229pp BM

2052   Cescinsky, Herbert.   The Gentle Art of Faking Furniture.
       London: Chapman & Hall, 1931; London: Eyre & Spottis-
       woode, 1969.   168pp, ill, 286 pls (How to detect genuine
       pieces from tool marks, wood types, etc.) DLC, NN

2053   Chancellor, Alfred Ernest.   Examples of Old Furniture.
       English and foreign, drawn and described....   London:
       Batsford, 1898.   28pp, 40 pls of measured drawings.
       MiGr, NN, DLC

2054   Church, Ella Rodman.   How to Furnish a Home.   New York:
       Appleton, 1883.   128pp, ill

2055   Clifford, Chandler Robbins.   Period Furnishings; an encyclo-
       pedia of historic furniture, decorations and furnishings,

fully illustrated. New York: Clifford & Lawton, 1911;
1914; rev. ed. 1915; 3rd ed. 1922; 4th ed. 1927; 5th ed.
rev., amended and supplemented, by William O. Hall.
New York: Hall Publishing, 1949. 238pp, ill, pls; ...;
...; ...; 250pp, ill, bib, tables tracing styles (400 B.C.
to end of 19th century) NN, DLC, MiGr

2056 The Collector. Monthly. London: Old Furniture, 1927-1930.
(Formerly Old Furniture; a magazine of domestic ornament) ill

2057 Cook, Clarence Chatham. The House Beautiful: essays on
beds and tables, stools and candlesticks. New York:
Scribner's, 1877; 1878; 1879; 1881; 1895. 336pp, ill,
color frontis DLC, NN, MiGr

2058 Cotchett, Lucretia Eddy. The Evolution of Furniture ...
illustrated with photographs of period houses and their
furniture. London: Batsford, 1938; New York: Scribner's, 1939. 118pp, ill, 94 pls CU, NN, DLC, NNC-
Ave

2059 Curtis, Richard Anthony (Tony). 'Ideal Home Magazine'
Antiques on a Budget--a guide to buying furniture. Galashiels, Scotland: Lyle Publications, 1973; as Antiques on
a Budget. New York: Scribner's, 1974. 127pp, ill, 8
color pls (12 articles reprinted)

2060 Davis, Frank. A Picture History of Furniture. New York:
Macmillan; London: Edward Hulton, 1958; as Furniture:
a picture history. London: Vista, 1962. 160pp, 404 ill

2061 _____. The Plain Man's Guide to Second-hand Furniture.
London: Michael Joseph, 1961. 95pp, pls

2062 De Mauny, F. Wood. London: Ginn, 1959; 1970. 32pp,
ill (Juvenile literature. To 1600)

2063 Denning, David. The Art and Craft of Cabinet-Making; a
practical handbook to the construction of cabinet furniture,
the use of tools, formation of joints ... Together with a
review of the development of furniture. London: Whittaker, 1891; Chicago: 1909; London; New York: Pitman,
1931. 320pp, 219 ill NN, DLC

2064 Douglas, Jane. Collectible Furniture. London: Longacre,
197-? ill

2065 *Dyer, Walter Alden. Handbook of Furniture Styles ... being
an abridged guide to the more important historic styles
of furniture, especially intended for ready reference. New
York: Century, 1918. 155pp, ill, pls, bib NN, MiGr

2066   Eberlein, Harold Donaldson, and Abbot McClure. The Practi-
       cal Book of Period Furniture, treating of furniture of the
       English, American colonial and post-colonial and principal
       French periods. Philadelphia; London: Lippincott, 1914.
       371pp, 250 ill, bib (Jacobean, 1603, to American Empire,
       1830) MiGr

2067   Erbe, Olga Adele. Bibliography of Modernist Furniture,
       1925-1935. New York: Columbia University School of
       Library Service, 1935. typescript NNC-Ave

2068   Examples of Art Workmanship of Various Ages and Countries.
       Decorative furniture, English, Italian, German, Flemish,
       etc. London: Arundel Society, under sanction of the
       Science and Art Department, South Kensington Museum,
       1871. pls

2069   Firth, Gay. Antiques Anonymous; a consumers' guide to old
       furniture. London: I. Allen, 1964. 80pp, ill, bib

2070   Freeman, Graydon La Verne. Period Antique Furniture.
       Watkins Glen, NY: Century, 1965. 75pp, pls

2071   Freeman, Ruth Sunderlin, and Larry Freeman. Antique Furni-
       ture Handbook. Watkins Glen, NY: Century, 1950. ill

2072   Friedman-Weiss, Jeffrey, Herbert H. Wise, and Andria Al-
       berts. Made With Oak. New York; London: Links, 1975.
       u.p., many color ill, 6pp catalog reprints (Chiefly furni-
       ture)

2073   Fry, Plantagenent Somerset (pseud. for Peter George Robin
       Somerset Fry). Antique Furniture. Feltham: Hamlyn,
       1971. 159pp, ill, bib (To ca. 1835)

2074   Furniture: a list of books in the Detroit Public Library,
       Fine Arts Department. Detroit: 1929. 65pp (Divided
       by period, country, individual pieces) NNC-Ave, MiD

2075   Furniture and Its Story. London: Evans Brothers, 1915;
       1920. 240pp (Earliest times to Napoleon) MiGr, BM

2076   Furniture History. Journal. Leeds, Eng: Furniture History
       Society, 1965- . ill

2077   Gayler, Julius F. Furniture, Yesterday and Today; the
       principal periods of furniture, with numerous illustrations
       of the best historical and modern examples, with a spe-
       cial note on finishes. New York: Currier & Harford,
       1926. 60pp, ill, 22 pls (Examples in the Metropolitan
       Museum, N.Y.) DLC, MiGr

2078   *Gloag, John Edwards. A Short Dictionary of Furniture, containing 1764 terms used in England and America. New York: Studio, 1951; London: Allen & Unwin, 1952; London; New York: Studio-Cromwell, 1955; New York: Holt, Rinehart, Winston, 1965; rev. abridged ed. London: 1966; rev. enl. ed. as A Short Dictionary of Furniture, containing over 2600 entries that include terms and names used in Britain and the United States of America. London: 1969. 565pp, 630 ill, bib; 1966: 279pp, ill; 1969: 813pp, ill, bib (Lists of makers and style tables included)

2079 _____. A Social History of Furniture Design, from B.C. 1300 to A.D. 1960. London: Cassell; New York: Crown, 1966. 202pp, 340 ill, 4 color pls, bib

2080 _____. Time, Taste and Furniture. London: Grant Richards; New York: F. A. Stokes, 1925; London: 1930; 1949. 330pp, ill, pls (End of Middle Ages to the 20th century) MiGr

2081 Gradmann, Erwin. Period Furniture. Tr. from the French adaptation of Andre Marthaler by M. Chisholm. London: Stanford, 1955. 64pp, 118 ill

2082 Great Styles of Furniture: English, Italian, French, Dutch, Spanish. London: Thames & Hudson; New York: Viking, 1963. 308pp, 800 ill (1500-1900)

2083 Habermann, Franz (Francois) Xavier, 1721-1796, and others. Models of Art Furniture in Rococo-style, designs of furniture of all periods, --church furniture included--of the 18th century. 2 vol. New York: Hessling & Spielmeyer, 1894? 64 pls MdBP, MiGr

2084 Harmes, Earl. Furniture of Yesterday and Today. Milwaukee; New York: Bruce, 1937. 63pp, ill NN

2085 Harris, M., and Sons. An Abridged Introductory Catalogue of Antique Furniture and Works of Art. London: M. Harris, 192-? 105pp, ill NN

2086 _____. A Catalogue and Index of Old Furniture and Works of Old Furniture and Works of Decorative Art, from late 16th century to early 19th century. 3 vols. London: Harris, 1932. MiGr

2087 Harrison, Molly. Furniture. London: Educational Supply Assoc., 1953; 4th ed. 1961. 89pp, ill, pls (Juvenile literature)

2088 Hayden, Arthur. Chats on Old Furniture: a practical guide for collectors. London: T. Fisher Unwin; New York: A. Stokes, 1905; London: 1912; 1920; 5th ed. ed. & rev. by Cyril G. E. Bunt. London: Benn, 1950. 283pp, ill,

pls, bib, gloss (European from Renaissance to Hepplewhite) MB, MiGr, DeWint

2089 Hayward, Charles Harold. Antique or Fake? The making
of old furniture. London: Evans Brothers, 1970; 1971.
256pp, ill, bib

2090 _____. Period Furniture Designs ... drawn from the
original pieces by the author. rev. ed. London: Evans,
1968. 111pp, chiefly ill

2091 Hayward, Helena, ed. World Furniture; an illustrated history.
Contributions by Douglas Ash and others. London: Hamlyn; New York: McGraw-Hill, 1965; London: 1969.
320pp, ill, 30 pls, bib (Ancient world through contemporary)

2092 Henderson, James. Furniture Collecting for Amateurs. London: Muller, 1967. 134pp, ill, 12 pls

2093 Hill, Conover. Antique Oak Furniture, an Illustrated Value
Guide. Paducah, Ky: Collector Books, 1974; 2nd ed.
1975. 124pp, ill

2094 _____. Antique Wicker Furniture, an Illustrated Value
Guide. Paducah, Ky: Collector Books, 1975. 136pp,
ill (700 pieces covered)

2095 *Hinckley, F. Lewis. A Directory of Antique Furniture; the
authentic classification of European and American designs
for professionals and connoisseurs. New York: Crown,
1953. text, 355pp of ill

2096 Historic Mahogany: monograph: period mahogany. New
York: Mahogany Assoc., 1924? (Characteristic forms
and designs of great designers from Chippendale on)
MiGr

2097 Historical Art Furniture: specimens of English, French,
German, and Italian workmanship from the Middle Ages,
Renaissance period, and epochs of Louis 13, Louis 14,
Louis 15, and Louis 16, drawn from originals in Euro-
pean museums and private collections. New York: Hel-
burn & Hagen, n.d.; 1889; 1912. 60 pls MB, MIGR

2098 Hoard, F. E., and A. W. Marlow. The Cabinetmakers'
Treasury. New York: Macmillan, 1952. 267pp, ill
(Essentially a guide to reproducing period furniture)

2099 Hodgson, Frederick Thomas, 1836- . The Practical Cabinet Maker and Furniture Designer's Assistant, with essays on the history of furniture, taste in design, color
and materials, with full explanation of the canons of good

taste in furniture. Chicago: F. J. Drake, 1910. 372pp, 200 ill NN, DeWint

2100   Hughes, George Bernard, and Therle Hughes. Small Antique Furniture. London: Lutterworth; New York: Macmillan, 1958; New York: Praeger, 1968. 219pp, 172 ill

2101   *Hunter, George Leland, 1867-1927. Decorative Furniture; a picture book of the beautiful forms of all ages and all periods: Egyptian, Assyrian, Greek, Roman, Byzantine, Chinese, Japanese, Persian, Romanesque Gothic, French Renaissance, Italian Renaissance, later Italian, Louis 13, 14, 15, 16, Directoire and Empire, Spanish, Portuguese, Flemish, Dutch, Swiss, Elizabethan, Jacobean, Charles 2, William and Mary, Queen Anne, early Georgian, Chippendale, Adam, Hepplewhite, Sheraton, American colonial, modern European and modern American, American Mission. Grand Rapids: Good Furniture Magazine; Philadelphia: Lippincott, 1923. 480pp, 900 ill, 23 color pls (Companion to Decorative Textiles) CU, ViU, DeWint

2102   Jacquemart, Albert. A History of Furniture, with chapters on tapestry, oriental embroidery and leather work, bronzes, ivories and other figures, clocks and time pieces, wrought iron, brass and other metal work, jewellery, gems and enamels, glass and ceramics, oriental lacquer and varnish, etc. Tr. from French (1876) by Mrs. Bury Palliser. London: Chapman & Hall, 1878; London: Reeves & Turner, 1907; 1908. 470pp, 170 ill PP, DLC, NN

2103   Jervis, Simon. Printed Furniture Designs Before 1650. Leeds: W. S. Maney, for Furniture History Society, 1974. 54pp, 372 pls

2104   *Johnson, Axel Petrus, and Marta K. Sironen, comp. Manual of the Furniture Arts and Crafts; furniture craftsmen, architects and artisans to the 20th century, with brief biographies. Ed. by William J. Etten. Grand Rapids, Mich: Johnson, 1928. 899pp, ill, bib (based on Grand Rapids Library collection) (Book contains general and technical descriptions, chapters on wood, machinery, construction, finishing, upholstery, lists of museums and craftsmen) DLC, NNC-Ave

2105   Joy, Edward Thomas. Furniture. London: Connoisseur, 1972. 226pp, ill, 8 pls, bib

2106   Katz, Laszlo. The Art of Woodworking and Furniture Appreciation. New York: Paul, Fay, Clara, 1970. 192pp, ill, bib

2107   Kimerly, William Lowing. How to Know Period Styles in

Furniture: a brief history of furniture from the days of
ancient Egypt to the present time. Grand Rapids, Mich:
Grand Rapids Furniture Record, 1912; 5th ed. 1921; 9th
ed. 1931. 147pp, ill MiGr

2108   Koues, Helen. How to Know Something About Antique Furni-
       ture. Chicago: Book Production Industries, 1946. 48pp,
       ill

2109   Lamb, George Newton. How to Know Period Furniture.
       Chicago: Mahogany Association, n.d. MiGr

2110   Lawford, Henry. The Cabinet of Practical, Useful and Deco-
       rative Furniture Designs. London; New York: J. S.
       Virtue, 1855; 1858. 9pp, 126 pls NNC-Ave, DLC

2111   Lazear, James, ed. The Wicker Revival. Antique Furniture
       Handbook No. 6. Watkins Glen, NY: Century, 1966.
       80pp, ill, bib (Early 19th to 20th century)

2112 *List of Books on Furniture with Descriptive Notes. Grand
       Rapids, Mich: Public Library, 1927. 143pp

2113 *List of Books on Furniture. Supplement. Grand Rapids,
       Mich: Public Library, 1954. 45pp (English and foreign
       language books. 1 page of periodicals)

2114   List of Books on Furniture in Library of Edinburgh Museum.
       Edinburgh, Scotland: 1890. BM

2115   Litchfield, Frederick. How to Collect Old Furniture. Lon-
       don: G. Bell, 1904; 1906; 1920. 169pp, ill, pls (Euro-
       pean from time of Renaissance) NN, MiGr

2116 *   . Illustrated History of Furniture from the Earliest
       to the Present Time. London: Truslove & Shirley, 1892;
       5th ed. London: Truslove; New York: J. Lane, 1903;
       7th ed. rev. & enl. London: Truslove & Hanson, 1922.
       280pp, ill, pls; 272pp, ill; 358pp, ill; 459pp, ill

2117   Little Books about Old Furniture. London: Heinemann, 1911.

2118   Lockwood, Luke Vincent. The Furniture Collector's Glossary.
       New York: Walpole Society, 1913; reprint. New York:
       Da Capo Pr, 1967. 55pp, ill MB, MiU, MiGr

2119   McClinton, Katharine Morrison (Kahle). An Outline of Period
       Furniture. New York: Putnam, 1929; reprint. New York:
       1972. 222pp, ill, pls, bib; 259pp, 195 ill, bib, gloss

2120   McDonald, John Wilson. Antique Furniture. London: Collins,
       1965. 160pp, ill

2121 MacMillan, Donald D. Great Furniture Styles, 1660-1830.
      New York: Odyssey Pr; London: Hamlyn, 1965. 47pp,
      ill

2122 Margon, Lester. World Furniture Treasures. Yesterday,
      today and tomorrow. New York: Reinhold; London:
      Chapman Hall, 1954. 186pp, ill

2123 Maskell, William, 1814?-1890. Industrial Arts; historical
      sketches. Furniture. South Kensington Museum. London:
      Chapman & Hall, 188-? 22pp, ill NN

2124 *Menzies, William Gladstone. Period Furniture for Everyman:
      a handbook for the amateur. London: Duckworth; New
      York: Scribner, 1939; new rev. ed. 1955. 155pp, ill, 32
      pls

2125 Mercer, Eric. Furniture, 700-1700. London: Weidenfeld &
      Nicolson, 1969. 183pp, ill, 128 pls, bib

2126 Miller, Herman, Furniture Company, Zeeland, Michigan. A
      History of Modern Furniture, from Prehistoric Times to
      the Post-War Era. Zeeland, Mich: 1948? ill MiGr

2127 Molesworth, Hender Delves, and John Kenworthy-Browne.
      Three Centuries of Furniture in Color. London: Joseph;
      New York: Viking, 1972. 328pp, chiefly ill, 544 color
      pls (1600-1900)

2128 Moore, Frank Frankfort. The Commonsense Collector; a
      handbook of hints on the collecting and the housing of
      antique furniture. London: Hodder & Stoughton, 1910;
      New York: Hodder & Stoughton, 1911. 220pp, ill, pls,
      color frontis MB, MiGr

2129 Moore, Hannah (N.) Hudson. The Old Furniture Book, with
      a sketch of past days and ways. New York: F. A. Stokes,
      1903; London: Hodder & Stoughton, 1906; New York: Tu-
      dor, 1937. 254pp, ill, 100 pls (European and American)
      MiGr, BM

2130 An Occasional Newsletter (of the Furniture History Society).
      Irregular. Leeds, Eng: the Society, School of History,
      the University, 1965- .

2131 O'Donnell, Erica. Furniture. London: Ginn, 1970. 32pp,
      ill (Juvenile literature. 1630-1970)

2132 Old Furniture: being examples selected from the works of
      the best known designers, from the 12th to the 18th cen-
      tury. Issued as supplements with the "Furniture Gazette."
      London: Wyman & Sons, 1883. 50pp BM

2133 Old Furniture; a magazine of domestic ornament. Monthly.
      London: Old Furniture Ltd., 1927-1930. (Title changed,
      1930, to The Collector) ill, color pls

2134 Philp, Peter. Antique Furniture for the Smaller Home.
      London; New York: Arco, 1962; London: Mayflower,
      1969. 172pp, ill, 8 pls, bib

2135 _____. Furniture of the World. London: Octopus, 1974.
      128pp, ill

2136 Plunkett, George Tindall. Furniture. General Guide ...
      Part 8, 3 chapters. Dublin: Science & Art Museum,
      1905-1911. ill (1. Italian; 2. French and Other Con-
      tinental; 3. English) BM

2137 Pocket Guides to Antique Furniture. Vol. I. Victorian (1840-
      1890); Vol. II. Primitive Pine; Vol. III. Federal-Empire
      (1810-1840); Vol. IV. Colonial; Vol. V. Mission and Art
      Nouveau; Vol. VI. Wicker Revival; Vol. VII. 1900 Edwardian
      Grand Rapids. Watkins Glen, NY: Century, 19- . 100pp
      each, ill

2138 Practical Collecting. London: Hodder & Stoughton, 1922.
      223pp, bib (Oak, walnut and mahogany furniture) MiGr

2139 Ramsey, L. G. G., and Helen Comstock, ed. "The Con-
      noisseur's" Guide to Antique Furniture. London: Connois-
      seur; as Antique Furniture; the guide for collectors, in-
      vestors, and dealers. New York: Hawthorn, 1969. 362pp,
      144 ill, 9 color pls, bib

2139a Reading Lists on Arts, Crafts. Furniture. Buffalo, NY:
      Grosvenor Public Library, 1900. MB

2140 Record, Nancy A. Coffers and Cabinets. Minneapolis: Ler-
      ner, 1968. 55pp, ill (Juvenile literature)

2141 Reeves, David Louis. Furniture: an explanatory history.
      London: Faber, 1947; 1948; 1959; 1965. 200pp, ill, 52
      pls NNC-Ave, MiGr

2142 [No entry.]

2143 Robie, Virginia Huntington. Historic Styles in Furniture.
      Chicago: House Beautiful, 1905; 2nd ed. 1910; Boston:
      Houghton, Mifflin, 1916. 196pp, many ill (Middle Ages
      in Europe to American Colonial) MiGr

2144 Robinson, Vincent Joseph. Ancient Furniture and Other Works
      of Art, illustrative of a collection formed by Vincent J.
      Robinson, of Parnham House, Dorset. London: B.

Quaritch, 1902. 84pp, ill, 74 pls (Also includes metal work, pottery, glass, etc.) MiGr

2145 *Roe, Frederick Gordon. A History of Oak Furniture. London: Connoisseur, 1920. 44pp, ill, 76 pls (Various European countries from the 13th century) MiGr

2146a Russell, Sir (Sydney) Gordon. Furniture. West Drayton, Middlesex: Penguin, 1947; rev. ed. as Looking at Furniture. London: Lund Humphries, 1964. 64pp, ill

2146b Saunders, Richard. Collecting and Restoring Wicker Furniture. New York: Crown, 1976. 200 ill

2147 Schiffer, Herbert F., and Peter B. Schiffer. Miniature Antique Furniture: including doll house and children's furniture from the United States and Europe. Wynnewood, Pa: Livingston Publishing, 1972. 264pp, 300 ill, bib

2148 *Schmitz, Hermann, comp. The Encyclopedia of Furniture: an outline history of furniture design in Egypt, Assyria, Persia, Greece, Rome, Italy, France, the Netherlands, Germany, England, Scandinavia, Spain, Russia, and in the Near and Far East up to the middle of the 19th century. Introd. by H. P. Shapland. London: E. Benn, 1926; London: A. Zwemmer, 1956; New York: Praeger, 1957. 63pp, 659 ill on 320 pls (No American)

2149 Shapland, Henry Percival. The Practical Decoration of Furniture. Vol. I. Veneering, inlay or marqueterie, gilding, painting; Vol. II. Moulding, pierced work, turned work, twisting, carving; Vol. III. Applied Metalwork, covering with leather and textiles, lacquering, and miscellaneous decoration. 3 vols. London: E. Benn, 1926-27. ill, pls DLC

2150 Singleton, Esther. Furniture. New York: Duffield, 1911; London: Chatto & Windus, 1913. 273pp, ill, 129 pls (Pieces from various countries, early times to mid-19th century, in European and American museums) MiGr

2151 Small, John William. Ancient and Modern Furniture; measured and drawn for the stone. Edinburgh: Mould & Tod, printers, 1883; Stirling, Scot: E. Mackay, 1903. 15pp, 50 pls; 29pp, 50 pls NNC-Ave

2152 Smith, Nancy A. Old Furniture: Understanding the craftsman's art. New York: Bobbs-Merrill, 1975. 200 ill (How old furniture was made)

2153 *Smith, Robert Henry Soden. List of Works on Furniture in the National Art Library. South Kensington Museum. London: 1878; 1885. 64pp

2154   Thompson, Frances. Wicker Furniture: illustrated price
          guide. Kermit, Tx: Collector's Weekly, 1973. 47pp,
          ill

2155   *Timms, William H., and G. Webb. The 35 Styles of Furni-
          ture. London: Timms & Webb, 1904. 86pp, ill (An-
          cient Egypt to L'Art Nouveau) NN, MiGr

2156   Wanscher, Ole. The Art of Furniture; 5000 years of furni-
          ture and interiors. Tr. from Danish (1966) by David
          Hohnen. New York: Reinhold, 1967; London: Allen &
          Unwin, 1968. 420pp, chiefly ill, bib

2157   Ward, James, 1851-1924. Furniture. Antique: Egypt, As-
          syria, Greece, and Rome; Byzantine, Romanesque, Sara-
          cencic, and the furniture of the Middle Ages. From Vol.
          II of Historic Ornament. London: Chapman & Hall, 1902.
          ill MiGr

2158   Warman, Edwin G., ed. Antique Furniture Guide; a guide to
          periods and styles from ancient times up to the Victorian
          era. Uniontown, Pa: Warman Publishing, 1971. 153pp,
          ill

2159   Way, Nelson E., and Constance Stapleton. Antiques Don't
          Lie. Garden City, NY: Doubleday, 1975. 150pp, ill
          (How to tell date, origin, etc. from details)

2160   Whiffen, R. B. A Pocket Compendium on Furniture and
          Terms Used in Valuations, Catalogues and Inventories.
          London: Estates Gazette, 1926; as The Chattel Auc-
          tioneer's Handbook on Furniture and Terms Used in Valu-
          ations, Catalogues and Inventories. London: Estates
          Gazette, 1937; 1947. 185pp; 349pp; 528pp, ill

2161   Williams, Guy Richard, and Edna Claughton. Collecting Old
          Furniture. London: Corgi, 1972. 125pp, ill (1500-1940)

AMERICAN FURNITURE

2162   Albers, Majorie K. Old Amana Furniture. Shenandoah,
          Iowa: Locust House, 1970. 85pp, pls (Amana Society,
          The Community of True Inspiration, 19th century)

2163   *American Antiques from the Israel Sack Collection. Ed. by
          Joseph H. Hennage. 4 vol. Washington, D.C.: High-
          land House, 1969, 1969, 1972, 1974. text, many ill,
          color pls (Israel Sack, Inc. began publishing in 1957,
          illustrated brochures entitled "Opportunities in American
          Antiques." Vol. I & II, Brochures #1-17; III, #18-21;
          IV, #22-25)

2164 American Art of the Colonies and Early Republic; furniture,
      paintings, and silver from private collections in the Chi-
      cago area. Exhibition. Chicago: Art Institute, 1971.
      84pp, ill

2165 American Cabinet-Maker and Upholsterer. Periodical. New
      York: J. H. Symonds, 189-?-1904.

2166 The American Furniture Gazette. Official organ of the furni-
      ture manufacturers of Chicago. Monthly. Chicago: 1883-
      1902.

2167 *Andrews, Edward Deming. The Community Industries of the
      Shakers. Albany: University of State of New York, 1932;
      Albany: NY State Museum of Natural History, 1933; re-
      print of 1933 ed. with new introd. by Cynthia Elyce Rubin.
      Charlestown, Mass: Emporium Publications, 196-?
      322pp, ill, bib; reprint: 307pp, ill, bib

2168 _____. The Hancock Shakers; the Shaker community at
      Hancock, Massachusetts, 1780-1960. Hancock: Shaker
      Community, 1961. 39pp, pls

2169 _____. The New York Shakers and Their Industries.
      Albany: NY State Museum, 1930. 8pp, ill

2170 *_____. The People Called Shakers: a search for a perfect
      society. New York: Oxford U Pr, 1953; new enl. ed.
      New York: Dover, 1963. 309pp, ill, bib; 351pp, ill, bib

2171 _____, and Faith Andrews. Fruits of the Shaker Tree of
      Life. Berkshire, Mass: Berkshire Traveller Pr, 1975.
      ill (Includes objects influencing the Andrews)

2172 *_____, and _____. Religion in Wood; a book of Shaker
      furniture. Bloomington; London: Indiana U Pr, 1966;
      1971. 106pp, ill, bib

2173 *_____, and _____. Shaker Furniture; the craftsmanship
      of an American communal sect. New Haven: Yale U Pr;
      London: H. Milford, Oxford U Pr, 1937; London: 1939;
      New York: Dover, 1950; 1967. 133pp, ill, 48 pls, bib
      (Definitive work)

2174 Baltimore Furniture; the work of Baltimore and Annapolis
      cabinetmakers from 1760 to 1810. Exhibition. February-
      April 1947. Baltimore: Museum of Art, 1947. 195pp,
      ill NNC-Ave, MiGr

2175 Barbour, Frederick K. The Stature of Fine Connecticut Furni-
      ture. n.p.: 1959. u.p., chiefly ill DeWint

2176 Barbour (Frederick K. and Margaret R.). Furniture Collection.

Hartford: Connecticut Historical Society, 1963; supplement. 19- . 71pp, ill; 31pp, ill

2177 Barnes, Jairus B., and Moselle Taylor Meals. American Furniture in the Western Reserve, 1680 to 1830. Exhibition. May-July 1972. Cleveland, O: Western Reserve Historical Society, 1972. 133pp, ill

2178 Bartlett, Lulu, ed. A Bit of Vanity, Furniture of 18th Century Boston. Exhibition sponsored by Department of American Decorative Arts, Museum of Fine Arts, Boston, and the Colonial Society of Massachusetts. May-June 1972. Boston: the Museum, 1972. 30pp, ill

2179 Baumann, Ludwig, and Co., New York. The 20th Century Ideal Furniture Made from the Prairie Grass of America. A novelty superseding rattan or willow ware.... New York: 191-? 19pp, pls (part color) DeWint

2180 Beck, Doreen. Book of American Furniture. Feltham: Hamlyn, 1973. 96pp, 102 (30 color) ill (1650 to present day)

2181 Beede, Carl Greenleaf. An Early American Queen Anne Escritoire, 1715-1730. Fore. by Ross H. Maynard. Boston: priv. printed, 1929. 10pp, pls DeWint, MiGr, DLC

2182 Berkley, Henry John. Register of the Cabinet Makers and Allied Trades in Maryland ... 1746-1820. Reprint from Maryland Historical Magazine, March 1930. Baltimore: 1930. MiGr

2183 Bishop, Robert Charles. American Furniture, 1620-1720. Dearborn, Mich: Greenfield Village, and Henry Ford Museum, 1975. 32pp, ill (From collections in both museums)

2184 _____. How to Know American Antique Furniture. New York: Dutton, 1973. 224pp, 300 (12 color) ill, bib (17th century to 1915)

2185 Bissell, Charles S. Antique Furniture in Suffield, Connecticut, 1670-1835. Hartford: Connecticut Historical Society, 1956. 128pp, ill, 61 pls

2186 *Bjerkoe, Ethel Hall, assisted by John Arthur Bjerkoe. The Cabinetmakers of America. Garden City, NY: Doubleday, 1957. 252pp, ill, bib, biogs (17th, 18th, 19th centuries)

2187 Bookout, Tim J. Western Shaker Furniture: Ohio and Kentucky. Atlanta, Ga: 1975. 23 pls in portfolio

2188 Boston Furniture of the 18th Century, a conference held by the Colonial Society of Massachusetts. Distributed by

U. Pr of Virginia, Charlottesville, 1974.   316pp, ill,
bib

2189   Brady, Nancy Hubbard, ed. Roycroft Hand Made Furniture;
a facsimile of a 1912 catalogue with other related material added--for the sake of interest.   East Aurora, NY:
House of Hubbard, 1973.   61pp, ill

2190   Brown, Mills. Cabinetmaking in the 18th Century.   Thesis.
Williamsburg, Va: 1959.   153pp DeWint

2191   The Buffalo Book of Prices for Manufacturing Cherry and
Black Walnut Cabinet Work, Supplementary to the New
York Book of Prices of 1834.   Buffalo Society of Journey-
men Cabinet Makers.   Buffalo: Steele, 1836.   39pp
NNC-Ave

2192   *Bulkeley, Houghton. Contributions to Connecticut Cabinet
Making.   Hartford: Connecticut Historical Society.   97pp,
ill, bib (Contains author's articles from the Society's
Bulletin, 1957 to 1966)

2193   *Burton, E. Milby. Charleston Furniture, 1700-1825.   Charleston, SC: Museum, 1955; 1970.   150pp of ill, bib, biogs

2194   *_____. Thomas Elfe, Charleston Cabinet-Maker.   Charleston, SC: Museum, 1952.   34pp, ill, pls (Thomas Elfe,
1719-1775) NN

2195   *Butler, Joseph Thomas. American Furniture from the First
Colonies to World War I.   London: Triune Books, 1974.
144pp, ill, bib

2196   Cabinet-Maker's Album of Furniture; comprising a collection
of designs for the newest and most elegant styles of furniture.   Philadelphia: H. C. Baird, 1868.   2pp, 48 pls
DeWint, NNC-Ave, MiGr

2197   Cabinet Making and Upholstery. A Journal of Industrial and
Decorative Art.   Monthly.   New York: 1884- .

2198   A Catalogue of American Antique Furniture, illustrated.   A
concise, simplified study of the styles and periods of
American furniture, with most of the articles of antique
furniture particularly described and illustrated so as to
enable the reader to identify them.   Strafford, Pa: Elf's
Head Pr, 1936.   51pp, ill

2199   Catalogue of an Exhibition of 18th Century Furniture, May
1952 under auspices of the National Park Service, Independence National Historical Park Project.   Philadelphia:
1952.   u. p.

2200 Catalogue of the Pendleton Collection of Colonial Furniture at
      the Rhode Island School of Design. Providence, RI: 1932.
      37pp, 6 pls

2201 *Cescinsky, Herbert, and George Leland Hunter. English and
      American Furniture; a pictorial handbook of furniture made
      in Great Britain and in the American Colonies, some in
      the 16th century, but principally in the 17th, 18th, and
      early 19th centuries. Grand Rapids, Mich: Dean-Hicks;
      Garden City, NY: Garden City Publishing, 1929. 312pp,
      400 ill, bib NN, DLC, MiGr, NNC-Ave

2202 Chamberlain House, restored and opened April 12, 1920, with
      an exhibition of missionary relics and early furniture.
      Honolulu: 1920. MH

2203 *Comstock, Helen. American Furniture; 17th, 18th, and 19th
      Century Styles. New York: Viking, 1962. 336pp, 700 ill,
      bib

2204 Connecticut Furniture: 17th and 18th Centuries. Hartford:
      Wadsworth Atheneum, 1967. 156pp, ill

2205 Cooper, Wendy Ann. The Furniture and Furnishings of John
      Brown, Merchant of Providence, 1736-1803. Thesis. 1971.
      191pp, ill DeWint

2206 *Cornelius, Charles Over. Early American Furniture. New
      York; London: Century, 1926; New York; London: D. Ap-
      pleton-Century, 1936? 278pp, ill, 63 pls, bib DLC, NN

2207 *   . Furniture Masterpieces of Duncan Phyfe. Garden
      City, NY: Doubleday, Page for Metropolitan Museum,
      NY, 1922; 1923; 1925; 1928; reprint. New York: Dover,
      1970. 86pp, ill, 63 photographs (Measured drawings by
      Stanley J. Rowland) DLC, ViU, NNC-Ave

2208 Country Style. (Exhibition of early American furniture.) New
      York: Brooklyn Institute of Arts and Sciences, 1956.
      43pp, ill

2209 Downs, Joseph. American Chippendale Furniture; a picture
      book. New York: Metropolitan Museum, 1942; 1946;
      1949. 3pp, 20 pls MiGr

2210 *   . American Furniture: Queen Anne and Chippendale
      periods in the Henry Francis du Pont Winterthur Museum.
      Fore. by Henry Francis du Pont. New York: Macmillan,
      1952; New York: Viking, 1967. v.p., 401 ill, 10 color
      pls, bib (Definitive work. 400 examples from Winterthur.
      Companion book to Charles F. Montgomery's American
      Furniture: the Federal period)

2211 _____ . A Picture Book of Philadelphia Chippendale Furniture, 1750-1780. Philadelphia: Pennsylvania Museum of
Art, 1931. 19pp, ill, pls

2212 _____ , and Ruth Ralston. A Loan Exhibition of New York
State Furniture, with Contemporary Accessories. February-April 1934. New York: Plandome Pr, Metropolitan
Museum, 1934. 28pp, 256 pieces catalogued, 23 pieces
ill, pls MiGr

2213 Dundore, Roy H. Pennsylvania German Painted Furniture.
Plymouth Meeting, Pa: Mrs. C. N. Keyser, 1944; 1946.
32pp, ill, pls; 38pp, ill, pls

2214 Dyer, Walter Alden. American Furniture of the 18th Century.
Pasadena, Cal: Esto Publishing, Pasadena Museum, 1934.
16pp NNC-Ave, MiGr

2215 Early Furniture Made in New Jersey, 1690 to 1870. Exhibition. October 1958-January 1959. Newark, NJ: Newark
Museum Association, 1958. 89pp, ill, pls

2216 Elder, William Voss, III. Baltimore Painted Furniture,
1800-1840. Exhibition. April-June 1972. Baltimore,
Md: Museum of Art, 1972. 132pp, ill, bib, makers'
list

2217 _____ . Maryland Queen Anne and Chippendale Furniture
of the 18th Century. Baltimore: NY Graphic Society,
Greenwich, Connecticut, for Baltimore Museum, 1968.

2218 Emerich, A. D., comp. Shaker Furniture and Objects from
the Faith and Edward Deming Andrews Collections, commemorating the bicentennial of the American Shakers.
Annotations by A. H. Benning. Washington, D.C.:
Smithsonian Institution Pr, for the Renwick Gallery, 1973.
88pp, ill, bib

2219 Erving, Henry Wood, 1851-1941. The Hartford Chest. New
Haven: Yale U Pr, for the Tercentenary Commission,
1934. 10pp, pls ViU, DLC

2220 _____ . Random Notes on Colonial Furniture. (A paper
read before the Connecticut Society of Sons of the Revolution in 1922.) Hartford: R. S. Peck, 1922; rev. ed.
Hartford: Connecticut Historical Society, 1931. 39pp,
ill; 60pp, ill, pls NN, DLC

2221 Fales, Dean A., Jr. Essex County Furniture: documented
treasures from local collections, 1660-1860. Exhibition.
June-October 1965. Salem, Mass: Essex Institute, 1965.
79pp, ill

2222 * _____, Robert Bishop, and Cyril I. Nelson. American
        Painted Furniture, 1660-1880. New York: Dutton, 1972.
        298pp, 577 (148 color) ill, bib (Many privately-owned
        pieces never before published)

2223 Fales, Martha Gandy. Regional Characteristics of Empire
        Furniture. Winterthur, Dela: Museum, 1954. 20pp, pls
        DeWint

2224 Fede, Helen Maggs. Washington Furniture at Mount Vernon.
        Mount Vernon, Va: its Ladies' Association of the Union,
        1966. 72pp, pls

2225 Finch, Elfreda. Flowers and Furniture in America's His-
        toric Homes. Fore. by Angela Place. New York: Hearth-
        side Pr, 1967. 117pp, ill

2226 Fisher, Leonard Everett. The Cabinet-makers. New York:
        F. Watts, 1966. 47pp, ill (Juvenile literature)

2227 Forman, Benno M. The 17th Century Case Furniture of
        Essex County, Massachusetts, and its Makers. Salem,
        Mass: 1968. 160pp, pls

2228 Forman, Henry Chandlee. Old Buildings, Gardens, and Fur-
        niture in Tidewater Maryland. Cambridge, Md: Tide-
        water, Publishers, 1967. 326pp, ill, bib

2229 Freeman, Graydon La Verne. Federal-Empire. Watkins
        Glen, NY: Century, 1956. 80pp, pls

2230 Freeman, John Crosby. Forgotten Rebel: Gustav Stickley
        and His Craftsman Mission Furniture. Watkins Glen, NY:
        Century, 1966. 120pp, ill, bib

2231 The Furniture and Cabinet Finisher. New York: Jesse Haney,
        1878. 98pp, ill

2232 A Furniture Festival; early American furniture from the col-
        lections in the Western Reserve. Exhibition. June-July
        1969. Fore. by Jairus Bronson Barnes. Cleveland, O:
        Western Reserve Historical Society, 1969. 50pp, ill

2233 Furniture Journal. Semi-monthly. Chicago: American
        Furniture Mart, 189- .

2234 The Furniture Manufacturer and Artisan. Monthly. Grand
        Rapids: Furniture Record Co, 1911-1926. (Formerly
        Michigan Artisan 1880-1910)

2235 Furniture News. Periodical. Minneapolis: 189- .

2236 Furniture Trade Review and Interior Decorator. Monthly.

New York: Review Publishing Co, 18- . (Merged with
Carpet and Upholstery Trade Review, November 1920)

2237   Furniture Worker. Semi-monthly. Cincinnati; Chicago:
       Spokesman Publishing, 1883-1922. (Continued as American
       Furniture Manufacturer)

2238   Furniture World. Bi-weekly. New York: Towse, 1895- .
       (Was American Cabinet Maker and Upholsterer)

2239   Gaines, Edith, and Dorothy H. Jenkins. (Woman's Day)
       Dictionary of Antique Furniture. Reprint of articles from
       the magazine. Princeton, NJ: Pyne Pr, 1974. 80pp,
       ill

2240   Gamon, Albert T. Pennsylvania Country Antiques. Engle-
       wood Cliffs, NJ: Prentice-Hall, 1968. 189pp, ill, bib
       (Chiefly furniture)

2241   Gilborn, Craig A. American Furniture, 1660-1725. London:
       Hamlyn, 1972. 64pp, 52 ill

2242   _____. Furniture and Furniture Production in Charleston,
       South Carolina. Student paper. 1960. 29pp DeWint

2243   _____. Furniture Production in the Connecticut River
       Valley: 17th century through Queen Anne style. Student
       paper. 1959. 32pp DeWint

2244   Ginsberg and Levy, Inc. English Sources of 18th Century
       American Furniture Design. Reprint from American Col-
       lector, June 1943. New York: 1943. 15pp, ill

2244a Good Furniture and Decoration, (title varies). Monthly. New
       York, etc.: National Trade Journals, 1913-1931. (Merged
       into Interior Architecture and Decoration)

2244b Gothic Album for Cabinet Makers; comprising designs for
       gothic furniture. Philadelphia: H. C. Baird, 1868. 2pp,
       23 pls MB, NN

2245   Gould, George Glen. Monograph on Period Furniture. (Ex-
       hibition.) New York: James McCreery, department store,
       1921. 48pp, ill, bib NN, MiGr

2246   _____, and Florence Gould. The Period Furniture Hand-
       book.... New York: Dodd, Mead; London: Lane, 1928.
       271pp, ill, pls NN, MB, MiGr

2247   Gowans, Alan. Images of American Living; four centuries
       of architecture and furniture as cultural expression.
       Philadelphia: Lippincott, 1963; 1964. 498pp, ill, bib

2248   Goyne, Nancy Ann. Furniture Craftsmen in Philadelphia,
        1760-1780; their role in a mercantile society. Thesis.
        1963. 218pp, pls DeWint

2249-50 [No entries.]

2251   Greenlaw, Barry A. New England Furniture at Williamsburg.
        Williamsburg, Va: Colonial Williamsburg Foundation, dist.
        by U. Pr of Virginia, Charlottesville, 1974. 195pp, ill
        of 164 pieces

2252   Gross, Katharine Wood. The Sources of Furniture Sold in
        Savannah, 1789-1815. Thesis. 1967. 189pp, pls DeWint

2253   Guild, Laurelle Van Arsdale. The American Home Course in
        Period Furniture. New York: Art Education Pr, 1932.
        27pp, ill ViU, MiGr

2254   Hall, John, architect. Cabinet Maker's Assistant. Embracing
        the most modern style of cabinet furniture: exemplified in
        new designs, practically aranged.... Baltimore: John
        Murphy, printer, 1840; 1853; facsimile reprint. New York:
        National Superior, Inc., 1944. 44 pls with 198 figures
        NN, DeWint

2255   Halsey, Richard Townley Haines, and Charles Over Cornelius.
        Loan Exhibition of Duncan Phyfe Furniture. Metropolitan
        Museum. October-December 1922. New York: 1922.
        10pp, ill

2256   Handberg, Ejner. Shop Drawings of Shaker Furniture and
        Woodenware; measured drawings. Stockbridge, Mass:
        Berkshire Traveller Pr, 1973. 81pp, ill

2257   Harkness, Douglas W. Catalogue of Unrecorded American
        Antique Furniture and Decoration. South Glens Falls,
        NY: 1964. 75pp, ill

2258   Heuvel, Johannes. The Cabinetmaker in 18th Century Wil-
        liamsburg, giving attention to the city's chief craftsmen
        in the furniture way.... Williamsburg, Va: Colonial
        Williamsburg, 1963. 40pp, pls

2259   Hill, John Henry. The Furniture Craftsmen in Baltimore,
        1783-1823. Thesis. 1967. 464pp DeWint

2260   Hodgson, Frederick Thomas, 1836-1919. Hints and Practical
        Information for Cabinet-Makers, upholsterers, and furni-
        ture men generally. New York: Author, 1884; Phila-
        delphia: McKay, 1910. 130pp ViU

2261   *Holloway, Edward Stratton. American Furniture and Decora-
        tion; Colonial and Federal. Philadelphia; London: Lippin-

cott, 1928; new ed. as The Practical Book of American
Furniture and Decoration, ... etc.   Garden City, NY:
Halcyon House, 1937; 1948.   191pp, 200 ill, 140 pls
MiGr, NNC-Ave

2262 *Hopkins, Thomas Smith, and Walter Scott Cox, comp. Colo-
        nial Furniture of West New Jersey.... Haddonfield, NJ:
        Historical Society of Haddonfield, by the Engle Pr, Phila-
        delphia, 1936.   113pp, ill DLC, MiGr

2263 *Hornor, William Macpherson, Jr. Blue Book, Philadelphia
        Furniture, William Penn to George Washington, with
        special reference to the Philadelphia-Chippendale School.
        (Cover title: Philadelphia Furniture, 1682-1807.) Phila-
        delphia: Author, 1935.   340pp, ill, pls, bib ViU, MiGr,
        NNC-Ave

2264 _____ . A Loan Exhibition of Authenticated Furniture of
        the Great Philadelphia Cabinet-Makers. April-May 1935.
        Philadelphia Museum of Art.   Philadelphia: Julian B.
        Slevin, 1935.   20pp, pls

2265 Horst, Melvin, photographer, and Elmer L. Smith. Early
        Country Furniture. Lebanon, Pa: Applied Arts Pub-
        lishers, 1970.   40pp, ill

2266 Hunter, Dard, Jr. David Evans, Cabinet Maker; His Life
        and Work. Thesis. 1954.   77pp, pls DeWint

2267 _____ . A Directory of the Cabinet Makers and Allied
        Trades in Philadelphia to 1820. Thesis, Part 2.   1954.
        195pp DeWint

2268 Hyde, Bryden Bordley. Bermuda's Antique Furniture and
        Silver. Hamilton, Bermuda: Bermuda National Trust,
        dist. by Maryland Historical Society, Baltimore, 1971.

2269 The John Brown House Loan Exhibition of Rhode Island Fur-
        niture, including some notable portraits, Chinese export
        porcelain, and other items. May-June 1965.   Providence,
        R.I. Historical Society, 1965.   178pp, pls

2270 Johnson, J. Stewart. New York Cabinetmaking Prior to the
        Revolution. Thesis. 1964.   123pp, pls DeWint

2271 The Journeymen Cabinet and Chair-Makers Philadelphia Book
        of Prices. 2nd ed. Philadelphia: Ormrod & Conrad, 1795;
        2nd corr. & enl. ed. 1795.   28pp; 82pp

2272 Kane, Patricia Ellen. Furniture of the New Haven Colony:
        the 17th century style. Pref. by Robert R. MacDonald.
        Exhibition. New Haven: New Haven Colony Historical
        Society, 1973.   93pp, ill, pls

2273 _____ . The 17th Century Case Furniture of Hartford
County, Connecticut, and its makers. Thesis. 1968.
196pp, pls DeWint

2274 *Kettell, Russell Hawes. The Pine Furniture of Early New
England. Garden City, NY: Doubleday, Doran, 1929;
reprint. New York: Dover, 1949; 1952; 1964. 477pp,
300 pieces ill; 618pp, 55 drawings, 230 photographs, bib

2275 Kimball, J. Wayland. Kimball's Book of Designs: furniture
and drapery. Boston: Kimball, 1876. 29pp, 27 pls
DeWint

2276 Kirk, John T. Connecticut Furniture: 17th and 18th centuries. Exhibition. November-December 1967. Hartford: Wadsworth Atheneum, 1967. 156pp, ill, bib

2277 _____ . Early American Furniture; how to recognize,
evaluate, buy, and care for the most beautiful pieces--
high-style, country, primitive, and rustic. New York:
Knopf, 1970; New York: Knopf, dist. by Random House,
1974. 208pp, 204 ill

2278 Kovel, Ralph, and Terry Kovel. American Country Furniture, 1780-1875. New York: Crown, 1965. 248pp, 700
ill, bib

2279 Litchfield Country Furniture. 1730-1850. Exhibition. July-
August 1969. Litchfield, Conn: County Historical Society,
1969. 125pp, ill

2280 A Loan Exhibition of Authenticated Furniture of the Great
Philadelphia Cabinet Makers. Pennsylvania Museum of
Art. Philadelphia: Julian B. Slevin, 1935. MiGr,
PPULC

2281 *Lockwood, Luke Vincent. Colonial Furniture in America;
the illustrated history of a great period of craftsmanship. New York: Scribner's, 1901; London: Batsford,
1902; new enl. ed. 2 vol. New York: 1913; 3rd ed.
enl. with supplementary chapters and now over 1000 illustrations. New York: 1926; reissued 1951; 2 vol in 1,
from 3rd ed. New York: Castle Books, 1957. 641pp,
293 ill, 12 pls (Includes architecture and interior woodwork)

2282 _____ . The Pendleton Collection. Providence: Rhode
Island School of Design, 1904. 416pp, ill (Charles L.
Pendleton catalogue) MiGr

2283 _____ . Three Centuries of Connecticut Furniture, 1635-
1935; an exhibition at the Morgan Memorial, Hartford.

Hartford: Case, Lockwood & Brainard, printers,
1935.

2284 Luther, Clair Franklin. The Hadley Chest. Hartford, Conn:
Case, Lockwood & Brainard, 1935. 144pp, ill, pls MB,
MiGr

2285 Lynch, Ernest Carlyle. Furniture Antiques Found in Virginia; a book of measured drawings. Milwaukee: Bruce
Publishing, 1954; New York: Bonanza, 1954. 95pp, ill,
bib

2286 *Lyon, Irving Whitall, 1840-1896. Colonial Furniture of New
England: a study of the domestic furniture in use in the
17th and 18th century. Boston: Houghton, Mifflin, 1891;
new ed. 1924. 285pp, ill, 113 pls MB, NNC-Ave, MiGr

2287 *McClelland, Nancy. Duncan Phyfe and the English Regency,
1795-1830. Fore. by Edward Knoblock. New York: W.
R. Scott, 1939. 364pp, 295 ill, bib NNC-Ave, MiGr

2288 Madigan, Mary Jean Smith. Eastlake-influenced American
Furniture, 1870-1890. Exhibition. November 1973-
January 1974. Yonkers, NY: Hudson River Museum,
1973. 66pp, ill, bib (Charles Lock Eastlake, 1833-
1906, British)

2289 Mallach, Stanley. Gothic Furniture Designs by Alexander
Jackson Davis. Thesis. University of Delaware. 1966.
text, ill, bib (Davis, architect, 1803-1892) NNC-Ave

2290 Margon, Lester. Construction of American Furniture
Treasures; measured drawings of selected museum pieces
with complete information on their construction and reproduction. New York: Home Craftsman, 1949; corrected
ed. with new essay "Brief Summary of Early American
Furniture Styles." New York: Dover, 1974. 167pp,
344 drawings, 54 photographs, 38 pls

2291 _____. Masterpieces of American Furniture, 1620-1860.
New York: Architectural Book Publishing, 1965. 256pp,
ill, measured drawings

2292 _____. More American Furniture Treasures, 1620-1840;
an anthology with photographs, measured drawings and
eclectic discussions. New York: Architectural Book Publishing, 1971. 256pp, ill

2293 Makers of Furniture of Quality: (catalogs of) Grand Rapids
Chair Co., Grand Rapids Fancy Furniture Co., Imperial
Furniture Co., the Luce Furniture Co., the Macey Co.,
Nelson Matter Furniture Co., John D. Raab Chair Co.,

Stickley Brothers Co.   Grand Rapids, Mich: The Guild,
1910. ill MiGr

2294   Maryland Queen Anne and Chippendale Furniture of the 18th
Century. New York: October House, for the Baltimore
Museum of Art, 1968. 128pp, ill

2295   Meader, Robert F. W. Illustrated Guide to Shaker Furniture.
New York: Dover; London: Constable, 1972. 129pp, ill,
18 pls (Includes 19th century forgeries; facsimile catalog
of R. M. Wagan, Mount Lebanon, N.Y., 1874?; details
of pieces)

2296   Millar, Donald. Colonial Furniture, Measured Drawings.
New York: Architectural Book Publishing, 1925. 31 pls
in portfolio MiGr

2297   *Miller, Edgar George, Jr. American Antique Furniture: a
book for amateurs. 2 vol. Baltimore: Lord Baltimore
Pr, 1937; reissue. New York: Barrows, 1948; 2 vol.
reprint. New York: Dover, 1966. 1106pp, 2115 ill (To
1840)

2298   *_____. The Standard Book of American Antique Furniture.
Abridgement of his American Antique Furniture. New
York: Greystone Pr, 1950. 856pp, ill

2299   Miller, V. Isabelle. Furniture by New York Cabinetmakers,
1650-1860. Exhibition. November 1956-March 1957.
New York: Museum of the City of NY, 1956. 84pp, ill

2300   *Montgomery, Charles F. American Furniture: the Federal
period in the Henry Francis du Pont Winterthur Museum.
Fore. by Henry Francis du Pont. New York: Viking,
1966; London: Thames & Hudson, 1967. 497pp, ill
(1788-1825. Companion to Joseph Down's American Furniture: Queen Anne and Chippendale)

2301   *Morse, Frances Clary. Furniture of the Olden Time. New
York: Macmillan, 1902; new ed. 1917; 1936; 1943; 1944.
371pp, ill; ...; ...; 470pp, ill; 450pp, 428 ill, gloss
(Classic on American Colonial and early Federal periods)
MiGr, MB

2302   Morse, John D., ed. Country Cabinetwork and Simple City
Furniture. 15th Winterthur Conference on Museum Opera-
tion and Connoisseurship. Charlottesville, Va: U. Pr of
Va., for Winterthur, 1970. 311pp, ill, bib

2303   *Nagel, Charles. American Furniture, 1650-1850; a brief
background and an illustrated history. London: Parrish;
New York: Chanticleer Pr, 1949. 112pp, ill, bib NNC-
Ave, DLC

2304   National Furniture Review. Monthly. Chicago: National
       Retail Furniture Association, 1927- .

2305   The New York Book of Prices for Manufacturing Cabinet and
       Chair Work. New York: Harper, for New York Society
       of Journeymen Cabinet Makers, 1834. 223pp, ill NNC-
       Ave

2306   New York Furniture Before 1840 in the Collection of the
       Albany Institute of History and Art. Albany: the Insti-
       tute, 1962. 63pp, ill

2307   Noel-Hume, Ivor. Williamsburg Cabinetmakers; the archaeo-
       logical evidence. Williamsburg, Va: Colonial Williams-
       burg Foundation, 1971. 48pp, ill

2308   Nutting, Wallace. Checklist of Early American Reproductions.
       Catalog. Saugus, Mass: Wallace Nutting, Inc., 1928;
       reprint with new introd. by John C. Freeman. Watkins
       Glen, NY: Century, 197-? 128pp, ill, bib (Nutting's
       reproductions of ironwork, brass, hardware, lighting,
       doorways, chairs, beds, etc.)

2309 *   . Furniture of the Pilgrim Century (of American
       Origin) 1620-1720, including Colonial utensils and hard-
       ware. Boston: Marshall Jones, 1921; rev. enl. ed. as
       Furniture of the Pilgrim Century ... 1620-1720, with
       maple and pine to 1800, including Colonial utensils and
       wrought iron house hardware into the 19th century.
       Framingham, Mass: Old America Co., 1924; rev. and
       enl. ed. 2 vol. New York: Dover, 1965. 587pp, 1000
       photographs; 716pp, 1559 ill of 2000 objects, pls (Pioneer,
       indispensable work)

2310 *   . Furniture Treasury, (mostly of American origin);
       all periods of American furniture with some foreign ex-
       amples in America, also American hardware and house-
       hold utensils. Drawings by Ernest John Donnelly. Vol.
       I & II. Cambridge, Mass: 1928, 1933; Vol. III. Framing-
       ham, Mass: Old America Co, 1933; New York; London:
       Macmillan, 1950; Vol. I & II reissued as 1 vol. New York:
       Macmillan, 1954; Vol. III reprint. New York: 1971; I &
       II. 1973. u.p., 5000 ill, each described

2311   . Photographs of Early Colonial Furniture. New
       York: mounted and bound by New York Public Library,
       1939. NN

2312   Nye, Alvan Crocker. A Collection of Scale-drawings, Details,
       and Sketches of What Is Commonly Known as Colonial
       Furniture, Measured and Drawn from Antique Examples.
       New York: W. Helburn, 1895. 55 pls MiGr

2313   O'Neill, James M.   Early American Furniture; designs in the
       Colonial style.   Bloomington, Ill: McKnight & McKnight,
       1963.   141pp, ill

2314   *Ormsbee, Thomas Hamilton.   Early American Furniture
       Makers; a social and biographical study.   New York: T.
       Y. Crowell, 1930; New York: Archer House, 1957.
       185pp, 122 ill, 67 pls, bib

2315   *   .   Field Guide to Early American Furniture.   Boston:
       Little Brown, 1951.   464pp, 360 ill   (To 1850)

2316   *   .   The Story of American Furniture.   New York:
       Macmillan, 1934; 1937; 1946.   276pp, 117 ill, 31 line
       drawings   DLC, BM

2317   Osburn, Burl Neff, and Bernice B. Osburn.   Measured
       Drawings of Early American Furniture.   Milwaukee:
       Bruce, 1926; enl. rev. ed. 1934; reprint of 1926 ed.
       New York: Dover, 1974.   82pp, ill, bib; 94pp, 150
       measured drawings, 32 photographs, bib   (1630-1825.
       Chiefly for schools)

2318   *Otto, Celia Jackson.   American Furniture of the 19th Cen-
       tury.   New York: Viking, 1965.   229pp, ill, 3 pls

2319   Parsons, Charles S.   The Dunlaps and Their Furniture.   Ex-
       hibition.   August-September 1970.   Manchester, NH: Cur-
       rier Gallery of Art, 1970.   310pp, ill, bib   (Major John
       Dunlap, 1746-1792)

2320   Philadelphia Cabinet and Chair Makers' Union Book of Prices
       for Manufacturing cabinet ware.   Philadelphia: printed
       for the Cabinet and Chair Makers, 1828.   MiGr

2321   Phin, John, 1830-1913, comp.   Hints and Practical Informa-
       tion for Cabinet-makers, Upholsterers, and Furniture men
       Generally.   New York: Industrial Publication Co, 1884.
       130pp

2322   Poesch, Jessie J.   Early Furniture of Louisiana.   Exhibition.
       February-July 1972.   Cabildo.   New Orleans: Louisiana
       State Museum, 1972.   85pp, ill, bib

2323   Polley, George Henry.   The Architecture, Interiors and
       Furniture of the American Colonies During the 18th Cen-
       tury.   Boston: Polley, 1914.   2pp, 90 pls in portfolio
       NNC-Ave, DLC

2324   _____, and Co.   Artistic Furniture and Architectural In-
       teriors, decorations, etc., during the last two and a half
       centuries.   By the most eminent artists of that period.
       Boston; New York: Polley, 1892.   1pp, 61 pls

2325   Ralston, Ruth.   The American High Chest.   New York:
          Metropolitan Museum, 1930.   2pp, 20 pls

2326   Randall, Richard H., Jr.   American Furniture in the Mu-
          seum of Fine Arts.   Boston: 1965.   276pp, ill

2327   _____.   The Furniture of H. H. Richardson.   Exhibition.
          January-February 1962.   Boston: Museum of Fine Arts,
          1962.   ill   (19th century)

2328   Rice, Norman S.   New York Furniture Before 1840 in the
          Collection of the Albany Institute of History and Art.
          Albany: 1962.   63pp, ill, bib

2329   *Sack, Albert.   Fine Points of Furniture: early American.
          Fore. by Israel Sack.   Introd. by John M. Graham III.
          New York: Crown, 1950; reprint.   New York: 1975.
          303pp, 800 ill

2330   Salomonsky, Edgar, and Verna Cook Salomonsky.   An Exem-
          plar of Antique Furniture Design; a collection of measured
          drawings accompanied by photographs and explanatory text,
          of pieces of furniture selected from those on exhibit in
          the Metropolitan Museum.   Grand Rapids, Mich: Periodical
          Publishing, 1923.   5pp, 25 pls   MiGr, NNC-Ave

2331   *Salomonsky, Verna Cook.   Masterpieces of Furniture Design;
          a collection of measured drawings ... of pieces of furni-
          ture ... on exhibition in the Metropolitan Museum of Art,
          the Brooklyn Museum of Arts and Sciences, the Rhode
          Island School of Design, and the Essex Institute.   4 port-
          folios.   Grand Rapids, Mich: Periodical Publishing, 1931;
          reprint. as Masterpieces in Furniture, in photographs and
          measured drawings.   New York: Dover, 1953.   101 pls,
          cased portfolios; reprint: 212pp, ill, bib by Adolph K.
          Placzek (Portfolios: 1. Index. Chairs, setees; 2. Chairs,
          tables; 3. Tables, sideboards, chests; 4. Desks, secre-
          taries, highboys, beds, miscellaneous)   NNC-Ave

2332   Schiffer, Herbert F.   Early Pennsylvania Furniture.   Whitford,
          Pa: Whitford Pr, 1966.   63pp, ill, bib

2333   Schiffer, Margaret Berwind.   Furniture and Its Makers of
          Chester County, Pennsylvania.   Philadelphia: U. of Pa.
          Pr, under auspices of Chester County Historical Society;
          London: Oxford U. Pr, 1966.   280pp, ill, 168 pls, bib

2334   Seymour's, (George Dudley), Furniture Collection in the
          Connecticut Historical Society.   Hartford: 1958.   141pp,
          ill

2335   Shea, John Gerald.   The American Shakers and Their Furni-
          ture; with measured drawings of museum classics.   New

York; London: Van Nostrand Reinhold, 1971. 168pp,
chiefly ill, gloss (Hundreds of pieces measured and illustrated to enable reproduction)

2336 *_____, and Paul Nolt Wenger. Colonial Furniture. Milwaukee; New York: Bruce, 1935. 180pp, ill, bib (Measured drawings) MiGr, NN

2337 Sigworth, Oliver F. The Four Styles of a Decade, 1740-
1750. New York: N.Y. Public Library, 1960. 33pp, ill
(Palladian, Chinese, rococo and gothic)

2338 *Singleton, Esther. The Furniture of Our Forefathers. Critical descriptions of plates by Russell Sturgis. 2 vol.
New York: Doubleday, Page, 1900-01; 1 vol. 1908; 1913;
1919; 1 vol. improved ed. New York: B. Blom, 1970.
663pp, 346 ill (Colonial times to early 19th century)
MiGr

2339 *Sironen, Marta Katrina. A History of American Furniture.
Ed. by N. I. Bienenstock. Commemorates 65th anni-
versary of continuous weekly publication of the "Furniture
World and Furniture Buyer and Decorator." East Strouds-
burg, Pa; New York: Towse, 1936. 150pp, ill NN,
MiGr

2340 Sloane, Samuel. Sloane's Homestead Architecture, containing
40 designs for villas, cottages, and farm houses, with
essays on style, construction, landscape gardening, furniture, etc. Philadelphia: Lippincott, 1861. 355pp, 200
engravings, 2 color pls NNC-Ave

2341 Snyder, John J., Jr. Philadelphia Furniture and Its Makers.
New York: Universe, Antiques Magazine, 1975. 160pp,
300 ill (18th and 19th century)

2342 Soderholtz, Eric Ellis. Colonial Architecture and Furniture.
Boston: Polley, 1895. 2pp, 60 pls MiGr

2343 Southern Furniture and Silver: the Federal period, 1788-1830.
Exhibition. September-November 1968. Baton Rouge, La:
Anglo-American Art Museum, Louisiana State U, 1968.
35pp, ill

2344 *Southern Furniture, 1640-1820. By the editors of Antiques
Magazine. Exhibition. January-March 1952. Museum of
Fine Arts, Richmond, Va. New York: 1952. 64pp, ill

2345 Steinfeldt, Cecilia, and Donald Stover. Early Texan Furniture
and Decorative Arts. Exhibition. June-December 1973.
Witte Memorial Museum. San Antonio, Tx: Trinity U.
Pr, for San Antonio Museum Assoc., 1973. 263pp, ill

2346   Stokes, J., of Philadelphia. The Cabinetmaker and Uphol-
       sters' Companion ... and a number of receipts....
       Philadelphia: H. C. Baird, 1850. 167pp, ill BM, DLC

2347   _____ . The Complete Cabinet-Maker and Upholsterer's
       Guide. n. p.: 1829; London: 1838; 1841. 16 pls; 5 pls;
       5 pls BM

2348   *Stoneman, Vernon C. John and Thomas Seymour, Cabinet-
       makers in Boston 1794-1816. Boston: Special Publica-
       tions, 1959; Supplement to John and Thomas Seymour.
       Boston: Author, 1965. 393pp, chiefly pls, bib

2349   Storrs, Alice K. Three Early American Furniture Makers,
       William Savery, 1722-1787; John Goddard, 1724-1785;
       Duncan Phyfe, 1768-1854; a bibliography. New York:
       School of Library Science, Columbia U., 1934. type-
       script NNC-Ave

2350   Swan, Mabel M. Samuel McIntire, Carver, and the Sander-
       sons, Early Salem Cabinet Makers. Salem, Mass: Essex
       Institute, 1934. 46pp, ill, pls (Extracts from invoices,
       etc.) MiGr, NNC-Ave

2351   Swift, Emma. A Selected List of Books on Early American
       Furniture Styles, Colonial, and Colonial Empire. New
       York: Columbia U., School of Library Science, 1935.
       13pp, typescript NNC-Ave

2352   Taylor, Henry Hammond. Knowing, Collecting and Restoring
       Early American Furniture. Philadelphia; London: Lippin-
       cott, 1930. 156pp, 22 line drawings, 59 ill NN

2353   *Taylor, Lonn, and David B. Warren. Texas Furniture. The
       cabinetmakers and their work, 1840-1880. Fore. by Ima
       Hogg. Austin, Tx: U. of T. Pr, with Bayou Bend Col-
       lection, Museum of Fine Arts, Houston, and the Winedale
       Museum, U. of T., 1975. 222 pieces ill (Includes tools
       and machinery)

2354   Theus, Mrs. Charlton M. Savannah Furniture, 1735-1825.
       Savannah?: 1967. 100pp, ill

2355   Thomas Day, 19th Century North Carolina Cabinetmaker.
       Permanent exhibition catalog. Raleigh, NC: N. C. Mu-
       seum of History, 1975. 75pp, 50 ill (Furniture and in-
       terior trim work by a free Black man)

2356   Three Centuries of Connecticut Furniture, 1635-1935. Fore.
       by Luke V. Lockwood. Exhibition. June-October 1935.
       Morgan Memorial, Hartford. Hartford: Connecticut
       Tercentenary Commission, Case, Lockwood & Brainard,
       printers, 1935. 41pp, ill MiGr, NNC-Ave

2357   True Gospel Simplicity. Exhibition. Hanover, NH: U. Pr
       of New England, 1974. ill (Shaker furniture in New
       Hampshire from 1774 on)

2358   Van Lennep, Gustave Adolphe, Jr. A Guide to (or A Catalog
       of) American Antique Furniture. Stratford, Pa: Elf's
       Head Pr, 1936; Philadelphia: Macrae, Smith, 1937. 51pp,
       ill; 95pp, ill MiGr

2359   Wallis, Frank E. Old Colonial Architecture and Furniture.
       Boston: George H. Polley, 1887. 4pp, 60 pls (Includes
       measured drawings) MiGr, NNC-Ave

2360   Walters, Betty Lawson. Furniture Makers of Indiana, 1793-
       1850. Indianapolis: Historical Society, 1972. 244pp, ill,
       pls

2361   _____. The King of Desks: Wooten's Patent Secretary.
       Washington, D.C.: Smithsonian, 1969. 31pp, ill

2362   Ware, William Rotch, 1848-1917, ed. Seats of the Colonists
       and Other Furnishings: illustrated largely with measured
       drawings by H. C. Dunham. Part 1. Boston: American
       Architect, 1904- . (No more published) 24pp, ill, 28
       pls (American and English chairs and furniture) MiGr

2363   Warrum, Richard L., ed. Indianapolis Collects. American
       Furniture, 1700-1850. Exhibition. January-February
       1972. Indianapolis: Speedway Pr, for Museum of Art,
       1972. 28pp, ill

2364   Watson, Aldren Auld. Country Furniture. New York: Thomas
       Y. Crowell, 1974. 274pp, 300 detailed pencil drawings
       (Chiefly the tools)

2365   *Wenham, Edward. The Collector's Guide to Furniture Design
       (English and American) from the Gothic to the 19th Cen-
       tury ... and showing the evolution of modern style. New
       York: Collectors Pr, 1928. 382pp, ill NN

2366   The White Directory of Manufacturers of Furniture and Kin-
       dred Goods of the United States and British Provinces.
       2nd enl. ed. Grand Rapids: White Printing, 1901. 396pp
       (Only one of numerous similar directories)

2367   Whitehill, Walter Muir, Brock Jobe, and Jonathan Fairbanks,
       eds. Boston Furniture of the 18th Century. Charlottes-
       ville, Va: U. Pr, 1974. ill

2368   Whitley, Edna Talbott. A Checklist of Kentucky Cabinetmakers,
       from 1775-1859. Paris, Ky: 1969. v.p., ill

2369   Williams, Henry Lionel. Country Furniture of Early America.

New York: Barnes, 1963; London: Yoseloff, 1964.
138pp, 300 ill (To 1800)

2370 Windsor, Henry H. Mission Furniture, How to Make It.
Chicago: Popular Mechanics, 1909-1912.

2371 Yarmon, Morton. Early American Antique Furniture. Greenwich, Conn: Sterling, for Fawcett Books, 1952; New York:
Arco, 1954. 144pp, ill

BRITISH ISLES FURNITURE

2372 Accounts of Chippendale, Haig and Company for the Furnishing of David Garrick's House in the Adelphi. V & A Museum, Department of Woodwork. London: HMSO, 1920.
MiGr

Ackermann, Rudolf. Fashionable Furniture. See: Pugin,
A. C., no. 2581.

2373 _____. The Upholsterer's and Cabinet-Maker's Repository.
London: Ackermann, 1823. ill, 44 color pls

2374 Adam, Robert, 1728-1792, and James Adam, d.1794. The
Architecture, Decoration and Furniture of Robert and
James Adam, selected from "Works in Architecture, "
published 1778-1822, and photo-lithographed from the
originals. Boston: G. H. Polley, 188-?; London: Batsford, 1880; New York: Helburn, n.d. (1881?); as Decorative Work; being a reproduction of the plates illustrating
decoration and furniture.... London: Batsford, 1891;
enl. ed. as The Decorative Work of Robert and James
Adam.... London: Batsford, 1900; 1901. 26 pls and
30 pls

2375 * _____, and _____. Works in Architecture. London:
printed for Authors, sold by T. Becket, 1773- ; 3 vol.
in 1 (published in parts). London: Priestley & Weale,
1773-1822; 2 vol. (published in 10 parts). London:
Authors, 1778-1786; reissue with added 3rd vol. London:
Priestly & Weale, 1822; London: E. Thezard Sons, 1902;
2 vol. reprint of original ed. Cleveland, Ohio: J. H.
Jansen, 1916; 3 vol. in 1. London: J. Tiranti, 1931;
Jersey City, NJ: H. C. Perleberg, n.d. (19-?). ill
with varying number of plates from 42 (Perlberg) to 107
(Thezard). A new ed. of 1822 was to have 125 plates.
(Volume I. Designs of Sion House, Middlesex) DLC, BM

2376 Adams, Maurice Bingham. Examples of Old English Houses
and Furniture, with some modern works from designs by
the author. London: Batsford, 1888. 9pp, 36 pls MB,
NNC-Ave

2377   Adams, Maurice Spencer Rowe. My Book of Furniture.
           London: M. Adams, Ltd., 1926. 108pp, ill (Furniture
           manufacturer)

2378   _____. My Connaught and Marlborough Furniture. Lon-
           don: M. Adams, 1928. 40pp, ill, pls MiGr

2379 *Adams-Acton, Murray. Domestic Architecture and Old Furni-
           ture. London: G. Bles, 1929. 123pp, ill, pls DeWint,
           NN, MiGr

2380   Allsopp, Harold Bruce. Decoration and Furniture. Vol. I.
           The English Tradition. Vol. II. Principles of Modern
           Design. 2 vol. London: I. Pitman, 1952-53. 233pp,
           205pp, ill, pls

2381   Artistic Furniture. London: J. Taylor, 1804. 98 color pls
           (Includes drapery) DeWint

2382   Ash, Douglas. Dictionary of English Antique Furniture.
           London: Muller, 1970. 164pp, ill, bib

2383   Aslin, Elizabeth. 19th Century English Furniture. London:
           Faber; New York: Yoseloff, 1962. 93pp, ill, bib

2384   Aveling, N. C. Dates in English Furniture from Gothic Times
           until the Commencement of the 19th Century. London: N.
           Clifford, 1911. 29pp

2385   Baker Furniture Company, Inc. A Collection of Drawings of
           Furniture of English 18th Century Styles as Well as Many
           Other Examples of Traditional and Contemporary Design
           both in Cabinet and in Upholstered Pieces. Holland, Mich:
           1950? chiefly pls MiGr

2386   Banks, J. Cabinet-Makers' New Guide. London?: 1829.
           SIB-1

2387   Barrett, Herbert Stanley. The ABC History of Antique Eng-
           lish Furniture. London: Old World Gallery, 1923; 1926.
           200pp V & A

2388   Barron, James. Modern and Elegant Designs of Cabinet and
           Upholstery Furniture, Supplied by James Baron ... Oxford
           Street, London, and Lower Temple Street, Birmingham.
           To be continued annually. London: W. M. Thiselton,
           printer, 1814. 7pp, 68 (65 color) pls (Drapery, furni-
           ture, roller and venetian blinds) DeWint

2389   Batley, H. H. A Series of Studies for Domestic Furniture
           Decoration, etc. London: Low, 1883. 10 plates in
           folio OC, SKM

2390 Bell, James Munro, ed. Chippendale, Sheraton, and Hepplewhite Furniture Designs, Arranged by J. M. Bell. London: Gibbings, 1900. 32pp, 246 ill (Designs without
text from Chippendale's Gentleman and Cabinet-Maker's
Director; Sheraton's Cabinet-Maker ... and his Designs
for Household Furniture; and Hepplewhite's Cabinet-Maker
and Upholsterer's Guide) MiGr, BM

2391 _____, ed. Furniture Designs, Arranged by J. Munro
Bell. Introd. and critical estimate by Arthur Hayden.
London: Gibbings, 1910; New York: McBride, 1912.
128pp of ill MiGr

2392 _____, ed. The Furniture Designs of Chippendale, Hepplewhite, and Sheraton. New York: McBride; London: Cresset Pr, 1938; New York: Tudor, 1940. 312pp, ill (Includes essays on these designers) MiGr

2393 _____. Furniture Designs of George Hepplewhite. Introd.
by Arthur Hayden. London: Gibbings, 1910. ill BM

2394 _____. Furniture Designs of Thomas Chippendale. Introd.
by Arthur Hayden. London: Gibbings, 1910. ill BM

2395 _____. Furniture Designs of Thomas Sheraton. Introd.
by Arthur Hayden. London: Gibbings, 1910. 128pp, ill
MiGr, BM

2396 Bell, Sam Hanna, N. A. Robb, and John Hewitt, eds. The
Arts in Ulster; a symposium. London: Harrap, 1951.
173pp, ill, pls, bib (Irish furniture, art, music, and
theater)

2397 Benn, H. Pringuer, and W. C. Baldock. Characteristics of
Old Furniture: styles in England, 1600-1800. London:
Simpkin, Marshall, Hamilton, Kent and Co., and Benn
Brothers, 1908. 79pp, ill BM

2398 _____, and Henry Percival Shapland. The Nation's
Treasures. Measured drawings of fine old furniture in
the V & A Museum. London: Simpkin, Marshall, and
Benn Brothers, 1910. 71pp, ill BM

2399 Benn, R. Davis. Style in Furniture. London; New York;
Bombay: Longmans, Green, 1904; 1910; 1911; London:
1912; London; New York; Bombay: 1920. 338pp, ill,
102 pls (English and French, 17th to 19th century) NN,
DLC, BM, MiGr

2400 Betts, J. (Collection of Furniture Designs.) London: n. d.
(1829?) 29 pls with many ill (Marlborough Rare Books,
Catalogue #73)

2401   Bickel, Thomas Harold. Chart of the History of English
       Furniture and Domestic Architecture. London: Benn,
       1953. 71pp, ill, bib

2402   Bitmead, Richard. The London Cabinet-Makers' Guide to the
       Entire Construction of Cabinet-Work, etc. 2 parts. Lon-
       don: Author, 1873; London: C. Lockwood, 1901; 1906;
       3rd ed. New York: Appleton, 1912; London: Technical
       Pr, 1948. 168pp, ill, pls NN, BM

2403   *Blake, John Percy, and Alfred Edward Reveirs Hopkins.
       English Furniture. Vol. I. Tudor to Stuart; Vol. II.
       Queen Anne; Vol. III. Chippendale and His School; Vol.
       IV. The Sheraton Period. Post-Chippendale Designers,
       1760-1820. 4 vol. London: Heinemann; New York: F.
       A. Stokes, 1911-22. 124pp; 115pp; 111pp; 135pp; all
       well-illustrated, color frontis's, pls BM

2404   _____, and _____. Old English Furniture for the Small
       Collector; its types, history and surroundings from Medi-
       eval to Victorian times. London: Batsford; New York:
       Scribner, 1930; 3rd rev. ed. 1948. 155pp, ill, pls MiGr,
       BM

2405   Bles, Arthur de. Old English Furniture Styles and How to
       Distinguish Them. New York: n.d. 30 blueprints in
       portfolio MiD

2406   Bly, John. Discovering English Furniture, 1500-1720. Tring:
       Shire Publications, 1971. 63pp, ill

2407   _____. Discovering English Furniture, 1720-1830. Tring:
       Shire Publications, 1971. 72pp, ill

2408   Bolton, Arthur Thomas. The Architecture of Robert and James
       Adam (1758-1794). 2 vol. London: Country Life; New
       York: Scribner, 1922. ill, bib, color frontis (Furniture
       included) NNC-Ave

2409   Booth, Lorenza. A Series of Original Designs for Decorative
       Furniture ... etc. London: Houlston & Wright, 1854;
       as The Exhibition Book of Original Designs for Decorative
       Furniture, etc., arranged for the hall, dining-room, draw-
       ing room, bed-room, boudoir, and library. London: 1863;
       1864. 46pp, 132 pls NN, BM

2410   Brackett, Oliver. Catalogue of English Furniture and Wood-
       work. V & A Museum. Late Stuart to Queen Anne.
       (Vol. III of 4.) London: HMSO, 1927.

2411 * _____. An Encyclopedia of English Furniture. A pictorial
       review ... from Gothic times to the mid-19th century.
       London: E. Benn; New York: McBride, 1927; 2nd ed. rev.

and ed. by H. Clifford Smith, as English Furniture Illustrated: a pictorial review of English furniture from Chaucer to Queen Victoria. London: Benn; New York: Macmillan, 1950; London: Spring Books, 1958. 14pp, ill, 310 pls; 300pp, ill, pls; 403pp, ill, pls

2412 _____ . English Furniture. London: E. Benn, 1928. 79pp, ill, bib BM

2413 * _____ . Thomas Chippendale: a study of his life, work and influence. London: Hodder & Stoughton, 1924; Boston: Houghton-Mifflin, 1925. 281pp, 9 ill, 76 pls, bib NN, DLC, BM

2414 Brett, Gerard. English Furniture and Its Setting from the Later 16th to the Early 19th Century. Illustrations from collection of the Royal Ontario Museum, University of Toronto. Toronto: U. of T. Pr, 1965. 117pp, ill, bib

2415 Bridgens, Richard. Designs for Grecian and Other Furniture with Candelabra, and Interior Decoration. London: William Pickering, 1838. 1pp, 60 pls (Also as Furniture with Candelabra ... etc.) PP, NN, BM

2416 Brodhurst, James George Joseph Penderel, and Edwin J. Layton. A Glossary of English Furniture of the Historic Periods. London: J. Murray, 1925. 196pp (Includes many biographies) MiGr

2417 Brown, Richard. The Rudiments of Drawing Cabinet and Upholstery Furniture. London: Author, 1820; 2nd ed. London: M. Taylor, 1822; 2nd improved ed. London: M. Taylor, 1835. 66pp, ill, pls; 87pp, 32 pls; 68pp, 25 pls (Includes interiors and draperies. Regency period) CtY, NN, DLC

2418 Buckby, Charles W. Introduction to English Furniture. London: Pitfield, 1948. 118pp, ill, pls, bib

2419 The Cabinet and Upholstery Advertiser--Modern Designs in Furniture and Upholstery. Periodical. London: 1877.

2420 Cabinet Maker. Monthly. London: Benn, 1880-date. (Now as Cabinet Maker and Retail Furnisher.)

2421 The Cabinet-Makers' Leeds Book of Prices, and designs of cabinet work, calculated for the convenience of cabinet makers in general, whereby the price of executing any piece of work, may be easily found. 2nd ed. Leeds: T. Gill, printer, 1804. 180pp, 29 pls MH-Ba

2422 The Cabinet-Maker's London Book of Prices, and designs of cabinet work in perspective. London: for the London

Society of Cabinet Makers, sold at White Swann, 1788;
2nd ed. with additions. 1793; Supplement, by G. Atkinson,
and W. Somerville. London: 1805. 143pp, 100 designs
on 20 pls; 266pp, 29 pls (Includes designs by Shearer,
Hepplewhite, Casement, and others) PPULC, MH-BA, BM

2423 The Cabinet-Makers' Manchester Book of Prices. Manchester,
      Eng: Russell, 1810; Supplement. Manchester: Pratt,
      1825. 59pp, ill NNC-Ave

2424 The Cabinet-Makers' Pattern Book, being examples of modern
      furniture of the character mostly in demand ... issued as
      supplements to the Furniture Gazette. London: Wyman,
      1873-1894. BM

2425 Candee, Helen Churchill. Jacobean Furniture and English
      Styles in Oak and Walnut. New York: F. A. Stokes,
      1916. 56pp, 43 ill, pls ViU, MiGr, PPL

2426 Catalogue of English Furniture and Woodwork. Vol. I. Gothic
      and Early Tudor, by Harold Clifford Smith; Vol. II. Late
      Tudor and Early Stuart, by H. C. Smith; Vol. III. Late
      Stuart to Queen Anne, by Oliver Brackett; Vol. IV. Georgian,
      by Ralph Edwards. 4 vols. London: V & A Museum,
      1923, 1930, 1927, 1931. ill, many pls BM

2427 Catalogue of Furniture From Montagu House, Devonshire
      House and Grosvenor House. 2nd ed. revised. London:
      HMSO, for V & A, 1919. u. p. MiGr

2428 *Cescinsky, Herbert. English Furniture of the 18th Century.
      3 vol. London: G. Routledge, 1909-11; New York: Funk
      & Wagnalls, 1909; London: Routledge, 1912; 1915; London:
      The Waverly Book Co, n. d. 384pp, 1166 ill, 11 pls
      (Hepplewhite, Adams, Chippendale, Sheraton, Locke, etc.)
      NN, MB

2429 *   . English Furniture from Gothic to Sheraton; a con-
      cise account of the development of English furniture and
      woodwork from the gothic of the 15th century to the classic
      revival of the early 19th. Grand Rapids, Mich: Dean-
      Hicks, 1929; 2nd ed. Garden City, New York: Doubleday,
      1937; reprint. New York: Dover, 1968. 438pp, 900 ill,
      bib; 406pp, 900 ill, bib PPULC, NN, MiGr

2430 *   . The Old-World House; its furniture and decoration.
      2 vols. London: A. & C. Black; New York: Macmillan,
      1924. many ill, text MiGr, NN, DLC

2431 *   , and Ernest R. Gribble. Early English Furniture
      and Woodwork. 2 vols. London: G. Routledge, 1922.
      text, 928 ill, 2 color frontis's (Earliest times to end of

17th century. Includes staircases, panellings, clocks, etc.) DLC, PPULC

2432 *_____, and George Leland Hunter. English and American Furniture; a pictorial handbook of furniture made in Great Britain and in the American colonies, some in the 16th century, but principally in the 17th, 18th, and early 19th centuries. Grand Rapids, Mich: Dean-Hicks; Garden City, NY: Garden City Publishing, 1929. 312pp, 400 ill, bib NN, DLC, MiGr

2433 Charles, Richard, and others. The Cabinet Maker: a journal of designs. For the use of upholsterers, cabinet-makers, decorators, carvers, gilders, and others. London: E. & F. N. Spon, 1868. 96 pls DLC, NNC-Ave

2434 _____. Cabinet Maker's Sketch Book. London: Author, 1866. 60 pls NNC-Ave, SKM

2435 _____. The Compiler. Furniture and decorations, choice and select designs from the best authors. London: 1879. 240pp, pls DeWint

2436 _____. Upholsterer's Design Book. London: Author, 1877. ill SKM

2437 *Chippendale, Thomas, 1718-1779. The Gentleman and Cabinet-Makers' Director: being a large collection of the most elegant and useful designs of household furniture, in the most fashionable taste. Including a great variety of chairs ... and other ornaments, to which is prefixed a short explanation of the five orders of architecture.... London: Author, 1754; 2nd ed. London: J. Heberkorn, 1775; 3rd ed. London: for Author, 1762; 3rd ed. 1768; facsimile reprint of 1762 ed. London: Hodder, 1894; 1910; facsimile reprint. New York: Towse, 1938; London: Tiranti, 1939; reprint with introd. by Ralph Edwards. London: Connoisseur, 1957. 34pp, ill, 161 pls (in 1st & 2nd ed.); 212 pls (3rd ed.)

2438 Clouston, K. Warren. The Chippendale Period in English Furniture. London: Edward Arnold, 1897; London: Debenham & Freebody; New York: E. Arnold, 1897. 224pp, ill, pls (William Chambers, Chippendale, Adam brothers, Shearer, Hepplewhite, Sheraton) ViU, NN, DLC

2439 *Clouston, R. S. English Furniture and Furniture Makers of the 18th Century. Partly reprinted from "The Connoisseur" and the "Burlington." London: Hurst & Blackett, 1906. 362pp, ill, folding pl (Sir William Chambers to Sheraton) MB, DLC, MiGr

2440 Coleridge, Anthony. Chippendale Furniture, Circa 1745-1765;

the work of Thomas Chippendale and his contemporaries
in the rococo taste: Vile, Cobb, Langlois, Channon,
Hallett, Ince and Mayhew, Lock, Johnson, and others.
New York: Potter; London: Faber, 1968. 229pp, ill,
420 pls, bib

2441 Complete Cabinet Maker and Upholsterer's Guide: comprising
the rudiments and principles of cabinet-making and upholstery with familiar instructions. London: Dean &
Munday, 1829. MiGr

2442 Cooper, Charles, 1844- . The English Table in History and
Literature. London: Low, 1929. 230pp, pls TxU, DLC,
NN

2443 Crawley, William. Is It Genuine? A guide to the identification of 18th century English furniture. London: Eyre &
Spottiswoode, 1971; New York: Hart, 1972. 156pp, ill;
188pp, ill

2444 Crunden, John, 1740-ca.1828. The Joyner and Cabinet
Maker's Darling, or Pocket Director. 60 new designs,
entirely new and useful. London: A. Webley, 1760; ...
66 new designs. London: 1765; 1770. 26 pls; BM

2445 *Dean, Margery. English Antique Furniture, 1450-1850. London: Merlin Pr; New York: Universe, 1969. 109pp, ill

2446 [No entry.]

2447 Early Chests in Wood and Iron. Public Record Office Museum.
London: HMSO, 1974. 12pp, ill

2448 *Eastlake, Charles Lock, 1833-1906. Hints on Household Taste
in Furniture, Upholstery and Other Details. Ed. by C.
C. Perkins. London: 1868; 2nd ed. rev. London: Longmans, Green, 1869; 3rd ed. London: Longmans, 1872;
Boston: James R. Osgood, 1872; 5th American ed. Boston:
1877; 4th rev. ed. London: Longmans, 1878; facsimile reprint of 1878 ed. New York: Dover; London: Constable,
1969. 306pp, ill; 1872: 300pp, 44 (14 color) pls including
wallpaper samples; 1969: 304pp, 35 pls, ill

2449 The Edinburgh Book of Prices for Manufacturing Cabinet-Work.
With various tables, as mutually agreed upon by the masters and journeymen. Edinburgh: J. Glass, printer, 1826.
44pp, pls DeWint

2450 Edis, Robert William, 1839-1927. Decoration and Furniture
of Town Houses. An address delivered before the Society
of Arts, 1880, amplified and enlarged. London: K. Paul;
New York: Scribner & Welford, 1881; facsimile reprint.

Wakefield, Eng: E P Publishing, 1972. 292pp, ill, 29 pls MB, MiGr, DLC

2451 _____. Healthy Furniture and Decoration. London: W. Clowes, printer, for the Executive Council of the International Health Exhibition, 1884. 75pp, ill NN, SKM

2452 *Edwards, Ralph. (Catalogue of English Furniture and Woodwork. V & A Museum.) Georgian Furniture. Vol. IV of 4. London: HMSO, 1931; supplement. 1947. 23pp, ill, 112 pls

2453 _____. Sheraton Furniture Designs from the Cabinet-Makers' and Upholsterers' Drawing-Book, 1791-1794. London: J. Tiranti, 1945; reissue. London: 1949. 92pp, 74 pls BM

2454 * _____. The Shorter Dictionary of English Furniture; from the Middle Ages to the Late Georgian period. Prepared from 1954 three-volume ed., text adjusted. London: Country Life, 1964. 684pp, 1900 ill, color frontis

2455 * _____, and Margaret Jourdain. Georgian Cabinet-Makers, ca1700-1800. London: Country Life, 1944; new rev. ed. 1946; 3rd ed. rev. 1955. 183pp, ill, pls, bib; 192pp; 247pp

2455a 18th Century English Furniture. London: Abbey Fine Arts, 1970. 71pp, ill

2456 *Ellwood, George Montague. English Furniture and Decoration, 1680-1800. Volume I. London: Batsford, 1899; 3rd ed. 1909; New York: Brentano, 19-?; 4th ed. London: 1933. 187-201pp of pls (No other volumes) NN, MiGr, NNC-Ave

2457 English Desks and Bureaux. V & A Museum. London: HMSO, 1968. 8pp, ill (See also: Hayward, John F.)

2458 English Household Furniture, mainly designed by Chippendale, Sheraton, Adam, and others of the Georgian period. Boston: Bates & Guild, 1900. 10pp, 100 pls showing 348 examples DeWint, MiGr

2459 Exhibition of Early English Needlework and Furniture. March 1928. Lond: 1928. DFo

2460 An Exhibition of Furniture by, and in the Manner of, Thomas Chippendale. (Held at Temple Newsom House.) Leeds: Leeds Art Collections Fund, 1951. 41pp, ill BM

2461 An Exhibition of Town and Country Furniture Illustrating the

Vernacular Tradition. July–August 1972. Stable Court
Galleries, Temple Newsam. Leeds: 1972. 64pp, ill

2462 Fashionable Furniture. London: R. Ackermann, 1809–1826.
      60 color pls (Plates from the Repository of Arts, Litera-
      ture, Fashions, etc.)

2463 Fashionable Furniture: a collection of 350 original designs
      representing cabinet work, upholstery, and decoration,
      by various designers, including 100 sketches by the late
      Bruce James Talbert; also a series of domestic interiors
      by Henry Shaw. Drawn, engraved, printed and published
      by "The Cabinet Maker and Art Furnisher." London: J.
      W. Benn, 1881; New York: J. O'Kane, 188-? 120pp, ill
      PPL, NN, MB, DLC

2464 *Fastnedge, Ralph. English Furniture Styles from 1500–1830.
      London; Baltimore: Penguin, 1955; London: Jenkins, 1962;
      New York: Barnes; Baltimore: Penguin, 1964. 321pp,
      101 ill, 64 pls, bib

2465 *_____, ed. Shearer Furniture Designs, from the Cabinet-
      Makers' London Book of Prices, 1788. Pref. and descrip-
      tive notes by R. Fastnedge. London: Tiranti, 1962.
      22pp, ill, pls, facsims

2466 *_____. Sheraton Furniture. London: Faber; New York:
      Yoseloff, 1962; London: 1968. 125pp, ill, 99 pls (some
      color) (1785–1810)

2467 Fenn, Frederick, and Bertie Wyllie. Old English Furniture.
      London: G. Newnes; New York: Scribners, 1904; London:
      1905; New York; London: 1913; New York: 1920; London:
      Batsford, 1920. 90pp, ill, 94 pls, bib; ...; 83pp, 104
      pls, bib DeWint, MiGr

2468 Fildes, George. On Elizabethan Furniture. A paper read
      at the Decorative Art Society, February 28, 1844. Lon-
      don: F. W. Calder, 1844. 37pp NN, BM

2469 Furniture: a series of outline plates. London: J. Betts,
      1830? 51 pls MdBP

2470 Furniture and Decoration. Weekly. London: 1890–

2471 Furniture Gazette: an illustrated journal, treating of all
      branches of cabinet-work, decoration, upholstery, and
      drapery. Weekly. London: 1872–1885; monthly. 1885–
      1893. (Published as Furniture and Decoration part of
      time) MiGr

2472 Fussell, George Edwin, 1889- . The English Rural

Labourer; his home, furniture, clothing and food, from
Tudor to Victorian times. London: Batchworth Pr, 1949.
164pp, ill, bib TxU, DeWint, DLC

2473 *Garside, Joshua T. Old English Furniture; a view of its
characteristics from Tudor times to the Regency, for the
use of collectors, designers and students. Part 1. London: Batsford; New York: Scribner's, 1924. ill, pls,
measured drawings NN, MiGr

2474 Gay, Eben Howard. The Chippendale Room from Woodcote
Park, Epsom, Surrey, England (ca1750). Boston: Museum of Fine Arts, 1928. 51pp, ill, pls, bib

2474a Genteel Household Furniture in the Present Taste, with an
addition of several articles never before executed, by a
Society of Upholsterers, Cabinet-makers, etc. London:
Robert Sayer, 1760; 2nd ed. 1765; 1785. 120 pls, over
350 designs MdBP, NN, PP

2474b Georgian Furniture. Introd. by Ralph Edwards. V & A Museum. London: HMSO, 1947; 1951; 1958; 3rd ed. rev.
by Desmond Fitz-Gerald. London: 1969. 20pp, 163 pls;
20pp, 171 pls; ...; 32pp, 278 (5 color) pls, bib

2475 Gilbert, Christopher. Late Georgian and Regency Furniture.
London: Hamlyn; Country Life, 1972. 64pp, ill (1760-
1830)

2476 Gillespie, James. Details of Scottish Domestic Architecture; a series of selected examples from the 16th and
17th centuries, of stonework, woodwork, furniture, plasterwork, and metalwork. Edinburgh: G. Waterston, 1922.

2477/9 Gillow, Messrs, decorator firm, London. Examples of Furniture and Decoration. London: Chiswick Pr, 1904? MiGr

2480 The Glasgow Book of Prices for Manufacturing Cabinet-Work,
with various tables. By a Committee of the Master
Cabinet-Makers and Journeymen. Glasgow: James Gurld,
printer, 1825. 48pp, ill DeWint

2481 *Gloag, John (Edwards). British Furniture Makers. London:
W. Collins; New York: Hastings House, 1945; London:
1946. 47pp, 25 ill, 8 color pls, bib NNC-Ave, DLC

2482 *_____. English Furniture. London: Black, 1934; 4th ed.
London: 1944; 1946; 1952; 5th ed. rev. & enl. 1965; 6th
ed. 1973. 199pp, ill, 24 pls; 180pp, 24 pls; ...; ...;
180pp, 109 ill, 24 pls, bib

2483 *_____. The English Tradition in Design. London; New

York: Penguin, 1947; enl. & rev. ed. London: A. & C. Black; New York: Macmillan, 1960. 76pp, 32 pp of ill, 40 pls

2484   _____. Guide to Furniture Styles--English and French, 1450-1850. London: A. & C. Black, 1972. 232pp, ill

2485   _____. Modern Home Furnishing. London: Macmillan, 1929. 127pp, ill NN

2486   _____, and Yvonne Hackenbroch. English Furniture with Some Furniture from Other Countries in the Irwin Unter- myer Collection. London: Thames & Hudson; Cambridge, Mass: Metropolitan Museum of Art, 1958. 95pp, 358 pls (part color)

2487   Godwin, Edward William, and others. Art Furniture ... with hints and suggestions on domestic furniture and decoration by William Watt. 2nd ed. London: Batsford, 1878. ill NN, SKM, MiGr

2488   Gordon, Hampden Charles. Old English Furniture, a Simple Guide. London: John Murray, 1948; New York: Dutton, 1949; reprint. 1962. 158pp, ill MiGr

2489   Gregory, Edward William. The Furniture Collector; an intro- duction to the study of English styles of the 17th and 18th century. London: H. Jenkins; Philadelphia: D. McKay, 1915. 299pp, 55 ill, pls, bib DLC, MiGr, NN

2490   Hackett, W. H. Decorative Furniture (English and French) of the 16th, 17th and 18th Centuries. Being a history of old furniture, and forming a concise guide to the best- known designs and styles. London: Estates Gazette, 1902. 263pp, ill, 15 pls CU, MB

2491   Harris, Eileen. The Furniture of Robert Adam. London: Tiranti, 1963; reprint. London: Academy Editions; New York: St. Martin's Pr, 1973. 110pp, ill, 155 pls, bib (Adam, 1762-1792)

2492   Harris, John, 1931- , comp. Regency Furniture. Designs from Contemporary Source Books 1803-1826; a collection of pattern-books, including sections from Thomas Sheraton (and others), with various comparative plates of 1744 to 1812. Chicago: Quadrangle; London: Tiranti, 1961. 108pp, ill (Sheraton, Hope, Ackerman, George Smith)

2493   Harris, M., and Sons, firm. Old English Furniture; its designers and craftsmen. London: M. Harris, 1935; 2nd ed. enl. 1938; 3rd ed. 1946. 69pp, ill; 107pp, ill, pls NN, MiGr, DLC

2494   Harrison, John Kirkbride.   A History of English Furniture.
       London: Mills & Boon, 1972. 184pp, ill, bib

2495   Harrison, Molly.   People and Furniture: a social background
       to the English home.   London: Benn; Totowa, NJ: Row-
       man & Littlefield, 1971. 160pp, ill, bib (ca1450-1970)

2496   *Hayden, Arthur.   Chats on Cottage and Farmhouse Furniture,
       with a chapter on old English chintzes by Hugh Phillips.
       New York: F. A. Stokes, 1911; 1912; London: T. Fisher
       Unwin, 1912; 1920; 2nd ed. rev. by Cyril G. E. Bunt, with
       a new chapter on 19th century furniture. New York: A.
       A. Wyn; London: Benn, 1950. 350pp, ill, 73 pls (17th,
       18th and 19th century. Includes ironwork and kitchen tools,
       etc.) DeWint, MOF, NN, MiGr

2497   Hayward, Charles Harold.   English Furniture at a Glance; a
       simple review in pictures of the origin and evolution of
       furniture from the 16th to the 18th century.   London:
       Architectural Pr, 1924; London; New York: Putnam, 1925.
       106pp, 100 ill MiGr

2498   * _____ .   English Period Furniture: an account of the evolu-
       tion of furniture from 1500-1850.   London: Evans, 1936;
       Philadelphia: Lippincott, 1949?; London: 1957; new enl.
       ed. London: 1966; New York: Arco, 1968; New York:
       Scribner, 1971. 229pp, ill; 245pp, ill; 263pp, ill; 271pp,
       ill, 16 pls

2499   Hayward, Helena.   Thomas Johnson and English Rococo.   Lon-
       don: Tiranti, 1964. 112pp, ill, 34 pls

2500   Hayward, John Forrest.   Chests of Drawers and Commodes in
       the Victoria and Albert Museum.   London: HMSO, 1960.
       44pp, ill, pls

2501   _____ , comp.   English Cabinets in the Victoria and Albert
       Museum.   London: HMSO, 1964; rev. ed. with added
       material by Phillis Rogers, as English Cabinets.   London:
       HMSO, 1972. 81pp, 34pp of ill (ca1600 to ca1900)

2502   _____ .   English Desks and Bureaux.   V & A.   London:
       HMSO, 1968. 22pp, ill, 40 pls (Portable desks to li-
       brary tables, 16th-19th century)

2503   _____ .   Tables in the V & A Museum.   London: HMSO,
       1961. 18pp, ill, 53 pls

2504   *Heal, Sir Ambrose, 1872- .   The Condon Furniture Makers
       from the Restoration to the Victorian Era, 1600-1840: a
       record of 2500 cabinet-makers, upholsterers, carvers
       and gilders, with their addresses and working dates,

illustrated by 165 reproductions of makers' tradecards; with chapters by R. W. Symonds on the problems of iden- tification of the furniture they produced.... London: Batsford, 1953; reprint. New York: Dover, 1972. 276pp, ill, bib

2505 Heaton, John Aldam, ed. Furniture and Decoration in Eng- land During the 18th Century. 2 vols in 4. London: John Bumpus, 1888; London: 1889-92. 200 facsim. pls from Chippendale, Adam, George Richardson, Hepplewhite, Sheraton, Pergolesi, etc. DeWint, MB, BM, MiGr

2506 *Hepplewhite, A(lice), and Co. The Cabinet-Maker and Up- holster's Guide; or, Repository of Designs for every article of household furniture, in the newest and most approved taste, by George Hepplewhite. London: 1788; 1789; 3rd ed. 1794; facsimile reprint from 3rd ed. London: Bats- ford, 1897; reprint with Supplement by Walter Rendell Storey. New York: Towse, 1942; reprint of 1794 ed. with pref. by Ralph Edwards. London: Tiranti, 1947; 1955; reprint with new introd. by Joseph Aronson. New York: Dover, 1969. 1788: 126 pls; 1789: 127 pls; 1897: 128 pls (Originally published by Hepplewhite's widow, Alice) MB, PPL, MiGr

2507 Hewitt, Linda. Chippendale and All the Rest, Some Influences on 18th Century English Furniture. New York: A. S. Barnes, 1974. 161pp, ill, bib

2508 Hildesley, Percival T. English Furniture Designs. Fore. by H. P. Shapland. London: Benn, 1923. 87pp, ill, scale drawings DLC, MiGr

2509 Hinckley, F. Lewis. A Directory of Queen Anne, Early Georgian, and Chippendale Furniture; establishing the pre- eminence of the Dublin craftsmen. New York: Crown, 1971. 277pp, 467 ill

2510 *History of English Furniture. V & A. London: HMSO, 1955. 26pp, 52 pls, bib

2511 Honour, Hugh. Cabinet Makers and Furniture Designers. London: Weidenfeld & Nicolson; New York: Putnam, 1969; Feltham: Spring Books, 1972. 320pp, 266 (35 color) ill, bib (1540-1957)

2512 Howard, Stanley. Our Furniture Through the Ages. London: Estates Gazette, 1950. 332pp, ill

2513 Hughes, Therle. Old English Furniture. London: Lutter- worth, 1949; New York: McBride, 1950; rev. ed. London: 1962; New York: Macmillan, 1963; New York: Praeger, 1969. 201pp, ill, 50 pls (To 1830)

2514 _____ . The Pocket Book of Furniture.   Feltham: Country
Life, 1968.   416pp, ill, bib

2515 Hunt, Thomas Frederick.   Examplars of Tudor Architecture,
adapted to modern habitations, with illustrative details selected from ancient edifices; and observations on the furniture of the Tudor Period.   London: Longman, Rees,
Orme, Brown, Green, & Longman, 1830; 1836; London:
Bohn, 1841; 1846.   200pp, 37 pls   IU, MH, NN, MiGr

2516 Hunter, Edmund.   The Story of Furniture.   Loughborough:
Wills & Hepworth, 1971.   52pp, 24 color ill   (Juvenile
literature.   To 1970)

2517 *Hurrell, John Weymouth.   Measured Drawings of Old Oak
English Furniture, also of some remains of architectural
woodwork, plasterwork, metalwork, glazing, etc.   London:
Batsford, 1902.   4pp, 110 pls   (Chiefly domestic and ecclesiastical)   MIU, MB, MiGr

2518 Hurt, Frederick C., and H. Nalder.   A Synopsis of English
Furniture from 1509 to 1820.   London: H. Nalder, 1928.
BM

2519 *Ince, William, fl.1762?, and John Mayhew.   The Universal
System of Household Furniture ... 300 designs in the most
elegant taste, both useful and ornamental ... English and
French.   London: Robert Sayer, 1759-1762; reprint with
pref. by Ralph Edwards.   Chicago: Quadrangle; London:
Tiranti, 1960.   11pp, 101 pls (Reprint has bib)   DLC, BM

2520 Jervis, Simon.   A Tortoiseshell Cabinet and Its Precursors.
Reprint from the Bulletin.   V & A.   London: HMSO, 1975.

2521 Joel, David.   The Adventure of British Furniture, 1851-1951.
London: Benn, 1953; rev. ed. as Furniture Design Set
Free: the British furniture revolution from 1851 to present
day.   London: Dent, 1969.   256pp, ill, pls; 108pp, ill,
128 pls

2522 Jones, Arthur J., Son and Co.   Description of a Suite of
Sculptured, Decorative Furniture, illustrative of Irish
history and antiquities, manufactured of Irish bog yew;
designed and executed by Arthur J. Jones, Son & Co.,
Dublin.   Dublin: Hodges, 1853- .   12pp, 7 pls   IU,
NNC-Ave, DeWint

2523 Jones, Barbara Mildred.   English Furniture at a Glance.
London: Architectural Pr; New York: Praeger, 1954;
rev. ed.   London: 1971.   96pp, ill; 100pp, ill   (1500 to
1920s)

2524 Jonquet, A.   Original Sketches for Art Furniture in the

Jacobean, Queen Anne, Adam, and other styles. London:
Batsford, 1879; 2nd ed. 1880.   60 pls; 2pp, 65 pls. MiGr,
DLC, MB

2525 *Jourdain, Margaret. Regency Furniture, 1795-1830. London:
Country Life; New York: Scribners, 1934; rev. enl. ed.
London; New York: 1948; 1949; rev. enl. ed. by Ralph
Fastnedge. London: Country Life, 1965. 111pp, ill;
188pp, ill; 116pp, 250 ill, bib

2526 _____ . Scottish Enterprise Furniture. Edinburgh: Scottish Commission of the Council of Industrial Design, 1947.
16pp (Includes history)

2527 _____ . Stuart Furniture at Knole. Rev. by F. M. Mason.
London: Country Life, 1952. 48pp, ill (Knole Park,
Sevenoaks, England)

2528 _____ , and F. Rose. English Furniture: the Georgian
period (1750-1830). Fore. by Ralph Edwards. London:
Batsford, 1953. 210pp, ill, bib (Companion to English
Interior Decoration, 1500-1830)

2529 Joy, Edward Thomas. Antique English Furniture. London:
Ward Lock; New York: Drake, 1972. 192pp, ill, pls,
bib (ca1600-1860)

2530 _____ . The Book of English Furniture (or The Country
Life Book ...). London: Country Life, 1964; South
Brunswick, NJ: A. S. Barnes, 1966. 104pp, 136 ill

2531 _____ . Chippendale. London; New York; Toronto; Sydney:
Hamlyn for Country Life, 1971. 63pp, ill

2532 _____ . English Furniture, A.D. 43 to 1950. London:
Batsford, 1962. 84pp, 199 ill

2533 Kenworthy-Browne, John Anthony. Chippendale and His Contemporaries. London: Orbis, 1973. 64pp, chiefly ill,
bib (1740-1800)

2534 King, Thomas, furniture pattern-drawer. The Cabinet Maker's
Sketch Book of Plain and Useful Designs. Volume I, chair
and sofa work; Volume II, Cabinet work generally. London: n.d. (ca1840). ill SKM

2535 _____ . Illustrations of Fashionable Cabinet Furniture.
London: Architectural & Scientific Library, 184-? 6pp,
61 designs on 33 pls NN

2536 _____ . King's Designs for Cabinet Makers and Upholsterers. London: 1835? (n.t.p.) 50 color pls MiGr

2537 _____. The Modern Style of Cabinet Work Exemplified
... Improved. London: Author, 1829; 2nd ed. 1832; 2nd
ed. with additions. London: H. G. Bohn, 1862. 5pp, 72
pls with 227 designs (part color) MiGr, DeWint, PU,
NNC-Ave

2538 _____. Original Designs for Cabinet Furniture. London:
Author, 1850? 42 pls (part color) MiGr, MdBP

2539 _____. Specimens of Furniture, in the Elizabethan and
Louis Quatorze Styles. London: n. d. (mid-19th century)
ill SKM

2540 _____. Supplementary Plates to the Work Entitled The
Modern Style of Cabinet Work Exemplified. The supplementary plates consist entirely of new designs ... being
articles of cabinet furniture of a description not contained
in the first work, and are added to complete the collection.
London: Author, 1834? 8pp, 28 pls (part color)

2541 *Laking, Guy Francis. The Furniture of Windsor Castle.
Published by command of His Majesty King Edward VII.
London: Bradbury, Agnew, 1905. 20pp, well-ill, 47
pls NNC-Ave, MiGr, PPPM

2542 Layton, Edwin J. Thomas Chippendale, a Review of His Life
and Origin. London: John Murray, 1928. 61pp MiGr

2543 *Lenygon, Francis Henry. Furniture in England from 1660 to
1760. London: Batsford; New York: Scribner, 1914;
London: 1915; 1920; 2nd rev. ed. London: 1924. 300pp,
ill, pls ("The actual writing of this work has been attributed to Margaret Jourdain." Library of Congress.) MiGr,
TxU, NN

2544 Light, Charles, and Robert Light. Designs and Catalogue of
Cabinet and Upholstery Furniture, Looking-Glasses, etc.
London: C. & R. Light, wholesale manufacturers, 1880.
435pp, ill BM

2545 Loan Exhibition of Furniture of the Gothic and Early Tudor
Periods. Luton, Eng: Public Museum, 1936. 16pp

2546 Lock, Matthew (or Matthias). Original Designs for Furniture.
1740 to 1765. London: 1863. ill SKM

2547 _____. Six Tables. London: 1746. 6 pls

2548 Lockwood, Luke Vincent, 1872-1951. A Collection of English
Furniture of the 17th and 18th Centuries. New York:
Robert Grier Cooke for Tiffany Studios, 1907. 479pp, ill
(This collection was made by Thomas B. Clarke, 1848-
1931)

2549   London Book of Prices for the Portable Desk Makers and
       Cabinet Small-Workers.   London: September 1, 1806.
       BM

2550   London Cabinet-Makers' Book of Prices, for the most im-
       proved extensible dining tables, with illustrative engrav-
       ings.   London: 1815; London: printed for a Committee
       of Masters and Journeymen, 1821.   ill MiGr

2551   London Cabinet-Makers' Book of Prices, for work not pro-
       vided in the Union Book, by a Committee.   London: 1831.
       BM

2552   The London Cabinet-Makers' Union Book of Prices.   London:
       Committee of Masters and Journeymen, Cabinet Makers'
       Union, 1811; 2nd ed. London: Stephen Couchman, 1824;
       3rd ed. 3 vol. London: 1831-46.   BM

2553   London Society of Cabinet-Makers' London Book of Prices
       and Designs of Cabinet-Work, calculated for the con-
       venience of cabinet-makers in general, whereby the price
       of executing any piece of work may be easily found ...
       containing ... various designs intended as a guide towards
       the prices. 3rd ed. with additions. London: C. Barber,
       1803; supplement by George Atkinson and William Somer-
       ville. London: 1805. MiGr

2554   Loudon, John Claudius, 1783-1843.   An Encyclopedia of Cot-
       tage, Farm, and Villa Architecture and Furniture.   2 vol.
       London: 1833; new ed. London: Longman, Rees, Orme,
       Brown..., 1835; new ed. ed. by Mrs. Loudon. London:
       F. Warne, 1844; as Cottage, Farm and Villa Architecture
       ... etc. New York: Scribner, Welford & Armstrong,
       1846?; New York: R. Worthington, 1883. 1138pp, 100
       lithographs, 2000 engravings, bib; 1846: 1317pp, ill DLC

2555   Loudon Furniture Designs, from the Encyclopedia of Cottage,
       Farmhouse and Villa Architecture and Furniture, 1839.
       Introd. by Christopher Gilbert. East Ardsley, Yorkshire:
       S. R. Publishers; London: Connoisseur, 1970. 135pp,
       ill

2556   McBride, Robert Medill, ed.   Furnishing with Antiques.
       New York: McBride, 1939. 112pp, ill MiGr

2557   Macdonald-Taylor, Margaret Stephens.   English Furniture
       from the Middle Ages to Modern Times. London: Evans
       Brothers, 1965; New York: Putnam, 1966. 299pp, ill,
       pls, bib

2558   _____ . Furniture.   London: Oxford U. Pr, 1961. 95pp,
       ill, bib

2559   Macnaghten, Patrick. Beginner's Guide to Collecting Antique
       Furniture. London: Pelham; New York: Hippocrene,
       1973. 153pp, ill, 16 pls (To 1900)

2560   Macquoid, Percy. English Furniture, Tapestry and Needle-
       work of the 16th to 19th Centuries. (Record of Lady Lever
       Art Gallery Collection.) London: Batsford, 1928. 155pp,
       116 pls

2561 *   . A History of English Furniture. The age of oak,
       1500-1660; the age of walnut, 1660-1720; the age of ma-
       hogany, 1720-1770; the age of satinwood, 1770-1820. 4
       vols. London; New York: Lawrence & Bullen, and Put-
       nam's, 1904-08; reprint. New York: Dover, 1972. 215
       ill, 15 color pls; 243 ill, 15 color pls; 254 ill, 15 color
       pls; 243 ill, 15 color pls (Pioneer work, now partly out
       of date because of modern research)

2562 *   , and Ralph Edwards. The Dictionary of English
       Furniture, from the Middle Ages to the Late Georgian
       Period. 3 vol. London: Country Life; New York:
       Scribner's, 1924-27; 2nd ed. rev. & enl. by Ralph Ed-
       wards. 3 vol. London: 1954. ill, 51 color pls; 3000
       ill, 43 color pls

2563   Malim, Margaret F. Old English Wood-Carving Patterns,
       from Oak Furniture of the Jacobean Period.... London:
       Batsford; New York: John Lane, 1906. 4pp, ill, 20 pls
       MiGr, DLC

2564   Mallett, W. E., furniture dealer. An Introduction to Old
       English Furniture. London: G. Newnes; New York:
       Scribner's, 1905; 1915. 144pp, 168 ill (Tudor period to
       ca1820) MB, MiGr

2565 *Marshall, Arthur. Specimens of Antique Carved Furniture
       and Woodwork, Measured and Drawn. London: W. H.
       Allen, 1888. 7pp, ill, 50 pls (15th to 18th century)
       NN, MiGr

2566   Marven, George, and Henry J. Story. Designs of Furniture.
       London: 1865. ill BM

2567 *Marx, Phyllis Emily, and Margaret Stephens Taylor. Mea-
       sured Drawings of English Furniture (The Oak Period)....
       London: E. Benn, 1931. 85pp, ill NN, MiGr

2568   Meyrick, Sir Samuel Rush, 1783-1848. Specimens of Ancient
       Furniture Drawn from Existing Authorities by Henry Shaw,
       with Descriptions. London: W. Pickering, 1836; London:
       Henry G. Bohn, 1866. 57pp, ill, 74 pls (part color)
       (Earliest period to Queen Anne. From English collections)
       TxU, NNC-Ave, MiGr

2569 *Musgrave, Clifford. Adam and Hepplewhite and Other Neo-
classical Furniture. London: Faber; New York: Taplinger, 1966. 223pp, ill, 177 (4 color) pls, bib (1760-
1820)

2570 _____. Regency Furniture, 1800-1830. London: Faber,
1961; New York: Yoseloff, 1962; 2nd rev. ed. London:
1970. 157pp, ill, 100 pls, bib

2571 *Nicholson, Peter, and Michael Angelo Nicholson. The Practical Cabinet-Maker, Upholsterer and Complete Decorator.
Parts 1-4 only. London: H. Fisher, 1826; 1843; facism.
reprint of 1826 ed. with new introd. by Christopher Gilbert. (Omits pp. 11-152 on Geometry) Wakefield: E P
Publishing, 1973. 152pp, 101 pls (some color); 1973:
12pp, 81 pls, bib DLC, BM

2572 Nickerson, David. English Furniture of the 18th Century.
New York: Putnam; London: Weidenfeld & Nicolson,
1963; as English Furniture. London: Octopus, 1973.
128pp, ill; 96pp, ill

2573 Ogden, William Sharp. Sketches of Antique Furniture Taken
from 80 Examples, Not Hitherto Illustrated, of Chiefly
17th Century English Carved Oak. London: Batsford;
London; Manchester: J. Heywood, 1888. ill ("The adoption of the word antique as a generic term for old furniture dates from" this book of drawings. Antiques, February 1956.)

2574 *Percival, MacIver. The Oak Collector, a guide to the collection of old oak and simple cottage furniture. London:
H. Jenkins; New York: Dodd, Mead, 1925. 282pp, ill,
31 pls, bib (V & A collection) NN

2575 *_____. Old English Furniture and Its Surroundings, from
the Restoration to the Regency. London: W. Heinemann;
New York: Scribner's, 1920. 208pp, ill, pls MiGr

2576 *_____. The Walnut Collector. London: H. Jenkins; New
York: Dodd, Mead, 1927. 294pp, ill, 31 pls NN

2577 Pollen, John Hungerford. Ancient and Modern Furniture and
Woodwork in the South Kensington Museum. London:
Chapman & Hall, 1874; New York: Scribner's, 1876;
rev. by T. A. Lehfeldt. London: HMSO, 1908. 143pp,
15 photographs, 42 woodcuts, color frontis NNC-Ave, BM

2578 _____. Catalogue of a Special Loan Collection of English
Furniture and Figured Silks Manufactured in the 17th and
18th Centuries. South Kensington Museum. London:
HMSO, 1896. 145pp

2579 _____. Furniture and Woodwork. London: 1876. See: Bevan, G. P., British Manufacturing Industries, Vol. 7.

2580 Portable Desk-Makers and Cabinet Small-Workers. Book of Prices. London: The Company, September 1, 1806. BM

2581 *Pugin, Augustus Charles. Modern Furniture from Designs by A. Pugin, J. Stafford of Bath, and others. London: M. A. Nattali, 1823. 52pp, 44 pls (Also issued by Acker- mann as Fashionable Furniture)

2582 Pugin, Augustus Welby Northmore. Gothic Furniture in the Style of the 15th Century. London: R. Ackermann, 1827; 1835. 24 or 26 pls BM, MiGr

2583 *Robinson, Frederick S. English Furniture. London: Methuen, 1905. 363pp, ill, 160 pls, bib (Saxon times to early 19th century) MiGr

2584 *Roe, Frederick Gordon. Ancient Coffers and Cupboards: their history and description from the earliest times to the middle of the 16th century. London: Methuen; New York: Dutton, 1902. 128pp, ill, 24 (2 color) pls MiGr

2585 * _____. Antique English Cottage Furniture. London: Phoenix, 1949; New York: M. McBride, 1950; new ed. rev. & enl. as English Cottage Furniture. London: Phoenix; New York: Roy Publishers, 1961. 128pp, 58 ill; 240pp, ill (Early times to late-Victorian)

2586 _____. Old English Furniture from Tudor to Regency.... London: National Magazine Company, 1948. 42pp, ill

2587 _____. Old Oak Furniture. London: Methuen, 1905; Chicago: A. C. McClurg, 1907. 339pp, ill, color frontis (Chiefly English) NN, MiGr

2588 _____. English Period Furniture. An introductory guide. London: Tiranti, 1946. 60pp, ill

2589 *Rogers, John Charles. English Furniture, Its Essentials and Characteristics Simply and Clearly Explained for the Stu- dent and Small Collector. Fore. by H. Avray Tipping. London: Country Life and G. Newnes; New York: Scrib- ner's, 1923; enl. & rev. by Margaret Jourdain. London; New York: 1950; rev. ed. London: Country Life, 1959; rev. ed. Feltham: Spring Books, 1967. 187pp, 244pp of pls (1450-early 19th century. Describes construction) MiGr

2590 _____. Modern English Furniture. London: Country Life; New York: Scribner's, 1930. 208pp, pls

2591   Sanders, William Bliss. Half-timbered Houses and Carved
        Oak Furniture of the 16th and 17th Centuries. London:
        Bernard Quaritch, 1894. 51pp, 30 pls MiGr

2592   Second Edition of Genteel Household Furniture ... containing
        upwards of 350 designs on 120 copper plates. London:
        Society of Upholsterers, Cabinet-Makers, etc., 1780.
        MiGr

2593   Seddon, John Pollard. King Rene's Honeymoon Cabinet.
        Illustrated from photographs of the panels painted by D.
        G. Rossetti, Sir Edward Burne-Jones, Ford Madox Brown,
        etc. London: Batsford, 1898. 16pp, ill NNC-Ave

2594   A Series, Containing 44 Engravings in Colours, of Fashionable
        Furniture; consisting of beds, sofas, ottomans, window-
        curtains, chairs, tables, book-cases, etc. London: R.
        Ackermann, 1823. 52pp, 44 color pls

2595   Shapland, Henry Percival. A Key to English Furniture. Lon-
        don; Glasgow: Blackie, 1938. 202pp, ill, 16 pls, bib
        MiGr

2596   *Shaw, Henry. Specimens of Ancient (or Famous) Furniture,
        drawn from existing authorities, with descriptions by Sir
        Samuel R. Meyrick. London: Pickering, 1836; London:
        Henry G. Bohn, 1866. 57pp, ill, 74 pls (11 color, al-
        though some special copies have all 74 plates colored)
        (Elizabethan & Jacobean) MiGr

2597   Shearer, Thomas. The Cabinet-Maker's London Book of
        Prices. London: 1788. ill SIB-1

2598   _____. Designs for Household Furniture. London: 1788.
        19pp, ill DKM

2599   Sheraton, Thomas, 1750-1806. The Cabinet Dictionary ...
        containing an explanation of all the terms used in the
        cabinet and upholstery branches.... London: W. Smith,
        1803; 2 vol. with new introd. by Wilford P. Cole, and
        Charles F. Montgomery. New York: Praeger, 1970.
        440pp, 88 pls NNC-Ave, BM

2600   _____. The Cabinet-Maker and Upholsterer's Drawing
        Book. 3 parts in 2 vol. London: Author, 1791-1793.
        Appendix.... London: 1793; Accompaniment.... London:
        n.d. (1794?); 3rd rev. ed. London: T. Bensley, 1802;
        facsimile reprint. Rev. & ed. by J. Munro Bell. Includes
        Appendix and Accompaniment. 1 vol. London: Gibbings,
        1895; reprint with new introd. by Joseph Aronson, of works
        between 1793 & 1802. New York: Dover, 1973. 65 pls;
        33 pls; 14 pls; 121 pls

2601 _____. Designs for Household Furniture Exhibiting a
Variety of Elegant and Useful Patterns in the Cabinet,
Chair, and Upholstery Branches. London?: 1812; re-
printed by J. Munro Bell, 1900. BM

2602 _____. Examples of Furniture and Decoration, containing
a selection of 167 typical specimens reproduced, on 16
plates, from his rare "Cabinet-Maker and Upholsterer's
Drawing Book" published 1791-1802. London: Batsford,
1906. MiGr

2603 A Short History of English Furniture. Introd. by Ralph Edwards. V & A. London: HMSO, 1966. 32pp, ill, 100
pls, bib (13th-late 19th century)

2604 Siddons, G. A. The Cabinet-Makers Guide. 5th augmented
ed. London: 1830. BM

2605 Simon, Constance. English Furniture Designers of the 18th
Century. Philadelphia: George W. Jacobs, 1904; London:
Batsford, 1905. 216pp, ill, pls (Includes Matthais Darly;
Chippendale school; Adam school; Harewood House, York-
shire; Stourhead, Bath; Rowton Castle, Salop; Hepplewhite
school; etc.) NN, MB, MiGr

2606 Singleton, Esther. French and English Furniture. New York:
McClure, Phillips, 1903. 394pp, ill, 68 pls (Louis 13
to Sheraton)

2607 Smith, Bernard E. Designs and Sketches for Furniture in the
Neo-Jacobean and Other Styles. London: Author, 1876;
Boston: 1877. ill MiGr, MB

2608 Stafford, Maureen. British Furniture Through the Ages.
Introd. by Robert Keith Middlemas. London: Barker;
New York: Coward-McCann, 1966. 112pp, ill

2609 The Story of English Furniture. Five centuries of craftsmanship. London; Maidstone: Greenly's, 1950. 27pp, ill

2610 *Symonds, Robert Wemyss. English Furniture from Charles 2
to George 2. A full account of the design, material and
quality of workmanship of walnut and mahogany furniture
of this period; and of how spurious specimens are made
... from collection of Percival D. Griffiths. London:
Connoisseur; New York: International Studio, 1929.
322pp, 259 ill, 4 color pls MiGr

2611 _____. English Furniture; a reader's guide. London:
Cambridge U. Pr, 1948; 2nd ed. London; New York:
Cambridge U. Pr, for National Book League, 1951. 19pp
(Includes 12pp of essay "English Furniture.") DLC, NNC-
Ave

2612 *   . Furniture Making in 17th and 18th Century Eng-
          land; an outline for collectors. London: Connoisseur,
          1955. 238pp, ill, 4 color pls

2613 *   . Masterpieces of English Furniture and Clocks; a
          study of walnut and mahogany furniture and of the asso-
          ciated crafts of the looking-glass maker and japanner, to-
          gether with an account of Thomas Tompion and other fa-
          mous clockmakers of the 17th and 18th century. London:
          Batsford, 1940. 172pp, 130 ill, 8 color pls

2614 *   . Old English Walnut and Lacquer Furniture. The
          present-day condition and value, and methods of the furni-
          ture-faker in producing spurious pieces. Fore. by Perci-
          val D. Griffiths. London: H. Jenkins; New York: 1923.
          176pp, ill, 65 pls

2615 *   . The Present State of Old English Furniture. New
          York: F. A. Stokes; London: Duckworth, 1921. 132pp,
          116 ill, 56 pls (1453-1807) MiGr

2616 *   . Veneered Walnut Furniture, 1660-1760. London:
          Alec Tiranti, 1946. 32pp, 52 pls MiGr

2617 *   , and Thomas Hamilton Ormsbee. Antique Furniture
          of the Walnut Period. New York: R. M. McBride, 1947.
          144pp, ill MiGr

2618 Tallboy (pseud.). Tallboy's Illustrated Table Showing the
          History of English Furniture and the Principal Characteris-
          tics of Period Furniture. Surbition: Tallboy's, 1928. BM

2619 Thomson, P. The Cabinet Maker's Sketch Book; a series of
          original details for modern furniture. Glasgow; Edinburgh:
          W. Mackensie, 1852-53. 45pp, 97 pls BM, DLC

2620 *Tipping, Henry Avray. English Furniture of the Cabriole
          Period. Boston: Small, Maynard; London: Cape, 1922.
          79pp, ill, 32 pls, bib (First half of 18th century) MiGr

2621 *   . Old English Furniture, its true value and function,
          being two lectures delivered at Messrs. Waring and Gil-
          low's on June 11 and 14th, 1928. London: Country Life,
          for Waring & Gillow, 1928. 24pp, pls MiGr

2622 Toller, Jane. Country Furniture. Newton Abbot: David &
          Charles, 1973; as English Country Furniture. South Bruns-
          wick, NJ: A. S. Barnes, 1973. 200pp, ill, pls, bib
          (1690-1840. Includes children's furniture)

2623 Tomlin, Maurice. Catalogue of Adam Period Furniture,
          V & A. London: HMSO, 1972. 207pp, ill, bib (1760-
          1800)

2624 _____ . English Furniture: an illustrated handbook. London: Faber, 1972. 180pp, ill, 128 pls, bib

2625 Town and Country Furniture: an exhibition ... illustrating the vernacular tradition. Temple Newsam, Stable Court Exhibition Galleries. July-August 1972. Leeds: the Galleries, 1972. 64pp, ill (To 1920)

2626 Turland, Frank. Furniture in England. London: Black, 1962. 64pp, 176 ill (Juvenile literature)

2627 Twiston-Davies, Sir Leonard, and Herbert Johnes Lloyd-Johnes. Welsh Furniture: an introduction. Cardiff: University of Wales, 1950. 55pp, ill, 72 pls

2628 Walton, Karin-M., comp. The Golden Age of English Furniture Upholstery, 1660-1840. Exhibition. Stable Court Exhibition Galleries. August-September 1973. Leeds: Temple Newsam House, 1973. 58pp, ill, bib

2629 *Ward-Jackson, Peter. English Furniture Designs of the 18th Century. V & A. London: HMSO, 1958. 68pp, 366 ill, 280 pls (Designs of 30 craftsmen)

2630 Waring, John Burley. Examples of Decorative Art in Furniture, selected from the Royal and other collections. London: Day, 1870. ill MiGr

2631 *Warne, E. J. Furniture Mouldings; full size sections of moulded details on English furniture from 1574 to 1820. Introd. by H. P. Shapland. London: E. Benn, 1923. 140pp of ill MiGr

2632 Watt, William. Art Furniture from Designs of E. W. Godwin, etc., with hints and suggestions on domestic furniture. London: Batsford, 1877. 20 pls BM

2633 Wells, Percy A., and John Hooper. Modern Cabinetwork, Furniture and Fitments: an account of the theory and practice in the production of all kinds of cabinetwork and furniture, with chapters on the growth and progress of design and construction.... London: Batsford, 1909; New York: John Lane, 1910; rev. ed. Philadelphia: Lippincott, 1918. 384pp, 1000 ill, 48 pls, bib, gloss NNC-Ave

2634 Wells-Cole, Anthony, comp. Oak Furniture from Lancashire and the Lake District. Exhibition. Stable Court Exhibition Galleries. September-October 1973. Leeds: Temple Newsam House, 1973. 29pp, ill, bib (ca1500 to 1742)

2634a Welsh Furniture from Tudor to Georgian Times. Exhibition.

May-September 1936.   Cardiff: National Museum of Wales,
1936.   28pp

2635 *Wenham, Edward.   The Collector's Guide to Furniture Design
(English and American) from the Gothic to the 19th Cen-
tury ... and showing the evolution of modern styles.   New
York: Collectors Pr, 1928.   382pp, ill   NN

2636 _____.   Old Furniture for Modern Rooms.   From the
Restoration to the Regency.   London: G. Bell, 1939; new
ed. London: Spring Books, 1964.   204pp, ill, 8 pls, bib;
198pp, ill, pls, bib

2637 [No entry.]

2638 *Wheeler, George Owen.   Old English Furniture of the 17th
and 18th Centuries; a guide for the collector.   With many
beautiful illustrations of representative pieces, and a
record of prices realized at auction.   London: Upcott
Gill; New York: Scribner's, 1907; 2nd ed. enl. as Old
English Furniture from the 16th to the 19th Centuries; a
guide for the collector.   London: Gill, 1909; 3rd ed.
"practically re-written, " as Old English Furniture of the
15th, 16th, 17th and 18th Centuries ... a guide....   London: Bazaar House, 1924.   480pp, ill, 8 pls; 748pp, ill,
pls; 617pp, ill, pls   MiGr

2639 Whitaker, Henry.   The Practical Cabinet Maker and Uphol-
sterer's Treasury of Designs, housefurnishing and deco-
rating assistant, in the Grecian, Italian, Renaissance,
Louis-Quatorze, Gothic, Tudor, and Elizabethan styles....
Parts 1-27. London: P. Jackson, 1847.   16pp, 110 pls
(Includes designs for Royal palaces, etc.)   BM

2640 Wileman, Edgar Harrison.   Early English Furniture.   Los
Angeles: Author, 1930.   8pp, ill   MiGr

2641 Williamson, George Charles, ed.   Handbooks of the Great
Craftsmen.   London: G. Bell, 1901- .

2642 Wills, Geoffrey.   Craftsmen and Cabinet-Makers of Classic
English Furniture.   Edinburgh: J. Bartholomew, 1974;
New York: St. Martin's, 1976.   136pp, ill, bib (1550-
1850)

2643 _____.   English Furniture, 1550-1760.   Enfield, Middlesex: Guinness Superlatives; Garden City, NY: Doubleday,
1971.   256pp, ill, bib

2644 _____.   English Furniture, 1760-1900.   Enfield: Guinness
Superlatives; Garden City, NY: Doubleday, 1971.   256pp,
ill, 4 pls, bib

2645   Wolsey, Samuel Wilfred, and R. W. P. Luft.   Furniture in
       England: the Age of the Joiner.   London: Barker, 1968;
       New York: Praeger, 1969.   105pp, 123 ill, 65 pls, bib
       (1550-1660)

2646   Wood, Henry, furniture designer.   A Useful and Modern Work
       on Cheval and Pole Screens, Ottomans, Chairs and Settees,
       for Mounting Berlin Needle Work.   London: Ackermann,
       1846.   colored ill   MiGr

2647   Woodforde, John.   The Observer's Book of Furniture from
       Tudor to Victorian Times.   London; New York: Warne,
       1964.   224pp, ill   (1603-1895)

2648   Yarwood, Doreen.   The English Home; a 1000 years of furni-
       ture and decoration.   London: Batsford; New York:
       Scribner, 1956.   393pp, ill

SPANISH AND PORTUGUESE FURNITURE

2649   Beckwith, John.   Caskets from Cordoba.   V & A.   London:
       HMSO, 1960.   72pp, ill, bib   (Carved wood)

2650   Burr, Grace Hardendorff.   Hispanic Furniture, from the 15th
       Through the 18th Century.   New York: Hispanic Society
       of America, 1941; 2nd ed. rev. & enl.   New York: Archive
       Pr, 1964.   231pp, ill, bib; 240pp, ill, bib

2651   *Byne, Arthur, and Mildred Stapley.   Spanish Interiors and
       Furniture: photographs and drawings.   2 vol.   New York:
       W. Helburn, 1921, 1925; New York; 1928; reprint.   1 vol.
       New York: Dover, 1969.   22pp, ill, 300 pls; reprint:
       326pp, 300 ill   MiGr, BM

2652   Domenech Gallisa, Rafael, and Luis Perez Bueno.   Antique
       Spanish Furniture.   Tr. from Spanish by Grace Harden-
       dorff Burr.   Bilingual ed. New York: Archive Pr, 1965.
       142pp, ill, 61 pls

2653   *Eberlein, Harold Donaldson, and Roger Wearne Ramsdell.
       The Practical Book of Italian, Spanish and Portuguese
       Furniture.   Philadelphia; London: Lippincott, 1927.
       254pp, 373 ill on 144 pls, color frontis   MiGr

2654   Emerson, William Ralph, 1833- .   The Architecture and
       Furniture of the Spanish Colonies During the 17th and 18th
       Centuries, including Mexico, Cuba, Porto Rico, and the
       Philippines.   Boston: G. H. Polley, 1901; 1902.   2pp,
       70 pls in folio   CU, NNC-Ave

2655   Peris, Nieves.   The Furniture of Antonio Gaudi.   Exhibition

of photographs. October-November 1973. New York:
Hastings Gallery of Spanish Institute, 1973. (Gaudi, 1852-
1926)

ITALIAN FURNITURE

2656 Albertolli, Professor Giacando, 1742-1839. The Architecture,
      Decoration and Furniture of the Royal Palaces of Milan.
      Reprint. New York: n.d. 36 pls in portfolio

2657 Bode, Wilhelm von. Italian Renaissance Furniture. Tr. by
      Mary E. Herrick. New York: Helburn, 1921. 48pp,
      134 ill, 71 pls

2658 *Eberlein, Harold Donaldson, and Roger Wearne Ramsdell.
      The Practical Book of Italian, Spanish, and Portuguese
      Furniture. Philadelphia; London: Lippincott, 1927. 254pp,
      373 ill on 144 pls, color frontis MiGr

2659 *Odom, William MacDougal. A History of Italian Furniture
      from the 14th to the Early 19th Century. 2 vol. Garden
      City, NY: Doubleday, Page, 1918, 1919; 2nd ed. New
      York: Archive Pr, 1966. ill (Standard work) DLC

2660 Pedrini, Augusto. Italian Furniture: interiors and decoration
      of the 15th and 16th centuries. New rev. ed. of Italian
      work. London: Tiranti, 1949. 256pp, ill MiGr

2661 Robinson, John Charles. Notice of Works of Medieval and
      Renaissance Sculpture, Decorative Furniture, etc., ac-
      quired in Italy, in the early part of the year 1859, for
      the South Kensington Museum. London: HMSO, 1860.
      BM

FRENCH FURNITURE

2662 Apra, Nietta. Empire Style, 1804-1815. Tr. from Italian
      (1970) Lond: Orbis, 1972. 64pp, 105 color illus

2663 _____. The Louis Styles: Louis 14, Louis 15, Louis 16.
      Tr. from Italian (1970). London: Orbis, 1972. 64pp,
      96 color ill (1634 to 1792)

2664 Bajot, Edouard. French Styles in Furniture and Architecture.
      Tr. from French. New York: Paul Wenzel, 189-?; 190-?;
      New York: C. Schenk, 1905? 60 pls, 1500 structural
      and ornamental details Gothic to modern CtY, MiGr

2665 Benn, R. Davis. Style in Furniture. London; New York;
      Bombay: Longmans, Green, 1904; 1910; New York:

Longmans, Green, 1911; London: 1912; London; New York: 1920. 338pp, ill, 102 pls (English and French, 17th to 19th century) MiGr, BM, NN, DLC

2666   Bonney, Mabel Therese, and Louise Bonney. Buying Antique and Modern Furniture in Paris. New York: R. M. McBride, 1929. 69pp, ill, pls

2667   Brackett, Oliver. Catalogue of the Jones Collection. Part I. Furniture (in the South Kensington Museum). London: HMSO, 1922. (18th century French) MiGr

2668   *Dilke, Lady Emilia Francis Strong. French Furniture and Decoration of the 18th Century. London: Bell, 1901. 260pp, ill, pls DLC, MiGr

2669   Dreyfus, Carle. French Furniture, Louis 14th, 15th and 16th periods. The Louvre Museum. Paris: A. Morance; New York: Brentano's, 1921. 56pp, ill, 88 pls, bib MiGr

2670   Dumonthier, Ernest. The Louis 16th Furniture. Chests of drawers, commodes and corner pieces. Mobilier National de France. Paris: Morance, 1922. 14pp, 54 pls MB

2671   Examples of Art Workmanship of Various Ages and Countries. Decorative furniture, French. London: Arundel Society, under sanction of South Kensington Museum, 1871. 8pp, 20 pls

2672   *Felice, Roger de. French Furniture in the Middle Ages and Under Louis 13th. Tr. by F. M. Atkinson. London: Heinemann, 1923; reissued. 1927. 152pp, ill, pls, bib, gloss NN, MiGr, BM

2673   *_____. French Furniture under Louis 14th. Tr. by F. M. Atkinson. London: Heinemann; New York: F. A. Stokes, 1922; reissued. 1927. 148pp, ill, color pls, gloss BM, NN, DeWint, MiGr

2674   *_____. French Furniture under Louis 15th. Tr. by Florence Simmonds. London: Heinemann; New York: F. A. Stokes, 1920; 1927. 132pp, color frontis, 64 pls, bib MB, DLC, MiGr, BM

2675   *_____. French Furniture under Louis 16th and the Empire. Tr. by F. M. Atkinson. London: Heinemann, 1920; New York: F. A. Stokes, 1921. 142pp, 99 ill on 64 pls DSI, NN, MiGr, BM

2676   *_____. Little Illustrated Books on Old French Furniture. 4 vol. See above.

2677   *Fregnac, Claude. French Cabinetmakers of the 18th Century.

Fore. by Pierre Verlet. Paris: Hachette; New York:
French and European Publications, 1965. 341pp, ill, list
of cabinetmakers

2678 French 18th Century Furniture Design: drawings from the
Musee des Arts Decoratifs, Paris. Exhibition. London:
Arts Council, 1960. 51pp, 8 pls

2679 Furniture Designs of a French Cabinet Maker. 2 vol. Paris:
ca1842-47. 381 color pls PBL

2680 Furniture. Plates from "l'Art Pour Tous," 1875. French,
German, English text. 2 vol. Paris: A. Morel, 1875?
76 pls NN, DLC

2681 Grandjean, Serge. Empire Furniture, 1800-1825. London:
Faber; New York: Taplinger, 1966. 120pp, ill, 99 (4
color) pls, bib

2682 Hessling, Egon, ed. Louis 15th Style Furniture in the Louvre.
Tr. from German. 2nd ed. Leipzig: A. Schumann's
Verlag, 1910? 11pp, ill, 28 pls (His work on Louis 16
and Directoire periods apparently not translated into English)

2683 _____, and Waldemar Hessling, ed. Louis 14th Style Furniture Contained in the Louvre and in the Museum of Decorative Arts. Tr. from German. 2nd ed. Leipzig: A. Schumann's Verlag, n.d. (1910?) 9pp, ill, 40 pls (Rococo)
NN

2684 Hinckley, F. Lewis. A Directory of Antique French Furniture,
1735 to 1800; over 300 illustrations of Provincial, Parisian,
and other European Antique furniture. New York: Crown,
1967. 214pp, 364 ill, bib

2685 Huth, Hans. Roentgen Furniture. Abraham and David Roent-
gen: European Cabinet-makers. New York: Sotheby Parke
Bernet, 1974. 260pp, 390 (3 color) ill (Roetgens born in
Germany, workshops in Germany and Paris. 18th century)

2686 Longnon, Henri Auguste, and Frances Wilson Huard. French
Provincial Furniture. Fore. by Richardson Wright. Phila-
delphia; London: Lippincott, 1927. 166pp, 71 ill, pls
DLC, MiGr

2687 Packer, Charles. Antique Paris Furniture by the Master
Ebenistes; a chronologically arranged pictorial review of
furniture by the master meniusiers-ebenistes from Boulle
to Jacob, together with a commentary on the styles and
techniques of the art. Newport, Monmouth, Eng: Ceramic
Book Co., 1956. 104pp, ill, bib (1710-1810)

2688 Ricci, Seymour de. Louis 16th Furniture. New York: Put-
     nam's, 1913; Stuttgart: J. Hoffmann, n.d. 480 ill on
     272 pls DLC, MiGr

2689 Saglio, Andre. French Furniture. New York: Scribner's;
     London: G. Newnes, 1907; London: Batsford, 1913.
     193pp, ill, 60 pls, bib (Earliest times to end of Napoleonic
     era) MiGr, NNC-Ave

2690 Singleton, Esther. French and English Furniture. New York:
     McClure, Phillips, 1903. 394pp, ill, 68 pls (Louis 13th
     to Empire and Jacobean to Sheraton) MiGr

2691 Souchal, Genevieve. French 18th Century Furniture. Tr.
     from French by Simon Watson Taylor. London: Weiden-
     feld & Nicolson; New York: Putnam, 1961. 128pp, 127
     ill

2692 Style Empire: historical furnitures, mostly executed for the
     personal use of Napoleon I and the Empress Josephine.
     New York: Hessling & Spielmeyer, 1895. MiGr

2693 Szabolcsi, Hedvig. French Furniture in Hungary. Tr. by
     Edna Lenart. Budapest: Corvina Pr, 1964. 48pp, ill,
     48 pls (17th and 18th century)

2694 Townsend, W. G. Paulson. Measured Drawings of French
     Furniture, from the collection in South Kensington Museum,
     Science and Art Department. Issued in 12 parts. London;
     New York: Truslove, Hanson & Combs, 1899. 121 pls
     (some color) NNC-Ave, MiGr

2695 Verlet, Pierre. French Royal Furniture; an historical survey
     followed by a study of 40 pieces preserved in Great Britain
     and the United States. Tr. by Michael Bullock. London:
     Barrie & Rockliff, 1963; New York: C. N. Potter, 1964.
     201pp, ill, 67 pls, bib (1663-1784)

2696 Viaux, Jacqueline. French Furniture. Tr. from French
     (1962) by Hazel Paget. New York: Putnam; London:
     Benn, 1964. 200pp, ill, 39 pls (9th century to 4th Re-
     public)

2697 *Watson, Francis John Bagott. Louis 16th Furniture. London:
     Tiranti; New York: Philosophical Library, 1960; London:
     Academy Editions; New York: St. Martin's Pr, 1973.
     162pp, ill, 203 pls, bib (1760-1792)

2698 _____ . French Furniture in the Wallace Collection.
     London: the Collection, 1956. 360pp, ill, 120 pls, bib
     (Catalogue raisonne)

GERMAN AND AUSTRIAN FURNITURE

2699 *Buchwald, Hans H. Form from Process--the Thonet chair;
      an exhibition of historic bentwood furniture from collection
      of John Sailer, Vienna. Fall and Winter 1967. Carpenter
      Center for the Visual Arts, Harvard University. Cam-
      bridge: Harvard U. Pr, 1967. 64pp, ill, bib

2700 The Cabinet Maker's Album; a selection of choice designs in
      rich and plain furniture for the use of cabinet makers and
      upholsterers. Tr. of German work. English, French
      and German. New York: E. Steiger, monthly 1871-1872.
      192pp, ill

2701 Himmelheber, Georg. Biedermeier Furniture. Tr. and ed.
      by Simon Jervis. London: Faber, 1974; New York:
      Scribner, 1975. 115pp, ill, 11 pls, bib (1810-1835.
      German and Austrian)

2702 Huth, Hans. Roentgen Furniture. Abraham and David Roent-
      gen: European cabinet-makers. New York: Sotheby Parke
      Bernet, 1974. 260pp, 390 (3 color) ill (Roentgens born
      in Germany, workshops in Germany and Paris, 18th cen-
      tury)

2703 Peasant Interiors and Peasant Furniture in the Alps. English
      adaptation by Richard Rickett. German, English and French
      text. Innsbruck: Penguin-Verlag; Frankfurt am Main:
      Umschau-Verlag, 1968. 116pp, chiefly ill

2704 Thonet, Gebruder, firm. Thonet Brothers ... inventors,
      manufacturers, and importers of Thonet bentwood furni-
      ture. New York: 1915. 163pp, chiefly ill NNC-Ave

2705 Thonet Furniture, 1830-1953. Exhibition. New York: Mu-
      seum of Modern Art, 1953. ill

FURNITURE OF MISCELLANEOUS COUNTRIES

2706 Atmore, M. G. Cape Furniture. Cape Town, South Africa:
      H. Timmons, 1965. 224pp, ill, pls

2707 Baraitser, Michael, and Anton Obholzer. Cape Country Furni-
      ture; a pictorial survey of regional styles, materials and
      techniques in the Cape Province of South Africa. Introd.
      by Mary Alexander Cook. Cape Town: Balkema, 1971.
      286pp, ill, bib

2708 Barany-Oberschall, Magda. Hungarian Furniture. Budapest:
      Officina Pr, 1939. 28pp, ill, 32 pls MiGr

2709 Clemmensen, Tove. Danish Furniture of the 18th Century.

Tr. from Danish (1945) by John R. B. Gosney. London: Committee of the Exhibition of Danish Art Treasures. Copenhagen: Gyldendal, 1948. 35pp, ill, bib

2710 Craig, Clifford, Kevin Fahy, and E. Graeme Robertson. Early Colonial Furniture in New South Wales and Van Diemen's Land. Melbourne, Aust: Georgian House, 1972. 220pp, ill, bib (New South Wales and Tasmania)

2711 Csillery, Klara K. Hungarian Village Furniture. Budapest: Corvina, 1972. 74pp, 56 pls (19th century benches, chests, sideboards, chairs)

2712 Domanovsky, Gyorgy. Hungarian Peasant Furniture. Budapest: Officina, 1948. 32pp, 32 pls DLC

2713 Dutch Furniture from the 15th to the 17th Century in the National Museum at Amsterdam. New York: Architectural Book Publishing, 19-? 38 mounted pls NNC-Ave

2714 Earnshaw, John. Early Sydney Cabinet-Makers 1804-1870; a directory with an introductory survey. Surry Hills, New South Wales, Aust: Wentworth Books, 1971. 55pp, ill

2715 Heinonen, Jorma. Old Finnish Furniture. Helsinki: 1969. ill

2716 Northcote-Bade, Stanley. Colonial Furniture in New Zealand. Wellington: Reed, 1971. 164pp, ill, bib

2717 Pearse, Geoffrey Eastcott. 18th Century Furniture in South Africa. Pretoria: J. L. Van Schaik, 1960. 193pp, ill, bib

2718 *Ritz, Gislind M. The Art of Painted Furniture. Tr. from German (1970) by Sigrid MacRae. New York; London: Van Nostrand Reinhold, 1970, 1971. 175pp, ill, 52 color pls, bib (of works 99 percent German) (16th century to 1900. Nordic countries, German-speaking countries, including Pennsylvania Dutch, Italy, Spain, Eastern Europe)

2719 Singleton, Esther. Dutch and Flemish Furniture. London: Hodder & Stoughton; New York: McClure, Phillips, 1907. 338pp, ill, 62 pls (Middle Ages to 19th century) MiGr

CANADIAN FURNITURE

2720 Dempsey, Hugh Aylmer. Ethnic Furniture. Calgary: Glenbow-Alberta Institute, 1970. 20pp, ill

2721 Dobson, Henry, and Barbara Dobson. The Early Furniture of Ontario and the Atlantic Provinces. Fore. by Dorothy

Duncan. Toronto: M. F. Feheley, 1975. 188pp, 209
ill

2722 Furniture and Upholstery Journal and Undertakers' Gazette.
Monthly. Toronto: James Acton, 1895- .

2723 Ingolfsrud, Elizabeth. All About Ontario Chests. Don Mills,
Ontario: House of Grant, 1973.

2724 *MacLaren, George E. G. Antique Furniture by Nova Scotian
Craftsmen. Toronto: Ryerson Pr, 1961. 146pp, ill
(To 1900)

2725 _____ . Nova Scotia Furniture. Halifax, N.S.: Petheric
Pr, 1969. 44pp, ill

2726 Minhinnick, Jeanne. Early Furniture in Upper Canada Village,
1800-1837. Toronto: Ryerson, 1964. 43pp, pls (Upper
Canada Village is a restoration)

2727 *Palardy, Jean. The Early Furniture of French Canada. Tr.
from French (1963) by Eric McLean. Toronto: Macmillan,
1963; 2nd ed. rev. Toronto: Macmillan; New York: St.
Martin's, 1965. 413pp, 600 ill, 11 pls, bib

2728 *Ryder, Huia Gwendoline. Antique Furniture by New Brunswick Craftsmen. Toronto: Ryerson, 1965; Toronto; New
York: McGraw Hill-Ryerson, 1973. 180pp, ill, bib,
makers' list (To 1900)

2729 Shackleton, Philip. The Furniture of Old Ontario. Toronto:
Macmillan of Canada, 1973. 399pp, ill

2730 Stevens, Gerald F. Early Ontario Furniture. Toronto:
Royal Ontario Museum, 1966. 16pp, ill, bib

2731 Stewart, Don R. A Guide to Pre-Confederation Furniture of
English Canada. Don Mills, Ontario: Longmans Canada,
1967. 150pp, ill

2732 Symons, Scott. Heritage; a romantic look at early Canadian
furniture. Greenwich, Conn: NY Graphic, 1971. 220pp,
ill, 47 pls

ORIENTAL FURNITURE

2733 Brohier, Richard Leslie. Furniture of the Dutch Period in
Ceylon. Colombo: National Museums of Ceylon Publication, 1969. 38pp, ill, 27 pls

2734 Cescinsky, Herbert. Chinese Furniture, a series of examples

from collections in France. London: Benn, 1922. 20pp,
10 ill, 54 pls NN, DLC, MiGr

2735 Drummond, William. Chinese Furniture. New York: Intercultural Arts Pr, 1969. 35 leaves, with slides

2736 Ecke, Gustav. Chinese Domestic Furniture. 2 vol in 1,
portfolio. Peking: Henri Vetch, 1944; facsimile reprint.
Rutland, Vt: Tuttle, 1963. 49pp, 161pp of ill, measured
drawings, bib (122 pieces) CU, NN, MiGr

2737 Ellsworth, Robert Hatfield. Chinese Furniture. Hardwood
examples of the Ming and early Ch'ing dynasties. New
York: Random House, 1971. 286pp, 151 ill, 31 pls, bib

2738 FitzGerald, Charles Patrick. Barbarian Beds; the origin of
the chair in China. London: Cresset Pr, 1965; South
Brunswick, NJ: A. S. Barnes, 1966. 85pp, ill, 17 pls,
bib (850 to 1100)

2739 Grilli, Elise. The Art of the Japanese Screen. New York:
Weatherhill, 1970; New York; Tokyo: Weatherhill, 1973.
288pp, 159 (48 color) ill (Late 16th to early 18th century)

2740 Kates, George Norbert. Chinese Household Furniture, from
examples selected and measured by Caroline F. Bieber,
and Beatrice Kates. New York; London: Harper, 1948;
reprint. New York: Dover, 197-? 125pp, ill, 112 pls,
bib; 205pp, 123 ill, bib NNC-Ave, MiGr

2741 Stone, Louise Hawley. The Chair in China. Toronto: Royal
Ontario Museum of Archaeology, 1932. 49pp, pls

VICTORIAN FURNITURE

2742 Andrews, John. The Price Guide to Victorian Furniture.
Woodbridge, Suffolk: Baron, 1973. 346pp, ill

2743 Bateman, Robert. Victorian Furniture Transformed, or the
art of improving the commonplace. London: S. Paul,
1971. 128pp, ill

2744 Bly, John. Victorian and Edwardian Furniture. London:
Shire, 1973. 72pp, 92 ill

2745 Cabinet-Maker's Assistant: a series of original designs for
modern furniture, with descriptions and details of construction.... Glasgow; London; New York: Blackie,
1853; 1863; reprint as The Victorian Cabinet-Maker's
Assistant; 418 original designs with descriptions and details of construction. Introd. by John Gloag. New York:

Dover, 1970. 60pp, 63pp of ill, 103 pls; 217pp, ill ViU, NN, MiGr

2746 Freeman, John Crosby, comp. Furniture for the Victorian Home; from A. J. Downing, American, Country Houses (1850) and John Claudius Loudon, English, Encyclopedia (1833). New introd. and index, by J. C. Freeman. Watkins Glen, NY: American Life Foundation, Century House, 1968. 212pp, ill

2747 Freeman, Ruth Sunderlin, and Larry Freeman. Victorian Furniture. Watkins Glen, NY: Century, 1950. 112pp, pls MiGr

2748 Hill, Conover. The Value Guide to Antique Oak Furniture. Paducah, Ky: Collector Books, 1972; 1974. 120pp, 888 ill (Turn of the century)

2749 Hopkinson, James. Victorian Cabinet Maker: the memoirs of James Hopkinson, 1819-1894. Ed. by Jocelyne Baty Goodman. London: Routledge & Paul, 1968. 138pp, ill, 20 pls

2750 Jervis, Simon. Victorian Furniture. London; Sydney: Ward Lock, 1968. 96pp, 97 pls

2751 *Ormsbee, Thomas H. A Field Guide to American Victorian Furniture. Boston: Little Brown, 1952. 428pp, 314 ill (1840-1880)

2752 *Roe, F. Gordon. Victorian Furniture. London: Phoenix House; New York: Roy, 1952. 160pp, ill

2753 *Symonds, Robert Wemyss, and Bruce Blundell Whineray. Victorian Furniture. London: Country Life, 1962. 232pp, 282 ill (To 1887)

2754 Vanderley Brothers, Inc., Grand Rapids, Michigan. Jewels of Victorian Furniture. Grand Rapids: James Bayne, 1947? MiGr

2755 Victorian Furniture. V & A. London: HMSO, 1962. 5pp, 27 pls

CHAIRS AND SEATING FURNITURE

2756 Alison, Filippo. Charles Rennie Mackintosh as a Designer of Chairs. Tr. from Italian (1973) by Bruno and Cristina Del Priore. London: Warehouse Publications, 1974. 104pp, ill, bib

2757 The American Chair; catalogue of exhibition. Fredericksburg,

Va: Connoisseurship, Research, and Gallery Course, Mary Washington College, 1972. 93pp, ill, bib

2758   Andrews, (A. H.) and Co., firm. The Evolution of the Chair. Chicago: Andrews, 1896. 62pp, ill

2759   Baroggio, Alexander. 200 Seating Furniture in Historical Styles, photographic reproductions from rare and characteristic specimens of chiefly English, French, Italian, Flemish, Spanish, and partly Oriental origin ... collected, classified and practically arranged. New York: A. Gerbel, 1909? 50 pls   DLC, MiGr

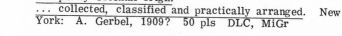

2760   Binstead, Herbert Ernest. English Chairs. With specimens illustrating the various periods from the 15th to the 19th century. 3 parts. London: J. Tiranti, 1923. 11pp, ill, 84 pls   NNC-Ave, BM

2761   Bishop, Robert Charles. Centuries and Styles of the American Chair, 1640-1970. New York: Dutton, 1972. 516pp, ill, bib (Wainscott, Windsor and Speaker's chairs, chair tables, modern furniture from 1915-1970. Private and public collections)

2762   Brazer, Esther Stevens. Early American Designs for Stenciled Chairs. Flushing, NY: Author, 1945. 9pp, 7 pls

2763   Buchwald, Hans H. Form from Process--the Thonet Chair. An exhibition of historic bentwood furniture from the collection of John Sailer, Vienna. Cambridge, Mass: Carpenter Center for the Visual Arts, Harvard, 1967. 64pp, ill, bib

2764   Connecticut Chairs in the Collection of the Connecticut Historical Society. Hartford: 1956. 67pp, ill, pls   CtY, DLC

2765   Cornelsen, R. Modern American Seating Furniture. 80 original designs for all kinds of modern American seating furniture, in the latest and most approved styles, showing the wood structure. New York: Hessling, n.d.; 18-?; 1897; 1910? 45 pls   MiD, MB, PP

2766   Darly, Matthew, fl.1778. A New Book of Chinese, Gothic and Modern Chairs. London: 1751. pls   DLC

2767 Darty, Peter. Chairs. A guide to choosing, buying and col-
          lecting. London: Barrie & Jenkins, 1972; Princeton,
          NJ: Pyne, 1974. 118pp, ill, 12 pls, bib (English,
          French and American. 15th-20th century)

2768 De Voe, Shirley Spaulding, 1899- . American Decorated
          Chairs. New Milford, Conn: Mock & Marsh, 1947.
          19pp, ill, bib DLC

2769 *Drepperd, Carl. Handbook of Antique Chairs. Garden City,
          NY: Doubleday, 1948. 275pp, ill

2770 Dumonthier, Ernest. Chairs by George Jacob. Louis 15,
          Louis 16, and Revolutionary Periods. Mobilier National
          de France. Paris: Morance, 1922. 13pp, 43 pls in
          portfolio DeWint, MiD

2771 _____. Chairs by the Jacob Brothers; Directory and Con-
          sulate Periods. Mobilier National de France. Paris:
          Albert Morance; New York: Brentano's, 1921. 14pp,
          42 pls DeWint

2772 *Dyer, Walter Alden, and Esther Stevens Brazer. The
          Rocking Chair, an American Institution. New York; Lon-
          don: Century, 1928; 1929. 127pp, ill, 29 pls (Boston
          Rocker, stencil decorations, advertisements from 1831,
          etc.) MiGr, DLC, PPL

2773 *Edwards, Ralph. A History of the English Chair. V & A
          Museum. London: HMSO, 1951; 1957; 2nd ed. 1965; 3rd
          ed. rev. by Desmond Fitz-Gerald, Simon Jervis, and J.
          Hardy, as English Chairs. London: HMSO, 1970. 30pp,
          ill, 120 pls; ...; 26pp, 120 pls, bib; 29pp, 130 pls, bib

2774 The English Chair, Its History and Evolution. London: Lund,
          Humphries, for M. Harris, 1937. 181pp, ill, 96 pls DLC

2775 English Chairs. London: V & A, 1950; 1970. 8pp, 129 ill
          (Originally part IV of A Picture Book of English Embroi-
          dery)

2776 English Chairs, with Specimens Illustrating the Various Periods
          from the 15th to the 19th Century. Introd. by Herbert E.
          Binstead. London: John Tiranti, 1923. 11pp, 84 pls
          MiGr

2777 FitzGerald, Charles Patrick. Barbarian Beds; the origin of
          the chair in China. London: Cresset Pr, 1965; South
          Brunswick, NJ: A. S. Barnes, 1966. 85pp, ill, 17 pls,
          bib (850-1100 A.D.)

2778 Frey, Gilbert. The Modern Chair: 1850 to Today. English
          version by D. Q. Stephenson. English, German and

French text. Teufen: Arthur Niggli; London: Tiranti;
New York: Architectural Book Co, 1970. 187pp, ill, bib

2779 Gillingham, Harrold Edgar. The Philadelphia Windsor Chair
and Its Journeyings. Reprint from Pennsylvania Magazine
of History and Biography, October 1931. Philadelphia:
Historical Society of Pa, 1931. 32pp (pp. 301-332)
DeWint

2780 Ginsburg and Levy, firm. A Century of American Chairs,
1720-1820. 30 illustrations ... with study of their
characteristics. Exhibition. New York: Ginsburg &
Levy Gallery, 1942. 40pp, chiefly ill, 30 pls NNC-Ave

2781 Gloag, John (Edwards). The Englishman's Chair; origins,
design, and social history of seat furniture in England.
London: Allen & Unwin, 1964; as The Chair, its origins
... etc. South Brunswick, NJ: A. S. Barnes, 1967.
307pp, ill, 64 pls, color frontis, bib

2782 Harris, M., and Sons, firm. Exhibition--The English Chair--
Its History and Evolution. May 1938. London: 1938.
29pp NN

2783 Heckscher, Morrison H. In Quest of Comfort: the easy chair
in America. Exhibition. New York: Metropolitan Museum, 1971. 15pp, ill

2784 Ingolfsrud, Elizabeth. All About Ontario Chairs. Don Mills,
Ontario: House of Grant, 1974.

2785 Iverson, Marion Day. The American Chair, 1630-1890. New
York: Hastings House, 1957. 241pp, ill

2786 Joy, Edward Thomas. The Country Life Book of Chairs.
London: Country Life, 1967. 96pp, 105 ill, bib

2787 Kane, Patricia Ellen. 300 Years of American Seating Furniture. Chairs and beds from the Mabel Brady Garvan and
other collections at Yale University. Fore. by Charles F.
Montgomery. Boston: N.Y. Graphic, 1976. 356pp, 400
ill, 18 color pls

2788 Kenney, John Tarrant. The Hitchcock Chair; the story of a
Connecticut Yankee. L(ambert) Hitchcock of Hitchcock-
ville--and an account of the restoration of his 19th century
manufactory. New York: Potter, 1971. 339pp, 400 ill,
11 color pls, bib

2789 King, Thomas. Original Designs for Chairs and Sofas, etc.
London: 1840? ill SKM

2790 Kirk, John T. American Chairs: Queen Anne and Chippendale. New York: Knopf, 1972. 208pp, ill, bib

2791   Lawford, Henry. The Chair and Sofa Manufacturer's Book of
       Designs. London: n.d. ill SKM

2792   Lea, Zilla Rider, ed. The Ornamented Chair; its develop-
       ment in America (1700-1890). Historical Society of Early
       American Decoration. Esther Stevens Brazer Guild. Rut-
       land, Vt: Tuttle, 1960. 173pp, chiefly ill, 300 photo-
       graphs, bib

2793   London Chair-makers' and Carvers' Book of Prices for Work-
       manship as Regulated and Agreed to by a Committee of
       Master Chair-manufacturers and Journeymen. London:
       T. Sorrell, 1802; Supplement. London: 1808; 2nd supple-
       ment. London: 1811; 2nd ed. London: T. Brettell, 1829;
       3rd supplement. London: Alfred Dodd, 1844; 4th ed.
       London: T. Brettell, 1871? ill MiGr

2794   Loring, J. N. The Anatomy of English Chair Types. A
       scientific classification of 18th century domestic styles.
       London: The Antique Collector, 1937; reprint. London:
       Hadden, Best, 1937. 22pp, ill NN, MiGr

2795   MacDonald, William H. Central New Jersey Chairmaking of
       the 19th century. Trenton, NJ: 1960. 59pp, pls

2796   MacLaren, George E. G. The Chair-Makers of Nova Scotia.
       Halifax: Nova Scotia Museum, 1966. 7pp, ill

2797   Manwaring, Robert. The Cabinet and Chair-Maker's Real
       Friend and Companion; or, The whole system of chair-
       making made plain and easy. London: 1765; abridged
       reprint from 1765 ed. London: J. Tiranti, 1937; 1948.
       40 pls; 3 pp, 38 pls BM

2798   _____. The Chairmaker's Guide. London: 1766. 75 pls
       SIB-2

2799   Mayes, Leonard John. The History of Chairmaking in High
       Wycombe. London: Routledge & Paul, 1960. 174pp, ill

2800   Meadmore, Clement. The Modern Chair: classics in produc-
       tion. London: Studio Vista, 1974. 191pp, ill (1876-
       1972)

2801   Modern Chairs, 1918-1970; an international exhibition pre-
       sented by the Whitechapel Art Gallery in association with
       the Observer. Arranged by the Victoria and Albert. Lon-
       don: the Gallery, 1970; London: Lund Humphries; Boston:
       Book and Art, 1971. 108pp, ill; 32pp, ill, 127 pls

2802   Moore, Mabel (Roberts). Hitchcock Chairs. New Haven:
       Yale U. Pr, 1933. 12pp, ill, pls MiGr

2803   Nutting, Wallace. Wallace Nutting Windsors; correct Windsor
        furniture. Saugus, Mass: Wallace Nutting Co, 1918.
        46pp, ill   NNC-Ave

2804 *   . A Windsor Handbook; comprising illustrations and
        descriptions of Windsor furniture of all periods, including
        side chairs, arm chairs, comb-backs, writing-arm
        Windsors, babies' high backs, babies' low chairs, child's
        chairs, also settees, love seats, stools and tables.   Sau-
        gus, Mass: Old America Company, Wallace Nutting, 1917;
        as American Windsors.   Framingham, Mass: Old America
        Co, 192-; reprint. Southampton, NY: Cracker Barrel Pr,
        1969; reprint. Rutland, Vt: Tuttle, 1973.   192pp, ill;
        208pp, ill

2805   101 Chairs and Stools Collected, with the assistance of the
        Furniture History Society, from Oxford District to show
        the historical evolution of chair design in Great Britain.
        Exhibition March 1968.   Divinity School.   Oxford: 1968.
        52pp, ill   DeWint

2806 *Ormsbee, Thomas Hamilton.   The Windsor Chair.   Great
        Neck, NY: Deerfield Books; New York: Hearthside Pr;
        London: W. H. Allen, 1962.   224pp, 80 chairs ill, bib

2807   Redwood, Sydney. The Crown Jewels and Coronation Chair.
        London: Westminster Pr, 1936; 2nd ed. 1937.   31pp,
        color pls

2808   Roe, Frederic Gordon.   Windsor Chairs.   London: Phoenix;
        New York: Pitman, 1953.   96pp, ill, bib

2809   Schwartz, Marvin D.   Please Be Seated; the evolution of the
        chair, 2000 B.C. to 2000 A.D.   New York: American
        Federation of Arts, 1968.   61pp, ill, bib

2810   A Selection of 19th Century American Chairs.   Exhibition.
        Hartford, Conn: Stowe-Day Foundation, 1973.   107pp,
        ill, bib

2811   Seven Decades of Design; a travelling exhibition.   Long Beach,
        Cal: Museum of Art, 1967.   u.p., ill

2812   Sparkes, Ivan George.   The English Country Chair: an illus-
        trated history of chairs and chairmaking.   Bourne End,
        Eng: Spurbooks, 1973.   160pp, ill, bib

2813   . The Windsor Chair.   An illustrated history of a
        classic English chair.   Bourne End: Spurbooks, 1975.
        143pp, ill, bib

2814   Stone, Louise Hawley.   The Chair in China.   Toronto: Royal
        Ontario Museum of Archaeology, 1932.   49pp, pls

2815   Thonet, Gebruder, firm.   Thonet Brothers ... Inventors,
          manufacturers, and importers of Thonet bentwood furni-
          ture.   New York: 1915. 163pp, chiefly ill

2816   Thonet Furniture, 1830-1953.   Exhibition.   Museum of Modern
          Art.   New York: 1953.

2817   Toms, W. Jr.   36 New, Original and Practical Designs for
          Chairs Adapted for the Drawing and Dining Room, Parlour
          and Hall.   Bath: J. Hollway, 1831? ill MiGr, SKM

2818   Van Why, Joseph S., and Anne S. MacFarland.   A Selection
          of 19th Century American Chairs.   Exhibition at Nook
          Farm Visitors' Center.   December 1973-March 1974.
          Hartford, Conn: Stowe-Day Foundation, 1973.   107pp, ill,
          8 pls, bib

2819   Ware, William Rotch, 1848-1917, ed.   Seats of the Colonists
          and Other Furnishings; illustrated largely with measured
          drawings by H. C. Dunham.   Part 1.   Boston: American
          Architect, 1904- . (No more published.) 24pp, ill, 28
          pls (American and English) MiGr

2820   The Washington Chair, Presented to the New York Historical
          Society by Benjamin Robert Winthrop, 1857.   New York:
          C. B. Richardson, 1857.   10pp, 2 pls

BEDS AND BEDROOM FURNITURE

2821   Beds--The Simmons Manufacturing Company.   1901-02 cata-
          logue.   Ed. by Robert J. Shepard.   Reprint.   Flushing,
          NY: Editor, 1974.   ill (Wood, brass, cradles and cribs
          and beds)

2822   Blyth, James N.   Notes on Beds and Bedding: historical and
          anecdotal.   London: Simpkin & Marshall, 1873.   90pp
          NB, SIB-1

2823   Broadbent, V. E.   Bedroom Furniture, Period and Modern.
          Milwaukee: Bruce, 1950.   122pp, ill NN, DLC

2824   Cook, Clarence Chatham.   The House Beautiful: essays on
          beds and tables, stools and candlesticks.   New York:
          Scribner, Armstrong, 1877; 1878; 1879; 1881; 1895.
          336pp, ill, color frontis

2825   Hardy, John, Sheila Landi, and Charles D. Wright.   A State
          Bed from Erthig.   London: V & A, 1972.   22pp, ill
          (Hanging-tester bed)

2826   Heal and Son, Ltd.   Simple Bedroom Furniture, illustrated by
          woodcuts from the original designs by Heal and Son.   An

essay by the late Mr. Gleson White on "Simplicity of Design" is reprinted at the end of this book.   London: 1899.   40pp, ill

2827   Illustrations and Descriptions of Cots, Solid Iron, Caned, and Corrugated, Angle Iron Bedsteads; also of convertible chairs, couches, etc.   London: 1870?   30 pls MB

2828   Kane, Patricia Ellen.   300 Years of American Seating Furniture.   Chairs and Beds from the Mabel Brady Garvan and other collections at Yale University.   Fore. by Charles F. Montgomery.   Boston: NY Graphic, 1976.   356pp, 400 ill, 18 color ill

2829   King, Thomas.   Decorations for Windows and Beds.   London: King, n. d.   pls (part color) PP

2830   _____ .   Fashionable Bedsteads with Hangings, etc.   London: n. d. (mid-19th century) ill SKM

2831   Mogg, Thomas and Company.   Ornamental Designs of Bed Room Furniture.   London: 1871.   portfolio of ill BM

2832   Pattern Book of Iron and Brass Bedsteads, of Parallel and Taper Tubing, with Dovetailed Joints and All the Latest Improvements.   London: 1861.   BM

2833   Record, Nancy A.   A Bed for the Night.   Minneapolis: Lerner, 1968.   55pp, ill

2834   Wright, Lawrence.   Warm and Snug: the history of the bed.   London: Routledge & K. Paul, 1962.   360pp, ill, bib

MIRRORS AND PICTURE FRAMES

2835   The Carver and Gilder's Guide, and Picture Frame Maker's Companion ... by a Practical Hand.   London: Kent & Co, 1873.   140pp BM

2836   Colonial Looking-Glasses and Mirrors.   Boston: Foster Brothers, 192-?   40pp, pls DeWint

2837   Comstock, Helen.   The Looking-Glass in America, 1700-1825.   Based on articles in "Antiques."   New York: Viking, 1968.   128pp ill

2838   Hasluck, Paul Nooncree.   Mounting and Framing Pictures.   London: Cassell, 1899; 1900; London; New York: 1903;...   160pp, ill NN

2839   Heydenryk, Henry.   The Art and History of Frames: an enquiry into the enhancement of paintings through the ages.

New York: Heinemann, 1963; London: Vane, 1964.
120pp, 100 ill, bib

2840   Johnson, Thomas, carver. Twelve Gerandoles. London:
       for R. Sayer, 1755; 1761. 12 pls or 8 pls NNC-Ave

2841   Jones, Inigo, 1573-1652. Designs for Chimney-Glasses and
       Chimney Pieces, of the Time of Charles I. Republished.
       London: 1858-1859. mainly ill IU, BM

2842   Lock, Matthew. A New Book of Ornaments for Looking Glass
       Frames, Chimney Pieces, etc., in the Chinese taste.
       London: 1768; London: for R. Sayer, 18-? MdBP

2843   . A New Book of Pier-Frames, Ovals, Gerandoles,
       Tables, etc. London: 1769. ill SKM

2844   Maryanski, Richard A. Antique Picture Frame Guide. Ed.
       by Anne Lunde. Niles, Ill: Cedar Forest Co, 1973.
       80pp, ill (Picture and mirror frames)

2845   Pineau, N., and L. Le Roux. Designs for Chimney-pieces,
       Wainscot-panels, Buffets, Pier Glasses, etc. n.p.: n.d.
       42 pls SKM

2846   The Plate-Glass-Book, Consisting of the Following Authentic
       Tables. I. The value of any looking-glass when finished,
       and fit for framing; II. The glass house table...; III. The
       Prices of Grinding. 3rd ed. enl. To which is added,
       the compleat appraiser ... with instructions for valuing
       of kitchen and household furniture. London: Author, 1760.
       170pp, 1 color pl DeWint

2847   *Roche, Serge. Mirrors. Tr. by Colin Duckworth. London:
       G. Duckworth, 1957. 38pp, ill, 294 (13 color) pls

2848   Sample Book of Designs of Looking Glass Frames, Cornices,
       Carved Chimney-pieces, and Other Art Specimens. Bir-
       mingham, Eng: Lee Eginton, 1780. MiGr

2849   Sims, George. New Designs, for carved frames, glasses,
       etc., as manufactured by George Sims, plate glass factor
       and wholesale carver and gilder. London: G. Sims,
       1825. MiGr

2850   Symonds, Robert Wemys. Masterpieces of English Furniture
       and Clocks; a study of walnut and mahogany furniture and
       of the associated crafts of the looking-glass maker and
       japanner, together with an account of Thomas Tompion and
       other famous clockmakers of the 17th and 18th centuries.
       London: Batsford, 1940. 172pp, 130 ill, 8 color pls

2851   Whitehead, J. Designs for Chimney and Pier Glasses,

Curtain Cornices, Candelabra, etc. London: n.d. ill
SKM

2852 Wills, Geoffrey. English Looking Glasses: a study of the
glass, frames, and makers, 1670-1820. London: Country
Life, 1965; South Brunswick, NJ: A. S. Barnes, 1967.
162pp, 164 ill, bib (Stuart-Regency)

2853 Zuccani, Ernest. Ernest Zuccani's New Designs of Gilt Chimney Glasses, etc. London: 1867.

2854 _____ . Newest Designs in Chimney Decoration, Mirrors,
Consoles, Girandoles, etc. London: 186-? 59 pls BPL

BATHS AND BATHROOMS

2855 Cross, Alfred William Stephens. Public Baths and Wash-
houses; a treatise on their planning, design, arrangement,
and fitting.... London: Batsford, 1906. 231pp, 274 ill,
144 plans (Includes equipment) DeWint

2856 Gerhard, William Paul, 1854-1927. Modern Baths and Bath
Houses. New York: J. Wiley, 1908. 311pp, ill, bib
BM, NN

2857 _____ . The Modern Rain Bath. Reprint from American
Architecture. New York: 1894. 15pp (Shower)

2858 _____ . On Bathing and Different Forms of Baths. New
York: 1895. NN

2859 Palmer, Roy. The Water Closet: a new history. Newton
Abbot: David & Charles, 1973. 141pp, ill

2860 Wright, Lawrence. Clean and Decent: the fascinating history
of the bathroom and the water closet, and of sundry habits,
fashions and accessories of the toilet, principally in Great
Britain, France and America. London: Routledge & K.
Paul; New York: Viking, 1960; London: 1966; Toronto:
U of Toronto Pr, 1967. 282pp, ill, bib

LIBRARY, SCHOOL, MUSEUM AND OFFICE FURNITURE AND FITTINGS

2861 Burgoyne, Frank James. Library Construction: architecture,
fittings, and furniture. London: G. Allen, 1897; 1898;
New York: Francis P. Harper, 1898; 2nd ed. London:
1905. 336pp, ill, pls TxU, NN, DLC

2862 Cameron, R. M., Edinburgh. Catalogue of School Furniture and Fittings for Board Schools, also school board books, forms and stationery. Edinburgh: 18-? 15pp, ill DeWint

2863   Clark, John Willis, 1833-1910. The Care of Books. An essay on the development of libraries and their fittings, from the earliest times to the end of the 18th century. Cambridge, Eng: U. Pr, 1901; 2nd ed. 1902; 1909. 330pp, ill; 352pp, ill, 52 pls, bib NN, DLC, PPL, ViU

2864   Drawings and Measurements of Furniture Used by the Museum. Drawings by Paul Bollo. New York: Metropolitan Museum, 1923; rev. ed. as Furniture, with drawings and measurements and various devices used by the museum. New York: 1930. 3pp, 40pp of ill; 4pp, 57pp of ill

2865   Elwell, Newton W. The Boston Public Library. Boston: G. H. Polley, 1896. 2pp, 26 pls ViU, DLC

2866   Johonnot, James, 1823-1883. Country School Houses; containing elevations, plans, and specifications, with estimates, directions to builders, suggestions to school grounds, furniture, apparatus, etc., and a treatise on schoolhouse architecture. New York: Ivison & Phinney, 1858; 1859; 1866; New York: J. W. Schermerhorn, 1871. 220pp, ill, 19 pls; ...; ...; 271pp, 42 (2 color) pls MiU, MH, NN

2867   Naudé, Gabriel. The Disposition, Ornament and Decoration of a Library: two chapters taken from John Evelyn's translation of 'Advis pour Dresser une Bibliothèque,' (Paris, 1627). Birmingham, Eng: School of Librarianship Pr, Polytechnic, 1970. 7pp

2868   _____ . Instructions Concerning Erecting of a Library. Tr. of entire Advis pour Dresser une Bibliotheque. London: G. Bedle, T. Collins and J. Crook, 1661; Cambridge, Eng: Riverside Pr, 1903. 96pp; 160pp

2869   Wallen, James. Things That Live Forever, being the story of office equipment from the dawn of thought to the age of art metal. Jamestown, NY: Roycrofters, for Art Metal Construction, 1921. 71pp

GARDEN AND STREET FURNITURE

2870   Collis, James. Remarks on Street Architecture. London: Atchley, 1838.

2871   Cottingham, Lewis Nockalls. The Smith's, Founder's, and Ornamental Worker's Director, comprising a variety of designs in the present taste for gates, piers, balcony railings, window guards, verandas, balustrades, vases,

etc; with various ornaments applicable to works in metal.
London: M. Taylor, 18-?; 182-? 45 pls IU, DLC

2872 Davison, Ralph C. Concrete Pottery and Garden Furniture.
New York: Munn, 1910; 1917. 196pp, ill NNC-Ave,
DLC

2873 Decorations for Parks and Gardens. Designs for gates,
garden seats, alcoves, temples, baths, entrance gates,
lodges, facades, prospect towers, cattle sheds, ruins,
bridges, greenhouses, etc. Also a hot house and hot
wall: with plans and scales on 55 plates. London: J.
Taylor, 18- . 1pp, 55 pls NNC-Ave, DLC

2874 Edwards, Paul Francis. English Garden Ornament. London:
G. Bell, 1965; South Brunswick, NJ: A. S. Barnes,
1967. 110pp, ill, 58 pls, bib

2875 Gothein, Marie Luise. A History of Garden Art. Ed. by
Walter P. Wright. Tr. from German by Mrs. Archer-
Hind. 2 vol. London; Toronto: J. M. Dent; New York:
Dutton, 1928; New York: Hacker Art Books, 1966. 600
ill, bib

2876 Grant White, John Ernest. Garden Art and Architecture.
London; New York: Abelard-Schumann, 1968. 110pp,
163 ill

2877 Hibberd, (James) Shirley, 1825-1890. Rustic Adornments
for Homes of Taste and Recreations of Town Folk in the
Study and Imitation of Nature. London: Groombridge,
1856; 2nd ed. 1857; new enl. & corrected ed. 1870; new
rev. ed. by T. W. Sanders. London: Collingridge, 1895.
353pp, ill, color pls; 508pp, ill, color pls; 402pp, 232
ill, 9 color pls (How to build and maintain aquariums,
gardens, aviaries, indoor plants, etc., with equipment)

2878 Hunt, Peter, ed. The Book of Garden Ornament. London:
Dent, 1974. 298pp, ill

2879 Janes, Kirtland and Company. 1870 catalog. Ornamental
Ironwork; fountains, statuary, vases, urns, lawn furniture, pedestals, baptismal fonts, animals veranda, summer house. Reprint with historical introduction. Princeton, NJ: Pyne Pr, 1971. u.p., ill of 167 items, bib

2880 Jekyll, Gertrude. Garden Ornament. London: Country
Life; New York: Scribner's, 1918; rev. ed. with Christopher Hussey. 1927. 460pp, ill, color frontis; 438pp, ill,
pls ViU, MiU

2881 McFarland, John Horace. Furnishing the Streets in Suburban

Communities. Washington, D.C.: American Civic Association, 1911; 1913. 4pp, ill NN, BPL, MB

2882 Mintons Flower Pots, Garden Seats, Jugs, etc., in rich coloured glazes, and new designs for fountains in majolica, and decorated earthenware for conservatories and public buildings. Stoke-on-Trent: Mintons China Works, 1887. ill

2883 Northend, Mary Harrod. Garden Ornaments. New York: Duffield, 1916. 178pp, ill, 31 pls DLC, NNC-Ave

2884 Robertson, William. Designs for Architecture, for garden chairs, small gates for villas, park entrances, aviarys, temples, boat houses, mausoleums, and bridges.... London: R. Ackerman, 1800. 24 color pls NNC-Ave

2885 Thonger, Charles. Book of Garden Furniture. London; New York: John Lane, 1903. 100pp, ill, 23 pls

2886 Underwood, Loring. The Garden and Its Accessories. Boston: Little, Brown, 1906. 215pp, ill

2886a Vardy, John. Some Designs of Mr. Inigo Jones and Mr. William Kent. London: 1744. 50 engraved pls (Chimney-pieces, garden seats and temples, chandeliers, tureens, silver standishes and cups, candlesticks, chairs, etc.)

2887 Weidenmann, Jacob. American Garden Architecture, designed and executed by J. Weidenmann, landscape architect. New York: 1877. ill

2888 Wrighte, William. Grotesque Architecture, or rural amusement, consisting of plans, elevations and sections, for huts, retreats, summer and winter hermitages, terminaries, Chinese, gothic and natural grottos, cascades, baths, mosques, moresque pavilions, grotesque and rustic seats, greenhouses, etc., many of which may be executed with flints, irregular stones, rude branches and the roots of trees. London: H. Webley, 1767; new ed. I. Taylor, 1790. 14pp, 28 pls NNC-Ave

2889 _____. Ideas for Rustic Furniture Proper for Garden Seats, summer houses, hermitages, cottages, etc., on 25 plates. Reprint from his Grotesque Architecture. London: M. Taylor, 1835; 1838. MiGr, DLC

2890 [No entry.]

SECTION VI

CERAMICS: POTTERY AND PORCELAIN

GENERAL WORKS

2891 Aldridge, Eileen. Porcelain. New York: Grosset & Dunlap, 1970. 159pp, ill (Juvenile literature)

2892 Arnoux, L. On Ceramic Manufactures, Porcelain, and Pottery. Lecture on result of Great Exhibition of 1851. London: Society for the Encouragement of Arts, Manufactures and Commerce, 1852. BM

2893 The Art and Technique of Ceramics. Exhibition. June-September 1937. Brooklyn Museum. New York: J. B. Watkins, printer, 1937; rev. ed. 1940. 111pp, ill, bib

2894 Ayer Antique China Company. Catalogue of Old Dark Blue Crockery and Old China, Delft, and other ware, wanted by the Ayer ... Company, with prices paid for same. Ayer, Mass: 18-? 23pp, ill DeWint

2895   Backlin-Landman, Hedy, and Edna Shapiro. The Story of
       Porcelain. New York: Odyssey Pr, 1965. 41pp, ill

2896   Barber, Edwin Atlee. The Ceramic Collector's Glossary.
       New York: Walpole Society, 1914; reprint. New York:
       Da Capo Pr, 1967. 119pp, many ill

2897   _____. Salt Glazed Stoneware. Germany, Flanders,
       England and the United States. Philadelphia: Museum
       of Art, 1906; enl. ed. Garden City, NY: Doubleday &
       Page; London: Hodder & Stoughton, 1907. 28pp, ill,
       pls; 32pp, ill, pls NN, BM

2898   _____. Tin Enameled Pottery, Maiolica, Delft and Other
       Stanniferous Faience. Philadelphia: Museum of Art,
       1906; Garden City, NY: Doubleday & Page, 1907. 39pp,
       ill, pls; 51pp, ill, 23 pls V & A, NN, BM

2899   Barnard, Harry. The Art of the Pottery: peeps at the art
       of the potter. London: A. & C. Black, 1932. 88pp,
       ill, 4 color pls, color frontis NN, BM

2900   Beckwith, Arthur. Pottery. Observations on the materials
       for the manufacturer of terracotta, stoneware, fire-brick,
       porcelain, earthenware, majolica, ... brick. Interna-
       tional Exhibition 1871, London. New York: D. Van Nos-
       trand, 1872. 101pp DeWint, DLC, BM

2901 *Berendsen, Anne A. J., Marcel K. Keezer, Sigurd Schoubye,
       Jaao Miguel dos Santos Simoes, and Jan Tichelaar. Tiles:
       a general history. Tr. from German (1964) by Janet
       Seligman. London: Faber; New York: Viking, 1967.
       286pp, ill, color pls, bib (First comprehensive history.
       2000 B.C. to present, all countries)

2902   Berges, Ruth. Collectors Choice of Porcelain and Faience.
       London: Yoseloff, 1967; South Brunswick, NJ: A. S.
       Barnes, 1968. 264pp, ill (part color), bib

2903 *   . From Gold to Porcelain; the art of porcelain and
       faience. New York; London: Yoseloff, 1963; 1964; 1965.
       239pp, 200 ill, 3 pls, bib (Faience, European porcelain,
       Oriental porcelain, majolica, etc.)

2904   Billington, Dora M. The Art of the Potter. London; New
       York: Oxford U Pr, 1937. 126pp, ill, 3 pls, bib

2905   Binns, Charles Fergus. The Potter's Craft. London: Con-
       stable; New York: Van Nostrand, 1910; 2nd rev. ed.
       New York: 1922; 3rd ed. 1947; 1950. 171pp, ill, 21
       pls; 206pp, ill, pls; 128pp, ill, pls DLC, NN, MiGr

2906   _____. The Story of the Potter; being a popular account of the rise and progress of the principal manufactures of pottery and porcelain of the world. London: G. Newnes, 1898; rev. ed. London; New York: Hodder & Stoughton, 1898; London: Newnes, 1905;... 248pp, 57 ill PPULC, CU

2907   Blake, William Phipps, 1826-   . International Exhibition, Vienna 1873. Ceramic Art: a report on pottery, porcelain, tiles, terra-cotta, and brick.... New York: D. Van Nostrand, 1875. 146pp, ill MB, BM

2908   *Boger, Louise Ade. The Dictionary of World Pottery and Porcelain: from prehistoric times to the present. New York: Scribner, 1971; London: A. & C. Black, 1972. 533pp, 562 photographs, 32 color pls, bib, 503 marks

2909   Bohn, Henry George, 1796-1881. A Guide to the Knowledge of Pottery, Porcelain, and Other Objects of Vertu. Comprising an illustrated catalogue of the Bernal Collection of works of art ... To which are added an introductory essay on pottery and porcelain and an engraved list of marks and monograms. London: G. Bell, 1857; 2nd corrected ed. London: Bohn, 1862; 1869; 3rd ed. 1876; London; New York: Bell, 1892; 1896; 1900; 1912. 504pp, 40 ill, 48 color pls, marks (4294 items covered) NN, BM, PPULC

2910   Borenius, Tancred. Catalogue of a Collection of Pottery Belonging to William Harrison Woodward. n.p.: priv. printed, 1928. 38pp, 25 pls

2911   Branner, John Casper. Bibliography of Clays and the Ceramic Art. Washington, D.C.: United States Geological Survey, 1896; 2nd ed. Columbus, O: American Ceramic Society, F. J. Heer, printer, 1906. 114pp, 451pp DLC, PPULC

2912   Bric-a-brac, a Handbook for the Use of Visitors to the Loan Collection in the Chicago Exposition for 1877. (Inter-state Industrial Exposition.) Chicago: Rand, McNally, 1877. 88pp (Chiefly pottery) DLC, MB

2913   Brooks, George Greaves. The China Collector's Assistant. London: Author, 1860. 15pp (Handbook of marks) NN, BM

2914   Buhler, Kathyrn C., and John C. Austin. The Campbell Museum Collection. Camden, NJ: Campbell Museum, 1969. 95pp, ill (some color), bib (Silver catalogued by Buhler; ceramic by Austin)

2915   Burgess, Frederick William. Old Pottery and Porcelain. London: Routledge; New York: Putnam's, 1916; 2nd impression. New York: 1924. 426pp, ill, pls, gloss PPULC, CU, NN

2916 *Burton, William. A General History of Porcelain. 2 vol.
      London: Chatto, 1920; London; New York: Cassell, 1921;
      New York: Funk, 1921. 204pp and 228pp, ill, 112 (32
      color) pls, bib BM, DLC

2917 *_____. Porcelain: a sketch of its nature, art and manu-
      facture. London; New York: Cassell, 1906; London:
      Batsford, 1906. 264pp, ill, 50 pls NN, CtY, BM

2918 _____, and Robert Lockhart Hobson. Handbook of Marks
      on Pottery and Porcelain. London: Macmillan, 1909;
      with additions. 1912; rev. enl. ed. 1928; 1929; reprint as
      Collector's Guide to Pottery and Porcelain Marks. Ed.
      by John Edwards. Stratford, Conn: J. Edwards, 1971.
      210pp, ill; 212pp, ill; 213pp, ill, bib DLC, PPULC

2919 Butterworth, Lionel Milner Angus. Pottery and Porcelain.
      Collins, 1964. 160pp, ill, 12 pls

2920 Byng-Hall, Major Herbert. The Adventures of a Bric-a-brac
      Hunter. London: Tinsley Brothers, 1868; 2nd ed. as
      The Bric-a-Brac Hunter: or, chapters on chinamania.
      London: Chatto & Windus; Philadelphia: Lippincott, 1875.
      212pp, ill; 290pp, ill NN, DLC

2921 Catalogue of the Objects of Ceramic Art and School of Design
      at the Melbourne Public Library. Melbourne, Australia:
      J. Ferris, 186-? 32pp

2922 Ceramic Age. Quarterly. Newark, NJ: Ceramics Publishing
      Co, 1921-24; monthly. 1924- .

2923 Ceramic Circle of Charlotte. Journal of Studies. Periodical.
      Charlotte, NC: 1971- .

2924 Ceramic Monthly. Chicago: 189-?-1900.

2925 Ceramics in Art and Industry. London: Doulton, 19-?

2926 Ceramics Monthly. Athens, O: 1953- .

2927 *Chaffers, William, 1811-1892. The Collector's Handbook to
      Keramics of the Renaissance and Modern Periods. Se-
      lected from "The Keramic Gallery." Pref. by Herbert
      M. Cundall. London: Gibbings; New York: Scribner's,
      1909. 316pp, 350 ill MiGr, DLC, PPULC

2928 *_____. The Keramic Gallery. Containing several hundred
      illustrations of rare, curious and choice examples of
      pottery and porcelain from earliest times to beginning of
      19th century. 2 vol. London: Chapman & Hall, 1872;
      2nd ed. rev. by H. M. Cundall. London: Gibbings; New
      York: Scribner's, 1907; 3rd rev. ed. by H. M. Cundall,

as The New Keramic Gallery, containing illustrations ...
to the beginning of the 20th century. With historical
notes. 2 vol. London: Reeves & Turner, 1926. ill,
227 pls; 468pp, ill, pls (5 color); 694pp, 700 ill, 8
color pls DLC, BM

2929 *_____. Marks and Monograms on Pottery and Porcelain,
with short historical notices of each manufactory, and an
introductory essay on the vasa fictilia of England. London:
J. Davy, 1863; also 2 vol. 1863; 3rd ed. rev. & augmented. 1870; 6th ed. rev. London: Bickers, 1876; 7th
ed. as Marks and Monograms on European and Oriental
Pottery and Porcelain.... London: Reeves & Turner,
1886; 8th ed. ed. by Frederick Litchfield. London:
Gibbings, 1897; 12th ed. with an increased number of
potter's marks and additional supplement. With a bibliography. London: Reeves & Turner, 1908; as The Collector's Handbook of Marks and Monograms.... 1914; rev.
ed. augmented by Frederick Litchfield, with upwards of
5000 marks. London: 1918; 1920; 1924; 1930; 1936;
1940; .. 1965. 256pp, ill; 1876: 1000pp, ill; 1912:
1079pp, ill, bib; The Handbook: 234pp to 367pp (Many
many editions of this standard work, and its abbreviated
form)

2930 Charleston, Robert J., ed. World Ceramics; an illustrated
history. Feltham: Hamlyn; New York: McGraw-Hill,
1968. 352pp, 1084 ill, bib

2931 China Classics Series. Ed. by Graydon La Verne Freeman.
6 vol. Watkins Glen, NY: Century, 1949- . ill, marks
(I. Majolica; II. Haviland-Limoges; III. European; IV.
Ironstone; V. Hand Painted; VI. English Staffordshire)

2932 The China Decorator. Monthly. New York: 1887-1901.

2933 Cohen, Hal L. Grosset's Complete Guide to Collectible
Plates. New York: Grosset & Dunlap, 1974. 244pp, ill,
bib

2934 Cooper, Emmanuel. A History of Pottery. London: Longman; New York: St. Martin's Pr, 1972. 276pp, ill, bib,
8 pls

2935 Cox, Warren Earle. The Book of Pottery and Porcelain.
2 vol. New York: L. Lee Shepard, dist. by Crown, 1944;
1945; 1946; 1949; rev. ed. 1966; 1970. ...; 1159pp, 3000
ill, color frontis, marks (Prehistoric to modern)

2936 Crockery and Glass Journal. Weekly. New York: G. Whittemore, 1874- . (First known as Crockery Journal)

2937 Cushion, John Patrick. Animals in Pottery and Porcelain.

London: Cory, Adams and Mackay; New York: October
House, 1966; New York: Crown, 1974. 72pp, ill, pls;
256pp, ill, 35 (3 color) pls, bib, gloss (Ancient Egypt
to present day)

2938 _____. Porcelain. London: Orbis, 1973. 64pp, chiefly
ill, bib (To 1860)

2939 _____. Pottery and Porcelain. London: The Connoisseur, 1972. 231pp, ill, 8 pls, bib

2940 _____, and W. B. Honey. Handbook of Pottery and Porcelain Marks. London: Faber, 1956; New York: Pitman,
1957; 2nd rev. ed. 1962; 3rd rev. ed. London: 1965.
476pp, ill, marks

2941 Darty, Peter. Pocketbook of Porcelain and Pottery Marks.
London: Dalton Watson, 1970. 183pp

2942 Design. Monthly. Columbus, O: Design Publishing, 1899-
1919. ill, pls

2943 Design. A monthly magazine devoted to the decorative arts.
Syracuse, NY: Keramic Studio, 19- .

2944 *Dillon, Edward. Porcelain. London: Methuen; New York:
Putnam's, 1904; London: 1909. 420pp, ill, 49 (19 color)
pls, bib

2945 _____. Porcelain and How to Collect It. London:
Methuen; New York: Dutton, 1910. 314pp, 32 pls MB,
NN

2946 Dodd, A. E. Concise Encyclopedic Dictionary of Ceramics.
2nd rev. ed. Amsterdam: Elsevier Publishing, 1967.
362pp

2947 Dudley, William Humble Ward, Earl of Dudley. Catalogue
of a Collection of Old Porcelain. London: 1886. 20pp

2948 Eames, Elizabeth Sara. Medieval Tiles: a handbook. London: British Museum, 1968. 34pp, ill, 20 pls, bib
(1220-1527)

2949 *Eberlein, Harold Donaldson, and Robert Wearne Ramsdell.
The Practical Book of Chinaware. Garden City, NY:
Halcyon House, 1925; 1942; Philadelphia; London: Lippincott, 1925; 1936; 1938; 2nd ed. Philadelphia: 1948.
325pp, ill, 116 pls, color frontis, bib

2950 Edwards, John, ed. Collector's Guide to Pottery and Porcelain Marks. Stratford, Conn: Author, 1928; reprint.
1971. 191pp, ill; 213pp, ill

2951 Elliott, Charles Wyllys. Pottery and Porcelain: from early
      times down to the Philadelphia Exhibition of 1876. New
      York: Appleton, 1878. 327pp, 165 ill, marks ViU, DLC

2952 Elward, Robert. On Collecting Engravings, Pottery, Porce-
      lain, Glass and Silver. London: E. Arnold, 1904; 1905.
      90pp, bib

2953 Evans, Lady Maria Millington. Lustre Pottery. London:
      Methuen, 1920; New York: Dutton, 1921. 148pp, 24 pls,
      bib NN, DLC

2954 John Evelyn and Co., London. A Book of Old China. Lon-
      don: Garden City Pr, printers, 1912. 53pp, ill DeWint

2955 Exhibition of Tiles. Philadelphia: 1915. 137 tiles ill

2956 Eyles, Desmond. Pottery Through the Ages. London:
      Doulton, 1950. 48pp, ill

2957 50 Masterpieces of Pottery, porcelain, glass vessels, stained
      glass, painted enamels. V & A. London: HMSO, 1950;
      2nd ed. 1964. 103pp, 50 ill BM

2958 Fisher, Stanley William. The China Collectors' Guide. Lon-
      don: Patina, 1957. 193pp, ill, bib

2959 Forman, Gordon Mitchell. 20th Century Ceramics, an inter-
      national survey of the best work produced by modern
      craftsmen, artists, and manufacturers. London; New
      York: Studio, 1936. 128pp, ill, pls

2960 *Fortnum, Charles Drury Edward. A Descriptive Catalogue of
      the Maiolica, Hispano-Moresco, Persian, Damascus, and
      Rhodian wares in the South Kensington Museum. With
      marks, monograms and historical notices. London: Chap-
      man & Hall, 1873. 700pp, ill, color pls, color frontis,
      bib BM

2961 _____. Maiolica. South Kensington Museum. London:
      Chapman & Hall, 1875; 1876; New York: Scribner, Wel-
      ford & Armstrong, 1876; 1877; London: 1882; 1892.
      192pp, ill MB, NN

2962 *   _____. Maiolica: a historic treatise on the glazed and
      enamelled earthen ware of Italy; with marks and mono-
      grams. Also some notes of Persian, Damascan, Rhodian,
      Hispano-Moresque wares. London; Oxford: Clarendon Pr,
      1896. 550pp, 21 pls, bib, marks MdBP

2963 Freeman, Graydon La Verne (Larry). Majolica. Watkins
      Glen, NY: Century, 1949. 88pp, ill

2964 Furnival, William James. Leadless Decorative Tiles, faience
      and mosaic; comprising notes and excerpts on the history,
      materials, manufacture and use of ornamental flooring
      tiles, ceramic mosaic and decorative tiles and faience,
      with complete series of recipes for tile-bodies, and for
      leadless glazes and art tile enamels. Stone, Stafford-
      shire: Author, 1904. 852pp ill, 37 pls (some color)
      (With notes by Stephen Bushell, C. Stanley Clarke, J. H.
      Marshall, Ambrose Wood) MB, DLC

2965 Giffin, Frank. Pottery and Porcelain. London: Muller,
      1967. 120pp, ill

2966 A Glossary of Ceramic Terms. Newark, NJ: Newark Mu-
      seum, 1952; 1954. 13pp, 264 terms defined

2967 Godden, Geoffrey Arthur. Antique China and Glass Under
      Five Pounds. London: Barker, 1966. 129pp, ill, 24
      pls, bib (1840-1914)

2968 _____. Antique Glass and China; a guide for the beginning
      collector. South Brunswick, NJ: A. S. Barnes, 1967.
      94pp, ill

2969 Haggar, Reginald George. Pottery Through the Ages. New
      York: Roy Publishing; London: Methuen, 1959. 74pp,
      ill, bib (Juvenile literature)

2970 Handbook of the Jones Collection in the South Kensington Mu-
      seum. London: Chapman & Hall, 1883. 160pp, ill
      (Sevres, Dresden, Chelsea, Oriental porcelain. Includes
      a few pieces of Louis 16 furniture inlaid with Sevres
      porcelain)

2971 A Handbook on Pottery and Glassware. Being a revised ed.
      of "A Textbook for (Pottery and Glass) Salespeople," 1923.
      London: Scott, Greenwood, 1933.

2972 [No entry.]

2973 Harbin, Edith, and Mary Joseph. Blue and White Pottery.
      Tenn: 1973. 21 color pls with notes, prices

2974 Harrison, Herbert Spencer, 1872- . Pots and Pans. The
      history of ceramics. London: G. Howe, 1928. 88pp,
      ill, bib MB, NN

2975 Hartman, Hazel. Porcelain and Pottery Marks. New York:
      1943. 128pp, marks (Italy, Holland, Germany, Eng-
      land, American)

2975a Haslam, Malcolm. Pottery. London: Orbis, 1972. 64pp,
      chiefly ill, bib

2976 Herring, James Vernon. Exhibition of Ceramics, Textiles,
      Metal and Wood Work from 450 B.C. to 1946. Howard
      University Gallery of Art. October-November 1947.
      Washington, D.C.: 1947. 20pp, ill

2977 Higgins and Seiter. China and Cut Glass/1889. Catalog re-
      print. Princeton, NJ: Pyne, 1971. 288pp, 1150 ill, bib
      (Limoges, Dresden, Bavarian, Austrian Imperial Crown,
      Cauldon china; Bohemian and gold glass; vases; Dutch
      pottery; cameo vases; steins, etc.; clocks, jardiniers,
      plaques)

2978 _____. China and Cut Glass, Limoges, Dresden, Bavarian,
      Austrian Imperial Crown ... etc. 1899. Catalog reprint.
      Princeton, NJ: Pyne, 1971. 275pp, ill, 20 pls, bib

2979 *Hillier, Bevis. Pottery and Porcelain 1700-1914: England,
      Europe and North America. London: Weidenfeld &
      Nicolson; New York: Meredith Pr, 1968. 386pp, ill
      (15 color), bib (Ceramics in their historic context)

2980 Hirst, Arlene. Every Woman's Guide to China, Glass, and
      Silver. New York: Arco, 1970. 126pp, ill

2981 Hobson, Robert Lockhart, 1872-1941. Porcelain (of All
      Countries): Oriental, Continental and British: a book of
      handy reference for collectors. London: Constable; New
      York: Dutton, 1906; London: 1908; New York: F. A.
      Stokes, 1910; 1917. 245pp, ill, 49 pls, marks ViU, BM

2982 _____, and Oliver Brackett. Catalogue of Porcelain,
      Furniture and other works of art in the collection of Lady
      Wantage ..., Lockinge House, Berks., and Overstone
      Park, Northants. Enfield: W. H. Fairbairns, 1912.
      111pp, pls DeWint

2983 Hodges, Henry. Pottery. Feltham: Hamlyn, 1972. 159pp,
      ill, bib

2984 Hodgson, Mrs. (A.) Willoughby. The Book of Old China.
      London: Bell, 1912. 135pp, marks, gloss

2985 _____. How to Identify Old China. London: Bell, 1904;
      1909; enl. rev. ed. London: Jenkins, 1928. 165pp, ill;
      ...; 183pp. ill, 40 pls, bib DLC, DeWint

2986 Hollowood, A. Bernard. Pottery and Glass. Harmondsworth,
      Eng: Penguin, 1947. 63pp, ill

2987 Honey, William Bowyer. The Art of the Potter; a book for
      the collector and the connoisseur. London: Faber, 1946;
      New York: Whittlesey, 1950?; New York: Beechhurst Pr,
      1955. 111pp, ill, 160 pls

2988 _____ . Pottery and Porcelain: a reader's guide. Cambridge: U Pr, for National Book League, 1950. 19pp,
bib

_____, and J. P. Cushion. Handbook of Pottery and Porce-
lain Marks. See: Cushion, J. P., no. 2940.

2989 Hooper, William Harcourt, and William Charles Phillips. A
Manual of Marks on Pottery and Porcelain. London:
Macmillan, 1876; 1877; new ed. 1879; 2nd ed. London;
New York: 1896; reprint. 1936. 238pp, ill

2990 Hughes, George Bernard. The Country Life Pocket Book of
China. London: Country Life, 1965; as The Collectors
Pocket Book of China. London: Hamlyn, 1965; New
York: Hawthorn, 1967; London: 1970. 376pp, ill, marks

2991 Jackson, Mary L. If Dishes Could Talk: the history and romance of old china. Boston: Meador, 1959; reprint.
Des Moines: Wallace-Homestead, 1971. 240pp, ill, gloss

2992 Jacquemart, Albert, 1805-1875. History of the Ceramic Art.
A Descriptive and philosophical study of the pottery of all
ages and nations. Tr. from French by Fanny (Mrs. Bury)
Palliser. London: Low, Marston, 1873; 2nd ed. 1877.
627pp, 200 ill, 12 color pls, 1000 marks TxU, DeWint,
ViU, DLC

2993 Jervis, William Percival. A Book of Pottery Marks. Philadelphia: Hayes Brothers, 1897; Philadelphia: Wright,
Tyndale & van Roden, 1898. 101pp, ill, several thousand
marks NN, DeWint

2994 _____ , comp. The Encyclopedia of Ceramics. New York:
1902. 673pp, ill, bib NN

2995 _____ . A Pottery Primer. New York: O'Gorman, 1911.
188pp, ill, pls NN

2996 Johnson, Stanley Currie. Collecting Old China. London:
Country Life, 1922. 32pp, ill NN

2997 Joyce, Max Wykes. 7000 Years of Pottery and Porcelain.
London: Peter Owen, 1958. 276pp, ill

2998 Katzenberg, Dena S. Blue Traditions; indigo dyed textiles
and related cobalt glazed ceramics from the 17th through
the 19th century. Exhibition. December 1973-January
1974. Baltimore: Museum of Art, 1973. 203pp, ill, bib

2999 Klein, William Karl. Repairing and Restoring China and
Glass: the Klein Method. New York: Harper & Row,
1962. 291pp, ill

3000 Kovel, Ralph M., and Terry Kovel. Dictionary of Marks;
      pottery and porcelain. New York: Crown, 1953; Cam-
      bridge: Heffer, 1954. 278pp, ill, bib, 5000 marks
      (American, English, European)

3001 Lancaster, H. Boswell. Talks on Pottery. Ed. by Vivian
      Brodzky. Leeds: Patina Pr, 1949. 63pp, pls

3002 Lane, (E.) Arthur. A Guide to the Collection of (Pottery)
      Tiles. V & A. London: HMSO, 1939; 2nd ed. 1961.
      75pp, 48 pls; 88pp, 49 pls, bib

3003 _____. Style in Pottery. London; New York: Oxford U
      Pr, 1948; 2nd ed. London: Faber, 1973; Parkridge, NJ:
      Noyes Pr, 1974. 63pp, pls; 80pp, ill, 1 pl

3004 Lee, Albert, 1868- . Portraits in Pottery, with Some
      Account of Pleasant Occasions Incident to Their Quest.
      Boston: Stratford, 1931. 272pp, pls, bib

3005 Lee, Ruth Wile. Exploring the World of Pottery. Chicago:
      Children's Pr, 1967. 93pp, ill (Juvenile literature)

3006 A List of Works on Pottery and Porcelain in the National Art
      Library. London: Eyre & Spottiswoode, 1875. 22pp BM

3007 *Litchfield, Frederick. Pottery and Porcelain: a guide to
      collectors. London: Bickers, 1879; London: Truslove,
      1899; London: A. & C. Black, 1925; 5th ed. enl and rev.
      by Frank Tilley. New York: M. Barrows; London:
      Black, 1951; 1953; 1963. 211pp, ill, pls; 362pp, 150 ill,
      46 pls, bib, marks

3008 Lockwood, Mary Smith. Hand-Book of Ceramic Art. New
      York: Putnam's, 1878. 137pp, frontis, bib BM

3009 Lunn, Richard. Pottery: a handbook of practical pottery for
      art teachers and students. 2 vol. London: Chapman &
      Hall, 1903-1910. 100pp, ill, bib PP

3010 *Marryat, Joseph. Collection (or Contribution) Towards a
      History of Pottery and Porcelain in the 15th, 16th, 17th
      and 18th centuries: with a description of the manufacture,
      a glossary, and list of monograms. London: J. Murray,
      1850; 2nd ed. augmented as A History of Pottery and
      Porcelain, medieval and modern. London: 1857; 3rd rev.
      ed. 1868. 381pp, ill, color pls; 472pp, ill, 12 color pls,
      color frontis; 549pp, 303 ill, 6 color pls BM

3011 Maskell, William. Pottery and Porcelain. South Kensington
      Museum. London: Chapman & Hall, 188-? ill NN

3012 Milward. List of Books on Pottery in the Hanley Museum.
      Hanley, Eng: 1905.

3013   Moffit, C., and R. Moffit. Old Chinaware Summary: an aid
       to identification. Boston?: Herman Publications, 1960.
       ill

3014   Moran, M. J. Porcelain Collecting for Beginners. London:
       Gifford, 1972. 117pp, ill, 16 pls

3015   Nichols, George Ward, 1837-1885. Pottery: how it is made,
       its shape and decoration, practical instructions for painting
       on porcelain and all kinds of pottery. New York: Put-
       nam's, 1879. 142pp, 42 ill, pls, bib DLC

3016   *Nichols, John Gough. Examples of Decorative Tiles Some-
       times Termed Encaustic ... in facsimile. London: J.
       B. Nichols, 1845. 19pp, 100 pls

3017   Nicholson, J. B. Catalogue of Books on Ceramics in the
       Manchester Free Library. Manchester, Eng: 1908.

3018   Noke, Charles John, and Harold J. Plant. Pottery: being a
       simple account of the history of pottery, and a description
       of some of the processes employed. London: Pitman,
       1924; 2nd ed. 1927. 136pp, ill; 148pp, ill BM

3019   *Norton, Edith M. Reading List on Arts and Crafts: Ce-
       ramics and glassware. new ed. Buffalo, NY: Grosvenor
       Library, 1907. 27pp (85% periodicals) NNC-Ave

3020   Old China. Monthly. Syracuse, NY: Keramic Studio,
       1901-04.

3021   Palliser, Fanny Marryat (Mrs. Bury). The China Collector's
       Pocket-Companion. London: Sampson Low, 1874; 3rd ed.
       1875. 136pp, ill, marks; 164pp, ill, marks

3022   Parsons, Claudia Sydney Maria, and F. H. Curl. China
       Mending and Restoration. London: Faber, 1963. 435pp,
       ill

3023   Peterson, E. Paul, and A. Peterson. Collector's Handbook
       of Marks on Pottery and Porcelain. Bridgeport, Conn:
       Associated Booksellers, 1974. 213pp (Italy, Germany,
       Holland, Scandinavia, Russia, France, Britain, Persia,
       Near East, China, Japan)

3024   Pier, Garrett Chatfield, 1875- . Catalogue of the Collection
       of Pottery, Porcelain and Faience. Metropolitan Museum.
       New York: 1911. 425pp, ill, 42 pls, bib

3025   Poche, Emanuel. Porcelain Marks of the World. New York:
       Arco, 1974. 255pp, marks

3026   The Potter. Periodical. London: 1893-94.

3027 Pottery and Porcelain: a Dictionary of Terms. New York: Hippocrene Books, 1974. ill

3028 Pottery and Porcelain Hand Book for the Use of Visitors Examining Pottery and Porcelain in the Metropolitan Museum. New York: 1875. 138pp, ill

3029 Pottery Gazette. Periodical. London: 1875- .

3030 Prime, William Cowper. Pottery and Porcelain of All Times and Nations, with tables of factories and artists' marks.... New York: Harper, 1878; 3rd ed. 1879. 531pp, ill, bib

3031 Rackham, Bernard. A Book of Porcelain. Fine examples in the Victoria and Albert Museum, painted by William Gibb. London: HMSO, A. & C. Black, 1910. 95pp, 28 color pls tipped in, marks (Chinese, Japanese, Italian, French, German and English)

3032 _____. A Key to Pottery and Glass. London; Glasgow: Blackie & Son, 1940; New York: Chemical Publishing, 1941. 180pp, ill, 16 pls

3033 Rhead, George Wooliscroft. The Earthenware Collector. London: Jenkins, 1920. 316pp, 60 ill, marks, bib

3034 Ripley, Mary Churchill. The Colour Blue in Pottery and Porcelain. Reprint from Old China. Syracuse, NY: 1902. 25pp, ill

3035 Roberts, William, 1862- . Rare Books and Their Prices; with chapters on pictures, pottery, porcelain, and postage stamps. London: G. Redway, 1896. 155pp

3036 Rose, Arthur Veel. Notes on Pottery of the 19th Century. New York: priv. printed, 1901; 2nd ed. New York; 1904. 47pp, marks

3037 Rust, Gordon A. Collector's Guide to Antique Porcelain. New York: Viking; London: Deutsch, 1973. 144pp, ill, bib

3038 Savage, George. Ceramics for the Collector; an introduction to pottery and porcelain. London: Rockliff, 1956. 224pp, ill, 1 color pl, bib

3039 * _____. Porcelain Through the Ages. Harmondsworth, Eng: Penguin, 1954; 2nd ed. London: Cassell, 1961; Baltimore; Penguin, 1963. 333pp, ill, bib; ...; 352pp, ill, bib (China, Europe, England to end of 19th century)

3040 * _____. Pottery Through the Ages. Harmondsworth, Eng: Penguin, 1959; London: Cassell, 1963. 247pp, ill, bib

3041 _____, and Harold Newman. An Illustrated Dictionary of
Ceramics: defining 3,054 terms relating to wares, materials, processes, styles, patterns, and shapes from
antiquity to the present day. Introductory list compiled
by John Cushion. London: Thames & Hudson; New York:
Van Nostrand Reinhold, 1974. 320pp, ill, 16 pls

3042 Schmidt, Robert, 1878-1952. Porcelain as an Art and Mirror
of Fashion. Tr. from German by W. A. Thorpe. London: Harrap, 1932. 336pp, 200 ill, 8 color pls, bib

3043 *Scott, Cleo M., and G. Ryland Scott, Jr. Antique Porcelain
Digest. Newport, Monm., Eng: Ceramic Book Co, 1961.
200pp, ill, 179 pls, bib (750 specimens ill)

3044 Searle, Alfred Broadhead, 1877- . An Encyclopedia of the
Ceramic Industries, being a guide to the materials,
methods of manufacture, means of recognition, and testing
the various articles in the clay-working and allied industries,
including clays, silica, felspar, bricks, tiles, pottery,
porcelain, pencils, refractory materials, ... for ... manufacturers, research workers, students, connoisseurs and
others. 3 vol. London: E. Benn, 1929-30. ill, bib

3045 Slosson, Mrs. A. The China-Hunters' Club. London?: 1878.
ill SIB-2

3046 Smith, Robert Henry Soden. A List of Works on Pottery and
Porcelain in the National Art Library, South Kensington
Museum. London: Eyre & Spottiswoode, 1875; 2nd ed.
as A List of Books and Pamphlets.... 1885. 22pp; 147pp

3047 Smith, Robert Murdoch. List of Books, etc., relating to
pottery and porcelain in the Library of the Edinburgh Museum of Science and Art. Edinburgh: 1893. 59pp

3048 *Solon, Louis Marc Emanuel. Catalogue of the Ceramic Li-
brary (Central School of Science and Technology, Stoke-on-
Trent), including the Solon Library, the Ceramic Society
Library, and the Library of the Pottery Department of the
School. Hanley, Eng: 1925; Supplement. 1930. ...; 98pp
V & A

3049 *_____. Ceramic Literature: an analytical index to the
works published in all languages on the history and the
technology of the ceramic art; also to the catalogues of
public museums, private collections and of auction sales
... and to the most important price-lists of the ancient
and modern manufactories of pottery and porcelain. London: Charles Griffin, 1910; Supplement: List of Books
on the History and Technology of the Ceramic Art. In
Ceramic Society Transactions, vol. 6, pp. 65-104.

Stoke-on-Trent: 1911-12. 660pp; 40pp (Absolute must. Exhaustive, all-language work with pungeant remarks) BM, NNC-Ave

3050 ———. Pottery Worship. 7 parts. London: Clowes, 1928.

3051 Sparkes, John Charles Lewis. Hints to China and Tile Decorators. Edited and revised by an American decorator, who has added designs of the principal borders, etc., used by the celebrated Wedgwood, and a list of all materials used in china and tile decoration. Boston: S. W. Tilton, 1877. 85pp, ill, 2 pls DLC

3052 ———, and Walter Gandy. Potters, Their Arts and Crafts. London: S. W. Partridge, 1896. 260pp, ill, pls

3053 Suttenfield, Elise. The Parade of Porcelain; a history. New York: Exposition Pr, 1963; 1964. 56pp, ill

3054 Theus, Will H. How to Detect and Collect Antique Porcelain and Pottery. New York: Knopf, 1974. ill, bib

3055 Thorn, C. Jordan. Handbook of Old Pottery and Porcelain Marks. New York: Tudor, 1949. 214pp, ill, 4000 marks and monograms arranged by country (From 15th century on)

3056 Trapnell, Alfred. Catalogues of the Trapnell Collection. Bristol: priv. printed, 1898.

3057 Treadwell, John H. A Manual of Pottery and Porcelain for American Collectors. New York: Putnam; London: Sampson Low, 1872. 161pp, ill, marks (Egyptian to European)

3058 Usher, James Ward. An Art Collector's Treasures, ... being a record historical and descriptive of the art collection formed by J. W. Usher (of Lincoln) 1886-1914. Introd. by George C. Williamson. London: Chiswick Pr, priv. printed, 1916. 223pp, 79 color pls (Chiefly porcelain--Chelsea, Worcester, Nankin, Sevres, Dresden, Derby, etc. Also French and English watches, Battersea enamels, miniatures, English silver, etc.)

3059 Vance-Phillips, L. Book of the China-Painter; a complete guide for the keramic decorator. New York: M. Marks, 1896. 311pp, ill

3060 *Waring, John Burley, ed. Pottery and Porcelain. Includes "Ceramic Art," by J. C. Robinson. London: Day & Son, 1857. 31pp, ill, color pls

3061 *Weale, James W. H. Classed Catalogue of Printed Books.
      Ceramics. National Art Library, South Kensington Mu-
      seum. London: Eyre & Spottiswoode, 1895.

3062 *Weiss, Gustav. The Book of Porcelain. Tr. from German
      by Janet Seligman. London: Barrie & Jenkins; New York:
      Praeger, 1971. 334pp, ill, pls, bib, 2500 marks (Orient
      and Europe to 1900)

3063 Westropp, Hodder Michael. Handbook of Pottery and Porce-
      lain, or history of those arts from earliest periods. Lon-
      don: Chatto & Windus; New York: R. Worthington, 1880.
      171pp, ill BM

3064 Whiteford, Sidney T. A Guide to Porcelain Painting. London:
      G. Rownew, 1877. 48pp, pls (part color), color frontis

3065 Whitehead, John W. Pottery and Porcelain: a brief account
      of the principal manufactures at home and abroad, with
      the most frequent marks. London: F. P. Wilson, 1898.
      308pp

3066 Williams, Guy Richard. Collecting Cheap China and Glass.
      London: Corgi, 1969. 125pp, ill, bib

3067 Wolseley, Cecilia. and Felicia Schuster. Those Minor Monu-
      ments: fresh lights on china appreciation. London:
      Angus & Robertson; New York: Arco, 1970. 115pp, ill,
      12 pls, bib

3068 Wood, Serry (pseud. for Graydon La Verne Freeman). Hand-
      painted China, including how-to-do section by S. S. Frackel-
      ton. Watkins Glen, NY: Century, 1953. 89pp, pls

3069 Wykes-Joyce, Max. 7000 Years of Pottery and Porcelain.
      London: Owen; New York: Philosophical Library, 1958.
      276pp, ill, 85 pls, bib

3070 Young, Jennie J. The Ceramic Art; a compendium of the
      history and manufacture of pottery and porcelain. New
      York: Harper, 1879. 499pp, ill, pls

3071 Zoellner, Adalbert. The Book of Porcelain. Tr. from Ger-
      man (1925). London: Methuen, 1927. 194pp, 32 pls

AMERICAN AND CANADIAN CERAMICS

3072 Adamson, Jack E. Illustrated Handbook of Ohio Sewer Pipe
      Folk Art. Barberton, O: 1973. 88pp, chiefly ill

3073 Alexander, Donald E. Roseville Pottery for the Collector.
      n.p.: Author, 1970. 78pp, ill, marks

3074 *Altman, Violet, and Seymour Altman. The Book of Buffalo
      Pottery. New York: Crown, 1969. 192pp, ill, bib

3075 American Ceramic Society Journal. Monthly. Easton, Pa:
      1918- . ill, pls

3076 The American Porcelain Tradition, 18th, 19th, 20th centuries.
      Loan exhibition from the New Jersey State Museum, May-
      June 1972. Shreveport, La: C. Young for Norton Art
      Gallery, 1972. 32pp, ill, bib

3077 American Pottery and Glassware Reporter. Weekly. Pitts-
      burgh: Journal of Industry, 1879-1882. (Continued as
      Pottery and Glassware Reporter)

3078 American Pottery Gazette. The monthly organ of the china,
      glass and kindred trades. Periodical. New York: Asso-
      ciated Trades Publishing, 1905-08.

3079 American Studio Pottery. V & A. London: HMSO, 1974.
      ill

3080 Barber, Edwin Atlee. Historical Sketch of the Green Point,
      New York, porcelain works of Charles Cartlidge and
      Company. Indianapolis: Clay-Worker, 1895. 59pp, ill

3081 _____ . Inscribed Pottery of the Pennsylvania Germans.
      Philadelphia: Museum of Art, 19-? PPPM

3082 _____ . Lead Glazed Pottery. Part first (Common Clays):
      plain glazed, sgraffito and slip-decorated wares. Phila-
      delphia: Museum of Art, 1907; Philadelphia: Hodder &
      Stoughton, 1908-; no more published. 32pp, ill, pls BM

3083 * _____ . Marks of American Potters. Philadelphia: Pat-
      terson & White, 1904; reprint. Southampton, NY: Cracker
      Barrel Pr, 1971? 174pp, ill, 1000 marks in facsimile
      NN

3084 * _____ . Pennsylvania Museum of School of Art. Catalog
      of American potteries and porcelain. Philadelphia: Mu-
      seum, 1893. 43pp, ill, color frontis

3085 * _____ . Pottery and Porcelain of the United States. An
      historical review of American ceramic art. London:
      Putnam's, 1895; 2nd rev. enl. ed. New York; London:
      Putnam's, 1901; 3rd ed. rev. & enl. 1909; reprint with
      a new introd. and bibliography. Watkins Glen, NY:
      Century, 1971. 446pp, 223 ill; 539pp, 277 ill; 621pp,
      335 ill; 450pp, ill, bib, 1000 marks

3086 * _____ . Tulip Ware of the Pennsylvania-German Potters:
      an historical sketch of the art of slip-decoration in the

United States. Philadelphia: Pennsylvania Museum of
Art, Patterson & White, 1903; 1926; reprint with introd.
by Henry J. Kauffman. New York: Dover; London: Constable, 1970. 233pp, 100 ill, 2 color pls

3087 _____. The Work of the Potteries of New Jersey from
1685-1876, being extracts from "The Pottery and Porcelain of the United States," by E. A. Barber, ... and
marks of New Jersey potteries as reproduced from "Pottery," published by the Thomas Maddock's Sons Co.
Newark, NJ: Museum Association, 1914. 34pp, ill

3088 Barnard, Julian. Victorian Ceramic Tiles. London: Studio
Vista; Greenwich, Conn: N.Y. Graphic Society, 1972.
184pp ill, pls, bib (Art tiles, 1830-1900. American
and English)

3089 Barons, Richard I. An Exhibition of 18th and 19th Century
American Folk Pottery. New Paltz, NY: 1969. 35pp,
ill

3090 *Barret, Richard Carter. Bennington Pottery and Porcelain.
A guide to identification. New York: Crown. 1958.
342pp, 450 pls of over 2000 pieces, 7 color pls (Definitive work by the curator of the Bennington Museum. Includes the Elizabeth McCullough Johnson Collection; the
collections at Bennington, notably the John Spargo Collection; and others)

3091 * _____. A Color Guide to Bennington Pottery. Manchester,
Vt: Forward Color Productions, 1966. 30pp, 200 pieces
ill, 14 color pls

3092 * _____. How to Identify Bennington Pottery. Brattleboro,
Vt: S. Greene Pr, 1964. 71pp ill (Comparison of
handles, bases, etc.)

3093 Bivins, John, Jr. The Moravian Potters in North Carolina.
Winston-Salem: U of N.C. Pr, for Old Salem, Inc.,
1972. 300pp, ill, bib

3094 Blair, C. Dean. The Potters and Potteries of Summit
County, 1828-1915. Akron, O: Summit County Historical
Society, 1965. 59pp, ill (Ohio)

3095 [No entry.]

3096 Case, Richard G. Onondaga Pottery. Catalog of exhibition,
December 1973-January 1974. Syracuse, NY: Everson
Museum of Art of Syracuse and Onondanga County, 1973.
10pp, ill

3097 Catalogue of Rookwood Art Pottery Shapes. Kingston, NY:
P-B Enterprises, 1971. u.p., ill

3098   Christensen, Erwin Ottomar. Early American Designs:
       Ceramics. New York: Pitman, 1952. 48pp, chiefly ill

3099   Clarke, John Mason. Swiss Influence on the Early Pennsyl-
       vania Slip Decorated Majolica. Albany, NY: J. B. Lyon,
       printer, 1908. 18pp, ill NN, DLC, MiGr

3100   Clay in the Hands of the Potter; an exhibition of pottery
       manufactured in the Rochester and Genesee Valley Region,
       ca.1793-1900. March-August 1974. Rochester, NY:
       Museum and Science Center, 1974. 56pp, ill, bib

3101   *Clement, Arthur Wilfred. Notes on American Ceramics,
       1607-1943. Handbook to the Museum Collections.
       Brooklyn, NY: Museum, 1944. 36pp, ill, pls, bib

3102   _____. Notes on American Pottery. Part 1. Some
       Early New Jersey Potteries. New York: Court Pr,
       1942- . ill

3103   _____. Notes on Early American Porcelain, 1738-1838.
       New York: Court Pr, priv. printed, 1946. 38pp DLC

3104   *   _____. Our Pioneer Potters. York, Pa: Maple Pr,
       1947; New York: priv. printed, 1947. 94pp, 24 ill,
       pls, bib DLC

3105   _____. Preliminary Notes for a Catalogue of Made-in-
       America Pottery and Porcelain Assembled for Exhibition
       at the Brooklyn Museum. Brooklyn: 1942. 32pp, bib

3106   *   _____, and Edith Bishop. The Pottery and Porcelain of
       New Jersey, 1688-1900. Exhibition. Newark, NJ:
       Newark Museum, 1947. ill

3107   Collard, Elizabeth. 19th Century Pottery and Porcelain in
       Canada. Montreal: McGill U Pr, 1967. 441pp, ill,
       pls, bib

3108   Collins, Steven N. Decorated Stoneware, the Art of the
       American Folk Potter. Exhibition. New Paltz, NY:
       College Art Gallery, State University College, 1974. ill
       (1795-1900)

3109   Crawford, Jean. Jugtown Pottery: History and Design.
       Winston-Salem, NC: John F. Blair, 1964. 127pp, ill,
       bib (Mid-18th century to present)

3110   Curtis, Phillip H. Tucker Porcelain 1826-1838; a re-ap-
       praisal. Thesis. 1972. 148pp, pls DeWint

3111   Du Tilleux, Jean. Roses in Porcelain. Exhibition. June-
       July 1973. Shreveport, La: R. W. Norton Art Founda-
       tion, 1973. 16pp, ill (American)

3112 *Earle, Alice Morse. China Collecting in America. New
        York: Scribner's, 1892; 1902; 1906; 1916; New York:
        Empire State Book Co, 1924; reprints. Detroit: Singing
        Tree Pr, 1970; (of 1892 ed.) Rutland. Vt: Tuttle, 1973.
        429pp, ill, pls (Colonial to 20th century)

3113 East Liverpool Pottery. Reprint of undated catalog. Chatta-
        nooga, Tenn: J & S Co, 197-? 89 ill (Ohio-made bowl
        and pitcher sets, plates, teapots, etc.)

3114 English and American Ceramics of the 18th and 19th Centuries;
        a selection from the collection of Mr. and Mrs. Harold G.
        Duckworth. December 1968-January 1969. Toledo, O:
        Toledo Museum, 1968. 53pp, ill, bib

3115 *Evans, Paul Frederic. Art Pottery of the United States. An
        encyclopedia of producers and their marks. New York:
        Scribner, 1974. 341pp, hundreds of ill, 23 color pls, bib,
        marks

3116 Exhibition of 18th and 19th Century Folk Pottery. February-
        March 1969. New Paltz, NY: State University College,
        Art Gallery, 1969. 61pp, ill

3117 Famous White House Chinaware ... an historical series of
        the chinaware of our Presidents. 32 parts in 1 vol.
        Newark, NJ: Ceramic Age, April 1935-September 1936.
        ill

3118 Fisher, Leonard Everett. The Potters. New York: F.
        Watts, 1969. 47pp, ill (Juvenile literature. Colonial
        period)

3119 Freeman, Graydon La Verne (Larry). Ironstone China. Wat-
        kins Glen, NY: Century, 1954; 1964. 79pp, chiefly ill,
        pls, marks

3120 Freeman, John Crosby. Blue-Decorated Stoneware of New
        York State. Watkins Glen, NY: Century; Yorker Yankee
        Museum Study Catalog, 19-? ill

3121 *Guilland, Harold Floyd. Early American Folk Pottery. Phila-
        delphia; London: Chilton Books, 1971. 322pp, 500 ill,
        16 pls, bib (Selections from the Index of American Design)

3122 Harris, W. B. The Potter's Wheel, and How It Goes Around.
        A complete description of the manufacture of pottery in
        America. Trenton, NJ: Burroughts & Mountford, 1886.
        63pp, ill NN

3123 Hawes, Lloyd E., and others. The Dedham Pottery. Dedham,
        Mass: Historical Society, 1968. 52pp, pls (Art pottery,
        1895-1943)

3124 *Henzke, Lucille. American Art Pottery. Camden, NJ: T. Nelson, 1970. 336pp, ill, gloss

3125 Hoffmann, Donald C. Why Not Warwick. Wheeling, W. Va: priv. printed, 1975. 116pp, ill, marks (Late 19th century china similar to Weller or Rookwood)

3126 Holmes, George Sanford. Lenox China; the story of Walter Scott Lenox. Trenton, NJ: Lenox, 1914; Philadelphia: priv. printed, 1924. 72pp, ill, pls (Lenox, 1859-1920) MiU

3127 Hood, Graham. Bonnin and Morris of Philadelphia; the first American porcelain factory, 1770-1772. Chapel Hill: U of N. Carolina Pr, for Institute of Early American History and Culture, Williamsburg, Va, 1972. 78pp, ill, bib

3128 Horney, Wayne B. Pottery of the Galena Area. Galena, Ill: 1965. 48pp, ill, color pls

3129 Hough, Walter. An Early West Virginia Pottery. Reprint from Report of the United States National Museum. Washington, D.C.: 1901. 10pp, ill, 18 pls (John Thompson's Morgantown pottery, 1800-1873. Includes plates of tools and moulds) MiU

3130 Huxford, Sharon, and Bob Huxford. The Collector's Encyclopedia of Roseville Pottery. Paducah, Ky: Collector Books, 1976; Price Guide. 1976. 184pp, ill of 2000 pieces

3131 *James, Arthur Edwin. The Potters and Potteries of Chester County, Pennsylvania. West Chester, Pa: Chester County Historical Society, 1945. 116pp, ill, pls, bib

3132 Johnson, Deb, and Gini Johnson. Beginner's Book of American Pottery. Des Moines: Wallace-Homestead, 1974; Price Guide, 1974. 119pp, hundreds of ill, 138 color ill

3133 Kamm, Minnie Watson. Old China. Grosse Pointe, Mich: Kamm Publications, 1951. 251pp, ill, marks (American and British, 1825-1890)

3134 Kendall, A. Harold. The Story of Hampshire Pottery. Keene, NH: 1963. 5pp (Hampshire Pottery, manufactured by J. B. Taft & Co., Keene)

3135 Keramic Studio. Periodical. Syracuse, NY: 19-?

3136 Ketchum, William C., Jr. Early Potters and Potteries of New York State. New York: Funk & Wagnalls, 1970. 278pp, ill, bib

3137 _____. The Pottery and Porcelain Collectors' Handbook;

a guide to Early American ceramics, from Maine to California. New York: Funk & Wagnalls, 1971. 204pp,
16pp of ill (Late 18th to early 20th century)

3138   Kircher, Edwin J. Rookwood Pottery: an explanation of its
       marks and symbols. Terrace Park?, O: priv. printed,
       1962. 20pp, ill, marks

3139   _____, and Barbara and Joseph Agranoff. Rookwood: its
       golden age of art pottery, 1880-1929. Cincinnati: Rook-
       wood Golden Era, 1969. 34pp, color pls

3140   Klamkin, Marian. American Patriotic and Political China.
       New York: Scribner, 1973. 215pp, ill, color ill

3141   _____. White House China. New York: Scribner, 1972.
       184pp, ill, bib

3142   Klapthor, Margaret Brown. Official White House China.
       Washington, D.C.: Smithsonian Institution Pr, 1975.
       284pp, 164 (81 color) ill, bib (George Washington to
       Lyndon Johnson)

3143   Kovel, Ralph, and Terry Kovel. Collector's Guide to Ameri-
       can Art Pottery. New York: Crown, 1974. 348pp, 700
       (100 color) ill, bib, marks (Plates, paperweights, medals,
       etc.)

3144   Lambart, Helen H. The Rivers of the Potters: the St.
       Charles and Cap-Rouge potteries in the late 19th century.
       Ottawa: National Museum of Canada, 1970. 30pp, ill,
       bib

3145   _____. Two Centuries of Ceramics in the Richelieu Val-
       ley; a documentary history. Ed. by Jennifer Arcand.
       Ottawa: National Museum of Canada, 1970. 34pp, ill,
       bib (Quebec)

3146   *McKearin, George Skinner. Loan Exhibition of Early Ameri-
       can Pottery and Early American Glass from Collection of
       G. S. McKearin, held 1931 at Grand Central Palace, New
       York. Hossick Falls, NY: Author, 1931. 56pp, ill

3147   Miller, J. Jefferson II, and Lyle M. Stone. 18th Century
       Ceramics from Fort Michilimackinac; a study in historical
       archaeology. Washington, D.C.: Smithsonian Institution,
       1970. 130pp, ill, bib

3148   Noel-Hume, Ivor. Pottery and Porcelain in Colonial Williams-
       burg Archaeological Collections. Williamsburg, Va: 1969.
       ill

3149   Osgood, Cornelius. The Jug and Related Stoneware of

Bennington. Rutland, Vt: Tuttle, 1971. 222pp, ill, 31
(8 color) pls, bib (19th century Norton potteries)

3150   Pappas, Joan, and A. Harold Kendall. Hampshire Pottery
       Manufactured by J. S. Taft and Co., Keene, New Hamp-
       shire. Manchester, Vt: 1971. 21pp, color pls

3151   *Peck, Herbert. Book of Rookwood Pottery. New York:
       Crown, 1968; Price Guide. 1969. 192pp, ill, marks
       (1880-)

3152   Pitkin, Albert Hastings, 1852-1917. Early American Folk
       Pottery, including the history of Bennington Pottery.
       Hartford, Conn: Case, Lockwood and Brainard, 1918.
       152pp, ill, pls

3153   Platt, Dorothy Pickard. The Story of Pickard China. Penn-
       sylvania: n.p., 1970. 87pp, ill, marks (1893 to present.
       Hand-painted pottery)

3154   Pocket Guide to Crockery and Silver Settings for the 1880
       Table. Reprint of material by Miss Maria Parloa, famous
       writer on domestic economy. Watkins Glen, NY: Century,
       1969. ill

3155   *The Potters and Potteries of Chester County, Pennsylvania.
       West Chester, Pa: Chester County Historical Society,
       1945.

3155a Pottery and Glassware Reporter. Weekly. Pittsburgh:
       Journal of Industry, 1879- . (Was American Pottery
       and Glass Reporter, before 1882)

3156   The Pottery and Porcelain of New Jersey Prior to 1876. Ex-
       hibition. February-March 1915. Newark, NJ: Museum
       Association, 1915. 32pp NN

3157   The Pottery and Porcelain of New Jersey, 1688-1900. Exhi-
       bition. April-May 1947. Newark: Museum Association,
       1947. 100pp, ill, bib

3158   [No entry.]

3159   Powell, Elizabeth A. Pennsylvania Pottery; tools and pro-
       cesses. Doylestown, Pa: Bucks County Historical So-
       ciety, 1972. 20pp, ill

3160   Purviance, Louise, Evan Purviance, and Norris F. Schneider.
       Roseville Art Pottery. Des Moines: Wallace-Homestead,
       1973; Price Guide. 197-? 51pp, 24 color pls

3161   _____, _____, and _____. Weller Art Pottery in

Color. Des Moines: Wallace-Homestead, 1975; Price
Guide, 197-? 48pp, ill, 24 color pls

3162 _____, _____, and _____. Zanesville Art Pottery in
Color. Leon, Io: Mid-America Book, 1968; Price Guide.
1968. 50pp, ill, 24 color pls, marks (Ohio: Zanesville,
Weller, Owen potteries)

3163 _____, _____, and _____. Zanesville Art Tile in
Color. Des Moines: Wallace-Homestead, 1975. 24
color pls (1874-1967)

3164 *Quimby, Ian M. G., ed. Ceramics in America. Winterthur
Conference Report 1972. Charlottesville, Va: U Pr of
Va, for the Henry Francis du Pont Winterthur Museum,
1973. 374pp, ill, bib

3165 *Ramsay, John. American Potters and Pottery. Boston:
Hale, Cushman & Flint, 1939; New York: Tudor, 1947.
304pp, 102 ill, bib, marks (19th century)

3166 Ray, Marcia. Collectible Ceramics. An encyclopedia of
pottery and porcelain for the American collector. New
York: Crown, 1974. 256pp, ill, 16 color pls (Chiefly
American art pottery)

3167 Raycraft, Donald R., and Carol Raycraft. American Country
Pottery. Des Moines: Wallace-Homestead, 1975. ill

3168 *Rice, Alvin H., and John Baer Stoudt. The Shenandoah Pottery. Strasburg, Va: Shenandoah Publishing, 1929.
277pp, ill, 7 color pls, marks (Shenandoah Pottery;
Bell Pottery; Eberly and Keister Potteries; early North
Carolina Moravians; etc.)

3169 The Rookwood Book. Cincinnati, O: Rookwood Pottery, 1905.

3170 Schneider, Norris F. Zanesville Art Pottery. Norwich, O:
priv. printed, 1963. ill (Weller, Owens, Roseville)

3171 *Schwartz, Marvin D. Collector's Guide to Antique American
Ceramics. Garden City, NY: Doubleday, 1969. 134pp,
ill

3172 _____, and Richard Wolfe. A History of American Art
Porcelain. New York: Renaissance Editions, 1967.
93pp, ill, bib

3173 Smith, Elmer Lewis, comp. Pottery: a utilitarian folk craft.
Lebanon, Pa: Applied Arts, 1972. 32pp, ill

3174 *Spargo, John, 1876- . The A.B.C. of Bennington Pottery

Wares. Bennington, Vt: Bennington Historical Museum, 1938; 1948. 38pp, ill, pls

3175 *_____. Early American Pottery and China. New York: Century, 1926; Garden City, NY: Garden City Publishing, 1948; reprint. Rutland, Vt: Tuttle, 1974. 393pp, ill, 64 pls, bib (Pre-Revolutionary to end of 19th century. Grotesqueries; slip-decorated and sgraffito ware; etc.)

3176 *_____. The Potters and Potteries of Bennington. Boston: Houghton Mifflin and Antiques Inc., 1926; facism. reprints. Southampton, NY: Cracker Barrel Pr, 1969; New York: Dover; London: Constable, 1972. 265pp, ill, 44 (8 color) pls, bib (Norton and Fenton Potteries)

3177 Stiles, Helen E. Pottery in the United States. Fore. by R. G. Cowan. New York: Dutton, 1941. 329pp, ill, bib

3178 Symonds, Richard, and Jean Symonds. Medalta Stoneware and Pottery for Collectors. Surrey, British Columbia: Symco Distributors, 1974. ill (Canadian Pottery)

3179 Taylor, David, and Patricia Taylor. The Hart Pottery. Picton, Ontario: Picton Gazette, 1966. 36pp, ill, pls (Samual Hart, late 1800s pottery)

3180 Taylor, R. C. Liberty China and Queen's Ware Manufactured and Sold Solely for the Benefit of Various Allied War Charities. New York: priv. printed, 1924. 45pp

3181 *Tucker China: 1825-1838. Exhibition. Philadelphia: Museum of Art, 1957. 36pp, ill (488 pieces)

3182 Watkins, C. Malcolm. Maryland-Made Pottery and Its Background. Baltimore: 1955? (Mid-18th century to 1930)

3183 *Watkins, Lura Woodside. Early New England Potters and Their Wares. Cambridge: Harvard U Pr, 1950; reprint. Hamden, Conn: Archon Books, 1968. 294pp, 136 ill, 62 pls, bib

3184 _____. Early New England Pottery. Sturbridge, Mass: Old Sturbridge Village, 1959. ill

3185 Webster, Donald Blake. The Brantford Pottery, 1849-1907; history and assessment of the stoneware pottery at Brantford, Ontario. Including results of excavations and analysis of products. Toronto: Royal Ontario Museum, 1968. 80pp, ill

3186 _____. Decorated Stoneware Pottery of North America. Rutland, Vt: Tuttle, 1971. 232pp, 300 ill, bib, gloss (Crocks, inkwells, porringers, etc.)

3187 _____. Early Canadian Pottery. Toronto: McClelland &
Stewart; Greenwich, Conn: N.Y. Graphic Society, 1971.
256pp, ill, bib

3188 Wetherbee, Jean. White Ironstones: a handbook on white
ironstone, with text and drawings. Canajoharie, NY:
1974. 100pp, 150 ill, bib

3189 White, Margaret E., comp. European and American Ceramics
in the Newark Museum Collections. Newark, NJ: 1952.
24pp, ill, bib

3190 *Wiltshire, William E. Folk Pottery of the Shenandoah Valley.
Introd. by H. E. Comstock. Fore. by Donald R. Webster.
Exhibition. Richmond, Va: Abby Aldrich Rockefeller Folk
Art Collection at Colonial Williamsburg; New York: Dutton,
1975. 130pp, ill, 60 color pls, bib, marks

3191 Wires, E. Stanley, Norris F. Schneider, and Moses Mesre.
Zanesville Decorative Tiles. Zanesville, O: 1972. 32pp,
ill, bib (American Encaustic Tiling Co., Zanesville)

BRITISH ISLES CERAMICS

3192 Ahlborn, Richard E. Inscribed English Delftware in the Henry
Francis du Pont Winterthur Museum. Paper for Museum
Laboratory Course, 1958. DeWint

3193 Aikin, Arthur. On Pottery. From Transactions of the Society
of Arts, Manufactures, Commerce, etc. London: J.
Moyes, 1832. 51pp BM

3194 Anderson, John Eustace. A Short Account of the Mortlake
Potteries. Richmond, Eng: Author, 1894. 14pp

3195 Arlidge, Dr. John Thomas. The True History and the Interesting Legend of the Willow Plate Pattern. Hanley, Eng:
priv. printed, 1882. 36pp

3196 Armistead, Kathleen M., and W. J. Grant-Davidson. Swansea
Pottery: catalogue of the Kildare S. Meager Bequest.
Swansea, Glamorgan: Glynn Vivian Art Gallery, 1968.
45pp, ill, 12 pls (Includes "A Short History of the Swansea
Potteries," by K. S. Meager)

3197 Arnoux, L. Pottery. London: 1876. See: Bevan, G. P.,
British Manufacturing Industries, vol. 7.

3198 Barker, Philip Arthur. The Medieval Pottery of Shropshire
from the Conquest to 1400. Shropshire, Eng: Archaeological Society, 1970. 80pp, ill (1066-1400)

3199 Barnard, Julian. Victorian Ceramic Tiles. London: Studio
Vista; Greenwich, Conn: N.Y. Graphic, 1972. 194pp,
ill, pls, bib (English and American art tiles, 1830-1900)

3200 *Barrett, Franklin Allen. Caughley and Coalport Porcelains.
Fore. by W. B. Honey. Leigh-on-Sea: F. Lewis, 1951.
108pp, ill, 80 pls

3201 * _____, and Arthur L. Thorpe. Derby Porcelain, 1750-
1848. London: Faber, 1971. 206pp, ill, 106 pls, bib

3202 Battie, David, and Michael Turner. The Price Guide to 19th
and 20th Century British Porcelain. London: Antique
Collectors Club, 1974. 440pp, 500 ill

3203 Beard, Charles Relly. Catalogue of the Collection of Martin-
ware Formed by Mr. Frederick F. John Nettlefold, together with a short history of the firm of R. W. Martin
and Brothers of Southall. London: Waterlow, printer,
1936. 252pp, 69 (31 color) pls V&A

3204 Bedford, John. Chelsea and Derby China. London: Cassell;
New York: Walker, 1967. 64pp, ill, 4 pls

3205 _____. Delftware. London: Cassell; New York: Walker,
1966. 64pp, ill, 2 color pls (Chiefly English delft, but
includes Dutch)

3206 _____. Old English Lustre Ware. London: Cassell,
1965; New York: Walker, 1966. 66pp, ill, 2 pls

3207 _____. Talking about Teapots; and thus about porcelain,
pottery, silver, Sheffield plate, etc. London: Parrish,
1964. 160pp, ill, bib

3208 *Bell, Robert Charles. Tyneside Pottery. London: Studio
Vista, 1971. 151pp, ill, pls (part color), bib (1740-1963)

3209 _____, and Margaret Anne Violet Gill. The Potteries of
Tyneside Upon Tyne. Newcastle upon Tyne: Graham,
1973. 40pp, ill, bib (1730-1950)

3210 Bemrose, Geoffrey J. V. Guide to the Collection of English
Lustre Ware, Given by the Countess of Munster, 1949.
Hanley, Stoke-on-Trent: Museum & Art Gallery, 1950.
ill

3211 * _____. 19th Century English Pottery and Porcelain.
London: Faber; New York: Pitman, 1952. 57pp, ill,
100 (4 color) pls, bib DLC, BM

3212 *Bemrose, William. Bow, Chelsea and Derby Porcelain.
Being further information relating to these factories,

obtained from original documents, not hitherto published.
London: Bemrose, 1898. 174pp, ill, 25 pls V&A, BM,
DLC

3213 * _____ . A Descriptive Catalogue of Porcelain and Other
Art Objects in the Collection of W. Bemrose. Derby;
London: priv. printed, 1898. 76pp, ill, 35 (3 color) pls,
marks BM

3214 [No entry.]

3215 Blacker, James F. The ABC of Collecting Old English
China. Giving a short history of the English factories,
and showing how to apply tests for unmarked china before
1800. 2nd ed. London: London Opinion Curio Club,
1908; London: Stanley Paul; Philadelphia: G. W. Jacobs,
1910; Boston: Cornhill; Philadelphia: Jacobs, 1911; London: S. Paul, 1915; 1916; 3rd ed. 1921. 142pp, ill;
386pp, ill, 66 pls NN, DLC, BM

3216 _____ . The ABC of Collecting Old English Pottery ...
with over 450 illustrations. London: S. Paul; Philadelphia:
S. Jacobs, 1910; 4th ed. London: 1923? 342pp, ill, 31
pls DLC, NN, BM

3217 * _____ . The ABC of English Salt-Glaze Stoneware, from
Dwight to Doulton. London: S. Paul, 1922. 243pp, 200
ill, pls DeWint

3218 * _____ . 19th Century English Ceramic Art. London: S.
Paul, 1911; 1912; as The ABC of 19th Century English
Ceramic Art. London: 1920; 1924. 534pp, 1200 ill
NN, BM, DLC

3219 Blake, Sylvia Dugger. Flow Blue China. Des Moines: Wallace-Homestead, 1971. 48pp, ill, 24 color pls (Chiefly
English)

3220 Blunt, Reginald, ed. The Cheyne Book of Chelsea China and
Pottery. (Catalog of 1924 exhibition.) London: G. Bles,
1924; Boston; New York: Houghton-Mifflin, 1925; 1929.
126pp, ill, pls, color frontis BM

3221 _____ . Red Anchor Pieces. London: Mills & Boon, 1928.
241pp, ill, pls (Chelsea china) BM

3222 *Boney, Knowles. Liverpool Porcelain of the 18th Century and
Its Makers. London: Batsford, 1957. 223pp, ill, 57 pls,
bib

3223 _____ . Richard Chaffers. A Liverpool potter. Liverpool:
Henry Young, 1960. 63pp, ill

3224 Bosanko, William. Collecting Old Lustre Ware. London:
      Heinemann, 1916; New York: Doran, 1917. 111pp, ill
      PPULC, DLC, NN

3225 Bourne, George. William Smith: potter and farmer, 1790-
      1858. London: Chatto & Windus, 1919. 230pp, ill BM

3226 *Bow Procelain 1744-1776. Exhibition of documentary ma-
      terial to commemorate the bicentenary of the retirement
      of Thomas Frye, manager of the factory and inventor and
      first manufacturer of porcelain in England. British Mu-
      seum, 1959-1960. London: 1959. 55pp, pls (Traces
      whole history on basis of the 26 known dated specimens)
      DeWint

3227 *Bradbury, Edward. Derby China: old and new. With a
      description of the Gladstone dessert service. London;
      Derby: Bemrose, 1883. 60pp

3228 Brears, Peter Charles David. A Catalogue of English Country
      Pottery Housed in the Yorkshire Museum, York. York:
      Yorkshire Philosophical Society, 1968. 40pp, ill (ca.1450-
      1905)

3229 _____. The Collector's Book of English Country Pottery.
      Newton Abbot: David & Charles, 1974. 207pp, ill, bib

3230 _____. The English Country Pottery: its history and
      techniques. Rutland, Vt: Tuttle; Newton Abbot: David
      & Charles, 1971. 266pp, ill, pl, bib

3231 _____. The Farnham Potteries. London; Chichester:
      Phillimore, 1971. 20pp, ill (Surrey, ca.1800 to ca.1970)

3232 Bruton, William Edward. Old English Willow Pattern Pottery;
      its romance, its history, and how to identify the old wares
      from the new. Rickmansworth, Hertfordshire: W. & D.
      Bruton, 1952. 16pp, ill BM, DLC

3233 *Bryant, Gilbert Ernest. The Chelsea Porcelain Toys. Scent
      bottles, bonbonnieres, etuis, seals and statuettes made at
      the Chelsea factory, 1745-1769, and Derby Chelsea, 1770-
      1784. London; Boston: Medici Society, 1925; 1929. 193pp,
      ill, 63 (47 color) pls, bib MdBP, NN, BM

3234 Buhler, Kathryn C. English Porcelain Figures, 1750-1775.
      Boston: Museum of Fine Arts, 1955. 32pp, ill (Museum's
      collection, many Chelsea)

3235 Bunt, John. Sir Leslie Joseph Loan Exhibition of Swansea
      Porcelain, June-August 1969. Swansea, Glamorgin: Glynn
      Vivian Art Gallery, 1969. 41pp, ill, 32 pls

3236 Burgess, William, 1857- . English Pottery and Pottery
       Trade. United States Consular Report, No. 136. Wash-
       ington, D.C.: GPO, 1892. 8pp

3237 Burnap Collection of English Pottery in the William Rockhill
       Nelson Gallery. Kansas City, Mo: Nelson Atkins, 1953;
       rev. enl. ed. by Ross E. Taggart. Kansas City: 1967.
       128pp, ill; 219pp, ill (988 specimens of slip wares, Delft,
       salt-glaze, Astbury, Agatewares, Whieldon, R. Wood,
       Wedgwood, Leeds, lustrewares, etc. Frank P. and Har-
       riet C. Burnap)

3238 *Burton, William. History and Description of English Earthen-
       ware and Stoneware to the Beginning of the 19th Century
       ... with reproductions of marks, etc. London; New York:
       Cassell, 1902; 1904. 192pp, ill, 58 (24 color), bib, gloss
       (1902 ed. had plates in gold and color) DLC, PPULC,
       BM

3239   . A History and Description of English Porcelain.
       London: Cassell, 1902; facsim. reprint with new introd.
       Wakefield: E P Publishing, 1972. 196pp, ill (some color),
       123 pls, bib BM

3240 Catalogue of Bristol and West of England Delft Collection.
       Bath, Eng: Victoria Art Gallery, 1929. 34pp

3241 Catalog of a Collection of Early English Earthenware and
       Other Works of Art. Introd. by R. L. Hobson, and J.
       W. L. Glaisher. London: Burlington Fine Art Clubs,
       1913. 159pp

3242 Catalogue of a Collection of Pottery and Porcelain, illustrating
       popular British history, lent by Henry Willett. South
       Kensington Museum. London: 1899. 123pp, ill

3243 Catalogue of the Exhibition of Swansea Pottery and Porcelain,
       Glynn Vivian Art Gallery, Swansea. Swansea, Wales:
       1951. 62pp

3244 Catalogue of the Greg Collection of English Pottery. Man-
       chester, Eng: Taylor, Garnett, Evans, printers, for the
       Art Gallery, 1924? 79pp, bib (Thomas Tylston Greg)
       DLC

3245 Cawley, M. Goss China Supplement. Newport, Monm:
       Ceramic Book Co, 1973. ill

3246   . A Pictorial Encyclopedia of Goss China. Newport,
       Monm: Ceramic Book Co, 1969. ill

3247 Celoria, Francis. Dated Post-Medieval Pottery in the London
       Museum. London: HMSO, 1966. 32pp, ill (1573-1887)

3248 *Charleston, Robert Jesse, ed. English Porcelain: 1745-1850.
      London: E. Benn; Toronto: U Pr, 1965. 183pp, ill, 76
      pls, bib

3249 Cheyne Book of Chelsea China and Pottery. London: Bles,
      1924; Boston; New York: Houghton-Mifflin, 1925; facsim.
      reprint ed. by Reginald Blunt. New introd. by J. V. G.
      Mallet. Wakefield: E P Publishing, 1973. 132pp, ill,
      51 pls, bib

3250 Christie, Brown and Co., Ltd. Biscuit Jars, Past and
      Present, from the Collection of Christie, Brown and Co.
      London: n.d. 27pp, ill (part color)

3251 *Church, Arthur Herbert, 1834-1915. Catalogue of the Speci-
      mens of Old English and Other Pottery in the Collection
      of A. H. Church. Cirencester, Eng: priv. printed, 1870.
      40pp ("A few copies of this catalogue are all that remain,
      as a fire destroyed the whole collection in 1873." Solon)
      ICN

3252 *_____. English Earthenware; handbook to the wares made
      in England during the 17th and 18th centuries. London:
      Chapman & Hall, 1884; rev. ed. 1904; rev. ed. 1911.
      123pp, ill, bib; 132pp, 67 pls, bib; 154pp, ill, 67 pls, bib
      BM

3253 *_____. English Porcelain: a handbook to the china made
      in England during the 18th century. London: Chapman &
      Hall, 1885; 1894; 1898; rev. ed. 1904; rev. ed. 1911; 1914.
      99pp, pls, bib; 1904: 113pp, 43 pls, bib; 120pp, 43 pls,
      bib BM

3254 Clarke, John Mason. English Gold Lustres. Albany, NY:
      J. B. Lyon, printers, for the Author, 1908. 15pp, ill,
      4 color pls (Semi-technical) DLC, NN

3255 William Cookworthy, 1705-1780: a commemorative exhibition
      of his Plymouth and Bristol porcelain. Plymouth, Eng:
      City Art Gallery, 1955. 31pp, ill

3256 Coxhead, J. R. W. The Romance of the Wool, Lace and
      Pottery Trades in Honiton, England. 6th ed. Honiton:
      Mrs. P. H. Thrower, 1968. 43pp, ill

3257 Coysh, Arthur Wilfred. Blue-Printed Earthenware, 1800-
      1850. Newton Abbot: David & Charles; Rutland, Vt:
      Tuttle, 1972. 112pp, ill, bib

3258 _____. Blue and White Transfer Ware, 1780-1840. New-
      ton Abbot: David & Charles, 1970. 112pp, ill, 51 pls,
      color frontis, bib (150 marked pieces ill and described)

3259   Crawley, James, ed. Potteries of Sunderland and District.
       A summary of their history and products. Sunderland:
       Museum & Art Gallery, 1951. 16pp, ill (Nearly all pink
       lustre) NN

3260   _____, ed. Rhymes and Mottoes on Sunderland Pottery.
       Sunderland: Free Library, Museum & Art Gallery, 1960.
       32pp, ill, 4 pls

3261   Cream-Coloured Earthenware. V & A. London: HMSO,
       1960. 31pp, 28 pls

3262   Crellin, J. K. Medical Ceramics: a catalogue of the English
       and Dutch collections in the Museum of the Wellcome In-
       stitute of the History of Medicine. London: The Institute,
       1969. 304pp, 490 ill, 2 pls, bib (Drug jars, pill slabs,
       etc.)

3263   Crisp, Frederick Arthur. Lowestoft China Factory and the
       Moulds Found There in December 1902. London: Grove
       Park Pr, priv. printed, 1907. 4pp, 21 pls DLC, NN

3264   _____. Catalogue of Lowestoft China in Possession of F.
       A. Crisp. London: Grove Park Pr, priv. printed, 1907.
       24pp, ill, 14 color pls

3265   _____. Porcelain and Pottery Bearing Arms of the Livery
       Companies of the City of London, in the possession of
       F. A. Crisp. London: Grove Park Pr, priv. printed,
       1911. 4pp, 6 color pls

3266   *Cushion, John Patrick. English China Collecting for Ama-
       teurs. London: Muller, 1967. 168pp, ill, 12 pls, bib
       (1630-1900)

3267   _____. Pocket Book of English Ceramic Marks and Those
       of Wales, Scotland and Ireland. London: Faber, 1959;
       new ed. 1965. 154pp, ill

3268   Dawson, Charles. Sussex Iron Work and Pottery. (With
       catalogue of exhibition of Lewes Castle, 1902.) Reprint
       from Sussex Archaeological Society's Collections. n. p.:
       1903. 62pp, ill

3269   De La Beche, Sir Henry Thomas, and Trenham Reeks. Cata-
       logue of Specimens Illustrative of the Composition and
       Manufacture of British Pottery and Porcelain from the
       Occupation of Britain, by Romans to the present time.
       Museum of Practical Geology. London: Eyre & Spottis-
       woode, for HMSO, 1855. ill

3270   Dennis, Richard. Catalogue of an Exhibition of Doulton

Stoneware and Terracotta 1870-1925. London: R. Dennis,
1971. 255pp, ill (675 items described)

3271 _____. William Moorcroft and Walter Moorcroft 1897-1973.
Exhibition. London: Fine Art Society, 1973. 128pp, ill
(482 items)

3272 *Dixon, Joseph Lawrence. English Porcelain of the 18th Century. London: Faber; New York: Pitman, 1952. 79pp,
ill, 99 (4 color) pls, bib

3273 Douglas, Jane. Collectible China. London: Longacre, 1961.
63pp, ill, bib

3274 Doulton and Co., Ltd. Royal Doulton: figures, animal
models, character and Toby jugs, flambe, veined sung,
rack plates. Burslem, Stoke-on-Trent: Doulton Fine
China, 1967. 109pp, chiefly ill

3275 *Dowman, Edward Andrews. Blue Dash Chargers and Other
Early English Tin Enamel Circular Dishes. London:
Werner Laurie, 1919. 185pp, many ill, pls, color frontis
PPL, DeWint, BM

3276 _____. English Pottery and Porcelain: being a concise
account of the development of the potter's art in England.
New enl. ed. London: Gill, 1899; 4th ed. enl. London:
Gill; New York: Scribner's, 1904; 5th ed. 1910; 6th ed.
rev. and enl. by Aubrey Gunn. London: The Bazaar,
1918. 190pp, ill; 324pp, ill; 436pp, ill, pls ("Reads
like an undisguised abridgment of L. Jewitt's Ceramic Art
of Great Britain." Solon) DeWint

3277 Duesbury, William, 1725-1786. List of the Principal Additions Made This Year to the New Invented Groups, jars,
vases, urns, beakers, cups, chalices, etc., of Mr. Duesbury's Derby and Chelsea Manufactory of porcelains, bis-
cuits and china ware. London: 1774? 15pp (Reprinted
in W. Bemrose's Bow, Chelsea and Derby Porcelain)

3278 William Duesbury's London Account Book (1751-53). Reprint.
London: English Porcelain Circle, 1931. ill (Duesbury's
outside work on Derby, Chelsea and Bow porcelains)

3279 Eaglestone, Arthur Archibald, and Terence Anthony Lockett.
The Rockingham Pottery. Clifton Park, Rotherham: Municipal Museum and Art Gallery, 1964; 1967; new rev. ed.
Rutland, Vt: Tuttle; Newton Abbot: David & Charles, 1973.
152pp, ill, 10 pls, bib; 159pp, ill, 16 pls, bib (To 1842)

3280 Eccles, Herbert, and Bernard Rackham. Analysed Specimens
of English Porcelain. V & A. London: HMSO, 1922.
53pp, 16 pls, bib

3281   Edwards, Rhoda. Lambeth Stoneware: the Woolley Collection,
       including Doulton Ware and products of other British pot-
       teries. London: Borough of Lambeth, 1973. 24pp, ill,
       24 pls (Art pottery by female decorators)

3282   18th Century English Porcelain: a picture book. Birmingham,
       Eng: City Museum & Art Gallery, 1964. 28pp, 25 ill
       (1751-1775)

3283   Elliott, Gordon Walter, comp. Some Descriptions of Pottery
       Making and Working Conditions, 1557-1844. Stoke-on-
       Trent: Ivy House Publications, 1970. 63pp, chiefly ill

3284   Emery, Norman. William Henry Goss and Goss Heraldic
       China. Stoke-on-Trent: Public Library, 1969. 44 leaves,
       ill, 2 pls, bib (1853-1906)

3285   English and American Ceramics of the 18th and 19th Centu-
       ries; a selection from the Collection of Mr. and Mrs.
       Harold G. Duckworth. December 1968-January 1969.
       Toledo, O: Toledo Museum, 1968. 53pp, ill, bib

3286   [No entry.]

       English Ceramic Circle. Transactions. See: English Porce-
       lain Circle, no. 3289.

3287   The English Ceramic Circle, 1927-1948. English pottery and
       porcelain. Commemorative catalogue of an exhibition held
       at the Victoria and Albert, May-June 1948. London:
       Routledge & K. Paul, 1949. 94pp, 123 pls

3288   English China and China Marks; being a guide to the principal
       marks found on English pottery and porcelain. London:
       Wyman, 1878. 35pp, ill BM

3289   *English Porcelain Circle. Transactions. No. 1-4. London;
       Aylesbury: English Ceramic Circle, 1928-1933; continued
       as English Ceramic Circle, Transactions. 1933- .

3290   English Porcelain 1743-1840: the Lucile Pillow Collection.
       Presented by Mrs. Howard W. Pillow to the Beaverbrook
       Art Gallery. Frederictown, New Brunswick, Can: 1959.
       38pp, pls

3291   *English Pottery and Porcelain. Exhibition. 1948. Victoria
       and Albert, by the English Ceramic Circle. London:
       Routledge & K. Paul, 1949. 94pp, ill (550 examples)
       BM

3292   English Pottery and Porcelain: being a concise account of
       the potter's art in England. By L. W. London: Bazaar,
       Exchange & Mart, 1874; 1880; new enl. ed. by Edward A.

Downman. London: Gill, 1896. 138pp, ill, pls; 190pp, ill, pls NN, MB

3293 English Pottery and Porcelain, 1300-1850. Exhibition. De-
      troit: Institute of Arts, 1954. 111pp, 138 ill

3294 English Pottery Industry: miscellaneous broadsides, 1833-1846.
      (46 broadsides in folder.) MH-BA

3295 English Pottery Old and New. Picture book of exhibition held
      in collaboration with the Council for Art and Industry, 1935.
      London: V & A, 1936. 56pp, ill, 40 pls BM

3296 Evans, William, of Shelton. Art and History of the Potting
      Business, compiled from the most practical sources, for
      the especial use of working potters, by their devoted friend.
      Shelton, Eng: Examiner's office, 1846. 72pp NN

3297 *Exhibition of Early English Earthenware. Introd. by R. L.
      Hobson, and J. W. L. Glaisher. London: Burlington
      Fine Arts Club, 1914. 150pp, ill, 50 fine pls (Out-
      standing private collections) NN, DLC

3298 Exhibition of English and Continental Porcelain of the 18th
      Century. June 1951. London: Antique Porcelain Co,
      1951. 95pp, chiefly ill, color pls

3299 Exhibition of Fulham Pottery and Prints. Fulham: Public
      Libraries, 1929. 36pp

3300 Exley, Clifford Landseer. A History of the Torksey and
      Mansfield China Factories. Lincoln, Eng: G. R. G.
      Exley, 1970. 82pp, ill, color frontis (Includes William
      Billingsley, 1758-1828)

3301 _____, Franklin A. Barrett, and Arthur L. Thorpe. The
      Pinxton China Factory. Derby, Eng: R. Coke-Steel,
      1963. 63pp, ill, pls (Billingsley's porcelain, etc. 18th
      century)

3302 *Eyles, Desmond. Royal Doulton, 1815-1965; the rise and ex-
      pansion of the Royal Doulton Potteries. London: Hutchin-
      son, 1965. 208pp, many ill

3303 Falkner, Frank. Catalogue of the Falkner-Sidebotham Collec-
      tion of English Pottery Figures ... in the Royal Museum,
      Peel Park. Manchester, Eng: 1906. 41pp, ill, 13 pls

3304 Fisher, Stanley William. British Pottery and Porcelain.
      London; New York: Arco, 1962; reprint. New York:
      Archer House, 1963; London: Mayflower, 1969. 162pp,
      ill, 8 pls, bib

3305 *   . The Decoration of English Porcelain; a description
           of the painting and printing on English porcelain of the
           period 1750-1850. London: D. Verschoyle, 1954. 213pp,
           ill, pls, bib

3306 *   . English Blue and White Porcelain of the 18th Cen-
           tury. An illustrated account of the early soft paste pro-
           ductions of Bow, Chelsea, Lowestoft, Derby, Longton Hall,
           Bristol, Worcester, Caughley, and Liverpool potters,
           ca.1740-1800. Fore. by Bernard Rackham. London:
           Batsford, 1947. 190pp, ill, pls, bib

3307   . English Ceramics: earthenware, delft, stoneware,
           creamware, porcelain, including a section on Welsh fac-
           tories. London; Melbourne: Ward Lock, 1966; New York:
           Hawthorn, 1967. 256pp, ill, color frontis, bib (To 1880)

3308   . English Pottery and Porcelain Marks. Slough;
           NY: Foulsham, 1970. 98pp, ill (Includes Scottish and
           Irish, ca.1750-1900)

3309   . A Start to Collecting English Pottery and Porcelain.
           London; New York: Foulsham, 1971. 90pp, ill, bib
           (ca.1600-1900)

3310 Fitz Randolph, Helen Elizabeth, and Mavis Doriel Hay. Deco-
           rative Crafts and Rural Potteries. Oxford: Clarendon,
           1927. 168pp, ill, pls (Weaving, lace, pottery)

3311 Fleming, John Arnold. Scottish Pottery. Glasgow: Maclehose,
           Jackson, 1923; facsim. reprint with new pref. by Peter
           Walton. Wakefield: E P Publishing, 1973. 299pp, ill,
           61 pls (To ca.1920)

3312 Fletcher, H. Morley. Investing in English Pottery and Porce-
           lain. London: Barrie & Rockliff; New York: C. N.
           Potter, 196-? ill

3313 Forsyth, Gordon Mitchell. Art and Craft of the Potter. Lon-
           don: Chapman & Hall, 1934. 98pp, ill, 63 pls MB

3314 *Franks, Augustus Wollaston, ed. Guide to the English Cera-
           mic Ante-Room and the Glass and Ceramic Gallery (in the
           British Museum). Introd. by E. A. Bond. London: 1888.
           18pp MH, BM

3315 *   . Notes on the Manufacture of Porcelain at Chelsea.
           Reprint from the Journal of the Archaeological Institute,
           Worcester. London: 1863. 10pp

3316 Freeth, Frank. Old English Pottery Collected and Catalogued
           by Mr. and Mrs. Freeth, with descriptions and illustrations
           of each object. London: Morgan, 1896. 80pp, pls IU

3317   Galpin, John. A Handbook of Goss China. Portsmouth, Eng:
       Author, 1972. 82pp, ill

3318   Garner, Frederick Harold. English Delftware. London:
       Faber; New York: Van Nostrand, 1948; 2nd ed. rev. &
       enl. by F. H. Garner and Michael Archer. London:
       Faber, 1972. 44pp, 100 pls, bib; 105pp, ill, 144 pls,
       bib

3319   Gatty, Charles Tindall. The Liverpool Potteries. Liverpool:
       Baker, 1882. 48pp (Supplements J. Mayer's work History
       of the Art of Pottery in Liverpool) MdBP

3320   Gaunt, William, and Maxwell, D. E. Clayton-Stamm. William
       De Morgan: pre-Raphaelite ceramics. Greenwich, Conn:
       N.Y. Graphic Society, 1971. 176pp, ill, bib

3321   Gautier, Louis. English Delft. London: Casa Rossa Gal-
       lery, 1929. 15pp, ill DeWint

3322   Gilhespy, Frank Brayshaw. Crown Derby Porcelain. Leigh-
       on-Sea: F. Lewis, 1951. 108pp, ill, pls, bib DLC

3323 * _____ . Derby Porcelain. London: MacGibbon & Kee,
       1961; London: Spring Books, 1965. 144pp, ill, 76 (13
       color) pls, bib, marks

3324   _____ , and Dorothy M. Budd. Royal Crown Derby China
       from 1876 to the Present Day, including Sampson Hancock
       (King Street) Derby, 1849-1935. London: C. Skilton, 1964.
       87pp, pls

3325   Gilruth, Mary Marjorie. The Importation of English Earthen-
       ware into Philadelphia, 1770-1800. Thesis. 1964. 192pp,
       pls DeWint

3326   Glover, Patricia E. The Development of English Porcelain,
       1744-1891. Exhibition. November-December 1972. Winni-
       peg, Can: Art Gallery, 1972. 30pp, ill, bib

3327   Godden, Geoffrey, A. British Porcelain, an illustrated guide.
       London: Barrie & Jenkins; New York: C. N. Potter, 1974.
       456pp, ill, 24 pls, bib, marks (40 factories from 1740s
       to present)

3328   _____ . British Pottery, an illustrated guide. New York:
       Crown, 1974. 452pp, 572 ill, 18 color pls (18th century
       to post-World War II studio pottery and reproductions)

3329   _____ . British Pottery and Porcelain, 1780-1850. New
       York: A. S. Barnes; London: A. Barker, 1963. 199pp,
       ill, 40 pls, bib

3330 *_____. Coalport and Coalbrookdale Porcelain. London:
Jenkins; New York: Praeger, 1970. 156pp, 232 ill, 155
(10 color) pls, bib

3331 *_____. Encyclopedia of British Pottery and Porcelain
Marks. London: Jenkins; New York: Crown, 1964; 2nd
ed. rev. London: 1968. 765pp, ill, 8 pls, bib, gloss
(300 years; over 4500 marks)

3332 _____. The Handbook of British Pottery and Porcelain
Marks. London: Jenkins, 1968; with revisions. London:
Barrie & Jenkins, 1972. 197pp, ill, bib (1776-1900)

3333 *_____. An Illustrated Encyclopedia of British Pottery and
Porcelain. London: Jenkins; New York: Crown, 1966.
390pp, 615 ill, 16 color pls, bib (1700-1900; 1000 marked
specimens illustrated) (Companion to his Encyclopedia of
British Pottery....)

3334 _____. An Illustrated Guide to Lowestoft (Soft Paste) Porcelain. London: Jenkins, 1969; New York: Praeger, 1970.
164pp, ill, 122 pls, bib

3335 _____. An Introductory Handbook to British China Marks
of the 19th Century. Bexhill, Sussex: Gardner's of Bexhill, 1962. 30pp, pls, bib

3336 _____. An Introduction to English Blue and White Porcelains. Sussex: Author, 1975. 79pp, ill

3337 *_____. Victorian Porcelain. Fore. by Hugh Wakefield.
London: H. Jenkins, 1961; New York: Universe, 1970.
222pp, ill, bib

3338 Grabham, Oxley. Yorkshire Potteries, Pots and Potters.
York, Eng: Yorkshire Philosophical Society, 1916; facsim.
reprint with new introd. by Peter Walton. Wakefield: S.
R. Publishers, 1971. 116pp, ill, bib (1800-1900) NN

3339 Greg, Thomas Tylston. A Contribution to the History of
English Pottery, with special reference to the Greg Collec-
tion. Lecture given at Manchester Art Gallery, 1906.
Manchester: Taylor, Garnett, Evans, 1908. 81pp DLC

3340 Grigaut, Paul L., comp. English Pottery and Porcelain, 1300-
1850. Exhibition. January-February 1954. Detroit:
Institute of Arts, 1954. 111pp, ill, bib

3341 Griggs, William, 1832-1911. Illustrations of Armorial China.
London: priv. printed, 1887. 26 leaves, 24 color pls in
portfolio DLC, DeWint

3342 Haberly, Lloyd. Mediaeval English Pavingtiles. Oxford: B.

Blackwell, for the Shakespeare Head Pr, 1937. 326pp,
ill, color pls, bib DLC, ViU

3343 Hackenbroch, Yvonne. Chelsea and Other English Porcelain,
Pottery, and Enamel in the Irwin Untermyer Collection.
Cambridge, Mass: Harvard U Pr, for Metropolitan Mu-
seum of Art, 1957. 286pp, ill, 146 pls (part color), bib

3344 Haggar, Reginald George. English Country Pottery. London:
Phoenix, 1950; as A New Guide to Old Pottery; English
country pottery. New York: McBride, 1950. 160pp, ill,
bib

3345 _____ . English Pottery Figures, 1660-1860. London: J.
Tiranti, 1947; 1952. 36pp, ill, 40 pls, bib

3346 Hancock, E. Campbell. The Amateur Pottery and Glass
Painter, with directions for gilding, chasing, burnishing,
bronzing and groundlaying. Illustrated, including facsimiles from sketch-book of N. H. J. Westlake, with an
appendix. London: Chapman & Hall, 1879;... 198pp,
ill, color pls NN, DLC

3347 _____ . China Colours; and how to use them. Worcester,
Eng: Hancock & Son; London: Reeves, 1880. 59pp, ill

3348 Hartley, Greens and Co. Pattern Book of the Leeds Pottery.
Designs of sundry articles of Queen's or cream-coloured
earthenware ... also with coats-of-arms, cyphers, landscapes, etc. Leeds: 1783; 1785; 1786; 1794; 1814. ill,
45 pls, 71 pls DeWint

3349 Haslam, Malcolm. English Art Pottery, 1865-1915. London:
Antique Collectors Club, 1975. 214pp, 200 (16 color) ill

3350 Haslem, John, 1808-1884. A Catalogue of China, Chiefly
Derby, of Enamels, and Other Paintings, the Property of
J. Haslem. Derby: R. Keene, priv. printed, 1879.
68pp, ill (Haslem was a Derby china painter)

3351 _____ . The Old Derby China Factory: the workmen and
their production. Containing biographical sketches of the
chief artist workmen, the various marks used, fac-similes
copied from old Derby pattern books, the original price
list of more than 400 figures and groups, etc. London:
G. Bell, 1876. 255pp, ill, 11 color pls, marks, facsimiles MiD, NN

3352 Hatton, Joseph, 1841-1907. Twyfords: a chapter on the
history of pottery. London: Virtue, 1898. 48pp, ill,
pls DeWint

3353 Hayden, Arthur. Chats on English China. (Also as Chats on

Old China.) London: Unwin; New York: F. A. Stokes, 1904; 2nd ed. London: 1906; 3rd ed. London: 1910; ...; London: Benn, 1947; 2nd ed. rev. by Cyril G. E. Bunt. London: Benn; New York: Wyn, 1952. 287pp, ill, 4 pls, bib; 1952: 168pp, ill, bib

3354 _____. Chats on English Earthenware. London: Unwin, 1909; 1919; as Chats on Old Earthenware. New York: F. A. Stokes, 1909; London: Unwin, 1922. 496pp, 150 ill, color frontis, bib, 200 marks, gloss PPL, NN, MB

3355 * _____. Old English Porcelain. The Lady Ludlow Collection. Introd. by W. Leslie Perkins. London: Murray, 1932. 191pp, hundreds of color ill, 132 pls (Lady Alice Sedgwick M. L. Ludlow's Chelsea, Bow, Worcester, etc., porcelain)

3356 Hinton, David Alban. Medieval Pottery of the Oxford Region. Oxford: Ashmolean Museum, 1973. 32pp, ill (ca. 1000-ca. 1500)

3357 Hobson, Robert Lockhart. Catalogue of the Collection of English Porcelain in the Department of British and Mediaeval Antiquities and Ethnography of the British Museum. Pref. by C. H. Read. London: 1905. 162pp, ill, 39 pls (part color) (Sir A. W. Franks Collection) BM

3358 * _____. Catalogue of the Collection of English Pottery in the Department of British and Mediaeval Antiquities and Ethnography of the British Museum. London: 1903. 310pp, ill, 42 pls (part color) (Very important work) BM

3359 _____. A Guide to the English Pottery and Porcelain in the Department of British and Mediaeval Antiquities ... British Museum. Pref. by C. H. Read. London: 1904; 2nd ed. 1910; 3rd ed. 1923. 127pp, 161 ill, 15 pls BM

3360 Hodgdon, Jeannette Rector. Collecting Old English Lustre. Portland, Me: Southworth-Anthoensen Pr, 1937. 44pp, ill, 14 pls

3361 Hodgkin, John Eliot, and Edith Hodgkin. Examples of Early English Pottery, Named, Dated and Inscribed. London: Cassell, 1891; facsim. reprint. Wakefield: E P Publishing, 1973. 187pp, 150 ill, color frontis (1571-1799, slip-decorated ware, saltglaze, English delft, stoneware) De-Wint

3362 Hodgson, Mrs. (A.) Willoughby. Old English China. London: G. Bell, 1913. 201pp, 64 ill, 16 color pls, color frontis

3363 [No entry.]

3364 Honey, William Bower. English Pottery and Porcelain. Lon-
      don: A. & C. Black, 1933; 2nd ed. 1945; 3rd ed. 1947;
      4th ed. 1949; 1952; 5th ed. rev. by R. J. Charleston.
      1962; 1964; 6th ed. rev. 1969. 270pp, ill, 24 pls, bib

3365 *   . Old English Porcelain; a handbook for collectors.
      London: G. Bell; New York: Harcourt Brace, 1928;
      London: 1931; New York: McGraw Hill, 1946; London:
      Faber, 1948; New York: 1949. 292pp, ill, 112 pls, bib

3366 Hood, Kenneth. English Pottery from the 15th to the 19th
      Century. National Gallery of Victoria. Melbourne; Lon-
      don: Oxford U Pr, 1966. 27pp, ill, 12 pls, bib

3367 Housman, H. Notes on the (Henry) Willett Collection of Pot-
      tery in the Brighton Museum. Together with the original
      catalogue of the collection. Brighton, Eng: W. J. Smith,
      1893. 100pp, ill

3368 *Hughes, George Bernard. English Pottery and Porcelain
      Figures. London: Lutterworth, 1964; New York: Praeger,
      1968. 224pp, ill, 48 pls, bib (1742-1900. Human, ani-
      mal and bird)

3369   . English and Scottish Earthenware, 1660-1860. Lon-
      don: Lutterworth; New York: Macmillan, 1961. 238pp,
      ill

3370 *   . Victorian Pottery and Porcelain. London: Country
      Life, 1959; New York: Macmillan, 1960; new ed. London:
      Spring, 1967. 184pp, 94 ill, 34 pls, bib

3371   , and Therle Hughes. The Collector's Encyclopedia
      of English Ceramics. London: Lutterworth Pr, 1956.
      172pp, 131 photographs, 80 drawings, marks, bib

3372 *   , and   . English Porcelain and Bone China,
      1743-1850. London: Lutterworth; New York: Macmillan,
      1955; New York: Praeger, 1968. 256pp, ill, pls

3373 Hughes, Peter. Welsh China: an illustrated handbook of
      pieces ... in the collection of the National Museum of
      Wales. Cardiff: the Museum, 1972. 28pp, ill, bib
      (1781-1915)

3374 Hurlbutt, Frank. Bow Porcelain. London: G. Bell, 1926.
      165pp, 64 (8 color) pls, bib

3375   . Bristol Porcelain. London; Boston: Medici So-
      ciety, 1928. 164pp, 64 pls (part color), bib

3376   . Chelsea China. Liverpool: U Pr of Liverpool,
      1937. 205pp, ill, 48 (8 color) pls DLC

3377 * _____. Old Derby Porcelain and Its Artist-Workmen.
       London: W. Laurie, 1925; 1928. 312pp, ill, 59 pls,
       color frontis, bib NN, DeWint

3378 Hyam, Edward E. The Early Period of Derby Porcelain,
       1750-1770. London: Hyam & Co., 1926. 29pp, pls
       NN, DeWint

3379 Illustrated Catalogue of the Knowles Boney Collection of Liver-
       pool Porcelain. Exhibition. Birkenhead, Eng: Winson
       Art Gallery & Museum, 1962. 32pp, 8 pls, bib (1756-
       1806)

3380 Illustrated Catalogue of the Loan Exhibition of Tournai and
       Chelsea Porcelain at the Belgian Institute, June-July 1953.
       London: the Institute, 1953. 47pp, ill

3381 Illustrated Guide to Irish Belleek Parian China. Los Angeles:
       1969. 82pp, ill, marks

3382 The Incomparable Art: English pottery from the Thomas Greg
       Collection. Manchester, Eng: City Art Gallery, 1969.
       79pp, 222 ill, bib

3383 Inventory Catalogue of the Specimens ... of earthenware,
       porcelain, glass, and enamels in the collection of the
       Museum of Irish Industry, Dublin. Part 1 of 3 parts.
       Dublin: the Museum, 1861. BM

3384 Irish Delftware: exhibition of 18th century Irish delftware at
       Castletown House, Celbridge, Country Kildare, head-
       quarters of the Irish Georgian Society. In association
       with Rosc 1971. October-December 1971. Dublin: Trinity
       College, 1971. 71pp, ill, pls, bib (1724-1800)

3385 Jenkins, Dilys. Llanelly Pottery. Swansea, Wales: Deb
       Books, 1968. 72pp, ill, 16 pls, bib

3386 Jenkins, Ellis. Swansea Porcelain. Reprint from Stewart
       Williams' Glamorgan Historian, Vol. 6. Cowbridge,
       Glamorgin: D. Brown, 1970. 80pp, color ill, 20 pls,
       bib

3387 Jewitt, Llewelyn Frederick William, 1816-1886. Ceramic
       Art of Great Britain, from prehistoric times to present
       day. Being a history of ancient and modern pottery and
       porcelain works of the Kingdom and of their productions
       of every class. 2 vol. London: Virtue; New York:
       Scribner's, 1878; new ed. London: 1883; 1887; new ed.
       rev. London: Ward Lock Reprints, 1970; reprint with
       new illustrations, and re-arranged by G. Godden, as
       Jewitt's Ceramic Art of Great Britain, 1800-1900. Lon-
       don: Barrie & Jenkins, 1972. 1100pp, 2000 ill, bib;

1972: 282pp, ill, 116 (20 color) pls, bib (Variously rated as a "fundamental work" by the Ceramic Book Company, and as a "babel of desultory information" by Solon)

_____ . The History of Ceramic Art in Great Britain. See: his Ceramic Art....

3388   _____ . A History of the Coalport Porcelain Works. Reprint from Art Journal. London: for Messrs Daniell, china dealers, 1862. 30pp, ill DLC

3389 *John, William David. Nantgarw Porcelain. Newport, Wales: R. H. Johns, 1948; Supplement No. 1. Newport: Ceramic Book Co, 1956; No. 2. with K. Coombes, Mackintosh' Nantgarw Porcelain Bird Services. Newport, Wales: 1969. 176pp, ill, 64 pls; 8pp, 4 pls, bib

3390 * _____ . Swansea Porcelain. Written with the assistance of Sidney Heath, Kildare S. Meager, Harry Sherman, B. A. Williams. Newport, Wales: Ceramic Book Co, 1957. 118pp, ill, 89 (20 color) pls, bib (450 specimens ill)

3391   _____ , and Warren Baker. Old English Lustre Pottery. Newport, Wales: R. H. Johns, 1951; new ed. Newport, Wales: Ceramic Book Co, 1962; 1966. 132pp, ill, 96 (14 color) pls, bib (Includes Anglo-American historical and naval-warfare lustrewares)

3392   _____ , and Katherine Coombes, and Gregory Coombes. An Illustrated Album of Superb Nantgarw Porcelain. Newport, Wales: Ceramic Book Co, 19-? ill

3393 * _____ , Anne Simcox, and Jacqueline Simcox. William Billingsley (1758-1828): his outstanding achievements as an artist and porcelain maker. An illustrated appendix by Sir Leslie Joseph (on) the Identification of Billingsley's painting on Swansea Porcelain. Newport, Wales: Ceramic Book Co, 1968. 97pp, 180 (40 color) ill, 74 pls (Derby flower-painter; Mansfield and Pinxton gilder; Nantgarw and Swansea decorator)

3394 Joseph, Felix. Tables of Monograms and Marks Placed on Various Potteries of Known Origins; arranged firstly by order of the pottery, and then geographically. London: priv. printed, 1857. ill SIB-2

3395 Kamm, Minnie Watson. Old China. Grosse Pointe, Mich: Kamm, 1951. 251pp, ill, marks (American and British, 1825-1890)

3396 Kidson, Joseph R., and Frank Kidson. Historical Notices of the Leeds Old Pottery, with a description of its Ware:

together with a brief account of the contemporary potteries
in the immediate vicinity. Leeds: Kidson, priv. printed,
1892; facsim. reprint. Wakefield: S. R. Publishing; London: Connoisseur, 1970. 162pp, ill, 22 pls ("Exhaustive" Solon)

3397 King, A. C. Notice of the Henri Deux Ware. London:
     Arundel Society, 1868. 8pp, 20 photographs

3398 *King, William, fl. 1921-31. Chelsea Porcelain. V & A.
     London: Bern Bros; New York: Scribner's, 1922.
     134pp, ill, 70 pls with 171 ill (7 color), bib

3399 *_____. English Porcelain Figures of the 18th Century.
     London; Boston: Medici Society, 1925. 15pp, 80 (8 color)
     pls, bib (Chelsea, Bow, Plymouth, Bristol, Derby) NN

3400 Lancaster, H. Boswell. Liverpool and Her Potters. Liver-
     pool: W. B. Jones, 1936. 94pp, ill, pls, bib

3401 Lane, (E.) Arthur. English Porcelain Figures of the 18th
     Century. London: Faber; New York: T. Yoseloff, 1961.
     148pp, ill, 96 pls (part color)

3402 Lardner, Dionysius. A Treatise on the Origin, the progres-
     sive improvement and present state of the manufacture of
     porcelain and glass. London: Longman, Rees; Phila-
     delphia: Carey, 1832. 334pp, ill

3403 Lawrence, Heather. Yorkshire Pots and Potteries. London:
     David & Charles, 1975. 112 examples ill, bib (Medieval
     to modern)

3404 Leach, Bernard Howell. The Leach Pottery, 1920-1952.
     London: Wightman, Mountain, printer, 1962. 13pp, ill

3405 _____, ed. A Potter's Portfolio. A selection of fine pots.
     London: Lund Humphries; New York: Pitman, 1951.
     28pp, 59 pls

3406 Levine, George Jacob. Inscribed Lowestoft Porcelain. Nor-
     wich, Eng: Author, 1968. 13 leaves, marks

3407 Lewer, Henry William. The China Collector. A Guide to
     the porcelains of English factories. London: Jenkins;
     New York: Dodd Mead, 1913; Philadelphia: D. McKay;
     Toronto: Bell & Cockburn, 1914. 347pp, 32 ill, bib,
     marks

3408 *Lewis, Griselda. Collector's History of English Pottery.
     London: Studio Vista; New York: Viking, 1969. 224pp,
     well ill

3409 _____ . English Pottery. New York: Pellegrini & Cudahy, 1950; as An Introduction to English Pottery. London: Art & Technics, 1950. 95pp, ill

3410 _____ . A Picture History of English Pottery. London: Hulton Pr, 1956; 1970. ill

3411 Lomax, Charles J. Quaint Old English Pottery. London: Sherratt & Hughes, 1909. 144pp, ill, pls (some color) (Also wrote Collection, treatment and disposal of town refuse, 1892. I wonder if he got his collecting start that way?) MiGr, MdBP, NN

3412 Luxmoore, Charles Frederick Coryndon. English Saltglazed Earthenware, "Saltglaze," or, the notes of a collector. 2nd ed. London; Exeter: W. Pollard, 1924. 65pp, 89 pls, color frontis NN

3413 Macalister, Donald Alexander, and Mrs. Donald A. Macalister. William Duesbury's London Account Book, 1751-1753. Fore. by R. L. Hobson. Facsimile reprint. London: English Porcelain Circle, 1931. 86pp, ill BM

3414 *McCauley, Robert Henry. Liverpool Transfer Designs on Anglo-American Pottery. Portland, Me: Southworth-Anthoensen Pr, 1942. 150pp, ill, 32 pls, bib

3415 Mackay, James Alexander. Commemorative Pottery and Porcelain. London: Garnstone Pr, 1971. 63pp, ill, bib (1600-1970)

3416 *Mackenna, Francis Severne. Champion's Bristol Porcelain. Leigh-on-Sea: F. Lewis, 1947. 107pp, ill, 117 pls, bib

3417 * _____ . Chelsea Porcelain: the gold anchor wares. (With a short account of the Duesbury period.) Leigh-on-Sea: F. Lewis, The Tithe House, 1952. 122pp, ill, 64 pls

3418 * _____ . Chelsea Porcelain: the red anchor wares. (With a short account of the Duesbury period.) Leigh-on-Sea: F. Lewis, Tithe House, 1951. 122pp, ill, 78 pls

3419 * _____ . Chelsea Porcelain: triangle and raised anchor wares. Leigh-on-Sea: F. Lewis, 1948; reprint. 1970. 90pp, ill, 56 pls, bib

3420 * _____ . Cookworthy's Plymouth and Bristol Porcelain. Leigh-on-Sea: F. Lewis, 1946. 109pp, ill, 58 pls, bib

3421 _____ . 18th Century English Porcelain. (Notes on various aspects of collecting.) Leigh-on-Sea: F. Lewis, 1970. 69pp, ill, 47 pls

3422 *_____ . The F. Severne Mackenna Collection of English
        Porcelains. Vol. I. Chelsea, 1743-1758; II. Plymouth
        and Bristol Porcelain; III. Worcester Porcelains. 3 vol.
        Leigh-on-Sea: F. Lewis, 1972. 186pp, chiefly ill; ill;
        162pp, ill

3423 Mackenzie, Compton. The House of Coalport, 1750-1950.
        London: Collins, 1952. 128pp, ill (Coalport China Co.,
        John Rose & Co. John Rose, 1772-1841)

3424 *Mankowitz, Wolf, and Reginald G. Haggar. The Concise
        Encyclopedia of English Pottery and Porcelain. London:
        A. Deutsch; New York: Hawthorn, 1957; New York:
        Praeger, 1968. 312pp, ill, 180 pls, bib (Chiefly V & A
        Collection)

3425 Maskell, William, 1814-1890. English Porcelain. Lon-
        don: Art Handbooks of South Kensington Museum,
        1885. 99pp

3426 _____ . Schreiber Collection Catalogue of English Porce-
        lain, enamels, etc. South Kensington Museum. London:
        1885. 241pp

3427 *Mawley, R. Pottery and Porcelain in 1876. An art student's
        ramble through some of the china shops of London. Lon-
        don: Field & Tuer, 1877. 82pp ("When one or 200 years
        have gone by, we can imagine what will be the rapture of
        the china collector--if any are left in that distant futurity--
        when he happens to have the good fortune of meeting with
        an odd copy of this most accurate and detailed record of
        the condition of the art china trade in England at that un-
        paralleled period of its prosperity." Solon, 1910)

3428 May, John, and Jennifer May. Commemorative Pottery, 1780-
        1900: a guide for collectors. London: Heinemann, 1972;
        New York: Scribner's, 1973. 180pp, 250 ill, 8 pls
        (Royal, military, political, railroad)

3429 Mayer, Joseph. History of the Art of Pottery in Liverpool.
        Liverpool: T. Brakell, printer, 1855; 2nd ed. with ill.
        Liverpool: D. Marples, 1871. 37pp, ill, pl; 55pp, ill
        MB, BM

3430 *_____ . On the Art of Pottery. (From a series of papers.)
        London: D. Marples, 1871; 2nd ed. as On the Art of Pot-
        tery, with a history of its progress in Liverpool. Liver-
        pool: D. Marples, 1873. 43pp, 97pp, ill

3431 _____ . A Synopsis of the History of the Manufacture of
        Earthenware; with reference to the specimens in the exhi-
        bition of the Liverpool Mechanics' Institution. Liverpool:
        Rockliff & Ellis, printers, 1842. 12pp MH-BA

3432   Meager, Kildare S.   The Swansea and Nantgarw Potteries,
       being (or together with) a record of the collection of
       Welsh pottery and porcelain ... Glynn Vivian Art Gallery,
       Swansea.   Swansea: 1949.   51pp, ill DLC

3433   Messenger, Michael.   Caughley Porcelains: exhibition,
       Shrewsbury Art Gallery.   Shrewsbury: Public Libraries,
       Museum and Art Gallery, 1972.   45pp, ill, 16 pls

3434   Mew, Egan.   Chelsea and Chelsea-Derby China.   Ed. by
       Thomas Leman Hare.   London: T. C. & E. C. Jack;
       New York: Dodd, Mead, 1909.   99pp, ill, 16 (8 color)
       pls, marks

3435   _____.   Old Bow China.   Ed. by Thomas Leman Hare.
       London: T. C. & E. C. Jack; New York: Dodd, Mead,
       1909.   111pp, ill, 16 (8 color) pls, bib, marks

3436   Miller, J. Jefferson II.   18th Century English Porcelain; a
       brief guide to the collection in the National Museum of
       History and Technology.   Washington, D.C.:   Smithsonian,
       1973.   95pp, ill, bib

3437   _____.   English Yellow-Glazed Earthenware.   Washington,
       D.C.:   Smithsonian, 1974.   125pp, 138 (64 color) ill
       (Leon Collection)

3438   Moore, Hanna (N.) Hudson.   Delftware, Dutch and English.
       London; Binghamton, NY: Hodder & Stoughton, 1909.
       78pp, ill, 58 pls, bib

3439 * _____.   The Old China Book, Including Staffordshire, Wedg-
       wood, Lustre, and Other English Pottery and Porcelain.
       New York: Grant Richards, 1903; London: Grant Richards,
       1904; London: Hodder & Stoughton, 1906; New York:
       Tudor, 1935; reprints. New York: 1944; Rutland, Vt:
       Tuttle, 1974.   283 to 312pp, 150 ill, bib (List of 711
       American, English and miscellaneous other views on china,
       18th and 19th centuries)

3440   Morley-Fletcher, Hugo.   Investing in Pottery and Porcelain.
       London: Barrie & Rockliff; New York: C. N. Potter,
       1968; London: Transworld, 1970.   160pp, 200 (16 color)
       pls   (1646-1918)

3441   Mount, Sally.   The Price Guide to 18th Century English Pot-
       tery.   Woodbridge, Suffolk: Antique Collectors' Club,
       Baron, 1972; Price Revision List. 1973.   427pp, ill, bib

3442   *Mundy, Robert Godfrey C.   English Delft Pottery.   London:
       Jenkins, 1928.   127pp, ill, 52 pls NN

3443   Murton, A. E.   Lowestoft China.   Lowestoft, Eng: 1932.
       67pp

3444 *Nance, Ernest Morton. The Pottery and Porcelain of Swansea
      and Nantgarw. Fore. by R. L. Hobson. London: Bats-
      ford, 1942. 579pp, 5000 ill, 196 pls, bib (Indispensable)

3445 Nightingale, James Edward. Contributions Towards the History
      of Early English Porcelain, from contemporary sources;
      to which are added reprints from Messrs. Christie sale
      catalogues of the Chelsea, Derby, Worcester and Bristol
      manufactories from 1769-1785. 3 parts. Salisbury: priv.
      printed, 1881; reprint in 1 vol. Wakefield, Eng: E P
      Publishing, 1973. 112pp, ill BM

3446 Nisbett, Marjorie. Pottery and Porcelain, Salisbury and
      South Wiltshire Museum. Salisbury: Museum, 1973.
      23pp, ill, bib (To 1850)

3447 Official Catalogue of the Exhibition of Decorative and Artistic
      Pottery, china and glass manufacture, in connection with
      the United Kingdom Section of the Imperial Institute, in-
      cluding particulars of a loan collection of china and pottery
      dating from the year 1600 A.D. London: 1894. 128pp

3448 Old English China. Its features, marks, and characteristics.
      By a collector. Hackney, Eng: G. Pite, 1907. 18pp BM

3449 Old English Porcelain. London: Stoner & Evans, 1909.
      (83)pp, pls with descriptive text BM

3450 Ormsbee, Thomas H. English China and Its Marks. Great
      Neck, NY: Channel, Deerfield Editions, 1959; rev. ed.
      London: W. H. Allen, 1962; Great Neck: 1967. 200pp,
      ill, 700 marks

3451 *Owen, Hugh. Two Centuries of Ceramic Art in Bristol, being
      a history of the manufacture of "the true porcelain," by
      Richard Champion; with an account of the Delft, earthen-
      ware, and enamel glass-works from original sources.
      London: Ball & Daldy, 1873. 402pp, 160 ill, pls (Au-
      thoritative) DLC

3452 Page, H. S. The Evolution of English Pottery During the
      18th Century. Brighton, Eng: 1911.

3453 Paul, Iain. The Scottish Tradition in Pottery. Edinburgh:
      T. Nelson, 1948. 8pp, 20 pls

3454 Perceval, S. G. On the Brislington Lustre Ware in the
      Bristol Art Gallery. Bristol: 1906. 8pp

3455 Phillips, P. W. A Short Account of Old English Pottery,
      and an introduction to the study of Chinese porcelain by

Rev. G. A. Schneider. Hitchin, Herts: 1901. 124pp, ill

3456 A Picture Book of Welsh Porcelain. Cardiff: National Museum of Wales, 1951. 32pp, chiefly ill NN

3457 Pinkham, Roger. Catalogue of Pottery by William DeMorgan. V & A. London: 1973. 115pp, ill, bib (William Frend De Morgan, 1839-1917)

3458 Porcelain Figures. V & A. London: HMSO, 1947; 2nd ed. 1968. 4pp, 30 ill, 28 pls

3459 *Porter, George Richardson, 1792-1852. A Treatise on the Origin, progressive improvement and present state of the manufacture of porcelain and glass. London: Longman, Rees, Orme, Brown & Green, 1830; 1832; Philadelphia: Carey & Lea, 1932; 1846. 252pp, ill, 14 woodcuts on porcelain-making, 36 on glass-making

3460 Pottery and Glass Trades' Review and Gazette, a Trade and Art Journal. London: 1877- .

3461 *Pountney, William Joseph. Old Bristol Potteries; being an account of the old potters and potteries of Bristol and Brislington, between 1650 and 1850, with some pages on the old chapel of St. Anne, Brislington. Fore. by R. L. Hobson, and B. Rackham. Bristol, Eng: Arrowsmith; London: Simpkin, Marshall, 1920; facsimile reprint with new introd. Wakefield, Eng: E P Publishing, 1972. 369pp, ill, 57 leaves of pls, color frontis (Gloucester potteries)

3462 Price, E. Stanley. John Sadler, a Liverpool Pottery Printer. (1720-1789.) West Kirby, Eng: 1949. 108pp, ill

3463 The Process of Making China. Illustrated with 12 engravings, descriptive of the works of the Royal China Manufactory, Worcester, etc. London: 1810. BM

3464 Pugh, Patterson David Gordon. Heraldic China Mementoes of the First World War. Newport, Monm: 1972. 50pp, ill, 54 pls, bib (Includes Goss heraldic porcelain)

3465 *_____, and Margery Pugh. Naval Ceramics. Newport, Monm: Ceramic Book Co, 1971. 113pp, ill, 133 pls, bib (1540-1940. English and American naval history depicted in china)

3466 *Rackham, Bernhard. Catalogue of English Porcelain, Earthenware, Enamels, etc., collected by Charles Schreiber, Esq.

and Lady Charlotte Elizabeth Schreiber, and presented to
the Museum in 1884. 3 vol. London: 1885; rev. ed.
Vol. I. London: V & A, 1915; Vol. II, III. London: 1930,
1924. text, hundreds of pls, marks

3467 * _____ . Catalogue of the Glaisher Collection of Pottery
and Porcelain in the Fitzwilliam Museum, Cambridge.
Vol. I. Text and color plates; II. Monochrome plates.
2 vol. Cambridge: U of C, 1935. ill, pls, color frontis, bib BM

3468 * _____ . Catalogue of the Herbert Allen Collection of English
Porcelain. London: V & A, 1917; 2nd ed. 1923. 168pp;
99 pls; 172pp, 99 pls, bib BM

3469 _____ . Medieval English Pottery. London: Faber, 1948;
2nd ed. rev. 1972. 34pp, ill, 90 pls; 40pp, ill, 96 pls
(Mostly pitchers, 13th-15th century. Full period: 1000-
1700)

3470 * _____ , and Herbert Read. English Pottery. Its development from early times to the end of the 19th century with
an appendix on the Wrotham potters by James W. L.
Glaisher. London: E. Benn, 1924; reprint with new introd. by Peter Walton. Wakefield, Eng: E P Publishing,
1972; Totowa, NJ: Rowman & Littlefield, 1973. 142pp,
ill, 115 (12 color) pls, bib

3471 _____ , and others. Victorian Exhibition, 1931. Victorian
crafts, etc. London: 1931. 45pp, ill BM

3472 Ramsey, L. G. G., ed. The Connoisseur New Guide to
Antique English Pottery, Porcelain, and Glass. Introd.
by G. Bernard Hughes. London: Connoisseur; New York:
Dutton, 1961. 192pp, ill, bib (1525-1860)

3473 Randall, John. The Clay Industries; including the fictile and
ceramic arts on the banks of the Severn; with notices of
the early use of Shropshire clays, the history of pottery,
porcelain, etc., in the district. Madeley, Eng: 1877.
56pp (Interesting for collectors of Sevres)

3474 Ray, Anthony. English Delftware Pottery, in the Robert Hall
Warren Collection at the Ashmolean Museum, Oxford.
Pref. by Nigel Warren. London: Faber; Boston: 1968.
248pp, ill, 112 (5 color) pls, bib

3475 _____ . English Delftware Tiles. London: Faber, 1973.
304pp, ill, 8 pls, bib (ca.1680-1790)

3476 Read, R. W. A Reprint of the Catalogue of the Chelsea
Porcelain Manufactory, 1756. London?: 1880. SIB-2

3477 Rees, Diana, and Marjorie G. Cawley. A Pictorial Encyclo-
       pedia of Goss China. Newport, Wales: Ceramic Book
       Co, 1970. 29pp, ill, 65 pls

3478 Regnard, Hella. A Pictorial Handbook of Goss Cottages and
       Buildings. (Cover title: W. H. Goss China Cottages.)
       Bath: Author, 1974. 48pp of ill

3479 Reynolds, Ernest Randolph. Collecting Victorian Porcelain.
       London: Arco, 1966; New York: Praeger, 1968. 128pp,
       ill, 32 pls, marks, gloss

3480 *Rhead, George Wooliscroft, 1854-1920. British Pottery
       Marks. London: Scott, Greenwood, 1910. 303pp, 14 ill,
       1200 marks

3481 *Rice, Dennis George. Illustrated Guide to Rockingham Pot-
       tery and Porcelain. London: Barrie & Jenkins; New
       York: Praeger, 1971. 194pp, ill, 112 pls, bib (Rice's
       is among the finest English collections)

3482 _____. Rockingham Ornamental Porcelain. London: Adam
       Publishing, 1965; Newport, Monm: Ceramic Book Co,
       1966. 167pp, 142 ill, 15 pls, bib

3483 Rose, Arthur Veel. Lancastrian "Lustred" Pottery. Reprint
       from American Pottery Gazette. New York?: 19-?
       (ca.1906). 5pp, 4 pls (Manchester, England)

3484 Rose, Muriel. Artist-Potters in England. London: Faber,
       1955; 2nd ed. 1970. 29pp, ill, 88 pls; 64pp, ill, 123
       pls, bib (1901-1953)

3485 The Royal Doulton Potteries; a brief summary of their rise
       and expansion during six reigns. Plaistow, Eng: Curwen
       Pr, n.d. 80pp, ill, pls

3486 Ruscoe, William. English Porcelain Figures, 1744-1848.
       London: J. Tiranti, 1947. 24pp, 40 pls

3487 Sandon, Henry. British Pottery and Porcelain for Pleasure
       and Investment. London: Gifford; New York: Arco,
       1969. 175pp, ill, 16 pls, bib

3488 *Savage, George. 18th Century English Porcelain. New York:
       Macmillan; London: Rockliff, 1952; new ed. London:
       Spring Books, 1964. 435pp, ill, 113 pls, bib

3489 * _____. English Pottery and Porcelain. London: Old-
       bourne Pr; New York: Universe, 1961. 432pp, 184 ill,
       bib (1200-1800)

3490 Sempill, Baroness Cecilia Alice F. English Pottery and

China. London: Collins, 1944; 1957. 47pp, 29 ill, 8 color pls, bib

3491   Series of 12 Delft Plates Illustrating the Tobacco Industry. Presented by J. H. Fitzhenry, etc. V & A. London: 1907. 28pp, 12 pls, color frontis BM, MiGr

3492   Sheppard, Thomas. Old Hull Pottery. Hull: Museum, 1902. 20pp, ill

3493   Shinn, Charles, and Dorrie Shinn. Illustrated Guide to Victorian Parian China. London: Barrie & Jenkins, 1971. 125pp, ill, 99 pls, bib (1842-1900)

3494   Shropshire Pottery and Porcelain. A brief guide to the collection displayed in Clive House Museum. Shrewsbury: Borough Council, 1969. 15pp, 3 ill, bib

3495   Smith, Alan. Illustrated Guide to Liverpool Herculaneum Pottery, 1796-1840. London: Barrie & Jenkins, 1970. 142pp, ill, 104 pls (Many with U.S. naval scenes and portraits)

3496   Smith, Robert H. Soden. Catalogue of the Collection of English Pottery and Porcelain Exhibited on Loan at the Alexandra Palace in 1873. London: 1873. 104pp (Before the exhibition opened, a fire destroyed nearly all the ceramics. The catalogue was still at the printers, and only a few copies were issued. Solon)

3497   *Solon, Louis Mark Emmanuel (sometimes M. L. or L. M.). The Art of the Old English Pottery; illustrated with 50 etchings of the author. London: Bemrose, 1882; 1883; 2nd rev. ed. Derby: Bemrose, 1885; New York: Appleton, 1886; facsim. reprint 1883 ed. New York: 1966; London: E P Publishing, 1973. 214pp, 50 ill; 269pp, ill; 209pp, ill, 48 (20 color) pls BM

3498   *_____. A Brief History of Old English Porcelain and Its Manufactories with an Artistic, industrial, and critical appreciation of their productions. London: Bemrose, 1903. 255pp, ill, bib BM

3499   _____. Salt-Glaze. Catalogue of a collection in the Hanley Technical Museum. Hanley: Albut & Daniel, 1890. 27pp, ill

3500   Spelman, W. W. R. Lowestoft China. Norwich, Eng: Jarrold, 1905. 78pp, ill, 97 pls (part color)

3501   Spero, Simon. The Price Guide to 18th Century English Porcelain. Woodbridge, Suffolk: Baron, Antique Collectors'

Club, 1971; Supplement. 1973. 448pp, chiefly ill of over 400 specimens, bib

3502 Stoner, Frank. Chelsea, Bow, and Derby Porcelain Figures: their distinguishing characteristics. Newport, Wales: Ceramic Book Co, 1955. 33pp, ill, 116 pls

3503 The Story of Coalport, the aristocrat of fine bone china. Stoke-on-Trent: Coalport China, Ltd., 1964. 15pp, ill

3504 [No entry.]

3505 Sugden, Alan Victor, and E. A. Entwisle. Potters of Darwen, 1839-1939. A Century of wallpaper printing by machinery. Manchester: 1939. 120pp

3506 Swansea and Nantgarw Porcelain from the Clyne Castle Collection. Swansea, Glamorgin: Glynn Vivian Art Gallery, 1954; 2nd ed. 1971. 33pp, ill

3507 Taggart, Ross E. The Frank P. and Harriet C. Burnap Collection of English Pottery in the William Rockhill Nelson Gallery. Rev. and enl. ed. Kansas City, Mo: The Gallery, 1967. 219pp, ill

3508 Tait, Hugh. Bow Porcelain, 1744-1776. A special exhibition of documentary material to commemorate the bi-centenary of the retirement of Thomas Frye ... October 1959-April 1960. London: British Museum, 1959. 55pp, ill

3509 Tapp, William Henry. Jefferyes Hamett O'Neale, 1734-1801, Red Anchor fable painter, and some contemporaries. London: U of London Pr, 1938. 66pp, 34 pls, color frontis, bib

3510 _____. A Selection from a Series of Articles Bearing on the History of the Old Porcelain Factory in Lawrence Street, Chelsea. Chosen by the Author as containing the most interesting and important information. n.p.: 1938-43. numerous ill, color pls

3511 Teulon-Porter, Noel. The N. Teulon-Porter Collection of Mocha Pottery. Exhibition. Stoke-on-Trent: Museum & Art Gallery, 1953. 16pp, ill

3512 Thomas, Leslie. The Story on the Willow Plate, Adapted from the Chinese Legend. New York: W. Morrow, 1940. 47pp, ill

3513 Thorne, Atwood. Pink Lustre Pottery. A Handbook for collectors. Pref. by Martin Buckmaster. London: Batsford, 1926. 38pp, ill, 21 pls, bib

3514 Tiffin, W. F. Chronograph of the Bow, Chelsea, and Derby
       Porcelain Manufactories, showing their simultaneous prog-
       ress and their various marks. Salisbury, Eng: 1847.
       14pp, marks

3515 Tilley, Frank. English Pottery and Porcelain of the 18th
       Century.... A preliminary guide for the collector, with
       over 50 illustrations. London: Connoisseur, 1947. 42pp,
       ill, bib

3516 _____. Marks on English Pottery and Porcelain of the
       18th Century and Early 19th: a selection of nearly 150
       marks more frequently found on English wares of this
       period. London: Antique Collector; Cambridge: Heffer,
       1954. 36pp, ill, bib

3517 Toppin, Aubrey J. British Pottery. British porcelain.
       General guide. Part 7. Dublin: Science & Art Museum,
       1904, 1905. 68pp; 45pp MiGr

3518 *Towner, Donald Chisholm. English Cream-Coloured Earthen-
       ware. London: Faber, 1957. 111pp, ill, 99 pls, bib
       (Drawings of spouts, handles, knobs, terminals)

3519 _____. Handbook of Leeds Pottery, and catalogue of the
       exhibited material at the Leeds City Art Gallery, 1951.
       Leeds: Municipal Art Gallery, 1951. 48pp, ill

3520 *_____. The Leeds Pottery. London: Cory, Adams &
       Mackay, 1963; New York: Taplinger, 1965. 180pp, ill,
       51 pls, bib (With complete factory patterns book)

3521 Transfer-printed Ware, gift of Mr. and Mrs. Harold G. Duck-
       worth. Columbus, O: Gallery of Fine Arts, 1973. 51pp,
       1 pl

3522 *The Trapnell Collection of Bristol and Plymouth Porcelain,
       with examples of Bristol glass and pottery. Bristol:
       priv. printed, 1905; as A Catalogue of Bristol and Ply-
       mouth Porcelain, with examples of Bristol glass and pot-
       tery, forming the collection made by Mr. Alfred Trapnell.
       2 vol. London: Albert Amor Gallery, 1912. 60pp, ill;
       34, 76pp, 58 pls, reprint of large sale catalog of Bristol
       porcelain at Christie & Ansell, 21 February 1780

3523 *Tudor-Craig, Sir Algernon. Armorial Porcelain of the 18th
       Century. Fore. by Sir Henry F. Burke. London: Cen-
       tury House, 1925. 136pp, ill, 57 (3 color) pls (Includes
       Chinese export ware)

3524 *Turner, William, F. S. S. The Ceramics of Swansea and
       Nantgarw; a history of the factories, with biographical
       notices of the artists and others, notes on the merits of

the porcelains, the marks thereon, etc., also an appendix on the mannerisms of the artists, by Robert Drane. London: Bemrose, 1897. 349pp, many ill, 34 (11 color) pls, marks (Standard work)

3525   . Transfer Printing on Enamel, Porcelain, and Pottery. Its origin and development in the United Kingdom. London; New York: Chapman & Hall, 1907. 175pp, ill, pls, bib

3526 *Wakefield, Hugh. Victorian Pottery. London: H. Jenkins, 1962; New York: Nelson, 1963; New York: Universe, 1970. 208pp, ill, bib, marks

3527 *Wallis, Alfred, and William Bemrose. The Pottery and Porcelain of Derbyshire: a sketch of the history of the fictile art in the county. Compiled from data hitherto unpublished, with biographical notices of the proprietors, artists, modellers. London: 1870. 52pp, 50 marks BM

3528 Watkins, C. Malcolm. North Devon Pottery and Its Export to America in the 17th Century. Paper 13 of the Museum of History and Technology. Washington, D.C.: Smithsonian, 1960. 60pp, ill, bib

3529 Watney, Bernard. English Blue and White Porcelain of the 18th Century. London: Faber, 1963; New York: T. Yoseloff, 1964; 2nd ed. rev. London: Faber, 1973. 137pp, ill, 99 pls, bib; 145pp, ill, 104 pls, bib (1750-1810)

3530 Way, J. P. A Short History of Old Bristol Pottery and Porcelain, Marks, etc. Bristol: 1908. 32pp, ill

3531 Westropp, Michael Seymour Dudley. Irish Pottery and Porcelain. General Guide to ... Pottery and Porcelain. Dublin: Science & Art Museum, 1935. 43pp, 13 pls

3532   . Notes on Pottery Manufacture in Ireland. Dublin: Royal Irish Academy Proceedings, Vol. 32, 1913. 27pp

3533 Wheatley, Henry Benjamin, 1838-1917. A Handbook of Art Industries in Pottery and the Precious Metals. London: Low, Searle & Rivington, 1886. 146, 124pp, 220 ill, 3 color pls DLC

3534   . Handbook of Decorative Art in Gold, Silver, Enamel on Metal, Porcelain, and Earthenware. London: Low, 1884. 149pp, ill

3535   , and Philip H. Delamotte. Art Work in Earthenware. London: Sampson Low, 1882; 2nd ed. with only Wheatley. 1886. ill

3536   _____, and _____. Art Work in Porcelain. London:
        Sampson Low, 1883; 2nd ed. with only Wheatley. 1886.
        ill

3537   White, Andrew John. Catalogue of Samian Potters' Stamps
        from Lancaster: a survey. Lancaster, Eng: Museum &
        Art Gallery, 1974. 9pp

        William Cookworthy, 1705-1780:.... See: no. 3255.

        William Duesbury's London Account Book. See no. 3278.

3538   Williams, Isaac J. A Guide to the Collection of Welsh Porce-
        lain (Nantgarw and Swansea); together with a catalogue and
        a botanical note on the flower-painting. Cardiff: National
        Museum of Wales, Press Board of U of Wales, 1931. 90pp,
        42 pls, color frontis, bib, dictionary of potters and painters
        DLC, NN, CU

3539   _____. The Nantgarw Pottery and Its Products: an exami-
        nation of the site. Cardiff: National Museum of Wales,
        1932. 40pp, ill, bib DLC

3540   Williams, Petra. Flow Blue China. 2 vol. Jeffersontown,
        Ky: Fountain House East, 1971; 1973. 217pp, 280pp, color
        ill, bib

3541   _____. Flow Blue China and Mulberry Ware, similarity and
        value guide. Jeffersontown, Ky: Fountain House East,
        1975. ill

3542   Williamson, Frederick. History and Classification of Derby
        Porcelain. Reprinted from The Museums Journal. London:
        1922. BM

3543   Wills, Geoffrey. The Book of English China. London: 1964;
        South Brunswick, NJ: A. S. Barnes, 1966. 96pp, 130 ill
        (1500-1800)

3544   _____. The Country Life Book of English China. London:
        Country Life, 1964. 96pp, ill

3545   _____. English Pottery and Porcelain. In 24 sections,
        available separately. London: Guinness Signatures, 1969.
        383pp, ill, bib (1600-1900)

3546   Wundt, L. English Pottery and Porcelain, being a concise
        account of the development of the potter's art in England.
        London: Bazaar, 1874; 1880. 138pp, ill

WEDGWOOD POTTERY, THOMAS BENTLEY,
AND THE TASSIES

3547   Ancient and Modern Wedgwood: exhibition at the Mortimer
       Museum, Hull, July-August 1932.   Hull, Eng: 1932.

3548   Archer, Stuart McDonald.   Josiah Wedgwood and the Potteries.
       London: Longman, 1973.   113pp, ill

3549   Archey, Gilbert.   Guide to the Josiah Wedgwood Bicentennary
       Exhibition, 1930.   Auckland, New Zealand: 1930.   15pp

3550   Barnard, Harry.   Artes Etruriae Renascunter.   A record of
       the works (of Josiah Wedgwood and Sons) at Etruria as
       they exist today, forming an unique example of an 18th
       century English factory.   London: Bemrose, 1920.   39pp,
       ill   DeWint, MH

3551   _____ .   Chats on Wedgwood Ware.   London: T. Fisher
       Unwin, 1924; New York: F. A. Stokes, 1925; London:
       1926; facsim. reprint of 1924 ed. with new introd. by
       Peter Walton.   Wakefield, Eng: E P Publishing, 1973.
       260pp, ill, 64 pls, color frontis   BM

3552   _____ .   Exhibition of Replicas of 18th Century Sculptured
       Miniatures: Wedgwood's portrait medallions of illustrious
       moderns made and finished by Bert Bentley.   n. p.:
       Josiah Wedgwood & Sons, 1922.   12pp

3553   _____ .   The Making of Wedgwood Pottery, Illustrated.
       Josiah Wedgwood and Sons, Ltd., Etruria, Stoke-on-
       Trent ... makers of china, earthenware, jasper, basaltes,
       cane red and Rockingham wares, mortars, etc.   Hanley,
       Eng: Webberley Ltd., 193-?   48pp, ill

3554   *Bartlett, William.   Catalogue of a Collection of Old Wedgwood
       Ware.   Liverpool: Lee & Nightingale, 1882.   126pp
       ("One of most complete collections in private hands."
       Solon)

3555   Bedford, John.   Wedgwood Jasper Ware.   London: Cassell,
       1964; New York: Walker, 1965.   64pp, ill, 2 pls

3556   Bentley, Richard.   Thomas Bentley, 1730-1780, of Liverpool,
       Etruria, and London.   Guildford, Eng: Billings & Sons,
       printer, 1927.   96pp, 1 ill (Wedgwood's business partner)
       CtY, MH

3557   *Burton, William.   Josiah Wedgwood and His Pottery.   Lon-
       don; New York: Cassell, 1922; New York: Funk & Wag-
       nalls, 1923.   195pp, ill, 105 (32 color) pls   ViU, DLC,
       BM

3558   Buten, Harry M. Wedgwood ABC But Not Middle E. Merion,
       Pa: Buten Museum of Wedgwood, 1964. 112pp, ill, bib

3559   _____ . Wedgwood and Artists. Merion, Pa: Buten Mu-
       seum of Wedgwood, 1960. 72pp, ill, bib

3560   _____ . Wedgwood Counterpoint. Five themes: Wedgwood
       anecdotes; unusually useful Wedgwood; Wedgwood chronology:
       an aid to dating Wedgwood ware, the philosophy of col-
       lecting; varieties of Wedgwood. Merion, Pa: Buten Mu-
       seum of Wedgwood, 1962. 256pp, ill, color pls

3561   _____ . Wedgwood Rarieties. Merion, Pa: Buten Museum
       of Wedgwood, 1969. 320pp, ill, pls (400 pieces ill)

3562   Catalogue of Works on Queen's Ware Patented for Messrs.
       Wedgwood by the Late Emile Lessore. On exhibition at
       Messrs. Mortlock's Galleries. London: 1876. 27pp
       (Lessore painted at Sevres, then Minton, then Wedgwood)

3563   Chaffers, William, 1811-1892. Catalogue of an Exhibition of
       Old Wedgwood Ware, at Messrs. Phillips' Ceramic Gal-
       leries, London. London: G. Davy & Sons, 1877. 49pp
       NN

3564   *Church, Sir Arthur Herbert. Josiah Wedgwood, master-
       potter. London: Seeley; New York: Macmillan, 1894;
       rev. enl. ed. London; New York: 1903; new rev. ed.
       1908. 103pp, ill, 4 pls, bib; 82pp, ill, pls, bib; 219pp,
       ill, pls, bib CU, NN

3565   Corkill, Margaret. Wedgwood and His Ware: a bibliography.
       Hatfield: Hertis, 1973. 39pp, ill

3566   Crowther, James Gerald. Josiah Wedgwood. London:
       Methuen, 1972. 46pp, ill

3567   18th Century Wedgwood at the Paine Art Center. May-June
       1965. Oshkosh, Wisc: 1965. 28pp

3568   Exhibition of Wedgwood at Kenwood House, Iveaugh Bequest,
       May-September 1954. London: County Council, 1954.
       16pp

3569   *Gatty, Charles T., comp. Catalogue of a Loan Collection of
       Works of Josiah Wedgwood Exhibited at the Liverpool Art
       Club, February 1879. Liverpool: 1879; rev. ill ed.
       Liverpool: 1879. 175pp; 190pp, 15 pls

3570   Gorely, Jean. A Selective Bibliography of Books and Maga-
       zine Articles on Wedgwood and Other Ceramics. A
       working list prepared by request for the Library of

Wellesley Collection. n.p.: Wellesley, 1953; with additions. 1956. (Wellesley, Mass.) 6 leaves BM

3571 _____. Wedgwood. New York: M. Barrows; New York: Gramercy Publishing, 1950. 190pp, 97 ill, pls DLC

3572 _____, and Marvin D. Schwartz. The Emily Winthrop Miles Collection: the works of Wedgwood and Tassie. Brooklyn: Institute of Arts and Sciences, 1965. 63pp, ill

3573 _____, and Mary Wadsworth. Exhibition: Old Wedgwood from bequest of Grenville Lindall Winthrop, June-September. Cambridge, Mass: Fogg Museum of Art, Harvard, 1944. 48pp

3574 Graham, John Meredith, II, and Hensleigh Cecil Wedgwood. Handbook Catalogue for the Brooklyn Museum Exhibition: Wedgwood, a living tradition. Brooklyn: Museum of Institute of Arts and Sciences; New York: Tudor, 1948; reprint as Wedgwood. New York: Arno Pr, 1974. 118pp, ill

3575 Gray, John Miller, 1850-1894. James and William Tassie. A biographical and critical sketch with a catalogue of their portrait medallions of modern personages. Edinburgh: W. G. Patterson, 1894. 174pp, pls (Many of the medallions prepared for Wedgwood. James Tassie, 1735-1799; William Tassie, 1777-1860) PPL, DeWint

3576 Gunsaulus, Frank Wakeley, comp. Old Wedgwood 1760-1795: a catalog of a collection of plaques, medallions, vases, figures, etc., in coloured jasper and basalte, produced by Josiah Wedgwood at Etruria ... 1760-1795. Chicago: Art Institute, 1912; 1916. 30pp, ill; 51pp, ill (Collections of Richard Tangye, Lord Tweedmouth, Arthur Sanderson, Frederick Rathbone)

3577 Hare, Thomas Leman. Wedgwood Porcelain. New York: Dodd, 1912.

3578 Hayden, Arthur. Catalogue of Wedgwood Exhibition Held in Conduit Street, London, December 1909. London: Josiah Wedgwood & Sons, 1909. 16pp

3579 Haynes, Denys Eyre Lankester. The Portland Vase. British Museum. London: HMSO, 1964. 48pp, pls (The original glass vase)

3580 *Heilpern, Gisela. Josiah Wedgwood, 18th century English

potter: a bibliography. Carbondale, Ill: Central Publications, Southern Illinois University, 1967. 66pp (Includes
works on Wedgwood's associates, painters, etc.)

3581 Hobson, Robert Lockhart. Chinese Porcelain and Wedgwood
Pottery, with other works of ceramic art, etc. (Record
of collections in Lady Lever Art Gallery.) Number 2 of
2 vol. London: Batsford, 1928. 227pp, ill, 103 pls
(part color) BM

3582 Honey, William Bowyer. Wedgwood Ware. London: Faber,
1948; New York: Van Nostrand, 1949; London: 1956.
35pp, ill, 100 pls (part color), bib

3583 Hower, Ralph M. The Wedgwoods: ten generations of potters.
Cambridge, Mass: Harvard U Pr, 1932. 58pp

3584 Hubbard, Elbert. Josiah and Sarah Wedgwood. East Aurora,
NY: Roycrofters, 1906. 27pp, 1 pl

3585 *Jewitt, Llewellyn Frederick William, 1818-1886. The Wedgwoods: being a life of Josiah Wedgwood with notices of
his works and their productions ... and a history of the
early potteries of Staffordshire. London: Virtue, 1865.
435pp, ill PPL

3586 John, William David, and Jacqueline Simcox. Early Wedgwood
Lustre Wares. Newport, Wales: Ceramic Book Company,
1963; 1966. 8pp, 52 ill, 13 pls; 1966: 66 ill on 12 pls
(Marked ware 1810-1815)

3587 Jonas, Maurice. Notes of an Art Collector. London: Routledge, 1907; 2nd ed. enl. with biographical notices and list
of medallions. London: 1908. 56pp, ill, 64 pls (Includes
illustrations of 65 early Wedgwood portrait medallions) MH

3588 Jones, Emily Beatrix Coursolles. Wedgwood Medallion. London: Chatto & Windus, 1922; New York: Holt, 1923.
302pp, ill NN, DLC

Josiah Wedgwood.... See: nos. 3638-3641.

3589 Kelly, Alison. Decorative Wedgwood in Architecture and
Furniture. London: Country Life, 1965. 147pp, ill, 34
(2 color) pls, bib

3590 _____, comp., in association with Josiah Wedgwood & Sons,
Ltd. The Story of Wedgwood. Rev. enl. ed. London:
Faber, 1962; New York: Viking, 1963. 80pp, ill, bib

3591 _____. Wedgwood Ware. London: Ward Lock, 1970.
96pp, ill, color frontis (1759-date)

3592 Klamkin, Marian. The Collector's Book of Wedgwood. Newton Abbot: David & Charles; New York: Dodd, Mead,
1971. 120pp, ill, bib, marks

3593 Lectures on Wedgwood, given at Wedgwood Memorial College.
Barlaston, Eng: 195-? ill

3594 Macht, Carol. Classical Wedgwood Designs; the sources and
their use and the relationship of Wedgwood jasper ware to
the classical revival of the 18th century. New York:
Barrows, 1957; reprint. 1958. 144pp, ill, bib; 131pp,
ill, 64 pls, bib

3595 Makeig-Jones, M. Some Glimpses of Fairyland. n.p.:
Josiah Wedgwood & Sons, 1921; reprint. Merion, Pa:
Buten Museum of Wedgwood, 1963. 50pp

3596 Mankowitz, Wolf. Collectors' Wedgwood Portfolio of Wedgwood Photographs Illustrating "Wedgwood." n.p.: 1953.
37pp, ill

3597 _____. The Portland Vase and the Wedgwood Copies.
London: A. Deutsch, 1952. 91pp, ill, bib

3598 * _____. Wedgwood. New York: Dutton; London: Batsford, 1953; reprint. London: Spring Books, 1966.
284pp, 116 ill, 8 color pls, bib

3599 *Meteyard, Eliza, 1816-1879. Choice Examples of Wedgwood
Art. A selection of plaques, cameos, medallions, vases,
etc., from the designs of Flaxman and others. London:
G. Bell, 1879. 28 pls NjP, BM

3600 * _____. The Life of Josiah Wedgwood (the Younger) from
His Private Correspondence and Family Papers, in the
possession of Joseph Mayer, F. Wedgwood, C. Darwin,
Miss Wedgwood and other original sources; with an intro-
ductory sketch of the art of pottery in England. 2 vol.
London: Hurst & Blackett, 1865, 1866; reprint with introd.
by R. W. Lightbown. London: Cornmarket, 1970; New
York: A. M. Kelley, 1971. 504pp, 643pp, 154 woodcuts
(Still the standard work, by the most respected of Wedg-
wood biographers)

3601 * _____. Memorials of Wedgwood. A selection from his
fine art works in plaques, medallions, figures and other
ornamental objects. London: Bell, 1874. 20pp, ill,
28 pls BM

3602 * _____. The Wedgwood Handbook. A manual for collectors.
Treating of the marks, monograms, etc. London: Bell,
1875; reprints. Peekskill, NY: Timothy Trace, 1963;
Detroit: Gale-Tower, 1970. 413pp; 427pp, gloss BM

3603 *_____. Wedgwood and His Work. A selection of his
            plaques, medallions, vases, etc., from the designs of
            Flaxman and others, with a sketch of his life and the
            progress of his fine art manufactures. London: Bell &
            Daldy, 1873; New York: Macmillan, 1876. 68pp, ill,
            28 pls (Includes collection of J. Falke) BM

3604 _____. Wedgwood Trio. Edited by Harry M. Buten.
            Merion, Pa: Buten Museum of Wedgwood, 1967. 280pp,
            ill

3605 *_____. Wedgwood's Catalogue of Cameos, Intaglios,
            Medals, Bas-reliefs, Busts and Small Statues. A reprint
            by Meteyard of an early (1787) original catalogue. Lon-
            don: Bell & Daldy, 1873. 108pp, ill

3606 *Moore, Hannah (N.) Hudson. Wedgwood and His Imitators.
            New York: F. A. Stokes, 1909; London: Hodder &
            Stoughton, 1910. 117pp, ill, 49 pls BM

3607 Nicholls, Robert. The Life of Josiah Wedgwood. Compiled
            from Miss Meteyard's biography--1865. Hanley, Eng:
            Webberley, 1930. 56pp BM

3608 Old Wedgwood. Periodical. Wellesley, Mass: Wedgwood
            Club, 1934-1947.

3609 Pargeter, Ph. Red House Glass Works, Stourbridge ...
            Reproduction of the Portland Vase in Glass by J. North-
            wood; with notes on Wedgwood's reproduction. Stour-
            bridge, Eng: 1877.

3610 Probert, J. L. The J. L. Probert Collection of Old Wedg-
            wood. n. p.: Author, 1882.

3611 Rathbone, Frederick. A Catalogue of a Collection of Plaques,
            Medallions, Vases, Figures, etc., in coloured jasper and
            basalte, produced by Josiah Wedgwood 1760-1795 ...
            property of Arthur Sanderson. Exhibition. Museum of
            Science and Art, Edinburgh. London: F. Rathbone;
            Edinburgh: T. & A. Constable, 1901; 2nd ed. rev. Lon-
            don: 1901; 1903. 69pp, ill

3612 _____. A Catalogue of a Collection of Plaques, Medallions,
            Vases, etc. ... by Josiah Wedgwood, 1760-1795, formed
            by Lord Tweedmouth. V & A. London: HMSO, 1905.
            58pp

3613 _____. Catalogue of the Wedgwood Museum at Etruria.
            Stoke-on-Trent: Josiah Wedgwood, Ltd., 1909. 116pp,
            ill

3614 _____. Centenary Year, 1895. Loan exhibition of selected pieces of old Wedgwood made at Burslem and Etruria. Exhibited at the Wedgwood Institute, Stoke-on-Trent. Burslem: Wedgwood Institute, 1895. 54pp, ill BM

3615 _____. Loan Exhibition of Selected Pieces of Old Wedgwood ... 1760-1793. London: 1893.

3616 * _____. Old Wedgwood; the decorative or artistic ceramic work in colour and relief, invented and produced by Josiah Wedgwood at Etruria in Staffordshire 1760-1794; ... biography and descriptive chapters, a list of marks, etc. (Also as Old Wedgwood. The English relief art work of the 18th century, made by Josiah Wedgwood at Etruria, 1760-1795.) 8 parts. London: B. Quaritch, 1893-1898. 102pp, ill; 94pp, 64 color pls, 2 color frontis (Essential work) BM, DLC

3617 _____. Old Wedgwood and Old Wedgwood Ware. Handbook to collection formed by Richard and George Tangye. With a sketch of Wedgwood's life and a chapter of marks used at Etruria. Birmingham: Museum and Art Gallery, 1885. 104pp, ill BM

3618 Reilly, Robin. Wedgwood Jasper. London: Charles Letts; New York: World, 1972. 80pp, ill, 58 color pls, bib, marks, gloss

3619 _____. Wedgwood--Portrait Medallions; an introduction. Exhibition. October 1973-January 1974. National Portrait Gallery. London: Barrie & Jenkins, 1973. 48pp, 120 ill

3620 _____, and George Savage. Wedgwood: the portrait medallions. London: Barrie & Jenkins, 1973. 379pp, 500 (13 color) ill, bib

3621 Rose, Arthur Veel. The Barberini Vase. New York: Tiffany, 1904. 53pp, ill (Glass Portland vase)

3622 Scheidemantel, Vivian J., comp. Josiah Wedgwood's Heads of Illustrious Moderns. Exhibition. November 1958-March 1959. Chicago: Art Institute, 1958.

3623 Singleton, Esther. Special Exhibition at Van Cortland House Museum (New York); Wedgwood cameo portrait medallions, china, portraits, and other 18th century articles. New York: Van Cortland Mansion, 1922. 42pp

3624 *Smiles, Samuel. Josiah Wedgwood, His Personal History. London: Murray, 1894; New York: Harper, 1895; London: 1897; New York: 1899; 1902; 1911; reprint. Detroit: Gale Research, 1971. 304pp; 316pp, 330pp; 304pp

3625 Smith, Charles B. 200 Years of Wedgwood Marks. 1759-1959. Philadelphia: Author, 1959? 15pp

3626 The Story of Wedgwood, 1730-1930. Fore. by Oliver Lodge.
      2nd ed. Wisbech, Eng: Balding & Mansell, 193-? 48pp,
      ill

3627 Tames, Richard Lawrence Amos. Josiah Wedgwood, 1730-
      1795; an illustrated life. Aylesbury: Shire Publications,
      1972. 48pp, ill, bib

3628 Townsend, Horace. Old Wedgwood, some notes on its history
      and its collection. New York: Phoenix Pr, 1907. 30pp,
      ill

3629 Vurpillat, Francis Jennings. A New Look at the Portland
      Vase and the Wedgwood Copies. Presented at the 2nd
      Wedgwood International Seminar, Cooper Union Museum....
      New York: 1957. 20pp

3630 Warrillow, Ernest James Dalzell. History of Etruria, Staf-
      fordshire, England, 1760-1951. Lloyds Bank, Hanley,
      Staffordshire: Etruscan Publications, 1952; 3rd ed. 1953.
      396pp, ill; 408pp, ill

3631 Wedgwood, Josiah. Museum Etruriae; or a catalogue of
      cameos, etc. Liverpool: G. F. Harris, for James
      Boardman, 1817. 149pp, ill (Reprint of 1787 catalogue,
      with brief history of English pottery and description of
      Portland Vase added)

3632 Wedgwood, Josiah, the Elder. A Catalogue of Cameos, Intag-
      lios, Bas-reliefs, Medallions, Busts, Vases, Statues ...
      now the joint property of Mr. Wedgwood and Mrs. Bentley.
      London: Christie & Ansell Sale Catalogue, 1781. 77pp

3633 _____ . A Catalogue of Cameos, Intaglios, Medals, and
      Bas Reliefs, with a general account of vases and other
      ornaments after the antique made by Wedgwood and Bent-
      ley. London: Cadel, 1773; 4th ed. with additions. Lon-
      don: 1777; 6th ed. enl. Etruria: 1787; reprint from 1787
      ed. ed. by E. Meteyard, with illustrations. London: Bell
      & Daldy, 1873. 60pp; 93pp; 73pp; 107pp, ill

3634 _____ . A Catalogue of Different Articles of Queen's Ware
      ... Manufactured by J. Wedgwood. n.p.: 1770? ill BM

3635 Wedgwood, Josiah Clement. A History of the Wedgwood
      Family. London: St. Catherine Pr, 1908. 325pp

3636 Wedgwood, Josiah, and Sons, Ltd. Early Wedgwood Pottery
      Exhibition at 34 Wigmore Street, London, 1951. Barlaston,
      Stoke-on-Trent: Wedgwood Museum, 1951. 110pp (Col-
      land Collection)

3637 _____ . The Story of Wedgwood, 1730-1930. Wisbech:

Balding & Mansell, 1930; rev. ed. Barlaston: 1946.
48pp; 47pp, ill

3638 Josiah Wedgwood and Sons, Ltd. Makers of china, earthenware, jasper, basalte, cane ware, red ware, Rockingham
ware, mortars. New Castle, Staffordshire: Wedgwood,
1908; Stoke-on-Trent: 1927? 50pp; 48pp

3639 Josiah Wedgwood Bicentenary. Commemorative exhibition of
ceramics, paintings, drawings, documents and maps.
Stoke-on-Trent: City Museum & Art Gallery, 1930. 36pp

3640 Josiah Wedgwood Catalogue of Cameos, Intaglios, Medals,
Bas-reliefs, Busts, Small Statues, Vases, etc. London:
1773; 2nd ed. in French. 1774; 3rd ed. French. 1775; 4th
ed. 1777; 5th ed. 1779; 6th ed. as Catalogue of Cameos,
intaglios, medals, bas-reliefs, busts, and small statues;
with a general account of tablets, vases, ecritoires, and
other ornamental and useful articles ... porcelain and
terra cotta. Etruria: 1787.

3641 Josiah Wedgwood, 1730-1795. A guide to an exhibition of
Wedgwood's works. Nottingham, Eng: Nottingham Castle,
Museum & Art Gallery, 1930. u. p.

3642 Wedgwood; an exhibition of Wedgwood pottery emphasizing the
works of Josiah Wedgwood. December 1956-January 1957.
Lawrence, Ks: U Museum of Art, 1957. 7pp

3643 Wedgwood Catalogue, Felix Joseph Bequest. Nottingham, Eng:
Nottingham Castle, Museum & Art Gallery, 1892. 68pp

3644 Wedgwood Collection of Mr. and Mrs. Samuel Oster. Philadelphia: Museum of Art, 1945.

3645 Wedgwood International Seminar. Annual. San Francisco:
1956- .

3646 Wedgwood Society Proceedings. Periodical. London: 1956- .

3647 Whinney, Margaret Dickens, and Rupert Gunnis. The Collection of Models by John Flaxman, at University College,
London; a catalogue and introduction. London: Athlone
Pr, 1967. 72pp, 24 pls (Flaxman, 1755-1826. Medal-
list, etc., for Wedgwood)

3648 Williamson, George Charles. The Imperial Russian Dinner
Service. The story of a famous work by J. Wedgwood.
London: G. Bell, 1909; or as The Wedgwood Imperial
Russian Dinner Service, copy of the unique example of
Bentley's original catalogue of the service, now pre-
served in Liverpool with the Mayer manuscripts, trans-
lated from the French. London: G. Bell, 1909. 114pp,

73 pls, color frontis, facsims   (The service made for
Catherine of Russia) MiGr

STAFFORDSHIRE POTTERY

3649 Andrade, Cyril. Astbury Figures: Old English Pottery. Exhibition at Dalmeny Galleries, October-November 1924.
London: Cyril Andrade, 1924. 39pp, ill, bib (John Astbury, 1688?-1743) DLC, BM

3650 Arman, David, and Linda Arman. Historical Staffordshire,
an Illustrated Check-list. Danville, Va: Arman Enterprises, 1975. 244pp, 400 ill, bib (2500 pieces)

3651 Ball, Abraham. The Price Guide to Pot-Lids and Other Under-
glaze Colour Prints on Pottery. Woodbridge, Suffolk:
Antique Collector's Club, Baron, 1970; Supplement Price
List. 1974. 496pp, 600 ill

3652 *Balston, Thomas. Staffordshire Portrait Figures of the Victorian Age. London: Faber; Newton, Mass: Branford,
1958; Supplement. London: J. Hall, 1963. 93pp, ill, 52
(4 color) pls; 16pp, 1 pl

3653 *Barber, Edwin Atlee. Anglo-American Pottery; old English
china with American views; a manual for collectors.
Indianapolis: The Clay-Worker, 1899; 2nd ed. enl. Philadelphia: Patterson & White, 1901. 161pp, 93 ill; 220pp,
135 ill, pls

3654 Bedford, John. Old Spode China. London: Cassell; New
York: Walker, 1967. 64pp, ill, 4 pls

3655 _____. Staffordshire Pottery Figures. London: Cassell,
1964; New York: Walker, 1965. 62pp, ill, 2 pls

3656a _____. Toby Jugs. London: Cassell; New York: Walker,
1968. 64pp, ill, 3 pls

3656b *Bemrose, William. Longton Hall Porcelain; being further information relating to this interesting fabrique. London:
Bemrose, 1906. 72pp, ill, 49 pls NN, V & A

3657 Burgess, William, 1857- . Staffordshire Versus American
Pottery. United States Consular Report, No. 132. Washington, D.C.: GPO, 1891. 23pp

3658 Butler, Joseph Thomas. Spatterware at Winterthur; an analysis of marks, forms, shapes, color and decoration. A
paper. 1957. 6pp typescript DeWint

3659 *Camehl, Ada Walker. The Blue China Book: early American

scenes and history pictured in the pottery of the time with supplementary chapter describing the celebrated collection of Presidential china in the White House..., and a complete checking list of known examples of Anglo-American pottery. New York: Dutton, 1916; 1937; New York: Tudor, 1946; New York: Dutton, 1948; 1950?; facsim. reprint of 1st ed. with additions by G. Godden. New York: Dover; London: Constable, 1971. ill; 327pp, 200 ill, 118 pls (1783-1850) PPULC, ViU

3660 Cannon, T(om?) G. Old Spode. London: W. Laurie; New York: F. A. Stokes, 1924; New York: 1925; London: 1927. 82pp, ill, 56 pls, color frontis, marks DLC, PPULC, NN

3661 Catalogue of the Morse Collection of American Historical Pottery. Worcester, Mass: American Antiquarian Society, 1916. 27pp (Emma De F. Morse)

3662 Clarke, Harold George. The Pot Lid Book, 1931. Resume of pot lid collecting, and detailed catalogue of all known pot lids from the pottery of Felix Edwards Pratt and Jesse Austin. London: Courier Pr, 1931. 184pp

3663 _____. The Pot Lid Recorder. A supplement (to Under-Glaze ...). London: Courier Pr, 1949.

3664 * _____. Under-Glaze Colour Picture Prints on Staffordshire Pottery (the centenary pot lid book). An account of their origin, and a descriptive catalogue compiled from the author's and the Lambert and Jenkins collections. London: Courier Pr, 1949; as The Pictorial Pot Lid Book.... London: 1955; 1960. 191pp, ill, pls; 293pp, ill, pls

3665 _____, and Frank Wrench. Colour Pictures on Pot Lids
      and Other Forms of 19th Century Staffordshire Pottery;
      an arranged and comprehensive guide to the collecting of
      the colour printed pictures of the 19th century on Stafford-
      shire pottery. London: Courier Pr, 1924. 205pp, ill,
      pls, color frontis

3666 Cooper, Ronald Glanville. English Slipware Dishes, 1650-
      1850. London: Tiranti, 1965; New York: Transatlantic
      Arts, 1968. 144pp, 333 ill, 160 pls, bib (Toft-Simpson
      ware)

3667 _____. The Pottery of Thomas Toft: a catalogue of Toft
      ware and slip decorated pottery, Leeds and Birmingham
      1952. Exhibition. Leeds: Art Gallery, 1952. 30pp, ill,
      bib (17th-century Staffordshire)

3668 Copeland, W. T., and Sons, Ltd. Famous Hunting Scenes on
      Spode China. A unique and permanent record of the art
      of John Frederick Herring. Leeds; London: Alf Cooke,
      ca.1955. 28pp, ill (Herring, 1795-1865)

3669 Dickens, Charles, 1812-1870. A Plated Article. With an
      introductory account of the historical Spode-Copeland China
      Works to which it refers. (Published in Household Words,
      1852.) Stoke-upon-Trent: W. T. Copeland & Sons, 1913?;
      1914?; New York: Tri-Arts Pr, 192-; Stoke-upon-Trent:
      1930? 20pp, 3 color ill, portrait (The Dickens) CtY,
      CU, MH

3670 Earle, Cyril. The Earle Collection of Early Staffordshire
      Pottery, illustrating over 700 different pieces. Introd. by
      Frank Falkner. Supplementary chapter by Thomas Shep-
      pard. London: A. Brown, 1915. 240pp, 270 ill, 10
      color pls, color frontis, bib (Includes Wedgwood)

3671 Eyles, Desmond. "Good Sir Toby." The Story of Toby jugs
      and character jugs through the ages. London: Doulton's
      Pottery; Leigh-on-Sea: F. Lewis, 1955. 108pp, ill, bib

3672 Falkner, Frank. The Wood Family of Burslem. Introd. by
      William Burton. London: Chapman & Hall, 1912; facsim.
      reprint with note on the author by Michael R. Parkinson.
      Wakefield, Eng: E P Publishing, 1972. 118pp, ill, 59
      pls, color frontis

3673 [No entry.]

3674 Fennelly, Catherine. Something Blue. Some American views
      on Staffordshire. Sturbridge, Mass: Old Sturbridge Vil-
      lage, 1955; 2nd ed. 1967. 36pp, chiefly ill, bib, marks

3675 Fletcher, Edward. Collecting Pot Lids. London: Pitman,
      1975. 114pp, ill

3676   Fox, Eleanor, and Edward G. Fox. Gaudy Dutch. Potts-
       ville, Pa: 1968; 1970. 37pp, ill, 16 color pls (ca.1800-
       1825)

3677   Freeman, Graydon La Verne (Larry). English Staffordshire.
       Watkins Glen, NY: Century, 1959. 95pp, pls

3678   Godden, Geoffrey Arthur. Illustrated Guide to Mason's Patent
       Ironstone China: the related ware--'stone china,' 'new
       stone,' 'granite china'--and their manufactures. London:
       Barrie & Jenkins; New York: Praeger, 1971. 175pp, ill,
       88 pls, bib

3679   _____. The Illustrated Guide to Ridgway Porcelains. Lon-
       don: Barrie & Jenkins, 1972. 93pp, ill, 96 pls, bib

3680   _____. Minton Pottery and Porcelain of the First Period,
       1793-1850. London: Jenkins, 1968; New York: Praeger,
       1970. 168pp, ill (some color), 94 pls, bib

3681 *Grant, Maurice Harold. The Makers of Black Basaltes.
       London; Edinburgh: Blackwood, 1910; facsim. reprint.
       London: Holland Pr, 1967. 400pp, ill, 96 pls (Wedg-
       wood, Turner, Palmer, Adams, etc. 300 pieces)

3682 *Greaser, Arlene, and Paul H. Greaser. Homespun Ceramics;
       a study of spatterware and spongeware. Allentown, Pa:
       1964; 2nd ed. 1964-65; 3rd ed. enl. 1967; 4th ed. enl.
       Des Moines, Io: Wallace-Homestead, 1973. 59pp, pls;
       90pp, pls; 123pp, ill, bib; 128pp, ill, bib

3683   Haggar, Reginald George. The Masons of Lane Delph and the
       Origin of Masons Patent Ironstone China. London: P. L.
       Humphries, for G. L. Ashworth, 1952. 104pp, ill, bib
       (Miles Mason, 1752-1822. So-called Gaudy Welsh)

3684 *_____. Staffordshire Chimney Ornaments. New York:
       Pitman; London: Phoenix, 1955. 158pp, ill, 103 (5 color)
       pls, bib

3685   Hall, John. Staffordshire Portrait Figures. London: Charles
       Letts; New York: World, 1972. 80pp, color ill, bib

3686 *Halsey, Richard Townley Haines. Pictures of Early New
       York on Dark Blue Staffordshire Pottery, together with
       pictures of Boston, New England, Philadelphia, the South,
       and West. New York: Dodd, Mead, 1899; reprint with
       new introd. by Marvin Schwartz. New York: Dover,
       1974. 329pp, 167 ill (many color), pls (1 color) DLC

3687   Hayden, Arthur. Spode and His Successors. A history of
       the pottery, Stoke-on-Trent, 1765-1865. Heaton Mersey,
       Eng: Cloister Pr, n.d.; New York: Tri-Arts, n.d.;

3688a Hillier, Bevis. Master Potters of the Industrial Revolution:
the Turners of Lane End. London: Cory, Adams and
Mackay, 1965. 96pp, 39 (3 color) pls, bib (John Turner,
1738-1787; William Turner, 1762-1835; John Turner, 1766-
1824)

3688b Holgate, David. New Hall and Its Imitators. London: Faber,
1971. 113pp, ill, 102 pls, bib (1781-1835)

3689 Hughes, George Bernard. The Story of Spode. n.p.: W. T.
Copeland, 1950. 36pp, ill

3690 Jones, Charles A. This 'n That and Where It's At in Early
Staffordshire Tableware. Homer, NY: Author, 1974.
42pp, ill (Index for locating published illustrations of
transferware patterns, spatterware and gaudy wares)

3691 Journal of Ceramic History. Periodical. Stafford, Eng:
George Street Pr, 1968- .

3692 Kelly, James Harold. Post Medieval Pottery ... (from
Stoke-on-Trent). Hanley, Stoke-on-Trent: Archaeological Society, City Museum & Art Gallery, 1975. 24pp,
ill (ca. 1600-1850)

3693 Laidacker, Samuel H. Prices for Historical Staffordshire
Realized at Auction Since the Publication of the Standard
Catalogue of Anglo-American China, 1810-1850, and
checked against the catalogue, containing the records of
the following collections: Mrs. John P. Coyle, William
Randolph Hearst, O. P. and M. J. Van Sweringen, and
several others. Scranton, Pa: Author, 1939. 22pp, ill

3694 *   . Standard Catalogue of Anglo-American China. I.
From 1810-1850; printed and decorative ware made in
England by the Staffordshire potteries for the American
trade; II. Other than American Views Appearing on Trans-
fer Decorated Wares Produced by Staffordshire and Other
English Potteries During the Period from 1815-1860. 2
vol. Scranton, Pa: 1938-51; 2nd rev. ed. of Part 1, as
Anglo-American Ware. Bristol, Pa: 1954. ill

3695 Lakin, Thomas. The Valuable Receipts of the Late Mr.
Thomas Lakin, with proper and necessary directions for
their preparation and use in the manufacture of porcelain,
earthenware and iron stone china. Leeds: E. Baines,
for Mrs. Lakin, 1824. 86pp (First time private recipes
of a manufacturer were printed for the common benefit
of all. Posthumous publication by destitute widow) NN

3696* Larsen, Ellouise Baker. American Historical Views on Staffordshire China. New York: Doubleday, Doran, 1939;
rev. enl. ed. 1950; corrected ed. with supplement and

145 additional illustrations. New York: Dover, 1974. 236pp, 133 (4 color) ill, bib; 317pp, ill; 345pp, ill, bib

3697 Latham, Bryan. Victorian Staffordshire Portrait Figures, for the Small Collector. London: A. Tiranti, 1953. 41pp, 71 ill

3698 Little, Wilfred Laurence. Staffordshire Blue: underglaze blue transfer-printed earthenware. London: Batsford; New York: Crown, 1969. 160pp, 120 ill, 64 pls, bib (Many American views)

3699 Lockett, Terence Anthony. Davenport Pottery and Porcelain, 1794-1887. Newton Abbot: David & Charles; Rutland, Vt: Tuttle, 1972. 112pp, pls, color frontis, bib

3700 Mackintosh, Sir Harold, Lord of Halifax. Early English Figure Pottery. A collection of Ralph Wood and contemporary pottery. Introd. by G. W. Horsfield. London: Chapman & Hall, 1938. 122pp, 16 (5 color) pls, bib (Ralph Wood, Astbury, Whieldon, including Tobys) DLC

3701 Meigh, William Alfred. Meigh's Lists. List No. 1. Alphabetical list of the Staffordshire potters, together with their dates and addresses. List No. 2. Alphabetical list of over 400 initials known to have been used by the Staffordshire potters. List No. 3. Alphabetical list of the names of Staffordshire potters, other than first name. List No. 4. Alphabetical dated list of the initials of all the Staffordshire potters. 4 parts. London: Forsbrook, V & A Department of British ... Antiquities, 1937.

3702 Minton, Herbert. Catalogue of Encaustic Tiles Manufactured by Minton, Hollins, and Wright, of Stoke-on-Trent. Stoke-on-Trent: 1844. 117 patterns for pavements

3703 Minton, Hollins and Co. Patent Tile Works. Stoke-on-Trent: 1877.

3704 Mintons' Breakfast, Tea, Dinner, and Toilet Patterns. Stoke-on-Trent: Minton China Works, 1888. ill

3705 Mintons' Secessionist Ware. Illustrated catalogue. Stoke-on-Trent: Mintons China Works, 1904. 28pp, ill

3706 Mintons' Selected Patterns of Enamelled Tiles ... etc. Stoke-on-Trent: 1870.

3707 Mountford, Arnold Robert. The Sadler Teapot Manufactory Site, Burslem, Stoke-on-Trent; ... Marquis of Granby Hotel Site; (and) Astbury-type pottery.... Hanley: City Museum & Art Gallery, 1974. 38pp, ill

3708   _____. The Illustrated Guide to Staffordshire Salt-Glazed
            Stoneware. London: Barrie & Jenkins; New York: Prae-
            ger, 1971. 88pp, ill, 136 pls, bib (Mid-18th century)

3709   _____, and F. Celoria. Some Examples of Sources in the
            History of 17th Century Ceramics. Stafford, Eng: George
            Street Pr, 1968. 27pp

3710   Nicholls, Robert, comp. 10 Generations of a Potting Family.
            Founded upon "William Adams, an old English Potter," by
            William Turner and other works on the Adams family.
            London: P. Lund, Humphries, 1931. 135pp, ill, 53 pls
            BM

3711   Oliver, Anthony. The Victorian Staffordshire Figure: a guide
            for collectors. London: Heinemann, 1971; New York:
            St. Martin's Pr, 1972. 179pp, 250 ill, 8 pls, bib

3712   Owen, Harold, 1872-1930. The Staffordshire Potter; with a
            chapter on the dangerous processes in the potting industry
            by the Dutchess of Sutherland. London: G. Richards,
            1901; reprint. Bath, Eng: Kingsmead Bookshop, 1970.
            357pp

3713   Peel, Derek Wilmot. A Pride of Potters. New York: R.
            Speller, 1957. 40pp, ill (Blue jasper ware by the Adams
            family)

3714   *Price, Robert Kenrick. Astbury, Whieldon and Ralph Wood
            Figures, and Toby Jugs. Introd. by Frank Falkner.
            London: Lane, 1922; 1938. 140pp, ill, 67 pls (part
            color) (Standard work)

3715   *Pugh, Patterson David Gordon. Staffordshire Portrait Figures,
            and Allied Subjects of the Victorian Era. London: Barrie
            & Jenkins, 1970. 688pp, 747 ill, 37 color pls, bib (1500
            figures)

3716   Rackham, Bernard, 1876- . Animals in Staffordshire Pot-
            tery. London: Penguin, 1953. 32pp, ill, 16 color pls
            BM

3717   *_____. Early Staffordshire Pottery. London: Faber,
            1951. 46pp, ill, 100 pls, bib (17th and 18th century)

3718   *Read, Herbert Edward. Staffordshire Pottery Figures. Lon-
            don: Duckworth, 1929. 24pp, ill, 76 (6 color) pls

3719   Rhead, George Wooliscroft, and Frederick Alfred Rhead.
            Staffordshire Pots and Potters. London: Hutchinson,
            1906. 384pp, 116 ill, 90 pen drawings, 4 color pls

3720   Rose, Arthur Veel. Antonin Boullemier. New York: priv.
            printed, 1900. 25pp, ill (Minton china painter)

3721   Scott, Amoret, and Christopher Scott. Discovering Stafford-
       shire Figures of the 19th Century. Tring: Shire Publica-
       tions, 1969. 67pp, ill

3722 *Shaw, Simeon. History of the Staffordshire Potteries and the
       Rise and Progress of the Manufacture of Pottery and Por-
       celain, with reference to genuine specimens and notices
       of eminent potters. Hanley, Eng: Author, 1829; facsimile
       reissue with introd. London: Scott, Greenwood, 1900; re-
       print. Newton Abbot: David & Charles; Wakefield: S. R.
       Publishers; New York: Praeger, 1970. 244pp (1690-
       1829) BM, DLC

3723   Smith, Mabel Woods. Anglo-American Historical China.
       Descriptive catalogue, with prices for which the pieces
       were sold at the New York Auction Art Galleries in the
       years 1920, 1921, 1922, and 1923. Chicago: R. O.
       Ballou, 1924. 119pp, ill

3724   Solon, Louis Mark Emanuel. Pate-sur-Pate. Newcastle:
       G. F. Bagguley, 1894; reprint. Newport, Monm: Ceramic
       Book Co, 1972. 13pp, ill (Solon himself describes the
       processes of raised white cameo engraving which he in-
       vented. 18 Minton vases)

3725   Stanley, Louis Thomas. Collecting Staffordshire Pottery.
       Garden City, NY: Doubleday; London: W. H. Allen,
       1963. 215pp, ill

3726   _____ . Collecting Staffordshire Pottery Figures. London:
       1971.

3727a Staffordshire Pottery Industry. Stafford: Staffordshire County
       Council, 1969. 35 leaves, ill, facsims, bib (1690-1860)

3727b *Stringer, George Eyre. New Hall Porcelain. London: Art
       Trade, 1949. 136pp, ill, marks, pattern numbers (De-
       finitive work)

3728   Thomas, John. The Rise of the Staffordshire Potteries.
       Pref. by G. D. H. Cole. Bath: Adams & Dart; New
       York: A. M. Kelley, 1971. 228pp, ill, 32 pls, bib
       (1710-1850)

3729   Transactions of the North Staffordshire Ceramic Society.
       Periodical. Tunstall: 1901- .

3730   Turner, Hugh Antony Ben. A Collector's Guide to Stafford-
       shire Pottery Figures. London: MacGibbon & Kee, 1971;
       Buchanan, NY: Emerson Books, 1974. 294pp, ill, 8
       color pls, bib (1740-1900)

3731   Turner, William, F. S. S. William Adams, the Life and

Work of an old English Potter; with an account of his
family and their productions. London; New York: Chapman & Hall, 1904. 252pp, ill, 72 pls

3732 200 Years of Spode. Exhibition. August-October 1970.
      Burlington House, London. London: Royal Academy,
      1970. 91pp, ill

3733 *Watney, Bernard. Longton Hall Porcelain. London: Faber;
      New York: Pitman, 1957. 72pp, ill, 80 (4 color) pls,
      bib (1750-1760)

3734 Weatherill, Lorna. The Pottery Trade and North Stafford-
      shire, 1660-1760. Manchester: U Pr; New York: A. M.
      Kelley, 1971. 174pp, ill, 7 pls, bib

3735 Wedgwood, Baron Josiah Clement. Staffordshire Pottery and
      Its History. London: Sampson Low; New York: McBride,
      1913; London: 1922. 229pp, ill; 240pp, ill BM

3736 *_____, and Thomas H. Ormsbee. Staffordshire Pottery.
      New York: McBride; London: Putnam, 1947. 174pp,
      ill (Part 1 is the 1913 book, Staffordshire Pottery ...
      History)

3737 Whitehead, James, and Charles Whitehead. Designs of Sundry
      Articles of Earthenware Manufactured by J. and Ch. White-
      head, Hanley, Staffordshire. At the same manufactory
      may be had a great variety of other articles; both useful
      and ornamental, as well as printed, painted, and enamelled,
      as likewise dry bodies, such as Egyptian, black, jasper,
      etc. Birmingham: 1798. ill

3738 *Whiter, Leonard R. Spode: a history of the family, factory
      and wares from 1733-1833. London: Barrie & Jenkins;
      New York: Praeger, 1970. 246pp, 250 ill, 313 (19 color)
      pls, bib, marks

3739 Williams, Sydney B. Antique Blue and White Spode. Fore.
      by Granville Fell. London: Batsford, 1943; 1947; 3rd
      ed. rev. & enl. London; New York: Batsford, 1949.
      242pp, 123 ill (Includes ware for American market)

3740 Williams-Woods, Cyril. Staffordshire Pot Lids and Their
      Potters. London: Faber, 1972. 173pp, ill, 72 pls, bib

3741 Wood, Richard, and Virginia A. Wood. Historical China Cup
      Plates: a catalogue. Baltimore: n.d. 22pp, ill of 134
      pieces

      Wood, Serry (pseud.). See: Graydon L. V. Freeman, no.
      3677.

3742 Woodhouse, Charles Platten. Old English Toby Jugs and Their Makers. London: Mountrose Pr, 1949. 48pp, ill, 12 pls

WORCESTER PORCELAIN

3743 Amor, Albert. The Collection of Old Worcester Porcelain, formed by the late Mr. R. Drane. London: A. Amor, Ltd., 1922. 80pp, 48 ill V & A

3744 Ballantyne, A. Randal. Robert Hancock and His Works, 1730-1817. London: Chiswick Pr, 1885. 50pp, ill, 14 pls (Engraver at Battersea and Worcester) V & A

3745 Barrett, Franklin Allen. Worcester Porcelain. London: Faber; New York: Pitman, 1953; 2nd ed. as Worcester Porcelain and Lund's Bristol. London: Faber, 1966. 53pp, 100 (4 color) pls, bib; 92pp, 103 (7 color) pls, bib

3746 Bedford, John. Old Worcester China. London: Cassell, 1966; New York: Walker, 1967. 63pp, ill, 2 pls (1753-1840)

3747 Binns, Richard William, 1819-1900. Catalogue of a Collection of Worcester Porcelain in the Museum at the Royal Porcelain Works. Worcester: the Company, 1882. 183pp, ill, pls (1900 items)

3748 * _____ . Catalogue of a Collection of Worcester Porcelain, and notes on Japanese specimens, in the Museum at the Royal Porcelain works. Worcester: Royal China Manufactory, 1882. 183pp, ill, pls BM

3749 * _____ . A Century of Potting in the City of Worcester, being the history of the Royal Porcelain Works, 1751-1851. London: B. Quaritch, 1865; 2nd ed. "to which is added a short account of the Celtic, Roman and medieval pottery of Worcester." London: 1877. 228pp, ill, color pls; 376pp, ill, pls (2nd ed. standard work) BM

3750 _____ . A Guide Through the Worcester Royal Porcelain Works, with a description of the various processes and manipulations used in the manufacture of porcelain. Worcester: F. Gosling, 1853; 1882; 1893. 35pp, ill; 48pp, ill

3751 * _____ . Worcester China. A record of the work of 45 years, 1852-1897. Ed. by C. F. Binns. London: B. Quaritch, 1897. 140pp, ill, 35 pls BM

3752 *Bins, W. Moore. The First Century of English Porcelain. London: Hurst & Blackett; Philadelphia: Lippincott, 1906. 251pp, 77 (46 color) pls, marks (Chiefly Worcester) MiGr

3753 *Cook, Cyril. The Life and Work of Robert Hancock; an ac-
       count of the life of the 18th century engraver and his de-
       signs on Battersea and Staffordshire enamels and Bow and
       Worcester porcelain. Knebworth, Herts: Author; London:
       Chapman & Hall, 1948; Supplement: an account of his en-
       gravings on 18th century Bow and Worcester porcelain,
       salt-glazed plates, and Battersea and Staffordshire enamels.
       Knebworth, Herts: Author, 1955. 255pp, ill, bib; 128pp,
       ill, bib NN, DLC

3754 Dykes, F. C. A Collection of Worcester Porcelain. Man-
       chester, Eng: Art Gallery, 1924. 42pp, ill

3755 _____. Some Thoughts on 18th Century English Porcelain.
       London: Westminster Pr, priv. printed, 1931. 40pp
       (Early Worcester, and early English transfer decoration)
       NN

3756 Fisher, Stanley W. Worcester Porcelain. London: Ward
       Lock, 1968. 96pp, chiefly ill, 1 color pl (Includes fakes
       and forgeries)

3757 *Godden, Geoffrey A. Caughley and Worcester Porcelains,
       1775-1800. London: Jenkins; New York: Praeger, 1969.
       161pp, 350 ill, 10 color pls, bib

3758 A Guide Through the Royal Porcelain Works ... Worcester.
       Worcester: Baylis, Lewis & Co, printers, 189-? 47pp,
       ill, 1 pl DLC

3759 Hobson, Robert Lockhart. Catalogue of the Frank Lloyd Col-
       lection of Worcester Porcelain of the Wall Period ... pre-
       sented in 1921. London: British Museum, 1923. 96pp,
       ill BM

3760 *_____. Worcester Porcelain. A description of the ware
       from the Wall period to the present day. London: B.
       Quaritch, 1910. 208pp, 16 ill, 92 collotype pls, 17 color
       pls, bib MB, PP

3761 *Mackenna, Francis Severne. Worcester Porcelain; the Wall
       period and its antecedents. Leigh-on-Sea: F. Lewis,
       1950. 193pp, ill, 81 pls, bib

3762 Marshall, Henry Rissik. Armorial Worcester Porcelain
       (First Period). Newport, Wales: Ceramic Book Co,
       1964. ill (24 colored armorials, 1751-1783)

3763 *_____. Coloured Worcester Porcelain of the First Period,
       (1751-1783). Newport, Wales: Ceramic Book Co, 1954.
       305pp, ill, bib (On display at Ashmolean Museum, Ox-
       ford)

3764 Sandon, Henry. The Illustrated Guide to Worcester Porcelain (1751-1793). London: Jenkins, 1969; New York: Praeger, 1970; rev. ed. 1975. 96pp, 159 (9 color) ill, bib (Royal Worcester Museum)

3765 _____. Royal Worcester Porcelain, from 1862 to Present Day. London: Barrie & Jenkins, 1973; rev. ed. New York: C. N. Potter, 1975. 265pp, 91 ill, 128 (19 color) pls, bib, marks

3766 Savage, George. The Story of Royal Worcester and the Dyson Perrins Museum. London: Pitkin, 1968; new ed. 1973. 24pp, ill

3767 Stieglitz, Marcel H. The Stieglitz Collection of Dr. Wall Worcester Porcelain. Exhibition. Chicago: Art Institute, 1947. 52pp, ill, bib

3768 Vizetelly, F. Catalogue of the Worcester Collection of Porcelain, divided into six classes or periods, and illustrating the progress of ceramic manufacture at Worcester from its earliest period (1751) to 1862. London: G. Unwin, 1865. 30pp

EUROPEAN, MEXICAN AND RUSSIAN CERAMICS

3769 Adams, Arthur Frederick, comp. Terra Cotta of the Italian Renaissance. Derby, Eng: Terra Cotta Association, 1928. 200 pls BM

3770 Amor, Albert. Catalogue of the Unique Collection of Early Dresden Figures Lent by Lord and Lady Fisher. London: A. Amor, Ltd., 1935. 8pp V & A

3771 Aslin, Elizabeth. French Exhibition Pieces, 1844-1878. Bethnal Green Museum. V & A. London: 1973. 36pp, chiefly ill (French ceramic wares, art metalwork, etc.)

3772 *Auscher, Ernest Simon. A History and Description of French Porcelain. Tr. and ed. by William Burton. London; New York: Cassell, 1905. 191pp, ill, 72 (24 color) pls, bib, marks BM

3773 Avery, Clara Louise. Masterpieces of European Porcelain. A catalogue of a special exhibition, March-May 1949. New York: Metropolitan Museum, 1949. 32pp, ill, 32 pls DLC, BM

3774 Bacci, Mina. European Porcelain. Tr. from Italian (1966) by Adeline Hartcup. Feltham; New York: Hamlyn, 1969; London: Hamlyn, 1974. 157pp, 69 color ill (1575-1800)

3775   Barber, Edwin Atlee.   Artificial Soft Paste Porcelain.   France,
          Italy, Spain and England.   Philadelphia: Pennsylvania Mu-
          seum of Art; Garden City, New York: Doubleday, 1907.
          40pp, ill, pls   BM, PPL

3776   _____ .   Catalogue of Mexican Maiolica Belonging to Mrs.
          Robert W. De Forest Exhibited by the Hispanic Society of
          America, February-March 1911.   New York: the Society,
          1911.   151pp, ill

3777   _____ .   The Emily Johnston De Forest Collection of Mexi-
          can Maiolica.   Metropolitan Museum.   New York: Gilliss
          Pr, 1918.   41pp, ill   (First exhibited at Hispanic Society,
          1911)

3778   _____ .   Hispano-Moresque Pottery in the Collection of the
          Hispanic Society of America.   New York: 1915.   278pp
          BM

3779   _____ .   The Maiolica of Mexico.   Philadelphia: Museum
          of Art, 1908.   115pp, ill, pls (part color), color frontis

3780   _____ .   Mexican Maiolica in the Collection of the Hispanic
          Society of America.   New York: 1915.   60pp, ill   BM

3781   _____ .   Spanish Maiolica in the Collection of the Hispanic
          Society of America.   New York: 1915.   150pp, ill   BM

3782   _____ .   Spanish Porcelains and Terra Cottas in the Collec-
          tion of the Hispanic Society of America.   New York: 1915.
          42pp, ill   BM

3783   Barton, Kenneth James.   Some Examples of Medieval Glazed
          Earthenware in Sweden.   Stockholm: Almquist & Wiksell,
          dist., 1968.   48pp, ill

3784   Bawo, and Dotter.   Limoges; its people, its china.   New
          York: 1901.   26pp, ill

3785   Beckwith, Arthur.   Majolica and Fayence: Italian, Sicilian,
          Majorcan, Hispano-Moresque, and Persian.   New York:
          D. Appleton, 1877.   185pp, ill, bib   BM, NN, DLC

3786   Berling, Karl.   Festive Publication to Commemorate the 200th
          Jubilee of the Oldest European China Factory, Meissen.
          Tr. from German (1900).   Leipzig: F. A. Brockhaus,
          1910; reprint as Meissen China: an illustrated History.
          New York: Dover; London: Constable, 1972.   191pp, ill
          (1709-1911)   BM

3787   *Blacker, James F.   The ABC of Collecting Old Continental
          Pottery.   London: S. Paul, 1913.   315pp, ill, 47 pls,
          marks   DKC, NN, BM

3788 Brightwell, Cecilia Lucy. Palissy: the Huguenot Potter.
London: Religious Tract Society, 1858; 1859; 1860; 1921.
176pp (Bernard Palissy, ca.1510-ca.1590. French)

3789 *Bristowe, William Syer. Victor China Fairings. London:
A. & C. Black, 1964; New York: Taplinger, 1965; new
enl. ed. 1971; 1973. 108pp, many ill; 115pp, ill (German, 1860-1910)

3790 Bubnova, Ed., ed. Old Russian Faience, with Factory Marks.
Moscow: Iskusstvo, 1973. 188pp, 142 ill, 40 color pls

3791 Buckley, John Joseph. French Pottery. General guide to
pottery and porcelain, chapter 3, part 7. Dublin: Science
& Art Museum, 1908; 1910. 32pp, 12 pls

3792 Caiger-Smith, Alan. Tin-Glaze Pottery in Europe and the
Islamic World: the tradition of 1000 years in maiolica,
faience and delft ware. London: Faber, 1973; New York:
Humanities Pr, 1974. 236pp, ill, 104 pls, bib

3793 Casey, Elizabeth Temple. The Lucy Truman Aldrich Collec-
tion of European Porcelain Figures of the 18th Century.
Providence: Rhode Island School of Design, Museum of
Art, 1965. 157pp, ill, pls

3794 Catalogue of an Exhibition of Royal Copenhagen Porcelain and
Copenhagen Art Faience. Brighton, Eng: Museum, 1915.
28pp

3795 *Charles, Robert Lonsdale. Continental Porcelain of the 18th
Century. London: E. Benn; Toronto: U Pr, 1964.
198pp, ill, 76 (12 color) pls, bib (Much on Meissen)

3796 Charleston, Robert Jesse, and John Ayers. The Waddesdon
Catalogue. Meissen and other European porcelain, by
Charleston. Oriental Porcelain, by Ayers. Fribourg:
Office du Lure; London: National Trust, 1971. 316pp,
ill, bib (James A. de Rothschild Collection at Waddesdon
Manor)

3797 Coenen, Frans. Essays on Glass, China, Silver, etc., in
connection with the Willet-Holthuysen Museum, Amsterdam. London: T. Werner Laurie, 1907. 62pp, 24 pls
NN

3798 *Cushion, John Patrick. Continental China Collecting for
Amateurs. London: Muller, 1970. 204pp, ill, 12 pls,
bib

3799 _____, comp. Pocket Book of French and Italian Ceramic
Marks. London: Faber, 1965. 199pp, ill

3800 _____ . Pocket Book of German Ceramic Marks and Those
of Other Central European Countries. London: Faber,
1961. 184pp, ill

3801 Dauterman, Carl Christian. Sevres. New York: Walker;
London: Studio Vista, 1969. 84pp, ill, bib

3802 Day, Colonel John. Dutch Pottery and Porcelain. General
guide to ... pottery and porcelain, chapter 6, part 7.
Dublin: Science & Art Museum, 1905. 16pp

3803 _____ . Flemish and German Stoneware. General guide to
... pottery and porcelain, chapter 7, part 7. Dublin:
Science & Art Museum, 1906. 16pp

3804 _____ . Porcelain, Northern, Central, and Eastern Europe.
General guide to ... pottery and porcelain, chapter 8,
part 7. Dublin: Science & Art Museum, 1906. 26pp

3805 de Guillebon, Regine de Plinval. Porcelain of Paris 1770-
1850. Tr. from French (1972) by Robin R. Charleston.
London: Barrie & Jenkins; New York: Walker, 1972.
362pp, 200 ill, 24 color pls, bib, 220 marks

3806 Delfts Aardewerk/Dutch Delftware. Dutch and English text.
Amsterdam: Rijksmuseum, 1967. 6pp, 35 pls

3807 Domanovszky, Gyorgy. Hungarian Pottery. Tr. from Hungarian by Istvan Farkas. Budapest: Corvina Pr, 1968.
78pp, ill, 48 pls

3808 Drake, Sir William Richard. Notes on Venetian Ceramics.
London: J. Murray; London: priv. printed, 1868. 40,
34pp, ill

3809 *Ducret, Siegfried. German Porcelain and Faience with Vienna,
Zurich and Nyon. Tr. from German by Diana Imber.
London: Oldbourne Pr; New York: Universe, 1962.
468pp, ill, 180 pls (part color), bib

3810 _____ . Unknown Porcelain of the 18th Century. Tr. by
John Hayward. Frankfurt am Main: L. Woeller Verlag,
1956. 142pp, ill, pls (part color), bib

3811 Earthenware from Castilla and Andalucia in the Collection of
the Hispanic Society of America. New York: 1931. 12pp,
ill, pls

3812 Earthenware from Spanish Galicia in the Collection of the Hispanic Society of America. New York: 1931. 12pp, ill,
pls, bib

3813 Eriksen, Svend. Sevres Porcelain. (James A. de Rothschild

Collection, Waddesdon Manor, Buckinghamshire.) Fribourg, Sweden: Office du Livre; London: National Trust,
1968. 339pp, ill

3814 Fajalanza Ware in the Collection of the Hispanic Society of
America. New York: 1930. pls

3815 Franks, Sir Augustus Wollaston. Catalogue of a Collection of
Continental Porcelain Lent and Described by Sir A. W.
Franks. Bethnal Green Museum, South Kensington Museum.
London: 1896. 109pp, 15 pls, marks

3816 Frantz, Henri. French Pottery and Porcelain. London: G.
Newnes, 1905; New York: Scribner's, 1906; London:
Batsford; New York: Scribner's, 1913. 177pp, ill, 77
(7 color) pls, bib MB, PP

3817 *Frothingham, Alice Wilson. Capodimonte and Buen Retiro
Porcelains; period of Charles III. New York: Hispanic
Society of America, 1955. 55pp, 55 ill, bib

3818 _____. Catalogue of Hispano-Moresque Pottery in the
Collection of the Hispanic Society of America. New York:
1936. 99 ill

3819 *_____. Lustreware of Spain. New York: Hispanic Society of America, 1951. 310pp, 221 ill, bib

3820 _____. Tile Panels of Spain, 1500-1650. New York:
Hispanic Society of America, 1969. 106pp, 178 ill, 6
color pls (Tile panels, ornamenting wainscots, altar-
pieces, etc.)

3821 Gardner, Paul Vickers. Meissen and Other German Porcelain in the Alfred Duane Pell Collection. Washington,
D.C.: Smithsonian, 1956. 66pp, ill, bib

3822 Garnier, Edouard, 1840- . The Soft Paste Porcelain of
Sevres, with an historical introduction. Tr. from French
by H. F. Anderson. London: Nimmo, 1889; 1892; New
York: Scribner's, 1901. 32pp, 50 large color pls of 250
specimens DLC

3823 Gasnault, Paul, and Edouard Garnier. French Pottery. Tr.
from French by M. P. Villars. South Kensington Museum.
London: Chapman & Hall, 1884; 1888. 183pp, ill, marks
DeWint

3824 Giacomotti, Jeanne. French Faience. Tr. from French by
Diana Imber. Pref. by George Savage. New York: Universe; London: Oldbourne, 1963; 1970. 266pp, 133 ill,
52 pls

3825 Godman, Frederick Du Cane, 1834-1919. Godman Collection
      of Oriental and Spanish Pottery. London: 1901. 78pp

3826 Goggin, John Mann. Spanish Majolica in the New World;
      types of the 16th to 18th centuries. New Haven: Depart-
      ment of Anthropology, Yale U, 1968. 240pp, ill, 18 pls

3827 Hackenbroch, Yvonne. Meissen and Other Continental Porce-
      lain, Faience and Enamel in the Irwin Untermyer Collec-
      tion. Cambridge, Mass: Harvard U Pr, for Metropolitan
      Museum, N.Y., 1956. 264pp, ill, 158 pls (some color)

3828 *Haggar, Reginald George. The Concise Encyclopedia of Con-
      tinental Pottery and Porcelain. London: Deutsch; New
      York: Hawthorn, 1960; New York: Praeger, 1968.
      545pp, ill, 183 (24 color) pls, bib, marks

3829 *Hannover, Emil. Pottery and Porcelain: a handbook for
      collectors. Tr. from Danish. Ed. and with notes by
      Bernard Rackham. Vol. I. Europe and the Near East;
      earthenware and stoneware; II. The Far East; III. Euro-
      pean Porcelain. 3 vol. London: Benn; New York:
      Scribner, 1925; reprint in 3 vol. New York: Dover,
      197-? 1944 ill, 11 color pls (Very comprehensive)

3830 Harris, Nathaniel. Porcelain Figures. New York: Golden
      Pr, 1974; London: Sampson Low, 1975. 80pp, chiefly
      ill (European)

3831 Haviland and Company, New York. Ceramics: a summary
      of leading facts in the history of ceramic art and in the
      composition and manufacture of pottery and porcelain.
      Boston, etc.: A. French; New York: Haviland, 1877.
      40pp, ill

3832 _____. Haviland China; a history. New York: Haviland
      & Co, n.d. 9pp, ill (Haviland was an American. The
      porcelain was made in Limoges)

3833 _____. The White House Porcelain Service. Designs by
      an American artist (Theodore R. Davis) illustrating ex-
      clusively American fauna and flora. New York: Haviland,
      1879. 88pp, ill (Made for Mrs. Rutherford B. Hayes)
      NN, MdBP

3834 Hayden, Arthur. Chats on Royal Copenhagen Porcelain.
      Abridged from author's Royal Copenhagen Porcelain ...
      1911. London: Fisher Unwin; New York: F. A. Stokes,
      1918. 360pp, ill, 56 pls, marks PPL, NN

3835 * _____. Royal Copenhagen Porcelain. Its history and
      development from the 18th century to the present day.

London: Fisher Unwin, 1911; New York: McBride, Nast,
1912.   452pp, 70 ill, 109 (5 color) pls

3836 *Hayward, John Forrest. Viennese Porcelain of the Du Paquier
Period. London: Rockliff, 1952. 218pp, ill, 76 (4 color)
pls, bib (18th century. Claude Du Paquier, d. 1751)

3837 Holl, Imre, and Pal Voit. Old Hungarian Stove Tiles. Budapest: Corvina, Clematis Pr, 1963. 80pp, 40 ill

3838 Holzbach, Wilfriede. Keramische Fliesen. Real Clay Tiles.
German, French, English text. Bonn: Domus, 1956.
135pp, ill

3839 *Honey, William Bowyer. Dresden China. An Introduction to
the study of Meissen porcelain. London: Black, 1934;
2nd ed. 1946; London: Faber, 1954. 233pp, ill, 61 pls
of 175 pieces, bib

3840 *_____. European Ceramic Art, from the end of the Middle
Ages to about 1815; a dictionary of factories, artists, tech-
nical terms. Vol. I. Illustrated Historical Survey of the
Wares of Meissen, Delft, Italian Majolica, Wedgwood,
Chelsea, etc.; II. Dictionary of Factories, artists, techni-
cal terms and general information. 2 vol. London: Faber;
New York: Van Nostrand, 1949-1952; 2nd ed. rev. by A.
Lane. London: Faber, 1952-1963. 86pp, 216 (24 color)
pls; text, ill, color frontis, marks, bib

3841 *_____. French Porcelain of the 18th Century. London:
Faber, 1950; 2nd ed. 1972. 79pp, ill, 104 pls, bib

3842 _____. German Porcelain. London: Faber; New York:
Pitman, 1947; London: 1949; 1954. 56pp, 157 ill, 4
color pls, bib

3843 Hughes, George Bernard. Meissen Porcelain Figures in the
Collection of the Honorable Mrs. Ionides. London:
Country Life, 1950. ill (English collection)

3844 Imber, Diana. Collecting Delft. London: Arco, 1968. 140pp,
57 ill, 25 pls, bib

3845 _____. Collecting European Delft and Faience. New York:
Praeger, 1958; 1968. 127pp, ill, bib; 139pp, ill, bib

3846 Jervis, William Percival. Rough Notes on Pottery. A complete history of pottery, ancient and modern. Appendix:
"Pate sur Pate," by M. L. Solon. Newark, NJ: 1896;
enl. ed. 1897; reissue as European China. Ed. by Serry
Wood (pseud. for Graydon La Verne Freeman). Omits
pages 87 to 102. Watkins Glen, NY: Century House,
1952; 1953. 112pp, ill, bib; ...; 87pp, ill

3847 *Jonge, Caroline Henriette de. Delft Ceramics. Tr. from
      Dutch by Marie-Christine Hallin. New York: Praeger;
      London: Pall Mall Pr, 1970. 168pp, ill, 20 pls, bib

3848 *_____. Dutch Tiles. Tr. from Dutch by P. S. Falla.
      London: Pall Mall Pr; New York: Praeger, 1971. 337pp,
      ill, 6 pls, bib (Decorative tiles, 1600-1970)

3849 *Justice, Jean. Dictionary of Marks and Monograms of Old
      Dutch Delft Pottery. Tr. from French (1901). London:
      Jenkins, 1930. 171pp, marks DLC, MB, DeWint

3850 Kidson, Henry E. About Old China. Being an account of the
      origin and manufacture of pottery and porcelain throughout
      Europe. Liverpool: Howell, 1908. 90pp, ill, 3 pls,
      marks NN

3851 Kiss, Akos. Baroque Pottery in Hungary; faience of Holics
      and Tata. Tr. by Zsuzsanna Horn. Budapest: Corvina
      Pr, 1966. 100pp, ill (18th century majolica factories)

3852 Knowles, William Pitcairn. Dutch Pottery and Porcelain.
      London: Newnes; New York: Scribner's, 1904; London:
      1905; London: Batsford; New York: Scribner's, 1913.
      122pp, 65 pls (part color) (Appendix on Delft pot-
      teries)

3853 Korf, Dingeman. Dutch Tiles. Tr. from Dutch (1960) by
      Marieke Clarke. London: Merlin Pr, 1963; New York:
      Universe, 1964. 136pp, ill, bib

3854 Laking, Guy Francis. Sevres Porcelain of Buckingham Palace
      and Windsor Castle. London: Bradbury, Agnew, 1907.
      203pp, ill, 63 pls

3855 Landais, Hubert. French Porcelain. Tr. from French by
      Isabel and Florence McHugh. London: Weidenfeld &
      Nicolson; New York: Putnam, 1961. 128pp, ill

3856 [No entry.]

3857 *Lane (E.) Arthur. French Faience. London: Faber; New
      York: Van Nostrand, 1948; London: 1953; 2nd ed. 1970;
      New York: Praeger, 1970. 49pp, ill, 96 pls, bib; 51pp,
      ill, 104 (8 color) pls, bib

3858 *_____. Italian Porcelain, with a note on Buen Retiro.
      London: Faber, 1954; New York: Pitman, 1955. 79pp,
      ill, 100 (4 color) pls, bib, marks

3859 *_____. Nevers Faience: the High Renaissance and baroque
      styles. Faenza: 1946.

3860 Liverani, Guiseppe. Five Centuries of Italian Majolica. New
      York: McGraw-Hill, 1960. 258pp, ill

3861 MacLellan, George B. A Guide to the MacLellan Collection
      of German and Austrian Porcelain. New York: priv.
      printed, 1946. 36pp, ill

3862 Majolica. Amsterdam: Rijksmuseum, 1961. 40pp, ill

3863 Maskell, William. Maiolica. South Kensington Museum.
      London: Chapman & Hall, 187-? 24pp, ill

3864 Mew, Egan. Dresden China. Ed. by Thomas Leman Hare.
      London: T. C. & E. C. Jack; New York: Dodd, Mead,
      1909. 92pp, ill, 16 (8 color) pls, marks

3865 _____. Royal Sevres China. Ed. by Thomas Leman Hare.
      London: T. C. & E. C. Jack; New York: Dodd, Mead,
      1905. 90pp, ill, 16 (8 color) pls, marks

3866 Mickenhagen, Richard. European Porcelain. Munich: n.d.
      80pp

3867 _____. German Porcelain: a guidebook in English and
      German. Munich: n.d. 56pp, marks

3868 Moody, C. W. Gouda Ceramics; the art nouveau era of Hol-
      land. San Francisco: 1970. 32 color pls, bib

3869 _____. Price Guide to Gouda Ceramics: the art nouveau
      era of Holland. San Francisco: 1973. 144pp, ill

3870 Morley, Henry, 1822-1894. Palissy the Potter. The life of
      Bernard Palissy of Saintes; his labours and discoveries in
      art and science. 2 vol. London: Chapman & Hall, 1852;
      Boston: Ticknor, Reed & Fields, 1858; 2nd ed. 1 vol.
      London: 1855; 3rd ed. 1869; London: Cassell, 1878.
      494pp, 4 ill; ...; 320pp, pls (Huguenot potter)

3871 _____. Meissen. London: Barrie & Jenkins, 1971; as
      Antique Porcelain in Color: Meissen. Garden City, NY:
      Doubleday, 1971. 119pp, chiefly ill (From 1710)

3872 Neurdenburg, Elizabeth. Old Dutch Pottery and Tiles. Tr.
      and annotated by Bernard Rackham. London: Benn; New
      York: Himebaugh, 1923. 155pp, 112 (8 color) ill, bib
      (Standard work) MB, NN

3873 Newman, Harold. Veilleuses, 1750-1860. South Brunswick,
      NJ: A. S. Barnes; London: Yoseloff, 1967. 258pp, 212
      ill, 8 pls, bib (Porcelain food warmers)

3874 Old, W(illiam?) W(atkins?). Indo-European Porcelain. Here-
      ford, Eng: 1882. 32pp

3875 Orsoy de Flines, E. W. van, ed. Guide to the Ceramic Col-
      lection (Foreign Ceramics). 2nd ed. Djakarta: Museum
      Pusat, 1969. 71pp, ill

3876 Partridge, R. W. Catalogue of the History and Unique Col-
      lection of Old Dresden Porcelain Exhibited at South Kensing-
      ton and Bethnal Green Museums since 1874. Purchased by
      R. W. Partridge, and now on exhibition in his galleries,
      May 1899. London: 1899. 52pp, ill

3877 Pauls-Eisenbeiss, Erika. German Porcelain of the 18th Cen-
      tury. Vol. I. Meissen from Beginning to circa 1760
      (1708-1760); II. Hochst, Frankenthal and Ludwigsburg.
      Tr. by Diana Imber. 2 vol. London: Barrie & Jenkins,
      1972. 750pp, ill, bib (Collection in Riehen, Switzerland)

3878 Penkala, Maria. European Porcelain, a Handbook for the
      Collector. Amsterdam: R. W. Haentjens Dekker, 1947;
      Darmstadt: 1951; 2nd ed. Rutland, Vt: Tuttle, 1968.
      314pp, ill; 256pp, ill

3879 _____ . European Pottery; 5000 marks on maiolica, faience
      and stoneware. Hengelo, Holland: H. L. Smit; London:
      Zwemmer, 1951; 2nd ed with 5780 marks. Rutland, Vt:
      Tuttle, 1968. 424pp, ill; 472pp, ill, pls, bib

3880 Pfungst, Henry Joseph. A Descriptive Catalogue of a Small
      Collection of Italian Maiolica, in the posession of H. J.
      Pfungst. London: 1890. ill

3881 Piccolpassi, Cipriano, 1524-1579. The Three Books of the
      Potter's Art Which Treat Not Only of the Practice, but
      also briefly of all the secrets of this art, a matter which
      ... has always been concealed. Tr. from Li Tre Libre
      dell 'Art del Vassio (1558) by Bernard Rackham and A.
      Van de Put. London: V & A, 1934. 85pp, 80 pls, bib
      (Majolica)

3882 Pickman, Dudley Leavitt. The Golden Age of European Porce-
      lain. Boston: 1936. 191pp, ill, color pls

      Plinval de Guilebon, Regine de. See: de Guillebon, R. d. P.

3883 Poche, Emanuel. Bohemian Porcelain. Tr. by Richard K.
      White. Prague: Artia, 1957? 69pp, ill, 176 (16 color)
      pls, marks (Czechoslovakian)

3884 *Rackham, Bernard. Catalogue of Italian Maiolica. 2 vol.
      London: V & A, 1940. text, ill, 222 pls, bib (Super-
      sedes the descriptive catalog of C. Drury E. Fortnum,
      1873) BM

3885 _____ . Dutch Tiles. The Van den Bergh Gift. A guide

with help of Herbert Read.   London: V & A, 1923; 2nd
ed. 1931.   32pp, 16 pls; 35pp, 20 pls

3886 _____.   Early Netherlands Maiolica.   With special reference
to the.tiles at the Vyne in Hapshire.   London: Bles, 1926.
136pp, ill

3887 _____.   Guide to the European Pottery and Porcelain in the
Fitzwilliam Museum, Cambridge.   Cambridge, Eng: 1935.
114pp

3888 _____.   Guide to Italian Maiolica.   V & A.   London: 1933.
97pp, 48 pls, bib

3889 * _____.   Italian Maiolica.   London: Faber, 1952; 2nd ed.
1963.   35pp, ill, 100 (4 color) pls, bib

3890 Raines, Joan, and Marvin Raines.   A Guide to Royal Bayreuth Figurals.   New City, NY: 1973.   45pp, chiefly
color ill, 20 color pls (300 pieces)

3891 Riano, Juan Facundo.   The Industrial Arts in Spain.   London:
South Kensington Museum, 1879; 1890.   276pp, ill, folding
pl (Golden ware of Calatayud, Hispano-Moresque faience,
Seville majolica, Valencia majolica, Buen Retiro, Alcora,
etc.)

3892 Ricci, Seymour de, comp.   A Catalogue of Early Italian
Majolica in the Collection of Mortimer L. Schiff.   New
York: priv. printed, 1927.   139 pls illustrating 111 speci-
mens

3893 Rickerson, Wildey C.   Majolica; collect it for fun and profit.
2nd ed.   Chester, Conn: Pequot Pr, 1972.   70pp, ill

3894 Ridout, William.   Catalogue of the Collection of Italian and
Other Maiolica, Medieval English Pottery, Dutch, Spanish
and French Faience, and Other Ceramic Wares, Formed
by W. Ridout of London and Toronto.   Prepared by Miss
F. U. Ridout with the help of W. B. Honey.   London:
priv. printed, 1934.   57pp, 64 pls

3895 Rosenfeld, David.   Porcelain Figures of the 18th Century in
Europe.   London; New York: Studio, 1949.   131pp, ill,
bib

3896 *Ross, Marvin Chauncey, and Marjorie Merriweather Post.
Russian Porcelains of the Gardner, Popov, Novyi, Iusupor,
Batenin, Sofronov, Michachevsky, Kornilov, Kisilov and
Kuznetsov factories.   Norman: U of Oklahoma Pr, 1968.
427pp, ill, pls

3897 Rostock, X.   The Royal Copenhagen Porcelain Manufactory and

the Faience Manufactory Aluminia, past and present.
Copenhagen: 1939. 76pp

3898 Russian Porcelain in the Hermitage Collection. Russian and
      English text. Moscow: 1973. 164 color pls, marks

3899 Salley, Virginia, and George H. Salley. Royal Bayreuth
      China. Portland, Me: 1969. 240 pieces ill, 17 color
      pls (18th century)

3900 *Savage, George. 18th Century German Porcelain. London:
      Rockliff; New York: Macmillan, 1958; London: Spring
      Books, 1967. 242pp, ill, 150 pls, bib (1710-1818)

3901 *_____. 17th and 18th Century French Porcelain. London:
      Barrie & Rockliff, 1960; New York: Macmillan, 1961;
      Feltham: Spring, 1969. 243pp, ill, 99 pls, bib

3902 Scavizzi, Giuseppe. Maiolica, Delft and Faience. Tr. from
      Italian (1966) by Peter Locke. Feltham: Hamlyn, 1970;
      1974. 157pp, ill (ca.1450-ca.1950)

3903 Schlegelmilch, Clifford J. Handbook of R. S. Prussia, R. S.
      Germany and Oscar Schlegelmilch porcelain marks. Flint,
      Mich: Schultz Printing, 1970; 2nd ed. 1971; 3rd ed. rev.
      as R. S. Prussia: handbook of Erdmann and Reinhold
      Schlegelmilch Prussia-Germany and Oscar Schlegelmilch
      Germany porcelain marks. Flint: 1973. 31pp, ill; 32pp,
      ill; 44pp, ill, color pls

3904 Schleiger, Arlene. 200 Patterns of Haviland China. 4 vol.
      Omaha: priv. printed, 1950-59; 3rd rev. ed. 1967; 1974.
      over 200 patterns each book

3905 Schmidt, Robert, 1878-1952. Early European Porcelain as
      Collected by Otto Blohm. Tr. by Marie Schuette and
      Klaus Knipping. Munich: F. Bruckmann, 1953. 284pp,
      ill (Chiefly German)

3906 Scott-Taggert, John. Italian Maiolica. Feltham: Hamlyn,
      1972. 64pp, ill, bib (1420-1565)

3907 Seger, Hermann August, 1839-1893. Collected Writings:
      prepared from the records of the Royal Porcelain Factory
      at Berlin. Tr. by member of the American Ceramic So-
      ciety, ed. by Albert Bleininger. 2 vol. Easton, Pa:
      Chemical Publishing, 1902. ill (Pottery, clay, bricks,
      etc.)

3908 Sitwell, Sacheverell. Theatrical Figures in Porcelain, Ger-
      man 18th Century. London: Curtain Pr, 1949. 43pp,
      ill DLC

3909 *Solon, Louis Mark Emmanuel (M. L.), 1835-1913. The Ancient Art Stoneware of the Low Countries and Germany: or "Gres de Flandres" and "Steinzeug"; its principal varieties, and the places where it was manufactured during the 16th and 17th centuries. 2 vol. London: Chiswick Pr, for Author, 1892. 386pp, 210 ill, 25 pls, bib

3910 _____. A History and Description of Italian Maiolica. Pref. by William Burton. London; New York: Cassell, 1907. 208pp, ill, 72 (24 color) pls, bib, 8pp of marks

3911 *_____. A History and Description of the Old French Faience. With an account of the revival of faience painting in France. Pref. by William Burton. London; New York: Cassell, 1903. 192pp, ill, 78 (24 color) pls, marks BM

3912 _____. The Old French Porcelaine, a historical and descriptive account of the chief manufactories and their artistic productions, from the end of the 17th to the beginning of the 19th century. (Unpublished ms.) 190? NNC-Ave

3913 *Stazzi, Francesco. Italian Porcelain of the 18th Century. Tr. from Italian (1964). London: Weidenfeld & Nicolson; New York: Putnam, 1967. 127pp, 135 ill

3914 Stiles, Helen E. Pottery of the Europeans. Introd. by Gordon M. Forsyth. New York: Dutton, 1940. 254pp, ill, pls, bib

3915 Strohmer, Erich. Old Viennese Porcelain. Tr. from German by Amethe von Zeppelin. 2nd ed. enl. Vienna: Kunstverlag Wolfrum, 1950. 30pp, ill

3916 Tait, Hugh. Porcelain. London: Hamlyn, 1962; rev. ed. London; New York: Hamlyn, 1972. 44pp, ill, 55 pls; 96pp, 200 ill, bib (European, 1575-1800)

3917 Tasnadine Marik, Klara. Viennese Porcelain. Budapest: Corvina, 1971. 56pp, 48 pls, bib (1718 on)

3918 Tilley, Frank. Principal Marks on Continental (European) Porcelain of the 18th Century; a selection of over 150 marks more frequently found at this period. London: Antique Collector, 1950. 41pp, ill, bib

3919 *Van DePut, Albert. Hispano-Moresque Ware of the 15th Century. A contribution to its history and chronology, based upon armorial specimens. London: Chapman & Hall, 1904; 2nd ed. with Supplementary Studies and Some Later Examples. 2 vol. in 1. London: 1911. 105pp, ill, 35 (3 color) pls; with 69 pls

3920   . The Valencian Styles of Hispano-Moresque Pottery,
              1404-1454, etc.; a companion to the Apuntes sobre cera-
              mica morisca of the late G. J. de Osma. New York:
              Hispanic Society of America, 1938. 99pp, 7 pls, bib

3921   , and Bernard Rackham. Catalogue of the Collection
              of Pottery and Porcelain in the Possession of Mr. Otto
              Beit. I. Hispano-Moresque Pottery, by Van DePut; II.
              Italian Majolica, and III. German and Other Porcelain, by
              Rackham. London: Chiswick Pr, priv. printed, 1916.
              168pp, 16 ill, 29 pls

3922 Voit, Pal, and Imre Holl. Old Hungarian Stove Tiles. Tr.
      by Lili Halapy. Budapest: Corvina Pr, 1963. 63pp, ill,
      48 pls, bib (Renaissance on)

3923 *von Erdberg, Joan Prentice, and Marvin C. Ross. Cata-
      logue of the Italian Majolica in the Walters Art Gallery.
      Baltimore: 1952. 58pp, ill

3924 Vydra, Josef, and Ludvik Kunz. Painting on Folk Ceramics.
      Tr. by Roberta Finlayson Samsour. London: Spring
      Books, 195-? 78pp, ill, bib (Moravian, majolica, Slo-
      vakian pottery)

3925 Vydrova, Jirina. Italian Majolica. Tr. by Ota Vojtisek.
      London: P. Nevill, 1960. 37pp, ill, 72 pls, bib

3926 Wallis, Henry. The Art of the Precursors: a study in the
      history of early Italian Maiolica. London: B. Quaritch,
      1901. 99pp, 75pp of color ill

3927   . Italian Ceramic Art. The Albarello. A study in
              early Renaissance maiolica. London: B. Quaritch, 1904.
              117pp of ill BM

3928   . Italian Ceramic Art. Examples of Maiolica and
              mezza-maiolica fabricated before 1500. London: priv.
              printed, 1897. 123pp, pls BM

3929   . Italian Ceramic Art. Figure design and other
              forms of ornamentation in 15th century Italian maiolica.
              London: B. Quaritch, 1905. 103pp, 101 ill, 4 color pls
              BM, NNC-Ave

3930   . Italian Ceramic Art. The maiolica pavement tiles
              of the 15th century. London: B. Quaritch, 1902. 87pp
              of ill BM

3931   . Oak-Leaf Jars. A 15th century Italian ware
              showing moresco influence. London: B. Quaritch, 1903.
              92pp of ill BM

3932 _____ . The Oriental Influence on the Ceramic Art of the
       Italian Renaissance. London: B. Quaritch, 1900. 50pp
       of ill BM

3933 _____ . 17 Plates by Nicola Fontana da Urbino at the
       Correr Museum, Venice: a study in early 16th century
       maiolica. London: Taylor & Francis, 1905 69pp, ill
       BM

3934 *Ware, George Whitaker. German and Austrian Porcelain.
       Frankfurt, Germany: Lothar Woeller Pr, 1952; London:
       Bailey & Swinfen, 1953; New York: Crown, 1963. 244pp,
       ill, 132 pls, bib

3935 Westropp, Michael Seymour Dudley. French Porcelain.
       General guide to ... pottery and porcelain, chapter 4,
       part 7. Dublin: Science & Art Museum, 1905; 2nd ed.
       1915. 37pp; 47 pp

3936 _____ . Italian Pottery and Porcelain. General guide to
       ... pottery and porcelain, chapter 9, part 7. Dublin:
       Science & Art Museum, 1907. 40pp

3937 _____ . Spanish Pottery and Porcelain. General guide to
       ... pottery and porcelain, chapter 5, part 7. Dublin:
       Science & Art Museum, 1906. 31pp MiGr

3938 Whishaw, Bernhard, 1857-1914, and Ellen Mary Whishaw.
       Illustrated Descriptive Account of the Museum of Anda-
       lusian Pottery and Lace, Antique and Modern.... Seville.
       London: Smith, Elder, 1913. 43pp, ill, pls

3939 White, Margaret E., comp. European and American Ceramics
       in the Newark Museum Collections. Newark, NJ: 1952.
       24pp, ill, bib

3940 Wood, Serry (pseud.). Haviland-Limoges China Classics II.
       Watkins Glen, NY: Century, 1951.

3941 Wylde, C. H. How to Collect Continental China. London:
       G. Bell, 1907. 253pp, ill, 40 pls, marks

3942 Wynter, Harriet. An Introduction to European Porcelain.
       London: Arlington House; New York: T. Y. Crowell,
       1971. 255pp, ill, 48 pls, bib

3943 Young, Harriet Gallagher. Grandmother's Haviland. Chicago:
       1962; rev. enl. Des Moines: Wallace-Homestead, 1970.
       99pp, ill, bib; 199pp, ill, bib

GENERAL ORIENTAL CERAMICS, INCLUDING THE NEAR EAST

3944   Allan, James Wilson. Medieval Middle Eastern Pottery. Ox-
       ford: Ashmolean Museum, 1971. 44pp, ill, bib (700 to
       1400)

3945   Blacker, James F. Chats on Oriental China. London: T.
       Fisher Unwin; New York: F. A. Stokes, 1908; London:
       1919. 408pp, ill, pls, color frontis, bib

3946 *Bushell, Stephen W. Oriental Ceramic Art ... With a com-
       plete history of Oriental porcelain, including processes,
       marks, etc. New York: Appleton, 1897. 400 ill, 116
       color pls (Fine Collection of William Thompson Walters)

3947   Carswell, John. Kutahya Tiles and Pottery from the Armenian
       Cathedral of St. James, Jerusalem. With Translations by
       C. J. F. Dowsett. Vol. I. The Pictorial Tiles and Other
       Vessels; II. A Historical Survey of the Kutahya Industry.
       A catalogue of the decorative tiles. 2 vol. Oxford:
       Clarendon, 1972. 112pp, ill, 46 pls; 179pp, ill, 43 pls,
       bib (Turkey, 12th century)

3948   Dimand, Maurice Sven. Islamic Pottery of the Near East.
       Metropolitan Museum. New York: Museum Pr, 1936;
       reprint with changes. 1941. 3pp, 20 pls

3949   _____. Loan Exhibition of Ceramic Art of the Near East.
       May-June 1931. New York: Metropolitan Museum, 1931.
       45pp, pls (Persia, Syria, Mesopotamia, Asia Minor, and
       Egypt during the Islamic period)

3950   Fehervari, Geza. Islamic Pottery: a comprehensive study
       based on the Barlow Collection. Fore. by Sir Harry
       Garner. London: Faber, 1973. 191pp, ill, 120 pls,
       bib (To ca. 1800)

3951   Franks, Augustus Wollaston. Catalogue of a Collection, of
       Oriental Porcelain and Pottery lent for exhibition by A.
       W. Franks. Bethnal Green Museum. London: Eyre &
       Spottiswoode, 1876; 2nd ed. 1878. 124pp, pls; 246pp,
       25 pls, marks, symbols

3952   Getz, John. An Illustrated and Descriptive Catalogue of the
       Rare Old Persian Pottery, with history and other notes
       pertaining to a private collection acquired by Messrs.
       H. O. Watson and Co. New York: Watson Galleries,
       J. J. Little, printer, 1908. 81pp, ill

3953   Godman, Frederick DuCane, 1834-1919. Godman Collection
       of Oriental and Spanish Pottery. London: 1901. 78pp

3954   Hobson, Robert Lockhart. A Guide to the Islamic Pottery

of the Near East. British Museum. London: 1932.
101pp, 73 ill, 40 pls

3955 * _____ . A Guide to the Pottery and Porcelain of the Far
East ... in the British Museum. London: 1924; later
ed. as A Handbook.... London: 1937; 3rd ed. 1948.
text, 230 ill, 14 pls; 180pp, 260 ill, 20 pls BM

3956 Kelekian, Dikran Khan. The Kelekian Collection of Persian
and Analogous Potteries. Paris: H. Clarke, 1910. 5pp,
112 pls DLC

3957 _____ . The Potteries of Persia; being a brief history of
the art of ceramics in the Near East. Paris: H. Clarke,
1909. 38pp, ill NN

3958 Koyama, Jujio, and John Figgess. 2000 Years of Oriental
Ceramics. New York: Abrams; London: Thames & Hudson, 1961. 379pp, 173 ill, 54 color pls, bib (To 1795)

3959 Lane, (Edward) Arthur. Early Islamic Pottery; Mesopotamia,
Egypt and Persia. London: Faber, 1947; New York:
Van Nostrand, 1948; New York: Pitman, 1949; London:
Faber, 1953; 1965. 52pp, ill, 100 (4 color) pls, bib
(Medieval pottery of Persia and other countries of Moham-
medan East)

3960 _____ . Later Islamic Pottery. London: Faber, 1957;
London: 1972. 125pp, ill, 100 pls, bib (Wares of
Persia, Syria, Turkey and adjoining countries)

3961 Locsin, Leandro, and Cecilia Locsin. Oriental Ceramics
Discovered in the Philippines. Rutland, Vt: Tuttle;
London: Prentice-Hall, 1967. 249pp, 223 ill, bib (1127-
1644)

3962 *Oriental Ceramic Society Transactions. Periodical. London:
1923- .

3963 *Oriental Ceramics: the world's great collections. 12 vol.
Tokyo: Kodansha; Rutland, Vt: Tuttle, 1976. 300pp each,
300 ill each, 100 color pls each (Tokyo National Museum;
British Museum; Musee Guimet; Freer Gallery; etc.)

3964 The Oriental Pottery and Porcelain. Tokyo: Meiji-Shobo,
1934. 2pp, 28 color pls DLC

3965 Penkala, Maria. Far Eastern Ceramics; marks and decoration. The Hague: Mouton, 1963. 263pp, ill

3966 Pier, Garrett Chatfield. Pottery of the Near East. New
York; London: Putnam's, 1909. 175pp, 64 ill, pls, bib

3967 [No entry.]

3968 Rackham, Bernard. Islamic Pottery and Italian Maiolica:
      illustrated catalogue of a private collection. London:
      Faber, 1959. 152pp, ill, 237 pls (part color), bib (1000
      to 1850)

3969 *Read, Sir Charles Herbert, 1857- . Exhibition of the Faience
      of Persia and the Nearer East. London: Burlington Fine
      Arts Club, 1907. 78pp, 27 pls (part color) NNC-Ave, BM

3970 Riefstahl, Rudolf Meyer. The Paris-Watson Collection of
      Mohammedan Potteries. New York: E. Weyhe, 1922.
      259pp, 94 pls (some color), bib

3971 Schuster, Felicia, and Cecilia Wolseley. Vases of the Sea,
      Far Eastern Porcelain and Other Treasures. London:
      Angus & Robertson; New York: Scribner's, 1974. 157pp,
      ill, 45 color pls, bib (China: Ming & Ch'ing; Japan:
      17th, 18th and 19th centuries)

3972 Shugio, H., comp. and ed. Catalogue of a Collection of ...
      Oriental Art Objects Belonging to T. E. Waggaman, of
      Washington. New York: 1893. 750 pieces of ceramics
      described

3973 *Wallis, Henry. The Godman Collection: Persian ceramic
      art in the Collection of F. DuCane Godman. The 13th
      Century lustred vases. London: Taylor & Francis, priv.
      printed, 1891. 50pp, 46 pls BM

3974 *   . The Godman Collection: Persian ceramic art in
      the collection of F. DuCane Godman with examples from
      other collections. The 13th century lustred wall-tiles.
      London: priv. printed, 1893; London: Taylor & Francis,
      1894. 37pp, ill, 42 pls BM

3975 _____. Persian Lustre Vases. London: Taylor & Fran-
      cis, priv. printed, 1919. 18pp, ill

3976 _____. Typical Examples of Persian and Oriental Ceramic
      Art. London: Lawrence & Bullen, 1893. ill

3977 _____. Notes on Some Early Persian Lustre Vases. 3
      vol. London: Quaritch, 1885-89. text, color ill, color
      pls

3978 Yoshida, Mitsukuni. In Search of Persian Pottery. Tr.
      by John M. Shields. Tokyo: Weatherhill & Tankosha,
      1972. 168pp, ill, color pls

CHINESE, KOREAN AND ANNAMESE CERAMICS

3979 *The Arts of the Ch'ing Dynasty. Exhibition. London: Orien-
       tal Ceramic Society, 1965. 80pp, 144 pls, bib

3980 *The Arts of the Ming Dynasty. Exhibition. Detroit: Institute
       of Arts, 1952. 48pp, ill

3981 *The Arts of the Ming Dynasty. An exhibition organized by
       the Arts Council of Great Britain and the Oriental Ceramic
       Society. November-December 1957. London: 1958.
       80pp, 104 pls, bib (Ceramics, lacquer, furniture, metal-
       work, jade, ivory, etc.)

3982 Ayers, John. The Baur Collection: Chinese ceramics. Vol.
       I. T'ang and Sung Period with Korean and Thai Wares;
       Vol. II. Ming Porcelains and Other Wares; Vol. III. Ch'ing
       Dynasty; Vol. IV. Painted and Polychrome Porcelains of
       the Ch'ing Dynasty. 4 vol. Geneve: Collections Baur;
       distributed by Kegan Paul, London and Boston, 1968-1974.
       228pp, 152 (28 color) ill, 108pp, ill, 82 pls; ...; 22,94pp,
       ill, 177 pls

3983 _____. The Seligman Collection of Oriental Art. 2 vol.
       Vol. I. see Hansford, S. Howard; Vol. II. Chinese and
       Korean Pottery and Porcelain. London: Arts Council of
       Great Britain, by Lund Humphries, 1957, 1964. 137pp,
       ill, 80 pls, bib (Vol. II)

3984 Bahr, A. W. Old Chinese Porcelain and Works of Art in
       China. Selected from an exhibition, held in Shanghai,
       November 1908, (Royal Asiatic Society). London; New
       York: Cassell, 1911. 160pp, 109 ill, 120 (12 color) pls
       CtY

3985 Barber, Edwin Atlee. Hard Paste Porcelain. 1st part.
       Philadelphia: Museum of Art, 1910- . pls

3986 Batz, Georges de. Exhibition of Chinese Ceramics and of
       European Drawings. March-April 1953. Boston: Museum
       of Fine Arts, 1953. 34pp, pls

3987 Bennett, Richard. Catalogue of the Collection of Old Chinese
       Porcelains Formed by Richard Bennett, Thornby Hall,
       Northhampton. Purchased and exhibited by Gorer, London.
       London: Menpes Printing, 1911. 79pp, 59 color pls

3988 *Beurdeley, Michel, and Cecile Beurdelay. Connoisseur's
       Guide to Chinese Ceramics. Tr. from French by Katherine
       Watson. New York: Harper, 1974; London: Connoisseur,
       197- . 317pp, ill (23 centuries)

3989 Blue-and-White Ware of the Ch'ing Dynasty. Compiled by the

National Palace Museum.   Vol. I.   K'ang-hsi and Yung-
cheng 1662-1735 a.d.; Vol. II.   Ch'ien-lung 1736-1795 a.d.
2 vol.   Kowloon: Cafa Company, 1968.   color pls

3990   Blue-and-White Ware of the Ming Dynasty.   National Palace
       Museum and the National Central Museum, Taichung, Tai-
       wan, Republic of China.   6 vol. in 7.   Kowloon, Hong-
       kong: Cafa Company, 1963.   ill, color pls

3991   Bluett, Edgar Ernest.   Chinese Pottery and Porcelain in the
       Collection of Mr. and Mrs. Alfred Clark.   Reprint from
       articles in Apollo, 1933-1934.   London: Hudson & Kearns,
       ca.1935.   50pp, ill   PPULC

3992   _____.   Ming and Ch'ing Porcelains, a short treatise con-
       cerning some dated specimens together with an account of
       their distinguishing features.   Fore. by George Eumorfo-
       poulos.   London: Chiswick Pr, 1933.   103pp, 19 pls, bib
       NN, DLC

       Boulay, Anthony du.   See: Du Boulay, Anthony.

3993   Brankston, Archibald Dooley.   Early Ming Wares of Ching-
       techen.   Hong Kong: Vetch, 1938; Hong Kong: Vetch &
       Lee; New York: Paragon Book Reprint Corp, 1970.   102pp,
       ill, color frontis, pls, bib   (Ching-te-chen)

3994   Brinkley, Frank.   Description of a Collection of Japanese,
       Chinese and Korean Porcelain, Pottery and Faience: made
       by Captain F. Brinkley.   Loaned to the Museum of Fine
       Arts, Boston.   New York: Edward Greey, 1876; 1885.
       118pp

3995   _____.   Description of "the Brinkley Collection" of Antique
       Japanese, Chinese and Korean Porcelain, Pottery, and
       Faience ... with a brief account of each ware, from his
       forthcoming "History of Japanese Keramics."   On exhibi-
       tion and for sale at the Art Gallery of Edward Greey.
       New York: 1885.   148pp

3996   Browning, Dr.   The Story of the Common Willow-pattern
       Plate.   Tr. from Chinese.   Liverpool: Hollingshead &
       Walker, 1882.   32pp, ill

3997   Burgess, William.   The Pottery Industry of Japan and China;
       being a report to the United States Potters' Association
       at Hotel Astor, New York, January 6, 1920.   New York?:
       1920.   36pp   NN

3998   Burton, Joseph.   Catalogue of Chinese Porcelain.   Wythen-
       shawe Hall, Northenden.   Manchester, Eng: Art Gallery,
       1931.   22pp, pls

3999 *Bushell, Stephen Wootton. Chinese Porcelain before the
Present Dynasty. Reprint from Journal of the Pekin
Oriental Society. Peking: Pie-T'ang Pr, 1886. 55pp
(Well-recommended by Solon) MB, DLC

4000 * _____, translator, ed. Chinese Porcelain; 16th century
coloured illustrations with Chinese manuscript text by
Hsiang Yuan-p'ien. Oxford: H. Frowde, Clarendon, 1908.
ill, 83 color pls (Solon recommends)

4001 _____. Description of Chinese Pottery and Porcelain;
being a translation of the T'ao Shuo, with introduction,
notes and bibliography. Oxford: Clarendon Pr, 1910.
(Shu, Yen)

4002 _____, and William M. Laffan. Catalogue of the Chinese
Porcelain in the J. Pierpont-Morgan Collection, New York.
New York: 1904; New York: Metropolitan Museum, 1907.
195pp, ill, 77 pls

4003 Carlyle, Richard Fredric. High Lights on Chinese Porcelain.
New Orleans: B. Mannheim Galleries, 1939. 70pp, ill,
pls, bib DLC

4004 Catalogue of an Exhibition of the Ceramic Art of China:
organized by the Arts Council of Great Britain and the
Oriental Ceramic Society to commemorate the Society's
founding, 1921. June-July 1971. V & A Museum. London: the Society, 1971. 61pp, ill, 66 pls (To 1850)

4005 Celadon Wares; catalogue of Exhibition. October-December
1947. London: Oriental Ceramic Society, 1948. 19pp,
ill

4006 Chinese Ceramic Figures; catalogue of exhibition held from
April-June 1947. London: Oriental Ceramic Society,
1948. 15pp, ill

4007 Chinese Ceramics, a catalogue of an anonymous loan collection. Exhibition. December 1944 to February 1945.
Brooklyn Museum. Brooklyn, NY: 1944. 34pp, ill

4008 Chinese, Corean and Japanese Potteries; descriptive catalogue
of loan exhibition of selected examples, the Chinese and
Corean authenticated by R. L Hobson ... the Japanese by
Edward S. Morse ... Under the auspices of the Japan Society, at the Galleries of M. Knoedler, New York. March
1914 ... with a Report on Early Chinese Potteries compiled from original sources by Rose Sickler Williams.
New York: Japan Society, 1914. 129pp, ill, color pls

4009 Christensen, Erwin Ottoman. Chinese Porcelains of the

Widener Collection. Washington, D. C.: National Gallery
of Art, 1947. 39pp, ill

4010   Collection of Rare Old Chinese Porcelains Collected by Sir
       William Bennett. London: Gorer, 1910. 14 color pls

4011   Davies, G. R. Collection of Old Chinese Porcelains Formed
       by G. R. Davies, formerly of Hartford, Cheshire, and
       now of Parton, N. B. London: Gorer, 1913. 25 pls

4012   Davis, Lucille, ed. Court Dishes of China; the cuisine of
       the Ch'ing Dynasty. Rutland, Vt: Tuttle, 1966. 243pp,
       ill (Includes ceramics)

4013   Day, Colonel John. Chinese Porcelain. General Guide to
       ... Pottery and Porcelain. Chapter 10, Part 7. Dublin:
       Science and Art Museum, 1905. 42pp

4014   *Donnelly, P. J. Blanc de Chine: the porcelain of Tehua in
       Fukien. London: Faber; New York: Praeger, 1969.
       407pp, ill, 166 (6 color) pls (Southeast China, Ming dynasty)

4015   *Du Boulay, Anthony. Chinese Porcelain. London: Weiden-
       feld & Nicolson; New York: Putnam, 1963; London: Octo-
       pus Books, 1973. 128pp, ill; 95pp, 132 (32 color) ill

4016   Duncan, Else Suenson. The Collector's First Handbook on
       Antique Chinese Ceramics. Chevy Chase, Md: Author,
       1933; Washington, D. C.: 1942. 3pp, ill, 29 pls; 2pp,
       54 pls   DLC, PPD

4017   Exhibition of Chinese Ceramics Lent by Mr. and Mrs. Eugene
       Bernat. September-October 1947. Boston: Museum of
       Fine Arts, 1947. 37pp, 13 pls

4018   Formed in Fire: Chinese porcelain. An exhibition. Museum
       of Fine Arts, St. Petersburg, and Cummer Gallery of Art,
       Jacksonville. St. Petersburg, Fla: 1970. 8pp, pls

4019   Frank, Ann. Chinese Blue and White. London: Studio Vista,
       1969; New York: Walker, 1970. 100pp, ill, bib

4020   *Garner, Sir Harry Mason. Oriental Blue and White. London:
       Faber, 1954; New York: Pitman, 1955; 3rd ed. London:
       1964; 1970; New York: Praeger, 1970. 86pp, ill, 103 pls,
       bib; 3rd ed.: 110 (10 color) pls including marks

4021   Gatty, Charles Tindal, comp. Catalogue of a Collection of
       Chinese Porcelain Lent for Exhibition to the Liverpool Art
       Club by George R. Davies. London: 1882. 39pp   BM

4022   Getz, John. A Catalogue of Chinese Porcelains Collected by
       Mr. and Mrs. Charles P. Taft, Cincinnati, Ohio, with

notes and illustrations. New York: priv. printed, De
Vinne Pr, 1904. 127pp, pls, bib DLC

4023   _____ . Catalogue of the (Frank Gair) Macomber Collection of Chinese Pottery. Boston: U. Pr, 1909. ill, 212
items cat'd

4024   _____ , comp. Hand-Book of a Collection of Chinese Porcelains Loaned by James Albert Garland. New York:
Metropolitan Museum, 1895.

4025 *Gompertz, Godfrey St. George Montague. Celadon Wares.
London: Faber, 1968; New York: Praeger, 1969. 104pp,
ill, 40 pls, bib

4026 * _____ . Chinese Celadon Wares. London: Faber, 1958.
72pp, ill (Japanese, American and English collections)

4027   _____ . Korean Celadon, and Other Wares of the Koryo
Period. London: Faber, 1963. 102pp, ill, 101 (6 color)
pls, bib

4028   _____ . Korean Pottery and Porcelain of the Yi Period.
London: Faber; New York: Praeger, 1968. 107pp, ill,
128 pls, bib (1392-1910)

4029   _____ , and Dr. Chewon Kim. The Ceramic Art of Korea.
n. p. 1960. ill

4030 *Gorer, Edgar, and J. F. Blacker. Chinese Porcelain and
Hardstones. Illustrated by 254 full page plates in color
of gems of Chinese ceramics and glyptic art. 2 vol.
London: Quaritch, 1911. 254 color pls DLC, NN

4031 *Gray, Basil. Early Chinese Pottery and Porcelain. New
York: Pitman, 1952; London: Faber, 1953. 48pp, ill,
100 pls, bib

4032 Grecy, E. Descriptions of a Collection of Japanese, Chinese
and Corean Porcelain, Pottery, and Faience of Captain E.
Brinkley of Yokohama. New York: 1885.

4033 Guide to Date Marks and Symbols on Chinese Porcelain and
on Chinese Art. Reprint from The Antique Collector.
London: Antique Collector; Cambridge: Heffer, 1954.
27pp, ill

4034 *Gulland, William Guiseppi. Chinese Porcelain. Notes by
T. J. Larkin. London: Chapman & Hall, 1898; 2nd ed.
1899; 2nd ed. 2 vol. 1902; 3rd ed. 1911; 4th ed. 1918;
5th ed. 1928-29. 270pp, ill, 131 pls; ...; ...; ...;
506pp, 896 ill, bib BM

4035 Handbook to the W. G. Gulland Bequest of Chinese Porcelain,
      etc. V & A Museum. London: 1950. 57pp, 48 pls

4036 Hare, Thomas Leman, ed. Old Chinese Porcelain. London:
      n. d. (1920s?) 100pp, ill, marks

4037 Hayashiya, Seizo, and Gakuji Hasebe. Chinese Ceramics.
      Tr. from Japanese by Charles Pomeroy. Rutland, Vt:
      Tuttle; London: Prentice-Hall, 1966. 102pp, ill, 113
      pls (To 1912)

4038 Hetherington, Arthur Lonsdale. Celadon Porcelain: its story
      and decorative value. Reprint from Old Furniture Maga-
      zine. London: 1928. 11pp, ill (1 color) MiU

4039 *_____. Chinese Ceramic Glazes. Cambridge, Eng: the
      U. Pr, 1937; 2nd ed. rev. South Pasadena, Cal: P. D.
      and Ione Perkins, 1948. 76pp, ill, 14 pls (part color),
      bib; 114pp, ill, bib (very valuable study)

4040 _____. The Early Ceramic Ware of China. Introd. by
      R. L. Hobson. London: Benn; New York: Scribner's,
      1922; popular abridged ed. London: Benn, 1924. 159pp,
      color frontis, 44 pls (part color), bib; 169pp, 31 pls
      DLC, TxU, MiU

4041 _____. The Pottery and Porcelain Factories of China....
      London: Kegan Paul; New York: Dutton, 1921. 15pp,
      map

4042 *Hippisley, Alfred E. Catalogue of the Hippisley Collection of
      Chinese Porcelain; with a sketch of the history of ceramic
      art in China. Reprint from Report of the Bureau of Eth-
      nology. Washington, D.C.: GPO, 1890; 2nd ed. with
      added plates. 1902. 105pp, 21 pls, 433 items (Solon
      recommends) NNC-Ave

4043 Hirth, Friedrich, 1845-1927. Ancient Porcelain: a study in
      Chinese mediaeval industry. Leipzig; Munich: G. Hirth,
      1888. 80pp DLC

4044 Hobson, Robert Lockhart. Catalogue of Chinese Pottery and
      Porcelain in the Collection of Sir Percival David. London:
      Stourton Pr, 1934. 180 pls (mostly color)

4045 _____. Catalogue of the Leonard Gow Collection of Chinese
      Porcelain. London: British Museum, 1931. 87 pls
      (Famille verte, famille noire, and famille jaune)

4046 _____. Chinese Porcelain and Wedgwood Pottery, with
      other works of ceramic art, etc. Record of collections
      in Lady Lever Art Gallery. Number 2 of 2 vol. London:
      Batsford, 1928. 227pp, ill, 103 pls (part color) BM

4047 * _____ . Chinese Pottery and Porcelain. An account of the
potter's art in China from primitive times to present day.
2 vol. London; New York: Cassell; New York: Funk &
Wagnalls, 1915; London: Cassell, 1950. 134 (40 color)
pls, bib, marks

4048 * _____ . The George Eumorfopoulous Collection. Catalogue
of the Chinese, Corean and Persian pottery and porcelain.
6 vol. London: Benn, 1925-28. text, pls, bib (Vol. I.
Chou-T'ang; II. T'ang-Ming. Ju, Kuan, Ko, Lung-ch'uan
and Chien Wares; III. T'ang-Ming. Chun, Ting, Tz'u-Chou
Wares; IV. Ming; V. Ch'ing Dynasty Porcelain, K'ang Hsi,
Yung Cheng, Ch'ien Lung; VI. Chinese Pottery, Corean and
Persian Wares) DLC, NN

4049 * _____ . The Later Ceramic Wares of China; being the blue
and white, famille verte, famille rose, monochromes, etc.,
of the K'ang Hsi, Yung Cheng, and Chien Lung and other
periods of the Ch'ing Dynasty. London: Benn; New York:
Scribner's, 1925. 155pp, ill, 76 (26 color) pls, bib (Sequel to Ming volume) TxU

4050 * _____ . The Wares of the Ming Dynasty. London: Benn;
New York: Scribner's, 1923; 1933; reprint. Rutland, Vt:
Tuttle, 1962. 240pp, 129 ill (12 color), 59 color pls, bib

4051 _____ , and A. L. Hetherington. The Art of the Chinese
Pottery from the Han Dynasty to the End of the Ming.
London: Benn; New York: Knopf, 1923. 20pp, ill, 152
pls (part color), color frontis (192 examples) MiU, NN

4052 _____ , Bernard Rackham, and William King. Chinese
Ceramics in Private Collections. London: Halton &
Truscott Smith, 1931. 239pp, ill (Collections of: Alex-
ander; H. J. Oppenheim; Oscar Raphael; Bloxam; H. B.
Harris; W. J. Holt; Charles Russell) BM, NN

4053 Hodgson, Mrs. (A.) Willoughby. How to Identify Old Chinese
Porcelain. London: Methuen, 1905; 2nd ed. 1906; Chicago: McClurg, 1907; London: 1920. 178pp, ill, 40
pls, bib; ...; ...; 196pp, ill, pls

4054 Holcombe, Chester. Ancient Chinese Porcelains and Other
Curiosities (or Curios) Belonging to George A. Hearn.
New York: 1894. 177pp, MiD, NN

4055 Hollingsworth, Alexander. Blue and White China; by Brother
A. Hollingsworth, Artificer to the Sette of Odd Volumes.
Delivered February 6, 1891. Appendix by Joseph Grego,
"Marks on Blue and White Nankin China." London:
Chiswick Pr, 1891. 70pp, ill, 18 color pls DLC, NN

4056 *Honey, William Bowyer. The Ceramic Art of China and

Other Countries of the Far East. London: Faber, 1944;
1945; 1946; 1954; New York: Beechurst Pr, 1954. 238pp,
ill, 196 (3 color) pls, bib

4057 _____. Corean Pottery. London: Faber, 1947; New York:
Van Nostrand, 1948; London: 1952; 1955. 19pp, ill, 100
(4 color) pls, bib

4058 * _____. Guide to the Later Chinese Porcelains, Periods of
K'ang Hsi, Yung Cheng and Ch'ien Lung. London: V & A
Museum, 1927. 123pp, 120 pls

4059 Jenyns, Roger Soame. Later Chinese Porcelain; the Ch'ing
Dynasty, 1644-1912. London: Faber, 1951; 2nd ed. 1959;
new. rev. ed. 1965; 4th rev. ed. 1971. 104pp, ill, 124
pls, bib; 111pp, ill, pls, bib; 111pp, ill, 128 pls, bib

4060 * _____. Ming Pottery and Porcelain. London: Faber,
1953; New York: Pitman, 1954. 160pp, ill, 124 pls, bib
(Sequel to Later Chinese Porcelain)

4061 Joseph, Adrian Malcolm. Chinese and Annamese Ceramics
Found in the Philippines and Indonesia. London: Hugh
Moss, 1973. 208pp, chiefly ill, bib (ca. 960-1350)

4062 _____. Ming Porcelains: their origins and development.
London: Bibelot, 1971. 78pp, ill, bib

4063 _____, Hugh Moss, and S. J. Fleming. Chinese Pottery
Burial Objects of the Sui and T'ang Dynasties. Exhibition.
London: Hugh M. Moss Ltd., 1970. 79pp, 118 ill, bib
(ca. 589-907)

4064 Kim, Chewon, and G. St. G. M. Gompertz, ed. The Ceramic
Art of Korea. New York; London: Yoseloff, 1961. 282pp,
ill, 100 pls (Celadon)

4065 Koyama, Fujio. A Selection of Outstanding Kinrande Porcelains in Japanese Collections. Kyoto: Unsodo, 1967.
55 color pls (16th century Ming, Ching Ching period
"gold brocade type" porcelain)

4066 Kuwayama, George. Chinese Ceramics: the Heeramaneck
Collection, a gift from Nasli M. Heeramaneck. Exhibition.
December 1973-March 1974. Los Angeles: County Mu-
seum of Art, 1973. 48pp, ill, bib (Pottery and porcelain)

4067 Laffan, William Mackay. Catalogue of the (J. Pierpont) Morgan Collection of Chinese Porcelains. Completed by
Thomas B. Clarke. 2 vol. New York: priv. printed,
1904-1911. ill BM

4068 Laufer, Berthold, 1874-1934. The Beginnings of Porcelain in

China. With a technical report by Henry W. Nichols.
Chicago: Field Museum, 1917; reprint. New York:
Kraus Reprint, 1967. 104pp (pp. 79-183), ill, 12 pls

4069 Lee, Sherman E. The Colors of Ink: Chinese paintings and
related ceramics from the Cleveland Museum of Art.
With catalogue contributions by James Robinson. Exhibition. Winter 1974. New York: Asia Society, dist. by
NY Graphic, Greenwich, 1974. 139pp, ill, bib

4070 Legeza, Ireneus Laszlo. A Descriptive and Illustrative Catalogue of the Malcolm Macdonald Collection of Chinese
Ceramics in the Gulbenkaian Museum of Oriental Art and
Architecture, University of Durham. Fore. by M. Macdonald. London: Oxford U. Pr, 1972. 112pp, ill, 166
pls, bib (To 1930)

4071 Loan Exhibition of Rare Chinese Porcelains.... January-
February ... at the Galleries of Duveen Brothers. New
York: J. J. Little, 1907?; 2nd ed. Preface signed J. G.
1907. 463pp; 224pp (Collection of George F. Kunz) NN

4072 Medcalf, Cyril Joseph Burr. Introduction to Chinese Pottery
and Porcelain. Fore. by Sir Alan Barlow. London:
Cresset Pr, for the Oriental Ceramic Society, 1955.
64pp, ill, bib

4073 Medley, Margaret. Illustrated Catalogue of Porcelains Decorated in Underglaze Blue and Copper Red in the Percival
David Foundation of Chinese Art, London School of Oriental and African Studies. London: P. David Foundation,
1963. 78pp, 24 pls, bib

4074 _____, comp. Illustrated Catalogue of the Percival David
Foundation of Chinese Art. (Section six: Ming and Ch'ing)
London: U. of London, School of Oriental and African
Studies, 196-? 63pp, ill, 14 pls

4075 _____. Illustrated Guide to the Collection. Percival David
Foundation of Chinese Art. London: the Foundation, 1974.
36pp, ill, 4 pls (Porcelain and pottery, 960-1795)

4076 Mew, Egan. Old Chinese Porcelain. London: T. C. & E. C.
Jack; New York: Dodd, Mead, 1909. 100pp, 16 (8 color)
pls, marks ViU, TU

4077 Mills, Richard, and W. C. Monkhouse. Catalogue of Blue
and White Oriental Porcelain Exhibited in 1895. London:
Burlington Fine Arts Club, 1895. 55pp, ill BM

4078 _____, and _____. Catalogue of Coloured Chinese Porcelain Exhibited in 1896. London: Burlington Fine Arts Club,
1896. 67pp, ill BM

4079   Ming Blue-and-White. Exhibition of Blue Decorated Porcelain
       of the Ming Dynasty. Philadelphia: Museum of Art, 1949;
       Chicago: Art Institute, 1949. 72pp, chiefly ill

4080   Ming Blue-and-White Porcelain. Catalogue of an exhibition.
       October-December 1946. London: Oriental Ceramic So-
       ciety, 1948. 14pp, ill

4081   *Monkhouse, William Cosmo. A History and Description of
       Chinese Porcelain. With notes by S. W. Bushell. Lon-
       don: Cassell, 1901. 176pp, ill, 72 (24 color) pls (Solon
       recommends) PP, DLC

4082   Monochrome Porcelain of the Ming and Manchu Dynasties;
       catalogue of an exhibition. October-December 1948.
       London: Oriental Ceramic Society, 1948. 22pp, ill DLC

4083   Monochrome Ware of the Ming Dynasty. Compiled by the Na-
       tional Palace Museum, Taipei, Taiwan, Republic of China.
       Vol. I. Yung-lo, Hstlan-te and Ch'eng-hua, 1403-1487 A.D.;
       Vol. II. Hung-ch'eh, Cheng-te, Chia-ching, Lung-ch'ing,
       and Wan-li, 1488-1620 A.D. 2 vol. Kowloon, Hongkong:
       Cafa Company, 1968. text, color pls

4084   Morgan, John Pierpont, 1837-1913. Catalogue of the Morgan
       Collection of Chinese Porcelains. With historic introduc-
       tion by Stephen W. Bushell. 2 vol. New York: priv.
       printed, 1904-1911. ill, 158 color pls

4085   Moss, Hugh Murray. Chinese and Annamese Ceramics. Lon-
       don: Bibelot, 1974. ill

4086   Osgood, Cornelius. Blue and White Chinese Porcelain; a study
       of form. New York: Ronald Pr, 1956. 166pp, ill

4087   *Pope, John Alexander. Chinese Porcelains from the Ardebil
       Shrine. Washington, D.C.: Freer Gallery, 1956. 192pp,
       ill, 142 pls, bib (14th, 15th and 16th century pieces --
       805 left of original 1162 -- deposited by Shah 'Abbas at
       the Shrine in 1611 A.D.)

4088   *_____. 14th-Century Blue and White: a group of Chinese
       porcelains in the Topkapu Sarayi Musei, Istanbul. Wash-
       ington, D.C.: Freer, 1952. ill

4089a*Prodan, Mario. The Art of the T'ang Potter. London:
       Hutchinson, 1960; New York: Viking, 1961. 186pp,
       color ill, pls, bib (618-907 A.D.) (Comprehensive)

4089b Rackham, Bernard. Catalogue of the Le Blond Collection of
       Corean Pottery. V & A. London: HMSO, 1918. 48pp,
       48 pls (Aubrey Le Blond)

4090 Read, Sir Charles Hercules, George Eumorfopoulos, and R.
       L. Hobson. Exhibition of Early Chinese Pottery and Por-
       celain, 1910. London: Burlington Fine Arts Club, 1910.
       97pp, 58 pls (part color) BM

4091 Reitz, S. C. Bosch. Catalogue of an Exhibition of Early
       Chinese Pottery and Sculpture. "Keramic Wares of the
       Sung Dynasty," by Rose Sickler Williams. New York:
       Metropolitan Museum, 1916. 139pp, pls

4092 Squiers, H. G. Illustrated Catalogue of the Noteworthy Col-
       lection of Beautiful Old Chinese Porcelain Formed by H.
       G. Squiers. New York: 1912.

4093 Sullivan, Michael. Chinese Ceramics, bronzes and jades in
       the Collection of Sir Alan and Lady Barlow. Ashmolean
       Museum, Oxford. London: Faber, 1963. 173pp, ill,
       160 pls, bib

4094 Sung Dynasty Wares: Ting, Ying Ch'ing and Tz'U Chou; cata-
       logue of exhibition.... November-December 1949. London:
       Oriental Ceramic Society, 1949. 15pp, ill DLC

4095 Thiel, Albert Willem Rudolf. Chinese Pottery and Stoneware.
       Los Angeles: Borden Publishing, 1953. 204pp, ill, pls

4096 Thompson, Sir Henry, 1820-1904. A Catalogue of Blue and
       White Nankin Porcelain, forming the collection of Sir H.
       Thompson. Pref. by Murray Marks. London: Ellis &
       White, 1878. 67pp, 26 pls

4097 Trapnell, Alfred. An Illustrated Catalogue of Chinese Porce-
       lain and Pottery, forming the Trapnell Collection. Bristol:
       priv. printed, 1901. 42pp, 72 pls, marks

4098 Tregear, Mary. Guide to the Chinese Ceramics. Oxford:
       Ashmolean Museum, 1966. 44pp, ill, bib

4099 Underglaze Red Ware of the Ming Dynasty. Compiled by the
       Joint Board of Directors of the National Palace Museum
       and the National Central Museum, T'ai-chung, Formosa.
       Hongkong: Cafa Company, 1963. 99pp, color pls

4100 Wares of the T'ang Dynasty; catalogue of exhibition ... April-
       June 1949. London: Oriental Ceramic Society, 1949.
       15pp, ill

4101 Warren, George B. Catalogue of Antique Chinese Porcelain
       Owned by G. B. Warren of Troy, New York. Boston:
       priv. printed, 1912. 85pp, pls

4102 *Williamson, George Charles, 1858- . The Book of Famille

Rose, Its History and Decoration. London: Methuen, 1927;
reprint. London: Kegan Paul, Trench; Rutland, Vt: Tuttle, 1970. 231pp, ill, 62 (19 color) pls (18th century)
BM

4103 Wirgin, Jan. Sung Ceramic Designs. Stockholm: 1970.
272pp, ill

CHINESE EXPORT PORCELAIN

4104 *Beurdeley, Michel. Chinese Trade Porcelain. Tr. by Diana
Imber. Rutland, Vt: Tuttle, 1962; 2nd ed. 1963; as
Porcelain of the East India Companies. London: Barrie
& Rockliff, 1962. 219pp, many ill, 24 pls, bib

4105 The China Trade and Its Influences. Exhibition. Metropolitan Museum. New York: Harbor Pr, printer, 1941.
21pp, 101 pls, bib

4106 *Crisp, Frederick Arthur. Armorial China; a catalogue of
Chinese porcelain with coats of arms, in the possession
of F. A. Crisp. 90pp, ill, 12 color pls DLC, NN

4107 Crossman, Carl L. A Design Catalogue of Chinese Export
Porcelain for the American Market. Salem, Mass: Peabody Museum, 1964. 48pp, pls

4108 Efird, Callie Huger, and Katherine Gross Farnham. Chinese
Export Porcelain from the Reeves Collection at Washington
and Lee University, High Museum of Art. Lexington, Va:
the University, 1973. 56pp, ill (Euchlin D. Reeves)

4109 Forbes, H. A. Crosby, and Carl I. Crossman. Boston: A
Key to Chinese Export Porcelain for the American Market.
Reprint from Ellis Memorial Antiques Show Catalogue.
Boston: 1972. 10pp, ill

4110 *Gordon, Elinor, ed. Chinese Export Porcelain: An Historical Survey. New York: Main Street Books, Universe,
1976. 184pp, 350 ill, 15 color pls (Originally in
Antiques)

4111 Gordon, Horace W., and Elinor Gordon. Oriental Lowestoft.
(Chinese Export Porcelain.) 3rd ed. Villanova, Pa:
Author, 1963. 51pp, pls

4112 *Howard, David Sanctuary. Chinese Armorial Porcelain.
London; New York: Faber, 1974. 1034pp, 2300 ill,
color pls (1695-1820, for British market. 1950 services
ill, and 3000 described)

4113 _____, and John Ayers. China for the West. London:
Sotheby Parke Bernet, 1976. ill (Mildred and Rafi Y.
Mottahedeh collection)

4114 *Hyde, John Alden Lloyd. Oriental Lowestoft; with special
reference to the trade with China and the porcelain
decorated for the American Market. New York: Scribner's, 1936; 2nd ed. as Oriental Lowestoft. Porcelaine
de la Cie des Indes, with special reference.... Newport, Eng: Ceramic Book Company; enl. rev. 3rd ed.
1964. 161pp, 30 pls; 166pp, pls; 168pp, 35 pls

4115 _____, and Ricardo R. Esperito Sainta Silva. Chinese
Porcelain for the European Market. Lisbon: Editions
R.E.S.M., 1956. 105pp, ill, 8 color pls

4116 Kernan, John Devereux. An Exhibition of China Trade
Porcelain Designed to Illustrate the Wares Imported to
the Port of New Haven. Historical introd. by Mary M.
Huber. Exhibition March-April 1968. New Haven: New
Haven Colony Historical Society, 1968. 99pp, ill, bib

4117 Le Corbeiller, Clare. China Trade Porcelain: Patterns of
Exchange. New York: Metropolitan Museum, 1974.
134pp, ill (16th-18th century. Exchange of pattern and
form ideas via merchant traffic between East and West)

4118 *Mudge, Jean McClure. Chinese Export Porcelain for the
American Trade, 1785-1835. Winterthur Series. Newark:
U. of Delaware Pr, dist. by Universe, New York, 1962.
284pp, ill, bib

4119 *Phillips, John Goldsmith. China-trade Porcelain; an account
of its historical background, manufacture and decoration,
and a study of the Helena Woolworth McCann Collection.
Cambridge, Mass: Harvard U. Pr, for the Winfield
Foundation and the Metropolitan Museum (N.Y.), 1956.
234pp, 104 ill, 14 color pls, bib

4120   Roth, Stig Adolf.   Chinese Porcelain Imported by the Swedish
       East India Company.   Tr. from Swedish by Mary G.
       Clarke.   Gothenburg: Historical Museum, 1965.   37pp,
       ill, bib

4121   Scheuleer, Lunsingh D.   Chinese Export Porcelain to Holland.
       London: Pitman, 1974.   text, ill

4122   Schiffer, Herbert, Peter Schiffer, and Nancy Schiffer.   Chinese
       Export Porcelain.   Standard Pattern and forms, 1780-1880.
       Exton, Pa: Schiffer Publishing, 1975.   256pp, 650 ill, 49
       color pls

4123   Staehelin, Walter August.   The Book of Porcelain; the manu-
       facture, transport, and sale of export porcelain in China
       during the 18th century.   Tr. from German by Michael
       Bullock.   New York: Macmillan; London: Lund, Humph-
       ries, 1966.   87pp, ill, 34 color pls, bib

4124   Wilson, Jane.   Canton China.   Essex, Conn: Riverside Pr,
       1961.   ill   (Shapes of blue and white export ware)

JAPANESE CERAMICS

4125   Asahi Shimbun Sha.   Japanese Coloured Porcelain, Kakiemon,
       Imari, Kutani, Nabeshima.   Tr. by Mutsuo Kakuzen and
       Francis B. Clapp.   Kyoto: Kyoto-Shoin, 1953.   31pp, ill

4126   *Audsley, George Ashdown, and James Lord Bowes.   The
       Keramic Art of Japan.   2 vol.   Liverpool; London: priv.
       printed, 1875-1880; abridged version, 1 vol.   London: H.
       Sotheran, 1881.   text, 67 (35 color) pls, marks; 304pp,
       ill, 32 pls (some color)   BM

4127   Bowes, James Lord.   Japanese Pottery, with notes describing
       the thoughts and subjects employed in its decoration ...
       (Bowes Collection).   Liverpool: Edward Howell, 1890.
       576pp, ill, 16 pls, color frontis   NNC-Ave, DLC, BM

4128   _____ .   A Vindication of the "Decorated Pottery of Japan."
       Liverpool: priv. printed, 1891.   63pp, ill, 3 (2 color)
       pls   (Answer to American press attack on his 1890 book)
       DLC, CtY, PP

4129   Brinkley, Frank.   Description of "the Brinkley Collection" of
       Antique Japanese, Chinese and Korean porcelain, pottery,
       and faience ... with a brief account of each ware, from
       his forthcoming "History of Japanese Keramics."   On exhi-
       bition and for sale at the Art Gallery of Edward Greey.
       New York: 1885.   148pp

4130   _____ .   Description of a Collection of Japanese, Chinese and Korean porcelain, pottery and faience: made by Captain F. Brinkley. Loaned to the Museum of Fine Arts, Boston. New York: E. Greey, 1876; 1885. 118pp

4131 _____ . Japan; its history, arts and literature. 9 vols. Boston; Tokyo: J. Millet, 1901. ill, text (Vol. 4, Pottery)

4132 Burgess, William. The Pottery Industry of Japan and China; being a report to the United States Potters' Association at Hotel Astor, New York, January 6, 1920. New York?: 1920. 36pp, NN

4133 Chinese, Corean and Japanese Potteries; descriptive catalogue of loan exhibition of selected examples, the Chinese and Corean authenticated by R. L. Hobson ... the Japanese by Edward S. Morse ... Under the auspices of the Japan Society, at the Galleries of M. Knoedler, N.Y., March 1914. With a report on early Chinese potteries compiled from original sources by Rose Sickler Williams. New York: Japan Society, 1914. 129pp, ill, color pls

4134 Cleveland, Richard S. 200 Years of Japanese Porcelain. Introd. by John A. Pope. Exhibition. St. Louis: 1970. 190pp, 142 ill (part color), bib

4135 *Franks, Augustus Wollaston, ed. Japanese Pottery. South Kensington Museum. London: Chapman & Hall, 1880; 2nd enl. ed. 1906. 112pp, ill, marks; 119pp, ill, marks, bib BM

4136 FuKui, Kikisaburo. Japanese Ceramic Art and National Characteristics. Japanese and English text. Tokyo: Ohashi, 1926; 1927. 195pp, 63 pls DeWint, NN

4137 Gorham, Hazel H. Japanese and Oriental Pottery. Yokohama: Yamagata Printing, 1949?; 195-?; 1952; reprint. Rutland, Vt: Tuttle, 1971. 256pp, ill, bib, marks

4138 Grecy, E. Description of a Collection of Japanese, Chinese and Corean Porcelain, Pottery, and Faience of Captain E. Brinkley of Yokohama. New York: 1885.

4139 Hare, Thomas Leman, ed. Japanese Porcelain. London: n.d. (1920s?) 96pp, ill, marks

4140 Japanese Pottery, Old and New. Exhibition, October-November 1950. Detroit: Institute of Arts, 1950; 2nd ed. 1952. 28pp, ill

4141 *Jenyns, Roger Soame. Japanese Porcelain. London: Faber; New York: Praeger, 1965; London: 1970; New York: 1971. 351pp, ill, 124 (4 color) pls, bib

4142 * _____. Japanese Pottery. London: Faber; New York:
       Praeger, 1971. 380pp, ill, 124 (4 color) pls, bib

4143 Katoh, Lynn W. Japanese Ceramics. Tokyo: Foreign Af-
       fairs Association of Japan, 1952; 1958? 34pp, ill

4144 Koyama, Fujio. The Heritage of Japanese Ceramics. Tr.
       and adapted by John Figgess. Introd. by John Alexander
       Pope. Tokyo: Weatherhill, 1973. 256pp, ill, bib (An-
       tiquity to present day)

4145 Lima, Paul, and Candy Lima. Enchantment of Nippon Porce-
       lain. Silverado, Cal: 1971; Price Guide. 1971. 15 color
       pls, marks; 8pp price guide (Late 19th century to 1940s)

4146 Mew, Egan. Japanese Porcelain. London: T. C. & E. C.
       Jack; New York: Dodd, Mead, 1909. 96pp, 16 (8 color)
       pls, marks NN, CU

4147 Meyer, Florence E. The Colorful World of Nippon. Des
       Moines: Wallace-Homestead, 1971; Price Guide. 1971.
       51pp, ill, 19 color pls, marks

4148 Mikami, Tsugio. The Art of Japanese Ceramics. Tr. by
       Ann Herring. New York: Weatherhill, 1972; Tokyo:
       Weatherhill & Heibansho, 1975. 188pp, 200 ill

4149 *Miller, Roy Andrew. Japanese Ceramics. Tokyo: Toto
       Shuppan, 1960. ill

4150 Mitsuoka, Tadanari. Ceramic Art of Japan. Tokyo: Japan
       Travel Bureau, 1949; 4th rev. ed. 1956. 190pp, ill; 184pp,
       ill

4151 Morse, Edward Sylvester, 1836-1926. Catalogue of the Morse
       Collection of Japanese Pottery. Boston Museum of Fine
       Arts. Cambridge, Mass: Riverside Pr, 1901; 2 vol. ed.
       1901. 384pp, ill, 68 pls, 1545 marks

4152 Munsterberg, Hugo. The Ceramic Art of Japan; a handbook
       for collectors. Rutland, Vt: Tuttle; London: Prentice
       Hall, 1964; Rutland: 1969. 272pp, 200 ill, 18 color ill,
       bib

4153 Okada, Yuzuru. History of Japanese Ceramics and Metalwork.
       Tr. by Masaaki Kawaguchi. Tokyo: Toto Shuppan; Rutland,
       Vt: Tuttle; London: Paterson, 1958. 168pp, 160 ill (To
       1868)

4154 Robinson, Dorothea. Nippon Hand-Painted China. 1972. 48pp,
       ill (Late 19th to early 20th century)

4155 Sato, Masahiko. Kyoto Ceramics: arts of Japan 2. Tr. by

Anne V. Towle, and Usher Coolidge.   Tokyo: Weatherhill
& Shibundo, 1973.   136pp, ill

4156   Sera, Yosuke.   Old Imari Blue and White Porcelain.   Japanese
with English summary and illustration descriptions.   Kyoto:
Hera do, 1959.   76, 38pp, pls

4157   Stitt, Irene.   Japanese Ceramics of the Last 100 Years.   New
York: Crown, 1974.   256pp, 325 ill, 22 color pls, bib,
gloss (Nippon, Kutani, Imari, Satsuma, "Made in Japan,"
and "Occupied Japan."   1868-1952)

4158   Volker, T.   The Japanese Porcelain Trade of the Dutch East
India Company after 1683.   Leiden, Holland: E. J. Brill,
1959.   92pp, ill, 24 pls

4159   Westropp, Michael Seymour Dudley.   Japanese Pottery and
Porcelain.   General Guide to Pottery and Porcelain,
Chapter 12, Part 7.   Dublin: Science and Art Museum,
1907.   44pp

POURING AND DRINKING VESSELS

4160   *Dimsdale, June.   Steins and Prices.   Kansas City?:   1970.
104pp, ill (Pewter, porcelain, glass, pottery.   Occupa-
tionals, characters, Mettlach, reproductions, etc.)

4161   Drinking Vessels from the Collection of the Darling Founda-
tion for New York Silver and Its Makers.   (Eggertsville,
N.Y.) Exhibition.   March-May 1960.   Buffalo: Historical
Society, 1960.   11pp, pls

4162   Fenwick, Paul E.   Mettlach Steins: prices and descriptions
of 1041 steins, over 500 steins illustrated.   Lee, Mass:
Author, 1974.   116pp, 500 ill

4163   Harrell, John L.   Regimental Steins of the Bavarian and Imperial German Armies.   Wurzburg, Germany: 1971.   67pp,
ill (550 pieces)

4164   Illustrated Catalog of German Steins.   Exhibition.   Oshkosh,
Wisc: Paine Art Center, 197-?   27 ill of 75 steins
(18th and 19th century)

4165   Jones, Edward Alfred.   Two Historic Welsh Cups.   London:
1935.

4166   Lowenstein, Jack, and Pat Clarke.   English Translation of
1899 Mettlach Catalog with Supplement Steins.   n.p.:
priv. printed, 1974.   64pp, no ill (700 pieces)

4167   McClenahan, Richard L.   Some Scottish Quaichs, a

Monograph. 2 vol. Skokie, Ill: Author, 1955. text,
ill DLC

4168 Mettlach Catalogue of 1899. Reprint. Rockford, Ill: R. H.
      Mohr, 19-? 34pp, ill (511 pieces)

4169 Mettlach Catalogue of 1901. Reprint. Rockford, Ill: R. H.
      Mohr, 19-? 24pp, 500 steins ill

4170 *Mohr, R(obert) H. Character Steins Pictured and Priced.
      Rockford, Ill: 1972. 54pp, ill, marks (115 steins)

4171 *   . Mettlach Steins and Their Prices. 5th ed. rev.
      Rockford, Ill: 1974; 6th ed. 1976. 127pp, ill (1095
      steins, 281 plaques, 73 beakers, 36 punch bowls)

4172 *Monson-Fitzjohn, Gilbert John. Drinking Vessels of Bygone
      Days, from the Neolithic Age to the Georgian Period.
      London: Herbert Jenkins, 1927. 144pp, ill (Glass,
      metal, wood)

4173 Pickman, Dudley Leavitt. Pouring Vessel Vagaries. Cam-
      bridge, Mass: the Mythology Co, 1938. 200pp, ill,
      color pls, color frontis (Pottery and silver examples
      from Boston Museum of Fine Art)

4174 Roberts, George Edwin, 1831-1865. Cups and Their Customs.
      London: 1863. SKM

4175 *Thomas, Terese. Mettlach Facsimile Catalog 1885-1905.
      (Cover title: Villeroy Boch Mettlach 1885-1905.) Wheel-
      ing, Ill: Hans J. Ammelounx, 1976. 368pp, 2000 ill,
      4 color pp, marks (Steins, beakers, pokals, pitcher sets,
      punch bowls, vases, plaques, etc. Catalog reprints in-
      cluding Old Frankonian and Delftware 1893; pink and ivory
      ware 1897, etc.)

4176 Wine Trade Loan Exhibition of Drinking Vessels, Also Books
      and Documents, etc. ... Held at Vintners' Hall, London.
      June-July 1933. London: J. Parry, 1933. 92pp, 136
      pls (381 pieces described)

SHAVING MUGS AND MUSTACHE CUPS

4177 Hammond, Dorothy. Mustache Cups: history and marks.
      Des Moines: Wallace-Homestead, 1972. 164pp, color
      ill, marks, bib (776 cups illustrated. Also mustache
      spoons, left-handed cups, and mustache curlers)

4178 Powell, Robert Blake. Antique Shaving Mugs of the United
      States. Hurst, Tx: Author, 1972. 272pp, ill (Mugs,
      razors and other barbering equipment)

4179   _____ .   Antique Shaving Mugs Price Guide.   Hurst, Tx:
          Author, 1972.

4180   Ware, William Porter.   Price List of Occupational and So-
          ciety Emblems Shaving Mugs.   Chicago: Lightner, 1949.
          96pp, ill

GLASS

GENERAL WORKS

4181 Art in Glass; a guide to the glass collections. Toledo, O:
        Museum of Art, 1969. 141pp, ill, bib

4182 Barff, F. S. Glass and Silicates. London: 1876. See:
        Bevan, G. P., British Manufacturing Industries, Vol. 7.

4183 *Belknap, Eugene McCamly. Milk Glass, etc. Introd. by
        George S. McKearin. New York: Crown, 1949; new ed.
        1959. 327pp, 450 ill, bib; 350pp, ill, bib (Milk and
        slag glass) BM, DLC

4184 Books on Glass, a Checklist of 183 Selected Titles. New
        York: Steuben Glass, 1946.

4185 Brothers, John Stanley, Jr. Thumbnail Sketches. Kalamazoo,
        Mich: Author, 1940. 477pp, ill (Articles from Hobbies
        magazine)

4186 *Buckley, Wilfred, (and continued by Bertha Terrell Buckley). The Art of Glass. Illustrated from Wilfred Buckley Collection in the Victoria and Albert. London: Phaidon, Allen & Unwin; New York: Phaidon, Oxford U Pr, 1939. 285pp, ill, 142 pls, bib NN, DLC

4187 Buechner, Thomas Scharman, and others, comp. Glass from the Corning Museum of Glass, a Guide to the Collections. Corning, NY: Museum, 19-?

4188 Catalogue of a Collection of Old Glass and Silver, loaned by Edward Holbrook, New York. March 1891. Chicago: Art Institute, 1891. 11pp MH

4189 Chaffers, William, 1811-1892. Catalogue of the Collection of Glass formed by Felix Slade (drawn up by Chaffers, added to and nearly re-written by W. A. Nicholls). With historical notes by Alexander Nesbitt.... London: 1871. BM

4190 Cornish, Derek Charles. The Mechanism of Glass Polishing; a history and bibliography. Chislehurst, Kent: British Scientific Instrument Research Association, 1961. 70pp

4191 Davis, Derek Cecil. Glass for Collectors. Feltham: Hamlyn, 1971. 159pp, ill, bib

4192 Davis, Frank. Antique Glass and Glass Collecting. Feltham: Hamlyn, 1973; New York: International Publications, 1974. 96pp, ill, bib (Arranged by country)

4193 _____. The Country Life Book of Glass. London: Country Life, 1966. 96pp, ill, bib

4194 A Decade of Glass Collecting; selections from the Melvin Billups Collection. Exhibition. Corning, NY: Museum of Glass, 1962. 64pp, ill

4195 Diamond, Freda. The Story of Glass. New York: Harcourt, Brace, 1953. 246pp, ill

4196 Diderot, Denis, 1713-1784. Encyclopedie, ou Dictionnaire Raisonne des Sciences.... Reprint of prints on glass manufacture, as "The Art of Glassmaking, 1751-1772." Corning, NY: Corning Glass Center, n.d. 6 pls NCorn

4197 *Dillon, Edward. Glass. London: Methuen; New York: Putnam's, 1907. 374pp, ill, 49 (12 color) pls, bib (British Museum and South Kensington Museum glass--Egyptian to 19th century. Early standard history) PP, NCorn

4198 Douglas, Jane. Collectible Glass. London: Longacre, 1961. 64pp, ill, bib

4199 Douglas, Ronald W., and Susan Frank. A History of Glass-
       making. Henley-on-Thames: Foulis, 1972. 213pp, ill,
       12 pls, bib, facsims

4200 Drake, Wilfred James. A Dictionary of Glasspainters and
       "Glasyers" of the 10th to 18th Century. New York:
       Metropolitan Museum, 1955. 224pp, ill, bib

4201 *Dreppard, Carl William. ABCs of Old Glass. Garden City,
       NY: Doubleday, 1949. 282pp, ill (Worldwide, but
       chiefly American) NN

4202 *Duncan, George Sang. Bibliography of Glass: from the
       earliest records to 1940. Fore. by W. E. S. Turner.
       Ed. by Violet Dimbleby. London: Dawsons of Pall Mall,
       for the Society of Glass Technology, 1960. 544pp, over
       16,000 entries

4203 Dunlop, Madeline Anne Wallace. Glass in the Old World.
       London: Field & Tuer; New York: Scribner & Welford,
       1882. 272pp, pls (part color)

4204 Duthie, Arthur Louis. Decorative Glass Processes. London:
       Constable, 1908; New York: D. van Nostrand, 1911; New
       York: 1916; London: 1919. 267pp, ill DLC, ViU

4205 *Eisen, Gustavus A., 1847-1940, and Fahim Kouchakji. Glass.
       Its origin, history, chronology, technic and classification
       to the 16th century. 2 vol. New York: Rudge, 1927.
       769pp, ill, pls (part color), color frontis DLC, NCorn

4206 *Elville, E. M. The Collector's Dictionary of Glass. London:
       Country Life, 1961; New York: Taplinger, 1962; 2nd ed.
       Feltham: Country Life, 1967. 194pp, 275 ill, pls, bib
       (British in emphasis; includes American, French, German,
       Dutch, Swedish and Venetian. Earliest to present time)

4207 Engle, Anita, comp. Readings in Glass History. Jerusalem:
       Phoenix, 1973- . ill, bib

4208 Evers, Jo. The Standard Cut Glass Value Guide. Paducah,
       Ky: Collector Books, 1975. 154pp, 2000 ill

4209 Fisher, Mary. Books on Glass; a check list of 256 selected
       titles. New York: Steuben Glass, 1947. 48pp (Follows
       her list of 1946 and G. J. L. Gomme's 1942 list)

4210 *Franks, Augustus Wollaston. Guide to the Glass Room in the
       British Museum. London: 1888.

4211 Freeman, (Graydon La Verne) Larry. Iridescent Glass.
       Introd. by Frederick Carter. Watkins Glen, NY: Century,
       1956. 128pp, ill

4212 Gandy, Walter. The Romance of Glass-Making. A sketch of
      the history of ornamental glass. London: 1892; London:
      S. W. Partridge, 1898. 160pp, ill NN, PPL

4213 Glass. Monthly. Norwood, Eng: 1923- .

4214 Glass; a complete magazine for the serious collector. Prince-
      ton, NJ: 1972.

4215 The Glass and Pottery World. Monthly. Chicago: Porter,
      Taylor, 1894- .

4216 The Glass Circle. Periodical. London: Oriel Pr, 1972- .

4217 The Glass Club Bulletin. Irregular periodical. Boston: Na-
      tional Early American Glass Club, 1938-1959.

4218 Glass from the Corning Museum of Glass; a guide to the col-
      lections. Corning, NY: 1955; 1958; 1965; 1974. 77pp,
      ill, bib; 96pp, ill, bib; 99pp, ill (some color), bib

4219 Glass Notes. Periodical. London: Arthur Churchill, Ltd.,
      1952.

4220 *Gomme, Geoffrey J. L. Books on Glass, a Check-list of
      80 Selected Titles. New York: Steuben Glass, 1942.
      23pp, annotated (See Mary Fisher)

4221 *Gros-Galliner, Gabriella. Glass: a Guide for Collectors.
      London: Muller; New York: Stein & Day, 1970. 176pp,
      ill, 28 pls, bib

4222 *Grover, Ray, and Lee Grover. Art Glass Nouveau. Rutland,
      Vt: Tuttle, 1967. 231pp, 423 color ill, bib, marks,
      ownership list (1870-1918)

4223 Haggar, Reginald George. Glass and Glass-Makers. London:
      Methuen, 1961; New York: Roy, 1962. 80pp, ill

4224 Harden, Donald Benjamin, and others, comp. Masterpieces
      of Glass: A Selection. Exhibition. London: British
      Museum, 1968. 199pp, 300 ill, 4 pls, bib (To 1862)

4225 Hartley, Julia M. Mills Glass Collection at Texas Christian
      University. Fort Worth: U Pr, 1975. ill

4226 *Haynes, Edward Barrington. Glass Through the Ages. Lon-
      don: Penguin, 1948; rev. ed. 1959; rev. ed. Harmonds-
      worth; Baltimore: Penguin, 1964. 304pp, ill, 96 pls, bib

4227 Hollowood, A. Bernard. Pottery and Glass. Harmondsworth,
      Eng: Penguin, 1947. 63pp, ill

4228 *Honey, William Bowyer. Glass. A Handbook for the Study
     of Glass Vessels of All Periods and Countries and a Guide
     to the Museum Collections. V & A. London: Ministry of
     Education, 1946. 169pp, ill, 72 pls, bib BM

4229 Hotchkiss, John F. Art Glass Prices. 2 vol. Rochester,
     New York: Hotchkiss House, 1966; 1967; 4th rev. ed.
     Art Glass Handbook and Price Guide. Rochester, NY:
     Hotchkiss House, 1972. 1972: 96pp, ill

4230 Janneau, Guillaume. Modern Glass. Tr. from French by
     Arnold Fleming. London: The Studio; New York: W. E.
     Rudge, 1931. 184pp, ill, pls, bib (1900-1925)

4231 Janson, S. E. Descriptive Catalogue of the Collection Illus-
     trating Glass Technology. London: Science Museum,
     HMSO, 1969. 55pp, 16 pls

4232 Jirik, Frantisek Xaver. Guide to the Glass Collection (in the
     Museum of Industrial Art, Prague). Tr. by Francis P.
     Marchant and Jaroslav Hokes. Prague: Obchodni a
     Zivnostenska Komora, 1934. 125pp, pls

4233 Johnson, Stanley Currie. Collecting Old Glassware. London:
     Country Life, 1922. 32pp, ill NN

4234 *Journal of Glass Studies. Annual. Corning, NY: Corning
     Museum, 1959- .

4235 *Kaemfer, Fritz, and Klaus G. Beyer. Glass: A World
     History. The story of 4000 years of fine glass-making.
     Tr. from German (1963) and rev. by Edmund Launert.
     London: Studio Vista, 1966; Greenwich, Conn: N.Y.
     Graphic Society, 1967. 314pp, 243 ill, 1 pl, bib

4236 Lagerberg, Ted, and Vi Lagerberg. Collectible Glass # One.
     New Port Richey, Fla: priv. printed, 1966; 1969; Price
     Guide. 196-? 207 color ill

4237 _____, and _____. Collectible Glass # Two. New
     Port Richey, Fla: priv. printed, 1966; Price Guide, 196-?
     389 color ill

4238 _____, and _____. A Color Picture Guide to over 100
     Types of Collectible Glass. New Port Richey, Fla:
     Modern Photographers, 1963. u.p., ill

4239 *Lewis, J. Sydney. Old Glass and How to Collect It. London:
     Laurie; Philadelphia: Lippincott, 1916; London: 1925;
     New York: Dodd Mead, 1925; 5th "Standard Ed." London:
     Laurie, 1939; New York: McBride, 1950. 225pp, ill,
     pls; 258pp, ill; 279pp, ill, pls; 188pp, ill, pls

4240   List of Books on Glass in Library of Edinburgh Museum.
       Edinburgh: 1893.

4241   McGrath, Raymond, and Albert Childerstone Frost.   Glass in
       Architecture and Decoration.   With a section on the nature
       and properties of glass.   London: Architecture Pr, 1937.
       664pp, hundreds of ill, bib

4242   Mariacher, Giovanni.   Glass from Antiquity to the Renais-
       sance.   Tr. from Italian (1966) by Michael Cunningham.
       Feltham: Hamlyn, 1970; 1974.   157pp, ill   (To ca. 1650)

4243   Middlemas, Robert Keith.   Antique Glass in Color.   Garden
       City, NY: Doubleday, 1971.   120pp, chiefly color ill

4244   Nesbitt, Alexander, 1817-1886.   A Descriptive Catalogue of
       the Glass Vessels of All Ages in the South Kensington Mu-
       seum.   London: Eyre & Spottiswoode, 1878.   218pp, ill
       (some color)   21 pls   BM

4245   _____ .   Glass (in the South Kensington Museum).   London:
       Chapman & Hall, 1878; New York: Scribner, 1879.   143pp,
       ill   NNC-Ave

4246   _____ .   Notes on the History of Glass-making Prepared as
       an Introduction to the Catalogue of the Collection of Glass
       of Various Periods Formed by Felix Slade and Bequeathed
       by Him to the British Museum.   London: Wertheimer,
       Lea, 1869.   50pp, bib (See W. Chaffers)

4247   O'Donnell, Erica.   Glass.   London: Ginn, 1964; 1970.   32pp,
       ill

4248   *Pellatt, Apsley, glass manufacturer.   Curiosities of Glass
       Making.   With details of the processes and productions of
       ancient and modern ornamental glass manufacture.   London:
       D. Bogue, 1849; Monmouth, Eng: Ceramic Book Co, 1969.
       146pp, ill, 5 color pls, color frontis

4249   _____ .   Memoir on the Origin, etc., of Glass-making.
       London: 1821.

4250   Perrot, Paul N.   A Short History of Glass Engraving.   New
       York: Steuben Glass, 1974.   50pp, ill

4251   Phillips, Charles John.   Glass: The Miracle Maker.   Its
       history, technology, and applications.   New York: Pit-
       man, 1941.   424pp, ill

4252   Polak, Ada Buch.   Glass: Its Tradition and Its Makers.
       New York: Putnam, 1975.   200 ill   (Late Roman Empire
       to Tiffany)

4253   _____ . Modern Glass. London: Faber; New York: Yose-
          loff, 1962. 94pp, ill, bib (Includes history)

4254 *Revi, Albert Christian. 19th Century Glass; its genesis and
          development. New York: T. Nelson, 1959; rev. ed.
          London; Camden, NJ: Nelson, 1967. 270pp, ill; 301pp,
          ill, gloss

4255 *Robertson, Richard Austin. Chats on Old Glass. London:
          Benn; New York: A. A. Wyn, 1954; rev. with new
          chapter on American glass by Kenneth M. Wilson. New
          York: Dover; London: Constable, 1969. 167pp, ill, bib;
          179pp, ill, 77 photographs, bib (140 pieces of Roman,
          Venetian, German, Victorian, American, etc., glass)

4256 Rogers, Frances, and Alice Beard. 5000 Years of Glass.
          New York: F. A. Stokes, 1937; Philadelphia: Lippincott,
          1948. 314pp, ill, pls

4257 Sauzay, Alexandre, 1804-1870. Marvels (or Wonders) of
          Glass-Making of All Ages. London: S. Low, Marston,
          1869; 1870; 1872; as Wonders of Glass-Making.... New
          York: Scribner, 1870; 1872; reprint as Wonders of Glass
          and Bottle Making in All Ages. Fort Davis, Tx: Fron-
          tier Pr, 1969. 272pp, 63 wood-engravings, 8 pls

4258 Savage, George. Glass. London: Weidenfeld & Nicholson;
          New York: Putnam, 1965; new ed. London: Octopus
          Books, 1972. 128pp, 141 ill; 97pp, ill

4259   _____ . Glass and Glassware. London: Octopus, 1973.
          128pp, ill (To 1972)

4260 Schrijver, Elka. Glass and Crystal. Tr. from German
          (1961). Vol. I. From Earliest Times to 1850; Vol. II.
          From the Mid-19th Century to the Present. London:
          Merlin Pr, 1963, 1964; New York: Universe Books,
          1964. 134pp, ill, bib; 94pp, ill, bib (I. includes Near
          East and Europe; II. includes Mexico and Israel)

4261 Shipley, Sylvia. Handbook of Glass. Exhibition "Glass
          Through Time." October-November 1944. Baltimore:
          Museum of Art, 1944. 28pp, ill

4262 Slade, Felix, 1790-1868. Catalogue of the Collection of
          Glass Formed by Felix Slade. With notes on the history
          of glass-making by Alexander Nesbitt, and an appendix
          containing a description of other works of art presented
          or bequeathed by Mr. Slade to the Nation, by Augustus
          W. Franks. London: priv. printed, 1871. 183pp, 40
          (22 color) pls, many woodcuts (British Museum Collec-
          tion)

4263 Smith, Robert Henry Soden. A List of Books and Pamphlets
      in the National Art Library ... illustrating glass, etc.
      South Kensington Museum. London: 1887. 47pp

4264 A Special Exhibition of Glass from the Museum Collections.
      Metropolitan Museum. October-November 1936. New
      York: 1936. 45pp, pls, color frontis

4265 Story of American Glass: the story of glass decoration: the
      story of English glass. Exhibitions 1953, 1954, 1955. 3
      vol. in 1. Corning, NY: Museum of Glass, 195-? ill

4266 Strauss, Jerome. Glass Drinking Vessels, from the Collec-
      tions of Jerome Strauss, and the Beth Bryan Strauss
      Memorial Foundation, a special exhibition, 1955. Corning,
      NY: Museum of Glass, 1955. 140pp, ill

4267 Studies in Glass History and Design. Periodical. Papers
      read at sessions of the International Congress on Glass.
      Sheffield: Society of Glass Technology, 196- .

4268 Treasures in Glass: on loan to Allentown Art Museum from
      the Corning Museum of Glass. October-December 1966.
      Kutztown, Pa: Kutztown Publishing, 1966. 95pp, ill

4269 *Vavra, Jaroslav Raimund. 5000 Years of Glass-making; the
      history of glass. Tr. by I. R. Bottheiner. Prague:
      Artia, 1954; Cambridge: Heffer, 1955. 195pp, ill, 204
      pls

4270 Von Saldern, Axel. Ancient Glasses in the Museum of Fine
      Arts. Boston: 1968. ill

4271 Vose, Ruth Hurst. Glass. London: Connoisseur, 1975;
      New York: Hearst, 1976. 222pp, 350 ill, 32 color pls

4272 *Wallace-Dunlop, Madeline Anne. Glass in the Old World.
      London: Field & Tuer; New York: Scribner & Welford,
      1882. 272pp, ill NNC-Ave

4273 *Weiss, Gustav. The Book of Glass. Tr. by Janet Seligman.
      New York: Praeger; London: Barrie & Jenkins, 1971.
      353pp, 200 ill, 298 (16 color) pls, bib (Western world
      chiefly. Beginnings to 20th century)

4274 Wyatt, Victor. From Sand-Core to Automation. A history
      of glass containers. London: Glass Manufacturers'
      Federation, 1966. 23pp, ill

AMERICAN GLASS

4275 Amberina; 1884 New England Glass Works, 1917 Libbey Glass

Co. Catalogs. Reprints. Toledo, O: Antique and Historic
Glass Foundation, 1970. 19pp, ill

4276 American Silver and Pressed Glass; a collection in the R. W.
      Norton Art Gallery. Shreveport, La: 1967. 68pp, ill

4277 Art in Crystal. A historical exhibition of Libbey Glass, 1818-
      1951. Toledo, O: Museum of Art, 1951. ill

4278 (M. J.) Averbeck Rich Cut Glass. Reprint of 1904 catalog.
      Berkeley, Cal: Cembura & Avery, 197-? ill

4279 Barber, Edwin Atlee, 1851-1916. American Glassware, old
      and new; a sketch of the glass industry in the United States
      and manual for collectors of historical bottles. Phila-
      delphia: D. McKay, 1900. 112pp, ill, pls DeWint

4280 Barret, Richard Carter. Blown and Pressed American Glass.
      Bennington, Vt: Bennington Museum, 1966. 30pp, 20
      color pls

4281 *_____. The Identification of American Art Glass. Vt?:
      priv. printed, dist. by Forward's Color Productions, Man-
      chester, Vt, 1964; new ed. as Collector's Handbook of
      American Art Glass. Manchester, Vt: Forward, 1971.
      30pp, color pls (Bennington Museum Collection)

4282 _____. Popular Ruby-Stained Pattern Glass. Manchester,
      Vt: Forward Color Productions, 1968. 31pp, color ill
      (From collections of Mr. and Mrs. C. Kenneth Vincent)

4283 Bennett, Harold, and Judy Bennett. Cambridge Glass Book.
      Leon, Iowa: Mid-America, 1968; Price Guide. Des
      Moines: Wallace-Homestead, 1970. 96pp, chiefly color
      ill; 8pp (Handmade glass, Cambridge, Ohio, 1901-1954)

4284 *Bishop, James W. The Glass Industry of Allegany County,
      Maryland: Cumberland, Mt. Savage, Lonaconing, Lavale.
      Cumberland, Md: 1968. 92pp, ill DeWint

4285 Bond, Marcelle. The Beauty of Albany Glass, 1893-1902.
      Berne, Ind: Publishers Printing House, 1972. 125pp,
      ill (Albany, Indiana)

4286 Bones, Francis. Collectibles of the Depression. Houston,
      Tx: 1971. 96pp, ill

4287 Boston and Sandwich Glass Co. Factory Catalogue. Ed. by
      Ruth Webb Lee. Wellesley Hills, Mass: Lee Publica-
      tions, 1969. ill

4288 Brahmer, Bonnie J. Custard Glass. Springfield?, Mo:

Author, 1966. 63pp, ill (First made at La Belle Glass
Works, Bridgeport, Ohio, 1886)

4289 Brown, Clark W. Salt Dishes; illustrations and descriptions
of 1359 different salt dishes. Ashland, Mass: Author,
1937; reprint. Leon, Iowa: Mid-America, 1968. 148pp,
ill

4290 _____. Supplement to "Salt Dishes." Des Moines: Wallace-Homestead, 1970. 107pp, ill of over 1000 pieces

4291 Burns, Charles. Glass Cup Plates. Philadelphia: Author,
1921.

4292 Butler Brothers, Chicago. 1905 Glassware Catalogue. Reprint. Chattanooga, Tenn: J. & S. Co, 197-? 27pp, ill

4293 _____. 1910 Glassware Catalogue. Reprint. Chattanooga,
Tenn: J. & S., 197-? 20pp, ill (Pressed and opalescent
glass)

4294 Chipman, Frank W. The Romance of Old Sandwich Glass,
with Dictionary of Old Sandwich Patterns. Sandwich,
Mass: Sandwich Publishing, 1932. 158pp, many ill.
patterns DLC, PPULC

4295 Coddington, Addison Epafro, and Elizabeth Maurer Coddington.
Old Salts. Indianapolis: Author, 1940. 6pp, 54 photographs

4296 Connelly, John. A Century-old Concern, business of Jones,
McDuffee and Stratton Co. Founded by Otis Norcross,
the elder, unbroken record of growth and progress, the
largest wholesale and retail crockery, china and glassware establishment in the country. Boston: H. G. Ellis,
printer, 1910. 52pp, ill (part color) DeWint

4297 The Corning Glass Center. Corning, NY: 1952; 1958. 45pp,
ill; 61pp, ill

4298 Cronin, J. R. 1966 Price Guide to Iowa City and Keota Glassware. Marshalltown, Io: Antique Publications Service,
1966. ill, price guide (Pattern glass)

4299 Cudd, Viola. Heisey Glassware. Brenham, Tx: 1969.
237pp, 195 pls

4300 Custard Glass Party Line. Ed. by O. Joe Olson. Monthly.
Kansas City, Mo: 19-?

4301 *Daniel, Dorothy. Cut and Engraved Glass, 1771-1905. The
collector's guide to American wares. New York: M.

Barrows, 1950.   441pp, 222 photographs, 55 drawings,
bib   (1800-1920s)

4302   Darr, Patrick T.   A Guide to Art and Pattern Glass.   Springfield, Mass: Pilgrim House, 1960.   120pp, ill

4303   Davidson, Marshall.   Early American Glass, a Picture Book.
Metropolitan Museum.   New York: Museum Pr, 1940;
reprint. 1942.   3pp, 20 pls

4304   Davis, Pearce.   The Development of the American Glass Industry.   New York: Russell & Russell, 1949.   316pp,
bib

4305   Delaplaine, Edward Schley.   John Frederick Amelung, Maryland Glassmaker.   Frederick, Md: Frederick News-Post,
1971.   16pp, ill   (New Bremen works, 1785-1797)

4306   *Di Bartolomeo, Robert E., ed.   American Glass, from the
Pages of Antiques; Vol. II, Pressed and Cut.   Princeton,
NJ: Pyne Pr, dist. by Scribner's, NY, 1974.   216pp, ill
(Salts, cup plates, compotes, candlesticks, goblets, etc.
Lacy pressed, post-lacy, cut and engraved.   See also
Marvin Schwartz, Vol. I.)

4307   Dooley, William Germain.   Enjoy Your Museum.   Old Sandwich glass.   Pasadena, Cal: Esto Publishing, for Pasadena Art Museum, 1934.   15pp DLC, NNC-Ave

4308   (C.) Dorflinger and Sons.   Cut Glass Catalogue, ca.1910.
Reprint with introd. by Albert C. Revi.   Hanover, Pa:
Spinning Wheel, 1970.   48pp, chiefly ill

4309   Doubles, Malcolm Ray.   Pattern Glass Checklist.   Richmond,
Va: 1959.   100pp

4310   Dunn, Jean W.   Glass; Lancaster and Lockport, New York.
Buffalo: Buffalo & Erie County Historical Society, 1971.
20pp, ill

4311   Ehrhardt, Alpha Lee.   Cut Glass Price Guide to 1500 Pieces.
Vol. I.   Kansas City, Mo: Heart of America, 1973.
120pp, 1500 pieces ill, marks, bib

4312   Eikelberner, George, and Serge Agadjanian.   American Glass
Candy Containers.   Belle Mead, NJ: S. Agadjanian, 1967.
120pp, 844 examples ill

4313   _____ , and _____ .   More American Glass Candy Containers.   Belle Mead, NJ: S. Agadjanian, 1970.   120pp,
843 examples ill

4314   Emanuele, Concetta.   Stems.   Sunol, Cal: Olive Tree Publications, 1970.   112pp, ill   (Stemware)

4315 Evers, Jo. Standard Cut Glass Value Guide. Paducah, Ky:
Collector Books, 1975. 155pp, 2000 ill

4316 Farrar, Estelle Sinclaire. H. P. Sinclaire, Jr., Glassmaker, Vol. I. The years before 1920. Garden City, NY:
Farrar Books, 1974; Vol. II. ... The Manufacturing Years,
1920-1927. Garden City, NY: Farrar, 1975. 146pp, ill
of 1200 items; 119pp, includes 70pp of ill, color pls, bib
(Henry Purdon Sinclaire, Jr.)

4317 Field, Anne E. On the Trail of Stoddard Glass. Dublin,
NH: William L. Bauhan, 1975. 110pp, 40pp of photographs, bib, gloss (Medicine and bitters bottles, 1842-
1873. Joseph Foster; Granite Glass; South Stoddard Glass;
New Granite Glass Works. New Hampshire)

4318 Fisher, Leonard Everett. The Glassmakers. New York: F.
Watts, 1964. 43pp, ill (Juvenile literature. Colonial
period)

4319 Florence, Gene. The Collectors Encyclopedia of Depression
Glass. Paducah, Ky: Collectors Books, 1973; 2nd ed.
1974. 142pp, 900 pieces ill (many color); 148pp, 1800
pieces ill, 3500 pieces described)

4320 _____. Encyclopedia of Akro Agate Glassware. Paducah,
Ky: Collectors Books, 197-? 80pp, color ill

4321 Fostoria Glass Company. 1901 catalog. Reprint. Paducah,
Ky: Collectors Books, 1971. 72pp, ill

4322 Gaupp, Polly, and Charles Gaupp. A Sandwich Glass Sampler.
East Sandwich, Mass: House of the Clipper Ship Pr, 1970.
u.p., ill

4323 Glass and You. Corning, NY: Corning Glass Center, 1953.
48pp, pls

4324 Glass; devoted to all manufactures of, dealers in and consumers of glass, glassware and kindred products ... including machinery. Monthly. New York: 1897-1898. ill

4325 Hand, Sherman. Carnival Glass Price Guide. Rochester,
NY: Hotchkiss House, 1973; 1975. 1973: 39pp

4326 _____. Colors in Carnival Glass. 4 vol. Rochester,
NY: Hotchkiss House, 1967-197- . 99pp each, color ill

4327 *Harrington, Jean Carl. Glass Making at Jamestown, America's first industry. Richmond, Va: Dietz Pr, 1952; rev.
ed. as A Tryal of Glasse, the story of glassmaking at
Jamestown. Richmond: 1972. 47pp, ill; 55pp, ill

4328 Hartley, Julia Magee. Old American Glass: the Mills

Collection at Texas Christian University. Fort Worth, Tx:
U Pr, 1975. 180pp, 38 (16 color) ill, bib (2721 pieces
of pressed, blown, art, and cut glass, also pottery and
porcelain, from 1607-present)

4329 Hartung, Marion T. Carnival Glass. 10 vol. Emporia, Ks:
Author, 1960-197- . (See following titles)

4330 _____. Carnival Glass in Color. Emporia, Ks: 1967.
u. p., ill, color pls (80 patterns)

4331 _____. Carnival Glass, 100 patterns. Salisbury?, NC:
1960; 2nd ed. Emporia, Ks: Author, 1965. 128pp, ill

4332 _____. Carnival Glass Price Guide. Emporia, Ks:
Author, 1965; 1966; 197- . 56pp; 62pp

4333 _____. Northwood Pattern Glass. Clear, colored, custard
and carnival. Emporia, Ks: Author, 1967; Price Guide.
197- . 100pp, ill

4334 _____. Opalescent Pattern Glass. Des Moines: Wallace-
Homestead, 1971; Price Guide. 1971. 112pp, ill, color
pls

4335 _____. Tenth Book of Carnival Glass. Emporia, Ks:
Author, 1974. 113pp, ill

4336 _____, and Ione E. Hinshaw. Patterns and Pinafores;
pressed glass toy dishes. Des Moines, Io: Wallace-
Homestead, 1971; Price Guide. 1971. 102pp, ill

4337 *Handbook of American Glass Industries; compiled for the
1936 exhibition of the American glass industries, Department of Industrial Art, Brooklyn Museum. Brooklyn:
Museum Pr, 1936. 117pp, ill (Contemporary glass)

4338 Heacock, William. The Encyclopedia of Victorian Colored
Pattern Glass. Vol. I. Toothpick Holders A to Z; Vol.
II. Opalescent Glass from A to Z. Jonesville, Mich:
Author, 197-, 1975. 400 pieces ill; 650 pieces ill

4339 *Heiges, George L. Henry William Stiegel and His Associates;
a story of Early American Industry. Manheim?, Pa:
1948. 227pp, ill, pls (Stiegel, 1729-1785) DeWint

4340 _____. Henry William Stiegel; the life story of a famous
American glassmaker. Manheim, Pa: Author, 1937.
80pp, 1 ill; pls, bib

4341 *Herrick, Ruth. Greentown Glass; the Indiana Tumbler and
Goblet Company and allied manufactures. Grand Rapids,

Mich: 1959. 40pp, ill (Golden Agate, Holly Amber, Chocolate Glass)

4342 Heisey Glassware Identification and Price Guide. Gas City, Ind: L-W Promotions, n. d. 48pp, 16pp of ill

4343 Heisey's Glassware: pressed ware catalogue no. 109. Reprint. Gas City, Ind: L-W Promotions, 1974. 152pp, ill, 4 color pls

4344 Heisey's Lead Blown Glassware (Some Pressed). Catalogue No. 14B. Reprint. Gas City, Ind: L-W Promotions, 1973. 80pp, ill, 4 color pls (Includes bar and restaurant ware)

4345 Hotchkiss, John F. Current Cut Glass Prices. Rochester, NY: Hotchkiss House, 1965. 56pp, ill

4346 _____. Cut Glass Handbook and Price Guide. 2nd ed. Rochester, NY: Hotchkiss House, 1970; Pittsford, NY: 1972. 124pp, ill; 128pp, ill (Contains reprint of Hawkes catalog)

4347 House, Caurtman G. Comparative Values of Patterned Glass; a check list with prices covering more than 6000 forms in the 200 most popular patterns of American pressed glass. Rochester, NY: E. Hart, printer, 1936; 1938; Supplement. Medina, New York: Author, 1939? 191pp; 7pp

4348 _____. Relative Values of Early American Patterned Glass, a check list with prices covering more than 7000 forms in the 200 most popular designs of American pressed glass. Albion, NY: Eddy Pr, 1944. 155pp

4349 Hull, Maude Pollard. Early Glassmaking in Virginia. Richmond: Jones Printing, 1933. 22pp ViU, DLC

4350 *Hunter, Frederick William, 1865-1919. Stiegel Glass. Boston; NY: Houghton Mifflin, 1914; with new introd. and notes by Helen McKearin. New York: Dover, 1950; 1967. 272pp, 159 ill, 12 color pls, bib (Stiegel, 1729-1785)

4351 Innes, Lowell. Early Glass of the Pittsburgh District, 1797-1890. Exhibition. Carnegie Museum. April 1949-May 1950. Pittsburgh: 1949; 2nd ed. 1950. 56pp, ill

4352 *Irwin, Frederick T. The Story of Sandwich Glass and Glass Workers. Manchester, NH: Granite State Pr, 1926. 99 pp, ill, pls (Boston Sandwich Glass Co) DeWint, DLC, NCorn

4353 *Jefferson, Josephine. Wheeling Glass. Mount Vernon, O: Guide Publishing Co, 1948. 86pp, ill

4354 Johnson, Virgil S. Millville Glass: The Early Days. Millville, NJ: Delaware Bay Trading Co, 1971. 128pp, ill

4355 Kamm, Minnie (E.) Watson, 1886- . Encyclopedia of Antique
       Pattern Glass. Ed. by Serry Wood (pseud.). 2 vol.
       Watkins Glen, NY: Century, 1961. ill (Beginnings to
       1915. Coordinates nomenclatures of the standard McKearin,
       Lee and Millard books)

4356 _____ . The Kamm-Wood Encyclopedia of Antique Pattern
       Glass. 2 vol. Watkins Glen, NY: Century, 1961.
       670pp, ill, 2500 patterns (Consolidation of the 8 Pattern
       Glass Pitcher books)

4357 * _____ . Patterns. 8 vol. Grosse Pointe, Mich, etc.:
       Kamm Publications, etc., 1939- . (See next eight titles,
       in chronological order)

4358 _____ . 200 Pattern Glass Pitchers. Detroit. Motschall,
       1939; 1941; 1946; 1952; reissue with new introd. by Serry
       Wood (pseud.). Watkins Glen, NY: Century, 1961. 138pp,
       ill

4359 _____ . A Second 200 Pattern Glass Pitchers. Detroit:
       Motschall, 1940; 1946; 3rd ed. Grosse Pointe Farms?,
       Mich: 1950. 141pp, ill

4360 _____ . A Third 200 Pattern Glass Pitchers. Detroit:
       Graphic Arts, 1943; Detroit: Motschall, 1946; 3rd ed.
       1953. 151pp, ill

4361 _____ . A Fourth Pitcher Book. Detroit: Motschall, 1946;
       Grosse Pointe Farms, Mich: 1950. 148pp, ill

4362 _____ . A Fifth Pitcher Book. Grosse Pointe Farms,
       Mich: 1948; 1952. 209pp, ill

4363 _____ . A Sixth Pitcher Book. Grosse Pointe Farms,
       Mich: 1949; 2nd ed. Detroit: Kamm, 1954. 97pp, ill,
       105 pls

4364 _____ . A Seventh Pitcher Book. Grosse Pointe Farms,
       Mich: 1953. 218pp, ill, 116 pls

4365 _____ . An Eighth Pitcher Book. Grosse Point Farms:
       1954. 218pp, ill, 116 pls

4366 Keefe, John Webster. Libbey Glass; A Tradition of 150
       Years, 1818-1968. Exhibition. Toledo, O: Museum of
       Art, 1968. 69pp, ill, bib

4367 Klamkin, Marian. The Collectors Guide to Carnival Glass.
       New York: Hawthorn, 1976. 230 ill, 32 color pls

4368 _____ . The Collector's Guide to Depression Glass. New
       York: Hawthorn, 1973; Depression Glass Collector's

Price Guide. 1974. 256pp, 239 ill, 44 color pls, bib,
gloss; 128pp, 150 ill (Federal, Macbeth-Evans, Jeannette,
Hazel Atlas, Hocking, Indiana companies)

4369 *Knittle, Rhea Mansfield. Early American Glass. Garden
City, NY: Garden City Publishing; New York; London:
Century, 1927; 1929; 1934; New York: Appleton-Century,
1937; 1939; Garden City, NY: 1948. 496pp, ill, 64 pls,
bib DeWint, NN

4370 Lagerberg, Ted, and Viola Lagerberg. Collectible Glass #
Three. Emil J. Larson and Durand glass. New Port
Richey, Fla: priv. printed, 1967; Price Guide, by John
F. Hotchkiss. Rochester, NY: 1967. u.p., 234 color
ill (Art Nouveau, American)

4371 Lane, Lyman, Sally Lane, and Joan Pappas. A Rare Collection of Keene and Stoddard Glass. Manchester, Vt: Forward's Color Productions, 1970. 4pp, 20 color pls (New
Hampshire glass)

4372 Lechler, Doris, and Virginia O'Neill. A Collector's Guide to
Children's Glass Dishes. Nashville, Tenn: T. Nelson,
1976. 200 ill (Late 19th to early 20th century)

4373 *Lee, Ruth Webb. Antique Fakes and Reproductions. Framingham Centre, Mass: 1938; Supplementary Pamphlet No. 1.
1940; 7th enl. rev. ed. Northborough, Mass: Author,
1950. 317pp, ill, 166 pls (Known reproductions of blown,
pressed, milk and Bohemian glass) DeWint

4374 _____. Current Values of Antique Glass: Victorian glass,
Sandwich glass, art glass, cup plates; the blue book of
valuations. Northborough, Mass: 1953; rev. ed. St.
Petersburg, Fla: 1957; rev. ed. Wellesley Hills, Mass:
Lee Publications, 1969. 339pp, ill

4375 * _____. Early American Pressed Glass. A Classification
of patterns collectible in sets together with individual
pieces for table decorations. Wellesley Hills, Mass:
Lee Publications, 1931; 4th ed. 1933; 22nd rev. ed.
Northborough, Mass: Author, 1946; 30th ed. 1949; still
in print. 630pp, ill; 683pp, ill; 666pp, ill

4376 * _____. Handbook of Early American Pressed Glass Patterns. Framingham, Mass: R. W. Lee, 1936. ill,
190 pls (Comprehensive check list. Reprint of plates
from Early American Pressed Glass)

4377 * _____. 19th-Century Art Glass. New York: M. Barrows,
1952; New York: 1966. 128pp, ill, 42 pls (Satin glass,
Amberina, Peachblow, spangled, Mary Gregory, Tiffany,
other iridescent, cameo, etc.)

4378 _____ . Price Guide to Pattern Glass. New York: M.
       Barrows, 1949; 1955; 3rd rev. ed. 1963. 1963: 331pp,
       ill

4379 * _____ . Sandwich Glass. The history of the Boston Sand-
       wich Glass Company. Framingham Centre, Mass: Author,
       1931; Wellesley Hills, Mass: 1947; reprint. Wellesley
       Hills, Mass: 1966; Handbook of Sandwich Glass. 1947;
       reprint. 196-? 590pp, 227 pls; Handbook has no text,
       only 238pp pls

4380 * _____ . Victorian Glass: specialties of the 19th century.
       Northborough, Mass: Author, 1944; 10th ed. 195-?; re-
       print. Wellesley Hills: 197-?; Handbook of Victorian
       Glass. 1946; reprint. 197-? 638pp, 260 bl/wh pls;
       Handbook has 275pp, pls only (Includes Sandwich and art
       glass)

4381 * _____ , and James H. Rose. American Glass Cup Plates.
       Wellesley Hills, Mass: Author, 1948; 3rd ed. 1952.
       445pp, 131 pls, 800 pieces ill

4382 Libbey Glass. 1896 catalog. Brilliant Cut Glass. Reprint.
       Toledo, O: Antique and Historic Glass Foundation, 1975.
       ill

4383 _____ . Cut Glass Catalog, 1896. Reprint. Toledo, O:
       Antique and Historic Glass Foundation, 1968. 25pp, ill

4384 Lindsey, Bessie M. Lore of Our Land Pictured in Glass.
       2 vol. Forsyth, Ill: Author, 1948, 1950; as American
       Historical Glass: historical association adds distinction
       to glassware. Rutland, Vt: Tuttle, 1966. 541pp, 530
       ill, bib (American history as pictured in glass, 1608-)

4385 McClinton, Katharine Morrison. (Collecting) American Glass.
       Cleveland: World, 1950; New York: Gramercy Pr, 1950.
       64pp, ill, bib (Earliest South Jersey to 19th century)

4386 *McKearin, George Skinner, and Helen McKearin. American
       Glass: the fine art of glassmaking in America. New
       York: Crown, 1941; 1946; 1948; 21st printing. 1971.
       634pp, 3000 ill (2000 photographs, 1000 drawings), bib
       (Definitive work, through 19th century)

4387 McKearin, Helen A. Exhibition of Mr. John Hays Hammond,
       Jr.'s Collection of Early American Glass, originally as-
       sembled by Mr. Leslie Buswell, shown through the cour-
       tesy of Mrs. William G. Walker.... November-December
       1930. New York: Art Center, 1930. 22pp, pls DeWint

4388 * _____ , and George S. McKearin. 200 Years of American
       Blown Glass. Garden City, NY: Doubleday, 1950; 6th ed.

1966; New York: Crown, 1966. 382pp, 105 (10 color)
ill, bib (Colonial days to modern time)

4389 McQuade, Arthur J. Illustrated Guide to Early American
Glass. Portland, Me: Portland Lithograph, 197-? 71pp,
ill

4390 Matthews, Robert T. Antiquers of Glass Candy Containers.
Glenelg, Md: n. p., 1970. v. p.

4391 _____ . A Collection of Old Glass Candy Containers; things
of the past illustrated in glass. Glenelg, Md: n. p.,
1966; 2nd ed. rev. & enl. 1967; 3rd rev. enl. ed. with
new supplement, Later Candy Containers. 1969. 45pp,
chiefly ill; ...; 62pp, ill, 8 pls

4392 _____ . Old Glass Candy Containers: price guide. Glenelg,
Md: 1966; 18pp, ill

4393 Metz, Alice Hulette. Early American Pattern Glass; identification and valuation of about 1500 patterns, clear photographs,
authoritative reproduction information, uses, terminology,
rarities, bargain patterns, plate numbers from standard
texts, accurate indexing. Westfield, NY: Guide Publishing,
1958; Book 2. Much More Early American Pattern Glass.
Westfield, NY: Guide, 1965; 2 vol. Columbus, O: Spen-
cer-Walker, 1968. 243pp, ill; ?pp, ill

4394 Mighell, Florence. A Collectors Book on Toothpick Holders.
Des Moines, Io: Wallace-Homestead, 1973. 60pp, ill,
30 color pls

4395 *Millard, Samuel Thomas. Goblets; a book intended primarily
to bring before the collector and dealer an accurate knowledge of the major portions of goblets existing and to establish a terminology for them that will be at once effective and uniform. Topeka, Ks: Central Pr, 1938; 1949.
142pp, ill

4396 * _____ . Goblets II. Holton, Ks: Gossip Pr, 1940. 123pp,
ill

4397 * _____ . Opaque Glass; a book showing a major portion of
opaque glass in their various forms. Topeka: Central
Pr, 1941; 1953; reprint. Des Moines: Wallace-Homestead, 1976. 247pp, ill, 325 pls

4398 Miller, Everett R., and Addie R. Miller. The New Martins-
ville Glass Story. Marietta, O: Richardson, 1972; Rives
Junction, Mich: Authors, 1974. 62pp, ill, pls (part
color); 550 ill (Peachblow)

4399 Miller, Robert William. The Art Glass Basket. Des

Moines: Wallace-Homestead, 1972. 32pp, 17 color pls
(1880-1890)

4400 _____ . Mary Gregory and Her Glass. Des Moines, Io:
Wallace-Homestead, 1972. 32pp, ill, 34 color ill (Mary
Gregory's work at Boston and Sandwich Glass Co., 1870-
1880)

4401 Mills, Flora Rupe. Excursions in Old Glass. San Antonio,
Tx: Naylor, 1961. 231pp, ill

4402 _____ . Potters and Glassblowers. San Antonio, Tx:
Naylor, 1963. 112pp, ill

4403 *Moore, Hannah (N.) Hudson. Old Glass, European and American. New York: F. A. Stokes, 1924; London: Hodder &
Stoughton, 1926; New York: 1931; 1935; 1946. 394pp,
265 ill DeWint, BM

4404 Murray, Dean L. Cruets Only. Phoenix, Ariz: 1969. ill,
18 pls

4405 _____ . More Cruets Only. Phoenix, Ariz: 1973; Price
Guide. 197-? 84pp, ill, many color pls; 8pp (533 pieces
from author's collection. Cut Velvet, majolica, Peachblow, etc.)

4406 Murray, Melvin L. History of Fostoria, Ohio Glass, 1887-
1920. Fostoria: Gray Printing, 1972. 57pp, ill, bib

4407 *Neal, Logan Wolfe, and D. B. Neal. Pressed Glass Salt
Dishes of the Lacy Period, 1825-1850. Philadelphia:
priv. printed, 1962. 465pp, hundreds measured drawings

4408 Noel-Hume, Ivor. Glass in Colonial Williamsburg; archaeological collection. Williamsburg, Va: Colonial Williamsburg, 1969. 48pp, ill

4409 Northend, Mary Harrod. American Glass. New York: Dodd
Mead, 1926; new ed. New York: Tudor, 1935; 1944; 1947.
209pp, many ill, color frontis (Author's collection)

4410 Notes for an Epicure, a Handbook on the Traditions of Service
of Wine and Other Beverages. Toledo, O: Libbey Glass,
1933. 44pp, ill, pls (part color) DeWint

4411 Owens, Richard E. Carnival Glass Tumblers. La Habra,
Cal: 1973. 128pp, color ill of 240 tumblers

4412 Papert, Emma. Illustrated Guide to American Glass. New
York: Hawthorn, 1972. 289pp, 250 ill, bib, gloss
(Stiegel, Tiffany, etc.)

4413 Pearson, J. Michael, and Dorothy T. Pearson. American
      Cut Glass for the Discriminating Collector. 2 vol. New
      York: Vantage Pr, 1965; 1969. 204pp, 600 ill; 190pp,
      ill (Includes trademarks)

4414 _____, and _____. Encyclopedia of American Cut Glass
      Patterns: geometric conceptions. Vol. I. Miami Beach,
      Fla: Author, 1975. ill

4415 _____, and _____. A Study of American Cut Glass
      Collections. Vol. I. Miami Beach, Fla: Author, 1969;
      Vol. II. New York: Vantage Pr, 1975. 200pp, ill (575
      pieces)

4416 Pennsylvania Glassware, 1870-1904. Pressed tumblers, stem
      ware, patterned sets, cruets, jars; etched and cut glass
      globes, shades, stalactites, balls; flint glass flasks, bran-
      dies, whiskeys, decanters, bitters, condiment bottles,
      jars; cut glass bowls, celeries, carafes, decanters, jugs,
      tankards, nappies, bon-bons, goblets, tumblers. Catalog
      reprint. Princeton, NJ: Pyne, 1972. 160pp, 500 ill
      (Plates from catalogs of Cascade Glassworks; Phoenix
      Glass, 1893; Agnew, 1894; T. B. Clark, 1896; U.S. Glass,
      1904)

4417 Pepper, Adeline. The Glass Gaffers of New Jersey, and
      Their Creations from 1739 to the Present. New York:
      Scribner, 1971. 330pp, 237 ill, bib, gloss (Over 30
      glassworks)

4418 Peterson, Arthur Goodwin. 400 Trademarks on Glass. Wash-
      ington, D.C.: Washington College Pr, 1967; De Bary,
      Fla: 1971. 52pp, ill

4419 _____. Glass Patents and Patterns. Sanford, Fla: Celery
      City Printing; De Bary, Fla: Author, 1973. 226pp, ill,
      bib

4420 _____. Glass Salt Shakers: 1000 Patterns. Des Moines:
      Wallace-Homestead, 1970. 196pp, ill

4421 _____. Salt and Salt Shakers; hobbies for young and old.
      Washington, D.C.: Washington College Pr, 1960. 148pp,
      ill, bib

4422 _____. 333 Glass Salt Shakers; a companion to 'Salt and
      Salt Shakers.' Takoma Park, Md: Washington College
      Pr, 1965. 28pp, 333 shakers ill, 260 others listed

4423 Pitkin and Brooks. Rich Cut Glass. 1907 catalog. Reprint.
      Berkeley, Cal: Cembura & Avery, 197-? ill

4424 Presznick, Rose M. Carnival and Iridescent Glass: Price
      Guide. 4 vol. Wadsworth, O: 1962-67; 1970. ill

4425 *Revi, Albert Christian. American Art Nouveau Glass. Cam-
      den, NJ: Nelson, 1968. 476pp, color ill, bib (Includes
      appendix of catalog reprints)

4426 _____. American Cut and Engraved Glass. New York: T.
      Nelson, 1965. 487pp, 500 ill, bib, marks

4427 * _____. Spinning Wheel's Collectible Glass. Hanover, Pa:
      Spinning Wheel, 1974. 160pp, ill (Articles from 30 years
      on early American, blown, art, cut, Art Nouveau, Art
      Deco, and modern glass)

4428 Righter, Miriam. Iowa City Glass. Des Moines: priv.
      printed, dist. by Mid-America Book, Leon, Iowa, 1966.
      ill

4429 Roberts, Darrah L. Art Glass Shades. Des Moines: Wallace-
      Homestead, 1968. 31pp, ill

4430 _____. Collecting Art Nouveau Shades. Des Moines:
      Wallace-Homestead, 1972. 118pp, 24 color pages

4431 Rose, James Harry. Cup Plate Discoveries Since 1948; the
      cup plate notes of J. H. Rose. Compiled by John E.
      Bilane. New York: J. E. Bilane, 1971. 41pp, ill

4432 * _____. The Story of American Pressed Glass of the Lacy
      Period, 1825-1850. Exhibition. June-September 1954.
      Corning, NY: Museum of Glass, 1954. 163pp, ill

4433 Sandwich Glass Museum Collection. Sandwich, Mass: 1969.
      71pp, ill, color pls (Boston & Sandwich Glass Co.)

4434 Schwartz, Marvin D., ed. American Glass, from the Pages
      of Antiques, Vol. I., Blown and Molded. Princeton, NJ:
      Pyne, 1974. 224pp, ill (See also: Di Bartolomeo, R.,
      Vol. II., no. 4306)

4435 _____. Collectors' Guide to Antique American Glass:
      History, Style, and Identification. Garden City, New
      York: Doubleday, 1969. 150pp, 100 ill

4436 Smith, Allan B., and Helen B. Smith. 1000 Individual Open
      Salts Illustrated. Litchfield, Me: Country House, 1972.
      u.p., ill, 72 pls, bib

4437 _____, and _____. 650 More Individual Open Salts
      Illustrated. A supplement. Litchfield, Me: Country
      House, 197-? 88pp, 40 (16 color) pls

4438 Smith, Don E. Findlay Pattern Glass. Fostoria, O: Gray
      Printing, 1970. 132pp, ill

4439   Stanley, Mary Louise.   A Century of Glass Toys.   Manchester,
       Vt: 1972; New York: Crown, 1972.   102pp, 33 pls,
       chiefly color (1250 toys--marbles, figural bottles, glass
       banks, etc.)

4440   Stout, Sandra McPhee.   The Complete Book of McKee Glass:
       A Comprehensive History.   Des Moines: Wallace-Home-
       stead, 197-?   150 ill

4441   .   Depression Glass in Color.   2 vol.   Des Moines:
       Wallace-Homestead, 197?.

4442   .   Depression Glass Price Guide.   Des Moines:
       Wallace-Homestead, 197-?   191pp

4443   Stuart, Anna Maude.   Bread Plates and Platters: Early
       American Pressed Glass Patterned Bread Plates and Plat-
       ters.   Hillsborough, Cal: Author, 1965.   163pp, ill,
       gloss

4444   *Swan, Frank Herbert.   Portland Glass.   Providence, RI:
       Roger Williams Pr, 1949; rev. and enl. by Marion Dana.
       Des Moines: Wallace-Homestead, 1974.   94pp, ill;
       106pp, ill (Portland Glass Company)

4445   Umbraco, Kitty, and Russell Umbraco.   Iridescent Stretch
       Glass.   Berkeley, Cal: Cembura & Avery, 197?.   ill

4446   Unitt, Doris Joyce, and Peter Unitt.   American and Canadian
       Goblets.   Peterborough, Ont: Clock House, 1970- .
       351pp, ill, bib (Over 1000 patterns stemware)

4447   Van Pelt, Mary.   Fantastic Figures.   Garden Grove, Cal:
       197?.   44pp (Imperial, Viking, Westmoreland, Jeannette,
       Erskine, Fenton, Lalique, Heisey, Martinsville)

4448   , and Wanda Huffman.   Animal Kingdom in Treasured
       Glass.   Garden Grove, Cal: 1972.   48pp, ill (Fostoria,
       Haley, Imperial, Fenton, Westmoreland, Cambridge)

4449   Van Tassel, Valentine.   American Glass.   New York: Bar-
       rows, 1950.   128pp, 75 ill (1632 to date)

4450   Warman, Edwin G.   American Cut Glass; a pattern book of
       the brilliant period, 1895-1915.   Uniontown, Pa: Warman,
       1954; reprint. 1970.   115pp, ill; 118pp, ill

4451   .   Milk Glass Addenda.   Uniontown, Pa: Warman,
       1952; 2nd ed. enl. & rev. 1959.   59pp, ill

4452   .   Milk Glass Price Guide; a guide to current values
       on more than 2000 different items.   Uniontown, Pa:
       Warman, 1952; ... 2100 items.   1960.   71pp, no ill

4453 _____. The Second Goblet Price Guide; current comparative values on more than 1700 goblets. Uniontown, Pa:
Warman, 1953. 37pp

4454 *Watkins, Lura Woodside. American Glass and Glassmaking.
London: M. Parrish; New York: Chanticleer Pr, 1950;
Southhampton, NY: Cracker Barrel Pr, 196-? 104pp,
ill, 55 color ill, bib

4455 *_____. Cambridge Glass, 1818-1888. The story of the
New England Glass Company. Boston: Marshall Jones,
1930; new ed. New York: Little Brown, 1953. 199pp,
80 ill DeWint

4456 _____. The Development of American Glassmaking; an
account of the fourth exhibition of the National Early
American Glass Club. Boston: 1935. 39pp, 16 pls

4457 Weatherman, Hazel Marie. Colored Glassware of the Depression Era. Book 1. Springfield, Mo: Midwest Litho,
printers, 1970; rev. enl. ed. 1972; Book 2. 1974. 240pp,
ill, 21 color pls; 400pp, ill (Both show 1000 pieces.
Book 1. 78 patterns; Book 2. 43 glass companies)

4458 _____. The First Fostoria Price Watch. Keyed to the
fully illustrated 'Fostoria: its first 50 years.' Springfield, Mo: Weatherman Glassbooks, 1974. 136pp, ill

4459 _____. Fostoria: Its First 50 Years. Springfield, Mo:
Weatherman Glassbooks, 1972. 320pp, 450 patterns ill,
8 color pp (Fostoria Glass Co., Moundsville, W. Va.,
1887-1942)

4460 _____. A Guidebook to Colored Glassware of the 1920s
and 1930s. Springfield, Mo: Fay Printing, 1969. 83pp,
ill

4461 _____. Price Trends for Colored Glassware of the Depression. Periodically revised. Springfield, Mo: 1970- .
80pp, ill; 1974/75: 124pp

4462 Welker, Mary, Lyle Welker, and Lynn Welker. Cambridge
Glass Company Catalog. Reprint of several catalogs.
Newark, O: Spencer Walker Pr, 197-? 120pp of ill
(Cambridge, Ohio. 1901-1954)

4463 _____, _____, and _____. Cambridge, Ohio, Glass
in Color. 2 vol. New Concord, O: 1969, 1973. 32pp,
ill; 15 color pls of 340 pieces

4464 Whitlow, Harry H. Art, Colored and Cameo Glass, Over
600 Examples. Riverview?, Mich: priv. printed, 1966.
52pp, chiefly color ill

4465 *Whitney Glass Works, Glassboro, New Jersey. Illustrated
      catalog and price list. 1904. Reprint with historical
      notes, 1900-1918, by Watson M. Lohmann. Pitman, NY:
      Author, 1972. 28, 64pp, ill, bib

4466 Wiggins, Berry. Stretch Glass in Color. Orange, Va: 1971.
      n.p., 38 color pls, catalog facsimiles (Fenton, Imperial,
      Northwood)

4467 Wiley, Franklin Baldwin. Flowers That Never Fade. An
      account of the Ware Collection of Blaschka glass models
      in the Harvard University Museum. Boston: B. Whid-
      den, 1897. 41pp, frontis (Leopold Blaschka, 1822-1895.
      Glass flowers.) NN

4468 Willey, Harold E. Heisey's Cut Handmade Glassware. Cata-
      log reprint. Des Moines: Wallace-Homestead, 1974.
      147pp, ill

4469 _____. Heisey's Deep Plate Etching, Etched and Carved,
      Pressed and Blown, Handmade Glassware. Des Moines:
      Wallace-Homestead, 1973. 39pp, ill

4470 Wilson, Kenneth M. Glass in New England. Sturbridge,
      Mass: Old Sturbridge Village, 1959. 34pp, ill (19th
      century)

4471 _____. New England Glass and Glassmaking. New York:
      Crowell, 1972. 401pp, 365 ill, bib

4472 Yeakley, Virginia, and Loren Yeakley. Heisey Glass in
      Color. Newark, O: 1970. 31pp, color ill

TIFFANY GLASS

4473 Amaya, Mario. Tiffany Glass. New York: Walker, 1967;
      London: Studio Vista, 1968. 84pp, ill

4474 Anderson, D. R. A Collectors Guide to Tiffany Lamps. n.p.
      ill

4475 The Art Work of Louis C. Tiffany. Garden City, NY: Dou-
      bleday Page, 1914. 90pp, pls (some color), color frontis

4476 Bing, Samuel, 1838-1905. Artistic America, Tiffany Glass
      and Art Nouveau. Chiefly a translation of La Culture
      Artistique en Amerique. Paris: 1896. Reprint, with
      introd. by Robert Koch. Cambridge, Mass; London:
      MIT Pr, 1970. 260pp, 100 ill, 6 pls

4477 Koch, Robert. Louis Comfort Tiffany, 1848-1933. Fore.
      by Thomas Tibbs; notes by Robert A. Laurer. Exhibition.

January-April 1958. New York: Museum of Contemporary
Crafts, 1958. 47pp, ill, bib

4478 *_____. Louis C. Tiffany, Rebel in Glass. New York:
Crown, 1963; 2nd ed. rev. 1966. 246pp, ill, bib
(Mostly biography)

4479 McKean, Hugh. The Arts of Louis Comfort Tiffany and His
Times. Exhibition. Sarasota, Fla: John and Mable
Ringling Museum of Art, 1975. ill

4480 *Neustadt, Egon. The Lamps of Tiffany. New York: Fair-
field Pr, 1970. 224pp, 300 (238 color) pls (Neustadt
Museum of Tiffany Art)

4481 Revolt in the Parlor. Fore. by Hugh F. McKean. Winter
Park, Fla: Parlor Pr, 1969. 84pp, ill (McKean Collection)

4482 Speenburgh, Gertrude. The Arts of the Tiffanys. Chicago:
Lightner, 1956. 120pp, ill

4483 Winter, Henry J. Francis. An Appreciation of Tiffany
Favrile Glass. Boston: Byron House, 1963. 27pp

4484 *_____. The Dynasty of Louis Comfort Tiffany. South
Hanover, Mass: 1968. 180pp, ill

4485 *_____. The Final Tiffany Dynasty Book. Boston: 1971.
280pp, ill

4486 _____. Louis Comfort Tiffany Commemorative Edition.
Boston: 1972. u.p., ill

STEUBEN GLASS

4487 Buechner, Thomas Scharman. Frederick Carder, His Life
and Work. Corning, NY: Museum of Glass, 1952. 23pp
NCorn

4488 Ericson, Eric E. A Guide to Colored Steuben Glass, 1903-
1933. 2 vol. Loveland, Col: Lithographic Pr, 1963,
1965. ill

4489 *Gardner, Paul Vickers. The Glass of Frederick Carder:
the life work of the famed Steuben technician and designer
including all his achievements in the world of glassmaking.
Introd. by Paul N. Perrot. New York: Crown, 1971.
373pp, 400 photographs, 7000 original factory line drawings, 80 color pls, bib, gloss (Carder's work at Steuben,
1903-1958)

4490   Hotchkiss, John F.   Carder's Steuben Glass; index and price
       guide.   Rochester, NY: Hotchkiss House, 1964; as Car-
       der's Steuben Glass Handbook and Price Guide.   Pittsford,
       NY: 1972.   1972: 119pp, ill

4491   Perrot, Paul N., Paul V. Gardner, and James S. Plaut.
       Steuben: 70 years of American glassmaking.   Pref. by
       Otto Wittmann.   New York: Praeger, for Toledo Museum
       of Art, 1974.   172pp, ill, 16 color pls (Works from
       1905-1973)

4492   Plaut, James Sachs.   Steuben Glass, a Monograph.   New
       York: Bittner, 1948; 2nd rev. enl. ed. 1951; 3rd rev.
       enl. ed. New York: Dover; London: Constable, 1972.
       30pp, ill, 61 pls; 30pp, ill, 68 pls; 111pp, ill, 79 pls

4493   Rockwell, Robert F.   Frederick Carder and His Steuben Glass
       1903-1933.   Corning, NY: Museum of Glass, 1968.   33pp,
       ill

4494   Steuben Crystal in Private Collections.   New York: Corning
       Glass Works, 1961.   64pp, chiefly ill

BRITISH ISLES GLASS

4495   Aitken, William Costen.   Glass Manufactures of Birmingham
       and Stourbridge, with some notes as to the introduction of
       the trade into the district.   Birmingham: 1851.   18pp

4496   Ash, Douglas.   How to Identify English Drinking Glasses and
       Decanters, 1680-1830.   London: Bell, 1962.   200pp, ill,
       24 pls, bib

4497   Ashdown, Charles Henry.   History of the Worshipful Company
       of Glaziers of the City of London, Otherwise the Company
       of Glaziers and Painters of Glass.   With contributory notes
       by Percy W. Berriman Tippetts.   London: Blades, East
       & Blades, printer, 1919; 192-? 163pp, ill

4498   Bacon, J. M.   English Glass Collecting for Beginners.   Lon-
       don: Penrith, 1942.   16pp

4499   *Barker, T. C.   Pilkington Brothers and the Glass Industry.
       London: Allen & Unwin, 1960.   296pp, pls

4500   *Bate, Percy.   English Table Glass.   London: Batsford; New
       York: Scribner's, 1905; London: Newnes, 1907; London:
       Batsford; New York: Scribner's, 1913.   130pp, ill, 67
       pls NN, DLC

4501   Beard, Geoffrey William.   19th Century Cameo Glass.   Fore.

by E. Barrington Haynes.   Newport, Eng: Ceramic Book
Co, 1956.   149pp, ill, bib   (Stourbridge)

4502   Bedford, John.   Bristol and Other Coloured Glass.   London:
       Cassell, 1964; New York: Walker, 1965.   64pp, ill, 2
       pls   (Bristol porcelain too)

4503   _____ .   English Crystal Glass.   London: Cassell, 1966;
       New York: Walker, 1967.   64pp, ill   (1680-1830)

4504   Bickerton, Leonard Marshall.   An Illustrated Guide to 18th
       Century English Drinking Glasses.   With a bibliography
       of English glass by D. R. Elleray.   London: Barrie &
       Jenkins, 1971; South Brunswick, NJ: Great Albion Books,
       1972.   101pp, ill, 143 pls, bib

4505 *Bles, Joseph.   Rare English Glasses of the 17th and 18th
       Century.   Includes "Commemorative Glass," by Sir John
       S. Risley.   London: Geoffrey Bles, 1924; Boston: Hough-
       ton Mifflin, 1925.   269pp, ill, 100 color pls, color frontis
       (Jacobite, King William, Anti-Jacobean glass)   PPULC,
       DLC

4506   Bradford, Betty.   Victorian Table Glass.   London: H. Jen-
       kins, 197-?   ill

4507   Buckley, Francis.   The Birmingham Glass Trade, 1740-1833.
       Sheffield: Society of Glass Technology, Transactions,
       1927.

4508 *_____ .   English Baluster-Stemmed Glasses of the 17th and
       18th Centuries.   Edinburgh: priv. printed, Ballanteyn Pr,
       1912.   29pp, 18 pls   NCorn, DeWint

4509 *_____ .   The Glass Trade in England in the 17th Century.
       London: priv. printed, Stevens & Sons, 1914.   64pp
       DeWint, NCorn

4510   _____ .   The Glasshouses of Dudley and Worcester.   Shef-
       field: Society of Glass Technology, Transactions, 1927.

4511 *_____ .   A History of Old English Glass.   Fore. by
       Bernard Rackham.   London: Benn; New York: Dingwall-
       Rock, 1925.   155pp, ill, 60 pls, bib   (Includes cut glass)

4512   _____ .   Notes on the Glasshouses of Stourbridge, 1700-
       1830.   Vienna: 1923; Sheffield, Eng: Society of Glass
       Technology, Transactions, 1927.

4513   _____ .   Old Lancashire Glasshouses.   Sheffield: Society
       of Glass Technology, Transactions, 1929.

4514 *_____ .   Old London Drinking Glasses.   Edinburgh: Ballan-
       tyne Pr, 1913.   37pp, 14 pls   NCorn

4515 *_____. Old London Glasshouses. London: priv. printed,
       Stevens & Sons, 1915. 42pp DeWint, NCorn

4516 _____. Old London Glasshouses. Southwark. Sheffield:
       Society of Glass Technology, Transactions, 1930.

4517 _____. The Taxation of English Glass in the 17th Century.
       London: priv. printed, Stevens, 1914. 74pp NN, DeWint

4518 *Buckley, Wilfred. Diamond Engraved Glasses of the 16th
       Century, with particular reference to five attributed to
       Giacomo Verzelini. London: Benn, 1929. 24pp, ill,
       33 pls DLC, NN, DeWint

4519 _____. Outlines of the History of Glass Making in England
       to Accompany Photographs of Glasses in the Collection of
       Mr. and Mrs. Wilfred Buckley, and of a few other glasses.
       n. p.: 1932. MH-FA

4520 Butterworth, Lionel Milner Angus. British Table and Orna-
       mental Glass. London: L. Hill, 1956. 123pp, ill
       (Bristol, Nailsea, Waterford, Jacobite, Stourbridge. Be-
       ginning to present day) NN

4521 _____. The Manufacture of Glass. London; New York:
       I. Pitman, 1948. 274pp, ill NN, DLC, BM

4522 Carson, Douglas. Antique Glass of England and Ireland. Re-
       print from American Ceramic Society Bulletin. Columbus,
       O: 1944. 4pp, ill NCorn

4523 Chance Brothers and Co., Ltd., manufacturers of window-
       glass, lighthouse engineers, and constructors, Birmingham.
       100 Years of British Glass Making, 1824-1924. London:
       1924. 23pp, ill (Smethwick, England and Glasgow, Scot-
       land factories)

4524 Charleston, Robert Jesse. English Glass. Exhibition. July-
       August 1968. V & A. 2 vol. London: HMSO, 1968.
       15pp, ill, 44 pls (1578-1835)

4525 Clarke, Harold George. The Story of Old English Glass Pic-
       tures, 1690-1810. London: Courier Pr, 1928. 107pp,
       44 pls, color frontis (Glass painting, staining, engraving)
       MB, DLC

4526 Comstock, Helen. Beilby Glass in America. Including some
       recent discoveries. Reprint from Connoisseur, June 1951.
       London: Connoisseur, 1951. 41pp, ill (Ralph Beilby,
       1743-1817; William Beilby, 1740-1819; and Mary Beilby,
       1749-1797) NCorn

4527 Cooper, William. The Crown Glass Cutter and Glazier's

Manual. Edinburgh: Oliver & Boyd; London: Simpkin,
Marshall, 1835. 125pp, pls DeWint

4528 Crellin, J. K., and J. R. Scott. Glass and British Pharmacy, 1600-1900: a survey and guide to the Wellcome
Collection of British glass. London: Wellcome Institute
of the History of Medicine, 1972. 72pp, ill, bib

4529 Crompton, Sidney, ed. English Glass. Contributors:
E. M. Elville; Euan Ross. London; Melbourne: Ward
Lock, 1967; New York: Hawthorn, 1968. 255pp, 206
ill, bib

4530 *Davis, Derek Cecil. English and Irish Antique Glass. London: Barker, 1964; New York: Praeger, 1965. 152pp,
ill, 40 pls, bib (1700-1850)

4531 _____, and Keith Middlemas. Coloured Glass. London:
Jenkins; New York: Crown, 1968. 119pp, chiefly ill
(96pp of color ill) (Roman imports to Art Nouveau)

4532 Davis, Frank. Early 18th-Century English Glass. Feltham;
New York: Hamlyn, 1971. 63pp, ill (1670-1745)

4533 Day, Colonel John. Glass. General Guide ... Part 9. Dublin: Science & Art Museum, 1906. 38pp

4534 Detailed Catalogue of the Exhibits of a Loan Exhibition of
Stourbridge Glass, covering three and a half centuries of
glass making by local glasshouses ... for the Stourbridge
Festival of Britain Exhibition, June 1951. Stourbridge:
Mark & Moody, printer, 1951. 27pp, pls

4535 Ebbott, Rex. British Glass of the 17th and 18th Centuries.
National Gallery of Victoria, Australia. Melbourne; London: Oxford U Pr, 1971. 31pp, ill, bib

4536 [No entry.]

4537 *Elville, E. M. English and Irish Cut Glass, 1750-1950.
London: Country Life, 1953. 95pp, ill

4538 *_____. English Table Glass. London: Country Life; New
York: Scribner's, 1951; rev. ed. London: 1960. 274pp,
ill, bib (Early to modern times)

4539 English Glass. Royal Scottish Museum. Edinburgh: HMSO,
1964. 32pp, ill (1685-1825)

4540 English 19th Century Cameo Glass, from the collection of
Mr. and Mrs. Albert Christian Revi; a special exhibition.
Corning, NY: Corning Glass Center, 1963. 43pp, 27 ill,
bib (Stourbridge glass)

4541 *Fleming, John Arnold. Scottish and Jacobite Glass. Fore.
by A. O. Curle. Glasgow: Jackson, 1938. 196pp, ill,
57 pls (Quaichs, rummers, glass cameos, finger-bowls,
wine-glasses, window-glass, milk bottles, etc.)

4542 Francis, Grant Richardson. Jacobite Drinking Glasses. Reprint from British Numismatic Journal, 1921-22. London:
Harrison, 1925. 37pp, ill, 12 pls NCorn

4543 * _____ . Old English Drinking Glasses. Their chronology
and sequence. London: H. Jenkins, 1926. 214pp, ill,
72 pls (385 glasses ill) (Standard work) DeWint

4544 _____ , and others. A Coronation Exhibition of Royal,
historical, political, and social glasses, commemorating
18th and 19th century events in English history, presented
by Arthur Churchill, Ltd. April-May 1937. London:
Churchill, 1937. 42pp, 44 pls; also 121pp, 61 pls NCorn

4545 Godfrey, Eleanor S. The Development of English Glassmaking,
1560-1640. New York: Norton, 1976. ill

4546 *Guttery, David Reginald. From Broad-Glass to Cut Crystal,
a History of the Stourbridge Glass Industry. London: L.
Hill, 1956. 161pp, ill, 69 pls

4547 Haden, Henry Jack. Notes on the Stourbridge Glass Trade.
Brierley Hill, Eng: Libraries and Arts Committee, 1949;
reprint with slight amendments. Dudley: Dudley Libraries,
Museums and Art Galleries, 1969. 37pp, ill, 6 pls
(1600-1900)

4548 _____ . The Stourbridge Glass Industry in the 19th Cen-
tury: (a study of the glass industry in Stourbridge,
Brierley Hill and Dudley). Tipton, Staffordshire: Black
Country Society, 1971. 39pp, ill, 2 pls, bib

4549 Hallen, Arthur Washington Cornelius, 1834-1899. French
'Gentlemen Glassmakers'; their work in England and Scot-
land. Edinburgh: T. & A. Constable, 1893. 16pp, ill
NCorn

4550 Harding, Walter. Old Irish Glass. The "W. Harding Collection" including old English and other pieces. n.p.: 1925;
Liverpool: Liverpool Printing, 1930. 121pp, ill

4551 *Hartshorne, Albert H. Old English Glasses, an Account of
Glass Drinking Vessels in England from Early Times to
End of 18th Century. London; New York: E. Arnold,
1897; reprint as Antique Drinking Glasses, a pictorial
history. New York; Boston: Brussel & Brussel, 1968.
490pp, 366 ill, 67 pls (English, Irish, Jacobite)

4552   Hayes, John T.   The Garton Collection of English Table Glass.
       London: London Museum,   HMSO, 1965.   40pp, ill, pls
       (1650-1782)

4553   *Honey, William Bowyer.   English Glass.   London: Collins,
       1946.   46pp, 26 ill, 8 color pls, bib

4554   *Hughes, George Bernard.   English Glass for the Collector,
       1660-1860.   New York: Macmillan; London: Lutterworth,
       1958; 1966; reprint. 1967; New York: Praeger, 1968.
       251pp, 56 ill, 47 pls, bib

4555   *   .   English, Scottish and Irish Table Glass, from the
       16th Century to 1820.   Boston: Boston Book and Art
       Shop; New York: Bramhall, 1956; as Table Glass in
       England, Scotland and Ireland from the 16th century to
       1820.   London: Batsford, 1956.   410pp, ill, bib

4556   Hulm, Edward Wyndham.   English Glass-Making in the 16th
       and 17th Centuries.   Excerpts from The Antiquary.   Lon-
       don: 1895.   NCorn

4557   (F. H.) John Collection of 18th Century Glass: English drink-
       ing glasses, coin jugs and tankards, Nailsea coloured glass
       jugs, pewter mounted spirit bottles: catalogue of the col-
       lection.   2nd ed. Royal Leamington Spa, Warwickshire:
       Public Library, Art Gallery and Museum, 1972.   18pp, ill

4557a John Northwood, his contribution to the Stourbridge flint glass
       industry, 1850-1902.   Stourbridge, Eng: Mark & Moody,
       1958.   134pp, ill   (Northwood, 1869-   )

4558   Kenyon, George Hugh.   The Glass Industry of the Weald (1350-
       1620).   Fore. by D. B. Harden.   Leicester: U Pr, 1967.
       231pp, ill, 23 pls, bib

4559   Lagerberg, Ted, and Viola Lagerberg.   Collectible Glass # 4.
       British Glass.   New Port Richey, Fla: Modern Photogra-
       phers, 1968; Price Guide, by John F. Hotchkiss.   Roches-
       ter, NY: Hotchkiss House, 1967.   u. p., 361 color ill
       (C. C. Manley Collection, Brierley Hill, England)

4560   Lloyd, Ward.   Investing in Georgian Glass.   London: Barrie
       & Rockliff; New York: Potter, 1969; London: Transworld,
       1971; as Collecting Georgian Glass.   South Brunswick, NJ:
       A. S. Barnes, 1971.   160pp, ill, 16 color pls (1714-1830,
       including American glass)

4561   Marson, Percival.   Glass and Glass Manufacture.   London;
       New York: I. Pitman, 1918; rev. enl. ed. by L. M.
       Angus Butterworth.   London: Pitman, 1932; 1936; 1949.
       127pp, ill, bib; 143pp, ill, bib   BM

4562 [No entry.]

4563 Now Thus, Now Thus, 1826-1926. St. Helena, Eng: 1926.
93pp, pls (Pilkington Brothers, Ltd.) DeWint

4564 O'Looney, Betty. Victorian Glass. V & A. London: HMSO,
1972. 45pp, chiefly ill

4565 Pargeter, Ph. Red House Glass Works, Stourbridge ... reproduction of the Portland Vase in glass by J. Northwood;
with notes on Wedgwood's reproduction. Stourbridge, Eng:
1877.

4566 *Percival, MacIver. The Glass Collector; a guide to old
English glass. London: H. Jenkins, 1918; New York:
Dodd Mead, 1919. 331pp, 70 ill, 30 pls, bib

4567 A Picture Book of English Glass. V & A. London: HMSO,
1926; 1929. ill

4568 Powell, Harry J. Glass-Making in England. London: Cambridge U Pr, 1923. 183pp, ill (Roman occupation to
1918)

4569 _____. Principles of Glass-Making, Together with Treatises on Crown and Sheet Glass, by Henry Chance, and
Plate Glass, by Henry G. Harris. London: G. Bell, 1883.
186pp, ill

4570 *Ramsey, William. History of the Worshipful Company of the
Glass Sellers of London. London: T. Connor, printer,
1898. 152pp, ill, pls, bib DLC

4571 Rohan, Thomas. Old Glass Beautiful, English and Irish.
London: Mills & Boon, 1930; New York: Dial Pr, 1931.
144pp, ill

4572 *Rush, James. The Ingenious Beilbys. London: Barrie &
Jenkins, 1973. 168pp, ill, pls (part color), bib (18th
century)

4573 Seaby, Wilfred Arthur. Irish Williamite Glass: (a study of
wheel-engraved examples from the 18th and early 19th
centuries). Belfast: Ulster Museum, 1965.

4574 _____, Catriona MacLeod, and Mary Boydell. Irish Glass;
from the 18th century to the present day. Exhibition.
October-December 1971. Limerick?, Ireland: City Art
Gallery, 1971. 27pp, ill, bib

4575 Simon, Andre Louis, 1877- . Bottlescrew Days; wine
drinking in England during the 18th century. London:

Duckworth, 1926. 273pp, pls, facsims (Includes chapters on wine glasses and bottles)

4576 Stannus, Mrs. Graydon. Old Irish Glass. London: Connoisseur, 1920; new rev. enl. ed. 1921. 115pp, ill; 60 pls

4577 Story of American Glass: the story of glass decoration: the story of English glass. Exhibitions 1953, 1954, 1955. 3 vol. in 1. Corning, NY: Museum of Glass, 195-? ill

4578 Thorpe, William Arnold. English and Irish Glass. London: Medici Society, 1927. 35pp, 65 pls (part color), bib

4579 *_____. English Glass. London: Black, 1935; 2nd ed. 1949; 3rd ed. 1961; New York: Macmillan, 1961. 302pp, 30 ill, 23 pls, bib (2nd century to present) DeWint

4580 *_____. A History of English and Irish Glass. 2 vol. London: Medici Society; Boston: Hale, Cushman & Flint, 1929; reprint. 1 vol. 1969. 372pp, 35 ill, 168 pls, bib (Includes chapter on tools; appendix on special glass toys used by glassmakers themselves in their public rituals)

4581 Turnbull, George, and Anthony Herron. The Price Guide to English 18th Century Drinking Glasses. Woodbridge, Suffolk: Baron, for the Antique Collectors Club, 1970; Supplement. 1973. 359pp, chiefly ill, bib

4582 Vincent, Keith. Nailsea Glass. London: David & Charles, 1975. 112pp, 60 ill, bib (Somerset, England)

4583 *Wakefield, Hugh. 19th Century British Glass. London: Faber; New York: Yoseloff, 1961. 64pp, ill, 99 (4 color) pls, bib

4584 _____. Victorian Glass. London: Circle of Glass Collectors, 1958? 3pp

4585 *Warren, Phelps. Irish Glass: The Age of Exuberance. London: Faber; New York: Scribner, 1970. 155pp, ill, 107 (4 color) pls, bib (200 pieces, 1780-1830)

4586 Webber, Norman W. Collecting Glass. Newton Abbot: David & Charles, 1972; Melbourne: Lansdowne, 1973. 196pp, ill, bib (To 1914)

4587 Westropp, Michael Seymour Dudley. English and Foreign Glass. General Guide to ... Glass. Part 9. 3rd ed. Dublin: Science & Art Museum, 1920. 64pp, 14 pls

4588 _____. Irish Glass. General Guide to Glass, chapter 2, part 9. Dublin: Science & Art Museum, 1913; 1918; 1920. 88pp, 20 pls

4589 *   . Irish Glass. An account of glass-making in Ire-
          land from the 16th century to present day. Dublin: Royal
          Irish Academy Proceedings, Vol. 29, 1911; London: Jen-
          kins, 1920; as Irish Glass. An account of its manufacture
          in Waterford, Cork, Dublin, Drumrea, Belfast, Newry and
          Londonderry. London: 1930. 206pp, ill; 40 pls of 188
          pieces and 220 patterns & designs DLC, BM

4590 Wilkinson, Oliver Nicholas. Old Glass: manufacture, styles,
          uses. London: Benn; New York: Philosophical Library,
          1968. 200pp, ill, 64 pls, bib

4591 Wilkinson, Reginald. The Hallmarks of Antique Glass. Lon-
          don: Richard Madley, 1968. 220pp, ill, pl

4592 Wills, Geoffrey. Antique Glass for Pleasure and Investment.
          London: Gifford, 1971; New York: Drake, 1972. 174pp,
          ill, 16 pls (1700-1800)

4593   . Candlesticks and Lustres. London: Guinness
          Signatures, 1968. 16pp, 17 ill (1685-1845)

4594   . Chandeliers. London: Guinness Signatures, 1968.
          16pp, 14 ill (1740-1830)

4595   . Commemorative Goblets. London: Guinness Sig-
          natures, 1968. 16pp, 15 ill (1581-1800)

4596   . The 'Country Life' Pocket Book of Glass. London:
          Country Life, 1966; as The Collector's Pocket Book of
          Glass. New York: Hawthorn, 1966. 317pp, ill, bib
          (Tableglass, pre-World War I)

4597   . Drinking Glasses. 2 parts. London: Guinness
          Signatures, 1968. 16pp, 18 ill; 16pp, 16 ill (English and
          Irish, 1667-1830)

4598   . 18th Century Coloured Glass. London: Guinness
          Signatures, 1968. 16pp, 16 ill (1675-1810. English
          and Irish)

4599   . Enamelled and Engraved Glass. London: Guin-
          ness Signatures, 1968. 16pp, 16 ill (Tableglass, 1676-
          1820. English)

4600   . English and Irish Glass. 16 parts, available
          separately. London: Guinness Signatures; Garden City,
          NY: Doubleday, 1968. 271pp, ill (See his Guinness
          Signature titles)

4601   . Ewers and Decanters. London: Guinness Signa-
          tures, 1968. 16pp, 15 ill (English, Irish, 1667-1830)

4602 _____ . Glass. London: Orbis, 1972. 64pp, chiefly ill,
       bib (To 1900)

4603 _____ . Irish Glass. London: Guinness Signatures, 1968.
       16pp, 13 ill (1745-1835)

4604 _____ . Modern Glass. Guildford: Guinness Signatures,
       1968. 16pp, 17 ill (English and Irish, 1903-1967)

4605 _____ . Novelties and 'Friggers.' London: Guinness
       Signatures, 1968. 16pp, 17 ill (English, Irish, 1788-
       1820)

4606 _____ . Table Wares. London: Guinness Signatures,
       1968. 16pp, 16 ill (English, Irish, 1667-1830)

4607 _____ . Victorian Glass. 2 parts. London: Guinness
       Signatures, 1968. 16pp, 13 ill; 16pp, 15 ill (English,
       Irish, 1837-1901)

4608 Wilmer, Daisy. Early English Glass: a guide for collectors
       of table and other decorative glass of the 16th, 17th and
       18th centuries. London: Upcott Gill, 1909; 2nd ed. 1911.
       272pp, ill; 282pp, ill

4609 Winbolt, Samuel Edward. Wealdon Glass. The Surrey-Sussex
       Glass Industry (A.D. 1226-1615). Hove, Eng: Combridges,
       1933. 85pp, 60 ill, bib

4610 Young, Sidney. History of the Worshipful Company of Glass
       Sellers of London. London: 1913. 76pp, pls

4611 Yoxall, James Henry. Collecting Old Glass, English and
       Irish. London: Heinemann, 1916. 109pp, ill

EUROPEAN, ORIENTAL AND CANADIAN GLASS

4612 Applegate, Judith. French Art Glass. Exhibition. April-
       May 1975. Boston: Museum of Fine Arts, 1975. 16pp,
       ill, bib, gloss (Emile Galle, Rene Lalique, Maurice
       Marinot)

4613 The Art of Glassblowing, or Plain instructions for making the
       chemical and philosophical instruments which are formed
       of glass. By a French artist. London: Bumpus & Grif-
       fin, 1831. 112pp, 4 pls BM

4614 Barber, Edwin Atlee. Spanish Glass in the Collection of the
       Hispanic Society of America. New York: Hispanic So-
       ciety; New York; London: Putnam's, 1917. 43pp, ill,
       pls, color frontis

4615 Blair, Dorothy. A History of Glass in Japan. New York:
      Kodansha International/USA; Charlottesville, Va: U Pr
      of Va, 1973. 479pp, ill, pls, bib

4616 Blount, Berniece, and Henry Blount. French Cameo Glass.
      Des Moines: Wallace-Homestead, 1968; Price Guide.
      1968. 160pp, 252 color pls, bib, 192 marks, (500 pieces)

4617 Bohemian Glass. V & A. London: HMSO, 1974. ill

4618 Bohemian Glass of the 17th and 18th Centuries. English and
      Czechoslovakian text. Prague: Obelisk, 1970. 172pp,
      pls

4619 Borsos, Bela. Glassmaking in Old Hungary. Tr. by Zsuz-
      sanna Horn. Budapest: Corvina; Boston: Branden, 1963.
      56pp, ill, 48 pls, bib (13th to 18th century)

4620 Buckley, Wilfred. Aert Schouman and the Glasses That He
      Engraved. With a supplementary note on glasses engraved
      by Frans Greenwood. London: Benn, 1931. 50pp, ill,
      30 pls, bib (Schouman, 1720-1792. The Hague)

4621 *   . European Glass. A brief outline of the history of
      glass-making, with notes on various methods of glass
      decoration. London: Benn; Boston; New York: Houghton-
      Mifflin, 1926. 96pp, ill, pls, bib (Includes essay on
      Dutch glass engravers by Dr. Ferand Hudig) NCorn, DLC,
      MiU

4622   . Notes on Frans Greenwood and the Glasses That
      He Engraved. London: Benn, 1930. 14pp, ill, 30 pls
      (Greenwood, 1680-1761. Holland) DLC

4623   . Outlines of the History of Glass Making in Various
      European Countries to Accompany Photographs in the Col-
      lection of Mr. and Mrs. W. Buckley, Moundsmere Manor,
      Basingstoke, and of a few other glasses. 15 vol. Basing-
      stoke, Hants: 1933. pls NCorn

4624   , (continued by Bertha Buckley). D. Wolff and the
      Glasses That He Engraved; with a supplementary note on
      a glass engraved by Frans Greenwood. London: Methuen,
      1935. 41pp, pls (David Wolff, 1732-1798, The Hague)

4625 Chance, Sir William Hugh Stobart. The Optical Glassworks
      at Benediktbeuern. Reprint from the Proceedings of the
      Physical Society. Cambridge, Eng: U Pr, 1937. 12pp,
      pl (Germany, 1806-1884) NCorn

4626 Davis, Frank. Continental Glass: From Roman to Modern
      Times. London: Barker, 1972. 125pp, ill, 64 pls, bib

4627   Dikshit, Moreshwar G. History of Indian Glass. Bombay:
       U of Bombay, 1969. 212pp, ill, 48 pls

4628   European Glass. Toledo, O: Museum of Art, 196-? 22pp,
       ill

4629   Exhibition of East Asiatic Glass; an Exhibition of glass from
       regions of Asia east of the Himalaya Mountains repre-
       senting 2500 years of East Asiatic interest in glass making.
       October 1948. Toledo: Museum of Art, 1948. 28pp, ill

4630   Frothingham, Alice Wilson. Barcelona Glass in Venetian
       Style. New York: Hispanic Society of America, 1956.
       49pp, ill

4631   _____. Hispanic Glass, with examples in the collection of
       the Hispanic Society of America. New York: 1941. 204pp,
       125 ill, pls, bib

4632 * _____. Spanish Glass. London: Faber, 1963; New York:
       Yoseloff, for the Hispanic Society of America, 1964. 96pp,
       96 ill, 4 color pls, bib

4633   Glass Vessels in Dutch Paintings of the 17th Century. Exhi-
       bition. August-October 1952. Corning, NY: Museum of
       Glass, 1952. 31pp, ill

4634   Grover, Ray, and Lee Grover. Carved and Decorated Euro-
       pean Art Glass. Rutland, Vt: Tuttle, 1970; Price Guide,
       by John F. Hotchkiss. Rochester, NY: Hotchkiss House,
       1970. 243pp, ill, 424 color pls, bib (1880-1930)

4635   Haudicquer de Blancourt, Jean, ca.1650-1704. The Art of
       Glass: shewing how to make all sorts of glass, crystal
       and enamel. Likewise ... pearls, precious stones, china
       and looking-glass ... Painting on glass and enameling ...
       with an appendix containing exact instructions for making
       glass-eyes of all colours. Tr. from French (1697). Lon-
       don: Brown, Bennet, Midwinter, Leigh, & Wilkin, 1699;
       reprint. London: Smith, Greenwood, 188-? 355pp, 9
       pls DeWint, NN, MiU, NjP

4636   Heller, David. In Search of V. O. C. Glass. Cape Town,
       South Africa: Maskew Miller; London: Bailey & Swinfen,
       1954. 103pp, ill (Dutch East India Company engraved
       tableglass)

4637   Hettes, Karel. Old Venetian Glass. Tr. by Ota Vojtisek.
       London: Spring Books, 1960. 46pp, ill, 72 pls, bib

4638   Lamm, Carl Johan. Glass from Iran in the National Museum,
       Stockholm. Stockholm: C. E. Fritzes K. Hovbokh, 1935.

21pp, ill, 48 pls, bib (Hannibal Collection of Medieval Glass)

4639 _____. Oriental Glass of Medieval Date Found in Sweden, and the early history of lustre-painting. Stockholm: Wahlstrom & Widstrand, 1941. 114pp, ill, 24 pls, bib ViU

4640 *McClinton, Katharine Morrison. Lalique for Collectors. New York: Scribner, 1975. 152pp, 148 (18 color) ill, bib, factory checklists (Rene Lalique, 1860-1945, Paris. Glass, gold, jewelry)

4641 MacLaren, George E. G. Nova Scotia Glass. Ed. by Barbara B. Smith. Rev. ed. Halifax: Nova Scotia Museum, 1968. 42pp, ill

4642 Mariacher, Giovanni. Italian Blown Glass, from ancient Rome to Venice. Tr. from Italian by Michael Bullock and Johanna Capra. London: Thames & Hudson; New York: McGraw-Hill, 1961. 248pp, ill, 84 pls, bib

4643 Marx, Robert F. Wine Glasses Recovered from the Sunken City of Port Royal: May 1966-March 1968. Kingston: Jamaica National Trust Commission, 1968. 35 leaves, chiefly ill, bib (Stemware. Port Royal sank in 1692 and again in 1907)

4644 *Middlemas, Robert Keith. Continental Coloured Glass. London: Barrie & Jenkins, 1971. 120pp, ill

4645 *Neri, Antonio. The Art of Glass: wherein are shown the ways to make and colour glass, pastes, enamels, lakes, and other curiosities; written in Italian, and translated in English by Christopher Merret. London: A. W., for Octavian Pulleyn, 1662; reprint, ed. by Sir Thomas Phillipps. Middle Hill, Worcestershire: priv. printed, Typis Medio-Montanis, 1826. 362pp, ill (Tr. of Nevi's L'arte Vetraria, 1612) NNC-Ave

4646 Pesatova, Zuzana. Bohemian Engraved Glass. Tr. from Czechoslovakian by Arnost Fappel. Feltham: Hamlyn, 1968. 63pp, ill, 110 pls, bib

4647 Pierce, Edith Chown. Canadian Glass. A footnote to history. Ontario: Ryerson Pr, 1954.

4648 Schmoranz, Gustav. Old Oriental Gilt and Enamelled Glass Vessels Extant in Public Museums and Private Collections.... Vienna; London: G. Norman & Son, printers, for Imperial Handels-Museum of Vienna, 1899. 75pp, 69 ill, 12 photographs, 32 color pls, bib

4649   Spence, Hilda, and Kevin Spence. <u>A Guide to Early Canadian</u>
       <u>Glass</u>. Toronto: Ryerson Pr, 1961; Don Mills, Ont:
       Longmans Canada, 1966. 184pp, ill; 112pp, ill

4650   Stevens, Gerald F. <u>Canadian Glass, 1825-1925</u>. Toronto:
       Ryerson Pr, 1967. 262pp, ill

4651   _____. <u>Early Canadian Glass</u>. Fore. by Lorne Pierce.
       Toronto: Ryerson Pr, 1960; 1961; reprint. 1967. 184pp,
       ill

4652   _____. <u>Early Ontario Glass</u>. Toronto: Royal Ontario
       Museum, 1965. 16pp, ill, bib

4653   _____. <u>The Edith Chown Pierce and Gerald Stevens Col-</u>
       <u>lection of Early Canadian Glass</u>. Exhibition. Toronto:
       Royal Ontario Museum, 1957. 22pp, ill

4654   <u>Three Great Centuries of Venetian Glass; a special exhibition.</u>
       Corning, NY: Museum of Glass, 1958. 116pp, ill, bib

4655   <u>A Tribute to Persia: Persian Glass</u>. Exhibition. Spring-
       Summer 1972. In honor of 2500th anniversary of the
       founding of the Persian Empire. Corning, NY: Museum
       of Glass, 1972. 18pp, ill, 1 pl, bib

4656   Unitt, Doris Joyce, and Peter Unitt. <u>American and Canadian</u>
       <u>Goblets</u>. Peterborough, Ont: Clock House, 1970. 351pp,
       ill, bib (Over 1000 patterns of stemware)

4657   _____, and _____. <u>Canadian Silver, Silver Plate and</u>
       <u>Related Glass</u>. Peterborough, Ont: Clock House, 1970.
       256pp, hundreds of ill, bib

4658   _____, and _____. <u>Treasury of Canadian Glass</u>. Peter-
       borough, Ont: Clock House, 1969. 280pp, bill, bib

4659   Uresova, Libuse. <u>Bohemian Glass</u>. V & A. London:
       HMSO, 1965. 18pp, 45 pls (Czechoslovakian)

4660   *von Saldern, Axel. <u>German Enamelled Glass, the Edwin J.</u>
       <u>Beinecke Collection and related pieces</u>. Corning, NY:
       Museum of Glass, 1965. 474pp, ill (some color) bib

4661   Waring, John Burley, ed. <u>Examples of Ornamental Art in</u>
       <u>Glass and Enamel, selected from collections of the Duke</u>
       <u>of Buccleuch, etc. ... with essay by A. W. Franks.</u>
       London: Day, 185-? 32pp, ill NNC-Ave

4662   Westropp, Michael Seymour Dudley. <u>English and Foreign</u>
       <u>Glass</u>. General guide to ... Glass, part 9. 3rd ed.
       Dublin: Science & Art Museum, 1920. 64pp, 14 pls

4663   White, Margaret E., comp. European and American Glass in
       the Newark Museum's Collections. Newark, NJ: 1955.
       32pp, ill, bib

BOTTLES, FLASKS AND FRUIT JARS

4664   Abbott, Allan L. Old Bottles; how and where to find them.
       Anaheim, Cal: Abbott & Abbott, 1970. 74pp, ill

4665   Adams, John Phillip. Bottle Collecting in America. Somers-
       worth, NH: New Hampshire Publishing, 1971. 133pp, ill

4666   _____. Bottle Collecting in New England; a guide to dig-
       ging, identification, and pricing. Somersworth: New
       Hampshire Publishing, 1969. 120pp, ill, pls

4667   Ashton, Robert J. The Bottle Collector's Price List for Em-
       bossed, Ink, and pontil-scarred bottles. New York: Ex-
       position Pr, 1972. 133pp

4668   Bailey, Shirley R. Bottle Town. Millville, NJ: 1968. 100pp,
       ill

4669   Baker, Oliver. Black Jacks and Leather Bottells; being some
       account of leather drinking vessels in England and inci-
       dentally of other ancient vessels. London: E. J. Burrow,
       printer, for W. J. Fieldhouse, Stratford-on-Avon, 1921.
       190pp, ill, 24 (3 color) pls DeWint

4670   Baldwin, Joseph K. (A Collector's Guide) to Patent and
       Proprietary Medicine Bottles of the 19th Century. New
       York: T. Nelson, 1973. 540pp, 800 bottles ill, 4000
       listed

4671   Ballou, Hazel, and Kaylen Alley. The Beginner's Book: Col-
       lecting jars and bottles for fun and money. Fort Scott,
       Kansas: Authors, 1966. ill

4672   Barber, Edwin Atlee. American Glassware, Old and New.
       A sketch of the glass industry in the United States, and
       manual for collectors of historical bottles. Philadelphia:
       Patterson & White, 1900; Philadelphia: D. McKay, 1900;
       reprint as Old American Bottles. Fort Davis, Tx: Fron-
       tier Pr, 1974. 112pp, ill, pls; 106pp, ill NN, BM

4673   Bartholomew, Ed Ellsworth. 1200 Old Medicine Bottles, with
       prices current. Fort Davis, Tx: Frontier Pr, 1970.
       120pp, ill

4674   Bates, Virginia T., and Beverly Chamberlain. Antique Bottle
       Finds in New England. Peterborough, NH: Noone House,
       1968. 80pp, ill, bib

4675   Beare, Nikki. Bottle Bonanza; a handbook for glass collectors.
       Miami: Hurricane House, 1965. 108pp, ill

4676   Beck, Doreen. The Book of Bottle Collecting. Feltham:
       Hamlyn, 1973. 96pp, ill, bib

4677   The Bertrand Bottles, a study of 19th century glass and ce-
       ramic containers. Washington, D.C.: GPO, 1974. 112pp,
       ill (19th century cargo of steamboat "Bertrand," sunk
       while headed for Montana goldfields in 1865)

4678   Bird, Douglas, Marion Bird, and Charles Corke. A Century
       of Antique Canadian Glass Fruit Jars. Lond, Ont: 1970.
       110pp, ill, bib

4679   Bird, Marion, and Douglas Bird. North American Fruit Jar
       Index. Orillia, Ont: Authors, 1968. u.p., ill

4680   Blumenstein, Lynn. Bottle Rush, U.S.A.; the story of our
       historic past through old time bottles. Salem, Ore: Old
       Time Bottle Publishing, 1966. 184pp, ill

4681   _____. Old Time Bottles, Found in Ghost Towns; pictures
       and prices of over 300 bottles in the 50 to over 100 year
       class that are to be found in the ghost towns of the West.
       Salem, Ore: Adolphson's Printing, 1963; rev. ed. Salem:
       Old Time Bottle Publishing, 1966. 74pp, ill; 80pp, ill

4682   _____. Redigging the West for Old Time Bottles. Salem,
       Ore: Old Time Bottle Publishing, 1965; rev. ed. 1966.
       183pp, ill; 199pp, ill

4683   _____. Wishbook 1865; relic identification for the year
       1865. Salem, Ore: Old Time Bottle Co, 1968. 144pp,
       ill

4684   Bottle News. Monthly. Kermit, Tx: Collector's Weekly,
       1973- .

4685   Boynton, Beatrice White. A Very Amateur Guide to Antique
       Bottle Collecting. Caldwell, Idaho: Caxton Printers, 1965.
       u.p., ill

4686   Brantley, William F. A Collectors Guide to Ball Jars. Fore.
       by Edmund F. Ball. Muncie, Ind: R. H. Martin, 1975.
       100pp, ill (some color), bib

4687   Brazeal, Frances. Old Bottles Sketched and Catalogued.
       Clovis, Cal: Clovis Printing, 1964. chiefly ill

4688   Bressie, Wesley, and Ruby Bressie. Ghost Town Bottle Price
       Guide. Eagle Point, Ore: 1964; 1966. 56pp, ill

4689   _____ , and _____ . 101 Ghost Town Relics; how to display, price guide. Yreka, Cal: Nolan's News-Journal, printer, 1967. 72pp, ill

4690   _____ , and _____ . Relic Trails to Treasure; the Americana price guide. Salem, Ore: Old Time Bottle Publishing, 1970. 192pp, ill

4691   Brise, Sheelah Maud Emily Ruggles. Sealed Bottles. London: Country Life; New York: Scribner's, 1949. 175pp, ill, 4 pls (1650 on) NN

4692   Burris, Ronald B. Collecting Fruit Jars, with price guide. No. 2. Visalia, Cal: Author, 1967. u.p., ill

4693   _____ . An Illustrated Guide for Collecting Fruit Jars. No. 1. Visalia, Cal: priv. printed, 1966; rev. ed. 1970. u.p., 121 ill, prices

4694   _____ . More Collectible Jars, with Price Guide. No. 3. Visalia, Cal: Author, 1971. u.p., ill

4695   _____ . Rare and Unusual Fruit Jars. Visalia, Cal: Author, 197-? u.p., ill

4696   Cleveland, Hugh. Bottle Pricing Guide. San Angelo, Tx: Cleveland Book Supply, 1975. 1000 ill

4697   Cohen, Hal L. Official Guide to Bottles, Old and New. New York: H-C Publishing, 1974; rev. ed. Florence, Alabama: House of Collectibles, 1975. 319pp, 850 ill, 16 color pls, bib; 400pp, 850 ill, pls, bib

4698   Colcleaser, Donald E. Bottles of Bygone Days; a guide book of modern bottles, 1850 to date. 2 vol. Klamath Falls, Ore: 1965, 1966. 91pp, ill; 58pp, ill

4699   _____ . Bottles; yesterday's trash--today's treasure. Napa?, Cal: 1967; Klamath Falls, Ore: 197-? 145pp, ill

4700   _____ . Dictionary of Soda and Mineral Water Bottles. Klamath Falls, Ore: 197-? 88pp, ill

4701   _____ . Dictionary of Spirits and Whiskey Bottles. Klamath Falls, Ore: 197-? 150pp, ill

4702   Covill, William E., Jr. Ink Bottles and Inkwells. Taunton, Mass: W. S. Sullwold, 1971. 431pp, ill of 1780 pieces

4703   Creswick, Alice M. Fruit Jars, a Price Guide and Descriptive Index to 1281 Fruit Jars. Grand Rapids: 1970. 72pp, ill

4704   _____, and Arleta Rodrigues. The Cresrod Blue Book of Fruit Jars; an index and price guide to 1035 fruit jars. Grand Rapids: Authors, 1969. 90pp, ill

4705   _____, and _____. The Cresrod Redbook of Fruit Jars. Grand Rapids: Authors, 1976. 102pp, ill (2036 jars)

4706   Davis, Derek Cecil. English Bottles and Decanters, 1650-1900. London: Charles Letts; New York: World, 1972. 80pp, ill, 60 color pls, bib

4707   Davis, Marvin, and Helen Davis. Antique Bottles. Pictures and prices of over 225 bottles. Medford, Ore: Gandee Printing Center, 1967. 62pp, ill

4708   _____, and _____. Bottles and Relics; pictures and prices of over 500 bottles, insulators and relics. Medford, Ore: Gandee, 1969. 155pp, ill

4709   _____, and _____. Collector's Price Guide to Bottles, tobacco tins, and relics. New York: Galahad Books, 1975. 208pp, ill, color pls

4710   Devner, Kay. Backward Through a Bottle. Tucson, Ari: Author, 1964. ill

4711   _____. Patent Medicine Bottles. Tucson: Author, 19-? 106pp, ill (1870s to 1920s)

4712   Edwards, Jack M. A Collectors Guide to the Whiskeys That Were. King City, Cal: 1967. 80pp, ill

4713   Elliott, Rex R. Hawaiian Bottles of Long Ago. Honolulu: Hawaiian Service, 1971. 93pp, ill

4714   Federation of Historic Bottle Clubs. Journal. Biannual. Memphis, Tenn: 197-?

4715   _____. Newsletter. Monthly. Memphis: 197-?

4716   Ferraro, Pat, and Bob Ferraro. A Bottle Collector's Book. Lovelock, Nev: 1966. 107pp, ill

4717   _____, and _____. The Past in Glass. Sparks, Nev: Western Printing, 1964. 95pp, ill

4718   Field, Anne E. On the Trail of Stoddard Glass. Dublin, NH: William L. Bauhan, 1975. 110pp, 40pp of photographs, bib, gloss (Medicine and bitters bottles, 1842-1873. Joseph Foster, Granite Glass, South Stoddard Glass, New Granite Glass Works)

4719   Fike, Richard E. Guide to Old Bottles, Contents and Prices;

illustrations and advertisements to over 250 bottles, plus
additional current price guide. 2 vol. Ogden, Utah:
1966. 48pp each, ill

4720 _____. Handbook for the Bottle-ologist; over 1000 bottles
listed including a background and description of those found
in the Great Basin. Ogden, Utah: 1965. 48pp, ill

4721 Fletcher, Edward. Bottle Collecting: Finding, Collecting and
Displaying Antique Bottles. London: Blandford Pr, 1972.
96pp, ill, 4 pls

4722 Foster, John Morrill. Old Bottle Foster and His Glass-
making Descendants. Fort Wayne, Ind: Keefer Printing,
1972. 104pp, ill, bib

4723 Foster, Kate. Scent Bottles. London: The Connoisseur,
Joseph, 1966. 111pp, 96 ill, 8 color pls, bib (Porcelain,
glass, enamel, silver, etc.)

4724 Fraser, Robert B. The South Carolina Dispensary Bottle.
n. p.: 1969. 8 leaves, ill

4725 Freeman, Graydon La Verne. Bitters Bottles, by James H.
Thompson (pseud.). Watkins Glen, NY: Century, 1947.
100pp, ill

4726 _____. Grand Old American Bottles; descriptive listings of
glass bottle types from Colonial times to the present.
Watkins Glen, NY: Century, 1964; reprint in 4 parts.
1. Liquors; 2. Medicinals; 3. Households; 4. Figurals.
Watkins Glen: 1975. 503pp, ill

4727 _____. The Medicine Showman. Watkins Glen, NY:
Century, 1949; 1957. 97pp, ill

4728 Gardner, Charles B., and J. Edmund Edwards. Collector's
Price Guide to Historical Bottles and Flasks. Stratford,
Conn: J. Edwards, 1970. 170pp, ill

4729 Glassware/1880, Whitall, Tatum and Co. Catalog reprint.
Princeton, NJ: Pyne, 1971. 88pp, ill (Bottles, chemical and pharmaceutical glass)

4730 Goodell, Donald. The American Bottle Collector's Price Guide
to Historical Flasks, Pontils, Bitters, Mineral Waters, Inks
and Sodas. Rutland, Vt: Tuttle, 1973. 144pp, ill, bib

4731 Hodges, Elizabeth. The Story of Glass; bottles and containers
through the ages. New York: Sterling, 1960. 47pp, ill
(Juvenile literature)

4732 Hotchkiss, John F., and Joan H. Cassidy. The New and

Revised Bottle Collecting Manual with Prices.   Rochester,
NY: Hotchkiss, Hawthorne, 1972.

4733   Huggins, Phillip K.   The South Carolina Dispensary: a bottle
collectors Atlas and history of the system.   Lexington,
SC: Sandlapper Pr, 1971.   ill

4734   Jensen, Al.   Old Owl Drug Bottles and Others.   Mountain
View, Cal: Author, 1967; 1968.   128pp, ill

4735   Jones, John Lemuel.   Soda and Mineral Water Bottles (Over
2000 Varieties).   Green, SC: Palmetto Enterprise, 1972.
163pp, ill

4736   Kauffman, Donald M., and June Kauffman.   Dig Those Crazy
Bottles; a handbook of pioneer bottles.   Cheyenne, Wyo:
1966.   64pp, chiefly ill

4737   Kendrick, Grace.   The Antique Bottle Collector; secrets re-
vealed to date and evaluate bottles of the 19th century.
Sparks, Nev: Western Printing, 1963; 1964; Price Supplement. 1965; 3rd ed. with Price Supplement. 1966.
68pp, ill; ...; 49pp, ill; 92pp, ill

4738   _____.   The Mouth-blown bottle.   Ann Arbor, Mich: Edwards Brothers, lithographers, 1968.   200pp, ill, bib

4739 *Ketchum, William C., Jr.   A Treasury of American Bottles.
New York: Bobbs-Merrill, 1975.   224pp, 300 ill, color
pls, gloss

4740   Kincade, Steve.   Early American Bottles and Glass.   Clovis,
Cal: Clovis Printing, 1964.   68pp, chiefly ill

4741   Klamkin, Marian.   The Collector's Book of Bottles.   New
York: Dodd, Mead, 1971.   248pp, 430 ill, bib   (Flasks,
bitters, medicines, inks, fruit jars, etc.)

4742   Kovel, Ralph M., and Terry H. Kovel.   The Official Bottle
Price List.   New York: Crown, 1971; 2nd ed. 1973.
219pp, ill, bib; 254pp, 400 ill, bib

4743   The Late Hiram Norcross Collection of Chestnut Bottles.   Exhibition.   April-September 1966.   Memphis: Brooks Memorial Art Gallery, 1966.   23pp, pls

4744   Launert, Edmund.   Scent and Scent Bottles.   London: Barrie
& Jenkins, 1975.   176pp, 200 (30 color) ill

4745   Lerk, James Andrew.   Bottles in Collection.   Bendigo, Victoria, Australia: Author, 1971.   60pp, ill

4746   Lief, Alfred.   A Close-up of Closures; history and progress.

New York: Glass Container Manufacturers Institute, 1965.
47pp, ill (Bottle seals)

4747   Lincoln, Gerald David. Antique Blob Top Bottles, Central
and Southern New England. Marlboro, Mass: 1970.
128pp, ill

4748   McKearin, Helen. Bottles, Flasks and Dr. Dyott. New York:
Crown, 1970. 159pp, ill, bib (Dyottville Glass Works,
1800-1850)

4749   _____. Price List of Bottles and Flasks; also a few of-
ferings in pewter, prints, cup plates and Anglo-American
pottery. New York: n.d. 23pp

4750 * _____. The Story of American Historical Flasks. Exhibition. Corning, NY: Corning Museum of Glass, 1953.
70pp, ill

4751   McMurray, Charles. Collector's Guide of Flasks and Bottles.
Dayton, O: 1927. 170pp, ill

4752   Maust, Don, ed. Bottle and Glass Handbook; a history of
bottles showing their various styles, types and uses from
ancient times to the present. Uniontown, Pa: E. G.
Warman, 1956; Bend, Ore: Bottle Digger's Library,
197-? 158pp, ill

4753   Meigh, Edward. The Story of the Glass Bottle. Stoke-on-
Trent: Ramsden, 1972. 86pp, ill, bib

4754   Monroe, Loretta. Old Bottles Found Along the Florida Keys.
Coral Gables, Fla: Wakebrook House, 1967. 216pp, ill

4755   Munsey, Cecil. Illustrated Guide to Collecting Bottles. Introd.
by Charles Gardner. New York: Hawthorn, 1970. 30pp,
over 1000 ill, bib, gloss (Ancient to modern)

4756   Nurnberg, John J. Crowns: The Complete Story. 4th ed.
Wilmington?, Del: Author, 1967. 495pp, ill (Bottle caps
and seals)

4757   Old Bottle Magazine. Monthly. Bend, Ore: Old Bottle Exchange, 19-?

4758   Paul, John Robert, and Paul W. Parmalee. Soft Drink Bot-
tling: a history with special references to Illinois. Springfield: State Museum Society, 1973. 121pp, ill, bib

4759   Phillips, Helen V. Antique Bottles. Cheyenne, Wyo: Logan
Printing, 1967. chiefly ill

4760   The Pontil. Periodical. Sacramento, Cal: Antique Bottle
Collector's Association of California, 19-?

4761   Proh, Stephen.   The Australian Bottle Collector.   Mt. Gravatt,
       Queensland: Bottle Collector's Review, 1973?   77pp, ill,
       bib

4762   Putnam, Hazel Elizabeth.   Bottled Before 1865.   Los Angeles:
       Rapid Blue Print, 1968.   100pp, ill

4763   _____ .   Bottle Identification.   Jamestown, Cal: 1965.
       u. p., 1000 ill from old catalogues, price guide

4764   Reed, Adele.   Old Bottles and Ghost Towns.   Bishop, Cal:
       Chalfant Pr, 1961; 1965.   55pp, ill

4765 *Revi, Albert Christian.   American Pressed Glass and Figure
       Bottles.   New York; London: T. Nelson, 1964; Camden,
       NJ: Nelson, 1970.   446pp, 600 ill, bib

4766   Rosenblum, Beatrice.   Field Guide to Orange County (New
       York) Bottles.   Middletown, NY: T. Emmett Henderson,
       1974.   123pp, ill

4767   _____ .   Handbook Guide to Orange County Bottles.   Middle-
       town, NY: T. E. Henderson, 1974.   228pp, ill

4768   [No entry.]

       Ruggles-Brise, Sheelah Maud Emily.   Sealed Bottles.   See:
       Brise, S. M. E. R.

4769   Seamans, Berna Mackey, and Mertie Mackey Robb.   Colorado
       Bottle History: When and Where?   Denver: R. & S.
       Publications, 1969.   71pp, ill

4770   Sellari, Carlo, and Dot Sellari.   Eastern Bottles.   3 vol.
       Waukesha, Wisconsin: Country Beautiful, 197-?; Price
       Guide. 197-?   ill; price guide has 3444 listings

4771 *_____ , and _____ .   The Illustrated Price Guide of
       Antique Bottles.   Waukesha, Wisconsin: Country Beauti-
       ful, 1975.   432pp, 3500 pieces ill, 50 color photographs
       (Fire grenades, bitters, poison, ink, perfume, pottery,
       barber, snuff, etc.   7000 bottles, chiefly pre-1903)

4772   Shroeder, Bill.   1000 Fruit Jars.   History of fruit jars.
       How to sell and ship.   Paducah, Ky: Collector Books,
       197-?   56pp, ill

4773   Thomas, John L.   Picnics, Coffins, Shoo-flies.   Weaverville,
       Cal: 1974.   92pp, ill

4774   Tibbitts, John C.   Chips from the Pontil.   Sacramento, Cal:
       J. C. Tibbits, 1963.   74pp, ill

4775 _____. John Doe, Bottle Collector. Sacramento, Cal:
Little Glass Shack, 1967. 123pp, ill

4776 _____. How to Collect Antique Bottles. Sacramento, Cal:
Little Glass Shack, 1969. 118pp, ill

4777 _____. 1200 Bottles Priced; a bottle price guide, catalog,
and classification system. Sacramento, Cal: Little Glass
Shack, 1964; 2 vol. new ed. with up-dated prices, and
index. Vol. II. by J. C. Tibbitts and Don Smith. 1970-
73. 164pp, ill

4778 Toulouse, Julian Harrison. Bottle Makers and Their Marks.
New York: T. Nelson, 1971. 624pp, ill, 900 older and
300 newer marks

4779 * _____. Fruit Jars, a Collectors Manual. Hanover, Pa:
Everybodys Pr, 1969. 542pp, 750 ill; 175 patent sketches
(1169 jars)

4780 Umberger, Arthur L., and Jewel Umberger. Collecting
Character Bottles. Tyler, Tx: Corker Book Co, 196-?
176pp, ill (500 figural bottles)

4781 _____, and _____. It's a Corker! Bottle Price Guide.
Tyler, Tx: Corker Book Co, 1966; rev. ed. 1968. 60pp,
ill (Over 400 bottles)

4782 *Van Rensselaer, Stephen. Checklist of Early American Bottles
and Flasks. New York: 1921; rev. ed. with checklist.
Peterborough, NH: Transcript Printing, 1926; rev. ed.,
ed. by J. Edmund Edwards. New introd. by Charles B.
Gardner. Stratford, Conn: J. E. Edwards, 1969; Southhampton, NY: Cracker Barrel Pr, 1969. 109pp, ill;
244, 320pp, ill; 313pp, ill

4783 Walbridge, William Spooner, 1854- . American Bottles Old
and New, a Story of the Industry in the United States.
Toledo, O: Caslon Pr, 1920. 112pp, ill DeWint

4784 Warman, Edwin G. Bottle Collector's Treasury; a collection
of information about classic and common bottles. Uniontown, Pa: E. G. Warman, 1972. 79pp, ill

4785 *Watson, Richard. Bitters Bottles. New York: T. Nelson,
1965; Supplement. Camden, NJ: T. Nelson, 1968. 304pp,
400 ill, bib; 160pp, ill, bib

4786 Wearin, Otha Donner. Statues That Pour: the story of
character bottles. Denver: Sage Books, 1965; reprint.
Des Moines: Wallace-Homestead, 1965. 208pp, ill, bib
(Character or figure bottles, glass and ceramic. European and American, old and new)

4787   Whitall Tatum and Company, 1880. Flint Glassware, blue
       ware, perfume and cologne bottles, show bottles and
       globes, green glassware, stoppers, druggists' sundries.
       Catalog reprint, with introduction. Princeton, NJ: Pyne,
       1971. 72pp, ill, 8 pls, bib

4788   _____. 1892 Catalog. Colognes, drug mills, bottles,
       scales, cork presses. Edited reprint. Millville, NJ:
       S. R. Bailey, 1969. 32pp, ill

4789   _____. 1902 Catalog. Edited reprint. Millville, NJ:
       S. R. Bailey, 196-? Chattanooga, Tenn: 1967. 64pp,
       ill

4790   Wills, Geoffrey. Bottles. 2 parts. Guilford, Surrey:
       Guinness Signatures, 1968. 16pp, 16 ill; 16pp, 11 ill
       (Part 1. To 1720; Part 2. From 1720. English and Irish
       bottles, 1650-1856)

4791   _____. English Glass Bottles for the Collector. Edin-
       burgh: J. Bartholomew, 1975. 82pp, ill

4792   Wilson Bill, and Betty Wilson. 19th Century Medicine in
       Glass. Amador City, Cal: 19th Century Hobby and
       Publishing, 1971. 147pp, ill

4793   _____, and _____. Spirits Bottles of the Old West.
       Santa Rosa, Cal: 1968. 180pp, ill, bib

4794   _____, and _____. Western Bitters. Santa Rosa, Cal:
       B & B Enterprises, 1969. 95pp, ill, bib

4795   Wood, Mabel C. Chemung County, New York: Bottles, Bot-
       tlers, and Their Stories; an interesting study and history
       of the area. Elmira Heights, NY: Golos Publishers,
       1973. 112pp, ill

4796   Yount, John T. Bottle Collector's Handbook and Pricing Guide.
       San Angelo, Tx: Action Printing, 1967; rev. ed. San
       Angelo, Tx: Educator Books, 1970. 89pp, ill; 145pp, ill

4797   Zimmerman, Mary I. Sun-colored Glass, Its Lure and Lore;
       the facts and the hobby of old purple glass. Amarillo, Tx:
       1964. 35pp, ill

PAPERWEIGHTS

4798   Bedford, John. Paperweights. London: Cassell; New York:
       Walker, 1968. 64pp, 68 ill, 4 pls

4799   *Bergstrom, Evangeline H. Old Glass Paperweights. Their

art, construction, and distinguishing features.   Chicago:
Lakeside Pr, 1940; London: Faber, 1947; New York:
1963.   132pp, 108 (20 color) pls   (French, English,
American)

4800 *Cloak, Evelyn Campbell.   Glass Paperweights of the Bergstrom Art Center; the complete collection of glass paperweights and related items.   Introd. by Helen McKearin.
London: Studio Vista; New York: Crown, 1969.   196pp,
color ill of 700 pieces, bib

4801 *Elville, E. M.   Paperweights and Other Glass Curiosities.
London: Country Life, 1954; new ed. London: Spring
Books, 1967.   116pp, ill, 16 pls, bib   (Chapters also on
lamps, candlesticks, mirrors, etc.)

4802 *Hollister, Paul M., Jr.   The Encyclopedia of Glass Paperweights.   New York: C. N. Potter, dist. by Crown, 1969.
312pp, 250 (140 color) ill, bib

4803 *_____.   Glass Paperweights of the New York Historical
Society.   New York: C. N. Potter, 1974.   230 (120 color)
ill of 549 pieces   (Catalogue raisonne)

4804 _____.   Glass Paperweights at Old Sturbridge Village; the
J. Cheney Wells Collection.   Sturbridge, Mass: 1969.
52pp, chiefly ill

4805 Jokelson, Paul.   Antique French Paperweights.   Scarsdale?,
NY: Author, 1955.   254pp, 360 ill, 8 color pls   (Bac-
carat, Clichy, Saint-Louis, etc.)

4806 _____.   100 of the Most Important Paperweights.   London:
John Wallace Printing, n.d.; Scarsdale, NY: 1966?   235pp,
100 color pls   NN

4807 _____.   Sulphides.   The Art of Cameo Incrustation.   New
York: Nelson, 1968.

4808 McCawley, Patricia Kathleen.   Antique Glass Paperweights
from France.   London: Spink, 1968.   92pp, ill   (1845-
1850)

4809 Mackay, James Alexander.   Glass Paperweights.   London:
Ward Lock; New York: Viking, 1973.   112pp, ill, bib

4810 Manheim, Frank J.   A Garland of Weights: some notes on
collecting antique French glass paperweights for those who
don't.   New York: 1967; London; Sydney: Bodley Head,
1968.   188pp, 43 color ill   (1845-1860)

4811 Melvin, Jean Sutherland.   American Glass Paperweights and
Their Makers; a story of glass-paperweight craftsmen of

the United States, their processes, and their products.
New York: T. Nelson, 1967; rev. enl. ed. Camden, NJ:
T. Nelson, 1970. 192pp, ill, 12 pls; 287pp, ill, bib,
gloss

4812 Paperweight Collectors' Association. Bulletin. Annual, irregular. Scarsdale, NY: 1954- .

4813 Selman, Laurence H. Catalog and Price Guide of Collectors'
Paperweights. Periodic catalog from dealer. Santa Cruz,
Cal: Author, 19- . 1975: 46pp, ill, color pls

4814 _____, and Linda Pope-Selman. Paperweights for Collectors. Santa Cruz, Cal: Paperweight Pr, 1975. 445
(225 color) ill (Antique and contemporary)

4815 Smith, Francis Edgar. American Glass Paperweights, giving
the types, origin, design, colors, names and dates, processes, methods, cuttings, catchwords, and other information now made available for dealers and collectors. Wollaston, Mass: Antique Pr, 1939. 187pp, ill, 30 pls

SILVER AND GOLD

GENERAL WORKS

4816 All That Glisters; 30 centuries of golden deception. Exhibi-
      tion. New York: Cooper Union Museum, 1950. 24pp,
      pls

4817 The Art of the Goldsmith and the Jeweler; a loan exhibition
      for the Benefit of the Young Women's Christian Association
      of the City of New York, November 1968. New York: A
      La Vieille Russie, 1968. 139pp, ill

4818 Bailey and Company, Gold and Silversmiths, Philadelphia.
      History of Silver, ancient and modern. Philadelphia:
      Rawley & Chew, printers, 1871. 47pp, ill PPL

4819 Blakemore, Kenneth. The Book of Gold. London: November
      Books; New York: Stein and Day, 1971. 224pp, ill, pls,
      bib (Gold products to 1970)

4820 Brunner, Herbert. Old Table Silver; a handbook for collectors
      and amateurs. Tr. from German (1964) by Janet Seligman.
      London: Faber; New York: Taplinger, 1967. 223pp, ill,
      2 color pls, bib (ca. 1450-1840)

4821 Buck, John Henry. Historical Sketch of Makers' Marks. New
      York?: Gorham?, 1903. DLC

4822 _____ . Old Plate, Ecclesiastical, Decorative and Domestic;
      its makers and marks. New York: Gorham Mfg. Co,
      1888; new & enl. ed. as Old Plate; its Makers and marks.
      New York: 1903. 268pp, 82 ill, marks; 327pp, many ill,
      bib, marks DLC, NN, PPL

4823 _____ . A Short Historical Sketch on Silver. New York:
      Author, 1895; published for benefit of the Art Loan Exhi-
      bition, April 1895. New York: Author, 1895. 21pp, 1
      pl; 28pp, ill NN, DLC

4824 Buhler, Kathryn C., and John C. Austin. The Campbell Mu-
         seum Collection. Camden, NJ: Campbell Museum, 1969.
         95pp, ill (some color), bib (Tureens. Silver, by Buhler;
         ceramic, by Austin)

4825 Came, Richard. Silver. London: Weidenfeld & Nicolson;
         New York: Putnam, 1961; new ed. London: Octopus,
         1972. 128pp, ill; 96pp, ill (1500-1800)

4826 Catalogue of Silver Presented to the Pennsylvania Museum by
         Samuel Rea. Philadelphia: the Museum, 1926. 19pp, ill

4827 Catalogue of the Exhibition of Goldsmiths' Art. With chapters
         on the history of the art by Edward Quaile. Liverpool:
         Liverpool Art Club, 1874. 54pp

4828 Chase, Sara Hannum. Silver: A First Book. New York:
         F. Watts, 1969; London: F. Watts, 1971. 87pp, ill
         (Juvenile literature)

4829 Cohen, Hal L. Official Guide to Silver and Silverplate.
         Florence, Alabama: House of Collectibles, 1974. 264pp,
         ill, marks (1840-1900)

4830 Culme, John, and John G. Strang. Antique Silver and Silver
         Collecting. Feltham; New York: Hamlyn, 1973. 96pp,
         ill, bib (1660-1971)

4831 Davis, Fredna Harris, and Kenneth K. Deibel. Silver Plated
         Flatware Patterns. Dallas: Bluebonnet Pr, 1973. 428pp,
         ill, bib (19th and 20th centuries)

4832 Dawson, Nelson. Goldsmiths' and Silversmiths' Work. Lon-
         don: Methuen; New York: Putnam, 1907. 266pp, ill,
         52 pls NN, DLC

4833 Delieb, Eric. Investing in Antique Silver. London: Barrie
         & Rockliff, 1967; as Investing in Silver. New York:
         Potter, 1967; London: Transworld, 1970. 152pp, ill, bib

4834 Dent, Herbert Crowley. Pique: a beautiful minor art. In-
         trod. by G. Reginald Grundy. London: Connoisseur, 1923.
         25pp, 36 pls (Wire inlay, gold and silver) NN, DLC

4835 A Descriptive Catalogue of Various Pieces of Silver Plate
         Forming the Collection of the New York Farmers. New
         York: priv. printed, 1932. 51pp, pls NN

4836 Douglas, Jane. Collectible Silver. London: Longacre, 196-?
         ill

4837 Fairholt, Frederick William. An Illustrated Descriptive

Catalogue of the Collection of Antique Silver Plate Formed by Lord Londesborough. London: 1860. ill

4838 Fletcher, Lucinda. Silver. London: Orbis, 1973. 64pp, chiefly ill, bib (ca.1400-1972)

4839 Foster, John Ebenezer, and T. D. Atkinson. An Illustrated Catalogue of the Loan Collection of Plate Exhibited in the Fitzwilliam Museum, May 1895. Cambridge: D. Bell & Macmilland & Bowes, for the Cambridge Antiquarian Society, 1896. 132pp, ill, 16 pls

4840 Grimwade, Arthur Girling, ed. Faber Monographs on Silver. London: Faber, 1959- .

4841 Harris, Ian. The Price Guide to Antique Silver. Woodbridge, Suffolk: Baron Publishing, Antique Collectors' Club, 1969; Price Guide Supplement, 1973. 532pp, 600 ill

4842 _____. The Price Guide to Victorian Silver. Woodbridge: Baron, 1971; Price Supplement. 1973. 280pp, ill

4843 *Hayden, Arthur. Chats on Old Silver. London: Fisher Unwin, 1915; London: E. Benn, 1928; 1949; 3rd ed. rev. & enl. ed. by Cyril G. E. Bunt. With new chapter on American Silver by Jessie McNab Dennis. New York: Dover; London: Constable, 1969. 424pp, ill, 99 pls, marks; 306pp, ill, marks; 371pp, ill, marks

4844 Henderson, James. Silver Collecting for Amateurs. London: F. Muller, 1965; London: Muller; New York: Barnes & Noble, 1968. 144pp, ill, 12 pls

4845 Holbrook, John Swift. The Art of the Silversmith and Its Development. New York: priv. printed, for Gorham Mfg. Co. 1918. 24pp, ill NN

4846 _____. Silver for the Dining Room. Selected periods. Cambridge, Mass: U. Pr, for Gorham Silver, 1912. 119pp, many ill, pls (Florentine, Louis 14, 15 and 16, Jacobean, early Georgian, mid and late Georgian, colonial, and martele periods; tureens, knives, forks, candelabra, coffee sets, etc.) PPL

4847 Holland, Margaret. Silver: An Illustrated Guide to Collecting Silver. London: Octopus, 1973. 144pp, ill

4848 Honour, Hugh. Goldsmiths and Silversmiths. London: Weidenfeld & Nicolson; New York: Putnam, 1971. 320pp, ill, color pls, bib (Biographies, 850-1945)

4849 How, George Evelyn Paget. Notes on Antique Silver, numbers

one to six inclusive; and a reprint of certain other published articles. Edinburgh: How, 1951. v.p., ill CtY

4850 Hughes, George Bernard. Modern Silver Throughout the
      World, 1880-1967. London: Studio Vista; New York:
      Crown, 1967. 256pp, 468 ill, 12 color pls, bib

4851 _____ . Small Antique Silverware. London: Batsford;
      New York: Macmillan, 1957. 224pp, ill (Vinaigrettes,
      mugs, fish slices, egg frames, buttons, buckles, candle-
      sticks, nutmeg graters, wine labels, toys, etc.)

4852 An Introduction to Silver; catalogue of an exhibition on view
      October 1953 to May 1954. Newark: Newark Museum
      Association, 1953. 59pp, ill

4853 Jones, Edward Alfred, 1872-1943. Catalogue of the Collec-
      tion of Old Plate of L. de Rothschild. London: Bemrose,
      1907. 41pp

4854 _____ . Catalogue of the Collection of Old Plate of William
      Farrer. London: St. Catherine Pr, 1924. 191pp, 93
      pls

4855 _____ . A Catalogue of the Objects in Gold and Silver and
      the Limoges Enamels in the Collection of the Baroness
      James de Rothschild. London: Constable, 1912. 200pp,
      101 pls

4856 _____ . Illustrated Catalogue of the Collection of Old Plate
      of J. Pierpont Morgan. London: priv. printed, Bemrose,
      1908. 108 leaves, 97 pls NN

4857 Lambert, George. A Paper on the Gold and Silversmiths'
      Art, in the main translated from ancient Greek, Roman,
      Flemish and French writers. Read before ... Society
      for the Encouragement of the Fine Arts. London: 1892.
      55pp BM

4858 Lowes, Emily Leigh. Chats on Old Silver. London:
      Fisher Unwin, 1908; New York: F. A. Stokes, 1909.
      320pp, ill, 54 pls, color frontis, bib NN

4859 Luddington, John. Antique Silver: a guide for would-be
      connoisseurs. London: Pelham, 1971. 126pp, ill, 16
      pls

4860 Luhrmann, Winifred Bruce. The First Book of Gold. New
      York: F. Watts, 1968; London: F. Watts, 1971. 66pp,
      ill (Juvenile literature)

4861 O'Donnell, Erica. Gold, Silver and Precious Stones. London:

Ginn, 1959; 1970. 32pp, ill (Juvenile literature. To
1600)

4862 Old Silver Dining Accessories. Williamstown, Mass: Sterling & Francine Clark Art Institute, 1965. 13pp, ill,
28 pls

4863 Oman, Charles Chichele. Medieval Silver Nefs. V & A.
London: HMSO, 1963. 30pp, ill, 24 pls

4864 Pollen, John Hungerford. Ancient and Modern Gold and Silver
Smiths' Work (in the South Kensington Museum). London:
Eyre & Spottiswoode, 1878. 415pp, ill BM

4865 _____. Gold and Silver Smiths' Work. New York: Scribner, 1879. 160pp, ill

4866 Read, Sir Charles Hercules, and Alec Bain Tonnochy. Catalogue of the Silver Plate, Mediaeval and Later, Bequested
to the British Museum by Sir Augustus Wollaston Franks,
with selected examples from other sources. London:
British Museum, 1928. 58pp, 62 pls, bib (Drinking vessels) BM, DLC

4867 Ricketts, Howard. Antique Gold and Enamelware in Color.
Garden City, NY: Doubleday, 1971; as Objects of Vertu.
London: Barrie & Jenkins, 1971. 124pp, chiefly color
ill, bib (Battersea, Bilston and Birmingham enamels;
French enamels, gold, tortoiseshell and horn, Faberge,
Dinglinger)

4868 Rowe, Robert. Silver in the City Museum and Art Gallery.
Birmingham, Eng: Museum and Art Gallery, 1954. 20pp,
ill

4869 Silver. Bimonthly. Portland, Ore: the Magazine Silver,
1968- . ill

4870 Silver Bulletin. Monthly. London: Art & Antiques Weekly,
1969- . ill

4871 Silver of the 17th, 18th and 19th Centuries: Exhibition, May
1952, Lawrence Hall, Williams College. Williamstown,
Mass: Sterling & Francine Clark Art Institute, 1952.
12pp, ill

4872 Smith, Robert Henry Soden. Examples of Art Workmanship
of Various Ages and Countries. Corporation and College
Plate. London: Arundel Society, under sanction of
Science and Art Department, South Kensington Museum,
1869. 20 pls (Probably mostly English)

4873 _____. List of Works on Goldsmiths' Work in the National

Art Library, South Kensington. South Kensington: Science
and Art Department of Committee of Council on Education,
1882; 2nd ed. as A List of Books and Pamphlets Illustrating Gold and Silversmiths' Work and Jewellery....
London: 1887. 62pp; 91pp BM

4874 Snell, Doris Jean. 100 Silver Collectibles. Des Moines:
Wallace-Homestead, 1973. 7pp, ill, 53 black/white pls

4875 _____. Silverplated Flatware. Des Moines: Wallace-
Homestead, 1971 56pp, ill

4876 Solis, Virgil, 1514-1562. Designs for Drinking Cups, Vases,
Ewers and Ornaments for Use of Gold and Silversmiths.
London: J. Rimell, 1862. ill NNC-Ave, SKM

4877 Steward, W. Augustus. Gold, Silversmithing and Horology,
at the Paris Exhibition, 1900. London: Heywood, 1900.
64pp, ill, color pl

4878 _____. Goldsmiths' and Silversmiths' Work: Past and
Present. Cantor Lecture. London: 1933. 45pp

4879 Studnitz, Arthur von. Gold: legal regulations for the standard of gold and silver wares in different countries. Tr.
from German. London: Chatto & Windus, 1877. 139pp
BM

4880 Sutherland, Carol Humphrey Vivian. Gold: Its Beauty, Power,
and Allure. London: Thames & Hudson, 1959; 2nd ed.
1960; 3rd ed. rev. & enl. 1969. 188pp, ill, 84 (15 color)
pls, bib; 196pp, ill, 47 pls, bib

4881 *Taylor, Gerald. Art in Silver and Gold. London: Studio
Vista; New York: Dutton, 1964. 160pp, ill

4882 Watts, William Walter. Works of Art in Silver and Other
Metals Belonging to Viscount and Viscountess (Arthur H.)
Lee of Fareham. London: priv. printed, 1936. ill BM

4883 Wenham, Edward. Old Silver for Modern Settings. London:
G. Bell, 1950; New York: Knopf, 1951; 1960; London:
Spring, 1964. 199pp, ill, 16 pls, bib (18th century)

4884 Wheatley, Henry Benjamin. Handbook of Decorative Art in
Gold, Silver, Enamel on Metal, Porcelain, and Earthenware. London: Low, 1884. 149pp, ill

4885 _____, and Philip H. Delamotte, 1821-1889. Art Work
in Gold and Silver; Medieval. London: Sampson Low;
New York: Scribner & Welford, 1882. 64pp, ill, color
frontis

4886 _____ , and _____ . Art Work in Gold and Silver; Modern. New York: Scribners; London: Sampson Low,
Marston, Searle & Rivington, 1882. 124pp, ill, color
frontis

4887 White, Benjamin. Gold: its place in the economy of mankind. London: Pitman, 1920. 130pp, ill, bib

4888 _____ . Silver: its history and romance. London; New
York: Hodder & Stoughton, 1917; London: Waterlow,
1920. 328pp, pls

4889 _____ . Silver: its intimate association with the daily life
of man. London; New York: Pitman, 1920. 144pp, ill,
bib

4890 White, Margaret E. An Introduction to Silver; catalogue of
an exhibition on view, October 1953-May 1954. Newark,
NJ: Museum Association, 1953. 59pp, pls

4891 Wigley, Thomas B. The Art of the Goldsmith and Jeweller:
a treatise on the manipulation of gold in the various processes of goldsmiths' work, and the manufacture of
personal ornaments, etc. London: 1898; 2nd ed. rev.
& enl. London: C. Griffin, 1911. 248pp, ill; 264pp, ill,
12 pls

4892 Williams, Guy Richard. Collecting Silver and Plate. London:
Corgi, 1971. 125pp, ill, bib

4893 Wills, Geoffrey. Silver for Pleasure and Investment. London: Gifford, 1969. 175pp, ill, 16 pls (1700-1800)

4894 *Wyler, Seymour B. The Book of Old Silver, English, American, foreign ... with all available hallmarks, including
Sheffield plate marks. New York: Crown, 1937; 1960;
24th printing. 1971. 447pp, ill, pls, bib (20,000 marks)

AMERICAN SILVER AND GOLD

4895 American Silver and Pressed Glass; a collection in the R. W.
Norton Art Gallery. Shreveport, La: the Gallery, 1967.
68pp, ill

4896 Andrus, Vincent D. Early American Silver, a picture book.
New York: Metropolitan Museum, 1955. 32pp, ill

4897 Avery, Clara Louise. American Silver of the 17th, and 18th
Centuries. A Study based on the Clearwater Collection.
Pref. by R. T. H. Halsey. New York: Metropolitan Museum, 1920. 216pp, ill, bib (Alphonso Trumpbour Clearwater) BM

4898 *_____. Early American Silver. New York; London: Century, 1930; reissue. New York: Russell & Russell, 1968.
378pp, ill, 63 pls, bib NN, DLC

4899 _____. An Exhibition of Early New York Silver. December 1931-January 1932. New York: Metropolitan Museum,
1931; reprint. New York: Arno, 1974. 25pp, 70pp of ill

4900 Barr, Lockwood Anderson. Checklist of Kentucky Silver and
Its Makers, 1790-1875. First published in Antiques, July
1945. New York: 1948. u. p.

4901 Beasley, Ellen. Samuel Williamson, Philadelphia Silversmith,
1794-1813. Thesis, 1964. 120pp, pls

4902 Beckman, E. D. Cincinnati Silversmiths, Jewelers, Watch
and Clock Makers. Fore. by Robert Alan Green. Harrison, NY: R. A. Green, 1975. 184pp, ill

4903 *Bigelow, Francis Hill. Historic Silver of the Colonies and Its
Makers. New York: Macmillan, 1917; 1925; 1931; reissued & rev. 1941; New York: Tudor, 1948. 476pp, 325
ill, bib, marks MH, BM, DLC

4904 Bohan, Peter J. American Gold, 1700-1800; a monograph
based on a loan exhibit, April-June 1963. Yale University
Art Gallery. New Haven: 1963. 52pp, ill, bib

4905 _____, and Philip Hammerslough. Early Connecticut Silver,
1700-1840. Middletown, Conn: Wesleyan U. Pr, 1970.
288pp, ill, bib

4906 Buck, John Henry. American Silver Work of 17th and 18th
Century Silversmiths. Exhibition. June-November 1906.
Boston: Museum of Fine Arts, 1906. 100pp, 29 pls

4907 _____. Loving Cups. New York: Gorham Manufacturing,
1898. 23pp, pls BM

4908 *Buhler, Kathryn C. American Silver. Cleveland: World,
1950. 64pp, ill, color pls, bib

4909 *_____. American Silver, 1655-1825, in the Museum of
Fine Arts, Boston. 2 vol. Boston: dist. by NY Graphic
Society, Greenwich, 1972. 708pp, ill, bib

4910 _____. French, English and American Silver; a loan exhibition in honor of Russell A. Plimpton, June-July 1956.
Minneapolis: Institute of Arts, 1956. 80pp, ill

4911 _____. Massachusetts Silver in the Frank L. and Louise
C. Harrington Collection. Worcester, Mass: Barre, 1965.
121pp, ill, 1 pl

4912 _____ . Masterpieces of Virginia Silver. Exhibited at Mu-
         seum of Fine Arts, January-February 1960. Richmond,
         Va: 1960. 99pp, ill

4913 _____ . Mount Vernon Silver. Mount Vernon, Va: Ladies'
         Association of the Union, 1957. 75pp, ill

4914 _____ . Paul Revere, Goldsmith, 1735-1818. Exhibition.
         Boston: Museum of Fine Arts, 1956. 42pp, pls

4915 * _____ , and Graham Hood. American Silver: Garvan and
         other collections in the Yale University Art Gallery.
         Vol. I. New England; Vol. II. Middle Colonies and South.
         2 vol. New Haven; London: Yale U. Pr, 1970. 344 and
         300pp, ill, bib (Francis Patrick Garvan)

4916 *Burton, E. Milby. South Carolina Silversmiths, 1690-1860.
         Charleston, S.C.: Charleston Museum, 1942; reprint.
         Rutland, Vt: Tuttle, 1968. 311pp, ill, pls, bib, marks
         BM, DLC

4917 Checklist of American Silversmith's Work, 1650-1850, in
         Museums in the New York Metropolitan area. (By stu-
         dents of the Metropolitan Museum and Columbia University.)
         New York: 1968. u.p., ill, bib NNC-Ave

4918 Christie, Ralph Aldreich. Silver Cups in Colonial Middletown.
         Middletown, Conn: Middlesex County Historical Society,
         1937. 26pp, 2 pls DLC

4919 *Clarke, Herman Frederick. John Coney, Silversmith, 1655-
         1722. Introd. by Hollis French. Boston: 1932. 92pp,
         31 pls (Massachusetts silversmith) BM

4920 * _____ . John Hull, a Builder of the Bay Colony. Portland,
         Me: Southworth-Anthoensen Pr, 1940. 221pp, ill, 15 pls,
         bib (Massachusetts silversmith, biography) DLC

4921 * _____ , and Henry Wilder Foote. Jeremiah Dummer:
         Colonial Craftsman and Merchant, 1645-1718. Fore. by
         E. Alfred Jones. Boston: Houghton Mifflin, 1935; re-
         print. 1970. 208pp, ill, 23 pls

4922 *Clayton, Michael. The Collectors' Dictionary of the Silver
         and Gold of Great Britain and North America. Fore. by
         A. G. Grimwade. Feltham; New York: Country Life;
         New York: World, 1971. 351pp, ill, bib (1150-1800
         A.D.)

4923 Collection of Early American Silver. New York: Tiffany
         Studios, 1920. 36pp

4924 *Cooper, Wendy Ann. Paul Revere's Boston, 1735-1818.

Introd. by Walter Muir Whitehill. Exhibition. April 1975.
Boston: Museum of Fine Arts, 1975. text, ill (some
color) (Paintings plus the Museum's collection of Boston
silver)

4925 *Currier, Ernest M., 1867-1936. Marks of Early American
Silversmiths, with notes on silver, spoon types, and list
of New York City silversmiths, 1815-1841. Ed. with
introd. by Kathryn C. Buhler. Portland, Me: South-
worth-Antheonsen; London: B. Quaritch, 1938; reprint
with publisher's foreword by Robert Alan Green. Harrison, NY: R. A. Green, 1970; reprint of 1938 ed. with
most of preliminary matter omitted and a new bibliography.
Watkins Glen, NY: American Life Foundation, 1970.
179pp, ill, 2 pls; ...; 177pp, ill, bib

4926 *Curtis, George Munson. Early Silver of Connecticut and Its
Makers. Meriden, Conn: International Silver Co, 1913.
115pp, ill, pls, marks MiU, DLC

4927 _____. Early Silversmiths of Connecticut. Meriden, Conn:
1911. 18pp DLC

4928 Cutten, George Barton. Silversmiths of Central New York.
Paper read at N.Y. State Historical Society Meeting, September 10. Hamilton?, NY: 1937. 5 leaves NN

4929 _____. Silversmiths of Georgia, together with watchmakers
and jewelers, 1733-1850. Savannah, Ga: Pigeonhole Pr,
1958. 154pp, pls

4930 _____. Silversmiths of North Carolina, 1696-1850. Raleigh, NC: State Department of Archives, 1948; exp. &
rev. by Mary Reynolds Peacock. Raleigh, NC: Historical Publications Section, State Department of Cultural
Resources, 1973. 93pp, ill, bib; 140pp, ill, bib

4931 _____. Silversmiths of Northampton, Massachusetts, and
Vicinity, Down to 1850. Northampton: 1942? 2 leaves
NN

4932 * _____. The Silversmiths of Virginia, together with watchmakers and jewelers, from 1694-1850. Richmond, Va:
Dietz Pr, 1952; reprint. Harrison, NY: Robert Alan
Green, 197-? 259pp, ill, bib, marks (More than 450
names)

4933 _____. The Silversmiths, watchmakers and jewelers of
the state of New York, outside of New York City. Hamilton, NY: priv. printed, 1939. 47pp (To 1850) NN, DLC

4934 _____. The Ten Eyck Silversmiths. Reprint from

Antiques.   Boston?:   1944?   10 leaves, ill   (Ten Eyck
family of silversmiths)   NN

4935 _____ .   Ten Silversmith Families of New York State.   Reprint from New York History.   New York: 1946?   13pp

4936 _____ , and Minnie Warren Cutten.   The Silversmiths of
Utica, with Illustrations of Their Silver and Their Marks.
Hamilton, NY: 1936.   67pp, ill, pls   (1799-1850)

4937 _____ , and Amy Pearce Ver Nooy.   The Silversmiths of
Poughkeepsie, N.Y.   Poughkeepsie: 1945?   23pp, ill

4938 Early Canadian Silver.   Exhibition.   Museum of Science, Halifax, and National Museum of Man, Ottawa.   Halifax, Nova
Scotia: 1971.   25pp, ill

4939 Early New England Silver, lent from the Mark Bortman Collection.   Exhibition February-March 1958.   Northampton,
Mass: Smith College Museum of Art, 1958.   23pp, ill

4940 Elias Pelletreau (1726-1810), Long Island Silversmith, and
His Sources of Design.   Exhibition.   Brooklyn, NY: Institute of Arts and Sciences Museum, 1959.   u.p., ill

4941 Elwell, Newton W., comp.   Colonial Silverware of the 17th
and 18th Centuries, comprising solid sets, small wares,
candelabras, communion services, etc.   Boston: G. H.
Polley, 1899.   2pp, 40 pls in portfolio   DLC, NN

4942-3[No entries.]

4944 Ensko, Robert.   Makers of Early American Silver.   New
York: Ensko, 1915.   46pp   DLC

4945 _____ .   17th and 18th Century American Silver.   New
York: Author, 1934.   25pp, ill, bib   MiD

4946 *Ensko, Stephen Guernsey Cook.   American Silversmiths and
Their Marks.   3 vol.   New York: Robert Ensko, Inc,
1927-1948; 2nd ed. Vol. II (1937) reprinted.   Southampton,
NY: Cracker Barrel Pr, 1969?   ill, bib; 82pp, ill, bib
ViU, DLC

4946a Exhibition of Silversmithing by John Coney, 1655-1722.   Boston: Museum of Fine Arts, 1932.   4 leaves

4946b Exhibition of Works in Silver and Gold by Myer Myers.   A
checklist of objects exhibited at the Brooklyn Museum,
February-March 1954.   Brooklyn: 1954.   10 mimeo-
graphed sheets

4947 Fales, Martha Gandy.   American Silver in the Henry Francis

Du Pont Winterthur Museum. Winterthur, Del: 1958.
142 pls

4948 *   . Early American Silver for the Cautious Collector.
London; New York: Funk & Wagnals, 1970; rev. enl. ed.
as Early American Silver. New York: Dutton, 1973.
329pp, ill, bib; 336pp, ill, bib, gloss

4949   . Joseph Richardson and Family, Philadelphia Silversmiths. Middletown, Conn: Wesleyan U. Pr, for Historical Society of Pa, 1974. 340pp, ill, 183 pls, bib
(Francis Richardson, 1681 1729; Francis, Jr., 1705-1782;
Joseph, 1711-1784; Joseph, Jr., 1752-1831; Nathaniel,
1754-1827)

4950   . Philadelphia Silver. Exhibition. Reprint from
Art Quarterly, Spring 1957. Detroit: Institute of Arts,
1957. 3pp (pp 45-47), pls

4951 Flynt, Henry N., and Martha Gandy Fales. The Heritage
Foundation Collection of Silver; with biographical sketches
of New England silversmiths, 1625-1825. Old Deerfield,
Mass: Heritage Foundation, 1968. 391pp, ill, bib, marks

4952 Fredyma, James P. A Directory of Maine Silversmiths and
Watch and Clock Makers. Hanover, NH: Marie-Louise
Antiques, 1972. 26pp, bib

4953 Fredyma, John J. A Directory of Connecticut Silversmiths
and Watch and Clock Makers. Hanover, NH: P.J. &
M.L. Fredyma, 1973. 600pp, bib

4954 Fredyma, Paul J., and Marie-Louise Fredyma. A Directory
of Boston Silversmiths and Watch and Clock Makers. Hanover, NH: M.-L. Fredyma, 1975. 46pp, bib

4955   , and   . A Directory of Massachusetts Silversmiths and Their Marks. White River Junction, Vt: Right
Printing Co, 1972. 27pp, bib

4956   , and   . A Directory of New Hampshire
Silversmiths and Their Marks. Orford, NH: Equity Pub.
Corp, 1971. 17pp, bib

4957   , and   . A Directory of Rhode Island Silversmiths and Their Marks. Hanover, NH: 1972. 21pp, bib

4958   , and   . A Directory of Vermont Silversmiths
and Watch and Clock Makers. Hanover, NH: M.-L.
Fredyma, 1975. 58pp, bib

4959 Freeman, Graydon La Verne (Larry). Early American Plated
Silver. Watkins Glen, NY: Century, 1973. 160pp, ill

4960   . Victorian Silver; plated and sterling; hollow and
flatware. Watkins Glen, NY: Century, 1967. 400pp, ill,
pls, bib (1000 patterns, 1830-1930)

4961   , and Jane Beaumont. Early American Plated Silver.
Watkins Glen, NY: Century, 1947; 1949; edited reprint.
1973. 239pp, ill; ...; 200pp, ill

4962 *French, Hollis. Jacob Hurd and His Sons, Nathaniel and
Benjamin, silversmiths of Boston, 1702-1781. Fore. by
Kathryn Buhler. Cambridge, Mass: Riverside Pr, for
Walpole Society, 1939; 1941; New York: 1947. 147pp,
28 pls, bib; 161pp, ill, bib (Jacob Hurd, 1703-1758;
Nathaniel, 1730-1777; Benjamin, 1739-1781)

4963   . A List of Early American Silversmiths and Their
Marks. Boston: Walpole Society, 1917; rev. & ed. by
Rita Benson, as The Encyclopedia of Early American
Silversmiths.... Harrisburg, Pa: Benson Gallery Pr,
1966. 164pp, ill, gloss

4964   . A Silver Collectors' Glossary and a List of Early
American Silversmiths and Their Marks. Boston: Walpole Society, 1917; reprint. New York: Da Capo Pr, 1967.
164pp, ill

4965 From Colony to Nation; an exhibition of American painting,
silver and architecture from 1650 to the War of 1812,
April-June 1949. Chicago: Art Institute, 1949. 140pp,
ill NNC-Ave

4966 Gerstell, Vivian S. Silversmiths of Lancaster, Pennsylvania,
1730-1850. Lancaster, Pa: County Historical Society,
1972. 145pp, ill, bib

4967 Gillingham, Harrold Edgar, 1864-1954. Cesar Ghiselin,
Philadelphia's First Gold and Silversmith, 1693-1733.
Reprint from the Pennsylvania Magazine of History and
Biography. Philadelphia: 1933. 15pp (pp. 244-259), ill,
pls DLC

4968   . Indian Ornaments Made by Philadelphia Silversmiths. New York: Museum of American Indian, Heye
Foundation, 1936. 26pp, ill, pl DLC, MB

4969 Goldsborough, Jennifer F. An Exhibition of New London
Silver, 1700-1835. October 1969. New London, Conn:
Lyman Allyn Museum, 1969. 40pp, pls

4970 Gourley, Hugh J., III. The New England Silversmith. An
exhibition of New England silver from mid-17th century
to the present selected from New England collections.

October-November 1965.   Providence, RI: School of Design, 1965.   40pp, pls

4971   Graham, James, Jr., 1877- , comp.   Early American Silver
Marks.   New York: 1936.   81pp, ill, marks   DeWint, MB

4972   Greene, Robert Alan, ed.   Maryland Silversmiths, 1715-1830.
Harrison, NY: Author, 197-?   ill   (Includes clockmakers)

4973   _____.   Ohio Silversmiths, 1787-1900.   Harrison, NY:
Author, 1975.   ill

4974   Halsey, Richard Townley Haines.   American Silver ... The
work of 17th and 18th century silversmiths.   Exhibition.
June-November 1906.   Boston: Museum of Fine Arts,
1906.   100pp, 29 pls

4975   _____.   Catalogue of an Exhibition of Silver Used in New
York, New Jersey and the South, with a note on early
New York silversmiths.   November-December 1911,
Metropolitan Museum.   New York: Gilliss Pr, 1911; re-
print.   New York: Arno, 1974.   97pp, ill, pls

4976   *Hammerslough, Philip H., and Rita F. Feigenbaum.   American Silver Collected by Philip H. Hammerslough.   Illustrated and indexed catalog of collection in the Wadsworth
Atheneum.   3 vol.   Hartford, Conn: priv. printed, 1958,
1960, 1965; supplements.   1965; 1967; 1970; 4th vol. 1974.
well ill, pls

4977   Harrington, Jessie.   Silversmiths of Delaware, 1700-1850,
and old Dutch silver in Delaware.   Wilmington: National
Society of Colonial Dames of America, Delaware, 1939.
132pp, pls, bib   PP, DLC

4978   Hiatt, Noble W., and Lucy F. Hiatt.   The Silversmiths of
Kentucky; together with some watchmakers and jewelers,
1785-1850.   Introd. by J. Winston Coleman, Jr.   Louisville, Ky: Standard Printing, 1954.   135pp, ill, pls, bib

4979   Hill, Harry Wilbur.   Maryland's Colonial Charm Portrayed
in Silver.   Baltimore: priv. printed by Waverly Pr, 1938.
269pp, pls, bib   (The silver service presented by citizens
of Maryland to the Cruiser Maryland in 1906, and trans-
ferred in 1921 to the Battleship Maryland)   DeWint, DLC

4980   *Hood, Graham.   American Silver.   A history of style, 1650-
1900.   New York: Praeger, 1970; London: Pall Mall,
1971; New York: 1972.   256pp, 286 ill, bib

4981   *Jones, Edward Alfred.   Old Silver of Europe and America
from Early Times to the 19th Century.   London: Batsford;
Philadelphia: Lippincott, 1928.   376pp, ill, 96 pls   NN

4982 Kauffman, Henry J. The Colonial Silversmith; his techniques and his products. Camden, NJ: Nelson, 1969. 176pp, ill, bib

4983 Knittle, Rhea Mansfield. Early Ohio Silversmiths and Pewterers, 1787-1847. Cleveland: Calvert Hatch, printers, 1943. 63pp, ill, bib

4984 Kovel, Ralph M., and Terry H. Kovel. A Directory of American Silver, Pewter, and Silver Plate. New York: Crown, 1961; New York: 1972. 352pp, ill, bib; 344pp, ill, bib (Before 1900)

4985 Langdon, John Emerson. Canadian Silversmiths and Their Marks, 1667-1867. Lunenburg, Vt: Stinehour Pr, 1960; enl. ed. as Canadian Silversmiths, 1700-1900. Toronto, Can: Stinehour, 1966. 190pp, ill; 249pp, ill, bib

4986 _____. Guide to Marks on Early Canadian Silver, 18th and 19th centuries. Toronto: Ryerson Pr, 1968. 104pp, ill

4987 Larus, Jane Bortman. Myer Myers, Silversmith, 1723-1795. Catalogue of the Bortman, Larus Collection of Myer Myers Colonial Silver. Klutznick Exhibit Hall, B'nai B'rith Building. Washington, D.C.: 1964. 12pp, ill

4988 McClinton, Katharine Morrison. Collecting American 19th Century Silver. New York: Scribner, 1968. 280pp, hundreds of ill, bib

4989 Mackay, Donald Cameron. Silvermiths and Related Craftsmen of the Atlantic Provinces. Halifax, Nova Scotia: Petheric Pr, 1973. ill

4990 McLanathan, Richard B. K., ed. Colonial Silversmiths, Masters and Apprentices. Introd. by Kathryn C. Buhler. Exhibition. Boston: Museum of Fine Arts, 1956. 98pp, ill

4991 Masterpieces of American Silver, the Virginia Museum of Fine Arts. January-February 1960. Richmond, Va: 1960. 99pp, ill

4992 Masterpieces of New England Silver, 1650-1800. Introd. by John Marshall Phillips. Exhibition. June-September 1939, Yale University Gallery of Fine Arts. Cambridge, Mass: Harvard U. Pr, 1939. 97pp, ill

4993 May, Earl Chapin. Century of Silver, 1847-1947; Connecticut Yankees and a Noble Metal. New York: R. M. McBride, for International Silver Co, 1947. 388pp, ill, 40 pls, bib

4994   Miller, V. Isabelle. New York Silversmiths of the 17th
       Century. Exhibition, December 1962-February 1963.
       New York: Museum of the City of NY, 1962. u.p., ill

4995   _____. Silver by New York Makers, Late 17th Century
       to 1900. Pref. by Luke Vincent Lockwood. Exhibition.
       Museum of City of New York, December 1937-January
       1938. New York: 1937. 71pp, ill, pls

4996   Miller, William Davis. The Silversmiths of Little Rest
       (Rhode Island). Boston: D. B. Updike, Merrymount Pr,
       1928. 50pp, ill, pls (Samuel Casey, 1724-ca.1773; John
       Waite, 1742-1817; Joseph Perkins, 1749-1789; Nathaniel
       Helme, 1761-1789; Gideon Casey, ca.1726-1786; William
       Waite, 1730-1826) MB

4997   Myer Myers, Goldsmith. Fore. by Stephen Ensko. Biography
       by Jeannette W. Rosenbaum. Philadelphia: 1954. 32 pls

4998   Natchez-made Silver of the 19th Century; an exhibition pre-
       sented by the Anglo-American Art Museum in cooperation
       with the Pilgrimage Garden Club of Natchez. January-
       March 1970. Baton Rouge, La: 1970. 48pp, ill

4999   New York State Silversmiths. Fore. by Kathryn C. Buhler.
       Eggertsville, NY: Darling Foundation of N.Y. State Early
       American Silversmiths and Silver, 1964. 228pp, ill, bib,
       marks

5000   Old English and Early American Silverwork; early silver in
       California collections. Los Angeles: Museum of Art,
       1962. 35pp, ill

5001   150 Years of American Craftsmanship in Silver from Samuel
       Kirk and Son. Exhibition, February-March 1967. Mem-
       phis, Tenn: Brooks Memorial Art Gallery, 1967. 20pp,
       pls (Baltimore silver)

5002   Outline of the Life and Works of Colonel Paul Revere; with a
       partial catalogue of silverware bearing his name. New-
       buryport, Mass: Towle Mfg. Co, 1901. 63pp, ill

5003   *Phillips, John Marshall. American Silver. New York: Chan-
       ticleer Pr; London: Max Parrish, 1949. 128pp, ill

5004   Piers, Harry, 1870-1940. Master Goldsmiths and Silversmiths
       of Nova Scotia and Their Marks. Comp. from unfinished
       manuscripts and notes with introduction and illustrations by
       Una B. Thomson and A. Matilda Strachan. Supple. by
       Donald C. Mackay. Halifax, Nova Scotia: Antiquarian
       Club, 1948. 161pp, ill

5005   *Pleasants, Jacob Hall, and Howard Sill. Maryland Silversmiths,

1715-1830. With illustrations of their silver and their marks, and with a facsimile of the design book of William Faris. Baltimore: Lord Baltimore Pr, 1930; reprint with foreword by Robert Alan Green. Harrison, NY: R. A. Green, 1972. 324pp, ill, 68 pls, marks (A definitive work)

5006 Prime, Mrs. Alfred Coxe. Three Centuries of Historic Silver. Philadelphia: Lippincott, 1938. many ill, marks

5007 Purtell, Joseph. The Tiffany Touch. New York: Random House, 1971. 309pp, ill

5008 *Rainwater, Dorothy T. American Silver Manufacturers, Their Marks, Trademarks and History. Hanover, Pa: Everybodys Pr, 1966; enl. & rev. ed. 1975. 240pp, ill, bib, 1500 trademarks from patent records, gloss (1842-1920. Spoons, napkin rings, flatware, trophies, etc.)

5009 _____, ed. Sterling Silver Holloware: tea, coffee services, pitchers and ewers, bookmarks, ash trays, candelabra, salts and peppers, desk sets and dressing sets, tea balls and bells, trays, flasks, match safes. Catalog reprints (Gorham Mfg. Co., 1888; Gorham Martele, 1900; Unger Brothers, 1904). Princeton, NJ: Pyne, 1973. 160pp, ill, bib

5010 _____, and H. Ivan Rainwater. American Silverplate. Nashville, Tenn: T. Nelson, 1968; Hanover, Pa: Everybodys Pr, 1972. 453pp, ill, bib; 480pp, ill, bib, gloss (Flatware and holloware. Includes lighting devices)

5011 Rice, Norman S. Albany Silver, 1652-1825. Exhibition, March-May 1964. Fore. by Laurence McKinney. Introd. by Kathryn C. Buhler. Albany, NY: Institute of History and Art, 1964. 81pp, ill

5012 *Rosenbaum, Jeanette W. Myer Myers, Goldsmith, 1723-1795. Fore. by Stephen Ensko; notes by Kathryn C. Buhler. Philadelphia: Jewish Publications Society of America, 1954. 141pp, ill, 30 pls, bib

5013 Samuel Kirk and Son: American Silver Craftsmen Since 1815. Traveling exhibit. Chicago: Historical Society, 1966. 31pp, pls

5014 Schild, Joan Lynn. Silversmiths of Rochester. Rochester, NY: Museum of Arts and Sciences, 1944.

5015 Schwartz, Marvin D. Collector's Guide to Antique American Silver: History, Style and Identification. Garden City, NY: Doubleday, 1975. ill

5016   Semon, Kurt M., ed. A Treasury of Old Silver. Drawn
       from issues of the American Collector. New York: R.
       M. McBride, 1947. 112pp, ill

5017   The Silver Thread Through Canadian History, "The Henry
       Birks Collection" of Canadian silver. Exhibition, La
       Maison Del Vecchio, Montreal. English and French text.
       Montreal: Canadian Industries Ltd, 1970. 20pp

5018   Smith, Sidney Adair. Mobile Silversmiths and Jewelers,
       1820-1867. Mobile, Ala: Historic Mobile Preservation
       Society, 1970. 15pp, ill

5019   Southern Furniture and Silver: the Federal period, 1788-
       1830. Exhibition. September-November 1968. Baton
       Rouge, La: Anglo-American Art Museum, Louisiana
       State U, 1968. 35pp, ill

5020   Southern Silver; an exhibition of silver made in the South prior
       to 1860. September-November 1968. Houston, Tex: Mu-
       seum of Fine Arts, 1968. 92pp, ill

5021   Spanish, French, and English Traditions in the Colonial silver
       of North America. Conference Report, 1968. Winterthur,
       Del: Henry Francis du Pont Winterthur Museum, 1969.
       109pp, ill

5022   Stow, Charles Messer. 17th and 18th Century American
       Silver. New York: R. Ensko, 1934. 30pp, ill, bib

5023   Stow, Millicent D. American Silver: Of the Colonies, in the
       New Nation, and Silver Today. New York: Barrow, 1950.
       170pp, ill, 83 pls, bib

5024   _____. Enjoy Your Museum; early American silver. Pasa-
       dena, Cal: Esto, 1936. ill

5025   *Thorn, C. Jordan. Handbook of American Silver and Pewter
       Marks. New York: Tudor, 1949. 289pp, ill

5026   Traquair, Ramsay. Old Silver of Quebec. Toronto: Art As-
       sociation of Canada, by Macmillan of Canada, 1940; re-
       issue, 1973. 169pp, 16pp of ill, bib

5027   Trudel, Jean. Silver in New France. Exhibition, 1974.
       Ottawa: National Gallery of Canada, 1974. 237pp, ill,
       bib, gloss (160 pieces)

5028   Turner, Noel D. American Silver Flatware, 1837-1910.
       South Brunswick, NJ: A. S. Barnes; London: Yoseloff,
       1972. 473pp, ill, bib, marks

5029   Unitt, Doris Joyce, and Peter Unitt. Canadian Silver, Silver

Plate and Related Glass. Peterborough, Ont: Clock
House, 1970. 256pp, hundreds of ill, bib

5030   Victorian Silverplated Holloware; tea services, caster sets,
       ice water pitchers, card receivers, napkin rings, knife
       rests, toilet sets, goblets, cups, trays and waiters,
       epergnes, butter dishes, pickle casters, salts, tureens,
       communion services. Catalog reprints (Rogers Brothers,
       1857; Meriden Britannia, 1867; Derby, 1883). Princeton,
       NJ: Pyne, 1972. 160pp, 800 ill

5031 *Wenham, Edward. Practical Book of American Silver. Phila-
       delphia: Lippincott, 1949. 275pp, ill, bib (To 1825)

5032   White, Margaret E., comp. European and American Silver
       in the Newark Museum Collection. Newark, NJ: 1953.
       33pp, ill, bib

5033 *Williams, Carl Mark. Silversmiths of New Jersey, 1700-
       1825, with some notice of clockmakers who were also
       silversmiths. Philadelphia: G. S. MacManus, 1949.
       164pp, ill, bib, marks (Silver utensils, clocks, etc.,
       arranged by county)

5034   Wise, William. Myer Myers: silversmith of old New York.
       New York: Jewish Publications, 1958. ill (Juvenile
       literature)

5035   Wroth, Lawrence Counselman, 1884- . Abel Buell of Con-
       necticut, Silversmith, Typefounder and Engraver. New
       Haven: Yale U. Pr, 1926; 2nd ed. rev. Middletown,
       Conn: Wesleyan U. Pr, 1958. 86pp, maps; 102pp, ill,
       bib (Abel Buell, 1742-1822)

5036 *Wyler, Seymour B. The Book of Old Silver, English, Ameri-
       can, Foreign ... with all available hallmarks, including
       Sheffield plate marks. New York: Crown, 1937; 1960;
       24th printing. 1971. 447pp, ill, pls, bib (20,000 marks)

AMERICAN AND CANADIAN CHURCH SILVER

5037   Berger, Florence Paull. The Early Plate in Connecticut
       Churches Prior to 1850, collected by the Connecticut So-
       ciety of the Colonial Dames of America. Exhibit, Morgan
       Memorial (Wadsworth Atheneum), May 1919. Hartford:
       1919. 12pp

5038   Buck, John Henry. The Early Church Plate of Salem, Massa-
       chusetts. Reprint from Essex Institute Historical Collec-
       tions. Salem: the Institute, 1907. 16pp

5039   Cruger, George A., ed. Church Silver of Colonial Virginia.

Exhibition, Virginia Museum, February-March 1970. Richmond, Va: 1970. 112pp, ill

5040 Curtis, George Munson. American Church Silver of the 17th and 18th Century, with a few pieces of domestic plate, exhibited at the Museum of Fine Arts, July-December 1911. Introd. "Early Silversmiths of Connecticut." Boston: 1911. 163pp, ill, 38 pls, gloss   NNC-Ave

5041 Elwell, Newton W., comp. Colonial Silverware of the 17th and 18th Centuries, comprising solid sets, small wares, candelabras, communion services, etc. Boston: G. H. Polley, 1899. 2pp, 40 pls in portfolio   NN, DLC

5042 Jones, Edward Alfred. Old Church Silver in Canada. Ottawa: Royal Society of Canada, 1918. 16pp (pp. 135-150)

5043 *   . The Old Silver of American Churches. Letchworth, Eng: Arden Pr, for Colonial Dames of America, 1913. 566pp, ill, 145 pls, marks   ViU, MdBP, DeWint, NNC-Ave

BRITISH ISLES SILVER AND GOLD

5044 Adam Silver. V & A Museum. London: HMSO, 1953. 4pp, ill, 28 pls

5045 Ancestral Plate. English silver 1660-1820. Exhibition arranged by the V & A Museum, London, for the Art Galleries and Museums Association, New Zealand. Auckland: Pelorus Pr, 1956. 29pp, ill

5046 Ash, Douglas. Dictionary of British Antique Silver. London: Pelham, 1972. 189pp, ill, bib (To 1837)

5047   . How to Identify English Silver Drinking Vessels, 600-1830. London: G. Bell, 1964. 159pp, ill, 24 pls, bib

5048 Ashbee, Charles Robert. Modern English Silverwork. London: Batsford, 1909. 34pp, ill, 100 pls (some color)

5049 Ashforth, Ellis, Wilson and Hawkesley Co., Sheffield, 1787-1811. "List of Pattern Book of Ashforth Ellis Wilson of Hawkesleys Plated Manufacture in Sheffield Upon a Scale of Six Inches to the Foot." Sheffield: 185? 29 pls DeWint

5050 Baggallay, A. Origin and History of Domestic Silver and Plate. Dulwich: priv. printed, 1910. 20pp

5051-2 [No entries.]

5053 Banister, Judith. Collecting Antique Silver. London: Ward
Lock, 1972. 128pp, chiefly ill (English, 1660-1880)

5054 _____. English Silver. London: Ward Lock, 1965; New
York: Hawthorn, 1966. 256pp, 140 ill, bib

5055 _____. English Silver. Originally published as Gli Argenti
Inglesi. Milan: 1966. London; New York: Hamlyn, 1969.
157pp, 71 color ill (1500-present)

5056 _____, ed. English Silver Hall-Marks: with lists of English, Scottish, and Irish hall-marks and makers' marks.
London; New York: Foulsham, 1970. 96pp, ill

5057 _____. An Introduction to Old English Silver. London:
Evans Brothers, 1964; as Old English Silver. New York:
Hawthorn, 1965. 287pp, ill, bib, marks (1500-1840)

5058 _____. Late Georgian and Regency Silver. Feltham:
Hamlyn, for Country Life, 1971. 63pp, ill (1775-1830
tableware)

5059 _____. Mid-Georgian Silver. Feltham: Hamlyn, for
Country Life, 1972. 64pp, ill (1727-1770 tableware)

5059a Barclay, George, engraver. Designs for Marking Silver
Plate. London: Author, 1860. BM

5059b _____. Monograms. London: G. Barclay, 1860-72.

5060 Bedford, John, and Derek Austin. Old Sheffield Plate. London: Cassell, 1966; New York: Walker, 1967. 63pp, ill

5061 Bennett, Douglas. Irish Georgian Silver. London: Cassell,
1972. 369pp, ill, bib (1700-1830)

5062 Bly, John. Discovering Hall Marks on English Silver. Tring:
Shire Publications, 1968. 56pp, ill

5063 Book of Engraved Designs for Articles in Sheffield Plate.
17-? 58 engraved pls, no text or title page PPULC

5064 Boutell, Charles. Gold Working. London: 1877. See also:
Bevan, G. P., British Manufacturing Industries, Vol. 11

5065 Bradbury, Frederick. British Assay Office Marks, 1544-
1928; old Sheffield plate makers' marks, 1743-1860.
Sheffield, Eng: Northend, 1928; 2nd ed. 1929; 3rd ed.
as British and Irish Silver Assay Office Marks 1544-
1932.... Sheffield: Northend; New York: Eilert Printing, 1932; 4th ed. British and Irish ... Marks 1544-
1936.... Sheffield: 1936; 5th ed. ... to 1939. Sheffield:

1939; ... 9th ed. ... to 1954.... Sheffield: 1955; 12th
ed. ... to 1968; with notes on gold markings, and marks
on foreign imported silver and gold plate; and old Sheffield.... Sheffield: 1968. 64pp, ill; 76pp, ill; 68pp;
ill; 84pp, ill, bib; 90pp, ill, bib; 93pp, ill, bib

5066 _____. Guide to Marks of Origin on British and Irish
Silver Plate. From mid-16th century to the year 1932.
Sheffield: Northend, 1932. 68pp PPULC

5067 * _____. History of Old Sheffield Plate: being an account
of the origin, growth, and decay of the industry and of the
antique silver and white or Britannia metal trade, with
chronological lists of makers' marks and numerous illustrations of specimens. London: Macmillan, 1912; Sheffield: Northend, 1968. 539pp, hundreds of ill, marks
NN, DLC, BM

5068 Bradbury, Thomas, and Sons, Ltd., Sheffield. Old Sheffield
Plate and An Old Sheffield Firm. Sheffield: 1924. 12pp,
ill DeWint

5069 Buckley, Francis. Old London Goldsmiths, 1666-1706, recorded in the newspapers. Uppermill: Moore & Edwards,
1926. 16pp

5070 _____. Sheffield Silver Platers, 1771-1805, recorded in
the London Gazette and directories. n.p.: Author, 1927.
15pp

5071 Buhler, Kathryn C. French, English and American Silver; a
loan exhibition in honor of Russell A. Plimpton, June-July
1956. Minneapolis: Institute of Arts, 1956. 80pp, ill

5072 Burgess, Frederick William. Silver: Pewter: Sheffield Plate.
New York: Dutton; London: Routledge, 1921; New York:
Tudor, 1937. 304pp, 85 ill, pls NN, DLC

5073 [No entry.]

5074 Bury, Shirley. Victorian Electroplate. London; New York:
Hamlyn, for Country Life, 1971. 63pp, ill, pl (1840-
1900)

5075 Caldicott, John William. The Values of Old English Silver
and Sheffield Plate, from the 15th to the 19th centuries.
Ed. by J. Starkie Gardner. (First edition of Values of
Antiques....) London: Bemrose, 1906. 293pp, ill, 87
pls, marks NN, DLC, BM

5076 Carrington, John Bodman, and George Ravensworth Hughes.
The Plate of the Worshipful Company of Goldsmiths. Oxford: U. Pr, 1926. 158pp, 83 pls BM

5077 Catalogue of a Loan Exhibition of Old English Plate and Deco-
      rations and Orders. Royal Northern Hospital. London:
      1929. 112pp, 81 ill

5078 Catalogue of an Exhibition of Royal Plate from Buckingham
      Palace and Windsor Castle. V & A Museum. London:
      1954. 50pp BM

5079 Catalogue of Silver from the Assheton Bennett Collection.
      Manchester: City Art Galleries, 1965. 79pp (Irish and
      French, 1350-1800)

5080 A Catalogue of the Ancient and Other Plate, tapestry, hearse-
      cloth, etc., belonging to the Worshipful Company of Vint-
      ners. London: 1911. 47pp

5081 Catalogue of the Exhibition of the Historic Plate of the City
      of London Exhibited at Goldsmiths' Hall, 1951; ... Illus-
      trations. 2 vol. London: Goldsmiths' Company, 1951.
      89pp, 2pp with 77 pls

5082 *Chaffers, William. Gilda Aurifabrorum. A history of English
      goldsmiths and plateworkers, and their marks stamped on
      plate, copied in fac-simile from celebrated examples; and
      the earliest records preserved at Goldsmiths' Hall, London,
      with their names, addresses, and dates of entry. Also
      historical accounts of the Goldsmiths' Company and their
      hall marks; the Regalia; the Mint; closing of the Exchequer;
      goldsmith-bankers; shop signs; a copious index, etc. Pre-
      ceded by an introductory essay on the goldsmiths' art.
      London: W. H. Allen, 1883; new ed. London: Reeves &
      Turner, 1899. 267pp, ill

5083 *_____. Hall Marks on Gold and Silver Plate, with tables
      of annual date letters employed in the principal assay of-
      fices of England, Scotland, and Ireland, from the earliest
      period of their use to the present day.... London: J.
      Davy, 1863; 2nd ed. enl. 1865; 3rd ed. 1868; 4th ed. rev.
      and "considerably augmented." London: 1872; 5th ed.
      "to which is now added a history of L'Orfevrerie Fran-
      caise." 2 parts. London: Bickers & Son, 1875; 6th ed.
      rev. 1883; 8th ed. with an introductory essay by Christo-
      pher A. Markham. London: Reeves & Turner, 1896;
      10th ed. enl., and "with a bibliography." Ed. by Major
      C. A. Markham. London: 1922; ed. and extended by
      Markham, as Chaffers' Hand Book to Hall Marks on Gold
      and Silver Plate.... London: Gibbings, for Reeves &
      Turner, 1897; reissue, 1902; etc. etc. under several
      titles, and edited by various people. Latest edition, cor-
      rected and revised by Cyril G. E. Bunt. London: Reeves,
      1966. 67pp; 88pp, 78pp, 112pp; 238pp; 322pp; etc. etc.

5084 Charles II Domestic Silver. V & A Museum. London: HMSO,
      1949. 32pp, ill

5085   Clark, Mark A. Paul Storr Silver in American Collections.
       Introd. by Judith Banister. Exhibition, February-March
       1972, Indianapolis Museum; March-April 1972, Dayton
       Art Institute. Indianapolis?: 1972. 20pp, ill (Paul
       Storr, 1771-1844)

5086   Collins, James E. The Private Book of Useful Alloys and
       Memoranda for Goldsmiths, Jewellers, etc. London:
       John C. Holten, 1872. 96pp BM

5087   Corporation Plate of England and Wales: catalogue of the
       exhibits (Goldsmiths' Hall); illustrations of some of the
       exhibits. 2 vol. London: Goldsmiths' Company, 1952.
       62pp; 2pp with 46 pls and ill

5088   Cripps, Wilfred Joseph, 1841-1903. College and Corporation
       Plate: a handbook to the reproductions of silver plate in
       the South Kensington Museum from celebrated English col-
       lections. London: HMSO, 1881. 155pp, 66 ill NN, MB

5089   _____ . English Plate Marks; giving tables of the alpha-
       betical date-letters and other hall-marks ... Extracted
       from Author's larger work. London: John Murray, 1882;
       3rd ed. as Old English Plate Marks. London: 1920;
       4th ed. 1930; ... 35pp; 7pp, 35 pls NN, BM

5090   _____ . Notes on Some Specimens of Ancient Plate in the
       Possession of the Worshipful Company of Merchant Taylors.
       London: 1877.

5091 * _____ . Old English Plate, ecclesiastical, decorative, and
       domestic; its makers and marks. London: John Murray,
       1878; ...; 5th ed. New York: Scribner, 1903; ...; ab-
       breviated ed. arranged by Percy Macquoid as The Plate
       Collector's Guide. London: Murray; New York: Scrib-
       ner's, 1908; ...; 11 revised & enl. impressions of 1878
       ed. up to 1926; reprint of 11th ed. London: Spring Books,
       1967. 133pp, ill; 432pp, ill; ...; 540pp, ill, bib, 2700
       marks facsims; Macquoid's arrangement has 200pp, 31 pls

5092   Curran, Mona. Collecting English Silver. London: Arco,
       1963; London: Mayflower, 1970. 132pp, ill, 8 pls, bib
       (To 1954)

5093   Delamer, Ida, ed. Irish Silver: exhibition of Irish silver
       from 1630-1820 at Trinity College, Dublin. October -
       December 1971. Dublin: 1971. 56pp, ill, bib

5094   Delieb, Eric. The Great Silver Manufactory; Matthew Boulton
       and the Birmingham Silversmiths, 1760-1790. Research
       collaboration by Michael Roberts. London: Studio Vista,
       1971; as Matthew Boulton, Master Silversmith. 1760-1790.

New York: Clarkson Potter, 1971. 144pp, ill, 16 pls, bib

5095   Dennis, Jessie McNab. English Silver. London: Studio
       Vista; New York: Walker, 1970. 84pp, ill, 1 pl, bib
       (1580-1820)

5096   Designs for Gold and Silversmiths. London: 1836. PPL

5097   Dixon, Stanley C. English Decorated Gold and Silver Trays.
       Monmouth, Wales: Ceramic Book Co., 1964. ill (1550-1850)

5098   Duckworth, Christian Leslie Dyce. Hall-marking of Gold and
       Silver Wares in Great Britain and Eire. Prescott, Lancs:
       Stephenson, 1953. 16pp, ill

5099   Duerden, Marilyn. Sheffield Silver 1773-1973: an exhibition to
       mark the bicentenary of the Sheffield Assay Office. Includes
       "Sheffield Silver and the Sheffield Assay Office, " by Molly
       Pearce. Sheffield: City Museum, 1973. 107pp, ill, bib

5100   Early Stuart Silver. V & A Museum. London: HMSO, 1950.
       32pp, ill

5101a Ebblewhite, Ernest Arthur, comp. Inventory of the Silver of the
       Company of Parish Clerks. London: 1923. 8pp, ill BM

5101b Ellenbogen, Eileen. English Vinaigrettes. Cambridge, Eng.:
       Golden Head, 1956. 39pp, ill, 16 pls, bib

5102   Ellis, Hubert Dynes. A Supplemental Description of Some of
       the Ancient Silver Plate Belonging to the Worshipful Com-
       pany of Armourers and Brasiers.... London: the Com-
       pany, 1910. 33pp, pls

5103   English and Scottish Silver. Royal Scottish Museum of Science
       and Art. Edinburgh: HMSO, 1954. 4pp, 25 pls (1557-1790)

5104   English Domestic Silver from Yorkshire Houses. Exhibit,
       July-September 1959. Leeds, Eng: Temple Newsam
       House, 1959. 30pp, ill

5105   English Medieval Silver. V & A Museum. London: HMSO,
       1952. 6pp, 25 pls

5106   English Silver; a catalogue to an exhibition of seven centuries
       of English domestic silver. January-March 1958. To-
       ronto: Royal Ontario Museum, 1958. 62pp, ill

5107   English Silver of Four Centuries, 1585-1835; a special exhi-
       bition. October 1969. Hartman Galleries. New York:
       1969. 66pp, ill

5108   English Silversmith's Work: Civil and domestic.   V & A
       Museum. London: HMSO, 1966. 8pp, ill

5109   Ensko, Stephen Guernsey Cook, and Edward Wenham.   English
       Silver, 1675-1825. New York: R. Ensko, 1937. 109pp,
       ill, bib DLC

5110   Examples of Art Workmanship of All Ages and Countries.
       Designs for Silversmiths. A series of 24 autotype repro-
       ductions of original designs for vases, ewers, salvers,
       etc. Science and Art Department, South Kensington Mu-
       seum. London: Arundel Society, 1871. 24 pls BM

5111   Exhibition of Historic Silver in Ulster. February-March 1956.
       Belfast: Museum and Art Gallery, 1956. 36pp, ill
       (1400-1837)

5112   Fairholt, Frederick William. An Illustrated Descriptive Cata-
       logue, of the collection of antique silver plate, formed by
       Albert, Lord Londesborough.... London: priv. printed
       by T. Richards, 1860. 27pp, ill, 20 pls NN

5113   Fallon, John Padraic. The Marks of the London Goldsmiths
       and Silversmiths, Georgian period (ca.1697-1837): a
       guide. Newton Abbot: David & Charles; New York:
       Arco, 1972. 420pp, ill, bib

5114 *Finlay, Ian. Scottish Gold and Silver Work. London: Chatto
       & Windus, 1956. 178pp, ill, 96 pls (Early Celtic to 19th
       century. Includes church plate, etc.)

5115   . The Scottish Tradition in Silver. Edinburgh:
       Thomas Nelson, 1948.

5116 *Frost, Thomas William. The Price Guide to Old Sheffield
       Plate. Woodbridge, Suffolk: Baron, for the Antique Col-
       lectors' Club, 1971; Revision List. 1972; Price Supple-
       ment. 1973. 396pp, chiefly ill

5117   Fry, Frederick Morris, and Roland Stuart Tewson. An Illus-
       trated Catalogue of Silver Plate of the Worshipful Company
       of Merchant Taylors. London: priv. printed, 1921.
       163pp, 47 pls BM

5118 *Gardner, John Starkie. Old Silver Work, Chiefly English,
       from the 15th to the 18th Centuries. A catalogue of the
       unique loan collection exhibited in 1902 at St. James's
       Court. Supplemented with some further fine specimens
       from the collections of the Dukes of Devonshire and Rut-
       land, Earl Cowper, and others. With historical and
       descriptive notes upon the objects illustrated, including
       references to further similar examples in the country, and

essays on some periods of the silversmiths' art. London:
Batsford; New York: S. Buckley, American agents, 1903.
198pp, ill, 121 pls DeWint, DLC, BM

5119 Gee, George Edward. The Goldsmith's Handbook. London:
Lockwood, 187-?; 2nd ed. 1881. 259pp, ill

5120 _____. The Silversmiths' Handbook. London: Lockwood,
1877; 2nd ed. 1885; 3rd ed. 1890; ... 221pp, 40 ill
DLC

5121 Gray, Percy Charles, and I. J. Swann. A Catalogue of the
Silver Plate in the Possession of the Master, Fellows
and Scholars of Trinity College, Cambridge. Cambridge:
1957. 72pp

5122 Greenwood, M. A. Ancient Plate of the Drapers' Company,
with some account of its origins, history, and vicissi-
tudes. London: Oxford U. Pr, 1930. 127pp, ill, pls
NN, PPL, BM

5123 Grimwade, Arthur Girling. The Queen's Silver; a survey of
Her Majesty's personal collection. London: Connoisseur,
1953. 120pp, ill, 64 pls TxU, DLC

5124 _____. Rococo Silver, 1727-1765. London: Faber, 1974.
74pp, ill, 96 pls, bib

5125 Hackenbroch, Yvonne. English and Other Silver in the Irwin
Untermyer Collection. New York: Metropolitan Museum,
1963; London: Thames & Hudson, 1964; rev. ed., dist.
by N.Y. Graphic Society, Greenwich, 1969. 96pp, ill,
201 pls, bib; 115pp, 200 pls, bib

_____. Finest English Silver. Catalogue of the collection
of the rare, early silver of Mr. Irwin Untermyer. See:
preceding title.

5126 Hayden, Arthur. Chats on Old Sheffield Plate. New York:
F. A. Stokes, 1918; London: Fisher Unwin, 1920; New
York: 1921; ...; facsim. reprint. Wakefield, Eng: E P
Pub, 1973. 302pp, ill, pls

5127 Hayward, John Forrest. The Courtauld Silver. New York:
Sotheby Park-Bernet, 1975. ill (18th century English.
Augustin and Samuel Courtauld)

5128 _____. Huguenot Silver in England, 1688-1727. London:
Faber, 1959. 89pp, ill, 96 pls, color frontis, bib

5129 *Heal, Sir Ambrose, comp. The London Goldsmiths, 1200-
1800. A record of the names and addresses of the

craftsmen, their shop-signs and trade-cards. Cambridge:
U. Pr, 1935; facsim. reprint. Newton Abbot: David &
Charles, 1972. 279pp, ill, 80 pls, facsims

5130 Herbert, William, 1771-1851. History of the Worshipful
      Company of Goldsmiths of London.... London: J. & C.
      Adlard, printers, 1837. 178pp (pp. 121-298) DLC

5131 Higgs, Percy Jackson. Assay Hall Marks on Old English
      Silver. Reprint of articles from Arts and Decoration.
      London: 1916. v.p., ill

5132 Holland, Margaret. Old Country Silver: an account of Eng-
      lish provincial silver, with sections on Ireland, Scotland,
      and Wales. Newton Abbot: David & Charles, 1971; as
      English Provincial Silver.... New York: Arco, 1971.
      240pp, ill, 1 pl, bib

5133 Horseman, W. A List of Hall Marks, as used on gold and
      silver plate, jewellery, etc., and employed in the assay
      offices of the United Kingdom; also descriptive notes of
      various foreign marks ... Including also marks used on
      porcelain. Rev. & Enl. ed. London: 1898; London:
      Simpkin & Marshall, for Assay Office, 1906. 20pp

5134 Howard, Montague. Old London Silver; its history, its
      makers, and its marks. New York: Scribner's, 1903.
      405pp, 200 ill, 5 color pls, color frontis, over 4000
      facsim. makers'- and hall-marks. PPL, DeWint

5135 Hughes, George Bernard. Antique Sheffield Plate. London:
      Batsford, 1970; as Sheffield Silver Plate. New York:
      Praeger, 1970. 300pp, 266 ill, 80 pls, bib

5136 *_____, and Therle Hughes. Three Centuries of English
      Domestic Silver, 1500-1820. London: Lutterworth, 1952;
      2nd impress. 1963; New York: Praeger, 1968. 248pp,
      ill, 46 pls

5137 Hughes, George Ravensworth. The Worshipful Company of
      Goldsmiths as Patrons of Their Craft, 1919-1953. Lon-
      don: the Company, 1965. 77pp, pls

5138 Irish Hall-Marks on Gold and Silver. Dublin: Company of
      Goldsmiths of Dublin, 1972. 19pp, ill (1638-1972)

5139 Irish Silver. V & A Museum. London: HMSO, 1959. 4pp,
      28 pls

5140 *Jackson, Sir Charles James, 1849-1923. English Goldsmiths
      and Their Marks; a history of goldsmiths and plate workers
      of England, Scotland, and Ireland. London: Macmillan,

1905; 2nd ed. rev. 1921; Los Angeles: Borden, 1921;
1948; 3rd ed. London: Batsford, 1949; 1964; New York:
Dover, 1964; 747pp, ill; 768pp, many ill

5141 * _____ . An Illustrated History of English Plate, ecclesiastical and secular, in which the development of form and
decoration in the silver and gold work of the British Isles,
from the earliest known examples to the latest of the
Georgian period, is delineated and described. 2 vol.
London: Batsford, Country Life, 1911; reprint. London:
Holland Pr, 1967; reprint of 1911 ed. New York: Dover,
1969. 1085pp, 1580 ill, 76 pls, color frontis, bib, marks
(The standard work)

5142 Jackson, Robert Wyse. Irish Silver. Cork: Mercier Pr,
1972. 86pp, 53 ill, pls, bib

5143 Jewitt, Llewellyn Frederick William. The Corporation Plate
and Insignia of Office of the Cities and Towns of England
and Wales. Ed. and compiled by W. H. St. John Hope.
2 vol. London: Bemrose, 1895. text, 400 ill (Vol. I.
Anglesey to Kent; Vol. II. Lancashire to Yorkshire) NN,
DLC

5144 Jones, Edward Alfred. Catalogue of the Plate Belonging to
the Duke of Portland at Welbeck Abbey. London: St.
Catherine Pr, 1935. 183pp, 21 pls

5145 _____ . Catalogue of the Plate of Clare College, Cambridge.
Cambridge: Eng: 1939. 87pp, 27 pls

5146 _____ . Catalogue of the Plate of Magdalen College, Oxford. Oxford: Oxford U. Pr, 1940. 103pp, 7 pls NN

5147 _____ . Catalogue of the Plate of Merton College, Oxford.
Oxford: U. Pr, 1938. 58pp, 12 pls NN

5148 _____ . Catalogue of the Plate of Oriel College, Oxford.
Oxford: U. Pr, 1944. 96pp, 20 pls NN

5149 _____ . Catalogue of the Plate of the Queen's College,
Oxford. Oxford: U. Pr, 1938. 87pp, 18 pls, bib

5150 _____ . The Gold and Silver of Windsor Castle. Letchworth: Arden Pr, 1911. 241pp, 103 pls NN

5151 _____ . Old English Gold Plate. London: Bemrose, 1907.
35pp, 38 pls DLC

5152 _____ . Old English Plate of the Emperor of Russia.
Letchworth; London: priv. printed, W. H. Smith, Arden
Pr, 1909. 115pp, 50 pls NN

5153 _____ . The Old Plate of the Cambridge Colleges. Cam-
        bridge: U. Pr, 1910. 125pp, 120 pls DLC, DeWint

5154 _____ . Old Oxford Plate. London: Constable, 1906.
        209pp, pls

5155 _____ . Old Royal Plate in the Tower of London, including
        the old silver communion vessels of the Chapel of St.
        Peter ad Vincula within the Tower. Oxford: Fox, Jones
        & Co, 1908. 79pp, 22 pls DLC, DeWint

5156 _____ . The Plate of Eton College. London: St. Catherine
        Pr, 1938. 71pp, 31 pls DLC

5157 _____ . Some Silver Wrought by the Courtauld Family of
        London, Goldsmiths of the City of London. Exhibition.
        Oxford: 1940. 129pp, 64 pls

5158 Keefe, F. D. Catalogue of the Clothworkers' Company Plate.
        London: the Company, 1969. 21pp, 9 ill, 8 pls (In-
        cludes gold and silver)

5159 Kennedy, Mary L. The Esther Thomas Hoblitzelle Collection
        of English Silver. Austin, Tex: 1957. 196pp, ill, color
        pls, bib

5160 Lawrance, David. English Silver from the 16th to the 19th
        Century. National Gallery of Victoria (Australia). Mel-
        bourne; London; New York: Oxford U. Pr, 1968. 31pp,
        ill, pls, bib (1500-1830)

5161 Lee, William. York Silver, 1475-1858: a short history of
        York silver, together with an illustrated catalogue of the
        W. Lee Collection now on permanent loan in the Treasury.
        York Minster Undercroft. York: Author, 1972. 40pp, ill

5162 Lever, Christopher. Goldsmiths and Silversmiths of England.
        London: Hutchinson, 1975. 256pp, ill, 32pp of pls

5163 Lightbourn, R. W. Tudor Domestic Silver. V & A Museum.
        London: HMSO, 1948; new ed. 1970. ...; 11pp, ill, 30
        pls (1490-1603)

5164 London Hall Marks, 1478-1898. Philadelphia: Bailey, Banks
        & Biddle, jewelers, 1913. 8pp

5165 Lutschaunig, Alfred. The Book of Hall Marks, or, Manual of
        reference for the gold and silversmith ... by the manager
        of the Liverpool Assay Office. London: J. C. Hotten,
        1872. 160pp, ill, 47 pls NN, SKM

        Macquoid, Percy, ed. The Plate Collector's Guide. See:
        Cripps, W. J.

5166 Mayne, Richard Harold. Old Channel Islands Silver: Its
      Makers and Marks. Pref. by Judith Banister. Jersey,
      Channel Islands: Print Holdings and Investments Ltd,
      1969. 96pp, ill, 72 pls, bib

5167 Mercers' Company Plate. London: Blades, East & Blades,
      for the Company, 1940. 85pp, pls NN

5168 Mid-Georgian Domestic Silver. V & A Museum. London:
      HMSO, 1952. 4pp, ill, 28 pls

5169 Mitchell, H. P. Catalogue of English Silversmiths' Work
      (with Scottish and Irish) Civil and Domestic. Introd. by
      William W. Watts. Pref. by Cecil H. Smith. V & A
      Museum. London: HMSO, 1920. 75pp, 64 pls, bib BM

5170 Moffatt, Harold Charles. Old Oxford Plate. London: Con-
      stable, 1906. 209pp, 98 pls

5171 Morgan, (Charles) Octavius (Swinnerton). Table of the Annual
      Assay Office Letters Used in Marking Plate from the
      Earliest Period of Their Use to the Present Time, to-
      gether with a reference to the various pieces of ancient
      plate which have been adopted as authorities for the same.
      London: Office of the Archaeological Institute of Great
      Britain and Ireland, 1853. 14pp DLC

5172 Norman-Wilcox, Gregor, ed. English Silver Cream Jugs of
      the 18th Century. Exhibition. Los Angeles: County Mu-
      seum, 1952. 46pp, ill (Collection of Mrs. William Ben-
      nett Munro)

5173 O'Donnell, Erica. Silver. London: Ginn, 1964; 1970. 32pp,
      ill (Juvenile literature. English silver 1660-1800)

5174 Okie, Howard Pitcher. Old Silver and Old Sheffield Plate; a
      history of the silversmiths art in Great Britain and Ireland,
      with ... 13,000 facsimile marks ... American silversmiths
      and their marks. Paris marks and ... date letters with a
      description of the methods of marking employed by Paris
      Guild ... Hallmarks and date letters ... of continental
      Europe ... History of old Sheffield Plate, ... list of every
      known maker.... Garden City, NY: Doubleday Doran,
      1928; 1936; 1938. 420pp, ill, pls DLC

5175 Old English and Early American Silverwork; early silver in
      California collections. Los Angeles: Museum of Art,
      1962. 35pp, ill

5176 Old Silver Platers and Their Marks. Sheffield: Parkin &
      Bacon, for Assay Office, 1908.

5177 *Oman, Charles Chichele. Caroline Silver, 1625-1688. London:
      Faber, 1970. 73pp, ill, 97 pls, bib

5178 _____ . A Catalogue of Plate Belonging to the Bank of
England. London: printed for the Governor of the Bank,
1939; London: the Bank, 1967. 42pp, 17 pls; 57pp, ill,
47 pls

5179 _____ . English Domestic Silver. London: A & C Black,
1934; new & rev. 4th ed. 1959; 5th ed. 1962; 7th ed. 1968.
240pp, 135 ill, 31 pls, bib (To 1830)

5180 _____ . English Silver from Charles II to the Regency.
A preliminary guide for the collector. London: Connoisseur, 1948. 41pp

5181 _____ . The English Silver in the Kremlin, 1557-1663.
London: Methuen, 1961. 94pp, ill, 55 pls, bib

5182 * _____ . English Silversmiths' Work, Civil and Domestic:
An Introduction. V & A Museum. London: HMSO, 1965.
16pp, 192 pls

5183 _____ . The Wellington Plate Portuguese Service (a baixela
Wellington). V & A Museum. London: HMSO, 1954.
11pp, ill, pls, bib (Silver)

5184 100 Years of English Silver, 1660-1760. Exhibition. Art
Museum. Austin: University of Texas, Printing Division,
1969? u.p., ill, 1 color pl

5185 Pairpont, Francis. Antique Plated Ware, a History of Old
Sheffield Plate. London: Pairpont, 1904; 1908; 4th ed.
1925. 24pp; 61pp; 66pp, ill DLC

5186 *Penzer, Norman Mosley. Paul Storr, the Last of the Goldsmiths. London: Batsford, 1954; new ed. as Paul Storr,
1771-1844. Silversmith and goldsmith. London: Spring
Books, 1971. 292pp, well-ill

5187 _____ . Regency Silver. London: Faber, 19-? ill

5188 Phillips, C. M. A Short Account of the Silver Plate and
Miscellaneous Articles Belonging to the Worshipful Com-
pany of Cooks, London. London: 1909. 31pp, ill, 4 pls
BM

5189 *Phillips, Philip A. S. Paul de Lamerie, Citizen and Goldsmith of London. A study of his life and work. A.D.
1688-1751. London: Batsford, 1935; facsim. reprint as
Paul de Lamerie, Silversmith of London 1688-1751. London: 1968. 115pp, ill, 164 pls

5190 Prideaux, Sir Walter S., comp. Memorials of the Goldsmiths'
Company. London: priv. printed, 1896.

5191   Pugin, Austus Charles, and Augustus Welby Northmore Pugin.
       Designs for Gold and Silversmiths. 2 parts. London: R.
       Ackermann, 1836. 27 pls BM

5192   Purchase, George Arthur R. The Story of the Corporation
       Plate ... City of Chichester. Chichester: Moore &
       Tillyer, 1954. 24pp, ill, bib

5193   Queen Anne Domestic Silver. V & A Museum. London:
       HMSO, 1951. 4pp, 28 pls

5194   Ramsey, L. G. G., ed. The Connoisseur New Guide to
       Antique English Silver and Plate. Introd. by Jonathan
       Stone. London: Connoisseur, 1962. 192pp, ill, bib

5195   Reddaway, Thomas Fiddian. The London Goldsmiths Circa
       1500. Royal Historical Society Transactions. London:
       1962. 14pp (pp. 49-62), bib

5196   Redman, William. Hall Marks, Illustrated. 1560-1915. A
       complete list of hall marks and date letters on gold and
       silver plate and jewellery ... And a list of the great
       diamonds of the world. London?: 1893?; Rev. by Edwin
       W. Streeter. Bradford, Eng: Author, 1915? ...; 48pp,
       ill

5197   Regency Domestic Silver. V & A Museum. London: HMSO,
       1952. 4pp, 22 pls (1800-1820)

5198   Ridgway, Maurice Hill. Chester Goldsmiths from Early
       Times to 1726. Fore. by Charles Oman. Altrincham:
       Sherratt, 1968. 198pp, ill, 37 pls (Chester, England)

5199   Robertson, Richard Austin. Old Sheffield Plate. London:
       Benn, 1957. 190pp, ill

5200   Rowe, Robert. Adam Silver, 1765-1795. London: Faber;
       New York: Taplinger, 1965. 94pp, ill, 97 pls, bib

5201   The Sheffield Assay Office Register. A copy of the register
       of the persons concerned in the manufacture of silver
       ware, 1773-1907. Sheffield: 1911. 104pp

5202   Sheffield Plate. V & A Museum. London: HMSO, 1955.
       5pp, 30 pls

5203   Shure, David Simon. Hester Bateman Silver, Queen of Eng-
       lish Silversmiths. London: W. H. Allen, 1959; Garden
       City, NY: Doubleday, 1960. 31pp, ill, 87 pls (Bateman,
       1709-1794)

5204   Sissons, W. Old Sheffield Plate. Sheffield: Pawson &
       Brailsford, 1901. 11pp, ill, 6 pls

5205   Slatter, John. Collecting Old Silver. Adelaide, Australia:
       Rigby, 1971; London: Hale, 1973. 64pp, ill (English,
       1702-1901)

5206   Smith, Sheena, comp. Norwich Silver, 1565/1706. Loan
       Exhibition, April 1-June 1966. Norwich: Castle Museum,
       1966. 39pp, 4 pls

5207   Stone, Jonathan. English Silver of the 18th Century. London:
       Cory, Adams & Mackay; New York: October House, 1965.
       72pp, ill, 39 (4 color) pls, bib

5208   Tatham, Charles Heathcote, 1771-1842. Designs for Orna-
       mental Plate, many of which have been executed in silver,
       from original drawings. London: for Thomas Gardiner
       by John Barfield, 1806. 3pp, ill, 41 pls DLC, NNC-Ave

5209   Taylor, Gerald. Elizabethan Silver. London: Faber, 19-?
       ill (Ashmolean Museum, Oxford)

5210   . Silver. An introduction to British Plate from the
       middle ages to the present day. Harmondsworth, Middle-
       sex: Penguin, 1956; 2nd ed. as Silver. Harmondsworth;
       Baltimore: Penguin, 1963; as Silver Through the Ages.
       New York: Barnes & Noble; London: Cassell, 1965.
       248pp, ill; 301pp, ill, 64 pls, bib

5211   Ticher, Kurt. Irish Silver in the Rococo Period. Shannon:
       Irish University Pr, 1972. 28pp, ill, 111 pls (1725-1775)

5212   , Ida Delamer, and William O'Sullivan. Hall-Marks
       on Dublin Silver 1730-1772. Dublin: National Museum of
       Ireland, 1968. 31pp, ill

5213   Torrey, Julia Whittemore. Old Sheffield Plate, its techniques
       and history as illustrated in a single private collection.
       Boston; New York: Houghton, Mifflin, 1918. 90pp, 65
       pls DLC

5214   Trade and Industry: Silver and Gold Wares. 2 vol. Shannon:
       Irish U. Pr, 1968-1971.

5215   Tremayne, Arthur. Hall Marks and Date Letters on Gold and
       Silver. London: N.A.G. Pr, 1944; rev. ed. by Eric
       Bruton. London: N.A.G. for Retail Jeweller, 1970.
       38pp, ill

5216   Veitch, Henry Newton. Sheffield Plate, its history, manu-
       facture and art; with makers' names and marks, also a
       note on foreign Sheffield Plate. London: G. Bell, 1908.
       359pp, ill, 75 pls DLC

5217   *Wardle, Patricia. Victorian Silver and Silver-Plate. Fore.

by Hugh Wakefield. London: H. Jenkins; New York: Nelson, 1963. 238pp, many ill, bib, marks (No flatware)

5218 Watts, William Walter. Catalogue of a Loan Exhibition of Silver Plate Belonging to the Colleges of the University of Oxford, November 1928. Oxford: U. Pr, 1928. 80pp, ill BM

5219 *_____. Old English Silver: Domestic and Ecclesiastical; from early times to the 19th century. London: E. Benn; New York: 1924. 148pp, 307 pls on 134pp of ill, bib (Standard work) NNC-Ave, BM

5220 Wenham, Edward. Domestic Silver of Great Britain and Ireland. New York; London: Oxford U. Pr, 1931; 1935. 186pp, ill, 95 pls, bib

5221 _____. Old Sheffield Plate; its romantic discovery and brief existence with a chapter on Britannia metal. London: Bell, 1955. 102pp, ill

5222 Westwood, Arthur. The Antiquity of Hall-Marking. Birmingham, Eng: Assay Office, 1935. 7pp

5223 Wilding, Peter. An Introduction to English Silver. London: Art & Technics, 1950. 119pp, ill

5224 Wilkinson, Wynyard R. T. Indian Colonial Silver: European Silversmiths in India (1790-1860) and Their Marks. London: Argent Pr, 1972. 171pp, ill, bib (Includes English and Scottish)

5225 Winter, C. Pattern Book for Jewellers, Goldsmiths.... London: n.d. ill SKM

5226 *Wyler, Seymour B. The Book of Old Silver, English, American, Foreign ... with all available hallmarks, including Sheffield plate marks. New York: Crown, 1937; 1960; 24th printing. 1971. 447pp, ill, pls, bib (20,000 marks)

5227 _____. The Book of Sheffield Plate, with all known makers' marks including Victorian plate insignia. New York: Crown, 1949. 188pp, ill

5228 Wyllie, Bertie. Sheffield Plate. London: Newnes; New York: Scribner's, 1908; London; New York: 1913. 116pp, 123 pls

5229 Young, W. A. The Silver and Sheffield Plate Collector. A guide to English domestic metal work. London: H. Jenkins, 1919. 320pp, 100 ill, 32 pls, bib, gloss

CHURCH SILVER OF THE BRITISH ISLES

5230   Ball, T. Stanley. Church Plate of the City of Chester. London: Sherratt & Hughes, 1907. 158pp, 12 pls

5231   Benton, Gerald Monatague, F. W. Galpin, and William James Pressey. The Church Plate of the County of Essex. Ed. by W. J. Pressey. Colchester, Eng: Benham, 1926. 335pp, ill, 27 pls

5232a   Buck, John Henry. Old Plate, Ecclesiastical, Decorative and Domestic; Its Makers and Marks. New York: Gorham, 1888; new & enl. ed. as Old Plate, Its Makers and Marks. New York: Gorham, 1903. 268pp, 82 ill, marks; 327pp, many ill, bib, marks DLC, NN, PPL

5232b   Burnes, Reverend Thomas. Old Scottish Communion Plate. Pref. by Reverend James Macgregor. Chronological tables of Scottish hall-marks by Alexander J. S. Brook. Edinburgh: R. & R. Clark, 1892. 651pp, ill, 84 pls NN, DLC

5233   Bury, Shirley. Copy or Creation: Victorian Treasures from English Churches. Fore. by John Betjeman. Exhibition organized by the Worshipful Company of Goldsmiths and the Victorian Society, May-June 1967, Goldsmiths' Hall. London: the Company, 1967. 48pp, ill, 4 pls, bib

5234   Carnegie, M. Church Plate in the Hundred of Blackheath. Blackheath: Blackheath Pr, 1939. 55pp, 21 pls

5235   Church Plate from the Midlands, 13th to 18th Century. Exhibition, April-May 1948. Birmingham: Museum and Art Gallery, 1948. 31pp, ill

5236   Cole, Marwood Anselm Rauceby Thorold, comp. Church Plate of the City of Bristol. Gloucester, Eng: Council of the Bristol and Gloucestershire Archaeological Society, 1932. pls DLC, NN

5237   Cooper, Reverend T. S. The Church Plate of Surrey. London: Roworth & Co, printer, for Surrey Archaeological Society, 1902. 383pp, pls

5238   Dawson, Ralph S. Silver Treasures of the Diocese of Salisbury. Exhibition, Salisbury Cathedral. Salisbury: 1958. 28pp

5239   Evans, John Thomas, 1869- . The Church Plate of Breconshire (Wales).... Stow-on-the-Wold: J. H. Alden, 1912. 160pp, 15 pls NN, DLC

5240   _____. The Church Plate of Cardiganshire (Wales)....

Stow-on-the-Wold: J. H. Alden, 1914. 163pp, ill, 20 pls NN, DLC

5241 _____ . Church Plate of Carmarthenshire (Wales)....
London: H. Gray, 1907. 148pp, ill, 14 pls DLC

5242 _____ . The Church Plate of Gloucestershire.... n. p.
(Bristol?): Council of the Bristol and Gloucestershire
Archaeological Society, 1906. 264pp, ill NN

5243 _____ . The Church Plate of Gowerland (Wales).... Stow-
on-the-Wold: J. H. Alden, 1921. 146pp, 39 pls NN

5244 _____ . Church Plate of Oxfordshire. Oxford: Alden Pr,
1928. 222pp, ill, 30 pls PP, DLC

5245 _____ . The Church Plate of Pembrokeshire (Wales)....
London: W. H. Roberts, 1905. 147pp, 10 pls DLC

5246 _____ . Church Plate of Radnorshire (Wales).... Stow-
on-the-Wold: J. H.: Alden, 1910. 160pp, ill, 6 pls

5247 Fallow, Thomas McCall, (finished by Hardy B. McCall).
Yorkshire Church Plate. 2 vol. Leeds: Yorkshire
Archaeological Society, 1912-1915. ill, pls NN, DLC

5248 Ferguson, Richard Saul, 1837-1900, ed. Old Church Plate
in the Diocese of Carlisle: with the makers and marks
... (also) municipal insignia and corporation and guild
plate of Carlisle. Carlisle: Thurman, 1882. 326pp, ill,
29 pls NNC-Ave, DLC

5249 Freshfield, Edwin Hanson, 1832-1918. Communion Plate of
the Churches of the City of London. London: priv.
printed, Rixon & Arnold, 1894. 152pp, ill, 15 pls, marks

5250 _____ . Communion Plate of the Parish Churches in the
County of London. London: priv. printed, Rixon &
Arnold, 1895. 111pp, 24 pls PPL

5251 _____ . Communion Plate of the Parish Churches in Essex. n. p. priv. printed, 1899. text, ill, 5 pls NN

5252 _____ . Communion Plate of the Parish Churches in the
County of Middlesex. London: priv. printed, Rixon &
Arnold, 1897. 83pp, ill, 15 pls MiD

5253 Gilchrist, James. Anglican Church Plate. London: Connoisseur, M. Joseph, 1967. 120pp, 75 ill, 8 pls, bib

5254 Jeavons, Sidney Aston. Church Plate of Warwickshire, Diocese of Coventry. Fore. by Charles C. Oman. Cheltenham,

Eng: Birmingham Archaeological Society, 1963. 92pp,
34 pls

5255 _____. The Church Plate of Derbyshire, 1491-1850. Pref.
by Charles C. Oman. Reprint from Journal, 1961. Sheffield, Eng: Derbyshire Archaeological Society, 1963.
84pp, 34 pls, marks

5256 Jones, Edward Alfred. Catalogue of the Plate of Christ
Church, Oxford. Oxford: Oxford U. Pr, 1939. 52pp,
18 pls DLC

5257 _____. Church Plate of the Diocese of Bangor. London:
Bemrose, 1906. 160pp, 34 pls NN

5258 _____. Old Church Plate of the Isle of Man. London:
Bemrose, 1907. 33pp, 20 pls, bib

5259 _____. Old Royal Plate in the Tower of London, including
the old silver Communion vessels of the Chapel of St.
Peter ad Vincula within the Tower. Oxford: Fox, Jones
& Co, 1908. 79pp, 22 pls DLC, DeWint

5260 _____. The Old Silver Sacramental Vessels of Foreign
Protestant Churches in England. London: Dent, 1907.
48pp, 22 pls DLC

5261 _____. The Plate of St. George's Chapel, Windsor Castle.
London: S.P.C.K., 1939. 37pp, ill MH

5262 Lea, William. Church Plate in the Arch-Deaconry of Worcester, being an inventory and notice of the sacred vessels in use in the different churches.... Worcester:
Deighton & Co, 1884. 80pp, ill, 5 pls MB, NNC-Ave

5263 *Markham, Christopher Alexander. Church Plate of the
County of Northampton. London: Simpkin, Marshall,
Hamilton, Kent & Co, 1894. 368pp, ill, 9 pls DLC

5264 Nightingale, James Edward. The Church Plate of the County
of Dorset.... Salisbury: Bennett Brothers, printers,
1889. 216pp, 14 ill, 3 pls, marks DLC, NNC-Ave

5265 _____. The Church Plate of the County of Wilts, including
that part of the county now in the diocese of Gloucester
and Bristol. Salisbury: Bennett Brothers, 1891. 256pp,
55 pls DLC

5266 *Oman, Charles C. English Church Plate, 597-1830. London;
New York: Oxford U. Pr, 1957. 326pp, ill, 199 pls, bib

5267 Peplow, William Augustus, and W. R. H. Peplow. Church
Plate of the Archdeaconry of Worcester and the Cathedral

Church. Stourbridge: Mark & Moody, 1967. 124pp, 59
ill, 36 pls

5268 Specimens of Ancient Church Plate; sepulchre crosses, etc.
Oxford: J. H. Parker, 1845. 10pp, ill, 50 pls DLC,
NNC-Ave

5269 Stanhope, Honorable Berkeley Lionel Scudamore, 1824-1919,
and Harold C. Moffatt. Church Plate of the County of
Hereford ... To which is added an inventory of church
goods in 6th and 7th Edward VI (i.e. 1552-1553). Westminster, England: A. Constable, 1903. 243pp, ill, 26
pls

5270 *Trollope, Reverend Andrew. An Inventory of the Church Plate
of Lancastershire. 2 vol. Leicester: Clarke & Hodgson,
1890. text, ill, 33 pls

5271 Walker, John William, and Margaret I. Walker. The Church
Plate of Berkshire. Winchester: priv. printed, 1927.
384pp, pls

5272 Watts, William Walter. Catalogue of Chalices and Other Communion Vessels. London: V & A, 1922. 78pp, ill, 28
pls BM

EUROPEAN AND RUSSIAN SILVER AND GOLD

5273 Andren, Erik. Swedish Silver. Tr. from Swedish (1947) by
Lillian Ollen. New York: Barrow, 1950. 160pp, 101
photographs (Old and new)

5274 *Bainbridge, Henry Charles. Peter Carl Faberge: goldsmith
and jeweller to the Russian Imperial Court and the principal crowned heads of Europe. An illustrated record and
review of his work, 1846-1920. Fore. by Sacheverall
Sitwell. London; New York: Batsford, 1949; London:
Spring Books, 1966. 169pp, ill, 128 pls (some color),
bib

5275 Belli-Barsali, Isa. Medieval Goldsmiths' Work. Tr. from
Italian by Margaret Crosland. Feltham; New York:
Hamlyn, 1969. 157pp, ill, 71 color pls (500-1500)

5276 Boeson, Gudmund, and Christen Anton Bøje. Old Danish
Silver. Tr. from Danish (1948) by Ronald Kay. Copenhagen: Hassing, 1949. 35pp, 210 pls, 496 illustrated
marks PPULC, DLC, BM

5277 Bøje, Christen Anton. Danish Silver Marks before 1870.
From the original 1946 work, and later revisions. Some

sections translated into English.   Copenhagen: Politikens
Forlag, 1954.

5278   Buhler, Kathryn C.   French, English and American Silver; a
       loan exhibition in honor of Russell A. Plimpton, June-
       July 1956.   Minneapolis: Institute of Arts, 1956.   80pp,
       ill

5279   Carre, Louis.   A Guide to Old French Plate.   Tr. from
       French.   Fore. by E. Alfred Jones.   London: Chapman
       & Hall; New York: Scribner's, 1931; reprint with fore.
       by Maurice Bouvier-Ajam.   London: Eyre & Spottiswoode,
       1971.   270pp, 100 ill, 32 pls, marks

5280   Catalogue of an Exhibition of a Collection of Silversmiths'
       Work of European Origin.   London: Burlington Fine Arts
       Club, 1901.   185pp, ill   BM

5281   Catalogue of Silver from the Assheton Bennett Collection.
       Manchester: City Art Galleries, 1965.   79pp   (Irish and
       French silver, 1350-1800)

5282   Cellini, Benvenuto, (1500-1571).   The Treatise of Benvenuto
       Cellini on Goldsmithing and Sculpture.   Tr. from Italian
       by C. R. Ashbee.   London: E. Arnold, 1898; reprint.
       New York: Dover, 1967.   164pp, ill, pls

5283   Churchill, Sidney John Alexander.   The Goldsmiths of Italy.
       Some account of their guilds, statues, and work, compiled
       from the published papers, notes and other material col-
       lected by the late S. J. A. Churchill, by Cyril George
       Edward Bunt.   London: Hopkinson, 1926.   182pp, 21 pls,
       bib   NN, DLC

5284   *Cripps, Wilfred Joseph.   Old French Plate: with tables of
       the Paris date-letters, and fac-similes of other marks.
       A handbook for the collector.   London: J. Murray, 1880;
       2nd ed. 1893; 3rd ed. 1920; facsim. reprint of 1880 ed.
       as Old French Silver.   Christchurch: Dolphin Pr, 1972;
       Boston: Newbury Books, 1973.   101pp, ill, 9 pls; 113pp;
       115pp

5285   Davis, Frank.   French Silver, 1450-1825.   London: Barker;
       New York: Praeger, 1970.   104pp, ill, 96 pls, bib

5286   Denaro, Victor F.   The Goldsmiths of Malta and Their Marks.
       Florence, Italy: L. S. Olschki, 1972.   241pp, ill, bib

5287   Dennis, Faith.   Three Centuries of French Domestic Silver:
       its makers and its marks.   2 vol.   New York: Metro-
       politan Museum, 1960.   ill, bib

5288   Examples of Art Workmanship of All Ages and Countries.

Decorative plate, chiefly Portuguese, German, and Italian.
London: Arundel Society, under sanction of Science and
Art Department, South Kensington Museum, 1869. pls
BM

5289 Fregnac, Claude. French Master Goldsmiths and Silversmiths
from the 17th to 19th Century. Pref. by Jacques Helft.
Tr. from French. New York: French & European Publications, 1966. 333pp, ill, bib

5290 French Domestic Silver. V & A Museum. London: HMSO,
1960. 32pp, ill, 26 pls

5291 Gardner, John Starkie. Exhibition of a Collection of Silversmiths' Work of European Origin. London: Burlington
Fine Arts Club, 1901. 185pp, 121 pls BM, NNC-Ave

5292 German and Swiss Domestic Silver of the Gothic Period.
V & A Museum. London: HMSO, 1961. 4pp, 27 pls
(1350-1521)

5293 German Domestic Silver of the 18th Century. V & A Museum.
London: HMSO, 1965. 32pp, 28 ill (1700-1775)

5294 German Domestic Silver, 1618-1700. V & A Museum. London: HMSO, 1967. 31pp, chiefly ill, 27 pls

5295 Gregoriette, Guido. Italian Gold, Silver and Jewelry. Their
history and centres. Milano: Alfieri & Lacroix, 1971.
178pp including pls, ill, bib

5296 Helft, Jacques. Exhibition of Old French Gold and Silver
Plate (16th to 18th Century). Held in galleries of Arnold
Seligman Rey, N.Y. Paris: Les Fils de Leon Helft,
1933. 52pp, 21 pls

5297   . French Master Goldsmiths and Silversmiths from
the 17th to the 19th Century. New York: French &
European Publications, 1966. 333pp, ill, bib (Louis
13th-Charles 10th)

5298 Hernmarck, Carl. The Art of the European Silversmith and
Goldsmith. 2 vol. London: 1974. about 500pp each
vol., ill, over 1000 pls, bib

5299 Italian Secular Silver. V & A Museum. London: HMSO,
1962. 4pp, 28 pls (1500-1805)

5300 Johnson, Ada Marshall. Hispanic Silverwork. New York:
Hispanic Society of America, 1944. 308pp, ill, pls, bib
(Includes catalogue of the Society's collection)

5301 *Jones, Edward Alfred. Old Silver of Europe and America

from Early Times to the 19th Century. London: Batsford; Philadelphia: Lippincott, 1928. 376pp, ill, 96 pls
NN

5302 Kolba, Judith H. Goldsmiths' Work. Budapest: Hungarian
National Museum, 1973. 46pp, 72pp of photographs, color
pl (10th-18th century, Museum's collection)

5303 Krohn-Hansen, Thorwald, and Robert Kloster. Bergen Silver
from the Guild Period. Summary in English. 2 vol.
Bergen, Norway: Museum, 1957. text, ill, bib

5304 Link, Eva Maria. The Book of Silver. Tr. from German
(1968) by Francisca Garvie. London: Barrie & Jenkins;
New York: Praeger, 1973. 301pp, 150 ill, 18 color pls,
bib, marks (European and American)

5305 Markham, Christopher Alexander, 1859- . Handbook to
Foreign Hall Marks on Gold and Silver Plate. (With the
exception of those on French plate.) London: Gibbings,
1898. 92pp, ill, 163 marks MB

5306 _____, ed. Hand Book to French Hall Marks on Gold and
Silver Plate. William Chaffer's L'orfevrerie Francais
was the foundation work. London: Reeves & Turner,
1899. 66pp, ill, bib NN

5307 Okie, Howard Pitcher. Old Silver and Old Sheffield Plate;
a history of the silversmiths' art in Great Britain and
Ireland, with ... 13,000 facsimile marks ... American
silversmiths and their marks. Paris marks and ... date
letters with a description of the methods of marking employed by Paris Guild ... Hallmarks and date letters ...
of continental Europe ... History of old Sheffield plate,
... list of every known maker.... Garden City, NY:
Doubleday Doran, 1928; 1936; 1938. 420pp, ill, pls
DLC

5308 Oman, Charles, comp. The Golden Age of Hispanic Silver,
1400-1665. V & A Museum. London: HMSO, 1968.
71pp, 280 ill, 180 pls, bib (Spain and Portugal)

5309 Scandinavian Silver. V & A Museum. London: HMSO, 1959.
32pp, ill

5310 Taylor, Gerald. Continental Gold and Silver. London: Connoisseur & Michael Joseph, 1967. 120pp, ill, 8 color pls,
bib

5311 Three Centuries of French Domestic Silver. Exhibition, May-
September 1938. New York: Metropolitan Museum, 1938.
20pp, ill, pls

5312   White, Margaret E., comp. European and American Silver
        in the Newark Museum Collection. Newark, NJ: 1953.
        33pp, ill, bib

5313   Wilkinson, Wynyard R. T. Indian Colonial Silver: European
        Silversmiths in India (1790-1860) and Their Marks. Lon-
        don: Argent Pr, 1972. 171pp, ill, bib (Also English
        and Scottish)

DUTCH SILVER

5314   Ash, Douglas. Dutch Silver. Cambridge, Eng: Golden Head
        Pr, 1965. 41pp, ill (1500-1800)

5315   Citroen, Karel A. Amsterdam Silversmiths and Their Marks.
        Partly tr. to English. Amsterdam: North-Holland Pub.
        Co, 1975. 1253 touch marks of gold and silversmiths.

5316   Duyvene de Wit-Klinkhamer, Theresa M., and Moses Heiman
        Gans. Dutch Silver. Tr. from Dutch (1958) by Oliver
        Van Oss. London: Faber, 1961. 97pp, ill, 144 pls, bib
        (1500-1800)

5317   *Frederiks, Johan Willem. Antique Dutch Silver. 4 vol. The
        Hague: M. Nijhoff, 1952-1965. text, 2000 specimens ill,
        bib (Standard work) See next listings.

5318   *_____. Dutch Silver; embossed plaquettes, tazze and
        dishes from the Renaissance until the end of the 18th cen-
        tury. The Hague: 1952. 538pp, ill, bib

5319   *_____. Dutch Silver; wrought plate of North and South
        Holland from the Renaissance until the End of the 18th
        Century. The Hague: 1958. 211pp, 313 pls

5320   *_____. Dutch Silver, wrought plate of the Central, North-
        ern and Southern provinces from the Renaissance until the
        end of the 18th Century. The Hague: 1960. 157pp, 332
        pls

5321   The Golden Age of Dutch Silver. V & A Museum. London:
        HMSO, 1953. 6pp, 30 pls (1590-1700)

SILVER FROM LATIN AMERICA, SOUTH AFRICA AND AUSTRALIA

5322   Albrecht, Kurt. 19th Century Australian Gold and Silver
        Smiths. Richmond, Victoria: Hutchinson Australia, 1969.
        69pp, ill

5323   Anderson, Lawrence Leslie. The Art of the Silversmith in

Mexico, 1519-1936. 2 vol. New York: Oxford U. Pr,
1941. text, ill, pls, bib, marks

5324   Cape Goldsmiths and Silversmiths Whose Initials Correspond
       to the Makers' Marks on Cape Silverware in the Africana
       Museum. Johannesburg: Africana Museum, 1946. 4pp

5325   *Hawkins, John B. Australian Silver, 1800-1900. Double
       Bay, Australia: Max Herford; dist. Robert Alan Green,
       NY, 1973. 85pp, ill, pls

5326   Heller, David. Further Researches in Cape Silver. Cape
       Town, South Africa: M. Miller; London: Bailey & Swin-
       fen, 1953. 179pp, ill, pls

5327   _____. A History of Cape Silver, 1700-1870. Capetown,
       Cape of Good Hope: D. Heller, 1949. 276pp, ill, bib

5328   Morrison, Mollie N. The Silversmiths and Goldsmiths of the
       Cape of Good Hope, 1652-1850. Johannesburg: 1936.
       84pp, 16 pls NN

5329   Oliver, H. G. A Catalogue of the Work in Silver, silver-
       gilt and gold by Cape Town craftsmen of the 18th and 19th
       centuries. Johannesburg: Africana Museum, 1946. 8pp

5330   Rosenthal, S. W. Jewelry and Silverware in Cuba. Washing-
       ton, D.C.: United States Bureau of Foreign and Domestic
       Commerce, 1919. 78pp

5331   _____. Silverware in China, Bolivia and Peru. Washing-
       ton, D.C.: United States Bureau of Foreign and Domestic
       Commerce, 1919. 115pp

5332   Three Centuries of Peruvian Silver; objects from the Vice-
       Royalty through early independence. Tr. by Ralph Sherrit
       and Hector Urquiaga. Exhibition. Lima: S. Valverde,
       1967? 63pp, ill

ORIENTAL SILVER AND GOLD†

5333   Forbes, H. A. Crosby, John Devereaux Kernan, and Ruth S.
       Wilkins. Chinese Export Silver, 1785-1885. Milton,
       Mass: Museum of the American China Trade, 1975.
       304pp, 303 ill, marks, bib (300 pieces)

---

†Much of the metalwork of the Orient, which is generally known as
a "minor art," can be found in this bibliography in Section IV under
Oriental Applied Arts.

5334 Gowland, William. Japanese Metallurgy. Part 1: gold and
      silver and their alloys. A paper read ... Society of
      Chemical Industry. London: Eyre & Spottiswoode, 1896.
      16pp, ill MdBP

5335 Gyllensvard, Bo. T'ang Gold and Silver. London: K. Paul,
      for Museum of Far Eastern Antiquities, 1957. 230pp, ill

5336 Rosenthal, S. W. Silverware in China, Bolivia and Peru.
      Washington, D.C.: United States Bureau of Foreign and
      Domestic Commerce, 1919. 115pp

5337 Roth, Henry Ling, 1855-1925. Oriental Silverwork, Malay
      and Chinese: a handbook for connoisseurs, collectors,
      students, and silversmiths. London: Truslove & Hanson,
      1910; Kuala Lumpur: U. of Malaya Pr, 1966; London:
      Oxford U. Pr, 1968. 300pp of ill (Also Siamese)

5338 Sasanian Silver: late antique and early medieval arts of
      luxury from Iran. Fore. by Charles H. Sawyer; historical
      survey by Martha Carter. Exhibition. August-September
      1967. Ann Arbor, Mich: University Museum of Art,
      1967. 158pp, ill, bib

5339 Singer, Paul. Early Chinese Gold and Silver. Exhibition.
      New York: China House Gallery, China Institute in
      America, 1971. 72pp, ill

5340 Tilly, Harry L. Modern Burmese Silverwork. Rangoon:
      Government Printing, 1904. 8pp, 14 pls

5341 _____. The Silverwork of Burma. Rangoon: Government
      Printing, 1902. 22pp, ill, 16 pls NN

SECTION IX

WOODWORK

WOODS AND WOODLAND INDUSTRIES

5342   Edlin, Herbert Leeson. Woodland Crafts in Britain: an account of the traditional uses of trees and timbers in the British countryside. London: Batsford, 1949; reprint. Newton Abbot: David & Charles, 1973. 182pp, ill, 81 pls, bib

5343   Fitz Randolph, Helen Elizabeth, and Mavis Doriel Haz. Timber and Underwood Industries and Some Village Workshops. Oxford: Clarendon, 1926. 239pp, pls

5344   Hetherington, Arthur Lonsdale, 1881- . British Empire Hardwoods from the Point of View of Turnery. Fore. by Major J. G. Holtzapffel Budd. London: HMSO, 1931. 34pp, pls NN

5345   Hinckley, F. Lewis. Directory of the Historic Cabinet Woods. New York: Crown, 1959. 186pp, 184 ill, bib (Hardwoods, 1460-1900)

5346 Hindle, Brooke, ed. America's Wooden Age: aspects of its early technology. Essays presented at a symposium, 1973. Essays by Charles F. Carroll; Silvio A. Bedini; Charles Howell; Louis C. Hunter; Nathan Rosenberg. Tarrytown, NY: Sleepy Hollow Restorations, 1975. 218pp, ill

5347 Holtzapffel, Charles, 1806-1847. Descriptive Catalogue of the Woods Commonly Employed in This Country for the Mechanical and Ornamental Arts ... An extract from "Turning and Mechanical Manipulation." London: Holtzapffel & Co., 1843; 1852. 7pp, 120 ill MH-A

5348 Hough, Romeyn Beck, 1857-1924. The American Woods, exhibited by actual specimens and with copious explanatory text. (Vol. 14 by Marjorie G. Hough.) 14 vol. Lowville, NY: Author, 1888-1928; 13 vol. as Hough's Encyclopedia of American Woods, by Ellwood S. Harrar. New York: R. Speller, 1957. ill, pls, samples

5349 Huggard, Eric Richard, and T. H. Owen. Forest Tools and Instruments. London: A. & C. Black, 1960. 119pp, ill

5350 The International Book of Wood. Fore. by Hugh Johnson. New York: Simon & Schuster, 1976. 150 color ill

5351 Levien, J. M. The Woods of New Zealand and Their Adaptability to Art Furniture. n.p.: 1861. 12 ill SIB-3

5352 *Payson, William Farquhar, ed. Mahogany, Antique and Modern; a study of its history and use in the decorative arts. New York: Dutton, 1926. 154pp, ill, pls ("In the Forest," by Payson; "Mahogany and the Cabinet-Maker," by K. Schmieg; "Mahogany in Architecture," by K. M. Murchison; "Marine Architecture and Boat Building," by H. B. Culver; "The Piano and its Prototypes," by Francis Morris; "Historic Furniture Styles," by C. O. Cornelius; "The Furniture of the Present Day," by Ralph Erskine.) NNC-Ave, MiGr

WOOD FINISHING

5353 The Cabinet-Makers' Guide: or, Rules and instructions in the art of varnishing, dying, staining, japanning, polishing, lackering and beautifying wood, ivory, tortoise-shell and metal.... London: J. Arliss, 1818; new ed. London: printed for Knight & Lacy; Greenfield, Mass.: Ansel Phelps, 1825; "from latest London edition." Concord, N.H.: Jacob B. Moore, printer, 1827. 36pp, 108pp; 120pp, with cover ill of piano CtY, NN, NNC-Ave

5354 The Carver and Gilder. London: Houlston & Stoneman, 184-? 80pp DeWint

5355   Crace, John Gregory. Some Account of the Worshipful Com-
       pany of Painters, Otherwise Painter-Stainers. London:
       the Company, 1880. 22pp BM

5356   Crease, James, inventor of cheap paint. Elegance, Amuse-
       ment and Utility: or the whole process of varnishing on
       wood. The 2nd edition to which is added gilding, working
       in black and gold, etc. London: Author, 1800; 3rd ed.
       Bath: Author, 1801?; 4th ed. 1802? 38pp NN, BM

5357   Darrow, Floyd Lavern. The Story of an Ancient Art, from
       the earliest adhesives to vegetable glue. Lansdale, Pa.;
       South Bend, Ind.: Perkins Glue Co., 1930. 94pp, ill,
       pls DeWint

5358   Englefield, William Alexander Devereux. The History of the
       Painter-Stainers Company of London. London: Chapman
       & Dodd, 1923; reissue with supplement. 1936. 248pp,
       pls BM

5359   The French Polishers Handbook, with a section on gilding and
       bronzing. London: P. Marshall, 1921. 114pp, ill DLC

5360   French Polisher's Manual. By a French Polisher. London;
       New York: E. & F. N. Spon, 1879; 1882; 1912; 2nd ed.
       rev. & enl. 1946. 31pp; ...; ...; 64pp, ill DLC, MiD

5361   The French Polisher's Trade Price List, showing at a glance
       the prices paid for labour only, and for labour and ma-
       terials combined, for french polishing every class of furni-
       ture, musical instruments, etc. London: Wyman & Sons,
       1885. 27pp, ill NN

5362   Gardner, Franklin B. Everybody's Paint Book. A complete
       guide to the art of outdoor and indoor painting. Designed
       for the special use of those who wish to do their own
       work, and consisting of practical lessons in plain painting,
       varnishing, polishing, staining, paper-hanging, kalsomining,
       etc. New York: M. T. Richardson, 1881; 1884; 1886;
       ...; 1892.... 188pp, ill NN, DLC, DeWint

5363   _____ . The Painters' Encyclopedia, containing definitions
       of all important words in the art of plain and artistic
       painting, with details in coach, carriage, railway car,
       house, sign and ornamental painting. New York: M. T.
       Richardson, 1887; 1891; 1894. 427pp, many ill MiD,
       NNC-Ave, DeWint

5364   Hasluck, Paul Nooncree, ed. Practical Graining and Marbling.
       London; New York: Cassell, 1902; 1904. 160pp, 79 ill
       DLC

5365   Howard, Thomas. The Improved Cabinet-Maker's Guide:

Comprising a collection of valuable receipts for dyeing, staining, varnishing, and beautifying of wood, ivory, tortoiseshell, brass, etc. London: n.p., 18-? 28pp

5366 Japanese Pattern Book of Veneers. 258 Original specimens of veneers. Index in Japanese and English. 2nd ed. Japan: 1878. 100 leaves

5367 Masury, John Wesley, 1820-1895. The American Grainers' Handbook: a popular and practical treatise on the art of imitating colored and fancy woods; with examples and illustrations. New York: Masury, 1872. 109pp, ill, 14 color pls ViU, NN

5368 Miller, Margaret M., and Sigmund Aarseth. Norwegian Rosemaling; decorative painting on wood. New York: Scribner, 1974. 211pp, ill, bib

5369 The Painter, Gilder, and Varnisher's Companion: containing rules and regulations in everything relating to the arts of painting, gilding, varnishing, and glass-staining. Philadelphia: H. C. Baird, 1850; ...; 27th ed., rev. enl., and in great part re-written. 1894. 189pp, ill; ...; 395pp, ill

5370 *Shapland, Henry Percival. The Practical Decoration of Furniture. I. Veneering, Inlay or Marqueterie, Gilding, Painting; II. Moulding, Pierced Work, Turned Work, Twisting, Carving; III. Applied Metalwork, Covering with Leather and Textiles, Lacquering and Miscellaneous Decoration. 3 vol. London: E. Benn, 1926-27. ill, pls DLC

5371 Soxhlet, D. H. The Art of Dyeing and Staining Marble, artificial stone, bone, horn, ivory and wood, and of imitating all sorts of wood; a practical handbook for the use of joiners, turners, manufacturers of fancy goods, stick and umbrella makers, comb makers, etc. Tr. from German by Arthur Morris and Herbert Robson. London: Scott, Greenwood, 1902. 168pp

5372 Standage, H. C., ed. Decoration of Metal, Wood, Glass, etc.; a book for manufacturers, mechanics, painters, decorators, and all workmen in the fancy trades. New York: J. Wiley, 1908. 228pp

5373 Tombor, Ilona R. Old Hungarian Painted Woodwork, 15th to 19th Century. Tr. by Lili Halapy. Budapest: Corvina Pr, 1967. 61pp, 51 pls

5374 Wall, William Edmund, 1858-1934. Graining, Ancient and Modern. Somerville, Mass.: Author, 1905; 2nd ed. rev. 1924; 3rd ed. rev. & enl. by Fred N. Vanderwalker.

Chicago: F. J. Drake, 1937. 137pp, 50 ill; 68 ill
(mostly color); 155pp, 75 ill (Illustrations of grained
doors and other objects, and tools used.)

5375 _____ . Practical Graining, with descriptions of colors
employed and tools used, illustrated by 47 color plates
representing the various woods used in interior finishing.
Philadelphia: House Painting and Decorating Publishing
Co., 1891. 59pp, 47 color pls

5376 *Whittock, Nathaniel. The Decorative Painters' and Glaziers'
Guide; containing the most approved methods of imitating
oak, mahogany, maple, rose, cedar, coral, and every
other kind of fancy wood; verd antique, dove sienna, por-
phyry, white veined, and other marbles; ... staining and
painting on glass ... and designs for decorating apartments; ... with directions for stenciling,... London:
I. T. Hinton, 1827. 332pp, 85 color pls

FRETWORK, BUHL WORK AND MARQUETRY

5377 Adamson, David. The Art of Fret Sawing and Marquetry
Cutting. A complete guide for amateurs and professionals,
containing full and practical instructions.... New York;
London: Ward, Lock, 1888. 158pp, 60 ill MiGr

5378 Bemrose, William, Jr. Fret Cutting and Perforated Carving,
with practical instructions. 2nd ed. London; Derby:
Bemrose, 1869; ...; 14th ed. London: Bemrose, 1875.
10pp, ill, pls; ...; 24pp, pls MiGr

5379 _____ . Manual of Buhl-Work and Marquetry ... with 90
colored designs. London: Bemrose, 1872; 1880?; 3rd
ed. 1887; ... 36pp, ill, 13 pls (some color) NN, BM

5380 (I. B.) Farrington's 1879 (Illustrated) Price List of Ornamental Designs for Scroll Sawing and All Kinds of Scroll
Saw Machines. Reprint. Levittown, NY: Early Trades
and Crafts Society, 1974. 16pp, ill   .

5381 Hope, Arthur. A Manual of Sorrento and Inlaid Work for
Amateurs, with Original Designs. Chicago: J. Wilkinson,
1876; New York: Putnam's, 1877; rev. ed. 1880. 47pp,
ill, 16 pls; ...; 84pp, ill, 20 pls ViU, DLC

5382 *Jackson, Frederick Hamilton, 1848-1923. Intarsia and Marquetry. London: Sands & Co, 1903. 152pp, ill, 55 pls
DeWint, NN

5383 Lawford, Henry. The Cabinet of Marquetry, Buhl, and Inlaid work. London: 1855; as Designs for Doors, corners,

panels ... bookcases, brass and china decorations, etc.
London: 1867. ill, 20 color pls NjP, DLC

5384 Sawyer, George A. Fret-Sawing and Wood-Carving, for
      Amateurs. Boston; New York: Lee & Shepard, 1875.
      63pp, drawings

5385 Williams, Henry T. Ornamental Designs for Fret-Work,
      Fancy Carving and Home Decorations. How to Use the
      Fret-Saw. 7 parts. New York: Author, 1875-1877.
      152 pls

WOODWORKING TOOLS, CARPENTRY AND JOINERY

5386 Alford, B. W. E., and Theodore C. Barker. A History of
      the Carpenters Company. London: Allen & Unwin, 1968.
      217pp, ill, 17 pls, bib

5387 *Arnold, Roy, and Philip Walker. The Traditional Tools of
      the Carpenter and Other Craftsmen. 4 vol. London:
      Arnold & Walker, 1974, 1975, 1976. ill (1. Mainly
      English metal planes. Includes supplement to W. L.
      Goodman's British Plane Makers from 1700. 2. Includes
      a bibliography. 3. Saws and other tools including plough
      planes. 4. Bits and planes.)

5388 Articles of the Carpenters' Company of Philadelphia: and
      their rules for measuring and valuing house-carpenters'
      work. Philadelphia: Hall & Sellers, printers, 1786; re-
      print as The Carpenters' Company ... 1786 Rule Book.
      Princeton, NJ: Pyne Pr, 1971; facsim. reprint, ed by
      Charles E. Peterson, as The Rules of Work of the Car-
      penters' Company of the City and County of Philadelphia,
      1786. Ambridge, Pa: Early American Industries Asso-
      ciation, 1975. 159pp, 36 pls

5389 Barras, Robert Thomas. The Sheffield Standard List: Prices
      and patterns of machinery, files, rasps, saws, joiners'
      tools, etc. Sheffield: R. T. Barras, 1862. ill, folio
      BM

5390 Blackburn, Graham. The Illustrated Encyclopedia of Wood-
      working Handtools, instruments and devices. New York:
      Simon & Schuster, 1974. 235pp, ill with drawings

5391 (G. W.) Bradley's Edge Tools. 1876 Catalog. Reprint.
      16pp, ill (Axes, adzes, draw knives, froes, coopers'
      tools, hoes, butchers' tools, etc.)

5392 Brombacher, A. F., and Co., Inc. Tools for Coopers and
      Gaugers, produce triers.... Catalogue No. 20. New

York: 1922; reprint. Philadelphia: A. M. Beitler, 1966.
36pp, ill

5393 Cavallini, William C., ed. Illustrated Catalogue of Carpen-
      ters' Tools: J. B. Shannon, Philadelphia, 1873. Reprint.
      West Harwick, Mass.: W. C. Cavallini, 1973.

5394 Chapin-Stephens Co., New Hartford, Conn. Catalogue No.
      114 (early-20th century). Reprint, with historical intro-
      duction. Fitzwilliam, N.H.: Ken Roberts, 1975. 88pp,
      ill (Planes, rules, marking gauges, levels, spoke-shaves,
      etc.)

5395 [No entry.]

5396 Davis Level and Tool Co. ca. 1880 catalog. Reprint. Lan-
      caster, Mass: Roger Smith, 1975. 76pp, ill

5397 Emerson, William Andrew, 1851- . Practical Instruction in
      the Art of Wood Engraving.... East Douglas, Mass.: C.
      J. Batcheller, 1876; new ed. as Handbook of Wood En-
      graving, with practical instruction in the art for persons
      wishing to learn without an instructor; containing a de-
      scription of tools and apparatus used and explaining the
      manner of engraving various classes of work.... Boston:
      Lee & Shepard; New York: C. T. Dillingham, 1881.
      52pp, ill, 2 color pls; 95pp, ill, color pls DLC, NN

5398 First Exhibition of Works in Wood Held at Carpenters'
      Hall ... 1884. London: 1884; Second Exhibition ...
      under auspices of ... Company of Carpenters and ...
      Company of Joiners ... 1888. London: 1888. BM

5399 *Goodman, William Louis. British Plane Makers from 1700.
      London: Bell, 1968. 135pp, ill, 8 pls, makers' list
      with marks & dates

5400 *   . The History of Woodworking Tools. London: G.
      Bell, 1964; New York: D. McKay, 1967. 208pp, ill, bib

5401 Hasluck, Paul Nooncree, ed. Cabinetwork and Joinery, com-
      prising designs and details of construction, with 2021
      working drawings. London; New York: Cassell, 1907;
      Philadelphia: McKay, 1908; London; New York: 1912.
      568pp, ill, 12 color pls NNC-Ave

5402 _____ . The Cabinet Workers' Handybook. A practical
      manual, embracing information on the tools, materials,
      appliances and processes employed in cabinet work. Lon-
      don: Crosby Lockwood, 1890; 1893; 4th ed. 1894; ...;
      7th ed. 1907. 140pp, ill MP, PPL, NN

5403 _____ , ed. The Handyman's Book of Tools, Materials,

and Processes Employed in Woodworking. London; New
York: Cassell, 1903; as Woodworking. A book of tools,
materials and processes for the handyman. London; New
York: 1906; Philadelphia: McKay, 1907; 1910; 1916.
760pp, 2545 ill ViU

5404 Hayes, M. Vincent. Artistry in Wood: ideas, history, tools,
techniques: carving, sculpture, assemblage, woodcuts,
etc. Newton Abbot: David & Charles, 1973. 127pp, ill,
bib

5405 Heckscher, Morrison H. The Organization and Practice of
Philadelphia Cabinet Making Establishments, 1790-1820.
Thesis. 1964. 216pp, pls DeWint

5406 Hendrick, Robert E. P. John Gaines II and Thomas Gaines I,
"Turners" of Ipswich, Massachusetts. Thesis. 1964.
386pp, pls DeWint

5407 Hewett, Cecil Alec. The Development of Carpentry, 1200-
1700; an Essex study. Newton Abbot: David & Charles;
New York: A. M. Kelley, 1969. 232pp, ill, bib

5408 Hibben, Thomas E. The Carpenters' Tool Chest. Philadelphia; London: Lippincott; London: Routledge, 1933.
209pp, ill PP, NN, DLC

5409 Horner, Joseph Gregory. Tools for Engineers and Woodworkers Including Modern Instruments of Measurement.
London: C. Lockwood, 1905; as Tools for Machinists
and Woodworkers; including modern instruments of
measurement; a practical treatise comprising a general
description and classification of cutting tools and tool
angles, allied cutting tools for machinists and woodworkers, shearing tools; scraping tools; saws, milling
cutters; drilling and boring tools; taps and dies; punches
and hammers; and the hardening, tempering, and grinding
of these tools. New York: N. W. Henley, 1906. 340pp,
456 ill MiU, MB, NN, PPD

5410 *Kilby, Kenneth. The Cooper and His Trade. London: J.
Baker, 1971. 192pp, ill, bib

5411 Lang and Jacobs--"Catalog and Price List"--Headquarters for
Coopers' Supplies and Cooperage Stock. 1884 Catalogue.
Reprint. 24pp, ill

5412 (Alex) Mathieson and Sons, Glasgow. 1899 Joiner and Cooper
Tools Catalogue. 8th ed. Reprint. Fitzwilliam, N.H.:
Ken Roberts, 1975. 64pp, 20 pls, over 527 full-size
moulding contours

5413 *Mercer, Henry Chapman, 1856-1930. Ancient Carpenters'

Tools, illustrated and explained, together with the implements of the lumberman, joiner, and cabinet maker in use
in the 18th century. Doylestown, Pa: Bucks County Historical Society, 1929; 2nd ed. 1951; 3rd ed. 1960; reprint
of 3rd ed. 1968. 331pp, 250 ill, bib

5414 Orr and Lockett Hardware Company. Mechanics Tools. 1898
Catalogue. Reprint. 208pp, ill (Woodworking tools,
drawing instruments, machines, stone cutters' tools, measuring tools, etc.)

5415 (The Arthur) Pascal Collection of Antique Woodworking Tools.
Montreal, Que: J. Pascal Hardware Co, 1975. 36pp,
ill, bib, gloss

5416 The Plane Facts. Levittown, NY: Early Trades & Crafts
Society, 197-?

5417 Richards, John. A Treatise on the Construction and Operation
of Wood-Working Machines: including a history of the
origin and progress of the manufacture of wood-working
machinery. London: E. & F. N. Spon, 1872. 283pp,
many ill, 23 pls NN

5418 _____. On the Arrangement, care, and operation of woodworking factories and machinery; forming a complete
operator's handbook. New York: E. & F. Spon, 1873.
189pp, ill NN

5419 _____. Wood Conversion by Machinery. London: Spon,
1876. 100pp, ill NN

5420 *Roberts, Kenneth D. Wooden Planes in 19th Century America.
Identification, classification, history, uses. Fitzwilliam,
N.H.: Ken Roberts, 1975. 160pp, 55 ill (Includes re-
prints of Arrowmammett Works, Middletown, Conn. Bench
Tools and Moulding Tools catalogue; also 32pp from C.
Holtzapffel's Turning and Mechanical Manipulation. London:
1858; also 32pp from Peter Nickolson's Mechanic's Com-
panion. Philadelphia: 1849.)

5421 * _____, and Jane W. Roberts. Planemakers and Other Edge
Tool Enterprises in New York State in the 19th Century.
Fitzwilliam, N.H.: Ken Roberts, for N.Y. State Historical
Association, and Early American Industries Association,
1971. 230pp, 120 pls (Excerpts from trade catalogues,
check lists, etc.)

5422 Robison, J., and T. Tredgold. Principles of Construction in
Carpentry and Joinery. London?: 1859. ill

5423 *Salaman, Raphael A. Dictionary of Tools Used in the Woodworking and Allied Trades, circa 1700-1900. London:
Allen & Unwin, 1975. 545pp, hundreds of ill, bib

5424 *Sayward, Elliot M. The Cooper and His Work; definitions,
      operations, materials, tools. 1969; reprint for the Early
      Trades and Crafts Society. Levittown, NY: 1972. 63
      leaves, ill

5425 *Sellens, Alvin. The Stanley Plane. A History and Descriptive
      Inventory. Ambridge, Pa: Early American Industries As-
      sociation, 1975. 216pp, 300 ill

5426 (J. B.) Shannon. Carpenters' Tools. 1873 Catalog. Reprint.
      97pp, ill

5427 *Sloan, Eric. A Reverence for Wood. New York: W. Funk,
      1965. 110pp, ill

5428 Stanley Rule and Level Co. 1859 Catalogue with 1855 price
      list. Reprint. 32pp, ill

5429 _____. January 1867 Price List. Reprint. Fitzwilliam,
      N.H.: Ken Roberts, 197-? 52pp, ill

5430 _____. Catalogue of Tools and Hardware, 1870. Price
      List of U.S. Standard Boxwood and Ivory Rules, levels,
      try squares, gauges, iron and wood bench planes, mallets,
      hand screws, spoke shaves, etc. Reprint. Bristol, Conn.:
      Ken Roberts, 1973. 96pp, ill, bib (Includes supplement of
      1871)

5431 _____. Price List of Tools and Hardware, 1879. Price
      List of U.S. Standard Boxwood and ivory rules, plumbs
      and levels, try squares, bevels, gauges, mallets, iron and
      wood adjustable planes, spoke shaves, screw drivers, awl
      hafts, handles, etc. Reprint with reprod. of additional
      pages of 2nd printing. Bristol, Conn: K. Roberts, 1973.
      68pp, ill

5432 _____. 1888 Catalog. Reprint. 68pp, ill

5433 _____. 1892 Catalog. Reprint. 65pp, ill

5434 _____. 1898 Catalog. Reprint. 70pp, ill

5435 _____. Catalogue # 102, 1909. Facs. reprint. Lan-
      caster, Pa: Roger Smith, 197-? 127pp, ill

5436 Stanley Works, Ltd. Great Britain. A Brief History of the
      Woodworker's Plane. Sheffield, Eng: Stanley Works,
      1961. 12pp, ill

5437 Stanley-Stone, Arthur Carlyon. The Worshipful Company of
      Turners of London. Its origin and history. London:
      Lindley-Jones, 1925. 337pp, pls, facsims BM

5438 Tompkins, C(harles) R. A History of the Planing-Mill, with
      practical suggestions for the construction, care, and man-
      agement of wood-working machinery. New York: J. Wiley,
      1889. 222pp NN

5439 Welsh, Peter C. Woodworking Tools, 1600-1900. "Contribu-
      tions from the Museum of History and Technology, Paper
      51." Washington, D.C.: Smithsonian Institute; GPO, 1966.
      48pp (pp. 179-227), ill, bib

5440 *Wildung, Frank H. Woodworking Tools at Shelburne Museum.
      Shelburne, Vt.: the Museum, 1957; new ed. by Carl Wil-
      dung. 197?. 70pp, ill; 77pp, ill

5441 (John) Wilkinson Company Price List No. 88 (1888). Tools
      and Machines for Metal and Woodworkers. Reprint. West
      Harwick, Mass: W. C. Cavallini, 1973. 36pp, ill

5442 Woodworking Machinery. The New York Public Library has
      bound together, without cataloguing, a collection of pam-
      phlets on this subject.

LATHES AND ORNAMENTAL TURNING

5443 Abell, Sydney George, John Leggat, and Warren Green Ogden,
      Jr. A Contribution Towards a Bibliography of the Writings,
      Special, General and Periodical Forming the Literature of
      the Art of Turning. n.p.: S. G. Abell, for the Society of
      Ornamental Turners, 1950; 2nd rev. & enl. ed. as A Bib-
      liography of the Art of Turning and Lathe and Machine
      Tool History, with additional references to books and
      periodical articles which are of interest in relation to these
      subjects. n.p.: Abell, 1956. 89pp

5444 Ash, James. The Art of Double-Counting on the Lathe; where-
      by a variety of patterns in the form of ellipses, triangles,
      squares, pentagons, hexagons, and octagons, three, four,
      six and eight-looped figures, besides others of a more
      complex character, may be produced by means of the com-
      mon eccentric chuck, used in combination with the division-
      plate and the eccentric and elliptical cutters. Appendix by
      John Jacob Holtzapffel. London: L. Booth, 1857; London:
      Holtzapffel, 1881. 131pp, 74 ill, pls NN

5445 Cavallini, William C., ed. Illustrated Catalogue of Scroll
      Saws, Lathes, Fancy Woods, Clock Movements, Pocket
      Cutlery, Mechanics' Tools, etc., etc. A. H. Pomeroy,
      Hartford, Conn. 1886. Reprint. West Harwick, Mass:
      W. C. Cavallini, 1973. 37pp, ill

5446 Engleheart, Nathaniel Brown. A Concise Treatise on Eccentric

Turning: to which are added practical observations on the
uses of the eccentric cutting frame, the drilling frame,
and the universal cutting frame. By an Amateur. London:
Pelham Richardson, 1852; London: 1867. 152pp, 50 pls
BM

5447 Evans, John Henry. Ornamental Turning. London: 1889;
      3 vol. Philadelphia: D. McKay, 1910. 282pp, ill

5448 The Handbook of Turning: containing instructions in concen-
      tric, elliptic, and eccentric turning; also various plates of
      chucks, tools, and instruments; and directions for using
      the eccentric cutter, drill, vertical cutter, and circular
      rest. London: Saunders & Otley, 1842; 1846; 1852; 1859;
      as The Turner's Companion. Philadelphia: 1868. 143pp,
      14 pls (Includes history of lathes) NN, DeWint, DLC

5449 Hasluck, Paul Nooncree, ed. Lathe-Work. A practical trea-
      tise on the tools, appliances, and processes employed in
      the art of turning. Including hand-turning, boring and
      drilling, the use of the slide rests, and overhead gear,
      screw-cutting by hand and self-acting motion, wheel-cut-
      ting, etc., etc. London: Lockwood, 18-?; 6th ed. 1898;
      8th ed. 1904; 11th ed. enl. & rev. New York: Van Nos-
      trand, 1923. 212pp, ill; ...; ...; ...; 232pp, ill NN,
      DLC

5450 _____ , ed. The Wood Turner's Handybook; a practical
      manual for workers at the lathe; embracing information on
      the tools, appliances and processes employed in wood
      turning. London: Lockwood, 18-?; 2nd ed. 1890; 6th ed.
      1901; ... 144pp, ill NN, MiU

5451 Hendrick, Robert E. P. John Gaines II and Thomas Gaines I,
      "Turners" of Ipswich, Massachusetts. Thesis. 1964.
      386pp, pls DeWint

5452 Hetherington, Arthur Lonsdale, 1881- . British Empire Hard-
      woods from the Point of View of Turnery. Fore. by Major
      J. G. Holtzapffel Budd. London: HMSO, 1931. 34pp, pls
      NN

5453 Holtzapffel, Charles, (and continued by John Holtzapffel).
      Turning and Mechanical Manipulation. Intended as a work
      of general reference and practical instruction, on the
      lathe.... 5 vol. (6 were intended). London: Holtzapffel
      & Co., 1843-1883. 3040pp, ill NN, DLC, DeWint, MdBP

5454 Holtzapffel, John. The Principles and Practices of Ornamental
      or Complex Turning. Vol. 5 of Turning and Mechanical
      Manipulation. London: Holtzapffel, 1894; reprint with a
      new introd. by Robert Austin. New York: Dover, 1973.
      656pp, 66 pls of 600 figures

5455 Horner, Joseph Gregory, 1847-1927. English and American
       Lathes. London; New York: Whittaker, 1900. 166pp, ill
       PP

5456 Ibbetson, John Holt. A Brief Account of Ibbetson's Geometric
       Chuck, manufactured by Holtzapffel and Company. With a
       selection of specimens illustrative of its powers. London:
       A. Hancock, printer, 1833. 47pp, ill NN, BM

5457 _____. Specimens in Eccentric Circular Turning, with
       practical instructions for producing corresponding pieces
       in that art. London: Author, 1817; 1818; new ed. Lon-
       don: W. Wetton, 1825; London: Longman, Orme, Brown,
       Green & Longman, 1838; 3rd ed. 1840; reissued. 1851.
       86pp, ill, 6 pls; ...; 100pp, ill, 6 pls; ...; 176pp, many
       ill, pls DeWint, NN, MB, BM

5458 Lukin, James. The Lathe and Its Uses; or, instruction in
       the art of turning wood and metal. Including a description
       of the most modern appliances for the ornamentation of
       plane and curved surfaces, an entirely novel form of lathe
       for eccentric and rose-engine turning; a lathe and planing
       machine combined. London: Trubner; New York: J.
       Wiley, 1868; 7th ed. London: K. Paul, Trench, Trubner,
       1891. 294pp, ill; 1891: 315pp, ill, pls ViU, PPH, De-
       Wint

5459 _____. Turning for Amateurs; being descriptions of the
       lathe and its attachments and tools; with minute instruc-
       tions for their effective use on wood, metal, ivory and
       other materials. London: L. U. Gill, 18- ; new ed.
       1884. 204pp, ill, 11 pls MiD, KRL

5460 _____, ed. Turning Lathes. London: E. & F. N. Spon,
       1888; 3rd ed. Colchester: Britannia Co, 1890; 5th ed.
       1899. 160pp, ill; 160pp, 19 pls; 228pp, 225 ill BM

5461 Northcott, William Henry. Examples of Lathes, Apparatus
       and Work. London: E. & F. N. Spon, 1889. 48pp, ill
       BM

5462 _____. Geometric Turning Simplified. London: E. &
       F. N. Spon, 1889. 62pp, ill

5463 _____. A Treatise on Lathes and Turning, Simple, Me-
       chanical, and Ornamental. London: 1868; 2nd ed. 1876.
       ill

5464 Savory, Henry Stiles. Geometric Turning; comprising a
       description of the new geometric chuck constructed by
       Mr. Plant, of Birmingham; with directions for its use.
       London: Longmans, Green, 1873. 78pp, ill, pls DeWint

5465 Small, Tunstall, and Christopher Woodbridge. Architectural
     Turned Woodwork of the 16th, 17th, and 18th Centuries.
     London: Architectural Pr; New York: Helburn, 1930.
     20 pls

5466 Woodbury, Robert S. History of the Lathe to 1850; a study
     in the growth of a technical element of an industrial
     economy. Cleveland: Society for the History of Tech-
     nology, 1961; Cambridge, Mass: MIT Pr, 1964. 124pp,
     ill, bib

WOODEN WARES AND TREEN

5467 Card, Devere A. The Use of Burl in America; a short dis-
     cussion of American treen. Utica, NY: Munson Williams-
     Proctor Institute, 1971. 30pp, ill

5468 Church, Sir Arthur Herbert. Old English Fruit Trenchers.
     Reprint from Portfolio, September, October, 1885. Lon-
     don: 1885. 20pp, ill CtY

5469 *Evan-Thomas, Owen. Domestic Utensils of Wood, 16th to 19th
     Century: a short history of wooden articles in domestic
     use from the 16th to the middle of the 19th century. Lon-
     don: Author, 1932; facsim. reprint. Wakefield, Eng: E P
     Publishing, 1973. 178pp, ill, 70 pls DLC, NN

5470 Gallatin, Albert Eugene. A 15th Century Mazer. Reprint
     from Art and Progress, May 1912. New York: De Vinne
     Pr, 1912. 7pp, 2 pls DLC, NN

5471 *Gould, Mary Earle. Early American Wooden Ware and Other
     Kitchen Utensils. Springfield, Mass: Pond-Ekberg, 1942;
     rev. ed. 1948; rev. enl. ed. Rutland, Vt: Tuttle, 1962.
     230pp, ill; 243pp, ill, 131 pls

5472 _____, and Kathleen Cairns. New York Use of Wooden
     Ware (Gould), and chairmaking in Orange County, New
     York (Cairns). New York: State Historical Association,
     1945. 9pp, ill NN

5473 James, William Thomas. Treen: A Book of Gougework.
     London: Pitman, 1950. 83pp, ill, bib

5474 Ketchum, William C., Jr. Basketry and Woodenware. A
     collector's guide. New York: Macmillan; London: Col-
     lier-Macmillan, 1974. 228pp, 83 ill, bib (Ca.1650-ca.
     1930)

5475 (L. H.) Mace and Company. 1883 catalog. Woodenware,
     meat safes, toys, refrigerators, children's carriages, and

house furnishings goods. Facsimile reprint. Princeton,
NJ: Pyne Pr, 1971. 70pp, ill, bib

5476 Maust, Don, ed. American Woodenware and Other Primitives;
a collection of essays on woodenware, treen, tin, brass,
copper, iron, pewter, and pottery; a practical reference.
Uniontown, Pa: E. G. Warman, 1974. 159pp, ill (Weathervanes, kitchen utensils, trunks, etc.)

5477 Nilsson, Ake R. Woodware. Tr. by D. Cook-Radmore. New
York: Drake, 1973. 88pp, ill

5478 Pinto, Edward Henry. A Short Guide to the Pinto Collection
of Wooden Bygones. Northwood, Middlesex: Pinto, 1955.
33pp, typescript BM

5479 *_____. Treen and Other Wooden Bygones: an encyclopedia
and social history. London: Bell, 1969. 458pp, ill, 239
pls, bib

5480 *_____. Treen, or small woodenware throughout the ages.
London; New York: Batsford, 1949. 120pp, ill

5481 *_____. Wooden Bygones of Smoking and Snuff Taking.
London: Hutchinson; Newton, Mass: C. T. Branford,
1961. 96pp, ill, 30 pls, bib

5482 *_____, and Eva Pinto. Tunbridge and Scottish Souvenir
Woodware. With chapters on bois durci and pyrography.
London: G. Bell, 1970. 149pp, 30 ill, 52 pls (19th
century. Includes tartan ware)

5483 Smith, William Hawkes. Description of an Ancient and Curious Wooden Tankard, or wassell bowl, in the possession
of the late Joseph Smith, Esq., of Bristol; with a short
account of the Glastonbury Cup, preserved at Wardour
Castle. Birmingham, Eng: Author, 1824. 4pp, ill BM

5484 Younghusband, Ethel. Mansions, Men, and Tunbridge Ware.
Trading Estate, Slough: Windsor Pr, 1949. 183pp, 21
ill (Tunbridge Wells, 1660-1900)

WOOD CARVING

5485 Agghazy, Maria G. Early Wood Carvings in Hungary. Tr.
by B. Baranyai. Budapest: Akademiai Kiado, Hungarian
Academy of Sciences, 1965. 38pp, 88 pls, bib

5486 Ahlborn, Richard E. Spanish Colonial Wood Carving in New
Mexico, 1598-1848. Thesis. 1959. 118pp, pls DeWint

5487 Anderson, Mary Desiree. The Medieval Carver. Pref. by

W. G. Constable. Cambridge, Eng: U Pr, 1935. 187pp, ill, 20 pls, bib BM

5488 Bemrose, William, Jr. Manual of Wood-Carving. Introd. by Llewellyn Jewitt. London; Oxford: J. M. Parker, 1862; 6th ed. 1868; 15th ed. London: Bemrose, 1880?; 23rd ed. London; Derby: Bemrose, 1906. 30pp, ill; 34pp, 14 pls; 72pp, ill, pls DLC, BM

5489 The Carver and Gilder. London: Houlston & Stoneman, 184-? 80pp DeWint

5490 Castilian Wood-Carvings of the Late Gothic Period in the Collections of the Hispanic Society of America. New York: 1927. 19pp, ill, 4 pls, bib MiU

5491 *Christensen, Erwin Ottomar. Early American Wood Carving. Cleveland: World, 1952; New York: Dover; London: Constable, 1972. 149pp, ill (some color); 160pp, ill, 9 pls, bib (17th century to present. Portraits, monuments, household articles, religious art, toys, decorations, decoys, etc.)

5492 *Cousins, Frank, and Phil M. Riley. The Woodcarver of Salem; Samuel McIntire, His Life and Work. Boston: Little, Brown & Co, 1916. 168pp, ill, 127 pls (McIntire, 1757-1811) NN, DLC

5493 Crallan, Franklyn A. Details of Gothic Wood Carvings ... being a series of drawings from original work chiefly of the 14th and 15th centuries. London: Batsford, 1896. 19pp, 34 pls MiGr

5494 Hasluck, Paul Nooncree, ed. Wood Carving: comprising practical instructions, examples and designs including 1146 working drawings and photographic illustrations. Philadelphia: McKay; London: Cassell, 1908; 1910. 568pp, 1146 ill (Includes "History of Wood Carving" by Herbert Turner) MiGr, DLC, NN

5495 Kimball, Sidney Fiske. Mr. Samuel McIntire, Carver, the Architect of Salem. Portland, Me: Southworth-Anthoensen Pr, for Essex Institute of Salem, 1940. 157pp, pls DLC

5496 MacLaren, George E. G. The Woodcarvers of Nova Scotia. Nova Scotia: Museum, 1971. 28pp, pls, bib

5497 *Maskell, Alfred. Wood Sculpture. London: Methuen, 1911. 425pp, 59 pls, bib TxU, MiU

5498 Miller, Fred, ed. Wood-Carving; practically, theoretically, and historically considered; with notes on design as applied to carved wood. London: Wyman, 1884?; 3rd ed. London: E. Menken, n.d. (1885?). 105pp, 65 ill (Tools and designs. Includes SKM Collection)

5499 Mudejar Wood-Carvings in the Collection of the Hispanic Society of America. New York: 1928. 63pp, ill, 16 pls, bib (Spanish-Mohammedan)

5500 Rogers, George Alfred. The Art of Wood-carving. Practical hints to amateurs, and a short history of the art. London: 1867. ill BM

5501 Rowe, Eleanor. French Wood Carvings from the National Museums. 3 vol. London: Batsford, 1896-97. 54 pls, bib (I. Late 15th and early 16th centuries; II. 16th century; III. 17th and 18th centuries)

5502 _____. Practical Wood-Carving: a book for the student, carver, teacher, designer, and architect ... old and modern examples. London: Batsford, 1907; rev. ed. 1918. 213pp, 114 ill, gloss

5503 _____, ed. Studies from the Museums, Woodcarving Details. Abridged ed. of 1890 original ed. London: J. Tiranti, 1928. 4pp, 28 pls MiGr

5504 Sanders, William Bliss. Examples of Carved Oak Woodwork in the Houses and Furniture of the 16th and 17th Centuries. London: B. Quaritch, 1883. 48pp, 25 ill MiGr

5505 Wood Carving; plates from "l'Art Pour Tous," 1866-79. Paris: A. Morel, 1879? 76 pls NN, DLC

SECTION X

METALWORK AND METALS

PEWTER, COPPER, BRASS, TIN AND ART METALWORK

5506 *Aitchison, Leslie. A History of Metals. 2 vol. London: Macdonald & Evens; New York: Interscience, 1960. 647pp, ill, pls, bib

5507 Aitken, William Costen. Brass and Brass Manufactures. The early history of the metal; the introduction of the manufacture of brass in England; its development; introduction into Birmingham; progressive and present condition of the manufacture. London: R. Hardwicke, 1866. 60pp (Extract from British Association for the Advancement of Science) DLC

5508 American Pewter (ca.1730-ca.1870) in the Collection of Dr. and Mrs. Melvyn D. Wolf. Loan exhibition. December 1973-January 1974. Flint, Mich: Institute of Arts, 1973. 40pp, ill, bib

5509 American Pewter from the Collection of Mrs. Robert D. Graff, Dr. Joseph H. Kler, Mr. John H. McMurray. Exhibition. January-September 1968. Trenton, NJ: State Museum, 1968. 16pp, ill

5510 *American Pewter in the Museum of Fine Arts, Boston, Department of American Decorative Arts and Sculpture. Introd. by Jonathan Fairbanks. Boston: the Museum, dist. by N.Y. Graphic Society, Greenwich, 1974. 119pp, ill, bib (342 pieces--half of them illustrated)

5511 American Pewterers and Their Marks. New York: Metropolitan Museum, 1940. 21pp

5512 Amiranashvili, Shalva IAsonovich. Georgian Metalwork, from Antiquity to the 18th Century. Tr. from Russian by Philippa Hentges. Feltham; New York: Hamlyn, 1971. 175pp, 109 color ill, bib (Georgia province)

491

5513   Andrews, Ruth. The Metal of the State. Exhibition. New
       York: Museum of American Folk Art, 1973. u. p., ill
       (196 items catalogued)

5514   Bedford, John. Pewter. London: Cassell, 1965; New York:
       Walker, 1966. 63pp, ill

5515   Bedinger, Margery, comp. A Selected List of Books on
       Metal. Denver: Denver Public Library, and American
       Society for Metals, 1943. 30pp

5516 *Bell, Malcolm. Old Pewter. London: Newnes Library of
       Applied Arts; New York: Scribner's, 1905; 1906; rev. ed.
       London: Batsford, 1913. 186pp, 106 pls, bib BM

5517   Blinn, Leroy J. A Practical Work Shop Companion for Tin,
       sheet iron and copper plate workers, containing rules for
       describing various kinds of patterns used by tin, sheet-
       iron and copper-plate workers; practical geometry, etc.
       Detroit: Henry E. Downer, 1864; Philadelphia: H. C.
       Baird, 1865; 1869; 1885; new enl. ed. 1891; 1900; new
       ed. as Tin, Sheet-iron and Copper-plate Worker.... New
       York: Baird, 1920. 178pp, ill; 184pp, ill; 296pp, 170
       ill; 334pp, 207 ill PPULC, DLC, NN

5518 *Bonnin, Alfred. Tutenag and Paktong, with notes on other
       alloys in domestic use during the 18th century. Oxford:
       H. Milford, Oxford U Pr, 1924. 98pp, ill, 29 pls NN,
       DLC

5519   Boyd, E. New Mexico Tinwork. Santa Fe: School of Ameri-
       can Research, 1953. 41pp, ill

5520   Brannt, William Theodore, ed. The Metal Worker's Handy-
       book of Receipts and Processes. Philadelphia: H. C.
       Baird, 1890; enl. ed. ed. by P. L. Tea. London: Hod-
       der & Stoughton, 1920. 538pp, ill; 582pp, ill

5521   Brass Candlesticks. ca.1797-1800 catalog facsimile reprint.
       Pref. by Rupert Gentle. Hungerford, Berks: Chilton
       Designs, Ltd, printer, 1973. 27 pls (24 candlesticks,
       3 bells) (From English brassfounder's catalog found in
       Philadelphia)

5522   The Brass Founders', Braziers', and Coppersmiths' Manual;
       containing a scientific description of brass-founding in all
       its several branches; valuable recipes for lackering; the
       rules and regulations of the Trade Society; and a complete
       list of all the master founders, braziers, and copper-
       smiths in the metropolis and its environs. London:
       Cowie & Strange, 1829. 79pp NN

5523 British Pewter. V & A. London: HMSO, 1960. 32pp, ill
(1300-1800)

5524 British Pewter, 1600-1850. Exhibition. April 1974. Manchester, NH: Currier Gallery, 1974. 42pp, ill, bib

5525 Burgess, Frederick William. Chats on Old Copper and Brass.
London: T. F. Unwin; New York: F. A. Stokes, 1914;
London: 1925; new rev. ed. by Cyril George E. Bunt.
London: Benn, 1954; New York: A. A. Wyn, 1955; re-
print of 1954 ed. Wakefield: E P Publishing, 1973.
400pp, ill; 1954: 184pp, ill, 47pp of pls NN, DLC, BM

5526 Butts, I. R. The Tinman's Manual and Builder's and Mechanic's Handbook designed for tinmen, japanners, coppersmiths, engineers, mechanics. 2nd ed. Boston: Author,
1860. 204pp, ill DeWint

5527 Byrne, Oliver. The Practical Metal-Worker's Assistant ...
with the application of the art of metallurgy to manufacturing
processes. Philadelphia: H. C. Baird, 1851. 557pp, ill
DeWint

5528 *Calder, Charles A. Rhode Island Pewterers and Their Work,
together with a list of American pewterers. Reprint from
the Rhode Island Historical Society Collections. Providence: A. A. Johnson, 1924. 39pp, ill, pls NN, PPULC

5529 Chubinashvili, Georgii N. Georgian Repousse Work, 8th to
18th Centuries. A selection of half-tone plates with annotations and an essay on the developmental history of the
art. (English, Russian, Georgian, German text.) Tbilisi,
USSR: State Pr of the Georgian SSR, 1957. 200 pls

5530 Cocks, Dorothy. The Pewter Collection of the New Canaan
Historical Society. New Canaan, Conn: 1967. 24pp, ill

5531 Copper Through the Ages. London: Copper Development Association, 1962.

5532 Cotterell, Howard Herschel. Bristol and West Country Pewterers. With illustrations of their marks. Bristol, Eng:
Museum & Art Gallery, 1918. 37pp, ill, pls, marks NjP

5533 * . National Types of Old Pewter. Boston: Antiques,
1925; rev. expanded ed. from articles in Antiques magazine, 1925-35. Princeton, NJ: Pyne Pr, 1972. 47pp,
ill; 160pp, ill (Western pewter)

5534 * . Old Pewter: its makers and marks in England,
Scotland and Ireland. An account of the old pewterer and
his craft, illustrating all known marks and secondary marks

of the old pewterer with a series of plates showing the chief types of their wares. London: Batsford, 1929; reprints. Rutland, Vt: Tuttle; London: Batsford, 1963; 1968; Rutland: 1971. 432pp, hundreds of ill, 82 pls, bib; 440pp, ill, 76 pls, bib; 1968: 448pp, 365 ill, bib

5535 *   . Pewter Down the Ages. From medieval times to the present day, with notes on evolution. Fore. by Antonio F. de Navarro. London: Hutchinson; Boston; New York: Houghton Mifflin, 1932. 237pp, ill, pls, marks

5536   . Pewter Down the Ages--marks most frequently found on old British pewter. Supplement in pocket of preceding title. London: Hutchinson, 1932. 23pp, pls

5537   . York Pewterers, 1272-1835. Gloucester, Eng: 1916. 15pp NjP

5538 Cottingham, Lewis Nockalls, 1787-1847. The Smith's and Founder's Director: containing a series of designs and patterns for ornamental iron and brass work. London: C. Hullmandel, for Author, 1823; 2nd ed. 1824. 2pp, 84 pls MdBP, NN

5539 Dalton, Ormonde Maddock. The Franks Bequest: the treasure of the Oxus, with other examples of early Oriental metalwork. British Museum. London: 1905; 2nd ed. 1926. 137pp, ill, 29 pls; 75pp, ill, 40 pls IU, DLC

5540 Davis, Watson. The Story of Copper. New York; London: 1924. 380pp, ill

5541 Day, Joan. Bristol Brass: A History of the Industry. London: David & Charles, 1973. 224pp, 30 ill, bib (Bristol, England)

5542 *Denman, Carolyn. A Bibliography of Pewter. Boston: Pewter Collectors' Club of America, 1945. 21pp (Includes longer, signed articles from Club's Bulletin) DLC, NNC-Ave

5543 *DeVoe, Shirley Spaulding. The Tinsmiths of Connecticut. Middletown, Conn: Wesleyan U Pr, for Connecticut Historical Society, 1968. 200pp, ill

5544 Dickinson, Henry Winram. Matthew Boulton. Cambridge, Eng: U Pr, 1937. 218pp, ill, pls (Boulton, 1728-1809. Includes "Memoirs of Boulton," by James Watt)

5545 *Dover Stamping Co. 1869. Tinware, tin toys, tinned iron wares, tinners' material, enameled stove hollow ware, tinners' tools and machines. Illustrated catalogue and

historical introduction.   Princeton, NJ: Pyne, 1971.
222pp, hundreds of ill, bib

5546   Downs, Joseph.   American Pewterers and Their Marks.   Ex-
       hibition.   March-April 1939.   New York: Metropolitan
       Museum, 1940; 2nd ed.   1942; reprint of 2nd ed.   Southamp-
       ton, NY: Cracker Barrel Pr, 1968.   2pp, ill, 21 pls

5547   Dunbar, Donald Earl.   The Tin-Plate Industry; a comparative
       study of its growth in the United States and in Wales.
       Boston; New York: Houghton Mifflin, 1915.   133pp, bib
       DLC, NN

5548   Ebblewhite, Ernest Arthur.   A Chronological History of the
       Worshipful Company of Tin Plate Workers Alias Wire
       Workers of the City of London from the Date of Its In-
       corporation to the Present Time.   London: priv. printed,
       1896.   133pp DLC, NN

5549   Ebert, Katherine.   Collecting American Pewter.   New York:
       Scribner, 1973.   163pp, 159 ill, bib, 368 marks, makers
       list   (1700-1860)

5550   Englefield, Elsie.   A Treatise on Pewter and Its Manufacture.
       Together with a brief account of the firm of Brown and
       Englefield, Ltd., the last of the great general pewter
       manufacturing firms of London.   London: Priory Pr,
       1933; London: Worshipful Co. of Pewterers, 1934; 2nd
       ed. London: Priory Pr, 1951.   85pp, ill, pls; 34pp, ill;
       72pp, pls DLC, NN, BM

5551   Evans, John J., Jr.   Early American Pewter.   Exhibition.
       January-March 1966.   Allentown, Pa: Art Museum, 1966.
       12pp, pls

5552   Exhibition of Art Brass Work and Arms, etc.   May 1890-92.
       London: Worshipful Co. of Armourers and Braziers,
       1890-92.

5553   Exhibition of Pewter, ... in association with the Society of
       Pewter Collectors.   September-October 1962.   Lincoln,
       Eng: Usher Art Gallery, 1962.   32pp, 4 pls   (English
       pewter)

5554   Fairbanks, Jonathan.   American Pewter in the Museum of
       Fine Arts, Boston.   Boston: 1974.   119pp, ill, bib

5555   50 Masterpieces of Metalwork.   London: V & A, 1951.
       103pp, ill, pls   BM

5556   Flower, Philip William.   History of the Trade in Tin; a short
       description of tin mining and metallurgy; a history of the

origin and progress of the tinplate trade.   London: G.
Bell, 1880.   219pp, ill NN, BM

5557 *Fuller, John, 1853- . The Art of Coppersmithing. A
      practical treatise on working sheet copper into all forms.
      New York: David Williams, 1894; 3rd ed. rev. 1904;
      4th ed. 1911. 327pp, ill, pls, diagrams NN, DeWint

5558 Gale, Edwards J. Pewter and the Amateur Collector. New
      York: Scribner's, 1909. 97pp, ill, 43 pls DLC, MB

5559 Gale, Walter Keith Vernon. Boulton, Watt and the Soho Un-
      dertakings. Appendix by W. A. Seaby. Birmingham,
      Eng: Museum & Art Gallery, 1952. 40pp, ill (Matthew
      Boulton, 1728-1809; James Watt, 1736-1819) DLC, NN

5560 Geerlings, Gerald Kenneth. Metal Crafts in Architecture;
      bronze, brass, cast iron, copper, lead, current develop-
      ments, tin, lighting fixtures, specifications. New York:
      Scribner, 1929; 1971. 202pp, 277 ill, bib

5561 *Gentle, Rupert, and Rachael Feild. English Domestic Brass
      1680-1810, and the history of its origins. London: Elek;
      New York: Dutton, 1975. 232pp, 366 ill

5562 Gibb, George Sweet. The Whitesmiths of Taunton. A History
      of Reed and Barton, 1824-1943. Cambridge, Mass: Har-
      vard U Pr, 1943; reprint. New York: Harper & Row,
      1969. 419pp, ill, pls, bib

5563 Goodison, Nicholas. Ormolu: The Work of Matthew Boulton.
      London: Phaidon; New York: Praeger, 1974. 398pp, ill,
      3 pls, bib

5564 Goodwin-Smith, R. English Domestic Metalwork. Leigh-on-
      Sea: F. Lewis, 1937; abridged ed. 1973. 101pp, ill,
      139 pls; 63pp, 95 pls (Gates, grilles, doors, lighting)

5565 *Gould, Mary Earle. Antique Tin and Tole Ware, Its History
      and Romance. Rutland, Vt: Tuttle, 1957; reprint, 1969.
      136pp, ill; 140pp, 255 pls

5566 Gowland, William, 1842-1922. The Art of Casting Bronze
      in Japan. From the Smithsonian Report, 1894. Washing-
      ton, D.C.: GPO, 1896. 43pp (pp. 609-651), ill, pls
      DLC

5567 _____. The Metals in Antiquity. Reprint from Journal.
      London: Royal Anthropological Institute of Great Britain
      and Ireland, 1912. 52pp (pp. 235-286), ill, pls NN

5568 Graham, John Meredith II, 1905- . American Pewter.
      Brooklyn: Museum, 1949. 36pp, ill

5569 Graham, Walter. The Brassfounder's Manual; instructions
      for modelling, pattern-making, moulding, alloying, turning,
      filing, etc. 2nd ed. rev. and with additions. London:
      Weale, 1868; 3rd ed. London: Strahan, 1870; 7th ed. rev.
      London: Crosby, Lockwood, 1887; 1911. 141pp, ill NN,
      DLC, BM

5570 _____. Brass Founding, tin plate and zinc working. Lon-
      don: 1876. See Bevan, G. P., British Manufacturing
      Industries, Vol. I.

5571 Griffiths, Thomas F. Griffiths and Browett, general iron
      and tin-plate workers, japanners of papier mache and
      iron trays, etc., manufacturers of tinned and enamelled
      wrought-iron hollow-ware, all kinds of tinmen's furniture,
      grocers' show vases, canisters, etc. Birmingham:
      ca.1850; 1860. 232pp, ill, pls; 356pp, ill, pls DeWint

5572 Haeberle, Arminius T. Old Pewter. Boston: R. G. Badger,
      1931. 128pp, ill, pls (Continental pewter) DLC, PP

5573 Haedeke, Hanns Ulrich. Metalwork. Tr. from German by
      Vivienne Menkes. London: Weidenfeld & Nicolson, 1969;
      New York: Universe, 1970. 227pp, ill, 128 (16 color)
      pls, bib

5574 *Hamilton, Henry, 1896- . The English Brass and Copper
      Industries to 1800. Introd. by William Ashley. London;
      New York: Longmans, Green, 1926; 2nd ed. with new
      introd. by J. R. Harris. London: Cass; New York: A.
      M. Kelley, 1967. 383pp, 8 pls, bib BM

5575 Harrison, John. The Decoration of Metals. Chasing, re-
      pousse and saw-piercing. London: Chapman & Hall,
      1894. 132pp, 180 ill, 7 pls MB

5576 Hatch, John Davis, Jr. Albany Pewter and Its Makers.
      Albany, NY: Institute of History and Art, 1942.

5577 Hatcher, John. English Tin Production and Trade Before
      1550. Oxford: Clarendon Pr, 1973. 219pp, ill, bib

5578 Hibben, Thomas. The Sons of Vulcan; the story of metals.
      Philadelphia; New York: Lippincott, 1940; London: T.
      W. Laurie, 1944. 259pp, ill; 224pp, ill (Juvenile litera-
      ture)

5579 Hiley, Edgar Nathaniel. Brass Saga. An account of the
      brassfounding industry. London: E. Benn, 1957. 166pp,
      pls

5580 Holmes, Frederic Morell, 1851- . The Marvels of Metals.
      London: Partridge, 1897. 160pp

5581   Hood, Graham. American Pew-
       ter; Garvan and other collec-
       tions at Yale. New Haven:
       1965. 59pp, ill, pls

5582   Jackson, Radway. English Pew-
       ter Touchmarks: including
       the marks of origin of some
       of the Scottish and Irish
       pewterers. Ed. by Ronald
       F. Michaeolis. London; New
       York: Foulsham, 1970.
       123pp, ill, bib

5583 *Jacobs, Carl. A Guide to
       American Pewter. New
       York: McBride, 1957.
       216pp, ill, marks

5584   Jacobs, Celia. Pocket Book of
       American Pewter; the makers
       and the marks. Springfield,
       Mass: 1960; 2nd ed. rev. & enl. Boston: Herman Pub-
       lishing, 1970. 85pp, ill; 93pp, ill

5585   John, William David, and Katherine Coombes. Paktong--
       Chinese Imperial Silver. Newport, Wales: Ceramic
       Book Co, 1969. ill

5586   _____, and _____. Paktong, the non-tarnishable Chi-
       nese 'silver' alloy used for 'Adam' firegrates and early
       Georgian candlesticks. Newport, Wales: Ceramic Book
       Co, 1970. 25pp, 50 pls, color frontis

5587 *_____, and Anne Simcox. Pontypool and Usk Japanned
       Wares, with the early history of the iron and tinplate
       industries at Pontypool. Newport, Wales: Ceramic Book
       Co, 1953; reprint with added illustrations. 1966. 88pp,
       ill, 26 (7 color) pls

5588   Johnson, Edmond. Description of Irish Antique Art Metal-
       work, etc. Dublin: Sealy & Bryers, 1893. 108pp

5589 *Kauffman, Henry J. American Copper and Brass. Camden,
       NJ: T. Nelson, 1968. 288pp, ill, bib

5590   _____. The American Pewterer, His Techniques and His
       Products. Camden, NJ: T. Nelson, 1970. 158pp, 115
       ill, bib, marks

5591   _____. Coppersmithing in Pennsylvania; being a treatise
       on the art of the 18th century coppersmith, together with

a description of his products and his establishments.
Pennsylvania German Folklore Society Publication Vol. II,
1946. 77pp (pp. 83-149), ill, bib NNC-Ave

5592 * _____ . Early American Copper, Tin, and Brass. New
York: McBride, 1950. 112pp, ill, bib

5593 _____ , and Zoe Elizabeth Kauffman. Pennsylvania German
Copper and Brass. Plymouth Meeting, Pa: Mrs. C. Naa-
man Keyser, 1947. 32pp, ill

5594 *Kerfoot, John B. American Pewter. Boston; New York:
Houghton Mifflin, 1924; New York: Crown, 1942; reprint.
1960. 239pp, 500 ill, marks (Author's collection.
Standard reference)

5595 Kolchin, Boris Aleksandrovich. Metallurgy and Metalworking
in Ancient Russia. Tr. from Russian. Jerusalem: Israel
Program for Scientific Translations, 1967. 112pp, ill

5596 Lambdin, Robert Lynn. Brass Through the Ages, from his
mural of the same name. Bridgeport, Conn: Bridgeport
Brass Co, 1944. 9 color pls NN

5597 Lardner, Dionysius. A Treatise on the Progressive Improvement and Present State of the Manufacture in Metal. 3
vol. London: Longman, Rees, Orme, and J. Taylor,
1831. ill (Part of the Cabinet Cyclopaedia)

5598 Larkin, James. The Practical Brass and Iron Founders'
Guide; a concise treatise on brass founding, moulding,
the metals and their alloys, etc. Philadelphia: A. Hart,
1853; 5th ed. rev. with additions. Philadelphia: H. C.
Baird, 1872; ...; 1907. 204pp, ill; 301pp, ill; 394pp, ill
NN, PPL, DeWint

5599 Lathrop, William Gilbert. The Brass Industry in Connecticut;
a study of the origin and development of the brass industry
in the Naugatuck Valley. Shelton, Conn: Author, 1909;
rev. enl. ed. as The Brass Industry in the United States;
a study of the origin and the development of the brass
industry in the Naugatuck Valley and its subsequent extension over the nation. Mount Carmel, Conn: W. G.
Lathrop, 1926; reprint. New York: Arno, 1972. 143pp,
pls, bib; 174pp, pls, bib

5600 *Laughlin, Ledlie Irwin. Pewter in America: its makers
and their marks. 2 vol. Boston: Houghton Mifflin,
1940; reprint with added material by author. 2 vol. in
1. Barre, Mass: Barre Publishers, 1969; Vol. III.
1971. I & II: 390pp, 78 pls, bib, marks; III: 276pp,
ill, marks, bib

5601   Lethaby, William Richard.   Leadwork, Old and Ornamental,
       and for the Most Part English.   London; New York: Mac-
       millan, 1893.   148pp, ill   DLC, PPL

5602 *Lindsay, John Seymour.   Iron and Brass Implements of the
       English House.   (or ... of the English and American
       Home.)   Introd. by Ralph Edwards.   London; Boston:
       Medici Society, 1927; rev. enl. ed.   Bass River, Mass:
       C. Jacobs; London: Tiranti, 1964.   211pp, drawings by
       author; 88pp, 473 ill   (Divided into: The Hearth; Cooking;
       Lighting; Tobacco Use; Miscellany; American Colonial
       Metalwork)   MiU, NNC-Ave, NN

5603   Lister, Raymond.   The Craftsman in Metal.   London: Bell
       1966; South Brunswick, NJ: A. S. Barnes, 1968.   208pp,
       ill, 24 pls, bib

5604   McDonald, Donald.   History of Platinum from the Earliest
       Times to the 1880s.   London: Johnson Matthey, 1960.
       254pp, ill, bib

5605   Manchester, Herbert (H.).   An Illustrated History of Mining
       and Metallurgy.   New York: Engineering & Mining
       Journal-Press, 1922.   48pp, ill   NN

5606   Marcosson, Isaac Frederick.   Copper Heritage.   The story
       of Revere copper and brass, Inc.   New York: Dodd,
       Mead, 1955.   254pp, ill

5607 *Markham, Christopher Alexander.   Pewter Marks and Old
       Pewter Ware, domestic and ecclesiastical, with about
       100 illustrations, 200 facsimile marks, and 1000 full
       descriptions of touches from the touch plates at Pewter-
       ers' Hall.   London: Reeves & Turner, 1909; 2nd ed.
       rev. & enl. 1928.   316pp, 100 ill, pls, marks; 355pp,
       188 ill, pls, marks   NN, MB

5608 *Massé, Henri Jean Louis.   Chats on Old Pewter.   London:
       T. F. Unwin, 1911; new ed. rev. by Ronald F. Michaelis.
       London: E. Benn, 1949; 3rd rev. ed. with new "Ameri-
       can Pewter in the 18th and 19th Centuries," by Henry J.
       Kauffman.   New York; Dover; London: Constable, 1971.
       422pp, ill, bib; 240pp, ill; 276pp, 67 ill, 44 pls, bib

5609 *_____.   The Pewter Collector; a guide to English pewter
       with some references to foreign work.   London: H.
       Jenkins, 1921; rev. ed. with additions by Ronald F.
       Michaelis.   London: Barrie & Jenkins, 1971.   314pp,
       ill, bib, makers lists; 280pp, ill, 17 pls, bib (English,
       Scottish, Irish)

5610 *_____.   Pewter Plate; a historical and descriptive

handbook. London: G. Bell, 1904; 2nd ed. 1910. 299pp,
ill, pls, bib; 331pp, ill, pls, bib (English and continental)
PP, MB

5611 Metal Work; plates from "l'Art Pour Tous." (1867-1880.)
German, French, English text. Paris: A. Morel, 1880?
117 mounted pls NN, DLC

5612 *Michaelis, Ronald Frederick. Antique Pewter of the British
Isles. A brief survey of what has been made in pewter
in England and the British Isles from the time of Queen
Elizabeth I to the reign of Queen Victoria. London: G.
Bell, 1955; London: Peter Smith, 1965; London: Con-
stable; New York: Dover, 1971. 118pp, ill, 40 pls, bib

5613 _____. British Pewter. London: Ward Lock; New York:
Drake, 1969. 96pp, ill, bib

5614 _____, comp. A Short History of the Worshipful Company
of Pewterers of London and a Catalogue of Pewterware in
Its Possession. London: Court of Assistants, 1968.
103pp, ill

5615 Miller, Fred. Barbotine Painting and Practical Hints on Brass
Repousse Work by Mrs. Ernest Peel. London: J. Heywood, 1885. 20pp

5616 Minchinton, Walter E. The British Tinplate Industry; a history. Oxford: Clarendon Pr, 1947; 1957. 286pp, ill

5617 Montgomery, Charles F. A History of American Pewter. A
Winterthur book. New York: Praeger, 1973. 246pp, ill,
bib, marks (Colonial to 19th century)

5618 *Moore, Hannah (N.) Hudson. Old Pewter, Brass, Copper, and
Sheffield Ware. New York: F. A. Stokes, 1905; London:
Hodder & Stoughton, 1906; 2nd ed. Garden City, NY: Gar-
den City Publishing, 1933; reprint of 1905 ed. with added
list of Continental, English, Scottish, and American names.
Rutland, Vt: Tuttle, 1972. 229pp, 105 ill. BM

5619 Mumford, John Kimberly. Outspinning the Spider; the story
of wire and wire rope. New York: Robert L. Stillson,
1921. 137pp, ill ViU, DLC

5620 Mundey, A. H. Tin and the Tin Industry. The metal history,
character and application. London; New York: I. Pitman,
1926. 130pp, ill

5621 *Myers, Louis Guerineau. Some Notes on American Pewterers.
Garden City, NY: Country Life, for Author, 1926. 96pp,
ill, pls, marks DLC, TxU

502

5622 Napier, James. Ancient Workers and Artificers in Metal. London: Griffin, 1857.

5623 *Navarro, Antonio de. Causeries on English Pewter. (Or ... on Old Pewter.) New York: Scribner's, 1911; London: Newnes, 1912; New York: 1924. 176pp, ill, 72 pls NN, PP

5624 Nunn, Elsa. Everyday Metals. London: Ginn, 1959; 1970. 32pp, ill (To 1600. Juvenile literature)

5625 Osborne, Arthur Dimon, 1828- . A Few Facts Relating to the Origin and History of John Dolbeare of Boston. New Haven: priv. printed, A. D. Osborne, 1893. 32pp, ill, pls (Pewterer)

5626 Pattern Book for Art-Metal-Workers. London: A. Fischer, 1882, 1883. 122pp BM

5627 Peal, Christopher Arthur. British Pewter and Britannia Metal for Pleasure and Investment. London: Gifford, 1971. 200pp, ill, 16 pls, bib

5628 People, Progress and Products; a story of 125 years of wire-making. Cleveland?: United States Steel Corp., American Steel and Wire Division, 1956? 24pp, ill

5629 *Percy, John, 1817-1889. Metallurgy: the art of extracting metals from their ores, and adapting them to various purposes of manufacture. Vol. I. Fuel; fire-clays; copper; zinc; brass; etc.; II. Iron and Steel; III. The Metallurgy of Lead, including desilverisation and cupellation; IV. Silver and Gold. 4 vol. London: J. Murray, 1861, 1864, 1870, 1880; rev. enl. ed. Vol. I. 1875. 635pp, ill; 934pp, ill, 4 pls; 567pp, ill; ill DLC

5630 Perry, Evan. Collecting Antique Metalware. Garden City, NY: Doubleday, 1974. 191pp, 211 ill (some color), bib

5631 *Perry, John Tavenor. Dinanderie; a history and description of medieval art work in copper, brass and bronze. London: G. Allen, 1910. 238pp, 71 ill, 48 pls, bib NNC-Ave

5632 Pewter Collectors' Club of America. Bulletin. Lexington, Mass: 1934-date.

5633 Pewter in America, 1650-1900. Manchester, NH: Currier Gallery of Art, 1968. 75pp, ill

5634 Phillips, John Arthur. Copper Smelting. London: 1876. See: Bevan, G. P., British Manufacturing Industries, Vol. I.

5635   Picard, Hugh K. Copper, from the Ore to the Metal. Lon-
       don: Pitman, 1916; 2nd ed. 1928. 130pp, ill; 134pp, ill

5636   Plunkett, George Tindall, and M. S. D. Westropp. Metal
       Work. General Guide ... Part 6. Dublin: Science &
       Art Museum, 1903, 1904; 1911.

5637   Pope-Hennessy, John Wyndham. Renaissance Bronzes from
       the Samuel H. Kress Collection: reliefs, plaquettes, uten-
       sils and mortars. London: Phaidon Pr, for the Founda-
       tion, Washington, D.C., 1965. 333pp, 616 ill

5638   Powers, Beatrice Farnsworth, and Olive Floyd. Early
       American Decorated Tinware: with designs and practical
       directions. Fore. by Katherine C. Buhler. New York:
       Hastings House, 1957. 267pp, ill, 79 pls, bib

5639   Pugin, Augustus Charles, and Welby Northmore Pugin. De-
       signs for Iron and Brass Work in the Style of the 15th
       and 16th Centuries. London: Ackermann, 1836. 27 pls
       BM

5640   *Redman, William. Illustrated Handbook of Information on
       Pewter and Sheffield Plate, with full particulars on touch
       marks, makers' marks, etc. London: Bradford, 1903.
       76pp, ill

5641   Revi, Albert Christian, ed. Spinning Wheel's Collecting Iron,
       Tin, Copper and Brass. Hanover, Pa: Spinning Wheel,
       1974. 160pp, ill

5642   Rhode Island Pewter, 1711-1856, from the collections of Dr.
       Madelaine Brown and Mr. J. K. Ott. Exhibition at John
       Brown House. Providence, RI: Historical Society, 1959.
       11pp, ill

5643   Rogers, Malcolm A., Jr. American Pewterers and Their
       Marks. 2nd ed. Southampton, NY: Cracker Barrel,
       1968. 22pp, marks

5644   *Rovenzon, John. A Treatise of Metallica. London: printed
       for Thomas Thorp, 1613; reprint. Wolverhampton: John
       N. Bagnall?, 1855. 30pp

5645   Savage, George. A Concise History of Bronzes. London:
       Thames & Hudson, 1968; New York: Praeger, 1969.
       264pp, 209 ill

5646   Scoffern, John, 1814-1882, W. C. Aitkin, W. Truran, and
       others. The Useful Metals and Their Alloys ... with
       their application to the industrial arts. London: 1857.
       (Part of Orr's Circle of the Industrial Arts) BM

5647 Shaw, Henry. Examples of Ornamental Metalwork. London:
      W. Pickering, 1836. 50 (2 color) pls BM

5648 Smith, Bertie Webster. 60 Centuries of Copper. London:
      Hutchinson, for Copper Development Association, 1965.
      96pp, ill, 32 pls with 64 ill, bib

5649 *Smith, Cyril Stanley. A History of Metallography: the de-
      velopment of ideas on the structure of metals before 1890.
      Chicago: U of C Pr, 1960; 1965. 293pp, ill

5650 Smith, Donald. Metalwork; an introductory historical survey.
      London; New York: Batsford, 1948. 64pp, ill

5651 Smith, R. H. S. A List of Books, Photographs, etc., in
      the National Art Library, Illustrating Metal Work. South
      Kensington Museum. London: 1883. 141pp BM

5652 Smyth, Warrington Wilkinson. Metallic Mining and Collieries.
      London: 1876; see Bevan, G. P., British Manufacturing
      Industries, Vol. 2.

5653 Sturtevant, Simon. Metallica, or the Treatise of Metallica.
      Briefly comprehending the doctrine of diverse new metal-
      lical inventions, but especially how to neale ... and worke
      all kinde of mettle-oares ... also a transcript of his
      Majesties letters patents.... London: G. Eld, 1612;
      reprint in Supplement to the Series of Letters Patent.
      London: HMSO, for Commissioner of Patents, 1858.
      (See also John Rovenzon) BM

5654 *Sutherland-Graeme, Alan Vincent. Old British Pewter from
      1500-1800; a preliminary guide for the collector with over
      40 illustrations. London: Connoisseur, 1951; London:
      National Magazine, 1952. 42pp, ill

5655 *Thorn, C. Jordan. Handbook of American Silver and Pewter
      Marks. New York: Tudor, 1949. 289pp, ill

5656 Treasures from Romania: a special exhibition held at the
      British Museum. Tr. by Richard Camber et al. London:
      the Museum, 1971; 2nd ed. rev. 1975. 111pp, ill, pls
      (To 1700)

5657 *Twopeny, William, 1797-1873. English Metal Work. Pref.
      by Laurence Binyon. London: Archibald Constable, 1904.
      15pp, 93 drawings DLC

5658 Ullyet, Kenneth. Pewter: A Guide for Collectors. London:
      Muller, 1973. 158pp, ill, 19 pls, bib

5659 _____. Pewter Collecting for Amateurs. London: Muller,
      1967. 147pp, ill, 12 pls (English)

5660   Verster, Arnoldus Johan George. Old European Pewter.
       Tr. from 2nd Dutch edition (1957). London: Thames &
       Hudson, 1958; New York: Viking, 1959. 80pp, ill, 117
       pls, bib (16th to 18th century)

5661   Vosburgh, H. K. Tinsmith's Helper and Pattern Book. Union-
       ville, Conn: Union Printing, 1879; 1901. 116pp, diagrams;
       120pp, diagrams NN

5662   Waring, John Burley. Examples of Metal-Work and Jewelry,
       selected from the Royal and other collections. With an
       essay by M. Digby Wyatt. London: n.d. (185?). ill,
       17 pls (some color)

5663   Weaver, Sir Lawrence, 1876- . English Leadwork: its art
       and history. London: Batsford, 1909. 268pp, 441 ill,
       bib

5664   Weiner, Pivoska. Old Pewter in Hungarian Collections. Tr.
       from Hungarian by E. Helvey. Budapest: Corvina, Cle-
       matis Pr, 1971. 102pp, 47 pls, marks

5665   *Welch, Charles. History of the Worshipful Company of
       Pewterers. 2 vol. London: Blades, East & Blades,
       1902. ill, 13 pls (part color), 3 color facsims

5666   Westropp, Michael Seymour Dudley. Metal Work. General
       Guide.... 5th ed. Dublin: Science & Art Museum, 1934.
       75pp, 22 pls

5667   Wilhelm, Donald George. The Book of Metals ... The stories,
       simply told, of the metals, their "characteristics," "be-
       haviorism," history, mining, refining, alloying and uses.
       New York; London: Harper, 1932. 341pp, pls (Including
       5 photographs by Margaret Bourke-White)

5668   *Wills, Geoffrey. The Book of Copper and Brass. Feltham:
       Country Life, 1968. 96pp, 115 ill, bib

5669   . Collecting Copper and Brass. London: Arco,
       1962; 1968; London: Mayflower, 1971. ...; 93pp, ill,
       bib; 157pp, ill, 8 pls, bib

5670   Wilson, David M. Anglo-Saxon Ornamental Metalwork, 700-
       1100, in the British Museum. Appendices by R. L. S.
       Bruce-Mitford, and R. I. Page. London: British Mu-
       seum, 1964. 248pp, ill, 34 pls

5671   *Wood, L. Ingleby. Scottish Pewter-Ware and Pewterers.
       London: Simpkins, Marshall; Edinburgh: G. A. Morton,
       1907. 223pp, ill, 35 pls

5672   Woolmer, Stanley Charles, and Charles H. Arkwright. Pewter

of the Channel Islands.   Edinburgh: J. Bartholomew,
1973.   159pp, ill, bib

5673   Wyatt, Sir Matthew Digby.   Metal Work, and Its Artistic Design.   London: Day & Son, 1852.   81pp, 50 pls (part
color)

5674   _____.   Observations on Metallic Art.   London: 1857.
color ill   V & A

5675   _____.   Specimens of Ornamental Art Workmanship in
Gold, Silver, Iron, Brass and Bronze, from the 12th to
the 19th Centuries ... Italy, England, France, Germany
and Spain.   London: Day, 1852.   81pp, ill

5676   Wylie, Walker Gill.   Pewter, Measure for Measure.   Miami,
Fla: Author, 1952.   68pp, ill (17th-20th century)

5677   Yalkert, Saul.   With Hammer and Tongs; malleable metals in
diverse designs.   Exhibition at Cooper Union Museum.
Boston: Merrymount Pr, 1941.   8pp, bib IU

5678   Yapp, George Wagstaffe, ed.   Art Industry: metal art-work
applied by the goldsmith, silversmith, jeweller, brass,
copper, iron and steel worker, bronzist, etc.   London:
J. Virtue, 1878-84.   76pp, 319 pls with 1200 ill   DLC,
V & A

5679   Young, W. A., comp.   Old English Pattern Books of the
Metal Trades, a descriptive catalogue.   Pref. by E. F.
Strange.   V & A.   London: 1913.   38pp, ill, 24 pls   BM

JAPANNING, TOLE AND PAINTED TINWARE

5680   Brown, William Norman.   A Handbook on Japanning and Enamelling for Cycles, Bedsteads, Tinware, etc.   London: Scott,
Greenwood, 1901; 2nd ed. rev. & enl. as A Handbook on
Japanning for Ironware, Tinware, Wood, etc., with Sections
on Tinplating and Galvanizing.   London: 1913.   52pp, ill;
69pp, ill

5681   Burney, Captain Henry, d. 1845?   Observations on the Lac-
quered or Japanned Ware of Ava.   n. p.:   1833.   (Ava is
part of Burma.   14th century on)   SIB-1

5682   Christensen, Erwin Ottomar.   Early American Designs: Tole-
ware.   New York: Pitman, 1952.   u. p., ill

5683   *Coffin, Margaret.   The History and Folklore of American
Country Tinware, 1700-1900.   Camden, NJ: T. Nelson,
1968.   226pp, ill, bib, gloss

5684 _____, and Charles Coffin. Painted Tinware We've Seen.
Vol. I. Pennsylvania and New York; Vol. II. Connecticut
and Maine. 2 vol. ill n. p.: n. d. ill

5685 Cox, Ralph. Victorian Tinware, with notes on a 19th century
catalogue. Stamford, Lincolnshire: Stamford Properties,
1970. 96pp, pls, facsims (Includes reprint of 1862 trade
catalog of J. H. Hopkins and Son, Birmingham, tin plate
workers and japanners)

5686 The Cabinet-Makers' Guide: or rules and instructions in the
art of varnishing, dying, staining, japanning, polishing,
lackering and beautifying wood, ivory, tortoiseshell and
metal.... London: J. Arliss, 1818; new ed. London:
printed for Knight & Lacy; Greenfield, Mass: Ansel
Phelps, 1825; "from latest London ed." Concord, NH:
Jacob B. Moore, printer, 1827. 36pp; 108pp; 120pp
with cover ill of piano CtY, NNC-Ave, NN

5687 *Gould, Mary Earle. Antique Tin and Tole Ware, Its History
and Romance. Rutland, Vt: Tuttle, 1957; reprint. 1969.
136pp, ill; 140pp, 255 pls

5688 Guide to the Collections of Pontypool and Usk Japan. Cardiff:
National Museum of Wales, 1926. 28pp

5689 *John, William David, and Anne Simcox. Pontypool and Usk
Japanned Wares, with the early history of the iron and
tinplate industries at Pontypool. Newport, Wales: Ceramic
Book Co, 1953; reprint with added illustrations, 1966.
88pp, ill, 26 (7 color) pls

5690 The Ladies' Amusement; or, whole art of japanning made
easy ... Drawn by Jean Nicolas Pillement and other
masters ... To which is added ... the most approved
methods of japanning. London: ca.1762; 2nd ed. facsimile reprint. Newport, Wales: Ceramic Book Co,
1959. 1959: 6pp, 200 pls with 1500 decoupage designs
(Jean Nicolas Pillement, 1719-1808; Robert Sayer; others)

5691 *Lawley, George T. History of Bilston, in the County of Stafford. A record of its archaeology, ecclesiology, paro-
chialia, folk lore, and bibliography. Bilston: 1893.
(Early English center of japanned tin-ware, near Wolverhampton) CtY

5692 *Mander, Gerald Poynton. Japanned Work in Wolverhampton.
Wolverhampton, Eng: 1925.

5693 Powers, Beatrice Farnsworth, and Olive Floyd. Early American Decorated Tinware: with designs and practical directions. Fore. by Katherine C. Buhler. New York: Hastings,
1957. 267pp, ill, 79 pls, bib

5694 *Stalker, John, and George Parker. A Treatise on Japaning
      and Varnishing. Being a compleat discovery of those arts.
      With the best way of making all sorts of varnish for japan,
      wood, prints, or pictures. The method of guilding, bur-
      nishing and lackering, with the art of guilding, separating,
      and refining metals: and of painting mezzo-tinto-prints.
      Also rules for counterfeiting tortoise-shell, and marble,
      and for staining or dying wood, ivory, and horn. To-
      gether with above an hundred distinct patterns for japan-
      work, in imitation of the Indians, for tables, stands,
      frames, cabinets, boxes, etc.... Oxford, Eng: for
      Authors, 1688. Reprint with pref. by H. D. Molesworth.
      London: Tiranti, 1960. 84pp, 24 pls DLC, BM

5695 Williams, Isaac J. Guide to the Collections of Pontypool and
      Usk Japan. Cardiff: National Museum of Wales; London:
      Milford, 1926. 28pp, ill, 8 pls, bib NN

IRONWORKS, FOUNDRIES AND STEEL

5696 The Art of Iron Moulding, in all its various branches. By
      an Experienced Workman. Boston: J. Philbrick, 1853.
      69pp DLC

5697 Bent, Quincy. Early Days of Iron and Steel in North America.
      New York: Newcomen Society in North America, 1950.
      24pp

5698 Bining, Arthur Cecil. The Iron Plantations of Early Penn-
      sylvania. Reprint from Pennsylvania Magazine of History
      and Biography. Philadelphia: Historical Society of Pa,
      1933. 21pp

5699 _____. Pennsylvania Iron Manufacture in the 18th Century.
      Harrisburg: Pennsylvania Historical Commission, 1938;
      1939; reprint. 1973. 227pp, ill, bib; 215pp, ill

5700 Boyer, Charles Shimer. Early Forges and Furnaces in New
      Jersey. Philadelphia: U. of Pa. Pr; London: H. Mil-
      ford, Oxford U. Pr, 1931. 287pp, ill, pls, bib

5701 Clarke, Mary Stetson. Pioneer Iron Works. Philadelphia:
      Chilton, 1968. 80pp, ill, 1 pl (Saugus, Massachusetts)

5702 Dunlap, Thomas, comp. and ed. Wiley's American Iron
      Trade Manual of the Leading Iron Industries of the United
      States, with a description of the iron ore regions, blast
      furnaces, rolling mills, Bessemer steel works, crucible
      steel works, car wheel and car works, iron bridge works,
      iron ship yards, pipe and tube works, and stove foundries
      of the country, giving their location and capacity of product.

2 parts. New York: J. Wiley, 1874. 554pp, 172pp, ill,
pls DLC, NN

5703 Fairbairn, Sir William, 1789-1874. Iron; its history, properties and process of manufacture. Edinburgh: A. & C.
Black, 1861; rev. & enl. ed. 1865; 3rd rev. & enl. ed.
1869. 235pp, ill; 293pp, ill; 338pp, ill BM, NN, MB

5704 Fell, Alfred. Early Iron Foundry of Furness and District:
an historical and descriptive account from earliest times
to the end of the 18th century, with an account of furness
ironmasters in Scotland, 1726-1800. Ulverston, Eng: H.
Kitchin, 1908; reprint. London: Cass; Clifton, NJ: Kelley,
1968. 464pp, pls, bib MB, NN

5705 French, Benjamin Franklin, 1799-1877. History of the Rise
and Progress of the Iron Trade of the United States, from
1621-1857. With numerous statistical tables, relating to
the manufacture, importation, exportation, price of iron
for more than a century. New York: Wiley & Halstead,
1858. 179pp DeWint, DLC

5706 Gale, Walter Keith Vernon. The Coneygre Foundry. Tipton,
Eng: Coneygre Foundry, 1954. 30pp, ill, bib

5707 _____. Iron and Steel. Harlow, Eng: Longmans, 1969.
132pp, 31 ill, 10 pls, bib (Industrial archaeology)

5708 Hartley, Edward Neal. Ironworks on the Saugus; the Lynn and
Braintree ventures of the Company of Undertakers of the
Ironworks in New England. Norman: U. of Oklahoma Pr,
1957. 328pp, ill

5709 Hood, Christopher. Iron and Steel: their production and
manufacture. London: Pitman, 1911. 150pp, ill BM

5710 *Howe, Henry Marion, 1848-1922. Metallurgy of Steel. Vol. I.
New York; London: Scientific Pub. Co, 1890; 2nd rev. &
enl. ed. 1891- . ill (Historical)

5711 Hunt, Robert Woolstan, 1838- . A History of Bessemer
Manufacture in America. The evolution of American rolling mills. New York: n.p., 1918. 54pp PBL

5712 Iron. A monthly review of metallurgy, mechanics, hardware,
machinery, and tools. Philadelphia: Iron Pub. Co, 18-?
ill DLC

5713 *The Iron Age (title varies). Weekly. New York: Chilton,
1855-date. ill

5714 *Iron Age Library Catalog. 1200 price lists and catalogues,

850 photos; 50 atlases and maps; 500 miscellaneous volumes. A collection of publications relating to American
geology, metallurgy, mechanics, engineering, the hardware and metal trades, and statistics of their allied industries. B.3, American Section, Exposition, Paris 1878.
Exhibited by David Williams, publisher of The Iron Age,
the Metallurgical Review and the Metal Worker. Poissy,
France: S. LeJay, 1878. 50pp DLC

5715   Iron. An Illustrated weekly journal for iron and steel manufacturers, metallurgists, mine proprietors, engineers,
shipbuilders, scientists, capitalists, etc. (title varies).
138 vol. London: Knight & Lacey, etc., 1823-1893;
continued as Industries and Iron. London: 1893. ill,
pls NN

5716   *Jeans, James Stephen, 1846-1913. Steel, its history, manufacture and uses. Lond: E. & F. N. Spon, 1880. 860pp,
ill, 24 pls, bib MiU, PPL, MB

5717   Keith, Herbert Cary, and Charles Rufus Harte. The Early
Iron Industry of Connecticut. Reprint from 51st Annual
Report. New Haven: Mack & Noel, for Connecticut So-
ciety of Civil Engineers, 1935. 69pp, ill (History and
relics (Keith); blast furnaces and furnace practice (Harte))
MB, DeWint

5718   *Needham, Joseph. The Development of Iron and Steel Technology in China. London: Newcomen Society, 1958.

5719   Pearse, John Barnard. A Concise History of the Iron Manufacture of the American Colonists up to the Revolution,
and of Pennsylvania until the present time. Philadelphia:
Allen, Land & Scott, 1876. BM

5720   Saugus Iron Works. Washington, D.C.: GPO, 1974. 20pp,
ill

5721   *Schubert, H. R. (John Rudolph Theodore). History of the
British Iron and Steel Industry from ca. 450 B.C. to A.D.
1775. Fore. by President of Iron and Steel Institute.
London: Routledge & K. Paul, 1957. 445pp, ill, bib

5722   Smiles, Samuel, 1812-1904. Industrial Biography: iron
workers and tool makers. London: J. Murray, 1863;
Boston: Ticknor & Fields, 1874; new ed. London: 1876;
Philadelphia: Lippincott, 1877; new ed. London: 1879;
reprint of 1863 ed. with additional illustrations, and a new
introduction by L. T. C. Bolt. Newton Abbot: David &
Charles, 1967. 342pp, 16pp of pls BM

5723   *Smith, Cyril Stanley. The Science of Steel: sources for the

history of iron and steel (1532-1786). Society for the
History of Technology monograph. Cambridge, Mass:
MIT Pr, 1968. 357pp, ill, bib

5724   Steel and Iron (title varies). Weekly. Pittsburgh: National
       Iron and Steel Pub., 1874-1914. ill (As American Manu-
       facturer and Trade of the West; also American Manufac-
       turer and Iron World, etc.)

5725   Steel Facts. Periodical. New York: American Iron & Steel
       Institute, 194-?

5726   Straker, Ernest. Wealden Iron ... A monograph on the
       former ironworks in the counties of Sussex, Surrey and
       Kent. London: G. Bell, 1931; reprint. Newton Abbot:
       David & Charles, 1969. 487pp, ill (300 years of iron
       manufacture)

5727   *Swank, James Moore, 1832-1914. History of the Manufacture
       of Iron in All Ages, and particularly in the United States
       for 300 years, from 1585 to 1885. Philadelphia: Author,
       1884; 2nd ed. rev. & enl. Philadelphia: American Iron
       and Steel Association, 1892. 428pp; 554pp

5728   Whiteley, B. Ironfounding. London; New York: Pitman,
       1921. 131pp, ill

5729   Williams, William Mattieu. Iron and Steel. London: 1876.
       See Bevan, G. P., British Manufacturing Industries,
       Vol. I.

5730   Worrilow, William H. A History of Steel Casting. Ed. by
       Arthur D. Graeff. Philadelphia: Steel Founders' Society
       of America, 1949. 167pp, ill

BLACKSMITHS

5731   Adams, Arthur James, comp. The History of the Worshipful
       Company of Blacksmiths from Early Times until the year
       1647. Being selected reproductions from the original
       books of the Company, an historical introduction, and
       many notes. London: priv. printed, Balding & Mansell,
       1937; as The History ... until the Year 1785.... London:
       Sylvan Pr, 1951. 66pp, ill; 207pp, ill

5732   Blacksmiths' Work Exhibition, under the auspices of the Wor-
       shipful Company of Blacksmiths, held at Ironmongers'
       Hall.... London: 1889. 8 leaves BM

5733   Dickinson, Henry Winram. John Wilkinson, ironmaster ...
       with numerous illustrations. Ulverston: Hume Kitchin,
       1914. 60pp, ill

5734 Gunnion, Vernon S., and Carroll J. Hopf, ed. The Black-
      smith: Artisan Within the Early Community. Fore. by
      Blanche K. Reigle. Introd. by John D. Tyler. Exhibi-
      tion. Harrisburg: Pennsylvania Historical and Museum
      Commission, 1972; Lancaster: Pennsylvania Farm Mu-
      seum of Landis Valley, 1973. 64pp, ill, bib

5735 Hasluck, Paul Nooncree, ed. Smiths' Work.... London;
      New York: Cassell, 1900; 1902; Philadelphia: McKay,
      1911. 160pp, ill, diags. MiU, PP, NN

5736 Hogg, Garry Lester. Hammer and Tongs: blacksmithing
      down the ages. London: Hutchinson, 1964. 160pp, ill,
      12 pls

5737 Longenecker, Elmer Z. The Early Blacksmiths of Lancaster
      County. Reprint from Community Historian, Vol. 10,
      December 1971. Lancaster: Community Historians, 1974.
      44pp

5738 Meyer, Franz Sales. A Handbook of Art Smithing for the Use
      of Practical Smiths, designers of ironwork, technical and
      art schools, architects, etc. Tr. from 2nd German ed.,
      and with an introd. by John Starkie Gardner. London:
      Batsford, 1896; New York: B. Hessling, 1906? 207pp,
      214 ill DLC, TxU

5739 Newman, Alfred A., and Co. The Old English Smithy. Lon-
      don: 1884. 14pp, ill DeWint

5740 Smith, H. R. Bradley. Blacksmiths' and Farriers' Tools at
      Shelburne Museum. Shelburne, Vt: the Museum, 1966;
      new ed. by Georgiana R. Smith. 1975. 262pp, ill; 272pp,
      ill

5741   Webber, Donald. The Village Blacksmith. London: David
       & Charles, 1971; Cranbury, NJ: Great Albion, 1972.
       160pp, 55 ill

5742   Welldon, William, and John Welldon. The Smith's Right Hand:
       or, A complete guide to the various branches of all sorts
       of iron work, etc. London: 1765. BM

DECORATIVE AND PRACTICAL IRON AND STEEL WORK

5743   Aesculapius Junior (pseud. for Shephard Thomas Taylor).
       Opercula (London Coal Plates). Introd. by Raymond
       Lister. London: 1929; reprint. Cambridge: Golden
       Head Pr, 1965. 32pp, ill with drawings

5744   Art in Iron. New York: The Wrot Iron Designers, 1932.

5745   Baines, John Manwaring. Wealdon Firebacks. Hastings,
       Eng: Science and Art School and Museum, 1958. 11pp,
       ill, 16 pls, bib

5746   Barnes, H. Jefferson. (Some Examples of) Ironwork and
       Metalwork by Charles Rennie Mackintosh in Glasgow
       School of Art Collection. Glasgow: the School, 1969.
       73pp of ill (MacKintosh, 1868-1928)

5747   *Byne, Arthur, and Mildred Stapley. Spanish Ironwork. New
       York: Hispanic Society of America, 1915. 143pp, 158
       ill, pls (Includes ecclesiastical work, and a catalogue of
       the Hispanic Society collection) NN, BM, MB

5748   Clarkson, Douglas A. Ancient Iron Work ... from the 13th
       Century. London: Atchley, 1860. 4pp, 48 pls

5749   Clouzot, Henri. Modern French Ironwork. Fore. by Max
       Judge. Tr. from French. London: J. Tiranti, 1928.
       5pp, 36 pls PPULC, DLC

5750   Curtis, Will, and Jane Curtis. Antique Woodstoves. Ash-
       ville, Me: Cobblesmith, 1975. 63pp, ill (Includes multi-
       plate stoves)

5751   *d'Allemagne, Henry Rene, 1863-1950. Decorative Antique
       Ironwork (in the Musee Le Secq des Tournelles, Rouen).
       Originally in two portfolios: Ferronnerie ancienne.
       Paris: J. Schemit, 1924. Reprint with introduction,
       bibliography and translation of captions by Vera K. Ostoia.
       New York: Dover, 1968. 417pp, chiefly ill, bib (4500
       objects, Roman times to 1850. Jewelry, sundials, clocks,
       utensils, tools, architectural ironwork, scissors, etc.)

5752   Davis, Myra Tolmach. Sketches in Iron: Samuel Yellin,

American Master of Wrought Iron, 1885-1940. Exhibition,
Dimock Gallery. Washington, D.C.: George Washington
University, 1971. 20pp, ill, pls, bib (Yellin, 1885-1940)

5753 Dawson, Charles. Sussex Iron Work and Pottery. With the
catalogue of the exhibition at Lewes Castle, 1902. Reprint from Sussex Archaeological Society's Collections.
1903. 62pp, ill

5754 Exhibition of Steel and Iron Work of European Origin. London:
Burlington Fine Arts Club, 1900. 82pp

5755 Erskine, F. J. Bent Ironwork. A practical manual of instruction for amateurs in the art and craft of making and
ornamenting light articles in imitation of the beautiful
mediaeval and Italian wrought iron work. London: Gill,
1892; 1894; London: Gill; New York: Scribner's, 1901?
54pp, ill DLC

5756 Ffoulkes, Charles John. Decorative Ironwork from the 11th
to the 13th Century. London: Methuen, 1913. 148pp,
ill, 81 diags, 32 pls, bib, names of smiths and ironworkers DLC, PP, MiU

5757 *Frank, Edgar Block. Old French Ironwork; the craftsman
and his art. Tr. from French (1948). Cambridge, Mass:
Harvard U. Pr; London: Oxford U. Pr, 1950. 221pp,
ill, 96 pls, bib

5758 _____. Small Gothic Ironwork. Offprint from Speculum,
October 1949. Cambridge, Mass: Medieval Academy of
America, n.d. 13pp (pp. 529-541), pls IU

5759 French, George Russell, 1803-1881, ed. A Catalogue of the
Antiquities, and Works of Art Exhibited at Ironmongers'
Hall.... May 1861. 4 parts. London: London & Mid-
dlesex Archaeological Society, 1869. BM

5760 Frey, Howard C. Conestoga Wagon Lore. Lancaster, Pa:
Pennsylvania Dutch Folklore Center, 1951. 20pp, ill

5761 Gardner, John Starkie. Exhibition of Chased and Embossed
Steel and Iron Work of European Origin. London: Burling-
ton Fine Arts Club, 1900. 82pp, ill, 70 pls NNC-Ave,
BM

5762 * _____. Ironwork. (Or Handbook on Ironwork.) Vol. I.
... From the earliest times to end of the mediaeval
period; Vol. II. ... Close of Mediaeval period to end of
18th century, excluding English work; Vol. III. Complete
survey of the artistic working of iron in Great Britain
from the earliest times. South Kensington Museum.

Vol. I and II. London: Chapman & Hall, 1893-97; 2nd ed.
2 vol., with Vol. II revised by William W. Watts as Continental Ironwork of the Renaissance and Later Periods.
London: HMSO, 1907; Vol. I, 3rd ed. Vol. III, 1st ed.
London: HMSO, 1914; 3 vol. London: 1922-30; Vol. I
& III. London: 1922-27; 4th ed. Vol. I. 1927. text, ill,
pls, bib DeWint, PPL, MiD, NN, DLC

5763 _____. Wrought Iron. London: 1887. MH

5764 Harris, John, 1931- , comp. English Decorative Ironwork
from Contemporary Source Books, 1610-1836; a collection
of drawings and pattern books including: A New Booke of
Drawings, by John Tijou, 1693; The Smith's Right Hand,
by W. J. Welldon, 1795; A Book of Designs, by J. Bottomley, 1793; etc. Chicago: Quadrangle, 1960. 18pp,
172 ill

5765 Hasluck, Paul Nooncree, ed. Bent Iron Work (Including Elementary Art Metal Work).... London; New York: Cassell, 1902; Philadelphia: McKay, 1903; 1906. 160pp, ill
NN, DLC

5766 Hayward, John Forrest. English Wrought-iron Work. V & A
Museum. London: HMSO, 1950. 32pp, ill, 27 pls, bib
NN

5767 Hendley, Thomas Holbein, 1847-1917. Damascening on Steel
or Iron, as Practiced in India. London: W. Griggs,
1892. 18pp, 32 color pls of 104 designs DLC, PP, MiU

5768 *Hoever, Otto. An Encyclopedia of Ironwork; examples of
hand wrought ironwork from the Middle Ages to the end
of the 18th century. New York: Weyhe; London: Benn,
1927; reprint as A Handbook of Wrought Iron from the
Middle Ages to the End of the 19th Century. Tr. from
German (1910) by Ann C. Weaver. London: Thames &
Hudson, 1962; as Wrought Iron; encyclopedia of ironwork.
New York: Universe, 1962; 1969. 20pp, ill, 320 pls

5769 Hollister-Short, Graham John. Discovering Wrought Iron.
Tring: Shire Publications, 1970. 72pp, ill, bib

5770 Horst, Melvin, photographer, and Elmer L. Smith. Early
Iron Ware. Lebanon, Pa: Applied Arts Pub, 1971.
32pp, ill

5771 Hummel, Charles F. Firebacks--an early Colonial craft.
n.p.: 1953. 9pp DeWint

5772 Iron Objects from the 14th to the 18th Centuries, Exhibition,
October-November 1967. Pennsylvania State University

College of Arts and Architecture presents works from the
Philadelphia Museum of Art. University Park, Pa: 1967.
12pp, ill

5773 Iron Work. Plates from l'Art Pour Tous. (1875). Paris:
A. Morel, 1875. 79 pls NN, DLC

5774 *John, William David, and Anne Simcox. Pontypool and Usk
Japanned Wares, with the early history of the iron and
tinplate industries at Pontypool. Newport, Wales:
Ceramic Book Co, 1953; reprint with additional illustrations. 1966, 88pp, ill, 26 (7 color) pls

5775 Jores, J. A New Book of Iron Work; containing a great
variety of designs (Useful for Painters, cabinet-makers,
carvers, smiths, fillegre-piercers, etc.) with gates of
various sorts, pilasters, fence for beaufets, tables, rails,
staircases, galleries, balconies, sign and lamp irons,
door-lights, gratings, brackets, pedestals, weather-cocks,
spindles, etc. London: Robert Sayer, 1759? 20 pls
NNC-Ave

5776 *Kauffman, Henry J. Early American Ironwork, Cast and
Wrought. Rutland, Vt: Tuttle; London: Prentice-Hall,
1966. 166pp, ill, bib (To 1900. Lamps, hardware, guns,
tools, locks, etc.)

5777 [No entry.]

Kowalczyk, Georg von. An Encyclopedia of Ironwork. See:
Hoever, O., no. 5768.

5778 Kuhn, Fritz. Wrought Iron. Tr. from German by Charles
B. Johnson. London: Harrap, 1965. 120pp, ill

5779 *Lamprecht Collection of Cast Iron Art. Birmingham, Ala:
American Cast Iron Pipe Co, 1941. 37pp, ill, bib (Origi-
nally collected by Gustav Lambrecht of the University of
Leipzig. Now on view at Birmingham Museum of Art.
Jewellery, stoves, candlesticks, sewing table gadgets, por-
traits, statuettes, toilette articles, plaques, etc.)

5780 Landis, Henry Kinzer. Conestoga Wagons and Their Ornamental Ironing. Allentown, Pa: Author, Pennsylvania
German Folklore Society, 1938. 15pp, ill NNC-Ave

5781 Lindsay, John Seymour. An Anatomy of English Wrought Iron.
London: Tiranti, 1964; New York: Taplinger, 1965. 60pp,
ill, 165 pls (1000-1800 A.D.)

5782 *_____. Iron and Brass Implements of the English House.
(Or, Iron and Brass Implements of the English and American

Home.) Introd. by Ralph Edwards. London; Boston: The Medici Society, 1927; rev. & enl. ed. Bass River, Mass: C. Jacobs; London: Tiranti, 1964. 211pp, many ill (drawings by author); 88pp, 473 ill (The hearth, cooking, lighting, tobacco use, miscellany, Colonial metal work, etc.)

5783 Lister, Raymond. Decorative Cast Ironwork in Great Britain. London: Bell, 1960. 258pp, ill, 24 pls, bib

5784 _____. Decorative Wrought Ironwork in Great Britain. London: Bell; Newton Centre, Mass: C. T. Branford, 1957; Newton Abbot: David & Charles, 1970. 267pp, ill, 28 pls, bib, gloss (Decorative, architectural, utilitarian)

5785 _____. Hammer and Hand: An Essay on the Ironwork of Cambridge. Cambridge, Eng: Author, 1969. 42pp, ill

5786 Luetke, Oscar. American Art in Wrought Iron, Exterior and Interior, 1886-1930. 2 vol. New York: Author, 1933. mounted ill (Marquees, hardware, flower stands, floor, bridge and table lamps, garden furniture, console tables, mirrors, andirons, etc.) NNC-Ave

5787 *Made of Iron. Exhibition, September-December 1966. Introd. by Stephen V. Grancsay; essay "On the Nature of Iron," by Cyril Stanley Smith. Houston: University of St. Thomas Art Department, 1966. 288pp, 290 ill, bib (All kinds of iron objects, all periods)

5788 Melnick, Robert, and Mimi Melnick. Manhole Covers of Los Angeles. Los Angeles: Dawsons Book Shop, 1974. 81pp, ill (Old and new)

5789 *Mercer, Henry Chapman. The Bible in Iron; pictured stoves and stoveplates of the Pennsylvania Germans; notes on Colonial firebacks in the United States, the ten-plate stove, Franklin's fireplace, and the tile stoves of the Moravians in Pennsylvania and North Carolina, together with a list of Colonial furnaces in the United States and Canada. Doylestown, Pa: Bucks County Historical Society, 1914; 2nd ed. rev. & enl. by Horace M. Mann, 1941; 3rd ed. rev., corr. & ed. by H. M. Mann, with further amendments and additions by Joseph E. Sandford. Doylestown: 1961. 174pp, ill; 256pp, ill; 100 pls of 409 ill

5790 _____. The Decorated Stove Plates of Durham, Pennsylvania. Doylestown: Bucks County Historical Society, 1897? 4pp DLC

5791 _____. The Decorated Stove Plates of the Pennsylvania Germans. Doylestown, Pa: McGinty's Job Press for

Bucks County Historical Society, 1899.   26pp, ill   DLC,
MB

5792   Murphy, Bailey Scott.   English and Scottish Wrought Iron-
       work: a series of examples of English ironwork of the
       best periods, together with most of the examples now
       existing in Scotland.   London: Batsford; Edinburgh:
       Waterston; New York: Scribner's, 1904.   14pp, mea-
       sured drawings, 80 pls   ViU, NNC-Ave, MB

5793   Museum Extension Project.   Pennsylvania.   Pennsylvania
       Wrought Iron.   Pittsburgh?: W.P.A., 1937?   95 pls
       (part color)

5794   Nutting, Wallace.   Early American Ironwork.   Saugus?,
       Mass: Author, 1919.   24pp, ill   DLC

5795   Ornamental Iron.   Monthly, then bi-monthly.   Chicago:
       Winslow Brothers, 1893-1895.

5796   Ornamental Iron, Bronze and Wire Bulletin.   Monthly.   Wash-
       ington, D.C., etc.: National Association of Ornamental
       Iron, Bronze and Wire Manufacturers, 1928- .

5797   Ornamental Ironwork/1870.   James, Kirtland & Co.   Cata-
       logue reprint.   Princeton, NJ: Pyne, 1971.   70pp, 110
       ill (Fountains, statuary, vases, urns, lawn furniture,
       etc.)

5798   Picture Book of English Wrought Iron Work.   V & A Museum.
       London: HMSO, 1929.   24pp, 20 ill

5799   Redfern, W. B.   Ancient Wood and Iron Work in Cambridge.
       Cambridge: W. P. Spaulding, 1886.   30 leaves, 28 pls
       NN

5800   Sanders, Amanda.   Bent Ironwork.   For beginners and pro-
       ficients.   London: Chapman & Hall, 1895.   48pp, ill

5801   Savage, Robert H.   Pennsylvania German Wrought Ironwork.
       Plymouth Meeting, Pa: Mrs. C. N. Keyser, 1947.   33pp,
       ill, bib

5802   *Shumway, George, Edward Durell, and Howard C. Frey.
       Conestoga Wagon 1750-1850.   Williamsburg, Va: Early
       American Industries Association, 1964; 2nd ed. York,
       Pa: E.A.I.A., 1966.   206pp, ill, bib; 281pp, ill, bib

5803   *Sonn, Albert H., 1867-1936.   Early American Wrought Iron.
       3 vol.   New York: Charles Scribner's, 1928.   ill, 320
       pls of drawings, bib (Tools, household utensils, etc.)

5804   Zimelli, Umberto, and Giovanni Vergerio.   Decorative

Ironwork. Tr. from Italian by Anthony Sutton. Feltham;
New York: Hamlyn, 1969. 159pp, ill (European ironwork to 1940)

ARCHITECTURAL IRONWORK

5805 Ayrton, Maxwell, and Arnold Silcock. Wrought Iron and Its
Decorative Use. London: Country Life; New York:
Scribner's, 1929. 496pp, 239 ill, bib (Most examples
from English country homes and churches) DeWint

5806 Bragg, Lillian Chaplin. Old Savannah Ironwork. Savannah,
Ga: 1957. 41pp, pls

5807 Byne, Arthur, and Mildred Stapley. Rejeria of the Spanish
Renaissance; a collection of photographs and measured
drawings, with descriptive text. New York: DeVinne Pr,
1914. 101pp, 26 pls, color frontis PP, DLC, CU

5808 Chatwin, Amina. Cheltenham's Ornamental Ironwork. Cheltenham, Glos: Author, 1975. 93pp, ill

5809 Cottingham, Lewis Nockalls. The Smith's, Founder's, and
Ornamental Worker's Director, comprising a variety of
designs in the present taste for gates, piers, balcony
railings, window guards, verandas, balustrades, vases,
etc., with various ornaments applicable to works in
metal. London: M. Taylor, 18-?; 182-? 45 pls IU,
DLC

5810 Deas, Alston. The Early Ironwork of Charleston. Introd. by
Albert Simons. Columbia, S.C.: Bostick & Thornley,
1941. 111pp, 64 ill (scale drawings), bib

5811 Ebbetts, Daniel John. Examples of Decorative Wrought Iron
Work of the 17th and 18th Century. Consisting of measured drawings of large and small gates, screens, grilles,
panels, ballustrading, etc., ... including a large number
of gates, etc., from London and its suburbs. 3pp, 15
pls in folio PP, DLC, BM

5812 *Gardner, John Starkie. English Ironwork of the 17th and 18th
Centuries; an historical and analytical account of the development of exterior smithcraft. London: Batsford, 1911;
reprint. New York: B. Blom, 1972. 336pp, 150 ill, 88
pls, list of smiths and designers (Lampholders, brackets,
signs, vanes, and architectural ironwork)

5813a Geerlings, Gerald Kenneth. Metal Crafts in Architecture.
Bronze, brass, cast iron, copper, lead, lighting fixtures,
tin, specifications. New York: Scribner's, 1929; reprint. 1957. 202pp, ill, bib

5813b*_____. Wrought Iron in Architecture: wrought iron crafts-
        manship; historical notes and illustrations of wrought iron
        in Italy, Spain, France, Holland, Belgium, England, Ger-
        many, America; modern wrought iron; lighting fixtures and
        knockers, specifications. New York: Scribner's, 1929;
        reprint. 1972. 202pp, ill, bib

5814   Gloag, John Edwards, and Derek L. Bridgwater. A History
        of Cast Iron in Architecture. Fore. by Sir Charles Reilly.
        London: Allen & Unwin, 1948. 395pp, ill, bib

5815   Kent, William Winthrop, 1860- . Architectural Wrought-
        Iron, ancient and modern. A compilation of examples
        from various sources, of German, Italian, Irish, English
        and American ironwork. New York: William T. Com-
        stock, 1888. 34pp, 35 pls PP

5816   Luetke, Oscar. American Art in Wrought Iron, Exterior and
        Interior, 1886-1930. 2 vol. New York: Author, 1933.
        mounted ill (Marquees, hardware, flower stands, floor,
        bridge and table lamps, garden furniture, console tables,
        mirrors, tables, candelabras, andirons, church metal
        work, etc.) NNC-Ave

5817   Robertson, Edward Graeme. Adelaide Lace. Adelaide,
        Australia: Rigby, 1973. 207pp, ill, bib

5818   _____. Ornamental Cast Iron in Melbourne. Melbourne:
        Georgian House, 1967; London: Routledge & K. Paul,
        1972. 229pp, chiefly ill (1870-1900)

5819   Small, Tunstall, and Christopher Woodbridge. English
        Wrought Ironwork, Mediaeval and Early Renaissance.
        London; New York: Architectural Pr, 1931. 4pp, 20
        pls

5820   _____, and _____. English Wrought Ironwork of the
        Late 17th and Early 18th Centuries. London: The Archi-
        tectural Pr; New York: Helburn, 1930. 20 pls

5821   Tijou, Jean. A New Booke of Drawings Invented and De-
        signed by J. Tijou. Containing severall sortes of iron
        worke as gates, frontispieces, balconies, staircases,
        pannells, etc., of which the most part hath been wrought
        at the Royall Building of Hampton Court ... All for the
        use of them that worke iron in perfection, and with art.
        London: Author, 1693; reproduced with an account of the
        author, and a description of the plates, by John Starkie
        Gardner. London: Batsford, 1896. 8pp, 20 pls

5822   *Wallace, Philip B. Colonial Ironwork in Old Philadelphia:
        the craftsmanship of the early days of the Republic.

Introd. by Fiske Kimball. New York: Architectural Book
Pub. Co, 1930; New York: Dover; London: Constable,
1970. 149pp of ill, bib (To ca.1800) (Railings, gates,
doorknockers, etc.)

5823 Weale, John, 1791-1862, ed. Designs of Ornamental Gates,
Lodges, Palisading and Iron Work of the Royal Parks
(adjoining the Metropolis); with some other designs. London: J. Weale, 1841. 20pp, ill, 50 pls BM

5824 Wickersham, John B. A New Phase in Iron Manufacture,
embracing a description of its uses for enclosing public
squares, cemetery lots, dwellings, cottages, offices,
gratings for stores, prisons, etc., window guards, bedsteads, tree boxes, verandas, etc. 2nd ed. New York:
William C. Bryant, 1853. 38pp, chiefly ill

HARDWARE AND DOOR KNOCKERS

5825 Aitken, William Costen. Guns, Nails, Locks, Wood Screws,
Railway Bolts and Spikes, Buttons, Pins, Needles, Sad-
dlery, and Electroplate. London: 1876. See: Bevan,
G. P., British Manufacturing Industries, Vol. 3.

Art Brass Co, Inc. See: Door Knockers..., no. 5831; A
History of Door Knockers, no. 5839.

5826 Blackall, Clarence Howard. Builders' Hardware; a manual
for architects, builders and house furnishers. Boston:
Ticknor, 1890. 322pp, ill, 4 double pls DeWint

5827 Carr, William H., and Co., Philadelphia. American Manufactured Hardware, etc., for sale.... Philadelphia:
William Brown, 1838; Reprint for Early American Industries Association from original in the library of Eleuthe-
rian Mills, with fore. by Richmond D. Wilkins. Wilmington, Del: 1972. 32pp, ill

5828 Chamberlain, Samuel. New England Doorways. New York:
Hastings House, 1939. 101pp, ill

5829 Cousins, Frank. 50 Salem Doorways. Garden City, NY:
Doubleday, Page, 1912. 50 pls

5830 Decorative French Hardware ... ornamental hardware employed in the interior decoration of apartments. Beginning from the Middle Ages up to the present time ...
selected from general catalogue of MM. Fontaine &
Vaillant of Paris, of which firm the Russell & Erwin
Manufacturing Company are sole United States Agents.
New York: 189-? ill, 36 pls NNC-Ave

5831 Door Knockers: the famous William Hall and Company Line,
       collected since 1843. New York: Art Brass Co, Inc.,
       1917. 23pp, ill, pls

5832 Hardware Age. Weekly. New York: David Williams, 1913.
       ill

5833 Hardware and Farm Equipment. Monthly. Kansas City:
       Western Retail Implement and Hardware Association,
       1895- . ill

5834 Hardware and Housewares. Periodical. Toronto: Wrigley,
       1909-1952. ill

5835 Hardware and Implement Trade, and Western Industrial
       Record. Weekly. Chicago: 1876- . ill

5836 Hardware Catalogues. A Miscellaneous collection. 11 vol.
       Milwaukee: 1851-1923. ill (Tools, cutlery, fences,
       building hardware, household utensils, lanterns, etc.) NN

5837 The Hardware Journal. Monthly. Melbourne, Australia:
       Trade Pr, 1886- . ill DLC

5838 Hardware Trade Journal. Weekly. London: Benn Brothers,
       1873- . ill DLC

5839 A History of Door Knockers. New York: Art Brass Co.,
       Inc., 1917. 8pp, ill

5840 Isham, Norman Morrison. A Glossary of Colonial Architec-
       tural Terms, with a bibliography of books 1880-1930, to
       which is added "The Dating of Old Houses," by Henry C.
       Mercer. New York: Walpole Society, 1939; reprint.
       Watkins Glen: Century, 1968. 56pp, ill (Mercer's
       article concerns dating nails, hardware, etc.)

5841 Messent, Claude John Wilson. The Old Door Knockers of
       Norwich, an alphabetical listing of 45 door knockers and
       sanctuary knockers in the city of Norwich and its most
       ancient suburbs. Norwich, Eng: Fletcher & Son, 1948.
       55pp, ill NNC-Ave, MB

5842 Nails: being a compilation of information on nails and nail-
       making from divers sources. Complement to a talk by
       Simeon Ross, February 1974. Levittown, NY: Early
       Trades and Crafts Society, 1974. 13pp, ill

5843 Rare Pattern Book of Door Furniture, handles, key plates....
       ca. 1790. ill MiGr

5844 Schiffer, Herbert F. Early Pennsylvania Hardware. Whitford,
       Pa.: Whitford Pr, 1966. 63pp, ill, bib

5845 Towne, Henry R. Locks and Builders Hardware, a Handbook
       for Architects. New York: 1904.

5846 Walker, J. General List of Prices of Hardwares, saddlery,
       plated and japanned wares, cutlery, etc. n. p. (England):
       1823. SIB-1

IVORY, JADE, LACQUER AND ENAMELS

GENERAL WORKS ON IVORY

5847 Alabaster, E. P. Ivories. General Guide, part 15. Dublin: Science & Art Museum, 1910. 54pp

5848 Beigbeder, Olivier. Ivory. London: Weidenfeld & Nicolson; New York: Putnam, 1965. 128pp, ill (to 1800)

5849 Beihoff, Norbert J. Ivory Through the Ages. Milwaukee, Wisc: Public Museum, 1961. 93pp, 109 ill

5850 Catalogue of an Exhibition of Carvings in Ivory. London: Burlington Fine Arts Club, 1923. 117pp

5851 Catalogue of Select Examples of Ivory-Carvings from the Second to the 16th Century; preserved in various public and private collections in England and other countries. London: Arundel Society, 1855. 28pp BM

5852 Howard, Wendell Stanton. The George Arnold Hearn Collection of Carved Ivories. New York: priv. printed, Gilliss Pr, 1908. 267pp, 214 ill MiU, MB

5853 Ivory Collection, Columbia Museum Catalog, Dubuque. Compiled by Iowa Writers' Project. Dubuque: 1940.

5854 Kunz, George Frederick. Ivory and the Elephant in Art, in Archaeology, and in Science. Garden City, NY: Doubleday, 1916. 128pp, ill, pls MiU, PPL

5855 Longhurst, Margaret Helen. Catalogue of Carvings in Ivory. Preface by Eric Maclagan. 2 vol. London: V & A Museum, 1927, 1929. ill, pls, bib BM

5856 Maskell, Alfred. Ivories. London: Methuen; New York: Putnam, 1905; Rutland, Vt.: Tuttle; London: Prentice-Hall, 1966. 551pp, 256 ill, 88 pls, bib

5857 Maskell, William, 1814-1890. A Description of the Ivories
      Ancient and Medieval in the South Kensington Museum.
      London: Chapman & Hall, 1872; 1875; New York: Scrib-
      ner, 1877. 124pp, ill BM, NN

5858 Williamson, George Charles. The Book of Ivory. London:
      F. Muller, 1938. 247pp, ill, 16 pls, bib (Ancient to
      medieval)

5859 Wills, Geoffrey. Ivory. London: Arco, 1968; South Bruns-
      wick, NJ: A. S. Barnes, 1969. 95pp, ill, 12 pls

5860 Wyatt, Sir Matthew Digby. Notices of Sculpture in Ivory,
      consisting of a lecture on the history, methods, and chief
      productions of the art ... at the Arundel Society ... and
      a catalogue of specimens of ancient ivory-carvings in
      various collections.... London: 1856. 54pp, ill, 9
      photos, bib

CHINESE AND INDIAN IVORY†

5861 Anand, Mulk Raj. Indian Ivories. Bombay: Marg Publica-
      tions, 1970. 50pp

5862 Chinese Ivories: catalogue and souvenir of the Grice Collec-
      tion. Sheffield, Eng: Graves Art Gallery, 1958. 72pp,
      ill, bib

5863 Cox, Warren Earle. Chinese Ivory Sculpture. New York:
      Crown, 1946. 112pp, ill

5864 Laufer, Berthold. Ivory in China. Chicago: Field Museum
      of Natural History, 1925. 78pp, ill, bib

5865 Lucas, Sydney Edward, comp. The Catalogue of Sassoon
      (Collection) Chinese Ivories. 3 vol. London: Country
      Life; New York: Scribner, 1950. 29pp, pls, bib

IVORY OF THE WESTERN WORLD

5866 Beckwith, John. Ivory Carvings in Early Medieval England.
      London: Harvey, Miller & Medcalf; Greenwich, Conn:
      NY Graphic Society, 1972. 168pp, ill, bib (700 to
      1200 A.D.)

5867 _____ . The Veroli Casket. V & A. London: HMSO,
      1962. 28pp, ill, 16 pls, bib (Byzantine ivory)

---

†Most Japanese ivories are in the form of netsukes, and are to be
found in that listing under Section XII.

5868   Carra, Massimo. Ivories of the West. Tr. from Italian by
       Raymond Rudorff. Feltham: Hamlyn, 1970. 160pp, ill
       (to 1718)

5869   Cust, Anna Maria Elizabeth. The Ivory Workers of the Mid-
       dle Ages. London: G. Bell, 1902; 1906; reprint. New
       York: AMS Pr, 1973. 169pp, ill, bib

5870   Ivory Carvings in Early Medieval England, 700-1200. Exhibi-
       tion May-July 1974, V & A Museum. London: Arts Coun-
       cil of Great Britain, 1974. 100pp, ill

5871   Longhurst, Margaret Helen. English Ivories. London: Put-
       nam, 1926. 171pp, ill, pls (part color), bib (Scholarly)
       NN, MiU

5872   Natanson, Joseph. Early Christian Ivories. London: J.
       Tiranti, 1953. 34pp, 51 pls, bib

5873   _____. Gothic Ivories of the 13th and 14th Centuries.
       London: Tiranti, 1951. 40pp, 64 pls, bib

5874   Westwood, John Obadiah, 1805-1893. A Descriptive Catalogue
       of the Fictile Ivories in the South Kensington Museum.
       With an account of the Continental collections of classical
       and mediaeval ivories. London: Eyre & Spottiswoode,
       1876. 547pp, ill, pls

AFRO-PORTUGUESE IVORY

5875   Fagg, W. P. Afro-Portuguese Ivories. London: Batchworth
       Pr, n.d. (195-?) 14pp, 46 pls, bib ("Hybrid" pieces
       carved by Africans for Portuguese to order. Salt cellars,
       spoons, forks, oliphants. 16th century)

5876   Read, Sir Charles Hercules, and O. M. Dalton. Antiquities
       from the City of Benin and from the other parts of West
       Africa, in the British Museum. London: 1899. ill
       (Includes the hybrid pieces)

GENERAL WORKS ON JADE AND OTHER HARDSTONES

5877   Bedford, John. Jade and Other Hardstone Carvings. London:
       Cassell; New York: Walker, 1969. 64pp, ill, 4 pls

5878   Bishop, Heber Reginald. The Bishop Collection. Investiga-
       tions and studies in jade. New York: 1900; New York:
       priv. printed, De Vinne Pr, 1906. 378pp, ill, bib

5879   The Bishop Collection of Jade and Other Hard Stones. New
       York: Metropolitan Museum, 190-? 104pp

5880 Denman, Carolyn. Jade, a Comprehensive Bibliography. Reprint from Journal of the American Oriental Society, vol.
65, April-June 1945. New Haven?: 1945. 10pp (pp.
117-126) DLC

5881 Getz, John. The Pratt Collection of Jades and Other Hard
Stones at Vassar College. New York: priv. printed,
Marion Pr, 1920. 62pp, ill

5882 _____. The (Robert B.) Woodward Collection of Jades and
Other Hard Stones. New York: priv. printed, De Vinne
Pr, 1913.

5883 Hansford, Sidney Howard. Jade: Essence of Hills and
Streams; the Von Oertzen Collection of Chinese and Indian
jades. Cape Town, S. Africa: Purnell; New York: American Elsevier Pub. Co., 1969. 220pp, ill, pls

5884 Heikenen, Patricia, ed. Jade as Sculpture. Exhibition, Minnesota Museum of Art, February-March; New York: Rare
Art Inc., April-June; Indianapolis Museum of Art, June-
August. Saint Paul, Minn.: 1975. 80pp, 103 ill, 6 color
pls

5885 Hemrich, Gerald I. The Handbook of Jade. Mentone, Cal:
Gembooks, 1966. 81pp, ill

5886 Kunz, George Frederick, 1856-1932, ed. The Bishop Collection. Investigations and Studies in Jade. 2 vol. New
York: priv. printed, DeVinne Pr, 1906. ill, 93 pls
(some color), bib (Includes mineralogical information)

5887 _____. The Printed Catalogue of the Heber R. Bishop
Collection of Jade. Supplement to the Bulletin of the
Metropolitan Museum, May 1906. New York: Gilliss Pr,
1906?

5888 Luzzatto-Bilitz, Oscar. Antique Jade. Tr. from Italian by
Francis Koval. London; New York: Hamlyn, 1969.
158pp, 71 color ill

5889 May, Evalyn. Jade for Beginners. Singapore: Moore for
Asia Pacific Pr, 1969. 65pp, ill

5890 Palmer, Jock Pegler. Jade. London: Spring Books, 1967.
44pp, ill, 54 pls

5891 Sakikawa, Noriyuki. Jade. Tokyo: Japan Publications, 1968.
61pp, ill

5892 Wills, Geoffrey. Jade. London; New York: Arco, 1964.
121pp, ill, 16 pls, bib

5893   _____. Jade of the East. Tokyo; New York: Weather-
            hill, 1972. 200pp, ill, bib (Asian and New Zealand art
            objects)

5894   Zara, Louis. Jade. London: Studio Vista; New York:
            Walker, 1969. 84pp, 53 ill, 2 pls, bib

CHINESE JADE AND OTHER HARDSTONES

5895   Davis, Frank Cecil Davis. Chinese Jade. Welwyn, Herts.,
            Eng: Author, 1935; 2nd ed. London: Commodore Pr,
            1944. 68pp, 19 pls

5896   De Tanner, P. Chinese Jade Ancient and Modern. Descrip-
            tive catalogue illustrating the most prominent pieces of a
            collection of jade articles, with special reference to sepul-
            chral jades. 2 vol. Berlin: Dietrich Reimer, Ernst
            Vohsen, 1925. BM

5897   Dohrenwend, Doris. Chinese Jades in the Royal Ontario Mu-
            seum. Toronto: 1971. 135pp, ill, bib

5898   Fuller, Richard E. Chinese Jades in the Seattle Art Museum.
            Seattle: 1971. 61 ill, text, introd. (Mr. & Mrs. Eugene
            Fuller Collection)

5899   Getz, John. Morgan Whitney Collection of Chinese Jades and
            Other Hard Stones Donated to the Isaac Delgado Museum
            of Art.... New Orleans: 1914. ill

5900   *Hansford, Sidney Howard. Chinese Carved Jades. Greenwich,
            Conn.: N.Y. Graphic; London: Faber, 1968. 131pp, ill,
            104 (8 color) pls, bib, gloss

5901   *_____. Chinese Jade Carving. London: Lund Humphries,
            1950. 145pp, 32 pls, color frontis, bib

5902   _____. Jade: Essence of Hills and Streams. The Von
            Oertzen Collection of Chinese and Indian Jades. New
            York: American Elsevier, 1969. 220pp, ill (part color),
            bib

5903   *Hartman, Joan Marcia. Chinese Jade of Five Centuries.
            Rutland, Vt.: Tuttle; Hemel Hempstead; Prentice-Hall,
            1969. 172pp, 55 ill (some color), bib, gloss (Ming-
            Ch'ing. 1368-1912)

5904   *_____. Three Dynasties of Jade. Exhibition. Indianapo-
            lis: Museum of Art, 1971. 43pp, ill

5905   Laufer, Berthold. Jade; a Study in Chinese archaeology and

religion. Chicago: Field Museum, 1912; 2nd ed. South
Pasadena, Cal.: P. D. & I. Perkins, 1946. 370pp, 68
(6 color) pls, bib

5906 Masterworks of Chinese Jade in the National Palace Museum.
Taipei, Taiwan, Republic of China: the Museum, 19-?;
Supplement. Ed. by Mai Ch-ch'eng. 1973. 50 color
pls (Shang-Ch'ing. 1766 B. C. -1911 A. D.)

5907 Nott, Stanley Charles, comp. A Catalogue of Rare Chinese
Jade Carvings (in the House of Jade). Introd. by Lieut. -
General Sir Sydney Lawford. St. Augustine, Fla: Record
Co., printer, 1940. 185pp, pls

5908 _____. Chinese Jade Throughout the Ages; a review of its
characteristics, decoration, folklore and symbolism. London: Batsford, 1936; 2nd ed. 1963; 4th printing. Rutland,
Vt.: Tuttle; London: Prentice-Hall, 1966; photo-reprint
of 1st ed. Rutland: 1973. 193pp, ill, 148 pls; 193pp,
134 pls, marks, bib (Asiatic, European & American collections. The authoritative volume. Has Chinese glossary)

5909 Pope-Hennesy, Dame Una. Early Chinese Jades. London:
Benn, 1923. 148pp, 64 pls (part color), bib

5910 Salmony, Alfred, 1890- . Archaic Chinese Jades from the
Edward and Louise B. Sonnenschein Collection. Catalog.
Chicago: Art Institute, 1952. ill

5911 * _____. Carved Jade of Ancient China. Berkeley, Cal.:
Gillick Pr, 1938. 85pp, 72 pls, bib

5912 Savage, George. Chinese Jade: a Concise Introduction.
London: Cory, Adams & Mackay, 1964; New York: October House, 1965; New York: British Book Center, 1974.
73pp, ill, 19 pls, bib (Earliest times to end of 18th C.)

GENERAL WORKS ON LACQUER

5913 Alabaster, E. P. Lacquer. General Guide to ... Japanese
Art. Chapter 1, Part 10. Dublin: Science & Art Museum, 1910.

5914 Audsley, George Ashdown. Descriptive Catalogue of Art
Works in Japanese Lacquer Forming Third Division of
the Japanese Collection of James Lord Bowes. London:
Chiswick Pr, 1875. 95pp NN, BM

5915 Bedford, John. Chinese and Japanese Lacquer. London:
Cassell; New York: Walker, 1969. 64pp, ill, 3 pls

5916   Bluett and Sons. Ming Lacquer. An exhibition. Introd. by
       Sir Harry Garner. London: Bluett, 1960. 29pp, pls

5917   *Boyer, Martha Hagensen. Japanese Export Lacquers from
       the 17th Century in the National Museum of Denmark.
       Copenhagen: 1959. 149pp, ill, 60 pls, bib

5918   Burney, Captain Henry, d. 1845?. Observations on the Lac-
       quered or Japanned Ware of Ava. n.p.: 1833. (Burmese)
       SIB-1

5919   Capey, Reco. Lacquer. Leicester: Dryad Handicrafts, 1928.
       25pp, pls

5920   *Fukushima, Oto, ed. Catalogue of the Collection of Japanese
       Lacquers of Martin John Desmoni. New York: priv.
       printed, 1947.

5921   Herberts, Kurt. Oriental Lacquer--Art and Technique. Lon-
       don: Thames & Hudson, 1962; 1963; 1967. 513pp, pls
       (part color)

5922   *Huth, Hans. Lacquer of the West; the History of a craft and
       an industry, 1550-1950. Chicago; London: U. of Chicago
       Pr, 1971. 158pp, 136 ill, 228 pls, bib (European &
       American)

5923   Jahss, Melvin, and Betty Jahss. Inro and Other Miniature
       Forms of Japanese Lacquer Art. London: K. Paul, 1970;
       Rutland, Vt.: Tuttle, 1971; London: 1972. 488pp, 256
       (76 color) pls, bib (Includes netsukes)

5924   Kanda, Matunosuke, ed. Japanese Lacquer. Tokyo: Meiji-
       Shobo, 1941. ill, 35 color pls in portfolio NN, NNC-Ave

5925   Koizumi, Gunji. Lacquer Work; a practical exposition of the
       art of lacquering together with valuable notes for the col-
       lector. Foreword by Lieut.-Col. E. F. Strange. Lon-
       don; New York: I. Pitman, 1923; New York: Putnam,
       1925. 45pp, ill, 47 pls MiGr, DLC

5926   Lee, Yu-Kuan. Oriental Lacquer Art. New York: Weather-
       hill for Oriental House Ltd., Tokyo, 1972. 394pp, ill of
       264 pieces, bib (China, Korea, Japan, and the Ryukyus)

5927   Luzzatto-Bilitz, Oscar. Oriental Lacquer. Tr. from Italian
       by Pauline L. Phillips. London; New York: Hamlyn,
       1969. 158pp, ill

5928   Okada, Yuzura. History of Japanese Textiles and Lacquer.
       Tr. by Charles S. Terry. Tokyo: Toto Shuppan; Rutland,
       Vt.: Tuttle; London: Paterson, 1958. 180pp, 165 ill
       (10 color)

5929   Orange, J.   A Small Collection of Japanese Lacquer.   Yoko-
       hama: 1910. 108pp

5930   Quin, John James, d. 1897.   The Lacquer Industry of Japan.
       n.p. 1881; Reprint in "Asiatic Society of Japan Transac-
       tions."   Vol. 9, Part 1.   Tokyo: 1906.   32pp (pp. 1-31)
       IC

5931   A Special Exhibition of Japanese Art; examples of screen
       painting, fan painting and lacquer-work from the collec-
       tions of museums and private owners. . . .   January 1938.
       Toledo, O.: Museum of Art, 1937.   52pp, ill, pls

5932   Stern, Harold P.   The Magnificent Three: Lacquer, Netsuke,
       and Tsuba.   Selections from the collection of Charles A.
       Greenfield.   Exhibit.   New York: Japan Society, 1972.
       141pp, ill, bib

5933   Strange, Edward Fairbrother.   Catalogue of Chinese Lacquer.
       V & A Museum.   London: HMSO, 1925.   36pp, 44 pls

5934   _____.   Catalogue of Japanese Lacquer.   V & A Museum.
       London: HMSO, 1924- .   with pls

5935   _____.   Chinese Lacquer.   New York: Scribner; London:
       E. Benn, 1926.   71pp, 54 pls (part color), bib   MiGr

5936   von Rague, Beatrix.   A History of Japanese Lacquerwork.
       Toronto: U. of T. Pr, 1975.

NEAR AND FAR EASTERN ENAMELS AND CLOISONNE

5937   Alexander, William Foster.   Cloisonné and Related Arts.
       Des Moines: Wallace-Homestead, 1972.   96pp, hundreds
       of ill

5938   Bowes, James Lord.   Japanese Enamels (from Bowes Collec-
       tion).   Liverpool: Author, 1884; reissue. London: B.
       Quaritch, 1886.   111pp, 20 (2 color) pls   BM

5939   _____.   Notes on Shippo.   A Sequel to "Japanese Enamels."
       Liverpool: Author, 1895; London: Kegan Paul, Trench,
       1895.   109pp, ill, 4 pls   (Cloisonné and glass-making)
       CU, CtY, BM, DLC

5940   Chu, Arthur, and Grace Chu.   Oriental Cloisonné and Other
       Enamels.   A Guide to collecting and repairing.   New York:
       Crown, 1975.   300 ill, bib

5941   Cosgrove, Maynard Giles.   The Enamels of China and Japan:
       champlevé and cloisonné.   London: Hale; New York: Dodd,
       Mead, 1974.   115pp, ill, 8 pls, bib

5942   Dalton, O(rmonde) M(addock), 1866-1945. Byzantine Enamels
       in Mr. Pierpont Morgan's Collection. With note by Roger
       Fry. London: Chatto & Windus for Burlington Magazine,
       1912. 16pp, 11 pls

5943   Fine-Enamelled Ware of the Ch'ing Dynasty. Yung-cheng
       period. National Palace Museum. 2 vol. Kowloon:
       Cafa Co., 1967. color pls.

5944   *Garner, Sir Harry Mason. Chinese and Japanese Cloisonné
       Enamels. London: Faber; Rutland, Vt.: Tuttle, 1962;
       2nd ed. London: 1970. 120pp, ill, 101 pls, bib (Chinese
       up to end of Ch'ing Dynasty. Includes western enamel
       decoration)

5945   Getz, John. Catalogue of the Avery Collection of Ancient
       Chinese Cloisonnés. Pref. by William H. Goodyear.
       Brooklyn: Museum of the Brooklyn Institute of Arts &
       Sciences, 1912. 72pp, ill (Includes history by Stephen
       W. Bushell) NN, DLC

5946   Jacobs, S.S., and Thomas Holbein Hendley. Jeypore Enamels.
       London: W. Griggs, 1886. 28 color pls with 120 designs

5947   Robinson, Basil William. Chinese Cloisonné Enamels. V &
       A Museum. London: HMSO, 1972. 12pp, chiefly color ill

5948   Wessel, Klaus. Byzantine Enamels, from the Fifth to the
       13th Century. Tr. from German (1967) by Irene R. Gib-
       bons. Greenwich, Conn.: N.Y. Graphic, 1968. 211pp,
       ill, 66 pls

EUROPEAN ENAMELS AND GENERAL WORKS

5949   Belli-Barsali, Isa. European Enamels. Tr. from Italian by
       Ramond Rudorff. Feltham; New York: Hamlyn, 1969.
       158pp, ill, 71 color pls (to 1700)

5950   Chamot, Mary. English Medieval Enamels. London: Benn,
       for University College of London, 1930. 49pp, 20 pls,
       bib NN, DLC

5951   Cunynghame, Harry Hardinge Samuel, 1848-1935. European
       Enamels. London: Connoisseur, Methuen; New York:
       Putnam's, 1906. 187pp, 57 (4 color) pls DLC, NN, MiGr

5952   Dalpayrat, L. Limoges Enamels; or, The processes of the
       early Limoges enamellers. Tr. by G. A. Bouvier. Lon-
       don: 1881.

5953   Dawson, Edith B. (Mrs. Nelson). Enamels. London: Methuen, 1906; Chicago: A. C. McClurg, 1908; 1910; 2nd ed. London: 1912. 207pp, 32 pls, bib MH, NN

5954 Day, Lewis Foreman. ... Enamelling, a comparative account of the development and practice of the art. London: Batsford, 1907. 222pp, 115 ill NNC-Ave

5955 Elward, Robert. On Collecting Miniatures, Enamels, and Jewellery. London: E. Arnold, 1905. 94pp, ill, bib

5956 Enamel, an Historic Survey to the Present Day. Exhibit. New York: Cooper Union, 1954. 28pp, ill, pls

5957 Forman, Werner. Limoges Enamels. Tr. by Ota Vojtisek. London: Hamlyn, 1962. 40pp, ill

5958 Gardner, John Starkie, comp. European Enamels from the Earliest Date to the End of the 17th Century, Exhibited in 1897. London: Burlington Fine Arts Club, 1897. 82pp, 72 pls BM

5959 Gauthier, Marie Madeleine, and Madeleine Marcheix. Limoges Enamels. Tr. from French by Ota Vojtisek. London: Hamlyn, 1963. 40pp, 57 pls (12th-14th centuries)

5960 Gilt-Metal and Enamel Work of the 18th Century: an exhibition, September-October 1967, of Georgian 'toys' chosen to illustrate the use made of gilt-metal, pinchbeck, painted enamel, silver and silver-coated copper. Private collections. Leamington Spa, Eng: Library, Art Gallery & Museum, 1967. 28pp, 8 pls, bib

5961 Hildburgh, Walter Leo. Medieval Spanish Enamels. Their Relation to the origin and the development of copper champleve enamels of the 12th and 13th centuries. London: Oxford U. Pr., H. Milford, 1936. 146pp, 24 pls, bib TxU, DLC

5962 Hughes, Therle, and Bernard Hughes. English Painted Enamels, from the collections of H. M. Queen Mary and Mrs. Ionides. London: Country Life; New York: Scribners, 1951; new ed. London: Spring Books, 1967. 156pp, ill, 4 color pls (Battersea boxes, etc. through 18th century)

5963 Kovacs, Eva. Limoges Champlevé Enamels in Hungary. Budapest: 1968. 103pp, ill (12th & 13th centuries)

5964 Lesley, Everett Parker. Enamel, an Historic Survey to the Present Day. New York: Cooper Union, 1954. 28pp, pls, bib

5965 Maskell, William, 1814?-1890. Enamels. South Kensington Museum. London: Chapman & Hall, 187-? 16pp, ill NN

5966   _____ . Schreiber Collection. Catalogue of English porce-
        lain, enamels, etc. London: South Kensington Museum,
        1885. 241pp

5967   Mew, Egan. Battersea Enamels. London; Boston: Medici
        Society, 1926. 27pp, 78 (6 color) pls NN, DLC

5968   Mihalik, Sandor. Old Hungarian Enamels. Tr. by Lily
        Halapy. Budapest: Corvina, 1961. 39pp, 48 pls

5969   Plunkett, George Tindall. Enamels. General Guide ...
        Part 5. Dublin: Science & Art Museum, 1902. 19pp

5970   Pollen, John Hungerford, ed. Catalogue of the Special Loan
        Exhibition of Enamels on Metal Held at the South Kensing-
        ton Museum in 1874. London: 1874; with plates. Lon-
        don: Chiswick Pr, 1875. 149pp, 15 pls

5971   The Raby Collection of Battersea and South Staffordshire
        Enamels. Manchester, Eng: City Art Gallery, 1955.
        40pp

5972   Ricketts, Howard. Antique Gold and Enamelware in Color.
        Garden City, NY: Doubleday; as Objects of Vertu. Lon-
        don: Barrie & Jenkins, 1971. 124pp, chiefly color ill,
        bib (Battersea, Bilston & Birmingham enamels, gold,
        tortoiseshell & horn, Faberge, Dinglinger)

5973   Rowe, Donald F. Enamels, the 12th-16th Century; a special
        exhibition at the Martin D'Arcy Gallery of Art. Chicago:
        Loyola University, 1970. 41pp, ill

5974   A Thousand Years of Enamel. Exhibit. May-June 1971.
        London: Wartski Gallery, 1971. 73pp, ill

5975   Verdier, Philippe. Catalogue of the Painted Enamels of the
        Renaissance. Baltimore: Walters Art Gallery, Trustees,
        1967. 423pp, ill

RUSSIAN ENAMELS (including Fabergé)

5976   Amiranashvili, Shalva IAsonovich. Medieval Georgian Enamels
        of Russia. Tr. by Francois Hirsch and John Ross. New
        York: H. N. Abrams, 1964. 126pp, ill

5977   Fabergé at Wartski (Gallery). May-June 1973. London:
        Wartski, 1973. 23 leaves

5978   Fabergé; the M. T. Heller II Collection. Exhibit at Phoenix
        Art Museum, October-November 1971. Phoenix, Ariz.:
        1971. 20pp, ill

5979 Hawley, Henry H. Fabergé and His Contemporaries; the India Early Minshall Collection of the Cleveland Museum of Art. Cleveland: 1967. 139pp, 64 ill, bib

5980 Ross, Marvin Chauncey. The Art of Karl Fabergé and His Contemporaries; Russian Imperial Portraits and Mementoes (Alexander III to Nicholas II), Russian Imperial Decoration and Watches. Collection of Marjorie Merriweather Post, Hillwood, Washington, D.C. Fore. by M. M. Post. Norman, Okla: U. of O. Pr, 1965. 238pp, ill, color pls, bib (Fabergé, 1846-1920)

5981 Snowman, Abraham Kenneth. The Art of Carl Fabergé. Boston: Boston Book & Art; London: Faber, 1953; rev. & enl. ed. 1962; 1964. 167pp, 434 ill; 186pp, 406 ill, 84 color pls. (The catalogue raisonné of the Imperial Easter eggs. 2nd ed. includes new photographs of the Kremlin collections, the Sandringham Royal Collection, etc.)

5982 Waterfield, Hermione. Fabergé. The Forbes Magazine Collection. Fore. by Malcolm Forbes, 1975. 116pp, 42 (32 color) pls

COSTUME AND FASHION

GENERAL WORKS

5983 Alexander, William, 1767-1816. The Costume of China.
      London: W. Miller, 1805. 5pp, 48 pls DeWint

5984 Allen, Agnes, and Jack Allen. The Story of Clothes. Lon-
      don: Faber, 1955; New York: Roy Publishers, 1958.
      260pp, ill (Juvenile literature)

5985 Andersen, Ellen Margrethe Dorothea. Danish Folk Costumes.
      Tr. from Danish by John R. B. Gosney. Copenhagen:
      Gyldendalske Boghandel Nordisk Forlag, 1948. 35pp, ill
      DLC

5986 *Anthony, Pegaret, and Janet Arnold. Costume: A General
      Bibliography. London: V & A, with the Costume Society,
      1966. 49pp

5987 Arnold, Janet. A Handbook of Costume. London: Macmillan
      London, 1975. 336pp, ill, bib (Costumes and accessories
      from collections in British Isles)

5988 Banateanu, Tancred, Gheorghe Fosca, and Emilia Ionescu,
      etc. Folk Costumes, Woven Textiles, and Embroideries
      of Rumania. Bucharest: State Publishing House for
      Literature and the Arts, 1958. 422pp, ill, 56 color pls

5989 Beard, Charles Relly. Catalogue of an Exhibition of Arms,
      Armour and Costumes in the Possession of Mr. C. An-
      drade. 5 parts. London: Wilkinson Brothers, 1922-
      1927.

5990 Bhushan, Jamila Brij. The Costumes and Textiles of India.
      Bombay: Taraporevala's Treasure House of Books, 1958.
      92pp, ill, pls (part color) DeWint, DLC

5991 Birrell, Verla Leone. Portfolio of Historic Design; practical
      plates for reference or for design application useful in

courses of art history, costume design, historic costume design, textile design, architectural design, applied art work. Provo, Utah: 1947. 36 pls

5992 Boucher, Francois Leon Louis. A History of Costume in the West. Tr. from French by John Ross. London: Thames & Hudson, 1967; as 20,000 Years of Fashion. The history of costume and personal adornment. New York: H. N. Abrams, 1967. 441pp, 1150 ill (Includes jewelry, fabrics, styles)

5993 Brooke, Iris. Dress and Undress, the Restoration and 18th Century. London: Methuen, 1958. 161pp, ill

5994 _____. English Children's Costume Since 1775. Introd. by James Laver. London: A & C Black, 1930. 86pp, ill, color frontis

5995 _____. English Costume in the Age of Elizabeth, the 16th Century. London: A & C Black, 1933; 1938; 2nd ed. London: 1950. 88pp, ill ViU, BM, DLC

5996 _____. English Costume of the 17th Century. London: A & C Black, 1947. 86pp, pls, color frontis

5997 _____. A History of English Costume. London: Methuen, 1937; 2nd ed. 1946; 3rd ed. 1949. 223pp, ill NN, BM, DLC

5998 Buck, Anne. Victorian Costume and Costume Accessories. London: H. Jenkins, 1961; New York: Nelson, 1962. 215pp, ill, bib

5999 *Burnham, Dorothy K. Cut My Cote. Toronto: Royal Ontario Museum, 1973. 34pp, ill (History of coats and shirts as related to loom size and type)

6000 Cammann, Schuyler. China's Dragon Robes. New York: Ronald Pr, 1952. 230pp, ill, bib

6001 Campbell, Lord Archibald. Highland Dress, Arms and Ornament. Westminster: Constable, 1899; reprint. London: Dawsons, 1969. 176pp, ill, 77 pls, bib NN, PPULC

6002 Catalogue of Early American Handicraft. Comprising costumes, quilts, coverlets, samplers, laces, embroideries, and other related objects. Fore. by Paul Jameson Woodward. Brooklyn: Museum Pr, 1924. 76pp, 16 pls DLC

6003 Chambers, Sir William, 1726-1796. Designs of Chinese Buildings, furniture, dresses, machines, and utensils. To which is annexed, a description of their temples,

houses, gardens, etc.   London: Author, 1757; reprint.
New York: B. Blom, 1968.   19pp, 21 engraved pls De-
Wint, DLC, MB

6004   Chandra, Moti.   Costumes, Textiles, Cosmetics and Coiffure
in Ancient and Medieval India.   General editor, S. P.
Gupta.   Delhi: Oriental Publishers for the Indian Archaeological Society, 1973.   248pp, ill, bib

6005   Collard, Eileen.   Early Clothing in Southern Ontario 1784-1867.
Burlington, Ont: Author, 1969.   27pp, ill

6006   _____.   From Toddler to Teens: An Outline of Children's
Clothing, Circa 1780-1930.   Burlington, Ont: Collard,
1973.   ill

6007   Conspicuous Waist; waistcoats and waistcoat designs, 1700-
1952.   Exhibition.   New York: Cooper Union Museum,
1952.   11pp, ill, bib

6008   Cruso, Thalassa.   Costume.   London Museum.   2nd ed.   London: Lancaster House, 1935; reprint.   1946.   211pp, pls

6009   Cunnington, Cecil Willett, and Phillis Cunnington.   Handbook
of English Costume in the 16th to 18th Century.   3 vol.
London: Faber, 1945-1957; with Vol. 4.   London: Faber;
Philadelphia: Dufour Editions, 1959.   ill; 1959: 606pp, ill

6010   Cunnington, Phillis Emily,
and Anne Buck.   Chil-
dren's Costume in Eng-
land, from the 14th to
the End of the 19th Cen-
tury.   New York: Barnes
& Noble, 1965.   235pp,
ill, 32 pls

6011   _____, and Catherine
Lucas.   Costumes for
Births, Marriages and
Deaths.   London: A &
C Black, 1972.   331pp,
ill, 64 pls, bib

6012   _____, and _____,
with chapters by Alan
Mansfield.   Occupational
Costume in England:
From the 11th Century
to 1914.   London: Black,
1967.   427pp, ill, 64 pls

6013   Davenport, Millia.   The Book of Costume.   2 vol.   New York:

Crown, 1948; 2 vol. in 1. New York: Crown, 195-?
958pp, 3000 ill, color frontis, bib (Includes jewelry,
ornament, coiffeur)

6014   Devere, Louis. Devere's Modern British Liveries. Comprising a large coloured plate ... representing all kinds
of livery for every class of man-servant ... also seven
plates of diagrams, containing patterns of a complete suit
for each servant, and a full letterpress description of all
the costumes. London: Simpkin, Marshall, 1863. 14pp,
color pls

6015   Dines, Glen. Sun, Sand, and Steel; costumes and equipment
of the Spanish-Mexican Southwest. New York: Putnam,
1972. 62pp, ill (Clothing, arms and accessories of ex-
plorers, priests, rancheros, soldiers and civilians, 1540-
1850)

6016   Douglas, Loudon Macqueen. The Kilt. A manual of Scottish
national dress. Edinburgh: Andrew Elliot, 1914. 49pp

6017   Drummond, James, 1816-1877. Ancient Scottish Weapons.
Introd. by Joseph Anderson. Edinburgh; London: G.
Waterston, 1881. 26pp, 54 color pls (Highland dress,
sporrans & pouches, brooches, musical instruments, agricultural and domestic implements, weapons, etc.)

6018   Dunbar, John Telfer. History of Highland Dress; a definitive
study of the history of Scottish costume and tartan, both
civil and military, including weapons. Appendix on dyes
by Annette Kok. Edinburgh: Oliver & Boyde, 1962;
Philadelphia: Dufour Editions, 1964. 248pp, ill, 58 pls,
bib

6019   Dunham, Lydia Roberts. Costume Collection. Denver: Art
Museum, 1962. 98pp, ill

6020   Earle, Alice Morse. Two Centuries of Costume in America,
1620-1820. 2 vol. New York; London: Macmillan, 1903;
2 vol. in 1. 1910; facsimile reprint. Rutland, Vt: Tuttle;
Hemel Hempstead: Prentice-Hall, 1971. 824pp, ill, 69
pls

6021   Egerton, Mary Margaret, Countess of Wilton. The Book of
Costume: or, Annals of Fashion, from the earliest period
to the present time. London: H. Colburn, 1846; new ed.
1847. 482pp, 200 ill

6022   Evans, Joan. Dress in Medieval France. Oxford: Clarendon
Pr, 1952. 94pp, ill, 84 pls, bib

6023   Evans, Mary. Costume Throughout the Ages. Philadelphia;

London: Lippincott, 1930; 2nd ed. rev. 1938; rev. ed.
Philadelphia: 1950. 360pp, ill, pls, color frontis, bib

6024 Fabri, Charles. History of Indian Dress. Calcutta: Orient
Longmans, 1960. 106pp, ill

6025 *Fairholt, Frederick William, 1814-1866. Costume in England;
a history of dress to the end of the 18th century, with a
glossary of terms for all articles of use or ornament worn
about the person. London: Chapman & Hall, 1846; 1860;
London: Bell & Daldy, 1866; 2 vol. enl. and rev. ed. by
H. A. Dillon. London: G. Bell, 1885; 1896; 1896-1909;
1 vol. reprint of 1885 ed. Detroit: Singing Tree Pr, 1968.
618pp, ill; 607pp, ill; 331pp, ill; 700 engravings, bib

6026 Fashion in Miniature. Manchester, Eng: Gallery of English
Costume, 1970. 28pp, chiefly ill (Dolls' clothing, 1700-
1905)

6027 Fernald, Helen Elizabeth. Chinese Court Costumes. Exhibition from Museum's Collection. November-December 1946.
Toronto: Royal Ontario Museum of Archaeology, 1946.
51pp, ill, 37 pls (part color), bib

6028 Flower, Cedric. Duck and Cabbage Tree; a pictorial history
of clothes in Australia, 1788-1914. Sydney: Angus &
Robertson, 1968. 157pp, ill

6029 *Frank Leslie's Lady's Journal. Weekly. New York: 1871-
1881. ill

6030 Fussell, George Edwin, 1889- . The English Rural Labourer;
his home, furniture, clothing and food, from Tudor to Victorian times. London: Batchworth Pr, 1949. 164pp, ill,
bib TxU, DeWint, DLC

6031 Gardiner, Florence Mary. The Evolution of Fashion. London: Cotton Pr, 1897. 91pp, ill MiD

6032 *Gibbs-Smith, Charles Harvard. Costume. An index to the
more important material in the Library, with annotations
and shelf-marks, together with a guide to other documentary material in the Museum. V & A. rev. ed.
London: HMSO, 1936.

6033 _____. The Fashionable Lady in the 19th Century. V &
A. London: HMSO, 1960. 184pp, chiefly ill

6034 Ginsburg, Madeleine. The Costume Court. V & A. London: HMSO, 1974.

6035 *Godey's Magazine. Monthly. 137 vol. New York: Godey
Company, 1830-1898.

6036   Gunsaulus, Helen Cowen. Japanese Costume. Chicago: Field
       Museum of Natural History, 1923. 26pp, pls

6037   Hansen, Henny Harald. Costumes and Styles. 685 examples
       of historic costumes in color. New York: Dutton, 1956.
       160pp, ill

6038   Hiler, Hilaire. From Nudity to Raiment; an introduction to
       the study of costume. London: W. & G. Foyle; London:
       S. Marshall; New York: F. Weyhe, 1929. 303pp, ill,
       pls, bib

6039 * _____, and Meyer Hiler, comp. Bibliography of Costume;
       a dictionary catalogue of about 8000 books and periodicals.
       Ed. by Helen Grant Cushing. New York: H. W. Wilson,
       1939; reprint. New York: B. Blom, 1967. 911pp

6040   Hill, Margot Hamilton, and Peter A. Bucknell. Fashion:
       Pattern and Cut from 1066 to 1930. London: Batsford;
       New York: Reinhold, 1967. 225pp, ill

6041   Holt, Ardern. Fancy Dresses Described; or, What to wear
       at fancy balls. 2nd ed. London: Debenham & Freebody,
       1880; 3rd ed. 1882; 5th ed. 1887; 6th ed. 1896. 105pp,
       16 pls; 168pp, pls; 253pp, color pls; 312pp, ill, pls NN,
       DeWint

6042   Huenefeld, Irene Pennington. International Directory of His-
       torical Clothing. Metuchen, NJ: Scarecrow Pr, 1967.
       175pp

6043   Hughes, Talbot. Dress Design. An account of costume for
       artists and dressmakers. New York: Macmillan; London:
       J. Hogg, 1913; London: Pitman, 1920. 362pp, ill, 35pp
       of pls

6044   Kelly, Francis Michael, and Randolph Schwabe. A Short
       History of Costume and Armour, Chiefly in England.
       (Cover title: A Short History of Costume and Armour,
       1066-1800.) 2 vol. London: Batsford, 1931; 2 vol.
       in 1. Reprint. New York: B. Blom, 1968; Newton Abbot:
       David & Charles, 1972. 261pp, ill, bib, gloss

6045   Kendrick, Albert Frank. Guide to the Collection of Costumes.
       V & A. London: 1924. ill

6046   Kup, Karl, and Muriel Baldwin. Costume, Gothic and Renais-
       sance. Some early costume books, by K. Kup. Costume:
       1400-1600, by M. Baldwin. New York: New York Public
       Library, reprint from Bulletin, 1937. 20pp, ill

6047   The Ladies' Cabinet of Fashion, Music, and Romance.

Monthly. 19 vol. London: G. Henderson, 182-?-1843. ill, color pls

6048 The Ladies' Hand-book of Millinery and Dress-making.... London: 1843; New York: J. S. Redfield, 1844. 60pp, ill BM, NN

6049 Laver, James. Children's Fashions in the 19th Century. London; New York: Batsford, 1951. 12pp, ill

6050 _____, ed. Costume of the Western World. Fashions of the Renaissance in England, France, Spain and Holland. New York: Harper; London: Harrap, 1951. 390pp, ill, pls

6051 _____, ed. Costume of the Western World: the Tudors to Louis 13. London: Harrap, 1952. v.p., 52 pls, bib

6052 _____. Taste and Fashion, from the French Revolution to the Present Day. London: Harrap, 1937; New York: Dodd, Mead, 1938; new rev. ed., including World War II. London; Toronto: Harrap, 1945; 1948. 271pp, ill, pls; 232pp, ill, pls (part color)

6053 Lester, Katherine Morris. Historic Costume; a resume of the characteristic types of costume from the most remote times to the present day. Peoria, Ill: Manual Arts Pr, 1925; 4th ed. enl. Peoria, Ill: C. A. Bennett, 1956; 5th ed. 1961. 244pp, ill; 269pp, ill, bib; 288pp, ill, bib

6054 Lister, Margot. Costumes of Everyday Life: an illustrated history of working clothes from 900 to 1910. London: Barrie & Jenkins, 1972. 178pp, ill, bib

6055 Little, Frances. 18th Century Costume in Europe, a Picture Book. New York: Metropolitan Museum, 1937. 3pp, 20 pls

6056 McClellan, Elizabeth. Historic Dress in America, 1607-1870. 2 vol. in 1. New York: B. Blom, 1969. ill

6057 McClintock, Henry Foster. Old Irish and Highland Dress, with notes on that of the Isle of Man. Dundalk, Ireland: Dundalgan Pr, 1943; 2nd enl. ed. with chapters on pre-Norman dress and early tartans. 1950. 188pp, ill, pls; 141, 87pp, ill, pls

6058 MacKinnon, C. R. Tartans and Highland Dress. Glasgow: Collins, 1960; 1961. 128pp, ill

6059 Mann, Kathleen. Peasant Costume in Europe. 2 vol. London: A & C. Black, 1931-36; 1 vol. London: Black; New

York: Macmillan, 1950. 191pp, 125 ill, 16 color pls,
color frontis

6060 Moore, Doris (Langley-Levy). The Child in Fashion. London:
      Batsford, 1953. 100pp, ill (Author's collection)

6061 Old English Costumes, selected from the collection ... (of)
      Talbot Hughes. A sequence of fashions through the 18th
      and 19th centuries. Presented to the V & A ... by Har-
      rods, Ltd. London: St. Catherine Pr, for Harrods, 1913.
      79pp, ill, 5 color pls DLC

6062 Perleberg, Hans Carl. Historical Russian Costumes, 14th to
      18th century, worn by the Russian Imperial Family and
      their guests at the Ball in the Winter Palace, St. Peters-
      burg, on February 27, 1903. New York: Author, 1923?
      50 pls in portfolio

6063 Priest, Alan Reed. Costumes from the Forbidden City. Ex-
      hibition. March-May 1945. New York: Metropolitan Mu-
      seum, 1945; New York: Arno Pr, 1974. 16pp, 56pp of ill
      (Chinese costume, textile, embroidery)

6064 _____. Japanese Costume. An exhibition of Nō robes and
      Buddhist vestments. New York: Metropolitan Museum,
      1935. 42pp, pls

6065 Reade, Brian. The Dominance of Spain, 1550-1660. London:
      Harrap, 1951. 27pp, ill

6066 Rhead, George Woolliscroft. Chats on Costume. London:
      T. F. Unwin, 1906. 304pp, 117 ill, bib

6067 Rozinskii, Lillian. 17th Century Costume. London: Pitman,
      1952. 42pp, ill

6068 The Scottish Clans and Their Tartans. History of each clan
      and full list of septs. 2nd ed. London: W. & A. K.
      Johnston; New York: Scribner's, 1892; 22nd ed. 1931;
      27th ed. 1939. 4pp, 96 color double pls; 58pp, 96 pls

6069 *Shaw, Henry. Dresses and Decorations of the Middle Ages,
      from the 7th to the 17th centuries. 2 vol. London:
      Pickering, 1843; 1858. 38 and 55 leaves of text, 128
      woodcuts, 94 hand-colored pls (Ruari McLean wrote, in
      his Victorian Book Design, "... it has a considerable
      claim to be called the most handsome book produced in
      the whole of the 19th century.") MB

6070 Sitwell, Sacheverell, and Doris Langley Moore. Gallery of
      Fashion, 1790-1822, from plates by Heideloff and Acker-
      mann. London; New York: Batsford, 1949. 12pp, ill

6071 *Smith, Robert Henry Soden. A List of Works on Costume in
      the National Art Library. South Kensington Museum.
      London: HMSO, 1881. 50pp

6072 Sronkova, Olga. Fashions Through the Centuries: Renais-
      sance, baroque, rococo. Tr. from Czechoslovakian by
      Till Gottheiner. London: Spring Books, 1959. 162pp,
      ill (Czech costume)

6073 Stone, Mrs. Elizabeth. Chronicles of Fashion from the Time
      of Elizabeth to the Early Part of the 19th Century, in
      Manners, Amusements, Banquets, Costumes, etc. 2 vol.
      London: R. Bentley, 1845. 15 pls DLC

6074 Tilke, Max. Costume Patterns and Designs. A survey ... of
      all periods and nations from antiquity to modern times.
      London: A. Zwemmer, 1956. 49pp, 128 pls

6075 Truman, Nevil. Historic Costuming. London: Pitman, 1936;
      1952. 152pp, ill

6076 Uzanne, (Louis) Octave. Fashion in Paris; the various phases
      of feminine taste and aesthetics from 1797 to 1897. Tr.
      from French by Lady Mary Loyd. London: W. Heine-
      mann; New York: Scribner's, 1898. 180pp, 250 ill, 100
      hand-colored pls DLC

6077 Wagner, Eduard, ill. Medieval Costume, Armour and Weap-
      ons, 1350-1450. Text by Zoroslava Drobna, and Jan
      Durdik. Tr. from Czechoslovakian by Jean Layton. Lon-
      don: Andrew Dakers, 1958. 72pp, 381 pls, bib

6078 Walker, Joseph Cooper. An Historic Essay on the Dress of
      the Ancient and Modern Irish ... to which is subjoined a
      memoir on the armour and weapons of the Irish. Dublin:
      Author, 1788. 180pp BM

6079 Walters, Helen. The Story of Caps and Gowns. Chicago;
      New York: E. R. Moore, 1939. 14pp, ill, color pl
      (Costume of universities and colleges)

6080 Waugh, Norah. The Cut of Men's Clothes, 1600-1900. Lon-
      don: Faber; New York: Theatre Arts Books, 1964.
      160pp, ill, 29 pls, bib

6081 Webb, Wilfred Mark. The Heritage of Dress; being notes on
      the history and evolution of clothes. London: E. G.
      Richards, 1907; new rev. ed. London: The Times, 1912.
      393pp, ill, 11 pls, bib; 299pp, ill, 12 pls, bib

6082 White, Margaret E. Costumes from the 1790s to 1937 in the
      Museum's Collection. Newark, NJ: 1954. 25pp, ill, bib

6083 Wilcox, Ruth Turner. The Mode in Furs; the history of
      furred costume of the world from the earliest times to
      the present. New York: Scribner, 1951. 257pp, ill, bib

6084 Williams, William Mattieu. The Philosophy of Clothing.
      London: T. Laurie, 1890. 155pp

ACCESSORIES AND MISCELLANEOUS ITEMS OF CLOTHING

6085 Beck, S. William. Gloves, Their Annuals and Associations:
      a chapter of trade and social history. London: Hamilton,
      Adams, 1883; reprint. Detroit; Singing Tree Pr, 1969.
      263pp, ill, pls

6086 Braun-Ronsdorf, Margarete. A History of the Handkerchief.
      Leigh-on-Sea: F. Lewis, 1967. 39pp, ill, 56 pls, bib

6087 Child, Theodore. Wimples and Crisping-Pins. Being studies
      in the coiffure and ornaments of women. New York:
      Harper, 1891; London: Osgood, McIwaine; New York:
      Harper, 1895. 209pp, ill, pls NN, DLC

6088 *Colle, Doriece. Collars, Stocks, Cravats; a history and
      costume dating guide to civilian men's neckpieces, 1655-
      1900. Emmaus, Pa: Rodale Pr, 1972. 255pp, ill, bib

6089 Collins, C. Cody. Love of a Glove; the romance, legends
      and fashion history of gloves and how they are made.
      New York: Fairchild, 1945; rev. ed. 1947. 128pp, ill,
      bib; 132pp, ill, bib DLC

6090 Crawford, Morris De Camp, and Elizabeth A. Guernsey.
      The History of Corsets in Pictures. New York: Fair-
      child, 1951. 41pp, ill

6091 _____, and _____. The History of Lingerie in Pic-
      tures. New York: Fairchild, 1952. 81pp, ill

6092 Dent, Allcroft and Co., Worcester, Massachusetts. A Brief
      Description of the Manufacture, History, and Associations
      of Gloves. Worcester: Bayles, Lewis, 189-? 32pp, ill
      DeWint

6093 Ellis, B. Eldred. Gloves and the Glove Trade. London:
      Pitman, 1921. 146pp, ill

6094 Fairholt, Frederick William. An Illustrated Glossary of
      Terms for All Articles of Use or Ornament Worn about
      the Person. Issued as Volume II. of Costume in England.
      London: Bell & Daldy, 1846. 272pp (pp. 335-607), ill

6095 Felkin, William. An Account of the Machine-Wrought Hosiery

Trade: its extent, and the condition of the framework-
knitters. 2nd ed. London: W. Strange, 1845. 50pp BM

6096 _____. History of the Machine-Wrought Hosiery and Lace
Manufactures. Cambridge, Eng: W. Metcalfe, printer,
1867; London: Longmans, Green, 1867; reprint centenary
ed., with essay on William Felkin by Stanley D. Chapman,
and a comprehensive index by Sheila M. Uppadine. Newton Abbot: David & Charles; New York: Burt Franklin,
for the American Society of Knitting Technologists, 1967;
reprint. Clifton, NJ: Kelley, 1974. 596pp, ill, 20 pls
BM, NN, DLC

6097 _____. Hosiery and Lace. London: 1876. DeWint See
also: Bevan, G. P., British Manufacturing Industries,
Vol. 6.

6098 Garsault, Francois Alexandre Pierre de, 1691?-1778. The
Art of the Wigmaker. Comprising: the shaping of the
beard; the cutting of the hair; the construction of wigs for
ladies and gentlemen; the renovator of wigs and the bath
and hat room proprietor. First published Paris: 1767;
tr. from French, ed. by J. Stevens Cox. London: Hair-
dressers' Registration Council, 1961. 44pp, 5 pls; 47pp,
pls DeWint

6099 Genders, Roy. Perfume Through the Ages. New York: Putnam, 1972. 238pp, ill, bib

6100 The History of the First Pair of Silk Stockings Made in This
Country and Worn by Queen Elizabeth; and of the great
invention of the stocking loom. 2 parts. London: John
Alexander, for the Worshipful Company of Frame-work-
knitters, 1884.

6101 Irwin, John. The Kashmir Shawl. V & A. London: HMSO,
1973. 61pp, ill, 54 pls, bib (To 1880)

6102 _____. Shawls; a study in Indo-European Influences.
V & A. London: HMSO, 1955. 66pp, ill, 54 pls, bib
(18th and 19th century Kashmir shawls of India, and
European imitations from Norwich, Edinburgh, France)

6103 [No entry.]

Joyce, Max Wykes. See: Wykes-Joyce, Max.

6104 Launert, Edmund. Scent and Scent Bottles. London: Barrie
& Jenkins, 1975. 176pp, 200 (30 color) ill

6105 Lester, Katherine Morris, and Bess Viola Oerke. An Illustrated History of Those Frills and Furbelows of Fashion

Which Have Come to be Known as: Accessories of dress.
Peoria, Ill: Manual Arts Pr, 1940; 2nd ed. Peoria: C.
A. Bennett, 1954. 587pp, ill, bib PP, TxU

6106 Manchester, Herbert (H.). The Evolution of Dress Fastening
Devices from the Bone Pin to the Koh-i-noor. Written
for Waldes and Company, Inc. Long Island City, NY:
1922; new ed. enl. as The Evolution ... to the Koh-i-noor
kover-zip. 1938. 22pp, ill; 40pp, ill NN, DLC, MiD

6107 Matthews, Leslie Gerard. The Antiques of Perfume. London:
Bell, 1973. 88pp, 36 pls, ill, bib (To ca.1900)

6108 Neckclothiana: or Tietania: being an essay on starchers.
By One of the Cloth. London: 1818. 1 pl (Neckties)
BM

6109 Noma, Seiroku. Masks. Tr. by Masaru Muro, and Yoshio
Tezuka. Rutland, Vt: Tuttle, 1957. 31pp, 44 pls

6110 Redfern, W. B. Royal and Historic Gloves and Shoes. London: Methuen, 1904. 110pp, 78 pls (some color), color
frontis

6111 Rock, C. H. Paisley Shawls: A Chapter of the Industrial
Revolution. Paisley, Scotland: Paisley Museum & Art
Galleries, 1966. 24pp, ill, bib

6112 Rundall, Myrtle Volora. A Book of Crochet Yokes for Corset
Covers, nightgowns, combination suits and vests. Marion,
Iowa: Needlework Co., 1915. ill

6113 Saint-Laurent, Cecil (pseud. for Jacques Laurent). A History
of Ladies Underwear. London: Joseph, 1968. 22pp, ill,
32 pls

6114 The Story of Hosiery. Burlington, N.C.: May Hosiery Mills,
193-? 101pp, ill

6115 Uzanne, (Louis) Octave. The Sunshade, the Glove, the Muff.
Tr. from French. London: J. C. Nimmo, 1883. 138pp,
ill DLC

6116 *Waugh, Norah. Corsets and Crinolines. London: Batsford,
1954; reprint. 1970. 176pp, ill, bib (16th to 19th century)

6117 Wykes-Joyce, Max. Cosmetics and Adornment: ancient and
contemporary usage. New York: Philosophical Library,
1961; Reprint. London: P. Owen, 197?. 190pp, ill, bib

CANES, WALKING STICKS AND UMBRELLAS

6118 Beach, David Nelson, Amanda B. Harris, Mary Wager-Fisher,

James L. Bowen, and others. Wonder Stories of Science.
Boston: Lothrop, 1885. 384pp, ill, pls (Juvenile literature. Includes: How Christmas cards are made, gloves,
umbrellas, fish-hooks, comb-makers, fishing rods, brooms,
dishes, lace, etc.)

6119 *Boehn, Max von. Modes and Manners: ornaments, lace, fans,
gloves, walking-sticks, parasols, jewelry and trinkets. Tr.
from German. London; Toronto: J. M. Dent; New York:
Dutton, 1929; reprint as Ornaments; lace, fans, gloves,
walking sticks, etc. New York: B. Blom, 1970. 273pp,
241 ill, 16 color pls

6120 Boothroyd, Albert Edward. Fascinating Walking Sticks. Ipswich, Suffolk: Viking Antiques, Salix Books, 1970; London: White Lion, 1973. 205pp, 63 ill, 76 pls

6121 Crawford, T. S. A History of the Umbrella. New York:
Taplinger; Newton Abbot: David & Charles, 1970. 220pp,
ill, bib

6122 French, Harry J. Umbrellas Past and Present. Leicester:
Kendall & Sons, 1923. 20pp, ill

6123 Grant, David, and Edward Hart. Shepherds' Crooks and
Walking Sticks. Clapham, Yorkshire: Dalesman, 1972.
49pp, ill

6124 Moxon, Stanley, comp. A Fox Centenary. Umbrella frames,
1848-1948. Stocksbridge, Eng: Samuel Fox and Co.,
1948. 55pp, ill, facsimiles NNC-Ave

6125 Sangster, William, 1808-1888. Umbrellas and Their History.
London: E. Wilson, 1855; another ed. with illustrations
by Bennett, etc. London; New York: Cassell, Petter &
Galpin, 1871. 64pp, ill; 80pp, ill DLC, BM

6126 Uzanne, (Louis) Octave. The Sunshade, the Glove, the Muff.
Tr. from French. London: J. C. Nimmo, 1883. 138pp,
ill

FANS

6127 *Armstrong, Nancy. A Collectors' History of Fans. New
York: C. N. Potter; London: Studio Vista, 1974. 208pp,
126 (16 color) ill, bib, makers' list

6128 Audsley, George Ashdown. Catalogue of Loan Collection of
Art Fans, etc. Liverpool: Liverpool Art Club, 1877;
Exhibition at Royal Scottish Museum. Edinburgh: Neill
& Co., for HMSO, 1878. 27pp BM

6129 *Boehn, Max von. Modes and Manners: ornaments, lace, fans, gloves, walking-sticks, parasols, jewelry and trinkets. Tr. from German. London; Toronto: J. M. Dent; New York: Dutton, 1929; as Ornaments; lace, fans, gloves, walking sticks, etc. New York: B. Blom, 1970. 273pp, 241 ill, 16 color pls

6130 Catalogue of Fourth Competitive Exhibition of Fans, etc. May 1897. London: Worshipful Company of Fan Makers, 1897. 58pp BM

6131 Chiba, Reiko. Painted Fans of Japan: 15 Noh drama masterpieces. Rutland, Vt: Tuttle, 1962. 41pp, color ill, bib

6132 Cust, Lionel Harry, comp. Catalogue of the Collection of Fans and Fan-Leaves, presented to the trustees of the British Museum by the Lady Charlotte Schreiber. London: 1893. 138pp

6133 De Vere Green, Bertha. A Collector's Guide to Fans over the Ages. London: 1974. ill, pls

6134 Examples of Art Workmanship of Various Ages and Countries. Fans of All countries. A series of 20 photographs of Spanish, French ... and English fans. Introd. by S. Redgrave. London: Arundel Society, under sanction of the Science and Art Department, South Kensington Museum, 1871. ill BM

6135 The Fan in All Ages. A Brief history of its evolution. To accompany an exhibition of fans, mostly French, of the 18th century. New York: Grolier Club, 1891. 21pp, ill

6136 Fan Leaves. Boston: Fan Guild of Boston, 1961. ill

6137 Flory, M. A. A Book About Fans: the history of fans and fan-painting, with a chapter on fan-collecting by Mary Cadwalader Jones. New York; London: Macmillan, 1895. 141pp, ill, pls MiU, DLC, PPL

6138 Holme, Charles, ed. Modern Design in Jewellery and Fans. London; New York: The Studio, 1902. 44pp, pls (part color) MiU

6139 Leary, Emmeline. Fans in Fashion. Exhibition. Stable Court Galleries, Temple Newsam, Leeds, and Gallery of English Costume, Platt Hall, Manchester. Leeds: City Art Gallery, 1975. 24pp, ill, pl, bib

6140 Percival, MacIver. The Fan Book. London: Fisher Unwin, 1920; New York: F. A. Stokes, 1921. 344pp, 18 ill, 32 pls, bib, list of painters, designers, printers (European 17th and 18th century) DLC

6141   Redgrave, S.   Catalogue of the Loan Exhibition of Fans, 1870.
         South Kensington Museum.   London: HMSO, 1870.   ill

         _____.   Fans of All Countries.   See: Examples of Art
         Workmanship, no. 6134.

6142   [No entry.]

6143 *Rhead, George Wooliscroft.   The History of the Fan.   London:
         K. Paul, 1910.   311pp, 83 ill, 127 (27 color) pls   (Italy,
         Spain, France, England, Holland, China, India)   DLC

6144   Salwey, Charlotte Maria Birch.   Fans of Japan.   Introd. by
         W. Anderson.   London: K. Paul, Trench, 1894.   149pp,
         39 ill, 10 color pls

6145   Schiffman, Maurice K.   Japan, the Land of Fans.   Tokyo:
         Foreign Affairs Assoc. of Japan, 1954.   23pp, ill   DLC

6146 *Schreiber, Lady Charlotte.   Fans and Fan-Leaves.   Vol. I.
         English; Vol. II. Foreign.   2 vol. London: J. Murray,
         1888, 1890.   ill, 314 pls   (Collection presented to the
         British Museum in 1891)

6147   Uzanne, (Louis) Octave, 1852-1931.   The Fan.   Tr. from
         French (1882).   London: J. C. Nimmo, 1884.   143pp,
         many ill

JAPANESE NETSUKE, INRO AND CHINESE TOGGLES

6148 *Barbanson, Adrienne.   Fables in Ivory; Japanese netsuke and
         their legends.   Pref. by Felix Tikotin.   Rutland, Vt:
         Tuttle; London: Prentice-Hall, 1961.   116pp, ill, bib

6149 *Brockhaus, Albert Eduard.   Netsukes.   Abridged and tr. from
         German (1905) by M. F. Watty.   Ed. by E. G. Stillman.
         London: G. Allen & Unwin, 1924; New York: Duffield,
         1924; reprint. 1969; Seattle: 1972.   175pp, ill, bib, gloss
         NN, DLC, BM

6150   Bushell, Raymond.   An Introduction to Netsuke.   Rutland, Vt:
         Tuttle, 1971.   78pp, 30 ill

6151   _____.   Collectors' Netsuke.   Tokyo: Weatherhill, 1970.
         200pp, ill, bib, gloss

6152   _____.   Netsuke Familiar and Unfamiliar: New Principles
         for Collecting.   New York: J. Weatherhill, 1976.   ill

6153 * _____.   The Netsuke Handbook of Ueda Reikichi.   Rutland,
         Vt: Tuttle, 19-?   325pp, 226 (24 color) ill, bib, gloss

6154 _____ . The Wonderful World of Netsuke, with 100 master-
       pieces of miniature sculpture in color. Rutland, Vt: Tut-
       tle; London: Prentice-Hall, 1964; Rutland: 1970. 71pp,
       ill (some color)

6155 Cammann, Schuyler. Substance and Symbol in Chinese Tog-
       gles. Chinese belt toggles from the C. F. Bieber Collec-
       tion. Philadelphia: Pa. U. Pr; London: Oxford U Pr,
       1962. 256pp, ill

6156 *Davey, Neil K. Netsuke: A Comprehensive Study. London:
       Faber; New York: Sotheby Parke Bernet, 1974. 584pp,
       1500 (63 color) ill (1300 netsuke assembled by Mark T.
       Hindson, from 1940 to 1965. Sold by Sotheby in London
       between 1967 and 1969)

6157 Gorham, Hazel H. Netsuke; their origin and development.
       Reprint from "Cultural Nippon." Tokyo: Central Federa-
       tion of Nippon Culture, 1940. 25pp, pls NN

6158 Hurtig, Bernard, comp. Masterpieces of Netsuke Art: 1000
       favorites of leading collectors. Tokyo; New York:
       Weatherhill, for International Netsuke Collectors Society,
       1973. 248pp, ill, bib

6159 Japanese Netsuke Formerly in the Collection of Robert L.
       Greene. Catalogue. London: K. Paul, 1973. 42pp

6160 *Jonas, Frank Morris. Netsuke. London: Kegan Paul,
       Trench & Trubner, 1928; reprint. Rutland, Vt: Tuttle;
       London: K. Paul, Trench, 1960. 185pp, ill, 55 pls
       (part color) DLC

6161 Lodge, John Ellerton. Japanese Netsuke. Unpublished gal-
       lery book. Boston: Museum of Fine Arts. 75 leaves

6162 Masterworks in Miniature: Japanese Netsuke; an exhibition
       of the G. H. Crone Collection at the Vancouver Art
       Gallery. November-December 1967. Vancouver: 1967.
       45pp, ill

6163 Meinertzhagen, Frederick. The Art of the Netsuke Carver.
       London: Routledge & Paul, 1956. 80pp, ill

6164 O'Brien, Mary Louise. Netsuke: A Guide for Collectors.
       Rutland, Vt: Tuttle; London: Prentice-Hall, 1965.
       245pp, 145 ill, gloss, list of carvers

6165 Okada, Yuzuru. Netsuke--a miniature art of Japan. Tr. by
       Ko Masuda. Tokyo: Japan Travel Bureau, 1953. 214pp,
       ill

6166 *Reikichi, Ueda. The Netsuke Handbook. Tr. by Raymond

Bushell. Rutland, Vt: Tuttle, 1964. 325pp, 226 ill
(By the greatest Japanese authority)

6167   Roosevelt, Cornelius V. S. Netsuke: A Bibliography. Wash-
       ington, DC: 1973. v.p.

6168   Roth, Stig Adolf. Netsuke in the Collections of the Rohss
       Museum of Arts and Crafts. Goteborg: the Museum, 1970.
       131pp, ill

6169   *Ryerson, Egerton. The Netsuke of Japan. Illustrating legends,
       history, folklore and customs. London: G. Bell, 1958;
       reprint. London: Yoseloff; South Brunswick, NJ: A. S.
       Barnes, 1967. 131pp, 249 photographs; 88pp, ill, 40 pls,
       bib

6170   Tollner, Madeline R. Netsuke. The Life and Legend of
       Japan in Miniature. San Francisco: Fearon, 1955; 1960.
       358pp, ill

6171   Vilimova, Lida, Werner Forman, and L. Bohackova. Japanese
       Netsuke. Tr. by Iris Urwin. London: Spring Books,
       1960. 2pp, 50 pls, bib

6172   Wrangham, Edward Addison. Inro: catalogue of an exhibition
       of Japanese inro from the collection of E. A. Wrangham
       at the Ashmolean Museum. October-November 1972. Ox-
       ford: the Museum, 1972. 46pp, ill, 56 pls, bib

BUTTONS

6173   Albert, Alphaeus Homer. Buttons of the Confederacy; a de-
       scriptive and illustrated catalogue of the buttons worn by
       the troops of the Confederate States of America, 1861-
       1865. Hightstown, NJ: 1963. 93pp, ill

6174   _____. Record of American Uniform and Historical But-
       tons ... 1775-1968. Boyertown, Pa: Boyertown Publish-
       ing, 1969; with supplement, 1968-1973. Boyertown: 1973.
       448pp, ill, bib

6175   Albert, Lillian Smith. A Button Collectors' Journal. Hights-
       town, NJ: 1941. 111pp, ill, bib

6176   _____. A Button Collectors' Second Journal. Hightstown,
       NJ; Yardley, Pa: Cook Printers, 1941. 333pp, ill, bib

6177   _____, and Jane Ford Adams. The Button Sampler. New
       York: Gramercy Publishing; New York: M. Barrows,
       1951. 143pp, ill; 185pp, ill

6178   _____, and Kathryn Kent (pseud.) The Complete Button

Book. Fore. by Carl W. Drepperd. Garden City, NY: Doubleday, 1949; reprint. Stratford, Conn: J. Edwards, 1971. 409pp, 5700 ill (part color) (Chiefly 18th and 19th centuries)

6179 Art in Buttons. Monthly. Rochester, NY: 1916.

6180 Betensley, Bertha L. Buttonhooks to Trade and Treasure. Westville, Ind: 1971. 37pp, ill

6181 Brown, Dorothy Foster. Button Parade. A book of button groupings. Chicago: Lightner, 1942; 2nd ed. 1942; rev. enl. ed. Des Moines, Iowa: Wallace-Homestead, 1968. 111pp, ill; 143pp, ill; 250pp, 2000 ill, bib, gloss

6182 _____, and George Elbert Adams. Backs of Buttons. Des Moines: Wallace-Homestead, 197-? 42pp, ill

6183 The Button Bulletin. Monthly. Springfield, Mass: National Button Society, 194-?

6184 Button Review. Monthly. St. Paul, Minn: 19-?-1945.

6185 Calver, William Louis. The British Army Button in the American Revolution. Reprint from New York Historical Society Quarterly Bulletin, 1923. New York: 1923. 29pp

6186 Chamberlin, Laura, Erwina B. Couse, and Marguerite Maple. Button Classics. Chicago: Lightner, 1941; 1948; reprint, with added material by P. S. Freeman, as Yesterday's Button Classics. Watkins Glen, NY: Century, 1970. 247pp, ill; 255pp, ill, 108 (3 color) pls

6187 _____, and Minerva Miner. Button Heritage. Sherburne, NY: F. E. Faulkner Printing, 1967. 247pp, ill

6188 Crummett, Polly De Steiguer. Button Collecting. Chicago: Lightner, 1939; rev. ed. ed. by P. S. Freeman, as Button Guide Book No. 1; their manufacture, use on costumes, and collectible types. Watkins Glen, NY: Century, 1969. 157pp, ill, bib; 96pp, ill

6189 Emilio, Luis Fenollosa, 1844- . The Emilio Collection of Military Buttons ... American, British, French and Spanish, with some of other countries, and non-military. Salem, Mass: Essex Institute, 1911. 264pp, 10 pls, ill'g 240 items

6190 *Epstein, Diana. Buttons. New York: Walker; London: Studio Vista, 1968. 84pp, ill

6191 Ertell, Viviane Beck. The Colorful World of Buttons.

Princeton: Pyne Pr, 1972; new ed. 1973. 192pp, ill
(17th, 18th and 19th century. Metal, ivory, Wedgwood,
porcelain, enamel, cloisonné, tortoise shell)

6192   Jarvis, Louise Huntington. Buttons Are Art. Grand Rapids:
Wobbema, printer, 1945? pls (Purpose "... to show how
many button designs have been taken from paintings, sculpture, and architecture ...") DeWint

6193   Johnson, David Funston. The American Historical Button.
6 vol. New Market, NJ: 194-? ill, pls

6194   _____. Uniform Buttons; American armed forces, 1784-
1948. 2 vol. Watkins Glen, NY: Century, 1948. text,
ill, values

6195   Jones, William Unite. The Button Industry. London: Pitman, 1924. 113pp, ill BM

6196   Lamm, Ruth, and others. Guidelines for Collecting China
Buttons. Hightstown, NJ: National Button Society of
America, 1970. 151pp, ill

6197   Luscomb, Sally C. The Collector's Encyclopedia of Buttons.
Reprint. New York: Crown, 1967. 242pp, ill

6198   _____. Just Buttons. Hartford, Conn: Author, 19-?

6199   _____, and Ethel Cassidy. The Old Button Box. Southing-
ton, Conn: 1951. 180pp, ill NN, DLC

6200   Nicholls, Florence Zacharie E. Button Hand Book. Comparative Values; serial numbers. Ithaca, NY: 1943; 1944.
128pp, ill, color frontis (1276 buttons)

6201   Olson, Lorraine. Old Buttons and Their Values. Chicago:
Lightner, 1940. 109pp, ill

6202   Peacock, Primrose. Buttons for the Collector. Newton
Abbot: David & Charles, 1972; as Antique Buttons; their
history and how to collect them. New York: Drake, 1972.
128pp, ill, bib

6203   Roberts, Catherine Christopher. Who's Got the Button? Old
and new angles to button collecting. New York: McKay,
1962. 97pp, ill

6204   Squire, Gwen. Buttons: A Guide for Collectors. London:
Muller, 1972. 213pp, ill

POLITICAL BUTTONS

6205 Albert, Alphaeus Home. Political Campaign and Commemorative
      Buttons; an illustrated catalogue with descriptions of the
      buttons used during the various political campaigns including
      the Washington Inaugural buttons and other commemorative
      and patriotic buttons. Hightstown, NJ: n. p., 1966. 76pp,
      ill

6206 Hake, Ted. Button Book. New York: Dafran, 1974. 224pp,
      thousands of ill

JEWELRY AND GEMS

6207 *Abbott, Henry G. (pseud. for George Henry A. Hazlitt). The
      American Watchmaker and Jeweler. An encyclopedia for
      the horologist, jeweler, gold and silver-smith. Containing
      hundreds of private receipts and formulas compiled from
      the best and most reliable sources. Complete directions
      for using all the latest tools, attachments and devices for
      watchmakers and jewelers. Chicago: G. K. Hazlitt & Co.,
      1891; 1892; 1894; 12th ed. 1898; Chicago: Hazlitt & Walker,
      1910. 310pp, ill; 354pp, ill; 1894: 354pp, 288 ill; 1898:
      378pp, ill; all with bib of books from 1639-1850

6208 American Jeweler. Monthly. Chicago: G. K. Hazlitt, 18- .
      ill, pls

6209 Antique Jewelry Price Guide. Gas City, Ind: L-W Promo-
      tions, 197-? 84pp, ill of over 1500 pieces (To 1890)

6210 Armstrong, Edmund Clarence Richard. Catalogue of Irish
      Gold Ornaments in the Collection of the Royal Irish Acad-
      emy. National Museum of Science & Art. 2nd ed. Dub-
      lin: HMSO, 1920. 104pp, ill, bib

6211 Armstrong, Nancy. Jewellery: An Historical Survey of
      British Styles and Jewels. Guilford: Lutterworth Pr,
      1973. 286pp, ill, 52 (10 color) pls, bib

6212 Bauer, J., and A. Bauer. A Book of Jewels. Tr. by Alz-
      beta Novakova. Prague: Artia, 1966. 143pp, 110 ill
      (Jewelry, objects, minerals)

6213 Beckman, E. D. Cincinnati Silversmiths, Jewelers, Watch
      and Clock Makers. Fore. by Robert Alan Green. Harri-
      son, NY: R. A. Green, 1975. 184pp, ill

6214 Berliner, Rudolf. Italian Drawings for Jewelry, 1700-1875;
      an introduction to an exhibition. September-October 1940.
      New York: Cooper Union Museum, 1940. 12pp, ill

6215 Bhushan, Jamila Brij. Indian Jewellery, Ornaments and
        Decorative Designs. Bombay: D. B. Taraporevala, 1955?;
        rev. ed. 1964. 168pp, ill, pls, bib; 189pp, ill, pls, bib

6216 A Bibliography on Beads, compiled from material provided by
        Alfred Buehler, Basel, Switzerland; Kenneth Kidd, Toronto,
        Canada; and others. Corning, NY: Corning Museum of
        Glass, 1962. 38 leaves

6217 Black, J. Anderson. The Story of Jewelry. New York:
        Morrow, 1974. 400pp, ill, bib

6218 Bradford, Ernle Dusgate Selby. English Victorian Jewellery.
        London: Country Life; New York: McBride, 1959; new
        ed. London: Spring Books, 1967. 141pp, ill, pls, bib

6219 _____ . Four Centuries of European Jewelry. London:
        Country Life; New York: Philosophical Library, 1953;
        reprint. London: Spring Books, 1967. 226pp, 108 ill,
        bib NN, DLC

6220 Burgess, Frederick William. Antique Jewellery and Trinkets.
        London: Routledge; New York: Putnam's, 1919; reprint.
        New York: Tudor; 1937; reprint. Detroit: Gale Research,
        1974. 399pp, 142 ill, pls (Includes tools, fans, watches,
        amulets, ancient jewelry) DLC, NN

6221 Burton, E. Milby. Hayden and Gregg, Jewellers of Charles-
        ton. Charleston, SC: Museum, 1938. 13pp, ill (Na-
        thaniel Hayden; William Gregg. 19th century) NN, BM

6222 Bury, Shirley. Jewellery. V & A. London: HMSO, 1972.
        19pp, chiefly ill, bib

6223 Carlisle, Lilian Baker. Vermont Clock and Watchmakers,
        Silversmiths, and Jewelers, 1778-1878. Shelburne, Vt:
        Shelburne Museum, 1970; Burlington, Vt: Dist. by the
        Stinehour Pr, Lunenburg, Vt., 1970. 313pp, ill, 989
        detailed biographies

6224 Castellani, Alessandro. Antique Jewelry and Its Revival.
        London: priv. printed; Philadelphia: J. H. Coats for
        the Pennsylvania Museum and School of Industrial Art,
        1862; Philadelphia: 1876. 27pp; 19pp; 19pp DLC, NB,
        NN

6225 _____ . Italian Jewelry as Worn by the Peasants of Italy
        as Collected for the South Kensington Museum. London:
        Arundel Society, 1868. 8pp, 12 pls SIB-1

6226 The Cheapside Hoard of Elizabethan and Jacobean Jewellery.
        London Museum. London: Lancaster House, 1928. 35pp,
        pls, color frontis DeWint

6227 Chinese Jewelry. New York: Metropolitan Museum, 1944.

6228 *Clifford, Anne. Cut-Steel and Berlin Iron Jewellery. Bath: Adams & Dart; South Brunswick, NJ: A. S. Barnes, 1971. 95pp, ill, 4 pls, bib (1795-1850)

6229 Cooper, Diana, and Norman Battershill. Victorian Sentimental Jewelry. Newton Abbot: David & Charles; New York: A. S. Barnes, 1972. 127pp, ill, bib

6230 Curran, Mona. Collecting Jewelry. London: Arco, 1963; as Collecting Antique Jewelry. New York: Emerson Books, 1964; New York: 1970. 153pp, ill, 4 pls, bib (English 18th and 19th century)

6231 _____. Jewels and Gems. London: Arco, 1961; as A Treasury of Jewels and Gems. New York: Emerson, 1962. 152pp, ill

6232 Darling, Ada W. Antique Jewelry. Watkins Glen, NY: Century, 1953. 200pp, ill, color pls

6233 _____. Antique Jewelry Identification with Price List. Des Moines: Wallace-Homestead, 1973. 48pp, 24 color pls

6234 _____. The Jewelled Trail; collecting antique jewelry. Des Moines: Wallace-Homestead, 1971. 163pp, ill, 16 color pls (Includes seals)

6235 *Davenport, Cyril James Humphries, 1848-1941. Cameos. London: Seeley; New York: Macmillan, 1900. 66pp, ill, 28 pls (Earliest work to Tassie and his contemporaries)

6236 _____. Cameos. Washington, DC: Smithsonian Report, 1904; facsimile reprint. Seattle: 1967. 6pp, ill, 4 pls

6237 _____. Cantor Lectures on the History of Personal Jewellery. From prehistoric times. Delivered before Society of Arts. London: W. Trounce, printer, 1902. 38pp, ill

6238 _____. Jewellery. London: Methuen, 1905; Chicago: A. C. McClurg, 1908; 1910; 2nd ed. London: Methuen, 1913. 166pp, ill, 25 pls, color frontis, bib NN

6239 Dennis, Faith. Renaissance Jewelry. Metropolitan Museum. New York: 1940. 3pp, 23 pls

6240 Dikshit, Moreshwar G. Etched Beads in India: decorative patterns and the geographical factors in their distribution. Poona: Post-Graduate & Research Institute, 1949. 79pp, ill, bib

6241   Dimand, Maurice Sven. Near Eastern Jewelry, a Picture
        Book. New York: Metropolitan Museum, 1944.

6242   Directory of Wholesale Dealers, manufacturers and jobbers
        of jewelry, watches, clocks, diamonds and precious stones,
        silver and silverplated ware, etc., in the United States.
        New York: 1885. many advertising ill

6243   Dongerkery, Kamala S. Jewelry and Personal Adornment in
        India. New Delhi: Indian Council for Cultural Relations,
        1970. 77pp, ill

6244   Elward, Robert. On Collecting Miniatures, Enamels, and
        Jewellery. London: E. Arnold, 1905. 94pp, ill, bib

6245   [No entry.]

6246   Erikson, Joan Mowat. The Universal Bead. New York:
        Norton, 1969. 191pp, ill

6247   *Evans, Joan. English Jewellery from the 5th Century A.D.
        to 1800. London: Methuen, 1921. 168pp, pls, bib

6248   *_____. A History of Jewellery, 1100-1870. London:
        Faber; New York: Pitman, 1953; 2nd rev. ed. London:
        Faber, 1970; Boston: Boston Book & Art, 1970. 240pp,
        ill, 13 color pls, bib; 224pp, ill, 204 pls, bib

6248a   Exhibition Catalogue of Gemstones and Jewellery. February-
        March 1960. 2nd ed. Birmingham, Eng: Museum & Art
        Gallery, 1960. 110pp, 12 pls

6249   Falkiner, Richard. Investing in Antique Jewellery. London:
        Barrie & Rockliff; New York: C. N. Potter, 1968; Lon-
        don: Corgi, 1971. 160pp, ill, 7 pls, bib (Includes
        Egyptian and Jewish jewellery)

6250   Flach, T. A Book of Jewellers Work. n.p.: 1736. 6 pls
        SIB-1

6251   Flower, Margaret Cameron Coss. Jewellery, 1837-1901.
        London: Cassell, 1968; New York: Walker, 1969. 64pp,
        ill, 4 pls, gloss

6252   _____. Victorian Jewellery. Fore. by Margaret J. Biggs.
        Chapter on collecting by Doris Langley Moore. London:
        Cassell; New York: Duell, Sloan, and Pearce, 1951; rev.
        ed. London: Cassell; South Brunswick, NJ: A. S. Barnes,
        1967; 1973. 271pp, ill, 10 pls, bib, gloss

6253   Fregnac, Claude. Jewelry from the Renaissance to Art Nou-
        veau. Tr. from French by Donald Law de Lauriston.

London: Weidenfeld & Nicolson, 1965; London: Octopus;
New York: Putnam, 1973. 127pp, 139 ill; 97pp, ill
(Ca. 1500-1900)

6254 Gatter, Robert S. Catalogue and Price List of Diamond, Gold-
plated Jewelry, and Silver Things. 1900. Reprint. Watkins Glen, NY: Century, 1969. 46pp, pls

6255 Gee, George Edward. The Hall-Marking of Jewellery....
London: C. Lockwood, 1882; 1883. 216pp, marks
DLC, ViU

6256 _____ . Jewellers' Assistant in the Art of Working in Gold,
etc. London: Lockwood, 1892; New York: 1892. 238pp,
tables MiD

6257 _____ . The Practical Gold-Worker, or, The Goldsmiths'
and Jeweller's Instructor in the art of allowing, melting,
reducing, colouring, collecting, and refining.... London:
Lockwood, 1877; 2nd ed. enl. as The Goldsmiths' Handbook.... London: 1881; 3rd ed. 1886; 4th ed. 1892;
...; rev. ed. London: Technical Pr, 1936; ... 229pp
to 263pp, tables

6258 Gere, Charlotte. American and European Jewelry, 1830-1911.
New York: Crown, 1975; as European and American Jewellery, 1830-1914. London: Heinemann, 1975. 240pp,
214 (64 color) ill, bib

6259 _____ . Victorian Jewelry Design. London: Kimber,
1972; Chicago: H. Regnery, 1973. 285pp, 156 ill, bib

Gerlach, Martin. See: Haberlandt, M., no. 6264.

6260 Giltay-Nijssen, L. Jewelry. New York: Universe, 1964.
112pp, ill

6261 Gregorietti, Guido. Jewelry Through the Ages. Fore. by
Erich Steingraber. Tr. from Italian by Helen Lawrence.
Feltham: Hamlyn; New York: American Heritage, 1969.
319pp, ill, bib (From ancient times)

6262 Guebelin Sohne. The House of Gübelin, 1854-1954. Ed. by
Eric Mann. Lucerne: 1954. ill NN, DLC

6263 The Gutman, (Melvin H.) Collection of Antique Jewelry. Exhibition. Norfolk, Va: Museum of Arts and Sciences,
1966. 45pp, ill, color pls

6264 Haberlandt, Michael, 1860-1940. Primitive and Folk Jewelry.
Ed. from German by Martin Gerlach. Reprint. New
York: Dover, 1971. 219pp of 1900 ill

6265   Halford, William, and Charles Young, jewellers. The Jew-
       ellers' Book of Patterns in Hair Work. Containing a great
       variety of copper-plate engravings of devices and pattern
       in hair; suitable for mourning jewellery, brooches, rings,
       guards.... London: William Halford and Charles Young,
       184-? 18 pls DeWint

6266   Heaton, Harriet A. The Brooches of Many Nations. Ed. by
       J. Potter Briscoe. Nottingham: Murray's Nottingham
       Book Co., 1904. 50pp, 31 pls MB, DLC, BM

6267   Heiniger, Ernst A., and Jean Heiniger. The Great Book of
       Jewels. Greenwich, Conn: N.Y. Graphic Society, 1975.
       300 color pls (Gems, jewelry, regalia and ceremonial
       jewelry, etc.)

6268   Hejj-Detari, Angela. Old Hungarian Jewelry. Tr. from
       Hungarian by Lili Halapy. Budapest: Corvina Pr, 1965.
       66pp, ill, 48 pls

6269   Hendley, Thomas Holbein. Indian Jewellery. Reprint from
       Journal of Indian Art. London: W. Griggs, 1909. 189pp,
       166 (33 color) pls (Indic) NN

6270   Howard, Montague. The Fashion of Wearing Earrings, Its
       Present Revival. New York: Howard & Co., n.d. u.p.,
       pls

6271   Hughes, Graham. The Art of Jewelry. New York: Viking,
       1972. 248pp, ill, bib (All ages and countries)

6272   _____. Jewelry. London: Studio Vista; New York: Dut-
       ton, 1966. 167pp, ill

6273   _____. Modern Jewelry, an International Survey, 1890-
       1967. New York: Crown, 1963; rev. ed. London: Studio
       Vista, 1966; 1968. 256pp, 415 ill, bib

6274   International Exhibition of Modern Jewellery, 1890-1961. 2
       vol. London: Worshipful Company of Goldsmiths, 1961.
       ill

       Jamila Brij Bhushan. See: Bhushan, J. B., no. 6215.

6275   Janson, Dora Jane. From Slave to Siren: the Victorian
       woman and her jewelry, from neo-classic to Art Nouveau.
       Exhibition. Durham?, NC: 1971. 111pp, ill

6276   Jet in the Collection of the Hispanic Society of America. New
       York: 1926. 20pp, ill, 6 pls, bib

6277   The Jewellers, Goldsmiths, Silversmiths, and Watchmakers'

Monthly Magazine. London: Henry Lea, 1863- . ill
DeWint, BM

6278 Jewelry History. Exhibition. Newark, NJ: Museum Association, 1914. 11pp, ill NN

6279 Jewelry in the Metropolitan Museum of Art. Supplement to
the Bulletin, June 1915. New York: 1915. 13pp, ill

6280 Jewelry; necklaces, La Alberca, Salamanca. New York:
Hispanic Society of America, 1931. 24pp, ill, pls

6281 Jones, John, watchmaker. The History and Object of Jewellery. London: by the Author at his Watch Manufactory,
1847. 69pp BM, NN

6282 Kaduck, John M. Collecting Watch Fobs. Cleveland, Ohio:
Author, 197-?; Collecting Watch Fobs: price guide. Des
Moines, Iowa: Wallace-Homestead, 1973. 100pp, ill;
98pp, ill

6283 Kendall, Hugh P. The Story of Whitby Jet: its workers from
earliest times. Whitby, Yorkshire: Whitby Museum,
Whitby Literary & Philosophical Society, 196-? 12pp, ill

6284 *King, Charles William, 1818-1888. The Natural History,
Ancient and Modern, of Precious Stones and Gems, and
of the Precious Metals. London: Bell & Daldy, 1865.

6285 Kunz, George Frederich, and Charles Hugh Stevenson. The
Book of the Pearl. The history, art, science and industry
of the queen of gems. London: Macmillan; New York:
Century, 1908. 548pp, ill, 102 pls, bib NN, MB

6286 Kuzel, Vladislav, and Emanuel Poche. A Book of Jewelry.
Tr. by Iris Urwin. London: Wingate, 1962. 104pp, ill,
pls (part color) (European)

6287 Lesley, Parker. Renaissance Jewels and Jeweled Objects,
from the Melvin Gutman Collection. Detroit: Institute
of Arts, 1961; Baltimore: Museum of Arts, 1968. ill,
bib

6288 Lewis, Malcolm David Samuel. Antique Paste Jewellery.
London: Faber, 1970. 80pp, ill, 57 pls, bib (1700 to
1865)

6289 *A List of Books and Pamphlets in the National Art Library,
South Kensington Museum, illustrating gold and silversmiths' work and jewellery. London: HMSO, 1887. 91pp

6290 Mason, Anita Frances. An Illustrated Dictionary of Jewellery.
Reading, Eng: Osprey Publishing, 1973. 390pp, ill, bib

6291 Meyer, Florence E. Pins for Hats and Cravats Worn by
      Ladies and Gentlemen. Des Moines: Wallace-Homestead,
      1974. u.p., ill, 13 color pls

6292 Mourey, Gabriel, and Aymer Vallance, et al. Modern De-
      signs in Jewellery and Fans. London: 1902; reprint as
      European (Art Nouveau) Jewellery and Fans. Watkins
      Glen, NY: Century, 1969; reprint as Art Nouveau Jewelry
      and Fans. New York: Dover; London: Constable, 1973;
      New York: 1975. 200pp, ill; 1973; 149pp, ill, 8 pls
      (W. Fred, Austrian; Chr. Ferdinand Morawe, German; F.
      Khnopff, Belgian; Georg Brochner, Dane; contributors)

6293 Osmun, William. 19th Century Jewelry, from the First Em-
      pire to the First World War. New York: Cooper Union
      Museum, 1955. 23pp, pls, bib by Whitney N. Morgan

6294 Oved, Sah. The Book of Necklaces: photographs from mu-
      seums and other sources. London: Barker, 1953. 111pp,
      ill, bib (Necklaces from last 25,000 years)

6295 Percival, MacIver. Chats on Old Jewellery and Trinkets.
      London: Fisher Unwin, 1912. 382pp, 300 ill, pls, bib,
      gloss DLC

6296 Peter, Mary. Collecting Victorian Jewellery. London: Mac-
      Gibbon & Kee, 1970; New York: Emerson Books, 1971.
      100pp, 30 ill, 33 pls

6297 Priest, Alan Reed. Chinese Jewelry; a picture book. New
      York: Metropolitan Museum, 1940. 3pp, 22 pls

6298 Read, Charles Hercules. The Waddeson Bequest. Collection
      of jewels, plate, and other works of art, bequeathed to
      the British Museum, by Baron Ferdinand Rothschild, 1898.
      London: The Trustees, 1899; 2nd ed. 1927. 48pp, ill,
      pls; 56pp, ill, 20 pls NN

6299 Renaissance Jewelry; a picture book. New York: Metropolitan
      Museum, 1943. 24pp, pls

6300 Roddin, (E. V.) and Co. Jewelry, Watches, and Silverware;
      bracelets, studs, toothpicks, paper cutters, earrings,
      thimbles, charms, chains, pins, plush boxes, silver plated
      ware, tortoise combs, hair pins, badges and medals, rings.
      Illustrated catalogue 1895. Reprint with introd. Princeton,
      NJ: Pyne Pr, 1971. 209pp, 3000 ill, bib

6301 Rogers, Frances, and Alice Beard. 5000 Years of Gems and
      Jewelry. New York: F. A. Stokes, 1940. 309pp, ill

6302 Rorimer, James Joseph. Mediaeval Jewelry. Metropolitan
      Museum. New York: 1940. 3pp, 20 pls

6303 Rossi, Filippo. Italian Jewelled Arts. Tr. from Italian by
      Elisabeth Mann Borghese. London: Thames & Hudson,
      1958. 233pp, 135 ill, bib

6304 Rowe, Donald F. The Art of Jewelry, 1450 to 1650. Exhi-
      bition. April-May 1975. Martin D'Arcy Gallery of Art.
      Chicago: Loyola U Pr, 1975. 68pp, 88 (5 color) ill, bib

6305 Saint, T. D. A New Book of Designs for Jewellers' Work.
      n. p.: 1770. ill SKM

6306 Seidler, Ned. Gems and Jewels. New York: Odyssey, 1964.
      45pp, ill

6307 Seyd, Mary. Introducing Beads. London: Batsford, 1973.
      96pp, ill, 4 pls, bib (Beadwork to 1900)

6308 Shipley, Robert Morrill, and others. Dictionary of Gems
      and Gemology, including ornamental, decorative, and
      curio stones; a glossary of over 4000 English and foreign
      words, terms, and abbreviations which may be encountered
      in English literature or in the gem, jewelry, or art trades.
      Los Angeles; Boston: Gemological Institute of America,
      1945; 5th ed. 1951. 254pp; 261pp

6309 *Smith, Harold Clifford. Jewellery. London; New York:
      Methuen; London: Connoisseur, 1908; reprint. Wake-
      field, Eng: E P Publishing, 1973. 410pp, ill, 53 pls,
      color frontis, bib

6310 Smith, Robert Henry Soden, ed. Catalogue of the Loan Exhi-
      bition of Ancient and Modern Jewellery and Personal Orna-
      ments 1872. South Kensington Museum, London: J.
      Strangeways, printer, 1873. 111pp, ill, 13 pls

6311 Sommerville, Maxwell, 1829-1904. Catalogue of a Cabinet
      of Gems, Cameos in Relief, and Other Engraved Stones,
      Ambers, Antique Pastes, Rings, etc., Collected in
      Europe, Asia, and Africa (by the Author). On view in
      the Centennial Loan Exhibition, etc. Philadelphia: Sher-
      man & Co, 1875; etc. 38pp; 67pp, ill; 66pp, ill

6312 Sorensen, Henry Richard, and Samuel J. Vaughn. Hand-
      wrought Jewelry. Milwaukee: Bruce, 1916. 102pp, ill
      (How-to)

6313 Steingraber, Erich. Antique Jewelery: its history in Europe
      from 800 to 1900. Tr. from German by Peter George.
      London: Thames & Hudson; New York: Praeger, 1957.
      191pp, 348 ill, bib

6314 Stopford, Francis Powys. The Romance of the Jewel. Lon-
      don: priv. printed, 1920. 96pp, 22 pls

6315 Thrasher, William, philo-astro-medicus. The Marrow of
      Chymical Physick; or, the practice of making chemical
      medicines. Divided in three books: ... A very rare way
      of making metaline glass of any colour whatsoever. Very
      useful for the making artificial rubies, saphirs, jacinths,
      etc. Likewise for the enamiling of rings, or for jewels;
      being very excellent and easie. London: T. J. for P.
      Parker, 1669. DLC

6316 Wallis, George. Jewellery. London: 1876. See also:
      Bevan, G. P., British Manufacturing Industries, Vol. 11.

6317 Weinstein, Michael. The World of Jewel Stones. New York:
      Sheridan House, 1958; London: Pitman, 1959. 430pp, ill,
      bib

6318 Williamson, George Charles, 1858- . The Book of Amber.
      Fore. by Edward Heron-Allen. London: E. Benn, 1932.
      268pp, pls, color frontis, bib

6319 _____, comp. Catalogue of the Collection of Jewels and
      Precious Works of Art the Property of J. Pierpont Morgan.
      London: priv. printed, Chiswick Pr, 1910. 183pp, ill,
      94 pls, 46 color pls

RINGS

6320 Braybrooke, Richard Cornwallis Neville (R. C. Neville),
      1820-1861. Romance of the Ring, or the history and
      antiquity of finger rings. Saffron Walden, Eng: 1856.
      SKM

6321 A Catalogue of the Paintings, Miniatures, Drawings, Engrav-
      ings, Rings and Miscellaneous Objects Bequeathed by ...
      Alexander Dyce. "Rings and Miscellaneous Objects" by
      Charles Christopher Black. South Kensington Museum.
      London: Eyre & Spottiswoode, for HMSO, 1874. 326pp

6322 Crisp, Frederick Arthur. Memorial Rings, Charles 2nd to
      William 4th, in Possession of F. A. Crisp. Introd. by
      Bower Marsh. London: Grove Park Pr, 1908. 373pp,
      ill DLC

6323 Dalton, Ormonde Maddock. Catalogue of the Finger Rings,
      Early Christian, Byzantine, Teutonic, Mediaeval and
      Later, Bequeathed by Sir Augustus Wollaston Franks ...
      in which are included the other rings of the same periods
      in the Museum. Pref. by C. H. Read. London: British
      Museum, 1912. 366pp, ill, bib NN, PP, BM

6324 Edwards, Charles, 1797-1868. The History and Poetry of

Finger-Rings. New York: Redfield, 1855; New York: A.
C. Armstrong, 1880; with a preface by R. H. Stoddard.
New York: J. W. Lovell, 189-? 239pp, ill, color frontis
NN, ViU, DLC

6325   Evans, Sir Arthur John. Posy-Rings. London: 1892. 30pp
       (English gold and silver)

6326   Evans, Joan. English Posies and Posy Rings; a catalogue with
       introduction. London: Oxford U. Pr, H. Milford, 1931.
       114pp DLC, CU

6327   Gatty, Charles Tindall. Catalogue of the Engraved Gems and
       Rings in the Collection of Joseph Mayer. London: Brad-
       bury, Agnew, printers, 1879.

6328   Jones, William, F.S.A. Finger-Ring Lore. Historical, leg-
       endary, anecdotal. London: Chatto & Windus, 1877; 2nd
       ed. rev. & enl. 1890; new ed. 1898. 545pp, many ill;
       567pp, ill TU, DeWint, SKM

6329   Kunz, George Frederick. Rings for the Finger from the
       Earliest Known Times to the Present ... origin, early
       making, materials, archaeology, history.... Philadelphia;
       London: Lippincott, 1917; facsimile reprint. New York:
       Dover; London: Constable, 1973. 381pp, 113 pls of 280
       ill (To 1916)

6330   McCarthy, James Remington. Rings Through the Ages, an
       Informal History. New York; London: Harper, 1945.
       202pp, pls, bib

6331   Oates, F. A. H. Catalogue of Finger Rings. n.p.: 1917.
       12pp

6332   *Oman, Charles Chichele. British Rings 800 to 1914. London:
       Batsford, 1973; Totawa, NJ: Rowman & Littlefield, 1974.
       146pp, ill, 100 pls, bib

6333   *   . Catalogue of Rings. London: V & A, 1930.
       154pp, 39 pls BM

SHOES AND BOOTS

6334   *Brooke, Iris. A History of English Footwear. London: St.
       Giles Publishing, 1949; rev. ed. as Footwear: a short
       history of European and American shoes. New York:
       Theatre Arts, 1971. 114pp, ill; 131pp, ill

6335   *Campion, Samuel Smith. Delightful History of Ye Gentle Craft:
       an illustrated history of feet costume. History of S. S.

Crispin and Crispianus and other noted shoemakers, with
many curious details from early records and tracts.
Originally published as a souvenir of the Northampton
Leather Work Exhibition, 1874. 2nd ed. Northampton:
Taylor & Son, 1876. 84pp, ill, 3 pls, frontis by George
Cruikshank MH, NN

6336   Devlin, James Dacre. The Shoemaker. 2 vol. London:
       Charles Knight, 1839, 1841. ill

6337   Dowie, James. The Foot and Its Covering, comprising a full
       translation of Dr. Camper's work on "The Best Form of
       Shoe." Tr. from German. London: R. Hardwicke,
       1861; 2nd ed. 1871. 204pp, ill, 3 pls; 287pp, ill NN

6338   Dutton, William Henry. The Boots and Shoes of Our Ances-
       tors as Exhibited by the Worshipful Company of Cord-
       wainers. With a brief history of the Company. London:
       Chapman & Hall, 1898. 13pp, ill, 30 pls BM

6339   Exhibition of Boots and Shoes Given by the Worshipful Company
       of Cordwainers at Their Hall, June 10 to 15, 1895, in-
       cluding a valuable loan collection.... London: 1895.
       35pp BM

6340   Greig, T. Watson. Ladies' Dress Shoes of the 19th Century.
       Edinburgh: David Douglas, 1900. 3pp, 63 color ill, color
       frontis

6341   _____. Ladies' Old-Fashioned Shoes. Edinburgh: David
       Douglas, 1885; Supplement. 1889. 9pp, 11 color pls;
       10pp (Mary, Queen of Scots, to end of 18th century;
       Author's collection) TxU, DeWint

6342   Hall, Joseph Sparkes. The Book of Feet: A history of boots and shoes with illustrations of the fashions of the Egyptians, Hebrews, Persians, Greeks, and Romans, and the prevailing style throughout Europe during the Middle Ages down to the present period.... London: Simpkin Marshall, 184-?; from 2nd Lond. ed. New York: William H. Graham, J. S. Redfield, 1847. 148pp, ill (part color); 216pp, ill, 4 color pls NN, DLC, DeWint

6343 Harding, J. S. The Boot and Shoe Industry. London: Pitman, 1918; 2nd ed. 1931. 130pp, ill; 212pp, ill BM

6344 Hughes, George Bernard, and Therle Hughes. Georgian Shoe Buckles; illustrated by the Lady Manfe Collection of Shoe Buckles at Kenwood. London: Greater London Council, 1972. 16pp, ill (1700-1800)

6345 Redfern, W. B. Royal and Historic Gloves and Shoes. London: Methuen, 1904. 110pp, 78 pls (some color), color frontis DLC

6346 Sulser, Wilhelm. The Bally Exhibition. Felsgarten House. Guide to the Shoe Museum of the Bally Shoe Factories Ltd. Tr. by F. S. Budgen. Schoenenwerd, Switzerland: 1948. 167pp, ill

6347 _____. A Brief History of the Shoe. Solothurn, Switzerland: Bally Shoe Museum, 1967? 16pp, ill

6348 Taylor, Walter C. The Shoe and Leather Lexicon; an illustrated glossary of trade and technical terms relating to shoes.... Boston: Boot & Shoe Recorder Publishing, 1912; rev. 10th ed. 1938. 72pp, ill; 86pp, ill

6349 *Wright, Thomas. The Romance of the Shoe; being the history of shoemaking in all ages, and especially in England and Scotland. London: C. J. Farncombe, 1922; reprint. Detroit: Singing Tree Pr, 1968. 323pp, 146 ill, pls

HATS AND HEADDRESSES

6350 Dony, John G. A History of the Straw Hat Industry. Luton, Eng: Gibbs, Bamforth, The Leagrave Pr, 1942. 219pp, pls, bib PPL

6351 Dunlap, Robert, and Co. A Short Treatise on Head Ware, Ancient and Modern. New York: Lockwood Pr, 1885. 32pp WaS

6352 Freeman, Charles Ernest. Luton and the Hat Industry. Luton, Eng: Museum and Art Gallery, 1953. 36pp, ill

6353 Genin, John Nicholas, 1819-1878. An Illustrated History of

the Hat, from the earliest ages to the present time.
Numerous illustrations of headwear. New York: J. N.
Genin, Importer & Manufacturer of Hats; New York:
Root & Tinker; New York: Bobbett & Edmonds; New
York: E. N. Grossman, printer, 1848; New York: 1850.
54pp, ill, pls   PPL, DLC, DeWint

6354   Giafferii, Paul Louis Victor de, comp.   Millinery in the
Fashion History of the World; from 5300 B.C. to the
present era.   72 centuries of head-dress, illustrated.
New York: Illustrated Milliner Co, 1927.   16 leaves,
16 color pls   NN

6355   Harrison, Michael.   The History of the Hat.   London: Jenkins, 1960.   188pp, ill

6356   The Hat Review.   Monthly.   New York: P. Bonfort, 1873- .
ill, pls   NN

6357   Howell, Mary J.   The Handbook of Millinery; comprised in
a series of lessons for the formation of bonnets, capotes,
turbans, caps, bows, etc.; to which is appended a treatise
on taste, and the blending of colours; also an essay on
corset making.   London: Simpkin, Marshall, 1847.   128pp,
ill   NN

6358   Inwards, Harry.   Straw Hats.   Their History and manufacture.
London: Pitman, 1922.   126pp, ill

6359   The Ladies' Hand-Book of Millinery and Dress-Making.   London: 1843; New York: J. S. Redfield, 1844.   60pp, ill
NN, BM

6360   Luton, Charles.   Luton and the Hat Industry.   Luton, Eng:
Museum and Art Gallery, 1953.   36pp, ill, bib

6361   Manchester, Herbert (H.).   The Hat in America and the Ferry
Hat Manufacturing Co., N.Y.   New York: 1926.   31pp,
ill

6362   _____.   The Romance of Men's Hats; written for E. V.
Connett & Company, from data and records in their possession.   New York: 1920.   38pp, ill   TxU

6363   _____.   60 Centuries of Hat Making; portrayed for E. V.
Connett Company from data and records in their possession.   New York: 1915.   40pp, ill

6364   The Romance of the Straw Hat.   Being a history of the industry and a guide to the collection.   Luton, Eng: Public
Museum, 1933.   48pp

6365   Sala, George Augustus (Henry).   The Hats of Humanity,

Historically, Humorously and Aesthetically Considered.
A homily.... Manchester, Eng: J. Gee, 1880? 60pp,
3 color pls NN

6366 Six Centuries of Headdress. Exhibition. April-May 1955.
Dallas, Tx: Museum of Fine Arts, 1955. 22pp, ill

6367 Weiss, Harry Bischoff, and Grace M. Weiss. The Early
Hatters of New Jersey. Trenton, NJ: Agricultural Society, 1961. 75pp, ill

6368 White, Margaret E. What's a Hat? The answer as found in
the Newark Museum Collection. Newark, NJ: n.p.,
1956. 20pp, ill, bib

SECTION XIII

CEREMONY AND OFFICIAL SYMBOLS

SEALS AND ENGRAVED GEMS

6369　Armstrong, Edmund Clarence Richard.　Irish Seal-Matrices
　　　and Seals.　Dublin: Hodges, Figgis, 1913.　135pp, 80 ill
　　　BM

6370　*Birch, Walter de Gray.　Catalogue of Seals in the Department
　　　of Manuscripts.　6 vol.　London:　British Museum, 1887-
　　　1900.　pls　NN, BM

6371　_____.　History of Scottish Seals.　Stirling: n.p., 1905.

6372　_____.　Seals.　London:　Methuen; New York:　Putnam's,
　　　1907.　327pp, 52 pls　NN, DLC

6373　Bloom, James Harvey.　English Seals.　London:　Methuen,
　　　1906; 1910.　274pp, 93 ill, bib　DLC, PPULC

6374　Boardman, John.　Engraved Gems:　the Ionides Collection.
　　　V & A.　Evanston, Ill:　Northwestern U Pr, 1968.　114pp,
　　　ill (9 color), bib

6375　Brindley, Harold Hulme, comp.　Impressions and Casts of
　　　Seals, coins, tokens, medals and other objects of art ex-
　　　hibited in the seal room, National Maritime Museum.
　　　Greenwich, Eng:　1938.　44pp, 4 pls　NN

6376　Buckley, Francis.　Fob Seals in the 17th Century.　Upper-
　　　mill:　Moore & Edwards, 1932.

6377　Caley, John.　Ancient Seals.　A catalogue of upwards of 1500
　　　impressions from ancient seals, in wax and sulphur.　Lon-
　　　don:　J. Rider, 183-?　61pp　(British Seals)　NN

6378　[No entry.]

　　　Catalogue of Seals.　London:　British Museum, 1887.　See:
　　　　Birch, W. d. G., above.

6379 Forrer, Leonard Steyning, comp. Biographical Dictionary of
Medallists, coin, gem and seal-engravers, mint-masters,
etc., ancient and modern, with references to their work,
B.C. 500-A.D. 1900. London: Spink & Son, 1902-03; 8
vol. reprint. New York: Burt Franklin, 1970. ill, pls,
bib

6380 Gatty, Charles Tindall. Catalogue of the Engraved Gems and
Rings in the Collection of Joseph Mayer. London: Bradbury, Agnew, printers, 1879.

6381 Goodell, Abner Cheney. Account of the Seals of the Courts
of the Colony of Massachusetts. Cambridge, Mass: 1883.
16pp, 2 pls NN

6382 Henfry, Henry William. Numismata Cromwelliana: or, the
medallic history of Oliver Cromwell, illustrated by his
coins, medals, and seals. London: J. R. Smith, 1877.
230pp, ill, 8 pls

6383 A History of Seals Used by the Senate of the United States,
1804-1952. Washington, D.C.: GPO, 1953. 34pp, ill

6384 Hope, William Henry St. John. The Seals of Armorial Insignia of the University of Cambridge. Part 1. London: W.
Satchell, 1883.

6385 *King, Charles William, 1818-1888. Antique Gems. London:
Bell & Daldy, 1866.

6386 *_____. Antique Gems and Rings. 2 vol. London: Bell
& Daldy, 1872. text, ill, 75 pls DeWint, SKM

6387 *_____. Handbook of Engraved Gems. London: Bell &
Daldy, 1866; 2nd ed. 1885. 396pp, pls; 282pp, 77pp of
pls MB, NjP

6388 Kingsford, Hugh Sadler. Seals. London: S.P.C.K.; New
York: Macmillan, 1920. 59pp, ill, bib NN

6389 Laing, Henry, 1803-1883. Descriptive Catalogue of Impressions from Ancient Scottish Seals. Royal, baronial, ecclesiastical, and municipal, embracing a period from A.D.
1094 to the Commonwealth. Edinburgh: T. Constable,
1840; 1850. 232pp, 30 pls; 32 pls NN, PPL, BM, MB

6390 _____. Supplemental Descriptive Catalogue of Ancient
Scottish Seals, royal, baronial, ecclesiastical, and mu-
nicipal ... A.D. 1150 to the 18th century. Edinburgh:
Edmonston & Douglas, 1866. 237pp, 15 pls NN, BM

6391 Lewis, John, 1675-1747. A Dissertation on the Antiquity and

Use of Seals in England. London: for W. Mount and T. Page, 1740. 31pp, ill, 1 pl NN, CtY, BM

6392 MacDonald, William Rae. Scottish Armorial Seals. Edinburgh: W. Green, 1904. 382pp, pls NN

6393 Madden, Sir Frederick. A Guide to the Autograph Letters, Manuscripts, Original Charters and Royal, Baronial and Ecclesiastical Seales.... London: British Museum, 1859; 1862. 41pp; 32pp NN

6394 Moring, Thomas, firm. Seal Engraving. London: T. Moring, 189-? 21pp, 7 pls, bib NN

6395 Osborne, Duffield, 1858-1917. Engraved Gems, Signets, Talismans and Ornamental Intaglios, Ancient and Modern. New York: H. Holt, 1912. 424pp, ill, 32 pls

6396 Parry, Hugh Lloyd. The Exeter Civic Seals. Exeter, Eng: James G. Commin, 1909. 35pp, pls

6397 Pedrick, Gale. Borough Seals of the Gothic Period: a series of examples, illustrating the nature of their design and artistic value. London: J. M. Dent, 1904. 141pp, 50 pls NN

6398 _____. Monastic Seals of the 13th Century.... London: De La More Pr, 1902. 144pp, 50 pls NN

6399 Porteous, Alexander. The Town Council Seals of Scotland, Historical, Legendary and Heraldic. Edinburgh: W. & A. K. Johnston, 1906. 300pp, ill NN

6400 Prime, William Cowper. Coins, Medals, and Seals, Ancient and Modern.... New York: Harper, 1861; 1864. 292pp, ill, 114 pls NN

6401 *Smith, Robert Henry Soden, ed. A List of Books and Pamphlets in the National Art Library ... Illustrating Seals. South Kensington Museum. London: Eyre & Spottiswoode, 1886. 46pp

6402 Sommerville, Maxwell. Engraved Gems: their place in the history of art. Philadelphia: Porter & Coates, 1877; enl. rev. ed. with catalog raisonné of Sommerville Collection. Philadelphia: Author, 1889. 71pp, pls; 783pp, ill, pls

6403 *Stevenson, John Horne, and Marguerite Wood. Scottish Heraldic Seals: royal, official, ecclesiastical, collegiate, burghal, personal. 3 vol. Glasgow: priv. printed, R. Maclehose & Coy, 1940. ill (Vol. I. Public Seals;

Vol. II. Personal Seals, A-J; Vol. III. Personal Seals, K-Z) NN

6404   Sutherland, Beth Benton. The Romance of Seals and Engraved Gems. Fore. by A. E. Alexander. New York: Macmillan, 1965. 174pp, ill, pls, bib

6405   *Tassie, James, 1735-1799. A Catalogue of Impressions in Sulphur, of antique and modern gems, from which pastes are made and sold. London: I. Murray, 1775. 99pp DLC

6406   * _____, and R. E. Raspe. Descriptive Catalogue of a General Collection of Ancient and Modern Engraved Gems, Cameos, Intaglios, taken from the most celebrated cabinets in Europe and cast in coloured pastes, white enamel and sulphur by James Tassie, modeller.... French and English text. 2 vol. London: 1791; abridged versions. 1816; 1830. 800pp, ill, 57 pls (Many of these were especially prepared for, and reproduced by J. Wedgwood)

6407   Taylor, Frank. Ecclesiastical, Monastic and Local Seals, 12th to 17th Century, from the Hatton Wood Manuscripts in the John Rylands Library. Manchester, Eng: 1947.

6408   _____. Selected Cheshire Seals, 12th to 17th century. Manchester, Eng: John Rylands Library Bulletin, 1942. 20pp

6409   Thompson, Sir E. M., ed. Guide to the ... Royal, Baronial and Ecclesiastical Seals. London: British Museum, 1886. 78pp

6410   Tonnochy, Alec Bain. Catalogue of British Seal-Dies in the British Museum. London: 1952. 212pp, ill, 32 pls, bib (Medieval British, Scottish, Irish and Welsh)

6411   Wadhams, Albert Ives, 1819-1884. An Essay upon the Origin and Use of Seals.... Albany, NY: W. C. Little, 1865. 39pp, ill, color pls NN

6412   Wyon, Alfred Benjamin. Great Seals of England, from the earliest period to the present time.... London: Chiswick, 1887. 217pp, 56 pls, bib NN

CROWN JEWELS AND REGALIA

6413   Broadley, Alexander Meyrick, 1847-1916. Garrard's, 1721-1911. Crown jewelers and goldsmiths during six reigns and in three centuries, with some account of the original seat of their business in the Haymarket and their new

home in Albemarle St.   London: Stanley Paul, 1912.
182pp, ill, pls NN, DLC

6414   Collins, Arthur Jefferies, ed.   Jewels and Plate of Queen
       Elizabeth I.   The inventory of 1574.   Edited from Harley
       Manuscript 1650 and Stowe Manuscript 555 in the British
       Museum.   London: the Museum, 1955.   599pp, ill

6415   Fillitz, Hermann.   Catalogue of the Crown Jewels and the
       Ecclesiastical Treasure Chamber.   Kunsthistoriches Mu-
       seum.   Tr. by Geoffrey Holmes.   Vienna: 1956.   64pp,
       32 pls   (Austrian, 9th century on)

6416   Fortnum, Charles Drury Edward.   Notes on Some of the An-
       tique and Renaissance Gems and Jewels in Her Majesty's
       Collection at Windsor Castle.   London: Nichols, 1876.
       28pp ICN

6417   Halls, Zillah.   Coronation Costume and Accessories, 1685-
       1953.   Introd. by Martin R. Holmes.   London Museum.
       London: HMSO, 1973.   70pp, ill, bib

6418   Hewitt, John, 1807-1878.   Crown Jewels.   London: HMSO,
       1841.   SKM

6419   Holmes, Martin Rivington.   The Crown Jewels in the Wakefield
       Tower.   London: HMSO, 1949; 1953; 2nd ed. 1955; 3rd ed.
       1967.   11pp; 26pp; 21 pp

6420   Jones, William, F.S.A.   Crowns and Coronations; a history
       of regalia.   London: Chatto & Windus, 1883; new ed.
       1898; 1902.   551pp, 91 ill, pls DLC

6421   Loftie, William John, 1839-1911.   Authorized Guide to the

Tower of London. London: HMSO, 1886; 2nd rev. ed.
1888; with a description of the Armoury by Viscount Dillon.
London: 1894. 152pp, ill, pls

6422   Meen, Victor Ben, and A. D. Tushingham. Crown Jewels of
Iran. Toronto: U of Toronto Pr, 1968. 159pp, ill, bib

6423   Redwood, Sydney. The Crown Jewels and Coronation Chair.
London: Westminster Pr, 1936; 2nd ed. 1937. 31pp,
color pls

6424   Sitwell, Hervey Degge Wilmot. The Crown Jewels and Other
Regalia in the Tower of London. Ed. by Clarence Winchester. London: Viscount Kemsley at Dropmore Pr,
1953. 116pp, pls, bib

6425   Twining, Edward Francis. The English Regalia and Crown
Jewels in the Tower of London. London: Street & Massey, 1935; 2nd ed. London: Lapworth, 1947. 72pp; 64pp

6426   _____. A History of the Crown Jewels of Europe. London: Batsford, 1960. 707pp, 230 pls, bib

6427   _____. The Scottish Regalia. London: Street & Massey,
1936. 33pp

6428   Younghusband, Sir George John, 1859- . The Jewel House.
An account of the many romances connected with the Royal
Regalia.... London: Jenkins; New York: George Doran,
1920. 256pp, pls, color frontis, facsims

6429   _____, and Cyril James Davenport. The Crown Jewels of
England. London; New York: Cassell, 1919. 84pp, 60
ill, 18 color pls

INSIGNIA OF OFFICE, TRUNCHEONS, AND MACES

6430   Browning, Alan Robert. The Mace; a brief history of the
mace and its use in House of Commons, the House of
Representatives, the Australian States and the Territory
of Papua and New Guinea. Canberra: Australian Government Printing Service, 1970. 24pp, bib

6431   Clark, Erland Fenn. Truncheons. Their romance and reality.
Over 100 plates illustrating more than 500 pieces, special
and Chief Constables' staves, tipstaves and truncheons;
early railway truncheons, "tythings," "hundreds," "Leets,"
ceremonial and bludgeons. Riots: wards; "patroles;"
portreeve. With a short sketch of Bow Street Runners,
Townsend, and the origin of the police. London: H.
Jenkins, 1935; 1952. 242pp, 100 pls

6432 Dicken, Eden Rowland Huddleston. The History of Truncheons.
      Ilfracombe, No. Devon: A. H. Stockwell, 1952. 136pp,
      ill (Types used by police, beadles, inns, navy, etc.)

6433 French, George Russell. On the Maces of the Corporation of
      Stratford-on-Avon, and the families of Quiney and Salder.
      Reprint from Stratford-on-Avon Herald, 1868.

6434 Fuller, Margaret D. West Country Friendly Societies: an
      account of village benefit clubs and their brass pole heads.
      Lingfield, Surrey: Oakwood Pr, for U of Reading, 1964.
      173pp, ill, bib

6435 Garstin, John Ribton. Irish State and Civic Maces, Swords,
      and Other Insignia. Dublin: 1898. 66pp

6436 Heckscher, William S. Maces; an exhibition of American
      ceremonial academic scepters in honor of the inauguration
      of President Terry Sanford, October-November 1970.
      Raleigh, NC: Litho Industries, for Duke University Mu-
      seum of Art, 1970. 55pp, ill, pls, bib

6437 Hope, William Henry St. John. The Stall Plates of the Knights
      of the Order of the Garter, 1348-1485. Westminster: A.
      Constable, 1901. 25pp, 90 color pls NN, DLC

6438 Jewitt, Llewellyn Frederick William. The Corporation Plate
      and Insignia of Office of the Cities and Towns of England
      and Wales. Ed. & comp. by W. H. St. John Hope. 2
      vol. London: Bemrose, 1895. 400 ill (I. Anglesey to
      Kent; II. Lancashire to Yorkshire) NN, DLC

6439 Lambert, George. Civic and Other Maces. Reprint from the
      Antiquary, February 1880. London: 1880? 15pp

6440 The Mace of the House of Representatives. Washington, D.C.:
      GPO, 1937; 3rd ed. prepared by Kenneth Romney. 1940;
      4th ed. rev. by Joseph H. Callahan, 1950. 12pp, 1 ill;
      15pp, ill; 15pp, ill ("Printed for the official use of the
      Sargeant of Arms")

6441 Milton, Roger. The English Ceremonial Book; a history of
      robes, insignia and ceremonies still in use in England.
      Newton Abbot: David & Charles; New York: Drake, 1972.
      216pp, ill, bib

6442 Oar Maces of Admiralty. National Maritime Museum. Lon-
      don: HMSO, 1966. 31pp, ill, bib

6443 Thorne, Peter. The Mace in the House of Commons. Lon-
      don: HMSO, 1957; rev. ed. 1971. 11pp, 1 pl

6444 Thorpe, Mary, and Charlotte Thorpe. London Church Staves, with some notes on their surroundings. London: E. Stock, 1895. 76pp, ill, pls NNC-Ave

6445 Watts, William Walter. Catalogue of Pastoral Staves. V & A. London: 1924. 40pp, ill, 20 pls, bib

6446 Williamson, George Charles. Notes on the Maces, Insignia of Office, and Town Plate of the Town of Guildford. Guildford: W. Matthews, 1896. 12pp

BIRTH, DEATH AND MARRIAGE OBJECTS

6447 Cunnington, Phillis, and Catherine Lucas. Costumes for Births, Marriages and Deaths. London: A. & C. Black, 1972. 331pp, ill, 64 pls, bib

6448 Curl, James Stevens. The Victorian Celebration of Death. Newton Abbot: David & Charles, 1972. 222pp, ill

6449 Davey, Richard Patrick Boyle, 1848- . A History of Mourning. London: Jay's, 1890. 111pp, ill, pls DeWint

6450 Freeman, Graydon La Verne (Larry). The American Life Collector, No. 10. Funerary Art. Watkins Glen, NY: Century House, 196-? 120pp, ill (Includes burial places, coffin plates, casket trimmings, burial rings and jewelry, mementos, sculpture and pictures, mourning ornaments and jewelry, and hearse ornaments)

6451 Freeman, Ruth Sunderlin, and Larry Freeman. O Promise Me; an album of wedding memories. Watkins Glen, NY: Century, 1954. 112pp, chiefly ill

6452 Goodman, L. B., ed. The American Life Collector, No. 8. Collectible Wedding Souvenirs, Past and Present. Watkins Glen, NY: American Life Foundation and Institute, dist. by Century, 1967. 128pp, ill (From collection of Dr. and Mrs. Larry Freeman. Bridal customs, wedding souvenirs, mementos and rings of 19th century)

6453 Hasluck, Paul Nooncree, 1854-1931, ed. Coffin-making and Undertaking; special appliances, Lancashire coffins, Southern Counties and other coffins. Children's coffins, adults' covered coffins, polishing coffins. Inscription plates, coffin furniture, trimming or lining, ornamented and panelled coffins; shells and outer coffins, lead coffins, undertaking. London; New York: Cassell, 1905. 96pp, ill MiD

6454 Jewitt, Llewellyn Frederick William. On Funeral Garlands. London: 1860. 11pp, ill, pl OCl

6455   Maskell, Joseph, 1829-1890. The Wedding-Ring; its history,
       literature and the superstitions respecting it.   A lecture.
       London: South Kensington Museum, 1868; 2nd ed. rev.
       London: H. Parr, 1888.   47pp; 60pp CtY, SKM

6456   Memento Mori.   200 years of funerary art and customs of
       Concord.   Concord, Mass: Antiquarian Society, 1967.
       35pp, ill

6457   Mourning Becomes America.   Exhibition.   March-May 1976.
       Harrisburg, Pa.; June-July, Albany, N.Y.   Harrisburg,
       Pa: William Penn Memorial Museum, 1976.   ill

6458   Roith, Cynthia.   Bygones--Love and Marriage Tokens.   Lon-
       don: Corgi, 1972.   95pp, ill (To 1900)

6459   White, Margaret E.   Bridal Gowns in the Museums' Collec-
       tion.   Newark, NJ: Newark Museum Association, 1954.
       20pp, ill, bib

MONUMENTAL BRASSES AND GRAVESTONE DESIGN

6460   Andrews, William Frampton.   Memorial Brasses in Hertford-
       shire Churches.   Hertford: S. Austin, 1866; Ware: G.
       Price, 1903.   54pp; 172pp BM

6461   Badger, Edward William.   Monumental Brasses of Warwick-
       shire.   Birmingham: Cornish Brothers, 1895.   66pp BM

6462   Beedell, Suzanne.   Brasses and Brass Rubbing.   Edinburgh:
       Bartholomew, 1973.   96pp, ill, bib

6463   Belcher, William Douglas.   Kentish Brasses.   2 vol.   Lon-
       don: Sprague, 1888, 1905.   plates with notes BM

6464 *Benton, Gerald Montague.   The Monumental Brasses of Cam-
       bridgeshire, Excluding Cambridge.   (An appendix in Rides
       Around Cambridge, by J. W. E. Conybeare.)   Cambridge,
       Eng: W. Heffer, 1902; 2nd ed. 1920.   ill BM

6465   Bertram, Jerome.   Brasses and Brass Rubbing in England.
       Newton Abbot: David & Charles, 1971.   206pp, ill, bib

6466   Bliss, Harry Augustus.   Memorial Art, Ancient and Modern:
       Illustrations and descriptions of the world's most notable
       examples of cemetary memorials.   Buffalo, NY: Bliss,
       1912.   240pp, ill, color frontis DeWint

6467   Bouquet, Alan Coates.   Church Brasses, British and Conti-
       nental; with some notes on incised stone slabs and indents.
       London: Batsford, 1956.   284pp, ill, bib

6468   Boutell, Charles. Monumental Brasses and Slabs: an histori-
       cal and descriptive notice of the incised monumental me-
       morials of the Middle Ages. London: G. Bell, 1847.
       235pp, ill, pls

6469   _____. The Monumental Brasses of England.... London:
       G. Bell, 1849. 53pp, pls SIB-1

6470   Brass Rubbings from Shakespeare's Countryside: a selection
       ... of rubbings. Stratford-upon-Avon: Edward Fox, 1970.
       28pp, chiefly ill

6471   Burgess, Frederick Bevan. English Churchyard Memorials.
       London: Lutterworth, 1963. 325pp, pls

6472   Busby, Richard James. Beginner's Guide to Brass Rubbing.
       London: Pelham, 1969; London: Mayflower, 1970. 128pp,
       ill, 16 pls

6473   _____. A Companion Guide to Brasses and Brass Rubbing.
       London: Pelham, 1973. 264pp, ill, bib

6474   Cameron, Hugh Keith. A List of Monumental Brasses on the
       Continent of Europe. Newport Pagnell, Bucks: Monu-
       mental Brass Society, 1970. 117pp, bib

6475   Catling, H. W. Notes on Brass Rubbing: with a list of some
       brasses in the Oxford Region and a summary of the re-
       maining figure brasses in the British Isles. 6th ed. rev.
       Oxford: U. of Oxford, Ashmolean Museum, 1969; 7th ed.
       1973. 89pp, ill, bib

6476   Chadwick, Harry, and Gilbert Wild. Brass Rubbing in York-
       shire. Clapham: Dalesman, 1975. 31pp, ill

6477   Christy, Miller, W. W. Porteous, and E. Bertram Smith.
       On Some Interesting Essex Brasses. Reprint from Trans-
       actions of the Essex Archaeological Society. Colchester:
       1898. 31pp BM

6478   Clarkson, Douglas A. New Designs for Monuments, Tombs,
       Mural Tablets, Crosses, Head Stones, and Ornamental
       Stone and Iron Work. 3 vol. London: Atchley & Co.,
       1852-65. ill BM

6479   Clayton, Henry James. The Ornaments of the Ministers as
       Shown on English Monumental Brasses. London: Alcuin
       Club Collections, vol. 22, 1919. 190pp, ill

6480   Clayton, Muriel. Catalogue of Rubbings of Brasses and In-
       cised Slabs. V & A Museum. London: HMSO, 1915; rev.
       ed. 1929; reissue. 1968. 251pp, ill, 72 pls

6481   The Complete Brass Rubbing Guide(s) to the Figure Brasses in
        ... Vol. I. ... Northamptonshire, Huntingdonshire, and
        Rutland; Vol. II. ... Nottinghamshire, Derbyshire and
        Leicestershire; Vol. III. ... Lincolnshire; Vol. IV. ...
        Norfolk; Vol. V. ... Suffolk. 5 vol. Norwich: Studio
        69, 1972.

6482   Connor, Arthur Bentley. Monumental Brasses in Somerset.
        Facsimile reprints of 22 papers (in) ... the Proceedings
        of the Somerset Archaeological and Natural History So-
        ciety, 1931-1953. Pref. by Paul Corbould. Bath:
        Kingsmead, 1970. 370pp, ill, 101 pls

6483   Cook, Malcolm. Discovering Brasses: A Guide to Monu-
        mental Brasses. Tring: Shire Pub, 1967. 48pp, ill

6484   Cotman, John Sell. Engravings of the Most Remarkable of
        the Sepulchral Brasses in Norfolk; tending to illustrate
        the ecclesiastical, military, and civil costume of former
        ages. London: J. & W. Freeman; Norwich: Author,
        1819; 2nd ed. as Sepulchral Brasses in Norfolk and Suf-
        folk includes Suffolk Brasses, with notes by Samuel Rush
        Meyrick, Albert Way, and N. Harris Nicolas. 2 vol.
        London: H. G. Bohn, 1837; 1838; 1839. 51pp, pls; text,
        173 pls (some color)

6485   _____ . Suffolk Brasses. London: J. & A. Arch; London:
        J. & W. Freeman; Norwich: Author, 1819. 42 pls

6486   Creeny, William Frederic. A Book of Facsimiles of Brasses
        on the Continent of Europe. Norwich: Author, 1884.
        73pp, ill

6487   _____ . Illustrations of Incised Slabs on the Continent of
        Europe. Norwich: Author, 1891. 71 facsims with notes
        BM

6488   Cutts, Edward Lewes. A Manual for the Study of the Sepulch-
        ral Slabs and Crosses of the Middle Ages. London; Ox-
        ford: John Henry Parker, 1849. 93pp, 83 pls BM

6489   Davis, Cecil Tudor. Monumental Brass in the Old or West
        Church, Aberdeen. Reprint from the Archaeological
        Journal. London: Harrison & Sons, 1894. BM

6490   _____ . The Monumental Brasses of Gloucestershire. Sup-
        plement to "Gloucestershire Notes and Queries," 1894-99.
        London: Phillimore, 1899. 230pp, ill BM

6491   _____ . Monumental Brasses of Herefordshire and Worces-
        tershire. Birmingham: 1885; 1887. 24pp, pls

6492   D'Elboux, Raymond Herbert, ed. The Monumental Brasses

of Essex.   Cambridge: U. of C, Monumental Brass Society, 1948.   BM

6493   Druitt, Herbert.   A Manual of Costume as Illustrated by
       Monumental Brasses.   London: A. Moring, 1906; reprint.
       Bath: Kingsmead, 1970.   384pp, ill, 99 pls

6494   Dunkin, Edwin Hadlow Wise.   The Monumental Brasses of
       Cornwall....   London: Spottiswoode, 1882; reprint.   Bath:
       Kingsmead, 1970.   107pp, 62 pls

6495   English Brass Rubbings.   Exhi-
       bition.   Brooklyn Museum,
       November 1935-January
       1936.   Brooklyn, NY: 1935.

6496   Farrer, Edmund.   Monumental
       Brasses in the County of
       Suffolk.   Norwich: Agas
       H. Goose, 1903.   93pp, ill

6497   Fisher, Thomas.   Drawings of
       Brasses in Some Kentish
       Churches.   Ed. by Ralph
       Griffin.   London: J. Bale,
       1913.   12 pls   BM

6498   Forbes, Harriette Merrifield.
       Gravestones of Early New
       England and the Men Who
       Made Them, 1653-1800.   Boston: Houghton Mifflin, 1927.
       141pp, pls   DLC, MB

6499   Franklyn, Julian.   Brasses.   London: Arco, 1964; 2nd ed.
       1969.   156pp, ill; 171pp, ill, 2 pls

6500   Gawthorp, Thomas John.   Designs and Examples of Monu-
       mental, Heraldic and Memorial Brasses....   London:
       Author, 1881.

6501   Gawthorp, Walter E.   The Brasses of Our Homeland Churches.
       London: 1923.   130pp, 62 pls

6502   Gibbs, John, architect.   Designs for Christian Memorials for
       Churchyards and Cemetaries.   Oxford: Author, 1868.
       10pp, 40 pls   MB

6503   Gillon, Edmund Vincent.   Early New England Gravestone Rub-
       bings.   New York: Dover, 1966.   195 pls

6504   _____.   Victorian Cemetery Art.   New York: Dover,
       1972.   173pp, 200 photographs

6505 Gittings, Clare. Brasses and Brass Rubbing. London:
      Blandford Pr, 1970. 104pp, ill

6506 Goss, Winifred Lane (Mrs. Charles Carpenter Goss). Colo-
      nial Gravestone Inscriptions in the State of New Hampshire.
      Dover, NH: Historic Archives Committee, National So-
      ciety of the Colonial Dames of America, 1942. 160pp, bib
      DLC

6507 Griffin, Ralph Hare, and Mill Stephenson. A List of Monu-
      mental Brasses Remaining in the County of Kent in 1922.
      Ashford: 1923. 245pp

6508 Haines, Herbert. A Manual of Monumental Brasses. 2 vol.
      London: J. H. & James Parker, 1861; reprint with introd.
      by Richard J. Busby. Bath: Adams & Dart, 1970. ...;
      286pp, ill

6509 Heape, Richard. Inscribed and Dated Stones and Sundials in
      and Adjoining the Ancient Parish of Rochdale. Cambridge,
      Eng: priv. printed, University Pr, 1926. 358pp

6510 Hoare, Captain Edward. On the Early Memorial Sepulchral
      Brass in Hayes Church.... London: 1881. 3pp

6511 Hudson, Franklin. The Monumental Brasses of Northampton-
      shire. London: 1853. 88 pls BM

6512 Hutchings, Peter Frank. Brass Rubbings in and Around
      Shakespeare's Stratford. Birmingham: Rodway, Drew &
      Hopwood, 1972. 24pp, ill

6513 Isherwood, Grace. Monumental Brasses in the Bedfordshire
      Churches. London: E. Stock, 1906. 68pp, ill

6514 Jacobs, G. Walker. Stranger Stop and Cast an Eye: A
      Guide to Gravestones and Gravestone Rubbing. Brattle-
      boro, Vt: Stephen Greene Pr, 1973. 123pp, ill, bib

6515 Jones, Barbara Mildred. Design for Death. Indianapolis:
      Bobbs-Merrill, 1967. 304pp, ill, bib

6516 Kate, Edward. The Monumental Brasses of Wiltshire:...
      13th to 17th centuries, accompanied with notices descrip-
      tive of ancient costume.... London: 1860; facsim. re-
      print. Bath: Kingsmead, 1969. 111pp, ill, 34 pls

6517 Le Strange, Richard. A Complete Descriptive Guide to
      British Monumental Brasses. London: Thames & Hudson,
      1972. 152pp, bib

6518 Lewis, John Masters. Welsh Monumental Brasses: A Guide.

Cardiff: National Museum of Wales, 1974. 113pp, ill,
pls

6519 Macklin, Herbert Walter. The Brasses of England. Northampton: Antiquary's Books, 1904; 1907; 1913. 336pp, 85 ill

6520 _____. Brasses of Huntingdonshire. Cambridge: Monumental Brass Society, 1900. 33pp

6521 _____. Macklin's Monumental Brasses.... London: Swan,
Sonnenschein, 1890; London: Allen & Unwin, 1913; 7th ed.
rev. and with new pref. by Charles Oman. London: Allen
& Unwin, 1953. 144pp, ill; 194pp, ill; 196pp, ill, pls, bib

6522 Mann, Sir James Gow. Monumental Brasses. Harmondsworth:
Penguin, 1957. 40pp, 32 color pls, bib

6523 Manning, Charles Robertson. A List of the Monumental
Brasses Remaining in England Arranged According to
Counties. London: 1846. BM

6524 Manual for the Study of Monumental Brasses. London: J. H.
Parker, 1848. ECB

6525 Monumental Brasses and Bronzes--a bibliography. London:
Copper Development Association, 1948.

6526 Monumental Brasses in Cambridgeshire and the Isle of Ely.
3rd ed. Cambridge: City Libraries, 1968. 29pp

6527 Morley, Henry Thomas. Monumental Brasses of Berkshire,
14th to 17th century. Reading: Electric Pr, 1924. 262pp,
ill

6528 Norris, Malcolm. Brass Rubbing. London: Studio Vista,
1965. 112pp, ill, bib

6529 _____, and Michael Kellett. Your Book of Brasses. London: Faber, 1974. 77pp, ill, 16pp of pls

6530 Notes of an Exhibition of Rubbings of Monumental Brasses.
South Kensington Museum. London: HMSO, 1918. 12pp

6531 Ogden, William Sharp. Christian Gravestones. London; Manchester: 1877. 150 examples ill

6532 Oliver, Andrew. Notes on Flemish Brasses in England. A
Lecture. St. Albans: W. Cartmel, 1889. 8pp

6533 Owen, Rupert K. W. Description of 25 Sussex Monumental
Brasses ... Hastings Museum. England: 1909. pls
BM

6534   The Oxford Portfolio of Monumental Brasses.   4 parts.   Ox-
       ford: Ashmolean Museum, 1951; 1952; 1954; 1955.   6 pls
       each part

6535   Page-Phillips, John, re-writer.   Macklin's Monumental
       Brasses: including a bibliography and a list of figure
       brasses remaining in churches in the United Kingdom.
       London: Allen & Unwin, 1969; 1972.   202pp, ill

6536   Palliser, Palliser and Co., firm of architects.   Palliser's
       Memorials and Headstones, together with the orders of
       architecture and a large number of miscellaneous designs
       and details of every description, making a most valuable
       and complete book for designers, cutters, carvers, and
       the general public.   New York: J. S. Ogilvie, 1891.
       140pp, 94 pls   DLC

6537   Sadler, Arthur George.   The Indents of Lost Monumental
       Brasses in Dorset and Hampshire: ... a record of re-
       maining indents or matrices.   Worthing, Sussex: Author,
       1975.   38pp, ill, bib

6538   _____.   The Lost Monumental Brasses of East Sussex....
       Worthing: Author, 1970.   55pp, ill

6539   Series of Photo-Lithographs of Monumental Brasses in West-
       minster Abbey.   King's Lynn: 1898.

6540   Simpson, Justin.   A List of the Sepulchral Brasses of Eng-
       land ... arranged in counties.   Stamford: 1857.   BM

6541   Staines, Edward Noel.   A Guide to the Monumental Brasses
       and Incised Slabs on the Isle of Wight.   London: Pinhorns,
       1972.   11pp, ill

6542   Stephenson, Mill, comp.   A List of Monumental Brasses in
       Surrey.   Pref. by J. M. Blatchly.   Surrey: Headley
       Brothers, 1921; 1926; reprint. Bath: Kingsmead, 1970.
       ...; 718pp, ill; 585pp, ill

6543   _____.   A List of Palimpsest Brasses in Great Britain.
       London: J. Bale, 1903.   232pp, ill

6544   Suffling, Ernest Richard.   English Church Brasses from the
       13th to 17th Centuries.   A Manual for antiquaries, archae-
       ologists and collectors.   London: L. Upcott Gill, 1910;
       facsim. reprint. Bath: Kingsmead, 1970.   456pp, 237 ill,
       bib

6545   Thornely, James L.   The Monumental Brasses of Lancashire
       and Cheshire: with some account of the persons repre-
       sented.   Hull: Andrews, 1893; facsim. reprint. Wakefield:
       E P, 1975.   322pp, ill; 314pp, ill

6546 *Trivick, Henry Houghton. The Craft and Design of Monumental Brasses. London: J. Baker; New York: Humanities, 1969. 152pp, 272 ill, 85 pls, bib

6547 _____. The Picture Book of Brasses in Gilt. London:
John Baker, 1971. 33pp, ill, 106 pls

6548 Waddington, William Angelo. Monumental Designs. Burnley,
Eng: 1875. BM

6549 Waller, John Green, and Lionel A. B. Waller. A Series of
Monumental Brasses from the 13th to the 16th Century.
London: 1842-1864. ill, 62 pls (some color) BM

6550 Ward, John Sebastian Marlow. Brasses. Cambridge Manuals
of Science and Literature. Cambridge: 1912. 159pp

6551 Wasserman, Emily. Gravestone Designs: Rubbings and
Photographs from Early New York and New Jersey. New
York: Dover; London: Constable, 1972. 33pp, 135 pls,
bib (1620-1825)

6552 Weaver, Sir Lawrence. Memorials and Monuments Old and
New: 200 subjects chosen from seven centuries. London:
Country Life; New York: Scribner's, 1915. 479pp, ill,
pls, bib

6553 Wheeldon, Jeremy. The Monumental Brasses in Saint Botolph's
Church, Boston. Boston, Lincolnshire, Eng: Richard Kay,
1973. 20pp, ill

6554 Winnington-Ingram, Arthur John. Monumental Brasses in
Hereford Cathedral. 3rd ed. rev. Hereford: 1972. 18pp,
ill

6555 Wright, James Stephen Nicholas. The Brasses of Westminster
Abbey. London: Baker, 1969. 48pp, ill

6556 Wust, Klaus German. Folk Art in Stone; southwest Virginia.
Edinburgh, Va: Shenandoah History, 1970. 28pp, ill
NNC-Ave

FLAGS AND BANNERS

6557 Balderston, Lloyd. The Evolution of the American Flag, from
materials collected by the late George Canby. Philadelphia:
Ferris & Leach, 1909. 144pp, ill, pls

6558 Bennett, Mabel R., comp. "... So Gallantly Streaming": the
story of Old Glory; the history and proper use of our flag
from 1776 to the present. New York: Drake, 1971; 1974.
104pp, ill, bib

6559   Bland, William, of Duffield. National Banners; their history
       and construction. n. p. (Eng.): 1892.   2pp, 1 color pl
       BM

6560   Cumberland, Frederick Barlow. Story of the Union Jack.
       Toronto: William Briggs, 1897; 2nd ed. rev. & enl.
       1900; London: Ward Lock, 1901; 3rd ed. rev. & enl.
       Toronto: 1909.   231pp, ill; 324pp, ill

6561   Green, Emanuel. The Union Jack. Exeter, Eng: priv.
       printed, 1891; 2nd ed. as The Union Jack: its history
       and development. London: Harrison & Sons, 1903.   20pp;
       33pp, color pls

6562   Griswold, Frank Gray. The House Flags of the Merchants of
       New York, 1800-1860. Norwood, Mass: Plimpton Pr,
       priv. printed, 1926.   48pp, color pls DeWint

6563   Harrison, Peleg Dennis. The Stars and Stripes and Other
       American Flags. Including their origin and history, army
       and navy regulations.... Boston: Little Brown, 1906;
       3rd ed. 1908; ...; 1914; ...   419pp, ill, 8 color pls;
       427pp, ill PP, NN, DeWint

6564   Hulme, Frederick Edward. The Flags of the World; their
       history, blazonry and associations. London; New York:
       F. Warne, 1897; 1915.   152pp, 26 color pls; text, over
       500 ill ViU, NjP

6565   MacGeorge, Andrew, 1810-1891. Flags: some account of
       their history and uses. London; Glasgow; Edinburgh:
       Blackie & Sons, 1881.   122pp, ill, 6 color pls PPL

6566   *Mastai, Boleslaw, and Marie-Louise D'Orange Mastai. The
       Stars and the Stripes; the American flag as art and as
       history from the birth of the Republic to the present.
       New York: Knopf, 1973.   238pp, color ill

6567   "Our Jack." The history of the Union Jack. London: 1897.
       15pp

6568   Preble, George Henry, 1816-1885. Our Flag. Origin and
       progress of the flag of the United States of America, with
       an introductory account of the symbols, banners, standards
       and flags of ancient and modern nations. Albany, NY:
       J. Munsell, 1872; 2nd ed. Boston: A. Williams, 1880;
       3rd ed. as Origin and History of the American Flag, and
       of the naval and yacht-club signals, seals and arms, and
       principal national songs of the United States. 2 vol.
       Philadelphia: N. L. Brown, 1917.   535pp, ill, 12 color
       pls; 815pp, ill, 10 color pls

6569   *Smith, Whitney. Flags Through the Ages and Across the

World. New York: McGraw Hill, 1975. 361pp, 3000 ill
(National and non-national flags, burgees, ensigns, gonfa-
lons, pennants, schivenkels, vexilloids, jockey silks)

6570 Winter, Eliza. The Making of Our Union Jack, 1707-1801.
Woodstock, Ontario: Express Book and Job Printer, 1911.
BM

CONJURING, MAGIC, AMULETS AND TALISMANS

6571 Beard, Charles Relly. Lucks and Talismans, a chapter of
popular superstition. London: Sampson Low, 1934. 258pp

6572 Conjuring Apparatus Up-to-Date. London; New York: Cassell,
1912; 1913; 1919. 152pp, 167 ill MdBE

6573 Conjuring; scarce items for collectors, catalogue No. 1. London: Daphne Lucille Barnett, 1938- . DLC

6574 *Evans, Joan. Magical Jewels of the Middle Ages and the
Renaissance, particularly in England. Oxford, Eng:
Clarendon Pr, 1922; reprint. Ann Arbor, Mich: Finch
Pr, 1974. 264pp, 3 pls

6575 Gregor, Arthur S. Amulets, Talismans, and Fetishes. New
York: Scribner's, 1975. ill (Juvenile literature. Through
the ages)

6576 Jones, William F.S.A. Credulities Past and Present, including the sea and seamen, miners, amulets and talismans,
rings, word and letter divination, numbers, trials, exor-
cising and blessing of animals, birds, eggs and luck. London: Chatto & Windus, 1880; 1898. 560pp, frontis DLC

6577 Kunz, George Frederick. The Curious Lore of Precious Stones;
being a description of their sentiments and folk lore, super-
stitions, symbolism, mysticism, use in medicine, protection,
prevention, religion and divinition, crystal gazing, birth-
stones, lucky stones and talismans, astral, zodiacal and
planetary. Philadelphia; London: Lippincott, 1913; New
York: Halcyon House, 1938. 406pp, ill, pls, color frontis

6578 _____. The Magic of Jewels and Charms. Philadelphia;
London: Lippincott, 1915. 422pp, many ill (some color),
pls ViU, CU

6579 Pavitt, William Thomas, and Kate Pavitt. A Book of Talismans, Amulets, and Zodiacal Gems. London: W. Rider,
1914; Philadelphia: D. McKay, 1915; 3rd rev. ed. New
York: S. Weiser, 1970; reprint of 1st ed. Detroit: Tower,
1971. 292pp, ill, 10 pls

6580   Peck and Snyder, New York.   1886 Catalog.   Sporting Goods;
       sports equipment and clothing, novelties, recreative sci-
       ence, firemen's supplies, magic lanterns and slides, plays
       and joke books, tricks and magic, badges and ornaments.
       Facsimile reprint with introd.   Princeton; New York:
       Pyne Pr, 1971.   u. p., ill

6581   Pitois, Christian, 1811-1877.   The History and Practice of
       Magic, by Paul Christian (pseud.).   Tr. from French by
       James Kirkup and Julian Shaw.   Ed. & rev. by Ross
       Nichols.   2 vol.   New York: Citadel Pr, 1963.   621pp,
       ill

6582   White, John, a lover of artificial conclusions, d. 1671.   A
       Rich Cabinet with Variety of Inventions; unlock'd and
       opened, for the recreation of ingenious spirits at their
       vacant hours.   London: 1651; 6th ed. 1689; another ed.
       as Hocus Pocus; or, a Rich cabinet of legerdemain curi-
       osities, etc.   London: 1715?   BM

ECCLESIASTICAL ANTIQUES

CHURCH DECORATION AND INTERIORS

6583 Anderson (afterwards Cox), Mary Desiree. Animal Carvings in British Churches. Cambridge, Eng: U. Pr, 1938. 99pp, ill, bib BM

6584 _____. Design for a Journey. Cambridge, Eng: U. Pr, 1940. 140pp, pls (Decoration and ornament)

6585 _____. Misericords, medieval life in English woodcarvings. Harmondsworth, Middlesex: Penguin, 1954. 30pp, ill, 48 pls (Choir-stalls)

6586 Andrews, William, 1848-1908, ed. Antiquities and Curiosities of the Church. London: W. Andrews & Co, 1897. 285pp, ill (Alms-boxes and alms dishes, collecting boxes, sundials, clocks, vanes, etc.) DLC, BM

6587 _____, ed. Ecclesiastical Curiosities. London: W. Andrews & Co, 1899. 250pp, ill, pls (Bells, chests, etc.) DLC

6588 Baker, James McFarlin, and Ralph Adams Cram. American Churches ... Articles on designing, planning, heating, ventilating, lighting and general equipment of churches. 2 vol. New York: American Architect, 1915. text, ill, pls

6589 Beesley, J. M., designer. Examples of Gas Fixtures and Other Metal Work for Ecclesiastical and Domestic Use. Designed after the manner of medieval art works. Philadelphia: Cornelius & Co., Mfrs., 1877. 13 leaves, ill DLC

6590 Bond, Francis. Screens and Galleries in English Churches. London; New York; Toronto: H. Frowde, 1908. 192pp, ill, bib DLC, PPULC

6591 _____. Wood Carvings in English Churches. Vol. I.
Misericords from the 13th to the 17th Century; Vol. II.
Stalls and Tabernacle Works; bishop's thrones and chancel;
chairs. 2 vol. London: Oxford U Pr; New York: Henry
Frowde, 1910. ill, bib DLC, BM

6592 A Boxwood Triptych in the Collection of the Hispanic Society
of America. New York: 1927. 11pp, ill, pl, bib DLC

6593 Bridgens, Richard. Sefton Church, with part of the interior
decorations. London: 1822. 2pp, 31 pls (Sefton, Lancashire) SKM

6594 Bullock, Albert Edward, ed. Grinling Gibbons and His Com-
peers ... Principal carvings in the churches of St. James,
Piccadilly and St. Paul's Cathedral.... London: Tiranti,
1914. 8pp, ill, 61 pls DeWint

6595 Byne, Arthur, and Mildred Stapley. Rejeria of the Spanish
Renaissance; a collection of photographs and measured
drawings, with descriptive text. New York: De Vinne
Pr, 1914. 101pp, 26 pls, color frontis (Church screens,
iron) PP, DLC, CU

6596 _____, and _____. Spanish Ironwork. New York: Hispanic Society of America, 1915. 143pp, 158 ill, pls (Includes ecclesiastical)

6597 Church Decoration; a practical manual of appropriate ornamen-
tation. Ed. by a Practical Illuminator. London: F.
Warne; New York: Scribner, Welford & Armstrong, 1874;
New York: Dutton, 1875; 1877. 84pp, ill, pls (part color)
MiD, NN, NNC-Ave

6598 Clinch, George. Old English Churches: their architecture,
furniture, decoration, vestments, plate, and monuments.
London: L.U. Gill, 1900; 2nd enl. ed. 1902; New York:
Scribner; London: Gill, 1903. 264pp, ill; 312pp, ill
BPL

6599 Cook, Gervis Frere-, ed. The Decorative Arts of the Christian Church. London: Cassell, 1972; as Art and Architecture of Christianity. Cleveland: Press of Case Western
Reserve U., 1972. 304pp, 320 (160 color) ill

6600 *Cox, John Charles. English Church Fittings, Furniture and
Accessories. Introd. by Aymer Vallance. London:
Batsford; New York: Putnam's, 1923; London: 1933.
320pp, ill, pls MiGr, NN, DLC, BM

6601 Crossley, Frederick Herbert. English Church Craftsmanship;
an introduction to the work of the mediaeval period and

some account of later developments. London; New York:
Batsford, 1941; 2nd ed. 1947. 120pp, ill, pls (2 color),
color frontis

6602 Cussans, John Edwin, 1837-1899. Inventory of Furniture and
Ornaments Remaining in All the Parish Churches of Hertfordshire in the Last Reign of King Edward the 6th. Oxford: J. Parker, 1873. 139pp MdBP, MH, SKM

6603 Cutts, Edward Lewes. An Essay on Church Furniture and
Decoration. London: J. Crockford, 1854. 143pp, ill,
9 pls (part color), color frontis NNC-Ave, TxU, SKM,
DLC

6604 _____. An Essay on the Christmas Decoration of Churches;
with an appendix on the decorations for Easter, the school
feast, harvest thanksgiving, confirmation, and for a marriage and a baptism. London: J. Crockford, 1859; 2nd ed.
London: Clerical Journal Office, 1863. 67pp, ill; 85pp,
ill, pl NNC-Ave

6605 Dillon, John, d.1831, comp. Inventory of the Ornaments,
Reliques, Jewels, Vestments, Books, etc., belonging to
the Cathedral Church of Glasgow.... Glasgow: for the
Maitland Club, 1831; reprint. New York: AMS Pr, 1974.
31pp DLC

6606 Duthie, Arthur Louis. Practical Church Decoration. A guide
to the design and execution of decoration of churches,
chapels and other ecclesiastical structures. London: Trade
Papers; New York: Painters' Magazine, 1907. 176pp, ill,
color pls DLC

6607 Ecclesiastical, Imperial, and Other Antiquities of the Russian
Empire. 6 vol. Moscow: 1849. ill, pls SKM

6608 Embury, Aymar. Early American Churches. Garden City,
NY: Doubleday, Page, 1914. 189pp, ill, pls (Includes
interiors) NN, DLC

6609 England, (John), Bishop of Charleston. Explanation of the
Construction, furniture and ornaments of a church, of the
vestments of the clergy.... Rome: 1833; another ed.
1845. BM

6610 French, Gilbert James. Practical Remarks on the Minor Accessories to the Services of the Church. Leeds, Eng:
1844. DLC

6611 Guide to Church Furnishing and Decoration. Chicago: 1876-
77. SKM

6612 Hole, William, 1710-1791. The Ornaments of Churches

Considered, with a particular view to the late decoration
of the Parish Church of St. Margaret, Westminster. To
which is subjoined ... history of said church; an account
of the altar-piece, and stained glass window.... Ed. and
with Introd. by Thomas Wilson. Oxford: W. Jackson,
printer, 1761. 143, 38, 8pp, 8 pls MdBP, DLC, DeWint

6613 Kidder, Frank Eugene, 1859-1903. Churches and Chapels.
Their arrangements, construction and equipment, supplemented by plans, interior and exterior views of numerous
churches of different denominations, arrangement and cost.
New York: Comstock, 1895; 2nd ed. rev. & enl. 1900;
3rd ed. 1906; 4th ed. rev. & enl. 1910. 55pp, ill; 157pp,
54 pls; 179pp, 200 ill, 67 pls; ... MiU, PP, DeWint

6614 King, A. C. Examples of Art Workmanship of Various Ages
and Countries. Ecclesiastical Metal Work of the Middle
Ages. London: Arundel Society, under sanction of Science
and Art Department, South Kensington Museum, 1868. ill,
pls BM

6615 Lasko, Peter. Ars Sacra, 800-1200. Harmondsworth: Penguin, 1972. 338pp, ill, 193 pls, bib (Christian art objects)

6616 Lupson, Edward John. St. Nicholas' Church, Great Yarmouth:
its history, organ, pulpit, library, etc.... Yarmouth,
Eng: Author, 1881. 250pp, ill, pl DLC

6617 Modern Churches, church furniture and decoration, containing
descriptions of the most beautiful churches of Europe, their
furniture, and decorations. London: H. Cox, 1867.
240pp, pls DeWint

6618 Natanson, Joseph. Early Christian Ivories. London: J. Tiranti, 1953. 34pp, 51 pls, bib

6619 Needham, Albert. How to Study an Old Church. Introd. by
John Littlejohn. London: Batsford, 1944; 2nd ed. rev. &
enl. 1945; 3rd ed. rev. & enl. 1948. 72pp, 450 drawings;
78pp, 480 drawings, 2 color pls; 88pp, ill, pls

6620 Oman, Charles Chichele. The Gloucester Candlestick. V & A
Museum. London: HMSO, 1958. 46pp, 36 ill, bib

6621 Peacock, Edward, ed. English Church Furniture, ornaments
and decorations, at the period of the Reformation, as exhibited in a list of goods destroyed in certain Lincolnshire
churches, A.D. 1566. London: John Camden Hotten, 1866.
271pp, ill MiGr

6622 Perkins, Jocelyn Henry Temple. Westminster Abbey, Its

Worship and Ornaments. 3 vol. London: Oxford U. Pr,
1938-1952. text, ill, pls

6623 Pugin, Augustus Welby Northmore. A Treatise on Chancel
      Screens and Rood Lofts, their antiquity, use, and symbolic
      signification. London: C. Dolman, 1851. 124pp, 14 pls

6624 Reliquary and Illustrated Archaeologist. Periodical. London:
      J. R. Smith, etc., 1860-1909. ill (Early Pagan and
      Christian Antiquities of Great Britain)

6625 Scheffer, Nathalie, comp. Russian Ecclesiastical Art; a
      descriptive catalogue of the (Eugene) De Savitsch Collec-
      tion. Washington, D.C.: 1951. 89pp, ill, bib (Icons,
      etc.)

6626 Shortt, Hugh de Sausmarez. Division in Salisbury Cathedral:
      a word about screens. Salisbury, Eng: Friends of ...
      Cathedral, 1970. 8pp, ill

6627 Smith, John Colin Dinsdale. Church Woodcarvings: a West
      Country survey. Newton Abbot: David & Charles; New
      York: A. M. Kelley, 1969. 112pp, chiefly ill (Medieval)

6628 Taralon, Jean. Treasures of the Churches of France. Tr.
      from French by Mira Intrator. London: Thames & Hud-
      son, 1966. 307pp, 288 ill, bib (Wood, ivory, textiles,
      etc.)

6629 Traquair, Ramsay. Old Churches and Church Carving in the
      Province of Quebec. Montreal: McGill University Pr,
      1928. 16pp, ill

6630 Unwin, Francis Sydney, 1885-1925. The Decorative Arts in
      the Service of the Church. London; Oxford: Mowbry;
      Milwaukee: Young Churchmen, 1912. 198pp, 45 pls

6631 Vallance, Aymer. English Church Screens; being great roods,
      screenwork and rood-lofts of parish churches in England
      and Wales. London: Batsford; New York: Scribner's,
      1936. 103pp, ill, pls (some color)

6632 _____ . Greater English Church Screens. Being great
      roods, screenwork and rood-lofts in cathedral, monastic
      and collegiate churches in England and Wales. London:
      Batsford, 1947. color frontis, 155 pls

CHURCH FURNITURE†

6633   Anson, Peter Frederick. Fashions in Church Furnishings, 1840-1940. London: Faith Pr, 1960; London: Studio Vista, 1965; New York: London House and Maxwell, 1966. 383pp, ill, bib

6634   Barr, James. Anglican Church Architecture, with some remarks upon ecclesiastical furniture. Oxford: J. H. Parker, 1842; 2nd ed. 1843; 3rd ed. 1846. 126pp, ill; 216pp, 88 ill V & A, DeWint, BM

6635   Beasley, E. A., comp. Burrow's Glossary of Church Architecture, Furniture and Fittings. A concise and reliable handbook for lovers of old churches. London: E. J. Burrow, 1937. 88pp, ill with drawings

6636 *Bond, Francis. The Chancel of English Churches; the altar, reredos, lenten veil, communion table, altar rails, houseling cloth, piscina, credence, sedilia, aumbry, sacrament house, Easter Sepulchre, squint, etc. London; New York: H. Milford, Oxford U. Pr, 1916. 274pp, ill, bib NN, DLC, NNC-Ave

6637   _____. Fonts and Font Covers. London; New York; Toronto: H. Frowde, Oxford U. Pr, 1908. 347pp, 426 ill, bib NN, DLC, BM

6638   _____. Wood Carvings in English Churches. Vol. I. Misericords from the 13th to the 17th Century; Vol. II. Stalls and Tabernacle Works; bishop's thrones and chancel; chairs. 2 vol. London; New York: Henry Frowde, Oxford U. Pr, 1910. ill, bib DLC, BM

6639   Boyd, Thomas M. Worship in Wood. Chicago: American Seating Co, 1927. 88pp, ill, pls (A history of furniture used in worship from the earliest times) PPULC, DLC, CU, MiGr

6640   Clinch, George. Old English Churches: Their Architecture, Furniture, Decoration, Vestments, Plate, and Monuments. London: L. U. Gill, 1900; 2nd ed. enl. 1902; New York: Scribner; London: Gill, 1903. 264pp, ill; 312pp, ill BPL

6641   Cox, George Henry, 1838-1928. Chancel and Its Furnishing. Gettysburg: Hammond, 1905. 14pp PPLT

---

†See also Shaker furniture entries listed under American furniture in Section V. Its design was closely linked to a deeply religious belief in "rightness" of form, and a simplicity completely free from worldliness and ostentation.

6642 Cox, John Charles, 1843-1919. Bench-ends in English Churches. London; New York: H. Milford, Oxford U. Pr, 1916. 208pp, 164 ill, bib MiGr

6643 * _____. English Church Fittings, Furniture and Accessories.... Introd. by Aymer Vallance. London: Batsford; New York: Putnam's, 1923; London: 1933. 320pp, ill, pls NN, DLC, MiGr, BM

6644 _____. Pulpits, Lecterns and Organs in English Churches. London; New York: Oxford U. Pr, 1915. 228pp, 155 ill NN, BM, MiGr

6645 _____, and Alfred Harvey. English Church Furniture, with 121 illustrations. London: Methuen; New York: Dutton, 1907; 2nd ed. London: 1908. 397pp, ill, 31 pls PPL, NN, MiGr

6646 Cussans, John Edwin, 1837-1899. Inventory of Furniture and Ornaments Remaining in All the Parish Churches of Hertfordshire in the Last Reign of King Edward the 6th. Oxford: J. Parker, 1873. 139pp MH, MdBP, SKM

6647 Cutts, Edward Lewes. An Essay on Church Furniture and Decoration. London: J. Crockford, 1854. 143pp, ill, 9 pls (part color), color frontis TxU, SKM, DLC, NNC-Ave

6648 Dearmer, Percy, 1867-1936. 50 Pictures of Gothic Altars. London; New York: Longmans, Green, 1910; London: A. R. Mowbray, 1922. 211pp, 50 pls DLC

6649 Delderfield, Eric R. A Guide to Church Furniture. Newton Abbot: David & Charles, 1966; New York: Taplinger, 1967. 157pp, 32 ill

6650 French, Gilbert James, 1804-1866. Illustrated Price List of Articles of Church Furniture in the Exhibition of 1851. Manchester, Eng: 1851. ill SKM

6651 Green, Edmund Tyrrell. Baptismal Fonts, Classified and Illustrated. London: S.P.C.K., 1928. 183pp, ill

6652 Heales, Alfred, 1827-1898. The Archaeology of the Christian Altar in Western Europe; with its adjuncts, furniture, and ornaments. London: Roworth & Co., printers, 1881. 96pp, ill MdBP

6653 _____. The History and Law of Church Seats, or pews. 2 vol. in 1. London: Butterworths, 1872. ill, text, bib (Primarily on pew-rights) TxU, DLC

6654 Hole, William, 1710-1791. The Ornaments of Churches

Considered, with a particular view to the late decoration
of the parish church of St. Margaret, Westminster. To
which is subjoined ... history of said church; an account
of the altar-piece, and stained glass window.... Ed. and
with Introd. by Thomas Wilson. Oxford: W. Jackson,
printer, 1761. 143, 38, 8 pp, 8 pls MdBP, DLC, DeWint

6655 Hope, William Henry St. John. English Altars from Illuminated Manuscripts. London: Alcuin Club, 1899. BM

6656 Howkins, Christopher. Discovering Church Furniture. Tring:
Shire Publications, 1969. 80pp, ill

6657 Instrumenta Ecclesiastica. Edited by the Ecclesiological Late
Cambridge Camden Society. London: J. Van Voorst,
1847; vol. II. 1856. no text, 72 pls--working drawings;
82 pls DeWint, DLC

6658 King, Harold Charles, 1869- . The Chancel and the Altar.
Pref. by Percy Dearmer. London; Oxford: Mowbray,
1911. 197pp, ill, 47 pls MB

6659 LeSage, Robert. Vestments and Church Furniture. Tr. from
French by Fergus Murphy. London: Burns & Oates, 1960.
155pp, bib

6660 *Lewer, Henry William, and James Charles Wall. The Church
Chests of Essex. London: Talbot, 1913. ill MH, NN

6661 Luebke, Wilhelm, 1826-1893. Ecclesiastical Art in Germany
During the Middle Ages. Tr. from 5th German ed. with
appendix by L. A. Wheatley. Edinburgh: T. C. Jack;
London: Cassell, 1870; 4th ed. Edinburgh: 1877. 299pp,
184 engravings, pls (2/3 of book devoted to furniture)
MiGr

6662 Lupson, Edward John. St. Nicholas' Church, Great Yarmouth: its history, organ, pulpit, library, etc.... Yarmouth, Eng: Author, 1881. 250pp, ill, pl DLC

6663 Modern Churches, Church Furniture and Decoration, containing
descriptions of the most beautiful churches of Europe, their
furniture and decorations. London: H. Cox, 1867. 240pp,
pls DeWint

6664 Morgan, Frederick Charles. Church Chests of Herefordshire.
Hereford, Eng: 1948. 22pp, ill DLC

6665 Needham, Albert. How to Study an Old Church. London:
Batsford, 1944; 2nd ed. rev. & enl. 1945; 3rd ed. rev.
& enl. 1948. 72pp, 450 drawings; 78pp, 480 drawings,
2 color pls; 88pp, ill

6666 Paley, F. A. Illustrations of Baptismal Fonts. London:
Van Voorst, 1844. ill ECB

6667 Peacock, Edward, ed. English Church Furniture, Ornaments
and Decorations, at the Period of the Reformation, as
exhibited in a list of goods destroyed in certain Lincolnshire churches, A.D. 1566. London: John Camden Hotten, 1866. 271pp, ill MiGr

6668 Petersen, Joan Margaret. Altar Frontals: their history and
construction, with special reference to English tradition
and practice. London: Church Information Office, 1962.
14pp, 6 pls

6669 Pocknee, Cyril Edward. The Christian Altar: In History and
Today. London: Mowbray, 1963. 112pp, ill, bib

6670 Pugin, Augustus Charles, and Augustus Welby Northmore Pugin.
Gothic Architecture Selected from Various Ancient Edifices
in England. Vol. 2 of 5 vol. London: 1831-1838; Re-
print without text of the 5 vol. in 2. Cleveland: D. H.
Dansen, 1914. (Vol. 2) 337 pls of church furniture
MiGr

6671 Roe, Frederick Gordon. Ancient Church Chests and Chairs
in the Home Counties Round Greater London; being the
tour ... through the churches of Middlesex, Hertfordshire,
Essex, Kent and Surrey. Fore. by C. Reginald Grundy.
London: Batsford, 1929. 130pp, 95 ill

6672 Sadlowski, Erwin L. Sacred Furnishings of Churches. Washington, D.C.: Catholic University of America, 1951.
176pp, ill

6673 Taylor, Florence. The Church and Its Furniture. London:
National Society, S.P.C.K., 1943; 1953. 48pp

6674 Wells-Cole, Anthony, and Richard Fawcett. Oak Furniture
from Yorkshire Churches. Exhibition, Temple Newsom
House, August-September 1971. Leeds: City Art Gallery,
1971. 54pp, ill (To 1700)

6675 Wright, John, 1836-1919. Some Notable Altars in the Church
of England and the American Episcopal Church. New
York: Macmillan, 1908. 383pp, 114 pls

ECCLESIASTICAL COSTUME AND NEEDLEWORK

6676 Clayton, Henry James. The Ornaments of the Ministers, as
shown on English monumental brasses. London: Alcuin
Club Collections, vol. 22, 1919. 190pp, ill BM

6677   Dearmer, Reverend Percy.   Linen Ornaments of the Church.
       London: Oxford U. Pr, Milford, 1929.   26pp, ill   DLC

6678   _____.   The Ornaments of the Ministers.   London: A. R.
       Mowbray, 1911; new ed.   London: Mowbray; Milwaukee:
       Morehouse, 1920; London: 1930.   194pp, 34 ill, 41 pls;
       136pp, 35 ill, 46 pls

6679   Dillon, John, d. 1831, comp.   Inventory of the Ornaments,
       Reliques, Jewels, Vestments, Books, etc., belonging to
       the Cathedral Church of Glasgow....   Glasgow: for the
       Maitland Club, 1831; reprint. New York: AMS Pr, 1974.
       31pp   DLC

6680   Dolby, Anastasia Marice.   Church Vestments: their origin,
       use, and ornament practically illustrated.   London: Chap-
       man & Hall, 1868.   208pp, ill, 37 pls, color frontis   BM

6681   French, Gilbert James.   The Tippets of the Canons Ecclesias-
       tical.   London: G. Bell, 1850.   28pp, ill   (Chaplains',
       priests' and choir tippets, scarfs, stoles)   CtY

6682   Hartshorne, Emily Sophia.   Designs for Church Embroidery
       and Crewel Work, from old examples.   London: Griffith
       & Farran; New York: Dutton, 1880.   45pp, 18 pls of 60
       patterns   CSmH

6683   Lambert, Miss (A.).   Church Needlework, by F. S.   London:
       1844.   BM

6684   LeSage, Robert.   Vestments and Church Furniture.   Tr. from
       French by Fergus Murphy.   London: Burns & Oates, 1960.
       155pp, bib

6685   Maclagan, Eric Robert Dalrymple.   English Ecclesiastical
       Embroideries, 13th to 16th century, in the V & A Museum.
       London: HMSO, 1907; rev. & reprinted. 1916; rev. by
       P. G. Trendell, with heraldic notes by A. Van de Put.
       London: 1930.   29pp, 3 ill; 45pp, 33 ill; 47pp, 35 ill,
       28 pls, bib; 68pp, ill, 40 pls, bib

6686   Museum Extension Project.   Pennsylvania.   Ecclesiastical
       Costumes.   Pittsburgh?:   1943.   44 color pls   (W. P. A.
       work)

6687   Pugin, Augustus Welby Northmore.   Glossary of Ecclesiastical
       Ornament and Costume, compiled from ancient authorities
       and examples.   London: 1841; 2nd ed. enl. & rev. by
       B. Smith. London: H. G. Bohn, 1846; 1868.   ...; 245pp,
       73 color pls

6688   *Raiment for the Lord's Service: a 1000 years of western

vestments. Fore. by John Maxon. Essay by Christa C.
Mayer-Thurman. Exhibition. November 1975-January
1976. Chicago: Art Institute, 1975. ill, bib, gloss
(Roman Catholic and Anglican, 12th to 20th century)

6689 Rock, Daniel. Textile Fabrics: a descriptive catalogue of
the collection of Church Vestments, dresses, silk stuffs,
needlework and tapestries in the South Kensington Museum.
London: HMSO, 1870. 353pp, 20 pls BM

6690 Tyack, George Smith. Historic Dress of the Clergy. London: W. Andrews, 1897. 134pp, ill

JUDAICA AND JEWISH CEREMONIAL OBJECTS

6691 Exhibition of Jewish Ceremonial Art, November-December
1951. Detroit: Institute of Arts, 1951. 45pp, ill, bib

6692 Freehof, Lillian B., and Bucky King. Embroideries and
Fabrics for Synagogue and Home; 5000 years of ornamental
needlework. New York: Hearthside Pr, 1966. 224pp, ill,
bib

6693 Grimwade, Arthur Girling, and others, comp. Treasures of
a London Temple; a descriptive catalogue of the ritual
plate, mantles, and furniture of the Spanish and Portuguese
Jews' Synagogue in Bevis Marks.... Introd. by S. Gaon.
Fore. by L. D. Barnett. London: Taylor's Foreign Pr,
1951. 68pp, ill, bib MiD, DLC

6694 Gutman, Joseph. Jewish Ceremonial Art. New York: T.
Yoseloff, 1964. 37pp, 60 pp of ill, bib

6695 Schoenberger, Guido, and Tom L. Freudenheim. Silver and
Judaica Collection of Mr. and Mrs. Michael Zagayski.
New York: Jewish Museum, 1963. ill

6696 Volavkova, Hana. The Synagogue Treasures of Bohemia and
Moravia. Tr. by G. Hort, and Roberta F. Samsour.
Prague: Sfinx, 1949. 38pp, ill (Includes Bohemian tex-
tiles)

SANTOS AND CHRISTIAN FOLK ART

6697 Boyd, E. (pseud.). New Mexico Santos. Santa Fe: Schools
of American Research, 1953. 4pp, ill

6698 _____ . New Mexico Santos: How to Name Them. Santa
Fe: Museum of New Mexico and International Folk Art
Foundation, 1966. chiefly ill

6699 _____. Saints and Saint Makers of New Mexico. Santa
      Fe: Laboratory of Anthropology, 1946. 139pp, ill, 24
      pls, bib

6700 Espinosa, Jose Edmundo. Saints in the Valley: Christian
      sacred images in the history, life and folk art of Spanish
      New Mexico. Albuquerque: U. of NM Pr, 1960. 122pp,
      ill, bib

6701 Frankenstein, Alfred Victor. Angels over the Altar; Christian
      folk art in Hawaii and the South Seas. Honolulu: U. of
      Hawaii Pr, 1961. 101pp, ill, pls, bib

6702 Giffords, Gloria Kay. Mexican Folk Retablos; masterpieces
      on Tin. Tucson: U. of Arizona Pr, 1974. 160pp, ill,
      bib

6703 Glubock, Shirley. The Art of the Spanish in the United States
      and Puerto Rico. New York: Macmillan, 1972. 48pp,
      ill (Juvenile literature)

6704 Mills, George Thompson. The People of the Saints. Colorado
      Springs: Taylor Museum, 1967. 71pp, 32 pls (New
      Mexico santos)

6705 Santos; an exhibition of the religious folk art of New Mexico,
      Amon Carter Museum of Western Art. Fort Worth, Tex:
      the Museum, 1964. 30pp, ill

6706 Santos of the Southwest. The Denver Art Museum Collection.
      Denver: Art Museum Winter Quarterly, 1953. 32pp, ill,
      bib

6707 Shalkop, Robert L. Wooden Saints; the santos of New Mexico.
      Feldafing: Buchheim Verlag, 1967? 63pp, ill, 16 pls

FOLK ART

Folk art is one of the most difficult terms to define. Some would remove the work of craftsmen--believing that skilled craft is the work only of trained craftsmen and that folk art is the product of untrained dabblers. Others concentrate on the art in folk art, and take what they will from arts and crafts as long as it mirrors a seeming personal view and, perhaps, a certain light-hearted even whimsical attitude.

European folk art differs from the more egalitarian American folk art because it is defined as having been made and used by peasants. (We have no peasants in America.)

Many people consider much of the handwork of the Shakers to be folk art. And yet the Shakers were skilled craftsmen and penultimate entrepreneurs. Many people consider anything done by the Pennsylvania Germans to be folk art--probably only because it was decorated in a pleasant "peasant-y" way with designs from the old country, done in bright colors.

The few tens of books on folk art included in this category are only part of the body of work on the subject as it is defined by a number of people. Inclusion here is based on the authors' use of "folk art." Other works, many on the same subjects, are to be found under various American arts, crafts and handicrafts: pottery, textiles, signs and signboards, toys, furniture, weathervanes, quilts, gravestones, and paper.

AMERICAN FOLK ART

6708   Abby Aldrich Rockefeller Folk Art Collection. Gallery Guide. Williamsburg, Va: Colonial Williamsburg, 1975. 32pp, ill of 30 pieces

6709   Adamson, Jack E. Illustrated Handbook of Ohio Sewer Pipe Folk Art. Barberton, Ohio: 1973. 88pp, chiefly ill

6710   American Folk Art; an exhibition in honor of Edith Gregor

Halpert. March-April 1973. Palm Beach, Fla: Society
of the Four Arts, 1973. 16pp, ill (Folk art from Halpert's collection)

6711 American Folk Art from the Abby Aldrich Rockefeller Folk
Art Collection. Catalog. Williamsburg, Va: Colonial
Williamsburg, 1959; rev. ed. 1966. 46pp, ill; 47pp, ill

6712 American Folk Art from the Shelburne Museum in Vermont.
Exhibition. Albright-Knox Art Gallery, Buffalo, December
1965-January 1966. Buffalo, NY: 1965. 36pp, ill

6713 American Folk Art; the art of the common man in America,
1750-1900. New York: Museum of Modern Art, 1932;
reprint. New York: Arno Pr, for MOMA, 1969. 52pp,
ill, pls, bib (Includes "American Folk Art," by Holger
Cahill)

6714 American Folk Art: the exhibit of 1932. A reassembly of
the first exhibit, January-March 1968. Abby Aldrich
Rockefeller Folk Art Collection. Williamsburg, Va: 1968.
19pp, ill, color pls

6715 American Heritage; an exhibition of paintings and crafts.
Denver Art Museum, March-April 1948. Denver: 1948.
28pp, ill

6716 Andrews, Ruth. The Metal of the State. Exhibition catalog.
New York: Museum of American Folk Art, 1973. u.p.,
ill, 196 pieces catalogued (New York State)

6717 *Bishop, Robert Charles. American Folk Sculptures. Gravestones, trade signs, weathervanes, scrimshaw, cigar store
Indians, decoys, whirligigs, chalk objects, handmade pottery, Mid- and Southwestern religious figures .., Of
special documentary interest: over 40 early photographs
and prints showing specific carvings in their early surroundings. Fore. by Mary Black. New York: Dutton,
1974. 392pp, 700 ill, 100 color pls, bib

6718 Boyd, E. (pseud. for Hall, Elizabeth Boyd White). New
Mexico Tinwork. Santa Fe: School of American Research,
1953. 41pp, ill

6719 _____. Popular Arts of Colonial New Mexico. Santa Fe:
Museum of International Folk Art, 1959. 51pp, ill, bib

6720 Brewington, Marion Vernon. Shipcarvers of North America.
Barre, Mass: Barre Publishing Co, 1962; New York:
Dover; London: Constable, 1972. 173pp, ill, bib (Ameri-
can & Canadian figureheads, etc., to 1900)

6721 Brill, Marna. Paper of the State. Works on Paper in New

York State. Exhibition. New York: Museum of American Folk Art, 1976. 16pp, 20 ill

6722 Buchert, Ilse, and Alexander Nesbitt. Weathercocks and
Weathercreatures; some examples of early American folk
art from the collection of the Shelburne Museum, Vermont.
Newport, RI: Third & Elm Pr, 1970. 46pp, ill

6723 [No entry.]

Cahill, Holger. See: American Folk Art; the art of the
common man....

6724 Carraher, Ronald George. Artists in Spite of Art. New
York; London: Van Nostrand Reinhold, 1970. 112pp
of ill

6725 Christensen, Erwin Ottomar. American Crafts and Folk Arts.
Washington, D.C.: R. B. Luce, 1964; Bombay: Vora,
1970. 90pp, ill, bib

6726 *_____. The Index of American Design. Introd. by Holger
Cahill. Washington, D.C.: The National Gallery; New
York: Macmillan, 1950. 229pp, 378 color ill, bib
(Government-sponsored W. P. A. research. Very fine.)

6727 _____. Popular Art in the United States, with illustrations
from the Index of American Design, National Gallery of
Art, Washington. London: Penguin, 1948. 30pp, 32 pls,
bib

6728 Cook, Gervis Frere-, ed. The Decorative Arts of the Mariner. London: Cassell; Boston: Little, Brown, 1966.
296pp, ill (Ship models, navigation instruments, scrimshaw, etc)

6729 An Eye on America. Folk Art from the Stewart E. Gregory
Collection. Fore. by Jean Lipman. Exhibition. New
York: Museum of American Folk Art, 1972. u. p., ill

6730 Fendelman, Helaine W. Tramp Art. An itinerant's folk art.
New York: Dutton, 1975. 127pp, 120 ill, 11 color pls,
bib (To accompany an exhibit at Museum of American
Folk Art, 1975. 1860s to 1930s)

6731 *Fitzgerald, Ken. Weathervanes and Whirligigs. New York:
Bramhall, C. N. Potter, 1967. 186pp, 180 ill

6732 [No entry.]

Foley, Daniel J. See: Priscilla Sawyer Lord. Folk Arts
and Crafts....

6733 Fried, Frederick. Artists in Wood; American carvers of
      cigar-store Indians, show figures, and circus wagons.
      New York: C. N. Potter, 1970. 297pp, 260 (30 color)
      ill, bib

6734 _____. Pictorial History of the Carousel. New York:
      A. S. Barnes, 1964; New York: Crown, 197-? 231pp,
      chiefly ill, bib (Band organs, carved wooden carousel
      animals)

6735 The Glen-Sanders Collection from Scotia, New York. Exhi-
      bition. Abby Aldrich Rockefeller Folk Art Collection,
      January-February 1966. Williamsburg, Va: Colonial Wil-
      liamsburg, 1966. 47pp, ill

6736 Glubock, Shirley. The Art of the Spanish in the United States
      and Puerto Rico. New York: Macmillan, 1972. 48pp,
      ill (Juvenile literature)

6737 Hall, Michael D. Folk Sculpture: the personal and the ec-
      centric. Exhibition. November 1971-January 1972.
      Bloomfield, Mich: Cranbrook Academy of Art, 1971.
      28pp, ill

6738 Halpert, Edith Gregor. Folk Art Collection: sculpture,
      weathervanes, paintings in oil, paintings in watercolors
      and pastels; needlework and painted textiles, fracturs and
      drawings, chalkware. New York: n.p., n.d. u.p., ill

6739 *Hemphill, Herbert W., Jr., ed. Folk Sculpture USA. Exhi-
      bition. March-May 1976, Brooklyn Museum; June- , Los
      Angeles County Museum. Brooklyn: 1976. 96pp, 107
      (16 color) ill, bib (Essays: 1. "Folk Sculpture without
      Folk," Daniel Robbins. 2. "A Sorting Process: the artist
      as collector," conversation between Sarah Faunce and
      Michael D. Hall. 3. "American Folk Sculpture: some
      considerations of its ethnic heritage," Michael Kan)

6740 _____, and Julia Weissman. Twentieth-century American
      Folk Art and Artists. New York: Dutton, 1974. 237pp,
      ill, color pl, bib

6741 Isaacson, Philip M. The American Eagle. Boston: N.Y.
      Graphic Society, 1975. text, 160 ill, 64 color pls

6742 Johnson, Bruce. American Cat-alogue. The Cat in American
      folk art. New York: Avon Books, in association with the
      Museum of American Folk Art, 1976. ill (some color),
      124 pieces

6743 Jones, Agnes Halsey, and Louis Clark Jones. New-found
      Folk Art of the Young Republic. Cooperstown, NY: State
      Historical Society, 1960. 35pp, pls

6744 Jones, Louis Clark. Outward Signs of Inner Beliefs: sym-
      bols of American patriotism. Exhibition. Fenimore
      House. Cooperstown, NY: NY State Historical Associa-
      tion, 1975. 76pp, 77 ill (16th-18th century)

6745 _____, and Marshall B. Davidson. American Folk Art in
      Fenimore House, Cooperstown, NY. New York: Metro-
      politan Museum, 1953. 29pp, color ill

6746 Kauffman, Henry J. Pennsylvania Dutch American Folk Art.
      Ed. by C. Geoffrey Holme. New York; London: America
      Studio Books, 1946; rev. & enl. New York: Dover, 1964.
      136pp, ill, pls, bib; 146pp, 275 ill, bib

6747 Kaye, Myrna. Yankee Weathervanes. New York: Dutton,
      1975. 236pp, drawings, bib

6748 Klamkin, Charles. Weather Vanes; the history, design and
      manufacture of an American folk art. New York: Haw-
      thorn, 1973. 209pp, 350 ill

6749 Klamkin, Marian. Hands to Work: Shaker folk art and indus-
      tries. New York: Dodd, Mead, 1972. 212pp, ill, bib

6750 _____. Marine Antiques. New York: Dodd, Mead, 1975.
      270 (23 color) ill

6751 _____, and Charles Klamkin. Woodcarving: an American
      folk art. New York: Hawthorn, 1974. 224pp, 360 photo-
      graphs

6752 Kranz, Jacqueline L. American Nautical Art and Antiques.
      New York: Crown, 1975. 248pp, 320 ill, color pls, bib

6753 *Laughton, (Leonard George) Carr. Old Ship Figure-Heads
      and Sterns, with which are associated galleries, hanging-
      pieces, catheads and diverse other matters that concern
      the "grace and countenance" of old sailing ships. London:
      Halton & T. Smith; New York: Minton, Balch, 1925.
      281pp, ill, 55 pls (part color), color frontis NN, NjP

6754 *Lichten, Frances. Folk Art of Rural Pennsylvania. New
      York; London: Scribner, 1946; reprint. 1963. 276pp, ill
      (part color)

6755 _____. Pennsylvania Dutch Folk Arts from the Geesey Col-
      lection and Others of Philadelphia. Philadelphia: Museum,
      195-? ill, bib

6756 Lipman, Jean. American Folk Art in Wood, Metal and Stone,
      1750-1850. New York: Pantheon, 1948; republication.
      New York: Dover; London: Constable, 1972. 193pp, ill,
      bib; 195pp, 183 ill, 4 color pls, bib

6757 _____. Provocative Parallels. Naive early Americans:
       international sophisticates. New York: Dutton, 1975.
       200 ill (Compares folk art and 20th century art)

6758 * _____, and Alice Winchester. The Flowering of American
       Folk Art 1776-1876. New York: Viking, 1974; London:
       Thames & Hudson, 1974. 288pp, ill (many in color), bib

6759 *Little, Nina Fletcher. The Abby Aldrich Rockefeller Folk Art
       Collection, a descriptive catalogue. Williamsburg, Va:
       Colonial Williamsburg, 1957. 402pp, ill, bib

6760 _____. Country Art in New England, 1790-1840. Stur-
       bridge, Mass: Old Sturbridge Village, 1960; 2nd rev. ed.
       1965. 32pp, ill; 40pp, ill

6761 Lord, Priscilla Sawyer, and Daniel J. Foley. The Folk Arts
       and Crafts of New England. Philadelphia: Chilton, 1965.
       282pp, ill, bib

6762 Louisiana Folk Art. Exhibition. October-December 1972. Baton
       Rouge: Anglo-American Art Museum, 1972. 44pp, ill

6763 Masterpieces of American Folk Art. Introd. by Thomas Arm-
       strong, III, and fore. by John Gordon. Exhibition. Lin-
       croft, NJ: Monmouth Museum, 1975. 132pp, 210 ill

6764 Nelson, Cyril I., comp. A Calendar of American Folk Art.
       (1976). New York: Dutton, 1975. 50 pieces ill

6765 Pendergast, Anthony W., and W. Porter Ware. Cigar Store
       Figures in American Folk Art. Chicago: Lightner Pub-
       lishing, 1953. 73pp, ill

6766 Pinckney, Pauline A. American Figureheads and Their Carvers.
       New York: W. W. Norton, 1940; Port Washington, NY:
       Kennikat Pr, 1969. 223pp, ill, bib

6767 Polley, Robert L., ed. America's Folk Art; treasures of
       American folk arts and crafts in distinguished museums
       and collections. Introd. by James A. H. Conrad. New
       York: Putnam, 1968. 189pp, ill

6768 Riccardi, Saro John. Pennsylvania Dutch Folk Art and Archi-
       tecture. A Selective Annotated Bibliography. (Reprint
       from Bulletin of the New York Public Library.) New York:
       NYPL, 1942. 15pp

6769 Robinson, Elinor. American Folk Sculpture, the work of 18th
       and 19th century craftsmen. Exhibition. October 1931-
       January 1932. Newark, NJ: Newark Museum, 1931.
       108pp, ill, pls, bib NNC-Ave

6770 Sabine, Ellen S. American Folk Art. Princeton, NJ: Van
       Nostrand, 1958. 132pp, 61 (11 color) ill

6771 Sanborn, Katherine Abbott, 1839-1917. Hunting Indians in a
       Taxi Cab. Boston: R. G. Badger, 1911. 74pp, ill, pls
       (Cigar store Indians) DLC

6772 Smith, Elmer Lewis. The Folk Art of Pennsylvania Dutch-
       land. Photos by Mel Horst. Witmer, Pa: Applied Arts,
       1966. 41pp, 100 ill

6773 Spencer, Corinne W., comp. Bibliography of Weathervanes.
       New York: Avery Library, Columbia U., 1938. 12pp type-
       script (Chiefly periodical literature references) NNC-Ave

6774 Stoudt, John Joseph. Consider the Lilies, How They Grow.
       Allentown, Pa: Pennsylvania German Folklore Society,
       2nd annual vol., 1937; rev. ed. as Pennsylvania Folk-Art;
       an interpretation. Allentown: Schlechter's, 1948. 402 pp,
       ill (some color), bib

6775 Turner, Robert P., ed., and Lewis Miller. Sketches and Chroni-
       cles. Princeton, NJ: Pyne Pr, 1968; 1972. 212pp, ill

6776 200 Years of American Sculpture. Whitney Museum, New
       York. Boston: Godine, 1976. 350pp, 414 (64 color) ill,
       bib (Includes folk sculpture)

6777 A Virginia Sampler: 18th, 19th and 20th century Virginia
       Folk Art. Exhibition. Roanoke, Va: Fine Arts Center,
       1976. 30 pieces ill

6778 Welsh, Peter C. American Folk Art: the art and spirit of a
       people; from the Eleanor and Mabel Van Alstyne Collection.
       Washington, D.C.: Smithsonian, 1965. u.p., ill, bib

FOLK ART OTHER THAN AMERICAN

6779   Arneberg, Halfdan. Norwegian Peasant Art. Vol. 1. Wo-
       men's Handicrafts. Vol. 2. Men's Handicrafts. 2 vol.
       Oslo: Fabritius, 1949-51. 15pp, 80 pls; 15pp, 110 pls

6780   Banateanu, Tancred, and M. Focsa. The Ornament in the
       Rumanian Folk Art. Bucharest: Meridiane Publishing
       House, 1963. 50pp, pls

6781   Bossert, Helmuth Theodor. Folk Art of Asia, Africa and the
       Americas. (Combined: Folk Art of Primitive Peoples
       and Decorative Art of Asia and Egypt.) New York: Prae-
       ger, 1964. 23pp, 80 color pls

6782   _____. Folk Art of Europe. Tr. by Sybil Moholy Nagy.
       2 parts. New York: Praeger, 1953; London: A. Zwem-
       mer, 1954; New York: 1964. 25pp, ill, 88 pls

6783   _____. Peasant Art in Europe, ... reproducing 2100 ex-
       amples of peasant ornament and handicraft taken directly
       from unpublished originals. Berlin: Wasmuth, 1926;
       London: E. Benn; New York: E. Weyhe, 1927. 45pp,
       ill, 132 pls (some color), bib   DLC, PPULC

6784   _____. Peasant Art in Europe; nearly 1900 examples of
       European folk-art products, especially ornaments, ceramics,
       embroideries, wickerwork and basketwork, fabrics, wood,
       glass and metalwork. London: Simpkin Marshall, 1938.
       55pp, 120 pls   BM

6785   _____. Peasant Art of Europe and Asia. New York:
       Praeger; Tubingen: E. Wasmuth, 1959. 16pp, ill,
       44 pls

6786   Buttitta, Antonino. Folk Art in Sicily. English ed. by Arthur
       Oliver and Michele Mignogna. Palermo: S. F. Flaccovio,
       1961. 327pp, ill

6787   Czarnecka, Irena, comp. Folk Art in Poland. Tr. from
       Polish (1957). Warsaw: Polonia, 1958. 234pp, chiefly
       plates

6788   Fel, Edit. Hungarian Peasant Art. Tr. from Hungarian.
       London: Batsford, 1961; 2nd ed. Budapest: Corvina,
       1969. 312pp, ill (Pottery, costume, furniture, carving,
       embroidery, musical instruments, buildings)

6789   _____. Saints, Soldiers, Shepherds. Budapest: Corvina,
       1966. 116pp, ill (Human figures in pottery, carved horn
       & wood, embroidery, and gingerbread molds)

6790   Feldon, Victoria. Lithuanian Folk Art. Los Angeles: 1966?
        77pp, pls

6791   Fletcher, Geoffrey S. Popular Art in England. London:
        Harrap, 1962. 78pp, ill

6792   Glubock, Shirley. The Art of the Spanish in the United States
        and Puerto Rico. New York: Macmillan, 1972. 48pp,
        ill (Juvenile literature)

6793   Hansen, Hans Jurgen, ed. European Folk Art in Europe and
        the Americas. Contributions by Peter Anker and others.
        Introd. by Robert Wildhaber. Tr. from German (1967)
        by Mary Whittall. London: Thames & Hudson, 1967;
        New York: McGraw-Hill, 1968. 288pp, 450 ill, 109 color
        pls, bib

6794   Hauglid, Roar, ed., and others. The Native Arts of Norway.
        Oslo: Mittel, 1953. 174pp, ill (Wood carving, rose
        painting, weaving, costumes)

6795   Holme, Charles, ed. Peasant Art in Austria and Hungary.
        Articles by A. S. Levetus, Michael Haberlandt, Aldar K.
        Koeroesfoel. London; New York: The Studio, 1911.
        54pp, ill, 106 (14 color) pls DeWint

6796   _____, ed. Peasant Art in Italy. Contributions by S. J.
        A. Churchill, V. Balzano, Elisa Ricci. London; New
        York: The Studio, 1913. 39pp, 91 pls MiU, NN

6797   _____, ed. Peasant Art in Russia. Articles translated
        by A. B. Boswell. London; New York: The Studio, 1912;
        reprint. 1942. 52pp, ill, 86 (12 color) pls (Includes
        Poland, Lithuania, the Russian Ukraine) MB, NjP

6798   _____, ed. Peasant Art in Sweden, Lapland and Iceland.
        Tr. by E. Adams-Ray. London; New York: The Studio,
        1910. 48pp, ill, 88 (12 color) pls NN, NjP

6799   Hungarian Decorative Folk Art. Budapest: Corvina, for the
        Hungarian Ethnographical (Neprajzi) Museum, 1954. 36pp,
        ill

6800   Il'in, Mikhail Andreevich. Russian Decorative Folk Art. Tr.
        from Russian by A. Shkarovsky. Ed. by J. Katzer.
        Moscow: Foreign Language Publishing House; London:
        Central Books, 1959. 136pp, ill

6801   Lambert, Margaret, and Enid Marx. English Popular and
        Traditional Art. London: Collins, 1946. 48pp, ill, 12
        color pls, bib (Paper, fabric, wood, pottery, straw,
        metal. Toys, valentines, figureheads, etc.) ViU

6802   _____, and _____. English Popular Art. London; New
        York: Batsford, 1951. 120pp, ill, 8 pls

6803   Manga, Janos. Herdsmen's Art in Hungary. Tr. by Kornel
        Balas. Budapest: Corvina, 1972. 85pp, ill, 58 pls, bib
        (19th century carvings)

6804   Miller, Margaret M., and Sigmund Aarseth. Norwegian Rose-
        maling; decorative painting on wood. New York: Scrib-
        ner, 1974. 211pp, ill, bib

6805   Mookerjee, Ajitcoomar. Folk Art of Bengal. Calcutta: U.
        of Calcutta, 1939; new & rev. ed. 1946. 50pp, ill, 42
        pls; 70pp, ill, pls

6806   Mrlian, Rudolf, ed. Slovak Folk Art. Tr. by Libuse Vok-
        rova-Ambrosova. Prague: Artia, 1953. ill

6807   Munsterberg, Hugo. The Folk Arts of Japan. Pref. by
        Soetsu Yanagi. Tokyo; Rutland, Vt: Tuttle, 1958. 168pp,
        ill, 10 color pls

6808   Okamura, Kichiemon, and Kageo Muraoka. Folk Arts and
        Crafts of Japan. Tokyo: Weatherhill & Heibonsha, 1975.
        168pp, ill

6809   Payant, Felix, ed. Primitive and Peasant Art, assembled
        from special issues of Design, a monthly magazine de-
        voted to the decorative arts. Syracuse, NY: Keramic
        Studio Publishing, 1932. 158pp, ill, pls (some color)

6810   Porter, Katherine Anne. Outline of Mexican Popular Arts
        and Crafts. (From the collection of Roberto A. Turnbull.)
        Los Angeles: Young & McCallister, 1922. 56pp, ill

6811   Reeves, Ruth. Folk Arts of India: metal, ceramics, jewelry,
        textiles and wood. Exhibition of the R. Reeves Memorial
        Collection at Syracuse University, and related works. Ed.
        & with introd. by Alexandra K. Schmeckebier. Syracuse:
        School of Art, the University, 1967. 93pp, ill

6812   Salvatori, Giuseppe. Rustic and Popular Art in Lithuania.
        Milano: Casa Editrice, Gea, 1925. 43pp, ill, pls (2
        color), bib

TEXTILES AND TEXTILE ARTS

TEXTILE FABRICS, MACHINERY AND FIBERS

6813 Ages, J. A. <u>Dutch Textiles</u>. Leigh-on-Sea: F. Lewis, 19-? pls

6814 Albrecht-Mathey, Elisabeth. <u>The Fabrics of Mulhouse and Alsace, 1750-1800</u>. Tr. from French by Cris Magdalino. Leigh-on-Sea: F. Lewis, 1968. 34pp, ill, 55 pls, bib

6815 <u>American Fabrics</u>. Quarterly. New York: Reporter Publications, 1946-date. ill, samples

6816 Archer, Thomas Croxen. <u>Wool, and Its Applications</u>. London: 1876. See: Bevan, G. P., <u>British Manufacturing Industries</u>, Vol. 5.

6817 Ardenne de Tizac, Jean Henri d'. <u>The Stuffs of China, Weavings and Embroideries</u>. London: Benn, 1924. 14pp, ill, 52 collotype pls (From French collections)

6818 Ashenhurst, Thomas R. <u>An Album of Textile Designs Containing Upwards of 7000 Patterns, suitable for fabrics of every description and an explanation of their arrangements and combinations</u>. Bradford, Eng: Author; Huddersfield, Eng: J. Broadbent, 1881; 2nd enl. ed. as <u>Design in Textile Fabrics</u>. London: Cassell, 1883; 1885; 3rd ed. 1888; London; New York: Cassell, 1899; 1907; ... 220pp, ill; 248pp, ill; 1899: 248pp, 10 color pls

6819 Ashton, Frederick T. <u>The Theory and Practice of the Art of Designing Fancy Cotton and Woollen Cloths from Sample</u>. Philadelphia: H. C. Baird, 1874. 62pp, ill

6820 *Bagnall, William R. <u>The Textile Industries of the United States, including sketches and notices of cotton, woolen, silk, and linen manufactures in the Colonial period</u>. Vol. I. 1639-1810. Cambridge, Mass: The Riverside Pr, 1893; (no more published). 613pp NN

6821   Baines, Sir Edward, 1800-1890. History of the Cotton Manu-
       facture in Great Britain, with a notice of its early history
       in the east and in all quarters of the globe; a description
       of the great mechanical inventions, which have caused its
       extension in Britain, and a view of the present state of the
       manufacture. London: H. Fisher, Fisher & Jackson,
       1835; 2nd ed. reprint with bibliographical introduction by
       W. H. Chaloner. London: Cass, 1966. 544pp, ill, 18
       pls, bib NN, BM

6822   Baldwin, Amos A. A Treatise on Designing and Weaving
       Plain and Fancy Woollen Cloths. New York: Peters &
       Richards, 1878. 53pp, 9 folding pls

6823   Banateanu, Tancred, Gheorghe Focsa, and Emilia Ionescu,
       and others. Folk Costumes, Woven Textiles, and Em-
       broideries of Rumania. Bucharest: State Publishing House
       for Literature and the Arts, 1958. 42pp, ill, 56 color pls

6824   Barker, Aldred Farrer. An Introduction to the Study of Tex-
       tile Design. London: Methuen; New York: Dutton, 1903;
       2nd ed. London: 1915; 3rd ed. 1919. 211pp, ill, pls

6825   _____. Ornamentation and Textile Design. London: Me-
       thuen; New York: F. A. Stokes, 1930. 31pp, ill, 94 pls,
       bib V & A, DeWint, NN

6826   Beaumont, Roberts. Color in Woven Design. London: Whit-
       taker, 1890; 2nd ed. Philadelphia: E. A. Posselt; London:
       Whittaker, 1912; 192-? 440pp, 203 ill, 32 color pls with
       126 designs; 372pp, ill, pls

6827   _____. The Finishing of Textile Fabrics--woollen, worsted,
       union and other cloths. London: Scott, Greenwood, 1909;
       2nd ed. enl. by Alexander Yewdall. London: 1926. 264pp,
       151 ill; 368pp, ill BM

6828   _____. Standard Cloths: structure and manufacture. Lon-
       don: Scott, Greenwood, 1916. 325pp, ill BM

6829   _____. Woven Fabrics at the World's Fair, Chicago.
       Manchester, Eng: Emmott, 1894. 121pp, 44 ill, 2 pls
       (Reprint from The Textile Manufacturer) NN

6830   _____, and Walter George Hill. Dress, Blouse and Cos-
       tume Cloths. London: Pitman, 1921. 579pp, 700 ill BM

6831   Beck, S. William. The Draper's Dictionary. A manual of
       textile fabrics: their history and applications. London:
       The Warehouseman & Draper's Journal, 1882. 377pp DLC

6832   Bendure, Zelma, and Gladys Pfeiffer. America's Fabrics.

Origin and history, manufacture, characteristics and uses.
New York: Macmillan, 1946; 1947. 688pp, many ill (some
color), color pls, bib

6833 Bentley, Phyllis Eleanor. Colne Valley Cloth from the Earliest
Times to the Present Day. Huddersfield, Eng: Chamber
of Commerce, Curwen Pr, 1947. 70pp, ill (Yorkshire)
NN

6834 Bhushan, Jamila Brij. The Costumes and Textiles of India.
Bombay: Taraporevala's Treasure House of Books, 1958.
92pp, ill, pls (part color) DeWint, DLC

6835 Birrell, Verla Leone. The Textile Arts, a handbook of fabric
structure and design processes: ancient and modern
weaving, braiding, printing, and other textile techniques.
New York: Harper, 1959. 514pp, ill, bib

6836 Bischoff, James, 1776-1845. A Comprehensive History of the
Woolen and Worsted Manufactures. 2 vol. London: Smith,
Elder, 1842; reprint. London: Cass, 1968. ill, bib

6837 Blum, Herman. The Loom Has a Brain; the story of the Jacquard weaver's art as applied to the modern Aubusson
tapestry. Philadelphia: Craftex Mills, 1957; rev. ed.
1959; rev. ed. 1966; rev. ed. Philadelphia: Blumhaven
Library & Gallery, 1970. 27pp; 84pp; 123pp, ill; 184pp,
ill NN, DLC

6838 Bolingbroke, Judith Mary. Carolinian Fabrics. Leigh-on-
Sea: F. Lewis, 1969. 20pp, 62 ill, 40 pls (1660-1685)

6839 _____. William and Mary Fabrics. Leigh-on-Sea: F.
Lewis, 1969. 20pp, ill, 40 pls (1688-1702)

6840 Bradbury, Fred. Jacquard Mechanism and Harness Mounting.
Belfast: Author, 1912. 355pp

6841 Branting, Agnes Margaretha Matilda, and Andreas A. F. Lind-
blom. Medieval Embroideries and Textiles in Sweden.
Tr. from Swedish (1928, 1929) by Mrs. S. J. Herrstrom.
2 vol. Uppsala: Almquist & Wiksells Boktryckeri-a.-b.,
1932. I. text; II. 220 pls (some color)

6842 Brett, Katharine B. Bouquets in Textiles; an introduction to
the textile arts. Toronto: Royal Ontario Museum, 1955.
20pp, pls MB

6843 Brief Guide to Persian Woven Fabrics. V & A. London:
1922; 1928; 1937; rev. ed. 1950. 14pp, ill, 16 pls; 20pp,
ill, 16 pls, bib; 31pp, ill BM

6844 Brief Guide to Turkish Woven Fabrics. V & A. London:

1923; 1931; rev. ed. 1950. 23pp, ill, 16 pls; 29pp, ill, 16 pls; 43pp, ill, 16 pls, bib

6845 British Sources of Art Nouveau; an exhibition of 19th and 20th century British textiles and wallpapers. March-May 1969. Manchester, Eng: Whitworth Art Gallery, Victoria U, 1969. 64pp, ill

6846 Britton, Nancy Pence. A Study of Some Early Islamic Textiles in the Museum of Fine Arts. Boston: 1938. 77pp, 100 ill, bib (Mohammedan and Egyptian textiles)

6847 Brockett, Linus Pierpont. The Silk Industry in America. A history prepared for the Centennial Exposition. New York: Silk Association of America, 1876. 237pp, 24 pls MiU, DLC, BM

6848 Bronson, J., and R. Bronson. The Domestic Manufacturers' Assistant and Family Directory in the Arts of Weaving and Dyeing, comprehending a plain system of directions applying to those arts and other branches nearly connected with them in the manufacture of cotton and woollen goods. Utica, NY: W. Williams, printer, 1817. 204pp, ill DeWint

6849 Buckle, John Staley. The Manufacturers' Compendium ... Tables for manufacturers of plain and fancy fabrics. 2 vol. London: Whittaker, 1864-66; 1 vol. Manchester: J. Galt, 1864. 374pp, colored specimens DP, BM

6850 Bunt, Cyril George Edward. Byzantine Fabrics. Leigh-on-Sea: F. Lewis, 1967. 11pp, 57 ill (Woven)

6851 _____. Chinese Fabrics. Leigh-on-Sea: F. Lewis, 1961. 11pp, 46 pls

6852 _____. Florentine Fabrics. Leigh-on-Sea: F. Lewis, 1962. 14pp, ill, 56 pls (Woven)

6853 _____. Hispano-Moresque Fabrics. Leigh-on-Sea: F. Lewis, 1966. 11pp, 44 pls (Woven fabrics, 900-1600)

6854 _____. Persian Fabrics. Leigh-on-Sea: F. Lewis, 1963. 9pp, 46 pls (Woven)

6855 _____. Sicilian and Lucchese Fabrics. Leigh-on-Sea: F. Lewis, 1961. 15pp, 65 ill, 48 pls

6856 _____. The Silks of Lyons. Leigh-on-Sea: F. Lewis, 1960. 15pp, 71 ill, 48 pls

6857 _____. Spanish Silks. Leigh-on-Sea: F. Lewis, 1965. 11pp, 48 pls (ca.1200-1800)

6858 _____ . Tudor and Stuart Fabrics. Leigh-on-Sea: F.
       Lewis, 1961. 15pp, 56 pls (1450-1680)

6859 _____ . Venetian Fabrics. Leigh-on-Sea: F. Lewis,
       1959. 15pp, 50 pls

6860 Burnley, James. The History of Wool and Woolcombing.
       London: S. Low, Marston, Searle & Rivington, 1889.
       487pp, ill, pls DeWint

6861 Butterworth, James, 1771-1837. The Antiquities of the Town,
       and a complete history of the trade of Manchester, with a
       description of Manchester and Salford: to which is added
       an account of the late improvements in the Town. Man-
       chester, Eng: C. W. Leake, for Author, 1822; as A
       Complete History of the Cotton Trade, including also, that
       of the silk, calico-printing, and hat manufactories; with
       remarks on their progress in Bolton, Bury, Stockport,
       Blackburn, and Wigan ... and the town of Manchester.
       Manchester: Leake, printer, 1823. 302pp, ill, pl DLC,
       MB

6862 _____ . The Fustian Manufacturer and Weaver's Complete
       Draught Book; containing 60 draughts for making so many
       different kinds of goods in the fustian manufacture ... to
       which are added a short account of the history of weaving,
       from the remotest period of antiquity, to the present time,
       and a description of the cotton tree. 2nd ed. Manchester:
       G. Bancks; London: C. Law, 18-? (1812?) 8pp, 3 pls
       ICJ, ICRL

6863 Candee, Helen Churchill. Weaves and Draperies, classic and
       modern. New York: F. A. Stokes, 1930. 300pp, 64 ill,
       color frontis, bib DLC, MB

6864 Catalogue of an Exhibition of Chinese and Japanese Brocades,
       1400-1812 A.D. ... collected by Shojiro Nomura; lent by
       Porter E. Sargent. December 1915-January 1916. Buf-
       falo: 1915. 16pp

6865 Catalog of the Special Loan Collection of English Furniture
       and Figured Silks Manufactured in the 17th and 18th Cen-
       tury. Introd. by John H. Pollen. London: Eyre &
       Spottiswoode, 1896. 145pp BM

6866 Cavallo, Adolph S. To Set a Smart Board: fashion as the
       decisive factor in the development of the Scottish linen
       damask industry. Reprint from Business History Review.
       Boston: 1963. 10pp (pp. 49-58)

6867 *A Century of British Fabrics, 1850-1950. Carpets, by J. H.
       Mellor; Printed and Woven Fabrics, by Frank Lewis; Wall

Papers, by E. A. Entwisle. Leigh-on-Sea: F. Lewis,
1955. 23pp, 100 ill, 64 pls

6868   Charlie, William Thomas. Flax and Its Products in Ireland.
London: Bell & Daldy, 1862. 191pp

6869   _____. Flax and Linen. London: 1876. See: Bevan,
G. P., British Manufacturing Industries, Vol. 5.

6870   Chase, William Henry. Five Generations of Loom Builders;
a story of loom building from the days of the craftsmanship of the hand loom weaver to the modern automatic
loom of Draper Corporation. With a supplement on the
origin and development of the arts of spinning and weaving.
Hopedale, Mass: Draper Corp, 1951. 87pp, ill, pls
DeWint

6871   Chat, Rosalyn, ed. Historic Fiberworks/Cranbrook; objects
in fiber from the 3rd to the 20th century. Exhibition.
March-October 1974. Bloomfield Hills, Mich: Cranbrook
Academy of Art, 1974. 19pp, ill

6872   *Ciba Review. Devoted to the history of dyeing, printing,
tanning, weaving, etc.... Monthly. Basle, Switzerland:
Society of Chemical Industry, 1937-date; Index. Vol. I, II.
1939- . ill

6873   Clarke, Leslie J. The Craftsman in Textiles. New York:
Praeger; London: Bell, 1968. 160pp, ill, 32 pls

6874   Cobb, B. F. Silk. London: 1876. See: Bevan, G. P.,
British Manufacturing Industries, Vol. 5.

6875   Cole, Alan Summerly. Ornament in European Silks. London:
Debenham & Freebody, 1899. 220pp, 169 ill, pls De-
Wint, DLC, CtY

6876   Cole, George S. A Complete Dictionary of Dry Goods and
History of Silk, cotton, linen, wool and other fibrous substances, including a full explanation of the modern processes of spinning, dyeing and weaving. Wichita, Kans:
Forest City Publishing, 1890; rev. ed. with an appendix
on window trimming. Chicago: W. B. Conkey, 1892;
rev. ed. Chicago: J. B. Herring, 1894; new rev. ed.
as Cole's Encyclopedia of Dry Goods.... New York:
Root Newspaper Association, 1900. 222pp; 584pp, ill,
pls; ...; 640pp, ill DLC, NN

6877   Colombo, Ruggero. Italian Textiles. Tr. by Sydney Webb.
Leigh-on-Sea: F. Lewis, 1953. 20pp, 70 pls

6878   Cooper, Grace Rogers. The Copp Family Textiles. Washington, DC: Smithsonian Institution Pr, 1971. 65pp, ill, pls

6879   Cowper, A. S., comp. Linen in the Highlands, 1753-1762.
       Edinburgh: College of Commerce, 1969. 54pp

6880   Cox, Ruth Yvonne. Textiles Used in Philadelphia, 1760-1775.
       Thesis. 1960. 258pp, pls DeWint

6881   Crawford, Morris De Camp. 5000 Years of Fibers and
       Fabrics. Exhibition. January-March 1946. Brooklyn:
       Museum, 1946. 34pp, ill, bib

6882   _____. The Heritage of Cotton, the fibre of two worlds
       and many ages. New York; London: Putnam's, 1924.
       244pp, 21 pls, color frontis, bib

6883   _____. The History of Silk and Its Development from
       3500 B.C. to the Present Time, 1923. Cincinnati: John
       Shillito, 1923. 15pp

6884   Donat, Franz. Large Book of Textile Designs. A collection
       of patterns for every textile specialist and a guide for the
       designing of textile fabrics. English translation by
       Rudolf Teltscher. English, French and German text.
       Vienna: A. Hartleben, 1904. 41pp, 301 color pls ill'g
       9015 different patterns, 6 samples DLC, NN

6885   Dunbar, Douglas L. The Story of Silk. New York: Japan
       Society of N.Y., 1927. 35pp

6886   Dunton, Nellie, comp. The Spanish Colonial Ornament and
       the Motifs Depicted in the Textiles of the Period of the
       American South West. Part 1. Philadelphia: H. C.
       Perleberg, 1935. ill, pls DLC, NN

6887   Dutch Textiles, in collaboration with 'International Textiles,'
       of Amsterdam. Leigh-on-Sea: F. Lewis, 1960. 21pp,
       76 ill, 54 pls NN

6888   Encyclopedia of Textiles, by Editors of 'American Fabrics
       Magazine;' illustrated and authoritative source book on
       textiles, presenting the complete and practical coverage
       of the entire field--its history and origins, its art and
       design, its natural and man-made fibers, etc. Engle-
       wood Cliffs, NJ; London: Prentice-Hall, 1960. 702pp,
       1000 ill

6889   Englestad, Helen. Norwegian Textiles. Leigh-on-Sea: F.
       Lewis, 1952. 16pp of pls

6890   English, Walter. The Textile Industry; an account of the
       early inventions of spinning, weaving, and knitting ma-
       chines. London; Harlow: Longmans, 1969. 242pp, pls

6891   Eumura, Rohuro. Persian Weaving and Dyeing. 2 vol.

Kyoto: Unsodo Publishing, 1962. 100 color pls (18th
and 19th century Persian, Indian, Turkestan and Caucasian)

6892   Evans, Mary. The Story of Textiles. Boston: Little, Brown,
1942. 64pp, ill (part color)

6893   An Exhibition of Antique and Modern Textiles. Newark, NJ:
Newark Museum Association, 1914. 15pp

6894   Falke, Otto von. Decorative Silks. Tr. from German (1913).
New ed. New York: Helburn, 1922; 3rd ed. London:
Zwemmer; New York: Helburn, 1936. 55pp, 126 (10
color) pls, 541 figures NN

6895   Fennelly, Catherine. Textiles in New England, 1790-1840.
Sturbridge, Mass: Old Sturbridge Village, 1961. 40pp,
ill

6896   Ferriere, Maud Trube. Swiss Textiles. Leigh-on-Sea: F.
Lewis, 1953. 20pp, pls

6897   Fifty Masterpieces of Textiles. V & A. London: HMSO,
1951. 103pp, ill BM

6898   Fischbach, Friedrich. The Most Important Textile Ornaments
Up to the 19th Century. 5 vol. Mainz: Mainzer verlagsanstalt und druckerei, 1902-1911? color pls CU

6899   _____. Ornament of Textile Fabrics. Text. by R. Potzke.
Tr. from German. London: B. Quaritch, 1883. 9pp,
160 color pls MB, NN

6900   Flanagan, James F. Spitalfields Silks of the 18th and 19th
Centuries. Leigh-on-Sea: F. Lewis, 1954. 23pp, ill,
pls

6901   *Flemming, Ernst Richard. An Encyclopedia of Textiles from
the Earliest Times to the Beginning of the 19th Century.
Tr. from German (1923). New York: E. Weyhe, 1927;
London: Benn, 1928; new ed. as Encyclopedia of Textiles:
decorative fabrics from antiquity to the beginning of the
19th century, including the Far East and Peru. Rev. with
introd. by Renate Jaques. London: Zwemmer; New York:
Praeger, 1958. 38pp, 328 (8 color) pls; 30pp, 304 (16
color) pls

6902   Frankl, Paul Theodore. American Textiles. Leigh-on-Sea:
F. Lewis, 1954. 20pp, 64pp of ill

6903   French, Gilbert James, 1804-1866. The Life and Times of
Samuel Crompton, inventor of the spinning machine called
the mule. With an appendix ... including a paper on the

origin of spinning by rollers, by Robert Cole. London:
Simpkin, Marshall, 1859; 2nd ed. Manchester: T. Din-
ham, 1860; 3rd ed. 1862. 299pp, ill, 2 pls; ...; 164pp,
ill (Crompton, 1753-1827) DLC, PPL

6904 The Franco-British Exhibition of Textiles. V & A. London:
HMSO, 1922. 26pp, 50 pls

6905 French Decorative Textiles. Philadelphia: H. C. Perleberg,
1938. 47 pls (some color) in portfolio MiD

6906 Gabor, Magda. Hungarian Textiles. Leigh-on-Sea: F.
Lewis, 1961. 19pp, ill

6907 Gallagher, Constance Dann. Linen Heirlooms; the story and
patterns of a collection of 19th century handwoven pieces
with directions for their reproduction. Newton Centre,
Mass: C. T. Branford, 1968. 209pp, ill, bib

6908 Geijer, Agnes. Oriental Textiles in Sweden. Copenhagen:
Rosenkilde, 1951. 139pp, ill, 104 pls, bib

6909 _____ . Textile Treasures of Uppsala Cathedral from Eight
Centuries. Stockholm: Almquist & Wiksell, 1964. 84pp,
ill, pls

6910 Geliazkova, Nevena. Bulgarian Textiles. Leigh-on-Sea: F.
Lewis, 1958. 23pp, ill, 56 pls

6911 Geoghegan, J. Silk in India. Calcutta: Office of the Superin-
tendant of Government Printing, 1872; 2nd ed. 1880. 126pp;
177pp MH-A

6912 Gilez, C. H. Spanish Textiles. Leigh-On-Sea: F. Lewis,
195-? pls

6913 Gill, Conrad, 1883- . The Rise of the Irish Linen Industry.
Oxford: Clarendon Pr, 1925; reprint. 1966. 359pp, ill,
pls, bib

6914 Gilroy, Clinton G., comp. The History of Silk, Cotton, Linen,
Wool, and Other Fibrous Substances: including observations
on spinning, dyeing and weaving. Also an account of the
pastoral life of the ancients, their social state and attain-
ments in the domestic arts, with appendices on Pliny's
Natural History; on the origin and manufacture of linen and
cotton paper; on felting, netting, etc.... New York:
Harper, 1845; New York: C. M. Saxton; New London,
Conn: E. R. Fellows, 1953. 464pp, 10 pls DLC, MB,
NN

6915 Glazier, Richard. Historic Textile Fabrics, a short history of

the tradition and development of pattern in woven and
printed stuffs. London: Batsford; New York: Scribner's,
1923. 119pp, 120 drawings, 83 pls, color frontis, bib
PP, ViU, DeWint

6916   Great Britain Patent Office. Patents for Inventions. Abridge-
       ments of Specifications Relating to Dressing and Finishing
       Woven Fabrics and Manufacturing Felted Fabrics. I. 1620-
       1866; II. 1867-1876. 2 vol. London: 1878, 1880. ill
       DeWint

6917   The Greenleaf Collection: textile arts from the 16th to early-
       19th century; bequest of the late Richard Cranch Greenleaf.
       New York: Cooper Union Museum, 1964. 38pp, ill, bib

6918   Gregory, Edward William. Canterbury Weavers, past and
       present. (1564-1905.) London: Press Printers, 1905.
       22pp, ill

6919   Guest, Richard. A Compendius History of the Cotton Manu-
       facture. Manchester: J. Pratt, printer, 1823; reprint.
       London: Cass, 1968. 70pp, 12 pls PPF, DLC

6920   Gulvin, Clifford. The Tweedmakers; a history of the Scottish
       fancy woollen industry 1600-1914. Newton Abbot: David
       & Charles; New York: Barnes & Noble, 1973. 240pp, ill,
       bib

6921   Gunsaulus, Helen C. Japanese Textiles. New York: priv.
       printed for the Japan Society of N.Y., 1941. 94pp, 16
       (8 color) pls, bib

6922   Hackenbroch, Yvonne. English and Other Needlework, tapes-
       tries and textiles in the Irwin Untermeyer Collection.
       Cambridge, Mass: Harvard U Pr, for the Metropolitan
       Museum of Art, N.Y., 1960. 80pp, ill, 182 pls (some
       color), bib

6923   Harte, N. B., and Kenneth G. Ponting, ed. Textile History
       and Economic History; essays in honour of Miss Julia de
       Lacy Mann. Manchester, Eng: U Pr, 1973. 396pp, ill,
       bib (Includes 15 essays on subjects such as "The Fan-
       tastical Folly of Fashion; the English Stocking Knitting In-
       dustry, 1500-1700," by J. Thirsk, and "The Undoing of
       the Italian Mercantile Colony in 16th Century London," by
       G. D. Ramsay)

6924   Heaton, Herbert. The Yorkshire Woollen and Worsted Indus-
       tries; from the earliest times up to the Industrial Revolu-
       tion. Oxford: Clarendon, 1920. 459pp, ill, bib NN

6925   Hemphill, Herbert. The Fabric of the State. Exhibition.

New York: Museum of American Folk Art, 1972. u.p.,
ill (212 items, New York state)

6926 Henere, Enrique. Spanish Textiles. Leigh-on-Sea: F. Lewis,
1955. 15pp, 57 pls

6927 Hennezel, Henri. Decorations and Designs of Silken Masterpieces, ancient and modern; original specimens in colours
belonging to the Textile History Museum of Lyon. New
York: French & European Pr, 1930. 10pp, 56 color pls
in portfolio NNC-Ave, PLF

6928 Hooper, Luther. Silk: its production and manufacture. London: Pitman, 1911; 2nd ed. enl. 1927. 126pp, ill; 138pp,
ill

6929 Horner, John. The Linen Trade of Europe During the Spinning
Wheel Period. Belfast: M'Caw, Stevenson & Orr, 1920.
591pp, ill, pls CU, DLC, DeWint

6930 *Hunter, George Leland. Decorative Textiles: an illustrated
book on coverings for furniture, walls and floors, including
damasks, brocades and velvets, tapestries, laces, embroideries, chintzes, cretonnes, drapery and furniture
trimmings, wall papers, carpets and rugs, tooled and illuminated leathers. Grand Rapids, Mich: Dean-Hicks;
Philadelphia; London: Lippincott, 1918. 457pp, 580 ill,
27 color pls, bib (Comprehensive treatise) PPL, MiGr,
DeWint

6931 Irwin, John, and P. R. Schwartz. Studies in Indo-European
Textile History. Ahmedabad, India: Calico Museum of
Textile, 1966. 124pp, color ill, bib

6932 James, John, 1811-1867. History of the Worsted Manufacture
in England. London: Longman, 1857; facsim. reprint.
London: Cass, 1968. 640, 40pp, 8 pls, bib

6933 Jenkins, John Geraint. The Welsh Woollen Industry. Cardiff:
National Museum of Wales, 1969. 410pp, ill

6934 Johnson, Arthur Henry, 1845-1927. The History of the Worshipful Company of the Drapers of London; preceded by an
introduction on London and her Gilds up to the close of
the 15th century. 5 vol. Oxford: Clarendon Pr, 1914-
1922. ill, pls DLC

6935 Johnston, Robert. Scotch-Tweed Designer's Handbook. 3rd
ed. Galashiels, Scotland: John Russell, 1879. 32pp, 12
pls NcRS

6936 Jourdain, Margaret. The Morant Collection of Old Velvets, damasks, brocades, etc... London; with a description of English upholstery during the 17th and 18th centuries. London: Virtue, 19-? 35pp, 14 pls DeWint

6937   Journal of Indian Textile History. Irregular periodical. Ahmedabad, India: Calico Museum of Textiles, 1955- . ill

6938   Kendrick, Albert Frank. Catalogue of Early Mediaeval Woven Fabrics. London: V & A, 1925. 73pp, 24 pls BM

6939   _____ . Catalogue of Muhammadan Textiles of the Mediaeval Period. V & A. London: HMSO, 1924. 74pp, 24 pls

6940 * _____ . English Decorative Fabrics of the 16th to 18th Centuries. Benfleet, Essex: Lewis, 1934. 88pp, ill, 52 pls (Carpet, embroidery, tapestry)

6941   La Prade, Marguerite Duguet de. French Textiles. Leigh-on-Sea: F. Lewis, 1955. 23pp, 92 ill, 64 pls

6942   Lardner, Dionysius. A Treatise on the Origin, progressive improvement and present state of the silk manufacture. London: Longman, Rees, 1831; Philadelphia: Carey & Lee, 1832; 1836. 339pp, ill; 276pp, ill

6943   Laufer, Berthold. Felt; how it was made and used in ancient times and a brief description of modern methods of manufacture and use. (Cover title: The Early History of Felt.) Chicago: Western Felt Works, 1930; 1937. 25pp, ill

6944   Lewis, Albert Easton. The Romance of Textiles. The story of design in weaving. New York: I. Pitman, 1937. 377pp

6945 *Lewis, Frank. British Textiles. Leigh-on-Sea: F. Lewis, 1951. 20pp, 99 ill

6946   _____ . Czechoslovak Textiles. Leigh-on-Sea: F. Lewis, 1962. 23pp, 150 ill, 64 pls

6947   _____ . James Leman (Working 1706-1718) Spitalfields Designer. Leigh-on-Sea: F. Lewis, 1954. ill (Biography)

6948   Lilly, Alfred Theodore. The Silk Industry of the United States from 1766-1874. New York: Jenkins & Thomas, printers, 1875; 1882. 12pp DLC

        Link, Pablo. South American Textiles. See: Pablo, Paul, below.

6949   [No entry.]

6950   Lipson, Ephraim. The History of the Woollen and Worsted

Industries. London: A. & C. Black, 1921. 273pp, frontis, bib NN

6951 _____. A Short History of Wool and Its Manufacture, Mainly in England. Cambridge: Harvard U Pr; London: Heinemann, 1953. 205pp

6952 List of Books on Textile Fabrics in Edinburgh Museum Library. Edinburgh: 1892.

6953 List of Prices in Those Branches of the Weaving Manufactory Called the Black Branch and the Fancy Branch. n.p.: 1769; or as List of the Prices in Those Branches of the Weaving Manufactory Called the Strong Plain, foot figured and flowered branches. n.p.: 1769. specimens latter belongs to RPB

6954 Lister, John. Cotton Manufacture: a manual of practical instruction in the processes of opening, carding, combing, drawing, doubling, and spinning of cotton, and the methods of dyeing and preparing goods for market. London: C. Lockwood, 1894. 222pp, numerous ill PP

6955 *Little, Frances (pseud.). Early American Textiles. New York; London: Century, 1931. 267pp, ill, pls, bib

6956 Lubell, Cecil. Textile Collections of the World. I. United States and Canada; II. United Kingdom. 2 vol. New York: Van Nostrand Reinhold, 1976.

6957 MacFarlane, David. The Damask and Imitation Shawl Manufacturers' Guide. Glasgow: 1821. SIB-1

6958 MacMillan, Donald D. The Tradition of French Fabrics, 1663-1863. Presented by Brunschwig & Fils, circulated by Smithsonian Institution. Exhibition. New York: 1963. 32pp, ill

6959 Majkowski, Karol. Polish Textiles. Leigh-on-Sea: F. Lewis, 1968. 14pp, 92 ill, 48 pls

6960 Manchester, Herbert (H.). The Story of Silk and Cheney Silks. South Manchester, Conn; New York: Cheney Brothers, Silk Manufacturers, 1916; rev. ed. with additions, 1924. 63pp, ill, color pls; 78pp, ill, color pls MB, NN

6961 Mann, Julia de Lacy. The Cloth Industry in the West of England from 1640 to 1880. Oxford: Clarendon Pr, 1971. 371pp, bib

6962 May, Florence Lewis. Silk Textiles of Spain, 8th to 15th

century. New York: Hispanic Society of New York, 1957.
286pp, ill

6963 Mayer, Christa Charlotte. Masterpieces of Western Textiles
      from the Art Institute. Chicago: 1969. 224pp, ill, bib

6964 *Mellor, John Hanson, and others. A Century of British Fab-
      rics, 1850-1950. Carpets by Mellor; Printed and Woven
      Fabrics, by Frank Lewis; Wall Papers by E. A. Entwisle.
      Leigh-on-Sea: F. Lewis, 1955. ill

6965 Mookerjee, Ajitcoomar. Designs on Indian Textiles. Calcutta:
      Indian Institute of Art in Industry, 19- . ill

6966 Moreau, Cesar, 1791-1860. Rise and Progress of the Wool
      Trade and Woollen Manufacture in Great Britain from the
      Earliest Period to the Present Time. Founded on official
      documents. London: Treuttel & Wurtz, 1828. 8pp

6967 Morgan, Frederick Charles. A Hereford Mercer's Inventory
      for the Year 1689, and the accounts for the years 1691
      to 1694 of John Noble, mercer. Hereford, Eng: Wool-
      hope Club, 1947. 24pp (pp. 187-210), ill DLC

6968 Morris, Barbara. Textiles. The early Victorian period,
      1830-1860. Ed. by Ralph Edwards and L. G. G. Ramsey.
      London: Connoisseur; New York: Reynal, 1958. ill

6969 Neppert-Boehland, Maria. German Textiles. Leigh-on-Sea:
      F. Lewis, 1955. 23pp, 63 pls

6970 Nisbet, Harry. Grammar of Textile Design. London: Scott,
      Greenwood; New York: D. Van Nostrand, 1906; 2nd ed.
      rev. & enl. London: 1919. 276pp, 490 ill; 504pp, 635 ill
      DLC

6971 Noma, Seiroku. Japanese Costume and Textile Arts. Tokyo:
      Weatherhill & Heibonsha, 1975. 160pp, ill

6972 Nomachi, Katsutoshi. Japanese Textiles. Leigh-on-Sea: F.
      Lewis, 1958. 23pp, ill, 56 pls

6973 North, Simon Newton Dexter, 1849-1924. A Century of Ameri-
      can Wool Manufacture, 1790-1890. Boston: Rockwell &
      Churchill Pr, 1895. 81pp NN

6974 Oelsner, Gustaf Hermann. A Handbook of Weaves, Trans-
      lated and Revised by Samuel S. Dale, including a supple-
      ment on the analysis of weaves and fabrics and 1875 illus-
      trated. New York: Dover, 1951. 402pp, ill

6975 Okada, Yuzura. History of Japanese Textiles and Lacquer.

Tr. by Charles S. Terry. Tokyo: Toto Shuppan; Rutland,
Vt: Tuttle; London: Paterson, 1958. 180pp, 165 (10
color) ill

6976   Old Textiles of India. Academy of Fine Arts. Calcutta: Ox-
        ford U Pr, 197-? 36pp, ill

6977   Oz, Tahsin. Turkish Textiles and Velvets. Ankara: Turkish
        Press, Broadcasting and Tourist Dept, 1950. ill (14th-
        16th centuries)

6978   Pablo, Paul (pseud.). South American Textiles. Leigh-on-
        Sea: F. Lewis, 1957. 23pp, ill, 54 pls

6979   Pajot-des-Charmes, C. The Art of Bleaching Piece-goods,
        cottons, and threads, of every description, rendered more
        easy and general by means of the oxygenated muriatic acid:
        ... silk, wool, ... paper. Tr. from French by William
        Nicholson. London: printed for G. G. & J. Robinson,
        1799. 351pp, 9 folding pls (of utensils and processes)
        DeWint

6980   Peckett, H. Early History of Cloth-Making. Huddersfield,
        Eng: Advertiser Pr, 1909. 22pp

6981   Peddie, Alexander. The Linen Manufacturer, Weaver and
        Warper's Assistant. 5th ed. Glasgow: W. Sommerville,
        1818. 292pp, 12 pls

6982   Perleberg, Hans Carl, comp. Persian Textiles. Introd. by
        John Cotton Dana. I. Original Persian and Paisley Shawls,
        tapestries and borders; II. Persian Decorative Art in Its
        Relation and Influence Upon Contemporary Art in Europe
        During the Years 1830 to 1850. 2 vol. Jersey City, NJ:
        Author, 1919. text, pls

6983   Petrescu, Paul, and Nicolae Rodna. Romanian Textiles.
        Leigh-on-Sea: F. Lewis, 1966. 23pp, ill, 48 pls

6984   Pollen, John Hungerford. Catalogue of a Special Loan Collec-
        tion of English Furniture and Figured Silks Manufactured
        in the 17th and 18th Centuries. South Kensington Museum.
        London: 1896. 145pp

6985   Poole, B. W. The Clothing Trades Industry. London: Pit-
        man, 1920. 100pp, ill

6986   Porter, George Richardson. A Treatise on the Origin, Pro-
        gressive Improvement, and Present State of the Silk Manu-
        facture. London: Longman, Rees, 1831. 339pp, ill

6987   Posselt, Emanuel Anthony, 1858- . Dictionary of Weaves;

a collection of all weaves from four to nine harness. 2000 weaves conveniently arranged for handy use.   London: S. Low, Marston, 1914.   85pp of ill

6988 _____. The Jacquard Machine Analyzed and Explained: with an appendix on the preparation of Jacquard cards, and practical hints to learners of Jacquard designing. Philadelphia: Pennsylvania Museum & School of Industrial Art, 1887.   127pp, 230 ill, pls   (Joseph Marie Jacquard, 1752-1834)

6989 _____. Manufacture of Narrow Woven Fabrics, Ribbons, Trimmings, Edgings, etc., ... construction of weaves and novelties, ... looms.   Philadelphia: Textile Publishing Co, 1917.   198pp, 240 ill

6990 _____. Recent Improvements in Textile Machinery Relating to Weaving.   Giving the most modern points on the construction of all kinds of looms, warpers, beamers, slashers, winders, spoolers, reeds, temples, shuttles, bobbins, heddles, heddle frames, pickers, jacquards, card stampers, etc., for the use of manufacturers, mill managers, designers, overseers, loomfixers, students and inventors. 3 vol.   Philadelphia: Posselt; London: Low, Marston, 1898-1905.   text, 600 ill

6991 _____. Technology of Textile Design: being a practical treatise on the construction and application of weaves for all textile fabrics, with minute reference to the latest inventions.   Philadelphia: Author; London: Low, Marston, 1889.   292pp, 1000 ill

6992 *Priest, Alan Reed.   Costumes from the Forbidden City.   Exhibition.   March-May 1945.   New York: Metropolitan Museum, 1945; reprint.   New York: Arno Pr, 1974.   16pp, 56pp of ill   (Costume, textiles, embroidery)

6993 * _____, and Pauline Simmons.   Chinese Textiles; an introduction to the study of their history, sources, techniques, symbolism, and use, occasioned by the exhibition of Chinese court robes and accessories.   December 1931-January 1932. Metropolitan Museum.   New York: 1931; new rev. ed. 1934.   88pp, ill, pls, bib; 96pp, ill, pls, bib

6994 Rasmussen, Steen Eiler.   Danish Textiles.   Leigh-on-Sea: F. Lewis, 1956.   27pp, 93 pls

6995 Reath, Nancy Andrews, and Eleanor B. Sacks.   Persian Textiles and Their Techniques from the 6th to the 18th century, including a system for general textile classification.   New Haven: Yale U Pr; London: H. Milford, 1937.   133pp, ill, pls

6996	Rock, Daniel. Textile Fabrics. South Kensington Museum
	Handbook. London: Chapman & Hall, 1876. 116pp, ill

6997	_____ . Textile Fabrics: a descriptive catalogue of the
	collection of church vestments, dresses, silk stuffs,
	needlework and tapestries in the South Kensington Museum.
	London: 1870. 353pp, 20 pls BM

6998	Rodier, Paul. The Romance of French Weaving. New York:
	F. A. Stokes, 1931; New York: Tudor, 1936. 356pp, 101
	(2 color) ill

6999	Saarto, Martha. Finnish Textiles. Tr. by Joy Silander-
	Lindfors. Leigh-on-Sea: F. Lewis, 1954. pls

7000	Sabin, A. K. The Silk Weavers of Spitalfields and Bethnal
	Green. With a catalogue and illustrations of Spitalfields
	Silks. V & A. London: HMSO, 1931. 39pp, 12 pls

7001	Sargent, Porter Edward. An Historical Sketch of Nishiki and
	Kinran Brocades with a Catalogue of 120 Rare Specimens
	Dating from 1400-1812, collected by Shojiro Nomura, to
	illustrate the historical development and varieties of weave
	and design. Boston: Copley Society, 1914. 43pp BM

7002	Sholl, Samuel. A Short Historical Account of the Silk Manu-
	facture in England. London: 1811. BM

7003	Short, Ernest Henry. Man and Wool. London: Hodder &
	Stoughton, 1921. 114pp, ill, pls (Wool manufacturing
	history)

7004	Simmonds, Peter Lund. Fibres and Cordage. London: 1876.
	See: Bevan, G. P., British Manufacturing Industries,
	Vol. 9.

7005	Simmons, Pauline. Chinese Patterned Silks. New York:
	Metropolitan Museum, 1948. 40pp, ill, bib NNC-Ave

7006	Slomann, Vilhelm. Bizarre Designs in Silks, Trade and Tra-
	ditions. Tr. from Danish by Eve M. Wendt. Copenhagen:
	E. Munksgaard, for the Ny Carlsberg Foundation, 1953.
	270pp, ill (1 color), bib

7007	Smith, A. D. Howell. Brief Guide to the Chinese Woven
	Fabrics. V & A. London: HMSO, 1925; 1938. 34pp,
	16 pls, bib BM

7008	_____ , and Albert James Koop. Guide to the Japanese
	Textiles. I. Textile Fabrics, by Smith; II. Costume, by
	Koop. 2 vol. in 1. V & A. London: HMSO, 1919,
	1920. ill, pls, bib

7009 Smith, (John), fl. 1747. Memoirs of Wool, Woolen Manu-
      facture, and Trade, (particularly in England) from the
      earliest to the present times. 2 vol. London: Author,
      1756-57. NN

7010 Spitalfields Silks of the 18th and 19th Centuries. Introd. by
      J. F. Flanagan. Leigh-on-Sea: F. Lewis, 1954. 23pp,
      94 ill, 64 pls

7011 Stellwag-Carion, Fritz. Austrian Textiles. Leigh-on-Sea:
      F. Lewis, 1960. 19pp, 99 ill, 56 pls

7012 Survey of World Textiles. 39 vols. Leigh-on-Sea: F. Lewis,
      1951- .

7013 Tann, Jennifer. Gloucester Woollen Mills. An account of
      the development of the woollen industry from 1550 to its
      collapse at the beginning of the 20th century. London:
      David & Charles, 1967; 1973. 254pp, 32 pls

7014 Textile Design; a bibliography and directory. Washington,
      D. C.: Textile Foundation, 1932. 29pp

7015 Textile History. Monthly. Newton Abbot, Eng: David &
      Charles, 1968- . ill

7016 Textile Machinery. Catalogue of the collections in the Science
      Museum, South Kensington. London: HMSO, 1921. 75pp,
      3 pls NN, DLC

7017 Textile Museum Catalogue Raisonné. Washington, D.C.:
      Textile Museum, 1952- .

7018 Textile Museum Journal. Annual. Washington, D.C.: Tex-
      tile Museum, 1962- . (Supersedes the Museum's Work-
      shop Notes, 1950-1961)

7019 The Textile Record of America. Periodical. Philadelphia:
      Textile Record, 1880-1903.

7020 Thompson, J. H. Canadian Textiles. Leigh-on-Sea: F.
      Lewis, 1963. 18pp, 114pp of pls

7021 *Thornton, Peter. Baroque and Rococo Silks. London: Faber;
      New York: Taplinger, 1965. 209pp, 124 pls of 248 ill,
      bib (1640-1770)

7022 Threads of History; the romance of fibers, natural and man-
      made, and the art of their use in decorative textiles. Ex-
      hibition circulated by the Decorative Arts Program of the
      American Federation of Arts. New York: 1965. 53pp,
      ill

7023   Thurston, V.   Short History of Decorative Textiles and Tap-
       estries.   Ditchling, Eng: 1934.   112pp

7024   Townsend, W. G. Paulson.   Modern Decorative Art in Eng-
       land; its development and characteristics.   London: Bats-
       ford, 1922.   ill, pls   (Woven and printed fabrics, wall
       papers, lace, embroidery, etc.)

7025   Tucker, Mae S., comp.   Textiles; a bibliography of the ma-
       terials in the "Textile Collection" at the Public Library
       of Charlotte and Mecklenburg County.   Charlotte, N.C.:
       1952.   49pp   DLC

7026   2000 Years of Silk Weaving.   Exhibition.   Los Angeles County
       Museum; Cleveland Museum of Art; Detroit Institute of
       Arts.   New York: E. Weyhe, 1944.   63pp, ill   NNC-Ave

7027   Uemura, Rokuro.   Old Art Treasures from Japan's Needles
       and Looms.   Tr. by Shiho Sakanishi.   Kyoto?:   Korinsha,
       1949.   13pp, ill

7028   Undi, Maria.   Hungarian Fancy Needlework and Weaving; the
       history of Hungarian decorative embroideries and weavings
       from the time of the occupation of Hungary by the Mag-
       yars till today.   Budapest: Author, 193-?   87pp, ill, bib

7029   Vacher, Sydney.   15th Century Italian Ornament, chiefly taken
       from brocades and stuffs found in pictures in the National
       Gallery, London.   London: B. Quaritch, 1886.   8pp, ill,
       30 color pls   NNC-Ave

7030   Vaclavik, Antonin, and Jaroslav Orel.   Textile Folk Art.   Tr.
       from Czechoslovakian by Helena Kaczerova.   London:
       Spring Books, 195-?   58pp, ill, 59 pls

7031   Verneuil, M(aurice) Pillard.   Japanese Textiles, Woven and
       Embroidered.   Introd. by G. Migeon.   4 vol.   London:
       Batsford, 1901.   80 color pls of 200 examples   (Museum
       and private collections)   BM

7032   Volbach, Wolfgang Friedrich.   Early Decorative Textiles.
       Tr. from Italian by Yuri Gabriel.   Feltham; New York:
       Hamlyn, 1969.   160pp, ill, 71 color pls   (To 1300)

7033   Wade, A. S.   Cotton Spinning.   London: Pitman, 1921.
       104pp, ill

7034   Walterstorff, Emilie von.   Swedish Textiles.   Stockholm:
       Nordiska Museet, 1925.   245 ill (many color)

7035   Wardle, Thomas, 1831-1909.   Handbook of the Collection
       Illustrative of the Wild Silks of India, in the South

Kensington Museum.   London: Eyre & Spottiswoode, 1881.
163pp, ill, 66 pls

7036   .   Monographs on the Tusser and Other Wild Silks of
India, descriptive of the objects and specimens exhibited
in the India section of the Paris Exhibition, and on the dye-
stuffs and tannin matters of India.   London: HMSO, 1878.
38pp

7037   .   Report on the Silks Exhibited in the Colonial Sections of the Colonial and Indian Exhibition, 1886.   London:
William Clowes, 1887.   BM

7038   Waring, John Burley, 1823-1875.   Examples of Weaving and
Embroidery.   London: 18-?

7039   Watson, John Forbes.   The Textile Manufacturers and the
Costumes of the People of India.   London: Eyre & Spottiswoode, for the Indian Office, 1866.   173pp, ill, 12 (9
color) pls DLC

7040   Watts, Isaac.   Cotton.   London: 1876.   See: Bevan, G.
P., British Manufacturing Industries, Vol. 5.

7041 *Weibel, Adele Coulin.   2000 Years of Textiles: the figured
textiles of Europe and the Near East.   New York: Pan-
theon, 1952.   169pp, ill, bib

7042   Weiss, Harry Bischoff, and Grace M. Ziegler (Weiss).   The
Early Woolen Industry of New Jersey.   Trenton, NJ:
Agricultural Society, 1958.   100pp, ill, bib

7043   West, Thomas Henry.   "The Loom Builders," the Drapers
as pioneer contributors to the American way of life.   New
York: Newcomen Society in North America, 1952.   36pp,
ill

7044   Wheeler, Monroe, ed.   Textiles and Ornaments of India, a
selection of designs.   New York: Museum of Modern Art,
1956.   93pp, ill, bib

7045 *White, George Savage, 1768-1835.   Memoir of Samuel Slater.
With a history of the rise ... of the cotton manufacture
in England and America.   2nd ed. Philadelphia: 1836.
448pp, pls (Slater was cotton manufacturer and fabric
printer) BM

7046   Woodhouse, Thomas, 1862-1933.   Artificial Silk; its manufacture and uses.   London; New York: Pitman, 1927.   137pp,
ill, color frontis

7047   .   Jacquards and Harnesses, card-cutting, lacing and repeating mechanism. London: Macmillan, 1923. 429pp, ill, pls

7048 _____, and Peter Kilgour. The Jute Industry from Seed to Finished Cloth. London; New York: Pitman, 1921. 133pp, ill

7049 Wool in History, British Wool Marketing Board. Wakefield, Eng: EP Publishing, 1972. 16pp, ill (To ca.1900)

7050 Wool Technology and the Industrial Revolution; an exhibition. North Andover?, Mass: Merrimack Valley Textile Museum, 1965. u.p., ill, facsims

7051 Woven Treasures of Persian Art; Persian textiles from the 6th to the 19th century. Exhibition. April-May 1959. Los Angeles: County Museum, 1959. 65pp, ill

7052 Wyckoff, William Cornelius, 1832-1888. The Silk Goods of America ... Improvements and advances of silk manufacture in the United States. New York: Van Nostrand, for Silk Association of America, 1879; 1880. 156pp

7053 Yamanobe, Tomoyuki. Textiles. Arts and Crafts of Japan. English adaptation by Lynn Katoh. Rutland, Vt: Tuttle; London: Paterson, 1957. 70pp, ill

SPINNING WHEELS, HAND LOOMS, NEEDLEWORK TOOLS
AND SEWING MACHINES

7054 *Andere, Mary. Old Needlework Boxes and Tools: their story and how to collect them. Newton Abbot: David & Charles; New York: Drake, 1971. 184pp, ill, pls, bib

7055 Catalogue of the Horner Collection of Spinning Wheels and Accessories. Belfast Public Art Gallery & Museum. Belfast: W. & G. Baird, 1909. 25pp, ill (John Horner) NN

7056 Channing, Marion L. The Textile Tools of Colonial Homes: from raw materials to finished garments before mass production in the factories. Marion, Mass: 1969. 64pp, ill, bib

7057 Chase, William Henry. Five Generations of Loom Builders; a story of loom building from the days of the craftsmanship of the hand loom weaver to the modern automatic loom of Draper Corporation. With a supplement on the origin and development of the arts of spinning and weaving. Hopedale, Mass: Draper Corp, 1951. 87pp, ill, pls DeWint

7058 Cooper, Grace Rogers. The Invention of the Sewing Machine.
      Bulletin 254. Washington, D.C.: Smithsonian Institution,
      1968. 156pp, ill, bib

7059 Ewers, William, and H. W. Baylor, with H. H. Kenaga.
      Sincere's History of the Sewing Machine. Phoenix, Ariz:
      Sincere Pr, 1970. 256pp, ill

7060 Gilbert, Keith Reginald. Sewing Machines. Science Museum.
      London: HMSO, 1970. 51pp, ill, 20 color ill (1830-
      1970)

7061 Groves, Sylvia. The History of Needlework Tools and Acces-
      sories. London: Country Life, 1966; 1968; Newton Abbot:
      David & Charles; New York: Arco, 1973. 136pp, 13 ill,
      60 pls; 136pp, ill, 64 pls, bib

7062 Herzberg, Rudolph. The Sewing Machine: its history, con-
      struction, and application. Tr. from German by U. Green.
      London: E. & F. N. Spon, 1864. 112pp, 7 folding pls
      BM, DLC

7063 Hoffmann, Marta. The Warp-Weighted Loom; studies in the
      history and technology of an ancient implement. Norsk
      Folk Museum. Oslo: Universitetsforlaget, 1964. 425pp,
      ill, bib

7064 Hooper, Luther. The Loom and Spindle: past, present and
      future. Reprint from Journal of the Royal Society of
      Arts, 1912, in the Smithsonian Institution Annual Report.
      Washington, D.C.: 1914. 50pp (pp. 629-78), ill, 11 pls
      DLC

7065 Lewton, Frederick L. The Servant in the House: a brief
      history of the sewing machine. From the Smithsonian
      Report. Washington, D.C.: 1930. 25pp (pp. 559-83),
      8 pls

7066 *Longman, Eleanor D., and Sophy Loch. Pins and Pincushions.
      London; New York: Longmans, Green, 1911. 188pp, 1
      ill, 43 pls MB, DLC, TxU

7067 Lundquist, Myrtle. The Book of a Thousand Thimbles. Des
      Moines: Wallace-Homestead, 1970. 91pp, ill (part
      color) (Gold, silver, porcelain, novelty, plastic)

7068 MacDonald, Dorothy K. Fibres, Spindles and Spinning-wheels.
      (History of the Textile Arts.) Toronto: Royal Ontario
      Museum of Archaeology, 1944; 2nd ed. 1950. 49pp, ill,
      bib

7069 Morrall, Michael Thomas. History and Description of Needle-making. Reprint from Hobson's Ashton Advertiser. (With tradecard and specimen needles.) London: Ashton-under-Lyne, 1852; 3rd ed. Manchester: 1862; ... BM

7070 Pennington, D., and M. Taylor. A Pictorial Guide to American Spinning Wheels. Ann Arbor, Mich: 1975. 100pp, ill

7071 Roth, H(enry) Ling. "Hand Card Making." Halifax: Bankfield Museum, Notes no. 11, 1912. 12pp, ill (Wool manufacturing) NN

7072 _____. "Hand Woolcombing." Halifax: Bankfield Museum, Notes no. 6, 1909. 10pp, ill (Wool manufacturing history) NN

7073 Salamon, N. The History of the Sewing Machine from 1750, with biography of E. Howe, Jr. London: 1863. BM

7074 Thompson, George B., comp. Spinning Wheels. (The John Horner Collection.) Belfast: Ulster Museum, 1964. 51pp, pls

7075 *Whiting, Gertrude. Tools and Toys of Stitchery. Partly reprinted from the Magazine Antiques. New York: Columbia U Pr, 1928; reprinted as Old-Time Tools and Toys of Needlework. New York: Dover, 1971. 357pp, 156 ill (Workbaskets, scissors, thimbles, measures, awls, needle books, pins, pincushions, bobbins, hoops, pinking blocks, spinning wheels, etc.)

PRINTED AND PAINTED FABRICS

7076 Albrecht-Mathey, Elisabeth. The Printed Fabrics of Mulhouse and Alsace, 1801-1850. Leigh-on-Sea: F. Lewis, 1968. text, 123 (3 color) ill

7077 American Scenes and Events on Textiles; an exhibition of printed cottons, linens, and silks from 1777-1941. September-November 1941. New York: N.Y. Historical Society, 1941. 1pp, 32 pls

7078 The Aniline Colours of the Badische Anilin- and Soda-Fabrik, Ludwigshafen o/Rhine, and their application on wool, cotton, silk and other textile fibres. Ludwigshafen: 1901. hundreds of actual wool, cotton, silk and other fabric samples

7079 Baker, George Percival. Calico Painting and Printing in the East Indies in the 17th and 18th Centuries. London: E. Arnold, 1921. 78pp, 9 (1 color) pls, portfolio of 37 (30 color) pls, bib V & A, DeWint

7080   Bancroft, Edward, 1744-1821. Experimental Researches
       Concerning the Philosophy of Permanent Colour; and the
       best means of producing them, by dying, callico printing,
       etc. London: for T. Cadell, Jun., and W. Davies,
       1794; 2nd ed. with additions. 2 vol. London: 1813; 2 vol.
       Philadelphia: T. Dobson, 1914. 456pp and 518pp NN

7081   Beer, Alice Baldwin. Trade Goods; a study of Indian chintz
       in the collection of the Cooper-Hewitt Museum of Decora-
       tive Arts and Design, Smithsonian Institution. Washington,
       D.C.: Smithsonian, 1970. 133pp, ill, bib

7082   Bemiss, Elijah. The Dyers' Companion in Two Parts: part
       first containing upward of 100 receipts for colouring woolen,
       cotton or silk cloths, ... second part containing directions
       for ... varnishing leather; to make oilcloth, lacker brass,
       and tin-ware. New London, Conn: Cady & Eels, printers,
       1806; 2nd ed. New York: Evert Duyckinck, 1815. 75pp;
       307pp DeWint

7083   Bindewald, Erwin, and Karl Kasper. Fairy Fancy on Fabrics.
       The wonderland of calico-printing. 2nd rev. ed. Braun-
       schweig: G. Westermann, 1951. 168pp, 180 ill (chiefly
       color), bib (History and modern practice) MiDa

7084   Bunt, Cyril George Edward, and Ernest Arthur Rose. Two
       Centuries of English Chintz, 1750-1950. As exemplified
       by the productions of Stead, McAlpin and Co. Leigh-on-
       Sea: F. Lewis, 1957. 80pp, ill, 63 pls

7085   Calvert, Frederich Crace. Dyeing and Calico Printing; in-
       cluding an account of the most recent improvements in the
       manufacture and use of analine colours. Ed. by John
       Stenhouse and Charles Edward Groves. Manchester, Eng:
       Palmer & Howe; London: Simpkin, Marshall, 1876; 2nd
       ed. Manchester: 1876; 3rd ed. 1878. 509pp, ill, speci-
       mens MH-BA, DLC, BM

7086   Capey, Reco. The Printing of Textiles. London: Chapman
       & Hall, 1930. 138pp, pls

7087   Catalogue of a Loan Exhibition of English Chintz. English
       printed furnishing fabrics from their origins until the
       present day. May-July 1960. V & A. London: HMSO,
       1960. 75pp

7088   Catalogue of a Retrospective Exhibition of Painted and Printed
       Fabrics. May-September 1927. New York: Metropolitan
       Museum, 1927. 95pp, ill

7089   Clark, Fiona. William Morris Wallpapers and Chintzes.
       Biographical note by Andrew Melvin. London: Academy

Editions; New York: St. Martin's Pr, 1973. 95pp, 91
ill, 8 pls, bib

7090   Clayton, Muriel. Brief Guide to the Western Painted, dyed
and printed textiles. Rev. from A. D. Howell Smith's
1924 ed. V & A. London: 1938. 32pp, 16 pls

7091   *Clouzot, Henri, and Frances Morris. Painted and Printed
Fabrics: the history of the manufactory at Jouy and other
ateliers in France, 1760-1815 (by Clouzot). Notes on the
History of Cotton Painting, especially in England and
America (by Morris). New York: Yale U Pr, for Metropolitan Museum, 1927. 108pp, ill, 92 pls, color frontis,
bib PPULC, NN, MiU, DLC

7092   *Cooper, Thomas, 1759-1839. A Practical Treatise on Dyeing
and Callicoe Printing; exhibiting the processes in the
French, German, English, and American practice of fixing
colours in woollen, cotton, silk and linen. Philadelphia:
William Fry, printer, for Thomas Dobson, 1815. 506pp,
ill MiU, DLC, DSI

7093   Cooper Union for the Advancement of Science and Art. Museum for the Arts of Decoration. Bibliography on Blue and
White Resist Printing. New York: 1956. 35pp

7094   Cox, Ruth Yvonne. Copperplate Textiles in the Williamsburg
Collection, Some Sources of Design. Williamsburg, Va:
Colonial Williamsburg, 1964. 23pp, ill, bib

7095   Crookes, Sir William. Dyeing and Tissue-Printing. London:
G. Bell, 1882. 418pp

7096   _____. A Practical Handbook of Dyeing and Calico Printing.
London: Longmans, Green, 1874. 730pp, 38 ill, 11 pls,
47 specimens, bib PP, DLC, BM

7097   Design by the Yard. Textile printing from 800 to 1956. Exhibition. New York: Cooper Union Museum, 1956. 24pp,
ill, bib

7098   The Dyer and Colour Maker's Companion: containing upwards
of 200 receipts for making colours on the most approved
principles, for all the various styles and fabrics now in
existence. Glasgow: W. Mackensie, for Author, 1849;
Philadelphia: H. C. Baird, 1850; new ed. Philadelphia:
1851; 1855; 1870; 1886; 1891; 1898. 96pp; 104pp MH,
DeWint, MB

7099   English Chintz. V & A. London: HMSO, 1955. 8pp, 32 pls

7100   English Chintz. Two centuries of changing taste. An exhibition at the Cotton Board Colour, Design and Style Center, Manchester. London: V & A, 1955. 58pp

7101   European Printed Textiles. V & A. London: HMSO, 1949. 16pp, ill, bib

7102   Floud, Peter, comp. English Printed Textiles, 1720-1836. London: V & A, 1960. 79pp, ill, bib

7103   Gilroy, Clinton G. A Practical Treatise on Dyeing and Calico-Printing; including the latest inventions and improvements; also a description of the origin, manufacture, uses, and chemical properties of the various animal, vegetable, and mineral substances employed in these arts. 2nd ed. rev. & enl. New York: Harper, 1846. 704pp, ill   NN

7104   Hurst, George Henry. Silk Dyeing, Printing and Finishing. Philadelphia: E. A. Posselt, 1882. 226pp, ill, 11 color pls with 66 patterns

7105   *Irwin, John, and Katharine B. Brett. Origins of Chintz; with a catalogue of Indo-European cotton-paintings in the Royal Ontario Museum, Toronto, and the Victoria and Albert Museum, London. London: HMSO, 1970. 144pp, ill, 166 pls, bib   (1600-1800)

7106   _____, and Margaret Hall. Indian Painted and Printed Fabrics. Ahmedabed: Calico Museum of Textiles, 1971. 203pp, 96pp of ill, 12 color pls

7107   The Journal of the Society of Dyers and Colourists, for all interested in the use or manufacture of colours, and in calico printing, bleaching, etc. Bradford, Eng: 1884-1919. ill, mounted specimens   DLC

7108   Kendrick, Albert Frank. Hand-painted Cottons of India. Reprint from Connoisseur. London: 1926. 10pp (pp. 80-89), ill, pl

7109   Lawrie, Leslie Gordon. A Bibliography of Dyeing and Textile Printing, comprising a list of books from the 16th century to the present time (1946). London: Chapman & Hall, 1949. 148pp, bib   DLC

7110   *Lewis, Frank. English Chintz, from earliest times until the present day. 2 vol. Benfleet, Essex: Lewis, 1935; rev. new ed. as English Chintz; a history of printed fabrics from earliest times to the present day. Leigh-on-Sea: F. Lewis, 1942. 36pp, 152 pls; 35pp, ill, 157 pls

7111   Montgomery, Florence M. Printed Textiles; English and American cottons and linens 1700-1850. A Winterthur Book. New

York: Viking; London: Thames & Hudson, 1970.   379pp,
ill, bib

7112 O'Brien, Charles. The Callico Printers' Assistant, ... including ... thoughts on genius and invention, suggestions
for an improved mode of printing, ... and a concise history of callicoe printing. 2 vol. London: 1789-92; Is-
lington: 1792; with new title page. London: Hamilson &
Co, 1795. BM

7113 O'Neill, Charles, 1831- . A Dictionary of Dyeing and Calico
Printing: containing a brief account of all the substances
and processes in use in the arts of dyeing and printing textile fabrics. Philadelphia: H. C. Baird, 1869. 491pp,
bib DLC

7114 _____. The Practice and Principles of Calico Printing,
bleaching, dyeing, etc. 2 vol. Philadelphia?: 1878.
SIB-1

7115 Osumi (or Ozumi), Tamezo. Printed Cottons of Asia: the
romance of trade textiles. Rev. & adjusted by George
Saito. Tokyo: Bijutsu Shuppan-Sha; Rutland, Vt: Tuttle;
London: Prentice-Hall, 1963. 187pp, 88 color pls, bib

7116 Percival, MacIver. The Chintz Book. London: Heinemann,
1923. 103pp, ill, pls (4 color), bib DLC

7117 Pettit, Florence Harvey. America's Indigo Blues; resist-
printed and dyed textiles of the 18th century. New York:
Hastings House, 1975. 251pp, ill, 8 color pls, gloss (65
examples ill)

7118 _____. America's Printed and Painted Fabrics, 1600-1900.
New York: Hastings House, 1970. 256pp, many ill, 6
color pls, bib

7119 Robinson, Stuart. A History of Printed Textiles. Cambridge,
Mass: MIT Pr, 1969. 152pp, ill, bib

7120 Sansone, Antonio. Dyeing: comprising the dyeing and bleaching
of wool, silk, cotton, flax, hemp, china grass etc. 2 vol.
Manchester, Eng: A. Heywood, 1888. 211 patterns on 29
pls; 45 pls (Vol. II. Patterns) DLC

7121 _____. Printing of Cotton Fabrics: comprising calico
bleaching, painting, dyeing. Manchester: A. Heywood,
1887. 385pp, ill, 42 colour printed patterns DLC

7122 Sims, T. Dyeing and Bleaching. London: 1876. See:
Bevan, G. P., British Manufacturing Industries, Vol. 6.

7123 Smith, A. D. Howell. Brief Guide to Oriental Painted, Dyed

and Printed Textiles. V & A. London: HMSO, 1924;
1950. 32pp, 16 pls; 20pp, 20 pls, bib

7124 _____ . Brief Guide to the Western Painted, Dyed and
Printed Textiles. London: V & A, 1924; rev. ed. ed.
by M. Clayton. London: 1938. 32pp, ill, 16 pls, bib
BM

7125 Tuchscherer, Jean Michel. The Fabrics of Mulhouse and Alsace, 1801-1850. Leigh-on-Sea: F. Lewis, 1972. 32pp,
52 pls, bib (Printed fabrics)

HANDWEAVING AND HANDWOVEN FABRICS

7126 Ackerman, Phyllis. Handwoven Textiles. Enjoy your museum
series. Pasadena, Cal: Esto Publishing, 1935. 16pp, ill

7127 Atwater, Mary Meigs. A Book of Patterns for Hand-Weaving,
designs from the John Landes drawings in the Pennsylvania
Museum. Cambridge, Mass: Shuttlecraft Guild, 1925. ill

7128 * _____ . The Shuttlecraft Book of American Hand-weaving,
being an account of the rise, development, eclipse and
modern revival of a national popular art, together with information of interest and value to collectors, technical
notes for the use of weavers, and a large collection of
historic patterns. New York: Macmillan, 1928; 1931;
1933; 1935; 1937; 1939; ...; rev. ed. 1951; 1954;...
1928-37: 275pp, ill; 1937-45: 281pp, ill; 1951-54: 341pp,
ill

7129 Barlow, Alfred. The History and Principles of Weaving by
Hand and by Power, with a chapter on lace-making machinery. London: S. Low, Marston, Searle & Rivington,
1876; London: S. Low; Philadelphia: H. C. Baird, 1878;
2nd ed. London: 1879; 3rd ed. 1884; 1898; Philadelphia:
1900. 443pp, ill, pls NN, SKM

7130 Bogdonoff, Nancy Dick. Handwoven Textiles of Early New
England: the legacy of a rural people, 1649-1880. Harrisburg, Pa: Stackpole, 1975. ill, color pls, bib

7131 Bowles, Ella Shannon. Homespun Handicrafts. Philadelphia;
London: Lippincott, 1931. 251pp, 60 ill NN, DLC, BM

7132 Brett, Katharine B. Ontario Handwoven Textiles; an introduction to hand-weaving in Ontario in the 19th century. Toronto: Royal Ontario Museum, 1956. 18pp, pls

7133 Gamble, William Burt. Hand-spinning and Hand-weaving. A
list of references in the New York Public Library. Reprint
from its Bulletin. New York: 1922. 41pp

7134   Gilroy, Clinton G.   The Art of Weaving, by Hand and by
       power; with an account of recent improvements in the art,
       and a sketch of the history of its rise and progress in
       ancient and modern times.   For the use of manufacturers
       and practical weavers, etc.   New York: G. D. Baldwin,
       1844; London: Wiley & Putnam, 1845; 2nd ed. London:
       Henry Washbourne, 1848.   574pp, ill, pls; 537pp, 34 pls;
       text, hundreds of ill, 30 pls

7135   Hooper, Luther.   Hand-Loom Weaving, plain and ornamental
       ... also ... several illustrations from ancient and modern
       textiles.   London: J. Hogg; New York: Macmillan, 1910;
       London; New York: Pitman, 1920; 1925; 1949.   341pp, ill,
       18 pls   BM, PPL, NN

7136   _____.   Weaving with Small Appliances.   3 vol.   London:
       Pitman, 1922-25.   ill   BM

7137   Reath, Nancy Andrews.   The Weaves of Hand-Loom Fabrics;
       a classification with historical notes.   Philadelphia: Penn-
       sylvania Museum, 1927.   64pp, ill (Weaves of cloth, twill,
       brocade, satin, velvet, etc.)   NN

EMBROIDERY, NEEDLEWORK, NEEDLEPOINT,
SAMPLERS AND CREWEL

7138   Ackerman, Phyllis.   Embroidery in Persia.   Reprint from
       Embroidery, December 1934.   New York: American Insti-
       tute for Persian Art and Architecture, 193-?   7pp, ill, pl

7139 *Alford, Marian Margaret.   Needlework as Art.   1 vol, or 1
       vol in 3.   London: Low, Marston, Searle, 1886; reprint.
       Wakefield, Eng: EP Publishing, 1975.   422pp, ill, 85 pls,
       bib

7140   Art and Ecclesiastical Embroidery.   London; New York: But-
       terick, 1898.   128pp, ill

7141   Ashton, Sir Arthur Leigh B.   Samplers.   London; Boston:
       Medici Society, 1926.   14pp, ill, 77 pls, color frontis, bib
       DeWint, BM

7142   _____, and Alan John B. Wace.   Brief Guide to the Persian
       Embroideries.   Pref. by Eric Maclagan.   London: V & A,
       1929; 1937; 1950.   19pp, ill, 16 pls, bib

7143   Baker, Muriel Lewis.   A Handbook of American Crewel Em-
       broidery.   Rutland, Vt: Tuttle; London: Prentice-Hall,
       1966.   67pp, ill, bib

7144   _____.   The XYZ's of Canvas Embroidery.   Sturbridge,
       Mass: Old Sturbridge Village, 1971.   pls

7145 Barber, Mary. Some Drawings of Ancient Embroidery, 30
      Specimens. Introd. by W. Butterfield. London; Man-
      chester: H. Sotheran, 1880. 29 (26 color) pls, color
      frontis NN, BM

7146 Barker, Aldred Farrer. Embroideries and Embroidery Ma-
      chines, etc. Reprint from The Textile Recorder, Vol.
      16, 1898. London; Manchester: Heywood, 1898. 71pp,
      pls NN

      Boler, James. See: Taylor, John, no. 7302.

7147 *Bolton, Ethel Stanwood, and Eva Johnston Coe. American
      Samplers. Pref. by Margaret Woodbridge Cushing.
      Boston: the Massachusetts Society of The Colonial Dames
      of America, 1921; reprints. Princeton, NJ: Pyne Pr,
      1973; New York: Dover; London: Constable, 1973. 416pp,
      ill, 126 pls, color frontis (To 1830)

7148 A Booke of Curious and Strange Inventions, called the first
      part of needleworkes, containing many singular and fine
      sortes of cut-workes, raisde-workes, stiches, and open cut-
      worke ... newlie augmented. First imprinted in Venice
      (C. B. Ciotti's Prima Parte de' Flori e disegni di varie
      sorti di ricami moderni) and now again newly printed in
      more exquisite sort, for the profit and delight of the gentle-
      women of England. London: William Barley, 1596. BM

7149 Books on Needlework in the New York Public Library. New
      York: Library's Bulletin iii, pp. 365-70, 1899.

7150 Brett, Gerard. Elizabethan Embroideries. London: V & A,
      1948. ill (Originally published as Part 1. of A Picture
      Book of English Embroideries)

7151   . Flowers in English Embroidery. London: V & A,
      1948. ill

7152 Brett, Katharine B. English Embroidery, 16th to 18th centu-
      ries; collections of the Royal Ontario Museum. Toronto:
      the Museum, 1972. 94pp, ill, color pls, bib

7153 Brief Guide to the Chinese Embroideries. V & A. London:
      HMSO, 1921; rev. ed. 1931. 12pp, ill, 8 pls BM

7154 Catalogue of a Collection of Old Embroideries of the Greek
      Islands and Turkey. London: Burlington Fine Arts Club,
      1914. 61pp BM

7155 Catalogue of Samplers. V & A. 2nd ed. London: 1915; 3rd
      ed. 1922. 47pp, 12 ill; 65pp, 16 ill, 12 pls, bib

7156 *Caulfield, Sophia Frances Anne, and Blanche C. Saward. The

Dictionary of Needlework. An encyclopedia of artistic, plain and fancy needlework. 6 vol. London: Upcott Gill, 1882; 2nd ed. 1 vol. 1887; facsim. reprint of 1882 ed. Feltham: Hamlyn; New York: Arco, 1972; 2 vol. reprint of 2nd ed. as Encyclopedia of Victorian Needlework. New York: Dover, 1972. 1887: 530pp, 822 ill, 41 color pls

7157   Cave, Oenone. English Folk Embroidery. London: Mills & Boon, 1965; New York: Taplinger, 1966. 101pp, ill, bib (Smocking)

7158   _____. Linen Cut-Work. New York: Hearthside Pr, 1963. 94pp, ill

7159   Christie, Grace (Mrs. Archibald H.), ed. Embroidery. A collection of articles on subjects connected with the study of fine needlework, including stitches, materials, methods of work, and designing, and history. With numerous illustrations and coloured plates, of modern work. London: J. Pearsall, 1909. 168pp, 116 ill, 30 (24 color) pls NN

7160   _____. Embroidery and Tapestry Weaving; a practical textbook of design and workmanship. London: J. Hogg, 1906; 4th ed. 1915; 4th ed. London; New York: Pitman, 1928; 1933. 403pp, ill, pls DLC, PPULC

7161 * _____. English Medieval Embroidery ... From the beginning of the 10th century until the end of the 14th: together with a descriptive catalogue of the surviving examples, etc. Oxford, Eng: Clarendon Pr, 1938. 224pp, ill, 160 pls, color frontis, bib BM

7162   _____. Samplers and Stitches, a handbook of the embroiderer's art. New York: Dutton, 1920; London: Batsford, 1921; 2nd ed. rev. & enl. New York; London: 1929; 3rd ed. London: 1934; 4th ed. London: 1948; 1950; New York: Hearthside, 1959. 142pp, 239 ill, 34 pls, color frontis PPULC, BM

7163   Church Embroidery: a manual of instructions for beginners in the art. London: Ward, Lock, 1886. 62pp, 7 pls NN

7164 *Colby, Averil. Samplers: yesterday and today. London: Batsford, 1964; as Samplers. Newton Center, Mass: C. T. Branford, 1965. 266pp, ill, bib

7165   Cole, Alan Summerly. Ancient Needlepoint and Pillow Lace, with notes on the history of lace making. London: Arundel Society, 1875. 12pp, ill, 20 pls (30 examples) PPULC, BM

7166   _____, ed. Catalogue of the Special Loan Exhibition of

Decorative Art Needlework Made Before 1800.   South
Kensington Museum.   London: 1873; 1874.   18 pls

7167   .   A Descriptive Catalogue of the Collections of
Tapestry and Embroidery in the South Kensington Museum.
London: SKM, 1888; A Supplemental Descriptive Catalogue
of Embroideries and Tapestry-woven Specimens.   Acquired
... between 1886 and June 1890.   London: Eyre & Spottiswoode, 1891; another supplement ... 1890-1894.   London: 1896.   432pp, bib; 48pp; 66pp   BM

7168   Crewel Craft: being a brief history of Ye Antient Craft.
Birkenhead: Bidston Hill, 1926.   23pp, ill, 5 color pls

7169   Crewel Embroidery, Old and New.   By editors of Weldons,
Ltd., London.   New York: Hearthside, 1963.   96pp, ill

7170   Davis, Mildred J.   Early American Embroidery Designs.
New York: Crown, 1969.   159pp, ill, bib

7171   .   Embroidery Designs 1780-1820.   New York: Crown,
1971.   92pp, chiefly ill   (From the manuscript collection,
the Textile Resource and Research Center, Valentine Museum, Richmond, Va.)

7172   Day, Lewis Foreman, and Mary Buckle.   Art in Needlework;
a book about embroidery.   London: Batsford, 1900; 1901;
3rd rev. ed. 1907; 3rd rev. & enl. ed. London: Batsford;
New York: Scribner, 1908; 4th ed. rev. London: 1914;
5th ed. rev. London: 193-?   262pp, ill; 274pp, ill   NN,
PP, NNC-Ave

7173   Delamotte, Freeman Gage.   The Embroiderers' Book of Design, containing initials, emblems, cyphers, monograms,
ornamental borders, ecclesiastical devices, mediaeval and
modern alphabets, and national emblems.   London: E. &
F. N. Spon, 1860; 4th ed. London: Crosby Lockwood,
1903.   2pp, 19 pls   NN

7174   The Delineator.   Monthly.   New York: Butterick, 1873-1937.
ill   (Needlework, dressmaking, etc.)

7175   Dolby, Anastasia Marice.   Church Embroidery, Ancient and
Modern.   London: Chapman & Hall, 1867.   176pp, ill,
20 pls, color frontis   DLC, BM

7176   Dongerkery, Kamala S.   The Romance of Indian Embroidery.
Bombay: Thacker, 1951.   62pp, ill

7177   Drew, Joan.   Embroidery and Design; a handbook of the principles of decorative art as applied to embroidery, illustrated
by typical designs.   Fore. by Miss M. M. Allan.   New

York: Dutton; London; New York: Pitman, 1916. 103pp,
ill MB, NN

7177a Edwards, Joan. Crewel Embroidery in England. New York:
William Morrow, 1975. 40 color pls

7178 The Embroiderers. Quarterly. London: Pearsall, 1923-29.
ill

7179 Embroidery. Quarterly. London: Embroiderers Guild, 1932- .

7180 Embroidery. The Ladies' Self Instructor in millinery and
mantua making, embroidery and applique, canvas-work,
knitting, netting and crochetwork. Philadelphia: J. &
J. L. Gihon, 1853. 207pp, pls (See The Ladies' Guide
in Needlework ...) DeWint

7181 The Embroidery Book, illustrating the Ladies' Home Journal
Embroidery Patterns. Monthly. New York: Home Pattern, 1909- .

7182 The Embroidery Magazine. Quarterly. New York: Pictorial
Review, 1909-1910.

7183 [No entry.]

7184 European Embroideries of the 16th and 17th Centuries. Exhibition. May-June 1941. Chicago: Art Institute, 1941.
8pp, 7 pls

7185 Exhibition of British Embroidery from the 13th to the 19th
Century. February-March 1959. Birmingham, Eng: Museum & Art Gallery, 1959. 54pp, 4 pls

7186 Exhibition of Early English Needlework and Furniture. March
1928. London: 1928. DFo

7187 Exhibition of English Embroidery Executed Prior to the Middle
of the 16th Century. Introd. by A. F. Kendrick. London:
Burlington Fine Arts Club, 1905. 87pp, ill, 30 (10 color)
pls BM

7188 The Fechimer Collection. A Picture book of English domestic
embroidery of the 16th to 19th centuries. Detroit: Institute of Arts, 1948. 40pp, ill (Emma S. Fechimer)

7189 Fel, Edit. Hungarian Peasant Embroidery. Tr. from Hun-
garian (1958) by Annie Barat and Lily Halapy. London:
Batsford, 1961; Budapest: Corvina, 1969; 2nd rev. ed.
London: Constable, 1971. 138pp, ill; 87pp, ill, 244 pls

7190 Finch, Lady E. The Sampler, a system of teaching plain

needlework in schools.   2nd ed.   London: 1855.   14 pls
BM

7191   Fitzwilliam, Lady Ada Wentworth, and A. F. Morris Hands.
       Jacobean Embroidery: its forms and fillings, including
       late Tudor.   London: K. Paul, 1912; 1913; 1928.   56pp,
       29 (4 color) pls

7192   Flowers in English Embroidery.   V & A.   London: HMSO,
       1963.   ill

       Frank Leslie's Ladies' Gazette of Fashion....   See: no. 7253.

7193   Freehof, Lillian B., and Bucky King.   Embroideries and
       Fabrics for Synagogue and Home; 5000 years of ornamental
       needlework.   New York: Hearthside, 1966.   224pp, ill, bib

7194   Freeman, Margaret Beam.   The St. Martin Embroideries; a
       15th-century series illustrating the life and legend of St.
       Martin of Tours.   New York: Metropolitan Museum, dist.
       by N.Y. Graphic Society, Greenwich, 1968.   131pp, ill,
       bib

7195   Fry, Gladys Windsor.   Embroidery and Needlework; being a
       textbook on design and technique, with numerous reproduc-
       tions of original drawings and works by the Author.   Lon-
       don: Pitman, 1935; 3rd ed. 1943; 1944; 1946.   278pp, ill,
       pls (part color)

7196   Georgian Embroideries.   London: V & A, 1928.   ill (Part
       III of A Picture Book of English Embroideries)

7197   Gilbert, Barbara L.   American Crewel-Work, 1700-1850.
       Thesis.   1965.   139pp, pls DeWint

7198   Gostelow, Mary.   A World of Embroidery.   New York: Scrib-
       ner, 1975.   170 photographs, 57 color pls, 235 diagrams,
       bib (Every country)

7199   Guide to the Collection of Samplers and Embroideries.   Cardiff:
       National Museum of Wales, 1939.   92pp

7200   Haggin, L.   Handbook of Embroidery.   London: 1880. SIB-2

7201   Hale, Lucretia Peabody, ed.   Designs in Outline for Art-
       Needlework.   Boston: S. W. Tilton, 1879.   pls

7202   _____.   More Stitches for Decorative Embroidery: contain-
       ing the Holbein, punto, tirato (drawn work)....   Boston:
       S. W. Tilton, 1879.   58pp, ill DLC

7203   _____, and Margaret E. White.   300 Decorative and Fancy

Articles for Presents, fairs, etc. Boston: S. W. Tilton, 1885. 206pp, ill DLC

7204 Hanley, Hope. Needlepoint. New York: Scribner, 1964. 156pp, ill, bib (Chiefly a how-to)

7205 * _____. Needlepoint in America. New York: Scribner, 1969. 160pp, ill, 6 color pls, bib

7206 *Harbeson, Georgiana Brown. American Needlework; history of decorative stitchery and embroidery from late 16th to 20th century. New York: Coward-McCann; New York: Bonanza, 1938; reprint. New York: 19-? 232pp, 400 ill, 6 color ill, bib

7207 Harris, Kathleen M. Embroidery, a Reader's Guide. London: Cambridge U Pr, for National Book League, 1950. 19pp (including 11 page introduction to subject of embroidery) NNC-Ave

7208 Hartland, H. R. Exhibition of British Embroidery from the 13th Century to the 19th Century. February-March 1959. Birmingham, Eng: Museum & Art Gallery, 1959. 54pp, ill

7209 Hartley, Florence. The Ladies' Hand Book of Fancy and Ornamental Work Comprising Directions and Patterns for Working in Applique, Beadwork, Braiding, etc. Compiled from the best authorities. Philadelphia: G. G. Evans, 1859; 1860; 1861. 240pp, ill, pls MB, DLC, PP

7210 Hartshorne, Charles Henry. English Mediaeval Embroidery, with a practical chapter by another hand. London; Oxford: J. H. Parker, 1845; 1848. ...; 132pp, 40 pls

7211 *Hawley, William H., ed., comp. Chinese Folk Design. A collection of cut-paper designs used for embroidery, together with 160 Chinese art symbols and their meanings. Hollywood, Cal: Author, 1949. u.p., ill of 300 designs plus 160 symbols ("Hua yang" designs) NN

7212 Head, Mrs. R. E. The Lace and Embroidery Collector: a guide to collectors of old lace and embroidery. New York: Dodd, Mead; London: Jenkins, 1922; reprints. Ann Arbor, Mich: Gryphon Books, 1971; Detroit: Gale Research, 1974. 252pp, 49 ill, bib, gloss (Includes samplers)

7213 Hedlund, Catherine A. A Primer of New England Crewel Embroidery. Sturbridge, Mass: Old Sturbridge Village, 1963; 1967; enl. ed. 1971; 1973. 47pp, ill; 64pp, ill; 76pp, ill; 73pp, ill

7214 *Higgin, Louis. Handbook of Embroidery. Ed. by Lady
      Marian Alford. Published by authority of the Royal School
      of Art Needlework. London: S. Low, Marston, Searle;
      New York: Scribner & Welford, 1880. 106pp, ill, 16
      pls (part color) MH, PPL

7215 Hill, Clare. Needlework. London: Chapman & Hall, 1903.
      312pp, ill, pls

7216 Holme, Geoffrey, 1887-1954, ed. A Book of Old Embroidery.
      With articles by A. F. Kendrick, L. F. Pesel, and E. W.
      Newberry. London; New York: The Studio, 1921. 40pp,
      97 (7 color) pls NN, DLC

7217 Hornor, Marianna Merritt. The Story of Samplers. Fore.
      by Evan H. Turner. Philadelphia: Museum of Art, 1971.
      18pp, 48 pls

7218 Howe, Margery Burnham. Early American Embroideries in
      Deerfield, Massachusetts. Deerfield: Heritage Founda-
      tion, 1963. 40pp, pls

7219 Hughes, Therle. English Domestic Needlework, 1660-1860.
      London: Lutterworth; New York: Macmillan, 1961.
      255pp, ill, 53 pls

7220 *Huish, Marcus Bourne. Samplers and Tapestry Embroideries.
      Also the stitchery of same by Mrs. Head.... London;
      New York: Longmans, Green, and the Fine Arts Society,
      1900; 2nd ed. 1913; reprint. New York: Dover, 1970.
      143pp, 77 ill, 56 (28 color) pls; 176pp, 101 (24 color) ill
      (250 years of samplers, embroideries, etc. Book is out-
      come of the 1900 exhibit at the Fine Art Society, London.
      2nd ed. contains some American samplers not in 1st)

7221 *Hunton, W. Gordon. English Decorative Textiles; tapestry
      and chintz, their design and development from the earliest
      times to the 19th century. London: J. Tiranti, 1930.
      9pp, ill, pls, bib DLC, MiU

7222 Illustrated Catalogue of English Samplers and Embroidery Pic-
      tures Shown in the Georgian House, Bristol. Bristol:
      City Art Gallery, 1951. 8pp, ill

7223 Instructions on Needle-work and Knitting, as derived from the
      practice of the Central School, Baldwin's Gardens, Gray's
      Inn Lane, London. London: Roake & Varty; C., J., G.,
      & F. Rivington; and Hatchard & Son, 1829. 26pp, 9 speci-
      mens of needlework (7 are miniature garments) DeWint

7224 Johnstone, Pauline. Greek Island Embroidery. London: Ti-
      ranti, 1964. 58pp, ill, 88 (4 color) pls

7225 _____ . A Guide to Greek Island Embroidery. V & A.
        London: HMSO, 1972. 111pp, chiefly ill, pls, bib

7226 Jones, Emily G. A Manual of Plain Needlework and Cutting-
        Out. London: J. Hughes, 1884; new rev. ed. by Miss
        Fanny Heath and Miss S. Lock. London: Longmans,
        Green, 1887. 112pp, ill, 5 pls; 128pp, ill, 7 pls

7227 *Jones, Mary Eirwen. British Samplers. Oxford, Eng: Pen-
        in-Hand Publishing, 1948. 85pp, pls DLC

7228 _____ . A History of Western Embroidery. London: Studio
        Vista; New York: Watson-Guptill, 1969. 159pp, 85 (12
        color) ill, bib

7229 Jourdain, Margaret. The History of English Secular Embroi-
        dery. London: K. Paul, Trench, Trubner, 1910; New
        York: Dutton, 1912. 202pp, ill, pls NN, DeWint

7230 The Journal of the Embroiderers' Guild. London: 1932- .

7231 Kassell, Hilda. Stitches in Time; the art and history of em-
        broidery. New York: Duell, Sloan & Pearce, 1966.
        108pp, ill (American embroidery)

7232 *Kendrick, Albert Frank. English Embroidery. London:
        Batsford; New York: Scribner, 1904; London: G. Newnes;
        New York: Scribner's, 1905; 1913. 126pp, ill, 65 (4
        color) pls, bib

7233 * _____ . English Needlework. London: A. & C. Black,
        1933; 2nd ed. rev. by Patricia Wardle. London: Black;
        New York: Barnes & Noble, 1967. 192pp, ill, 24 pls;
        212pp, ill, 31 pls, bib (14th-19th century)

7234 * _____ , Louisa F. Pesel, and E. W. Newberry. A Book of
        Old Embroidery. Ed. by Geoffrey Holme. London: Studio,
        1921. 40pp, ill, 87 (7 color) pls, color frontis, bib (The
        whole world)

7235 Kergman, Marie Louise, ed. Punto-tirato, or drawn work.
        Brooklyn: Henry Bristow, 1883. 31pp, ill DeWint

7236 King, Donald. Opus Anglicanum; English medieval embroidery.
        Exhibition. V & A. London: Arts Council, 1963. 64pp,
        ill, pls

7237 _____ . Samplers. V & A. London: HMSO, 1960. 62
        pls, bib (Early 17th to mid 19th century)

7238 Kocsis (later Foris), Maria. History of Folk Cross Stitch.
        Ed. by Andreas Foris. Tr. and introd. by Heinz Edgar

Kiewe. Nuremberg: Sebaldus-Verlag, 1950; 2nd ed. as
Folk Cross Stitch; 278 color charts collected from countries
along the Danube. Nuremberg: Sebaldus-Verlag; Oxford:
Art Needlework Industries, 1955. 77pp, ill

7239 The Ladies' Guide in Needlework. A gift for the industrious,
containing instructions in canvas work, knitting, netting,
and crochet work, millinery and mantua-making, embroidery and applique. American ed. Philadelphia: W. A.
Leary, 1850. ill (See Embroidery; the Ladies' Self Instructor ...)

7240 The Ladies' Handbook of Baby Linen: containing plain and
ample instructions for the preparation of an infant's ward-
robe. London: 1843; New York: J. S. Redfield, 1844.
60pp, ill BM

7241 The Ladies' Hand-Book of Embroidery on Muslin, lace work,
and tatting.... London: 1843; New York: J. S. Redfield,
1844. 60pp, ill CtY, BM

7242 The Ladies' Hand-Book of Fancy Needle Work and Embroidery
.... London: 1842; New York: J. S. Redfield, 1844.
60pp, ill NN, BM

7243 The Ladies' Hand-Book of Needlework. Cincinnati: J. Shillito,
1879. 32pp, ill DLC

7244 The Ladies' Hand-Book of Plain Needlework. London: 1842;
American ed. by an American Lady. New York: Redfield,
1844. 60pp, ill BM

7245 The Ladies' Work-Book, containing instructions in knitting,
netting, point-lace, embroidery, crochet, etc. London:
Cassell, 1852; 1854? 98pp, ill MB, BM

7246 The Ladies' Work-Table Book; containing instructions in plain
and fancy needle-work, embroidery, etc. New York: J.
Winchester, 1844; Philadelphia: G. B. Zeiber, 1845; 3rd
ed. London: 1850; Philadelphia: T. B. Peterson, 185-?;
1863? 168pp, ill ViU, NN, BM

7247 The Lady's Handbook of Fancy Needlework. Containing 400
new designs in ornamental needlework. London: Ward,
Lock, 188-? 383pp, ill

7248 The Lady's Keepsake; or, Treasures of the needle. Pref. by
Aiguillette. London: Darton, 1851. ill DLC

7249 Lambert, Miss A. The Hand-Book of Needlework, by F. S.
London: 1842; 3rd ed. with illustrations and additions.
London: J. Murray, 1843; as The Ladies' Complete Guide

to Needlework and Embroidery. Philadelphia: T. B.
Peterson, 1859. ...; 400pp, ill; 327pp, ill BM

7250   Landon, Mary Taylor, and Susan Burrows Swan. American
       Crewelwork. New York: Macmillan, 1970. 192pp, ill
       (part color)

7251   Lane, Rose Wilder. Woman's Day Book of American Needle-
       work. New York: Simon & Schuster, 1974. 208pp, 140
       color ill

7252   Lefebure, Ernest. Embroidery and Lace: their manufacture
       and history from the remotest antiquity to the present day.
       A handbook for amateurs, collectors, and general readers.
       Tr. and enl. by Alan S. Cole. London: H. Grevel, 1888;
       1889; Philadelphia: Lippincott, 1889. 326pp, 156 ill

7253   Frank Leslie's Ladies' Gazette of Fashion and Fancy Needle-
       work. Monthly. New York: 1854- .

7254   Lessing, Julius. Old German Patterns for Linen Cross Stitch
       Work. 3 vol. Berlin: Lipperheide, 1880. ill PP

7255   Levey, Santina. Discovering Embroidery of the 19th Century.
       Tring: Shire Publications, 1971. 64pp, ill (English
       1800-1900)

7256   List of Books on Needlework in Edinburgh Museum Library.
       Edinburgh: 1892.

7257   A List of Samplers in the Victoria and Albert Museum. Lon-
       don: 1906; 2nd ed. 1915; 3rd ed. 1922. 21pp; 47pp, 12
       ill; 65pp, 12 ill

7258   Lockwood, Mary Smith, and Elizabeth Glaister. Art Embroi-
       dery. A treatise on the revived practice of decorative
       needlework. London; Belfast: Marcus Ward, 1878. 83pp,
       ill, 19 color pls PPL

7259   Manual of English Mediaeval Embroidery. London: J. H. &
       J. Parker, 1848. ill

7260   *Marshall, Frances, and Hugh Marshall. Old English Embroi-
       dery: its technique and symbolism. London: H. Cox,
       1894. 138pp, 31 ill, 17 pls MB

7261   Masé, E. (pseud. for Eliza Mary Ann Savage). Art-Needle-
       work; a guide to embroidery in crewels, silks, applique,
       etc. London: Home Help Series, 1877.

7262   May, Florence Lewis. Catalogue of Laces and Embroideries
       in the Collection of the Hispanic Society of America. New
       York: 1936. 147pp, 48 pls, bib TxU

7263 Meulenbelt-Niewburg, Albarta. Embroidery Motifs from Old
         Dutch Samplers. New York: Scribner's, 1975. (Over 700
         cross-stitch patterns)

7264 Morris, Barbara J. History of English Embroidery. V & A.
         London: HMSO, 1951. 48pp, ill, bib

7265 *_____. Victorian Embroidery. Fore. by Hugh Wakefield.
         London: Jenkins, 1962; New York: Nelson, 1963. 238pp,
         19 ill, 71 pl, bib (Includes the Work Societies, Irish
         lace making and embroidery schools, also American work)

7266 Moura, Maria Clementina C. de. Traditional Embroidery of
         Portugal, Complete with Designs. London; New York:
         Batsford, 1952. 58pp, ill NN, DLC

7267 Needle and Bobbin Club Bulletin. Semi-annual. New York:
         1916- .

7268 Needle and Brush: Useful and Decorative. New York: But-
         terick, 1889. many ill (Embroidery, piano covers, table
         covers, lambrequins, quilts, frames and cases for photo-
         graphs, fans, baskets, pincushions, painting on glass and
         china, etc.)

7269 The Needle's Excellency. Exhibition. V & A. London:
         HMSO, 1973. 56pp, ill, bib (ca. 1570-ca. 1700)

7270 Needlework and Allied Crafts in Guilford Museum. Guilford,
         Surrey: Guilford Corporation, 1972. 22pp, ill, 6 pls, bib

7271 *Nevinson, John Lea. Catalogue of English Domestic Embroi-
         dery of the 16th and 17th Centuries. V & A. London:
         HMSO, 1938; 1950. 107pp, ill, 72 pls, color frontis, bib
         BM

7272 Notes on Applied Work and Patchwork. V & A. London:
         HMSO, 1938; 2nd ed. 1949. 18pp, 16 pls, bib (English)

7273 Owen, Mrs. H. Illuminated Book of Needlework, preceded by
         a history of needlework. London?: 1847. SIB-2

7274 Palliser, Mrs. Bury (Fanny Marryat). A Descriptive Cata-
         logue of the Lace and Embroidery in the South Kensington
         Museum. London: 1871; 2nd ed. 1873; 3rd ed. rev. &
         enl. by Alan S. Cole. 1881. 14 ill BM

7275 Payne, F. G. Guide to the Collection of Samplers and Em-
         broideries. Cardiff: National Museum of Wales, and the
         Press Board of the University of Wales, 1939. 92pp, 21
         pls NN

7276 A Picture Book of English Domestic Embroidery of the 16th to

the 19th Century.   Detroit: Institute of Arts, 1948.   40pp,
ill

7277   A Picture Book of English Embroideries.   4 parts.   London:
       V & A, 19- . (1. Elizabethan Embroideries, by G.
       Brett; 2. Stuart Embroideries; 3. Georgian Embroideries;
       4. English Chairs, by Ralph Edwards)

7278   Porter, Anna M.   Norwegian Drawn Work (Hardanger) ...
       Gittertyl, Filet.   Asbury Park, NJ: Kinmouth Pr, 1905.
       40pp, ill DLC

7279   Proctor, Molly Geraldine.   Victorian Canvas Work: Berlin
       wool work.   London: Batsford, 1972.   160pp, 87 ill, 4
       color pls, bib

7280   Pullan, Mrs. Matilda Marian Chesney.   The Lady's Manual
       of Fancy-Work: a complete instructor in every variety of
       ornamental needle-work: including applique, bead-work,
       Berlin-work, braiding, bobbin-work ... and a glossary of
       French and German terms used in needle-work, not to be
       found in any dictionary.   New York: Dick & Fitzgerald,
       1859.   300 ill, 8 folding pls, "The Ladies Lexicon of Fancy
       Needlework" DLC

7281   Reed, John Q., and Eliza M. Lavin.   Needle-craft: artistic
       and practical.   New York: Butterick, 1889.   320pp, ill
       DLC

7282   Ring, Betty, ed.   Needlework, an Historical Survey.   Articles
       reprinted from the Magazine Antiques.   New York: Uni-
       verse, Main Street, 1975.   176pp, 300 ill

7283   Risley, Christine.   Machine Embroidery.   With an historic
       survey by Patricia Wardle.   Newton Centre, Mass: C. T.
       Branford, 1961.   128pp, ill

7284   Samplers.   V & A.   London: HMSO, 1947.   ill

7285   Schiffer, Margaret Berwind.   Historical Needlework of Penn-
       sylvania.   New York: Scribner, 1968.   160pp, ill

7286   A Schole-house for the Needle.   Book u Here Followeth Cer-
       taine Patternes of Cut Workes.   England: R. Schorleyken,
       1627.

7287   Schuette, Marie, and Sigrid Muller-Christensen.   A Pictorial
       History of Embroidery.   Tr. by Donald King.   New York:
       Praeger, 1964; as The Art of Embroidery.   London:
       Thames & Hudson, 1964.   336pp, 464 ill, 300 pls (To
       1900)

7288   Schwab, David E.   The Story of Lace and Embroidery and

Handkerchiefs. New York: Fairchild, 1957. 80, 35pp,
ill

7289 *Seligman, G. Saville, and Talbot Hughes. Domestic Needle-
      work: its origins and customs throughout the centuries.
      London: Country Life, 1931. 95pp, 131 (31 color) pls,
      color frontis (500 objects illustrated. Gloves, stockings,
      purses, caps, shoes, boxes, book covers, cushions, etc.)

7290 Smith, A. D. Howell. Catalogue of Algerian Embroideries.
      V & A. London: 1915; rev. ed. by A. J. B. Wace.
      London: 1935. 14pp, 3 pls; 38pp, pls, bib BM

7291 Smith, Robert Henry Soden. A List of Books and Pamphlets
      in the National Art Library ... Lace and Needlework.
      South Kensington Museum. London: 1879; A List ...
      illustrating textile fabrics, ... lace and needlework. Lon-
      don: 1888. ...; 85pp

7292 *Snook, Barbara. English Historical Embroidery. London:
      Batsford, 1960; reprint as English Embroidery. London:
      Mills & Boon, 1974. 136pp, ill, bib

7293 _____. Florentine Embroidery. New York: Scribner,
      1967. 160pp, ill, bib

7294 Stapley, Mildred. Popular Weaving and Embroidery in Spain.
      New York: W. Helburn, 1924. 60pp, 175 ill, 124 (3
      color) pls DLC

7295 Stearns, Martha Genung. Homespun and Blue; a study of
      American crewel embroidery. London; New York: Scrib-
      ner's, 1940; New York: 1963. 96pp, ill, pls

7296 *Stone, Mrs. Elizabeth. The Art of Needlework, from the
      earliest ages; including some notices of the ancient histori-
      cal tapestries. London: 18-?; 2nd ed. by Countess Mary
      Margaret Wilton. London: H. Colburn, 1840; 3rd ed.
      1841; 1844. 405pp SKM

7297 Stuart Embroideries. London: V & A, 1927.

7298 Swain, Margaret Helen. The Flowerers; the origins and
      history of Ayrshire Needlework. London: W. & R.
      Chambers, 1955. 62pp, ill

7299 _____. Historical Needlework: a study of influences in
      Scotland and Northern England. London: Barrie & Jenkins;
      New York: Scribner, 1970. 140pp, ill, 52 pls, bib (To
      1860)

7300 *_____. The Needlework of Mary Queen of Scots. New
      York; London: Van Nostrand Reinhold, 1973. 128pp, ill,

bib   (Mary, 1542-1587)

7301 *Symonds, Mary, and Louisa Preece. Needlework Through the
      Ages. A short survey of its development in decorative art
      with particular regard to its inspirational relationship with
      other methods of craftsmanship. London: Hodder &
      Stoughton, 1928; 1938. 350 specimens ill, 104 (8 color)
      pls

7302 *Taylor, John, the Water Poet. The Needles Excellency; a
      new book wherein are divers admirable workes wrought
      with the needle, newly invented and out in copper for the
      pleasure and profit of the industrious. London: James
      Boler, 1631; 10th ed. 1626; 12th ed. 1640; 1646; photo-
      static copy of Harvard copy. London: 1949. 8pp, 14 pls
      (imperfect, wanting 8pp and 12 pls); 8pp, 31 pls (imper-
      fect); 42 leaves, ill BM, V & A, MH

7303 Tillett, Leslie. American Needlework, 1776-1976. Fore. by
      Rose Kennedy. New York: Little Brown, 1975. ill

7304 Townsend, W. G. Paulson, and Louisa F. Pesel. Embroidery;
      or, the craft of the needle. Pref. by Walter Crane. Lon-
      don; New York: Truslove, Hanson & Comba, 1899; new
      ed. 1907. 115pp, ill; 328pp, 86 ill, pls

7305 Vinciolo, Federico. Renaissance Patterns for Lace and Em-
      broidery; an unabridged facsimile of the "Singuliers et
      Nouveaux Portraicts" of 1587. Tr. by Stanley Appelbaum.
      New York: Dover, 1971. 93pp, ill

7306 Wace, Alan John Bayard. Catalogue of Algerian Embroideries.
      Rev. ed. London: V & A, 1935. 38pp, ill BM

7307 * _____ . Mediterranean and Near Eastern Embroideries
      from the Collection of Mrs. F. H. (Beatrice) Cook. 2
      vol. London: Halton, 1935. I. 87pp, 8 ill, bib; II. 135
      (56 color) pls

7308 Wandel, Gertie. Danish Embroidery. English and Danish
      text. London: Batsford, 1959. 210pp, ill, 4 color pls

7309 *Wardle, Patricia. Guide to English Embroidery. V & A.
      London: HMSO, 1970. 40pp, ill, 57 pls, bib

7310 Wheeler, Candace Thurber, 1827-1923. The Development of
      Embroidery in America. London; New York: Harper,
      1921. 151pp, ill, pls (part color) (Needles, Puritan
      crewel, Moravian work, samplers, quilts, lace, French
      embroidery, tapestry, Berlin work, etc.)

7311 Wiczyk, Arlene Zeger, comp. A Treasury of Needlework

Projects from Godey's Lady's Book.   New York: Arco, 1972.   320pp, ill

7312   Wingfield Digby, George Frederick.   Elizabethan Embroidery. London: Faber, 1963; New York: Yoseloff, 1964.   151pp, ill, 84 pls, bib

7313   Worthley, A. C., comp.   Needlework: a classified list of books in the State Library of South Australia, together with selected periodical articles.   Adelaide: State Library, 1968.   25pp

LACE

7314   Bath, Virginia Churchill.   Lace, history and guide.   Chicago: Regnery, 1974.   320pp, ill, bib

7315   Beebe, Mrs. C. D.   Lace Ancient and Modern; comprising a history of its origin and manufacture, with instructions concerning the manner of making it.   New York: Sharpes, 1880.   256pp, ill NN, DLC

7316   Birnbaum, Leon.   Legacy in Lace.   New York: Fairchild Publications, 1968.   92pp, ill

7317   Blum, Clara M.   Old World Lace; or, a guide for the lace lover.   New York: Dutton, 1920.   85pp, ill DLC, NN, PPULC

7318   A Book of Engraved Lace Patterns.   London?:   1600?   pls only MiU

7319   Boyle, Elizabeth.   The Irish Flowerers.   Holywood, County Down: Ulster Folk Museum; Belfast: Queen's University, 1971.   160pp, ill, 16 pls, bib   (Lace industry in Ireland, 1600-1920)

7320   Briscoe, John Potter, and S. J. Kirk.   Contributions Towards a Bibliography of Lace.   Nottingham: Free Public Libraries, 1896.   16pp   BM

7321   Catalogue of a Loan Collection of Ancient Lace.   Liverpool: Art Club, 1882.   39pp

7322   Catalogue of the MacCallum Collection of Old Laces and Embroideries, of laces shown by the Bric-a-Brac Club, and of other textiles exhibited at the Museum.   Boston: Museum of Fine Arts, 1878.   39pp

7323   Catalogue to the Collection of Lace.   Dublin: Science and Art Museum, 1937.   74pp

7324 Clifford, Chandler Robbins. The Lace Dictionary. Pocket
      edition including historic and commercial terms, technical
      terms, native and foreign. New York: Clifford & Lawton,
      1913. 156pp, ill NN, NNC-Ave

7325 Cole, Alan Summerly. Ancient Needlepoint and Pillow Lace.
      With notes on the history of lace making. London: Arun-
      del Society, 1875. 12pp, ill, 20 pls (30 examples) BM,
      PPULC

7326 _____ . Catalogue of Lace. General Guide to ... Lace and
      Embroidery. Chapter 1, Part 4. Dublin: Science & Art
      Museum, 1899. 23pp

7327 _____ . Catalogue of the Special Loan Collection of Ancient
      Lace and Fine Art Needlework (at the Midland Counties
      Art Museum). Birmingham, Eng: 1878. SIB-3

7328 _____ . A Supplemental Descriptive Catalogue of Specimens
      of Lace Acquired for the South Kensington Museum between
      1880 and June 1890. London: 1891; supplement ... be-
      tween June 1890 and June 1895. London: 1895. 48pp;
      57pp

7329 _____ , ed. Handmade Laces from the Museum. London:
      V & A, 1890. ill

7330 _____ . A Renascence of the Irish Art of Lace-Making.
      London: Chapman & Hall, 1888. 40pp, 12 pls DLC

7331 Devonia (pseud.). Honiton Lace Making: being full instruc-
      tions for acquiring this beautiful art. London: The Ba-
      zaar, 1873; 2nd enl. ed. as The Honiton Lace Book. 1875.
      ill; 83pp, ill

7332 Douglas, Mrs. The Imperial Macrame Lace Book. Illustra-
      tions and instructions. London: 1879. ill SKM

7333 Fischbach, Friedrich, 1839-1908. Lace Album; a series of
      26 plates of designs for lace. St. Gall, Switzerland?:
      priv. printed, 1878. 26 pls DP

7334 Freeman, Charles Ernest. Pillow Lace in the East Midlands.
      Luton: Museum and Art Gallery, 1958. 51pp, ill, 14 pls,
      bib

7335 Hale, Lucretia Peabody, ed. Point-Lace: a guide to lace-
      work; containing instructions in numerous lace-stitches,
      ... with descriptions of how to copy and imitate old point
      lace. Boston: S. W. Tilton, 1879. 40pp, ill, 6 pls
      NN, DLC

7336 Halls, Zillah. Machine Made Lace in Nottingham in the 18th

and 19th Century.   Nottingham: Art Galleries & Museums
Committee, 1964.   52pp, ill

7337   Hawkins, Daisy Waterhouse.   Old Point Lace and How to Copy
       and Imitate It.   London: Chatto & Windus, 1878.   21pp,
       5 ill, 17 pls MiD

7338   Head, Mrs. R. E.   The Lace and Embroidery Collector: a
       guide to collectors of old lace and embroideries.   London:
       Jenkins; New York: Dodd, Mead, 1922; reprints.   Ann
       Arbor, Mich: Gryphon Books, 1971; Detroit: Gale Re-
       search, 1974.   252pp, 49 ill, bib, gloss   (Includes sam-
       plers)

7339   Henneberg, Alfred von.   The Art and Craft of Old Lace.
       Introd. by Wilhelm Pinder.   London: Batsford; New York:
       E. Weyhe, 1931.   49pp, 182 (8 color) pls, bib   NN

7340   Huetson, T. L.   Lace and Bobbins; a history and collector's
       guide.   Newton Abbot: David & Charles; South Brunswick,
       NJ: A. S. Barnes, 1973.   187pp, ill, bib

7341   Inder, Pamela Mary.   Honiton Lace.   Exeter, Devon: Exeter
       Museums & Art Gallery, 1971.   36pp, ill, bib   (To 1970)

7342   Irish Lace.   Report upon visits to convents, classes, and
       schools where lacemaking and designing for lace are taught
       ... with illustrations of specimens of recently produced
       laces.   London: Eyre & Spottiswoode, for Privy Council,
       1887.

7343   *Jackson, Emily Nevill.   A History of Hand-made Lace.
       Dealing with the origin of lace, the growth of great lace
       centres, the mode of manufacture, the methods of dis-
       tinguishing, and the care of various kinds of lace.   With
       supplementary information by Ernesto Jesurum.   London:
       L. U. Gill; New York: Scribner's, 1900; reprint. Detroit:
       Gale-Tower, 1971.   245pp, 225 ill, 19 pls, 6 pls with 12
       samples of real lace, bib, gloss   DLC, BM

7344   Jones, Mary Eirwen.   The Romance of Lace.   London: Spring,
       1951; London; New York: Staples, 1952.   171pp, ill

7345   *Jourdain, Margaret.   Old Lace, a handbook for collectors; an
       account of the different styles of lace, their history, char-
       acteristics and manufacture.   London: Batsford, 1908;
       1909.   121pp, 95 pls of 163 examples   MB

7346   Kellogg, Charlotte (Hoffman).   Bobbins of Belgium; a book of
       Belgian lace, lace-workers, lace-schools and lace-villages.
       New York; London: Funk & Wagnalls, 1920.   314pp, ill,
       pls   TU, PP, DeWint

7347 The Lace with the Delicate Air. Exhibition. New York:
      Brooklyn Institute of Arts & Sciences Museum, 1956. ill

7348 The Lady's Lace Book; a collection of new designs in point
      lace, Renaissance work, guipure and punto-tirato. Lon-
      don: Ward, Lock, 18-? 95pp

7349 List of Books on Lace in the Library of the Edinburgh Mu-
      seum. Edinburgh: 1892.

7350 Loan Collection of the History of French Laces. Bulletin no.
      5, January 1930. New York: Museum of French Art,
      French Institute in the United States. 1930. DLC

7351 Lochhead, Jessie Helen. Lace-Making in Hamilton. Hamil-
      ton, Scotland: Public Libraries & Museum, 1971. 20pp,
      8 ill, 8 pls, bib (ca.1550-1900)

7352 Longfield, Ada K. Guide to the Collection of Lace, National
      Museum of Ireland. Dublin: Stationery Office, 1970.
      46pp, pls

7353 Lowes, Emily Leigh. Chats on Old Lace and Needlework.
      London: Fisher Unwin; New York: F. A. Stokes, 1908;
      ...; 1925. 386pp, 76 ill, pls, color frontis, bib

7354 May, Florence Lewis. Catalogue of Laces and Embroideries
      in the Collection of the Hispanic Society of America. New
      York: 1936. 147pp, 48 pls, bib TxU

7355 _____. Hispanic Lace and Lace Making. New York: His-
      panic Society of America, 1939. 417pp, 432 ill, pls, bib

7356 Meulen-Nulle, L. W. van der. Lace. Tr. from Dutch. New
      York: Universe, 1964. 79pp, ill

7357 Modern Bobbin Lace in the Collection of the Hispanic Society
      of America. New York: 1931. 24pp, ill, bib (Spanish
      lace)

7358 Moody, A. Penderel. Devon Pillow Lace: its history and how
      to make it. London; New York: Cassell, 1908. 160pp,
      ill DLC

7359 _____. Lace Making and Collecting; an elementary hand-
      book. London: Cassell, 1909. 111pp, ill

7360 *Moore, Hannah (N.) Hudson. The Lace Book. New York:
      F. A. Stokes, 1904; London; Cambridge, Mass: Chapman
      & Hall, 1905; London; Cambridge, Mass: Hodder &
      Stoughton, 1908; New York: Tudor, 1937. 206pp, 70 en-
      gravings BM

7361   Morris, Frances. Notes on Laces of the American Colonists:
       with plates explanatory of lace technique from antique
       laces of the American collectors. New York: William
       Helburn, for Needle & Bobbin Club, 1926. 14pp, 30 pls

7362   _____, and Marian Hague. Antique Laces of American
       Collectors. Exhibition. Metropolitan Museum. 1919.
       New York: William Helburn, for Needle & Bobbin Club,
       1920. ill, pls (Italy, France, Netherlands. 16th-18th
       centuries) NN

7363   *Palliser, Mrs. Bury (Fanny Marryat). A Descriptive Cata-
       logue of the Laces and Embroidery in the South Kensington
       Museum. London: SKM, 1871; 2nd ed. 1873; 3rd ed. rev.
       & enl. by A. S. Cole. 1881. 14 ill BM

7364   *   _____. History of Lace. London: 1865; 2nd ed. 1869;
       3rd ed. 1875; 4th ed. rev. by Margaret Jourdain and Alice
       Dryden. New York: Scribner's, 1902; 3rd ed. facsim.
       reprint. Detroit: Gale-Tower, 1971. 454pp, 169 ill, bib;
       4th ed.: 536pp, 266 ill

7365   Pollen, Maria Margaret (Mrs. John Hungerford). Seven Cen-
       turies of Lace. Pref. by Alan Cole. London: Heinemann;
       New York: Macmillan, 1908. 59pp, 120 pls DLC

7366   Pond, Gabrielle. An Introduction to Lace. London: Garn-
       stone Pr, 1968; 1973. 76pp, ill

7367   Portier, Louise W. Medici Lace and the Art of Making It.
       New York?: 1908. 16pp, ill

7368   Powys, Marian. Lace and Lace Making. Boston: C. T.
       Branford, 1954. ill

7369   The Queen Lace Book. A historical and descriptive account
       of the hand-made antique laces of all countries. London:
       HMSO, 1874. ill SKM

7370   Ricci, Elisa. Old Italian Lace. 2 vol. London: W. Heine-
       mann; Philadelphia: Lippincott, 1913. 716 ill, pls DLC

7371   Schwab, David E. The Story of Lace and Embroidery and
       Handkerchiefs. New York: Fairchild, 1957. 80, 35pp,
       ill

7372   Sharp, Mary. Point and Pillow Lace; a short account of
       various kinds, ancient and modern, and how to recognize
       them. 2nd ed. New York: Dutton; London: J. Murray,
       1905; reprint. Detroit: Gale-Tower, 1971. 202pp, ill,
       43 (4 color) pls, bib, gloss (Italian, French, Flemish,
       English, Irish. Hand and machine)

7373 *Smith, Robert Henry Soden. A List of Books and Pamphlets
      in the National Art Library ... Lace and Needlework.
      South Kensington Museum. London: 1879; as A List of
      Books ... illustrating textile fabrics, ... lace.... Lon-
      don: Eyre & Spottiswoode, 1888. ...; 85pp

7374 Sylvia. Book of Macrame Lace. London: 1885. 5pp

7375 Trendell, P. G. Guide to the Collection of Lace. V & A.
      London: HMSO, 1930. 18pp, 32 pls, bib

7376 Vinciolo, Federico. Renaissance Patterns for Lace and Em-
      broidery; an unabridged facsimile of the "Singuliers et
      Nouveaux Portraicts" of 1587. Tr. by Stanley Applebaum.
      New York: Dover, 1971. 93pp, ill

7377 Wardle, Patricia. Victorian Lace. London: Jenkins, 1968;
      New York: Praeger, 1969. 286pp, ill, bib (English,
      French, Belgian)

7378 Whiting, Gertrude. A Lace Guide for Makers and Collectors.
      With bibliography and five-language nomenclature. New
      York: Dutton, 1920. 415pp, many ill, bib BM

7379 Wright, Thomas, 1859-1936. The Romance of the Lace Pil-
      low: being the history of lace-making in Bucks., Beds.,
      Northants. and neighbouring counties, together with some
      account of the lace industries of Devon and Ireland. Olney:
      H. H. Armstrong, 1919; facsim. reprint. Chicheley: Paul
      P. B. Minet, 1971; McMinville, Ore: Robin & Russ, 1974.
      271pp, ill, 48 pls, bib

KNITTING, KNOTTING, NETTING, TATTING,
CROCHET, MACRAME AND ROPEWORK

7380 The Art of Crochet, with directions for the various stitches,
      and elegant and useful articles, embellished with numerous
      beautiful designs. Ramsgate, Eng: I. Hope, 1846. 80pp,
      ill BM

7381 The Art of Knitting. London; New York: Butterick, 1897.
      152pp, ill

7382 Baynes, Mrs. Godfrey John. The Album of Fancy Needle-
      work. 4 parts. London: Simpkin, Marshall; Gravesend:
      G. J. Baynes, 1847-48. 24pp, 24pp, 24pp, 38pp, ill, pls
      V & A

7383 Bickford, Dana. Illustrated Instruction Book for the Bickford
      Family Knitting Machine. New York: D. Bickford, 1873;
      1875. 59pp, ill DLC

7384   C., M. H. The Old Art of Tatting. By an Englishwoman.
        (Signed: M. H. C.) Bath: Hollway & Son, 1870? 36pp

7385   Douglas, Mrs. The Imperial Macrame Lace Book. Illustra-
        tions and Instructions. London: 1879. ill SKM

7386   Drew, James Meddick. Ropework; knots, hitches, splices,
        halters. Saint Paul, Minn: Webb Book Publishing, 1936.
        69pp, ill DLC

7387   Every, S. F. The Art of Netting; with the method of making
        and mending fishing nets practically explained and illus-
        trated. London: Author, 1845. 54pp, pls MH, DeWint

7388   Gifford, Virginia Snodgrass. An Annotated Bibliography on
        Hand Knitting with an Historical Introduction. Washington,
        D.C.: 1969. 38 leaves

7389   Graumont, Raoul, and John Hensel. Encyclopedia of Knots
        and Fancy Rope Work. New York: Cornell Maritime Pr,
        1939; 1942; rev. enl. ed. 1943; ... 615pp, ill, pls; ...;
        663pp, ill, pls DLC, PP, ViU

7390   _____, and _____. Square Knot, Tatting, Fringe and
        Needle Work. New York: Cornell Maritime Pr, 1943;
        1946. 113pp, ill

7391   Hale, Lucretia Peabody, ed. The Art of Knitting. Containing
        careful directions for beginners as well as instruction in a
        variety of knitting stitches. Boston: S. W. Tilton, 1881.
        103pp, ill DLC

7392   A Handbook of Crochet, Useful and Ornamental. Philadelphia:

G. S. Appleton; New York: D. Appleton, 1949. 64pp
DeWint

7393 Hartley, Marie, and Joan Ingilby. The Old Hand-Knitters of
       the Dales, with an introduction to the early history of
       knitting. Clapham, Lancaster: Dalesman Publishing,
       1951; 1969. 128pp, ill, pls; 80pp, ill, 8 pls BM

7394 *Henson, Gravenor, 1785-1852. The Civil, Political and Me-
       chanical History of the Framework Knitters, in Europe
       and America ... and an account of the rise, progress,
       and present state of the machinery for superseding human
       labors. Vol. 1. Nottingham: R. Sutton, 1831; reprint,
       with new introd. by Stanley D. Chapman, and an excerpt
       from previously unpublished 2nd volume, plus an index.
       New York: A. M. Kelley; Newton Abbot: David & Charles,
       1970. 425pp; 449pp (From William Lee's invention of the
       stocking frame in 1589 to ca.1790) MH-BA

7395 Jutsom, Captain James Netherclift. The Sailor's Book of
       Knots, Bends, Splices, etc., Shown in Colours. With
       tables of strength of ropes, etc., and wire rigging. Glas-
       gow: J. Brown, 1903; 3rd ed. as Knots, Bends, Splices....
       Glasgow: 1906; rev. enl. ed. 1912. 69pp, 115 diagrams;
       ...; 86pp, ill NN

7396 Kiewe, Heinz Edgar. The Sacred History of Knitting. Ox-
       ford, Eng: Art Needlework Industries, 1967; 2nd ed. 1971.
       114pp, 88 pls; 124pp, ill, 114 pls

7397 Knitting, Netting, and Crochet Work. A winter gift for ladies
       ... containing the newest and most fashionable patterns.
       From the latest London edition. New York: Burgess &
       Stringer, 1844; Philadelphia: G. B. Zieber, 1847, 1848.
       65pp, ill NN, DLC

7398 The Ladies' Knitting and Netting Book. London: 1837; 3rd
       ed. with additions. London: 1839. BM

7399 The Ladies' Netting Work Book. New ed. Kilmarnock:
       Thomsons Brothers, 1850? BM

7400 Ladies' Work-box Companion. A handbook of knitting, netting,
       tatting, and Berlin work. Containing entirely new receipts.
       New York: G. A. Leavitt, 187-? 64pp NN

7401 Lambert, Miss A. Instructions for Making Miss Lambert's
       Registered Crochet Flowers. London: 1852. BM

7402 _____. My Knitting Book. London: John Murray, 1843;
       4th ed. 1844. ...; 108pp

7403 Lonely Hours. A text book of knitting, by an American lady.

In two parts. Containing 27 patterns and directions for the most useful and fashionable articles of knitting now in use. Philadelphia: E. Gaskill, 1849. 72pp PP, NjP, DeWint

7404   Severn, William. Rope Roundup; the lore and craft of rope and roping. New York: D. McKay, 1960. 237pp, ill, pls (Making and using rope from earliest times to now)

7405   Spencer, Charles Louis, 1870-   . Knots, Splices and Fancy Work. Glasgow: Brown, Son, and Ferguson, 1934; New York: Kennedy Brothers, 1938. 138pp, ill; 193pp, ill ("The whole of Captain Jutsum's book, Knots and Splices, has been incorporated in this volume.")

7406   Sylvia. Book of Macrame Lace. London: 1885. 5pp

7407   Watson, Marcia L., comp. Needles and Hooks and What Is Made with Them. 2 vol. Lynn, Mass: Home Cheer, 1890-91. ill (Knitting and crocheting)

7408   Weldon's Practical Crochet. London: Weldon & Co, 1895; reprint as Victorian Crochet. With new introd. by Florence Weinstein. New York: Dover, 1975. 228pp, ill

7409   The Work Box and Needles; or, rules and directions for netting, knitting, tatting, Berlin and lace work. New York: Coast City, 1886. 64pp

STEVENGRAPHS

7410   Baker, Wilma Sinclair Le Van. The Silk Pictures of Thomas Stevens; a biography of the coventry weaver and his contribution to the art of weaving, with an illustrated catalogue of his work. New York: Exposition Pr, 1957. 147pp, ill (part color), pls (Thomas Stevens, 1828-1888)

7411 *Godden, Geoffrey Arthur. Stevengraphs and Other Victorian Silk Pictures. London: Barrie & Jenkins; Rutherford, NJ: Fairleigh Dickinson U Pr, 1971. 492pp, 340 ill, 12 color pls, bib

7412   Sprake, Austin. The Price Guide to Stevengraphs, Stevens Silk Postcards, Bookmarkers. Woodbridge, Suffolk: Antique Collectors Club, Baron Publishing, 1971; 1972. 80pp, 208pp, ill

7413   _____, and Michael Darby. Stevengraphs: the reference book on Thomas Stevens' mounted silk woven pictures and silk woven bookmarkers. Part 1. The Mounted Silk Woven Pictures and Portraits, Sprake; Part II. The Silk Woven

Bookmarkers, Darby. Guernsey, Eng: Authors, 1968.
156pp, ill

BED COVERINGS AND QUILTS

7414 American Coverlets of the 19th Century from the Helen Louise
Allen Textile Collection. Exhibition. Madison: U of Wis-
consin, Elvehjem Art Center, 1975. 96pp, ill, bib

7415 Bacon, Lenice Ingram. American Patchwork Quilts. New
York: William Morrow, 1973. 190pp, ill, bib

7416 Bed Ruggs, 1722-1833. Loan exhibition. November-December
1972. Hartford, Conn: Wadsworth Atheneum, 1972. 80pp,
ill

7417 *Bishop, Robert Charles. New Discoveries in American Quilts.
New York: Dutton, 1975. 127pp, 240 (160) ill, bib

7418 Burnham, Harold B., and Dorothy K. Burnham. "Keep Me
Warm One Night"; early handweaving in Eastern Canada.
Toronto: U of Toronto Pr, with the Royal Ontario Museum,
1972. 387pp, ill, bib

7419 Carlisle, Lilian Baker. Pieced Work and Applique Quilts at
Shelburne Museum. Shelburne, Vt: the Museum, 1957.
95pp, ill

7420 Catalogue of Early American Handicraft. Comprising costumes, quilts, coverlets, samplers, laces, embroideries,
and other related objects. Fore. by Paul Jameson Woodward. Brooklyn: Museum Pr, 1924. 76pp, 16 pls DLC

7421 *Colby, Averil. Patchwork. London: Batsford, 1958; 1965;
Newton Centre, Mass: C. T. Branford, 1965. 201pp, ill

7422 _____. Patchwork Quilts. London: Batsford, 1965; New
York: Scribner, 1966. 94pp, ill (some color)

7423 Cummings, Abbott Lowell. Bed Hangings; a treatise on fabrics and styles in the curtaining of beds, 1650-1850.
Boston: Society for the Preservation of New England Antiquities, 1961. 60pp, pls

7424 Davison, Mildred. American Quilts from the Art Institute of
Chicago. Chicago: 1966. 9pp, 39 pls

7425 _____. Early American Hand-woven Coverlets, in the collections of the Art Institute of Chicago. Chicago: 1946.
15pp, ill, bib

7426 _____, and Christa Mayer-Thurman. Coverlets: a handbook

on the collection of woven coverlets in the Art Institute of
Chicago. Chicago: 1973. 228pp, ill, bib

7427 DeGraw, Imelda G. Quilts and Coverlets. Exhibition. Denver: Art Museum, 1974. 160pp, ill, bib

7428 Dunham, Lydia Roberts. Quilt Collection. Exhibition. Denver: Art Museum, 1963. 120pp of ill (some color), bib

7429 *Dunton, William Rush, Jr. Old Quilts. Cantonsville, Md:
Author, 1945; 1946; 1947. 278pp, 125 pls, color frontis,
bib

7430 *Finley, Ruth Ebright. Old Patchwork Quilts and the Women
Who Made Them. Philadelphia; London: Lippincott; New
York: Grosset & Dunlap, 1929; New York: 1950; Newton
Centre, Mass: C. T. Branford, 1970. 202pp, 96 pls,
color frontis, 100 diagrams

7431 Fitzrandolph, Mavis. Traditional Quilting, its story and its
practice. London: Batsford, 1954. 168pp, ill

7432 Graeff, Marie Knorr. Pennsylvania German Quilts. Plymouth Meeting, Pa: Mrs. C. Naeman Keyser, 1946.
32pp, pls (How-to)

7433 The Great American Cover-up: counterpanes of the 18th and
19th centuries. Introd. by Dana S. Katzenberg. Baltimore, Md: Museum of Art, 1971. 48pp, ill, pls

7434 Haas, Louise Krause, and Robert Barlett Haas. Quilts,
Counterpanes, and Related Printed Fabrics. Santa Monica,
Cal: 1956. 24pp, pls

7435 Haders, Phyllis. Sunshine and Shadow. The Amish and their
quilts. New York: Universe, 1976. 72pp, 48 (12 color)
ill, (calendar)

7436 *Hake, Elizabeth. English Quilting--old and new, with notes
on its West Country tradition. London: Batsford; New
York: Scribner, 1937. 23pp, ill, pls (West of England,
Herefordshire, Wiltshire, Leicester, North of England,
and Wales) MB, DLC, NN

7437 *Hall, Carrie A., and Rose Good Kretsinger. The Romance
of the Patchwork Quilt in America. Caldwell, Idaho:
Caxton Printers, 1935; 1936; 1947; reprint. New York:
Bonanza, 1969? 299pp, many ill, bib (Part I. History
and Quilt Patches; II. Quilts--antique and modern; III.
Quilting and Quilting Designs) DeWint

7438 *Holstein, Jonathan. Abstract Design in American Quilts.

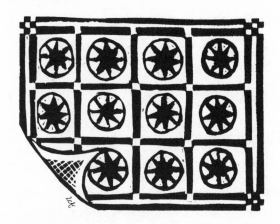

New York: Whitney Museum of American Art, 1971.
15pp, ill, 1 pl

7439   . American Pieced Quilts. Exhibition. Lausanne
Musee des Arts Decoratifs, and Renwick Gallery. New
York: Viking, 1973. 94pp, ill, bib (Largely from col-
lections of Gail Van der Hoof and the Author)

7440 *   . The Pieced Quilt: an American design tradition.
Greenwich, Conn: N.Y. Graphic Society; Toronto: Mc-
Clelland & Stewart, 1973. 192pp, ill, 100 color pls, bib
(Holstein mounted the 1971 Whitney Museum show with
Gail Van der Hoof with quilts from their collections)

7441 *Ickis, Marguerite. The Standard Book of Quilt Making and
Collecting. New York: Dover; New York: Greystone Pr,
1949; reprint. New York: Dover, 1959. 276pp, 483 ill

7442 Jeffery, G. G. Rugs and Quilts from Shreds and Patches.
London; New York: Oxford U Pr, 1943. 47pp, ill, diagrams

7443 Jones, Stella M. Hawaiian Quilts. Honolulu: Academy of
Arts, 1930; reprint and 2nd rev. ed. Includes catalog of
exhibition, "The Quilt--a Hawaiian Heritage," Honolulu
Academy. Honolulu: Daughters of Hawaii, 1973. 53pp,
ill, pls; 78pp, ill (150 years of quilts to 1917) DLC, NN

7444 Maclagan, Eric Robert Dalrymple. Notes on Quilting. V &
A. London: 1932; 1934; 1949. 14pp, 16 pls, bib

7445 Museum Extension Project. Pennsylvania Quilts, Pieced and
Appliqued. District 2, Pennsylvania: W. P. A., n.d.
20 color pls

7446 Obenchain, Eliza Caroline Calvert, 1856- . Hand-woven
        Coverlets. By Eliza Calvert Hall (pseud.). Boston:
        Little Brown, 1912; 1925; as A Book of Handwoven Cover-
        lets. Rutland, Vt: Tuttle; London: Prentice-Hall, 1966.
        279pp, ill, pls; 411pp, ill

7447 Old Quilts. Watkins Glen, NY: Century House for American
        Life Foundation, 19-?

7448 150 Years of American Quilts. Lawrence: U of Kansas, Mu-
        seum of Art, 1973. 56pp, ill, bib

7449 *Orlofsky, Patsy, and Myron Orlofsky. Quilts in America.
        New York: McGraw Hill, 1974. 368pp, 300 ill, 48 color
        pls, bib (ca.1704-present. Includes tools and equipment)

7450 *Peto, Florence. American Quilts and Coverlets. New York:
        Parrish, 1949. 104pp, 36 (4 color) pls

7451 *_____ . Historic American Quilts. New York: 1939. ill

7452 Plews, Edith Rice. Hawaiian Quilting on Kauai. Kauai,
        Hawaii: the Kauai Museum, 1973. ill

7453 Plummer, Alfred, ed. The Witney Blanket Industry; the
        records of the Witney blanket weavers, edited. London:
        G. Routledge, 1934. 284pp, pls, facsims

7454 The Quilt Engagement Calendar. New York: Dutton, Sunrise,
        1974. 57 color photographs

7455 *Rabb, Kate Milan. Indiana Coverlets and Coverlet Weavers.
        Indianapolis: Indiana Historical Society, Vol. 8, no. 8,
        1928. 39pp (pp. 395-433), pls

7456 *Reinert, Guy F. Coverlets of the Pennsylvania Germans.
        Allentown, Pa: Pennsylvania German Folklore Society,
        1949.

7457 *Robertson, Elizabeth Wells. American Quilts. New York:
        Studio, 1948. ill

7458 *Safford, Carleton L., and Robert Charles Bishop. America's
        Quilts and Coverlets as Design: a survey of American bed-
        covers. New York: Dutton, 1972. 313pp, 462 (100 color)
        ill, bib (Includes bed rugs, linsey-wolsey, etc.)

7459 *Swygert, Mildred (Mrs. Luther M.), ed. Heirlooms from Old
        Looms; a catalog of coverlets owned by the Colonial Cover-
        let Guild of America and its members. Chicago: the
        Guild, 1940; rev. ed. 1955. 406pp, ill

7460 Vote, Marjean. Patchwork Pleasure: a pattern identification

guide. Des Moines: Wallace-Homestead, n.d. (197-?)
83pp, ill

7461 *Webster, Marie D. Quilts--their story and how to make
them. Garden City, NY: Doubleday, 1915; New York:
Tudor, 1943; reprint. Detroit: Gale, 1975. 178pp, 97
ill, pls (part color), bib, list of quilt names

7462 White, Margaret E. American Hand-Woven Coverlets in the
Newark Museum. Newark, NJ: Museum Association,
1947. 83pp, ill, bib

7463 _____, comp. Quilts and Counterpanes in the Newark Museum. Newark, NJ: 1948. 90pp, ill, bib

GENERAL WORKS ON CARPETS AND RUGS

7464 Achdjean, Albert. The Rug: a fundamental art. Introd. by
Arnold van Gennep. French and English text. Paris:
Author, 1949. 287pp, ill, 105 (23 mounted color) pls,
bib (Egypt, Armenia, Persia, Arabia, Turkestan, China,
Turkey, the Balkans, Poland, Spain, Portugal) BM

7465 American Carpet and Upholstery Journal. Monthly. Philadelphia: 1890-1909? ill

7466 The American Carpet and Upholstery Journal. Oriental and
Domestic rugs. Supplement. Philadelphia: 1903. 100pp,
pls DLC

7467 Beaumont, Roberts. Carpets and Rugs. Pref. by Frank
Beaumont. London: Scott, Greenwood, 1924. 410pp,
190 ill, 15 (14 color) pls DeWint

7468 Bowles, Ella Shannon. Handmade Rugs. Boston: Little,
Brown; Garden City, NY: Garden City Publishing, 1927;
Garden City: 1937. 205pp, ill, pls, color frontis, bib
NNC-Ave, DLC, BM

7469 Bradbury, Fred. Carpet Manufacturer. Belfast, Ireland:
Author, dist. by J. Heywood, London, Lord & Nagle,
Boston, 1904. 301pp, ill, pls DeWint

7470 Campana, P. Michele. European Carpets. Tr. from Italian
(1966) by Margaret Crosland. Feltham; New York: Hamlyn, 1969. 160pp, ill, 70 color ill (ca. 1500-ca. 1900)

7471 Carwitham, John, fl. 1730. Floor-Decoration of various
kinds, both in plano and perspective. Adapted to the
ornamenting of halls, rooms, summer houses, etc., in
24 copper plates. A work entirely new, and as serviceable

to gentlemen and workmen by the perspective views in ye
several head-pieces as entertaining to the ladies in coloring them. London: by J. Carwitham, sold by R. Caldwell at Mercer's Hall, Cheapside, 1739; 2nd ed. as Various Kinds of Floor-Decorations ... for ornamenting the
floors of halls, rooms ... whither in pavements of stone,
or marble, or with painted floor cloths. London: for
John Bowles at the Black Horse in Cornhill, 1745. 1pp,
24 pls NN, DLC, MH, BM

7472 Clifford, Chandler Robbins. The Rug Dictionary. 2nd ed.
      New York: Clifford & Lawton, 1926. 69pp, ill DLC

7473 Cole, Alan Summerly. Ornamentation of Rugs and Carpets.
      Reprint from Journal of the Society of Arts, London:
      July 1910. Washington, D.C.: Smithsonian Institution
      Annual Report, 1911.

7474 Concerning Carpets. London: 1884. 99pp

7475 Cook, Alexander N., ed. A Century of Carpet and Rug
      Making in America, 1825-1925. New York: Bigelow-
      Hartford Carpet Co, 1925. 97pp, ill, pls NN

7476 *Faraday, Cornelia Bateman. European and American Carpets
      and Rugs; a history of the hand-woven decorative floor
      coverings of Spain, France, Great Britain, Scandinavia,
      Belgium, Holland, Italy, Balkans, Germany, Austria, and
      early America; and of the machine-made carpets and rugs
      of modern Europe and the United States. Grand Rapids,
      Mich: Dean-Hicks, 1929. 382pp, 370 ill, 32 color pls
      NN, DLC, PP

7477 *Franses, Jack. European and Oriental Rugs: For Pleasure
      and Investment. London: Gifford, 1970; rev. ed. 1973.
      176pp, ill, 16 pls, bib; 180pp, ill, 16 pls, bib

7478 Franses, Michael. An Introduction to the World of Rugs: an
      exhibition at the Hugh Moss Gallery, December 1973.
      London: Hugh M. Moss, Ltd., 1973. 108pp, chiefly ill
      (ca.1630-ca.1920)

7479 Grierson, Ronald. Woven Rugs. 3rd ed. Leicester, Eng:
      1967. 51pp, ill, 8 pls, bib

7480 Griffitt, J. R. G. Turkey Carpets and Their Manufacture.
      London: 1884. 22pp

7481 Haggard, William. The Little Rug Book. London: Cassell,
      1972. 40pp, ill, 8 pls

7482 Hall, Philip A. The Rug and Carpet Industry of Philadelphia.
      Philadelphia: Hardwick & Magee, 1917.

7483   History and Manufacture of Floor Coverings. New York: Re-
       view Publishing, 1899. 98pp, ill, pls NN

7484   Holt, Rosa Belle. Rugs: Oriental and Occidental, Antique
       and Modern. Chicago: A. C. McClurg, 1901; 1908; new
       rev. ed. Garden City, NY: Garden City Publishing, 1937.
       167pp, pls, color frontis, bib; 201pp, ill, 33 (11 color)
       pls, bib; 208pp, ill, 33 (12 color) pls, bib

7485   Home Industries and Domestic Manufactures. New York: The
       Association Artists, 189-? 42 leaves (Rag carpet weaving,
       homespun woolen rugs, homespun cotton rugs, linsey
       woolsey)

7486   Jacobs, Bertram. Axminster Carpets (Hand-made), 1755-
       1957. Leigh-on-Sea: F. Lewis, 1970. 79pp, 90 ill,
       48 pls, bib

7487   _____. The Story of British Carpets. London: Carpet Re-
       view, 1968. 188pp, ill

7488   Jarry, Madeleine. The Carpets of Aubusson. Tr. from
       French by C. Magdalino. Leigh-on-Sea: F. Lewis, 1969.
       67pp, 92 ill, 64 pls

7489   _____. The Carpets of the Manufacture De la Savonnerie.
       Tr. from French by C. Magdalino. Leigh-on-Sea: F.
       Lewis, 1966. 47pp, 26 ill, 70 pls

7490   Kemp, F. F. A Few Hints and a Little Advice on the Care
       and Preservation of Old Rugs. London: Jekyll's, 1934.
       20pp

7491   Kendrick, Albert Frank. Guide to the Collection of Carpets.
       V & A. London: 1915; 2nd rev. ed. 1920; 3rd ed. rev.
       by C. E. C. Tattersall, 1931. 96pp, 47 pls; 88pp, 48
       pls; 68pp, 52 pls

7492   _____. Guide to an Exhibition of Tapestries, Carpets, and
       Furniture Lent by the Earl of Dalkeith. March-May 1914.
       V & A. London: HMSO, 1914; 2nd ed. 1914. 27pp, 15
       pls

7493   _____, and Creassey Edward Cecil Tattersall. Fine Car-
       pets in the Victoria and Albert Museum; 20 examples, re-
       produced for the first time in colour, of old carpets from
       Persia, India, Caucasia, Armenia, Turkey, China, Spain
       and England. London: E. Benn; New York: Scribner,
       1924. 26pp, 20 color pls

7494 * _____, and _____. Hand-woven Carpets, Oriental and
       European. 2 vol. London: Benn; New York: Scribner's,

1922; reprint in 1 vol. New York: Dover, 1973. ill,
205 (19 color) pls, bib; 388pp, ill, bib NNC-Ave

7495 Kenyon, Otis Allen. Carpets and Rugs: how they are made,
how to select them, how to care for them. Canton, O:
Hoover Co, 1923. 158pp, ill

7496 Kuehnel, Ernst. Catalog of Spanish Rugs, 12th Century to
19th Century. Technical analysis by Louisa Bellinger.
Washington, D.C.: Textile Museum, by National Publishing Co, 1953. 64pp, ill, 44 pls, bib (Catalogue raisonne)

7497 Lanier, Mildred B. English and Oriental Carpets at Williamsburg. Charlottesville, Va: U Pr of Virginia, 1974. 132pp,
ill, color pls, bib (57 examples, 17th, 18th, 19th centuries)

7498 Little, Nina Fletcher. Floor Coverings in New England before
1850. Sturbridge, Mass: Old Sturbridge Village, 1967.
82pp, ill

7499 Loan Exhibition of Tapestries, Carpets, and Silk Fabrics from
the Mobilier National, Paris. Introd. by Cecil Smith.
July-October 1912. V & A. London: HMSO, 1912. 11pp,
4 pls

7500 Mathews, Sibyl Irene. Needle-Made Rugs. London: Mills &
Boon, 1960. 128pp, ill, bib

7501 Mayorcas, Mondo J. English Needlework Carpets, 16th to
19th Century. Leigh-on-Sea: F. Lewis, 1963. 62pp, ill,
94 pls

7502 Nairn, (Michael) and Co. Linoleum, Manufactured by M.
Nairn. Kirkcaldy, Scotland: 188-? 55 color pls DLC,
MB

7503 O'Brien, Mildred Richmond Jackson. The Rug and Carpet
Book. New York: M. Barrows, 1946. 166pp, ill, 20 pls,
bib NNC-Ave

7504 Pontremoli, J. M. The Pontremoli Collection of Carpets and
Textiles. Introd. and descriptive notes by Frank Lewis.
Leigh-on-Sea: F. Lewis, 1942. 16pp, 59 pls NNC-Ave

7505 Riefstahl, Rudolf Meyer. A Short Bibliography for the Student
of Oriental and Western Hand-Knotted Rugs and Carpets.
New York: N.Y.U. Pr Bookstore, 1926. 23pp

7506 *Ries, Estelle H. American Rugs. Cleveland: World Publishing, 1950. 63pp, ill, bib

7507 *Roth, Rodris. Floor Coverings in 18th Century America.

Bulletin 250. Washington, D.C.: Smithsonian Pr, 1967.
64pp, ill

7508 Sautier, Albert. Italian Peasant Rugs. Milan: Gli editori
Piantanida-Valcarenghi, 1923. 45pp, 31 pls (part color),
bib NN

7509 Schlosser, Ignaz. The Book of Rugs, Oriental and European.
Tr. from German. New York: Crown; London: Batsford, 1963. 318pp, ill, bib

7510 Sirelius, Uuno Taavi, 1872- . The Hand-Woven Rugs of
Finland. Helsinki: Government Printing Office, 1925.
14pp, ill, 2 color pls NN

7511 *   . The Ryijy-Rugs of Finland; an historical study.
Tr. by Alexander Matson. Helsinki: Otava Publishing,
1926. 251pp, 334 ill, 94 color pls NN

7512 (A. F.) Stoddard and Co., Ltd. The Carpet Makers; 100
years of designing and manufacturing carpets of quality.
Historical section by C. A. Oakley. Elderslie, Johnstone,
Scotland: Newman Neame for Stoddard, 1962. 70pp,
chiefly ill (part color), pls

7513 *Tattersall, Creassey Edward Cecil. A History of British
Carpets, from the introduction of the craft until the
present day. Benfleet, Essex: F. Lewis, 1934; new ed.
rev. & enl. by Stanley Reed. Leigh-on-Sea: F. Lewis,
1966. 182pp, 116 (54 color) pls, color frontis; 139pp,
176 pls

7514 *   . Notes on Carpet-Knotting and Weaving. V & A.
2nd ed. London: HMSO, 1927; 3rd ed. 1933; 1939; reprint. 1950; 1969. 50pp, 12 pls; 49pp, 12 pls; 42pp, 12
pls BM

7515 Taylor, A. History of the Carpet Trade. London: 1874.
SIB-1

7516 United States Library of Congress. Division of Bibliography.
List of References on the Carpet and Rug Industry of the
United States. Select List ... no. 681. Washington, D.C.:
GPO, 1922. 6 leaves NN

7517 Viale Ferrero, Mercedes. Rare Carpets: from East and
West. Tr. from Italian (1969). London: Orbis Books,
1972. 64pp, chiefly ill, bib

7518 *Walker, Mrs. Lydia Le Baron. Homecraft Rugs; their historic background, romance of stitchery and method of
making. New York: F. A. Stokes, 1929. 421pp, ill, 21
pls, bib

7519   Weeks, Jeanne G., and Donald Treganowan. Rugs and Car-
       pets of Europe and the Western World. London; Phila-
       delphia: Chilton, 1969. 251pp, ill, 17 color pls, bib
       (Includes American)

7520   Whytock, A. Carpet Manufacture and Design. London?:
       1856. SIB-1

7521   Young, Fred Henry, d. 1943. A Century of Carpet Making,
       1839-1939. Glasgow: James Templeton, Mfr., 1944.
       80pp, pl

ORIENTAL, CAUCASIAN, INDIC AND PERSIAN RUGS

7522   Amir, M. K. Zephyr. Supreme Persian Carpets; oriental
       carpets. Rutland, Vt: C. E. Tuttle, 1972. 138pp, color
       ill

7523   Ancient Berber Tapestries and Rugs and Ancient Moroccan
       Embroideries. Exhibition. October-November 1952. Ox-
       ford, Eng: Maison Francaise, 1952. 28pp, ill, bib

7524   Antique Chinese Rugs. (Tiffany Studios, New York City.)
       Rutland, Vt: C. E. Tuttle, 1969. 96pp, ill

7525   Antique Oriental Rugs and Period Furniture. Exhibition.
       March 1915. Detroit: Museum of Art, 1915. 75pp, ill

7526   Ararat (pseud.). Oriental Carpets and Rugs. London: 1891.
       BM

7527   The Art of the Oriental Rug; a loan exhibition of rugs from
       the Postian Collection held in the McIntosh Gallery of the
       University of Western Ontario, February 1969. London,
       Ontario: 1969. 22pp, ill

7528   Aslanapa, Oktay. Turkish Arts: Seljuk and Ottoman Carpets,
       tiles and miniature paintings. Tr. by Herman Kreider.
       Rev. by Sheila M. O'Callaghan. Istanbul: Dogan Kardes
       Kayinlari, n.d. (pre-1956); 1961? 147pp, ill

7529   Ballard, James Franklin. Catalogue of Oriental Rugs in the
       Collection of James F. Ballard. Exhibition. October-
       December 1924. Indianapolis: John Herron Art Institute,
       by Hollenbeck Pr, 1924. 206pp, ill, 1 color pl, bib

7530   _____. Descriptive Catalogue of an Exhibition of Oriental
       Rugs from the Collection of J. F. Ballard. Chicago:
       Art Institute, 1922; San Francisco: The Museum, 1923.
       90pp, ill, bib

7531   _____. Ghiordes Rugs of the 17th and 18th Centuries from

the Collection of J. F. Ballard. St. Louis: Oriental
Publishing, 1916. 77pp, ill

7532 Bennett, Ian. Book of Oriental Carpets and Rugs. Feltham:
Hamlyn, 1972. 128pp, ill, 60 color pls

7533 Bidder, Hans. Carpets from Eastern Turkestan, Known as
Khotan, Samarkind and Kansu Carpets. Tr. by Grace
Marjory Allen. New York: Universe, 1964. 96pp, 46
ill, 20 color pls, bib

7534 *Bode, Wilhelm von. Antique Rugs from the Near East. Tr.
by Rudolf M. Riefstahl. 190-?; 3rd ed. with contributions
by Ernst Kuhnel. New York: E. Weyhe, 1922; 4th ed.
rev. Tr. by Charles Grant Ellis. Berlin: Klinkhardt &
Biermann, 1955; 1958; London: Bell, 1970. ...; 65pp,
ill, 96 pls, color frontis; 184pp, ill, 4 pls (13th-17th
century) PPULC, DLC

7535 Bogolyubov, Aleksandr Aleksandrovich. Carpets of Central
Asia. Ed. by J. M. A. Thompson. Tr. of Tapis de
l'Asie Centrale. 2 vol. St. Petersburg: 1908, 1909;
London: Crosby Pr, 1973. 59 pls

7536 Breck, Joseph. Loan Exhibition of Oriental Rugs from the
Collection of James F. Ballard of St. Louis, Missouri.
October-December 1921. New York: Metropolitan Museum, 1921. 27pp, pls (Collection given to Museum in
1922)

7537 _____, and Frances Morris. The James F. Ballard Collection of Oriental Rugs. Metropolitan Museum. New
York: 1923. 71pp, ill, 129 pls

7538 Calatchi, Robert de. Oriental Carpets. Tr. from French
(1967) by Valerie Howard. Rutland, Vt: C. E. Tuttle,
1967. 223pp, ill, pls

7539 Campana, P. Michele. Oriental Carpets. Tr. from Italian
(1945) by Adeline Hartcup. London; New York: Hamlyn,
1969. 157pp, 66 color ill

7540 Caucasian Rugs. Exhibition of rugs and saddlebags owned
by Rug-society members. Washington, D.C.: Textile
Museum, 1975. 40pp, ill

7541 Chattopadhyaya, Kamaladevi. Carpets and Floor Coverings
of India: An Historical Review. Bombay: Taraporevala,
1969. 68pp, ill, pls (1 color), bib

7542 Clark, Hartley. Bokhara, Turkoman and Afghan Rugs. London: John Lane, 1922. 130pp, ill, 25 (17 color) pls
PP, MiU, MH

7543 Cliff, Vincent D., comp. Loan Exhibition of Antique Oriental
      Rugs. January 1921. Detroit: Institute of Arts, 1951.
      75pp, ill

7544 Clifford, Chandler Robbins. Rugs of the Orient. New York:
      Clifford & Lawton, 1911. 108pp, ill, pls DLC, NNC-Ave

7545 Con, Jessica Meyer. Carpets from the Orient. Tr. from
      Dutch by Marieke Clarke. London: Merlin; Singapore:
      Moore, 1966; New York: Universe, 1967. 63pp, ill, 24
      pls, bib

7546 Coxon, Herbert. Oriental Carpets, How They Are Made and
      Conveyed to Europe. London: T. F. Unwin, 1884. 75pp,
      10 pls DLC, SKM

7547 Cselenyi, Ladislav. Oriental Rugs from the Collection of Mr.
      John Schorsher. Toronto: Royal Ontario Museum, 1971.
      96pp, ill, bib (Chiefly R. S. Williams Collection)

7548 Davenport, Michael A. One Knot at a Time; a story of tra-
      dition. Portland, Ore: S. A. Kahl, 1953? 16pp, ill

7549 De Calatchi, Robert. Oriental Carpets. Rutland, Vt: Tuttle,
      1970. 236pp, 78 (48 color) pls, bib

7550 Denwood, Philip. The Tibetan Carpet. Warminster, Wilts:
      Aris & Phillips, 1975. 101pp, ill, 25 color pls, bib,
      gloss

7551 Dilley, Arthur Urbane. An Exhibition of Oriental Rugs Lent
      by James Franklin Ballard. November 1923-January 1924.
      Pittsburgh: Carnegie Institute, 1923. 17pp, pls

7552 _____. The Garden of Paradise Rug and the Holy Carpet
      of the Mosque at Ardebil, reproduced with variations in
      silk. New York: priv. printed by Donchian & Co, 1924.
      31pp, 6 pls NN

7553 _____. Oriental Rugs. Boston: A. U. Dilley & Co, 1909.
      80pp, ill DLC

7554 * _____. Oriental Rugs and Carpets; a comprehensive study.
      New York; London: Scribner, 1931; rev. by Maurice S.
      Dimand. Philadelphia: Lippincott, 1959. 303pp, ill, 79
      pls; 289pp, 66 ill, 14 color pls CU, DLC

7555 Dimand, Maurice Sven. The Ballard Collection of Oriental
      Rugs in the City Art Museum of St. Louis. St. Louis:
      priv. printed, 1935. 216pp, ill

7556 _____. An Early Cut-Pile Rug from Egypt. Reprint from

Metropolitan Museum Studies, March 1933. New York: 1935. 12pp (pp. 151-162), ill, color pls, bib

7557   . A Guide to the Exhibition of Oriental Rugs and Textiles. Metropolitan Museum. May-September 1935. New York: E. L. Hildreth, Brattleboro, Vt., printer, 1935. 36pp, 35 pls

7558   . The Kevorkian Foundation Collection of Rare and Magnificent Oriental Carpets: special loan exhibition; a guide and catalog. New York: 1966. 35pp, ill, 17 pls

7559   . Oriental Rugs in the Metropolitan Museum of Art. With chapter and catalogue of rugs of China and Chinese Turkestan by Jean Matley. New York: Metropolitan Museum, dist. by N.Y. Graphic, Greenwich, Conn., 1973. 353pp, ill, bib

7560 Donchian, John B. Threads from the Oriental Loom; a series of intimate notes and sketches helpful and interesting to students, connoisseurs and collectors. New York?: 1901; 1913. ...; 101pp, ill

7561 *Dunn, Eliza (pseud. for Edith Eliza Norton). Rugs in Their Native Land. New York: Dodd, Mead, 1910. 155pp, ill, color pls (Oriental rugs) DLC

7562 Dwight, Harrison Griswold, 1875- . Persian Miniatures. Garden City, New York: Doubleday, Page, 1917. 328pp, ill, bib

7563 *Edwards, Arthur Cecil. The Persian Carpet. A survey of the carpet weaving-industry of Persia. London: Duckworth, 1953; 1967; new ed. with plates. 1974; 1975. 384pp, 200 ill

7564 Eiland, Murray L. Oriental Rugs: A Comprehensive Study. Greenwich, Conn: N.Y. Graphic Society, 1973. 196pp, ill, bib

7565 Ellis, Charles Grant. Early Caucasian Rugs. Exhibition. Washington, D.C.: Textile Museum, 1975. 112pp, ill (16 color) (So-called "Kuba" rugs)

7566 Ellwanger, William DeLancey, 1854-1913, ed. The Oriental Rug; a monograph on Eastern rugs and carpets, saddlebags, mats and pillows. With a consideration of kinds and classes, types, borders, figures, dyes, symbols, etc. New York: Dodd, Mead, 1903; London: Gay & Bird, 1904; New York: 1909. 154pp, ill, 12 color pls DLC, CU

7567 Erdmann, Kurt. Oriental Carpets: an essay on their history.

Tr. by Charles G. Ellis.   New York: Universe, 1960;
1962; as Oriental Carpets: an account of their history.
London: Zwemmer, 1961.   78pp, 189 ill, bib

7568 _____ .   700 Years of Oriental Carpets.   Ed. by Hanna
Erdmann.   Tr. from German by May H. Beattie and
Hildegard Herzog.   London: Faber; Los Angeles: U of
California Pr, 1970.   238pp, 286 ill, 20 color pls, bib

7569 Formenton, Fabio.   Oriental Rugs and Carpets.   Tr. from
Italian by Pauline L. Phillips.   Feltham; New York:
Hamlyn, 1972; New York: McGraw-Hill, 1972.   252pp,
ill, color pls, bib

7570 Franses, Jack.   Tribal Rugs from Afghanistan and Turkestan.
London: Franses of Piccadilly, 1973.   64pp, chiefly ill

7571 Gans-Ruedin, Erwin.   The Connoisseur's Guide to Oriental
Carpets.   Tr. from French by Valerie Howard.   Rutland,
Vt: Tuttle, 1971; as Modern Oriental Carpets.   London:
Thames & Hudson, 1971.   431pp, 466 ill, bib

7572 Gould, George Glen.   Monograph on Chinese Rugs.   New
York: J. McCreery, 1921; 2nd ed. Washington, D.C.:
Woodward & Lothrop, 1926.   20pp, ill, color pl, bib
DLC

7573 Gregorian, Arthur T.   Oriental Rugs and the Stories They
Tell.   Boston: Taylor Pr, 1949; Boston: Nimrod Pr,
1967.   94pp, ill; 230pp, ill, bib

7574 Griggs, William, 1832-1911.   An Account of the Unique North
Indian Carpet Presented to the Worshipful Company of
Girdlers by the Master, Robert Bell.   London: Griggs,
1904?   text, color facsims

7575 _____ .   Asian Carpets.   16th and 17th century designs
from the Jaipur Palaces.   Text by Thomas H. Hendley.
London: W. Griggs, lithographer to the King, 1905.
20pp, 145 pls (chiefly color), bib   CU, NN, DLC, MB

7576 Grote-Hasenbalg, Werner.   Carpets of the Orient.   Tr. from
German.   Leipzig: Schmidt, 1936; 1939.   23pp, ill, 48
color pls

7577 * _____ .   Masterpieces of Oriental Rugs.   Tr. from German
by G. Barry Gifford.   Berlin: Scarabaeus, 1922?; 2nd
ed. 3 vol. Berlin: W. Mueller, 1925.   121pp, ill, 120
color pls in 2 portfolios   NN, DLC

7578 Gurdji, V.   Oriental Rug Weaving.   New York: Neely, 1900;
2nd ed. 1901; facsimile reprint. Seattle: 1966.   94pp, ill

7579 _____. Threads from the Oriental Loom. A series of
intimate notes and sketches helpful and interesting to
students, connoisseurs and collectors. Rev. by John B.
Donchian. New York?: 1913. 101pp, pls DeWint

7580 *Haack, Hermann. Oriental Rugs; an illustrated guide. Ed.
and tr. from German by George and Cornelia Wingfield
Digby. London: Faber; Newton, Mass: C. T. Branford,
1960. 76pp, ill, 44 pls, bib

7581 Hackmack, Adolf. Chinese Carpets and Rugs. Tr. from
German (1921) by Miss L. Arnold. Tientsin, China: La
Librairie Francaise, 1924; reprint. New York: Dover;
London: Constable, 1973. 48pp, ill, 27 pls (part color);
78pp, ill

7582 Harris, Henry T. Monograph on the Carpet Weaving Industry
of Southern India. Madras: Government Pr, 1908. 72pp,
ill, 30 pls CU

7583 Hand-book for Lovers of Oriental Rugs. Philadelphia: Fritz
& LaRue, 1925. 87pp, ill PP

7584 Hawley, Walter Augustus, 1863-1920. Oriental Rugs, Antique
and Modern. New York; London: John Lane, 1913; New
York: Dodd, 1922; 1925; New York: Tudor, 1937; New
York: Dover, 1970. 320pp, 80 ill, 11 color pls

7585 Hendley, Thomas Holbein, 1847-1917. Asian Carpets. 16th
and 17th century designs from the Jaipur Palaces, etc.
2 vol. London: W. Griggs, 1905. 20pp, 145 pls (chiefly
color), bib CU, NN, DLC, MB

7586 Hopf, Albrecht. Oriental Carpets and Rugs. Tr. from the
German by Daphne Woodward. New York: Viking; London:
Thames & Hudson, 1962. 140pp, ill, 62 color pls

7587 Hopf, Carl. Old Persian Carpets and Their Artistic Values;
a study. Munich: F. Bruckmann, 1913. 40pp, ill, color
pls, color frontis PP, DeWint, NN

7588 Hubel, Reinhard G. The Book of Carpets. Tr. from German
by Katherine Watson. New York: Praeger, 1970; London:
Barrie & Jenkins, 1971. 348pp, 200 ill, pl, bib (Oriental
to 1900)

7589 *Humphries, Sydney, 1862-1941. Oriental Carpets, Runners,
and Rugs, and Some Jacquard Reproductions. London:
A. & C. Black, 1910. 427pp, ill, 29 (24 color) pls (including 8 color pls of Jacquard carpets) (Joseph Marie
Jacquard, 1752-1834) MiU, NNC-Ave

7590 Indian Carpets. Bombay: Marg Publications, 1966. 45pp, ill

7591 Jacobsen, Charles Wells. Check Points on How to Buy Orien-
      tal Rugs. Rutland, Vt: Tuttle; London: Prentice-Hall,
      1969. 208pp, ill

7592 _____. Facts About Oriental Rugs. Syracuse, NY: 192-?;
      Rochester, NY: Du Bois Pr, 1931; Syracuse: 1952. 152pp,
      ill, pls

7593 _____. Oriental Rugs--a complete guide. Tokyo; Rutland,
      Vt: Tuttle; London: Prentice-Hall, 1962. 479pp, 245 ill,
      39 color pls, bib

7594 Jacoby, Heinrich. About Oriental Carpets. New York: H.
      Wickenhauser, 19-? 23pp, color ill NN

7595 _____. How to Know Oriental Carpets and Rugs. Tr.
      from German by R. J. La Fountaine. London: Allen &
      Unwin, 1952. 148pp, ill, pls (2 color), bib

7596 Kalman, Michael. Oriental Rugs; the Kalman Collection.
      Toronto: Royal Ontario Museum, 1959. 31pp, pls

7597 Kendrick, Albert Frank, Arthur Upham Pope, and William G.
      Thomson. The Emperor's Carpet (from the Hapsburg Col-
      lection) and Two Others. London: Cardinal & Harford,
      192-? 23pp, ill

7598 *Kuehnel, Ernst, and Louise Bellinger. Cairene Rugs and
      Others Technically Related, 15th Century to 17th Century.
      Washington, D.C.: Washington National Publishing, for
      Textile Museum, 1957. 90pp, ill, 50 pls (Egyptian)

7599 Kybalova, Ludmila. Carpets of the Orient. Tr. from
      Czechoslovakian by Till Gottheiner. London; New York;
      Toronto: Hamlyn, 1969. 61pp, ill, 75 pls

7600 Landreau, Anthony N., and W. R. Pickering. From the
      Bosporus to Samarkind; flat-woven rugs. Exhibition.
      Washington, D.C.: Textile Museum, 1969. 112pp, ill,
      bib

7601 Langton, Mary Beach. How to Know Oriental Rugs. A Hand-
      book.... New York: D. Appleton, 1904; 1911; New York;
      London: 1916; 1926; 1933; etc. 244pp, 20 (12 color) pls
      DLC, NN

7602 Larson, Knut. Rugs and Carpets of the Orient. London: F.
      Warne, 1967. 219pp, ill

7603 Leitch, Gordon B. Chinese Rugs. New York: Dodd, Mead,
      1928; New York: Tudor, 1928; new ed. 1935. 171pp,
      ill, pls, color frontis, bib MiU, MB

7604 Lessing, Julius. Ancient Oriental Carpet Patterns After Pictures and Originals of the 15th and 16th Centuries. London: H. Sotheran, 1879. 25pp, 30 color pls PPL, NN

7605 Lewis, Frank. Oriental Rugs and Textiles: the Perez Collection; with a commentary and descriptive notes. Leigh-on-Sea: F. Lewis, 1953. 16pp, 64 pls (Includes some European rugs)

7606 Lewis, George Griffin. The Mystery of the Oriental Rug. Philadelphia: Lippincott, 1914. 30 ill, color frontis

7607 _____. The Practical Book of Oriental Rugs. Philadelphia: Lippincott, 1911; new ed. rev. & enl. Philadelphia; London: Lippincott, 1913; 1916; 5th ed. with additional chapter on Chinese rugs and extra plates. 1920; 6th ed. rev. Philadelphia; New York: 1945; ... 359pp, ill, pls; 375pp, ill, 92 (32 color) pls

7608 Liebetrau, Preben. Oriental Rugs in Colour. Tr. from Danish by Katherine John. New York: Macmillan, 1963; 9th printing. 1971. 131pp, ill, 64 pls, bib

7609 Lion Rugs from Fars Province in Iran. Introd. by Richard Ettinghausen. Text by Parviz Tanavoli. Technical notes by Anthony N. Landreau. Travelling exhibition arranged by the Smithsonian Institution, 1974-77. Washington, D.C.: Textile Museum, 1974. 62pp, ill, 29 color pls (Lion motif rugs from southwestern Iran)

7610 Loan Exhibition of Persian Rugs of the So-called Polish Type. June-September 1930. Metropolitan Museum. New York: 1930. 14pp, ill, 8 pls, bib

7611 Lorentz, H. A. A View of Chinese Rugs from the 17th to 20th Century. London; Boston: Routledge & K. Paul, 1972. 194pp, ill, bib

7612 Macey, Roy Edgar Gene. Oriental Prayer Rugs. Leigh-on-Sea: F. Lewis, 1961. 24pp, ill, 65 pls

7613 McMullan, Joseph V. Islamic Carpets. Fore. by Ernst J. Grube. New York: Near Eastern Art Research Center, 1965. 385pp, ill, pls

7614 _____. Turkish Rugs. The Rachel B. Stevens Memorial Collection. Exhibition. September-December 1972. Washington, D.C.: Textile Museum, 1972. 63pp, ill

7615 _____. Turkoman Rugs. Exhibition. Harvard University, William Hayes Fogg Art Museum. Cambridge, Mass: 1966. 63pp, ill

7616 Martin, Fredrik Robert, 1888-1933. History of Oriental Car-
      pets Before 1800. Vienna: F. R. Martin, 1908. 159pp,
      ill, 33 pls (part color), bib DLC, NN, BM

7617 Masterpieces of Iranian Rugs and Textiles. Exhibition. June-
      September 1964. Washington, D.C.: Textile Museum,
      1964. 12pp, ill

7618 *May, C. J. Delabere. How to Identify Persian Rugs and
      Other Oriental Rugs. London: G. Bell, 1920; 1931; rev.
      enl. ed. London: Bell, 1952; New York: Crowell, 1953.
      133pp, 15 pls; 152pp, 27 pls

7619 Mumford, John Kimberly, 1863-1926. Chinese Rugs. New
      York: Mentor Association, 1916. 11pp, ill, 6 color pls
      NN

7620 _____. Oriental Rugs. New York: Scribner's, 1900;
      1901; 1912; 4th ed. 1929. 278pp, ill, 26 pls (some color)

7621 _____. The Yerkes Collection of Oriental Carpets. New
      York: Knapp, 1910. 31 leaves, 27 color pls (Charles
      Tyson Yerkes, 1837-1905)

7622 Mustafa, Muhammad. Turkish Prayer Rugs. Tr. by Abd
      El-Rahman F. Mohamed. Cairo: 1953. 78pp, ill DLC

7623 Oriental Rugs; the Kalman Collection. Exhibition. Toronto:
      Royal Ontario Museum, 1956? 47pp, ill

7624 Perez, Elia. Oriental Rugs and Textiles, the Perez Collec-
      tion. Leigh-on-Sea: F. Lewis, 1953. 10pp, ill

7625 *Pope, Arthur Upham. Catalog of a Loan Exhibition of Early
      Oriental Carpets from Persia, Asia Minor, the Caucasus,
      Egypt and Spain. January 1926. Arts Club of Chicago.
      New York: Night & Day Pr, printers, 1926. 122pp, ill,
      bib

7626 *Raphaelian, Harry M. The Hidden Language of Symbols in
      Oriental Rugs. New York: Anatol Sivas, 1953. 230pp,
      ill

7627 Reed, Stanley. All Colour Book of Oriental Carpets and Rugs.
      London: Octopus, 1972. 72pp, 100 color ill

7628 _____. Oriental Rugs and Carpets. London: Weidenfeld
      & Nicolson; New York: Putnam, 1967; London: Octopus,
      1972. 120pp, ill; 96pp, ill

7629 Revault, Jacques, and Louis Poinssot. Designs and Patterns
      from North African Carpets and Textiles. Tr. from

French (1950-57) by Stanley Appelbaum. New selection of
plates from the four portfolios of Tapis Tunisiens. New
York: Dover; London: Constable, 1973. 121pp, chiefly
ill, 2 pls

7630 A Rich Inheritance: oriental rugs of the 19th and early 20th
centuries. Exhibition. November 1974-January 1975.
Omaha, Neb: Joslyn Art Museum, 1974. 75pp, ill, color
pls

7631 Riefstahl, Rudolf Meyer. Turkish "Bird" Rugs and Their Design. Reprint from Art Bulletin. New York: N.Y.U.,
1925. 5pp (pp. 91-95), pls

7632 Ripley, Mary Churchill. The Chinese Rug Book. New York:
F. A. Stokes, 1927. 66pp, 17 ill, pls NN

7633 _____. Oriental Rug Book. New York: F. A. Stokes,
1904; new ed. New York: Tudor, 1936. 310pp, 164 ill,
85 (7 color) pls

7634 Robinson, Vincent Joseph. Eastern Carpets, 12 Early Ex-
amples with Descriptive Notices. Pref. by Sir George C.
M. Birdwood. London: 1882-96. 24 color pls NNC-
Ave

7635 The Rug Primer. New Edition--1904. A little booklet of
definitions for the buyer and seller of rugs. Republished
from the Upholsterer. (Cover title: Oriental Rugs.)
New York: Clifford & Lawton, 1904. 47pp

7636 Rugs and Carpets from the Orient, 1907. Compliments of the
H. B. Chaflin Company, N.Y. New York: 1907. 111pp,
ill NN

7637 Rugs of the Near and Middle East from the Collections of
Arthur D. Jenkins and H. McCoy Jones. Exhibition.
June-September 1963. Washington, D.C.: Textile Mu-
seum, 1963. 18pp, ill

7638 Saad, De Mitry Georges. Art in Oriental Rugs. Hot Springs
National Park, Arkansas: Tanner, the Printer, 1927.
127pp, pls DLC

7639 Sarre, Friedrich. Ancient Oriental Carpets, by the Imperial
Royal Austrian Museum of Art and Industry, Vienna; being
a supplement to the Oriental Carpets, published 1892 to
1896 by the Imperial Royal Austrian Commercial Museum.
Pref. by A. von Scala. Introd. by Wilhelm Bode. Ed.
by Arthur von Scala. Leipzig: K. W. Hiersemann, 1908.
10pp, 25 color pls DLC

7640 _____, and Hermann Trenkwald. Old Oriental Carpets.

Austrian Museum for Art and Industry. Tr. by A. F.
Kendrick. 2 vol. Vienna: A. Schroll, 1926-29. ill,
120 pls, bib

7641 Schuermann, Ulrich. Caucasian Rugs: a detailed presentation of the art of carpet weaving in the various districts
of the Caucasus during the 18th and 19th century. Tr.
from German (1965) by A. Grainge. London: Allen &
Unwin; Braunschweig: Linkhardt & Biermann, 1965;
Braunschweig: 1971? 359pp, 160 color ill

7642 _____. Central Asian Rugs: a detailed presentation of
the art of rug weaving in central-Asia in the 18th and 19th
century. With a historical review by Hans Konig. Tr.
from German by Alan Grainge. London: Allen & Unwin,
1970. 176pp, color ill, bib

7643 _____. Oriental Carpets: an introduction. Tr. from
German by James Clark. London: Hamlyn, 1966. 80pp,
70 color ill, bib

7644 *Tattersall, Creassey Edward Cecil. The Carpets of Persia;
a book for those who use and admire them. London:
Luzac, 1931. 52pp, ill, 32 pls

7645 Thacher, Amos B. Turkoman Rugs: an illustrative monograph. New York: Hajji Baba Club, 1940. 55 pls

7646 The Tiffany Studios Collection of Antique Chinese Rugs. New
York: Tiffany, 1908; as Antique Chinese Rugs. Rutland,
Vt: Tuttle; London: Prentice-Hall, 1969. 96pp, ill,
32 pls

7647 Tschebull, Raoul. Kazak; carpets of the Caucasus. Introd.
by Joseph V. McMullan. Exhibition. New York: Near
Eastern Art Research Center, 1971. 104pp, 40 pls

7648 Turkhan, Kudret H. Islamic Rugs. Ed. by Lynne Thornton.
London: Barker, 1968; New York: Praeger, 1969. 112pp,
ill, pls (part color)

7649 Valentiner, Wilhalm Reinhold. Catalogue of a Loan Exhibition of Early Oriental Rugs. November 1910-January
1911. New York: Gilliss Pr, for Metropolitan Museum,
1910. 62pp, ill, bib

7650 Williams, Moddie Jeffries. A Primer of Facts about Oriental
Rugs. New York: Carlton Pr, 1967. 144pp, ill, 24
pls

7651 Winters, Lawrence. Rugs and Carpets from the Orient. New
York: H. B. Claflin, 1890? 112pp, ill

7652 Wolfe, Freida, and A. T. Wolfe. How to Identify Oriental
      Rugs. London: T. Fisher Unwin, 1927. 54pp, ill, 45
      pls (part color)

HOOKED RUGS

7653 (Edward Sands) Frost Hooked Rug Patterns. Greenfield,
      Mass: Charlotte K. Stratton, 1952. 63pp, ill (part color)
      DeWint

7654 (Edward Sands) Frost Hooked Rug Patterns. Greenfield Vil-
      lage and Henry Ford Museum. Dearborn, Mich: Edison
      Institute, 1970. 6pp, ill DeWint

7655 (Edward Sands) Frost & Co, Biddeford, Maine. Descriptive
      Circular. Turkish Rug Patterns. Colored rug or mat
      patterns. Biddeford, Me: 1884. 24pp, ill DeWint

7656 *Kent, William Winthrop. The Hooked Rug; a record of its
      ancient origin, modern development, methods of making,
      sources of design, value as a handicraft, the growth of
      collections, probable future in America, and other data.
      Fore. by Will H. Low. New York: Dodd, Mead, 1930;
      New York: Tudor, 1930; 1937; 1941; reprint. Detroit:
      Gale-Tower, 1971. 210pp, 173 ill, color frontis

7657 _____ . Hooked Rug Design. Showing 28 reproductions of
      the author's own designs, ... 150 other examples from
      many co-operative sources. Springfield, Mass: Pond-
      Ekberg, 1949. 190pp, ill (some color), bib

7658 * _____ . Rare Hooked Rugs and Others Both Antique and
      Modern from Cooperative Sources. Critique by Hazel
      Boyer Brown. Springfield, Mass: Pond-Ekberg, 1941.
      227pp, 240 ill, pls (part color), color frontis

7659 *Kopp, Joel, and Kate Kopp. American Hooked and Sewn Rugs.
      Folk art underfoot. New York: Dutton, 1975. 128pp,
      213 (100 color) ill, bib

7660 * _____ , and _____ . Hooked Rugs in the Folk Art Tradi-
      tion. Exhibition catalog of the show at the Museum of
      American Folk Art, New York. September 1974–January
      1975. New York: the Museum, 1974. 29pp, ill, bib
      (77 rugs listed)

7661 McGown, Pearl Kinnear. The Dreams Beneath Design. A
      story of the history and background of the designs of
      hooked rugs. Boston: B. Humphries, 1939. 96pp, ill
      (By a foremost rug & pattern designer)

7662 * _____ . The Lore and Lure of Hooked Rugs. West Boyl-
      ston, Mass: Author, 1966. 310pp, ill

7663 Martin, Shirley Ann. "Hooked Rugs." Lecture, notes and
      bibliography. n. d. DeWint

7664 Rex, Stella Hay. Choice Hooked Rugs. New York: Prentice-
      Hall, 1953; London: Bailey & Swinfen, 1955. 250pp, ill,
      17 pls, bib

7665 *Waugh, Elizabeth, and Edith Foley. Collecting Hooked Rugs.
      New York; London: Century, 1927. 140pp, ill, pls

7666 Zarbock, Barbara Johnston. The Complete Book of Rug
      Hooking. Princeton, NJ; London: Van Nostrand, 1962.
      120pp, ill, 16 pls, bib

TAPESTRIES

7667 Ackerman, Phyllis. Catalogue of the Retrospective Loan Ex-
      hibition of European Tapestries. Pref. by J. Nilsen Laur-
      vik. San Francisco: Museum of Art, 1922.

7668 _____ . The Rockefeller-McCormick Tapestries. Three
      early 16th century tapestries, with a discussion of the
      history of the tree of life. New York: Oxford U Pr,
      1932. 48pp, ill

7669 _____ . Tapestries. Enjoy Your Museum Series. Pasa-
      dena, Cal: Esto Publishing, 1938. 14pp, ill

7670 _____ . Tapestry, the Mirror of Civilization. New York;
      London: Oxford U Pr, 1933; reprint: AMS Pr, 1970.
      451pp, ill, 48 pls, bib

7671 Alexander, Edward Johnston, and Carol H. Woodward. The
      Flora of the Unicorn Tapestries. Reprint. New York:
      N.Y. Botanical Garden Journal, 1941; 2nd ed. New York:
      Metropolitan Museum, 1947. 28pp, ill DLC

7672 *Belloc, Hilaire. The Book of the Bayeaux Tapestry. Pre-
      senting the complete work in a series of colour facsimiles.
      London: Chatto & Windus, 1913; New York: Putnam's,
      1914; 1916. 76pp, 38 color pls

7673 Birrell, Francis Frederick Locker. Guide to the Bayeux
      Tapestry. London: South Kensington Museum, 1914; 2nd
      ed. 1921; 3rd ed. 1931. 42pp, 11 pls; 34pp, 12 pls;
      135pp, 12 pls BM

7674 Biryukova, N. Y. Gothic and Renaissance Tapestries. The
      Hermitage, Leningrad. London: Hamlyn, 1966. 128pp,
      206 ill, pls, bib (1450-1519)

7675 Calvert, Albert Frederick. The Spanish Royal Tapestries.

London; New York: J. Lane, 1921. 67pp, ill, 277 pls
NN

7676 Candee, Helen Churchill. The Tapestry Book. New York:
      F. A. Stokes, 1912; reprint. New York: Tudor, 1935.
      275pp, 99 ill, 4 color pls MiD, DLC, NN

7677 Catalogue of Books, etc., on Tapestry in the Library of F.
      G. Macomber. Boston: 1895.

7678 Catalogue of a Loan Exhibition of French Gothic Tapestries.
      Introd. by Joseph Breck. May-September 1928. New
      York: Metropolitan Museum, 1928. 25pp, 2 pls

7679 Catalogue of an Exhibition of Tapestries. January-February
      1893. Boston Museum of Fine Arts. Boston: A. Mudge,
      1893. 46pp, ill

7680 A Catalogue of the Ancient and Other plate, tapestry, hearse-
      cloth, etc., belonging to the Worshipful Company of Vint-
      ners. London: 1911. 47pp BM

7681 Champeaux, Alfred de. Tapestry. (South Kensington Museum.)
      Tr. from French by Mrs. Richard Forster Sketchley.
      London: Chapman & Hall, 1877; 1878; New York: Scrib-
      ner, Welford & Armstrong, 1878; London: 1887. 78pp,
      ill, pls, bib (History)

7682 *De Hulst, Roger Adolf. Flemish Tapestries. Tr. from Dutch
      by Frances J. Stillman. New York: Universe, 1967. ill

7683 Ffoulke, Charles Mather. The Ffoulke Collection of Tapestries.
      Comp. by E. Verlant. New York: Priv. printed, 1913.
      346pp, 74 (4 color) pls NN

7684 _____. Monograph on the Judith and Holofernes Series,
      consisting of eight Flemish tapestries with original borders.
      Washington, D.C.: 1907. 28pp of pls DLC

7685 Forman, Werner, and B. Forman. A Book of Tapestries.
      Text by J. Blazkova. Tr. by Hedda Vesela-Stranska.
      London: Spring, 1958? 62pp, 74 ill, bib (History of
      Czechoslovakian tapestry)

7686 400 Years of English Tapestries on Exhibition at the Vigo-
      Sternberg Galleries. November 1971. London: 1971.
      66pp, pls, bib

7687 *Fowke, Frank Rede. The Bayeaux Tapestry: a history and
      description. London: Bell, 1875; 2nd ed. London: Bell,
      1898; 1913. 139pp, 79 pls

7688 Franses, Jack. Tapestries and Their Mythology. New York:

Drake, 1975. 160pp, ill, color pls, bib, signs and symbols (English, Scottish, Irish and American)

7689   French, Gilbert James, 1804-1866. On the Banners of the
       Bayeaux Tapestry and Some of the Earliest Heraldic
       Charges. London: 1857. BM

7690   Fry, Frederick Morris. A Historical Catalogue of the Pic-
       tures, herse-cloths and tapestry at Merchant Taylors'
       Hall, with a list of sculptures and engravings. London:
       Chapman & Hall, 1907; Supplement. London: 1928. 167pp,
       ill; 3 pls CtY, NN, BM

7691   Getz, John. A Short Historical Sketch on Tapestry and Em-
       broidery. Published for the benefit of the Art Loan Exhi-
       bition. April 1895. 36pp, ill NN

7692   Godon, Julien. Painted Tapestry and Its Application to In-
       terior Decoration; practical lessons in tapestry painting
       with liquid colour. Tr. by B. Bucknall. London:
       Lechertier, Barbe, 1879. 89pp, ill (part color) DLC,
       DeWint

7693 *Goebel, Heinrich. Tapestries. Vol. I. The Lowlands. Tr.
       by Robert West (pseud.). Printed in Germany for Bren-
       tano, N.Y., 1924; 1947. 97pp, ill, pls

7694   Great Periods of Tapestry. Exhibition. February 1961.
       Allentown, Pa: Art Museum, 1961. 61pp, 31 ill

7695   Handbook to the Loan Exhibition of French Tapestries, medi-
       aeval, Renaissance and modern, from the public and pri-
       vate collections of France. November 1947-February 1948.
       New York: Metropolitan Museum, 1947. 47pp, ill, bib

7696   Heinz, Dora. Medieval Tapestries. Tr. from German (1965)
       by J. R. Foster. London: Methuen, 1967. 56pp, 20
       pls, bib (1385-1513)

7697   Hulst, Roger Adolf d'. Flemish Tapestries from the 15th to
       the 18th Century. Fore. by H. Liebaera. Tr. from
       Dutch by Frances J. Stillman. Brussels: Editions Ar-
       cade; New York: Universe, 1967. 324pp, ill, bib

7698   Hunter, George Leland. Catalogue of a Loan Exhibition of
       Gothic, Renaissance, Baroque, 18th century and modern
       American tapestries. October-November 1914. Buffalo;
       New York: Buffalo Fine Arts Academy, Albright Art
       Gallery, 1914. 42pp, bib DLC

7699   _____. The "Parnassus" Tapestry in the New York Public
       Library. Reprint from the Bulletin. New York: N.Y.P.L.,
       1915. 5pp, pl

7700 _____ . The Practical Book of Tapestries. Philadelphia;
        London: Lippincott, 1925. 302pp, 228 (8 color) ill, bib
        PPL, ViU

7701 _____ . Tapestries; their origin, history and renaissance.
        New York: John Lane, 1912; London: Lane, 1913. 438pp,
        147 ill, 4 color pls, bib NN, PPL

7702 Jarry, Madeleine. World Tapestry, from its origins to the
        present. New York: Putnam, 1969. 358pp, ill, bib

7703 Jobe, Joseph, ed. Great Tapestries; the web of history from
        the 12th to the 20th century. By Pierre Verlet and others.
        Tr. by Peggy Rowell Oberson. Lausanne: Edita, 1965;
        as The Art of Tapestry. London: Thames & Hudson, 1965.
        278pp, ill, bib

7704 Jones, Mary Eirwen. British and American Tapestries. Had-
        leigh, Eng: Tower Bridge Publications, 1952. 98pp, ill
        DLC

7705 Kendrick, Albert Frank. Catalogue of Tapestries. V & A.
        London: HMSO, 1914; 2nd ed. with supplementary notes
        by A. Van de Put. 1924. 104pp, 18 pls; 102pp, 36 pls,
        bib BM

7706 Lejard, Andre, ed. French Tapestry. London: P. Elek,
        1946. 107pp, ill, color pls, bib

7707 LJsselsteyn, Gerardina Tjebberta van. Tapestry. The most
        expensive industry of the 15th and 16th centuries. A re-
        newed research into technique, origin and iconography.
        The Hague: Brussels van Goor, 1969. 232pp, ill, 102pp
        of photographs, bib

7708 Loan Exhibition of French and Flemish Tapestries. Assembled
        and arranged by George Leland Hunter. Avery Library,
        Columbia University, N.Y., 1914. New York: Institute of
        Arts and Sciences, 1914; Philadelphia: Museum of Art,
        1915; etc. 16pp, ill

7709 McCall, George Henry. The Joseph Widener Collection.
        Tapestries at Lynnewood Hall, Elkins Park, Pennsylvania,
        with historical introduction and descriptive notes. Phila-
        delphia: priv. printed; New York: Rogers-Kellogg-Stillson,
        printers, 1932. 89pp, ill, 25 (11 color) pls, bib

7710 McCormick, Edith (Rockefeller), 1872-1932. The Rockefeller
        McCormick Tapestries. Three early 16th century tapes-
tries, tries, with a discussion of the history of the Tree of Life.
        New York: Oxford U Pr, 1932. 48pp, 43 pls (part color)
        ViU, DLC

7711 Macquoid, Percy. English Furniture, Tapestry and Needle-
      work of the 16th to 19th Centuries. (Record of Lady
      Lever Art Gallery Collection.) London: Batsford, 1928.
      155pp, 116 pls

7712 Mailey, Jean. Chinese Silk Tapestry. K'o-ssu from private
      and museum collections. New York: China Institute in
      America, 1971. 60pp, ill

7713 Marillier, Henry Currie. English Tapestries of the 18th
      Century; a handbook to the Post-Mortlake productions of
      English weavers. London: Medici Society, 1930. 128pp,
      ill, 48 pls

7714 _____. Handbook to the Teniers Tapestries. London:
      Oxford U Pr, 1932. 114pp, ill, 72 pls (David Teniers,
      the Younger, 1610-1690. Brussels)

7715 _____. History of the Merton Abbey Tapestry Works,
      founded by William Morris. London: Constable, 1927.
      37pp, ill (Morris, 1834-1896)

7716 _____. The Tapestries at Hampton Court Palace. Lon-
      don: HMSO, for the Ministry of Works, 1951; rev. ed.
      1962. 31pp, ill, 29 pls

7717 Masterpieces of French Tapestry, Medieval, Renaissance,
      Modern. Exhibition. V & A Museum and the Arts Coun-
      cil of Great Britain. London: the Council, 1947; sepa-
      rate book of illustrations. London: 1947; Chicago: Art
      Institute, 1948. 32pp; ill

7718 *Medieval Tapestries, a picture book. New York: Metropoli-
      tan Museum, 1947.

7719 Mercedes, Viale Ferrero. Tapestries. London: Hamlyn,
      1974. 160pp, color ill

7720 Muentz, Eugene, 1845-1902. A Short History of Tapestry
      from the Earliest Times to the End of the 18th Century.
      Tr. from French by Miss Louisa J. Davis. London;
      New York: Cassell, 1885. 399pp, ill MB

7721 Pianzola, Maurice, and Julian Coffinet. Tapestry. English
      version by Julian Snelling and Claude Namy. Geneve:
      Editions de Bonvent, 1971; New York: Van Nostrand
      Reinhold, 1974. 128pp, ill, bib

7722 Ricci, Seymour de. Catalogue of 20 Renaissance Tapestries
      from the J. Pierpont Morgan Collection. Pairs: Typog-
      raphie P. Renouard, 1913. 51pp, 20 pls

7723 Rorimer, James Joseph. The Unicorn Tapestries at the

Cloisters, a picture book. New York: Metropolitan Museum, 1938; 4th rev. ed. New York: 1962. 38pp, ill (Flemish)

7724 Sevensma, W. S. Tapestries. Tr. from Dutch by Alexis Brown. London: Merlin; New York: Universe, 1965. 110pp, ill, pls, bib

7725 Souchal, Genevieve. Masterpieces of Tapestry from the 14th to 16th Century. Tr. by Richard A. H. Oxby. Fore. by Thomas Hoving. Introd. by Francis Salet. Exhibition. New York: Metropolitan Museum, 1974. 222pp, ill, bib (Originally exhibited in Paris, Grand Palais, 1973)

7726 Szablowski, Jerzy, Sophie Schneebalg-Perelman, and Adelbrecht L. J. Van de Wall. The Flemish Tapestries at Wawel Castle in Cracow. Treasures of King Sigismund Augustus Jagiello. English version by Haakon Chevalier. Antwerp: Fond Mercator, 1972. 501pp, ill, bib

7727 Tapestries and Carpets from the Palace of the Prado, woven at the Royal Manufactory of Madrid.... Exhibition. Hispanic Society of America, N.Y. New York: Putnam, 1917. ill

7728 The Tapestries of the Vienna Imperial Court. Vienna: Krystallverlag, G. m. b. H., 1922. 20pp, ill

7729 *Thomson, William George, 1865- . A History of Tapestry from the Earliest Times until the Present Day. New York: Putnam's; London: Hodder & Stoughton, 1906; rev. ed. London: 1930; New York: Putnam, 1931; 3rd ed. rev. & ed. by Frances Paul Thomson, and Ester Sylvia Thomson. London: E. P. Publishing, 1973. 506pp, ill, 74 pls; 550pp, 128 pls, bib; 596pp, ill, 131 pls, bib NN

7730 _____ . Tapestry Weaving in England from the Earliest Times to the End of the 18th Century. London: Batsford; New York: Scribner's, 1914. 172pp, ill, 3 color pls, bib

7731 2000 Years of Tapestry Weaving; a loan exhibition. December 1951-January 1952, Wadsworth Atheneum; February-March 1952, Baltimore Museum of Art. Hartford?, Conn: 1951. 86pp, ill

7732 Wace, Alan John Bayard. The Marlborough Tapestries at Blenheim Palace and Their Relation to Other Military Tapestries of the War of the Spanish Succession. London; New York: Phaidon, 1968. 146pp, ill, bib (Flemish)

7733 *Weigert, Roger Armand. French Tapestry. Tr. from French (1956) by Donald and Monique King. London:

Faber; Newton, Mass: C. T. Branford, 1962. 214pp,
ill, 68 pls, bib

7734 Wingfield Digby, George Frederick. The Devonshire Hunting
       Tapestries. V & A. London: HMSO, 1971. 92pp, ill,
       47 pls, bib (ca.1430-ca.1445)

7735 _____. French Tapestries, from the 14th to the 18th
       Century. London; New York: Batsford, 1951. 12pp, ill

DRAPERY, WINDOW ORNAMENT AND UPHOLSTERY

7736 Arrowsmith, James. An Analysis of Drapery, or the Up-
       holster's assistant, ... shewing the proportions for cutting
       130 various sized festoons. London: M. Bell, 1819.
       31pp, 20 pls DeWint

7737 Bartol, Samuel F. Practical Hints on the Subject of Window
       Ornaments. By S. F. Bartol, window shade manufacturer,
       and depot of cornices, tassels and decorations. New York:
       C. Willets, printer, 1849. 24pp DeWint

7738 Blyth and Sons. Designs of Cabinet Furniture, Chimney
       Glasses, Draperies, etc., manufactured by Blyth and
       Sons ... Chiswell Street, London. 2 parts. Liverpool;
       Manchester: A. Macgregor, 1869; with price list. 1879.
       247 pls BM

7739 Booth, Lorenza. Original Design Book for Cornices and
       Draperies. London: Palmer & Cottrell, 18-? 24 pls

7740 Brightman, Anna. Fabrics and Styles of Colonial Window
       Hangings as Revealed Through Boston and Salem, Massa-
       chusetts, records, 1700-1760. A dissertation submitted
       to the Graduate School of Florida State University. Ann
       Arbor, Mich: University Microfilms, 1966. Xeroxed
       copy, 219pp, pls

7741 _____. Window Treatments for Historic Homes, 1700-
       1850. Washington, D.C.: National Trust for Historic
       Preservation, 1966. 15pp, pls

7742 Charles, Richard. 300 Original Designs for Window-Draperies,
       fringes, and mantle-board decorations. London: Author,
       1874. ill, 100 pls MiD, SKM

7743 The Development of Various Decorative and Upholstery Fabrics.
       New York: F. Schumacher, 1924. color ill

7744 Dubois, Marius Joseph. Curtains and Draperies; a survey of
       the classic periods. Tr. from French by Violet M.

Macdonald. London: Batsford; New York: Viking, 1967. 252pp, ill (1747-1900)

7745 Jonquet, A. 30 Original Designs for Window Draperies. London: Batsford, 1877. 30 pls SKM

7746 Kimball, J. Wayland. Kimball's Book of Designs: furniture and drapery. Boston: Kimball, 1876. 29pp, 27 pls DeWint

7747 King, Thomas. Decorations for Windows and Beds. London: King, n.d. pls (part color) (19th century) PP

7748 _____. The Upholsterer's Accelerator, being rules for cutting and forming draperies, valances, etc. London: G. Taylor, printer, 1833; London: Architectural & Scientific Library, 184-? 36pp, 35 pls MB, DeWint

7749 _____. Upholsterer's Guide: rules for cutting and forming draperies, valances, etc. London: J. Weale, 1848. 37pp, ill, pls MH-BA, SKM

7750 _____. The Upholsterer's Sketch Book ... for fashionable draperies, etc. London: Weale, Simpkin, Marshall, 1839; Part II. ... Window Curtains and Beds in the Elizabethan and French Styles. London: 184-? ill; 16 color pls SKM

7751 Martin, Thomas, of New York. Awnings. How to Measure for Rise and Fall Awnings, slide awnings, awnings between iron columns, window awnings, roller and tie-down awnings. New York: 1878. 22pp, ill DLC

7752 A Series, containing 44 engravings in colours, of fashionable furniture; consisting of beds, sofas, ottomans, window-curtains, chairs, tables, book-cases, etc. London: R. Ackerman, 1823. 52pp, 44 color pls

7753 The Upholsterer, devoted to the upholstery arts. Monthly. New York: Clifford & Lawton, 1902- . ill

WALL COVERING, WALLPAPER AND WALL DECORATION

7754 Ackerman, Phyllis. Wallpaper, Its History, Design and Use. New York: F. A. Stokes; London: Heinemann, 1923; reprint. New York: Tudor, 1938. 268pp, ill, color frontis, bib

7755 Allen, Edward B. Early American Wall Paintings, 1710-1850. New Haven: Yale U Pr; London: H. Milford, Oxford U Pr, 1926; reprint with additions. Watkins Glen, NY: Century, 1971. 110pp, ill, pl; 112pp, ill

7756   (Fr.) Beck and Co, NY. <u>Artistic Wall Papers Designed and</u>
       <u>Manufactured.</u> 1. Henry Wadsworth Longfellow, and his
       work, by Lymon Abbott; 2. Dado, screen, and frieze.
       New York: 1881. 8pp, ill DeWint

7757   Bles, Arthur de. <u>Walls and Their Decoration.</u> New York:
       Wallpaper Guild of America, 1925. 23pp, ill NN

7758   <u>A Book of Designs.</u> (Taken from old French wall-coverings
       of the period 1790-1850.) Leigh-on-Sea: F. Lewis, 1943.
       ill BM

7759   Bradshaw, William Richard. <u>Wall Paper: its history, manu-</u>
       facture and decorative importance. New York: J. P.
       McHugh, 1891. 21pp, frontis NN, DLC

7760   Brightling, Walter Reade. <u>Wall-Paper Influence Upon the</u>
       <u>Home.</u> Montreal: Watson Foster, 1908. BM

7761   Clark, Fiona. <u>William Morris Wallpapers and Chintzes.</u>
       Biographical note by Andrew Melvin. London: Academy
       Editions; New York: St. Martin's Pr, 1973. 95pp, 91 ill,
       8 pls, bib

7762   Cook, Clarence Chatham. <u>"What Shall We Do with Our Walls?"</u>
       New York: Warren, Fuller, 1880; 1881; 2nd ed. 1883;
       1884. 35pp, ill, 5 pls (gold and color), color frontis
       (Illustrated with wallpaper designs by Samuel Colman and
       Louis C. Tiffany) NN, DLC

7763   Crace, John Gregory. <u>"The Crace Papers."</u> Two lectures
       on the history of paperhangings delivered by J. G. Crace
       to the Royal Institution of British Architects on 4th and
       18th February, 1839. Birmingham, Eng: J. G. Hammond,
       1839. 55pp, ill BM

7764   Entwisle, Eric Arthur. <u>The Book of Wallpaper; a history and</u>
       an appreciation. Introd. by Sacheveral Sitwell. London:
       A. Barker, 1954; rev. ed. Bath: Kingsmead Reprints,
       1970. 151pp, ill, 66 pls, bib

7765   _____. <u>French Scenic Wallpapers, 1800-1860.</u> Leigh-on-
       Sea: F. Lewis, 1972. 63pp, ill, 44 pls, bib

7766 * _____. <u>A Literary History of Wallpaper.</u> London: Bats-
       ford, 1960. 211pp, 127 ill

7767 * _____. <u>Wallpapers of the Victorian Era.</u> Leigh-on-Sea:
       F. Lewis, 1964. 55 pp, ill, 48 pls (1839-1899)

7768   _____, and John Mellor, and Frank Lewis. <u>A Century of</u>
       <u>British Fabrics, 1850-1950.</u> Leigh-on-Sea: F. Lewis,
       1955; 1961. ill (Wall-papers by Entwisle)

7769 Exhibition of Wall Paper, Historical and Contemporary. De-
      cember 1937-January 1938. Buffalo, NY: Buffalo Fine
      Arts Academy, Albright Art Gallery, 1937. 50pp, ill, bib

7770 Hathaway, Calvin Sutliff. Wall-papers in the Museum's Col-
      lections, Produced Before 1900. New York: Cooper Union
      Museum Chronicle, 1938. pp. 115-167, ill NN

7771 Historic Wallpapers in the Whitworth Art Gallery, from the
      collection presented to the Gallery in 1967 by the Wall
      Papers Manufacturers Ltd. Manchester, Eng: Victoria
      U of Manchester, Whitworth Art Gallery, 1972. 59pp,
      ill, bib

7772 Jennings, Arthur Seymour. Practical Paper-hanging; a hand-
      book on decoration in paper and other materials with
      practical instructions on hanging them. New York: W.
      T. Comstock, 1892. 116pp, ill MiD

7773 _____. Wall-paper Decoration. A practical guide to the
      selection, use and hanging of wall-paper and other portable
      decorations. London: Trade Papers Publishing; New
      York: Clifford & Lawton, 1906; London: 1907. 177pp,
      143 ill, 8 color pls, color frontis, 6 samples NN

7774 _____. Wallpapers and Wall Coverings. A practical book
      for decorators, paperhangers, architects, builders and
      houseowners. London: Trade Papers Publishing, 1902;
      New York: W. T. Comstock, 1903. 161pp, many ill
      (some color), 3 samples PP, MB

7775 Katzenbach, Louis, and William Katzenbach. The Practical
      Book of American Wallpaper. Introd. by Nancy V. Mc-
      Clelland. Philadelphia: Lippincott, 1951. 142pp, 114
      pls, 14 samples

7776 *Little, Nina Fletcher. American Decorative Wall Painting
      1700-1850. Sturbridge, Mass: Old Sturbridge Village,
      with Studio Publications, 1952; enl. ed. New York: Dut-
      ton, 1972. 145pp, ill, bib

7777 *McClelland, Nancy. Historic Wall-Papers, from their in-
      ception to the introduction of machinery. Introd. by Henri
      Clouzot. Philadelphia; London: Lippincott, 1924. 458pp,
      245 ill, 12 color pl, bib MB, ViU

7778 _____. The Practical Book of Decorative Wall-Treatments.
      Philadelphia; London: Lippincott, 1926. 273pp, 206 ill,
      8 color pls, bib ViU, PP

7779 McClelland, Nancy, Inc. Wall-papers Old and New. Ex-
      clusive designs. New York: 1930. 68pp, ill MB

7780   Melvin, Andrew, ed. Wallpapers and Designs by William
       Morris. London: Academy Editions, 1971. 103pp,
       chiefly ill

7781   Morton, George H. The History of Paper-hangings, with a
       review of other modes of mural decoration. Read before
       the Architectural and Archaeological Society of Liverpool.
       Liverpool: G. H. Morton, 1875. 45pp DLC

7782   Northend, Mary Harrod. Wall-papers from New England
       Homes. Salem, Mass: M. H. Northend, 19-? 17 pls
       NN

7783   Oman, C. C. Catalogue of Wall-papers. V & A Museum,
       Department of Engraving, illustration and design. London:
       Board of Education, 1929. 114pp, ill, 24 pls, bib DLC

7784   Sanborn, Katherine Abbott. Old Time Wall Papers, an ac-
       count of the pictoral papers on our forefathers' walls, with
       a study of the historical development of wall paper making
       and decoration. Greenwich, Conn; New York: The Literary
       Collector Pr, 1905. 116pp, ill, 83 pls

7785   Sanderson, Arthur, and Sons, Ltd., wallpaper manufacturers.
       A Century of Sanderson, 1860-1960. London: Sanderson,
       1960. 39pp, ill (Section on wallpaper and chintzes by
       Sacheverall Sitwell)

7786   *Sugden, Alan Victor, and J. L. Edmonston. A History of
       English Wallpaper, 1509-1914. London: Batsford, 1925;
       New York: Scribner, 1926. 281pp, 190 ill, 70 color pls,
       31 portraits, bib NN

7787   Wallpaper, a picture book of examples in the Collection of the
       Cooper Union Museum. New York: its Chronicle, 1961.
       46pp, ill

7788   Ward, George Whiteley. Wall Paper, Its Origin, Development
       and Manufacture. London; New York: Pitman, 1922.
       100pp, ill

7789   Wearne, Harry, 1852-1929. Harry Wearne, a short account
       of his life and work, with 63 reproductions of his designs
       in full color. New York: Thomsen-Ellis, 1933. 179pp,
       ill, color pls (Includes wallpaper designs)

LEATHERWORK, LEATHER MANUFACTURE AND TOOLS

7790   Baker, Oliver. Black Jacks and Leather Bottells; being some
       account of leather drinking vessels in England and inci-
       dentally of other ancient vessels. London: E. J. Burrow,

printer, priv. printed for W. J. Fieldhouse, Stratford-on-
Avon, 1921.   190pp, ill, 24 (3 color) pls

7791 Collins, James. Hides and Leather. London: 1876. See
also: Bevan, G. P., British Manufacturing Industries,
Vol. 9., no. 43.

7792 Davis, Charles Thomas. The Manufacture of Leather: being
a description of all of the processes for the tanning, taw-
ing, currying, finishing, and dyeing of every kind of leather
... with special reference to the best American practice.
To which are added complete lists of all American patents
for materials, processes, tools, and machines for tanning,
currying, etc. Philadelphia: H. C. Baird, 1885; 2nd ed.
1897.   824pp, ill, pls, 12 specimens   BM, DLC, DeWint

7793 Exhibit of Leathercraft Through the Ages.   London: Museum
of Leathercraft, 1951.   68pp, ill   BM

7794 Leather in the Decorative Arts. Exhibition. New York:
Cooper Union Museum for Arts of Decoration, 1950.   15pp,
ill, pls, bib

7795 Leathercraft Through the Ages: an historical survey. Exhibition. London: Museum of Leathercraft, 1951.   49pp, ill

7796 Nothing Takes the Place of Leather. Exhibition. Newark:
Museum, 1926.   32pp, ill, bib   DLC

7797 (C. S.) Osborne & Company. Standard Tools 1911. Catalog
reprint. Early Trades and Crafts Society, Mid-West Tool
Collectors, Early American Industries Association. South
Burlington, Vt: EAIA, 1976.   63pp, 190 ill (Leather
working tools, also tools for carpet layer, caulker, plumber,
tinsmith, upholsterer, etc. Also icepicks, can openers,
champagne nippers, cigar box openers, etc.)

7798 Stevens, John W.   Leather Manufacture ... containing illustrations of machinery, etc. London; Chicago: Sampson Low,
1891.   240pp, ill

7799 Waterer, John William. Leather. London: Ginn, 1959; 1970.
32pp, ill (Juvenile literature. Leather ware to 1800)

7800 _____ . Spanish Leather: a history of its use from 800 to
1800 for mural hanging, screens, upholstery, altar frontals,
ecclesiastical vestments, footwear, gloves, pouches and
caskets. London: Faber, 1971.   130pp, ill, 81 pls (some
color), bib

MISCELLANEOUS RAW MATERIALS

RUBBER, WAX, TORTOISESHELL, PLASTIC AND AMBER

7801 The Art of Making Wax Flowers. 2nd ed. Boston: P. Mason, 1874. 27pp, ill DLC

7802 Beadle, Clayton, and Henry Potter Stevens. Rubber. Production and utilization of the raw product. London: Pitman, 1911. 132pp

7803 Catalogue of the Exhibition of Works in Horn, ancient and modern, held at the Mansion House, October 1882. London: Worshipful Company of Horners, 1882; rev. ed. 1882. 48pp BM

7804 Collins, James. Guttapercha and Indiarubber. London: 1876. See: Bevan, G. P., British Manufacturing Industries, Vol. 9, no. 43.

7805 Dards, Mrs. A Catalogue of Shell-work, etc., by Mrs. Dards, consisting of a great variety of beautiful objects, equal to nature, minutely described; comprehending a new system, which will be highly gratifying to every lover of natural history. Exhibited at No. 52, Bankside, Southwark. London: 1798. 9pp DeWint

7806 DuBois, J. Harry. Plastics History U.S.A. Boston: Cahners Books, 1972. 448pp, ill, bib

7807 Francis, George William, 1800-1865. The Art of Modelling Wax Flowers, fruit, etc., etc. London: Simpkin, Marshall, 1849; 3rd ed. 1851; improved ed. 1853. 55pp, ill; ...; 78pp, ill DeWint

7808 The Hand-book of Useful and Ornamental Amusements and Accomplishments, including artificial flower making, engraving, etching, painting in all its styles, modelling, carving in wood, ivory and shell. By a Lady. London: Smith, Elder, 1845. 315pp, pls DeWint

7809   Hasluck, Paul Nooncree, 1854-1931, ed. Bamboo Work, com-
       prising the construction of furniture, household fitments
       and other articles in bamboo. London; New York; Mel-
       bourn: Cassell, 1901; Philadelphia: McKay, 1903; New
       York; London: Cassell, 1911;... 160pp, ill NN, PP

7810   Kaufman, Morris. The First Century of Plastics; celluloid
       and its sequel. London: Plastics Institute, 1963. 130pp,
       ill

7811   Marble in the Home and Garden. Cleveland, O: National
       Association of Marble Dealers, 1928. 63pp, ill, pls

7812   Mumford, John Kimberly. The Story of Bakelite. New York:
       Robert L. Stillson, 1924. 80pp, ill, pls PU, DLC

7813   Peachey, Mrs. E. The Royal Guide to Wax Flower Modelling.
       London?: Author, 1851. 4 hand-colored pls

7814   Phillips, Philip A. S. John Obrisset, Hugenot carver, medal-
       list, horn and tortoiseshell worker and snuff box maker,
       with examples of his work dated 1705-1728. London:
       Batsford, 1931. 74pp, 104 ill, facsims

7815   Pyke, E. J. A Biographical Dictionary of Wax Modellers.
       Oxford: Clarendon Pr, 1973. 216pp, ill, 79 pls, bib

7816   Seeligmann, T., G. Lamy Torrilhon, and H. Falconnet.
       Indiarubber and Gutta Percha: a complete practical trea-
       tise on Indiarubber and gutta percha in their historical,
       botanical, aboricultural, mechanical, chemical, and elec-
       trical aspects. Tr. from French by John G. McIntosh.
       London: Scott, Greenwood, 1903; 2nd ed. rev. & enl.
       1910. 402pp, 86 ill, bib; 408pp, 145 ill, tables, bib
       DLC

7817   Simmonds, Peter Lund. The Commercial Products of the
       Animal Kingdom Employed in the Arts and Manufactures,
       shown in the collection of the Bethnal Green Branch of
       the South Kensington Museum. London: HMSO, 1880.
       BM

7818   Sloane, Thomas O'Conor. Rubber Hand Stamps and the
       Manipulation of Rubber; a practical treatise on the manu-
       facture of India rubber hand stamps, small articles of
       India rubber, the hektograph, special inks, cements, and
       allied subjects. New York: Hanley, 1891; 2nd ed. ...
       also giving the sources of India rubber and its history.
       New York: 1900; 3rd rev. ed. ...includes "rubber in
       surgery and dentistry, rubber tires." New York: 1912;
       4th rev. ed. includes "rubberized fabrics, raincoats,
       gloves, garden and fire hose." New York: 1927. 146pp,
       ill; ...; 167pp, ill; 222pp, ill

SECTION XVIII

PAPER

HISTORY AND MANUFACTURE OF PAPER AND WATERMARKS

7819 Adams, Charles M. Some Notes on the Art of Marbling Paper
      in the 17th Century. Reprint from Bulletin, July 1947.
      New York: New York Public Library, 1947. 14pp

7820 Archer, Thomas Croxen. Paper. London: 1877. See: Bevan,
      G. P., British Manufacturing Industries, Vol. 8, no. 43.

7821 Balston, Thomas. William Balston, Paper Maker, 1759-1849.
      London: Methuen, 1954. 171pp, ill, watermark facsims

7822 Beadle, Clayton. Chapters on Papermaking. 5 vol. London:
      H. H. Grattan, 1904-1908. BM

7823 Bofarull y Sans, Francisco de Asis de, 1843-1936. Animals
      in Watermarks. Ed. and with a supplement by E. J.
      Labarre. Tr. by A. J. Henschel. Hilversum, Holland:
      Paper Publications Society, 1959. 66pp, ill DeWint

7824 *Butler, Frank O. The Story of Paper-Making. An account
      of paper-making from its earliest known record down to
      the present time. Chicago: J. W. Butler Paper Co, 1901.
      136pp, ill ViU

7825 Chalmers, Thomas Wightman. Paper Making and Its Ma-
      chinery. London: Constable, 1920. 178pp, 144 ill, 6 pls

7826 *Churchill, William Algernon. Watermarks in Paper in Hol-
      land, France, England in the 17th and 18th Centuries and
      Their Interconnection. Amsterdam: M. Hertzberger,
      1935. 96pp, 432pp of watermark reproductions, bib ViU,
      DLC, TxU

7827 Clapperton, Robert Henderson. Paper. Historical account of
      its making by hand from the earliest times down to the
      present day. Oxford: Shakespeare Head Pr, 1934. 158pp,
      ill, pls, bib MiU, NN, CtY

7828 _____ . The Paper-Making Machine, its invention, evolution and development. Oxford; New York: Pergamon Pr,
1967. 365pp, ill, pls

7829 Davis, Charles Thomas. The Manufacture of Paper: being
a description of the various processes for the fabrication,
coloring, and finishing of every kind of paper.... Philadelphia: H. C. Baird; London: Low, Marston, 1886.
608pp, ill BM

7830 Day, Frederick T. An Introduction to Paper, Its Manufacture
and Use. London: Newnes, 1962. 125pp, ill, bib, gloss

7831 Eineder, Georg. The Ancient Paper-Mills of the Former
Austro-Hungarian Empire and Their Watermarks. Tr. by
E. J. Labarre. Hilversum, Holland: Paper Publications
Society, 1960. 182pp, pls

7832 Ewald, Alexander Charles. Paper and Parchment: historical
sketches. London: Ward & Downey, 1890. 335pp

7833 Heawood, Edward. Watermarks, Mainly of the 17th and 18th
Centuries. Hilversum, Holland: Paper Publications Society, 1950. 154pp, 533 pls

7834 *Herring, Richard. Paper and Paper Making, Ancient and
Modern. Introd. by Reverend George Croly. London:
Longman, Brown, Green, etc., 1856. 125pp, ill, 30
paper specimens ViU

7835 A History of Paper. New York: Fraser Paper Co, 1964.
121pp, ill, 2 pls

7836 *Hunter, Dard, 1883- . Chinese Ceremonial Paper; a monograph relating to the fabrication of paper and tin foil and
the use of paper in Chinese rites and religious ceremonies.
Chillicothe, O: The Mountain House Pr, 1937. 79pp, ill,
pls, specimens, bib CU, PP, ICN

7837 _____ . The Dard Hunter Paper Museum. Appleton, Wis-
consin: Institute of Paper Chemistry, n.d. 10pp, pls
(Museum is at M.I.T., Boston) InU

7838 _____ . 15th Century Papermaking. New York: Press of
Ars Typographica, 1927. 17pp, ill NN

7839 * _____ . Handmade Paper and Its Water Marks; a bibliography. Marborough-on-Hudson, NY: Technical Association
of the Pulp and Paper Industry, 1916; 1917; reprint. New
York: Burt Franklin, 1967. 22pp NN

7840 _____ . The Literature of Papermaking, 1390-1800.

Chillicothe, O: 1925; Reprint. New York: Burt Franklin,
1971. 47pp, ill, pl, mounted facsims. ViU, TxU

7841   . Old Papermaking. Chillicothe, O: 1923. 112pp,
ill, pls, facsims. TxU, DLC, DeWint

7842 *   . Old Papermaking in China and Japan. Chillicothe,
O: Mountain House Pr, 1932. 71pp, ill, pls (part color),
samples DeWint, DLC

7843   . Old Watermarks of Animals. New York?: 191-?
4pp, ill BM

7844 *   . Papermaking by Hand in America. Chillicothe, O:
Mountain House Pr, 1950. 326pp, color frontis, pls,
samples NN, DeWint

7845   . Papermaking by Hand in India. New York: Pynson, 1939. 129pp, pls, bib MB, DLC

7846   . Papermaking in Indo-China. Chillicothe, O:
Mountain House Pr, 1947. 102pp, ill, 2 samples DLC,
DeWint

7847 *   . Papermaking in Pioneer America. Philadelphia:
University of Pa. Pr; Oxford, Eng: U. Pr, 1952; 1954.
178pp, ill (1690-1817) TxU, CU

7848   . Papermaking in Southern Siam. Chillicothe, O:
Mountain House Pr, 1936. 34pp, color frontis, pls,
samples NN

7849   . A Papermaking Pilgrimage to Japan, Korea and
China. New York: Pynson Printers, 1936. 148pp, ill,
pls, specimens, bib ViU, NjP

7850 *   . Papermaking: the history and technique of an
ancient craft. New York: Knopf, 1943; 2nd ed. rev. &
enl. 1947; London: Cresset Pr, 1947; rev. & enl. ed.
1957; New York: Knopf, 1967. 398pp, ill, specimens,
bib; 611pp, ill, pls, bib TxU, ViU, MB

7851 *   . Papermaking Through 18 Centuries. New York:
W. E. Rudge, 1930; reprint. New York: Burt Franklin,
1971. 358pp, ill, pls

7852   . Romance of Watermarks; a discourse on the origin
and motive of these mystic symbols which first appeared
in Italy near the end of the 13th century. And a biographical sketch of the author by Katherine Fisher. Cincinnati: Stratford Pr, 1939? 34pp NNC-Ave, DLC

7853 Irogami. (Plain tinted Japanese paper. Before 1878.) 30pp,
no text, 81 specimens MB

7854   Jenkins, Rhys. Paper-Making in England, 1495-1788. Reprint from Library Association Record, 1900-1902. London: Association of Assistant Librarians, 1958. 33pp

7855   Maddox, Harry Alfred. Paper: its history, sources and manufacture. London: Pitman, 1916; 2nd ed. 1928;... 159pp; 168pp

7856   Narita, Kiyofusa. Patterned Paper, Ebosho, and Watermarked Paper. Tokyo: Paper Museum, 1961. 12pp, ill

7857   Newman, Thelma Rita, Jay Hartley Newman, and Lee Scott Newman. Paper as Art and Craft: the complete book of the history and processes of the paper arts. New York: Crown; London: Allen & Unwin, 1973. 308pp, ill, 5 pls, bib

7858   Papermaking: Art and Craft; an account derived from the exhibition presented at the Library of Congress, April 1968. Washington, D.C.: 1968. 96pp, ill, facsims

7859   Seki, Yoshikuni. Collection of Pictures of Old and New Papermaking for Hand-made Paper and of Old Paper-shop with 175 Specimens of Actual Hand-made Paper. 2 vol. Japan: 1965. Portfolio of samples in case

7860   Smith, David Clayton. History of Papermaking in the United States (1691-1969). New York: Lockwood, 1970. 693pp, ill

7861   Sommerville, William, and Son, Ltd. Watermarks--a brief history and survey of the techniques. South Croyden: W. Sommerville, 1973. 14pp, ill, samples, bib

7862   Spicer, Albert Dykes. The Paper Trade; a descriptive and historical survey of the paper trade from the commencement of the 19th century. London: Methuen, 1907. 282pp, diags, bib

7863   Voorn, Hendrick. Old Ream Wrappers; an essay on early ream wrappers of antiquarian interest. North Hills, Pa: Bird and Bull, 1969. 110pp, ill

7864   Weeks, Lyman Horace. A History of Paper Manufacturing in the United States, 1690-1916. New York: Lockwood Trade Journal, 1916; reprint. New York: Burt Franklin, 1969. 252pp, ill, bib

7865   West, Clarence Jay, comp. Pulp and Paper Manufacture; Bibliography and United States Patents. Annual. New York: Technical Association of the Pulp and Paper Industry, 1932- .

PAPERWORKS AND STENCILS

7866 Brill, Marna. Paper of the State. Works on paper in New
      York State. Exhibition. New York: Museum of American
      Folk Art, 1976. 16pp, 20 ill

7867 Cohen, Hal L. Official Guide to Paper Americana. New
      York: House of Collectibles, 1972. 320pp, ill, 8 color
      pp of ill (Catalogs, greeting cards, advertising cards,
      etc.)

7868 Hechtinger, Adelaide, and Wilbur Cross. The Complete Book
      of Paper Antiques. New York: Coward, McCann &
      Geoghegan, 1972. 220pp, ill, bib (Valentines, playbills,
      posters, etc.)

7869 Hollingsworth and Whitney Co., Boston. Paper Bags, 1860-
      1891. Boston: 1891? 21pp, pls DeWint

7870 Kuo, Nancy. Chinese Paper-cut Pictures, Old and Modern.
      New York: Taplinger, 1965. 20pp, ill, 75 pls

7871 Laliberte, Norman, and Alex Mogelon. The Art of Stencil;
      history and modern uses. New York: Van Nostrand Rein-
      hold, 1971. 104pp, ill

7872 Lambert, Frederick Charles, and Charles Godfrey Leland.
      Paperwork, Decorative and Useful. London: Dawbarn &
      Ward, n.d. (ca.1900). 24pp, ill, pl

7873 McClinton, Katharine Morrison. The Chromolithographs of Louis
      Prang. New York: Clarkson Potter, 1973. 246pp, ill

7874 Proudfoot, W. B. The Origin of Stencil Duplicating. London:
      Hutchinson, 1972. 128pp, ill, bib (History of stencils
      and stencil cutting)

7875 *Tuer, Andrew White, 1838-1900. The Book of Delightful and
      Strange Designs; being 100 facsimile illustrations of the
      art of the Japanese stencil-cutter. In English, French,
      German. London: Leadenhall; New York: Scribner's,
      1893; reprint as Japanese Stencil Designs; 100 outstanding
      examples. New York: Dover, 1967. 24, 27, 26pp, 104
      designs; 24pp, 112 pls

7876 Yamanashi, Taeko. Paper Dolls of Old Japan. Tr. by G.
      A. Pomeroy. Tokyo: Toto Shuppan; Rutland, Vt: Tuttle,
      1961. 49pp, ill

PAPIER MACHE AND DECOUPAGE

7877 Barnard, J., London firm. Paper Mache: with clear

directions for decoration and inlaying it with pearl. London: Adams & Gee, printers, 188-? 8pp DeWint

7878 Bielefeld, Charles Frederick. On the Use of the Improved Papier Mache in Furniture, in the interior decoration of buildings, and in works of art. London: Rickerby, 1840; London: J. B. Nichols & Son, ca.1842; new ed. 1850. 11pp, 116 pls; 11pp, 128 pls NN, DLC, BM

7879 Boileau, Daniel. Papyro-plastics, or, The art of modelling in paper; being an instructive amusement for young persons of both sexes. London: Boosey & Sons, 18-?; 2nd enl. ed. 1925. 102pp, 22 pls DeWint, BM

7880 *DeVoe, Shirley Spaulding, 1899- . English Papier Mache of the Georgian and Victorian Period. London: Barrie & Jenkins; Middletown, Conn: Wesleyan U. Pr, 1971. 193pp, 180 ill, bib (Wolverhampton-Birmingham districts)

7881 *Dickinson, George. English Papier-Mache: its origin, development and decline. London: Courier Pr, 1925. 135pp, ill, 31 pls (some color) DLC, MB

7882 Gerken, Jo Elizabeth. Wonderful Dolls of Papier Mache. Lincoln, Neb: Doll Research Associations, 1970. 227pp, ill

7883 An Introduction to Decoupage and Related Paper Work at the Wenham Museum, Wenham, Massachusetts. Exhibition. n.p.: 1954. 8pp, ill, bib

7884 Jackson, George and Sons, London. The Collection of George Jackson and Sons, manufacturers of composition and improved papier mache. 2 vol. in 1. London: 1836-39. ill (Part 1. First Part of the Collection of Detached Enrichments, and various articles of taste and furniture; Part 2. Second Part....) NNC-Ave

7885 _____. Part of the Collection of Relievo Decorations as Executed in Papier Mache and Carton Pierre. London: J. Weale, 1849. 66 pls (1 color) MH, CtY

7886 Jervis, Simon. 19th Century Papier-Mache. V & A Museum. London: HMSO, 1973. 13pp, color ill (English, ca.1810-1854)

7887 Lindsey, George. Pens and Papier Mache. London: 1876. See: Bevan, G. P., British Manufacturing Industries, Vol. 3, no. 43.

7888 Sommer, Elyse. Decoupage Old and New. New York: Watson-Guptill, 1971. 175pp, ill

7889   Toller, Jane. Papier-Mache in Great Britain and America.
       London: Bell; Newton, Mass: C. T. Branford, 1962.
       126pp, ill, 32 pls

SILHOUETTES, FRAKTURS
AND SCHERENSCHNITTE

7890 *Boehn, Max von. Miniatures and
       Silhouettes. Tr. by E. K.
       Walker. London; Toronto:
       J. M. Dent; New York: Dut-
       ton, 1928; New York: B.
       Blom, 1970. 214pp, ill

7891   Bolton, Ethel Stanwood. Wax
       Portraits and Silhouettes.
       Introd. by Charles Henry Hart.
       Boston: National Society of the
       Colonial Dames of America,
       1914; 2nd ed. 1915; enl. ed.
       as American Wax Portraits....
       Boston; New York: Houghton-Mifflin, 1929.   88pp, ill,
       pls NN, PPL, DLC, BM

7892   Borneman, Henry Stauffer. Pennsylvania German Illuminated
       Manuscripts: a classification of fraktur-schriften and an
       inquiry into their history and art. Norristown, Pa: Ger-
       man Society, Proceedings and Papers, Vol. 46, 1937; re-
       print. New York: Dover; London: Constable, 1973. 61pp,
       ill, 38 (36 color) pls (1507-1841)

7893 *Carrick, Alice Van Leer. Shades of Our Ancestors; American
       profiles and profilists. Boston: Little Brown, 1928; re-
       print as A History of American Silhouettes; a collector's
       guide, 1790-1840. Rutland, Vt: Tuttle, 1968. 205pp, ill,
       color frontis, pls, bib; 332pp, ill, bib

7894   Church, Frederick Stuart. Silhouettes. New York: Valen-
       tine, 1876. 16 leaves of ill

7895   _____. Silhouettes, first series. Boston: Estes & Lauriat,
       1878. 12 leaves of ill

7896   Coke, Desmond. The Art of Silhouette. London: M. Secker,
       1913; reprint. Detroit: Singing Tree Pr, 1970. 230pp,
       ill, pls

7897   Edouart, Augustin A. C. F., 1789-1861. A Treatise of Sil-
       houette Likenesses. London: Longman & Co, 1835.
       122pp, 18 pls

7898 Froelich, K. <u>Frolics with Scissors and Pen.</u> Tr. by Mdme.
de Chatelain. <u>London?:</u> 1860. SIB-1

7899 Hickman, Peggy. <u>Silhouettes.</u> New York: Walker; London:
Cassell, 1968. 60pp, ill, 4 pls

7900 _____. <u>Silhouettes: A Living Art.</u> Fore. by Roy Strong.
New York: St. Martin's Pr, 1975. 96pp, ill (From the
Caves of Lascaux to 20th century)

7901 _____. <u>Two Centuries of Silhouettes. Celebrities in Profile.</u> London: A. & C. Black, 1971. 155pp, ill

7902 Hopf, Claudia. <u>Scherenschnitte, the Folk Art of Scissors
Cutting.</u> Lancaster, Pa: John Paer's Sons, 1974. ill

7903 *Jackson, Emily Nevill. <u>Ancestors in Silhouette, Cut by
August Edouart.</u> London; New York: John Lane, 1921.
239pp, ill (Lists 11,600 portraits cut by this artist, including 3600 of American subjects) PPL, BM

7904 * _____. <u>Catalogue of 5200 Named and Dated English Silhouette Portraits by August Adouart, 1789-1861.</u> London:
Wallbrook, 1911. 56pp, ill NN, BM

7905 * _____. <u>Catalogue and Supplement: 5800 named and dated
silhouette portraits by A. Edouard, 1789-1861.</u> Bath,
Eng: Harding & Curtis, 1914; Chelsea, Eng: J. B.
Shears, 192-? 56pp, ill BM, DLC

7906 * _____. <u>Catalogue of 3800 Named and Dated American
Silhouette Portraits by August Edouart, 1789-1861.</u>
Kensington, Lond: Wakeham, 1926. 31pp, ill TxU,
DLC

7907 * _____. <u>The History of Silhouettes.</u> Fore. by Dorothy
Nevill. London: The Connoisseur; New York: J. T.
Gleason, 1911. 121pp, ill, 74 (2 color) pls, 6 color
facsimiles, bib (On glass, porcelain and paper) NN, BM

7908 * _____. <u>Silhouette: notes and dictionary.</u> London:
Methuen; New York: Scribner's, 1938. 154pp, ill, 103
(10 color) pls (On porcelain, glass, ivory, paper, and
jewellery) DLC

7909 Laliberte, Norman, and Alex Mogelon. <u>Silhouettes; shadows
and cutouts: history and modern use.</u> New York: Reinhold, 1968. 112pp, ill

7910 Leslie, Hubert. <u>Silhouettes and Scissor-Cutting.</u> London:
Lane, 1939. 79pp, 42 ill DLC

7911 Lister, Raymond. Silhouettes; an introduction to their history
         and to the art of cutting and painting them. Fore. by
         Simon Lissim. London; New York: Pitman, 1953. 76pp,
         ill, bib

7912 London, Hannah Ruth. Miniatures and Silhouettes of Early
         American Jews. 2 vol. in 1. Rutland, Vt: Tuttle, 1970.
         ill

7913 Mayne, Arthur. British Profile Miniaturists. Boston: Boston
         Book and Art, 1970. 131pp, ill, pls

7914 Pennsylvania German Fraktur and Color Drawings, Exhibited
         at Pennsylvania Farm Museum of Landis Valley, May-
         June 1969. Lancaster: the Museum, 1969. 72pp, ill

7915 Roe, Frederick Gordon. Women in Profile: Study in Silhouette.
         London: J. Baker, 1970. 69pp, ill, 32 pls

7916 Shelley, Donald. The Fraktur-Writings or Illuminated Manu-
         scripts of the Pennsylvania Germans. Allentown, Pa:
         Pennsylvania German Folklore Society, 1961. 375pp, ill,
         facsims (some color), bib

7917 Townshend, B. A. Groups of Figures from Cuttings in Black
         Paper. London?: 1808. 6 pls SIB-1

7918 _____. Introduction to the Art of Cutting Groups of Figures
         in Black Paper. London?: 1815. 13 pls SIB-1

7919 Valentine and Company, varnish works, New York. Silhouettes.
         New York: 1876. 16 pls

7920 Vernay, Arthur Stannard. The Silhouette. New York?: 1911.
         20pp, pls

7921 Woodiwiss, John. British Silhouettes. London: Country Life,
         1965. 96pp, ill (18th and 19th century British)

CARDS

GREETING CARDS AND STATIONERY

7922 Buday, Gyorgy (George). The History of the Christmas Card. London: Rockliff; New York: Pitman, 1954; new ed. London: Spring Books, 1964. 304pp, ill, pls, bib NN, DLC

7923 _____. The Story of the Christmas Card. London: Odhams Pr, 194-?; 1951. 43pp, ill NN, DLC, BM

7924 Chase, Ernest Dudley. The Romance of Greeting Cards; an historical account of the origin, evolution, and development of the Christmas card, Valentine, and other forms of engraved or printed greetings, from the earliest days to the present time. Introd. by Harry W. Brown. Cambridge, Mass: U. Pr, 1926; reprint. Detroit: Tower, 1971. 255pp, ill, pls DLC

7925 Ettlinger, L. D., and R. G. Holloway. Compliments of the Season. London: Penguin, 1947. ill

7926 Freeman, Graydon La Verne, ed. A Century of American Greeting Cards. Honoring Louis Prang and his followers. A brief memorial issue for students and card collectors. Watkins Glen, NY: Century, 1974. ill, samples, bib

7927 Freymann, Sara Jane, comp. Season's Greetings. New York: Harmony Books, dist. by Crown, 1974. 24 cards, reprinted in facsimile, which can be torn out and used.

7928 *Lee, Ruth Webb. A History of Valentines. New York: Studio 1952; London: Batsford, 1953. 239pp, ill, color pls (Standard reference)

7929 Lyons, Forrest, Jr. Collectors Guide to Postcards. Gas City, Ind: L-W Promotions, 1974. 128 pp, ill (2000 cards, including greeting cards)

7930 The Quiver of Love. A Collection of valentines, ancient and

modern; with illustrations in color from drawings by Walter
Crane and Kate Greenaway. London: Marcus Ward, 1876.
152pp, 8 color pls (Crane, 1845- ; Greenaway, 1846-
1901) DLC

7931 Stone, Lillian Newton. A Showing of Sentimental Valentines
from the ... Stone Collection. Newark, NJ: Museum Association, 19-?

7932 Tiffany, Louis, and Co. Stationery, Invitations, Notes and
Letter Paper of English and French Manufacture, visiting
cards, arms, crests, monograms, etc. Engraved on
metal or stone. New York: Tiffany, 1875. 17 pls

7933 White, Gleeson, 1851-1898. Christmas Cards and Their Chief
Designers. London: The Studio, 1894; 1895. 56pp, ill,
pls

PLAYING CARDS AND TAROT CARDS

7934 Beal, George. Discovering Playing-Cards and Tarots. Aylesbury: Shire Publications, 1972. 56pp, ill, bib

7935 _____. Playing Cards and Their Story. New York: Arco,
1975. 120pp, 91 ill, 37 (8 color) pls

7936 *Benham, Sir William Gurney. Playing Cards. History of
the pack and explanations of its many secrets. London;
Melbourne: Ward, Lock, 1931; London: Spring Books,
1957. 195pp, 242 ill NN, DLC

7937 Braun, Franz. Playing Cards Since 1850. English text form
by Fred G. Bower. Cologne, Germany: 1970-72. facsimile in case, bib

7938 The Cardboard Court; playing cards through history. Exhibi-
      tion. Baltimore: Peabody Institute Library, 1960. 43pp,
      ill

7939 *Cary, Melbert B., Jr. War Cards: a prolusion. New York:
      Press of the Woolly Whale, 1937. ill

7940 *Catalogue of the Collection of Playing Cards of Various Ages
      and Countries: formed by Henry D. Phillips (Master of
      the Worshipful Company of Makers of Playing Cards 1896-
      97). London: priv. printed, 1903. ill

7941 *Chatto, William Andrew. Facts and Speculations on the Origin
      and History of Playing Cards. London: J. R. Smith,
      1848. 343pp, ill, pls (some color), bib TxU, CtY

7942 Clark, Freida. Playing Card Collectors Handbook. Descrip-
      tions and check lists. English royalty and cards issued
      by Worshipful Company of Makers of Playing Cards. n.p.
      (London): 1954? 64pp BM

7943 Coleman, Stanley Jackson. Romance, History and Mystery
      of Playing Cards and Cartomancy. Douglas, Isle of Man:
      Folklore Academy, 1962. 14pp

7944 Culin, (Robert) Stewart, 1858-1929. Chess and Playing Cards.
      Catalogue of games and implements for divination exhibited
      by the United States National Museum at the Cotton States
      and International Exposition, Atlanta, Georgia, 1895. Re-
      print from Annual Report of United States National Museum,
      1896. Washington, D.C.: Smithsonian, 1898. 277pp
      (pp. 665-942), ill, 50 pls (part color) PP, DLC, NN

7945 *Franks, Augustus Wollaston, ed. Playing Cards of Various
      Ages ... selected from collection of Lady Charlotte Schrei-
      ber. 3 vol. London: J. Murray, 1892-95. (Vol. I.
      ... English and Scottish, Dutch and Flemish. Vol. II.
      ... French and German. Vol. III. ... Swiss, Swedish,
      Russian, Polish, Italian, Spanish, and Portuguese; to-
      gether with a supplement of other countries.) 447 pls

7946 Guerrier, Dennis. Solo Boxes. London: Panther, 1969.
      144pp of ill (19th century card game with counters)

7947 _____ . Solo Naughts and Crosses. London: Panther,
      1969. 128pp of ill

7948 *Hargrave, Catherine Perry. A History of Playing Cards and
      a Bibliography of Cards and Gaming. Compiled and illus-
      trated from the old cards and books in the collection of
      the United States Playing Card Company in Cincinnati.
      Boston; New York: Houghton-Mifflin, 1930; reprint. New

York: Dover; London: Constable, 1966. 468pp, 1462 ill,
4 color pls, 78pp bib

7949   Hoffmann, Detlef. The Playing Card; an illustrated history.
Tr. from German. Greenwich, Conn: N.Y. Graphic Society, 1973. 96pp, ill, bib

7950   Horr, Norton Townshend, 1862-1917, comp. Bibliography of
Card-Games and of the History of Playing-Cards. Cleveland, O: C. Horr, 1892. 79pp DLC

7951   Huson, Paul. The Devil's Picturebook. London: Abacus,
1972. ill

7952   *Jessel, Frederick. Bibliography of Works in English on
Playing Cards. London; New York: Longmans, Green,
1905. 312pp, 1733 titles DLC, TxU

7953   Kursrock, Lawrence. United States Playing Cards, Priced
Catalogue. New York: Author, 1965.

7954   Mann, Sylvia. Collecting Playing Cards. London: Arco;
New York: Crown, 1966; London: H. Baker, 1973.
215pp, ill, 8 pls, bib

7955   _____. The Dragons of Portugal. Farnham, Eng: Sandford, for The Playing Card Society, 1973. ill

7956   _____. The William Penn Collection of Playing Cards.
Rye, Eng: Author, 1966. ill

7957   Mayer, Leo Ary. Mamluk Playing Cards. Leiden: Brill,
1971. 61pp, ill ("Mameluke." History of Islamic playing
cards)

7958   Moakley, Gertrude. The Tarot Cards Painted by Bonifacio
Bembo for the Visconti-Sforza Family; an iconographic and
historic study. New York: New York Public Library,
1966. 124pp, ill

7959   Morley, Henry Thomas. Old and Curious Playing Cards: their
history and types from many countries and periods. London: Batsford, 1931; reprint. Detroit: Gale, 197-?
235pp, ill, color frontis, bib BM, NN

7960   Moxon, Joseph. The Use of the Astronomical Playing-Cards.
Teaching and ordinary capacity by them to be acquainted
with all the stars in heaven. London: J. Moxon, printer,
1692. 59pp, with catalogue of globes, maps, sea-plates,
mathematical instruments, and books

7961   O'Donoghue, Freeman M., comp. Catalogue of the Collection

of Playing Cards Bequeathed to the Trustees of the British
Museum by the Late Lady Charlotte Schreiber. London:
Longmans, Green, 1901. no ill

7962   (Pardon, George Frederick.) Whist: its history and prac-
       tice. By an amateur. London: Bell & Wood, 1843; new
       ed. London: D. Bogue, 1844. 99pp BM

7963   Pettigrew, J. T. (Possibly T. J.). On the Origin and An-
       tiquity of Playing Cards and Description of a Pack of the
       Time of the Commonwealth. London?: 1853. ill SIB-3

7964   Singer, Samuel Weller. Researches into the History of Play-
       ing Cards; with illustrations of the origin of printing and
       engraving on wood. London: B. Triphook, 1816. 373pp,
       pls (some color)

7965   Taylor, Edward Samuel, ed., and others. History of Playing
       Cards.... London: J. C. Hotten, 1865; reprint. Rut-
       land, Vt: Tuttle, 1973. 530pp, ill, 48 pls, bib BM

7966   Tilley, Roger. A History of Playing Cards. London: Studio
       Vista; New York: C. N. Potter, 1973. 192pp, ill, bib

7967   _____. Playing Cards. London: Weidenfeld & Nicolson;
       New York: Putnam, 1967; London: Octopus, 1973. 120pp,
       ill; 97pp, ill

7968   Van Rensselaer, Mrs. John King. The Devil's Picture Books.
       London: T. Fisher Unwin, 1892. ill

7969   _____. Prophetical, Educational and Playing Cards. Lon-
       don: Hurst & Blackett, 1912. ill (Chiefly tarot)

7970   Wayland, Virginia, and Harold Wayland. Of Carving, Cards
       and Cookery. Arcadia, Cal: Raccoon Pr, 1962. 52 ill
       (Moxon's deck showing methods of cutting meat, fish,
       fowl. Various editions between 1677 and 1717)

7971   Willshire, William Hughes. A Descriptive Catalogue of Play-
       ing and Other Cards in the British Museum, accompanied
       by a concise general history of the subject and remarks
       on cards of divination and of a politico-historical character.
       London: HMSO, 1876; supplement. 1877. 360pp, bib;
       87pp, 23 pls (some color) BM, DLC, PPULC, CtY, NN

PICTURE POSTCARDS

7972   Alderson, Frederick. The Comic Postcard in English Life.
       Newton Abbot: David & Charles; Rutland, Vt: Tuttle,
       1970. 112pp, ill (part color)

7973 American Postcard Journal. Bi-monthly. West Haven, Conn:
      Roy and Marilyn Nuhn, 197-?- .

7974 Beckley, W. Bourcy, and M. Ruth Duke. Handbook for Post-
      card Collectors. Illustrated with over 75 pictures from
      photographs of postcards used throughout the world in both
      the 19th and 20th century; giving a double system of clas-
      sification and covering more than 40 different types. Los
      Angeles: L. B. Harrison, 1949; 2nd ed. Los Angeles:
      Bourcy-Beckley, 1954. 51pp, ill, bib; 72pp, ill, bib

7975 Burdick, Jefferson R. The American Card Catalog. (The
      Standard Guide on all collected cards and their values.)
      Syracuse, NY: Author, 1946; supplement. 1949; New
      York: Author, 1953; reprint. 1956; ...; 1967. 144pp,
      ill; 168pp, ill, bib; 225pp, ill, bib

7976 _____. The Detroit Index. A numerical listing of post-
      cards published by the Detroit Publishing Company, com-
      prising the regularly numbered cards from number one
      through 72,275, as known to date. Great Kills, NY: John
      Sperling, 1955. 216pp

7977 _____. The Handbook of Detroit Publishing Company Post
      Cards; a guide for collectors with a detailed checklist of
      the later contract issues and all unnumbered cards. Syra-
      cuse?, NY: Burdick?, 1954; supplement. 1955. u.p., ill

7978 _____. Pioneer Post Cards; the story of mailing cards to
      1898, with an illustrated checklist of publishers and titles.
      Syracuse, NY: Nostalgia Pr, 1957; supplement. 1958.
      144pp, ill; 66pp (American and foreign)

7979 _____, comp. The United States Card Collectors Catalogue.
      Syracuse, NY: J. R. Burdick, 1939. 87pp, pls NN

7980 Butland, Arthur James, and Edward Aubrey Westwood. Pic-
      ture Post Cards and All About Them. Teddington, Eng:
      Postcard Collector's Guide and News, 1959. 34pp

7981 Caley, George L. Post Cards of Yesteryear: 1893-1926;
      Delaware and elsewhere. Smyrna, Del: Shane Quality
      Pr, printers, 1973. 92pp, 280 ill

7982 Carline, Richard. Pictures in the Post; the story of the pic-
      ture postcard and its place in the history of popular art.
      Bedford, Eng: G. Fraser, 1959; London: Gordon Fraser
      Gallery, 1971; 1972. 71pp, ill; 128pp, ill, bib

7983 Cole, George Watson, 1850-1939. Postcards: the world in
      miniature. A plan for their systematic arrangement.
      Pasadena: priv. printed, 1935. 27pp NN, DLC

7984   Corson, Walter. Know Your Cards and Their Value. Glen
       Moore, Pa: Author, 1965. mimeographed list

7985   _____. Publisher's Trademarks Identified. Folsom, Pa:
       Better Post Card Collectors' Club, 1962.

7986   French Postcards. New York: Avon, 1954. 125pp, ill

7987   Freymann, Sarah Jane, ed. Hearts and Flowers: 28 romantic
       postcards from the turn of the century. New York: Crown,
       1975. 28 cards to tear out and use.

7988   Hewlett, Maurice Raymond, comp. Picton's Priced Catalogue
       of British Pictorial Postcards and Postmarks, 1894-1939.
       2nd ed. Chippenham?, Eng: B.P.H. Publications, 1971.
       77pp, ill, bib

7989   Hill, Cuthbert William. Discovering Picture Postcards. Fol-
       som, Pa: Deltiologists of America, 1970; Tring, Eng:
       Shire Publications, 1970. 64pp, ill, pls, bib

7990   Holt, Tonie, and Valmai Holt. Picture Postcards of the
       Golden Age: a collector's guide. Folsom, Pa: Deltiolo-
       gists of America, 1971; London: MacGibbon & Kee, 1971.
       214pp, pls

7991   International Postcard Market. Periodical. London: J. H. D.
       Smith, 1968- .

7992   Jenkinson, David H. A Checklist of Post Cards Published by
       the Edward H. Mitchell Company ... 1898-1915. Rev. ed.
       New Haven, Conn: 1975.

7993   Kaduck, John M. Mail Memories. Cleveland: Author, 1971.
       68pp, 1500 ill

7994   _____. Patriotic Postcards. Des Moines: Wallace-Home-
       stead, 1974. 65pp, ill

7995   _____. Rare and Expensive Postcards. Des Moines:
       Wallace-Homestead, 1974. 85pp, ill

7996   Klamkin, Marian. Picture Postcards. New York: Dodd,
       Mead; Newton Abbot: David & Charles, 1974. 192pp, ill,
       bib

7997   Lackey, Bernard B. Edward H. Mitchell, Publisher Handbook.
       North Springfield, Va: 1975. 48pp

7998   Lauterbach, Carl, comp. Postcard Album; also a cultural
       history. Tr. from French and German by Judith Bogianc-
       kino-Matthais, and Elizabeth Earl. New York: Universe,
       1961. 64pp, ill

7999 Lowe, James L. Bibliography of Postcard Literature; a list
      of references pertaining to the publishing and collecting of
      picture post cards. Folsom, Pa: Deltiologists of America,
      1969. 10pp, ill

8000 _____. Lincoln Postcard Catalogue; a check list of Lincoln
      postcards, old and new. Folsom, Pa: Better Postcard
      Collectors' Club, 1967; rev. ed. 1973. 65pp, ill

8001 _____. Standard Postcard Catalog; a price guide for col-
      lectors. Folsom, Pa: Better Postcard Collectors' Club,
      1968. 64pp, ill

8002 _____. Washington Postcard Catalogue; a checklist of
      Washington postcards, old and new. Newtown Square, Pa:
      1974. ill

8003 _____, and Ben Papell. Detroit Publishing Company Col-
      lector's Guide. Newtown Square, Pa: 1975. ill

8004 Lyons, Forrest D., Jr. The Artist Signed Postcard. Gas
      City, Ind: L-W Promotions, 1975. 88pp, 1250 ill, prices

8005 _____. Collectors Guide to Postcards. Gas City, Ind:
      L-W Promotions, 1974. 128pp, ill (2000 cards including
      greeting cards, advertising cards, etc.)

8006 Metropolitan Post Card Collectors Club. Bi-monthly bulletin.
      New York: the Club, 1948-date.

8007 Miller, George, and Dorothy Miller. Picture Postcards in the
      United States: 1893-1918. New York: C. N. Potter, 1976.
      text, 145 (71 color) ill

8008 Nørgaard, Erik. With Love: The Erotic Postcard. London:
      MacGibbon & Kee, 1969; as With Love to You; a history
      of the erotic postcard. New York: C. N. Potter, 1969.
      120pp, chiefly ill

8009 Ouelette, William. Fantasy Postcards. Introd. by Barbara
      Jones. New York: Doubleday, 1975. ill (some color)

8010 Postcard Collector's Guide and News. Periodical. Tedding-
      ton, Eng: 195- .

8011 Stadtmiller, Bernard. Postcard Collecting: A Fun Invest-
      ment. Palm Bay, Fla: Author, 1975. 80pp, ill

8012 Staff, Frank. The Picture Postcard and Its Origins. Lon-
      don: Lutterworth; New York: Praeger, 1966. 95pp, ill

8013 Wall, Edward John, and Henry Snowden Ward. The

Photographic Picture Post-Card for Personal Use and for
Profit. London: Dawburn & Ward, 1906. 104pp

TRADE, ADVERTISING, SAILING AND CIGARET CARDS, AND CIGAR LABELS

8014 Album Containing a Collection of Over 300 Trade Cards of the
Romantic Period, 1840-1855. 68 leaves DLC

8015 Bagnall, Charles Lane, and Edward C. Wharton-Tigar.
British Cigarette Card Issues. 2 parts in 4 vol. London:
Longon Cigarette Card Co, 1950. 54pp; 160pp, ill; 84pp;
158pp, ill (Part I. 1888-1919. Vol. I. Catalogue of Com-
parative Values. Vol. II. Handbook. Part II. 1920-1940.
Vol. I. Catalogue. Vol. II. Handbook)

8016 Bagnall, Dorothy. Collecting Cigarette Cards and Other Trade
Issues. London: Arco, 1965. 112pp, 16 pls

8017 Baker Furniture Company, Inc. A Small Collection of London
Tradesmen's Cards of the 18th Century. Holland, Mich:
Baker Furniture, 1940? 2pp, 20 pls

8018 Bell, Robert Charles. Tradesmen's Tickets and Private Tokens: 1785-1819. Newcastle-upon-Tyne: Corbitt & Hunter,
1966. 316pp, ill, bib

8019 Calvert, Henry Reginald. Scientific Trade Cards in the Science Museum Collection. London: HMSO, 1971. 57pp,
ill, 61 pls (1650-1880)

8020 Cartophilic Notes and News. Bi-monthly. Brentford, Eng:
Cartophilic Society of Great Britain, 1965- . (Includes
cigarette and other trade cards)

8021 Cartophilic Reference Book. London: Cartophilic Society of
Great Britain, 1942- .

8022 The Cigarette Card Issues of John Player and Sons: an official checklist. Windsor, Berkshire: E. F. Pressey, for
Cartophilic Society of Great Britain, 1950. 44pp, ill

8023 Cigarette Card News. Monthly. London: London Cigarette
Card Co, 1933- . ill

8024 Cope Brothers and Company. Cope's Cigar Box Decorations.
2 parts. Liverpool: 1868. BM

8025 _____ . Cigar Brands and Cigar Box Decorations. Liverpool: for the Proprietors, by John Fraser, 1885. 442pp
BM

8026   Cruse, Alfred James. Cigarette Card Collecting. (Including
       a short history of tobacco.) London: Vawser & Wiles,
       1948; 2nd ed. 1951. 172pp, ill

8027   _____. Match-box Labels of the World; with a history of
       fire-making appliances from primitive man to the modern
       match, together with a history of the world's labels. Lon-
       don: R. Ross, 1946. 127pp, ill, color frontis, pls TxU,
       DLC

8028   Davis, Alec. Package and Print; the development of container
       and label design. London: 1967; New York: Potter,
       1968. 112pp, ill, pls, bib

8029   Faber, A. D. Smokers' Segars and Stickers. Watkins Glen,
       NY: Century, 1949. 80pp, ill with drawings (Cigar
       labels)

8030   Forbes, Allan. The Story of Clipper Ship Sailing Cards. Re-
       print from American Antiquarian Society Proceedings, 1949.
       Worcester, Mass: the Society, 1950. 50pp (pp. 225-274),
       ill (part color)

8031   _____, and Ralph M. Eastman. Yankee Ship Sailing Cards.
       Presenting reproductions of some of the colorful cards
       announcing ship sailings in the days when Boston ships
       and Boston men were known in every port of the Seven
       Seas. 3 vol. Boston: State Street Trust Company, 1948,
       1949, 1952. 76pp, pls (part color); 111pp, ill;   TxU,
       MH, DLC, DeWint

8032   Gillingham, Harold Edgar. Old Business Cards of Philadel-
       phia. Reprinted from Pennsylvania Magazine of History
       and Biography, July 1929. Philadelphia: Historical So-
       ciety of Pa, 1929. 26pp (pp. 203-229), ill, pl NN, De-
       Wint

8033   Gower, F. C. The First Subject Catalogue of Cigarette
       Cards. London: Croyden, 1941. 47 leaves

8034   Gurd, Eric. Cigarette Cards: an outline. London: Carto-
       philic Society of Great Britain, 1942. 12pp

8035   *Heal, Sir Ambrose. London Tradesmen's Cards of the 18th
       Century; an account of their origin and use. London:
       Batsford; New York: Scribner's, 1925; reprint. New York:
       Dover, 1968. 110pp, 100 pls (Includes some by Hogarth)

8036   _____. Old London Bridge Tradesmen's Cards and Tokens.
       Reprint from Old London Bridge, by Gordon Cochrane
       Home. London: John Lane, 1931. 27pp (pp. 305-331),
       ill ICN, BM

8037 _____. Samuel Pepys: his trade cards. Reprint from article. London: The Connoisseur, 1933. 7pp BM

8038 _____. The Trade Cards of Engravers.... Reprint from The Print Collector's Quarterly. London: Hudson & Kearns, 1927. 34pp, ill ICN, BM

8039 Jenny, Adele. Early American Trade Cards from the Collection of Bella C. Landauer. New York: New York Historical Society, 1927. 25pp, color frontis, 44 pls

8040 Landauer, Bella Clara. Gilbert and Sullivan Influence on American Tradecards. New York: priv. printed, 1936. 15pp, ill, pls

8041 _____. The Indian Does Not Vanish in American Advertising from the Bella C. Landauer Collection, New York Historical Society. New York: 1940. 2pp, 23 pls

8042 _____. Some Early American Lottery Items. New York: priv. printed, Harbor Pr, 1928. 19pp, ill

8043 _____. Some Embossed American Tradecards. New York: priv. printed, Harbor Pr, 1941. 18pp, pls

8044 _____. Some Terpsichorean Tradecards from the Landauer Collection.... New York: New York Historical Society, 1940. 2pp, 20 pls

8045 _____. Some Tradecards from the Landauer Aeronautical Collection. New York: New York Historical Society, 1940. 2pp, 8 pls

8046 Rendell, Joan. Collecting Matchbox Labels. London: Arco, 1963. 158pp, ill

8047 _____. Matchbox Labels. New York: Praeger; Newton Abbot: David & Charles, 1968. 112pp, ill

8048 [No entry.]

8049 Wharton-Tigar, Edward C. The Cigarette Card Issues of W. D. and H. O. Wills: an official checklist. Parts 1, 2 and 3 revised. 4 parts. Clewin, Eng: E. F. Pressey, for Cartophilic Society of Great Britain, 1950. ill

8050 The World Tobacco Issues Index: an authentic catalogue, without prices, of cigarette cards issued anywhere in the world up to the end of 1956. Windsor, Berkshire: Cartophilic Society of Great Britain, 195-?; First Supplement. 1965. 452pp, ill

GAMES AND TOYS

GAMES

8051 Bartlett, Vernon. <u>The Past of Pastimes</u>. London: Chatto
& Windus; Hamden, Conn: Archon, 1969. 160pp, ill,
16 pls, bib (History of games)

8052 Baumann, Paul. <u>Collecting Antique Marbles</u>. Leon, Iowa:
Prairie Winds Pr, 1970; Price Guide. 197-? 86pp, color
ill; 15pp

8053 Culin, (Robert) Stewart. <u>Chinese Games with Dice</u>. Read
before the Oriental Club of Philadelphia, March 14, 1889.
Philadelphia: Franklin Printing, 1889. 21pp, ill, color
pl NN, DLC

8054 _____. <u>Chinese Games with Dice and Dominoes</u>. (Enlarged from <u>Chinese Games with Dice</u>.) United States
National Museum. Washington, D.C.: GPO, 1895. 48pp
(pp. 489-537), ill, 12 (1 color) pls NjP, DLC

8055 _____. <u>The Game of Ma-Jong; its origin and significance</u>.
Brooklyn, NY: Museum Quarterly, 1924. 16pp, ill, pl

8056 _____. <u>Korean Games</u>. Philadelphia: 1895; reissued as
<u>Games of the Orient</u>. Rutland, Vt: Tuttle, 1958. ill
(Includes kites)

8057 Durant, John, and Otto Bettmann. <u>Pictorial History of
American Sports, from Colonial Times to the Present</u>.
New York: A. S. Barnes, 1952. 280pp, ill

8058 _____, and Alice Durant. <u>Pictorial History of the American Circus</u>. New York: A. S. Barnes, 1957. 328pp,
ill (part color)

8059 Ferretti, Fred. <u>The Great American Marble Book</u>. New
York: Workman, 1973. 157pp, ill

8060 Francis, Philip Harwood. A Study of Targets in Games: (tournaments, field sports, baseball, cricket, football, hockey, golf, lawn tennis, bowls, etc.) London: Mitre Pr, 1951. 235pp, ill (Symbology, folklore and history of targets)

8061 Freeman, Graydon La Verne (Larry), ed. Yesterday's Games. Watkins Glen, NY: Century House, 1970. 160pp, ill (Includes board and table games)

8062 Garsault, Francois Alexandre Pierre, 1691?-1778. The Art of the Tennis-Racket-Maker and of Tennis. Originally published in French in 1767, and now translated into English for the first time by Catherine W. Leftwich. Harrow Weald, Eng: priv. printed, Raven Printers, 1938. 45pp, 4 pls NN

8063 Gibson, Nevin H. A Pictorial History of Golf. Rev. ed. South Brunswick, NJ: A. S. Barnes, 1974. 282pp, ill, bib

8064 Game of Billiards. New Instructions for Playing the Game of Billiards ... To which is prefixed an historical account of the game. By an amateur. London: T. Hurst, 1801. 72pp BM

8065 Grant, John Gordon. The Complete Curler; being the history and practice of the game of curling. London: A. & C. Black, 1914. 220pp, 16 ill, diags

8066 *Hannas, Linda. The English Jigsaw Puzzle, 1760-1890: with a descriptive checklist of puzzles in the Museums of Great Britain and the Author's Collection. London: Wayland, 1972. 164pp, ill, 37 (2 color) pls, bib, facsims

8067 Hart, Clive. Kites: An Historical Survey. London: Faber; New York: Praeger, 1967. 196pp, ill, 35 pls, bib

8068 Hilton, Harold Horsfall, and Garden Grant Smith. The Royal and Ancient Game of Golf. London: Golf Illustrated, 1912. 275pp, ill BM

8069 Ingraham, Clara. Collector's Encyclopedia of Antique Marbles. Paducah, Ky: Collector Books, 1972. 24pp, ill, color pls, prices

8070 Lillie, Arthur. Croquet, its history, rules and secrets. London: 1897. 264pp BM

8071 Marble Mania. Newsletter. Trumbull, Conn: Marble Collector's Society of America, 1976- .

8072 Monthly Weather Review. Periodical. Washington, D.C.: especially 1895 to 1915. (Many articles on kites)

8073 Morrison, Mel, and Carl Terison. Marbles, Identification and Price Guide. Falmouth, Me: Authors, 197-? 17pp, ill

8074 Naismith, James, 1861-1939. Basketball, its origin and development. New York: Associated Pr, 1941. 198pp, pls

8075 Patterson, Jerry E. Antiques of Sports. New York: Crown, 1975. 250 items ill (Includes firearms)

8076 Peck and Snyder, New York. 1886 catalog. Sporting Goods; sports equipment and clothing, novelties, recreative science, firemen's supplies, magic lanterns and slides, plays and joke books, tricks and magic, badges and ornaments. Facsimile reprint with introd. Princeton, NJ: Pyne Pr, 1971. 336pp, ill

8077 Play Ball. Books, pictures and relics of ball games of many kinds. Exhibition. March-May 1963. Baltimore: Peabody Institute Library, 1963. 28pp

8078 Sang, Ly Yu. Sparrow: the Chinese Game called ma-ch'iau; a descriptive and explanatory story. New York: Long Sang Ti Chinese Curios, 1923. 128pp, ill (Mah jong)

8079 Scott, Tom. The Story of Golf; from its origins to the present day. London: A. Barker, 1972. 166pp, ill, bib

8080 Simpson, Sir Walter Grindlay. The Art of Golf. Edinburgh: D. Douglas, 1887; 1892. 186pp BM

8081 Sportsmen's Exposition, 1895. Sporting and Athletic Goods in Hardware Stores. Compiled from the "Iron Age" series of articles illustrating methods of hardware store arrangement. New York: Williams, 1895. 30pp, ill DLC

8082 Streeter, Tal. The Art of the Japanese Kite. Tokyo: John Weatherhill, 1974. 184pp, ill (History and folklore)

8083 Three Centuries of Golf: the story of golf and catalogue of exhibits and illustrations from the Spalding Golf Museum, Dundee. Dundee, Scotland: Dundee Corporation, Art Galleries and Museums, 1968. 12pp, ill

8084 Tingay, Lance. History of Lawn Tennis in Pictures. Fore. by Sir Carl Aarvold. London: T. Stacey, 1973. 144pp, ill

8085 Weiss, Harry Bischoff. Something About Jumping Jacks and the Jack-in-the-Box. Trenton, NJ: Edwards Brothers, printers, Ann Arbor, Mich, 1945. 84pp, ill, bib

8086 Wymer, Norman. Sport in England; a history of 2000 years of games and pastimes. London: Harrap, 1949. 271pp, pls, bib

CHESS AND BOARD GAMES

8087   Allen, George, 1808-1876. Catalogue of My Chess Collection.
        Philadelphia: 1858. 11pp manuscript (See also Jackson,
        F. A.) OCI

8088   Bell, Robert Charles. Board and Table Games from Many
        Civilizations. London; New York: Oxford U. Pr, 1960;
        2nd ed. 2 vol. London: Oxford U. Pr, 1969. 210pp, ill,
        22 pls, bib; 155pp, ill, 19 pls, bib

8089   _____. Discovering Old Board Games. Aylesbury: Shire
        Publications, 1973. 79pp, ill, bib

8090   Culin, (Robert) Stewart, 1858-1929. Chess and Playing Cards.
        Catalog of games and implements for diviniation exhibited
        by the United States National Museum at the Cotton States
        and International Exposition, Atlanta, Georgia, 1895.
        Washington, D.C.: Smithsonian, Annual Report, 1896;
        reprint. 1898. 277pp (pp. 665-942), ill, 50 pls (part
        color) PP, DLC, NN

8091   Falkener, Edward, 1814-1896. Games Ancient and Oriental,
        and How to Play Them. Being the Games of the Ancient
        Egyptians, the leira gramme of the Greeks, the ludus
        latrunculorum of the Romans and the oriental games of
        chess, draughts, backgammon and magic squares. Lon-
        don; New York: Longmans, Green, 1892. 366pp, ill,
        pls DLC, DeWint

8092   Freeman, Graydon La Verne (Larry), ed. Yesterday's
        Games. Watkins Glen, NY: Century, 1970. 160pp, ill
        from old catalogs (Includes board games)

8093 Gizycki, Jerzy. A History of Chess. Tr. from Polish (1960) by A. Wojciehowski, D. Ronowicz, and W. Bartoszewski. Ed. by B. H. Wood. London: Abbey Library, 1972. 375pp, ill, 9 pls

8094 Graham, F. Lanier. Chess Sets. New York: Walker, 1968. 82pp, 79 ill, 2 pls, bib

8095 Hammond, Alex. The Book of Chessmen. New York: W. Morrow; London: Arthur Barker, 1950. 160pp, ill, 62 pls (Ivory, bone, metals, ceramics, wood, etc.)

8096 Jackson, Francis Aristide, and Gregory Bernard Keen. Catalogue of the Chess Collection of the Late George Allen. Philadelphia: J. Meichel, printer, 1878. 89pp (Collection bought by the Philadelphia Library Company) NjP, NN

8097 Katz, Emile. History of Chessmen. London: Hugh Evelyn, 1963. 38pp, 23 pls

8098 Mackett-Beeson, Alfred Ernest James. Chessmen. London: Weidenfeld & Nicolson; New York: Putnam, 1968; London: Octopus, 1973. 120pp, ill; 97pp, ill

8099 Meadows, Joseph Kenny, illustrator. Backgammon, Its History and Practice. London?: 1844.

8100 Murray, Harold James Ruthven. A History of Board Games Other than Chess. Oxford, Eng: Clarendon, 1952. 267pp, ill, bib

8101 _____. History of Chess. Oxford: Clarendon, 1913; reprint. 1962. 900pp, ill, pls, bib

8102 (Pardon, George Frederick.) Backgammon: its history and practice. London: 1844. 79pp, ill BM

8103 Whitehouse, Francis Reginald Beaman. Table Games of Georgian and Victorian Days. London: Garnett, 1951; rev. 2nd ed. Royston, Herts: Priory Pr, 1971. 102pp, ill, 38 pls

8104 Wichmann, Hans, and Siegfried Wichmann. Chess, the Story of Chesspieces from Antiquity to Modern Times. Tr. by Cornelia Brookfield and Claudia Rosoux. London: P. Hamlyn, 1960; New York: Crown, 1964. 328pp, ill, pls (part color), bib

DOLLS AND DOLLS' HOUSES

8105 Ackley, Edith Flack. Paper Dolls, their history and how to

make them. New York: F. A. Stokes, 1930; 1939.
107pp, ill, pl

8106   American Made Dolls and Figurines. Boston: Doll Collec-
       tors of America, 1940; Supplement. 1942. 42pp, ill; 87pp,
       ill

8107   Anderton, Johana G. More 20th Century Dolls. Riverdale,
       Md: Hobby House, 1974. 720pp, ill, facsims

8108   _____. 20th Century Dolls: From Bisque to Vinyl. River-
       dale, Md: Hobby House, 1971. 464pp (1900 to 1970.
       1300 bisque, china, rubber, wood, rag and vinyl dolls)

8109   Angione, Genevieve. All-bisque and Half-bisque Dolls. Cam-
       den, NJ: T. Nelson, 1969. 357pp, over 400 ill, marks
       (French and German)

8110   Bachmann, Manfred, and Claus Hansmann. Dolls the Wide
       World Over: An Historical Account. Tr. from German
       (1971) by Ruth Michaelis-Jena. London: Harrap; New
       York: Crown, 1973. 204pp, ill, bib (18th, 19th and
       20th century. 432 dolls)

8111   Baker, Roger. Dolls and Dolls' Houses: A Collector's Intro-
       duction. Fore. by Patrick Murray. London: Orbis, 1973.
       64pp, chiefly ill, bib (To 1935)

8112   Bateman, Thelma. Blue Book of Dolls and Values. Washing-
       ton, D.C.: Hobby House, 1971. 194pp, ill (Antique and
       "collectible")

8113   _____. Delightful Dolls, Antique and Otherwise. Washing-
       ton, D.C.: Hobby House Pr, 1966. 237pp, ill, bib

8114   Benson, Arthur Christopher, and Sir Lawrence Weaver. The
       Book of the Queen's Dolls' House, and the Book of the
       Queen's Dolls' House Library. Ed. by E. V. Lucas. 2
       vol. London: Methuen, 1924. 92pls; 123 ill, 11 pls
       (Queen Mary) DLC, NN, BM

8115   _____, and _____, ed. Everybody's Book of the Queen's
       Dolls' House. An abbreviation by F. V. Morley of The
       Book of the Queen's Dolls' House. London: The Daily
       Telegraph, 1924. 150pp, 123 ill, 11 pls ViU, DLC, NN

8116   *Boehn, Max von. Dolls. Tr. by Josephine Nicoll. (Origi-
       nally Vol. I of Dolls and Puppets.) New York: Dover,
       1972. 269pp, ill, 15 pls, bib (European dolls, doll
       houses and furniture)

8117 * _____. Dolls and Puppets. Tr. from German (1929) by
       Josephine Nicoll, with a note on puppets by George Bernard

Shaw. London: G. G. Harrap, 1932; new and rev. ed.
with additions by Luella Hart and Lili Criswell. Boston:
C. T. Branford, 1956; reprint. New York: Cooper Square
Publishers, 1966. 521pp, ill, 30 pls BM

8118 Bradford, Faith. The Dolls' House. Washington, D.C.:
      Smithsonian, 1965. 32pp, ill

8119 Butler Brothers Catalogue. Christmas 1910. Dolls, toys
      and games. Reprint. Chattanooga, Tenn: J. & S. Co,
      1967. 39pp, ill

8120 The Carlisle Collection of Miniature Rooms. The National
      Trust. London: the Trust, 1973. 10pp, ill, 4 pls
      (Dolls' houses)

8121 Catalogue of the Greg Collection of Dolls and Dolls' Houses.
      Manchester, Eng: R. Bates, printer, for the Art Gallery,
      19-? 37pp (Thomas Tylston Greg) DLC

8122 Cole, Adeline P., comp. Notes on the Collection of Dolls
      and Figurines at the Wenham Museum, Claflin-Richards
      House, Wenham, Massachusetts. Wenham: Historical
      Association, 1951. 171pp, ill, bib

8123 Coleman, Dorothy S. "My Darling" Dolls, Kammer and
      Reinhardt, 1927. Princeton, NJ: Pyne, 1972. 80pp, ill

8124 _____. Prices for Dolls. n.p.: priv. printed, 1975.
      30pp

8125 * _____, Elizabeth A. Coleman, and Evelyn J. Coleman.
      The Collector's Encyclopedia of Dolls. New York: Crown,
      1968; London: Hale, 1970. 697pp, 2000 ill, pls, bib,
      marks (To 1925)

8126 * _____, _____, and _____. The Collector's Book of
      Doll Clothes. Costumes in Miniature: 1700-1929. New
      York: Crown, 1975. 700pp, 1000 ill, 160 pp of patterns

8127 _____, _____, and _____. Dolls: Makers and
      Marks. Washington, D.C.: 1963; Addenda. 1966; 1971.
      97pp, ill; 56pp, ill; 122pp, ill

8128 Coleman, Evelyn, Elizabeth Coleman, and Dorothy Coleman.
      The Age of Dolls. Washington, D.C.: D. S. Coleman,
      1965. 138pp, ill, gloss

8129 Cramer. China Heads. 80pp, 189 ill (Doll heads)

8130 Cusset, J. The Jumeau Doll Story. Tr. from French (1885).
      n.p.: N. S. Davies, 1957. 79pp, ill PP

8131   Darrah, Marjorie Meritt. Dolls in Color. Des Moines:
       Wallace-Homestead, 1971. 24 color pls

8132   Desmonde, Kay. All Color Book of Dolls. London: Octopus,
       1974. 72pp, 100 color pls

8133   _____. Dolls and Dolls Houses. London: Charles Letts,
       1972. 80pp, ill, 59 color photographs, bib (1745-1930)

8134   Doll Collectors of America. Periodical. Boston: 1940- .

8135   Doll Collectors Manual. Periodical. Boston?: Doll Collec-
       tors of America, 1949- . ill

8136   The Doll House of Colleen Moore, a Fairyland Castle. Chicago:
       Museum of Science and Industry, 1950. 32pp, ill

8137   Doll News. Irregular periodical. Brooklyn: National Doll
       and Toy Collectors Club, 1941- . ill

8138   Doll Talk for Collectors; magazine for the Doll Hobby Club.
       Irregular periodical. Independence, Mo: Kimport Dolls,
       1936- . ill

8139   Dolls. V & A Museum. London: HMSO, 1960; 2nd ed. 1969.
       7pp, 28 ill, 28 pls, bib

8140   Dolls and Dolls' Houses. Text by M. W. London: V & A
       Museum, 1950. ill, 28 pls, bib

8141   Early, Alice Kate. English Dolls, Effigies, and Puppets.
       London: Batsford; New York: R. M. McBride, 1955.
       226pp, ill, bib

8142   Eaton, Faith. Dolls in Color. New York: Macmillan, 1976.
       80pp of color ill

8143   Eldridge, Charlotte B. The Godey Lady Doll; the story of
       her creation with patterns for dresses and doll furniture.
       New York: Hastings, 1953. 209pp, ill

8144   Ellenburg, M. Kelly. Effanbee-the dolls with the golden
       hearts. Riverdale, Md: Hobby House, 1973. 200pp, ill
       (Old catalog photographs)

8145   Fashion in Miniature. Manchester, Eng: Gallery of English
       Costume, 1970. 28pp, chiefly ill (Dolls' clothing, 1700-
       1905)

8146   Fawcett, Clara Evelyn Hallard. Dolls: a guide for collectors.
       New York: H. L. Lindquist, 1947; Boston: C. T. Bran-
       ford, 1964. 194pp, ill, bib; 282pp, ill, bib (Includes
       puppets and marionettes)

8147   First Doll Exhibition. Winchester Public Library, Massa-
       chusetts. May 1938. Sponsored by Doll Collectors of
       America, Boston. Winchester: 1938. 20pp, ill

8148   Flick, Pauline. The Dolls' House Book. London: Collins,
       1973. 126pp, ill, 12 pls (To 1972)

8149 *Fox, Carl. The Doll. New York: Abrams, 1972; new
       shorter ed. 1973. 343pp, 191 (70 color) pls, bib; 143pp,
       ill, 145 (52 color) pls, bib

8150 *Fraser, Antonia. Dolls. London: Weidenfeld & Nicolson;
       New York: Putnam, 1963; London: Octopus, 1973.
       128pp, ill; 96pp, ill (18th, 19th and 20th century)

8151   Freeman, Ruth Sunderlin. American Dolls. Watkins Glen,
       NY: Century, 1952. 71pp, ill

8152   _____. American Dolls Encyclopedia. Watkins Glen, NY:
       Century, 1962; 3rd rev. ed. 1973. 96pp, ill

8153   _____. How to Mend and Dress Old Dolls. Watkins Glen,
       NY: Century, 1960. 48pp, ill

8154   Gerken, Jo Elizabeth. Wonderful Dolls of Wax. Lincoln,
       Neb: Doll Research Associates, 1964. 135pp, 96 ill, bib

8155   Gordon, Lesley. A Pageant of Dolls. A brief history of
       dolls showing the national costumes and customs of many
       lands. Leicester: Edmunde Warde, 1948; New York:
       A. A. Wyn, 1949. 132pp, ill, 16 color pls, bib

8156   Greene, Vivien. English Dolls Houses of the 18th and 19th
       Centuries. London: Batsford, 1955. 224pp, 147 ill

8157   _____. Family Dolls' Houses. London: Bell; Newton,
       Mass: C. T. Branford, 1973. 176pp, ill, 8 pls, bib

8158   Hart, Luella Tilton. Complete French Doll Directory, 1801-
       1964; covers early doll makers, sellers, trademarks,
       patents. n.p.: 1965. 125pp, ill

8159   _____. Directory of British Dolls. n.p.: 1964. 52pp,
       ill (Patent and trademark directory)

8160   _____. Directory of German Dolls Trademarks, 1875-
       1960. n.p.: 1964. 75pp, ill

8161   _____. Directory of United States Doll Trademarks, 1888-
       1968. n.p.: 1968. 90pp, ill

8162   _____. The Japanese Doll. Middletown, Conn: E. A.
       Fisher, printer, 1952. 92pp, ill

8163 Hillier, Mary. Dolls and Doll-makers. London: Weidenfeld
      & Nicolson; New York: Putnam, 1968. 256pp, ill

8164 Holt, Florrie Bell. Antique Turpin Dolls. Cincinnati (Tala-
      ria), O: 1961. 94pp, ill

8165 Hopkinson, Isabella, and William Hopkinson. Dolls and Minia-
      tures with Their Prices at Auction. Concord, NH: Rum-
      ford Pr, 1970. 51pp, color ill

8166 *Jacobs, Flora Gill. Dolls' Houses in America, Historic
      Preservation in Miniature. New York: Scribner's, 1974.
      395pp, 416 (16 color) ill, bib (1744 to present. 114
      houses, handcrafted and commercially made)

8167 *_____. A History of Doll Houses; four centuries of the
      domestic world in miniature. New York: Scribner's,
      1958; rev. & enl. ed. as A History of Dolls' Houses.
      1965. 322pp, ill, bib; 342pp, ill, bib (Standard work)

8168 _____, and Estrid Faurholt. A Book of Dolls and Doll
      Houses. Rutland, Vt: Tuttle, 1967. 224pp, ill (Dolls
      by Faurholt; houses by Jacobs)

8169 Jendrick, Barbara Whitton. A Picture Book of Paper Dolls
      and Paper Toys. Pittsford, NY: Author, 1975. 400 ill
      (European and American)

8170 Johl, Janet Pagter. The Fascinating Story of Dolls. New
      York: H. L. Lindquist, 1941; reissue with new material
      and eliminations of some material. Ed. by Ruth S.
      Freeman. Watkins Glen, NY: Century, 1970. 270pp, ill

8171 _____. More About Dolls. New York: Lindquist, 1946.
      309pp, ill

8172 _____. Still More About Dolls. New York: Lindquist,
      1950. 300pp, ill

8173 _____. Your Dolls and Mine; a collectors' handbook.
      New York: Lindquist, 1952. 384pp, ill

8174 Johnston, La Vaughn C. Open Mouth Dolls. Downey, Cal:
      E. Quinn, printer, 1974. 152pp, chiefly ill (A private
      collection)

8175 Ketterman, Marie. 200 Years of Pennsylvania Dolls. Ply-
      mouth Meeting, Pa: Mrs. C. Naaman Keyser, 1954.
      132pp, ill

8176 King, Eileen. Toys and Dolls for Collectors. London:
      Hamlyn, 1973. 159pp, ill, bib

8177   Kramer, Vera. Dolls in Wonderland. Museum Catalogue.
       Brighton, Eng: 197-?

8178   Kredel, Fritz. Dolls and
       Puppets of the 19th
       Century, as Delineated
       in 24 Drawings. Lex-
       ington, Ky: Gravesend
       Pr, 1958. 19pp, ill

8179   Latham, Jean. Dolls'
       Houses: A Personal
       Choice. London:
       Black; New York:
       Scribner, 1969.
       200pp, 180 ill, 12
       color ill

8180   Leuzzi, Marlene. An-
       tique Doll Price Guide.
       2nd ed. Englewood,
       Col: 1972; 3rd ed.
       197-? 176pp, 300 ill;
       192pp, ill of 700 dolls

8181   _____. Kewpies in Action. Englewood, Col: 1973.
       121pp, ill, 16 color pls

8182   _____, and Robert Kershner. Price Guide to Collectible
       Dolls: Composition to Vinyl. Englewood, Col: 1973.
       128pp, ill

8183   Lovett, Edward. The Child's Doll, its origin, legend, and
       folk-lore. London: Evans, 1915. 16pp, ill OCI, BM

8184   _____. Handbook to the Exhibition of the Lovett Collec-
       tion of Dolls. April-May 1914. Cardiff: National Mu-
       seum of Wales, 1914. 24pp, 6 pls MH-P

8185   Low, Frances H. Queen Victoria's Dolls. London: G.
       Newnes, 1894. 40 color ill NN

8186   Manos, Susan. Schoenhut Dolls and Toys, a Loving Legacy.
       Paducah, Ky: Collector Books, 1976. hundreds of ill

8187   Marion, Frieda. China Half-figures, Called Pincushion Dolls.
       Newburyport, Mass: Rowley Printing, for Author, 1974.
       ill (ca. 1900-1925)

8188   Merrill, Madeline O., and Nellie W. Perkins. Handbook of
       Collectible Dolls. 3 vol. Melrose?, Mass: 1969, 1970,
       1972. 253pp; 168pp; 312pp; all ill

8189 Miller, Robert W., comp. Wallace-Homestead Price Guide to
      Dolls. Des Moines: 1975. 850 dolls ill'd and priced; 4
      color pls

8190 Mills, Winifred Harrington, and Louise M. Dunn. The Story
      of Old Dolls and How to Make New Ones. New York:
      Doubleday, Doran, 1940. 234pp, ill, pls, bib

8191 Musgrave, Clifford. Queen Mary's Dolls' House and Dolls
      Belonging to Her Majesty the Queen. London: Pitkin
      Pictorials, 1967. 24pp, ill

8192 Noble, John. Beautiful Dolls, an appreciation of the most
      beautiful dolls made in America and Europe during the
      18th, 19th and 20th centuries. New York: Hawthorn,
      1971. 205pp, 196 (46 color) pls

8193 _____. Dolls. New York: Walker, 1967. 84pp, ill

8194 _____. A Treasury of Beautiful Dolls. Fore. by Dorothy,
      Elizabeth and Evelyn Coleman. New York: Hawthorn,
      1971. 210pp, ill

8195 O'Brien, Marian Maeve. The Collectors Guide to Dollhouses
      and Dollhouse Miniatures. (Part I. Dollhouses; Part II.
      Dollhouse miniatures, antiques, reproductions, and mod-
      ern.) New York: Hawthorn, 1974. 213pp, 230 photo-
      graphs, 17 color pls, bib

8196 Poppenhuizen/Dolls' Houses. Dutch and English text. Am-
      sterdam: Rijksmuseum, 1967. 8pp, 33 pls

8197 Record of United States Patents. Boston: Doll Collectors of
      America, 1944.

8198a Robinson, Joy. Warwick Doll Museum: the story of dolls
      and the Joy Robinson Collection. Warwick, Eng: Oken's
      House, the Museum, 1955. 17pp, ill

8198b Rosner, Bernard, and Joy Beckerman. Inside the World of
      Miniatures and Dollhouses: a comprehensive guide to col-
      lecting and creating. New York: McKay, 1976. 200 ill

8199 St. George, Eleanor. Dolls of Three Centuries. New York:
      Scribner's, 1951. 205pp, ill

8200 _____. The Dolls of Yesterday. New York: Scribner's,
      1948; 1964? 204pp, ill, pls (Over 450 American and
      European dolls. Two centuries)

8201 _____. Old Dolls. New York: Barrows, 1950. 176pp,
      77 ill

8202   Schroeder, Joseph J., comp. The Wonderful World of Toys,
        Games and Dolls, 1860-1930. Northfield, Ill: Digest
        Books, 1971. 256pp, ill, 1 pl (Catalogue reprints)

8203   Shea, Ralph A. Doll Mark Clues. I. Dictionary of Antique
        Doll Marks; II. Numbers in Antique Doll Marks (Part A);
        III. Numbers in Antique Doll Marks (Part B); IV. Numbers
        in Antique Doll Marks. 4 vol. Ridgefield, NJ: Author,
        1967; 1968; 1974; 1975. 281pp; 296pp; 295pp; 295pp; with
        prices

8204   Singleton, Esther. Dolls. New York: Payson & Clarke,
        1927. 167pp, 80 pls, color frontis

8205   Smith, Patricia R. Antique Collectors' Dolls. Paducah, Ky:
        Collector Books, 1975. 306pp, 1000 ill, 16 color pp
        (1850-1935)

8206   _____. Armand Marseille Dolls. Paducah, Ky: Collector
        Books, 1976. 144pp, 75pp of color pictures (1865-1928)

8207   The Standard Antique Doll Identification and Value Guide.
        Paducah, Ky: Collector Books, 1976. hundreds of ill
        (To 1935)

8208   Tavares, Olinda. The Armchair Museum of Dolls. New
        York: Vantage Pr, 1973. 138pp, ill

8209   Toys and Dolls, a Bibliography. Tunbridge Wells, Kent:
        Public Library and Museum, 1974. 11pp

8210   White, Gwen. A Book of Dolls. London: A. & C. Black;
        New York: Macmillan, 1956. 108pp, ill

8211 * _____. Dolls of the World. London: Mills & Boon;
        Newton Centre, Mass: C. T. Branford, 1962. 256pp,
        ill of 268 dolls, bib

8212   _____. European and American Dolls and Their Marks
        and Patents. London: Batsford; New York: Putnam,
        1966. 274pp, ill, bib, 625 marks (To 1910)

8213   _____. A Picture-Book of Ancient and Modern Dolls.
        London: A. & C. Black; New York: Macmillan, 1928.
        44pp, ill, color pls BM

8214   Worrell, Estelle Ansley, and Norman Worrell. The Doll
        Book. Princeton, NJ: Van Nostrand, 1966. 135pp, ill
        (Juvenile literature)

8215   Young, Helen. The Complete Book of Doll Collecting. New
        York: Putnam, 1967. 312pp, ill

8216 _____. Here Is Your Hobby: Doll Collecting. New York:
       Putnam, 1964. 128pp, ill, bib

PUPPETS AND MARIONETTES

8217 *Baird, Bill. The Art of the Puppet. New York: Macmillan,
       1965. 251pp, many ill (most color) (Ancient to modern,
       world-wide)

8218 *Boehn, Max von. Dolls and Puppets. Tr. from German
       (1929) by Josephine Nicoll, with a note on puppets by
       George Bernard Shaw. London: G. G. Harrap, 1932;
       new rev. ed. with additions by Luella Hart and Lili Cris-
       well. Boston: C. T. Branford, 1956; New York: Cooper
       Square, 1966. 521pp, ill, 30 pls BM

8219 _____. Puppets and Automata. Tr. by Josephine Nicoll.
       Originally Vol. II. of Dolls and Puppets. New York:
       Dover, 1972. 257pp, ill, bib

8220 Bohmer, Gunter. Puppets. Tr. from German (1969) by
       Gerald Morice. London: Macdonald, 1971; as The Wonder-
       ful World of Puppets. Boston: Plays, Inc., 1971. 156pp,
       ill (Based on puppet collection of City of Munich)

8221 Byrom, Michael. Punch and Judy: Its Origin and Evolution.
       Aberdeen: Shiva Publications, 1972. 87pp, ill, 24 pls,
       bib

8222 Coleman, Stanley Jackson, comp. Puppets of Many Races;
       collected, collated and edited. Douglas, Isle of Man:
       Folklore Academy, 1957. 15pp, typescript

8223 Currell, David. The Complete Book of Puppetry. London:
       Plays, Inc., 1975. 206pp, ill

8224 Dunn, Charles James. The Early Japanese Puppet Drama.
       London: Luzac, 1966. 154pp, 12 pls, bib

8225 Fawcett, Clara Evelyn Hallard. Dolls: a guide for collec-
       tors. New York: H. L. Lindquist, 1947; Boston: C. T.
       Branford, 1964. 194pp, ill, bib; 282pp, ill, bib (In-
       cludes puppets and marionettes)

8226 McPharlin, Paul. The Puppet Theatre in America: a his-
       tory, 1524-1948. New York: Harper, 1949; 2nd ed. with
       Supplement: puppets in America since 1948, by Marjorie
       Batchelder McPharlin. Boston: Plays, Inc., 1969. 506pp,
       ill; 734pp, ill

8227 _____. Puppets in America, 1739 to today. With an

account of the first American Puppetry Conference. Birmingham, Mich: Puppetry Imprints, 1936; 1948. 64pp,
ill

8228 _____. Puppets in American Life, 1524-1915. Thesis.
U. of Michigan, 1940. 299pp, bib

8229 Morse, Richard E. Small Wonders; puppets and marionettes.
Exhibition. New York: Cooper Union Museum, 1949?
7pp, bib MiU

8230 Seijiro, Saito, Yamaguschi Hiroichi, and Yoshinaga Takao.
Masterpieces of Japanese Puppetry, sculptured heads of the
Bunraku theatre. English adaptation by Roy Andrew Miller.
Rutland, Vt: Tuttle, 1958. 91pp, ill

8231 Sibbald, Reginald S. Marionettes in the North of France.
Thesis. Philadelphia: U. of Pa, 1936; London: H. Milford, Oxford U. Pr, 1936. 134pp, frontis, bib

8232 Speaight, George. The History of the English Puppet Theatre.
London: G. G. Harrap; New York: J. de Graff, 1955.
350pp, ill, bib

8233 _____. The History of the English Toy Theatre. London:
Macdonald, 1946; rev. ed. London: Studio Vista; Boston:
Plays, Inc., 1969. 255pp, ill, color pls

8234 Tilakasiri, J. The Puppet Theatre of Asia. Colombo: Department of Cultural Affairs, 1968. 166pp. ill

8235 Wilson, Albert Edward, 1885- . Penny Plain and Twopence
Coloured, a history of juvenile drama. Fore. by Charles
B. Cochran. London: G. G. Harrap, 1932; Index to Illustrations, by Charles Dewhurst Williams. 19-? 117pp,
83 ill, pls

MISCELLANEOUS HUMAN FIGURES

8236 Bleier, Paul, and Meta Bleier. John Rogers' Groups of Statuary; a pictorial and annotated guide for the collector.
North Woodmere?, NY: 1971. 218pp, ill, bib (Rogers,
1829-1904) (Included because these Rogers' groups were
de rigueur in some Victorian parlors)

8237 Gatacre, E. V. Madame Tussaud's. London: Madam Tussaud's, 1972. 40pp, ill, facsims

8238 Sala, George Augustus Henry. Madame Tussaud's Exhibition.
Catalogue. London: 1909; 1918. BM

8239   Scott, Amoret, and Christopher Scott. Dummy Board Figures.
       Cambridge, Eng: Golden Head Pr, 1966. 21pp, 15 pls

TOYS, MODEL SOLDIERS, BABY RATTLES
AND NURSERY ANTIQUES

8240   Baldet, Marcel. Lead Soldiers and Figurines. Fore. by
       Peter J. Blum. Tr. by E. Stanton Russell. New York:
       Crown, 1961. 126pp, ill, pls (some color), bib (Euro-
       pean)

8241   Barenholtz, Edith F., ed. The George Brown Toy Sketch-
       book. See: Brown, George.

8242   Bartley, Sir George Christopher Trout. Toys. London:
       1876. See: Bevan, G. P., British Manufacturing Indus-
       tries, Vol. 8, no. 43.

8243   Blum, Peter. Military Miniatures. New York: Odyssey,
       1964. 34pp, ill, color pls (English, American, Russian,
       French and Indian)

8244   *Brown, George W., 1830-1889, toy designer. The George
       Brown Toy Sketchbook. Reprint ed. with introd. by Edith
       F. Barenholtz. Princeton, NJ: Pyne Pr, 1971. 144pp,
       ill, 58 color pls (American)

8245   Bull, Peter. The Teddy Bear Book. New York: Random
       House, 1970. 207pp, ill

8246   Butler Brothers Catalogue. Christmas 1910. Dolls, Toys
       and Games. Reprint. Chattanooga, Tenn: J. & S. Co,
       1967. 39pp, ill

8247   Cook, Catherine, and Edith Morris. Fascinating Tin Toys
       for Girls, 1820-1920. Oak Bluffs, Mass: E. Morris,
       1975. 64pp, ill, bib

8248   Cranmer, Don. Cast Iron and Tin Toys of Yesterday, with
       Price Guide. Gas City, Ind: L-W Promotions, 1974.
       108pp, ill (500 old toys--cast iron cars, trucks, tractors,
       wind-ups, etc.)

8249   Culff, Robert. The World of Toys. Feltham: Hamlyn, 1969.
       140pp, chiefly ill

8250   Daiken, Leslie Herbert. Children's Toys Throughout the
       Ages. London: Batsford; New York: Praeger, 1953;
       new & rev. ed. London: Spring, 1963; 1965. 207pp, ill,
       bib

8251   *_____. World of Toys; a guide to the principal public and

private collections in Great Britain of period toys, dolls
and dolls' houses, games, puppets and marionettes, toy
soldiers; musical boxes and automata; also modern toys
... etc. Kent, Eng: Lambarde Pr, 1963. 271pp, ill,
32 pls, bib

8252   Dongerkery, Kamala Sunderrao. A Journey Through Toyland.
       Bombay, India: Popular Book Depot, 1954. 118pp, ill,
       bib (Chiefly Indian toys)

8253   Ehrich Brothers, New York. Toy Price List, Winter 1882.
       Catalog reprint. New York: Burton E. Purmell, 19-?
       20pp, pls

8254   Feeny, William F. Later Toys. n.p.: Author, 1971.
       78pp, ill (Catalog reprints, 1915-1930)

8255   Flick, Pauline. Discovering Toys and Toy Museums. Tring,
       Eng: Shire Publications, 1971. 63pp, ill, bib

8256   *Foley, Daniel J. Toys Through the Ages ... Story of play-
       things filled with history, folklore, romance and nostalgia.
       Philadelphia: Chilton, 1962. 145pp, ill, bib

8257   Fraser, Antonia. A History of Toys. New York: Delacorte;
       London: Weidenfeld & Nicolson, 1966; new ed. London;
       New York: Spring Books, 1972. 256pp, 302 ill, bib

8258   Freeman, Graydon La Verne, and Ruth Freeman. Yesterday's
       Toys; one of a series on bygone Americana. Watkins Glen,
       NY: Century, 1962; 1968. 127pp, ill

8259   Freeman, Ruth Sunderlin, and Larry Freeman. Calvacade of
       Toys. Watkins Glen, NY: Century, 1942. 399pp, ill, bib

8260   Fritzsch, Karl Ewald, and Manfred Bachmann. An Illustrated
       History of Toys. Tr. from German by Ruth Michaelis-
       Jena, with Patrick Murphy. London: Abbey Library (Mur-
       ray's Book Sales), 1966; Leipzig: Edition Leipzig, 1968.
       87pp, ill, 106 pls, bib

8261   Gamage's Christmas Bazaar, 1913. Catalog reprint. Newton
       Abbot: David & Charles, 1974. 28, 472pp, ill (A. W.
       Gamage, Ltd.)

8262   *Garratt, John G. Model Soldiers; a collectors Guide. Lon-
       don: Seeley Service, 1959. 239pp, ill

8263   Gordon, Lesley. Peepshow into Paradise; a history of chil-
       dren's toys. London: Harrap, 1953; New York: J. De
       Graff, 1954. 264pp, ill, 6 color pls, bib (4500 years of
       worldwide toys)

8264   Gould, Douglas W. The Top: Universal Toy, Enduring Pas-
       time. New York: C. N. Potter, 1973. 274pp, ill, bib

8265   *Groeber, Karl. Children's Toys of Bygone Days. A history
       of playthings of all peoples from prehistoric times to the
       19th century. Tr. from German (1928) by Philip Here-
       ford. London: Batsford; New York: F. A. Stokes, 1928;
       London: 1932. 61pp, 306 pls (some color), bib (Very
       important work) DLC, PP, MB

8266   Harris, Henry Edward David. Model Soldiers. London:
       Weidenfeld & Nicolson; New York: Putnam, 1962. 128pp,
       ill (some color)

8267   Hercik, Emanuel. Folk Toys, les jouets populaires. English
       and French text. Tr. by R. Finlay Samsourova. Prague:
       Orbis, 1951. 66pp, ill, 176 color pls, bib (Czechoslo-
       vakian toys and folk art)

8268   Hertz, Louis Heilbroner. The Handbook of Old American
       Toys. Wethersfield, Conn: M. Haber, 1947. 119pp, ill,
       catalog facsim. reprints (Chiefly metal)

8269   _____. Messrs. Ives of Bridgeport; the saga of America's
       greatest toymakers. Wethersfield, Conn: M. Haber, 1950.
       159pp, ill, pls, bib (Edward Riley Ives, 1839-1918; Henry
       Candee Ives, 1867-1936)

8270   _____. The Toy Collector. New York: Funk & Wagnalls,
       1969. 304pp, 139 ill, 24 color pls, bib

8271   Hillier, Mary. Pagaent of Toys. London: Elek, 1965; New
       York: Taplinger, 1966. 155pp, ill, 4 color pls, bib

8272   His, Hans Peter. Altes Spielzeug aus Basel, ... Old Toys
       from Basle. German, French and English text. Basel:
       Stiftung fur das Historische Museum, 1973. 49pp, ill
       (Collection exhibited at the Kirschgarten of the Museum)

8273   Holme, Geoffrey, ed. Children's Toys of Yesterday. Lon-
       don; New York: The Studio, 1932. 128pp, ill, color pls
       MiU, DLC

8274   Hornby, John. Toys Down the Ages. London: Chatto, Boyd
       & Oliver, 1972. 48pp, ill

8275   Hubley Manufacturing Co., Lancaster, Pa. "The "Lancaster"
       Iron Toys. Lancaster: 190-?; catalog reprint. Lancaster:
       M. M. Davison, 1964. 20pp, ill DeWint

8276   Hutchings, Margaret. The Book of the Teddy Bear. Boston:
       C. T. Branford, 1964. 283pp, ill

8277 *Jackson, Emily Neville. Toys of Other Days. London:
      Country Life; New York: Scribner's, 1908; New York:
      B. Blom, 1968. 309pp, ill, bib MB, BM

8278 Jacoby, Daniel S., ed. and comp. The Amazing Catalogue
      of the Esteemed Firm of George Heironimus Besteleier;
      selective excerpts from editions 1793 and 1807. Reprint.
      New York: Merrimack Publishing, 1971. 82pp, chiefly
      ill (German toys)

8279 Jendrick, Barbara Whitton. A Picture Book of Paper Dolls
      and Paper Toys. Pittsford, NY: Author, 1975. 400 ill
      (European and American)

8280 Kelley, Dale, ed. Marshall Field Toy Catalog 1892-1893.
      Catalog reprint. Des Moines: Wallace-Homestead; Leon,
      Iowa: Mid-America Book Co, 1969. 36pp, ill

8281 King, Eileen. Toys and Dolls for Collectors. London:
      Hamlyn, 1973. 159pp, ill, bib

8282 Landells, Ebenezer, 1808-1860. The Boy's Own Toy-Maker.
      A practical illustrated guide to the useful employment of
      leisure hours. Boston: Shepard, Clark & Brown, 1859;
      New York: D. Appleton; London: Griffith & Farran,
      1860; 6th ed. London: 1863; New York: Appleton, 1865.
      153pp, 250 ill DeWint

8283 _____, and Alice Landells (daughter). The Girl's Own
      Toy-Maker. 4th ed. New York: Dutton; London: Grif-
      fith & Farran, 1863; London: 1880. 154pp, well ill
      (Paper toys, doll furniture and clothing, etc.) NN

8284 Long, Ernest A. Dictionary of Toys Sold in America: ref-
      erence book for dealers and collectors. n.p.: 1971.
      83pp, ill (1400 toys, 1870-1930)

8285 Lukin, James. (Toys and Toymaking.) Toy Making for
      Amateurs: being instructions for the home construction
      of simple wooden toys, and of others that are moved or
      driven by weights, clockwork, steam, electricity, etc....
      London: L. U. Gill, 1882. 276pp, ill NN, PPL

8286 McClintock, Inez Bertail, and Marshall McClintock. Toys
      in America. Washington, D.C.: Public Affairs Pr, 1961.
      480pp, ill

      Marshall Field 1892-1893 catalog. See: Kelley, Dale, above.

8287 Mookerjee, Ajitcoomar. Folk Toys of India. Calcutta; New
      Delhi: Oxford Book and Stationery Co, 1956. 30pp, ill,
      66 pls, bib (Ceramic toys of traditional forms)

8288 Murray, Patrick. Toys. London: Studio Vista, 1968. 160pp, chiefly ill

8289 Nicollier, Jean. Collecting Toy Soldiers. Rutland, Vt: Tuttle, 1967. ill

8290 Nisizawa, Tekiho. Japanese Folk-Toys. Tokyo: Tourist Library, 1939. 82pp, color ill

8291 Ortmann, Erwin. The Collector's Guide to Model Tin Figures. Tr. by Ruth Michaelis-Jena, and Patrick Murray. New York: Putnam's, 1974. 199pp, ill, bib (Middle Ages to present. Includes French lead soldiers)

8292 Perelman, Leon J. Perelman Antique Toy Museum. Des Moines: Wallace-Homestead, 1972. 24pp of color pls

8293 Playthings of the Past; 19th and early 20th century toys from the collection of the Louisiana State Museum. New Orleans: 1969. 25pp, ill

8294 Remise, Jac, and Jean Fondin. The Golden Age of Toys. English text by D. B. Tubbs. Lausanne: Edita, dist. by N.Y. Graphic, Greenwich, Conn, 1967. 252pp, ill (99 percent French and German toys, dolls, trains, boats, clockwork toys, cars, etc.)

8295 *Richards, Leonard William. Old British Model Soldiers, 1893-1918: an illustrated reference guide for collectors. London: Arms and Armour Pr, 1970; New York: Tricorn Pr, 197-? 75pp, chiefly ill

8296 Roith, Cynthia. Bygones--games and toys of long ago. London: Corgi, 1972. 94pp, ill, bib (To 1900)

8297 Rothera, Diana. Antique Rattles: some examples from the collection, 1748-1920. Cambridge, Eng: Dian F. Boyes, 1970. 73pp, ill

8298 Sakamoto, Kazuya, text, and Kiyoshi Sonobe, photographer. Japanese Toys: playing with history. Tr. from Japanese by Charles A. Pomeroy. Tokyo: Bijutsu Shuppan-Sha; Rutland, Vt: Tuttle; London: Prentice-Hall, 1965. 516pp, ill, pls

8299 Schroeder, Joseph J., comp. The Wonderful World of Toys, Games and Dolls, 1860-1930. Northfield, Ill: Digest Books, 1971. 256pp, ill, 1 pls (Catalog reprints)

8300 Shishido, Misako. The Folk Toys of Japan. Tr. by Tatsuo Shibata. Rutland, Vt: Japan Publishing Trading, 1963. 71pp, ill

8301   Sloane, Thomas O'Conor. Electric Toy Making for Amateurs;
       including batteries, magnets, motors, miscellaneous toys
       and dynamo construction. New York: N. W. Hendley,
       1892; ...; 15th ed. rev. & enl. 1903; 21st ed. 1923.
       140pp, ill; 183pp, ill; 254pp, ill

8302   Smith, Leonora M. Nodders. Des Moines: Wallace-Home-
       stead, 1973. 6pp of color pls

8303   Symons, Harry. Playthings of Yesterday; Harry Symons in-
       troduces the Percy Band Collection, Pioneer Village.
       Toronto: Ryerson, 1963. 96pp, ill, pls

8304   Tomlinson, Charles. The Magnet: familiarly described and
       illustrated by a box of magnetic toys. London: Joseph
       & Myers, 1857. 47pp (BM has without the toys)

8305   Toys. Exhibition. Bethnal Green Museum. London: HMSO,
       1967. 28pp, ill (ca. 1800-1920)

8306   Toys in the London Museum. London: HMSO, 1969. 24pp,
       chiefly ill

8307   Washington Model Soldier Society Bulletin. Periodical. 13
       numbers in 1 vol. Annapolis, Md: 1955-1957. NN

8308   Weiss, Harry Bischoff, 1883- . American Baby Rattles
       from Colonial Times to the Present ... Silver, terra
       cotta, tin, wood, celluloid and plastic rattles. Trenton,
       NJ: priv. printed, 1941. 59pp, 97 ill on 16 pls, bib

8309   White, Gwen. Antique Toys and Their Background. London:
       Batsford; New York: Arco, 1971. 260pp, over 1000 ill,
       8 pls, bib (Antiquity through early 20th century)

8310   _____. A Book of Toys. New York; Harmondsworth:
       Penguin, 1946. 63pp, ill

8311   Young, Rachel M. R. Teaching Toys in the Norwich Museums
       Collection. Norwich, Eng: Castle Museum, 1966. 19pp,
       4 pls, bib

RAILROAD AND AIRPLANE MODELS

8312   Carlisle & Finch Co., 1911 Model Railroad Catalogue. Re-
       print. 36pp, ill

8313   Carstens, Harold H. The Trains of Lionel's Standard Gauge
       Era; history of Lionel standard gauge, toy trains of yester-
       year. Ramsey, NJ: Model Craftsmen Pub Co, 1964.
       35pp, ill

8314 Carter, Ernest Frank. The Model Railway Encyclopedia.
      London: Burke, 1950. 496pp, ill, bib

8315 Collins, Francis Arnold. The Boys' Book of Model Aero-
      planes; how to build and fly them. New York: Century,
      1910; 1914; rev. ed. 1921; 1923; new & rev. ed. New
      York; London: Century, 1929; 1936; 4th ed. rev. 1941;
      1943. 308pp, ill, pls; 264pp, ill, pls;...

8316 Ellis, Cuthbert Hamilton. Model Railways, 1838-1939. Lon-
      don: Allen & Unwin, 1962. 139pp, ill

8317 Greenly, Henry, 1876-1947. Model Electric Locomotives and
      Their Construction; a practical manual on the design and
      building of electric railway models. London: Model Rail-
      ways Pr, 1911. 142pp, ill, 2 pls NN

8318 _____ . Model Electric Locomotives and Railways, their
      details and practical construction. London; Cassell: 1922?
      311pp, 326 ill NN, DLC

8319 _____ . The Model Locomotive, Its Design and Construction;
      a practical manual on the building and management of
      miniature railway engines. London: P. Marshall, 1904.
      276pp, 370 ill, 9 folding pls NN, DLC

8320 _____ . Model Steam Locomotives, their details and prac-
      tical construction. London; New York: Cassell, 1922;
      1925; new ed. 1929; 1932; rev. by Ernest A. Steel. Lon-
      don: 1951. 311pp, ill; ...; ...; ...; 320pp, ill

8321 Hertz, Louis Heilbroner. Collecting Model Trains. New
      York: Simmons-Boardman, 1956. 352pp, ill

8322 Jeanmaire, Claude, comp. Bing, die modellbahnen unserer
      grossvater; die geschichte des hauses Bing, Nurnberg,
      von 1866-1933-1966.... Bing, Granddad's model railway.
      In German, French, English. Villigen: Verlag Eisenbahn,
      1972. 399pp, chiefly ill, facsim. from Bing catalogues

8323 _____ . Die Grossen Spurweiten. The Railway models of
      Marklin ... 1891-1968. In German and English. Basel:
      Verlag Eisenbahn, 1969. 254pp, ill (Marklin-Spielzeu-
      geisenbahn model railway)

8324 Johnson, Valentine Edward. Modern Models, including full
      instructions for making and using model aeroplanes, dirigi-
      bles, hydro-aeroplanes, mono-rail models, wireless teleg-
      raphy, x-ray apparatus, etc. London: C. A. Pearson,
      1914. 126pp, 8 pls

8325 Kowal, Case. Toy Trains of Yesteryear. Newton, NJ:

Carstens; Ramsey, NJ: Model Craftsman, 1971. 50pp, ill

8326 Levy, A. A Century of Model Trains. 2nd ed. in English and German. Newton, NJ: Carstens; 1974. ill

8327 The Model Railroader. Monthly. Milwaukee, Wisc: Kalmbach, 1934- . ill

8328 Readers' Guide to Model Railroad Literature with Buyers' Guide. Milwaukee, Wisc: Kalmach, 1934- . NN

8329 *Reder, Gustav. Clockwork, Steam and Electric: A History of Model Railways. Tr. from German (1969) by C. Hamilton Ellis. London: Allan, 1972. 216pp, ill, facsims, bib

8330 Train Collectors Quarterly. Pittsburgh: Train Collectors Association, 1955- . ill

MODELS AND MINIATURES

8331 Banks, Jonathan. Models, machines and instruments made use of by Mr. (John) Banks in his course of lectures, 1790. Drawings by his son Jonathan. (Mr. John Banks, fl. 1795- , lectured on machines, engines, mills, bellows, cranks, etc.) MH

8332 Boileau, Daniel. The Art of Working in Pasteboard, upon scientific principles: to which is added, an appendix containing directions for constructing architectural models. Compiled from the German of B. H. Blasche. London: Boosey & Sons, 1827. 114pp, pls BM, DeWint

8333 Catalogue of Models of Machinery, drawings, tools, etc., in the South Kensington Museum, with classified table of contents, and an alphabetical list of exhibitions and subjects. London: Eyre & Spottiswoode, for HMSO, 1880. 194pp DLC

8334 Catalogue of the Exhibition of Paintings, curiosities, models, apparatus ... for the benefit of the Mechanics' Institution. Leeds: E. Baines, 1839. 31pp BM

8335 Caunter, Cyril Francis. Model Petrol Engines. London: P. Marshall, 1922; 2nd ed. 1934. 68pp, ill; 73pp, ill DLC, NN

8336 Davidson, Ellis A., d. 1878. The Boy Joiner and Model Maker, containing practical directions for making numerous articles for use and ornament. London: Cassell, 18- . 211pp, 200ill, pls

8337 Descriptive Catalogue of the Mining, metallurgical, geological,
      and agricultural models, the National Museum. Melbourne,
      Australia: J. Ferres, 1871. 80pp, 15 pls (Machinery
      models)

8338 Fisher, Elizabeth Andrews. Miniature Stuff. Middletown,
      Conn: 1964. 128pp, ill

8339 Fisher, J., ed. An Illustrated Record of the Retrospective
      Exhibition Held at South Kensington, 1896. Containing 256
      illustrations of designs, models ... for which gold and
      silver medals have been awarded by the Department of
      Science and Art. London: Chapman & Hall, for Educa-
      tion Committee, Privy Council, 1897. 156pp, 256 ill

8340 Gosner, Kenneth L. Mechanical Models; a collection of the
      Newark Museum. Newark: 1954. 20pp, ill, bib

8341 Greenly, Henry. Model Engineering; a guide to model work-
      shop practice, with working drawings of engines, boilers,
      rolling stock, cannon, electric machines, etc. London;
      New York: Cassell, 1915; 5th impression. 1930. 407pp,
      724 drawings, 85 pls DLC

8342 _____. Model Steam Engines, how to understand them and
      how to run them. London: P. Marshall, 1906; 5th ed.
      19-? 60pp, ill; 87pp, ill NN

8343 Hasluck, Paul Nooncree. The Model Engineer's Handybook.
      A Practical manual on model steam engines. Embracing
      information on the tools, materials and processes em-
      ployed in their construction. London: Lockwood, 1889;
      7th ed. 1902; New York: Van Nostrand, 1902;... 144pp,
      ill, pls (Includes pattern-making) MiU, MB, NN

8344 Hughes, George Bernard, and Therle Hughes. Collecting
      Miniature Antiques: a guide for collectors. London:
      Heinemann, 1973. 184pp, ill, 8 pls, bib (ca.1500-ca.
      1900)

8345 Kent, George Henry. The Ware Collection of Blaschka Glass
      Flower Models; a short description of their makers and
      their making. Cambridge, Mass: Author, 1908. 42pp,
      3 pls (Harvard's Ware Collection. Leopold Blaschka,
      1822-1895) MB, NN

8346 Latham, Jean. Miniature Antiques. London: A. & C.
      Black, 1972; as Collecting Miniature Antiques. New York:
      Scribner, 1973. 177pp, ill, 4 pls, bib

8347 McClinton, Katharine Morrison. Antiques in Miniature. New
      York: Scribner, 1970. 182pp, ill (Medium-size minia-
      tures in pottery, porcelain, glass, metal, wood)

8348   Marshall, Percival, ed. Wonderful Models; the romance of
       the world in miniature and a complete encyclopedia of
       model craft, comprising the construction and use of repre-
       sentative and working models in advertising, architecture
       and building, civil and mechanical engineering, naval
       architecture, and railway engineering, and the applications
       of electricity to their operation; also the romance of his-
       toric models and the modern development of model en-
       gineering as an aid to invention, as a recreation, and as
       an essential element in education. 2 vol. London: P.
       Marshall; New York: Spon & Chamberlain, 1928. ill,
       18 folding pls ViU, NN, MB

8349   Sandham, Henry, ed. Catalogue of Models of Machinery,
       Drawings, Tools, etc. in the South Kensington Museum.
       London: 1875; 2nd ed. 1880. 194pp BM

8350   Smith, Frank R., and Ruth E. Smith. Miniature Lamps.
       New York: Nelson, 1968. 285pp, 641 (11 color) ill, bib
       (Under 10" high)

8351   Toller, Jane. Antique Miniature Furniture in Great Britain
       and America. London: Bell; Newton Centre, Mass: C.
       T. Branford, 1966. 112pp, 60 ill, 32 pls, bib (1700-
       1900)

8352   Worrell, Estelle Ansley. Americana in Miniature. New York:
       Van Nostrand Reinhold, 1973. 64pp, ill

8353   Yates, Raymond Francis. Model Making, including workshop
       practice, design and construction of models.... New
       York: Norman W. Henley, 1919; 2nd ed. 1925. 390pp,
       300 ill; 428pp, ill

BICYCLES AND TRICYCLES

8354   Alderson, Frederick. Bicycling: A History. New York:
       Praeger, 1972. 214pp, ill

8355   Bottomley, Joseph Firth. The Velocipede, Its Past, Its
       Present and Its Future. London: Simpkins, Marshall,
       1869. 105pp, ill, pls NN, CtY

8356   Caunter, Cyril Francis. The History and Development of
       Cycles, as illustrated by the collection of cycles in the
       Science Museum. 2 vol. London: HMSO, 1955-58. ill
       (Vol. I. Bicycles & Tricycles; Vol. II. Motorcycles)

8357   Davis, Alexander. The Velocipede; its history, and practical
       hints how to use it. London: 1869. 21pp, ill MiD

8358 Grew, W. F. The Cycle Industry. London: Pitman, 1921.
      123pp, ill BM

8359 Griffin, Harry Hewitt. Bicycles and Tricycles of the Year
      1878/79; being a chronicle of the new inventions and im-
      provements introduced each season and a permanent record
      of the progress in the manufacture of bicycles and tri-
      cycles; designed also to assist intending purchasers in the
      choice of a machine. London: "The Bazaar," 1879;
      ... the Year 1877. London: Gill, 1887; ... the Year
      1889;... 116pp, ill; ...

8360 _____ . Bicycles and Tricycles of the Year 1886. Cata-
      logue. London: 1886; reprint with introd. by Noel Marsh-
      man. Otley: Olicana Books, 1971. 198pp, ill

8361 _____ . Cycles and Cycling. With a chapter for ladies,
      by Miss L. C. Davidson. New York: F. A. Stokes,
      1890; London: G. Bell, 1893; 3rd ed. London: 1897; ...
      120pp, ill; 124pp, ill; 150pp, 77 ill NN, MiD

8362 Leek, Stephen, and Sybil Leek. The Bicycle--that curious
      invention. Nashville: T. Nelson, 1973. 144pp, ill
      (Juvenile lit.)

8363 Monroe, Lynn Lee. Boneshakers and Other Bikes. Minnea-
      polis: Lerner Publications, 1973. 32pp, ill (Juvenile
      lit.)

8364 *Oliver, Smith Hempstone, and Donald H. Berkebile. Catalog
      of the Cycle Collection of the Division of Engineering,
      United States National Museum. Washington, D.C.: GPO,
      1953; as Wheels and Wheeling; the Smithsonian Cycle Col-
      lection. Washington, D.C.: Smithsonian Institution Pr,
      1974. 104pp, ill, bib

8365 Sturmey, Henry. Tricyclists' Annual. Periodical. London:
      Iliffe, 1880- .

8366 Woodforde, John. The Story of the Bicycle. London: Rout-
      ledge & K. Paul, 1970; New York: Universe, 1971.
      175pp, ill

SHIPS, RAILROADS AND AUTOMOBILES

SHIPS' EQUIPMENT AND DECORATION†

8367 Greenhill, Basil, and Ann Gifford. Travelling by Sea in the 19th Century. Interior design in Victorian passenger ships. London: A & C Black, 1972; New York: Hastings, 1974. 168pp, ill (Includes chapter on 18th century)

8368 Overton, George Leonard. Water Transport. Catalogue of the collections in the Science Museum, South Kensington. London: HMSO, 1923- . pls DLC, NN

8369 _____, and Hereward Philip Spratt. Handbook of the Collections Illustrating Marine Engines. Science Museum. Vol. I. History and Development, Overton; Vol. II. Descriptive Catalogue, Spratt. 2 vol. London: HMSO, 1935-38; Vol. II. reprint. 1953. text, pls, bib DLC, NN

8370 Schult, Joachim. Curious Boating Inventions. Tr. from German (1971) by Inge Moore. London: Elek, 1974. 150pp, ill (1790-1968)

8371 _____. Curious Yachting Inventions. Tr. from German (1971) by Inge Moore. Introd. by Dougal Robertson. London: Elek, 1974. 139pp, ill (1878-1968)

MODELS OF SHIPS, BOATS AND JUNKS

8372 Anderson, Roger Charles. Catalogue of Ship Models (Scale), National Maritime Museum, Greenwich. London: HMSO, 1952. 133pp, ill

8373 Bathe, Basil W. Ship Models. Science Museum. 4 vol.

_____

†See also Instruments of Precision in Section XXXI for books on navigation equipment.

London: HMSO, 1963-66; 2nd ed. in 1 vol. as Ship
Models: sailing ships and small craft. London: 1966.
text, ill (some color); 188pp, ill (Earliest times to 1700)

8374   Biddle, Tyrrel E. A Treatise on the Construction, rigging
and handling of model yachts, ships and steamers. London: Charles Wilson, 1879; 2nd ed. enl. London: Norie
& Wilson, 1883; reissue. London: 1896. 107pp, 10 pls
BM

8375   Bowen, Frank Charles. From Carrack to Clipper; a book of
sailing ship models. rev. ed. London; New York: Halton,
1948. 74pp, ill (part color)

8376   Catalogue of the Henry Huddleston Rogers Collection of Ship
Models, United States Naval Academy Museum. Annapolis,
Md: Naval Institute Pr, 1954; 1958; rev. ed. 1971. 115pp,
ill; 137pp, ill

8377   Catalogue of the Naval and Marine Engineering Collection in
the Science Division of the V & A Museum. With descriptive and historical notes. London: HMSO, 1899; 2nd ed.
with supplement containing illustrations. London: 1911.
311pp: 407pp, 12 pls (Includes ship models)

8378   Catalogue of the Naval Models in the South Kensington Museum.
Part 1. Admiralty Collection of Models, etc. 2. Collec-
tion of Models from Private Sources. 2 parts. London:
HMSO, 1865. 279pp, photographic ill

8379   Catalogue of Ship Models and Marine Engineering in the South
Kensington Museum. London: Eyre & Spottiswoode, for
HMSO, 1878; 1889. 167pp, 352pp DLC

8380   Chatterton, Edward Keble. Sailing Models, Ancient and Modern. London: Hurst & Blackett, 1934. 95pp, 161 ill,
4 color pls NN, DLC

8381   _____ . Ship-models. London: The Studio, 1922; ed. by
Geoffrey Holme. London: 1923; reprint of 77 plates.

New York: H. C. Perleberg, n.d.   53pp, 142 pls (part
color)   PPULC, DLC

8382 _____. Steamship Models. London: W. T. Laurie, 1924.
      84pp, 128 (8 color) pls

8383 Clowes, Geoffrey Swinford Laird.   Sailing Ships: their history
      and development as illustrated by the collection of ship-
      models in the Science Museum.   London: HMSO, 1930;
      2nd ed. 2 vol. London: 1931, 1932; 2nd ed. with additions,
      London: 1936; 3rd ed. 2 vol. in 1. (Vol. I from 1932 ed.,
      Vol. II revised by Ernest William White.) London: 1947-
      48; 4th ed. exp. & rev. by E. W. White. London: 1951-
      52; reprint. 1962. ill, pls (Vol. I. Historical Notes;
      Vol. II. Catalogue of Exhibits with Descriptive Notes) CU,
      NN, BM

8384 Culver, Henry Brundage.   Contemporary Scale Models of Ves-
      sels of the 17th Century, being a collection of illustrations
      of authentic productions of the model makers' art of that
      period, gathered from many sources; together with brief
      descriptions and identifications thereof where possible, pre-
      pared for the Ship Model Society. New York: Payson &
      Clarke, 1926. 2pp, ill, 50 pls MB, DLC

8385 Emmons, Conant H.   Bottled Ships and Other Objects: Their
      History and Usage, Including Some Unusual Models.   Lus-
      by, Ind: Ship in Bottle Pr, 1969. 93pp, ill

8386 Exhibition of Models of Cargo-carrying Steamers, 1876-1930;
      catalogue.   February-May 1933. Cardiff: National Mu-
      seum of Wales, and the Press Board of the University of
      Wales, 1933. 26pp NN, MiD

8387 Freeston, Ewart Cecil.   Prisoner-of-War Ship Models, 1775-
      1825. Lymington, Eng: Nautical Pub Co; Annapolis, Md:
      Naval Institute Pr, 1973. 174pp, ill, bib, gloss (Pris-
      oners of war in England)

8388 Hasluck, Paul Nooncree, ed.   Building Model Boats, including
      sailing and steam vessels. London: Cassell, 1899; Lon-
      don; New York: Cassell, 1901; Philadelphia: McKay,
      1906. 160pp, ill MB, PPL

8389 Illustrated Catalogue of the "Maze Collection" of Chinese Junk
      Models in the Science Museum, London.   London: printed
      in Shanghai, 1939. ill

8390 Lauder, J. P., and R. H. Biggs.   Ships in Bottles. London:
      Marshall, 1949; rev. ed. London: 1962. 74pp, ill

8391 Marshall, Percival, 1870- , ed.   Machinery for Model

Steamers; a practical handbook on the design and construction of engines and boilers for model steamers, the use of liquid fuel, and the proportions of machinery for model boats. London: P. Marshall, 1903. 45pp, ill NN

8392 Naish, G. P. B., comp. A Picture Book of Ship-Models (in the Greenwich National Maritime Museum). London: HMSO, 1953. 30pp, 32 ill

8393 Oude Schepen. Old Ships, with English text. Catalogue. Amsterdam: Rijks-Museum, 1957. ill

8394 Parker, Captain Harry. A Chat on Old Ship Models. London: Parker Gallery, 1952. 27pp, ill

8395 Sandham, Henry, ed. Catalogue of Mercantile Marine and Naval Models in the South Kensington Museum. London: HMSO, 1874.

8396 _____. Catalogue of Ship Models and Marine Engineering in the South Kensington Museum. London: 1878; 2nd ed. 1889. ...; 352pp

8397 Ships Models. Edinburgh: Museum of Science & Art, 1956. ill

8398 Spratt, Hereward Philip. Handbook of the Collections Illustrating Merchant Steamers and Motor-Ships. Science Museum. 2 parts. London: HMSO, 1949- . descriptive catalog, pls, bib CU, NN

SCRIMSHAW, ARTS OF MARINERS AND SHIPS' CARVING

8399 Banks, Steven. The Handicrafts of the Sailor. Newton Abbot: David & Charles, 1974. 96pp, ill, bib (ca.1600-ca.1900)

8400 Barbeau, Charles Marius. 'All Hands Aboard Scrimshawing.' Reprint from The American Neptune, April 1952. Salem, Mass: Peabody Museum, 1966. 26pp, pls

8401 Barnes, Clare, Jr. John F. Kennedy: Scrimshaw Collector. Boston: Little, Brown, 1969. 127pp, ill (34-piece collection)

8402 Brewington, Marion Vernon. Shipcarvers of North America. Barre, Mass: Barre Publishing Co, 1962; New York: Dover; London: Constable, 1972. 173pp, ill, bib (Canadian & American figureheads, etc. to 1900)

8403 Cook, Gervis Frere-, ed. The Decorative Arts of the Mariner. London: Cassell; Boston: Little, Brown, 1966. 296pp, ill (Ship models, navigational instruments, carvings)

8404 Crosby, Everett Uberto. Susan's Teeth and Much About
      Scrimshaw. Nantucket Island, Mass: Tetaukimmo Pr,
      1955. 62pp, ill (Seven whales' teeth carved on the ship
      Susan, Nantucket 1828. Reprint of articles by Frank
      Wood, Arthur C. Watson, Marius Barbeau)

8405 Earle, Walter K. Scrimshaw, Folk Art of the Whalers.
      Cold Spring Harbor, NY: The Whaling Museum Society,
      1957. 36pp, ill, pls

8406 Flayderman, E. Norman. Scrimshaw and Scrimshanders;
      whales and whalemen. Ed. by R. L. Wilson. New Mil-
      ford, Conn: Author, 1972. 293pp, ill, bib

8407 Hansen, Hans Jurgen, ed. Art and the Seafarer: a historical
      survey of the arts and crafts of sailors and shipwrights,
      with contributions by Edward H. H. Archibald, and others.
      Tr. by James and Inge Moore. New York: Viking, 1968.
      292pp, ill, pls, bib

8408 Klamkin, Marian. Marine Antiques. New York: Dodd, Mead,
      1975. 270 (23 color) ill

8409 Kranz, Jacqueline L. American Nautical Art and Antiques.
      New York: Crown, 1975. 248pp, 320 ill, color pls, bib
      (Paintings, prints, lights, foghorns, flags, tools, maps,
      scrimshaw, ship models, etc.)

8410 *Laughton, (Leonard George) Carr. Old Ship Figure-Heads
      and Sterns, with which are associated galleries, hanging-
      pieces, catheads and diverse other matters that concern
      the "grace and countenance" of old sailing ships. London:
      Halton & T. Mith; New York: Minton, Balch, 1925. 281pp,
      ill, 55 pls (part color) NN, NjP

8411 Randier, Jean. Nautical Antiques, for the Collector. Prince-
      ton, NJ: Pyne Pr, 1976. ill

8412 Scrimshaw. Tasmania Museum and Art Gallery. Hobart,
      Tasmania: the Museum, 1963. 23pp, ill.

8413 Stackpole, Edouard A. Scrimshaw at Mystic Seaport, featuring
      objects from the Nynett, Howland, Townshend and White
      collections. Mystic, Conn: Marine Historical Association,
      1958. 53pp, pls

AUTOMOBILE AND RAILWAY COLLECTIBLES

8414 Ballou and Wright. Ballou-Wright Automobile Supplies Cata-
      log, 1906. Reprint. With preface by Ron Brantano.
      Portland: Oregon Historical Society, 1971. 58pp, ill

8415   Burkhalter, Agnes S.   Historical Railroad Lanterns.   Win-
       chester, Tenn: 1971.   ill of 80 items

8416   The Equipment on the "Lake Shore Ltd.," the new 24-hour
       train between Chicago and New York, via the New York
       Central and Lake Shore and Michigan Southern Railways.
       New York?:   N.Y. Central Railroad Co, 189-?   11 mounted
       photographs (Furniture and accessories)   NNC-Ave

8417   Fahnestock, Murray.   Those Wonderful Unauthorized Acces-
       sories for Model A Fords.   Compiled principally from the
       Collection of M. Fahnestock.   Arcadia, Cal: Post Motor
       Books, 1971.   250pp, ill

8418   Johnson, Howard.   Railroad Collectibles: A Price Guide.
       Gas City, Ind: L-W Promotions, 1973.   80pp, ill (Lan-
       terns, keys, books, timetables, locks, lamps, oilers,
       postcards, etc.)

8419   Morgan, Brian Stanford.   Railway Relics.   Shepperton, Eng:
       Allan, 1969.   128pp, ill, 40 pls (Industrial archaeology)

8420   Smith, Donald John.   Discovering Railwayana.   Tring: Shire
       Publications, 1971.   63pp, ill, bib (Equipment and sup-
       plies)

SECTION XXII

MUSIC

GENERAL WORKS ON MUSICAL INSTRUMENTS

8421 Armstrong, Robert Bruce. Musical Instruments. 2 vol.
Vol. I. Edinburgh: D. Douglas, 1904; Vol. II. Edinburgh:
T. & A. Constable, 1908. ill (Vol. I. The Irish and the
Highland Harp; Vol. II. English and Irish Instruments)

8422 Audel, Stephane. Musical Instruments. Tr. from French by
Arethusa Ewbank. London: Harrap, 1961. 16pp, ill
(Juvenile literature)

8423 Baines, Anthony Cuthbert. European and American Musical
Instruments. London: Batsford, 1966. 174pp, 825 photographs, 112 pls, bib

8424 _____. Musical Instruments Through the Ages. Harmondsworth, Eng; Baltimore: Penguin, for the Galpin Society,
1961; rev. ed. London: Faber; New York: Walker, 1966.
383pp, ill, 32 pls; 344pp, ill, pls, bib

8425 Bessaraboff, Nicholas. Ancient European Musical Instruments; an organological study of the musical instruments in the Leslie Lindsey Mason Collection at the Museum of Fine Arts. Pref. by Edwin J. Hipkiss. Fore. by Francis W. Galpin. New York: October House, for Boston Museum of Fine Arts, 1941; Cambridge, Mass: Harvard U. Pr, for the Museum, 1941. 503pp, ill, 16 pls, bib

8426 Boulton, Laura Theresa. Musical Instruments of World Cultures; from the ... Boulton Collection. New York: Intercultural Arts Pr, 1972. 80pp, ill

8427 Boyden, David Dodge. Catalogue of the Hill Collection of Music Instruments in the Ashmolean Museum, Oxford. London; New York: Oxford U. Pr, 1969. 54pp, ill, 57 pls, bib (Chiefly string instruments, 1500-1820)

8428 British Musical Instruments: an exhibition ... with the Arts Council of Great Britain, August 1951. Ilford, Essex: Galpin Society, 1951. 35pp, ill

8429 Brown, Crosby. The Crosby Brown Collection of Musical Instruments of All Nations. Vol. I. Keyboard Instruments. Vol. II. Wall Cases (contents of). 2 vol. New York: Metropolitan Museum, 1903- . 313pp, 134 pls; text, pls

8430 _____. The Crosby Brown Collection of Musical Instruments of All Nations, prepared under the direction, and issued with the authorization of the Donor (Mrs. Mary Elizabeth A. Brown). 4 vol. in 5. New York: Metropolitan Museum, 1902-1907. pls, charts, bib (I. Europe; II. Asia; III. Instruments of Savage Tribes and Semi-Civilized Peoples. Part 1. Africa; Part 2. Oceania; IV. Historical Groups.

8431 *Buchner, Alexandr. Musical Instruments Through the Ages. Tr. by Iris Urwin. London: Spring Books, 1957. 44pp, 323 ill, 224 pls

8432 Catalogue of a Special Exhibition of Ancient Musical Instruments. South Kensington Museum. London: J. Strangeways, 1872. 48pp, 16 pls

8433 Catalogue of the Music Library. The Hague. Gemeentemuseum. New York: Da Capo Pr, 1969. ill (Instruments)

8434 Catalogue of the Stearns Collection of Musical Instruments. Ann Arbor: U. of Michigan, 1918. 260pp

8435 Checklist of the Yale Collection of Musical Instruments. New Haven: Yale U. Pr, 1968. 43pp

8436   Clemencic, Rene. Old Musical Instruments. Tr. by David
       Hermges. London: Weidenfeld & Nicolson; New York:
       Putnam's, 1968. 120pp, ill

8437   de Lange, Margaret M., comp. Catalogue of the Musical
       Instruments in the Collection of Percival R. Kirby.
       Johannesburg: Africana Museum, 1967. 155 leaves

8438   Densmore, Frances. Handbook of the Collection of Musical
       Instruments in the United States National Museum. Wash-
       ington, D.C.: GPO, 1927; reprint. New York: Da Capo
       Pr, 1971. 164pp, 49 pls

8439   Engle, Carl, 1818-1882. Examples of Art Workmanship of
       Various Ages and Countries. Musical Instruments in the
       South Kensington Museum. With descriptions. London:
       HMSO, 1869; 2nd ed. as A Descriptive Catalogue of Musi-
       cal Instruments.... London: 1870; 1874; New York:
       Scribner, Welford and Armstrong, 1876; 1877; London:
       Wyman & Sons, 1908; reprint of 2nd ed. New York: B.
       Blom, 1971. 128pp, ill; 82pp, ill; ...; ...; ...; 146pp,
       ill; 402pp, ill NN, DLC

8440   Fox, Lilla Margaret. Instruments of Parade Music. New
       York: Roy, 1967. 126pp, ill

8441   _____. Instruments of Religion and Folklore. London:
       Letterworth, 1969; New York: Roy, 1970. 135pp, ill

8442   _____. Instruments of Popular Music: a history of musical
       instruments. London: Letterworth, 1966; New York: Roy,
       1968. 112pp, ill

8443   Gabry, Gyorgy. Old Musical Instruments. Tr. from Hun-
       garian by Eva Racz. Budapest: Corvina Pr, 1969. 42pp,
       55 pls

8444   Galpin, Francis William. Old English Instruments of Music.
       London: Methuen, 1910; Chicago: McClurg, 1911; 3rd
       ed. rev. 1932; 4th rev. ed. with notes by Thurston Dart.
       London: Methuen; New York: Barnes & Noble, 1965.
       327pp, 46 ill, 56 pls, bib; ...; 254pp, ill, bib

8445   _____. A Textbook of European Musical Instruments, their
       origin, history, and characteristics. London: Williams
       & Norgate; New York: Dutton, 1937; London: 1946; New
       York: J. De Graff, 1956. 256pp, ill, 10 pls, bib

8446   Gammond, Peter. Musical Instruments in Color. New York:
       Macmillan, 1976. 80pp of color ill

8447   Geiringer, Karl. Musical Instruments. Their history from

the Stone Age to the present day. Tr. by Bernard Miall.
London: Allen & Unwin, 1943; 2nd ed. 1945; New York:
Oxford U. Pr, 1945; London: 1949. 339pp, 65 pls, color
frontis, bib; ...; 278pp, ill, 26 pls, bib

8448 Germaine, Joseph. A Short History of Musical Instruments.
More particularly showing the origin of the modern harp
and pianoforte from the ideas of archaic times. London:
S. & P. Erard, 1897. 32pp BM

8449 Gillingham, Harrold Edgar. Some Early Philadelphia Instrument Makers. Reprint from Pennsylvania Magazine of
History and Biography. Philadelphia: Historical Society
of Pa, 1927. 22pp, ill PPL

8450 Harrison, Frank Llewellyn, and Joan Rimmer. European
Musical Instruments. London: Studio Vista; New York:
W. W. Norton, 1964. 210pp, ill

8451 Hipkins, Alfred James. Musical Instruments: historic, rare
and unique, ... Edinburgh; London: A. & C. Black, 1888;
1921; 1945. 107pp, ill, 50 color pls MB, DLC

8452 Instruments of Music. History and Development. Glasgow:
Kelvingrove Art Gallery and Museum, 1941. 17pp

8453 International Loan Exhibition of Musical Instruments, 1900.
Sydenham, Eng: Crystal Palace, 1900. 55pp

8454 Jenkins, Jean. Musical Instruments: Handbook to the Collection. Horniman Museum, London. London: London
County Council, 1958; 2nd ed. London: Inner London
Educational Authority, 1970. 109pp, ill, pls, bib; 104pp,
ill, 32 pls, bib

8455 Kallmann, Helmut. Canadian-built 19th Century Musical Instruments; checklist. 2nd ed. Edmonton, Alberta: Edmonton Publishing, 1966. 7 leaves

8456 Kendall, Alan. The World of Musical Instruments. London:
Hamlyn, 1972. 128pp, 152 (32 color) ill

8457 Krishnaswami, S. Musical Instruments of India. Delhi:
Ministry of Information and Broadcasting, 1965. 102pp,
ill

8458 Lacey, Marion. Picture Book of Musical Instruments.
Boston; New York: Lothrop, Lee & Shepard, 1942.
55pp of ill

8459 Lachmann, Erich. Catalogue of the Lachmann Collection of
Historical Musical Instruments. Los Angeles, Cal:
193-? 12pp, pls NN

8460   Lang, Paul Henry, and Otto Bettmann.   A Pictorial History
       of Music.   New York: Norton, 1960.   242pp, ill

8461   Leeuwen Boomkamp, Carel van, and J. H. van der Meer.
       The Leeuwen Boomkamp Collection of Musical Instruments.
       Amsterdam: Knuf, 1971.   190pp, ill, bib

8462   Marcuse, Sibyl.   Musical Instruments at Yale; a selection of
       western instruments from the 15th to 20th century.   Exhi-
       bition.   February-March 1960.   New Haven: Yale Art
       Gallery, 1960.   47pp, ill

8463   Melville-Mason, Graham, ed.   An Exhibition of European
       Musical Instruments.   Galpin Society, Reid School of
       Music, Edinburgh University.   August-September 1968.
       London: Galpin Society, 1968.   100pp, ill, 40 pls

8464   Musical Instruments.   Catalog.   Cincinnati: Art Museum,
       1949.   23pp, ill, bib

8465   Musical Instruments as Works of Art.   V & A Museum.   Lon-
       don: HMSO, 1968.   101pp of ill

8466   Musical Instruments in the Royal Ontario Museum.   Toronto:
       1971.   96pp, ill

8467   Paetkau, David H.   The Growth of Instruments and Instru-
       mental Music.   New York: Vantage Pr, 1962.   393pp, ill

8468   Paganelli, Sergio.   Musical Instruments from the Renaissance
       to the 19th Century.   Tr. from Italian by Anthony Rhodes.
       Feltham: Hamlyn, 1970.   157pp, ill

8469   Piggott, Sir Francis Taylor.   The Music and Musical Instru-
       ments of Japan, with notes by T. L. Southgate.   London:
       Batsford, 1893; 2nd ed. Yokohama: Kelly & Walsh, 1909;
       reprint. New York: Da Capo Pr, 1971.   230pp, 16 pls;
       196pp, ill, 5 pls

8470   Powne, Michael.   Ethiopian Music, an Introduction; a survey
       of ecclesiastical and secular Ethiopian music and instru-
       ments.   London: Oxford U. Pr, 1966; New York: Oxford
       U. Pr, 1968.   160pp, ill, 11 pls

8471   Pulver, Jeffrey.   Dictionary of Old English Music and Musical
       Instruments.   London: K. Paul; New York: Dutton, 1923.
       247pp, ill, pls

8472   Rimbault, Edward Francis.   Musical Instruments.   London:
       1876.   See: Bevan, G. P., British Manufacturing Indus-
       tries, Vol. 11, no. 43.

8473   Rokseth, Yvonne Rihouet.   Musical Instruments in the 15th

Century Church. Cambridge, Eng: Bois de Boulogne, 1968. 5pp

8474 Russell, Raymond, and Anthony Baines. Catalogue of Musical Instruments in the V & A. Vol. I. Keyboard Instruments, by Russell; Vol. II. Non-Keyboard Instruments, by Baines. 2 vol. London: HMSO, 1968. 94pp, ill, 61 pls, bib; 1212pp, ill, 96 pls, bib

8475 Sachs, Curt, 1881- . The History of Musical Instruments. New York: W. W. Norton, 1940; London: Dent, 1942. 505pp, 24 pls, bib

8476 Schwartz, Harry Wayne. The Story of Musical Instruments from Shepherd's Pipes to Symphony. Freeport, NY: Books for Libraries, 1970. 365pp, ill

8477 Singleton, Esther. The Orchestra and Its Instruments. New York: Symphony Society of New York, 1917. 312pp, pls, music

8478 Stainer, Sir John, 1840-1901. The Music of the Bible, with an account of the development of modern musical instruments from ancient types. London: Novello, Ewer, 1879; new ed. with additions by F. W. Galpin. London: Novello; New York: H. W. Gray, 1914. 186pp, ill; 230pp, ill, pls

8479 Thibault, G. (Mme de Chambure), Jean Jenkins, and Josiane Bran-Ricci. 18th Century Musical Instruments: France and Britain. Exhibition. V & A Museum. English and French text. London: HMSO, 1974. 229pp, chiefly ill (Many pieces from Conservatoire National Superieur de Musique, Paris; V & A Museum; Horniman Museum, London)

8480 Thornton, Peter. Musical Instruments as Works of Art. 2 vol. Catalogue and Picture Book. London: HMSO, 19-? (V & A Museum)

8481 Wiant, Bliss. The Music of China. Hong Kong: Chung Chi Publications, Chung Chi College, 1965. 161pp, ill

8482 Willson, Robina Beckles. Musical Instruments. Edinburgh; London: Oliver & Boyd, 1964. 64pp, ill (Juvenile literature)

8483 Winternitz, Emanuel. Musical Instruments of the Western World. London: Thames & Hudson; New York: McGraw-Hill, 1967. 259pp, 59 ill, 100 pls, bib

KEYBOARD INSTRUMENTS

8484   Bie, Oskar.   A History of the Pianoforte and Pianoforte
       Players.   Tr. and rev. from German by E. E. Kellett,
       and E. W. Naylor.   London: J. M. Den; New York:
       Dutton, 1899.   336pp, ill, 5 pls   NN, DLC

8485   Boalch, Donald Howard.   Makers of the Harpsichord and
       Clavichord, 1440-1840.   London: G. Ronald, 1950; Lon-
       don: G. Ronald; New York: Macmillan, 1956.   169pp,
       ill, 32 pls, bib

8486   Boddington, Henry.   Catalogue of the Instruments Principally
       Illustrative of the History of the Pianoforte.   Manchester: G.
       Falknew, Dunsgate Pr, 1888.   42 pls (Property of Author,
       formerly collection of J. Kendrick Pyne)   CtY, PPULC

8487   Brinsmead, Edgar.   The History of the Pianoforte, with an
       account of ancient music and musical instruments.   Lon-
       don: Cassell, 1868; London: Cassell, Petter & Galpin,
       1870; 1876; with "Inventions Patented between the Years
       1693-1876."   1877; new ed. as The History of the Piano-
       forte, with an account of the theory of sound and also of
       the music and musical instruments of the ancients.   Lon-
       don: Novello, Ewer, 1879; 30,000th.   London: Simpkin,
       Marshall, 1889; 1897.   80pp, ill; 1879: 204pp, ill; 1889:
       254pp, ill, pls   PP, MiD, BM

8488   Broadwood, James Shudi.   Some Notes on the Harpsichord and
       Pianoforte Made by J. S. Broadwood, 1838.   With observa-
       tions and elucidations by Henry Fowler Broadwood.   London:
       W. S. Johnson, 1862.   14pp

8489   Broadwood Collection of Antique Instruments; forerunners of the
       modern pianoforte, on view at (John) Broadwood & Sons
       Galleries.   London: 1910?   16pp

8490   Carmi, Avner, and Hannah Carmi.   The Immortal Piano.
       (The Siena Piano.) London: Redman, 1961. 286pp, ill

8491   Closson, Ernest. History of the Piano. Tr. from French
       (1944) by Delano Ames. London: Paul Elek, 1947; 2nd
       ed. ed. & rev. by Robin Golding. London: Elek, 1974.
       168pp, ill, bib; 154pp, ill, bib

8492   Dolge, Alfred. Pianos and Their Makers: a comprehensive
       history of the development of the piano from the mono-
       chord to the concert grand player piano. 2 vol. Covina,
       Cal: Covina Publishing, 1911-1913; reprint. New York:
       Dover; London: Constable, 1972. 478pp, ill, pls; 581pp,
       ill

8493   The English Harpsichord Magazine and Early Keyboard Instru-
       ment Review. Biannual. Chesham Bois, Bucks: Edgar
       Hunt, 1974- .

8494   Germaine, Joseph. A Short History of Musical Instruments.
       More particularly showing the origins of the modern harp
       and pianoforte from the ideas of archaic times. London:
       S. & P. Erard, 1897. 32pp BM

8495   Harding, Rosamond Evelyn Mary. The Piano-forte; its history
       traced to the Great Exhibition of 1851. London?: 1933;
       reprint. New York: Da Capo Pr, 1973. 432pp, ill, pls,
       bib

8496   The Harpsichord Magazine. Chesham Bois, Bucks: Edgar
       Hunt, 1973-1974. (Became The English Harpsichord...)

8497   *Hipkins, Alfred James, 1826-1903. A Description and History
       of the Pianoforte and of the Older Keyboard Stringed In-
       struments. London; New York: Novello Ewer, 1896; 1929.
       128pp, ill, pls MiU, DLC

8498   _____ . History of the Pianoforte. London: Novello?,
       1883. 16pp

8499   Hirt, Franz Josef. Stringed Keyboard Instruments, 1440-1880.
       Tr. from German (1955) by M. Boehme-Brown. Boston:
       Boston Book and Art Shop, 1968. 465pp, ill

8500   Hollis, Helen. Pianos in the Smithsonian Institution. Wash-
       ington, D.C.: its Press, 1973. 47pp, ill, bib

8501   Hoover, Cynthia A. Harpsichords and Clavichords. Washing-
       ton, D.C.: Smithsonian Institution Pr, 1969. 43pp, ill,
       bib

8502   Hubbard, Frank. Three Centuries of Harpsichord Making.

Cambridge, Mass: Harvard U Pr; London: Oxford U Pr,
1965. 472pp, 41 pls, bib (16th, 17th and 18th century
Italian, Flemish, French and German)

8503 James, Philip Brutton. Early Keyboard Instruments; from
their beginnings to the year 1820. London: Peter Davies;
New York: F. A. Stokes, 1930; London: Holland Pr,
1967; London: Tabard Pr, 1970. 153pp, ill, 66 pls, bib,
list of British makers (Spinet, virginal, clavichord,
harpsichord, pianoforte)

8504 Krehbiel, Henry Edward. The Pianoforte and Its Music. New
York: Scribner's, 1911. 314pp, ill, bib

8505 List of Pianofortes, and of various samples and models, intended to illustrate the principles of their manufacture.
Exhibited by J(ohn) Broadwood & Sons ... with an historical introduction. (International Exhibition of 1862.) London: 1862. BM

8506 Loesser, Arthur. Men, Women and Pianos: a social history.
New York: Simon & Schuster, 1954. 654pp, ill, bib

8507 Michel, Norman Elwood. Historical Pianos, Harpsichords
and Clavichords. Pico Rivera, Cal: 1963; Supplement.
1963?; 1970. 209pp, ill; 8pp; 236pp, ill

8508 Newman, Sidney, and Peter Williams, comp. The Russell
Collection and Other Early Keyboard Instruments in Saint
Cecilia's Hall, Edinburgh. Edinburgh: U. Pr, 1968.
79pp, ill

8509 Pierce, Bob. Pierce Piano Atlas. Long Beach, Cal: priv.
printed, 1966. (Lists piano makers, city and dates)

8510 *Rimbault, Edward Francis. The Pianoforte; its origin, progress and construction with some accounts of instruments
of the same class which preceded it: viz. the clavichord,
virginal, spinet, harpsichord, etc. London: Robert Cocks,
1860. 420pp, ill, color frontis BM

8511 Russell, Raymond. Catalogue of the Benton Fletcher Collection of Early Keyboard Instruments at Fenton House,
Hampstead. London: Country Life, 1957. 26pp, ill

8512 _____. Early Keyboard Instruments. V & A Museum.
London: HMSO, 1959. 32pp, ill

8513 _____. The Harpsichord and Clavichord: an introductory
study. London: Faber, 1959; New York: October House,
1965; 2nd ed. rev. by Howard Schott. London: 1973.
208pp, ill, 103 pls, bib (To ca.1900)

8514   , and Anthony Baines. Catalogue of Musical Instruments in the V & A Museum. Vol. I. Keyboard Instruments, by Russell; Vol. II. Non-Keyboard Instruments,
by Baines. 2 vol. London: HMSO, 1968. 94pp, ill,
61 pls, bib; 121pp, ill, 96 pls, bib

8515 Shortridge, John D. Italian Harpsichord-building in the 16th
and 17th Century. (Paper 15.) Washington, D.C.: Smithsonian, 1960; 1970. 10pp, ill; 13pp, ill, bib

8516 Steinert, Morris, 1831-1912. The M. Steinert Collection of
Keyed and Stringed Instruments. A catalogue with various
treatises on the history of the instruments. (World's
Columbian Exposition, 1893.) New York: C. F. Tretbar,
1893. 170pp, ill

8517 Stephen, James L., comp. Collections of Catalogues, Drawings, Diagrams, and Descriptions of Pianofortes--English
and foreign, and player pianos. (12 collections in the
British Museum)

8518 Sumner, William Leslie. The Pianoforte. London: Macdonald,
1966; 1967; 3rd ed. with corr. and add. London: Macdonald; New York: St. Martin's Pr, 1971. 223pp, ill, 32
pls, bib

8519 Van Atta, Harrison Louis, ed. A Treatise on the Piano and
Player Piano; explanatory of its principles.... Dayton,
O: Ohio Printing Co, 1914. 151pp, ill, pl DLC

8520 Wier, Albert Ernest. The Piano. Its history, makers,
players and music. London; New York: Longmans, 1940.
467pp, bib

8521 Winternitz, Emanuel. Keyboard Instruments in the Metropolitan Museum of Art; a picture book. New York: 1961.
48pp, ill

PLUCKED STRINGED INSTRUMENTS

Harps

8522 Armstrong, Robert Bruce. Irish and Highland Harps. Introd. by Seoirse Bodley. Edinburgh: D. Douglas, 1904;
facsim. reprint. Shannon: Irish U. Pr. 1969. 199pp,
ill, pls

8523 Hayward, Richard. The Story of the Irish Harp. Belfast,
Ire: Author, 1954; London: A. Guinness, 1954. 24pp,
ill, pls NN

8524 Rensch, Roslyn. The Harp: its history, technique and

repertoire.   London: Duckworth,   1969.   246pp, ill, 40
pls, bib

8525   Thomas, A.   History of the Harp.   London: 1859.   SIB-3

Guitars, Mandolins, etc.

8526   Appleby, Wilfred M.   The Evolution of the Classic Guitar: a
tentative outline.   Cheltenham: International Classic Guitar
Association, 1966.   40pp of ill

8527   Azpiazu, Jose de.   The Guitar and Guitarists from the Beginning to the Present Day.   London: G. Ricordi, 1960.
39pp, ill

8528   Grunfeld, Frederic V.   The Art and Times of the Guitar: an
illustrated history of guitars and guitarists.   New York:
Macmillan; London: Collier-Macmillan, 1969.   340pp, ill,
bib

8529   Gulik, Robert Hans van.   The Lore of the Chinese Lute; an
essay in Ch'in ideology.   Tokyo: Sophia U, 1940.   224pp,
ill, pls, bib

8530   Steinert, Morris.   Catalogue of the Morris Steinert Collection
of Keyed and Stringed Instruments ... exhibited as a loan
collection at the World's Columbian Exposition by its proprietor M. Steinert ... International Exposition for Music
and Theater, Vienna, 1892.   New Haven: Tuttle, Morehouse & Taylor, 1893.

8531   Winder, John Geldart.   J. C. Winder's Illustrated and Descriptive Catalogue of English Made Mandolines, banjoes, guitars, etc.   London: J. G. Winder, 1897.

ORGANS AND FAIRGROUND ORGANS

8532   Armstrong, William H.   Organs for America--the life and
work of David Tannenberg.   Philadelphia: U. of Pa. Pr,
1967.   154pp, 21 pls, bib

8533   The Art Organ; modern aspects of organ building for private
residences, concert halls and churches, with special
reference to the Orgue de Salon, the ideal chamber organ.
Paris; New York: The Art Organ Co, 1907.   44pp, pls

8534   Audsley, George Ashdown.   The Art of Organ-Building; a
comprehensive historical, theoretical and practical treatise
on the tonal appointment and mechanical construction
of concert-room, church, and chamber organs.   2 vol.
in 4.

London: Low, Marston, 1905; 2 vol. New York: Dodd,
Mead, 1905. text, many ill, 15 pls

8535   Azevedo, Carlos de. Baroque Organ-Cases of Portugal. Amsterdam: Uitgeverij Frits Knuf, 1972. 130pp, ill, bib

8536   Barnes, William Harrison, and Edward B. Gammons. Two
Centuries of American Organ Building; "from tracker to
tracker." Glen Rock, NJ: J. Fischer, 1970. 142pp, ill

8537   Beaumont, Anthony. Fair Organs; 50 pictures. Hemel Hempstead: Model Aeronautical Pr, 1968. 6pp, 56pp of ill
(A mechanical instrument)

8538   Boston, Noel, and Lyndesay G. Langwill. Church and Chamber
Barrel-Organs. Their origin, makers, music and location;
a chapter in English church music. Edinburgh: L. G.
Langwill, 1967; 2nd rev. ed. enl. by Langwill. 1970.
120pp, ill; 125pp, ill

8539   Clutton, Cecil, and George Dixon. The Organ; its tonal structure and registration. London: Grenville, 1950. 172pp,
bib

8540   _____, and Austin Niland. The British Organ. London:
Batsford, 1963. 320pp, ill, bib

8541   Cockayne, Eric Victor. The Fair Organ: how it works: an
introduction to the mechanical organ of the fairground.
Manchester, Eng: Fair Organ Preservation Society, 1967.
40pp, ill

8542   _____. The Fairground Organ: its music, mechanism and
history. Appendix by Ronald Leach. Newton Abbot: David
& Charles, 1970. 239pp, ill, bib

8543   Elvin, Laurence. Forster & Andrew: organ builders, 1843-
1956. A chapter in English organ building. Fore. by
W. L. Sumner. Lincoln, Eng: L. Elvin, 1968. 78pp,
ill, 16 pls

8544. Engel, David Hermann, 1816-1877. Remarks on the State of
the Art of Organ-Building. Tr. from German by David
Hamilton. London: Addison, 1856. 20pp NN

8545   Fesperman, John T. A Snetzler Chamber Organ of 1761.
Washington, D.C.: Smithsonian, 1970. 56pp, ill, pls

8546   Freeman, Andrew. Church Organs and Organ Cases. London:
S.P.C.K., 1942. 32pp, pls DLC

8547   _____. English Organ-Cases. London: G. A. Mate & Son,
1921. 132pp, ill, 47 pls MB, NN

8548   . Father Smith, otherwise Bernard Schmidt, being
an account of a 17th century organ maker. Prologue by
M. R. James. London: Office of "Musical Opinion,"
1926. 80pp, pls, bib (Schmidt, 1630?-1708) CU, NN

8549 Gellerman, Robert F. The American Reed Organ, its history,
restorations, and tuning with descriptions of some outstanding collections, including a stop dictionary and a
directory.... New Haven, Conn: Edgewood Pr, 19- ;
Vestal, NY: Vestal Pr, 1973. 173pp, ill, bib

8550 Goodrich, Wallace. The Organ in France: a study of its
mechanical construction, tonal characteristics and literature. Boston: Boston Music Co, 1917. 168pp, ill

8551 Haacke, Walter, photographer. Organs of the World. Tr.
from German by Marcus Wells. London: Allen & Unwin,
1966. 112pp of ill

8552 Hill, Arthur George. Organ Cases and Organs of the Middle
Ages and Renaissance; the art archaeology of the organ.
2 vol. London: D. Bogue, 1883-1891. 134pp; 102pp;
39 pls NN

8553 Hopkins, Edward John, and Edward Francis Rimbault. The
Organ, Its History and Construction. A comprehensive
treatise on the structure and capabilities of the organ ...
with an entirely new history of the organ, memoirs of the
most eminent builders of the 17th and 18th centuries, and
other matters of research.... London: R. Cocks; New
York: H. Balliere, 1855; 1870; 1877; reprint with new
pref. and corrections by William Leslie Sumner. London:
McDonald, 1973. 112 and 596pp, ill; ...; ...; 796pp,
180 ill, 1 folding pl

8554 Matthews, Enid Noel. Colonial Organs and Organbuilders.
Carlton, Victoria, Australia: Melbourne U. Pr, 1969.
277pp, ill

8555 Michel, Norman Elwood. Michel's Organ Atlas; organs,
melodeons, harmoniums, church organs, lap organs,
barrel organs. Pico Rivera, Cal: Author, 1969. 128pp,
ill

8556 Norbury, John. The Box of Whistles: an illustrated book on
organ cases, with notes on organs at home and abroad.
London: Bradbury, Agnew, 1877; 1878. 32pp, 20 color
pls BM, DLC

8557 Organ Parade. Manchester: Fair Organ Preservation Society, 1973. 108pp, chiefly ill (Fairground organs)

8558 Organs, Rides and Engines on Parade. 2 vol. Manchester,

Eng: Fair Organ Preservation Society, 19?-1972. ill; 40pp of ill

8559 Perkins, Jocelyn Henry Temple. The Organs and Bells of Westminster Abbey. London: Novello, 1937. 109pp, ill

8560 Perrot, Jean. The Organ, from Its Invention in the Hellenistic Period to the End of the 13th Century. Tr. from French by Norma Deane. London; New York: Oxford U. Pr, 1971. 317pp, ill, 28 pls

8561 Rimbault, Edward Francis. The Early English Organ Builders and Their Works, from the 15th century to the period of the Great Rebellion; an unwritten chapter in the history of the organ. London: 1865; ... a Lecture. London: William Reeves, 1925? ; 111pp, 1 pl BM

8562 _____. The Organ, Its History and Construction. n. p. (London?): 1855; 1870; 1887. BM

8563 Sayer, Michael. Samuel Renn: English Organ Builder. London: Phillimore, 1974. 133pp, ill

8564 *Sumner, William Leslie. The Organ: its evolution, principles of construction and use. London: Macdonald, 1952; 1955; 3rd rev. ed. New York: Philosophical Library; London: 1962. 466pp, ill, 24 pls, bib; ...; 544pp, ill, 35 pls, bib

8565 Wedgwood, James Ingall. Some Continental Organs (Ancient and Modern) and Their Makers, with specifications of many ... fine examples in Germany and Switzerland. London: William Reeves, 1910. 69pp BM

8566 Whitworth, Reginald. The Electric Organ, a historical introduction and a comprehensive description of modern usage of electricity in organ building.... London: "Musical Opinion," 1930. 202pp, 92 ill, 8 pls

8567 Williams, Charles Francis Abdy. The Story of the Organ. London: W. Scott; New York: Scribner's, 1903; reprint. Detroit: Singing Tree Pr, 1972. 327pp, ill, pls, bib

8568 Williams, Peter Fredric. The European Organ, 1450-1850. London: Batsford, 1966. 336pp, ill, 54 pls, bib

8569 *Wilson, Michael. The English Chamber Organ: History and Development, 1650-1850. Fore. by W. L. Sumner. Oxford: Cassirer; Columbia, SC: U. of South Carolina Pr, 1968. 148pp, ill, 43 pls, bib

BOWED INSTRUMENTS

8570 Bachmann, Alberto Abraham. An Encyclopedia of the Violin.
      Introd. by Eugene Ysaye. Tr. by F. H. Martens. Ed.
      by Albert Wier. New York; London: Appleton, 1925;
      1926; New York: 1937; reprint with new pref. by Stuart
      Canin. New York: Da Capo Pr, 1966. 470pp, ill, color
      pls, bib NN, DLC

8571 Bachmann, Werner. The Origins of Bowing and the Develop-
      ment of Bowed Instruments up to the 13th Century. Tr.
      from German by Norma Deane. London: Oxford U. Pr,
      1969. 178pp, ill, 41 pls

8572 Balfour, Henry. The Natural History of the Musical Bow: a
      chapter in the developmental history of stringed instru-
      ments of music. Oxford: Clarendon, 1899. 87pp (Primi-
      tive stringed instruments) NN, BM

8573 Broadhouse, John. Facts about Fiddles, Violins, Old and
      New. London: William Reeves, 1879; 3rd ed. 1889; 4th
      ed. enl. 1890. 20pp; ...; 24pp PP, NN, BM

8574 Broadley, Arthur. The Violincello: its history, selection
      and adjustment. London: H. Marshall; New York: Scrib-
      ner's, 1921. 111pp, pls TxU, NN

8575 Clarke, A. Mason. The Violin and Old Violin Makers. Being
      an historical and biographical account of the violin. With
      facsimiles of labels of the old makers. London: W.
      Reeves, 1910. 120pp, ill DLC

8576 *Doring, Ernest N. How Many Strads? Our heritage from the
      master. A tribute to the memory of a great genius....
      Being a tabulation of works believed to survive produced
      in Cremona by Antonio Stradivari between 1666 and 1737
      including relevant data ... of his two sons Francesco and
      Omobono. Chicago: William Lewis, 1945. 379pp, ill

8577 Edgerly, Beatrice. From the Hunter's Bow. The history and
      romance of musical instruments. New York: Putnam's,
      1941; 2nd ed. 1942. 491pp, ill, bib

8578 Engel, Carl. Researches into the Early History of the Violin
      Family. London: Novello, Ewer; Boston: Ditson, 1883.
      168pp, ill CU, DLC

8579 Farga, Franz. Violins and Violinists. Tr. from German
      (1940) by Egon Larsen. Chapter on English violin-makers,
      by E. W. Lavender. London: Rockliff; New York: Mac-
      millan, 1950; 1951; 1955. 223pp, ill

8580 Fetis, Francois Joseph, 1784-1871. Notice of Antonio

Stradivarius, the celebrated violin-maker: preceded by historical and critical researches on the origin and transformation of bow instruments. Tr. by J. Bishop. London: R. Cocks, 1864; London: William Reeves, 192-?; 194-? 132pp, ill (Stradivarius, 1644-1737) NN, BM

8581 Fleming, James M., 1839- . The Fiddle Fancier's Guide, a manual of information regarding violins, violas, basses and bows of classical and modern times.... London: Haynes, Foucher, 1892. 310pp, ill, 10 pls CU, NN, DLC

8582 _____. Old Violins and Their Makers, including some references to those of modern times. London: L. Upcott Gill, 1883; 1886; 1890; 1897. 331pp, ill, list of makers English and foreign (Illustrations include sound holes, violin tickets, etc.) MiU, DLC, MB

8583 Foucher, Georges. Treatise on the History and Construction of the Violin, etc. London: E. Shore, 1894; rev. ed. 1897; new and rev. ed. London: Haynes, 1899. 82pp PP, DLC

8584 Freeman, Jay C. All About the Violin, the king of instruments. Chicago: E. T. Root, 1889. 12pp

8585 Goffrie, Charles. The Violin: a condensed history of the violin. Its perfection and its famous makers. Philadelphia: G. Andre, 1876; 1879. 32pp DLC

8586 Goodkind, Herbert K. Violin Iconography of Antonio Stradivari, 1644-1737; treatises on the life and work of the patriarch of the violin-makers. Inventory of 700 known or recorded Stradivari string instruments. Index of 3,500 names of past or present Stradivari owners. Photographs of 400 Stradivari instruments with 1500 views. Larchmont, NY: 1972. 780pp, ill, bib

8587 Hamma, Fridolin. German Violin Makers: a critical dictionary of German Violin makers, with a series of plates illustrating characteristic and fine examples of their work. Tr. from German (1948) by Walter Stewart. London: William Reeves, 1961. 51pp, 78 pls

8588 Hart, George, violin maker. The Violin; its famous makers and their imitators. Philadelphia: n.d.; London: Dulau, 1875; New York: Bouton, 1876; ...; with additions by author's son and Towry Piper. London: Dulau, 1909. ...; 184pp, ill, 24 pls; 310pp, ill, pls; ...; 526pp, ill, pls BM, PP

8589 Hayes, Gerald Ravenscourt. Musical Instruments and Their

Music, 1500-1750. Vol. I. London: H. Milford, Oxford
U. Pr, 1928- . ill, 11 pls, bib NN, ViU, MB

8590 Hill, William Henry, Arthur F. Hill, and Alfred E. Hill.
Antonio Stradivari, his life and work (1644-1737). London: W. E. Hill, 1902. 303pp, ill, 30 pls DLC

8591 _____, _____, and _____. The Violin Makers of
the Guarneri Family: 1626-1762, their life and work.
Introd. by Edward Dent. London: W. E. Hill, 1931.
181pp, ill, 60 pls (some color)

8592 Jalovec, Karel. Beautiful Italian Violins. Tr. by J. B.
Kozak. London: Hamlyn, 1964. 111pp, ill (1650-1850)

8593 _____. German and Austrian Violin-Makers. Tr. from
Czech by George Theiner. Ed. by Patrick Hanks. London: Hamlyn, 1967. 439pp, 800 ill, 16 pls

8594 * _____. Italian Violin Makers. Prague: Orbis; Cambridge,
Eng: Heffer, 1952; London: Anglo-Italian Publications,
1958; rev. ed. London: P. Hamlyn, 1964. 656pp, ill;
440pp, 32 pls, bib (1,850 specimens)

8595 _____. The Violin Makers of Bohemia, including craftsmen of Moravia and Slovakia. London: Anglo-Italian
Publications, 1960. 128pp, ill

8596 Lachmann, Erich. Erich Lachmann Collection of Historical
Stringed Musical Instruments. Los Angeles: U. of
Southern California, Allan Hancock Foundation, 1950.
53pp, chiefly ill

8597 Lyon and Healy, firm. Catalogue of the Lyon and Healy Collection of Rare Old Violins, violas, and violoncellos (!),
also bows of rare makes. Chicago: Lyon & Healy, 1892;
...; 35th ed. 1929. 110pp, ill, 6 pls; ...; 122pp, ill

8598 _____. The (Royal De Forest) Hawley Collection of Violins;
with a history of their makers and a brief review of the
evolution and decline of the art of violin-making in Italy,
1540-1800. Chicago: 1904. 105pp, 36 pls (part color)
ViU, MiU

8599 Moeller, Max, the Younger. The Violin-Makers of the Low
Countries--Belgium and Holland. Amsterdam: Author,
1955. 165pp, ill

8600 Morris, Reverend William Meredith. British Violin-Makers,
classical and modern. London: 1904; 2nd ed. 1920. ill,
33 pls V & A

8601   Oakes, William W.   A Review of Ancient and Modern Violin
       Making.   Seattle: Metropolitan Printing, 1899.   113pp,
       pls   DLC

8602   Retford, William Charles.   Bows and Bow Makers.   London:
       Strad, 1964.   86pp, ill

8603   *Sandys, William, 1792-1874, and Simon Andrew Forster, 1801-
       1870.   History of Violins and Other Instruments Played on
       the Bow from the Remotest Times to the Present, also an
       account of the principal makers, English and foreign.   Lon-
       don: John Russell Smith, 1864.   390pp, ill, 2 pls, color
       frontis   ViU, BM

8604   Stainer, Miss Cecie.   A Dictionary of Violin Makers, com-
       piled from the best authorities.   London: Novello, 1896;
       rev. ed. 190-?   ; 102pp, bib

WIND INSTRUMENTS

8605   Badger, Alfred G.   Illustrated History of the Flute ... with
       a description of the new or Boehm flute.   New York:
       Firth, Pond; Boston: O. Ditson, 1853; New York: 1854;
       reprint of 2nd ed. New York: G. W. Averell, 1861.
       48pp, ill; 54pp, ill; 50pp, ill   BM

8606   Baines, Anthony Cuthbert.   Bagpipes.   Oxford, Eng: Pitt-
       Rivers Museum, 1960.   140pp, ill, 16 pls, bib

8607   .   Woodwind Instruments and Their History.   Fore.
       by Sir Adrian Boult.   London: Faber, 1957; 1962; 3rd
       ed. 1967.   384pp, 79 ill, 32 pls, bib

8608   Balfour, Henry.   The Old British "Pibcorn" or "Hornpipe,"
       and its affinities.   Reprint from the Journal Anthropologi-
       cal Institute, Vol. XX.   London: Harrison & Sons, 1890.
       13pp, pls   MH

8609   Bate, Philip.   The Flute: a Study of Its History, Develop-
       ment and Construction.   London: Benn; New York: W.
       W. Norton, 1969.   268pp, ill, 23 pls, bib

8610   .   The Oboe: outline of its history, development and
       construction.   London: Benn; New York: Philosophical
       Library, 1956; 2nd rev. ed. 1962.   195pp, ill, bib

8611   .   The Trumpet and Trombone: an outline of their
       history, development and construction.   London: Benn;
       New York: Norton, 1966; 2nd ed. 1972.   272pp, ill, 18
       pls, bib; 272pp, ill, 32 pls, bib

8612   Bonner, Stephen, ed. Aeolean Harp. I. Design and Con-
       struction, by Jonathan Mansfield; II. History and Organology,
       by Stephen Bonner; Aeolian Harp in European Literature,
       1591-1892, by Andrew Brown. 3 vol. Cambridge, Eng:
       Bois de Boulogne, 1968, 1968, 1970. 37pp, ill, facsims,
       bib; 94pp, ill, 8 pls, bib; 93pp, ill

8613   Carse, Adam von Ahn. Musical Wind Instruments. A history
       of the wind instruments used in European orchestras and
       wind-bands from the later Middle Ages up to the present
       time.... London: Macmillan, 1939. 381pp, ill, 30 pls
       of 183 instruments, bib   MB, BN, DLC

8614   _____. A List of Instruments in the Adam Carse Collec-
       tion of Musical Wind Instruments. Horniman Museum and
       Library. London: 1947. 16pp   DLC

8615   _____. The Adam Carse Collection of Old Musical Wind
       Instruments. Horniman Museum and Library. London:
       County Council, 1951. 88pp, ill   BM

8616   Collinson, Francis. The Bagpipe: The History of a Musical
       Instrument. London: Routledge & K. Paul, 1975. 257pp,
       ill, 16pp of pls, bib

8617   Daubeny, Ulric. Orchestral Wind Instruments, Ancient and
       Modern; being an account of the origin and evolution of
       wind instruments from the earliest to the most recent
       times. London: William Reeves, 1919; reprint. Freeport,
       NY: Books for Libraries Pr, 1970. 147pp, ill, 10 pls,
       bib

8618   Eliason, Robert E. Graves and Company, Musical Instru-
       ment Makers. Dearborn, Mich: Henry Ford Museum,
       1975. 21pp, ill

8619   _____. Keyed Bugles in the United States. Washington,
       D.C.: Smithsonian, 1972. 44pp, ill

8620   Fitzpatrick, Horace. The Horn and Horn-playing, and the
       Austro-Bohemian tradition from 1680 to 1830. London:
       Oxford U. Pr, 1970. 256pp, ill, 17 pls, bib

8621   Fox, Lilla Margaret. Instruments of Processional Music.
       London: Lutterworth Pr, 1967. 127pp, ill

8622   Langwill, Lyndesay Graham. The Bassoon and Double Bas-
       soon; a short history of their origin, development and
       makers. London: Hinrichsen, 1948; 1955. 40pp, ill,
       bib

8623   _____. The Curtal (1550-1750), a chapter in the evolution

of the bassoon. Reprint from Musical Times. London:
1937. 7pp, ill DLC

8624   . List of Some 1800 Wood-wind and Brass Instrument-
makers and Inventors. Edinburgh: Author, 1941-43; as
Index of Musical Wind-Instrument Makers. Edinburgh:
Author, 1962; 3rd ed. rev., enl. and ill. 1972. ...; ...;
232pp, ill, bib

8625   . A List of Wind Instrument Makers Arranged Alphabetically under the Towns in Which They Worked. Edinburgh: 1949. 29pp NN

8626   . A 17th Century Wood-Wind Curiosity. Reprint from
Musical Times. London: 1938. 2pp, ill DLC

8627   . A Short History of the Bassoon. Reprint from
Musical Progress and Mail. n. p. (London?): 1939. 4pp,
ill DLC

8628 A List of Instruments Included in the Adam Carse Collection
of Musical Wind Instruments. London: Horniman Museum,
1947. 16pp

8629 Morley-Pegge, Reginald Frederick. The French Horn; some
notes on the evolution of the instrument and its technique.
New York: Philosophical Library; London: Benn, 1960;
2nd ed. 1973. 222pp, ill, 8 pls, bib; 2nd ed: 17 pls

8630 Rendall, Francis Geoffrey. The Clarinet: some notes upon
its history and construction. London: Williams & Nor-
gate; New York: Philosophical Library, 1954; rev. 2nd
ed. London: Benn, 1957. 184pp, ill, bib

8631 Ridley, E. A. K. The Ridley Collection of Musical Wind
Instruments in Luton Museum and Art Gallery. A history
and catalog. Luton, Bedfordshire: Public Museum, 1957.
32pp, ill, 8 pls

BELLS AND CHURCH BELLS

8632 Andrews, William, 1848-1908. History of Bells. Paisley:
1885. bib NRB

8633 Anthony, Dorothy Malone. The World of Bells. 2 vol. Des
Moines: Wallace-Homestead, 1971, 1974. 49pp each, ill,
color pls (Porcelain, glass, silver, brass, etc.)

8634 Beamont, William. A Chapter on Bells, and inscriptions
upon some of them. Warrington, Eng: Pease, 1888.
43pp MB

8635   Beckett, Sir Edmund. Lectures on Church-building: with
        some practical remarks on bells and clocks. By Edmund
        Beckett Denison. 2nd ed. enl. London: Bell & Daldy,
        1856. 309pp, ill, pls NN, MdBP

8636   _____. A Rudimentary Treatise on Clocks, Watches and
        Bells for Public Purposes. Mostly reprinted from 7th,
        1883, ed. New preface and new list of great bells, and
        an appendix on weathercocks. 8th ed. London: Crosby,
        Lockwood, 1903; facsim. reprint. Wakefield, Eng: EP
        Publishing, 1974. 404pp, ill

8637   Bells and Carillons. A scrapbook, compiled by the Music
        Department. Boston: Boston Public Library, 1942.
        111pp, ill, bib

8638   Benson, George. The Bells of the Ancient Churches of
        York. York, Eng: W. Pickwell, 1885. 16 pls BM

8639   Briscoe, John Potter. Curiosities of the Belfry. London:
        Hamilton, Adams, 1883. 156pp, 12 ill (some by Cruik-
        shank) (Bells)

8640   Caulfeild, Sophia Frances Anne. House Mottoes and Inscrip-
        tions. London: E. Stock, 1902. 146pp, ill (Sun dials,
        posie rings, bells, etc.)

8641   Cheetham, Frank Halliday. The Church Bells of Lancashire.
        4 parts. Manchester, Eng: Richard Gill, Sherratt &
        Hughes, 1915-21.

8642   Cocks, Alfred Heneage. The Church Bells of Buckingham-
        shire. Their inscriptions, founders, users and traditions.
        London: Jarrold, 1897. 760pp, ill, 33 pls, bib NN,
        DLC

8643   Colchester, Walter Edmund. Hampshire Church Bells: their
        founders and inscriptions. Winchester, Eng: 1920. 116pp

8644   *Coleman, Satis Narrona Barton. Bells; their history, legends,
        making and uses. Fore. by Otis W. Caldwell. New
        York; Chicago: Rand McNally, 1928; Chicago: Rand Mc-
        Nally; Detroit: Tower, 1971; Westport, Conn: Greenwood
        Pr, 1971. 462pp, ill, bib

8645   Descriptive Souvenir of the Columbian Liberty Bell and Silver
        Model of United States Treasury Building. World's Colum-
        bian Exposition, 1893. Chicago: W. B. Conkey, 1893.
        20pp DLC

8646   Designs, Priced, for Bells, Cranks, Screws, and Other Domes-
        tic and General Tools, etc., by Denison(?). London:
        1770? SKM

8647 Downman, Edward Andrews. Ancient Church Bells in England; their inscriptions, founders' trade marks, and measurements, together with some notice of the early bell founders. Advance ed. Wickford?, Essex: 1898; 2nd ed. Laindon, Essex: Author, 1899. 226pp, ill BM, CU, MH, NN

8648 Dunkin, Edwin Hadlow Wise. The Church Bells of Cornwall. Their archaeology and present condition. London; Derby: Bemrose, 1898. 94pp, ill, 3 pls NN, BM

8649 Eeles, Francis Carolus. The Church and Other Bells of Kincardineshire. Being a complete account of all the bells in the county, their history, uses, and ornaments; with notices of their founders, and an article on the more interesting belfries. To which is prefixed a short general survey of bells in Scotland. Aberdeen: W. Jolly; London: E. Stock, 1897. 50pp, pls DLC

8650 _____. The Church Bells of Linlithgowshire. Edinburgh: J. Orr, 1913. 34pp, ill NN

8651 Ellacombe, Henry Thomas, 1790-1885. The Bells of the Cathedral Church at St. Peter, Exon. Exeter: William Pollard, for Author, 1874. 40pp, ill PP

8652 _____. The Church Bells of Devon: with a list of those in Cornwall, to which is added a supplement on various matters relating to the "Bells of the Church." 2 vol. in 1. Exeter: W. Pollard, for Author, 1872. ill, 36 (1 color) pls, bib DLC, NN

8653 _____. Church Bells of Gloucestershire. Exeter: W. Pollard, for Author, 1881. 207pp, ill, 10 pls DLC

8654 _____. The Church Bells of Somerset, to which is added an Olla Podrida of bell matters of general interest. Exeter: W. Pollard, for Author, 1875. 148pp, ill, 14 pls DLC

8655 Gatty, Alfred, 1813-1903. The Bell: its origin, history and uses. London: George Ball, 1847; 1848. 47pp, frontis; 117pp, ill BM

8656 Goss, Elbridge Henry. Early Bells of Massachusetts. Reprint from Historical and Geneological Register, April and July 1874. Boston: D. Clapp, printer, 1874. 34pp BM, DLC

8657 Hatch, Eric. The Little Book of Bells. Sketches by Eric Sloane. New York: Duell, Sloan & Pearce, 1964. 85pp, ill

8658 Hotchkiss, Justus Street. Bells. A paper read before the

New Haven Colony Historical Society, December 1888.
New Haven: Tuttle, Morehouse & Taylor, printers, 1889.
25pp CtY

8659 Jennings, Trevor Stanley. A History of Staffordshire Bells.
      London: Author, 1968. 119pp

8660 L'Estrange, John, 1836-1877. The Church Bells of Norfolk;
      where, when, and by whom they were made: with the
      inscriptions on all the bells in the county. Norwich, Eng:
      Miller & Leavins, 1874. 255pp, many ill MdBP

8661 Llewellins and James, Bristol. Bells and Bellfounding, a
      practical treatise upon church bells, by X-Y-Z. Bristol:
      J. W. Arrowsmith, 1879; reprint. Bath, Eng: Kings-
      mead Reprints, 196-? 57pp, ill

8662 Lomax, Benjamin. Bells and Bellringers. London: H. J.
      Infield, 1879. 119pp

8663 Lukis, William C(ollings), 1817-1892. An Account of Church
      Bells with Some Notices of Wiltshire Bells and Bell-
      Founders ... and inscriptions from nearly 500 parishes
      in various parts of the Kingdom. London; Oxford: J. H.
      Parker, 1857. text, 7 pls, bib by H. T. Ellacombe

8664 Madge, Sidney Joseph. Moulton Church and Its Bells, with
      a complete summary of the bells in the several parishes
      of Northamptonshire; also a comprehensive bibliography
      on "bells." London: E. Stock, 1895. 98pp, ill, bib
      MB, TxU

8665 Meyer, Adolph C. Bell Collectors of America; some recent
      additions to the pamphlet, "A Selected Number of Bells
      and Gongs,".... St. Louis, Mo: 194-? 20pp, ill, bib

8666 _____ . A Selected Number of Bells and Gongs from the
      Collection of Mr. and Mrs. A. C. Meyer. St. Louis?:
      194-? 23pp, ill

8667 _____ . Travel Search for Bells. Chicago: Lightner,
      1944. 197pp, ill, pls NN

8668 Morris, Ernest. Bells of All Nations. London: Hale, 1951.
      212pp, ill, bib, music

8669 _____ . Tintinnabula. Small bells, etc. London: Robert
      Hale, 1959. 175pp, ill, 20 pls (Handbells, animal bells,
      non-metallic, etc.)

8670 _____ . Towers and Bells of Britain. London: Hale,
      1955. 270pp, ill (Church bells)

8671   Nichols, Arthur Howard. The Bells of Harvard College. Boston: Clapp & Son, 1911. 11pp, pls

8672   . (Revere Bells). Bells of Paul and Joseph W. Revere. Boston: 1911. 40pp, pls (Paul Revere, 1735-1818; Joseph Revere, 1777-1868)

8673   . Christ Church Bells. Boston: 1904. 11pp, pl DLC

8674   . Early Bells of Paul Revere. Boston: 1904. 9pp, ill DLC

8675   Nichols, John Roberts. Bells Thro' the Ages. The founders' craft and ringers' art. London: Chapman & Hall, 1928. 320pp, ill, pls BM, DLC

8676   North, Thomas, 1830-1884. Church Bells of Bedfordshire; their founders, inscriptions, traditions, and peculiar uses; with a brief history of bells in that county. London: E. Stock, 1883. 217pp, ill

8677   . Church Bells of Hertfordshire; their founders, inscriptions, traditions.... London: E. Stock, 1886. 252pp, ill

8678   . The Church Bells of Northamptonshire ... with chapters on bells and the Northants Bell Founders. Leicester: S. Clarke, 1878. 471pp, ill

8679   . The Church Bells of Rutland.... Leicester, Eng: S. Clarke, 1880. 172pp, ill, 7 pls DLC

8680   . The Church Bells of the County and City of London.... Leicester: S. Clarke, 1882. 780pp, ill, 28 pls DLC

8681   . English Bells and Bell Lore. A book on bells by the late Thomas North, ed. by Reverend William Beresford. Leek: W. H. Eaton, printer, 1888. 206pp, ill DLC

8682   Owen, Reverend Theodore Montague Nugent. The Church Bells of Huntingtonshire, their inscriptions, founders, uses, traditions.... London: Jarrold & Sons, 1899. 154pp, ill DLC

8683   Park, G. R. The Church Bells of Holderness. London: 1898. 83pp

8684   Perkins, Jocelyn Henry Temple. The Organs and Bells of Westminster Abbey. London: Novello, 1937. 109pp, ill

8685   Raven, John James. The Bells of England. Northampton?:
       1904; London: Methuen, 1906. 338pp, ill, pls BM

8686   _____. Church Bells of Cambridgeshire ... with a list of
       inscriptions. Lowestoft: S. Tymms, 1869; 2nd ed. with
       a supplement. Cambridge: Antiquarian Society, 1881-82.
       36pp, pls; 220pp, ill, pls BM

8687   _____. The Church Bells of Suffolk ... list of inscriptions
       and historical notes. London: Jarrold, 1890. 266pp, ill,
       8 pls BM

8688   Rosewater, Victor. The Liberty Bell. Its history and sig-
       nificance. New York; London: D. Appleton, 1926. 246pp,
       pls, bib

8689   Sharpe, Frederick. The Church Bells of Berkshire: their
       inscriptions and founders, arranged alphabetically by
       parishes. Reprint from Berkshire Archaeological Journal,
       1939-1957. Fore. by Bishop of Oxford. Bath, Eng:
       Kingsmead Reprints, 1970. 404pp, ill, 64 pls

8690   _____. The Church Bells of Guernsey, Aldernay and Sark;
       their inscriptions and founders. With notes on the medie-
       val Exeter foundry by John G. M. Scott. Brockley, Eng:
       Smart, 1964. 78pp, ill

8691   _____. The Church Bells of Herefordshire, Oxfordshire,
       Radnorshire ... their inscriptions and founders. 4 vol.
       Launton, Oxon: Author, 1946-195-? 592pp, ill, bib

8692   Sloane, Eric. The Sound of Bells. Garden City, NY: Double-
       day, 1966. 58pp, ill

8693   Springer, L. Elsinore. The Collector's Book of Bells. New
       York: Crown, 1972. 244pp, 450 ill, bib

8694   Stahlschmidt, J. C. L. Church Bells of Kent: their inscrip-
       tions, founders, uses, and traditions. London: E. Stock,
       1887. 455pp, ill, 4 pls

8695   _____. Surrey Bells and London Bell Founders. A con-
       tribution to the comparative study of bell inscriptions.
       London: E. Stock, 1884. 230pp, ill, 15 pls

8696   Stoudt, John Baer, 1878- . The Liberty Bells of Pennsyl-
       vania; presented to the Pennsylvania-German Society....
       Norristown, Pa: Norristown Pr, 1930. 204pp, ill

8697   Tyack, George Smith. A Book About Bells. London: W.
       Andrews, 1898; reprint. Ann Arbor, Mich: Gryphon
       Books, 1971. 307pp, ill, pls

8698   Tyssen, Amherst Daniel, 1843-1930. The Church Bells of
        Sussex. Lewes: Farncombe, 1915. 215pp

8699   Walters, Henry Beauchamp. Church Bells. London: A. R.
        Mowbray, 1908. 160pp, 39 ill, pl

8700   _____. Church Bells of England. London: H. Frowde,
        1912. 400pp, pls, color frontis, bib, list of bell-founders
        DLC

8701   _____. The Church Bells of Shropshire. London: Shrews-
        bury, 1902-11; Cardiff: U. of Wales, 1915. 482pp, ill,
        26 pls

8702   _____. The Church Bells of Somerset. Taunton, Eng:
        1920. ill

8703   _____. The Church Bells of Wiltshire: their inscriptions
        and history. 3 parts. Devizes: Wiltshire Archaeological
        Society, 1927-29; facsimile reprint. Bath, Eng: Kings-
        mead Reprints, 1969. 350pp, ill, pls

8704   _____. The Church Bells of Worcestershire: their in-
        scriptions and history. Worcester, Eng: 1925. ill

8705   _____. The Gloucestershire Bell-Foundries. Bristol: J.
        W. Arrowsmith, 1912. 10pp

8706   _____. London Church Bells and Bell-Founders. London:
        Harrison, 1907.

8707   _____. Some Notes on Worcestershire Bell-Founders.
        London: Harrison, 1906.

8708   _____. Some 13th-Century English Bells. n. p.: 1926.

MUSIC BOXES AND MECHANICAL INSTRUMENTS

8709   Bowers, Q. David. Encyclopedia of Automatic Musical Instru-
        ments. Including a dictionary of automatic musical instru-
        ment terms. Vestal, NY: Vestal Pr, 1967; 1972. 1008pp,
        ill

8710   _____. Put Another Nickel In. A history of coin-operated
        pianos and orchestrions. Vestal, NY: Vestal Pr, 1966;
        New York: Bonanza-Crown, 197-? 248pp, 500 ill, many
        facsims

8711   _____. A Tune for a Token. Thiensville, Wisc: Token
        and Medal Society, 1975. 80pp, ill (Tokens to operate
        nickelodeons, music boxes, etc.)

8712 Buchner, Alexandr. Mechanical Musical Instruments. Tr.
        by Iris Urwin. London: Batchworth Pr, 1959; New York:
        Tudor, 1960. 110pp, ill, 174 pls, bib

8713 Bulletin of the Musical Box Society International (U.S.A.).
        n. p.: 1965- .

8714 Catalog of Timepieces. Exeter, NH: Adams Brown, 1969.
        60pp, ill (Tools, music boxes, clocks, barometers, etc.)

8715 *Clark, John Ernest Thomas. Musical Boxes. Birmingham,
        Eng: Cornish Brothers, 1948; as Musical Boxes; a history
        and an appreciation. London: Fountain Pr, 1952; 3rd ed.
        London: Allen & Unwin, 1961. 72pp, pls; 236pp, ill, pls;
        264pp, ill, 24 pls, bib

8716 De Waard, Romke. From Music Boxes to Street Organs. Tr.
        from Dutch by Wade Jenkins. Vestal, NY: Vestal Pr,
        1967. 264pp, ill

8717 Fallis, David. Music Boxes: A Guide for Collectors. New
        York: Stein & Day, 1971. 143pp, ill, bib, gloss

8718 Givens, Larry. Re-enacting the Artist; a story of the Ampico
        Reproducing Piano. Vestal, NY: Vestal Pr, 1970. 136pp,
        ill

8719 Hoke, Helen, and John Hoke. Music Boxes, Their Lore and
        Lure; a book that tells their story--how they began in bell
        towers and moved into clocks and watches and snuff boxes--
        their whole bright history and their present renaissance.
        New York: Hawthorn, 1957. 94pp, ill, phonodisc in pocket

8720 Hoover, Cynthia A. Music Machines--American Style; a cata-
        logue of the exhibition. Introductory notes by Erik Barnouw
        and Irving Kolodin. Washington, D.C.: Smithsonian Insti-
        tution Pr, for the National Museum of History and Tech-
        nology, 1971. 139pp, ill

8721 Karshner, Roger. The Music Machine. Los Angeles, Cal:
        Nash, 1971. 196pp, ill

8722 Mosoriak, Roy. The Curious History of Music Boxes. Chi-
        cago: Lightner, 1943. 242pp, ill, bib PP

8723 The Music Box--Journal of the Musical Box Society of Great
        Britain. Periodical. London: 1962- .

8724 Music Boxes. Symphonion and polyphone, 1894-95. Catalog
        reprint. Vestal, NY: Vestal Pr, 197-? ill

8725 Music Machines--American Style. Washington, D.C.: GPO,

1971. 139pp, ill (Barrel organs, nickelodeons, phonographs, jukeboxes, etc.)

8726 Nicole Freres Ltd. Music Box Catalogue, 1901. Reprint.
Vestal, NY: Vestal Pr, 197-? 39pp, ill (Regina, Poly-
phon and Harmonia)

8727 Ord-Hume, Arthur Wolfgang J. G. Clockwork Music: an
illustrated history of mechanical musical instruments from
the music box to the pianola from automaton Lady Virginal
Players to orchestrions. New York: Crown; London:
Allen & Unwin, 1973. 334 pp, ill

8728 _____. Collecting Musical Boxes, and How to Repair Them.
London: Allen & Unwin; New York: Crown, 1967. 140pp,
ill, 44 pls, bib

8729 _____. Player Piano: the history of the mechanical piano
and how to repair it. London: Allen & Unwin, 1970; South
Brunswick, NJ: A. S. Barnes, 1971. 296pp, ill, 64pp of
pls

8730 The Regina and the Regina-phone. 1908 catalog reprint. Vestal, NY: Vestal Pr, 197-? 20pp, ill

8731 Regina Music Box Catalog. 190-? Reprint. Vestal, NY:
Vestal Pr, 197-? 16pp, ill (9 disc-type music boxes)

8732 Roehl, Harvey N. Keyes to a Musical Past; player pianos
and music boxes, being an illustrated treatise on the
various types of mechanical musical instruments ... which
have enlightened the spirits of mankind over many decades
... pictures and advertising material.... Vestal, NY:
Vestal Pr, 1968. 48pp, ill

8733 _____, and Marion Roehl. Player Piano Treasury. Vestal,
NY: Vestal Pr, 1961; 1964; 2nd ed. 1973. ill with old
catalog reprints

8734 Seeburg Automatic Pianos. Catalog reprint. Vestal, NY:
Vestal Pr, 197-? ill of 315 coin-operated pianos

8735 The Story of the Music Box; 19 lovely melodies of antique
music boxes from the authentic Brown Collection and a
charmingly illustrated history of the music box. 19th
century originals. New York: Caedmon Records, 196-?
8pp, ill, with phonodisc

8736 Tallis, David. Music Boxes: A Guide for Collectors. New
York: Stein & Day; London: Muller, 1971. 143pp, ill,
color pls, bib, gloss

8737 Templeton, Alec Andrew. Alec Templeton's Music Boxes, as told to Rachael Bail Baumel.   New York: W. Funk; London: Mayflower Publishing, 1958.   164pp, ill, 16 pls

8738   Tiffany and Company.   A Few Remarks Concerning Makers of Singing Bird Boxes of the 18th and 19th Centuries.   New York: Tiffany, 1910.   26pp, pls (Pierre Jaquet-Droz, Henri Louis Jaquet-Droz, Charles Bruguier, etc.)

8739   Webb, Graham.   The Cylinder Musical Box Handbook.   London: Faber, 1969; New York: Farnhill, 1969.   176pp, ill (How to rebuild, restore and collect)

8740   _____.   The Disc Musical Box Handbook.   London: Faber, 1971.   323pp, ill, 20 pls

8741   Welte Orchestrion Catalog.   Reprint.   Vestal, NY: Vestal Pr, 19- .   ill (German firm of M. Welte and Sons)

8742   Wilson, D. Miller.   The "Player Piano;" its construction, how to play--what to play and how to preserve it....   London; New York: Pitman, 1922?   104pp, ill

SECTION XXIII

COMMUNICATION AND IDENTIFICATION

SIGNS AND SIGNBOARDS

8743   Benham, Sir William Gurney. Inn Signs and Their Meaning.
       London: Brewers' Society, 1939. 16 leaves, color ill
       NN

8744   Brainard, Morgan B. Morgan B. Brainard's Tavern Signs:
       a collection. Hartford: Connecticut Historical Society,
       1958. 86pp, chiefly ill NN

8745   Chapin, Howard Millar. Early American Signboards. Provi-
       dence: Rhode Island Historical Society, 1926. 24pp, ill
       DLC, CtY

8746   Christy, Miller. The Trade Signs of Essex: a popular ac-
       count of the origin and meanings of the public house and
       other signs now or formerly found in the county of Essex.
       Chelmsford, Eng: E. Durant; London: Griffith, Farran,
       1887. 184pp, ill, bib MH

8747   A Collection of Drawings of Inn Signs, with newspaper cuttings
       and other relevant historical material, formed by Mr. G.
       Creed. 14 vol. n. p. (London?): 1855? BM

8748   Cornman, Frederick. Some Old London Shope Signes and
       Streete Tablets of the 16th, 17th and 18th Centuries. 1st
       series. London: priv. printed, 1891. 2pp, 40 leaves,
       color ill DLC

8749   _____ . Some Old London Streete Signs. Also facsimiles
       of trademens curious and quaint illustrated advertisements,
       and some notable olde houses of the 17th and 18th cen-
       turies. 3rd series. London: priv. printed, 1900. pls
       MH

8750   Creux, Rene. Old Inn-signs in Switzerland. English adapta-
       tion by R. A. Langford. Zurich: Swiss National Tourist
       Office, 1962. 76pp, chiefly ill

779

8751   Crosby, Everett Uberto. Books and Baskets, Signs and Silver
       of Old-time Nantucket. Nantucket, Mass: Inquirer & Mir-
       ror Pr, printer, 1940. 72pp, ill DLC

8752   Delderfield, Eric R. British Inn Signs and Their Stories.
       Dawlish, Eng: David & Charles, 1965. 160pp, ill

8753   _____ . Introduction to Inn Signs. Newton Abbot: David &
       Charles; New York: Arco, 1969; London: Pan Books,
       1971. 176pp, ill; 142pp, 16 pls

8754   *Endell, Fritz August Gottfried. Old Tavern Signs: an ex-
       cursion in the history of hospitality. Boston: Houghton
       Mifflin, 1916; reprint. Detroit: Singing Tree Pr, 1968.
       303pp, ill, pls, bib

8755   Fletcher, Mark Henry Washington. Inns and Inn Signs of
       Dudley. Netherton, Eng: Author, 1953. 51pp, ill

8756   Fothergill, George Algernon. A North Country Album. Notes
       of the signs and sundials in North Yorkshire and Durham.
       Darlington, Eng: 1901. 126pp

8757   Graham, Frank. North Country Inn Signs. Newcastle-upon-
       Tyne: Author, 1968. 73pp, ill

8758   Hasluck, Paul Nooncree, ed. Glass Writing, Embossing and
       Fascia work; including the making and fixing of wood
       letters and illuminated signs. London; New York: Cas-
       sell; Philadelphia: McKay, 1906; 1907; New York: Funk
       & Wagnals, 192-? 160pp, ill NCorn, NN

8759   Heal, Sir Ambrose. London Shop-Signs, other than those
       given by Larwood and Hotten in their "History of Sign-
       boards,".... London: Batsford?, 1939. 76pp BM

8760   _____ . The Signboards of Old London Shops. A review
       of shop signs employed by the London Tradesmen during
       the 17th and 18th centuries. (Compiled from Author's
       collection of contemporary trade-cards and billboards.)
       London: Batsford, 1947; reprint. New York: B. Blom,
       1972. 220pp, ill BM

8761   Hopkins, Robert Thurston. The Lure of London. (Contains
       portions of author's This London, 1927.) London: C.
       Palmer, 1929. 290pp, ill, pls NN

8762   Inn Signs: Their History and Their Meaning. London: The
       Brewers' Society, 1969. 35pp, chiefly ill

8763   Inwards, Jabez. Pictures of the Traffic; consisting of re-
       marks on public house signs. London: 1851? 34pp BM

8764 Knittle, Rhea Mansfield. Early Ohio Taverns, tavern-sign,
       stage-coach, barge, banner, chair and settee painters.
       Ashland: Calvert-Hatch, 1937. 46pp, bib

8765 Lamb, Cadbury, and Gordon Wright. Discovering Inn Signs.
       Tring: Shire Publications, 1968. 64pp, ill

8766 Larwood, Jacob (pseud. for Herman Diederik Johan Von
       Schevichayen) 1827-1918, and John Camden Hotten, 1832-
       1873. The History of Signboards. London: J. C. Hotten,
       1866; as The History of Signboards, from the earliest
       times to the present day. London: 1866; 1867. 536pp,
       100 ill, 19 pls BM

8767 _____, and _____. English Inn Signs. Being a revised
       and modern version of History of Signboards. Chapter on
       modern inn signs by Gerald Millar. London: Chatto &
       Windus, 1951. 336pp, ill, bib BM

8768 Lillywhite, Bryant. London Signs: a reference book of Lon-
       don Signs from earliest times to about the mid-19th cen-
       tury. London: Allen & Unwin, 1972. 696pp, ill, 25 pls

8769 Lloyd, Llewelyn C. The Inns of Shrewsbury. Their signs
       and their stories. Shrewsbury: priv. printed, 1942.
       65pp, ill

8770 Longman, Charles James, 1852-1934. The House of Longman,
       1724-1800; a bibliographic history with a list of signs used
       by booksellers of that period. Ed., with introd. by John
       E. Chandler. London; New York: Longmans, Green,
       1936. 488pp NN, TU

8771 Meadows, Cecil Austen. Trade Signs and Their Origins.
       London: Routledge & K. Paul, 1957. 177pp, ill, bib

8772 Monson-Fitzjohn, Gilbert John. Quaint Signs of Old Inns.
       London: H. Jenkins, 1926. 157pp, ill

8773 Museum Extension Project. Pennsylvania. Tavern Signs;
       historical backgrounds. Sign boards from Colonial inns
       and taverns. Willow Grove, Pa: WPA, 195-? 37 leaves,
       31 color pls, bib

8774 Norman, Philip, 1842-1931. London Signs and Inscriptions.
       Introd. by Henry B. Wheatley. London: E. Stock, 1893;
       reprint. Detroit: Singing Tree, 1968. 237pp, ill DLC

8775 Patty, C. The Signboards of England. London: Cuthbert Pr,
       1912.

8776 Plumtree, H. Public House Signs. Their history and signifi-
       cance. 1934. 16pp MiGr

8777   Price, Frederick George Hilton. The Signs of Old Lombard
       Street. London: Field & Tuer, 1887; rev. and smaller
       ed. London: Simpkin, Marshall; New York: Scribner's,
       1902. 112 leaves, ill; 207pp, 70 ill (Goldsmiths' signs)

       Schevichayen, Herman Diederik Johan Von. See: Larwood,
       Jacob (pseud.), no. 8766.

8778   Sherlock, Helen Travers. The Rising Sun. A study of inn
       signs. Oxford, Eng: B. Blackwell, 1937.

8779   Signs and Symbols, U.S.A., 1780-1960. Exhibition. March-
       April 1963. New York: Downtown Gallery, 1963. u.p.,
       ill

8780   Stevens, Joseph. A Paper on the Hampshire Inn Signs and
       Their Probable Origin. Winchester, Eng: Jacob &
       Johnson, 1879. 56pp

8781   Swift, Charles Robert. Inns and Inn Signs. Sacred and
       secular. St. Albans: C. R. Swift, 1947. 47pp, ill

8782   Tate, William Edward. Inns and Inn Signs in and Near
       Burslem, in Stoke-on-Trent. Burslem: W. Savage, 1944.
       46pp, ill, color frontis

8783   Turnor, Reginald. The Spotted Dog; a book of English inn
       signs. London: Sylvan Pr, 1948. 128pp, ill

8784   Usherwood, Stephen. Inns and Inn Signs. London: Ginn,
       1971. 16pp, ill (Juvenile literature)

8785   Wagner, Charles Louis Henry. The Story of Signs; an outline
       history of the sign arts from the earliest recorded times
       to the present "Atomic Age." Boston: MacGibbon, 1954.
       123pp, ill

ADVERTISING COLLECTIBLES

8786   Cope, Jim. Collectable Old Advertising, with Current Prices
       and Photos. Orange, Tex: 1971. ill

8787   Cornman, Frederick. Some Illustrations of Olde London as
       Quaintly Illustrated Advertisements, shoppe signs and
       curious old houses of the 18th century. 2nd series. Lon-
       don: Author, 1894. 69 leaves, color ill and frontis
       NNC-Ave, DLC

8788   _____. Some Olde London Streete Signs. Also facsimiles
       of tradesmens curious and quaint illustrated advertisements,
       and some notable olde houses of the 17th and 18th centuries.
       3rd series. London: priv. printed, 1900. pls MH

8789 Davis, Alec. Package and Print; the development of con-
      tainer and label design. London: 1967; New York: C.
      N. Potter, 1968. 112pp, ill, pls, bib (Includes tin
      containers)

8790 de Vries, Leonard, and Ilonka Van Amstel, comp. The Won-
      derful World of American Advertisements, 1865-1900.
      Chicago: Follett, 1972; London: J. Murray, 1973. 144pp,
      chiefly ill

8791 Drepperd, Carl William, comp. Early American Advertising
      Art; a collection of wood cut and stereotype illustrations
      used in American newspaper, almanac and magazine ad-
      vertising, 1750-1850. New York: Youth Group of Maga-
      zines, 1943. 48pp, chiefly ill DLC, PP, DeWint

8792 Hake, Ted. A Treasury of Advertising Collectibles. New
      York: Dafran, 1974. 224pp, ill (Postcards, shoe horns,
      serving trays, etc.)

8793 *Hornung, Clarence Pearson. Handbook of Early American
      Advertising Art. New York: Dover, 1947; 2nd ed. rev.
      & expanded. 2 vol. New York: Dover, 1953. 176pp,
      ill, bib; text, ill, pls, bib

8794 Kaduck, John M. Collecting Advertising Mirrors. Des Moines:
      Wallace-Homestead, 1973. 56pp, ill of 200 mirrors

8795 Klug, Ray. Antique Advertising. Vol. I. Signs, tins, dye
      cabinets, trays, etc.; Vol. II. Signs, tins, trays, pocket
      mirrors, matchholders, etc.; Vol. III. Signs, tins, trays,
      tobacco packets, country store items, etc. 3 vol. Gas
      City, Ind: L-W Promotions, 1972- . 132pp each, hun-
      dreds of ill

8796 Muzio, Jack. Collectable Tin Advertising Trays. Santa Rosa,
      Cal: 19? 12 color pls (1886-?)

8797 Polansky, Tom. Advertising Trays. Loma Linda, Cal: 1971.
      100pp, ill (Beer, whiskey, soda water, change, and Vienna
      art trays)

8798 Presbrey, Frank Spencer. The History and Development of
      Advertising. With more than 350 illustrations. Garden
      City, NY: Doubleday, 1929; reprint. New York: Green-
      wood Pr, 1968. 642pp, 350 ill, pls

8799 Schuwer, Philippe. History of Advertising. Tr. from French
      by Joan White. London: Leisure Arts, 1967. 112pp, ill,
      facsims

8800 Sinel, Joseph, comp. A Book of American Trade-Marks and

Devices. New York: Knopf, 1924. 64 leaves, numerous ill (some color), trademark facsims

8801 Weaver, Sir Lawrence. Exhibitions and the Arts of Display. London: Country Life; New York: Scribner's, 1925. 106pp, 162 pls (part color), color frontis

8802 Zucker, Irving. A Source Book of French Advertising Art: ... with over 5000 illustrations from the turn of the century. London: Faber, 1964. 256pp, ill (1890-1910)

BOTTLE TICKETS

8803 Bottle Tickets. V & A. London: HMSO, 1958. 6pp, 26 pls (Metal, ceramics, etc.)

8804 Dent, Herbert Crowley. Wine, Spirit and Sauce Labels of the 18th and 19th Centuries. Norwich, Eng: H. W. Hunt, 1933. 15pp, 6 pls, color frontis NN, DLC

8805 Penzer, Norman Mosley. The Book of the Wine Label. Fore. by Andre L. Simon. London: Home & Van Thal, 1947; reprint. London: White Lion, 1974. 144pp, ill, 28pp of pls, bib (Battersea enamel, silver, pearl, Sheffield plate, etc.)

8806 Whitworth, Eric Watkinson. Wine Labels. London: Cassell, 1966. 63pp, ill (Chiefly silver)

TELEPHONES, TELEGRAPH AND RADIO

8807 Baldwin, Francis George C. The History of the Telephone in the United Kingdom. Fore. by Frank Gill. London: Chapman & Hall, 1925; 1938. 728pp, pls DLC

8808 Brooks, John. Telephone: The First 100 years. New York: Harper & Row, 1976. 369pp, ill

8809 Casson, Herbert Newton. History of the Telephone. Chicago: A. C. McClurg, 1910; 3rd ed. 1910; 4th ed. 1911; 6th ed. 1917. 315pp, ill, 26 pls NN, CU, MB

8810 Davis, Daniel. Book of the Telegraph. With "catalogue of apparatus to illustrate magnetism" manufactured and sold by D. Davis ... 1848. 2 parts. Boston: 1848. ill BM

8811 _____. Book of the Telegraph. Boston: Author, 1852; 2nd ed. rev. by T. Hall. Boston: Palmer & Hall, 1858. 44pp, ill; 78pp, ill DLC

8812 Denman, Roderick Peter G., comp. Electrical Communication.

Catalogue of the Collections in the Science Museum, South
Kensington. 2 vol. London: HMSO, 1926. ill, pls
(I. Line Telegraphy and Telephony; II. Wireless Telephony)
DLC, MiU

8813 Du Moncel, Theodore Achille Louis. The Telephone, the
Microphone, and the Phonograph. Tr. from French, with
add. & corr. London: 1879. ill

8814 Fahie, John Joseph. Historic Notes on the Telephone. Reprint from The Electrician. London: J. Gray, 1883.
8pp BM

8815 _____. A History of Electric Telegraphy to the Year 1837.
London: E. & F. N. Spon, 1883. 542pp BM

8816 _____. A History of Wireless Telegraphy, 1838-1899....
Edinburgh; London: W. Blackwood, 1899; 2nd rev. ed.
1901. 325pp; 348pp

8817 Houston, Edwin James, 1847-1914. The Electric Transmission of Intelligence, and other advanced primers of electricity. New York: W. J. Johnston, 1893. 330pp, ill
(Electric telegraph, cable telegraphy, annunciators and
alarms, telephone, batteries, welding, etc.) PPL, DLC

8818 _____, and Arthur Edwin Kennelly. The Electric Telephone.
New York: W. J. Johnston, 1896; 2nd enl. ed. New York:
Electrical World & Engineer, 1902. 412pp, ill

8819 Lardner, Dionysius. The Electric Telegraph. New ed. rev.
& rewritten by Edward B. Bright. London: J. Walton,
1867. 272pp, 140 ill

8820 O'Dea, William T. Handbook of the Collections Illustrating
Radio Communication; its history and development. Fore.
by G. R. M. Garratt. Science Museum. London: HMSO,
1934; 1949. 94pp, pls, bib MiD

8821 Osborne, Albert E. Why Man Has Used Pictures, and a comparison between the telephone and the stereoscope. Introd.
by J. E. Lough. New York: Underwood, 1904. 58pp

8822 Poole, Joseph. Telegraphy, Telephony, and Wireless. London: Pitman, 1921. 120pp, ill

8823 Rhodes, Frederick Leland. Beginnings of Telephony. Fore.
by General John J. Carty. New York; London: Harper,
1929. 261pp, ill, pls, bib

8824 Sabine, Robert. The History and Progress of the Electric
Telegraph. 2nd ed. London; New York: Virtue, 1869.
280pp BM

8825 _____. Telegraphy. London: 1876. See: Bevan, G. P.,
       British Manufacturing Industries, Vol. 10, no. 43.

8826 Shepardson, George DeFrees. Telephone Apparatus, an intro-
       duction to the development and theory. New York: Apple-
       ton, 1917. 337pp, 115 ill, bib

8827 Story, Alfred Thomas. A Story of Wireless Telegraphy.
       New York: Appleton, 1904. 215pp, 57 ill

8828 Terry, Astley C., and William Finn. Illustrations and De-
       scriptions of Telegraphic Apparatus. Buffalo, NY: A. C.
       Terry, 1884. 91pp, ill

8829 Zeda, Umberto. Telephones and Lightning Conductors. Tr.
       from Italian by S. R. Bottone. London: G. Pitman, 1907.
       100pp, 60 ill BM

PHONOGRAPHS AND MICROPHONES

8830 Chew, V. K. Talking Machines, 1877-1914: some aspects
       of the early history of the gramophone. Science Museum.
       London: HMSO, 1967. 81pp, ill

8831 Du Moncel, Theodore Achilles Louis. The Telephone, the
       Microphone, and the Phonograph. Tr. from French with
       additions and corrections. London: 1879. ill

8832 Edisonia, Ltd., London. Phonographs, Graphophone Records,
       Supplies: price list, 1898. Facsimile reprint. South-
       bourne, Bournemouth: City of London Phonograph and
       Gramophone Society, 1965. 20pp, ill

8833 Frow, George L., comp. A Guide to the Edison Cylinder
       Phonograph: a handbook for collectors containing details
       of the spring-driven models produced from 1895 to 1929,
       with some notes on the earlier models manufactured by
       the North American Phonograph Company, the National
       Phonograph Company, and later Edison companies at
       Orange, New Jersey, U.S.A. St. Austell, Eng: Antony,
       1970. 64pp, ill

8834 Gelatt, Roland. The Fabulous Phonograph: the story of the
       gramophone from tin foil to high fidelity. Philadelphia:
       Lippincott, 1955; London: Cassell, 1956; rev. ed. as The
       Fabulous Phonograph; from Edison to Stereo. New York:
       Appleton-Century, 1966. 320pp, ill; 336pp, ill

8835 Mitchell, Ogilvie. Talking Machines. London: Pitman, 1922.
       120pp, ill

8836 Music Machines--American Style. Washington, D.C.: GPO,

1971. 139pp, ill (Barrel organs, nickelodeons, phonographs, jukeboxes, etc.)

8837   The Phonograph and How to Use It; being a short history of
       its invention and development, containing also directions,
       helpful hints and plain talks as to its care and use, etc.
       Including also a reprint of the Openeer Papers and phono-
       graph short stories. New York: A. Becker, 1900.
       181pp, ill

8838   The Phonoscope; a monthly journal devoted to scientific and
       amusement inventions appertaining to sight and sound.
       New York: Phonoscope Publishing Co, November 1896- .
       ill, pls DLC

8839   Read, Oliver, and Walter L. Welch. From Tin Foil to Stereo:
       evolution of the phonograph. Indianapolis: H. W. Sams,
       1959. 524pp, ill, pls, bib

8840   Talking Machine News. Periodical. London: 19- . BM

PHOTOGRAPHY AND CAMERAS

8841   *Auer, Michel. The Illustrated History of the Camera from
       1839 to the Present. Boston: N.Y. Graphic Society,
       1975. 285pp, 535 ill, 70 color pls

8842   Barnes, John. Barnes Museum of Cinematography, catalogue
       of the collection. 5 vol. St. Ives, Cornwall: Barnes
       Museum, 1970. (Part 2. "Optical Projection: the
       history of the magic lantern from the 17th to the 20th
       century, including an account of the illuminants used in
       projection....") 70pp, ill

8843   Bisbee, A. The History and Practice of Daguerreotyping.
       n.p. 1853; New York: Arno, 1973. 104pp, 8 pls

8844   Bliven, Floyd Edward. The Daguerrotype Story. New York:
       Vantage Pr, 1957. 22pp, ill

8845   Bolton, Henry Carrington. Notes on the History of the Magic
       Lantern. New York?: 190-? NN, PPULC

8846   Boni, Albert. Photographic Literature; an international bib-
       liographic guide to general and specialized literature on
       photographic processes, techniques, theory, chemistry,
       physics, apparatus, materials and applications, industry,
       history, biography, aesthetics. New York: Morgan &
       Morgan, 1962. 335pp

8847   Brewster, Sir David, 1781-1868. The Stereoscope. Its
       history, theory and construction with its application to the

fine and useful arts and to education. London: John
Murray, 1856; London: Hotten, 1870; reprint of 1856 ed.
Dobbs Ferry, NY: Morgan, 1971. 235pp, ill NN, BM

8848 Cameras/1898. Rochester Optical Company. Catalog reprint.
Princeton, NJ: Pyne, 1971. 118pp, ill

8849 Castle, Peter. Collecting and Valuing Old Photographs. London: Garnstone Pr, 1973. 176pp, ill, bib

8850 Cook, Olive. Movement in Two Dimensions, a study of the
animated and projected pictures which preceded the invention of cinematography. London: Hutchinson, 1963.
142pp, ill, bib

8851 Cotter, Alan, and Paulette Cotter. Reflecting on Photography,
1839-1902; a catalogue of the Cotter collection. Santa
Barbara, Cal: National Directory of Camera Collectors,
1973. 139pp, ill, bib

8852 Darrah, William Culp. Stereo Views. Gettysburg, Pa:
priv. printed, 196-? ill

8853 Dollond, George, 1774-1852. Description of the Camera Lu-
cida. London?: n.p., ca.1830. 1 pl SIB-1

8854 Elmendorf, Dwight Lathrop. Lantern Slides: how to make
and color them. New York: E. & H. T. Anthony, 1895;
1897; 1900. 68pp, ill, pls (Includes illustrated pieces
of equipment used)

8855 Foster, Peter Le Neve. Photography. London: 1877. See:
Bevan, G. P., British Manufacturing Industries, Vol. 8.

8856 Gamble, William. Photography and Its Applications. London:
Pitman, 1920. 132pp, ill

8857 Gernsheim, Helmut, and Alison Gernsheim. The History of
Photography from the Earliest Use of the Camera Obscura
in the 11th Century up to 1914. London: Oxford U. Pr,
1955; rev. & enl. ed. as The History of Photography ...
to the Beginning of the Modern Era. London: Thames
& Hudson; New York: McGraw-Hill, 1969. 395pp, ill,
bib; 599pp, ill, bib

8858 _____, and _____. Louis Jacques Mande Daguerre
(1787-1851), the world's first photographer. Cleveland:
World, 1956; 2nd rev. ed. as L. J. M. Daguerre (1787-
1851), the history of the diorama and the daguerretype.
New York: Dover, 1965. 216pp, ill; 226pp, 124 ill,
pls, bib

8859 Gilbert, George. Collecting Photographica. The images and

equipment of the first 100 years of photography. New
York: Hawthorn, 1976. 302pp, ill, bib

8860   , comp. Photographic Advertising from A-to-Z.
From the Kodak to the Leica. Actual size from the pages
of the leading magazines of America from the 1880s to
the 1920s ... cameras, plates, novelties, schools, shutters. New York: Yesterday's Cameras, 1970. 192pp,
chiefly ill

8861 Graphic Antiquarian. Quarterly. Indianapolis: Graphic Enterprises, 1970- . (Camera collecting, etc.)

8862 Gross, Harry I. Antique and Classic Cameras. New York:
American Photography Book Company, 1965; another issue.
Philadelphia: Chilton, 1965. 192pp, ill

8863 Hasluck, Paul Nooncree, ed. Optical Lanterns and Accessories; how to make and manage them, including instructions on making slides. London; New York: Cassell,
1901; Philadelphia: McKay, 1903. 160pp, ill DLC, TxU

8864   , ed. Photographic Cameras and Accessories, comprising how to make cameras, dark slides, shutters, and
stands.... London; New York: Cassell, 1901;... Philadelphia: McKay, 1909;... 160pp, many ill ViU, DLC

8865 Holmes, Edward. An Age of Cameras. Hertfordshire, Eng:
Fountain Pr, Argus Books, 1974. 159pp, ill (some color)

8866 Hunt, Robert, 1807-1887. A Popular Treatise on the Art of
Photography, including daguerreotype, and all the new
methods of producing pictures by the chemical agency of
light. Glasgow: R. Griffon, 1841. 96pp, ill DLC, MB

8867 Illustrated Catalogue of Photographic Equipment and Materials
for Amateurs. 1891. Facsimile reprint. Hastings-on-
Hudson, NY: Morgan & Morgan, n.d. (197?) 128pp, ill

8868 Jenkins, Charles Francis, 1869-1934. Animated Pictures:
an exposition of the historical development of chronopho-
tography. Its present scientific applications and future
possibilities, and of the methods and apparatus employed
in the entertainment of large audiences by means of projecting lanterns to give the appearance of objects in motion. Washington: H. L. McQueen, 1897. 118pp, ill,
pls DLC, PPF

8869   . Picture Ribbons: an exposition of the methods
and apparatus employed in the manufacture of the picture
ribbons used in projecting lanterns to give the appearance
of objects in motion. Washington, D.C.: H. L. McQueen,
1898. 56pp, ill, pls NN, DLC

8870   Jenkins, Harold F.   Two Points of View; the history of the
          parlor stereoscope.   Uniontown, Pa: E. G. Warman,
          1973.   75pp, ill   (Viewers, cameras and cards)

8871   Lager, James L.   Leica Illustrated Guide.   1925-1975.   Dobbs
          Ferry, NY: Morgan & Morgan, 1975.   64pp, ill

8872   Lahue, Kalton Carroll, and Joseph A. Bailey.   Collecting
          Vintage Cameras.   Vol. 1.   The American 35mm.   Garden
          City, NY: American Photographic Pub, 1972.   159pp, ill

8873   Lardner, Dionysius.   Light, Colour, Solar Microscope, Cam-
          era Lucida, Camera Obscura, Magic Lantern.   London:
          Walton & Maberly, 1869.   202pp, ill

8874   Lothrop, Eaton S., Jr.   A Century of Cameras from the Col-
          lection of the International Museum of Photography at
          George Eastman House.   Dobbs Ferry, NY: Morgan &
          Morgan, 1973.   150pp, ill, bib

8875   McKeown, Jim.   Price Guide to Antique and Classic Still
          Cameras.   Grantsburg, Wisc: Centennial Photo Service,
          1974.   59pp, 1000 items priced

8876   Meteyard, Eliza.   A Group of Englishmen (1795-1815); being
          a record of the Younger Wedgwoods and their friends, em-
          bracing the history of the discovery of photography, and a
          facsimile of the first photograph.   London: Longmans,
          Green, 1871.   416pp, ill   (Solon commented: "a few
          'drawing room' experiments conducted on principles long
          before laid down ... do not establish a claim to the in-
          vention of photography...")

8877   Miller, Russell.   Click.   New York: Arco, 1974.   120pp,
          color ill   (History of photography)

8878   *Newhall, Beaumont.   The History of Photography from 1839
          to the Present Day.   New York: Museum of Modern Art,
          1964; rev. & enl. ed. London: Secker & Warburg, 1972.
          ...; 216pp, ill, bib

8879   _____ .   The Daguerretype in America.   New York: Duell,
          Sloane & Pearce, 1961.   176pp, ill

8880   Osborne, Albert E.   The Stereograph and the Stereoscope ...
          What they mean for individual development.   What they
          promise for the spread of civilization.   New York: Under-
          wood, 1909.   288pp, ill

8881   _____ .   Why Man Has Used Pictures, and a comparison be-
          tween the telephone and the stereoscope.   Introd. by J.
          E. Lough.   New York: Underwood, 1904.   58pp

8882   Permutt, C.   Collecting Old Cameras.   n. p. , 1975.   80 ill

8883   The Photographic Collector's Newsletter.   Quarterly.   Brook-
       lyn?:   1971-?

8884   Photographica.   Monthly.   New York: Photographic Historical
       Society of New York, 196-?   ill

8885   Pollack, Peter.   The Picture History of Photography, from
       the earliest beginnings to the present day.   rev. & enl.
       ed. New York: Abrams, 1969.   708pp, ill

8886   Rinhart, Floyd, and Marion Rinhart.   American Daguerreian
       (!) Art.   New York: Potter, 1967.   135pp, ill

8887 * _____ , and _____ .   American Miniature Case Art.
       South Brunswick, NJ: A. S. Barnes; London: Yoseloff,
       1969.   205pp, 229 ill, 4 pls, bib   (Cases used by early
       photographers)

8888   Rochester Optical Company 1898.   The Premo Camera.
       Catalog reprint, with historical introduction.   Princeton,
       NJ: Pyne Pr, 1971.   108pp, ill, bib

8889   Rudisill, Richard.   Mirror Image; the influence of the daguer-
       reotype on American Society.   Albuquerque: U. of New
       Mexico Pr, 1971.   342pp, ill, 202 pls

8890   Seely, Charles A. , and Henry Garbanati.   A Description of
       Some Important Improvements in the Processes and Ap-
       paratus Designed for the Use of Photographers, with illus-
       trations and confirmative testimony. New York: American
       Journal of Photography, 1859.   24pp, ill   DLC

8891   Snelling, Henry Hunt, b. 1817.   A Dictionary of the Photo-
       graphic Art ... Together with a list of articles of every
       description employed in its practice.   New York: H. H.
       Snelling, 1854.   235, 56pp, ill, pls   DLC

8892   _____ .   The History and Practice of the Art of Photography
       ... Containing all the instructions necessary for the com-
       plete practice of the daguerrean and photogenic art.   New
       York: Putnam, 1849; reprint with introd. by Beaumont
       Newhall.   Hastings-on-Hudson, New York: Morgan &
       Morgan, 1970.   139pp, ill, pls

8893   Sobieszek, Robert A. , comp.   The Collodion Process and the
       Ferrotype: three accounts, 1854-1872.   Reprint.   New
       York: Arno, 1973.   100, 27, and 80pp, ill   (1. The
       Collodion Process on Glass, F. S. Archer, 1854; 2. On
       the Intervention of Art in Photography, L. D. Blanquart-
       Evrard, 1864; 3. Trask's Practical Ferrotyper, A. K. P.
       Trask, 1872.)

8894   Stokes, Isaac Newton Phelps.   The Hawes-Stokes Collection
       of American Daguerreotypes by Albert Sands Southworth,
       and Josiah Johnson Hawes.   Metropolitan Museum.   New
       York: Museum Pr, 1939.   21pp, 24 pls

8895   Story, Alfred Thomas.   The Story of Photography.   New York:
       Appleton, 1898; 1902; New York: McClure, Phillips, 1904;
       New York: 1913; 1915; reprint of 1904 ed.   Rochester,
       NY: Visual Studies Workshop, 1974.   169pp, 38 ill, bib

8896   Thomas, David Bowen.   Cameras: photographs and acces-
       sories.   Science Museum.   London: HMSO, 1966.   47pp,
       ill

8897   _____ .   The Science Museum Photography Collection: a
       catalogue.   London: HMSO, 1969.   113pp, ill, 4 pls

8898   Tissandier, Gaston, 1843-1899.   A History and Handbook of
       Photography.   Tr. from French and ed. by J. Thomson.
       London: S. Low, 1876; 2nd ed. with appendix by H. F.
       Talbot.   London: S. Low, Marston, Searle, Rivington,
       1878.   326pp, 21 pls; 400pp, 70 ill   BM

8899   Towne, Thomas.   The Automatical Camera Obscura.   Ex-
       hibiting scenes from nature, etc.   4 vol.   London:
       Fletcher, 1821-1823.   BM

8900   Wall, Edward John, writer on photography, and Henry Snow-
       den Ward.   The Photographic Picture Post-Card for Per-
       sonal Use and for Profit.   London: Dawburn and Ward,
       1906.   104pp

8901   Welling, William.   Collectors' Guide to 19th Century Photo-
       graphs.   New York: Macmillan, 1976.   204pp, 300 ill

8902   Wolf, Myron, comp.   Directory of Collectable Cameras.
       Originally in Popular Photography.   Lexington, Mass:
       1972.   101pp, ill

8903   [No entry.]

SECTION XXIV

WRITING: BY HAND AND MACHINE

WRITING IMPLEMENTS, PRINTING MACHINERY
AND ENGRAVING TOOLS

8904 Bloy, C. H. A History of Printing Ink, Balls and Rollers,
      1440-1850. London: Evelyn Adams & Mackay, 1967; 1972.
      147pp, pls; 172pp, ill, facsims

8905 Bore, Henry. The Story of the Invention of the Steel Pen,
      with a description of the manufacturing process by which
      they are produced. London: Perry & Co, 1886; New
      York: Ivison, Blakeman, 1890; 3rd ed. London: Perry,
      1892. 52pp; 64pp; 67pp NN, DLC, BM

8906 Bullen, George, ed. Caxton Celebration, 1877. Catalogue
      of the loan collection of antiquities, curiosities, and ap-
      pliances connected with the art of printing. South Kensing-
      ton Museum. London: Elzevir Pr, 1877; London: N.
      Trubner, 1877. 404pp; 472pp PPULC, NN, CtY

8907 Catalogue of the Collection of Items at the Printer's Devil,
      Fetter Lane, London EC4, illustrating the history of
      printing. London: Whitbread, 1955. 98pp, ill

8908 Caxton Magazine and British Stationer. Monthly. London:
      East & Blades, 1901-1910. ill, pls

8909 Covill, William E., Jr. Ink Bottles and Inkwells. Taunton,
      Mass: W. S. Sullwold, 1971. 431pp, ill of 1780 pieces

8910 Dickinson, Henry Winram, 1870-1952. A Brief History of
      Draughtsmen's Instruments. To be read at the Science
      Museum, London, February 8, 1950. London: Newcomen
      Society for the Study of the History of Engineering and
      Technology, 1950. 16pp, bib NNC-Ave

8911 Emerson, William Andrew, 1851- . Practical Instruction in
      the Art of Wood Engraving.... East Douglas, Mass: C.

J. Batcheller, 1876; new ed. as Handbook of Wood Engraving, with practical instruction in the art for persons
wishing to learn without an instructor; containing a description of tools and apparatus used and explaining the manner
of engraving various classes of work.... Boston: Lee &
Shepard; New York: C. T. Dillingham, 1881. 52pp, ill,
color pl, color frontis; 95pp, ill, color pls NN, DLC

8912 Faber, J. L. The Lead Pencil Manufactory at Stein near
Nurnberg, Bavaria. Historical Sketch. n.p. 1861. 9 pls

8913 Faithorne, William, ca.1626-1691. The Art of Graveing and
Etching, wherein is exprest the true way of graveing in
copper, also the manner and method of that famous Callot,
and Mr. Bosse, in their several ways of etching. London:
Author, 1662. 48pp, 4 leaves, 10 pls (Includes tools)

8914 Foley, John. History of the Invention and Illustrated Process
of Making Foley's Diamond Pointed Gold Pens, with complete illustrated catalogue. New York: Mayer, Merkel &
Ottomann, 1876. 77pp, ill DeWint, DLC

8915 Glass, James. Pens and Pen-making. Edinburgh; New York:
Ormiston & Glass, 1889. 21pp

8916 Guppy, Henry. Human Records: a survey of their history
from the beginning. Reprint from Bulletin of John Rylands
Library. Manchester: U. Pr, 1943. 43pp, bib DLC

8917 Kelly, Rob Roy. American Wood Type: 1828-1900. New
York: Van Nostrand Reinhold, 1969. ill

8918 Lewis, James Henry, 1786-1853. The Best Method of Pen-
making.... Leeds: Author, 1820; London: 1826; reprint.
Calcutta: 1826; as The Art of Making a Good Pen. Bristol: Author, 1825?; London: Author, 1828. 32pp, 4 pls;
...; 24pp, pls;... NN, BM

8919 Lindsey, G. Pens and Papier Mache. London: 1876. See
also: Bevan, G. P., British Manufacturing Industries,
Vol. 3, no. 43.

8920 A List of Printing Materials, second hand types, bookbinders'
tools, etc. n.p.: 18-? u.p., ill NN

8921 McGraw, Vincent D. McGraw's Book of Antique Inkwells.
Minneapolis: 1972. 430pp, 1780 items illustrated

8922 Moran, James. The
        Composition of Read-
        ing Matter; a history
        from case to com-
        puter. London:
        Wace, 1965. 84pp,
        ill, bib (Typesetting
        machines)

8923 _____. Printing
        Presses: their
        history and develop-
        ment from the 15th century to modern times.   London:
        1973. 312pp, 177 ill

8924 Office Appliances; the magazine of office equipment.   Periodi-
        cal. New York; Chicago: Patterson, 1904- .

8925 Palatino, Giovanni Battista. The Instruments of Writing;
        translated from the writing book of G. Palatino, Rome,
        1540, by Henry K. Pierce. To which is added a partial
        translation of Ludovico degli Arrighi's The Method of
        Cutting a Pen, Rome, 1523, by Erich A. O'D. Taylor,
        and technical notes by John Howard Benson. Newport,
        R.I.: Berry Hill Pr, 1953. 26pp, ill DeWint

8926 Parker, T. N. Description of an Ink-glass in Which the Sup-
        ply of Ink is Regulated by a Float. n.p.: 1816. SIB-1

8927 Pencil Points. A journal for the drafting room. Monthly.
        Stamford, Conn: the Architectural Review, 1920- .

8928 Pride, B. The Art of Pen-Cutting. Comprising an history
        of the invention and the first use of pens, etc. London:
        1812. 1 pl BM

8929 Rivera, Betty, and Ted Rivera. Inkstands and Inkwells: a
        collector's guide. New York: Crown, 1973. 192pp, 140
        ill, 8 color pls, bib (17th century to Art Deco)

8930 Smith, Howard B. A History of the Shorthand Writing Ma-
        chine (Stenotype) and Machine-Written Shorthand (Stenotypy).
        Washington, D.C.: Author, 1942. 32 leaves

8931 Spawn, Willman, and Carol Spawn. Aitken Shop; identifica-
        tion of an 18th century bindery and its tools. Reprint
        from Papers of the Bibliographical Society of America,
        Vol. 57, 1963. 16pp (pp. 422-437), ill DeWint

8932 Stewart, Alexander A., comp. Compositors' Tools and Ma-
        terials, a primer of information about composing sticks,

galleys, leads, brass rules, cutting and mitering machines, etc. Chicago: United Typothetae of America, 1918. 38pp, ill

8933 _____, comp. Imposing Tables and Lock-up Appliances, describing the tools and materials used in locking up forms for the press, including some modern utilities for special purposes. Chicago: United Typothetae of America, 1918. 50pp, ill

8934 _____, comp. Type Cases and Composing-Room Furniture, a primer of information about type cases, work stands, cabinets, case racks, galley racks, standing galleys, etc. Chicago: United Typothetae of America, 1918. 34pp, ill

8935 Strange, Edward Fairbrother. Tools and Materials Illustrating the Japanese Method of Colour-printing. A descriptive catalogue of a collection exhibited in the Museum. South Kensington Museum. London: HMSO, 1913. 22pp, 3 pls

8936 Thompson, John Smith. History of Composing Machines. A complete record of the art of composing type by machinery.... Chicago: Inland Printer, 1904. 200pp, ill NN

8937 Tools and Materials Used in Etching and Engraving; a descriptive catalogue of a collection exhibited at the Museum. V & A Museum. 3rd ed. London: HMSO, 1914. 18pp

8938 *Tuer, Andrew White. History of Horn-books. 2 vol. London: Leadenhall; New York: Scribner's, 1896; 1 vol. London; New York: 1897. (1 volume edition, 486pp), 300 ill, pls, 3 facsimile hornbooks BM

8939 Walter, Leo G. Walter's Inkwells of 1885. Akron, O: 1968. 51pp, ill (Glass and cast iron)

8940 Webster, William, writing master. The Description and Use of a Complete Sett or Case of Pocket Instruments. 2nd ed. London: 1739; 4th ed. 1768. 3 pls BM

8941 *Whalley, Joyce Irene. Writing Implements and Accessories from the Roman Stylus to the Typewriter. Detroit: Gale, 1975. 144pp, ill (Ink wells, pounce pots, paperweights, pens, pencils, etc.)

TYPEWRITERS

8942 Adler, Michael H. The Writing Machine. London: Allen & Unwin, 1973. 381pp, ill, bib

8943 *Beeching, Wilfred A. Century of the Typewriter. London:

Heinemann, 1974; New York: St. Martin's Pr, 1975. 276pp, ill

8944 *Bliven, Bruce Ormsby. The Wonderful Writing Machine. New York: Random House, 1954. 236pp, ill

8945 Current, Richard Nelson. The Typewriter and the Men Who Made It. Urbana: U. of Illinois Pr, 1954. 149pp, ill NN, TxU, PP

8946 Densmore, Yost and Co., New York. The Typewriter! A machine to supersede the pen. New York: Densmore, Yost, 1875? 7pp, ill (Includes: "What 'Mark Twain' Says About It") CtY

8947 The Evolution of the Typewriter. New York: Royal Typewriter Co, 1921. 52pp, ill NN

8948 Foulke, Arthur Toye. Mr. Typewriter; a biography of Christopher Latham Sholes. Boston: Christopher Publishing, 1961. 134pp, ill, bib (Sholes, 1819-1890)

8949 Gamble, William Burt, comp. List of Works Relating to the Development and Manufacture of Typewriting Machines. Reprint from Bulletin. New York: New York Public Library, 1913. 18pp

8950 Gould, Rupert Thomas. The Story of the Typewriter. From the 18th to the 20th centuries. Ed. by Dudley W. Hooper. Fore. by Mancell Gutteridge. London: Office Control and Management, 1949. 48pp, ill MH, NN

8951 *Herrl, George, comp. The Carl P. Dietz Collection of Typewriters. Milwaukee: Public Museum, 1965. 103pp, chiefly ill of 308 specimens (Most comprehensive collection of typewriters in America, probably the world)

8952 The History of Touch Typewriting. New York: Wyckoff, Seamans & Benedict (owners of Remington Typewriter Company), 1900? 31pp, ill NN

8953 Jenkins, Henry Charles. Cantor Lectures on Type-writing Machines ... April and May 1894. London: W. Trounce, for the Society for the Encouragement of Arts, Manufactures and Commerce, 1894. 27pp, ill, bib NN

8954 Jones, C. LeRoy. Typewriters Unlimited. Springfield, Mo: Rocky's Technical Publications, 1956. 76pp, ill

8955 Mares, George Carl. The History of the Typewriter: being an illustrated account of the origin, rise and development of the writing machine. London: G. Pitman, 1909. 318pp, ill BM, NN

8956   Manual of the Typewriter.   London: Pitman, 1893.   93pp
        BM

8957   Morton, Arthur E.   Questions and Answers on Typewriting
        and Office Procedure, with sections on the history and
        development of the typewriter.   London: I. Pitman, 1928.
        145pp, pl NN

8958   Oden, Charles Vonley.   Evolution of the Typewriter.   New
        York: J. E. Hetsh, printer, 1917.   154pp, ill, pls,
        facsims NN

8959   Richards, George Tilghman.   Handbook of the Collection Illus-
        trating Typewriters: a brief outline of the history and de-
        velopment of the correspondence typewriter with reference
        to the National Collection, and descriptions of the exhibits.
        Science Museum.   London: HMSO, 1938; reprint. 1948;
        2nd ed. as The History and Development of Typewriters.
        1964.   57pp, 10 pls; 49pp, ill, 8 pls DLC, NN

8960   The Story of the Typewriter, 1873-1923.   Published in com-
        memoration of the 50th anniversary of the invention of the
        writing machine.   Herkimer, NY: Herkimer County His-
        torical Society, 1923.   142pp, ill, pls NN

8961   United States Patent Office.   Book Typewriter Patents.   Ex-
        tracts from Patent Office specifications.   Vol. 1- .
        Washington, D.C.: GPO, 1843-93.   NN, DLC

8962   Weller, Charles Edward.   The Early History of the Type-
        writer.   La Porte, Ind: Chase & Shepherd, printers,
        1918.   87pp, ill, pls NN

8963   Zellers, John Adam.   The Typewriter; a short history, on
        its 75th anniversary.   1873-1948.   An Address.   New
        York: Newcomen Society of England, American Branch,
        1948.   20pp, ill (Remington typewriters) NN

SECTION XXV

ANIMALS AND AGRICULTURE

IMPLEMENTS AND MACHINERY OF AGRICULTURE,
GARDENING AND ANIMAL HUSBANDRY

8964 *Andrews, George Henry, 1816-1898. Rudimentary Treatise
     on Agricultural Engineering. 1. Buildings; 2. Motive
     powers and machinery of the steading; 3. Field machines
     and implements. 3 vol. in 1. London: J. Weale, 1852.
     ill DeWint

8965 *Ardrey, Robert L. American Agricultural Implements; a re-
     view of invention and development in the agricultural imple-
     ment industry of the United States. Chicago: Author,
     1894; reprint. New York: Arno, 1972; reprint. Wilmington,
     Del: Scholarly Resources, 1975. 236pp, 200 ill (Part 1.
     General History of Invention and Improvement; Part 2.
     Pioneer Manufacturing Centers)

8966 Bagster, Samuel, Jr. The Management of Bees, with a de-
     scription of "The Ladies' Safety Hive." London: Bagster

799

& Pickering, 1834; 2nd ed. London: Saunders & Otley, 1838; 3rd ed. 1865. 244pp, ill, color frontis; ...; 240pp, numerous woodcuts, hand-colored frontis MH, DLC

8967 Bailey, Robert C. Farm Tools and Implements before 1850. Spring City, Tenn: Hillcrest Books, 1973. 72pp, ill (Reproduced from old advertising material)

8968 Baker, John Wynn. A Short Description and List, with the prices of the instruments of husbandry, made in the factory at Laughlinstown near Celbridge, in the County of Kildare. Dublin: Author, under patronage of the Dublin Society, 1767; 3rd ed. enl. & amended, 1769. 32pp; 54pp BM

8969 Barker, Albert Winslow. Typical Farm Buildings and Farm Implements of Eastern Pennsylvania in the 19th Century. Survey and drawings. Moylan, Pa: Rose Valley Pr, 1934. ill DLC

8970 Beecham, Helen Audrey, and John Walter Yeoman Higgs. The Story of Farm Tools. London: Evans Brothers, for National Federation of Young Farmers' Clubs, 1951; rev. ed. 1961. 48pp, ill, bib

8971 A Book of Patterns of Household, Garden, Carpenter's and Other Objects. n.p. (England): n.d. SKM

8972 Bradley, Richard, 1688-1732. New Improvements of Planting and Gardening, both philosophical and practical. 5th ed. London: for W. Mears, 1726. 608pp, pls

8973 Breck, Joseph, 1794-1873. Catalogue of Horticultural and Agricultural Implements and Tools. Boston: 1845. 32pp, woodcut ill MH

8974 _____, and Co., firm, Boston. Catalogue of Vegetable, herb, tree, flower and grass seeds, bulbous flower roots ... agricultural tools ... implements and tools for sale at the New England Agricultural Warehouse and Seed Store, connected with the New England Farmer. 7th ed. Boston: the Farmer, 1838. 80pp, ill MiU-C

8975 *Brown, Reginald Allen. The History and Origin of Horse Brasses, (the symbolic reasons for many of the designs). Lewes, Eng: W. E. Baxter, printer, 1949; reprint. London: R. A. Brown, 1963. 64pp, ill; 88pp, ill

8976 Burgh, Nicholas Procter. The Manufacture of Sugar, and the Machinery Employed for Colonial and Home Purposes. Read before the Society of Art Adelphi. London: Trubner, 1866. 31pp

8977 _____. A Treatise on Sugar Machinery. Including the

process of producing sugar from the cane, refining moist
and loaf sugar, home and colonial; the practical mode of
designing, manufacturing, and erecting the machinery....
London: E. & F. N. Spon, 1863. 64pp, 16 pls MB

8978 Casson, Herbert Newton. The Romance of the Reaper. New
York: Doubleday, Page, 1908. 184pp, pls PP, DLC

8979 Catalogue of the Various Agricultural Implements ... Exhibited
... 1846-1938. (Annual exhibition catalogues.) London:
Royal Agricultural Society, 1846-1938. BM

8980 Clarke, Cuthbert. The True Theory and Practice of Husbandry ... to which is annexed, a compendium of mechanics; calculated to assist the husbandman in the choice
and construction of every implement peculiar to his business. London: for Author, 1777; 1781. 363pp, pls BM

8981 Common, R. F. J. The History of the Invention of the
Reaping Machine. Bedford, Eng: G. H. Stonebridge,
printer, 1907. 46pp, ill (Cyrus Hall McCormick, 1809-
1884; John Common, b.1778) BM, CU

8982 The Country Gentlemen's Catalogue of Requisites for the House,
field, farm, garden, stable, kennel, etc., to which is
added a notebook, prize record and directory specially
compiled for the use of country gentlemen. Published an-
nually. London: Eden Fisher, 1894; reprinted. London:
Garnstone, 1969. 314pp, ill

8983 Cousins, Peter. Hog Plow and Sith: cultural aspects of early
agricultural technology. Dearborn, Mich: Greenfield Village and Henry Ford Museum, 1973. 20pp, ill (Early
wooden moldboard plow and a Flemish scythe used in
America)

8984 Davis, Alexander. A Treatise on Horse Saddles and Bridles;
their history and manufacture. London: 1867. CtY

8985 Dearborn, Ned. ... Bird Houses and How to Build Them.
Washington, D.C.: GPO, 1914; reprint. 1917; rev. ed.
1918. 19pp, ill

8986 Dickson, Adam. A Treatise of Agriculture. Edinburgh:
Author and A. Donaldson, 1762; 2nd ed. 1765; new ed.
2 vol. London: T. Longman; T. Caddel; Edinburgh: A.
Kincaid & J. Bell, 1770. 427pp, folding pls BM

8987 *Edwards, Everett Eugene. A Bibliography of the History of
Agriculture in the United States. Washington, D.C.: De-
partment of Agriculture, GPO, 1930; reprint. New York:
Burt Franklin, 1970. 307pp

8987a Evans, Benjamin Lindsay. A History of Farm Implements
      and Implement Firms in New Zealand. Feilding, N. Z.:
      Fisher Printing, 1956. 104pp, ill

8988 The Evolution of the Reaping Machine in the United States.
      Department of Agriculture, Office of Experimentation Bul-
      letin No. 103. Washington, D. C.: GPO, 1902.

8989 An Exhibition of the Rural Arts Held in Connection with the
      75th Anniversary of the Founding of the Department of
      Agriculture, 1862-1937. November 1937. Washington,
      D. C.: GPO, 1937. 76pp, ill NNC-Ave

8990 [No entry.]

8991 Farmer's and Mechanics' Journal. Devoted to Agriculture,
      horticulture, and the mechanic arts. Chagrin Falls, Ohio:
      1842-1843.

8992 Farmer's Complete Guide Through All the Articles of His Pro-
      fession. n. p. (England?): 1760. OED

8993 Flower, Edward Fordham, 1805-1883. Bits and Bearing
      Reins; with observations on horses and harness. New
      York; London: Cassell, Petter & Galpin, 1875. 55pp

8994 French, Henry Flagg, 1813-1885. English Plows and Plowing.
      In United States Patent Office Report, 1859, pp. 239-260.
      Washington, D. C.: 1860.

8995 *Fussell, George Edwin. The Farmer's Tools, 1500-1900:
      the history of British farm implements, tools and ma-
      chinery before the tractor came. London: A. Melrose,
      1952. 246pp, ill, 111 pls, bib TxU, NNC-Ave, MiD

8996 Gailey, Alan, and Alexander Fenton, ed. The Spade in
      Northern and Atlantic Europe. Holywood, Ireland: Ulster
      Folk Museum; Belfast: Queen's University of Belfast,
      1970. 257pp, ill, 24 pls

8997 Grancsay, Stephen Vincent. A Loan Exhibition of Equestrian
      Equipment from the Metropolitan Museum of Art. May-
      July 1955. Louisville, Ky: J. B. Speed Art Museum,
      1955. u. p., pls

8998 Hardware and Farm Equipment. Monthly. Kansas City:
      Western Retail Implement and Hardware Association,
      1895- . ill

8999 Hartfield, George. Horse Brasses. London; New York:
      Abelard-Schuman, 1965. 62pp, ill

9000 Hasluck, Paul Nooncree, ed. Beehives and Bee Keepers'

Appliances. London; New York: Cassell, 1905; Philadelphia: McKay, 1905; 1907. 160pp, ill ViU, MB

9001 _____. Harness Making. London; New York: Cassell,
1904; reprinted with Saddlery, as Saddlery and Harness
Making. London: J. A. Allen, 1971. 160pp, ill; 320pp,
ill

9002 _____, ed. Saddlery. London; New York: Cassell, 1904;
Philadelphia: McKay, 1904. 160pp, many ill (See preceding title) MB, DLC

9003 Haug, LeRoy C., and Gerhard A. Malm. Bible of Bridle
Bits. Valley Falls, Kansas: Authors, 1975. 850 types
illustrated

9004 Hawke, Peter, ill. Text by Emma Wood. Our Agricultural
Heritage: a selection of farm machinery restored. London: Queen Anne Pr, 1971. 48pp, ill, bib (To 1935)

9005 Hill, James R., and Co. Harness Makers and Dealers Supply
Catalog, ca.1910. Reprint. 197-? 42pp, ill

9006 Holbrook, Stewart. Machines of Plenty: pioneering in American agriculture. New York: Macmillan, 1955.

9007 The Horseshoers' and Blacksmiths' Journal. Monthly. De-
troit: Master Horseshoers' and Blacksmiths' National
Protective Association of America, 1875-1924. ill, pls
NN

9008 Houghton, John, ed. A Collection of Letters for the Improvement of Husbandry and Trade. Periodical publications.
2 vol. London: 1681-1683; as A Collection for Improvement of Husbandry and Trade. No. 1-582. London: 1692-
1703; rev. with preface and indexes by R. Bradley. 4 vol.
London: 1727-28. BM

9009 Jones, Louis Clark. The Farmers' Museum. Operated by
the New York State Historical Association. Cooperstown,
NY: the Museum, 1948. 48pp, ill NN

9010 Keegan, Terry. The Heavy Horse; its harness and harness
decoration. London: Pelham, 1973; South Brunswick, NJ:
A. S. Barnes, 1974. 217pp, ill, bib

9011 Kline, John B. Tobacco Farming and Cider Making Tools.
Reamstown, Pa: Author, 1975. 52pp, ill

9012 Lacy, Charles de Lacy. The History of the Spur. Partly
reprinted from Country Life, 1904. London: The Connoisseur, 1911. 81pp, 50 pls TxU, DLC

9013   Lambert, Frederick. Tools and Devices for Coppice Crafts.
       London: Evans Brothers, for National Federation of Young
       Farmers' Clubs, 1957. 48pp, ill

9014   Lettermann, Edward J. Farming in Early Minnesota. St.
       Paul: Ramsey County Historical Society, 1969; rev. ed.
       1971. 97pp, ill

9015   A List of Bygones (ie. Rural Implements) in the Possession
       of the Museum. Alton, Hampshire, Eng: Curtis Museum,
       1941. 36pp

9016   McCormick, Cyrus, Jr., 1890- . The Century of the Reaper
       (1831-1931); an account of Cyrus Hall McCormick, the in-
       ventor of the reaper ... of the ... harvesting machine....
       Boston; New York: Houghton Mifflin, 1931. 307pp, pls
       (McCormick, 1809-1884)

9017   Martin, J. Lynton. The Ross Farm Story; a brief history of
       agriculture in Nova Scotia with particular emphasis on life
       on the small upland farm. Halifax: Nova Scotia Museum,
       1972. 41pp, ill

9018   Massingham, Harold John, 1888-1952. Country Relics. An
       account of some old tools and properties once belonging to
       English craftsmen and husbandmen, saved from destruction,
       and now described with their users and their stories.
       London: Cambridge U. Pr, 1939. 239pp, ill with draw-
       ings DLC

9019   Michelsen, Peter. Danish Wheel Ploughs. An illustrated
       catalogue. Copenhagen: Publications from the Interna-
       tional Secretariat for Research on the History of Agri-
       cultural Implements, 1959. ill

9020   Morgan, Frederick Charles. Inventories of a Hereford Sad-
       dler's Shop in the Years 1692 and 1696. Hereford, Eng:
       1947. 16pp (pp. 253-268) ICN

9021   New Improvements of Planting and Gardening. 6th ed. Lon-
       don: printed for J. and J. Knapton, 1731. BM

9022   Partridge, Michael. Early Agricultural Machinery. London:
       Hugh Evelyn, 1969. 72pp, 16 color ill

9023 * _____ . Farm Tools Through the Ages. Reading, Eng:
       Osprey; Boston: 1973. 240pp, ill, facsims, bib (To
       1900)

9024   Passmore, John B. The English Plough. Oxford: Oxford U
       Pr, 1930. 84pp, ill, 13 pls, bib MH, DLC, NN

9025   Plat (or Platt), Sir Hugh. The New and Admirable Arte of

Setting of Corne: with all the necessary tooles and other circumstances belonging to the same: the particular titles whereof are set downe in the page following. London: Peter Short, 1600; 1601. 32pp DLC, BM

9026 Richards, Hubert S. All About Horse Brasses. A collector's complete guide, incorporating "Horse Brass Collections" and "Horse Brasses." London: Wylde Green, 1942. 55pp, ill

9027 _____ . Horse Brass Collections. Birmingham, Eng: 1944. pls (The Clifton Collection and the Marshfield Collection)

9028 _____ . Horse Brasses, Figure Subjects. A collector's guide. London: Wylde Green, 1937. 24pp

9029 _____ . More Horse Brasses. London: Wylde Green, 1938. 24pp

9030 Roberts, Sonia. Bird-keeping and Birdcages: a history. New York: Drake, 1973. 138pp, ill

9031 Rockley, Alicia Margaret. A History of Gardening in England. 2nd ed. London: B. Quaritch, 1896; 3rd ed. London: J. Murray, 1910; reprint. Detroit: Singing Tree Pr, 1969. 405pp, ill, bib

9032 Schlebecker, John T. Agricultural Implements and Machines in the Collection of the National Museum of History and Technology. Washington, D.C.: Smithsonian, 1972. 57pp, ill

9033 Sharp, James. Descriptions of Some of the Utensils in Husbandry, rolling carriages, cart rollers, and divided rollers for land or gardens, ... made and sold by J. Sharp. London: 1773; 1777. ...; 58pp, pls; another 1777 has 93pp, pls BM, DeWint

9034 Sinclair, Sir John, 1754-1835. An Account of James Small, and of his improvements in the construction of agricultural implements. Edinburgh: Abernethy & Walker, printers, 1811. 13pp, pls NN

9035 Slight, James, and Robert Scott Burn. The Book of Farm Implements and Machines. Ed. by Henry Stephens. Edinburgh; London: Blackwood, 1858. 648pp, ill, 40 pls

9036 Sloane, Eric. The Seasons of America's Past. New York: W. Funk, 1958. 150pp, ill (Agricultural tools)

9037 Small, James, 1740?-1793. Treatise of Ploughs and Wheel Carriages. Edinburgh: Author, 1763; 1784. 1784: 255pp, 5 pls NN

9038   Smith, Harris Pearson. Farm Machinery and Equipment.
       New York: McGraw Hill, 1929; 2nd ed. New York; Lon-
       don: 1937. 448pp, ill; 460pp, ill

9039   Smith, James, of Coventry. Remarks on Thorough Draining
       and Deep Plowing. Extracted from the third report of
       Drummond's Agricultural Museum. (A catalogue of imple-
       ments, seeds, etc.) 6th ed. Stirling; Edinburgh: W.
       Drummond & Sons, 1843; 7th ed., with notes. 1844.   BM

9040   Spenser, Arthur John, and John B. Passmore. Handbook of
       the Collections Illustrating Agricultural Implements and
       Machinery; a brief survey of the machines and implements
       which are available to the farmer, with notes on their
       development. Science Museum. London: HMSO, 1930.
       94pp, 16 pls, bib   DLC, NN

9041   Steffen, Randy. United States Military Saddles, 1812-1943.
       Norman: U. of Oklahoma Pr, 1973. 158pp, ill

9042   Stephens, Henry, 1795-1874. The Book of the Farm: detailing
       the labours of the farmer, steward, plowman, hedger,
       cattle-man, shepherd, field-worker, and dairymaid ... with
       notes by John S. Skinner. 2 vol. London; Edinburgh:
       Blackwood; New York: Greeley & McElrath, 1847; 2nd
       ed. London; Edinburgh: 1852; 5th ed. rev. and largely
       rewritten by James Macdonald, as Stephen's Book of the
       Farm.... Vol. I. Land and Its Equipment; Vol. II. Farm
       Crops; Vol. III. Farm Live Stock. 3 vol. in 5. London;
       Edinburgh: 1908-09. ill, 21 pls   DLC

9043   Taylor, J. Neufville. Guide to the Collection of Bygone Agri-
       cultural Implements. Gloucester, Eng: Folk Museum,
       1950. 19pp, ill

9044   Taylor, John Ellor, 1837-1895. The Aquarium: its inhabi-
       tants, structure, and management. New ed. London:
       W. H. Allen, 1884. 316pp, ill   DLC

9045   Thomas, John Jacob, 1810-1895. Farm Implements; and the
       principles of their construction and use; an elementary ...
       treatise on mechanics.... New York; London: 1855; new
       ed. New York: 1861; New York: O. Judd, 1869; new ed.
       rev. & enl. 1879; new ed. 1886. 302pp, ill; 312pp, ill;
       316pp, ill   BM

9046   Tools and Tillage. Annual. Copenhagen: G. E. C. Gad
       Publishers, 1968- .   ill

9047   Tull, Jethro, 1674-1741. Horse-shoeing Husbandry: or, An
       essay on the principles of tillage and vegetation. Wherein
       is shewn a method of introducing a sort of vineyard-culture

into the cornfields, in order to increase their product, and
diminish the common expence, by the use of instruments
described in cuts. London: Author, 1733; Supplement.
1736; 3rd ed. ... with descriptions and cuts of the instruments. London: printed for A. Millar, 1751;... 200pp,
6 pls; 65pp, 432pp, 7 pls DLC, DeWint

9048 Tylden, Major G. Horses and Saddlery: an account of the
animals used by the British and Commonwealth armies
from the 17th century to the present day, with a description of their equipment. London: J. A. Allen, with the
Army Museums Ogilby Trust, 1965. 276pp, ill, 81 pls,
color frontis

9049 Vince, John Norman Thatcher. Discovering Horse Brasses.
Tring: Shire Publications, 1968. 46pp, ill, bib

9050 _____. Vintage Farm Machines. Aylesbury: Shire Publications, 1973. 33pp, ill, bib (English, ca.1800-1972)

9051 Ward, Gordon Reginald. On Dating Old Horse-Shoes. Hull:
Museum, 1939. pls BM, V & A

9052 West, L. A. Agriculture: Hand Tools to Mechanization.
Science Museum. London: HMSO, 1967. 47pp, ill (20
color) (To 1913)

9053 Wheelhouse, Frances. Digging Stick to Rotary Hoe: men and
machines in rural Australia. Fore. by J. R. A. McMillan.
Melbourne; London: Cassell, 1966. 222pp, ill, bib

9054 Wilson, John, professor of agriculture. Agricultural Products
and Implements. Lecture, before Royal Society for the
Encouragement of Arts, Manufactures and Commerce, as
a result of the Great Exhibition. London: 1852.

9055 Wilson, John Marius, ed. The Rural Cyclopedia; or a general
dictionary of agriculture, and of the arts, sciences, instruments, and practice, necessary to the farmer, stockfarmer,
gardener, forester, landsteward, farrier, etc. 4 vol.
Edinburgh: 1847-49. text, 63 engraved pls of plants,
birds, landscapes, farm equipment, etc.

9056 Worlidge, John, fl. 1669-1698. Systema Agriculturae, the
mystery of husbandry discovered, wherein is treated of
the several new and most advantagious ways of tilling,
planting, sowing: all sorts of gardens ... and coppices,
as also of fruits, corn, grain ... cattle, fowl, beasts,
bees, silk-worms, etc. With an account of the several
instruments and engines used in this profession.... London: T. Johnson, for S. Speed, 1669; 2nd ed. enl. &
corr. London: J. C., for T. Dring, 1675; 3rd ed. 1681;

5th ed. rev., corr., enl. as The Gentleman's Companion
in the Business and Pleasures of Country Life.... London: E. Curll & J. Pemberton, 1716. 278pp, ill; 324pp,
ill; 334pp, ill, pl; 504pp, ill

9057   Wright, Philip Arthur. Old Farm Implements. London: A.
       & C. Black, 1961; London: David & Charles, 1975.   95pp,
       ill, 23 pls

9058   Wrightson, Professor John. Agricultural Machinery. London:
       1876. See: Bevan, G. P., British Manufacturing Indus-
       tries, Vol. 10, no. 43.

BARBED WIRE

9059   *Allison, Vernon. Barbed Wire and Related Fencing Items.
       Fort Worth, Tx: 19? ill

9060   Clifton, Robert T. Barbs, Prongs, Points, Prickers, and
       Stickers; a complete and illustrated catalogue of antique
       barbed wire. Norman: U. of Oklahoma Pr, 1970; reprint.
       1974. 418pp, ill

9061   _____. Field Guide for Barbed Wire Collectors. Denton,
       Tx: Acobac Pr, 1966. 84pp, ill

9062   *Glover, Jack. "Bobbed" Wire. Sunset, Tx: Cow Puddle Pr,
       1966; 2nd ed. as More Bobbed Wire, 1969; as The "Bobbed"
       Wire II Bible, 1971; 4th ed. as The "Bobbed" Wire III
       Bible, 1972. u.p., ill

9063   International Barbed Wire Gazette. Monthly periodical. Arling-
       ton, Tx: J. Glover, 197-?- .

9064a James, Jesse S. Early United States Barbed Wire Patents.
       Maywood, Calif: 1966. 291pp, ill

9064b Jenkins, Jay. Old West Barb Wire Guide Book. Fort Worth,
       Tx: 19?

9065   Little, Joe Dean. Joe's Antique Barbed Wire Manual. Tex-
       line, Tx: Rabbit Ear Pub. Co, 1971. 140pp, ill

9066   McCallum, Henry D., and Frances T. McCallum. The Wire
       That Fenced the West. Norman: U. of Oklahoma Pr,
       1965; reprint. 1972. 285pp, ill

9067a Maurer, Albert. Barb Wire: Collectors Identification Guide.
       Phoenix, Ariz: 1970. 24pp, chiefly ill

9067b Rock, Herbert. Barbed Wire Identification Hand Book. Bak-
       ersfield, Calif: 19? 80pp, ill

9068   Suggested Price Guide for Barbed Wire Collectors.   Texline,
         Tx: Rabbit Ear Pub. Co, 1971. 12pp, ill

9069   Turner, Thomas Edward.   Barbed Wire; handbook and pricing
         guide.   San Angelo, Tx: Educator Books, 1969.   102pp,
         ill

DAIRIES AND BUTTER MAKING

9070   Moseley and Stoddard Catalog, 1896.   Reprint.   Levittown,
         NY: Early Trades and Crafts Society, 1975.   32pp, 77
         ill (Tools and machinery for dairy, creamery & cheese
         factory)

9071   Powell, Elizabeth A.   Pennsylvania Butter Tools and Processes.
         Doylestown, Pa: Bucks County Historical Society, 1975.
         28pp, ill, bib (Collection of the Mercer Museum)

9072   Smith, Elmer Lewis, comp.   Early American Butter Prints;
         a collection of rural folk art, designs illustrated from hand
         carved butter molds and prints.   Witmer, Pa: Applied
         Arts, 1968.   42pp, ill (Rubbings and illustrations of over
         100 designs)

9073   Smith, Richard Flanders.   Pennsylvania Butter Prints.   Eph-
         rata, Pa: Science Press, 1970.   36pp, ill, color pls

9074   Trice, James E.   Butter Molds; a primitive art form.   Des
         Moines: Wallace-Homestead, 1973.   100pp, ill

9075   Willard, Xerxes Addison, 1820-1882.   Willard's Practical
         Butter Book: a complete treatise on butter-making at
         factories and farm dairies, including the selection ... of
         stock ... --with plans for dairy rooms and creameries,
         dairy fixtures, utensils, etc.   New York: Rural Pub. Co,
         1875.   171pp, ill DLC

9076   _____.   Willard's Practical Dairy Husbandry: a complete
         treatise on Dairy Farms and Farming..., --history and
         mode of organization of butter and cheese factories, --
         dairy utensils, etc., etc.   New York: D. D. T. Moore,
         1872.   546pp, ill, 1 pl DLC

SECTION XXVI

EQUIPMENT OF SPORT AND WEAPONS OF WAR

FISHING

9077 "All About Fishing and Fishing Apparatus." International
Fisheries Exhibition, London, 1883. Selected papers.
London: 1883. BM

9078 Audrey-Fletcher, Henry Lancelot. Halcyon; or, Rod-fishing
with fly, minnow and worm. To which is added a short
and easy method of dressing flies, with a description of
the materials used, by Henry Wade. London: Bell &
Daldy, 1861. 212pp, 12 pls (part color)

9079 Chitty, Edward, 1804-1863. The Fly Fishers' Text Book, by
Theophilis South (pseud.). London: R. Ackermann, 1841;
as The Illustrated Fly Fisher's Text Book; a complete
guide to the science of fly-fishing for salmon, trout, gray-
ling, etc. London: H. G. Bohn, 1845. 231pp, ill, 23
engraved pls (Implements, appliances & artificial flies)
CU, NN, MH, CtY

9080 Collins, Joseph William. Catalogue of the Collection Illustrating the Fishing Vessels and Boats, and their equipment,
... anglers' outfits, etc. Great International Fisheries
Exhibition, London 1883. Washington, D.C.: GPO, 1883.
DLC, BM

9081 The Complete Family-Piece: and, Country Gentleman, and
farmer's best guide. In three parts. Part 1. Containing
a ... collection of above 1000 well-experienced family
receipts ... Part 2. Containing 1. full instructions to be
observed in hunting, coursing, setting and shooting ...
2. cautions, rules, and directions to be taken and observed
in fishing; with the manner of making and preserving of
rods, lines, floats, artificial flies, etc. ... 3. ... gardens
... Part 3. ... practical rules, and methods for the improving of land, and managing a farm. 2nd ed. London:
for A. Bettesworth & C. Hitch, 1737. 526, 62pp DeWint

9082   Davis, F. M. An Account of the Fishing Gear of England and
       Wales. London: HMSO, 1923; 3rd rev. ed. 1937. 101pp,
       ill; 139pp, ill, bib NN

9083   Dennys, John, d. 1609. The Secrets of Angling: teaching the
       choicest tooles, baytes and seasons, for the taking of any
       fish, in pond or river: practiced and familiarly opened in
       three bookes.... London: for Roger Jackson, 1613; Lon-
       don: by Augustine Matthews for Roger Jackson, ca. 1620;
       reprints. London: 1877; London: W. Satchell, 1883.
       62pp; ...; 62pp, ill (In verse)

9084   Dewar, George Albemarle Bertie. The Book of the Dry Fly.
       London: Lawrence & Bullen, 1897; new ed. London: A.
       & C. Black, 1910. 238pp, pls; 277pp, 8 color pls

9085   Evans, W. The Art of Angling; or, Complete fly-fisher:
       describing the different kinds of fish, their haunts, places
       of feeding, etc.... kinds of baits, and ... flies ... with
       ample directions for making artificial flies. Uxbridge,
       Eng: William Lake, printer, sold at all the fishing tackle
       shops in London, 1820? 95pp, frontispiece MH, NN

9086   Hills, John Waller, 1867-1938. A History of Fly Fishing for
       Trout. London: P. Allen; New York: F. A. Stokes,
       1921; reprint. Rockville Centre, NY: Freshet Pr, 1971.
       244pp, ill, bib

9087   MacClelland, Harry G. The Trout Fly Dressers' Cabinet of
       Devices; or, How to tie flies for trout and grayling fishing.
       London: Sampson, Low, 1899;... London: Fishing Ga-
       zette, 1909;... 137pp, ill NN

9088   *McDonald, John Dennis. Quill Gordon. New York: Knopf,

1972. 195pp, ill, 11 color pls, bib (Includes modern version of A Treatyse of Fysshynge with an Angle, by Juliana Berners, and an edited version of Charles Cotton's contribution to The Compleat Angler) (History of artificial flies)

9089 Marburg, Mrs. Mary (Orvis). Favorite Flies and Their Histories.... Boston; New York: Houghton, Mifflin, 1892; 1896. 522pp, ill, pls (32 color) DeWint

9090 Mascall, Leonard, d. 1589. A Booke of Fishing with Hook and Line, and of all other instruments thereunto belonging. Another of sundrie engines and trappes to take polcats, buzards, rattes, mice and all other kindes of vermine and beasts. London: John Wolfe, printer, 1590; reprint with pref. and glossary by Thomas Satchell. London: Satchell, 1884. 92pp, ill, folding pl; 52pp, ill MiU, MH, CtY, NN

9091 Melner, Samuel, and Hermann Kessler, comp. Great Fishing Tackle Catalogs of the Golden Age. Commentary by Sparse Grey Hackle. New York: Crown, 1972. 344pp, ill

9092 *Orvis, Charles F., and A. Nelson Cheney. Fishing with the Fly, sketches by lovers of the art, with illustrations of standard flies. Manchester, Vt: Orvis, 1883. 299pp, color pls

9093 Overfield, T. Donald. Famous Flies and Their Originators. London: A. & C. Black, 1972. 186, 16pp, ill, pls

9094 Pennell, Harry Cholmondeley, 1837-1915. Modern Improvements in Fishing Tackle and Fish Hooks. London: Sampson Low, 1887. 194pp, ill BM

9095 _____, and others. Fishing. 2 vol. London: Longmans, Green, 1887, 1896. ill, pls (Includes implements and tackle)

9096 Pritt, Thomas Evan. Yorkshire Trout Flies.... Leeds: Goodall & Suddick, 1885; 2nd ed. as North Country Flies. London: Sampson, Low, 1886. 47pp; 63pp BM

9097 Smith, Onnie Warren, 1872-1941. Casting Tackle and Methods. Reprint from "Outdoor Life." Cincinnati: Stewart & Kidd, 1920. 257pp, pls

9098 Theakston, Michael. British Angling Flies. Rev. by F. M. Walbran. Ripon, Eng: William Harrison, 1883. 145pp, ill

9099 Walker, Charles Edward. Old Flies in New Dresses. London: Lawrence & Bullen, 1898. 116pp, 3 pls BM

9100 *Walton, Sir Izaak, 1593-1683. The Compleat Angler, or,
      The contemplative man's recreation, being a discourse
      of fish and fishing, not unworthy of the perusal of most
      anglers. London: T. Maxey, printer, for R. Marriot,
      1653; 2nd ed. enl. 1655; 7th ed. amended and improved
      by Izaak Walton and Charles Cotton, as The Compleat
      Angler ... in two parts. I. Being a discourse of rivers,
      fish-ponds, fish and fishing. II. Instructions How to Angle
      for a Trout or a Grayling.... London: H. Kent, 1759;
      2 vol. in 1. London: for T. Hope, 1760; ed. by John
      Major. Boston: Little, Brown, 1866; etc. etc. 246pp,
      ill; 355pp, ill; ...; 340pp, ill, pls; 1866: 445pp, ill, pls
      (fishing implements are illustrated)

9101 Webster, David. The Angler and the Loop-Rod. Edinburgh:
      W. Blackwood, 1885. 340pp BM

9102 Wells, Henry P. Fly-Rods and Fly-Tackle. Suggestions as
      to their manufacture and use. London: Sampson Low,
      1884; New York: Harper, 1885. 364pp, ill BM

9103 West, Leonard. The Natural Trout Fly and Its Imitation.
      Being an angler's record of insects seen at the waterside
      and the method of making their imitations. St. Helens:
      Author, 1912. 144pp, 13 color pls

9104 Wilcocks, James C. The Sea-Fisherman, or Fishing Pilotage.
      Comprising the chief methods of hook and line fishing in
      the British and other seas, a glance at nets, and remarks
      on boats and boating. Guernsey, Eng: S. Barbet, for
      Author, 1865; 3rd ed. much enl., rewritten as The Sea-
      Fisherman ... profusely illustrated with woodcuts of leads,
      baited hooks, knots, nets, boats, etc., and detailed de-
      scriptions of same. London: Longmans, Green, 1875.
      196pp, ill, pls; 323pp, ill, pls

ARCHERY

9105 The Archer's Guide: containing full instructions for the use
      of that ancient and noble instrument, the bow ... accom-
      panied by a sketch of the history of the long-bow. (By
      an old Toxophilite.) London: T. Hurst, 1833; facsimile
      reprint. London: Tabard Pr, 1970. 178pp, ill, color
      frontis, bib DeWint

9106 A Book on the Excellence of the Bow and Arrow. Arabic
      manuscript, circa 1500 A.D., in Garrett Collection,
      Princeton University Library. Tr. and ed. by Nabih
      Amin Faris, and Robert Potter Elmer. Princeton, NJ:
      U. Pr, 1945. 182pp, pls

9107 Burke, Edmund H. The History of Archery. Westport,
      Conn: Greenwood Pr, 1957. 224pp, ill

9108 Chenevix Trench, Charles Pocklington. A History of Marks-
      manship. London: Longman, 1972. 319pp, ill (Fire-
      arms and bows and arrows)

9109 Cosson, Baron Charles Alexander de. The Crossbow of
      Ulrich V, Count of Wurtemberg, 1460, with remarks on
      its construction. n. p. : 1892? 20pp (pp. 445-464), ill
      InU

9110 Featherstone, Donald Frederick. The Bowmen of England:
      the story of the English longbow. London: Jarrolds,
      1967. 200pp, 8 pls, bib

9111 Hansard, George Agar. The Book of Archery, being the com-
      plete history and practice of the art, ancient and modern.
      London: Longman, Orme, etc., 1840; London: H. G.
      Bohn, 1841. 456pp, pls NjP, DLC, MiU

9112 Hand-book of Archery; wherein are described the various im-
      plements used in the art, with directions for their use,
      etc., also the laws of archery. 2nd ed. London: R.
      Tyas, n. d. 61pp, frontispiece NjP

9113 Heath, Ernest Gerald. The Grey Goose Wing. Reading, Pa:
      Osprey, 1971. 343pp, ill, 17 pls

9114 _____ . A History of Target Archery. Newton Abbot:
      David & Charles, 1973. 208pp, ill, bib

9115 Hurley, Vic. Arrows Against Steel: The History of the Bow.
      New York: Mason & Charter, 1975. ill

9116 Oxley, James Edwin. The Fletchers and Longbowstringmakers
      of London. London: Worshipful Co. of Fletchers, 1968.
      160pp, 6 ill, 9 pls, bib

9117 Payne-Gallwey, Sir Ralph. The Projectile-throwing Engines
      of the Ancients. London: Longman, 1907; facsimile re-
      print with new introd. by E. G. Heath. Wakefield, Eng:
      E P Publishing, 1973. 44pp, ill, 26 pls (Oriental bows
      and arrows, ca. 1400-ca. 1900)

9118 Pope, Saxton Temple. A Study of Bows and Arrows. Berke-
      ley, Cal: Cal. U. Pr, 1923; reprint, with fore. by
      Robert F. Heizer, as Bows and Arrows. Berkeley; Lon-
      don: Cambridge U. Pr, 1962. 83pp, 20 pls

DECOYS

9119 *Barber, Joel David. Wild Fowl Decoys. New York: Derry-
       dale Pr; New York: Windward House, 1934; New York:
       Dover, 1954. 156pp, ill, 140 (4 color) pls, color frontis
       (Duck, swan and geese)

9120 Cheever, Byron. Mason Decoys. Heber City, Utah: Hill-
       crest, 1974. 166pp, ill (Mason's Decoy Factory products)

9121 *Colio, Quintina. American Decoys: ducks, eiders, scoters,
       geese, brant, swan, and other unusual decoys, from 1865
       to 1920. Ephrata, Pa: Science Pr, 1972. 96pp, ill

9122 Decoy Collector's Guide. Annual. Burlington, Iowa: 196-?-

9123 Earnest, Adele. The Art of the Decoy: American Bird
       Carvings. New York: Potter, 1965. 170pp, 208 ill, bib

9124 *Mackey, William J., Jr. American Bird Decoys. With a
       chapter on American decoys as folk art by Quintina Colio.
       New York: Dutton, 1965. 256pp, 188 ill, 8 color pls

9125 Parmalee, Paul Woodburn, and Forrest D. Loomis. Decoys
       and Decoy Carvers of Illinois. DeKalb: Northern U. Pr,
       1969. 506pp, 426 ill, bib

9126 Smith, Elmer Lewis. American Wildfowl Decoys from Folk
       Art to Factory: a sampler of collectibles. Lebanon, Pa:
       Applied Arts, 1974. 32pp, chiefly ill

9127 Starr, George Ross, Jr. Decoys of the Atlantic Flyway.
       New York: Winchester Pr, 1974. 350 decoys ill, 60 in
       color (Includes "stick-up" decoys. Pieces from Starr
       Collection)

9128 Webster, David S., and William Kehoe. Decoys at Shelburne
       Museum. Shelburne, Vt: the Museum, 1961. 129pp, ill,
       pls

GENERAL WORKS ON ARMS AND ARMOR

9129 Akehurst, Richard. Antique Weapons for Pleasure and Invest-
       ment. London: Gifford; New York: Arco, 1969. 174pp,
       128 ill, 22 pls (18th century to present day)

9130 _____. Sporting Guns. London: Weidenfeld & Nicolson,
       1968; London: Octopus, 1972. 96pp, ill, 24 color pls
       (18th century to present day)

9131 _____. The World of Guns. Feltham; New York: Hamlyn,
       1972. 127pp, ill (Small guns to 1971)

9132   Alexander, S. G. B.   Antique Pistols.   New York: Arco,
       1964.   55pp, color ill, bib

9133   Allen, G. W. B.   Pistols, Rifles and Machine-guns.   London:
       English U Pr, 1953.   ill

9134   Antique Arms Annual.   Waco, Tx: S. P. Stevens, 1971-   .

9135   Arms and Armour.   Hazel Grove, Cheshire: Arms and
       Armour Society, Northern Branch, 1968.   39pp, chiefly ill

9136   Arms and Armour: the journal of the Arms and Armour So-
       ciety.   Monthly.   Leatherhead, Eng: 1953-   .

9137   The Arms Collector.   Periodical.   East Syracuse, NY: Ameri-
       can Arms Collectors Association, 1938-   .

9138   Ashdown, Charles Henry.   Armour and Weapons in the Middle
       Ages.   London: Harrap;   New York: Brentano's, 1925.
       219pp, ill, bib

9139 *   .   British and Foreign Arms and Armour ... illus-
       trated ... from actual examples, missals, illuminated
       manuscripts, brasses, effigies, etc., and from original
       research in the British Museum, the Tower of London,
       Wallace Collection, Rotunda at Woolwich, many private
       collections, etc.   London; Edinburgh: T. C. Jack, 1909;
       as Arms and Armour ... etc.   New York: Dodge, 1909;
       reprint as British and Continental Arms and Armour.   New
       York: Dover, 1970.

9140   Bailey, De Witt, and others.   Guns and Gun Collecting.   Lon-
       don: Octopus, 1972.   128pp, ill   (To ca.1950)

9141   Ball, William, Jr.   The Checklist of Auction Sale Catalogues
       of Firearms.   West Chester, Pa: 1939.   7pp   DeWint

9142 *Barwick, Humphrey.   A Breefe Discourse, concerning the
       force and effect of all manuall weapons of fire, and the
       disability of the long bowe or archery, in respect of others
       of greater force now in use....   (A criticism of Sir John
       Smythe's "Certain Discourses," and Sir Roger Williams'
       "A Briefe Discourse of Warre.")   London: For Richard
       Oliffe, 1594?; reprint in Bow Versus Gun.   Introd. by
       Ernest Gerald Heath.   Wakefield, Eng: E P Publishing,
       1973.   35 leaves; (Reprint, which includes Smythe's book,
       is 219pp, ill) BM

9143   Basco, Jean.   The Armour Court; a general guide.   Royal
       Ontario Museum.   Toronto: 1970.   24pp, ill

9144   Baxter, D. R.   Superimposed Load Firearms, 1360-1860.

Hong Kong: South China Morning Post, 1966. 536pp, ill, bib

9145 Beard, Charles Relly. Catalogue of an Exhibition of Arms, armour and costumes in the possession of Mr. C. Andrade. 5 parts. London: Wilkinson Brothers, 1922-1927.

9146 _____ . Notes on the Barberini and Some Allied Armours. Blackburn, Eng: priv. printed, 1924. 48pp, 3 ill

9147 Beardmore, John. A Catalogue with Illustrations of the Collection of Ancient Arms and Armour, at Uplands, near Fareham, Hampshire. London: Boone, printer, 1844. 29pp, 17 pls

9148 Belote, Theodore Thomas. American and European Swords in the Historical Collections of the United States National Museum. Washington, D. C. : GPO, 1932. 163pp, pls, bib

9149 Belous, Russell E. , ed. A Distinguished Collection of Arms and Armor on Permanent Display. Museum of Natural History, Los Angeles. Los Angeles: Ward Ritchie Pr, 1968. 128pp, ill

9150 Blackmore, Howard Loftus. Arms and Armour. London: Studio Vista; New York: Dutton, 1965. 160pp, ill

9151 _____ . Firearms. London: Studio Vista; New York: Dutton, 1964. 158pp, ill, pls

9152 _____ . Guns and Rifles of the World. London: Batsford; New York: Viking, 1965. 134pp, ill, pls (1 color), bib

9153 _____ . Hunting Weapons. London: Barrie & Jenkins, 1971. 401pp, ill, 40 pls, bib (ca. 1600-1900)

9154 Blair, Claude. European and American Arms, Circa 1100-1850. New York: Crown, 1962. 134pp, ill, pls, bib

9155 _____ . European Armour, Circa 1066 to Circa 1700. London: Batsford, 1958. 248pp, 299 ill, bib

9156 _____ . Pistols of the World. London: Batsford, 1968. 823 ill

9157 Boehret, Paul C. The Ax and Its Variations, Military and Civil. Easton, Pa: Hobson Printing, 1966. 79pp, ill

9158 *Boothroyd, Geoffrey. The Handgun. London: Cassell, 1970. 584pp, 850 ill

9159 Bow Versus Gun. Introd. by Ernest Gerald Heath. Wakefield,

Eng: E P Publishing, 1973. 219pp, ill (Reprint of
Humphrey Barwick's A Breefe Discourse..., and Sir John
Smythe's Certain Discourses)

9160 Bowman, Hank Wieand. Antique Guns. Ed. by Lucian Cary.
Greenwich, Conn: Fawcett; New York: Arco, 1953.
144pp, ill

9161 _____. Famous Guns from Famous Collections. Greenwich, Conn: Fawcett, 1957. 144pp, ill, pls

9162 _____. Famous Guns from the Smithsonian Collection.
Greenwich, Conn: Fawcett, 1966; New York: Arco, 1967.
112pp, ill

9163 Brett, Edwin John. A Pictorial and Descriptive Record of
the Origin and Development of Arms and Armour. To
which are appended plates specially drawn from the Author's
collection, at Oaklands, St. Peter's, Thanet, and Burleigh
House, London. London: Low, Marston, 1894. 128pp,
133 pls with 1000 figures MiD, PPL, BM

9164 Brown, John Brewer. Sword and Firearm Collection of the
Society of Cincinnati in the Anderson House Museum,
Washington, D.C. Washington: the Society, 1965. 120pp,
ill

9165 *Burton, Richard F. The Book of the Sword. London: Chatto
& Windus, 1884. 299pp

9166 Calvert, Albert Frederick. Spanish Arms and Armour: account of the Royal Armoury of Madrid. London; New
York: J. Lane, 1907. 142pp, 386 ill, 248 pls (Based
on the catalogue prepared in 1898 by the Conde de Valencia de San Juan) NN

9167 Carman, W. Y. A History of Firearms from Earliest Times
to 1914. London: Routledge & Paul, 1955. 207pp, ill

9168 Carter, Anthony. The Bayonet: a history of knife and sword
bayonets, 1850-1970. London: Arms and Armour Pr,
1974. 128pp, ill

9169 Chapel, Charles Edward. Gun Collecting. New York: Coward-
McCann, 1939; 2nd ed. rev. 1947; reprint as The Complete
Book of Gun Collecting. New York: 1960. 232pp, ill, 14
pls, bib

9170 _____. The Gun Collector's Handbook of Values. San
Leandro, Cal: Author, 1940; rev. ed. New York: Coward-
McCann, 1947; rev. ed. 1951; rev. ed. 1955; 7th rev. ed.
1966; 8th ed. rev. by Mrs. C. E. Chapel. 1968; 9th ed.

1970; etc. 220pp, ill, 32 pls; 412pp, ill, 48 pls, bib; 403pp, ill, pls, bib; 398pp, ill, 49 pls, bib; etc.

9171 Chenevix Trench, Charles Pocklington. A History of Marks-manship. London: Longman, 1972. 319pp, ill (Fire-arms and bows and arrows)

9172 Cleator, Philip Ellaby. Weapons of War. London: Hale, 1967; New York: Crowell, 1968. 224pp, ill, 32 pls

9173 Cripps-Day, Francis Henry, ed. Fragmenta Armamentaria. 5 vol. Frome, Eng: Author, 1934-1950. (An Introduc-tion to the Study of Greenwich Armour. Part 2-4 (1 never published). 1934-45; A Sale of Armour by Lottery in 1586. Vol. 2, part 2. 1938, 54pp; Collection of Armour of Ferdinand, Archduke of the Tirol, at Ambras. Vol. 2, part 4. 1950, 187pp; The Past is Never Dead. Vol. 5. 1941, 216pp, 9 pls)

9174 _____. A Record of Armour Sales, 1881-1924. London: G. Bell, 1925. 327pp, ill (See also: Laking, Sir G. F., A Record of European Armour and Arms....) ViU, DLC

9175 *Dean, Bashford. Catalogue of European Arms and Armour. New York: Metropolitan Museum, 1905. 215pp, ill, bib

9176 *_____. Catalogue of European Court Swords and Hunting Swords, including the Ellis, de Dino, Riggs, and Reubell Collections. New York: Metropolitan Museum, 1929. 86pp, 101 pls, color frontis

9177 *_____. Catalogue of a Loan Exhibition of Arms and Armor. February-April 1911. Metropolitan Museum. New York: Gilliss Pr, 1911. 85pp, ill, pls

9178 _____. The Collection of Arms and Armor of Rutherford Stuyvesant, 1843-1909. New York: priv. printed, De Vinne Pr, 1914. 174pp

9179 *_____. Handbook of Arms and Armor, European and Ori-ental. Metropolitan Museum. New York: Gilliss Pr, 1915; 4th ed. with additions and corrections and chapter on the Bashford Dean Memorial Gallery, by Stephen V. Grancsay. New York: 1930. 161pp, 65 pls; 331pp, 149 ill

9180 *_____. Helmets and Body Armor in Modern Warfare. New Haven: Yale U. Pr, for Metropolitan Museum, New York, 1920. 325pp, ill

9181 *_____. Notes on Arms and Armor. Metropolitan Museum. New York: 1916. 149pp, ill, pls

9182 *Demmin, Auguste Frederic, 1823?-1898. Weapons of War;
      being a history of arms and armour from the earliest
      period to the present time. Tr. from French (1870) by
      Charles C. Black. London: Bell & Daldy, 1870; as An
      Illustrated History of Arms and Armour ... etc. London:
      G. Bell, 1877; 1894; 1901; 1911. 595pp, 2000 ill NN,
      DLC, ICRL

9183 de Reuck, A. V. S. The Art of the Armourer. An exhibi-
      tion of armour, swords and firearms. April-May 1963.
      London: V & A, 1963. 100pp, pls

9184 Dufty, Arthur Richard. European Armour in the Tower of
      London. London: HMSO, 1968. 25pp, ill, 165 pls

9185 Ellacott, Samuel Ernest. Armour and Blade. London; New
      York: Abelard-Schuman, 1962. 191pp, ill

9186 _____. Collecting Arms and Armour. London: Arco,
      1964. 128pp, ill

9187 _____. Guns. London: Methuen, 1955. 76pp, ill

9188 Ellis, John. The Social History of the Machine Gun. New
      York: Pantheon, 1976. 186pp, ill, bib

9189 Espingarda Perfeyta, or, The perfect gun. Ed. and tr. by
      Rainer Daehnhardt, and W. Keith Neal. Originally pub-
      lished in Lisbon, 1718. London; New York: Sotheby
      Parke Bernet, 1975. 466pp, ill (Includes gunsmith's
      tools)

9190 Exhibition of Spanish Royal Armour in Her Majesty's Tower
      of London. April-September 1960. London: HMSO, 1960.
      24pp, ill, 16 pls

9191 *Ffoulkes, Charles John, 1868-1947. Armour and Weapons.
      With pref. by Viscount Dillon. Oxford: Clarendon, 1909;
      reprint. Wakefield, Eng: E P Publishing, 1973; reprint.
      Totowa, NJ: Rowman & Littlefield, 1974. 112pp, ill,
      11 pls, bib

9192 * _____. The Armourer and His Craft from the 11th to the
      16th Century. London: Methuen; Boston: Small, Maynard,
      1912; reprint. New York: B. Blom; New York: F. Ungar,
      1967. 199pp, ill, 32 pls, 104 reproductions of marks

9193 _____. Arms and Armour in the Banqueting Hall, Edin-
      burgh Castle. Edinburgh: HMSO, 1930; 1936. 16pp, ill
      CU

9194 _____. European Arms and Armour. London: Bell, for
      the Historical Association, 1932. 16pp MiU, DLC

9195 _____. European Arms and Armour in the University of
Oxford. Principally in the Ashmolean and Pitt-Rivers
Museums. Oxford: Clarendon, 1912. 64pp, ill, 19 pls
DLC

9196 _____. Tower of London; guide to the armouries. London: HMSO, 1924; 1930; 1936. 24pp; 25pp; 28pp, all ill
NNC-Ave

9197 Frith, James, and Ronald Andrews. Antique Pistol Collecting
(1400-1860). London: Holland Pr, 1960. 122pp, ill, 25
pls

9198 Frodelius, Ron, and R. E. Burt. The Trap Collectors Guide.
Dalton, NY: R. E. Burt, 1975. 78pp, 300 ill, 1500 items

9199 Fryer, Douglas John. Antique Weapons A to Z. London:
Bell, 1969; New York: T. Nelson, 1971. 114pp, ill, bib

9200 Gardner, John Starkie. Foreign Armour in England. London: Seeley; New York: Macmillan, 1898. 96pp, ill,
pls (8 color)

9201 Gilchrist, Helen Ives. A Catalogue of the Collection of Arms
and Armor Presented to the Cleveland Museum of Art by
Mr. and Mrs. John Long Severance; 1916-1923. Cleveland:
the Museum, 1924; 2nd ed. 1948. 294pp, ill DLC

9202 Grancsay, Stephen Vincent. The Armor of Galio de Genouilhac.
New York: Plantin Pr, for Metropolitan Museum, 1937.
36pp, ill, 28 pls, bib DLC

9203 * _____. Arms and Armour. New York: Odyssey, 1964;
London: Hamlyn, 1965. 46pp, ill

9204 * _____. The Bashford Dean Collection of Arms and Armor
in the Metropolitan Museum of Art. Introd. by Carl Otto
von Kienbusch. Portland, Me: Southworth Pr, for the
Armor and Arms Club of N.Y.C., 1933. 270pp, 63 pls,
bib

9205 _____. Catalogue of Armor. Worcester, Mass: John
Woodman Higgins Armory, 1961. 127pp, pls

9206 _____. Historical Armor, a picture book. New York:
Metropolitan Museum, 1944. ill

9207 _____. Historic Arms and Armor. Metropolitan Museum.
New York: Museum Pr, 1935; 2nd ed. 1938. 8pp, 20 pls

9208 _____. Loan Exhibition of European Arms and Armor.
Metropolitan Museum. August-September 1931. New York:
1931. 120pp, pls

9209   _____   .   Loan Exhibition of Medieval and Renaissance Arms
and Armor from the Metropolitan Museum, New York.
Los Angeles: County Museum; Pittsburgh, Pa: Carnegie
Institute, etc., 1953. v.p., ill

9210   _____   .   Master French Gunsmiths' Designs of the 17th to
19th Centuries, reproduced in facsimile. New York:
Greenberg, 1950; New York: Winchester Pr, 1970. 208pp,
ill

9211   _____   .   Sculpture in Arms and Armor; a picture book.
New York: Metropolitan Museum, 1940. ill

9212   Greener, William, d. 1869. The Gun and Its Development;
with notes on shooting. London; New York: Cassell,
1881; 2nd ed. enl. 1884; 3rd. ed. 1885?; 9th ed. 1910;
9th ed. reprints. New York: Bonanza, 1967; London:
Arms and Armour Pr, 1972; Detroit: Gale, 1975. 674pp,
ill; 740pp, ill; 768pp, ill; 9th ed.: 830pp, ill

9213   _____   .   The Gun; or, A treatise on the various descriptions of small fire-arms. London: Longman, 1835.
240pp, ill, pls NN

9214   _____   .   The Science of Gunnery, as applied to the use and
construction of fire arms. London: Longman, 1841; new
ed. enl. London: E. Churton, 1846; as Gunnery in 1858:
being a treatise on rifles, cannon, and sporting arms; explaining the principles of the science of gunnery, and describing the newest improvements in fire-arms. London:
Smith, Elder, 1858. 324pp, ill, pls; 478pp, ill, pls; ...;
439pp, ill, 5 pls DLC

9215   *Greener, William Oliver, 1862- . A Bibliography of Guns
and Shooting. Being a list of ancient and modern English
and foreign books relating to firearms and their use, and
to the composition and manufacture of explosives; with an
introductory chapter on technical books and the writers of
them, firearms inventions, and the history of gunmaking
and the development of the art of wing shooting. Comp.
and rev. to date by Wirt Gerrare (pseud.). Westminster,
Eng: Roxburghe Pr, 1896. 216pp, 2500 titles ViU

9216   Greener, William Wellington, 1834-1921. The Breechloader,
and How to Use It. New York: Forest & Stream, 1892;
2nd ed. 1893; London: Cassell, 1894. 288pp, ill; 276pp,
ill; 351pp, ill PPL

9217   _____   .   Choke-bore Guns, and how to load for all kinds
of game. London; New York: Cassell, 1876. 215pp,
ill, 3 pls

9218   _____   .   Modern Breech-Loaders; sporting and military.

London; New York: Cassell, 1871; reprint with new introd.
by Donald B. McLean. Forest Grove, Ore: Normount
Technical Publications, 1971. 242pp, 123 ill, pls; 256pp,
ill NN

9219 _____. Modern Shotguns. London; New York: Cassell,
1888; 2nd ed. rev. 1891. 192pp, ill; 202pp, ill, 1 pl
(Includes ammunition and accessories)

9220 Grose, Francis, 1731-1799. A Treatise on Ancient Armour
and Weapons. Illustrated by plates taken from the original
armour in the Tower of London and other arsenals, museums, and cabinets. London: S. Hooper, 1785; 1786;
Supplement. 1789; reprint. Glendale, NY: Benchmark Publishing, 1970. 49 pls; 118pp, 62 pls, bib; Supplement:
10pp, 12 pls; reprint: 118pp, 62 pls

9221 The Gun Digest Treasury; the best from ten years of the Gun
Digest. Ed. by John T. Amber. Northfield, Ill: Gun
Digest, 1956.

9222 Guns from Long Island Collections; an exhibition of guns and
memorabilia ca.1609 to 1900. March-July 1961. Stony
Brook, NY: Suffolk Museum, 1961. 53pp, pls

9223 Gyngell, Dudley Stuart Hawtrey. Armourers Marks. Being a
compilation of the known marks of armourers, swordsmiths
and gunsmiths. London: Thorsons, 1959. 131pp, ill, bib

9224 Handbook of the Severance Collection of Arms and Armor. Includes "History of Armor, " by Helen I. Gilchrist. Cleveland, O: Museum of Art, 1925; 2nd ed. 1948. 71pp, ill

9225 Harrison, Herbert Spencer. A Handbook to the Weapons of War
and the Chase. Horniman Museum and Library. London:
Southwood, Smith, printer, 1908; rev. 2nd ed. as War and the
Chase. A Handbook to the Collection of weapons of savage,
barbaric and civilized peoples. London: 1929. 73pp, 2 pls,
bib; 85pp, 2 pls, bib MiU, DLC

9226 Hawkins, Peter. The Price Guide to Antique Guns and Pistols.
Woodbridge, Eng: Antique Collectors Club, 1973. 380pp,
chiefly ill (To ca.1900)

9227 *Hayward, John Forrest. The Art of the Gunmaker. 2 vol.
London: Barrie & Rockliff, 1962, 1963; 2nd ed. 1965.
Vol. I. 1500-1660. 303pp, 67 pls; 332pp, 83 pls; Vol. II.
1660-1830. (Includes American.) 379pp, 100 pls, bib

9228 *_____. European Armour. V & A. London: HMSO, 1951;
1965. 28pp, 32 pls, bib

9229 *_____. European Firearms. V & A. London: HMSO,

1955; 2nd ed. 1969.   53pp, ill, 34 pls, bib; 65pp, ill, 43 pls, bib

9230 *_____. Swords and Daggers. V & A. London: HMSO, 1951; 1955. 10pp, 32 pls

9231 *Held, Robert. The Age of Firearms: a pictorial history from the invention of gunpowder to the advent of the modern breechloader. New York: Harper, 1957; new. rev. ed. by Joseph J. Schroeder, Jr. Northfield, Ill: Gun Digest, 1970. 192pp, ill

9232 Henderson, James. Firearms Collecting for Amateurs. London: Muller, 1966. 143pp, ill, 12 pls

9233 _____. Sword Collecting for Amateurs. London: Muller, 1969. 144pp, ill, 8 pls, bib (Author's collection)

9234 Hewitt, John, 1807-1878. Ancient Armour and Weapons in Europe; from the iron period of the northern nations to the end of the 17th century: with illustrations from contemporary monuments. Vol. I. To end of 13th century; II. The 14th century; III. Supplement--15th, 16th and 17th centuries. 3 vol. Oxford; London: J. Henry & J. Parker, 1855-1860; Facsimile reprint with pref. by Claude Blair. Graz: Akademische Druck u. Verlagsanstalt, 1967. 1228pp, 140 ill, 232 pls NNC-Ave, MdBP

9235 _____. Official Catalogue of the Tower Armories. London: Eyre & Spottiswoode, 1859; 1870. 141pp NN

9236 _____. The Tower: its history, armouries, and antiquities ... accompanied with an essay on English armour from

the time of the Conquerer till its final disuse. A sketch
of the history of gun-founding ... with an historical notice
and description of the Crown Jewels. London: 1841; 2nd
ed. enl. 1845; 3rd ed. 1854? 282 pls, 51 portraits (Ex-
tra-illustrated copy in NN); 133pp, ill; 113pp, ill, pls
NN, MiD

9237 Historical Firearms Society of South Africa. Journal. Capetown, South Africa: the Society, 1958- .

9238 The History of Guns. Introd. by Frederick Wilkinson. Tr.
from Italian (1972). London: Orbis, 1973. 64pp, chiefly
ill, bib (To 1880)

9239 Hobart, Frank William Archer. Pictorial History of the Sub-
machine Gun. London: Ian Allen, 1971; 1973. 224pp, ill

9240 Hoff, Arne. Airguns and Other Pneumatic Arms. London:
Barrie & Jenkins, 1972. 99pp, ill, 40 pls (To 1900)

9241 Hogg, Ian Vernon. German Pistols and Revolvers, 1871-1945.
London: Arms and Armour Pr, 1971. 160pp, ill

9242 Hunter, Edmund. The Story of Arms and Armour. Loughborough: Wills & Hepworth, 1971. 52pp, 24 color ill
(Juvenile literature)

9243 Hutchison, Lt.-Col. Graham Seton. Machine Guns: their
history and tactical employment.... London: Macmillan,
1938. 349pp, ill, pls NN, CtY

9244 Jackson, Herbert J. European Hand Firearms of the 16th,
17th and 18th Centuries. With a treatise on Scottish firearms, by C. E. Whitelaw. London: Lee Warner, 1923;
reprint. London: Holland Pr; Chicago: Quadrangle,
1959. 108pp, ill, 71 pls (Includes powder flasks, etc.)

9245 James, Philip. Christian Warfare and Armour. London:
Victory Pr, 1972. 128pp

9246 Johnson, Derek Ernest. Collecting Militaria. London: Barker,
1971. 124pp, ill, bib DLC

9247 Johnson, Stanley Currie. Chats on Military Curios. London:
Unwin; New York: Stokes, 1915. 342pp, pls, bib (Includes medals, prisoner of war curios, etc.) DLC, NN

9248 Joubert, F. Catalogue of the Collection of European Arms
and Armour Formed at Greenock by R. L. Scott. 3 vol.
Glasgow: priv. printed, 1924. 126 pls

9249 The Journal of the Historical Breechloading Smallarms

Association. Biannual. London: Imperial War Museum, H.B.S.A., 1973- .

9250   Kennard, Arthur Norris. French Pistols and Sporting Guns. Feltham; New York: Country Life, 1972. 64pp, ill (To 1850)

9251   Kiesling, Paul. Bayonets of the World. Kedichem: Military Collectors Service, 1973- .

9252   Kist, Johannes Bastiaan. Dutch Muskets and Pistols. English, Dutch and German text. London: Arms and Armour Pr, 1974. 176pp, ill, 8 pls

9253   Klein, Walter. The Muzzle Loading Rifle. n.p.: 1942.

9254   Lack, Dennis. Discovering Antique Firearms. Tring: Shire Publications, 1971. 64pp, ill, bib (ca.1350-1862)

9255   Lake, William Robert. Patents for Inventions Relating to Machine-guns and Automatic Breech Mechanisms. London: Haseltine, Lake, 1896. 106pp, ill NN

9256   Laking, Guy Francis, 1875-1919. The Armoury of Windsor Castle; European section. London: Bradbury, Agnew, 1904. 283pp, 39 pls NN

9257 *   . Catalogue of European Armour and Arms in the Wallace Collection at Hertford House. London: HMSO, 1900; 2nd ed. 1901; 4th ed. 1910. 356pp, ill (1343 items described) DLC

9258   . A Catalogue of the Armour and Arms in the Armoury of the Knights of Saint John of Jerusalem, now in the Palace, Valetta, Malta. London: Bradbury, Agnew, 1903. ill

9259 *   . A Record of European Armour and Arms Through Seven Centuries. Introd. by the Baron de Cosson. 5 vol. London: G. Bell, 1920-22. ill, pls, bib PPL

9260   Latham, John Wilkinson. Early Breech-loaders. Edgware, Middlesex: Arms and Armour Pr, 1966. 21pp, 3 pls

9261   . Discovering Edged Weapons. Tring: Shire Publications, 1972. 64pp, ill, bib

9262   . Pictorial History of Swords and Bayonets Including Dirks and Daggers. London: Allan, 1973. 88pp, ill, pls, bib

9263   Lavin, James D. A History of Spanish Firearms. New York: Arco; London: 1965. 304pp, 26 ill, 122 pls, marks

9264 Lenk, Torsten Rickard. The Flintlock: Its Origin and De-
velopment. Tr. from Swedish Flintlaset (1939) by G. A.
Urquart. Ed. by John F. Hayward. London: Holland
Pr, 1965. 188pp, ill, 134 pls

9265 Letosnikova, Libuse. The Armoury at Konopiste Castle. Tr.
from Czeckoslovakian by F. Nebel. Prague: Odeon, 1970.
74pp, ill

9266 Lindsay, Merrill. 100 Great Guns: An Illustrated History of
Firearms. New York: Walker, 1967; London: Blandford,
1968. 379pp, ill, bib

9267 Linsey, Martin, and Norma J. Roberts. Arms and Armor in
the Cleveland Museum of Art. Cleveland: 1974. 20pp, ill,
bib

9268 List of Books Relating to Weapons and Armour. Edinburgh:
Museum, 1891. BM

9269 Lister, John E. Sketch Book of Hand Guns. Philadelphia?:
1954. 30 leaves, ill

9270 Loftie, William John, 1839-1911. Authorized Guide to the
Tower of London. London: HMSO, 1886; 2nd rev. ed.
1883; with a description of the armoury by Viscount Dillon.
London: HMSO, 1894. 152pp, ill, pl

9271 *Lonstaff, Frederick Victor, 1879-1961, and A(ndrew) Hilliard
Alleridge. The Book of the Machine Gun. London: Hugh
Rees, 1917. 337pp, pls, bib of books 1860-1915.

9272 Lugs, Jaroslav. Firearms Past and Present: a complete review of firearm systems and their histories. Tr. from
Czechoslovakian. 2 vol. London: Grenville, 1973. ill,
bib

9273 Maeurer, Herman A. Military Edged Weapons of the World,
1880-1965; a private collection. College Point, NY:
Author, 1967. 151pp, ill

9274 Magazine of Antique Firearms. Monthly. Athens, Tenn:
1911-1912.

9275 Mann, Sir James Gow. The Etched Decoration of Armour.
A Study in classification. (Henriette Hertz Fund Annual
Lecture, 1940.) London: H. Milford, 1940; 1944. 31pp,
21 pls NN

9276 _____. European Arms and Armour. Text with historical
notes and illustrations. 2 vol. London: Wallace Collection, Hertford House, 1962. 239pp, ill, 104 pls; 474pp,
ill, 103 pls, bib

9277   Martin, Paul. Armour and Weapons. Tr. from French by
       Rene North. London: Jenkins, 1968; as Arms and Armour,
       from the 9th to the 17th century. Rutland, Vt: Tuttle,
       1968. 298pp, 240 ill, 2 color pls, bib

9278   Mayer, Joseph Ralph. Five Centuries of Gunsmiths, Sword-
       smiths and Armourers, 1400-1900. Columbus, O: Walter
       F. Heer, 1948.

9279   Metscl, John. Rudolph J. Nunnemacher Collection of Projec-
       tile Arms. 2 parts. Milwaukee: Public Museum, 1928.
       ill

9280   Meyrick, Sir Samuel Rush. Engraved Illustrations of Antient
       Arms and Armour, from the Collection of Llewelyn Meyrick
       ... at Goodrich Court, Herefordshire. 2 vol. London:
       Oxford U. Pr, 1830. 150 or 151 pls DLC

9281   _____. Observations upon the History of Hand Fire-Arms
       and Their Appurtenances. London: Society of Antiquaries,
       'Archaeologia,' Vol. 22, 1828. Facsimile reprint with
       new introd. Richmond, Surrey: Richmond Publishing,
       1971. 49pp

9282   *A Military Dictionary, explaining and describing the technical
       terms, phrases, works, and machines, used in the science
       of war; embellished with copper-plates of all the common
       works used in military architecture: as well as the uten-
       sils employed in attacks and defence; with references for
       their explanation.... London: G. Robinson, etc., 1778.
       184pp, 2 folding pls DeWint

9283   A Miscellany of Arms and Armor, presented by fellow mem-
       bers of the Armor and Arms Club to Bashford Dean in
       honor of his 60th birthday, October 28, 1927. New York:
       priv. printed, W. E. Rudge, 1927; for public sale. New
       York: Rudge, 1928. 109pp, ill, pls, bib (Essays on
       many subjects, including The Barbute, pirate and bucca-
       neer weapons, American military pike of 1776, Oriental
       weapons, etc.)

9284   Mollo, Eugene. Russian Military Swords, 1801-1917. London:
       Historical Research Unit, 1969. 56pp, chiefly ill

9285   *Nearing, Jane, comp. Bibliography of Gun Books, some very
       rare and valuable, some out of print. Richardson, Tx:
       Public Library, 1974.

9286   Nickel, Helmut. Warriors and Worthies; arms and armor
       through the ages. New York: Atheneum, 1969; rev. ed.
       as Arms and Armour Through the Ages. London: Collins,
       1971. 122pp, ill, bib

9287   Nicolle, Patrick. A Book of Armour. Harmondsworth:
       Penguin, 1954. 30pp, ill

9288   Nonte, George Charles. Firearms Encyclopedia. New York:
       Harper & Row; London: Wolfe, 1973. 341pp, ill, bib

9289   Norman, Alexander Vesey (Bethune). Arms and Armour.
       London: Weidenfeld & Nicolson; New York: Putnam,
       1964. 128pp, ill

9290   _____ . The Mediaeval Soldier. London: Barker; New
       York: Crowell, 1971. 278pp, ill, bib

9291   _____ . Small Swords and Military Swords: the develop-
       ment and dating, from the middle of the 17th century to
       the early 19th century. Reprint from Antiques International,
       1966. London: Arms and Armour Pr, 1967. 24pp, ill

9292 *Oakeshott, Ronald Ewart. The Archaeology of Weapons:
       arms and armour from pre-history to the Age of Chivalry.
       London: Lutterworth Pr, 1960; New York: Praeger, 1963.
       359pp, 179 ill, 20 pls, bib (To 1325)

9293   _____ . The Sword in the Age of Chivalry. London: Lut-
       terworth, 1964. 152pp, ill, 48 pls, bib (European, 900-
       1550)

9294   Olson, Ludwig. Mauser Bolt Rifles. 2 vol. Aberdeen
       Proving Ground, Md: Author, 1950, 1951; rev. ed. 1956.
       1956: 200pp, 200 ill, pls (German)

9295   Pakula, Marvin H. Heraldry and Armor of the Middle Ages.
       South Brunswick, NJ: A. S. Barnes, 1972. 264pp, ill,
       bib

9296   Papers of the Armor and Arms Club of New York City. Oc-
       casional periodical. New York: 1940- .

9297   Peirce, P. C. A Handbook of Court and Hunting Swords,
       1660-1820. London: Quaritch, 1937. 100pp

9298 *Peterson, Harold Leslie, ed. Encyclopedia of Firearms.
       London: Connoisseur; New York: Dutton, 1964. 367pp,
       ill, 8 color pls, bib

9299   _____ . A History of Body Armor. New York: Scribner,
       1968. 64pp, ill (Juvenile literature)

9300   _____ . A History of Firearms. New York: Scribner,
       1961. 56pp, ill (Juvenile literature)

9301   _____ . Pageant of the Gun: a treasury of stories of

firearms. Their romance and lore, development, and use
through 10 centuries. Garden City, NY: Doubleday, 1967.
352pp, ill

9302   _____ . The Treasury of the Gun. New York: Golden
Pr, 1962. 249pp, ill, pls, bib

9303   _____ , and Robert Elman. The Great Guns. New York:
Ridge Pr; Feltham: Hamlyn, 1971. 252pp, ill, bib (To
1900)

9304 Pollard, Hugh Bertie Campbell. Automatic Pistols. London;
New York: I. Pitman, 1920. 110pp, 15 pls

9305   _____ . The Book of the Pistol and Revolver. London:
McBride, Nast, 1917. 230pp, ill, 37 pls

9306   _____ . A History of Firearms. London: G. Bles; Boston:
Houghton Mifflin, 1936; reprint. New York: Burt Franklin,
1973. 320pp, ill, 41 pls, bib

9307   _____ . Shot-Guns; their history and development. London;
New York: I. Pitman, 1923. 121pp, ill

9308 Pope, Dudley. Guns; from the invention of gunpowder to the
20th century. New York: Delacort Pr; London: Weidenfeld & Nicolson, 1965. 254pp, ill, pls

9309 Quick, John. Dictionary of Weapons and Military Terms.
New York: McGraw Hill, 1973. 515pp, ill, bib

9310 Reid, William. Arms Through the Ages. New York: Harper,
1976. 800 ill (By Director of London's Army Museum)

9311 Ricketts, Howard. Firearms. London: Weidenfeld & Nicolson, 1962; London: Octopus Books, 1972. 128pp, 140 ill;
97pp, ill (To 1866)

9312 *Riling, Raymond Lawrence Joseph. Guns and Shooting, a selected chronological bibliography ... for the arms collector, etc.... New York: Greenberg, 1951. 434pp, ill

9313 Rumford, Sir Benjamin Thompson, 1753-1814. The Complete
Works of Count Rumford. 4 vol. Boston: American
Academy of Arts and Sciences, 1870-75. ill, 61 pls
(Gunnery, heating, fireplaces, kitchen utensils, etc.)

9314 Rywell, Martin. Gun Collectors' Guide; old guns for profit;
complete guide to antique gun collecting. 5th ed. Harriman, Tenn: Pioneer, 1961. 128pp, ill

9315 Sandham, Henry, ed. Catalogue of the Collection of Munitions

of War ... in the South Kensington Museum.   London:
HMSO, 1875.

9316 Satterlee, Leroy De Forest.   A Catalogue of Firearms for
      the Collector.   Detroit: priv. printed, 1927; 2nd ed.
      1939.   242pp, ill, pls, bib; 334pp, ill, bib (See also:
      Gluckman, Arcadi no. 9432-9434)

9317 *Schoebel, Johannes.   Princely Arms and Armour: a selection
      from the Dresden Collection.   (Historiches Museum.)   Tr.
      from German (1973) by M. O. A. Stanton.   Pref. by
      Claude Blair.   London: Barrie & Jenkins, 1975; as Fine
      Arms and Armour: treasures in the Dresden Collection.
      New York: Putnam's, 1975.   255pp, 178 (48 color) pls

9318 A Selection from the William Randolph Hearst Collection of
      Arms and Armor in the Detroit Institute of Arts.   Detroit:
      1954.   35pp, ill

9319 Serven, James Edsall, ed.   The Collecting of Guns.   Harris-
      burg, Pa: Stackpole, 1964.   272pp, ill, bib (Contributing
      authors include William A. Albaugh III)

9320 _____, and others.   Guns of the World; the complete col-
      lectors' and traders' guide.   Los Angeles: Petersen
      Publishing, 1972.   400pp, ill

9321 Shepperd, Gilbert Alan.   Arms and Armour, 1660-1918: the
      soldier and his weapons.   London: Hart-Davis, 1971; as
      A History of War and Weapons, 1660-1918; arms and
      armour from the Age of Louis 14th to World War I.   New
      York: Crowell, 1972.   224pp, ill

9322 Skelton, Joseph.   Engraved Illustrations of Antient Arms and
      Armour, from the collection at Goodrich Court, Hereford-
      shire; after the drawings, and with the descriptions of Dr.
      (Samuel Rush) Meyrick.   2 vol.   London: Oxford, 1830.
      151 pls   DLC

9323 Small Arms Profile.   Monthly.   Windsor, Berkshire: Profile
      Publisher, 1971- .

9324 Smith, James A.   The Antique Pistol Book.   n. p. : Speed-
      well, 1948.   ill with drawings

9325 Smith, Joseph Edward.   Small Arms of the World; a basic
      manual of small arms.   The classic by W. H. B. Smith.
      8th ed. completely rev. by J. E. Smith.   Harrisburg, Pa:
      Stackpole, 1968.   768pp, ill

9326 Smith, Robert Henry Soden.   A List of Books and Photographs
      in the National Art Library, illustrating armour and

weapons, etc.   South Kensington Museum.   London: HMSO,
1883. 68pp

9327 *Smith, Walter Harold Black, 1901-1959.   A Basic Manual of
Military Small Arms.   Harrisburg, Pa; Washington, D.C.:
Military Service Publishing, 1943; 8th ed. rev. & enl. by
Joseph E. Smith.   (See above) 213pp, ill; 735pp, ill

9328 [No entry.]

9329 _____. Mannlicher Rifles and Pistols; original drawings by
von Kromar from the Steyr Armory.   Famous sporting and
military weapons.   Harrisburg, Pa; Washington, D.C.:
Military Service Publishing, 1947.   239pp, ill (Pre-Russian
occupation of Austria)

9330 _____. Mauser Rifles and Pistols.   Washington, D.C.: Military Service Publishing, 1947.   (German/World War II)

9331 _____. The N. R. A. Book of Small Arms.   Harrisburg,
Pa: 1946; rev. & enl. as The Book of Pistols and Revolvers, with supplement by Kent Bellah.   4th ed. Harrisburg, Pa: Stackpole, 1960.   718pp, ill

9332 *Smythe, Sir John, 1534?-1607, Knight.   Certain Discourses
Concerning the Formes and Effects of Divers Sorts of
Weapons ... and chiefly of the Mosquet, the Caliver and
the Long-bow, etc.   London: R. Johnes, 1590; reprinted
in Bow Versus Gun.   Wakefield: E P Publishing, 1973.
BM

9333 Special Exhibition of Swordguards at the Museum of Fine Arts,
Boston.   Boston: 1907.   ill

9334 State Armoury in the Moscow Kremlin.   Moscow: Izobrazitel-
noye Iskussfvo, 1969.   204pp, ill

9335 Steinwedel, Louis W.   The Gun Collector's Fact Book.   New
York: Arco, 1975.   217pp, ill

9336 Stelle, James Parish, and William B. Harrison.   Gunsmiths'
Manual.   1883.   Reprint as How to Be a Gunsmith; or Gun-
smiths' Manual.   Ed. by Martin Rywell.   Harriman, Tenn:
Pioneer Pr, 1955.   376pp, ill

9337 Stephens, Frederick John.   A Collector's Pictorial Book of
Bayonets.   London: Arms & Armour Pr; Harrisburg, Pa:
Stackpole, 1971.   127pp, chiefly ill, bib (ca.1670-1964)

9338 *Stone, George Cameron.   A Glossary of the Construction,
Decoration and Use of Arms and Armor in All Countries
and in all times, together with some closely related

subjects. Portland, Me: Southworth Pr, 1934; New York: Brussel, 1961. 694pp, 875 ill of over 3500 pieces, bib

9339 Swenson, George Watts Parks. Pictorial History of the Rifle. Shepperton: Allan, 1971. 184pp, ill, bib (To 1970)

9340 Tarassuk, Leonid. Antique European and American Firearms of the Hermitage Museum. Tr. by R. Drapkin. Leningrad: Iskusstvo Publishing, 1971; New York: n.d. 212pp, 541 ill, color pls, marks, makers

9341 _____. Russian Pistols of the 17th Century. York, Pa: Stackpole, 1968. 35pp, ill

9342 Taylerson, Anthony William Finlay. Revolving Arms. London: Jenkins; New York: Walker, 1967. 123pp, ill, 32 pls

9343 _____, James Frith, and Ronald A. N. Andrews. The Revolver: 1818-1914. Vol. I. 1818-1865; Vol. II. 1865-1888; Vol. III. 1889-1914. 3 vol. London: Jenkins; New York: Crown, 1966; London: 1970; New York: 1971. 360pp, ill, pls, bib; 292pp, ill, bib; 324pp, ill, pls, bib

9344 Tennent, Sir James Emerson, 1804-1869. The Story of the Guns. London: Longman, 1864; facsimile reprint with new introd. by W. S. Curtis. Richmond, Surrey: Richmond Publishing Co, 1972. 364pp, ill, pls, bib

9345 Thomas, Bruno, Ortwin Gamber, and Hans Schedelmann. Arms and Armour. Masterpieces by European craftsmen from the 13th to 19th century. Tr. from German by Ilse Bloom and William Reid. London: Thames & Hudson; New York: McGraw Hill, 1964. 252pp, ill, 46 color pls, bib

9346 Thordeman, Bengt J. N., Poul Norlund, and Bo E. Inglemark. Armour from the Battle of Wisby, 1361. 2 vol. Stockholm: Kungl. vitterhets historie och antiqvitets akademien, 1939-40. 426pp, 145 pls, bib (Wisby, Sweden)

9347 Toller, Jane. Prisoners-of-War Work, 1756-1815. Cambridge, Eng: Golden Head Pr, 1965. 23pp, ill, 13 pls, bib

9348 Toman, Karel. A Book of Military Uniforms and Weapons, an illustrated survey of military dress, arms and practice through the ages. Tr. from Czechoslovakian by Alice Denesova. London: Hamlyn & Wingate, 1964. 166pp, ill

9349 Tunis, Edwin. Weapons, a Pictorial History. Cleveland: World, 1954. 151pp, ill

9350 Valentine, Eric. Rapiers: an illustrated reference guide to
      the rapiers of the 16th and 17th centuries; with their com-
      panions. London: Arms & Armour Pr, 1968. 74pp,
      chiefly 58 ill, bib

9351 Wagner, Eduard, ill. Medieval Costume, Armour and Weap-
      ons, 1350-1450. Text by Zoroslava Drobna and Jan Durdik.
      Tr. from Czechoslovakian by Jean Layton. London:
      Andrew Dakers, 1958. 72pp, 381 pls, bib

9352 Waller, John Green. Arms and Armour. A lecture, delivered
      at the London Institution. London: priv. printed, 1871.
      31pp, ill BM

9353 Walsh, John Henry, 1810-1888. The Shot-Gun and Sporting
      Rifle: and the dogs, ponies, ferrets, etc. used with them
      in the various kinds of shooting and trapping. London;
      New York: Routledge, Warne & Routledge, 1859; 2nd ed.
      1862. 448pp, many ill, pls; 496pp, ill, pls DLC

9354 Westropp, Michael Seymour Dudley, 1868- . Arms and
      Armour (European). General guide to Art Collection.
      Chapters 1 and 2, Part 10. Dublin: Science & Art Mu-
      seum, 1906. 29pp and 46pp

9355 Wilkinson, Frederick John. Antique Arms and Armour. Lon-
      don: Ward Lock; New York: Drake, 1972. 192pp, ill,
      bib

9356 *   . Antique Firearms. 16 sections, available sepa-
      rately. London: Guinness Signatures, 1969; 1 vol. Garden
      City, NY: Doubleday, 1969. 255pp, ill, bib

9357 *   . Edged Weapons. Garden City, NY: Doubleday;
      London: Guinness Signatures, 1970. 256pp, ill, 14 pls

9358   . Flintlock Guns and Rifles: an illustrated reference
      guide. London: Arms & Armour Pr, 1971. 80pp, chiefly
      ill, bib

9359   . Flintlock Pistols: an illustrated reference guide
      to flintlock pistols from the 17th to 19th centuries. Lon-
      don: Arms & Armour Pr, 1969. 75pp, chiefly ill, bib
      (1610-1830)

9360   . Guns. New York: Grosset & Dunlap, 1971.
      158pp, ill (Juvenile literature)

9361   . Let's Look at Arms and Armour. London: Mul-
      ler, 1968; 2nd ed. as Arms and Armour. London: Black,
      1969. 64pp, ill (Juvenile literature)

9362   . Small Arms. London: Ward Lock, 1965; New
      York: Hawthorn, 1966. 256pp, 173 ill, bib

9363 * _____. Swords and Daggers. London: Ward Lock, 1967.
        256pp, 195 ill, bib

9364 Wilkinson, Henry. Engines of War: or, Historical and experi-
        mental observations on ancient and modern warlike ma-
        chines and implements, including the manufacture of guns,
        gunpowder and swords, with remarks on bronze, iron,
        steel, etc. London: Longman, 1841; reprint with new
        introd. by W. S. Curtis. Richmond, Eng: Richmond
        Publishing, 1973. 269pp, bib BM

9365 _____. Observations on Swords; addressed to officers and
        civilians, but especially to those who prefer a good sword
        to a bad one. 8th ed. London: Author, 1862. 24pp BM

9366 Williams, Sir Roger. A Briefe Discourse of Warre.... Lon-
        don: T. Orwin, 1590. manuscript notes (See no. 9149
        and no. 9152) BM

9367 Winant, Lewis. Early Percussion Firearms: a history of
        early percussion ignition--from Forsyth to Winchester.
        44/40. Jenkins, 1961; Feltham: Spring Books, 1970.
        190pp, ill, 89 pls, bib (1806-1886)

9368 _____. Firearms Curiosa. New York: Greenberg; New
        York: St. Martin's Pr, 1955. 281pp, ill of 300 pieces
        (Firearms hidden in canes, knives, ploughs, keys, sun-
        dials, etc.)

9369 _____. Pepperbox Firearms. New York: Greenberg,
        1952. 177pp, 92pp of pls

9370 Wintringham, Thomas Henry. The Story of Weapons and Tac-
        tics from Troy to Stalingrad. Boston: Houghton Mifflin,
        1943; as Weapons and Tactics. London: Faber, 1943;
        Freeport, NY: Books for Libraries Pr, 1971. 208pp, ill,
        pls

9371 Wise, Terence. European Edged Weapons. London: Almark
        Publishing, 1974. 96pp, ill

9372 Wolff, Eldon G. Air Gun Batteries. Milwaukee: Public Mu-
        seum, 195-? 28pp, 38 ill, 18 figures

9373 _____. Air Guns. Milwaukee: Public Museum, 1958.
        198pp, 66 ill

9374 *Wynn, Kenneth G., comp. Arms and Armour: (A list of
        articles and notes which appeared in 'The Connoisseur,'
        1901-1960.) Hayes, Middlesex: K. G. Wynn, 1961. 44pp

9375 Young, Peter. The Machinery of War: An Illustrated History
        of Weapons. London: Hart-Davis, MacGibbon, 1973.
        128pp, ill

AMERICAN ARMS AND ARMOR

9376   Abels, Robert. Early American Firearms. Cleveland:
       World, 1950. 63pp, ill, 7 color pls, bib

9377   Albaugh, William A. Confederate Edged Weapons. New York:
       Harper, 1960. 198pp, ill

9378   _____. Handbook of Confederate Swords. Union City, Tenn:
       Pioneer Pr, 1951. ill

9379   _____. A Photographic Supplement of Confederate Swords.
       Washington?: 1963. 205pp, ill, pls

9380   _____. Tyler, Texas, C. S. A. Harrisburg, Pa: Stack-
       pole, 1958. 235pp, pls (Confederate ordnance works)

9381   _____, Hugh Benet, and Edward N. Simmons. Handguns:
       concerning the guns, the men who made them, and the
       times of their use. Philadelphia: Riling & Lentz, 1963.
       250pp, ill, pls

9382   _____, and Richard D. Steuart. The Original Confederate
       Colt; the story of the Leech and Rigdon and Rigdon-Ansley
       revolvers. New York: Greenberg, 1953. 62pp, ill

9383   Altmayer, Jay P. American Presentation Swords. Rankin Pr,
       1958. ill (Post-Revolutionary War to close of Spanish
       American War)

9384   The American Gun. Vol. I, parts 1-3. Madison Books, 1961.
       ill (many color) (Originally published as magazines)

9385   American Military Insignia, 1800-1851. Washington, D.C.:
       Smithsonian, 1963. ill

9386   Annis, Philip Geoffrey Walter. Naval Swords: British and
       American naval edged weapons, 1660-1815. London: Arms
       & Armour Pr, 1970. 80pp, ill, bib (United States, 1776-
       1815)

9387   Bady, Donald B. Colt Automatic Pistols: 1896-1955. Fadco
       Publishing, 1956.

9388   Bailey, DeWitt. Percussion Guns and Rifles; an illustrated
       reference guide. Harrisburg, Pa: Stackpole; London:
       Arms & Armour Pr, 1972. 79pp, ill, bib

9389   Baird, John D. Hawken Rifles, the Mountain Man's Choice.
       Franklin, Indiana: Franklin Printing, 1968. 95pp, ill
       (Samuel T. Hawken, 1792-1884; Jacob Hawken, 1786-
       1849)

9390   Behn, Jack. '45-70' Rifles. Harrisburg, Pa: Stackpole,
       1956. ill (1873-1898. Author's collection)

9391   Belote, Theodore Thomas. American and European Swords
       in the Historical Collections of the United States National
       Museum. Washington, D.C.: GPO, 1932. 163pp, pls,
       bib

9392   Benet, S. V. Description and Rules for the Management of
       the Springfield Rifle, Carbine, and Army revolvers, Cali-
       ber 45. Springfield, Mass: National Armory, 1882.
       (Army manual)

9393   Boehret, Paul C. Arming the Troops, 1775-1815. Easton,
       Pa: Hobson Printing, 1967- . ill, bib

9394   Bowman, Hank Wieand. Antique Guns from the Stagecoach
       Collection; early self-contained cartridge firearms, single
       and multi-shot pistols, percussion Colts, Allens and Whee-
       locks, Colt Dragoons, Remingtons, fine cased and one-of-
       a-kind weapons. New York: Arco; Greenwich, Conn:
       Fawcett, 1953; Greenwich: 1964; New York: 1969. 144pp,
       ill

9395   Brinckerhoff, Sidney B., and Pierce A. Chamberlain. Spanish
       Military Weapons in Colonial America, 1700-1821. Harris-
       burg, Pa: Stackpole, 1972. 159pp, ill, bib

9396   Brown, J., and C. Gentry. John M. Browning: American
       gunmaker. New York: Doubleday, 1964. ill

9397   Brown, Rodney Hilton. American Polearms, 1526-1865; the
       lance, halberd, spontoon, pike, and naval boarding weapons.
       New Milford, Conn: N. Flayderman, 1967. 198pp, ill,
       bib

9398   Browning, (J. M. & M. S.) Co. A History of Browning Guns
       from 1831. Ogden, Utah: 1942. 62pp, ill

9399   *Bruce, Robert V. Lincoln and the Tools of War. Fore. by
       Benjamin P. Thomas. Indianapolis: Bobbs-Merrill, 1956.
       368pp, ill, pls (Study of Union equipment, rifles to ships)

9400   Butler, David F. United States Firearms: The First Century,
       1776-1875. New York: Winchester Pr, 1971. 249pp, ill

9401   Calver, William Louis, and Reginald Pelham Bolton. History
       Written with Pick and Shovel; military buttons, belt-plates,
       badges, and other relics excavated from Colonial, Revolu-
       tionary, and War of 1812 camp sites, by the Field Ex-
       ploration Committee of the New York Historical Society.
       Compiled and indexed by Roberta Leighton. New York:
       the Society, 1950. 320pp, ill, bib PPULC, DLC

9402   Carey, Arthur Merwyn. American Firearms Makers: when,
       where, and what they made from the Colonial Period to
       the end of the 19th century. New York: Crowell, 1953.
       146pp, ill, bib NN, DLC, TxU

9403   Chapel, Charles Edward. Guns of the Old West. New York:
       Coward-McCann, 1961. 806pp, ill, bib

9404   *Coggins, Jack. Arms and Equipment of the Civil War.
       Garden City, NY: Doubleday, 1962. 160pp, ill

9405   Colby, Carroll B. Civil War Weapons: small arms and
       artillery of the Blue and Gray. New York: Coward-
       McCann, 1962. 48pp, ill (Juvenile literature)

9406   _____. Fighting Gear of World War I: equipment and
       weapons of the American Doughboy. New York: Coward-
       McCann, 1961. 48pp, ill (Juvenile literature)

9407   _____. Firearms by Winchester: a part of United States
       history. New York: Coward-McCann, 1957. 48pp, ill
       (Juvenile literature)

9408   _____. Musket to M-14: pistols, rifles and machine guns
       through the years. New York: Coward McCann, 1960.
       48pp, ill (Juvenile literature)

9409   _____. Revolutionary War Weapons: pole arms, hand
       guns, shoulder arms and artillery. New York: Coward-
       McCann, 1963. 48pp, ill (Juvenile literature)

9410   _____. Six-Shooter; pistols, revolvers, and automatics,
       past and present. New York: Coward-McCann, 1956.
       48pp, ill (Juvenile literature)

9411   _____. Two Centuries of Firearms. New York: Coward-
       McCann, 1975. ill

9412   Cromwell, Giles. The Virginia Manufactory of Arms. Char-
       lottesville, Va: U. Pr, 1975.

9413   Curry, (N.) and Brother, San Francisco. Price List 1884.
       Reprint. Berkeley, Cal: Paradox Pr, 1965. 60pp, ill
       (Firearms)

9414   *Curtis, John Obed, and William H. Guthman. New England
       Militia Uniforms and Accoutrements. A pictorial survey.
       Sturbridge, Mass: Old Sturbridge Village, 1971. 102pp,
       ill, bib (Uniforms, swords, knapsacks, belts, drums,
       horse equipment, etc.)

9415   Demeritt, Dwight Burgess, Jr. Maine Made Guns and Their

Makers. Hallowell Me: P. S. Plumer, Jr., printer, for
Maine State Museum, 1973. 209pp, ill, bib

9416 Dexter, F. Theodore. Forty-two Years' Scrapbook of Rare
      Ancient Firearms. Warren F. Lewis, 1954.

9417 _____. Half Century Scrapbook of Vari-type Firearms.
      Weaver Publishing, 1960. ill (Frank C. Bivens, Jr.
      Collection)

9418 Deyrup, F. J. Arms Making in the Connecticut Valley. York,
      Pa: Shumway, 1970.

9419 Dillin, John Grace Wolfe, 1860- . The Kentucky Rifle; a
      study of the origin and development of a purely American
      type of firearm, together with accurate historical data
      concerning early Colonial gunsmiths.... Washington, D.C.:
      National Rifle Assoc., 1924; 3rd ed. includes "Kentucky
      Pistol," by George N. Hyatt. New York: Ludlum &
      Beebe, 1946; 4th ed. New York: Trimmer, 1959. 124pp,
      126 pls; 136pp, pls; 154pp, 126 pls

9420 Dunathan, Arni T. The American B. B. Gun: a collector's
      guide. South Brunswick, NY: A. S. Barnes; London:
      Yoseloff, 1971. 154pp, ill

9421 Edwards, William B. The Story of Colt's Revolver; the biog-
      raphy of Colonel Samuel Colt. Harrisburg, Pa: Stackpole,
      1953. 470pp, ill, pls, bib

9422 Fluck, John J. Colt-Root Model 1853; an illustrated mono-
      graph. F. Theodore Dexter, 1950. ill (Study of classi-
      fication made possible by Fluck's finding of the first
      model)

9423 Folger, William M. Description of the Hotchkiss Magazine
      Rifle. Navy model.--caliber .45. Washington, D.C.:
      GPO, 1879. 22pp NN

9424 _____. Machine Guns: the Gatling. The Hotchkiss Re-
      volving Cannon. 1880. Washington, D.C.: Navy Ord-
      nance Office, 1880. 32pp NN

9425 Fuller, Claud E. The Breech-Loader in the Service, 1816-
      1917; a history of all standard and experimental United
      States breechloading and magazine shoulder arms. Topeka,
      Kansas: Arms Reference Club of America, 1933; reprint.
      New Milford, Conn: N. Flayderman, 1965. 381pp, ill,
      pls, bib

9426 _____. The Rifled Musket. Harrisburg, Pa: Stackpole,
      1958. 302pp, ill

9427 _____ . Springfield Muzzle-loading Shoulder Arms; a de-
        scription of the flint lock muskets, musketoons and car-
        bines and the special models from 1795 to 1865, with
        ordnance office reports.... New York: F. Bannerman,
        1930. 176pp, ill, pls

9428 _____ . The Whitney Firearms. Huntington, W. Va:
        Standard Publications, 1946. 335pp, ill (Eli Whitney,
        1765-1825)

9429 _____ , and Richard D. Steuart. Firearms of the Confed-
        eracy; the shoulder arms, pistols and revolvers of the
        Confederate soldier, including the regular United States
        models, the imported arms, and those manufactured within
        the Confederacy. Huntington, W. Va: Standard Publica-
        tions, 1944. 333pp, ill, pls

9430 *Gavin, William G. Accoutrement Plates, North and South,
        1861-1865. Fore. by Stephen V. Grancsay. Philadelphia:
        Riling & Lentz, 1963. 217pp, ill, pls (Belt plates and
        clasps)

9431 Gill, Harold B. , Jr. The Gunsmith in Colonial Virginia.
        Williamsburg, Va: Colonial Williamsburg, by U. Pr of
        Va. , Charlottesville, 1974. 139pp, 6 pls, bib

9432 Gluckman, Arcadi. United States Martial Pistols and Re-
        volvers. Buffalo, NY: Otto Ulbrich, 1939; reprint. 1944;
        reprint. Harrisburg, Pa: Stackpole, 197-? 249pp, ill,
        29 pls, bib

9433 _____ . United States Muskets, Rifles and Carbines. Buf-
        falo, NY: Otto Ulbrich, 1948; Harrisburg, Pa: Stackpole,
        1959. 447pp, ill, bib

9434 _____ , and Leroy De Forest Satterlee. American Gun
        Makers. Buffalo, NY: Otto Ulbrich, 1940; 1945; 2nd ed.
        includes Supplement of American Gun Makers. Harris-
        burg, Pa: Stackpole, 1953. 186pp, bib; 243pp, bib

9435 Grancsay, Stephen Vincent. American Engraved Powder Horns.
        New York: Metropolitan Museum, 1945; Philadelphia: R.
        Riling Arms Books, 1946; 1965. 96pp, ill, 47 pls, bib
        (Based on J. H. Grenville Gilbert Collection)

9436 Grant, James J. Single Shot Rifles. New York: Morrow,
        1947; supplement as More Single Shot Rifles. 1959. 385pp,
        ill (Ballard, Stevens, Remington, Sharps, Winchester, F.
        Wesson, Maynard & Wurfflein. Chiefly American)
        DLC

9437 Great Western Gun Works, 1888-89. Catalog reprint. Victoria,
        Tx: Victoria Daily News, 1969. 46pp, ill

9438 Guthman, William H. United States Army Weapons, 1784-
      1791. Cincinnati, O: The American Society, 1975. 94pp,
      ill (Includes scrimshaw powder horns, axes, swords,
      firearms)

9439 Hanson, Charles E. The Northwest Gun. Lincoln: Nebraska
      State Historical Society, 1955. 85pp, ill

9440 Hatch, Alden. Remington Arms in American History. New
      York: Rinehart, 1956; rev. ed. Bridgeport?, Conn: 1972.
      359pp, ill; 364pp, ill

9441 *Haven, Charles Tower, and Frank A. Belden. A History of
      the Colt Revolver, and other arms made by Colt's Patent
      Fire Arms Manufacturing Company from 1836 to 1940.
      Fore. by Stephen V. Grancsay. New York: W. Morrow,
      1940. 711pp, ill, gloss, facs. of documents

9442 Haythornthwaite, Philip. Uniforms of the Civil War, 1861-
      1865. New York: Macmillan, 1976. 150 color ill

9443 Hellstrom, Carl Reinhold. "S & W," 100 years of gunmaking,
      1852-1952. New York: Newcomen Society in North
      America, 1952. 33pp, ill (Smith and Wesson) DeWint

9444 Helmer, William J. The Gun That Made the Twenties Roar.
      New York: Macmillan, 1969. 286pp, ill

9445 Hibbard, Spencer, Bartlett and Company. 1884. Catalog
      reprint. 96pp, ill

9446 Hicks, James C. U.S. Firearms, 1776-1956. Notes on U.S.
      Ordnance. Vol. I. Fadco Publishing, 195-?

9447 Holloway, Carroll C. Texas Gun Lore. San Antonio: Naylor,
      1951. 238pp, ill, bib

9448 Hornor, James Crawford. Hand "Gonnes" and Other Weapons
      of the Colonial Period, 1607-1770. Philadelphia: Society
      of Colonial Wars in the Commonwealth of Pa., 1972. 10pp

9449 Hutsler, Donald A. A Checklist of Ohio Gunsmiths, and related
      tradesmen, of the 18th and 19th centuries. Worthington, O:
      Golden Age Arms Co, 1970. 69pp

9450 _____ . Gunsmiths of Ohio: 18th and 19th Centuries. Vol.
      I. Biographical data. York, Pa: George Shumway, 1973.
      444pp, ill, bib

9451 Illustrated Catalogue of United States Cartridge Company's Col-
      lection of Firearms; the most complete collection in the
      United States. Old Greenwich, Conn: WE, Inc., 1920; as

Pictorial History of Firearms to 1905; the United States
Cartridge Company Collection. With introd. by Donald B.
McLean. Forest Grove, Ore: Normount Technical Publi-
cations, 1971. 140pp of ill; 143pp, ill

9452 Kalman, James M., and C. Meade Patterson. A Pictorial
History of United States Single Shot Martial Pistols. New
York: Scribner, 1957. 21pp, 44 color pls, bib

9453 Karr, Charles Lee, Jr. Remington Handguns. Harrisburg,
Pa: Stackpole, 1956.

9454 Kauffman, Henry J. Early American Gunsmiths, 1650-1850;
illustrated and documented. New York: Bramhall House;
Harrisburg, Pa: Stackpole, 1952. 94pp, ill

9455 _____. The Pennsylvania-Kentucky Rifle. Harrisburg, Pa:
Stackpole, 1960. 367pp, 293 ill, bib, gloss

9456 Kennet, Lee, and James L. Anderson. The Gun in America.
Westport, Conn: Greenwood, 1975. ill

9457 Kerksis, Sydney C. Plates and Buckles of the American Military, 1795-1874. Kennesaw, Ga: Gilgal Pr, 1974. 548pp,
ill, bib

9458 Kindig, Joe. Thoughts on the Kentucky Rifle in Its Golden
Age. Ed. by Mary Ann Cresswell. Research by Samuel
E. Dyke and Henry J. Kauffman. Wilmington, Del: G.
N. Hyatt, 1960. 561pp, ill

9459 Kirkland, Turner. Southern Derringers of the Mississippi
Valley. 2nd ed. Union City, Tenn: Pioneer Pr, 1972.
102pp, ill

9460 Koury, Michael J. Arms for Texas; a study of the weapons
of the Republic of Texas. Fort Collins, Col: Old Army
Pr, 1973. 94pp, ill, bib (1836-1846)

9461 Landis, Henry Kinger, and George Diller Landis. Lancaster
Rifle Accessories. Allentown, Pa: Pennsylvania German
Folklore Society, Vol. 9, 1944. 78pp (pp 107-184), ill

9462 _____, and _____. Lancaster Rifles. Allentown, Pa:
Pennsylvania Folklore Society, 1943. 51pp (pp 107-157),
pls NNC-Ave

9463 Lindsay, Merrill. The Kentucky Rifle. New York: Arms Pr,
and the Historical Society of York County, Pa., 1972. ill
(Pennsylvania, Virginia, North Carolina, Kentucky and
Maryland)

9464 *Lord, Francis Alfred. Civil War Collectors Encyclopedia;

arms, uniforms, and equipment of the Union and Confederacy. Harrisburg, Pa: Stackpole, 1965. 360pp, 350
ill, bib; Vol. II. West Columbia, S.C.: Lord Americana
and Research, 1975. 210pp, ill, bib

9465 _____. Civil War Sutlers and Their Wares. New York:
Yoseloff, 1969. 162pp, ill, bib (Supplied necessities--
food, tobacco, etc.)

9466 Lovell, (John P.) Arms Company. 1890 Catalogue. Guns
and Hunting Supplies. Reprint. Princeton, NJ: Pyne
Pr, 1971. 75pp, ill

9467 McHenry, Roy C., and Walter Roper. Smith and Wesson
Handguns. Huntington, W. Va: Standard Publications,
1945. 233pp, ill, pls DLC, NN

9468 Madis, George. The Winchester Book. Dallas, Tx: 1961.

9469 Mayer, Joseph Ralph. Early Virginia Gunlocks. Reprint
from "American Collector." Rochester, NY: Museum of
Arts & Sciences, 1939. 7pp, ill

9470 _____. Flintlocks of the Iroquois, 1620-1687. Rochester,
NY: Rochester Museum of Arts & Sciences, 1943. 59pp,
ill, bib DLC

9471 Moore, Warren. Weapons of the American Revolution ... and
accoutrements. New York: Funk & Wagnalls, 1967.
225pp, ill

9472 Mouillesseaux, Harold R. Ethan Allen, Gunmaker: his
partners, patents and firearms. Ottawa: Museum Restoration Service, 1973. 170pp, ill (Ethan Allen, 1806-1871)

9473 Neumann, George C. Firearms of the American Revolution,
1775-1783. Washington, D.C.: American Ordnance Association, 1973. 16pp, ill, bib

9474 _____. The History of Weapons of the American Revolution. New York: Harper & Row, 1967. 373pp, ill

9475 _____. Swords and Blades of the American Revolution.
Harrisburg, Pa: Stackpole, 1973. 288pp, 1600 ill, bib

9476 _____, and Frank J. Kravic. Collector's Illustrated Encyclopedia of the American Revolution. Harrisburg, Pa:
Stackpole, 1975. 286pp, ill of 2300 items, bib (Includes
ammunition, weapons, wigs, writing instruments, etc.)

9477 Parsons, John E. Catalogue of a Loan Exhibition of Percussion Colt Revolvers and Conversions, 1836-1873.

February-May 1942. New York: Harbor Pr, for Metropolitan Museum, 1942. 39pp, 40 pls

9478 _____ . The First Winchester; the story of the 1866 repeating rifle. New York: Morrow, 1955. 207pp, ill

9479 _____ . Henry Deringer's Pocket Pistol. New York:
Morrow, 1952. 255pp, 70 ill, bib

9480 _____ . The Peacemaker and Its Rivals: an account of
the single action Colt. New York: Morrow, 1950; 1953.
184pp, ill, facsims, bib

9481 _____ . Smith and Wesson Revolvers, the pioneer single
action models. New York: W. Morrow, 1957. ill, docu-
ment facsims

9482 _____ , and John de Mont. Firearms in the Custer Battle.
Harrisburg, Pa: Stackpole, 1953. 59pp, ill, pls, bib

9483 Peterson, Harold Leslie. American Indian Tomahawks; with
an appendix, The Blacksmith Shop, by Milford G. Chandler.
New York: Museum of American Indian, 1965. 142pp,
314 axes ill, pls, bib, makers' list of those not made by
Indians

9484 _____ . The American Sword, 1775-1945. A Survey of the
swords worn by the uniformed forces of the United States
from the Revolution to the close of World War II. New
Hope, Pa: Robert Halter, 1954; new ed. rev., includes
Catalogue of exhibit of author's American silver mounted
swords, 1700-1815. Philadelphia: Ray Riling Arms Books,
1965. 274pp, ill; 286, 60pp, ill

9485 * _____ . Arms and Armor in Colonial America, 1526-1783.
Harrisburg, Pa: Stackpole; New York: Bramhall House,
1956. 350pp, ill, bib

9486 _____ . Arms and Armor of the Pilgrims, 1620-1692. Plymouth, Mass: Plimoth Plantation and the Pilgrim Society,
1957. 28pp, ill (British-made, but used in America)

9487 _____ . The Fuller Collection of American Firearms,
America's Military Long Arms. Philadelphia: Eastern
National Park & Monument Association, 1967. 63pp, ill

9488 _____ . The Remington Historical Treasury of American
Guns. Edinburgh; New York: T. Nelson; New York:
Grosset & Dunlap, 1966. 154pp, ill

9489 Roberts, Ned Henry. The Muzzle-loading Cap Lock Rifle.
Manchester, NH: Granite State Pr, 1940; 2nd ed. enl.

Manchester: Clarke Pr, 1944; 3rd ed. 1947. 432pp, ill, makers; 528pp, 157 ill, makers; 308pp, ill, pls, makers

9490 Russell, Carl Parcher. Firearms, Traps, and Tools of the Mountain Men. New York: Knopf, 1967. 448pp, ill (Mountain men in the West)

9491 _____. Guns on the Early Frontiers. Berkeley: U California Pr, 1957.

9492 Rywell, Martin. American Antique Guns and Their Current Prices; catalog of United States pistols and revolvers that lists, describes, and gives up-to-date prices on every American make, model and type from flintlock through automatics; over 2000 firearms. Harriman, Tenn: Pioneer Pr, 1950; 1951; etc. ill, bib

9493 _____. Colt Guns. Harriman, Tenn: Pioneer Pr, 1957. 134pp, ill

9494 _____. Confederate Guns and Their Current Prices ... handguns and shoulder firearms made or used by the Confederacy.... Harriman, Tenn: Pioneer Pr, 1952. 54pp, ill

9495 _____. Fell's Collector's Guide to American Antique Firearms. New York: F. Fell, 1963. 215pp, ill

9496 _____. Smith and Wesson: the story of the Revolver. Union City, Tenn: Pioneer Pr, 1953. ill (Includes "100 Years of Gun Making" by Carl Hillstrom)

9497 _____. United States Military Muskets, rifles, carbines, and their current prices ... all United States martial shoulder arms ... from 1795 through World War II. Harriman, Tenn: Pioneer Pr, 1951. 46pp, ill

9498 Saterlee, L. D. 14 Old Gun Catalogs for the Collector. Northfield, Ill: Gun Digest Co, 1953. ill (Facsimiles of eight Sharps catalogs, 1859-1880; plus four other catalogs)

9499 Sawyer, Charles Winthrop. Our Rifles. Boston: Williams Book Store, 1941. 412pp, 450 ill, pls, makers list (1800-1919) (Also published as Vol. III of author's Firearms in American History, 1910-1920)

9500 Serven, James Edsell. Colt Cartridge Pistols. Foundation Pr, 1952.

9501 _____. Colt Dragoon Pistols; a saga of the six-shooter, and the trails it blazed. Dallas, Tx: C. Metzger, 1946. 55pp, ill

9502 _____ . Colt Firearms, 1836-1958. Santa Ana, Cal: 1958;
        1960. 387pp, ill, pls

9503 _____ . Colt Percussion Pistols; a pictorial review of
        model variations; facts about their manufacture and use.
        Dallas, Tx: C. Metzger, 1947. 59pp, ill

9504 _____ . Guns on the Arizona Frontier. Tucson: Arizona
        Pioneer's Historical Society, 1965. 20pp, ill, bib

9505 _____ . Paterson Pistols: first of the famous firearms
        patented and promoted by Samuel Colt. Dallas, Tx: Carl
        Metzger, 1946.

9506 _____ . 200 Years of American Firearms. Chicago: Fol-
        lett, 1975. ill

9507 *Sharpe, Philip Burdette. The Rifle in America. Introd. by
        Julian S. Hatcher. New York: W. Morrow, 1938; 2nd
        ed. rev. and enl. New York: Funk & Wagnalls, 1947;
        3rd ed. with supplement. New York: Funk & Wagnalls,
        1953; 1958. 641pp, ill, pls; 782pp, ill, pls; 800pp, ill,
        pls; 833pp, ill, pls

9508 Shields, Joseph W., Jr. From Flintlock to M-1. New York:
        Coward-McCann, 1954. 220pp, ill

9509 Shumway, George. Longrifles of Note, Pennsylvania. York,
        Pa: Early American Industries Association, 1968; as
        Longrifles of Note. London: Arms & Armour Pr, 1968.
        72pp, ill (1750-1850)

9510 Simmons, Richard F. Custom Built Rifles. New York:
        Stackpole & Heck, 1949; 2nd ed. 1955. 184pp, ill

9511 Steffen, Randy. United States Military Saddles, 1812-1943.
        Norman: U. of Oklahoma Pr, 1973. 158pp, ill

9512 *Vandiver, Frank Everson. Ploughshares into Swords; Josiah
        Gorgas and Confederate ordnance. Austin: U of Texas
        Pr, 1952. 349pp, pl

9513 Van Rensselaer, Stephen. American Firearms; an histology
        of American gunsmiths, arms manufacturers and patentees
        with detailed description of their arms. Watkins Glen,
        NY: Century, 1947; The Colt Supplement. 1948. 288pp,
        ill; 94pp, ill

9514 _____ . American Fire Arms. Vol. I. Colt Arms; II.
        Other American Gunsmiths ... from Colonial days to
        present. 2 vol. Watkins Glen, NY: Century, 19-?
        125 ill

9515 Wahl, Paul, and Donald R. Toppel. The Gatling Gun. New
      York: Arc, 1965; London: H. Jenkins, 1966. 168pp,
      ill, pls, bib

9516 Watrous, George R. Winchester Rifles and Shotguns. New
      Haven: Winchester, 1943; 2nd ed. 1950; 3rd ed. as The
      History of Winchester Firearms, 1866-1966. New Haven:
      1966; 4th ed. as The History ... 1866-1975. New York:
      Winchester Pr, 1975. ...; 188pp, ill; 229pp, ill

9517 Webster, Donald Blake, Jr. American Socket Bayonets, 1717-
      1873. Ottawa, Ont: Museum Restoration Service, 1964.
      47pp, ill

9518 _____. Suicide Specials. Harrisburg, Pa: Stackpole,
      1958. ill (Small revolvers after Civil War)

9519 West, Bill. Browning Arms and History, 1842-1973. Azuza,
      Cal: B. West, 1972. u.p., ill

9520 _____, comp. Hartley and Graham. Arms and ammuni-
      tion, 1895-99, sporting goods catalogs. Illustrated: rifles,
      carbines, pistols, shotguns, cannon, cartridges, gun sights,
      cases, traps, loaders, tools, etc. Other Americana: bi-
      cycles, whistles, dog sundries, compasses, knives, cups,
      decoys, flasks, axes, lanterns, golf equipment, leather
      goods. Azuza, Cal: Author, 1972. 112pp, ill

9521 _____.. Know Your Winchesters: General Use, All Models
      and Types, 1849-1969. Azuza, Cal: Author, 1970. ill

9522 _____. Marlin and Ballard, Arms and History, 1861-1971.
      Azuza, Cal: Author, 1968; 1972. u.p., ill

9523 _____. Remington Arms and History, 1849-1971. Azuza,
      Cal: Author, 1970. u.p., ill

9524 _____. Remington Arms Catalogues, 1877-1899; rifles,
      carbines, muskets, pistols and shotguns, illustrated car-
      tridges, sights, parts, and accessories. Azuza, Cal:
      Author, 1970. 42, 48, 43pp, ill

9525 _____. Savage and Stevens, Arms and History, 1849-1971.
      Whittier, Cal: Stockton-Doty, printer, 1971. u.p., ill

9526 _____. Winchesters, Cartridges and History. Azuza, Cal:
      Author, 197-? u.p., ill

9527 Whelen, Townsend. The American Rifle. New York: Cen-
      tury, 1923. ill

9528 Wilkinson, Frederick John. British and American Flintlocks.
      Feltham: Hamlyn for Country Life, 1971. 63pp, ill

9529   Williamson, Harold Francis. Winchester: the gun that won
          the west. Washington, D.C.: Combat Forces Pr, 1952.
          494pp, 200 ill, bib

9530   Wilson, Robert Lawrence. The Arms Collection of Colonel
          (Samuel) Colt. Wadsworth Atheneum, Hartford, Connecti-
          cut. Bullville, NY: H. Glass, 1964. 132pp, ill (Colt,
          1814-1862)

9531   _____. Samuel Colt Presents: a loan exhibition of pre-
          sentation percussion Colt firearms, Wadsworth Atheneum,
          November 1961-January 1962. Pref. by C. C. Cunning-
          ham. Fore. by John S. deMont. Hartford, Conn: 1961.
          293pp, ill, bib CU

9532   Wolff, Eldon G. Ballard Rifles in Henry J. Nunnemacher
          Collection. Milwaukee: Public Museum, 1945; 2nd ed.
          1961. 77pp, 27 pls

9533   _____. Guns, the story behind the Nunnemacher Collec-
          tion. Milwaukee: Public Museum, 1961. 17pp, 17 ill

9534   _____. The Nye-Terry Breech-Loader Complex. Mil-
          waukee: Public Museum, 1961. 19pp, 17 ill, figures

9535   _____. Revolver Classification. Milwaukee: Public Mu-
          seum, 1950. 16pp, 2 pls

9536   _____. Wyatt Atkinson, Riflesmith. Milwaukee: Public
          Museum, 1964. 16pp, 21 ill

ARMS AND ARMOUR OF THE BRITISH ISLES AND CANADA

9537   Anderson, Joseph, 1832-1916. Ancient Scottish Weapons. A
          series of drawings by the late James Drummond. Edin-
          burgh; London: G. Waterston, 1881. 200pp, ill DLC,
          BM

9538   *Annis, Philip Geoffrey Walter. Naval Swords: British and
          American Naval edged weapons, 1660-1815. London:
          Arms & Armour Pr, 1970. 80pp, ill, bib (American,
          1776-1815)

9539   Arms and Armour in the Banqueting Hall, Edinburgh Castle.
          Edinburgh: Dept. of Ancient Monuments and Historic
          Buildings, 1936. 16pp

9540   *Ashdown, Charles Henry. Arms and Armour ... illustrated
          ... from actual examples, missals, illuminated manu-
          scripts, brasses, effigies, etc., and from original re-
          search in the British Museum, the Tower of London,

Wallace Collection, Rotunda at Woolwich, many private collections, etc. London: T. C. & E. C. Jack; New York: Dodge, 1909; as British and Continental Arms and Armor. New York: Dover, 1970. 384pp, 450 ill, 42 pls

9541 Aylward, James De Vine. The Small Sword in England; its history, its forms, its makers, and its masters. London: Hutchinson, 1945; new rev. ed. 1960. 132pp, ill, pl, bib; 176pp, ill, 24 pls, bib

9542 Bailey, De Witt. British Military Longarms, 1815-1865. London: Arms & Armour Pr, 1972. 79pp, ill

9543 _____. British Military Longarms, 1715-1815. London: Arms & Armour Pr, 1971; Harrisburg, Pa: Stackpole, 1972. 80pp, ill

9544 Beard, Charles Relly. The Clothing and Arming of the Yeomen of the Guard, 1485-1685. London: 1928. 60pp, 25 ill V & A

9545 Blackmore, Howard Loftus. British Military Firearms 1650-1850. London: Jenkins, 1961. 33 ill, 83 pls, bib

9546 _____. Royal Sporting Guns at Windsor. London: HMSO, 1968. 69pp, ill, 53 pls

9547 Blair, Claude. The Emperor Maximilian's Gift of Armour to Henry 8th and the Silvered and Engraved Armour at the Tower of London. Oxford: U. Pr, 1965. 13 pls

9548 _____. Three Presentation Swords in the Victoria and Albert, and a group of English enamels. Exhibition. London: V & A, 1972. 53pp, ill, bib

9549 Blanch, H. J. A Century of Guns: a sketch of the leading types of sporting and military small arms. London: H. J. Blanch & Sons, 1900; 1909; reprint, ed. by Martin Rywell, as English Guns and Gun Makers, (including Century of Guns). Harriman, Tenn: Pioneer Pr, 1956. 153pp, ill, 21 pls; 1956: 160pp, 140pp of ill (1500 to date. English, Scottish and Irish)

9550 Campbell, Lord Archibald. Highland Dress, arms and ornament. Westminster: Constable, 1899; reprint. London: Dawsons, 1969. 176pp, ill, 77 pls, bib NN, PPULC

9551 _____. Notes on Swords from the Battlefield of Culloden. London: C. J. Clark, 1894. 24pp, 4 ill BM

9552 Carey, Arthur Merwyn. English, Irish, and Scottish Firearms Makers: when, where, and what they made, from

the middle of the 16th century to the end of the 19th
century. New York: Crowell, 1954; London; Edinburgh:
Chambers, 1955; 2nd ed. Edgware, Eng: Arms & Armour
Pr; New York: Arco, 1967. 121pp, ill, 8 pls, bib

9553   Catalogue of a Most Splendid and Instructive Collection of
       Antient Armour, exhibiting at Oplotheca (London) ...
       forming a series from the Norman Conquest; including the
       greatest variety of fine shields, helmets, swords, guns, etc.,
       etc. London: Smith & Davy, printers, 1816. 31pp MiU

9554   Cosson, Baron Charles Alexander de, and W. Burges. Ancient
       Helmets and Examples of Mail. A catalogue of objects ex-
       hibited in the rooms of the Royal Archaeological Institute,
       1880. London: 1881. 15 pls

9555   Cripps-Day, Francis Henry. Arms and Armour in Churches
       in England. Reprint from the "Archaeological Journal."
       London: 1934.

9556   Dillon, Viscount Harold Arthur Lee. An Almain Armourer's
       Album. Selections from an original manuscript in the
       Victoria and Albert Museum, South Kensington. Repro-
       duced. Reprint from "Archaeological Journal" Vol. 52,
       1895 and Vol. 60, 1903. London: W. Griggs, 1905; re-
       print as Armour. An Elizabethan armourer's album and
       armour notes. London: Arms and Armour Pr; York,
       Pa: G. Shumway, 1968. 75pp, ill (Album possibly by
       Jacob Topf)

9557   Dixon, Norman. Georgian Pistols: the art and craft of the
       flintlock pistol, 1715-1840. London: Arms & Armour Pr,
       1971. 184pp, ill

9558   Drummond, James, 1816-1877. Ancient Scottish Weapons.
       Introd. by Joseph Anderson. Edinburgh; London: G.
       Waterston, 1881. 26pp, 54 color pls (Highland dress,
       musical instruments, agricultural and domestic imple-
       ments, weapons, etc.) DLC

9559   Dunham, Keith. The Gun Trade of Birmingham; a short his-
       torical note of some of the more interesting features of a
       long-established local industry. Birmingham, Eng: Mu-
       seum and Art Gallery, 1955. 43pp, ill, bib NN

9560   Early Firearms of Great Britain and Ireland from the Collec-
       tion of Clay P. Bedford. Metropolitan Museum of Art.
       New York: dist. by N.Y. Graphic Society, Greenwich,
       Conn., 1971. 187pp, ill, 4 pls

9561   Ffoulkes, Charles John. Arms and Armament. An historical
       survey of the weapons of the British Army. Fore. by

Claud W. Jacob.   London: Harrap, 1943; 1945; 1947.
158pp, ill, bib

9562 _____ .   Arms and the Tower.   Imperial War Museum.
London: J. Murray, 1939.   246pp, pls

9563 _____ .   The Gun-Founders of England, with a List of
English and Continental gun-founders from the 14th to the
19th centuries.   Pref. by Lord Cottesloe.   Cambridge,
Eng: U. Pr, 1937; reprint.   York, Pa: G. Shumway,
1969.   133pp, ill, 15 pls, bib

9564 _____ .   Inventory and Survey of the Armouries of the
Tower of London.   2 vol.   London: HMSO, 1916.   ill,
38 pls

9565 _____ , and E. C. Hopkinson.   Sword, Lance and Bayonet;
a record of the arms of the British Army and Navy.   2nd
ed. Edgware, Eng: Arms & Armour Pr; New York: Arco,
1967.   145pp, ill, 3 pls, bib

9566 Gardner, John Starkie, 1844-1930.   Armour in England from
the Earliest Times to the 17th Century.   I. Armour made
in England or for Englishmen; II. Foreign Arms in England.
2 parts in 1.   London: Seeley; New York: Macmillan,
1898.   96pp, 81 ill, 16 color pls   TxU, CU, PP

9567 _____ .   Armour in England to the Reign of James I.   London: Seeley; New York: Macmillan, 1897.   100pp, ill,
12 color pls   DLC, PPD

9568 George, John Nigel.   English Guns and Rifles; being an account of the development, design, and usage of English
sporting rifles and shotguns--from their introduction during
the 15th century until the advent of the metallic cartridges
in the 19th century--together with notes on muskets, service rifles, blunderbusses, and other arms, including also
various historical notes and accounts regarding individual
makers and users of these arms.   Harrisburg, Pa: Stackpole, 1947.   344pp, ill, bib   DLC, TxU, NN

9569 _____ .   English Pistols and Revolvers; an historical outline
of the development and design of English hand firearms
from the 17th century to the present day.   London: Holland Pr, 1938.   256pp, ill   DLC

9570 Glendenning, Ian.   British Pistols and Guns, 1640-1840.   London: Cassell, 1951; facsimile reprint.   London: Arms &
Armour Pr; New York: Arco, 1967.   195pp, ill

9571 Gooding, Sidney James.   The Canadian Gunsmiths, 1608-1900.
West Hill, Ontario: Museum Restoration Service, 1962.
308pp, ill, bib

9572 _____ . An Introduction to British Artillery in North
America. Ottawa, Ontario: Museum Restoration Service,
1965. 54pp, ill

9573 Grancsay, Stephen V., and Merrill Lindsay, comp. and ed.
Illustrated British Firearms Patents, 1714-1853. New
York: Winchester Pr, 1969. v.p., ill

9574 Holmes, Martin Rivington. Arms and Armour in Tudor and
Stuart London. V & A. London: HMSO, 1957; 2nd ed.
1970. 39pp, ill, 20 pls (1485-1685)

9575 Jackson, Melvin H., and Carel de Beer. 18th Century Gun-
founding: the Verbruggens at the Royal Brass Foundry, a
chapter in the history of technology. Washington, D.C.:
Smithsonian, 1974. 183pp, ill, bib (Woolwich, England.
Royal Arsenal)

9576 Kelly, Francis Michael, and Randolph Schwabe. A Short
History of Costume and Armour, chiefly in England.
(Cover title: A Short History of Costume and Armour,
1066-1800.) 2 vol. London: Batsford, 1931; 2 vol. in
1. New York: B. Blom, 1968; Newton Abbot: David &
Charles, 1972. 261pp, ill, bib, gloss

9577 Kingsland, Peter William, and Susan Keable. British Military
Uniforms and Equipment, 1788-1830. Researched under
supervision of the National Army Museum, London. London: Guiness Button Holdings, 1971. ill, color pls

9578 Latham, John Wilkinson. British Cut and Thrust Weapons.
Newton Abbot: David & Charles; Rutland, Vt: Tuttle,
1971. 112pp, ill, bib

9579 _____ . British Military Bayonets from 1700 to 1945. London: 1967; New York: Arco, 1969. 94pp, ill, bib

9580 _____ . British Military Swords: from 1800 to the present
day. London: Hutchinson, 1966. 91pp, ill, 32 pls, bib

9581 Majendie, Vivian Dering, and C. Orde Browne. Military
Breech-Loading Rifles: (with detailed notes on) the Snider,
the Martini-Henry and Boxer Ammunition. Woolwich, Eng:
Boddy & Co, for Royal Artillery Institution, 1870; facsimile reprint. London: Arms & Armour Pr, 1973.
129pp, ill, 13 pls MB

9582 Mann, Sir James Gow. An Outline of Arms and Armour in
England from the Early Middle Ages to the Civil War.
(Tower of London Collection.) London: HMSO, 1960;
2nd ed. rev. by A. R. Dufty. London: 1969. 44pp,
ill, bib

9583   Mayer, Joseph Ralph. Celtic Art on Scottish Pistols. New
       York: Armor & Arms Club, 1940. 10pp, ill DLC

9584   *Meyrick, Sir Samuel Rush, 1783-1848. A Critical Enquiry
       into Antient Armour, as it existed in Europe, but par-
       ticularly in England, from the Norman Conquest to the
       Reign of King Charles 2nd: with a glossary of military
       terms of the middle ages. 3 vol. London: 1824; 2nd
       ed. corr. & enl. by Meyrick, Albert Way, Douce and
       others. London: Henry Bohn, 1842. 90 (80 color) pls
       of knights and soldiers dressed in complete armour and
       carrying their weapons. NjP, MB, NN

9585   Neal, William Keith, and D. H. L. Back. Forsyth & Com-
       pany: Patent Gunmakers. London: Bell, 1969. 280pp,
       ill, 68 pls (Early 19th century)

9586   _____, and _____. Great British Gunmakers, 1740-
       1790: the history of John Twigg and the Packington Guns.
       New York: Sotheby Parke Bernet, 1975. ill (Includes
       the Packington Collection)

9587   _____, and _____. The Mantons: Gunmakers. New
       York: Walker, 1966; London: Jenkins, 1967. 300pp, ill,
       86 pls

9588   Norman, Alexander Vesey Bethune, and Don Pottinger. A
       History of War and Weapons, 449 to 1660; English warfare
       from the Anglo-Saxons to Cromwell. London: Barker;
       New York: Crowell, 1966. 224pp, ill

9589   Nye, Nathaniel. The Art of Gunnery. Wherein is described
       the true way to make all sorts of gunpowder, gun-match,
       the art of shooting in great and small ordnance ... to
       make divers sorts of artificall fireworks. 2 parts. Lon-
       don: 1647; 1648. BM

9590   Roads, C. H. The British Soldier's Firearm, 1850-1864.
       London: Jenkins, 1964. 332pp, ill, bib

9591   Tout, Thomas Frederick, 1855-1929. Firearms in England
       in the 14th Century. Reprint from his "English Historical
       Review," Vol. XXVI, 1911, with introd. by Claude Blair.
       London: Arms & Armour Pr, 1968. 57pp, ill

9592   Tylden, Major G. Horses and Saddlery: an account of the
       animals used by the British and Commonwealth Armies
       from the 17th century to the present day, with a descrip-
       tion of their equipment. London: by J. A. Allen, with
       the Army Museums Ogilby Trust, 1965. 276pp, ill, 81
       pls, color frontis

9593   Walker, James, inventor of the Improved Patent Copper

Gunpowder barrels. Remarks ... on the safe conveyance
and preservation of gunpowder. London: J. Darling,
printer, 1814. 95pp

9594 Wallace, John. Scottish Swords and Dirks: an illustrated
reference guide to Scottish edged weapons. London:
Arms & Armour Pr; Harrisburg, Pa: Stackpole, 1970.
80pp, ill

9595 Wilkinson, Frederick John. British and American Flintlocks.
Feltham: Hamlyn, for Country Life, 1971. 63pp, ill

9596 Wyatt, Robert John. Collecting Volunteer Militaria. Newton
Abbot, Eng; North Pomfret, Vt: David & Charles, 1974.
160pp, ill (British volunteer unites ... badges, uniforms,
etc.)

ORIENTAL ARMS AND ARMOUR

9597 Anderson, Leonard John. Japanese Armour: an illustrated
guide to the work of the Myochin and Saotome families
from the 15th to the 20th century. London: Arms &
Armour Pr; Harrisburg, Pa: Stackpole, 1968. 84pp, ill,
bib

9598 Catalogue of an Exhibition of the Arms and Armour of Old
Japan, held by the Japan Society. London: The Society,
1905. 147pp, 40 pls

9599 Church, Sir Arthur Herbert. Japanese Sword Guards; Some
tsuba in the collection of A. H. Church. Reading, Eng:
priv. printed, 1914. 80pp, 40 pls MiD

9600 Dean, Bashford. Catalogue of the Loan Collection of Japanese
Armor. New York: Metropolitan Museum, 1903. 71pp,
ill, pls

9601 Dobree, Alfred. Japanese Sword Blades. Edgware, Middle-
      sex: Arms & Armour Pr, 1967; rev. ed. York, Pa:
      Armor and Arms Pr, 1971. 39pp, ill, 15 pls; 73pp, ill,
      marks

9602 The Egerton Collection of Oriental Armour. Manchester,
      Eng: Garnet, Evans, for the Art Gallery, 19-? 60pp
      (Earl Wilbraham Egerton Egerton) DLC

9603 Egerton, Lord Wilbraham, 1832-1909. A Description of
      Indian and Oriental Armour. 2nd ed. London: Allen &
      Unwin, 1896; 2nd ed. reprinted with introd. by H. Russell
      Robinson. London: Arms & Armour Pr; Harrisburg,
      Pa: Stackpole, 1968. 178pp, ill, 24 (2 color) pls, bib
      (South Kensington Museum's and Author's collections) BM

9604 _____. An Illustrated Handbook of Indian Arms; being a
      classified and descriptive catalogue of the arms exhibited
      at the India Museum.... London: W. H. Allen, 1880;
      new ed. as A Description of Indian and Oriental Armour.
      London: Allen, 1896. 162pp, ill; 178pp, ill BM

9605 Foreman, Werner. Swords and Daggers of Indonesia. Lon-
      don: Spring, 19-? ill (many color)

9606 German, Michael Cyril. A Guide to Oriental Daggers and
      Swords. London: Author, 1967. 59pp, ill

9607 Gunsaulus, Helen Cowen. The Japanese Sword and Its Decora-
      tion. Chicago: Field Museum of Natural History, 1924.
      21pp, pls

9608 _____. Japanese Sword-mounts in the Collections of Field
      Museum. Chicago: the Museum, 1923. 195pp, 61 pls

9609 Hamilton, John. Collection of Japanese Sword Guards with
      Selected Pieces of Sword Furniture. Hanover, NH: U.
      Pr of New England, 1974.

9610 Hawley, Willis Meeker. Japanese Swords. Hollywood, Cal:
      1945. ill chart

9611 Japanese Sword Guards. Boston: Museum of Fine Arts,
      192-? 35 pls, unpublished

9612 *Japanese Works of Art; armour, weapons, sword-fittings,
      lacquer, pictures, textiles, colour-prints, selected from
      the Mosle Collection. Ed. by Alexander George Mosle.
      2 vol. Leipzig: 1914. 204 (4 color) pls

9613 Joly, Henri L. Japanese Sword Fittings. Catalogue of Col-
      lection of George Herbert Naunton. London: priv. printed,
      Tokio Pr, 1912; Reading, Pa: 1922. 317pp

9614 _____, comp. Japanese Sword-Mounts. A catalogue of
      the collection of John Clarke Hawkshaw. London: 1910.
      300pp, ill, 50 pls

9615 _____. List of Names, kakihan, collected from sword-
      mounts, etc. Supplementary to Shinkichi Hara's "Meister...".
      London: 1919. 134pp of manuscript, photostated (About
      2950 names) MH

9616 Kozan, Sakakibara. The Manufacture of Armour and Helmets
      in 16th Century Japan. Rutland, Vt: Tuttle, 1963. 144pp,
      ill, bib

9617 Laking, Guy Francis. Catalogue, Oriental Arms and Armour.
      Wallace Collection, Hertford House. London: HMSO, 1914.
      pls

9618 Lyman, Benjamin Smith, 1835-1920. Japanese Swords. Read
      before the Numismatic and Antiquarian Society of Philadel-
      phia, 3 April, 1890. Reprint from "Proceedings." Phila-
      delphia: 1892. 38pp, ill DLC

9619 _____. Metallurgical and Other Features of Japanese
      Swords. (Abstract.) Philadelphia: 1896. 14pp BM,
      MH-P

9620 Okabe-Kakuya. Japanese Sword Guards. Boston: Museum of
      Fine Arts, 1908. 139pp, ill DLC

9621 Payne-Gallwey, Sir Ralph. The Projectile-throwing Engines of
      the Ancients. London: Longman, 1907; facsimile reprint,
      with new introd. by E. G. Heath. Wakefield, Eng: E P
      Publishing, 1973. 44pp, ill, 26 pls (Oriental bows and
      arrows ca.1400 to ca.1900)

9622 Rawson, Philip Stanley. The Indian Sword. London: Jenkins,
      1968. 108pp, ill, 48 pls, bib

9623 *Robinson, Basil William. Arms and Armour of Old Japan.
      V & A. London: HMSO, 1951. 44pp, 26 ill

9624 _____. The Arts of the Japanese Sword. London: Faber,
      1961; 2nd ed. 1970. 110pp, ill, 100 pls; 2nd ed. 120 pls

9625 Robinson, Henry Russell. Japanese Arms and Armor. New
      York: Crown; London: Arms & Armour Pr, 1969. 54pp,
      112 ill, 29 color pls

9626 _____. Oriental Armour. London: Jenkins; New York:
      Walker, 1967. 257pp, ill, 32 pls, bib

9627 _____. A Short History of Japanese Armour. London:
      HMSO, 1965. 47pp, ill, bib, gloss

9628   Rucker, Robert Hamilton. Catalogue of a Loan Exhibition of
       Japanese Sword Fittings. Introd. by Howard Mansfield.
       August-December 1922. New York: R. A. Haag, printer,
       for Metropolitan Museum, 1924. (19)pp, 59 leaves, 43 pls

9629   _____, comp. Catalogue of a Loan Exhibition of Japanese
       Sword Guards. July-October 1921. New York: R. A.
       Haag, printer, for Metropolitan Museum, 1922. 21pp,
       73 pls

9630   _____. The Gōda Collection of Japanese Sword Fittings.
       Metropolitan Museum. New York: 1924. 93pp, ill, bib

9631   Solc, Vaclav. Swords and Daggers of Indonesia. Tr. from
       Czechoslovakian by Till Gottheiner. London: Spring,
       1958. 13pp, 34 pls

9632   Stern, Harold P. The Magnificent Three: lacquer, netsuke,
       and tsuba; selections from the collection of Charles A.
       Greenfield. Exhibition. New York: Japan Society, 1972.
       141pp, ill, bib

9633   Suzuki, Katei. Tanto (Japanese Daggers). English tr.
       Berkeley?, Cal: Japanese Sword Society of United States,
       1973. 86pp, marks

9634   To-ken Catalogue; an exhibition of Japanese Swords and other
       items representing the martial arts from the 4th to the
       20th centuries. Abingdon, Eng: To-ken Society of Great
       Britain, 1968. 90pp, ill

9635   Yamanaka, Sadajiro. Exhibition of Japanese Armour and
       Horse Ornaments. New York: Yamanaka & Co, 1933.
       64pp, ill, 3 pls (Originally Collection of Kametaro Hamano)

9636   Yumoto, John Masayuki. The Samurai Sword: a handbook.
       Rutland, Vt: Tuttle, 1958. 191pp, ill, bib (900 A.D. on)

DAGGERS AND KNIVES

9637   Cheney, William Murray. Pocket Knives. 2nd ed. Los
       Angeles: Author, 1968. 51pp

9638   Cole, M. H. A Collection of United States Military Knives,
       1861-1968. Birmingham, Ala: Economy Pr, printer,
       1968. 85pp, ill

9639   *Dean, Bashford. Catalogue of European Daggers, 1300-1900,
       including the Ellis, De Dino, Riggs and Reubell Collections.
       Metropolitan Museum. New York: 1929. 196pp, ill, 85
       pls, bib

9640   Ehrhardt, Larry. Encyclopedia of Pocket Knives: Winchester
       and Marbles Hardware Collectibles, Book 3. Kansas City:
       Heart of America Pr, 1974. ill

9641   Ehrhardt, Roy. Encyclopedia of Old Pocket Knives. Kansas
       City: Heart of America Pr, 1973. 96pp, ill of 336 knives

9642   Ferguson, Dewey P. Romance of Knife Collecting. n. p. :
       19-? 99pp, ill (W. R. Case & Sons; Winchester; Utica;
       Shapleigh Hardware; Standard; Remington; Keen Kutter, etc.)

9643   Frazier, Charles. The Knife Collector's Handbook; a pictorial
       and written guide to the collecting of pocket knives and
       their value. Middletown, O: Author, 1969. 237pp, ill

9644   Janes, Edward C. The Story of Knives. New York: Putnam,
       1968. 127pp, ill (Juvenile literature)

9645   *Mercer, Henry Chapman. The Bowie and Other Knives.
       Doylestown, Pa: 1917. 15pp

9646   *Peterson, Harold Leslie. American Knives: the first history
       and collectors' guide. New York; London: Scribner, 1958;
       reprint. 1975. 178pp, 186 ill (No table or kitchen cut-
       lery)

9647   _____ . Daggers and Fighting Knives of the Western World,
       from the Stone Age till 1900. London: Jenkins, 1968;
       New York: 1970. 90pp, ill, 32 pls, bib

9648   _____ . A History of Knives. New York: Scribner, 1966.
       64pp, ill (Juvenile literature)

9649   Thorp, Raymond W. The Bowie Knife. Albuquerque: U of
       New Mexico Pr, 1948. 167pp, ill, pls, bib

PUNISHMENTS

9650   Andrews, William, 1848-1908. Bygone Punishments. London:
       W. Andrews, 1899; 2nd ed. London: P. Allan, 1931.
       311pp, ill, pls; 292pp, ill, pls DLC

9651   _____ . Old-Time Punishments. Hull: W. Andrews, 1890.
       251pp, ill DLC

9652   _____ . Punishments in the Olden Time: being an histori-
       cal account of the ducking stool, brank, pillory, stocks,
       drunkard's cloak, whipping post, riding the stang, etc.
       London: W. Stewart, 1881? 76pp, ill DLC

CONTAINERS, LOCKS AND KEYS

BASKETS

9653 Ashley, Gertrude, and Mildred Ashley. Raffia Basketry as a Fine Art. Deerfield, Mass: 1915. 45pp, 16 ill, color frontis

9654 *Bailey, Richard C. Collectors' Choice; the McLeod Basket Collection. Bakersfield, Cal: Kern County Historical Society Museum, 1951. 36pp, ill, bib (Edwin Lincoln McLeod)

9655 Bobart, Henry Hodgkinson. Basketwork Through the Ages. London: Oxford U Pr, H. Milford; New York: Oxford U Pr, 1936; reprint. Detroit: Singing Tree Pr, Gale Research, 1971. 174pp, 86 ill, bib

9656 _____, comp. Records of the Basketmakers' Company. London: Dunn, Collin, 1911. 183pp, ill DLC, TxU

9657 Christopher, F. J. Basketry. Ed. by Marjorie O'Shaughnessy. London: W. & G. Foyle, 1951; rev. ed. New York: Dover, 1952. 108pp, 155 ill (Chiefly how-to)

9658 Crampton, Charles. Canework ... with an introduction to the history of basket-making and some notes on cane and its uses by H. H. Peach. Leicester: Dryad Pr, 1924; 2nd ed. 1926; 6th rev. ed. 1933; 10th ed. 1948; 12th ed. 1951;... 63pp; 67pp; 96pp; 135pp; all ill, bib MiD, TxU

9659 Firth, Annie. Cane Basket Work: a practical manual on weaving useful and fancy basket. London: L. U. Gill, 1897; 2 vol. London: Gill; New York: Scribner's, 1899-1901; 2 vol. London: 1905. 88pp, 80 ill, 1 pl NN, MB, TxU

9660 Fitz Randolph, Helen Elizabeth, and Mavis Doriel Hay. Osier-Growing and Basketry and Some Rural Factories. Oxford: Clarendon Pr, 1926. 159pp, pls

9661   Hasluck, Paul Nooncree, ed.   Basket Work of All Kinds.
       London; New York: Cassell, 1902; Philadelphia: McKay,
       1903; 1914. 160pp, ill MB, DLC

9662 *Ketchum, William C., Jr.   American Basketry and Wooden-
       ware, a collector's guide.   New York: Macmillan; Lon-
       don: Collier Macmillan, 1974.   228pp, 83 ill, bib
       (ca.1650-ca.1930)

9663   A List of the Sizes of Skips, Baskets and Hampers, with the
       journeyman's prices affixed for Lancaster, Cheshire, etc.
       England: 1845. SIB-2

9664   Otty (afterwards Williamson), Isabel A.   English Basketry on
       Wood Bases. Leeds: E. J. Arnold, 1913. 62pp

9665   Rossbach, Ed.   Baskets as Textile Art.   New York: Van
       Nostrand Reinhold, 1973. 199pp, ill, bib (Old and new,
       all over world)

9666 *Seeler, Katherine, and Edgar Seeler.   Nantucket Lightship
       Baskets.   Nantucket, Mass: Deermouse, 1972. 116pp,
       ill, 51 pls

9667 *Teleki, Gloria Roth.   The Baskets of Rural America.   New
       York: Dutton, 1975. 202pp, 94 ill, bib (Shaker, Appa-
       lachian, etc. Includes tools)

9668   Tinsley, Laura Rollins.   Practical and Artistic Basketry.
       New York; Chicago: 1904. 142pp, 112 ill

TRUNKS AND BOXES

9669   Bedford, John.   All Kinds of Small Boxes.   London: Cassell,
       1964; New York: Walker, 1965. 68pp, ill, 2 pls

9670   Carlisle, Lillian Baker.   Hat Boxes and Bandboxes at Shel-
       burne Museum.   Shelburne, Vt: 1960. 196pp, ill, pls

9671   Delieb, Eric.   Silver Boxes.   London: Jenkins; as English
       Silver Boxes.   New York: C. N. Potter, 1968. 120pp,
       chiefly ill

9672   Hill, Henry David, and Sidney Hill, (pseud. Henry and Sidney
       Berry-Hill).   Antique Gold Boxes: Their lore and their
       lure.   New York: Abelard, 1954. 223pp, ill, bib

9673   Klamkin, Marian.   The Collector's Book of Boxes.   New York:
       Dodd, Mead, 1970; Newton Abbot: David & Charles, 1972.
       145pp, 182 ill, bib

9674   Labuda, Martin, and Maryann Labuda.   Antique Trunks; how to decorate, repair and restore. Cleveland: Antique Trunk Co, 1968. 24pp, ill

9675 _____, and _____. Price and Identification Guide to Antique Trunks; their history and current values, with value-increasing tips n' hints. Cleveland: Antique Trunk Co, 1972. 24pp, ill, 85 photographs

9676 Ryerse, Phyllis. A Guide to the History and Restoration of Antique Trunks. Freehold, NJ: Ryerse, 1974. ill

9677 Snowman, Abraham Kenneth. 18th Century Gold Boxes of Europe. Fore. by Sacheverell Sitwell. Appendix by F. J. B. Watson. London: Faber, 1966; 1968. 192pp, 750 (130 color) ill, bib (Includes boxes from Leningrad Hermitage)

SAFES, MONEY PROTECTORS, MECHANICAL AND STILL BANKS

9678 Bellows, Ina Hayward. Old Mechanical Banks. A comprehensive study of the subject of mechanical banks. Chicago: Lightner, 1940; 1954. 150pp, many ill, pls DLC

9679 Cranmer, Don. Still Banks of Yesterday. Gas City, Ind: L-W Promotions, 197-? 88pp, ill (450 banks--cast iron, glass, tin, pot metal)

9680 Griffith, F. H. Mechanical Banks. New ed. Sea Girt, NJ: Author, 1972. 32pp, 297 banks ill

9681 Hertz, Louis Heilbroner. Mechanical Toy Banks. Wethersfield, Conn: M. Haber, 1947. 146 leaves

9682 Hopkinson, Isabella, and William P. Hopkinson. Toys and Banks with Their Prices at Auction. Concord, NH: Rumford Pr, 1970. 50pp, color ill (1000 19th and early-20th century pieces)

9683 Ibbetson, John Holt. A Practical View of an Invention for the Better Protecting Bank Notes against Forgery. London: Wetton & Jarvis, 1820. 68pp BM

9684 Kraske, Robert. Silent Sentinels; the story of locks, vaults, and burglar alarms. Garden City, NY: Doubleday, 1969. 127pp, ill (Ancient Egypt to present)

9685 The Mechanical Banker. Newsletter. Ed. by H. E. Mihlheim and Steve Steckbeck. Allegan, Mich: Mechanical Bank Collectors of America, 19- .

9686 Meyer, John Daniel. A Handbook of Old Mechanical Penny

Banks. Tyrone, Pa: 1948; 2nd ed. 1952. 107pp, ill;
119pp, ill, bib

9687 _____, and Larry Freeman. Old Penny Banks: Mechanical. (by Meyer.) Stills. (by Freeman.) Watkins Glen:
Century House, 1960. 130pp, ill

9688 *Price, George. A Treatise on Fire and Thief-Proof Deposi-
tories, and locks and keys. London: Simpkin, Marshall,
1856; 1858. 916pp, 450 ill (most scale diagrams), 1 color
pl (First English language work on subject) NN, DLC

9689 _____. A Treatise on Gun-powder-proof Locks, gun-powder-
proof lock-chambers, drill-proof safes, etc. London: E.
& F. N. Spon, 1860. 116pp, ill NN

9690 Sala, George Augustus (Henry), 1828-1895. The Battle of the
Safes; or British Invincibles versus Yankee Ironclads.
With appendix containing official report of R. Mallet ...
R. F. Fairlie, etc. London: 1868. BM

9691 Whiting, Hubert B. Old Iron Still Banks. Manchester, Vt:
Forward's Color Productions, 1968. u.p., color ill

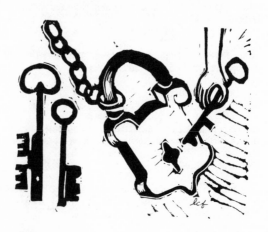

LOCKS AND KEYS

9692 Aitken, William Costen. Guns, nails, locks, wood screws,
railway bolts and spikes, buttons, pins, needles, saddlery,
and electroplate. London: 1876. See also: Bevan, G. P.,
British Manufacturing Industries, Vol. 3., no. 43.

9693 *Antique Locks from the Collection of Josiah Parks and Sons,
Ltd. Willenhall, Staffordshire: 1955.

9694 Arnall, Franklin M. The Padlock Collector. Menstone, Cal:
      1973. 61pp, ill of 350 padlocks

9695 Buehr, Walter. The Story of Locks. New York: Scribner,
      1953. 45pp, ill

9696 Collectors Guide to Locks and Keys. Gas City, Ind: L. W.
      Promotions, n.d. (197-?) 60pp, ill (Over 400 items--
      padlocks, chest locks, door and railroad locks, and keys)

9697 *Eras, Vincent J. M. Locks and Keys Throughout the Ages.
      Amsterdam: H. H. Fronczek; London: Bailey & Swinfen,
      1957. 194pp, ill

9698 Hobbs, Alfred Charles, 1812-1891. Rudimentary Treatise on
      the Construction of Locks. Compiled by George Dodd from
      materials furnished by A. C. Hobbs. Ed. by Charles
      Tomlinson. London: Weale, 1853; as Rudimentary Treatise
      on the Construction of Door Locks, for commercial and
      domestic purposes. Compiled by G. Dodd, ed. by Charles
      Tomlinson. 2nd issue with Mr. Smyth's letter on the
      Bramah locks. London: Weale, 1858-9; as Locks and
      Safes. The Construction of Locks ... To which is added
      a description of J. B. Fenby's Patent Locks, and a note
      upon iron safes, by R. Mallet. London: Weale, 1868.
      172pp, ill; 174pp, ill MB, CtY, NN, MB

9699 Hogg, Garry. Safe Bind, Safe Find; the story of locks, bolts
      and bars. London: Phoenix House, 1961; New York:
      Criterion Books, 1968. 126pp, ill; 158pp, ill

9700 *Hopkins, Albert Allis, 1869-1939. The Lure of the Lock. A
      Short Treatise on Locks to Elucidate the John M. Mossman
      Collection of Locks in the Museum of the General Society
      of Mechanics and Tradesmen in the City of New York, in-
      cluding some of the "Mossman Papers." New York: the
      Society, 1928. 246pp, 500 ill (Mostly 1850-1912) ViU,
      MiU, DLC

9701 Monk, Eric. Keys: Their History and Collection. Boston:
      Newbury, 1975. 64pp, ill, bib

9702 Pitt-Rivers, Augustus Henry Lane-Fox. On the Development
      of Primitive Locks and Keys. London: Chatto & Windus,
      1883. 31pp, pls (The Pitt-Rivers collection)

9703 Stephen, John. The Story of Locks and Keys. London:
      Oak Tree Pr; New York: Sterling, 1962. 48pp, ill
      (Juvenile literature)

9704 Tomlinson, Charles, ed. Rudimentary Treatise on the Con-
      struction of Locks. London: Weale, 1853. See: Hobbs,
      A. C., no. 9698.

9705 Towne, Henry R. Locks and Builders' Hardware, a handbook
      for architects. New York: 1904. NN

9706 Yale, Linus, Jr., 1821-1868, locksmith. A Dissertation on
      Locks and Lock-picking, showing the advantages attending
      the use of the magic infallible bank lock.... Philadelphia:
      1856. (By co-founder of Yale & Towne Mfg. Co.) BM

9707 Zara, Louis. Locks and Keys. New York: Walker, 1969.
      82pp, ill, 2 pls, bib

CANS AND TIN CONTAINERS

9708 Bitting, A. W. Appertizing, or the art of canning: its history
      and development. San Francisco: 1937.

9709 Carbonated Beverages in the United States: historical review.
      Greenwich, Conn: Marketing Research-Packaging, Ameri-
      can Can Co, 1972. 50pp, ill (Chiefly color)

9710 Clemens, Kaye. Tobacco and Food Tins. Paducah, Ky:
      Collector Books, 1974. ill

9711 Davis, Marvin, and Helen Davis. Collector's Price Guide to
      Bottles, Tobacco Tins, and relics. New York: Galahad
      Books, 1975. 208pp, ill, color pls

9712 _____, and _____. Tobacco Tins; pictures and prices
      of over 150 tobacco tins. Medford, Ore: Grandee
      Printing Center, 1970. 61pp, ill

9713 May, Earl Chapin. The Canning Clan; a pageant of pioneering
      Americans. New York: Macmillan, 1937. 487pp, ill,
      bib NN, DLC

9714 Pettit, Ernest L. The Book of Collectible Tin Containers
      with Price Guide. 3 vol. Manchester, Vt: Forward's
      Color Productions, 1967-1970. ill, color pls

9715 A Pictorial History of the Metal Can from Its Earliest Begin-
      nings to the Present Day. Washington, D.C.: Can Manu-
      facturers Institute, 196-? 24pp, ill

9716 Polansky, Tom. Advertising Tin Containers (that aren't in
      the other books). Vol. II. Loma Linda, Cal: 1972.
      50pp, ill (Late 1800s-1930)

SECTION XXVIII

IN THE HOME

HOUSEHOLD TOOLS AND APPLIANCES

9717　Adamson, Gareth. Machines at Home. London: Lutter-
　　　worth, 1969. 48pp, ill

9718　Art in Everyday Use in Early New England. Exhibition.
　　　July-September 1939. George Walter Vincent Smith Art
　　　Gallery. Springfield, Mass: 1939.

9719　Bayne-Powell, Rosamond. Housekeeping in the 18th Century.
　　　London: Murray, 1956. 208pp, ill

9720　Beecher, Catherine Esther, 1800-1878, and Harriet Beecher
　　　Stowe, 1811-1895. The American Woman's Home: or,
　　　principles of domestic science; being a guide to the forma-
　　　tion and maintenance of economical, healthful, beautiful,
　　　and Christian homes. New York: Ford; Boston: H. A.
　　　Brown, 1869. 500pp, ill

9721　Beeton, Isabella Mary. The Book of Household Management;
　　　comprising information for the mistress, housekeeper,
　　　cook, kitchen-maid, butler, footman, coachman, valet....
　　　London: S. O. Beeton, 1861; rev. ed. London: Ward
　　　Lock, 1880; facsim. reprint of 1861 ed. New York: Far-
　　　rar, Straus & Giroux, 1969. 1112pp, ill (part color);
　　　1296pp, pls; 1112pp, ill

9722　Bertram, (C.) Anthony G. The House: a machine for living
　　　in; a summary of the art and science of homemaking con-
　　　sidered functionally. London: A. & C. Black, 1935; 2nd
　　　ed. as The House; a summary of the art and science of
　　　domestic architecture, 1945. 115pp, ill, bib; 114pp, ill,
　　　bib

9723　Bowlin, Opal M. Antique Sad Irons: a description and
　　　history of irons. Yucca Valley, Cal: priv. printed,
　　　1965. 39pp, many ill

9724   Brooke, Sheena. Hearth and Home: a short history of do-
           mestic equipment. London: Mills & Boon, 1973. 168pp,
           ill, 8 pls, bib (To 1973)

9725   Buehr, Walter. Home Sweet Home in the 19th Century. New
           York: Crowell, 1965. 159pp, ill, bib

9726   Cassell's Household Guide: being a complete encyclopedia of
           domestic and social economy, and forming a guide to every
           department of practical life. 4 vol. London; Paris; New
           York: Cassell, Petter, & Galpin, 187-? text, pls (part
           color) DeWint

9727   Earle, Alice Morse. Customs and Fashions in Old New Eng-
           land. London: D. Nutt; New York: Scribner's, 1893;
           New York: 1894; 1899; 1902; 1904; 1909; 1911;... 387pp
           ViU, CtY

9728   _____. Home Life in Colonial Days ... illustrated by
           photographs ... of real things, works and happenings of
           olden times. New York; London: Macmillan, 1899; New
           York: 1900; 1902; ...; 1913; 1926; 1933; 1935; 1946; re-
           print with new preface. Stockbridge, Mass: Berkshire
           Traveller Pr, 1975. 470pp, 150 ill, pls

9729   Electrical Dealer. Monthly. Chicago: Haywood Publishing,
           1928- . ill (Electric home equipment and appliances)

9730   Glissman, A. H. Evolution of the Sad Iron. Carlsbad, Cal:
           Author, 1969; Oceanside, Cal: MB Printing, 1970. 282pp,
           378 ill

9731   Gregory, Edward William, 1871- . The Art and Craft of
           Home-Making, with an appendix of 200 household recipes.
           London: T. Murby, 1913; 2nd ed. rev. & enl. 1925; 1927.
           190pp, ill, 16 pls; 224pp, ill, pls (some color) MB, NN

9732   Hankenson, Dick. Trivets. Maple Plain, Minn: Author,
           1963. ill

9733   _____. Trivets, Book 1. Des Moines: Wallace-Home-
           stead, 1972. 107pp, ill

9734   _____. Trivets, Old and New Reproductions. Book 2.
           Des Moines: Wallace-Homestead, 1972. 144pp, ill

9735   Hardware and Housewares. Toronto: Wrigley, 1909-1952.

9736   Harrington, Ida (Schwedler). Modern Appliances in the Home.
           Albany, NY: Agriculture Department, New York State,
           1913. 9pp (pp. 1856-66) NN

9737   Harrison, Herbert Spenser, 1872- . A Handbook to the Cases

Illustrating Stages in the Evolution of the Domestic Arts.
Horniman Museum and Library. 2 parts in 1 vol. Lon-
don: London County Council, 1911?; 2nd ed. 1924; 2 vol.
London: 1924-25. 39pp, 2 pls, 54pp, 2 pls; 44pp, pls;
77pp, pls (Chiefly primitive. Part 1. Agriculture, prepa-
ration of food, firemaking (including notes on the Andaman
Collection); 2. Basketry, pottery, spinning, weaving, etc.)
DLC, CU

9738   Hasluck, Paul Nooncree, ed. Domestic Jobbing: the repair
       of household articles. London; New York: Cassell, 1907;
       Philadelphia: McKay, 1907. 160pp, many ill NN

       Holloway, Laura C. See: Langford, L. C. H., no. 9746.

9739   Home Furnishings Daily. Chicago: National Housewares
       Manufacturing Association, 1934-date.

9740   Hoover, Frank Garfield. Fabulous Dustpan: the story of the
       Hoover Company. New York; Cleveland: World, 1955.
       250pp, ill (Vacuum cleaners)

9741   The Household Companion; comprising a complete cook book--
       practical household recipes, aids and hints for household
       decorations; the care of domestic plants and animals....
       Ed. by Alice A. Johnson, Janet McKensie Hill, Henry
       Hartshorne, etc. 6 parts in 1 vol. Philadelphia: The
       Uplift Publishing Co, 1909; Toronto: John C. Winston,
       1913. ill, color pls (First published as The Standard
       Book of Recipes and Housewife's Guide, 1901)

9742   Jekyll, Gertrude. Old English Household Life. Some account
       of cottage objects and country folk. London: Batsford;
       New York: Putnam, 1925; 1933; 2nd ed. rev. with addi-
       tions of suggestions by Herbert Batsford on village crafts-
       manship, and observation and drawings by Sydney R. Jones.
       London: Batsford; New York: Scribner's, 1939; London:
       1945. 222pp, many ill; 120pp, ill, pls (1 color) ViU,
       NN, PPL

9743   Jewry, Mary, ed. Warne's Model Cookery and Housekeeping
       Book, containing complete instructions in household manage-
       ment. London: F. Warne; New York: Scribner, Welford,
       & Armstrong, 1868; new ed. London: 1871?; 1899;...
       156pp, ill, color pls MB, NN, DeWint

9744   Johnson, Helen Louise. The Enterprising Housekeeper.
       Philadelphia: Enterprise Manufacturing Co, 1898. ill

9745   The Ladies' Home Journal. Monthly. Philadelphia: Curtis
       Publishing, 1883-date. ill

9746   Langford, Laura Carter Holloway, 1848- . The Hearthstone,

or life at Home, a household manual. Containing hints
and helps for home making; home furnishing; decorations;
amusements ... together with a complete cookery book.
Philadelphia: Bradley, 1883. 582pp, ill, pls DLC, ViU

9747 *Lifshey, Earl. The Housewares Story; a history of the
      American housewares industry. Chicago: National House-
      wares Manufacturers Association, 1973. 384pp, ill, bib

9748 Our English Home; its early history and progress. With
      notes on the introduction of domestic inventions. Oxford;
      London: 1860. BM

9749 Pearsall, Ronald. Collecting Mechanical Antiques. Newton
      Abbot: David & Charles; New York: Arco, 1973. 197pp,
      ill, bib (1830-1880. Household appliances, machinery,
      inventions)

9750 Peet, Louise Jenison, and Lenore E. Sater Thye. Household
      Equipment. New York: J. Wiley; London: Chapman &
      Hall, 1934; 2nd ed. 1940. 315pp, ill, bib; 391pp, ill, bib

9751 Rihn, Gerald J. A Pictorial History of Antique Irons. Glen-
      shaw, Pa: Gerald J. Rihn, 197-? 400 ill (Includes
      miniature irons and trivets)

9752 *Schaefer, Herwin. The Roots of Modern Design. Functional
      Tradition in the 19th century. London: Studio Vista,
      1970. 211pp, 289 ill, bib

9753 Smith, Robert Paul. Lost and Found; an illustrated compen-
      dium of things no longer in general use: the hatpin, the
      icebox, the carpet beater, and oven; household posses-
      sions they don't make that way any more. New York:
      Charterhouse, 1973. 158pp, ill

9754 Stoudt, John Joseph. Sunbonnets and Shoofly Pies. A Penn-
      sylvania Dutch Cultural history. Cranbury, NJ: A. S.
      Barnes, 1973. 272pp, ill

9755 Thompson, Frances. Mountain Relics. Cranbury, NJ: A.
      S. Barnes, 1976. 400 ill (Implements of farm and
      frontier life)

9756 Tryon, Rolla Milton. Household Manufacturers in the United
      States, 1640-1860. Chicago: U of Chicago Pr, 1917;
      reprint. New York: Johnson Reprint, 1966. 413pp,
      bib

KITCHENS AND COOKING ANTIQUES

9757 Barton, William. Descriptive List of Patent Circular Front
      Cooking Apparatus, manufactured by W. Barton. London:
      Gadsby & Arnold, 1868. 36pp   BM

9758 Booth, Sally Smith. Hung, Strung and Potted; a history of
      eating in Colonial America. New York: C. N. Potter,
      1971. 238pp, ill, bib, gloss (includes utensils)

9759 Cook, Mary Alexander. The Cape Kitchen; a description of
      its position, lay-out, fittings and utensils. Stellenbosch,
      South Africa: Stellenbosch Museum, 1973? 112pp, ill

9760 The Country Kitchen, 1850. Scotia, NY: American Review,
      1965. 31pp, ill with facsimile advertisements

9761 Curtis, Will, and Jane Curtis. Antique Woodstoves. Ash-
      ville, Me: Cobblesmith, 1975. 63pp, ill (Multi-plate
      stoves, cooking ranges, toy stoves, etc.)

9762 Dickson, Paul. The Great American Ice Cream Book. New
      York: Atheneum, 1972. 206pp, ill (Includes utensils
      and tools)

9763 Douglass, Robert G. Collectors Manual to Fruit Jar Wrenches
      and Canning Utensils. Norris City, Ill: Author, 1976.
      49pp, ill

9764 Ellacott, Samuel Ernest. The Story of the Kitchen. London:
      Methuen, 1953; 1955; 1960. 76pp, ill, bib (Juvenile
      literature)

9765 Enchantment of Enameled "Cook Ware." Kermit, Tx: Col-
      lectors Weekly Books, 1974. hundreds of ill

9766 Ewbank, Thomas, 1792-1870. Transactions of the Society of
      Literary and Scientific Chiffoniers: being essays on primi-
      tive art in domestic life. The spoon. By Habbakuk O.
      Westman (pseud.) Issued in 4 parts. New York: Harper,
      1844; as The Spoon: primitive, Egyptian, Roman, Medie-
      val, and Modern. London: Wiley & Putnam, 1845. 288pp,
      100 ill, 8 pls

9767 *Franklin, Linda Campbell. From Hearth to Cookstove: a
      history of American kitchen collectibles from 1700-1930.
      (America in the Kitchen.) Florence, Ala: House of Col-
      lectibles, 1976. 271pp, 1155 ill, bib, guide to restora-
      tions

9768 Garrett, Theodore Francis, ed. The Encyclopedia of Practi-
      cal Cookery: a complete dictionary of all pertaining to
      the art of cookery and table service. 4 vol. New York:
      J. Arnot Penman, n.d.; London: L. U. Gill, 1890?;
      Hyde Park, Mass: G. T. King, 1898; 2 vol. London:
      1898.   ill, pls (Some ill's by George Cruikshank)

9769 Gould, Mary Earle. When We Were Young. South Brunswick,
      NJ: A. S. Barnes, 1969. 297pp, ill (Includes utensils
      and tools)

9770 *_____ . Early American Wooden Ware and Other Kitchen
      Utensils. Springfield, Mass: Pond-Ekberg, 1942; rev.
      ed. 1948; rev. & enl. ed. Rutland, Vt: Tuttle, 1962.
      230pp, ill; ...; 243pp, ill, 131 pls

9771 _____ , and Kathleen Cairns. Wooden Ware (Gould), and
      Chairmaking in Orange County, New York (Cairns). New
      York: State Historical Association, 1945. 9pp, ill NN

9772 Gray, Dorothy. Gone With the Hearth. Millbrae, Cal:
      Celestial Arts/Les Femmes, 1976. 225pp, ill (Utensils,
      foods, cookbooks)

9773 Greaser, Arlene, and Paul H. Greaser. Cookie Cutters and
      Molds; a study of cookie cutters, turk's head molds, butter
      molds, and ice cream molds. Allentown, Pa: Authors,
      1969. 171pp, ill (some color), bib

9774 Harrington, Ida (Schwedler). Choice and Care of Utensils.
      Ithaca, NY: College of Agriculture, Cornell U, 1912;
      Supplement. 1912. 22pp (pp. 18-40); 4pp NN

9775 *Harrison, Molly. The Kitchen in History. Reading, Eng:
      Osprey, 1972; New York: Scribner's, 1973. 142pp, ill,
      32 pls, bib (British, to 1971)

9776 *Herman, Judith, and Marguerite Shalett Herman. The

Cornucopia: being a kitchen entertainment and cook book
...1390-1899. New York; London: Harper, 1973. 297pp,
ill, bib (Recipes, cooking implements and lore)

Horst, Melvin. See: Elmer L. Smith, no. 9809.

9777 *Hough, Walter, 1859-1935. Collection of Heating and Lighting
Utensils in the United States National Museum. (Smithsonian.) Washington, D.C.: GPO, 1928. 113pp, many
ill, 99 pls (Includes cooking utensils) DLC, ViU

9778 Hume, Abraham, 1814-1884. Remarks on Quernes, Ancient
and Modern. Liverpool?, Eng: 1851. SIB-1

9779 *John, William David, and Jacqueline Simcox. English Decorated Trays (1550-1850). Newport, Eng: Ceramic Book
Co, 1964. 213pp, 455 ill (Silver, gilt, Paktong, Pontypool, papier-mache, ceramic, marquetry, Tunbridge,
straw, etc.)

9780 *Kauffman, Henry J. American Copper and Brass. Camden,
NJ: T. Nelson, 1968. 288pp, ill, bib

9781 *_____. Early American Copper, tin, and brass. New
York: McBride, 1950. 112pp, ill, bib

9782 _____, and Q. David Bowers. Early American Andirons
and Other Fireplace Accessories. Nashville, Tenn: T.
Nelson, 1974. 192pp, ill (17th-20th century. All kinds
of utensils for cooking)

9783 *Landis, Henry Kinzer. Early Kitchens of the Pennsylvania
Germans. A paper read 1935. Norristown, Pa: Pennsylvania German Society, 1939. 130pp, ill DLC

9784 *Lantz, Louise K. Old American Kitchen-Ware, 1725-1925.
Camden, NJ: T. Nelson, 1972. 288pp, 250 ill, bib
(Also includes much that's not kitchenware)

9785 _____. Price Guide to Old Kitchenware. Hydes, Md:
Author, 1965; rev. 1970; rev. 1974. 39pp, ill; 40pp, ill

9786 *Lea, Zilla R., ed. The Ornamented Tray 1720-1920. His-
torical Society of Early American Decoration. Rutland,
Vt: Tuttle, 1971. 252pp, 506 ill, 7 color pls, bib
(Based on Esther Stevens Brazer Photographic Collection)

9787 *Lindsay, J. Seymour. Iron and Brass Implements of the
English House. London; Boston: Medici Society, 1927;
new ed. as Iron and Brass Implements of the English and
American House. Bass River, Mass: C. Jacobs, 1964.
88pp, plus 374 drawings (Six sections: The Hearth;

Cooking; Lighting; Tobacco Use; Miscellany; American
Colonial Metalwork)

9788   MacSwiggan, Amelia E.   Fairy Lamps; evening's glow of
          yesteryear.   Introd. by Marjorie Smith.   New York:
          Fountainhead, 1962.   170pp, ill (Includes teapots and
          food warmers heated on night lights)

9789   Manchester, Herbert (H.).   The Evolution of Cooking and
          Heating.   Troy, NY: Fuller & Warren, 1917.   35pp, ill
          NN

9790   Masters, Thomas.   A Short Treatise Concerning Some Patent
          Inventions for the Production of Ice and Artificial Cold,
          lemonade, nectar, and all aerated beverages; also the
          newly improved rotary knife cleaning machine, and im-
          proved culinary utensils; being also a handbook of instruc-
          tion, to guide the uninitiated in the uses of various ma-
          chines and apparatus;...   London: Patent Journal Printing
          Office, 1850.   120pp, ill   DLC, NN, BM

9791   Matthews, Mary Lou.   American Kitchen Collectibles, identi-
          fication and price guide.   Gas City, Ind: L-W Promo-
          tions, 1974.   81pp of ill (chiefly catalog reprints)

9792   Maust, Don, ed.   American Woodenware and Other Primi-
          tives; a collection of essays on woodenware, treen, tin,
          brass, copper, iron, pewter, and pottery; a practical
          reference.   Uniontown, Pa: E. G. Warman, 1974.
          159pp, ill

9793   Miles, Elizabeth B.   The English Silver Pocket Nutmeg
          Grater; a collection of 50 examples from 1693-1816.
          Shaker Heights?, O: 1966.   81pp, ill

9794   Miller, Robert William.   American Primitives.   Des Moines:
          Wallace-Homestead, 1972.   109pp, ill (Museum of Appa-
          lachia, Norris, Tennessee Collection)

9795   *Norwak, Mary.   Kitchen Antiques.   London: Ward Lock;
          New York: Praeger, 1975.   135pp, 120 ill, 8 color pls,
          list of restorations (American and English.   Includes
          household account books and manuscript recipes)

9796   *Objects for Preparing Food.   Ed. by Mimi Shorr (Sheraton);
          introd. by Sandra R. Zimmerman; essay by Yukihisa
          Isobe.   Exhibition organized by the Renwick Gallery,
          Washington, and the Museum of Contemporary Crafts,
          New York.   September 1972-January 1973; February-
          April 1973.   Washington, D.C.: 1972.   u.p., many ill
          (Old and new)

9797   O'Connor, Hyla.   The Early American Cookbook.   New York:

Rutledge Pr, and Prentice-Hall, 1974. 160pp, ill (Includes utensils, dishes and food)

9798   Papin, Denis. A New Digester or Engine for Softening
       Bones Containing the Description of Its Make and Use in
       These Particulars, viz: cookery, voyages at sea, con-
       fectionary, making of drinks, chymistry, and dying.
       London: 1681; facsimile reprint. London: Dawsons of
       Pall Mall, 1966. 54pp, folding pl (The first pressure
       cooker!)

9799   *Phipps, Frances. Colonial Kitchens, Their Furnishings, and
       Their Gardens. New York: Hawthorn, 1972. 346pp, 30
       ill, bib

9800   Pope-Hennessy, John Wyndham. Renaissance Bronzes from
       the Samuel H. Kress Collection; Reliefs, plaquettes, uten-
       sils and mortars. London: Phaidon Pr, for Kress Foun-
       dation, Washington, D.C., 1965. 333pp, 616 ill

9801   Porter, Enid M. The Hearth and the Kitchen. Guidebook.
       Cambridge, Eng: Cambridge & County Folk Museum,
       1971. 19pp, ill

9802   Powell, Elizabeth A. Pennsylvania Butter Tools and Processes.
       Doylestown, Pa: Bucks County Historical Society, 1975.
       28pp, ill, bib (Mercer Museum Collection)

9803   Raycraft, Donald R., and Carol Raycraft. Early American
       Kitchen Antiques. Des Moines: Wallace-Homestead, 1972.
       50pp, ill, 24 color pls

9804   Robinson, William, F. L. S. My Wood Fires and Their
       Story. Showing the beauty and use of the wood fire....
       London: Country Life & Newnes; New York: Scribner's,
       1917. 54pp, ill, pls (Utensils and equipment included)
       NNC-Ave

9805   Rumford, Sir Benjamin Thompson, 1753-1814. Essays, Politi-
       cal, Economical, and Philosophical. 3 vol. London: T.
       Cadell, Jr., and W. Davies, 1796-1802; 1st American ed.
       from 3rd London. Boston: D. West, 1798-1804. ill
       (Vol. I. Includes "Of Chimney Fireplaces." Vol. III. "On
       the Construction of Kitchen Fireplaces and Kitchen Utensils
       ... (and) supplementary observations concerning chimney
       fireplaces."

9806   _____ . The Complete Works of Count Rumford. 4 vol.
       Boston: American Academy of Arts and Sciences, 1870-75.
       ill, 61 pls (Gunnery, heating, fireplaces, kitchen utensils,
       ranges, etc.)

9807   Schnadig, Victor K. American-Victorian Figural Napkin Rings.

Des Moines: Wallace-Homestead, 1971. 153pp, 500 rings ill (1780-1900)

9808   Sharp, James. An Account of the Principle and Effects of the Pensilvanian Stove Grates ... commonly known by the name of American Stoves. London: B. White, 1782?; 10th ed. as An Account ... of the Air Stove-Grates.... London: 1785? 14pp, pls; 18pp, pls BM

9809   Smith, Elmer Lewis, comp., ed., and Melvin Horst, photographer. Early American Butter Prints; a collection of rural folk art, designs illustrated from hand-carved butter molds and prints. Witmer, Pa: Applied Arts, 1968. 42pp, 100 designs in rubbings and photographs

9810 *   , and   . Tinware: Yesterday and Today. Lebanon, Pa: Applied Arts, 1974. 40pp, ill

9811 *   , and   . Early Iron Ware. Lebanon, Pa: Applied Arts, 1971. 32pp, ill

9812   Smith, Harold Clifford. A Catalogue Raisonné of the Principal Articles of Furniture and Other Objects of Artistic and Historical Importance at the Mansion House, London. Including the clocks, barometers, cut crystal-glass, chandeliers, busts, statuary, and Royal Windsor tapestries. Together with descriptions of surviving examples of the ancient fittings and equipment of the Great Kitchen. London: Corporation of London for General Purposes Committee, 1954. 37pp, typescript BM

9813   Smith, Richard Flanders. Pennsylvania Butter Prints. Ephrata, Pa: Science Pr, 1970. 36pp, ill, color pls

9814 *Soyer, Alexis, d. 1858. The Gastronomic Regenerator: a simplified and entirely new system of cookery with nearly 2000 practical receipts suited to the income of all classes. Illustrated with numerous engravings and correct and minute plans how kitchens of every size, from the kitchen of a royal palace to that of a humble cottage, are to be constructed and furnished. London: Simpkin, Marshall, 1846; 8th ed. 1852. 720, 18, 30pp, ill, pls

9815 *   . The Modern Housewife, or ménagère. Comprising nearly 1000 receipts for the economic and judicious preparation of every meal of the day, and those for the nursery and sick room; ... illustrated with engravings, including the modern housewife's unique kitchen, and magic stove. 11 thousandth. London: Simpkin, Marshall, 1849; 20 thousandth. 1851; 32 thousandth. 1856;... 434pp, ill; 450pp, ill, pls; 508pp, ill

9816 *   . The Pantropheon; or, History of food, and its

preparation, from the earliest ages of the world ...
Plates, illustrating the greatest gastronomic marvels of
antiquity. London: Simpkin, Marshall, 1853. 474pp,
42 pls, bib (Contains 3000 references to various authors)
BM, DLC

9817   Thompson, Frances. Mountain Relics. Cranbury, NJ: A.
        S. Barnes, 1976. 400 ill

9818   Trice, James E. Butter Molds; a primitive art form. Des
        Moines: Wallace-Homestead, 1973. 100pp, ill

9819   Weiner, Piroska. Carved Honeycake Moulds. Tr. by Pal
        Morvay. Budapest: Corvina Pr, 1964. 50pp, ill, 48
        pls (Hungarian)

9820   Wright, Lawrence. Home Fires Burning: the history of do-
        mestic heating and cooking. London: Routledge & K.
        Paul, 1964. 219pp, ill, bib

COFFEE AND TEA SERVICES

9821   Bedford, John. Talking about Teapots; and thus about porce-
        lain, pottery, silver, Sheffield plate, etc. London: Par-
        rish, 1964. 160pp, ill, bib

9822   Folger Coffee Company Collection of Antique English Silver
        Coffee Pots. Exhibition. October-November 1959.
        Kansas City, Mo: William Rockhill Nelson Gallery of
        Art, and Mary Atkins Museum of Fine Arts, 1959. (Other
        museums too) v.p., ill

9822a   Fujioka, Ryoichi. Tea Ceremony Utensils. New York:
        Weatherhill, 1973. 128pp, 208 (19 color) ill

9822b   Fukukita, Yasunosuke. Cha-no-yu; tea cult of Japan, an
        aesthetic pastime. Tokyo: Maruzen Co, 1932; New York:
        Japan Society of N.Y., 1935; 1936. 111pp, ill, pls, bib;
        ...; 138pp, ill, pls (part color), bib

9822c   Hayashiya, Tatsusaburo, Masao Nakamura, and Seizo Haya-
        shiya. Japanese Arts and the Tea Ceremony. Tokyo:
        Weatherhill & Heilbonsha (Survey of Japanese Art), 1975.
        196pp, ill

9823   The Lipton Collection: antique English silver designed for the
        serving of tea. Exhibition. Portland, Ore: Portland Art
        Museum, 1954; Dayton, O: Dayton Art Institute, 1958;
        etc. 103pp, ill

9824   Mountford, Arnold Robert. The Sadler Teapot Manufactory

Site, Burslem, Stoke-on-Trent; ... Marquis of Granby
Hotel Site; ... Astbury-type pottery.... Hanley, Stoke-
on-Trent: City Museum and Art Gallery, Archaeological
Society, 1974. 38pp, ill

9825 One Hundred and Eleven Coffee Cups. Preston, Lancs: Harris Museum and Art Gallery, 1953. 19pp, ill, 16 pls

9826 Roth, Rodris. Tea Drinking in 18th Century America: its
etiquette and equipage. Smithsonian Institution. Bulletin
225. Washington, D.C.: GPO, 1961. 31pp (pp. 61-91),
ill

9827 *Sandon, Henry. Coffee Pots and Teapots for the Collector.
Edinburgh: J. Bartholomew, 1973; New York: Arco,
1974. 128pp, ill, 162 pls, bib (ca.1700-1972)

9828 Taggart, Ross E., ed. Antique English Silver Coffee Pots,
Folger Coffee Company Collection. Minneapolis: Institute
of Arts, 1962. 84pp, ill (Queen Ann to early 19th
century)

9829 Teapots in Pottery and Porcelain. V & A. London: HMSO,
19-? 28 pls

9830 *Tilley, Frank. Teapots and Tea. Newport, Monm, Eng:
Ceramic Book Co, 1957. 135pp, 200 ill, 75 (10 color)
pls (Evolution of teapots, including micro-analyses and
fluorescences of English porcelains)

9831 *Twining, R. The Book of the Tea-pot and of some tea-cup
times, with pictures of tea-pots of many periods and
places. London: R. Twining & Co, 1899. 64pp, ill

9832 Wedgwood, G. R. The History of the Tea-Cup: with a descriptive account of the potters' art. London: Wesleyan
Conference Office, 1878. 154pp, ill BM

9833 Yena, Louise. The Handbook of Antique Coffee and Tea Collectibles; price guide. Vol. I. San Antonio, Tx: 1971.
ill, bib

9834-6 [No entries.]

TABLE CUTLERY, RAZORS AND SHEFFIELD TRADE†

9837 Aldridge, Joseph. Illustrated Furnishing Guide and General
List of Furnishing Ironmongery, table cutlery, etc. London: A. Gadsby, 1866. 120pp, ill BM

†See also Knives and Daggers in Section XXVI and works on Sheffield
plate under British Isles Silver and Gold in Section VIII.

9838 *Bailey, Charles Thomas Peach. Knives and Forks. London;
       Boston: Medici Society, 1927. 15pp, ill, color frontis,
       72 pls, bib (15th-18th century) NN, BM, DeWint

9839 Bement, Lewis D. The Cutlery Story: a brief history of the
       romance and manufacture of cutlery from the earliest
       times to modern methods of manufacture. Deerfield,
       Mass: Associated Cutlery Industries of America, 1950;
       reprinted 1972. 35pp, ill NN, BPL

9840 Callis, F. Cutlery. London: 1878. See also: Bevan, G.
       P., British Manufacturing Industries, Vol. 11, no. 43.

9841 Cutlery, a Bibliography. Sheffield, Eng: Libraries, Art
       Galleries & Museums Committee, 1960. 30pp, ill DLC

9842 Defenbacher, D. S. Knife, Fork, Spoon; the story of our
       primary eating implements and the development of their
       form. Exhibition, sponsored by Towle Silversmiths.
       Minneapolis: Walker Art Center, 1951. 63pp, ill, bib
       NN

9843 A Directory of Sheffield, containing the names and residence
       of the merchants, manufacturers, tradesmen, and principal
       inhabitants; an historical sketch and description of the
       town and neighbourhood; the marks struck by the manu-
       facturers, and every other necessary information respecting
       the trade and the place. Sheffield: James Montgomery,
       printer, for John Robinson, 1797. 180pp

9844 *A Directory of Sheffield, including the manufacture of the ad-
       jacent villages, with the several marks of the cutlers,
       scissor and file-smiths, edge tool and sickle-makers.
       Sheffield: Gales & Martin, 1787; Sheffield: J. Robinson,
       1797; reprint of 1787 ed. New York: Da Capo Pr, 1969.
       85pp, ill (Anvils, hammers, pen and pocket knives, saws,
       etc., etc.)

9845 *A Directory of Sheffield, published by Gales and Martin in
       1787. Reprinted in facsimile, with an introduction by
       Sidney Oldall Addy. Sheffield: Pawson & Brailsford,
       1889. 100pp, ill CU

9846 Hayward, John Forrest. English Cutlery: 16th to 18th cen-
       tury. V & A Museum. London: HMSO, 1956; 1957.
       18pp, ill; text, 24 pls

9847 *Himsworth, Joseph Beeston. The Story of Cutlery, from flint
       to stainless steel. London: Benn, 1953. 208pp, ill
       NN, DLC

9848 Kingsbury, Benjamin. A Treatise on Razors; in which the
       weight, shape, and temper of a razor, the means of

keeping it in order, and the manner of using it are particularly considered. London: 1797; 5th ed. 1806; 7th
ed. London: E. Blackader, printer, 1814; 8th ed. London: Kerwood & Fox, printer, 1820; 12th ed. London:
J. S. Hodson, 1842;... 59pp; 47pp; ...; ...; 46pp; etc.
(Includes advertisements, even for toothbrushes) DeWint,
DLC

9849 Leader, Robert Eadon. History of the Company of Cutlers
      in Hallamshire. 2 vol. Sheffield: printed by Pawson &
      Brailsford, 1905-1906. ill DLC

9850 Shroeder, Bill. 1000 Razors. Paducah, Ky: Collector Books,
      197-? 71pp, ill

9851 Singleton, H. Raymond. A Chronology of Cutlery. Sheffield:
      Sheffield City Museum, 1973. 7pp, ill, 5pp of pls

9852 Smith, Joseph. Explanation, or Key, to the various manufac-
      tories of Sheffield with engravings of each article, designed
      for the utility of merchants, wholesale ironmongers, and
      travellers. Sheffield: H. A. Bacon, printer, 1816; re-
      print. South Burlington, Vt: Early American Industries
      Association, 1975. 110 pls (Part I. Tools for carpenters,
      joiners, coopers, curriers, farmers; II. Cutlery trade;
      III. Surgical and dental instruments.)

9853 Taber, Martha Van Hosen. A History of the Cutlery Industry
      in the Connecticut Valley. Northampton, Mass: Smith
      College Studies in History, XLI, 1955. 138pp, bib

9854 Walker, J. General List of Prices of Hardwares, Saddlery,
      Plated and Japanned Wares, Cutlery, etc. n.p. (Eng.):
      1823. SIB-3

9855 Welch, Charles, 1845-1924. History of the Cutlers' Company
      of London and of the Minor Cutlery Crafts. With biographi-
      cal notices of early London cutlers. Vol. I. Early times
      to the year 1500; II. From 1500 to modern times. 2 vol.
      London: priv. printed for the Company, 1916; 1923. pls,
      facsims BM

SPOONS

9856 Betensley, Bertha L. 104 Spoon Patents. Westville, Ind:
      1972. 48pp, ill

9857 Buckley, Francis. 17th Century Spoons. Uppermill, Eng:
      Moore & Edwards, 1928. pls

9858 The Collection of Spoons Made by Mrs. S. P. (Mary Ann

Ogden) Avery, 1867-1890; presented by her to the Metropolitan Museum of Art, 1897. New York: the Museum,
1899. 23pp, 9 pls

9859 Crosby, Everett Uberto. The Spoon Primer; or, An easy and
        pleasant guide for determining the approximate dates of
        the making of old American silver spoons. Adorned with
        cuts, to which is added a chart which records the dates of
        changes in spoon styles.... Nantucket, Mass: Inquirer
        & Mirror Pr, printer, 1941. 26pp, ill   DLC

9860 Currier, Ernest M, 1867-1936. Early American Silversmiths;
        the Newbury Spoonmakers. New York: Currier & Roby,
        1930. 15pp, ill

9861 Defenbacher, D. S. Knife, Fork, Spoon; the story of our
        primary eating implements and the development of their
        form. Minneapolis: Walker Art Center, 1951. 63pp,
        ill, bib (Exhibition sponsored by Towle Silversmiths)
        NN

9862 Gask, Norman. Old Silver Spoons of England, a practical
        guide for collectors. London: H. Jenkins, 1926; facsim.
        reprint. London: Spring Books, 1973. 189pp, ill, 32
        pls (Master spoons, Hanoverian patterns, medicine, rat-
        tail, straining, Bhudda & York, punch ladles, etc., to
        ca.1830) NN. DLC

9863 Greene, Robert Alan. Coin Silver Spoonmakers. Long Lake,
        NY: 1968. 13pp, ill

9864 Hardt, Anton. Adventuring Further in Souvenir Spoons, with
        a first glimpse of the Tiffany souvenir spoons. New York:
        Author, 1965. 107pp, ill (catalogue reprints)

9865 _____, comp. Souvenir Spoons of the Nineties, as pictured
        and described in The Jewelers' Circular and the (George
        B.) James Catalogue in 1891. New York: Author, 1962;
        197-? 269pp, ill; 288pp, ill

9866 _____. A Third Harvest of Souvenir Spoons. New York:
        Author, 1969; 197-? 141pp, ill; 152pp, 167 ill (Ameri-
        can)

9867 [No entry.]

9868 Homer, Ronald F. Five Centuries of Base Metal Spoons.
        New York: Price Glover, 1975. 59pp, ill, bib, marks
        (Pewter and latten up to 18th century)

9869 *How, George Evelyn Paget, and Jane Penrice How. English
        and Scottish Silver Spoons. Medieval to late Stuart and

pre-Elizabethan hall-marks on English plate. 3 vol. London: Authors, 1952-1957; 1964. text, ill, 306 pls of hundreds of spoons

9870   Owen, Trefor Meredith, ed. The Story of the Lovespoon. Swansea: Celtic Educational, 1973. 98pp, ill (Welsh wooden spoons)

9871   *Price, Frederick Hilton. Old Base Metal Spoons. With illustrations and marks. London: Batsford, 1908. 99pp, 39 ill, 16 pls, marks

9872   *Rainwater, Dorothy T., and Donna H. Felger. American Spoons, Souvenir and Historical. Camden, NJ: T. Nelson, 1969; Hanover, Pa: Everybodys Pr, 1971. 416pp, 600 ill, bib

9873   *Rupert, Charles Gideon. Apostle Spoons. Their evolution from earlier types, and the emblems used by the silversmiths for the Apostles. London: Oxford U. Pr, 1929. 36pp, ill, 23 pls

9874   Snodin, Michael. English Silver Spoons. London: Letts, 1974. 79pp, color ill, bib

9875   Stutzenberger, Albert. The American Story in Spoons; with an historical sketch of the spoon through the ages. Louisville, Ky: 1953; reprint as American Historical Spoons; the American story in spoons. Rutland, Vt: Tuttle, 1971. 535pp, ill, bib

HEATING, LIGHTING, REFRIGERATION
AND ELECTRICITY; SOME THINGS
THAT SMOKE AND BURN

FIREMAKING AND MATCHES

9876 *Christy, Miller, comp. Fire-Making Appliances. Catalogues
for the exhibition in the private museum of Bryant and
May, London. London: Simpkin, Marshall, Hamilton,
Kent, for the Museum, 1926; Supplement. London: 1928.
192pp, 410 ill; 74pp, pls (Wood-friction, flint & pyrites,
flint & steel, tinders, optical & chemical methods, friction
matches, etc.) DeWint, NN, MdBP

9877 Cort, R. Instantaneous Light and Fire Machines. A description of the principle, application, and management of the
newly-invented light and fire machines. Together with
some thoughts upon the establishment of a society for the
further encouragement of the arts. London: J. M. Richardson, by Ballintine & Law, printers, 1809. 42pp NN

9878 Cruse, Alfred J. Match-box Labels of the World; with a history of fire-making appliances from primitive man to the
modern match, together with a history of the world's labels. London: R. Ross, 1946.

9879 Dixon, William Hepworth. The Match Industry. Its origin
and development. London: Pitman, 1925. 150pp BM

9880 Heavisides, Michael. The True History of the Invention of
the Lucifer Match, by John Walker, of Stockton-on-Tees,
in 1827; with an account of the ancient modes of procuring
light or fire. Stockton-on-Tees: Heavisides & Sons, 1909.
32pp, ill (John Walker, 1781-1859) DLC, BM

9881 Hough, Walter. Fire as an Agent in Human Culture. Washington, D.C.: United States National Museum, 1926.
270pp, many ill, 41 pls

9882 _____ . Fire-making Apparatus in the United States National

Museum. In its Proceedings, vol. 73. Washington, D.C.:
1928. 72pp, ill, 11 pls NN

9883 Manchester, Herbert (H.). The Diamond Match Co.; a century of service, of progress, and of growth, 1835-1935.
New York; Chicago: 1935. 108pp, ill

9884 _____. Fifty Years of Match Making. New York: Diamond
Match Co, 1928. 20pp, ill

9885 _____. The Romance of Fire Making. From Prehistoric
Ages to the Eddy Match. Montreal: Eddy Match Co, 1931.
25pp, ill NN

9886 _____. The Romance of the Match. New York; Chicago:
Diamond Match Co, 1926. 45pp, ill MB, DLC

9887 *Mercer, Henry Chapman. Light and Fire Making, with 45 illustrations explaining the rubbing of fire from wood, the
striking of flint and steel, and some of the lamps, candles,
torches and lanterns of the American pioneer. Contributions to American History by Bucks County Historical Society. Philadelphia: MacCalla & Co, printers, 1898.
29pp NN, DLC

9888 O'Dea, William T. Making Fire. Science Museum. London:
HMSO, 1964. 48pp, ill

9889 Thomas, Doreen. Strike a Light: John Walker, 1781-1859.
Middlesborough, Yorkshire: Teesside Museums, 1971.
62pp, ill, bib (History of matches)

9890 Tidy, Charles Meymott, 1843-1892. ... The Story of a Tinder-
box. A course of lectures delivered ... 1888/89. London:
SPCK, 1897. 105pp, ill (Juvenile literature) NN

9891 Watson, Warren Neal. Early Fire-making Methods and Devices. From the Stone Age until the introduction of the
match. Washington, D.C.: Smithsonian, 1939. 75pp, ill,
pls NN

FIREPLACES AND HEARTHS

9892 (Boyd, Alexander and Son.) The English Fireplace: its advantages, its objections and its rivals. Considered with a
view to ... economy. London: J. Bumpus, 1871. 40pp,
ill NN

9893 Boyd, R. W. An Illustrated History of the English Fireplace
from the Period at which Chimneys were First Used in
England, down to the present time. London: Batsford,
19-? 1pp, 13 pls DeWint

9894   Buchanan, Robertson, 1770-1816. Practical and Descriptive
       Essays on the Economy of Fuel, and management of heat,
       with an appendix containing observations on chimney fire-
       places, particularly those used in Ireland, on stoves, on
       gas-lights, on lime-kilns, on furnases and chimneys used
       for rapid distillation in distilleries of Scotland.... Glas-
       gow: Author, by Longman, Hurst, Rees & Orme; London:
       J. Anderson, 1810; Glasgow: 1815. 253pp; 364pp, 5 pls

9895   Burgess, Joseph Tom, 1826-1886. English Hearths and Irish
       Homes: life scenes from an editor's note book.... New
       ed. of "Leaves from an Editor's Note-Book." London:
       1868. ill (Includes firebacks) DLC

9896   Catalogue of Register Grates, interiors, dog grates, hob
       grates, mantel grates, fire dogs, fire backs, casings,
       fenders and fire-irons. Carron Company of London, late
       Longden and Co. Stirlingshire: Carron Works, 1911.
       113 pls NNC-Ave

9897   *Edwards, Frederick. Our Domestic Fireplaces. On the eco-
       nomical use of fuel, and the prevention of smoke in domes-
       tic fireplaces.... London: Hardwicke, 1864; 1865; new
       rev. & enl. ed. London: Longmans, Green, 1870; 1876.
       82pp, pls; 47pp, pls; 110pp, 16 pls; 168pp, 24 pls DLC,
       MH, BM

9898   Fireplaces, Chimney Pieces, Fireplace Accessories. Photo-
       graphs from the collections in the V & A Museum. n.p.:
       n.d. (mounted and bound by the New York Public Library,
       1938). 85 photographs NN

9899   Franklin, Benjamin. Observations on Smoky Chimneys, their
       causes and cure; with consideration on fuel and stoves.
       London: I. & J. Taylor, 1793; 2nd ed. Philadelphia:
       printed; London: re-printed for J. DeBrett, 1787. 80pp,
       2 folding pls; 56pp, ill, pl

9900   Franklin, Linda Campbell. From Hearth to Cookstove; Col-
       lectibles of the American Kitchen 1700-1930. Florence,
       Ala: House of Collectibles, 1976. 271pp, 1155 ill, bib

9901   Gillespie, G. Curtis, comp. Rumford Fireplaces and How
       They are Made, containing Benjamin, Count of Rumford's
       essay on "Proper Fireplace Construction." New York:
       W. T. Comstock, 1906. 198pp, ill, pl (Many pictures
       of fireplace equipment) NNC-Ave

9902   Gould, Mary Earle. The Early American House; household
       life in America, 1620-1850. New York: McBride, 1949;
       rev. ed. as The Early American House; Household life in
       America with special chapters on the construction and evo-
       lution of old American homes, fireplaces and iron utensils,

and hearthside and barnyard activities. Rutland, Vt:
Tuttle, 1965. 143pp, ill; 152pp, ill, bib

9903 Kauffman, Henry J. The American Fireplace: Chimneys,
Mantlepieces, Fireplaces and Accessories. Introd. by
Joe Kindig III. Nashville, Tenn: T. Nelson, 1972.
352pp, ill, bib

9904 *_____, and Q. David Bowers. Early American Andirons
and Other Fireplace Accessories. Nashville: T. Nelson,
1974. 192pp, ill (17th-20th century. Skillets, waffle
irons, bellows, etc.)

9905a Kelly, Alison. The Book of English Fireplaces. Feltham:
Country Life Books, 1968. 96pp, 111 ill (Roman times
to 20th century)

9905b *Mercer, Henry C. The Bible in Iron. Pictured Stoves and
Stoveplates of the Pennsylvania Germans. Doylestown,
Pa: Bucks County Historical Society, 1914; 2nd ed. rev.
corr. & enl. by Horace M. Mann. 1941; 3rd ed. ed. &
enl. by Joseph E. Sandford. 1961. 174pp, 240 pl; 216pp,
316 pl; 256pp, 409 pl

9906 Orton, Vrost. Observations on the Forgotten Art of Building
a Good Fireplace; the story of Sir Benjamin Thompson,
Count Rumford, ... and his principles of fireplace design.
Dublin, NH: "Yankee" Magazine, 1969. 60pp, ill DeWint

9907 *Peirce, Josephine Halverson. Fire on the Hearth; the Evolution and romance of the heating stove. With 145 illustrations from photographs and drawings showing an amazing
variety of heating devices; also entertaining anecdotes,
excerpts from old diaries and other papers, alluring advertisements and interesting bits of information pertaining
to their manufacture and use. Introd. by Robert W. G.
Vall. Springfield, Mass: Pond-Ekberg, 1931; 1952.
254pp, 145 ill, bib DeWint

9908 *Putnam, John Pickering, 1847-1917. The Open Fire-place in All
Ages. For "The American Architect & Building News." Boston: J. R. Osgood, 1881; new ed. rev. & enl. 20 new designs
of chimney-pieces and interior decorations. Boston: Tichnor,
1882; new ed. rev. & enl. 1886. 212pp, 269 ill, 35 pls; 204pp,
300 ill; 207pp, 245 ill, 55 pls NNC-Ave, NN

9909 Robinson, William, F. L. S. My Wood Fires and Their Story,
showing the beauty and use of the wood fire.... London:
Country Life, Newnes; New York: Scribner's, 1917. 54pp,
ill, pls (Fireplaces, utensils) NNC-Ave

9910 Rumford, Sir Benjamin Thompson. Essays, political, economical, and philosophical. 3 vol. London: T. Cadell, Jr.,

and W. Davies, 1796-1802; 1st American ed. from 3rd London. Boston: D. West, 1798-1804. ill (Vol. I. Includes
"Of Chimney Fireplaces." Vol. III. "On the Construction
of Kitchen Fireplaces and Kitchen Utensils..." supplementary observations concerning chimney fireplaces)

9911   . ... Of Chimney Fire-Places, with proposals for
improving them, to save fuel; to render dwelling-houses
more comfortable and salubrious, and effectually to pre-
vent chimnies from smoking. 3rd ed. London: printed
for T. Cadell Jr., and W. Davies, 1797. ill NNC-Ave

9912 *Shuffrey, L. A. The English Fireplace; a history of the development of the chimney, chimney-piece and firegrate,
with their accessories, from the earliest times to the beginning of the 19th century. London; New York: Batsford,
1912. 234pp, 200 ill, 130 pls DLC, NNC-Ave

9913 Smith & Anthony Stove Co., Boston. Some Artistic Fire
Places and Their Surroundings; containing illustrations of
special designs and inventions for the artistic and practical treatment of the fireplace. Boston: the Manufacturers,
1885; 1887; 1890. 39pp, ill; 47pp, ill; 52pp, ill DLC

9914 United States. Library of Congress. Division of Bibliography.
... Brief List of References on Fireplaces. Select List
of References no. 585. Washington, D.C.: 1921. 6 leaves
typescript. NN

CHIMNEY PIECES AND MANTELS

9915 Adam, Robert, and James Adam. A Book of Mantels: 37
drawings in color reproduced from recently discovered
originals by Robert and James Adam. New York: Architectural Book Co, 1915. 2pp, ill, 19 color pls BM

9916 Barbet, J., fl. ca.1635. A Booke of Archetecture Containing
Seeling Pieces, chimny peeces and several sorts usefull
for carpenters, joyners, carvers, painters. London: Are
to be sould by Robert Pricke in Whitecross-Street, 1670.
1pp, 28 pls DeWint

9917 Buck, C. C. Album of Mantels in Wood, stone, slate and
brick. New York: J. O'Kane, 1883. 2pp, 60 pls DeWint

9918 Clarkson, Douglas A. Fonts, Mural Tablets, Chimney Pieces,
and Balustrades. London: Atchley, 1860. ill

9919 Dawson, Naismith. Some Old London Mantels From the 16th
to the 18th Centuries. New York: Dawson, n.d. (ca.1918).
48 pls (Includes fireplace equipment) NNC-Ave

9920 Designs for Chimney-Pieces, with mouldings and bases at large,
      on 24 plates.   London: for I. & J. Taylor, 179-?   24 pls
      NNC-Ave

9921 Fireplaces, Chimney Pieces, Fireplace Accessories.   Photo-
      graphs from the collections in the V & A Museum.   n.p.;
      n.d. (mounted and bound by the New York Public Library,
      1938).   85 photographs   NN

9922 Guillaume, L.   Guillaume's Interior Architecture, containing
      12 folio plates, showing 12 designs and eight sections for
      doors, stairs, window-finish, mantels, wainscotting, etc....
      New York: A. J. Bicknell, 1875.   1pp, 12 pls   DLC, De-
      Wint

9923 Jones, Inigo, 1573-1652.   Designs for Chimney-Glasses and
      Chimney-Pieces, of the time of Charles I.   Republished.
      London: 1858-59.   chiefly ill   IU, BM

9924 Kauffman, Henry J.   The American Fireplace: chimneys,
      mantlepieces, fireplaces and accessories.   Introd. by Joe
      Kindig III.   Nashville, Tenn: T. Nelson, 1972.   352pp,
      ill, bib

9925 Lock, Matthew.   A New Book of Ornaments for Looking Glass
      Frames, chimney pieces, etc. in the Chinese taste.   Lon-
      don: 1768; London: For R. Sayer, 18-?   ill   MdBP

9926 Milton, Thomas, 1743?-1827.   The Chimney-piece-maker's
      Daily Assistant, or, A treasury of new designs for chim-
      ney-pieces ... in the antique, modern, ornamental and
      gothic taste, from the original drawings by Thomas Milton,
      John Crunden, and Placido Columbani....   London: H.
      Webley, 1766.   54 pls   DLC, NNC-Ave

9927 Pineau, N., and L. Le Roux.   Designs for Chimney-pieces,
      wainscot-panels, buffets, pier glasses, etc.   n.p., n.d.
      42 pls   SKM

9928 *Putnam, John Pickering.   The Open Fireplace in All Ages.
      Boston: J. R. Osgood, 1881; new rev. & enl. ed. with
      20 new plates of designs of chimney-pieces and interior
      decoration.   Boston: Ticknor, 1882; 1886.   207pp, 245
      cuts, 55 pls   NNC-Ave

9929 Rothery, Guy Cadogan.   Chimneypieces and Ingle Nooks, Their
      Design and Ornamentation.   New York: F. A. Stokes, 1911.
      239pp, ill, 31 pls, bib   (From ancient Greece & Rome to
      current practice)   MiGr

9930 _____.   English Chimney-Pieces, Their Design and Develop-
      ment from the Earliest Times to the 19th Century.   London:

J. Tiranti; New York: Architectural Book Publishing Co,
1927. 16pp, ill, pls

9931 Sample Book of Designs of Looking Glass Frames, cornices,
carved chimney-pieces, and other art specimens. Birmingham, Eng: Lee Eginton, 1780. MiGr

9932 *Shuffrey, L. A. The English Fireplace; a history of the development of the chimney, chimney-piece and firegrate,
with their accessories, from the earliest times to the beginning of the 19th century. London; New York: Batsford,
1912. 234pp, 200 ill, 130 pls NNC-Ave, DLC

9933 Swan, Abraham. The British Architect: or, The builder's
treasury of staircases, arches, doors, windows, ... new
and curious chimney-pieces, corbels, shields, and other
beautiful decorations. London: printed for Author, 1745;
1750; 1758; Philadelphia: R. Bell, 1775; Boston: 1794.
20pp, 60 pls; ...; ...; 17pp, 60 pls

9934 _____. Upwards of 150 New Designs, for chimney pieces;
from the plain and simple, to the most superb and magnificent.... London: printed for Robert Sayer, 1768. ill
NNC-Ave

9935 Vardy, John. Some Designs of Mr. Inigo Jones and Mr. William Kent. London: 1744. 50 engraved plates (Chimney-
pieces, garden seats and temples, chandeliers, tureens,
silver standishes and cups, candlesticks, chairs, etc.)

9936 Waite, Diana S., ed. & comp. Architectural Elements: the
technological revolution; galvanized iron roof plates and
corrugated sheets; cast iron facades, columns, door and
window caps, sills and lintels; galvanized cornices; mar-
bleized slate mantels; plumbing and heating supplies and
fixtures; staircases, balconies, newels and balustrades in
wood and iron; cut and etched glass transoms and side-
lights. Princeton, NJ: Pyne Pr, 1972. v.p., ill, bib
(Facsimile reprints of plates from manufacturer catalogues:
Marshall, Lefferts & Brother, 1854; Buffalo Eagle Iron
Works, 1859; Morris, Tasker & Company, 1860; Philadelphia Architectural Iron Co., 1872; Keystone Mantel and
Slate Works, 1872; George O. Stevens, 1879.)

HEATING, VENTILATION AND PLUMBING

9937 Buchanan, Robertson, 1770-1816. Practical and Descriptive
Essays on the Economy of Fuel, and Management of Heat,
with an appendix containing observations on chimney fireplaces, particularly those used in Ireland, on stoves, on
gas-lights, on lime-kilns, on furnases and chimneys used

for rapid distillation in distilleries of Scotland.... Glasgow: Author, by Longman, Hurst, Rees & Orme; London: J. Anderson, 1810; Glasgow: 1815. 253pp, 364pp, 5 pls (Includes steam pipes, gauge-cocks, safety valves; 10pp devoted to gas illumination and its apparatus) MB, DLC, NN

9938 Curtis, Will, and Jane Curtis. Antique Woodstoves. Ashville, Maine: Cobblesmith, 1975. 63pp, ill (Includes baseburners, multi-plate stoves, cooking ranges, and toy stoves)

9939 Edwards, Frederick, Jr. On the Ventilation of Dwelling-Houses. London: Hardwicke, 1858; London: Longmans, Green, 1867; 1868; 2nd ed. rev. London: Longmans, 1880; 1881. 168pp, ill, pls; 178pp, 17 pls DLC, NN, BM

9940 *Hough, Walter, 1859-1935. ... Collection of Heating and Lighting Utensils in the United States National Museum. Washington, D.C.: GPO, 1928. 113pp, many ill, 99 pls (Stoves, lamps, candlesticks, roasters, etc.) DLC, ViU

9941 MacLaren, George E. G. Romance of the Heating Stove. A History of Everyday Things, No. 3. Halifax: Nova Scotia Museum, 1972. u.p., ill

9942 Manchester, Herbert (H.). The Evolution of Cooking and Heating. Troy, NY: Fuller & Warren, 1917. 35pp, ill NN

9943 *Peirce, Josephine Halverson. Fire on the Hearth; the evolution and romance of the heating-stove. With 145 illustrations from photographs and drawings showing an amazing variety of heating devices; also entertaining anecdotes, excerpts from old diaries and other papers, alluring advertisements and interesting bits of information pertaining to their manufacture and uses. Introd. by Robert W. G. Vall. Springfield, Mass: Pond-Ekberg, 1931; 1952. 254pp, ill, bib DeWint

9944 Plumbers' Work: Past and Present. A brief commentary and a descriptive account of the Museum and workshops established by the Worshipful Company of Plumbers at King's College, London. London: C. Cull & Co, 1896. 35pp, pls BM

9945 Tomlinson, Charles. Rudimentary Treatise on Warming and Ventilation. London: Weale, 1850-58.

9946 Waite, Diana S., ed. & comp. Architectural Elements: the technological revolution; galvanized iron roof plates and corrugated sheets; cast iron facades, columns, door and

window caps, sills and lintels; galvanized cornices; mar-
bleized slate mantels; plumbing and heating supplies and
fixtures; staircases, balconies, e.. etc. Princeton, NJ:
Pyne Pr, 1972. v.p., ill, bib (Facsimile reprints from
trade catalogues. Marshall, Lefferts and Brother, 1854;
Buffalo Eagle Iron Works, 1859; Morris, Tasker & Co,
1860; Philadelphia Architectural Iron Company, 1872; Keystone Mantel and Slate Works, 1872; George O. Stevens,
1879)

9947 Wright, Lawrence. Home Fires Burning: the history of domestic heating and cooking. London: Routledge & K. Paul,
1964. 219pp, ill, bib DLC

LIGHTING

9948 Accum, Friedrich Christian, 1769-1838. A Practical Treatise
on Gas-Light; Exhibiting a summary description of the apparatus and machinery best calculated for illuminating
streets, houses and manufactories, with carburetted hydro-
gen, or coal-gas; with remarks on the utility, safety, and
general nature of this new branch of civil economy. London: G. Hayden for R. Ackermann, 1815; 2nd ed. London:
Longman, 1815; 3rd ed. London: Davies, Michael and
Hudson for R. Ackermann, 1816; 4th ed. 1818. 186pp,
ill, 7 color plates; 194pp, ill, plates;... (Gaswork apparatus, globes, domestic gas fittings) DeWint, DLC

9949 Anthony, T. Robert. 19th Century Fairy Lamps. Manchester,
Vt: 38pp, 18pp of color pls

9950 Barrows, Benjamin H. Evolution of Artificial Light, from a
pine knot to a Pintsch Light. Compliments Passenger Department, Union Pacific System, Omaha. Chicago: Knight,
Leonard, printers, 1893. 107pp, ill

9951 Battersby, D. I. Miniature Lamp Price Guide. Arcadia, Cal:
Author, 1975. (Cued to F. R. & R. E. Smith's Miniature
Lamps)

9952 *Beneschi, Ladislaus Edler von, 1845- . The Lighting Fix-
ture From the Middle Ages to the Middle of the 19th Century; illustrated by 989 specimens (divided into 21 groups).
Tr. from Das Beleuchtungswesen, 1905. Philadelphia:
192-?; as A Revue of the Development of the Lighting Fix-
ture From the Middle Ages to the Middle of the 19th Century.... Philadelphia: Perleberg, 1933; as Old Lamps of
Central Europe and Other Lighting Devices. Tr. & ed. by
Leroy Livingston Thwing. Rutland, Vt: Tuttle for The
Rushlight Club, 1962, 1963. 32pp, ill, 60 pls, bib (Grease
and oil lamps, candleholders, wood-burning devices, lamps,
15th-19th century) NN, DLC, CtY

9953   Brewster, Sir David.   The History of the Invention of the
       Dioptric Lights and Their Introduction into Great Britain.
       London: J. Murray, 1865; 1876.   48pp; 64pp   (Lighthouse
       lighting)   NN

9954   Burkhalter, Agnes S.   Historical Railroad Lanterns.   Win-
       chester, Tenn: 1971.   80 items ill

9955   Catalogue of Apparatus Suitable for Lectures and Class In-
       struction in Group III.   Subject 1.   Acoustics, light, heat.
       2. Magnetism and electricity.   8th ed.   South Kensington
       Museum.   London: Eyre & Spottiswoode for HMSO, 1865.
       22pp

9956   Chandler, Dean.   Outline of History of Lighting by Gas.
       Fore. by Dr. Charles Carpenter.   London: South Metro-
       politan Gas Co., 1936.   279pp, ill, color pls   CU

9957   Cooke, Lawrence S., ed.   Lighting in America from Colonial
       Rushlights to Victorian Chandeliers.   New York: Main
       Street Books, Universe, 1976.   160pp, 350 ill

9958   Cooper, Thomas.   Some Information Concerning Gas Lights.
       Philadelphia: J. Maxwell, printer, for John Conrad, 1816.
       190pp, ill, 2 pls   DLC, NN

9959   Cort, R.   Instantaneous Light and Fire Machines.   A descrip-
       tion of the principle, application, and management of the
       newly-invented light and fire machines.   Together with
       some thoughts upon the establishment of a society for the
       further encouragement of the arts.   London: J. M.
       Richardson, by Ballintine & Law, printers, 1809.   42pp
       NN

9960   Courter, J. W.   Aladdin, the Magic Name in Lamps: Aladdin
       Kerosene Mantle Lamps, Aladdin Electric Lamps, and
       Alacite by Aladdin.   Simpson, Ill: 1971; Des Moines: Wal-
       lace-Homestead, 1971; Manual and Price Guide, 197-?
       168pp, 80 ill, 12 color pls, bib; Price Guide, 11pp

9961   Curtis, J. Arthur.   Lamp Collectors' Handbook, miniature
       night lights, early grease lamps....   Newark, Ohio:
       Barnacle Wharf Trading Co, 1969.   200pp, pls

9962   Darbee, Herbert C.   A Glossary of Old Lamps and Lighting
       Devices.   Nashville, Tenn: American Association for
       State and Local History, Technical Leaflet, 1965.   16pp,
       ill

9963   Delmore, Mrs. Edward J.   Victorian Miniature Oil Lamps.
       Manchester, Vt: Forward's Color Productions, 1968.
       chiefly ill, 14 pls

9964   Early Lighting; a pictorial guide.   Boston: The Rushlight
            Club, 1972.   129pp, ill, bib

9965   Electricity and Electric Illumination.   Arc and Incandescent
            Systems; Their origin and history.   Boston: 1883.   PPWa

9966   Freeman, Graydon La Verne (Larry).   Collecting Old Lamps.
            Catalog and Study Guide No. 3 of the American Life Foun-
            dation.   new ed.   Watkins Glen, NY: Century House,
            1968.   48pp, ill   (Argands and Astrals, pattern glass,
            whale and coal oil, miniature, GWTW's and banquets,
            pattern glass shades for electric and gas, art glass shades,
            store, car and outdoor lamps)

9967   _____ .   Light on Old Lamps.   Watkins Glen, NY: Century
            House, 1944; rev. & enl. ed. 1946; 5th ed. 1955; enl. &
            rev. ed. as New Light on Old Lamps.   Watkins Glen, NY:
            Century, 1968.   112pp; 116pp; 128pp; 220pp; all ill, bib
            (18th & 19th century.   1946 ed. includes Art Nouveau;
            1968 ed. includes early gas and electric)

9968   Gerhard, William Paul.   On Gas Burners, gas pressure
            regulators and governor burners, gas globes and globe
            holders, and gas fixtures.   Philadelphia: Franklin Insti-
            tute, 1894.   39pp

9969   Gould, George Glen, and Florence Gould.   Period Lighting
            Fixtures.   New York: Dodd, Mead, 1928.   274pp, many
            ill, color frontis   (Italy, Spain, France, England, America,
            medieval days to 19th century)   MiGr

9970   Hammer, William Joseph.   The William J. Hammer Collection
            of Incandescent Electric Lamps; being the report of the
            Committee on Science and the Arts on the Historical Col-
            lection of Incandescent Electric Lamps made and exhibited
            at the St. Louis Exposition of 1904.   Philadelphia: Franklin
            Institute, 1906; New York: 1915?   8pp, pl   NN

9971   Hauksbee, Francis, d. 1713?   Physico-mechanical Experiments
            on Various Subjects.   Containing an account of several sur-
            prizing phenomena touching light and electricity, producible
            on the attrition of bodies.   With many other remarkable
            appearances, not before observ'd: together with the ex-
            planations of all the machines, (the figures of which are
            curiously engraved on copper) and other apparatus us'd in
            making the experiments.   London: R. Brugis, Printer,
            for Author, 1709; 2nd ed. London: J. Senex, 1719.   194pp,
            pls; 336pp, 8 folding pls   NN, MB, MiU, NjP, ViU, PPL

9972   *Hayward, Arthur H.   Colonial Lighting.   Boston: B. J.
            Brimmer, 1923; new & rev. ed. Boston: Little Brown,
            1927; 3rd ed. enl. with new introd. and supplement,

"Colonial Chandeliers," by James R. Marsh, as Colonial
and Early American Lighting. New York: Dover; London:
Constable, 1962. 159pp, ill, pls; 198pp, 168 ill (Dover)
(1620-1800)

9973 Heavisides, Michael. The True History of the Invention of
      the Lucifer Match, by John Walker, of Stockton-on-Tees,
      in 1827. With an account of the ancient modes of pro-
      curing light or fire. Stockton-on-Tees: Heavisides &
      Sons, 1909. 32pp, ill DLC, BM

9974 Hebard, Helen Brigham. Early Lighting in New England,
      1620-1861. Rutland, Vt: Tuttle, 1964. 88pp, ill, pls,
      bib

9975 Hough, Walter, 1859-1935. ... Collection of Heating and
      Lighting Utensils in the United States National Museum.
      Washington, D.C.: GPO, 1928. 113pp, many ill, 99 pls
      (Stoves, lamps, candlesticks, roasters, etc.) DLC, ViU

9976 Hubbard, Howard G. A Complete Checklist of Household
      Lights Patented in the United States, 1792-1826. South
      Hadley, Mass: 1935. 24pp mimeographed NN, DeWint

9977 Hunt, Charles, 1842- . Gas Lighting. Vol. III of Chemical
      Technology, ed. by C. E. Groves, and William Thorpe.
      London: Churchill; Philadelphia: P. Blakiston's, 1900.
      312pp, ill, pls NN

9978 _____. History of the Introduction of Gas Lighting. Lon-
      don: W. King, 1907. 150pp, ill, pls DLC

9979 Kaempffert, Waldemar Berhnard. Ornamental Street Lighting:
      a municipal investment and its return. New York: Na-
      tional Electric Light Association, 1912. 47pp, ill NN

9980 Koch, Robert. Louis C. Tiffany's Glass-Bronzes--Lamps, a
      complete collector's guide. New York: Crown, 1971.
      201pp, 350 ill

9981 Lamps and Lighting Through the Ages. Specimens exhibited
      at Cumberland House, Southsea. Portsmouth, Eng: Free
      Public Library, 1934.

9982 Lamps and Other Lighting Devices, 1850-1906. Compiled by
      editors of Pyne Press. Catalogues of Seven Companies:
      Archer & Warner; Cornelius & Sons; Hitchcock Lamp Co.;
      King Glass; Bellaire Goblet; Macbeth-Evans; Fostoria
      Glass. Princeton, NJ: Pyne Pr, 1972. 160pp, ill, bib

9983 Levy, Stanley Isaac. Incandescent Lighting. London: Pitman,
      1922. 129pp, ill

9984 Lighting. Science Museum. London: HMSO, 1966. ill

9985 Luckiesh, Matthew, 1883- . The Lighting Art; its practice
       and possibilities. New York: McGraw Hill, 1917. 229pp,
       ill

9986 _____. Lighting Fixtures and Lighting Effects. New York:
       McGraw Hill, 1925. 330pp, ill

9987 _____. Lighting the House. New York: Century, 1920.
       289pp, ill, pls (Electric incandescent)

9988 _____. Portable Lamps, Their Design and Use. New
       York: Dutton, 1924. 144pp, ill

9989 _____. Torch of Civilization. The story of man's conquest
       of darkness. New York: Putnam's, 1940. 269pp, pls

9990 *MacSwiggan, Amelia E. Fairy Lamps; evening's glow of
       yesteryear. Introd. by Marjorie Smith. New York:
       Fountainhead, 1962. 170pp, ill (Victorian night lights,
       tea pots & food warmers)

9991 Meadows, Cecil Austin. Discovering Oil Lamps. Aylesbury:
       Shire Publications, 1972. 48pp, ill

9992 *Mercer, Henry Chapman. Light and Fire-Making, with 45
       illustrations explaining the rubbing of fire from wood, the
       striking of flint and steel, and some of the lamps, candles,
       torches and lanterns of the American pioneer. Contributions
       to American History by Bucks County Historical Society.
       Philadelphia: MacCalla & Co, printers, 1898. 29pp NN,
       DLC

9993 Mitchell, Ray. The Study Book of Lamps and Candles. Lon-
       don: Bodley Head, 1959. 47pp, ill

9994 Noreen, Sarah Pressey. Public Street Lighting in Washington,
       D.C.; an illustrated history. Washington: George Wash-
       ington University, 1975. 55pp, ill, bib

9995 O'Dea, William T. Darkness into Daylight; an account of the
       past, present and future of man-made illumination. (Hand-
       book for the exhibition at the Science Museum, South
       Kensington. April-September 1948.) London: HMSO,
       1948. 34pp, ill, bib

9996 _____. Electric Illumination; an account of the principles,
       applications and development of electric lighting. Science
       Museum. London: HMSO, 1936. 39pp, ill, pls, bib

9997 _____. Lighting. Science Museum. 2 vol. London:

HMSO, 1966-67. 20 color ill (Oil lamps, candles, gas, mineral oil, electric lamps, etc., other than in the home)

9998 _____. A Short History of Lighting. Rev. and brought up to date. London: HMSO, 1958. 39pp, ill

9999 * _____. The Social History of Lighting. London: Routledge & K. Paul, 1958. 254pp, ill

10000 Patterson, Robert Hogarth. Gas and Lighting. London: 1876. See: Bevan, G. P., British Manufacturing Industries, Vol. 4, no. 43.

10001 Percival, G. Arncliffe. The Electric Lamp Industry. London: Pitman, 1920. 112pp, ill

10002 Perry, David H. Out of Darkness: a history of lighting; an exhibition held at the Rochester Museum and Science Center, February-June 1969. Rochester, NY: Museum, 1969. 22pp, ill

10003 Pohs, Henry A. Early Underground Mine Lamps: Mine lighting from antiquity to Arizona. Tucson: Arizona Historical Society, Museum Monograph No. 6, 1974. 108pp, ill, bib (Oil and electric)

10004 Pricing Old Lamps. Guide No. 3. Watkins Glen, NY: Century House, Yorker Yankee Museum Catalog, 197-? ill

10005 Raycraft, Donald R., and Carol Raycraft. Early American Lighting. Des Moines: Wallace-Homestead, 1974. 52pp, ill, 24 color pls (Grease lamps, iron holders, rushlight stands, street lights, candle holders, tin lanterns, etc., 1783-1865)

10006 Robins, Frederick William. The Story of the Lamp (and the Candle). London: Oxford U. Pr, 1939; reprint. Bath: Kingsmead Reprints, 1970. 153pp, ill, 50 pls, bib (500 specimens from author's collection. Includes street lighting and light houses)

10007 Roith, Cynthia. Bygones--Lamps and Lighting. London: Corgi, 1972. 95pp, ill with drawings

10008 *The Rushlight. Periodical. Boston, etc.: Rushlight Club, 1934-35; 1936-date. ill (History of lighting)

10009 Rushlight Society Journal. Periodical. Boston: Rushlight Club, 193-?-

10010 Russell, Loris Shano. A Heritage of Light: lamps and

lighting in the early Canadian home. Toronto: U. of
Toronto Pr, 1968. 344pp, 200 ill, bib

10011 St. Aubin, Louis O., Jr. Pairpoint Lamps. New Bedford,
Mass: Brookside Antiques, 1974. ill (139 lamps, 1890-
1920s)

10012 Silverberg, Robert. Light for the World! Edison and the
Power. New York: Van Nostrand, 1967. 281pp, ill

10013 Spenser, Arthur John, comp. Miners' Lighting Appliances.
Catalogue of the Collections in the Science Museum, South
Kensington. London: HMSO, 1926. 56pp, ill, 6 pls

10014 Thompson, J. H., and B. Redwood. The Petroleum Lamp:
its choice and use. London: 1902. 104pp

10015 *Thwing, Leroy. Flickering Flames. A history of domestic
lighting through the ages. Rutland, Vt: Tuttle, for the
Rushlight Club, 1958; London: Bell, 1960; London: Prentice-Hall, 1967; Rutland: 1972. 138pp, ill, 96 pls, bib,
gloss (Basic introduction to all kinds of lighting except
gas and electric)

10016 _____. A Glossary of Old Lamps and Lighting Devices.
Technical Leaflet No. 30. Nashville, Tenn: American
Association for State and Local History, 197-? ill, bib

10017 * _____, and Julius Daniels. A Dictionary of Old Lamps
and Other Lighting Devices. Cambridge, Mass: Authors,
1954. 15pp, ill

10018 Whipple, Fred H. Municipal Lighting. Detroit: Free Press,
1880; 1889. 257pp, ill; 333pp, 24pp of ill BPL

CANDLES AND CANDLEHOLDERS

10019 Archer, Margaret, and Douglas Archer. Glass Candlesticks,
with current values. Paducah, Ky: Collector Books,
1975. 112pp, ill

10020 Brass Candlesticks. ca.1797-1800 catalogue. Facsimile reprint, with pref. by Rupert Gentle. Hungerford, Berks,
Eng: Chilton Designs Ltd., printer, 1973. 27 pls--24 of
candlesticks, 3 of bells

10021 Bridgens, Richard. Designs for Grecian and Other Furniture
with Candelabra, and interior decoration. London: William Pickering, 1838. 1pp, 60 pls PP, NN, DLC, BM

10022 *Butler, Joseph Thomas. Candleholders in America: 1650-

1900; a comprehensive collection of American and European candle fixtures used in America. New York: Crown, 1967. 178pp, 136 ill, bib

10023 Designs for Candlesticks, Urns, and Various Table Furniture. n.p. (London?): 1780. 141pp of ill SKM

10024 Dummelow, John. The Wax Chandlers of London: a short history of the Worshipful Company of Wax Chandlers. Chichester: Phillimore, 1973. 204pp, ill, 10 pls, bib

10025 *Gentle, Rupert. G. Dallas Coons Candlestick Collection. Exhibition of the collection of G. D. Coons given to the Valentine Museum. January-March 1975. Richmond, Va: Valentine Museum, 1975. 48pp, ill (English & Continental, 1200-1800)

10026 Grove, John Robert. Antique Brass Candlesticks, 1450-1750. Queen Anne, Md: 1967. 140pp, chiefly ill

10027 Johnson, Thomas, carver. Twelve Gerandoles. London: for R. Sayer, 1755; 1761. 12 pls or 8 pls (Wood-carving) NNC-Ave

10028 Lock, Matthew (or Matthias). A New Book of Pier-Frames, Ovals, Gerandoles, Tables, etc. London: 1769. ill SKM

10029 Michaelis, Ronald Frederick. Base Metal Candlesticks. London: Antique Collectors Club, 1975. 200pp, 250 ill (Brass, pewter, bronze up to mid-19th century)

10030 Monier-Williams, Randall. The Tallow Chandlers of London. Vol. I. Mystery in the Making; Vol. II. Crown, the City

and the Crafts; Vol. III.   3. vol. London:
Kaye & Ward, 1970-73. 96pp, ill; 144pp, ill; 160pp, ill,
5 pls

10031 Oman, Charles Chichele. The Gloucester Candlestick.
V & A Museum. London: HMSO, 1958. 46pp, 36 ill,
bib (Ecclesiastical candlestick)

10032 Pearson, John Caler. The Rowfant Candlesticks. Cleveland:
Rowfant Club, 1959. 355pp, chiefly ill (Extensive collection)

10033 Thomas, William George Mackay. English Candlesticks before 1600. London: Metropolitan Stationery Co., 1954.
131pp, ill

10034 Vardy, John. Some Designs of Mr. Inigo Jones and Mr.
William Kent. London: 1744. 50 engraved plates
(Chimney-pieces, garden seats and temples, chandeliers,
tureens, silver standishes and cups, candlesticks, chairs,
etc.)

10035 Whitaker, Henry. Antique Candelabra, Tazze, etc. London:
H. Whitaker, 1827. ill

10036 Williams, William Mattieus. Oils and Candles. London:
1876. See: Bevan, G. P., British Manufacturing Industries, Vol. 4, no. 43.

10037 *Wills, Geoffrey. Candlesticks. Newton Abbot: David &
Charles; New York: C. N. Potter, 1974. 120pp, 110
(9 color) ill, bib (Metal, glass, pottery, porcelain to
ca.1880)

10038 Wilson, George Fergusson, 1822-1902. On the Manufacturers
of Prices' Patent Candle Company. A lecture ... with an
account of the introduction and some of the uses of glyc-
erine. London: W. H. Smith, 1856. 63pp

FIREWORKS AND EXPLOSIVES

10039 The Art of Making All Kinds of Fireworks ... to which is
added the history of Guy Fawkes, and Gunpowder Plot....
3rd ed. London: W. Mason, 1813. 26pp

10040 Brown, W. H. Firework Making for Amateurs: being complete and explicit instructions in the art of pyrotechny.
London: Upcott Gill, 18-? 200pp, pls DeWint

10041 Grotz, Christopher. The Art of Making Fireworks, detonating
balls, etc., containing plain and easy directions for mixing

and preparing the ingredients, and making and finishing the most simple devices in this ingenious art: together with how to make and fill air and fire balloons; and how to prepare and make detonating balls, spiders, segars, boots and shoes, Waterloo crackers, etc.... London: Dean & Munday, 1819?; New York: S. King, 1821; 1822;... 26pp, color frontis, ill CtY, PP

10042 _____ . The Art of Making Fireworks, improved to the modern practice; from the minutest to the highest branches: containing plain and easy directions for mixing and preparing the ingredients, with instructions for making squibs, crackers, serpents, wheels, roman candles, rockets, etc. Derby, Eng: Thomas Richardson, 18-? 24pp, folding color frontis NN

10043 Select List of References on Fireworks. Washington, D.C.: Library of Congress, 1911; Additional References.... 1929. 6pp; 3pp

10044 Williams, William Mattieu. Explosive Compounds. London: 1876. See: Bevan, G. P., British Manufacturing Industries, Vol. 2, no. 43.

USE OF TOBACCO AND SNUFF

10045 Apperson, George Latimer, 1857- . The Social History of Smoking. London: M. Secker, 1914; New York: Putnam's, 1916. 254pp (Includes tobacconists' signs) NN

10046 *Arents, George, Jr. Tobacco. Its History Illustrated by the Books, Manuscripts and Engravings in the Library of George Arents, Junior. Together with an introductory essay, a glossary and bibliographic notes by Jerome E. Brooks. 5 vol. New York: The Rosenbach Co, 1937-1952; supplement as Tobacco, A catalogue of the books, manuscripts and engravings acquired since 1942 in the Arents Tobacco Collection at the New York Public Library, from 1507 to the present. Compiled by Sarah Augusta Dickson (Parts I-VII) and Perry Hugh O'Neill (Parts VIII-X). 10 parts. New York: NYPL, 1958-1969. Vol. I. 1507-1615. 543pp, ill (some color), color frontis; Vol. II. 1615-1698. 564pp, ill, pls; Vol. III. 1698-1783. 542pp, ill, color frontis; Vol. IV. 1784-1800. Addenda: 1554-1942. 485pp, ill; Vol. V. Index, compiled by Anne M. Nill. 2 parts: Index of names, index of subjects. 327pp. Parts I-X. 650pp, pls of title pages, bound in two volumes by NYPL. (This remarkable catalogue raisonné contains a 173-page introduction; many illustrations of pipes, and other paraphernalia; and an index which covers thoroughly everything from clay pipes, clyster pipes, snuff bottles and boxes, tobacco pipes, tobacco jars to wooden Indians, etc.) NN

10047 Barber, Edwin Atlee. Antiquity of the Tobacco-Pipe in
Europe. n.p.: 1879; n.p.: n.d.; Part II. Switzerland.
n.p.: 1882. 6pp BM

10048 _____. Catalogue of the Collection of Tobacco Pipes Deposited by Him in the Pennsylvania Museum and School of
Industrial Art. Fairmount Park, Memorial Hall. Philadelphia: 1882. 13pp BM, MH

10049 *Bragge, William. Bibliotheca Nicotiana: a catalogue of
books about tobacco; together with a catalogue of objects
connected with the use of tobacco in all its forms. Birmingham, Eng: Author, 1850; 1874; Birmingham: priv.
printed by Hudson & Son, 1880. 248pp;... (1874 - 169
titles. 1880 - 409 titles and classified catalogue of 13,000
objects (pipes, snuff mills, snuff rasps, snuff bottles,
tinder boxes, etc.--a collection sold in 1882) ViU, DLC,
CU, PPULC

10050 _____. Guide to the Loan Collection of Objects Connected
with the Use of Tobacco and Other Narcotics. See: Muston, C. N. B., no. 10081.

10051 Brongers, Georg A. Nicotiana Tubacum; the history of tobacco and tobacco smoking in the Netherlands. Tr. from
Dutch by W. C. ter Spill. Amsterdam: H. J. W. Becht's
Uitgeversmaatschappij, dist. by Wittenborn, New York,
1965. 259pp, ill (part color), bib

Brooks, Jerome E. See: Arents, George, Jr., above.

10052 Bumstead, George. Specimen of a Bibliography of Old Books
and Pamphlets, illustrative of the mug, glass, bottle, the
loving cup, and the social pipe.... Diss, Eng: for compiler by Lusher Brothers, 1885. 144pp NN

10053 Catalogue of Specimens of Art Work in Chinese Snuff Bottles,
and other articles ... connected with the use of tobacco
... collection of William Bragge. Liverpool: Liverpool
Art Club, 1878. 48pp

10054 Chatto, William Andrew. A Paper:--of tobacco; treating of
the rise, progress, pleasures, and advantages of smoking.
With anecdotes of distinguished smokers, mems on pipes
and tobacco-boxes, and a tritical essay on snuff. By
Joseph Fume (pseud.) London: Chapman & Hall, 1839.
165pp, ill, pls NN, DLC

10055 Chinese Snuff Bottles: a magazine for the collector and student of Chinese snuff bottles. periodical. London: 1964-

10056 Clemens, Kaye. Tobacco and Food Tins. Paducah, Ky:
Collector Books, 1974. ill

10057 Corti, Count Egon Caesar. History of Smoking. Tr. from
       German (1928) by Paul England. London: Harrap, 1931;
       New York: Harcourt, Brace, 1932. 295pp, 64 pls, bib
       DLC

10058 Crone, Ernst. Pieter Holm and His Tobacco Box. Tr. by
       Dirk Brouwer. Introd. by Edwin Pugsley. Mystic, Conn:
       Marine Historical Association, 1953. 22pp, ill

10059 *Curtis, Mattoon Monroe. The (Story) Book of Snuff and
       Snuff Boxes, with 119 rare and unusual reproductions of
       snuff boxes in vari-coloured gold, silver, ivory, and
       precious woods and stones. New York: Liveright, 1935;
       London: Peter Owen, 1956. 149pp, ill, bib NN, CU

10060 Davis, Marvin, and Helen Davis. Tobacco Tins; pictures
       and prices of over 150 tobacco tins. Medford, Ore:
       Grandee Printing, 1970. 61pp, ill

10061 Dunhill, Alfred Henry. The Gentle Art of Smoking. London:
       Reinhardt; New York: Putnam, 1954. 146pp, ill, bib;
       177pp, ill (Snuff, matches, lighters, pipes, etc.)

10062 _____. The Pipe Book. London: A. & C. Black, 1924;
       rev. ed. 1960; London: Barker; New York: Macmillan,
       1969. 262pp, 230 ill, 28 (4 color) pls

10063 An Exhibition of Chinese Snuff Bottles, June 1970. London:
       Hugh M. Moss, Ltd., 1970. 93pp, chiefly ill

10064 Exhibition of Chinese Snuff Bottles of the 17th Century and
       the 18th Century from the Collection of Mr. and Mrs.
       Martin Schoen, China Institute in America, December 1952-
       January 1953. New York: 1952. 30pp, ill

10065 Forrester, Alfred Henry, 1804-1872. A Few Words About
       Pipes, Smoking and Tobacco, by Alfred Crowquill (pseud.).
       Reprint from notes, 1839-1840. New York: Arents To-
       bacco Collection, New York Public Library, 1947. 91pp,
       ill NN

10066 Goldring, William. The Pipe Book; a history and how-to.
       New York: Drake, 1973. 140pp, ill

10067 Gordon, Robert. Pipes. San Antonio, Tx: Author, 197-?
       120 pieces from Gordon Collection

10068 Greg, Thomas Tylston. Catalogue of a Collection of Brass
       Tobacco Boxes, 1760-1780, and other trophies made to
       celebrate the battles in the Silesian and Seven Years' War.
       Manchester, Eng: Art Gallery, 1922? 55pp, pls DLC,
       NN

10069   Harley, Laurence Shepheard. The Clay Tobacco-Pipe in
        Britain; with special reference to Essex and East Anglia.
        London: Essex Field Club, 1963. 41pp, ill, 9 pls, bib

10070   Herment, Georges. The Pipe; a serious yet diverting treatise
        on the history of the pipe and all its appurtenances. ...
        Tr. from French by Arthur L. Hayward. Fore. by
        Stephen Potter. London: Cassell, 1954. New York:
        Simon & Schuster, 1955. 164pp, ill

10071   Hitt, Henry C. Old Chinese Snuff Bottles. Notes, with a
        catalogue of a modest collection. 2nd ed. Bremerton,
        Wash: Author, 1945. 110pp, ill, 4 pls MB, NN

10072   _____, ed. Snuff Bottle Analecta. Periodical. Bremer-
        ton, Wash: 1946- . ill MB, NN

10073   _____. Register of Painted Inside Chinese Snuff Bottles.
        Bremerton, Wash: 1947. 18pp, pls

10074   Hughes, George Bernard. English Snuff-boxes. London:
        MacGibbon & Kee, 1971. 143pp, ill, 32 pls (ca.1600-
        1850)

10075   Huish, Marcus Bourne, 1845-1921. Chinese Snuff Bottles
        of Stone, Porcelain, and Glass utilized to uprear a fabric
        of fancies concerning China and the Chinese. London:
        Chiswick Press for Sette of Odd Volumes, 1895. 51pp,
        ill, color frontis, pls NN, DLC

10076   Jewitt, Llewellyn Frederick William. A Few Words on
        "Fairy Pipes;" with a plate of old English tobacco pipes
        made at Broseley, Shropshire. Reprint from "The Reli-
        quary." London: 1862. ill

10077   Le Corbeiller, Clare. European and American Snuff Boxes,
        1730-1830. London: Batsford; New York: Viking, 1966.
        120pp, 102 pls, marks, bib, gloss

10078   McCausland, Hugh. Snuff and Snuff Boxes. London: Batch-
        worth, 1951. 144pp, ill, bib

10079   Moss, Hugh Murray. Chinese Snuff Bottles of the Silica or
        Quartz Group. London: Bibelot Publishers, 1971. 84pp,
        221 ill

10080   _____. Snuff Bottles of China. London: Bibelot Pub-
        lishers, 1971. 158pp, ill, bib

10081   Muston, C. N. B. Guide to the Loan Collection of Objects
        Connected with the Use of Tobacco and Other Narcotics
        ... lent by Mr. William Bragge. Introd. by T. C. Archer.

Edinburgh Museum of Science and Art.   Edinburgh: Neill
& Co, for HMSO, 1880.   20pp   DLC

10082   Myer, Reginald.   Chats on Old English Tobacco Jars, with
a reprint of a book on the Westminster Tobacco Box,
published in 1824.   Introd. by Charles R. Beard.   London:
S. Low; Philadelphia: Lippincott, 1930.   111pp, 130 ill,
62 pls   NN   (See no. 10093.)

10083 *Norton, Richard, and Martin Norton.   A History of Gold
Snuff Boxes.   London: S. J. Phillips, 1938.   115pp, 43
pls   DLC, NN

10084   Perry, Lilla S.   Chinese Snuff Bottles; the adventures and
studies of a collector.   Tokyo; Rutland, Vt: Tuttle; London: Prentice-Hall, 1960; Rutland: 1973.   158pp, 162 ill,
bib   (Jade, quartz, glass, etc.)

10085 *Pinto, Edward H.   Wooden Bygones of Smoking and Snuff
Taking.   London: Hutchinson; Newton, Mass: C. T.
Branford, 1961.   96pp, ill, 30 pls, bib

10086   Price, Frederick George Hilton, 1842-1909.   Notes Upon
Some Early Clay Tobacco Pipes from the 16th to the 18th
Centuries Found in the City of London, in the possession
of the author.   Reprint from "Archaeological Journal."
London: 1900.   16pp

10087 *Pritchett, Robert Taylor.   Smokiana.   Historical and Ethno-
graphical.   (Ye pipes of all nations.)   London: Quaritch,
1890.   101pp, ill (some color)

10088   Reynolds, J. C.   The Tobacco Pipe, Pipe Clays and Tobacco.
London: Reynolds Tobacco Pipe Manufactory, 1862.   16pp,
ill

10089   Scott, Amoret, and Christopher Scott.   Discovering Smoking
Antiques.   Tring: Shire Publications, 1970.   56pp, ill,
bib

10090   _____, and _____.   Tobacco and the Collector.   London: Parrish, 1966.   178pp, ill, 4 pls, bib

10091   Shepherd, Cecil William.   Snuff Yesterday and Today.   London: G. Smith, 1963.   92pp, ill, 8 pls, bib

10092   Sheppard, Thomas, 1876- .   Early Hull Tobacco Pipes and
Their Makers.   Hull: Museum, 1902.   28pp, ill (One
of the most complete collections of 17th century pipes)

10093   Stephenson, Simon, comp.   Representation of the Embossed,
chased, and engraved subjects and inscriptions which

decorate the tobacco box and cases, belonging to the Past
Overseers Society of the Parishes of St. Margaret and St.
John, Westminster. London: J. Clark, 1824; reprints.
London: Waterlow, 1887; London: 1913. 11pp, 34 pls
("Depicts a remarkable series of boxes and caskets which
grew around a small horn tobacco box. An engraved
silver plate commemorating important topical events was
added each year." B. Quaritch, Catalogue No. 906, 1971)

10094   Watson, Francis John Bagott. The Choiseul Box. London;
        New York: Oxford U. Pr, 1963. 21pp, pls (Snuff box)

10095   West, Gordon. 400 Years of Smoking. London: "Tobacco,"
        1953. 80pp, ill

10096   Winckworth, (John) Peter. The Westminster Tobacco Box.
        London: Past Overseers' Society of St. Margaret and St.
        John in collaboration with "The Connoisseur," 1966. 35pp,
        ill

ELECTRICITY, MOTORS AND MAGNETISM

10097   Bakewell, Frederick Collier. Electric Science; its history,
        phenomena, and application. London: Ingram, Cooke &
        Co, 1853; 3rd ed. rev. & enl. as A Manual of Electricity,
        practical and theoretical. London; Glasgow: R. Riffin,
        1859. 199pp, pls; 314pp, pls BM

10098   The Beginnings of the Incandescent Lamp and Lighting System.
        Dearborn, Mich: Greenfield Village and Henry Ford Mu-
        seum, 1976. 33pp, many ill (From writings of Thomas
        A. Edison)

10099   Catalogue of Apparatus Suitable for Lectures and Class In-
        struction in Group III. Subject 1. Acoustics, light, heat.
        2. Magnetism and electricity. South Kensington Museum.
        8th ed. London: Eyre & Spottiswoode, HMSO, 1865.
        22pp BM

10100   A Chronological History of Electrical Development. New
        York: 1946. 106, 38pp (History of 462 American elec-
        trical equipment manufacturers)

10101   Electrical Designs; comprising instructions for constructing
        small motors, testing instruments, and other apparatus;
        with working drawings for each design. Reprint from
        "The American Electrician," New York: 1901. 262pp,
        ill, diags DLC, NN

10102   Electrical Instruments. Illustrated catalogues, 1882-1928;
        1889-1910. Bound. Philadelphia: Franklin Institute,
        1931, 1932. v.p. PPF

10103 Electrical World. Weekly. London: 188-?

10104 Electricity and Electric Illumination. Arc and Incandescent
       Systems; their origin and history. Boston: 1883. PPWa

10105 Francis, George William, 1800-1865. Electrical Experi-
       ments, illustrating the theory, practice and application of
       the science of free or frictional electricity: containing
       the methods of making and managing electrical apparatus
       of every description. London: D. Francis, 1844; 5th ed.
       1850; 7th ed. 1854;... u.p., ill; 91pp, ill NNC-Ave,
       PPF

10106 Gray, John, B. SC., F. R. A. I. Electrical Influence Ma-
       chines. A full account of their historical development and
       modern forms, with instructions for making them. London:
       Whittaker, 1890; 2nd ed. enl. & rev. London; New York:
       Whittaker, 1903. 237pp, 89 ill, 4 pls; 296pp, 105 ill, 2
       pls MiD, DLC

10107 Hammer, William Joseph, 1858-1934. "Edison and His In-
       ventions." A lecture before the Franklin Institute. Phila-
       delphia: 1889. 30 leaves DLC

10108   . The W. J. Hammer Collection of Incandescent
       Electric Lamps; being the report of the Committee on
       Science and the Arts on the historical collection of incan-
       descent electric lamps made and exhibited at the St. Louis
       Exposition of 1904. Philadelphia: Franklin Institute,
       1906; New York: 1915? 8pp, pl NN

10109 Hartley, F. Saint A., comp. Electrical Engineering. Cata-
       logue of the collections in the Science Museum, South
       Kensington. London: HMSO, 1927. 116pp, ill, 14 pls
       (See also: O'Dea, William T.) DLC, CU

10110 Hauksbee, Francis, d. 1713?. Physico-mechanical Experi-
       ments on Various Subjects. Containing an account of
       several surprizing phenomena touching light and electricity,
       producible on the attrition of bodies. With many other
       remarkable appearances, not before observ'd: together
       with the explanations of all the machines, (the figures of
       which are curiously engraved in copper) and other appara-
       tus us'd in making the experiments. London: R. Brugis,
       printer, for Author, 1709; 2nd ed. London: J. Senex,
       1719. 194pp, pls; 336pp, 8 folding pls ViU, NN, MB,
       MiU, PPL, NjP

10111 Houston, Edwin James. Electricity in Everyday Life. 3 vol.
       New York: P. F. Collier, 1905. text, ill, pls (part
       color), color frontis NjP, NN

10112 _____. Electricity 100 Years Ago and Today. New York: W. J. Johnston, 1894. 199pp, ill PPL, NN

10113 _____. Recent Types of Dynamo-electric Machinery; a complete guide for the electrician, engineer, student and professor, being a valuable history ... of American dynamo machines and their application. New York: Collier, 1897; ...; 1902. 612pp, ill ViU, NjP

10114 Levy, Stanley Isaac. Incandescent Lighting. London: Pitman, 1922. 129pp, ill

10115 Luckiesh, Matthew. Lighting Fixtures and Lighting Effects. New York: McGraw Hill, 1925. 330pp, ill

10116 _____. Lighting the Home. New York: Century, 1920. 289pp, ill, pls (Electric incandescent)

10117 O'Dea, William T. Electric Illumination; an account of the principles, applications and development of electric lighting. Science Museum. London: HMSO, 1936. 39pp, ill, pl, bib

10118 _____. Handbook of the Collections Illustrating Electrical Engineering. Science Museum. Vol. I. London: HMSO, 1933- . pls (Electric power, history & development) DLC

10119 Percival, G. Arncliffe. The Electric Lamp Industry. London: Pitman, 1920. 112pp, ill

10120 Silverberg, Robert. Light for the World! Edison and the Power. New York: Van Nostrand, 1967. 281pp, ill

10121 Sloane, Thomas O'Conor. Electric Toy Making for Amateurs; including batteries, magnets, motors, miscellaneous toys and dynamo construction. New York: N. W. Hendley, 1892; ... 15th ed., rev. & enl. 1903; ...; 21st ed. 1923. 140pp, ill; 183pp, ill; 254pp, ill

10122 Tomlinson, Charles. The Magnet: familiarly described and illustrated by a box of magnetic toys. London: Joseph & Myers, 1857. 47pp (The copy in the British Museum without toys)

10123 Watson, Sir William, M.D. Experiments and Observations Tending to Illustrate the Nature and Properties of Electricity. London: Davis, 1745. BM

10124 _____. A Sequel to the Experiments and Observations to Illustrate the Nature and Properties of Electricity, with a copperplate of the machine. London: Davis, 1746. 78pp, pl

ICE AND REFRIGERATION

10125   Anderson, Oscar Edward. Refrigeration in America; a his-
        tory of a new technology and its impact. Princeton, NJ:
        Princeton U. Pr, for U. of Cincinnati, 1953. 344pp, ill,
        bib

10126   Crawhill, Thomas Currah, and B. Lentaigne. Refrigeration
        Exhibition (April-August 1934); a brief account of the
        historical development of mechanical refrigeration and a
        descriptive catalog of the exhibits. Science Museum.
        London: HMSO, 1934. 27pp, ill NN

10127   Cummings, Richard Osborn. The American Ice Harvests; a
        historical study in technology, 1800-1918. Berkeley: U.
        of Cal. Pr, 1949. 184pp, ill, bib

10128   Hall, Henry, 1845-1920. The Ice Industry of the United
        States, with a brief sketch of its history. Report for the
        10th Census of the U.S., 1880. Washington, D.C.: GPO,
        1888; facsim. reprint. Ambridge, Pa: Early American
        Industries Association, 1975. 43pp, 51 ill (Includes tools)

10129   Hiles, Theron L. The Ice Crop: how to harvest, store,
        ship and use ice, a complete practical treatise for ... all
        interested in ice houses, cold storage and the handling or
        use of ice in any way, including many recipes for iced
        dishes and beverages. New York: O. Judd, 1893. 122pp,
        ill ViU, PPL, DLC, DeWint

10130   Masters, Thomas. The Ice Book: being a compendius ...
        history of everything connected with ice; from its introduc-
        tion in Europe as an article of luxury to the present time;
        with an account of the artificial manner of producing pure
        and solid ice; and a valuable collection of ... recipes for
        ... water-ices and ice-creams. London: 1844. 198pp,
        6 pls BM, DLC

10131   _____. A Short Treatise Concerning Some Patent Inven-
        tions for the Production of Ice and Artificial Cold, lemon-
        ade, nectar, and all aerated beverages; also the newly im-
        proved ꞓotary knife cleaning machine, and improved culi-
        nary utensils; being also a handbook of instruction, to
        guide the uninitiated in the uses of various machines and
        apparatus.... London: Patent Journal Printing Office,
        1850. 120pp, ill DLC, BM, NN

10132   Springett, Bernard H. Cold Storage and Ice-making. Lon-
        don: Pitman, 1921. 122pp, ill

10133   Wood, William T., and Co. Price List 1894-95. Reprint
        as Price List William T. Wood & Co. Manufacturers of
        Finest Quality Ice Tools, Arlington, Mass. Levittown,
        NY: Early Trades and Crafts Society, 1974.

FIREFIGHTING AND FIREMARKS

EQUIPMENT AND FIRE INSURANCE MARKS

10134 American Fire Marks. The Insurance Company of North
        America Collection. Philadelphia: 1933. 133pp, many
        ill (Various company marks)

10135 *Bulau, Alwin E. Footprints of Assurance. New York:
        Macmillan, 1954. 319pp, ill, color pls, bib (Definitive
        work on firemarks) DeWint, DLC, NN

10136 Daly, Georg Anne, and John J. Robrecht. An Illustrated
        Handbook of Fire Apparatus, with emphasis on 19th
        century pieces. Philadelphia: Insurance Company of
        North America Corp., Archives Dept., 1972. 128pp, ill,
        pl (Fire-fighting)

10137 Dunshee, Kenneth Holcomb. Enjine! Enjine! A Story of
        Fire Protection. New York: H. V. Smith, 1939. 63pp,
        ill DeWint, NN, DLC

10138 Firefighting at the Turn of the Century. Lebanon, Pa: Ap-
        plied Arts, 196-? ill

10139 Fothergill, George Algernon. British Fire-marks from 1680.
        Edinburgh: W. Green, 1911. 185pp, 60 ill, bib DeWint

10140 Gilbert, Keith Reginald. Fire Engines and Other Fire-
        fighting Appliances. Science Museum. London: HMSO,
        1966. 48pp, ill (19 color)

10141 Gillespie, George Cuthbert, and Stevenson Hockley Walsh.
        Fire Insurance House Marks of the United States, with
        illustrations from the original marks. Philadelphia: priv.
        printed, Lippincott, 1915. 16pp, 24 pls NN

10142 Gillingham, Harrold Edgar. Fire Marks of American Fire
        Insurance Companies. Philadelphia: 1914. 40pp, ill
        PP

10143 _____ . Foreign Fire Marks. Philadelphia: 1916. u.p.
      PP

10144 Gray, Jerome B. 100 Years: being a short history of
      fires, and the methods of fighting fires during the past
      100 years, together with some interesting facts about
      fires of ancient times. Philadelphia: Franklin Fire In-
      surance Company, 1929. 82pp, ill, pls TxU, DeWint

10145 Holmes, Frederick Morell, 1851- . Firemen and Their
      Exploits: with some account of the rise and development
      of fire-brigades, of various appliances for saving life at
      fires and extinguishing the flames. London: S. W. Par-
      tridge, 1899. 167pp, ill, pls DLC

10146 McCosker, M. J. The Historical Collection of the Insurance
      Company of North America. Philadelphia: the Company,
      1945; 2nd ed. 1967. 173pp, ill, color frontis, pls; 213pp,
      pls

10147 The (H. V.) Smith Museum, the Home Insurance Company
      Building. New York: 1941. 8 leaves, ill, pl (Handbook
      of museum of fire prevention and extinction) NN

10148 Swigart, W. Emmert. Old Fire Marks. Reprint from
      "Bulletin" of the Historical Society of Montgomery County,
      Pa. West Chester, Pa: Penn Mutual Fire Insurance
      Company, 1946. 15pp, pls

10149 Williams, Bertram. Fire Marks and Insurance Office Fire
      Brigades. London: C. & E. Layton, 1927. 85pp, ill
      NN, DeWint

10150 _____ . Insurance Office Signs. 2nd ed. London: Post
      Magazine & Insurance Monitor, 1929? 59pp, ill NN

10151 _____ . Specimens of British Fire Marks. London: C.
      & E. Layton, 1934. 129pp, ill NN

WEIGHING AND MEASURING

INSTRUMENTS OF PRECISION

10152   Adams, George, d. 1773, the Elder.   The Description and
        Use of a New Sea Quadrant.   London: John Hart, 1748.
        40pp   BM

10153   Adams, George, 1750-1795, the Younger.   Geometrical and
        Graphical Essays, containing a description of the mathe-
        matical instruments used in geometry, civil and military
        surveying, levelling and perspective....   London: Author,
        1791; 2nd ed. corr. & enl. by William Jones.   London:
        W. & S. Jones, 1797.   500pp, 32 pls   BM

10154   .   A Short Dissertation on the Barometer, thermo-
        meter, and other meteorological instruments: together
        with an account of the prognostic signs of the weather.
        London: Author, 1790.   60pp   BM

10155   .   (32 Plates Illustrating Instruments Such as Pro-
        tractors and Surveying Tools.)   London: 1791.   DeWint

10156   Anderson, Robert Geoffrey William, comp.   The Mariner's
        Astrolabe: exhibition at the Royal Scottish Museum,
        August-September 1972.   Edinburgh: the Museum, 1972.
        36pp, ill

10157   Asprey & Co.   The Clockwork of the Heavens.   Exhibition
        of Astronomical clocks, watches and allied scientific in-
        struments, presented by Asprey with help of Harriet
        Wynter, and collaboration of various museums and private
        collections.   London: Asprey, 1973.   92pp, ill, bib   (to
        1854)

10158 *Babbage, Charles, 1792-1871.   History of (His) Calculating
        Engines.   London: n.d.; reprinted by Henry Prevost
        Babbage in Babbage's Calculating Engines; being a collec-
        tion of papers relating to them, their history and

construction.   London: E. & F. N. Spon, 1889.   342pp,
ill

10159   Bedini, Silvio A.   The Borghesi Astronomical Clock.   Washington, D.C.: Smithsonian, GPO, 1964.   75pp, ill, bib

10160 *Bell, Geoffrey Howard, and Ellen Florence Bell.   Old English
Barometers.   Winchester, Eng: Warren, 1952; reprint.
1971.   42pp, ill, 39 pls, bib

10161 *Bion, Nicolas.   The Construction and Principal Uses of
Mathematical Instruments.   Translated from the French
of M. Bion, Chief Instrument-Maker to the French King.
To which are added, the construction and uses of such
instruments as are omitted by M. Bion; particularly of
those invented or improved by the English.   By Edmund
Stone.   London: printed by H. W. for John Senex and
William Taylor, 1723; 2nd ed. with supplement "... some
of the most useful mathematical instruments as now improved."   London: printed for J. Richardson, 1758.
264pp, 26 folding pls of instruments; 325pp, pls (Drawing,
measuring, surveying and navigating instruments) MH,
NNC-Ave, DLC, PP, CtY, CU

10162   Bolton, Henry Carrington.   Evolution of the Thermometer,
1592-1743.   Easton, Pa: The Chemical Publishing Co,
1900.   98pp, ill, bib DLC, NN, PPULC

10163   Brewington, Marion Vernon.   The Peabody Museum Collection of Navigating Instruments with Notes on Their Makers.
Salem, Mass: the Museum, 1963.   154pp, 57 pls

10164   Brewster, Sir David, 1781-1868.   Description of Several New
Micrometers, for various purposes in the Arts and Sciences.   3 parts.   Edinburgh: W. Harris, 1813.   ill

10165   Catalogue of Optical and General Scientific Instruments.   London: printed for the Optical Convention, 1912.   400pp,
many ill (Telescopes, binoculars, microscopes, meteorological, mathematical and surveying instruments, cameras, etc.)

10166   Catalogue of Timepieces.   Exeter, NH: Adams Brown, 1969.
60pp, ill (Tools, music boxes, clocks, watches, barometers)

10167   Chaldecott, J. A.   Handbook of the Collection Illustrating
Temperature Measurement and Control.   Science Museum.
Catalogue of Exhibits with Notes.   Part 2.   London:
HMSO, 1955- .   ill, pls NN

10168   Dent, Edward John, 1790-1835.   On the Construction and

Management of Chronometers, Clocks, and Watches. London: Author, 1844; 1846; 1851; reprint. 1955; reprint of 1844 ed. Exeter, NH: Adams Brown, 197-? 32pp, 12 ill

10169   . A Treatise on the Aneroid, a newly invented portable barometer with a short historical notice on barometers in general, their construction and use. London: Author, 1849; 1850; 1852; 1859; republished. Philadelphia: M'Allister & Bro., 1860. 34pp, ill DLC, NN, MB

10170 Dick, Thomas, 1774-1857. The Practical Astronomer. Comprising illustrations of light and colours--practical descriptions of all kinds of telescopes--the use of the equatorial-transit-circular, and other astronomical instruments, a particular account of the Earl of Rosse's large telescopes, and other topics.... London: Seeley, Burnside, & Seeley, 1845; Philadelphia: Biddle, 1848; 1850; New York: 1855; Philadelphia: 1856; New York: Harper, 1872. 567pp, ill; 437pp, ill; 396pp, ill; ...; 437pp, 100 ill ViU, MH

10171 Dollond, Peter. A Description of the Girometer, Made and Sold by Peter and George Dollond. London: 1811. BM

10172   , and George Dollond. Description and Use of the Mathematical Drawing Instruments, and of the lines on the plain scale, the sector, the proportional compasses, and the gunners callipers; with a practical application. London: 1819. 35pp, pls BM

10173   , and   . The Description of a Binnacle Compass Illuminated by Prismatic Reflection ... made and sold by P. & G. Dollond. London: 1812.

10174 Dondi, Giovanni de. The Planetarium of G. de Dondi, citizen of Padua: a manuscript of 1397. Translated from Latin by Granville Hugh Baillie; with additional materials from another Dondi manuscript translated from Latin by Herbert Alan Lloyd. Ed. by F. A. B. Ward. London: Antiquarian Horological Society, 1974. 156pp, ill (some color) (Astronomical clocks)

10175 Ebel, Otto. The Metronome and Its Use. Brooklyn, NY: Chandler & Hall Music Co, 1903. 15pp

17176 Electrical Measuring Instruments. Illustrated Catalogues, 1879-1915. Bound. Franklin Institute, Philadelphia, 1931. v.p. PPF

10177 Englefield, Sir Henry Charles. Description of a New Transit Instrument, improved by ... Englefield, ... made and sold by Thomas Jones. London: 1814. pls (Surveying)

10178 Fayerman, Edmund Reynolds. Description of the Music

Timekeeper. Patented by E. R. F., 16 July, 1853.
London: R. Clay, printer, 1853. 8pp, ill, 4 pls (Metronome) DLC

10179 Fox, Philip. Adler Planetarium and Astronomical Museum.
An Account of the optical planetarium and a brief guide to
the museum. Chicago: Lakeside Pr, R. R. Donnelley,
1933; 4th ed. Chicago: F. J. Ringley, 1937. 62pp, ill
(Astronomical models and instruments, planispheres, etc.)

10180 Frazier, Arthur H. Joseph Saxton and His Contribution to
the Medal Ruling and Photographic Arts. Washington,
D.C.: Smithsonian, 1975. (Precision and artists' instruments)

10181 _____. Water Current Meters in the Smithsonian Collections. Washington, D.C.: 1974. 95pp, ill, bib

10182 Goodison, Nicholas. English Barometers, 1680-1860; a
history of domestic barometers and their makers. New
York: Potter, 1968; London: Cassell, 1969. 353pp,
158 ill, 3 color pls, bib (Chiefly mercurial barometers.
Includes clockmakers and instrument makers)

10183 Gould, Rupert Thomas. John Harrison and His Timekeepers.
Reprint from the "Mariner's Mirror," April 1935. London:
1935; London: National Maritime Museum, 1958. 24pp,
ill, 9 pls (Chronometers. Harrison worked 1729-1776)
NN

10184 _____. The Marine Chronometer, Its History and Development. Fore. by Sir Frank W. Dyson. London: J. D.
Potter, 1923; reprint. London: Holland Pr, 1971. 287pp,
85 ill, 39 pls

10185 Gunter, Edmund, 1581-1626. The Description and Use of a
Portable Instrument ... known ... [as] G[unter]'s Quadrant ... To which is added the use of Nepiars [sic] Bones
in multiplication, division, and extraction of roots. 2 parts.
London: William Leybourn, 1685. (John Napier, 1550-
1617, inventor of logarithms) BM

10186 _____. De Sectore and Radio. The Description and Use
of the Sector ... the description and use of the cross-
staffe.... London: William Jones, 1623; 2nd ed. as The
Description and Use of the Sector, Crosse-Staffe, and
Other Instruments.... London: 1836; 3rd ed. including
"... the further use of the quadrant," by S. Foster.
London: 1653; 4th ed. 1662; facsim. reprint as Use of
the Sector, Crosse-Staffe.... Amsterdam: Theatrum
Orbis Terrarum; New York: Da Capo, 1971. 143 and
216pp, ill BM

10187   Gurley, W., and L. E. Gurley. <u>Gurley Manual of Surveying</u>
        <u>Instruments ... or, Manual of the principal instruments</u>
        <u>used in American engineering and surveying....</u> (title
        varies) Troy, NY: Gurley, 1855-1949. ill TxU, NN,
        DLC, DeWint

10188   *Guye, Samuel, and Henri Michel. <u>Time and Space: Mea-</u>
        <u>suring Instruments from the 15th to the 19th Century.</u> Tr.
        from French by Diana Dolan. London: Pall Mall Pr,
        1970; New York: Praeger, 1971. 289pp, ill, 140 pls
        (Clocks, watches & instruments)

10189   Harrison, John, 1693-1776. <u>A Description Concerning Such</u>
        <u>Mechanism as Will Afford a Nice, or true mensuration of</u>
        <u>time; together with some account of the attempts for the</u>
        <u>discovery of the longitude by the moon: as also an ac-</u>
        <u>count of the discovery of the scale of musick.</u> London:
        Author, 1775. 108pp (Chronometer) MH, DLC

10190   _____ <u>The Principles of Mr. Harrison's Time-Keeper.</u>
        Preface and notes by Nevil Maskelyne, Astronomer Royal.
        London: W. Richardson & S. Clark, printers, 1767.
        31pp, 10 pls NNC-Ave, DLC, MH

10191   _____. <u>Remarks on a Pamphlet Lately Published by the</u>
        <u>Reverend Mr. Maskelyne, under the authority of the</u>
        <u>Board of Longitude.</u> London: W. Sandby, 1767. 34pp
        NN

10192   Heather, John Fry. <u>A Treatise on Mathematical Instruments,</u>
        <u>including most of the instruments employed in drawing; for</u>
        <u>assisting the vision; in surveying and levelling, in practical</u>
        <u>astronomy and for measuring the angles of crystals.</u> Lon-
        don: 1849; ...; 7th ed., with appendices. London: 1864;
        enl. ed. 3 vol. London: J. Weale, 1871; 14th ed. rev.
        London: Crosby Lockwood, 1888. text, pls BM

10193   Hoare, Charles. <u>The Slide-Rule and How to Use It.</u> London:
        Weale, 1868.

10194   Horsburgh, Ellice Martin, ed. <u>Handbook of the Exhibition of</u>
        <u>Napier Relics and of Books, instruments, and devices for</u>
        <u>facilitating calculation.</u> (Napier Tercentenary Celebration.)
        Edinburgh: Royal Society of Edinburgh; London: G. Bell,
        1914. 343pp, ill, pls NN, MiU, DLC

10195   _____, ed. <u>Modern Instruments and Methods of Calcula-</u>
        <u>tion: a handbook of the Napier Tercentenary Exhibition,</u>
        <u>Edinburgh.</u> London: G. Bell, 1914. 343pp

10196   Hulme, Frederick Edward. <u>Mathematical Drawing Instru-</u>
        <u>ments and How to Use Them.</u> London; Edinburgh: Young

Mechanics Series, 1879; New York: Bicknell, 1880; 2nd
ed. New York: William T. Comstock, 1884; 1892. 152pp,
ill, 10 pls BM, MiD, PPL

10197 Jagger, Cedric. Paul Philip Barraud: a study of a fine
chronometer maker, and of his relatives, associates and
successors in the family business, 1750-1929. Fore. by
H. Quill. London: Antiquarian Horological Society, 1968.
177pp, ill, 1 pl, facsims. (Dating and serial numbers of
clocks, watches and chronometers)

10198 Jenkins, Henry. A Description of Several Astronomical and
Geographical Clocks; with an account of their motions and
uses; and a short account [of] a marine regulator. 2nd ed.
with additions. London: 1778. 129pp

10199 Jones, Thomas, 1763-1831, mathematical instrument maker.
A Companion to the Mountain Barometer, consisting of
tables, whereby the operation of computing heights with
that instrument is rendered ... easy ..; with a description of the Englefield Mountain Barometer. London: 1817;
2nd ed. enl. (1820?) u.p. (Henry Charles Englefield)
CtY, BM

10200 _____. Description and Use of the Pocket Case of Mathematical Instruments; wherein are particularly explained the
nature and use of all the lines contained on the plain scale,
the sector, the gunter, and proportional compasses....
new ed., with corr. London: W. & S. Jones, 1797.
19pp, pls

10201 _____. The Description and Use of the Sea Octant, commonly called Hadley's Quadrant.... London: Author,
1777-?; 2nd ed. 1795; 3rd ed. 1813. 28pp, diagrams
NN, MB

10202 _____. Description and Use of "The Sectograph," principally designed for the purpose of dividing right lines into
equal parts. London: 1814. BM

10203 *Kiely, Edmond Richard. Surveying Instruments. Their
history and Classroom use. (Also as a thesis.) New
York: Teachers College, Columbia University, 1947.
411pp, ill, bib NNC-Ave

10204 Lancaster-Jones, Ernest, comp. Geodesy and Surveying.
Catalogue of the collections in the Science Museum, South
Kensington. London: HMSO, 1925. 110pp, ill, 7 pls
DLC, NN

10205 Leybourn, William, 1626-1700? The Description and Use of
a Portable Instrument, vulgarly known by the name of

Gunter's Quadrant, by which is performed most proposi-
tions in astronomy.... London: T. B. for H. Sawbridge
at the Bible on Ludgate-Hill, 1685; 2nd ed. London: for
J. Wilcox, 1721; 4th ed. To which is added, The Use of
the Universal Ring-Dial. London: John Gilbert, 1771.
70pp, folding diagrams MiU, NNC-Ave

10206 List of Apparatus Available for Scientific Researches Involving
Accurate Measurements; and contained in different Ameri-
can laboratories. Republished from Bulletin of the Library
of Harvard University, nos. 11 & 12. Introd. by Wolcott
Gibbs, Edward C. Pickering, John Trowbridge. Cambridge,
Mass: Harvard U. Pr, 1879. 10pp MiU

10207 Lyman, Benjamin Smith. Notes on Mine-Surveying Instruments, with special reference to Mr. Dunbar D. Scott's
paper on their evolution, and its discussion. New York:
Transactions of the American Institute of Mining Engineers,
vol. 31, 1900. 54pp, ill

10208 _____. An Old Japanese Foot Measure. Reprint from
Proceedings of the Numismatic and Antiquarian Society of
Philadelphia 1887/89. Philadelphia: 1890. 12pp (pp.
68-76), ill MH

10209 Mahan, Dennis Hart, 1802-1871. Industrial Drawing: comprising the description and uses of drawing instruments,
the construction of plane figures, the projections and sections of geometrical solids.... New York: J. Wiley,
1852; 2nd ed. 1855; 2nd ed. rev. & corr. 1863; 1871;
rev. & enl. by Dwinel F. Thompson. 1877;...; 156pp;
...; 209pp, ill, 30 pls (all illustrated) NN, MiU

10210 Marcosson, Isaac F. Wherever Men Trade. History of the
National Cash Register Company. New York: 1945.
263pp, ill

10211 Marshall, Alfred William, and George Gentry. Micrometers,
Slide Gauges, and Calipers, Their Construction and Use;
a handbook on appliances used in engineering workshops for
fine mechanical measurements. 2nd ed. London: P.
Marshall, 1915; rev. & enl. 1939. 77pp, ill NN

10212 Mathematics. Catalogue of the Collections in the Science
Museum, South Kensington. London: HMSO, 1926- .
ill DLC, NN

10213 May, William Edward. A History of Marine Navigation.
With a chapter on modern developments by Leonard Holder.
Henley-on-Thames: Foulis, 1973. 280pp, ill, bib

10214 *Mayer, Leo Ary. Islamic Astrolabists and Their Works.
Geneva: A. Kundig, 1956. ill

10215 *Mercer, Vaudrey. Jon Arnold and Son, Chronometer
       Makers 1762-1843. Introd. by Anthony Randall. London:
       Antiquarian Horological Society, 1972. 300pp, ill, bib

10216 Meteorology. Catalogue of the Collections in the Science
       Museum, South Kensington. London: HMSO, 1922.
       107pp, ill, 6 pls NN, DLC

10217 Middleton, George Alexander Thomas. Surveying and Sur-
       veying Instruments. London: Whittaker, 1894; 2nd ed.
       rev. & enl. London; New York: Whittaker, 1902; London:
       Pitman, 19-? 116pp, pls; 150pp, 8 pls ViU, CU

10218 Middleton, William Edgar Knowles. Catalogue of Meteorologi-
       cal Instruments in the Museum of History and Technology.
       Washington, D.C.: Smithsonian Institution Pr, 1969.

10219 *_____. The History of the Barometer. Baltimore: Johns
       Hopkins Pr, 1964. 516pp, 196 ill (English & American)

10220 *_____. The History of the Thermometer and Its Uses in
       Meteorology. Baltimore: Johns Hopkins Pr, 1966. 249pp,
       ill

10221 _____. Invention of the Meteorological Instruments.
       Baltimore: Johns Hopkins Pr, 1969. 362pp, 233 ill, bib

10222 Moon, Parry Hiram. The Abacus: its history, its design,
       its possibilities in the modern world. New York: Gordon
       & Breach Science Publications, 1971. 179pp, ill

10223 Mudge, Thomas, Jr., 1760-1843. ... A Narrative of Facts
       Relating to Some Timekeepers Constructed by Thomas
       Mudge (senior) for the Discovery of the Longitude at Sea,
       etc.,... London: T. Payne, 1792. 171pp, 1 pls DLC

10224 Needham, (Noel) Joseph (T. M.), Wang Ling, and Derek J.
       de Solla Price. Heavenly Clockwork. The Great Astro-
       nomical Clocks of medieval China. Cambridge, Eng: Uni-
       versity Pr in association with the Antiquarian Horological
       Society, 1960. 253pp, ill, bib

10225 Nelthropp, Henry Leonard. A Catalogue Chronologically Ar-
       ranged of the Collection of Clocks, watches, chronometers,
       movements, sundials, seals, etc., etc., presented to the
       Worshipful Company of Clockmakers. London: Blades,
       East & Blades, 1895; 2nd ed. 1900. 85pp, bib BM

10226 Pullan, J. M. The History of the Abacus. London: Hutch-
       inson, 1968; New York: Praeger, 1969. 127pp, ill

10227 Richeson, Allie Wilson. English Land Measuring to 1880;

instruments and practices. Cambridge, Mass: Society for the History of Technology and M. I. T. Pr, 1966. 214pp, ill, bib

10228 Robertson, John, Librarian to the Royal Society. A Treatise of Such Mathematical Instruments as are Usually Put into a Portable Case ... To which is prefixed a short account of the authors who have treated on the proportional compasses and sector. London: 1747; 2nd ed. enl. London: T. Heath & J. Nourse, 1757. 7 pls; 188pp, ill

10229 Saul, Edward. An Historical and Philosophical Account of the Barometer or Weather-Glass. London: 1730; corr. ed. London: 1735; 3rd ed. London: 1766. BM

10230 Saunders, Harold Nicholas. The Astrolabe: a brief account of its history and construction together with practical instructions showing how it was used and can still be used for solving many astronomical problems. Bude, Cornwall: Author, 1971. 35pp, ill, bib

10231 Scott, Dunbar D., and others. The evolution of Mine-Surveying Instruments, comprising the original papers of Mr. Scott on the subject, together with the discussion thereof, and independent contributions on the subject. New York: American Institute of Mining Engineers, 1902. 324pp, ill DLC

10232 Simms, Frederic Walter, 1803-1865. A Treatise on the Principal Mathematical Instruments Employed in Surveying, levelling, and astronomy: explaining their construction, adjustments and use. 6th ed. London: Troughton & Simms, 1844. 130pp, ill DLC

10233 Smith, John, clockmaker. A Compleat Discourse of the Nature, use and right managing of that wonderfull instrument the baroscope or quick-silver weather glass. London: 1688. BM

10234 Stanley, William Ford. A Descriptive Treatise on Mathematical Drawing Instruments, their construction, uses, qualities ... and suggestions for improvement; with hints upon drawing and colouring. London: 1866; 2nd ed. 1868; 5th ed. London: E. & F. N. Spon, 1887; 6th ed. as Mathematical Drawing and Measuring Instruments. 1888.   ;   ; 307pp; 346pp

10235 _____. Surveying and Levelling Instruments Theoretically and Practically Described. London: E. & F. N. Spon, 1890; 3rd ed. 1901. 552pp; 562pp BM

10236 Stephan, W. G. Drawing Instruments. London: E. & F. N. Spon, 1908.

10237   Sturmy, Samuel. The Mariners Magazine, or Sturmy's
        Mathematical and Practical Arts. Containing, The de-
        scription and use of the scale of scales...; The art of
        navigation...; A new way of surveying the land...; The
        art of gauging all sorts of vessels...; The art of dial-
        ling.... 7 parts. London: E. Cotes, 1669; 3rd ed.
        corr. by J. Colson, ... with The making and use of
        divers mathematical instruments.... 2 parts. London:
        1684, 83. v.p. BM

10238   *Taylor, Eva Germaine Rimington. The Haven Finding Art:
        a history of navigation from Odysseus to Captain Cook.
        Fore. by K. St. B. Collins. London: Hollis & Carter,
        1956; New York: Abelard-Schuman, 1957. 295pp, ill;
        310pp, 25 pls (Includes appendix on Chinese medieval
        navigation, based on research by Joseph Needham) NN

10239   *   . The Mathematical Practitioners of Hanoverian
        England, 1714-1840. London: Cambridge U. Pr, for
        the Institute of Navigation, 1966. 503pp, ill, 12 pls,
        bib (Includes a catalog of makers and users)

10240   *   . The Mathematical Practitioners of Tudor and
        Stuart England, 1485-1714. London: Cambridge U. Pr,
        for the Institute of Navigation, 1954. 443pp, ill, 12 pls,
        bib (Includes 400 users and makers)

10241   *   , and M. W. Richey. The Geometrical Seaman: a
        book of early nautical instruments. London: Hollis &
        Carter, for Institute of Navigation, 1962. 112pp, 37 pls
        (Compasses, sextants, chronometers, etc.)

10242   Thompson, Silvanus Phillips, 1851-1916. The Rose of the
        Winds: the origin and development of the compass-card.
        London: H. Milford, Oxford U. Pr, for the British
        Academy, 1914. 81pp, ill, 6 color pls, bib

10243   Tyas, Robert. The Weather Glass: concise description of
        the barometer.... London: 1871; A Companion to the
        Weather Glass. Periodical. London: 1868- .

10244   Vance, David, and Cornelia Corson. Computers in the Mu-
        seum. White Plains, NY: International Business Ma-
        chines Corp., 1973. 69pp, ill, bib

10245   *Waters, David Watkin. The Art of Navigation in England
        in Elizabethan and Early Stuart Times. London: Hollis
        & Carter; New Haven: Yale U. Pr, 1958. 696pp, ill,
        pls, bib

WEIGHTS, MEASURES AND SCALES

10246   Barker, William Robert. Ancient Standard Weights and
        Measures of the City of Bristol. Bristol, Eng: J. W.
        Arrowsmith, 1908. 27pp, pls, facsims of marks V & A

10247   Bendick, Jeanne. How Much and How Many: the story of
        weights and measures. New York: Whittlesey House,
        1947; rev. & enl. ed. Leicester: Brockhampton Pr; New
        York: Whittlesey, 1960; 2nd rev. ed. 1970. 188pp, ill,
        bib (Juvenile literature)

10248   Berriman, Algernon Edward. Historical Metrology; a new
        analysis of the archaeological and the historical evidence
        relating to weights and measures. London: Dent; New
        York: Dutton, 1953; New York: Greenwood, 1969. 224pp,
        65 ill, bib

10249   *Chisholm, Henry William, 1809- . On the Science of
        Weighing and Measuring and Standards of Measure and
        Weight. New York; London: Macmillan, 1877. 192pp,
        ill NN, CU, PPL

10250   Cleland, James, 1770-1840. An Historical Account of the
        Local and Imperial Weights and Measures of Lanark
        (County) and an Inventory of Those Belonging to the Cor-
        poration of Glasgow. Glasgow: J. Smith (?), 1832. DLC

10251   Dent, Herbert Crowley, 1860- . Old English Bronze Wool-
        Weights. Norwich: H. W. Hunt, 1927. 32pp, 29 pls NN

10252   Details of Weights and Measures Exposed at the World's
        Columbian Exposition by the Bureau of Commerce and
        Industry ... Japan. Tokyo: M. Onuki, printer, 1903
        (i.e. 1893). 9pp DeWint

10253   Ellis, Keith. Man and Measurement. London: Priory Pr,
        1973. 128pp, ill, bib

10254   Graham, John Thomas. Weights and Measures Then and
        Now. Exeter, Eng: Wheaton, 1964. 113pp, ill (Juvenile
        literature)

10255   *Irwin, Keith Gordon. The Romance of Weights and Measures.
        New York: Viking, 1960. 144pp, ill

10256   *Kisch, Bruno. Scales and Weights; a historical outline.
        New Haven; London: Yale U. Pr, 1966. 297pp, ill, bib
        (From earliest times)

10257   Lane-Poole, Stanley. Catalogue of Arabic Glass Weights in
        the British Museum. Ed. by Reginald S. Poole. London:
        The Trustees, 1891. 127pp, 9 pls PPULC, DLC, BM

10258   Langwith, Benjamin, 1684?-1743.   Observations on Doctor
        Arbuthnot's Dissertation on Coins, Weights, and Measures.
        London: D. Browne, 1747.   43pp   MiU

10259   Mattimoe, George E., and Robert H. Nagao.   A Brief
        History of Weights and Measures in Hawaii.   Honolulu:
        Weights and Measures Branch, State Department of Agri-
        culture, 1967.   85 leaves, ill

10260   *Pioneers in Industry.   Chicago: Fairbanks, Morse & Co,
        1945.   (Manufacturers of scales)

10261   Sheppard, Thomas, and J. F. Musham.   Money Scales and
        Weights.   London: Spink & Co, 1923.   221pp, ill   (In-
        cludes English coin weights, Edward III to Victorian, in
        Hull Museum)

10262   Skinner, Frederick George.   Weights and Measures: Their
        ancient origins and their development in Great Britain up
        to A.D. 1855.   Science Museum.   London: HMSO, 1967.
        117pp, ill, 16 pls

10263   Walker, James, M. A.   The Theory and Use of a Physical
        Balance.   Oxford, Eng: Clarendon Pr, 1887.   40pp, ill

10264   Zupko, Ronald Edward.   A Dictionary of English Weights
        and Measures; from Anglo-Saxon times to the 19th century.
        Madison: U. of Wisconsin Pr, 1968.   224pp, bib

WEATHERVANES, WHIRLIGIGS AND LIGHTNING RODS†

10265   Anderson, Richard.   Lightning Conductors, their history,
        nature, and mode of application.   London; New York: E.
        & F. N. Spon, 1879, 1880; 3rd ed. enl. 1885.   256pp,
        ill, bib; 470pp, ill   BPL, BM

10266   Buchert, Ilse, and Alexander Nesbitt.   Weathercocks and
        Weathercreatures; some examples of early American folk
        art from the collection of the Shelburne Museum, Vermont.
        Newport, RI: Third & Elm Pr, 1970.   46pp, ill

10267   Fiske, J. W., 1893 Catalog: Copper weathervanes, bannerets,
        lightning rods, stable fixtures.   Facsim. reprint with intro-
        duction.   Princeton, NJ: Pyne Pr, 1971.   152pp, ill

10268   *Fitzgerald, Ken.   Weathervanes and Whirligigs.   New York:
        Bramhall, C. N. Potter, 1967.   186pp, 180 drawings

†Most of the books on American folk art in Section XV include
weathervanes and whirligigs.

10269   Hands, Alfred. Lightning and the Churches. London: J.
         W. Gray, 1909; 2nd ed. 1910. 92pp, ill DAS

10270   _____. Scientific Protection. A guide to the proper ap-
         plication of lightning conductors. n.p.: 1902. u.p.
         DAS

10271   Henry, Alfred Judson, 1858-1931. Lightning and Lightning
         Conductors. Washington, D.C.: GPO, 1909. 20pp, ill
         NN, DLC

10272   Kaye, Myrna. Yankee Weathervanes. New York: Dutton,
         1975. 236pp, drawings, bib

10273   Klamkin, Charles. Weather Vanes; the history, design and
         manufacture of an American folk art. New York: Haw-
         thorne, 1973. 209pp, 350 ill, bib

10274   Lightning Conductors!!! Otis's patent insulated lightning
         conductor. New York: Lyon Manufacturing, 1854; as
         Lightning Conductors!!! ... The only method of absolute
         protection against lightning, as demonstrated by science
         and experience. New York: Lyon, 1858. 28pp, ill;
         36pp, ill NN, DLC

10275   Lodge, Sir Oliver Joseph, 1851-1940. Lightning Conductors
         and Lightning Guards. A treatise on the protection of
         buildings, of telegraph instruments and submarine cables,
         and of electric installations generally, from damage by
         atmospheric discharges. London: Whittaker; New York:
         Macmillan, 1885; 1892. 544pp, ill, 19 pls BM, PPL,
         NjP, ViU

10276   Lyon, Lucius, 1817-1892. A Treatise on Lightning Conductors;

compiled from a work on thunderstorms, by Sir William
S. Harris, F. R. S., and other standard authors. New
York: Putnam, 1853; 2nd ed. 1855. 191pp, ill; 240pp,
ill CU, NN

10277   Messent, Claude John Wilson. The Weather Vanes of Norfolk
        and Norwich. Norwich, Eng: Fletcher & Son, 1937.
        127pp, 112 ill DLC

10278   Needham, Albert. English Weathervanes; their stories and
        legends from medieval to modern times. Haywards
        Heath, Sussex: C. Clarke, 1953. 102pp, 275 drawings

10279   Pagdin, William Edward. The Story of the Weathercock;
        all illustrated by the author. Stockton-on-Tees: Author,
        by E. Appleby, 1949. 99pp, ill DLC

10280   Quimby, A. M., and Son, New York. Circular of A. M.
        Quimby and Son, dealers in Quimby's improved lightning
        rods for houses and vessels ... a review of the merits
        of several modes of constructing lightning rods, together
        with some information of general interest. New York:
        Baker & Godwin, printers, 1862. 18pp DLC

10281   _____. A Description of Quimby's Improved Lightning
        Rods.... New York: Quimby, 1852. 14pp DLC

10282   Spencer, Corinne W., comp. Bibliography of Weathervanes.
        New York: Avery Library, Columbia U., 1938. 12pp
        typescript (Mainly periodical literature references) NNC-
        Ave

10283   Watson, Sir William, M.D. Observations Upon the Effects
        of Lightning, with an account of the apparatus proposed to
        prevent its mischiefs to buildings. London: 1764. BM

        Weathervanes/1893. See: Fiske, J. W. ..., above.

10284   Zeda, Umberto. Telephones and Lightning Conductors. Tr.
        from Italian by S. R. Bottone. London: Pitman, 1907.
        100pp, 60 ill BM

SUNDIALS

10285 *The Book of Old Sundials and Their Mottoes. Illustrated by
        Alfred Rawlings and Warrington Hogg. "Old Sundials,"
        by Launcelot Cross. Boston; London: T. N. Foulis, 1914;
        reprint. London; Boston: 1917; Edinburgh; London: 1922.
        102pp, 36 ill, 8 col pls NN, CtY, DLC

10286   Cousins, Frank W. Sundials: The Art and Science of

Gnomics. New York: Universe, 1970. 247pp, drawings,
bib

10287 Dawbarn, Albert Yelverton. The Sun-Dial. Explanation of
the Principle, construction, and use of the sun-dial. London: 1891. BM

10288 Dolan, Winthrop W. A Choice of Sundials. Brattleboro, Vt:
Stephen Greene Pr, 1975. 148pp, ill, bib (European and
American)

10289 *Earle, Alice Morse. Sun-Dials and Roses of Yesterday;
garden delights which are here displayed in every truth and
are moreover regarded as emblems. New York; London:
Macmillan, 1902; 1922; reprint. Detroit: Singing Tree Pr,
1969; Rutland, Vt: Tuttle, 1971. 461pp, many ill, pls

10290 Fale, Thomas, fl. 1604. Horologiographia;/The art of dialling:/Teaching an easie and perfect way/to make all kinds
of dials upon any/ plaine plat howsoever placed:/ with the
drawing of the twelve signes, and/ houres unequall in them
all. / Whereunto is annexed the making and use of other
dials and instruments, whereby the houre of the day and
night is known. London: printed by Thomas Orwin, dwelling in Pater-noster Rowe against the signe of the Checker,
1593; London: F. Kyngston, 1626; 1627; 1633; 1652;....
facsim. reprint. Amsterdam: Theatrum Orbis Terrarum;
New York: Da Capo Pr, 1971. 40pp, 60 pls; ...; ...;
...; 60pp, ill, 16 leaves NN, MiU, DFo

10291 Ferguson, James, 1710-1776. Select Mechanical Exercises:
shewing how to construct different clocks, orreries, and
sun-dials, on plain and easy principles ... with tables....
London: printed for W. Strahan; ... T. Cadell (Cadeli?),
1773; 2nd ed. London: 1778; 3rd ed. London: for W.
Strahan and T. Cadeli, 1790. ...; ...; 272pp, 9 folding
pls MH, DLC, DeWint

10292 Fothergill, George Algernon. A North Country Album. Notes
of the signs and sundials in North Yorkshire and Durham.
Darlington, Eng: 1901. 126pp

10293 *Gatty, Margaret Scott (Mrs. Alfred). The Book of Sun-Dials.
London: Bell & Daldy, 1872; new & enl. ed. by H. K. F.
Gatty and Eleanor Lloyd, with appendix on construction of
dials by W. Richardson. London: G. Bell, 1889; 3rd ed.
enl. 1890; 4th ed. enl. & re-ed. by Horatia K. F. Eden
and Eleanor Lloyd, with "Portable Sundials," by Lewis
Evans. London: Bell, 1900. 156pp, 5 pls; 502pp, ill;
578pp, ill; 529pp, ill, 9 pls DeWint, ViU, DLC

10294 Good, John, fl. 1706-1733, teacher of mathematics. The

Art of Shadows: or, Universal-dialling; with tables exactly
calculated for the latitude of 51 degrees 30 minutes, viz.
London. Teaching any person to draw a true sun-dial....
2nd ed. London: J. Robinson, 1711; 3rd ed. London: R.
Mount, 1721; 3rd ed. London; Page, 1731. ; 184pp, 2
pls CtY, PP

10295 Gorham Company. Crehore Sun-Dial, a new sun-dial that
tells standard time. New York: Gorham, 192-? 7pp,
ill (Inventor: Albert C. Crehore) NNC-Ave

10296 Gunter, Edmund. The Description and Use of His Majesties
Dials in White-Hall Garden. London: B. Norton & J.
Bill, 1624. 59pp BM

10297 Heape, Richard. Old Sun-dials In or Near the Ancient Parish
of Rochdale. Rochdale, Eng: J. D. Howarth, 1920. 15pp

10298 Henslow, Thomas Geoffrey Wall. Ye Sun-dial Booke. Fore.
by Beverley Nichols. London: W. & G. Foyle, 1914;
1935. 422pp, 350 drawings, 2 pls (Chiefly verses & mottoes) MiU, NN

10299 Herbert, Alan Patrick. Sundials Old and New, or, Fun with
the sun. Introd. by D. W. Waters. London: Methuen,
1967. 198pp, ill

10300 Horne, Ethelbert. Primitive Sun Dials or Scratch Dials.
Pref. by John Charles Cox. Taunton, Eng: Barnicott &
Pearce, 1917. 90pp, pls BM

10301 _____. Scratch Dials: their description and history.
London: S. Marshall, 1929. 62pp, ill NN, BM

10302 Leybourn, William, 1626-1700? The Art of Dialing: plain,
concave, convex, projective, reflective, refractive. Shewing how to make all such dials, and to adorn them with
all useful furniture, relating to the course of the sun,
performed, arithmetically, geometrically, instrumentally
and mechanically. London: S. G. & B. G., printers for
B. Tooke and T. Sawbridge, 1669; 2nd ed. 1681; London:
for A. Churchill, 1682. 175pp, diagrams; ...; 308pp, ill,
pls NNC-Ave, DLC, PBL

10303 MacGibbon, David, and Thomas Ross. Castellated and Do-
mestic Architecture of Scotland from the 12th to 18th
Century. 5 vol. Edinburgh: Douglas, 1887-1892. ill
(Vol. 5 includes 157 page section "Scottish Sundials") NN,
MB

10304 Marshall, Roy Kenneth. Sundials. New York: Macmillan;
London: Collier-Macmillan, 1963. 127pp, ill

10305 Mayall, Robert Newton, and Margaret Mayall. Sundials; how to know, use, and make them. Boston: Hale, Cushman, Flint, 1938. 197pp, ill, pls (Includes description of the David Eugene Smith Collection of Astronomical Instruments)

10306 Rawlings, Alfred. A Little Book of Sundial Mottoes. London; Boston: T. N. Foulis, 1914; 1923. 37pp, ill, 4 color pls

10307 Rohr, Rene R. Sundials: history, theory and practice. Tr. from French by Gabriel Goden. Toronto: U. of Toronto Pr, 1970. 142pp, ill

10308 Shephard, Geoffrey Colin. Queens' College Dial: a short description of the sun dial.... Cambridge: Author, 195-?; 1957; 1972. ; 11pp, ill; 14pp, ill

10309 *Spackman, Henry Spicer. The Timepiece of Shadows, a history of the sun-dial. New York: W. T. Comstock, 1895. 110pp, ill

10310 *Ward, Francis Alan Burnett. Timekeepers: clocks, watches, sundials, sand-glasses. Science Museum. London: HMSO, 1963. 46pp, ill (1500-1764)

10311 Young, Francis Chilton, ed. Mechanical Work in Garden and Greenhouse. 3 parts. 1. Geometry for Gardeners, F. C. Young. 2. Sundials and Dialling, Arthur Yorke. 3. Greenhouse Building and Heating, various writers. London: Ward & Lock, 1893. 105pp, ill

GENERAL WORKS ON CLOCKS AND WATCHES

10312 *Abbott, Henry George (pseud.). Antique Watches and How to Establish Their Age. Portraits and brief biographical sketches of the celebrated watchmakers of the world, and a directory of over 6,000 names of English, French, German, Dutch, Swiss and American watch and clock makers who were in business prior to the year 1850.... Chicago: G. K. Hazlitt, 1897. 204pp, many ill, pls BM

10313 _____ . History of Time Measurement and of Time-Measuring Instruments; an historical sketch of horology from the earliest ages to the present time--world-famed workers in their field and their achievements. New York: Calculagraph Co, 1913. 38pp

10314 Aked, Charles Kenneth, comp., with Mrs. R. K. Shenton. Horology in Provincial and Rural Museums. Wadhurst, Sussex: Antiquarian Horological Society, 1974. 46pp, bib

10315 All Sorts of Files, Tools, and Engines for Clock and Watch
       Makers, Gold and Silversmiths, and Jewellers' Tools,
       Engine, Oval, and Common Lathes, Rollers or Flatting
       Mills, etc. Made and sold by Ford, Whitmore, and
       Brunton. Birmingham, Eng: n. d. ill SKM

10316 *Allix, Charles. Carriage Clocks, Their History and Develop-
       ment. Woodbridge, Suffolk: Baron, Antique Collectors
       Club, 1974. 484pp, 500 ill, 15 color pls, gloss (French,
       English, Swiss, German, Japanese, Italian, Argentinian,
       and American portable clocks)

10317 Antiquarian Horology, and the Proceedings of the Antiquarian
       Horological Society. Quarterly. London: 19?- .

10318 Asprey & Co. The Clockwork of the Heavens. Exhibition of
       astronomical clocks, watches, and allied scientific instru-
       ments, presented by Asprey with the help of Harriet Wyn-
       ter, and collaboration of various museums and private col-
       lections. London: Asprey, 1973. 92pp, ill, bib (To
       1854)

10319 Bailey, Roy Rutherford. Romance and History of Time.
       2 vol. Chicago: Elgin National Watch Co, 1922. color
       ill, text

10320 _____ . Through the Ages with Father Time. A series
       of world-wide adventures on the road from long ago to
       now. Chicago: Wells, 1922. 192pp, ill, pls (Watches,
       clocks, sundials, etc. from prehistoric times to 1921)

10321 Baillie, Granville Hugh. Clocks and Watches; an historical
       bibliography. Fore. by Harold Spencer-Jones. London:
       N. A. G. Pr, 1951. 414pp, ill NN, DLC

10322 _____ . Watches--their history, decoration, and mechanism.
       London: Methuen, 1929. 383pp, ill, color frontis, 75 pls
       (some color), bib BM

10323 * _____ . Watchmakers and Clockmakers of the World.
       London: Methuen, 1929; 2nd ed. London: N. A. G. Pr,
       1947; 3rd enl. ed. London: 1953. 415pp, bib; 388pp;
       388pp (Information on 36, 000 makers to 1825) NN, BM

10324 Bain, Alexander, electrician. Short History of Electric
       Clocks. London: Chapman & Hall, 1852; facsim. reprint.
       ed. by W. D. Hackmann. London: Turner & Devereux,
       1973. 32pp, ill (Clocks manufactured by Bain)

10325 Barr, Lockwood Anderson. The Origin of the Clock Label.
       Reprint from the Bulletin of the National Association of
       Watch and Clock Collectors, December 1955, Vol. 7, no.
       61. Columbia, Pa: 1955? 8pp

10326   _____. Women Clockmakers. New York: n.d. typescript PPF

10327 *Bassermann-Jordon, Ernst Von. The Book of Old Clocks
and Watches. Germany: 1914; 1920; 1922; 4th ed. rev.
by Hans von Bertele. Tr. from German by H. Alan
Lloyd. London: Allen & Unwin; New York: Crown, 1964.
523pp, ill, 20 pls, bib (Essential, standard work)

10328 Beckett, Sir Edmund. Clock and Watch Work. From the
8th edition of the Encyclopaedia Britannica. Edinburgh:
A. & C. Black, 1855. 144pp, ill NN, DLC

10329   _____. Clocks and Locks. From the Encyclopaedia
Britannica. 2nd ed. with a full account of the great clock
at Westminster. Edinburgh: A. & C. Black; London:
Longmans, 1857. 236pp, ill (Clocks, locks & keys,
"Big Ben")

10330   _____. Lectures on Church Building, Bells and Clocks.
London: Bell & Daldy, 1856. ECB

10331 * _____. A Rudimentary Treatise on Clock and Watch
Making: with a chapter on church clocks; and an account
of the proceedings respecting the Great Westminster Clock.
London: J. Weale, 1850; ...; 4th ed. enl. 1860; 5th ed.
London: Virtue, 1868; ...; 8th ed. with a new preface
and new list of great bells, and an appendix on weather-
cocks, etc. London: Crosby Lockwood, 1903; as A Rudimentary Treatise on Clocks, watches and bells for public
purposes. London: Virtue, 1862; ...; 7th ed. 1883; 8th
ed. 1903; facsim. reprint of 8th ed. Wakefield, Eng: EP
Pub, 1974. 279pp, ill; 434pp, ill; 424pp, ill; 404pp, 81
ill; 404pp, ill

10332 Beevers, S. Benson, comp. The John Gershom Parkington
Memorial Collection of Time Measurement Instruments.
Reprint from Connoisseur Yearbook. Parkeston, Eng:
Beevers, 1958. 15pp, ill

10333 Benson, James William. Time and Time-Tellers. (On
dials, clocks and watches.) London: Robert Hardwicke,
1875; London: J. W. Benson, 1902. 189pp, ill; 136pp,
ill NN, DLC, BM

10334   _____. Turret Clocks. London: 1882. 70pp

10335 Bentley, W. J. (pseud. for Ullyett, Kenneth.) Looking for
Clocks and Watches. London: Corgi, 1973. 94pp

10336   _____. The Plain Man's Guide to Antique Clocks. London: Joseph, 1963. 96pp, ill, 20 pls

10337   Borland, Kathryn Kilby, and Helen Ross Speicher. <u>Clocks,</u>
        <u>from Shadow to Atom.</u> Chicago: Follett, 1969. <u>62pp,</u>
        <u>ill, 2 pls</u>

10338   *Brearley, Harry Chase. <u>Time Telling Through the Ages.</u>
        New York: Doubleday, Page, for Robert H. Ingersoll Co,
        1919. 294pp, ill, pls, bib (Includes appendix of well-
        known private and public collections) NN, DLC

10339   *Britten, Frederick James, 1843-1913. <u>Former Clock and</u>
        <u>Watchmakers and Their Work. Including an account of</u>
        <u>the development of horological instruments from the</u>
        <u>earliest mechanisms, with portraits of masters of the art,</u>
        <u>a directory of over 5000 names, and some examples of</u>
        <u>modern construction.</u> London: F. N. Spon; New York:
        Spon & Chamberlain, 1894. 397pp, ill MiD, NN, PPULC

10340   *_____. <u>Old Clocks and Watches and Their Makers; a his-</u>
        <u>torical and descriptive account of the different styles of</u>
        <u>clocks and watches of the past in England and abroad con-</u>
        <u>taining a list of nearly 8000 (10,000; 11,000; 12,000;</u>
        <u>14,000) makers.</u> London: Batsford; New York: Scrib-
        ner's, 1899; 2nd ed. 1904; 3rd ed. London: 1911; 4th ed.,
        comprising the chapters on old clocks from "Old Clocks
        and Watches and Their Makers," together with the com-
        plete list of makers from the same, with add. & corr.
        London: Batsford; New York: Scribner, 1919; 5th ed.
        London: E. & F. N. Spon, 1922; Deluxe 6th ed. com-
        bines 4th and 5th ed.; 7th ed. by G. H. Baillie, C. Clut-
        ton, and C. A. Ilbert. New York: Dutton; London: E.
        & F. N. Spon, 1956; Facsim. reprint of 6th ed. Wake-
        field, Eng: S. R. Publishers, 1971; 8th ed. new and enl.
        by Cecil Clutton. London: Eyre Methuen, 1973. 500pp,
        ill; 735pp, 700 ill; 790pp, ill; 597pp, ill; 822pp, 859 ill;
        899pp, ill; 518pp, ill; 586pp, 278 (4 color) pls; all with
        bib and gloss

10341   _____. <u>The Watch Repairers' Instructor; a practical</u>
        <u>handybook on cleaning, repairing and adjusting....</u> Based
        on P. N. Hasluck's <u>The Watch Jobbers' Handy Book...,</u>
        no. 10393.

10342   Bruton, Eric. <u>Clocks and Watches.</u> Feltham, Eng: Ham-
        lyn, 1968. 140pp, ill

10343   _____. <u>Clocks and Watches, 1400-1900.</u> London: Barker;
        New York: Praeger, 1967. 208pp, ill, 40 pls

10344   _____. <u>Dictionary of Clocks and Watches.</u> London:
        1962; New York: Archer House, 1963. 210pp, ill

10345   _____. <u>The Long Case Clock.</u> London: Arco, 1964;

New York: Praeger, 1968; 1974. 146pp, ill; ...; 156pp, 49 ill

10346 _____. The True Book About Clocks. London: F. Muller, 1957. 144pp, ill

10347 Buck, John Henry. Collection of Watches Loaned to the Metropolitan Museum of Art ... by Mrs. George A. Hearn. New York: priv. printed, Gilliss Pr, 1907. many ill (87 watches)

10348 Buckley, Francis. Old Watchmakers. Uppermill: Moore & Edwards, 1929. 6pp, pls

10349 Carpenter, William Benjamin, 1813-1885. Mechanical Philosophy, Horology, and Astronomy; being an exposition of the properties of matter and of their mode of action; the construction of instruments for the measurement of time; and a description of the heavenly bodies. London: W. S. Orr, 1843; 1844; 1848; 1850; new ed. London: H. G. Bohn, 1857; new ed. London: G. Bell, 1877. 575pp, 175 ill DLC, PPULC

10350 Catalogue of the Clocks, etc., in the Wallace Collection. London: Hertford House, 1905. 404pp (Strong on French clocks)

10351 Catalogue of Timepieces. Exeter, NH: Adams Brown, 1969. 60pp, ill (Tools, music boxes, clocks, watches, barometers)

10352 Chamberlain, Paul Mellen. It's About Time. New York: Richard R. Smith, 1941; reprint. London: Holland Pr, 1964. 490pp, ill, bib (Three parts: 1. escapements; 2. experiments and unusual timepieces; 3. famous watchmakers, histories and descriptions. Book compiled from articles published before his death)

10353 *Chapuis, Alfred, and Eugene Jaquet. The History of the Self-Winding Watch, 1770-1931. English adaptation by R. Savare Grandvoinet. Neuchatel: Editions du Griffon; London: Batsford, 1956. 246pp, 154 ill, color frontis

10354 Cipolla, Carlo Maria. Clocks and Culture, 1300-1700. London: Collins; New York: Walker, 1967. 192pp, ill. 6 pls, bib (Relationship in Europe between mechanical clocks and science and philosophy)

10355 Clock Guide: identification with prices. Des Moines: Wallace-Homestead, 1955. 121pp, ill (some color)

10356 Clocks and Watches. (Prepared with the cooperation of the

Science Service.) Garden City, NY: Doubleday, 1968.
64pp, ill

10357 *Clutton, Cecil, and George Daniels. Watches of Europe
and America. London: Batsford; London: Studio Vista;
New York: Viking, 1965; 2nd ed. as Watches. London:
Batsford, 1971. 159pp, 597 ill, 84 pls; 260pp, 624 ill
(Mid-16th to mid-19th century, emphasis on 1780-1830)

10358 Collectors' Pieces: clocks and watches. Exhibition. Science Museum, London, May-August 1964. London: Antiquarian Horological Society, May 1964; 2nd ed. rev. July
1964. 91pp, ill, bib

10359 Crom, Theodore R. Horological Wheel Cutting Engines,
1700-1900. Gainesville, ?: 1970. 150pp, ill, bib

10360 Cumhaill, P. W. (pseud.) Investing in Clocks and Watches.
London: Barrie & Rockliff; New York: Potter, 1967;
London: Corgi, 1971. 159pp, 200 ill, 16 color pls, bib
(ca.1430-ca.1900)

10361 Cumming, Alexander, 1733-1814. The Elements of Clock
and Watch Work, adapted to practice. In two essays.
London: Author, 1766. 192pp, ill, 16 pls NN, BM

10362 Cunynghame, Sir Henry Hardinge Samuel. Time and Clocks:
ancient and modern methods of measuring time. London:
Constable; New York: Dutton; 1906; reprint. Detroit:
Singing Tree Pr, 1970. 200pp, ill, 1 pl PPL, DLC, NN

10363 Cuss, Theodore Patrick Camerer. The Country Life Book
of Watches. London: Country Life, 1967. 128pp, ill,
4 pls

10364 _____ . Early Watches. Feltham: Hamlyn, for Country
Life, 1971. 63pp, ill (1500-1715)

10365 * _____ . The Story of Watches. London: MacGibbon &
Kee; New York: Philosophical Library, 1952. 176pp, ill,
bib NN, DLC

10366 Daniels, George. English and American Watches. London;
New York: Abelard-Schuman, 1967. 128pp, ill, bib

10367 De Carle, Donald. Clocks and Their Value: illustrated guide
to ancient and modern clocks with a unique chart of all
known Tompion clocks. London: N. A. G. Pr, 1968;
2nd ed. 1971. 144pp, ill, bib; 159pp, ill, bib

10368 _____ . Watchmakers' and Clockmakers' Encyclopedic Dictionary. London: N.A.G. Pr, 1950. 252pp, ill

10369 *Dent, Edward John, 1790-1835. On the Construction and
      Management of Chronometers, clocks and watches. Lon-
      don: Author, 1844; 1846; 1851; reprint. 1951; reprint of
      1844 ed. Exeter, NH: Adams Brown, 197-? 32pp, 12
      ill

10370 Derham, William, M. A. (or F. R. S.) The Artificial
      Clock-Maker. A treatise of watch, and clock-work: where-
      in the art of calculating numbers for most sorts of move-
      ments is explained ... Also the history of clockwork ....
      by W. D. London: James Knapton, 1696; 2nd ed. enl.
      2 parts and supplement. 1700; ...; 4th ed. as The Artifi-
      cial Clock-maker, a treatise of watch and clock-work,
      shewing to the meanest capacities the art of calculating
      numbers to all sorts of movements, the way to alter clock-
      work, to make chimes and set them to musical notes, and
      to calculate and correct the motion of pendulums: also
      numbers for divers movements; with the antient and modern
      history of clock-work; and many instruments, tables and
      other matters.... London: James, John and Paul Knapton,
      1734. 132pp; ...; 140pp BM

10371 Dondi, Giovanni de. The Planetarium of G. de Dondi, Citizen
      of Padua: a manuscript of 1397. Tr. from Latin by Gran-
      ville Hugh Baillie; with additional material from another
      Dondi manuscript translated from Latin by Herbert Alan
      Lloyd. Ed. by F. A. B. Ward. London: Antiquarian
      Horological Society, 1974. 156pp, ill (some color)

10372 DuPuis, Nathan Fellowes, 1836-1917. The Measures and the
      Measurement of Time. Reprint from "Queen's Quarterly."
      Kingston, Ontario: Jackson Pr, 1915; 1940. 147pp

10373 Edwardes, Ernest Lawrence. Weight-Driven Chamber Clocks
      of the Middle Ages and Renaissance 1350-1680; with some
      observations concerning certain larger clocks of medieval
      time. Vol. I. of Old Weight-Driven Chamber Clocks,
      1350-1850 series. Altrincham, Eng: J. Sherratt, 1965.
      160pp, ill, 52 pls, bib

10374 Ehrhardt, Roy. The Pocket Watch Guide. Kansas City:
      Heart of America Pr, 1972; Book 2. 1974. 120pp, 4pp of
      pictures (2600 watches & prices)

10375 _____ . The Timekeeper. Kansas City: Heart of America
      Pr, 1972.

10376 _____ . Trade Marks on Watch Cases, Pocket Watches,
      Gold Rings. Kansas City: Heart of America Pr, 1975.
      44pp, ill

10377 Electric Clocks and Chimes; a practical handbook giving

complete instructions for the making of successful electrical timepieces, synchronised clock systems, and chiming
mechanisms. London: P. Marshall, 1921; rev. ed. 1929.
159pp, ill, diag. NN, DLC

10378   Ferguson, James, 1710-1776. Select Mechanical Exercises:
shewing how to construct different clocks, orreries, and
sun-dials, on plain and easy principles ... with tables....
London: printed for W. Strahan; and T. Cadell, 1773;
2nd ed. London: 1778; 3rd ed. London: for Strahan and
Cadeli (?), 1790. ...; ...; 272pp, 9 folding pls MH,
DLC, DeWint

10379   Fleet, Simon. Clocks. London: Weidenfeld & Nicolson;
New York: Putnam, 1961; London: Octopus, 1972. 128pp,
135 ill; 96pp, ill

10380   400 Years of Watchmaking. Exhibition. Rolex Watch U.S.A.,
Inc. New York: Rolex, 1974. ill (Primarily collection
of Anthony A. Benis. 1580-1939)

10381   Fried, Henry B. Calvacade of Time; a visual history of
watches. From the private collection of the Zale Corporation. Dallas: 1968. 126pp, color ill

10382   . The James W. Packard Collection of Unusual and
Complicated Watches, owned and presented by the Horological Institute of America. Indianapolis?: the Institute,
1959. 44pp, ill

10383   Gazeley, William John. Clock and Watch Escapements. London: Heywood, 1956. 294pp, ill

10384   . Watch and Clock Making and Repairing; dealing
with the construction and repair of watches, clocks and
chronometers. London: Heywood; New York: Van Nostrand, 1953. 440pp, ill

10385   Gillingham, Harrold Edgar. Early Time Telling Devices.
An address ... Bucks County Historical Society, September 26, 1936. n.p.: 1937. 12pp PHi

10386   *Goodrich, Ward L. The Modern Clock. A Study of time
keeping mechanism; its construction, regulation and repair.
Chicago: Hazlitt & Walker, 1905; 2nd ed. Chicago: North
American Watch Tool & Supply Co, 1950; 9th printing.
Chicago: 1970. 502pp, many ill

10387 *   . The Watchmakers Lathe, its use and abuse; a
story of the lathe in its various forms, past and present,
its construction and proper uses.... Chicago: Hazlitt &
Walker, 1903; Chicago: 1952; reprint. 1972. 264pp, ill
DLC, MB

10388 Gordon, George Francis Carter. Clockmaking Past and
       Present. With which is incorporated the more important
       portions of "Clocks, Watches, and Bells," by the Late
       Lord Grimthorpe, relating to turret clocks and gravity
       escapements. London: C. Lockwood, 1925; London:
       Technical Pr, 1928; 1946; 2nd ed. enl. by Arthur V. May.
       London: Technical Pr, 1949. ...; ...; ...; 232pp, ill,
       bib NN

10389 Great Britain. Patent Office. Library. Subject List of
       Works on Horology (comprising determination and division
       of time, dialing, clocks, watches, and other time-keepers)
       in the Library of the Patent Office. London: HMSO, 1912.
       56pp DLC

10390 *Guye, Samuel, and Henri Michel. Time and Space: measur-
       ing instruments from the 15th to the 19th century. Tr.
       from French by Diana Dolan. London: Pall Mall Pr,
       1970; New York: Praeger, 1971. 289pp, ill, 140 pls
       (London), 20 pls (NY)

10391 Hagans, Orville Roberts. Horological Collection, Clock
       Manor Museum, Evergreen, Colorado. Denver: Golden
       Bell Pr, 1964. 72pp, ill, pls (Collection of O. R. Ha-
       gans and Josephine Hagans)

10392 Hasluck, Paul Nooncree, ed. The Clock Jobbers' Handybook.
       A Practical Manual on cleaning, repairing and adjusting:
       embracing information on the tools, materials, appliances
       and processes employed in clockwork. London: Lockwood,
       189-?; 2nd ed. 1893; 4th ed. 1896; ...; 12th ed. rev. by
       F. W. Britten. London: Technical Pr, 1948. 159pp, 105
       ill PPL, MiD, NB

10393 _____, ed. The Watch Jobbers' Handy Book. A practical
       manual on cleaning, repairing and adjusting: embracing in-
       formation on the tools, materials, appliances and processes
       employed in watchwork. London: Lockwood, 1889; 6th ed.
       1896; 8th ed. 1902; New York: Van Nostrand, 1902;...
       15th printing. London: Technical Pr, 1936. 144pp, 106
       ill (See: Britten, F. W., no. 10341.) MB, MiU, NN

10394 Haswell, J. Eric. Horology; the science of time measure-
       ment and the construction of clocks, watches and chronome-
       ters. London: Chapman & Hall, 1928; New York: N. W.
       Henley, 1929; with supplement. London: 1937; 1947;...
       267pp, ill, 19 pls; ...; 288pp, ill, 19 pls NN, DLC

10395 Hatton, Thomas, watch-maker. An Introduction to the Me-
       chanical Part of Clock and Watch Work.... London: T.
       Longman and G. Robinson, P. Law, and Co., 1773. 400pp,
       18 pls CtY, DeWint

10396   Hering, Daniel Webster. Key to the Watches in the James
        Arthur Collection of Clocks and Watches. Addendum to
        the Lure of the Clock. New York: NY U. Pr, 1934.
        23pp, pls DLC, ViU

10397   _____ . The Lure of the Clock; an account of the James
        Arthur Collection of Clocks and Watches at New York Uni-
        versity. New York: NYU. Pr; London: Milford, Oxford
        U. Pr, 1932; reprint. New York: Crown, 1963.   121 pp,
        ill, pls (part color) MB, ViU, DLC

10398   Howard, Wendell Stanton. Collection of Watches Loaned to
        the Metropolitan Museum of Art, NY, by Mrs. George
        Arnold Hearn. New York: priv. printed, Gilliss Pr,
        1907; 1917.   34pp, 100 pls DLC, NN

10399   Howse, Derek, and Beresford Hutchinson. The Clocks and
        Watches of Captain James Cook, 1769-1969.   London:
        Antiquarian Horological Society, 1970.   67pp, ill

10400   Horological Journal. Monthly. London: Kent & Co, for
        British Horological Institute, 1858- .   ill

10401   Horological Review. Collector's Edition. Reprint of rare
        issues from 1916-1916. London(?): N.A.G. Pr(?), 1958.
        72pp (Curious clocks, enamel dials, famous old English
        clocks, alarm clocks for the deaf, etc.)

10402   Jagger, Cedric. Clocks. London: Orbis Books; New York:
        1973. 64pp, 80 color pls, bib, gloss (To ca. 1960)

10403   Jenkins, Henry. A Description of Several Astronomical and
        Geographical Clocks; with an account of their motions and
        uses; and a short account (of) a marine regulator.   2nd
        ed. with additions. London: 1778. 129pp

10404   Johnson, Chester. Clocks and Watches. New York: Odys-
        sey Pr, 1964; London: Hamlyn, 1965. 44pp, ill

10405   Kendal, James Francis. A History of Watches and Other Time-
        keepers. London: C. Lockwood, 1892. 252pp, ill DLC

10406   "Kinostan" (pseud.). Electric Clocks; principles, construc-
        tion and working. London: Cassell, 19-?; 1920; London;
        NY: 1921; 1923; 8th ed. 1936. 152pp, 213 ill MiD, NN

10407   Leiter,   , and Alma Helfrich-Dorner. Die Uhr (The Clock).
        English translation laid in. Germany: 1967. 360pp, ill
        (500 years of masterpieces)

10408   *Lloyd, Herbert Alan. Chats on Old Clocks. (First written
        by Arthur Hayden in 1917.) London: Benn, 1951; 2nd ed.

New York: Wyn, 1952; 2nd ed. rev. & reset. as Old
Clocks. London: Benn, 1958; Fair Lawn, NJ: Essential
Books, 1959; 3rd ed. rev. London: 1964; 4th ed. rev. &
enl. London: Benn; New York: Dover, 1970. 186pp, ill;
176pp, 54 pls, bib; ...; 4th ed. 216pp, 270 ill, 80 pls

10409   _____ . The Collector's Dictionary of Clocks. London:
Country Life, 1964; South Brunswick, NJ: A. S. Barnes,
1965. 214pp, ill, bib

10410   _____ . The Complete Book of Old Clocks. New York:
Putnam, 1965. 176pp, ill, bib

10411   _____ . Some Outstanding Clocks Over 700 Years, 1250-
1950. London: L. Hill, 1958. 160pp, ill, 173 pls, bib

10412   Loomes, Brian. The White Dial Clock. New York: Drake,
1975. 172pp, ill, bib (Grandfather clocks with painted
dials, ca.1770-1870)

10413   Lyon and Scott. Evolution of the Timepiece. Ottumwa,
Iowa: Lyon & Scott, 1895. 31pp, ill DLC

10414   MacCarthy, James Remington. A Matter of Time. The
Story of the Watch. New York; London: Harper, 1947.
230pp, ill, bib

10415   Maloney, Terry. The Story of Clocks. N.Y.: Sterling, 1960;
Lond: Oak Tree Pr, 1962. 48pp, ill (Juvenile literature)

10416   *Milham, Willis I. Time and Timekeepers, including the
history, construction, care, and accuracy of clocks and
watches. New York: Macmillan, 1923; reprint. 1929;
1941; 1942; 1944; 1945; 1947. 616pp, ill, bib (Comprehensive, clear book based on course taught by author at
Williams College)

10417   Miller, Robert William. Clock Guide Identification with
Prices. Des Moines: Wallace-Homestead, 1971. 123pp,
112pp of photographs

10418   *Moore, Hannah (N.) Hudson. The Old Clock Book. New
York: F. A. Stokes, 1911; London: Heinemann, 1912.
339pp, 104 ill, list of makers BM

10419   Morgan, (Charles) Octavius (Swinnerton). Observations on
the Classification and Arrangement of a Collection of
Watches. Caerloon: Antiquarian Association, 1875.

10420   Naylor, Arthur Henry. The Study Book of Time and Clocks.
Lond: Bodley Head, 1959; 1965. 47pp, ill (Juvenile literature)

10421   Nelthropp, Henry Leonard. Treatise on Watchwork, past and

present. London; New York: E. & F. N. Spon, 1873.
310pp, ill ViU, BM

10422 Nicholls, Andrew. Clocks in Color. New York: Macmillan,
       1976. 80pp of color ill

10423 *Nutting, Wallace. The Clock Book; being a description of
       foreign and American clocks. Framingham, Mass: Old
       America Co, 1924; expanded ed. as The Complete Clock
       Book, by William B. Jacobs, Jr., and John E. Edwards.
       Stratford, Conn: Edmund-Bradley, 197-?; facsim reprint.
       Greens Farms, Conn: Modern Farms and Crafts, 1975.
       312pp, ill of 250 clocks; 483pp, 550 ill

10424 Overton, George Leonard. Clocks and Watches. London;
       New York: Pitman, 1922. 127pp, ill

10425 Palmer, Brooks. The Romance of Time. New Haven: C.
       Schaffner Advertising Agency, 1954. 54pp, ill, bib

10426 Parr, W. A Treatise on Pocket Watches. London?: 1804.
       1 pl SIB-1

10427 Pertuch, Walter Albert Richard, and Emerson W. Hilker,
       comps. Horological Books and Pamphlets in the Franklin
       Institute Library. Philadelphia: the Institute, 1956; 2nd
       ed. Philadelphia: 1968; 197-? 50pp, 109pp PPF

10428 Pippa, L. Masterpieces of Watchmaking. Lausanne: 1967.
       319pp, ill (English, German, Italian, French and Swiss)

10429 Pocket Timepieces of New York Chapter Members. New
       York: National Association of Watch and Clock Collectors,
       1968. 36pp, ill

10430 Proctor, (Frederick T.), Collection of Antique Watches and
       Table Clocks. Utica, NY: 1913. ill

10431 Reid, Thomas. Treatise on Clock and Watch Making, theo-
       retical and practical. 2nd ed. Glasgow, etc.: Blackie &
       Son, 1844; 4th ed. 1849. 466pp, 19 pls, bib

10432 *Richardson, Albert Deane, 1833-1869. Ancient and Modern
       Time-Keepers, containing ... notice of works of the
       National Watch Company, Elgin, Illinois. Reprint from
       Harper's Monthly Magazine, 1869. New York: 1870.
       16pp, ill

10433 *Robertson, John Drummond, 1857- . The Evolution of
       Clockwork, with a special section on the clocks of Japan.
       With a comprehensive bibliography of horology. London:
       Cassell, 1931; facsim. reprint. Wakefield, Eng: S. R.

Pub, 1972. 358pp, 101 ill, bib (Author's collection. Bibliography of over 600 authors)

10434 Robertson, W. B., and F. Walker. The Royal Clocks in Windsor Castle, Buckingham Palace, St. James' Palace and Hampton Court. London: 1904. 42pp

10435 *Royer-Collard, Frederick Bernard. Skeleton Clocks. London: N.A.G. Pr, 1969. 154pp, 200 ill

10436 Scherer, Josef Otto. Old Clocks. Berne: Hallwag, 1964. 9pp, ill, 19 color pls

10437 Seibel, Emanuel, and Orville Roberts Hagans, eds. & tr. Complicated Watches. Denver, Colo: Press of Roberts Pub. Co, 1945. 136pp, ill, diags (On the repair of them)

10438 Smith, Alan. Clocks and Watches. London: Connoisseur, 1975; New York: Hearst, 1976. 222pp, 400 ill, 26 color pls, bib (European, English, American and Japanese clocks, middle ages to present day)

10439 Smith, Eric. Repairing Antique Clocks: a guide for amateurs. Newton Abbot: David & Charles, 1973. 231pp, ill

10440 Smith, John (?), clockmaker. Horological Dialogues ... shewing the nature, use and right managing of clocks and watches, with an appendix containing Mr. Oughtred's method for calculating of numbers. By J. S., clock-maker. London?: 1675. BM

10441 _____ . Horological Disquisitions Concerning the Nature of Time, and the reasons by all days, from noon to noon, are not alike 24 hours long, ... with a table of pendulums, shewing the beats that any length makes in an hour, to which is added ... Rules for ... the ... use of the quicksilver and spirit weather-glasses. London: Richard Cumberland, 1694; 2nd ed. corr. 1708. 82pp, pls BM, DeWint

10442 *Smith, Grace Howard, and Eugene Randolph Smith. Watch Keys as Jewelry. Collecting Experiences of a Husband and Wife. Syracuse, NY: Syracuse U. Pr, 1967. 137pp, ill (some color)

10443 Smith, Simon Harcourt. A Catalogue of Various Clocks, watches, automata, and other miscellaneous objects of European workmanship dating from the 18th and the early 19th centuries, in the Palace Museum and the Wu Ying Tien, Peiping. Peking: Palace Museum, 1933. 32pp, pls

10444 Sobol, Ken. The Clock Museum. New York: McGraw-Hill, 1967. 48pp, color ill (Juvenile literature)

10445 *Spear, Dorothea E. American Watch Papers, with a descriptive list of the collection in the American Antiquarian
Society. Reprint from the Society's Proceedings. Vol.
61. Worcester, Mass: the Society, 1952. 76pp, ill, pls

10446 Tait, Hugh. Clocks in the British Museum. London: HMSO,
1968. 55pp, ill, 48 pls, bib (1300-1734. Ilbert Collection)

10447 Terwilliger, Charles. The Horolovar Collection, a comprehensive history and catalogue of 400-day clocks, 1880-
1912. Bronxville, NY: Horolovar Co, 1962. 143pp, ill

10448 Thomson, Adam. Time and Timekeepers. London: T. &
W. Boone, 1842. 195pp, ill BM, DLC

10449 Tripplin, Julien S. Report on the Exhibits in Class 96:
clocks, watches and timepieces. Paris Exhibition, 1900.
London: Wyman & Sons, 1901.

10450 _____. Watch and Clock Making in 1889: being an account of the exhibits in the horological section of the
French International Exhibition. London: Crosby Lockwood, 1890. 142pp

10451 *Tyler, Eric John. The Craft of the Clockmaker. London:
Ward Lock, 1973; New York: Crown, 1974. 96pp, 235
ill, bib (14th century to present. Includes tools)

10452 Ullyett, Kenneth. Clocks and Watches. Feltham: Hamlyn,
1971. 159pp, ill, bib (To 1970)

10453 _____. The Plain Man's Guide to Antique Clocks. By
W. J. Bentley (Pseud.). London: M. Joseph, 1963.
96pp, ill

10454 _____. In Quest of Clocks. London: Rockliff, 1951;
1962; new ed. Feltham: Spring Books, 1968. 264pp, ill,
pls; 269pp, 44 pls

10455 _____. Watch Collecting. London: Muller, 1970. 144pp,
ill, 20 pls (Welsh, Irish, English, American and Continental watches)

10456 Vulliamy, Benjamin Lewis, 1780-1854. On the Construction
and Regulation of Clocks for Railway Stations. London:
W. Clowes, 1845. 16pp DLC

10457 _____. Some Considerations on Public Clocks, Particularly Church Clocks. Supplement. 2 parts. London:
1828-30; 2nd ed. London: priv. printed, 1831. BM

10458 Ward, Francis Alan Burnett. Clocks and Watches. Vol. I.

Weight-Driven Clocks; Vol. II. Spring-Driven Clocks.
2 vol. London: Science Museum, HMSO, 1973, 1972.
48pp, ill; 48pp, ill (1550-1818)

10459 _____ . Descriptive Catalogue of the Collection Illustrating
Time Measurement. (Cover title: Time Measurement.)
Science Museum. London: HMSO, 1966. 151pp, ill, 12
pls

10460 _____ . Handbook of the Collections Illustrating Time
Measurement. Part 1. London: HMSO, 1936; Part 2.
1950; 3rd ed. 2 vol. 1947-55; 4th ed. 1958; in 1 vol.
1966. ill, pls, bib; 1966 ed. 151pp, 12 pls (Part 1.
Historical Review. 2. Illustrations of Collection)

10461 _____ . Timekeepers: clocks, watches, sundials, sand-
glasses. Science Museum. London: HMSO, 1963. 46pp,
ill (1500-1764)

10462 The Watch Dial. Monthly. Cincinnati: 1887-1890. ill

10463 Watches. The Paul Mellen Chamberlain Collection at the
Art Institute of Chicago. (Lent by the Chamberlain Memorial Museum.) Chicago: 1921. u.p., ill, pls

10464 The Watchmaker and Jeweler. Monthly. New York: E.
Albert, 1870- . ill

10465 Way, Robert Barnard, and Noel D. Green. Time and Its
Reckoning. New York: Chemical Pub. Co, 1940. 137pp,
ill, color frontis

10466 Welch, Kenneth Frederick. Time Measurement: An Introductory History. London: David & Charles, 1972; as
The History of Clocks and Watches. New York: Drake,
1972. 128pp, ill, bib

10467 Williamson, G(eorge) C(harles), comp. Catalogue of the
Collection of Watches, the property of J. Pierpont Morgan.
London: priv. printed, Chiswick Pr, 1912. 244pp, ill,
92 pls, bib NjP

10468 Willsberger, Johann. Clocks and Watches. Introd. by
Arnold Toynbee. New York: Dial Pr, 1975. color ill
of 130 pieces (15th to 20th century)

10469 *Wood, Edward J. Curiosities of Clocks and Watches from
the Earliest Times. London: Richard Bentley, 1866;
facsim. reprint. with new introduction by Richard Good.
Wakefield, Eng: EP Pub; New York: Beekman, 1973;
reprint of 1866 ed. Detroit: Gale, 1975. 443pp, ill

10470 Worswick, G., comp. Watches in the Usher Collection.

Usher Gallery, Lincoln.   Lincoln, Eng: 1973. 13pp, ill,
bib (ca. 1620-1850)

10471   Wright, Lawrence.   Clockwork Man: the story of time, its
        origins, its uses, its tyranny.   London: Elek, 1968; New
        York: Horizon, 1969.   260pp, ill, 16 pls, bib

10472   Wyatt, Sir Matthew Digby, 1820-1877.   The History of the
        Manufacture of Clocks.   Reprint from the Clerkenwell
        News.   London: 1870?   32pp BM

AMERICAN AND CANADIAN CLOCKS AND WATCHES

10473 *Abbott, Henry G. (pseud. for Hazlitt, George Henry A.).
        The American Watchmaker and Jeweler.   An encyclopedia
        for the horologist, jeweler, gold and silver-smith.   Con-
        taining hundreds of private receipts and formulas compiled
        from the best and most reliable sources.   Complete di-
        rections for using all the latest tools, attachments and
        devices for watchmakers and jewelers.   Chicago: G. K.
        Hazlitt, 1891; 1892; 1894; 12th ed. 1898; ...; Chicago:
        Hazlitt & Walker, 1910.   310pp, ill; 354pp, ill; 354pp, 288
        ill; 378pp, ill; ...; all with bibliography of books from
        1639-1850.   (First book on tools)

10474 *_____.   The Watch Factories of America, past and present.
        A complete history of watchmaking in America, from 1809
        to 1888 inclusive.   Chicago: G. K. Hazlitt, 1888; re-
        printed & rev. from Watch Factories ... as A Pioneer
        History of the American Waltham Watch Company.   Chi-
        cago: American Jeweler Printing, 1905; reprint. Exeter,
        NH: Adams Brown, 197-?   144pp, 50 ill, pls; 109pp, 32
        ill, pls

10475   American Clock Company. Catalogue 1878. Reprint. St.
        Louis: American Reprints, 196-? 88pp, many ill (Seth
        Thomas, New Haven, E. N. Welch, Welch Spring & Co.,
        Briggs Rotary)

10476   American Waltham Watch Company. Materials sold by Rob-
        bins and Appleton, general agents. New York: American
        Waltham, 1885; facsim. reprint. Bristol, Conn; London:
        Ken Roberts, 1972. 112pp, ill

10477   Ansonia Clock Co. Catalogue 1886/87. Reprint. St. Louis:
        American Reprints, 196-? 96pp, 315 ill (Calendar novel-
        ties, swinging arm, carriage and cottage clocks, etc.)

10478   _____ . Catalogue 1914. Reprint. St. Louis: American
        Reprints, 19-? 140pp, ill (Automobile, gallery, hall,
        marine lever, novelty, mantle, regulators, etc.)

10479   Avery, Amos Geer. New England Clocks at Old Sturbridge
        Village; the Cheney Wills collection. 2nd ed. Sturbridge,
        Mass: 1966. ill

10480   Bailey, Chris H., comp. Seth Thomas Clock Company. Il-
        lustrated catalogue of clocks, regulators, and time pieces,
        made and manufactured by the Seth Thomas Clock Company,
        Plymouth Hollow, Connecticut, 1863, with additions 1864-
        1872, also tower clocks 1874. Reprint. Bristol, Conn:
        Ken Roberts, 1973. 68pp, ill, bib

10481   _____ . 200 Years of American Clocks and Watches.
        Englewood Cliffs, NJ: Prentice-Hall, 1975. 254pp, ill

10482   Barr, Lockwood Anderson. Eli Terry Pillar and Scroll
        Shelf Clocks. Columbia, Pa?: National Association of
        Watch & Clock Collectors, 1952; reprint. Exeter, NH:
        Adams Brown, 1956? 13pp, ill; 16pp, 16 ill

10483   _____ . Index to Chauncey Jerome's Autobiography. Pel-
        ham Manor, NY: 1947.

10484   Battison, Edwin A., and Patricia E. Kane. The American
        Clock, 1725-1865: the Mabel Brady Garvan and other col-
        lections at Yale University. Fore. by Charles F. Mont-
        gomery; Introd. by Derek de Solla Price. Greenwich,
        Conn: N.Y. Graphic Society, 1973. 176pp, 150 ill, bib,
        gloss (Pictures insides and outsides of tall, shelf and
        wall clocks)

10485   Beckman, E. D. Cincinnati Silversmiths, Jewelers, Watch
        and Clock Makers. Fore. by Robert Alan Green. Harri-
        son, NY: R. A. Green, 1975. 184pp, ill

10486   Booth, Mary Louise, comp. New and Complete Watchmaker's

Manual with an Appendix Containing a History of Clock and
Watch Making in America. Tr. from French. New York:
J. Wiley, 1860; 1863; 1869; 1872; ...; 1889. 294pp, ill,
12 pls (Tools, and French, Swiss and English pieces) NN,
DLC, BM

10487 Boston Clock Company. Illustrated Catalogue, 1881. Reprint.
Exeter, NH: Adams Brown, 197-? 43pp, ill (Onyx and
gilded shelf clocks, travelling clocks, etc.)

10488 _____. Catalogue 1890. Reprint. Exeter, NH: Adams
Brown, 197-? 48pp, ill of 40 clocks

10489 Burrows, G. Edmond. Canadian Clocks and Clockmakers.
Oshawa, Ontario: Kalabi, 1973. 500pp, ill

10490 Camp, Hiram, 1811-1893. A Sketch of the Clock Making
Business, 1792-1892. New Haven, Conn: n.d. 8pp De-
Wint

10491 Carlisle, Lilian Baker. Vermont Clock and Watchmakers,
Silversmiths, and Jewelers, 1778-1878. Shelburne, Vt:
Shelburne Museum, 1970; Burlington, Vt: Dist. by the
Stinehour Pr, Lunenburg, Vt, 1970. 313pp, ill, 989 de-
tailed biographies

10492 Chandlee, Edward E. Six Quaker Clockmakers. Philadelphia:
The Historical Society of Pennsylvania, 1943. 260pp, ill,
pls, bib (Abel Cottey; Benjamin Chandlee; Benjamin Chandlee, Jr.; Goldsmith Chandlee; Ellis Chandlee; Isaac Chandlee) PP, DLC, NNC-Ave

10493 Clock Makers of Concord, Massachusetts, as gathered at the
Concord Antiquarian Museum, April-May 1966. Concord,
Mass: 1966. 36pp, pls

10494 Collectors Guide to Clocks, Price Guide. Gas City, Ind: L.
W. Promotions, 1973. 61pp, ill (Schiller, Welch, An-
sonia, Gilbert, Lasallita, Seth Thomas, Tiger, Waterbury,
Ironclad, Ingraham, Ithaca)

10495 Conrad, Henry Clay. Duncan Beard, Clockmaker; an address
delivered at Old Drawyers Meeting House, in St. George's
Hundred, New Castle County, Delaware. June 3, 1928.
n.p.: n.d. (1928) 8pp DeU

10496 _____. Old Delaware Clock-Makers. Wilmington, Del:
The Historical Society, 1898. 34pp, pls, primarily biographies DLC, NN

10497 Criss, David. Collector's Price Guide to American Pocket
Watches. Imlay City, Mich: Author, 1975. 160 ill

10498   Crossman, Charles S.   A Complete History of Watch and
        Clock Making in America.   New York: Jewelers Circular-
        Keystone, serialized 1889-91; first in book form as re-
        print.   Exeter, NH: Adams Brown, 1970.   213pp   NN

10499   *Drepperd, Carl William.   American Clocks and Clockmakers.
        Garden City, NY: Doubleday; Boston: Branford, 1947;
        2nd ed. enl.   Boston: 1955; reprint of 2nd ed.   Boston:
        Branford; London: Bailey & Swinfen, 1958.   312pp, ill,
        bib, gloss; 364pp (includes 52pp supplement), 400 ill, bib,
        gloss, list of makers

10500   Drost, William E.   Clocks and Watches of New Jersey.
        Elizabeth, NJ: Engineering Pub, 1966.   291pp, ill   (Last
        250 years)

10501   *Dworetsky, Lester, and Robert Dickstein.   Horology Ameri-
        cana.   Roslyn Heights, NY: Horology Americana, 1972.
        212pp, ill   (Private collection from early Colonial days on)

10502   Eckhardt, George H.   Early Pennsylvania Clocks.   Lancaster:
        North Museum Commission, 1938.   22pp

10503   *_____.   Pennsylvania Clocks and Clockmakers; an epic of
        early American science, industry and craftsmanship.   New
        York: Devin-Adair, Bonanza, 1955.   229pp, ill   (Includes
        watch papers)

10504   _____.   United States Clock and Watch Patents, 1790-1890;
        the Record of a century of American horology and enter-
        prise.   New York: 1960.   231pp, ill

10505   Ehrhardt, Roy.   American Pocket Watch Identification and
        Price Guide.   Book II.   Kansas City: Heart of America
        Pr, 1975.   192pp, ill   (Old catalogue pages reprinted)

10506   Fennelly, Catherine.   New England Clocks: the J. Cheney
        Wells Collection.   Sturbridge, Mass: Old Sturbridge Vil-
        lage, 1955.   32pp, ill

10507   Fredyma, James P.   A Directory of Maine Silversmiths and
        Watch and Clock Makers.   Hanover, NH: Marie-Louise
        Antiques, 1972.   26pp, bib

10508   Fredyma, John J.   A Directory of Connecticut Silversmiths
        and Watch and Clock Makers.   Hanover, NH: P.J. and
        M-L Fredyma, 1973.   600pp, bib

10509   Fredyma, Paul J., and Marie-Louise Fredyma.   A Directory
        of Boston Silversmiths and Watch and Clock Makers.   Han-
        over, NH: M-L Fredyma, 1975.   46pp, bib

10510   _____, and _____.   A Directory of Vermont Silversmiths

and Watch and Clock Makers.   Hanover, NH: M-L Fredyma, 1975. 58pp, bib

10511   Gibbs, James W. Buckeye Horology. A Review of Ohio
clock and watchmakers. Columbia, Pa: Art Crafters,
1971. 128pp, ill, 58 photographs

10512   _____. The Life and Death of the Ithaca Calendar Clock
Company. Bulletin Supplement. Philadelphia: National
Association of Watch and Clock Collectors, 1960. 80pp,
ill

10513   Gilbert, (William L.), Clock Company. Illustrated Catalogue
1901/02. Reprint. Exeter, NH: Adams Brown, 197-?
120pp, ill

10514   *Hoopes, Penrose Robinson. Connecticut Clockmakers of the
18th Century. New York: Dodd Mead; Hartford, Conn:
E. V. Mitchell, 1930; rev. ed. together with Some Minor
Connecticut Clockmakers. Reprints. New York: Dover,
1974; Rutland, Vt: Tuttle; Gloucester, Mass: Peter
Smith, 1975. 182pp, 56 ill, pls, bib, biogs

10515   _____. Early Clockmaking in Connecticut. New Haven:
Tercentenary Commission, 1934. 26pp

10516 * _____. Shop Records of Daniel Burnap, clockmaker.
Hartford: Connecticut Historical Society, 1958. 188pp,
many ill, pls (Most complete record of an 18th century
craftsman known)

10517   Howard, (Edward), and Co. Illustrated Catalogue of Clocks
Manufactured by the Howard Watch and Clock Company,
Boston, 1874. Facsim. reprint. Bristol, Conn; London:
Ken Roberts, 1972. 63pp, ill (Office and bank regulators,
astronomical clocks, electrical watch clocks, sidewalk
clocks, etc.)

10518   _____. Catalogue of Hall Striking Clocks, 1888. Reprint. Bristol, Conn: American Clock and Watch Museum, 1963. 27pp, ill

10519   _____. New Electric Watchman's Clock. 1888. Reprint.
Exeter, NH: Adams Brown, 1966. 20pp, ill

10520   _____. 1889 Catalogue of Fine Regulators, bank and office clocks. Reprint. Exeter, NH: Adams Brown, 1966.
43pp, ill (Figure 8, keyhole, regulators, electric, marine
& locomotive clocks)

10521   _____. Watch Catalogue 1909, with supplements 1912-1921.
Reprint. St. Louis: American Reprints, 1975. 48pp, ill

(Includes years under Keystone Watch Case Co.; also the Edward Howard chronometer)

10522 Ingersol, Robert H. and Brothers. 1914 catalogue. Reprint. St. Louis: American Reprints, 1970; 1972; 1973. 32pp, ill

10523 Ingraham, (E.), and Co. Illustrated Catalogue and Price List of Clocks Manufactured by E. Ingraham and Co., Bristol, Connecticut, 1880. Introductory historical sketch of Elias Ingraham.... Bristol; London: Ken Roberts, 1972. 63pp, ill

10524 James, Arthur Edwin. Chester County Clocks and Their Makers. West Chester, Pa: Chester County Historical Society, 1947. 205pp, ill, bib

10525 *Jerome, Chauncey. History of the American Clock Business for the Past 60 Years, and life of Chauncey Jerome, written by himself. New Haven, Conn: F. C. Dayton, Jr., 1860; reprint. Exeter, NH: Adams Brown, 197-? 144pp; 59pp (See also: Barr, L. A., above)

10526 Jerome & Co., Philadelphia, manufacturers and wholesale clock dealers. Catalogue. Philadelphia: Young & Duross, 1852; reprint. Bristol, Conn: American Clock and Watch Museum, 1964. 24pp, ill

10527 Johnson, Marilyn Ann. Clockmakers and Cabinetmakers of Elizabethtown, New Jersey, in the Federal Period. Thesis. 1963. 260pp, pls DeWint

10528 The Lancaster Watch Co., 1889-1910. 1. Essay, by Alan Smith; 2. A Trade Catalogue; 3. Papers, by Harry G. Abbott. 3 parts in 1 vol. Fitzwilliam, NH: Ken Roberts, 1973. 88pp, ill

10529 Lavoie, Paul L. Clocks Made in Canada by the Arthur Pequegnat Clock Co., Berlin-Kitchener, Ontario. Guelph, Ont: Author, 1973. ill

10530 Maust, Don, comp. Early American Clocks. A collection of essays on early American clocks and their makers, a practical reference. 2 vol. Uniontown, Pa: E. G. Warman, 1971, 1973. 79pp each, ill, bib

10531 Milham, Willis Isbister. The Columbus Clock. Williamstown, Mass: 1945. 34pp, ill, bib (This clock was first sold at the Chicago World's Fair, 1884)

10532 *Miller, Andrew Haynes, and Dalia Maria Miller. Survey of American Clocks: Calendar clocks. Elgin, Ill: Antiquitat, 1972. 159pp, 500 ill including patent drawings (47 kinds of clocks)

10533 New Haven Clock Company. 1886 Catalog. Reprint with
       1887 price list supplement. Bloomsburg, Pa: G. & G.
       Enterprises, 197-? 168pp, ill

10534 _____ . 1889/90 Catalogue. Reprint. Exeter, NH:
       Adams Brown, 1974. 206pp, ill

10535 _____ . 1906/07 New Design Catalogue. Reprint. Haga-
       man, NY: Merrill Dye, 1968. 40pp, ill

10536 Niebling, Warren H. History of the American Watch Case.
       Philadelphia: Whitmore, 1971. 192pp, ill

10537 *Palmer, Brooks. The Book of American Clocks. (Illustrated
       by Wallace Nutting and Author.) New York: Macmillan,
       1950; 11th printing. 1972. 318pp, 312 ill, bib, 6000 clock
       and watchmakers (Since 1650)

10538 * _____ . A Treasury of American Clocks. New York:
       Macmillan; London: Collier-Macmillan, 1967; 5th printing.
       1973. 384pp, chiefly ill (559 ill); 1973 printing includes
       49pp list of makers and corrections to earlier list

10539 The (James Ward) Packard Watch Collection Owned by the
       Horological Institute of America. Presented as a Com-
       plete Exhibit at the fourth annual jewelry show, August
       1929, at Chicago ... courtesy ... Webb C. Ball Watch
       Co. Cleveland, O: W. C. Ball, 1929. 4 leaves NN

10540 Prentiss Clock Improvement Company. 1897 catalogue. Re-
       print. St. Louis: American Reprints, 1969; 1972. 53pp,
       ill (Office clocks, calendars, regulators and synchronizers,
       8-, 60-, and 90-day movements)

10541 *Richardson, Albert Deane, 1833-1869. Ancient and Modern
       Time-Keepers. Containing ... notice of works of the
       National Watch Company, Elgin, Illinois. From Harper's
       Monthly Magazine, 1869. New York: 1870. 16pp, ill

10542 *Roberts, Kenneth D. Contributions of Joseph Ives to Con-
       necticut Clock Technology, 1810-1862. Bristol, Conn:
       Ken Roberts, 1970. 338pp, ill; 352pp, 175 ill, 44 pls

10543 * _____ . Eli Terry and the Connecticut Shelf Clock.
       Bristol, Conn: Ken Roberts, 1973. 320pp, many ill,
       bib (Late 1700s to early 1800s)

10544 Rosenberg, C. American Pocket Watches; their source and
       their identity. Hollywood, Cal: 1965. 64pp, ill

10545 St. Louis Clock and Silver Ware Co., 1904 catalog. St.
       Louis: American Reprints, 1975. 88pp, 574 ill (An-
       sonia, Sempire, Waterbury, Gilbert, Ingraham, Newman,

G. & K. Swarzwald, Seth Thomas)

10546 Sanderson, R. L. Waltham Industries. Waltham, Mass:
      1957. 164pp, ill (American Waltham Watch Co., U.S.
      Watch Co., tool and jewel factories)

10547 Sands, Anna B. Time Pieces of Old and New Connecticut. Hart-
      ford, Conn: Manufacturers Association, 1926. 33pp, ill

10548 Schwartz, Marvin D. Collector's Guide to Antique American
      Clocks: history, style, identification. Garden City, NY:
      Doubleday, 1975. ill (17th century to 1940s)

10549 Seth Thomas Clock Company. 1879 Catalogue. Reprint.
      St. Louis: American Reprints, 1974. ill

10550 Seth Thomas Clocks. 1884/5. Catalog reprint. St. Louis:
      American Reprints, 1973. 128pp, 125 ill (Includes "Seth
      Thomas, the Conservative Clockmaking Yankee," by Chris
      H. Bailey)

10551 Seth Thomas Clock Co. Illustrated Catalogue of Clocks,
      1892-1893. Reprint. Exeter, NH: Adams Brown, 197-?
      136pp, ill (Marine, alarm, lever, shelf, wall regulator,
      hall and tower. Three pages of watches)

10552 _____. 1904/05 Catalog. Reprint. St. Louis: Ameri-
      can Reprints, 1974. 144pp, ill

10553 _____. Factory List of Seth Thomas Clock Movements.
      1907 Catalogue. Reprint. Exeter, NH: Adams Brown,
      197-? 25pp, 3pp of movements (175 movements before
      1908)

10554 The Story of Edward Howard and the First American Watch.
      Boston: E. Howard Watch Works, 1910. 24pp, color pls

10555 Terry, Henry. American Clock Making; its early history
      and present extent of business. Waterbury, Conn: J.
      Giles & Son, 1870; 1885; reprint of 1885 ed. as American
      Clock Making; its early history. Also, illustrated cata-
      logue of clocks, manufactured by the Terry Clock Co,
      Pittsfield, Mass. Bristol, Conn: American Clock and
      Watch Museum, 1974. 24pp, ill; ...; 94pp, ill, bib

10556 Thomson, Richard. Antique American Clocks and Watches.
      Princeton, NJ; London: Van Nostrand, 1968. 192pp, 67
      ill

10557 Townsend, George E. Almost Everything You Wanted to Know
      about American Watches and Didn't Know Who to Ask.
      Vienna?, Va: 1971. 92pp, 200 scale drawings (1809-1900)

10558 _____ . Encyclopedia of Dollar Watches. Vienna, Va:
          1974. 400pp, 100 scale drawings (1877-1974)

10559 Unitt, Doris, and Peter Unitt. Arthur Pequegnat Clocks with
          History and Price Guide. Peterborough, Ont: Clock
          House, 1973. ill (Canadian clocks)

10560 Unitt, Peter, and Doris Unitt. Peter's Clock Book. Peter-
          borough, Ont: Clock House, 1969. ill (Canadian clocks)

10561 Von Hohenhoff, Elsa. American Clocks and Clockmaking to
          1860; an annotated, selected bibliography. 1942. 10pp
          typescript, bound NNC-Ave

10562 Warman, Edwin G. Early American Clocks. 3 vol. Union-
          town, Pa: Warman Pub Co, 197-? ill

10563 Watch-making in America. Embodying the history of watch-
          making as an invention, and as an industry. Reprint
          from Appleton's Journal, July 2, 9, 1870. Boston: Ap-
          pleton, 1870. 2pp, ill

10564 *Waterbury Clock Company. 1867 Catalog. Reprint. St.
          Louis: American Reprints, 1973. 132pp, ill (Iron front
          clocks, Blinking Eye, Sambo, Topsey, continental and
          organ grinder, cottage, steeple, sharp and gothic)

10565 _____ . 1881 Catalogue. Reprint. St. Louis: American
          Reprints, 1973. 122pp, ill

10566 _____ . 1908/09 Catalogue. Reprint. St. Louis: Ameri-
          can Reprints, 197-? 88pp, ill of over 350 clocks

10567 Welch, (E. N.), Manufacturing Co. Catalogue 1885. Reprint.
          Exeter, NH: Adams Brown, 1970. 63pp, ill (Regulators,
          calendars, alarms, ship bell, cottage, etc.)

10568 Wells, Joel Cheney, 1874- . New England Clocks at Old
          Sturbridge Village: the J. Cheney Wells Collection. Stur-
          bridge Village, Mass: 1955. 32pp, chiefly ill, bib

10569 *Willard, John Ware. A History of Simon Willard, inventer
          and clockmaker, together with some account of his sons--
          his apprentices--and the workmen associated with him,
          with ... other clockmakers of the family name. Boston:
          E. O. Cockayne, 1911; reprint. New York: 1968. 133pp,
          ill, pls (Simon Willard, 1753-1848)

BRITISH ISLES CLOCKS AND WATCHES

10570 *Atkins, Samuel Elliott, and William Henry Overall. Some

Account of Worshipful Company of Clockmakers of the City of London. London: Blades, East & Blades, 1881. 346pp, pls BM, DeWint

10571 Baillie, Granville Hugh. Guide to the Museum of the Clock-makers' Company of London. London: Frome, Butler & Tanner, for the Company, 1939. 73pp, ill (Not confined to British pieces) MH, BM

10572 Bain, Alexander, electrician. Short History of Electric Clocks. London: Chapman & Hall, 1852; facsim. reprint ed. by W. D. Hackmann. London: Turner & Devereux, 1973. 32pp, ill (Clocks manufactured by Bain)

10573 Beeson, Cyril Frederick Cherrington. Clockmaking in Oxford-shire, 1400-1850. Banbury, Eng: Banbury Historical Society; Enfield: Antiquarian Horological Society, 1962; re-print with add. of Part 3. Oxford: Museum of the History of Science, 1967. 160pp, ill, pls; 193pp, 34 pls, bib

10574   . English Church Clocks, 1280-1850. London: An-tique Horological Society; Chichester: Phillimore, 1971. 132pp, ill, bib

10575 Bellchambers, Jack Kenneth. Devonshire Clockmakers. Totnes, Devon: Midland Bank Chambers, 1962. 41pp, ill, 12 pls (Good listing not in Baillie)

10576   . Somerset Clockmakers. London: Antiquarian Horological Society, 1968. 79pp, ill, 22 pls

10577 Bird, Anthony. English Furniture for the Private Collector, including antique clocks. London: Batsford, 1961; New York: Hearthside Pr, 1962. 216pp, ill

10578 *   . English House Clocks, 1600-1850: an historical survey and guide for collectors and dealers. Newton Ab-bot: David & Charles, 1973; as Illustrated Guide to House Clocks, 1600-1850; an historical survey and guide for col-lectors and dealers. London; New York: Arco, 1973. 313pp, ill, 45 pls (Discusses links of American and Eng-lish with French and Dutch, and includes hints on fakes and marriages)

10579 Brazil, Walter Henry. Old English Clocks. Excerpt from The Coventry Bookshelf, vol. 12, no. 6. Coventry: 1934. 15pp, ill, pl NN

10580 British Clockmaker's Heritage Exhibition. May-September 1952. Science Museum. London: HMSO, 1952; Illustrated Catalogue of Exhibit. 1952. 93pp; 93pp, ill

10581 *Britten, Frederick James. Old English Clocks. (The David

Arthur F. Wetherfield Collection). London: Lawrence & Jellicoe, 1907. 113pp, ill (1675-1775) BM

10582 Brown, Howard Miles. Cornish Clocks and Clockmakers. Dawlish, Devon: David & Charles, 1961; 2nd ed. Newton Abbot: David & Charles, 1970. 80pp, ill; 94pp, ill, 8 pls, bib (Over 400 makers to 1850)

10583 Buckley, Francis. Old Manchester Clock and Watch Makers, 17th and 18th centuries. Uppermill: Moore & Edwards, 1929. 6pp

10584 Catalogue of the Museum of the Worshipful Company of Clockmakers of London, preserved in the Guildhall Library, London. 2nd ed. London: Blades, East & Blades, 1902. 95pp, bib (See also: Baillie, G. H.; Clutton, C.) BM

10585 *Cescinsky, Herbert. The Old English Master Clockmakers and Their Clocks, 1670-1820. London: Routledge; New York: F. A. Stokes, 1938. 182pp, 275 ill NN, DLC

10586 *_____, and Malcolm R. Webster. English Domestic Clocks. London: Routledge, 1913; 2nd ed. 1914; reprint. Feltham; New York: Spring Books, 1969. 353pp, 400 ill, pls, color frontis (Bracket, long-case, lantern, wall, cartel clocks, 1630-1850) DLC, MdBP, PPULC

10587 Clutton, Cecil, and George Daniels. Clocks and Watches in the Collection of the Worshipful Company of Clockmakers, City of London Guildhall. London: Sotheby Parke-Bernet, 1975. text, 200 pieces ill (Includes additions to collection since 1949)

10588 Congreve, Sir William, 1772-1828. William Congreve and His Clock: a (facsimile) reprint of the patent granted to Congreve in 1808, with an introductory note. London: Turner & Devereux, 1972. 24pp, ill

10589 Daniell, J. A. The Making of Clocks and Watches in Leicestershire and Rutland. Leicester: Archaeological Society, 1952. 36pp, ill (List of makers)

10590 Dawson, Percy George. The Design of English Domestic Clocks, 1660-1700. Based on a lecture. London: Antiquarian Horological Society, 1956. 23pp, pls

10591 De Carle, Donald. Clocks and Their Value: illustrated Guide to ancient and modern clocks with a unique chart of all known Tompion Clocks. London: N.A.G. Pr, 1968; 2nd ed. 1971. 144pp, ill, bib; 159pp, ill, bib

10592 Dinsdale, Norman Vincent. The Old Clockmakers of Yorkshire.

Clapham, Yorkshire: Dalesman Pub. Co, 1946. 82pp, ill

10593   Edwardes, Ernest Lawrence. The Grandfather Clock; an
        archaeological and descriptive essay on the English long-
        case clock with its weight-driven precursors and contem-
        poraries. With notes on some Scottish, Welsh and Irish
        examples. Altrincham: Sherratt, 1949; new ed. rev. &
        enl. 1952; 3rd ed. enl. & rev. 1971. 253pp, ill, 54 pls;
        270pp, ill, 193 pls, bib (ca.1658-1840)

10594   English Clocks and Watches and Their Makers. London:
        Horological Journal, 1924. BM

10595   English Watches. V & A Museum. London: HMSO, 1969.
        86pp, ill

10596   Exhibition of British Watches and Clocks. Birmingham, Eng:
        Museum of Science and Industry, 1953. 20pp

10597   Fennell, Geraldine A. A List of Irish Watch and Clock-
        makers. Dublin: Stationery Office, 1963. 42pp

10598   Five Centuries of British Timekeeping: an exhibition of
        modern clocks and watches by the British Clock and Watch
        Makers Association together with historical specimens by
        the old master clockmakers, Goldsmiths' Hall, October
        1955. London: N.A.G. Pr, 1955. 69pp, ill

10599   Goaman, Muriel. English Clocks. London: The Connois-
        seur, Joseph, 1967. 119pp, ill, 8 pls, bib

10600   Green, F. H. Old English Clocks. Being a collector's ob-
        servations on some 17th century clocks. Ditchling: priv.
        printed, St. Dominic's Pr, 1931. 89pp, ill, 50 pls DLC,
        NN

10601   Hawkes, Arthur John. The Clockmakers and Watchmakers of
        Wigan, 1650-1850. Wigan, Eng: Author, 1950. 84pp, ill

10602   *Hayden, Arthur. Chats on Old Clocks. London: Fisher Un-
        win, 1917; 1918; New York: F. A. Stokes, 1918; London:
        1925; 1928. 302pp, 80 ill, pls (Brass lantern clocks,
        long case, bracket and provincial clocks, Scottish and Irish
        clocks and watches, bit on American clocks) PPL, NN

10603   Hayward, John Forrest. English Watches. V & A Museum.
        London: HMSO, 1954; rev. ed. London: 1956; 2nd ed.
        1969. 10pp, ill, 47 pls, bib; ...; 14pp, 59 pls, bib

10604   Hill, R. Noel. Early British Clocks from Circa 1600 to
        Circa 1800.... A preliminary guide for the collector.
        London: Connoisseur, 1949. 42pp, 40 ill, pls

10605   Joy, Edward Thomas. The Country Life Book of Clocks.
        London: Country Life, 1967. 96pp, 16 ill, 80 photo-
        graphs, bib (Chiefly English (some European) from 1500-
        1900. Tompion, East, Knibb, Quare, Graham, etc.)

10606   Lee, Ronald Alfred. The Knibb Family Clockmakers: or,
        Automatopael Knibb familiael. Byfleet, Eng: Manor
        House, 1964. 188pp, ill (Knibb family--1655-1720)

10607   Little, John Egram, and D. F. Nettell. Uffington Church
        Clock: a short technical and historical account of the
        Uffington Church clock A.D. 1701. Uffington: John E.
        Little, 1969. 11pp, ill, 4 pls

10608 *Lloyd, H. Alan. The English Domestic Clock, Its Evolution
        and History; a brief guide to the essential details for
        dating a clock. London: Silk & Terry, for Author, 1938.
        28pp, 57 ill NNC-Ave

10609   Loomes, Brian. Westmorland Clocks and Clockmakers.
        London: David & Charles, 1974. 112pp, 11 ill

10610   _____ . Yorkshire Clockmakers. Lancaster: Dalesman,
        1972. 192pp, 56 ill, bib (Clocks, cases, dials. 1700
        makers listed to 1860)

10611   Mason, Bernard. Clock and Watchmaking in Colchester,
        England. A history of provincial clockmaking from the
        15th to the 19th centuries in the oldest recorded town in
        Great Britain. London: Country Life, 1969. 436pp, ill
        (1460-1875)

10612   Mudge, Thomas, 1717-1794. Description with Plates of the
        Time-Keeper Invented by the Late Mr. Thomas Mudge,
        with a narrative by his son. London: Author, 1799.
        176pp, 9 pls NN, MB

10613   Mudge, Thomas, Jr., 1760-1843. ... A Narrative of Facts
        Relating to Some Timekeepers Constructed by Thomas
        Mudge (senior) for the discovery of the longitude at sea,
        etc.... London: T. Payne, 1792. 171pp, 1 pl DLC

10614   Nelthropp, Henry Leonard. A Catalogue Chronologically Ar-
        ranged of the Collection of Clocks, watches, chronometers,
        movements, sundials, seals, etc., etc., presented to the
        Worshipful Company of Clockmakers. London: Blades,
        East & Blades, 1895; 2nd ed. 1900. 85pp, bib BM

10615   Nixseaman, A. J. First Production: Tompion's great clock.
        Biggleswade, Beds.: C. Elphick, 1953. 64pp, ill (Thomas
        Tompion, 1639-1713)

10616   Overall, William Henry. A Catalogue of Books, Manuscripts,

Clocks, Watches, ... in the library and museum of the Worshipful Company of Clockmakers. London: E. J. Francis, 1875. 116pp, bib RNB, BM

10617 Peate, Iorwerth Cyfeiliog. Clock and Watch Makers in Wales. Cardiff: National Museum of Wales, 1945; 2nd ed. Cardiff: Welsh Folk Museum, 1960. 85pp, ill; 108pp, 18 ill (Includes sundials)

10618 Rees, Abraham. (The Cyclopedia). Rees's Clocks, Watches and chronometers, 1819-1820; a selection from 'The Cyclopedia; or, Universal dictionary of arts, sciences and literature,' by Abraham Rees. (First published London, 1819.) Facsim. reprint of extracts. Newton Abbot: David & Charles, 1970. 295pp, ill

10619 Reid, C. L. North Country Clockmakers of the 17th, 18th, and 19th centuries. Newcastle-upon-Tyne: 1925. 140pp

10620 *Smith, John, another clockmaker, comp. A Handbook and Directory of Old Scottish Clockmakers from 1540 to 1850 A.D. Edinburgh: W. J. Hay, 1903; 2nd ed. rev. & enl. as Old Scottish Clockmakers from 1453 to 1850. Edinburgh: Oliver & Boyd, 1921. 97pp, ill; 436pp, pls DLC

10621 *Symonds, Robert Wemyss. A Book of English Clocks. 2nd ed. London: Penguin, 1950. 80pp, ill

10622 _____. A History of English Clocks. London; New York: Penguin, 1947. 79pp, 72 pls

10623 * _____. Masterpieces of English Furniture and Clocks; a study of walnut and mahogany furniture and of the associated crafts of the looking-glass maker and japanner, together with an account of Thomas Tompion and other famous clock-makers of the 17th and 18th centuries. London: Batsford, 1940. 172pp, 130 ill, 8 color pls

10624 * _____. Thomas Tompion: His life and work. London: Batsford, 1951; reprint. Feltham: Spring Books, 1969. 320pp, ill, 276 (4 color) pls; 320pp, ill, 152 (4 color) pls

10625 Tribe, Tom, comp. Dorset Clock and Watchmakers. Sturminster Newton, Dorset: T. Tribe, 1970. 12 leaves (1612-1939)

10626 Turner, A. J., ed. Maurice Wheeler's Account of the Inclined Plane Clock, 1684: reproduced from 'Philosophical Transactions,' No. 161, July 20, 1684. With an introduction. Facsim. reprint. London: Turner & Devereux, 1972. 24pp, 1 ill

10627 Ullyett, Kenneth. British Clocks and Clockmakers.... London: Collins, 1947. 47pp, ill

10628   Vernay, Arthur Stannard. The Wetherfield Collection of
        English Clocks. New York: 1928. 100 clocks ill (David
        Arthur F. Wetherfield) (See also: Britten, F. J.)

10629   Waters, Ivor. A Note on Chepstow Clock and Watch Makers.
        Chepstow, Eng: Author, 1952. 7pp, bib

10630   *Wenham, Edward. Old Clocks for Modern Use; with a guide
        to their mechanism. London: G. Bell, 1951; New York:
        Studio-Crowell, 1952. 174pp, 70 ill, 26 photographs, bib

10631   White, William Douglas. Derbyshire Clockmakers Before
        1850: The Whitehurst family. Duffield, Eng: Derbyshire
        Archaeological and Natural History Society, 1958. 15pp
        typescript, bib

EUROPEAN AND ASIAN CLOCKS AND WATCHES

10632   Bassermann-Jordan, Ernst von. The Clock of Philip the
        Good of Burgundy. Leipzig: W. Diebener g. m. b. h.,
        1927. 43pp, 40 ill, color pls, bib (Duke of Burgundy,
        1396-1467) DLC

10633   Bedini, Silvio A. The Borghesi Astronomical Clock. Wash-
        ington, D.C.: Smithsonian, GPO, 1964. 75pp, ill, bib

10634   _____. Johan Philipp Treffler, Clockmaker of Augsburg.
        Ridgefield, Conn: Author, 1957. 41pp, ill (Treffler,
        1625-?)

10635   Bonnant, Georges. The Introduction of Western Horology in
        China. La Chaux-de-Fonds, Switzerland: La Suisse Hor-
        legere, 1960. 11pp, ill

10636   Breguet, C. A. L. Breguet, Horologer. Tr. from French.
        Enfield: 1963. 30pp, ill (Abraham Louis Breguet, 1747-
        1823. Detailed listing of his inventions)

10637   Chenakal, Valentine L. Watchmakers and Clockmakers in
        Russia, 1400-1850. Tr. from Russian by W. F. Ryan.
        London: Antiquarian Horological Society, 1972. 64pp, ill

10638   Crommelin, Claude August. The Clocks of Christiaan Huy-
        gens. London?: 1950. 7pp, ill (Huygens, 1629-1695)

10639   _____. Descriptive Catalogue of the Huygens Collection
        in the Rijksmuseum voor de Geschiedenis der Natuurweten-
        schapen (History of Science) at Leiden. Leiden, Holland:
        1949. 31pp, 4 pls, bib (Includes optical instruments) DLC

10640   Daniels, George. The Art of Breguet--Master Horologist.

London: Sotheby Parke Bernet, 1974. 400pp, 115 (25 color) ill

10641 Edey, Winthrop. French Clocks. New York: Walker; London: Studio Vista, 1967. 83pp, ill (1660-1789)

10642 Jagger, Cedric. Paul Philip Barraud: a study of a fine chronometer maker, and of his relatives, associates and successors in the family business, 1750-1929. Fore. by H. Quill. London: Antiquarian Horological Society, 1968. 177pp, ill, 1 pl, facsims. (Dating and serial numbers of clocks, watches, chronometers)

10643 Jaquet, Eugene, and Alfred Chapuis. Technique and History of the Swiss Watch from its Beginnings to the Present Day. Tr. from French (1945) by D. S. Torrens and C. Jenkins. Published under the auspices of Swiss Society of Chronometry and the Swiss Watch Chamber. Bern: Urs Graf-Verlag, 1953; rev. ed.. ed. by Samuel Gute. Feltham: Spring Books, 1970. 278pp, ill (part color), 236 pls; rev. ed. 172pp (1510-1968)

10644 Mody, N. H. N. A Collection of Japanese Clocks. London: Kegan Paul, 1932; reprint. Rutland, Vt: Tuttle, 1967. 27pp, ill, 135 pls; 69pp, ill

10645 Mortensen, O. The Copenhagen Clock. Jen Olsen's Clock. Copenhagen: 1959. 157pp, ill

10646 Needham, (Noel) Joseph (T. M.), Wang Ling, and Derek J. de Solla Price. Heavenly Clockwork. The Great Astronomical Clocks of Medieval China. Cambridge, Eng: University Pr in Association with the Antiquarian Horological Society, 1960. 253pp, ill, bib

10647 *Ross, Marvin Chauncey. The Art of Karl Fabergé and His Contemporaries; Russian Imperial portraits and mementoes (Alexander III to Nicholas II), Russian Imperial Decoration and watches. Collection of Marjorie Merriweather Post, Hillwood, Washington, D.C., and foreword by her. Norman, Okla: U. of O. Pr, 1965. 238pp, ill, color pls, bib (Faberge, 1846-1920)

10648 Sellink, J. L. Dutch Antique Domestic Clocks, ca.1670-1870. A Catalogue of the main collection in the Oegstgeest Museum of Clocks. Leiden: Stenfert Kroese, 1973. 465pp, 400 photographs, bib

10649 *Tyler, Eric John. European Clocks. London: Ward Lock, 1968. 258pp, ill, bib (Includes tools)

AUTOMATA AND GAMBLING MACHINES

10650   Archer, Mildred. Tippoo's Tiger. London: V & A Mu-
        seum, 1959. 30pp, 22 pls

10651   Bradford, Gamaliel, 1795-1839. The History and Analysis
        of the Supposed Automaton Chess Player of M. de Kempe-
        len, now exhibiting in this country by Mr. Maezel; with
        lithographic figures illustrative of the probable method by
        which its motions are directed. Boston: Hilliard, Gray,
        1826. 24pp, ill DeWint

10652a *Chapuis, Alfred, and Edmond Droz. Automata; a historical
        and technological study. Tr. by Alec Reid. Neuchatel:
        Editions du Griffon; London: Batsford; New York: Central
        Book Co, 1958. 407pp, 488 ill, 18 color pls (Includes
        much on clocks)

10652b Christensen, David G. Slot Machines; a pictorial review.
        Vestal, N.Y.: Vestal Pr, 1976. 120pp, 60 ill (gambling
        machines; one-arm bandits)

10653   Cohen, John. Human Robots in Myth and Science. London:
        Allen & Unwin, 1966; South Brunswick, NJ: A. S. Barnes,
        1967. 156pp, 16 pls, bib

10654   Cooke, Conrad William, 1843- . Some Works on Automata;
        automata old and new. Odde Volume Brotherhood, opus-
        cula, no. XXIX. London: Chiswick Pr, 1893. 117pp, pls
        (A Bibliography) TxU, DLC

10655   Cox, James, fl. 1769. A Description of a Most Magnificent
        Piece of Mechanism and Art. London: 1769. 14pp (bound
        with other pamphlets) MiU

10656   _____. A Descriptive Catalogue of the Several Superb and
        Magnificent Pieces of Mechanism and Jewellery, exhibited
        in the Museum, at Spring Gardens, Charing-Cross. Lon-
        don: 1772; 1772; 1773. 28pp; 20pp; 31pp (Cox was a
        jeweller and the proprietor) NN, CtY

10657a _____. A Descriptive Inventory of the Several Exquisite
        and Magnificent Pieces of Mechanism and Jewellery, com-
        priz'd in the schedule ... for enabling Mr. James Cox, of
        the City of London, Jeweller, to dispose of His Museum
        by Way of Lottery. London: H. Hart, printer, 1773; 1774.
        46pp, plate (Quaritch reports 71pp) (56 pieces described:
        musical cabinets, automata, chiming clocks, cage of singing
        birds, etc.) MH-BA, NN

10657b Directions for Operating Mills, Operator's Bell, Counter O.K.
        Mint Vender, Front O.K. Mint Vender. Reprint. Vestal,
        NY: Vestal Pr, 197-? ill

10658a Heyl, Edgar G. An Unhurried View of Automata. Baltimore: Author, n. d. 4 leaves

10658b Instructions for the Dewey and Chicago Machines. Mills Novelty Company. Reprint. Vestal, NY: Vestal Pr, 197-? 12pp, ill

10659 A Loan Exhibition of Antique Automatons, for the Benefit of the Pestalozzi Foundation of America. November-December 1950. New York: A La Vieille Russie, 1950. 69pp, ill (part color) DeWint

10660 Mills Gambling Machine Catalog, 1918. Reprint. Vestal, NY: Vestal Pr, 197-? 24pp, ill

10661 Smith, Simon Harcourt. A Catalogue of Various Clocks, watches, automata, and other miscellaneous objects of European workmanship dating from the 18th and the early 19th centuries, in the Palace Museum and the Wu Ying Tien, Peiping. Peking: Palace Museum, 1933. 32pp, pls

10662 Vaucanson, Jacques de. An Account of the Mechanism of an Automaton Playing on the German Flute, (and other figures). Tr. from French by J. T. Desaguliers. London: 1742. 23pp BM

10663 *Wood, Edward J. Curiosities of Clocks and Watches from the Earliest Times. London: Richard Bentley, 1866; facsim. reprint, with new introd. by Richard Good. Wakefield, Eng: EP Pub; New York: Beekman, 1973; Detroit: Gale Pr, 1975. 443pp, ill

SECTION XXXII

PHILOSOPHIE AND SCIENCE

SCIENTIFIC INSTRUMENTS

10664   Accum, Friedrich Christian, 1769-1838. A Descriptive
        Catalogue of the Apparatus and Instruments Employed in
        Experimental and Operative Chemistry, in analytical min-
        eralogy, and in the pursuits of the recent discoveries of
        Voltaic electricity. London: G. Hayden, printer, 1817.
        59pp   DLC

10665   _____ . Dictionary of the Apparatus and Instruments Em-
        ployed in Operative and Experimental Chemistry. London:
        1821; 2nd ed. as An Explanatory Dictionary of the Appara-
        tus and Instruments Employed in the Various Operations of
        Philosophical and Experimental Chemistry. London: T.
        Boys, 1824.   ; 295pp, ill, 17 folding copperplates DLC

10666   Allen, Cecil John. A Century of Scientific Instrument Making,
        1853-1953. A History of W(illiam) F(ord) Stanley and
        Company. London: Harley, for Stanley, 1953. 64pp, ill
        BM, DLC

10667   The Art of Glassblowing, or, Plain instructions for making
        the chemical and philosophical instruments which are
        formed of glass. By a French Artist. London: Bumpus
        & Griffin, 1831. 112pp, 4 pls BM

10668   Barclay, Alexander, comp. Chemistry. Catalogue of the
        collections in the Science Museum, South Kensington.
        London: HMSO, 1927. 76pp, ill, 10 pls

10669   _____ . Early American Scientific Instruments and Their
        Makers. Museum of History and Technology, Smithsonian.
        Washington, D.C.: GPO, 1964. 184pp, ill, pls, bib

10670   Campbell, Rosemae (Wells). Tops and Gyrascopes. New
        York: Crowell, 1959. 174pp, ill

10671   Catalogue of a Special Loan Collection of Scientific Apparatus

at the South Kensington Museum, 1876. 3rd ed. London:
Eyre & Spottiswoode, for HMSO, 1877; Conferences Held
in Connection with the Exhibit. London: Chapman & Hall,
for HMSO, 1877. 1084pp, ill, 6 pls; 441pp, ill

10672 A Catalogue of an Exhibition of Apparatus Illustrating the Application of Scientific Principles to Aeronautics. Science
Museum. London: Eyre & Spottiswoode, for HMSO, 1912.
20pp, pls DLC

10673 Catalogue of Apparatus Suitable for Lectures and Class Instruction in Group III. Subject 1. Acoustics, light, heat.
2. Magnetism and electricity. South Kensington Museum.
London: Eyre & Spottiswoode, for HMSO, 1865. 22pp

10674 Catalogue of the Science Collections for Teaching and Research in the V & A Museum. 4 parts. London: HMSO,
1892, 1891-1895.

10675 Chaldecott, J. A. The King George III Collection of Scientific Instruments; a brief outline of the history of the collection together with notes on personalities involved and
points of interest in connection with objects shown in a
special exhibition.... Science Museum ... 1949. London: HMSO, 1949; Handbook of the King George III Collection of Scientific Instruments. Catalogue of exhibits with
descriptive notes. London: HMSO, 1951. 13pp, ill; 92pp
BM, NN, DLC

10676 Cohen, I. Bernard. Some Early Tools of American Science;
an account of the early scientific instruments and mineralogical and biological collection in Harvard University.
Fore. by Samuel Eliot Morison. Cambridge, Mass: Harvard U. Pr, 1950; New York: Russell & Russell, 1967.
201pp, ill, bib DLC, TxU

10677 Crommelin, Claude August. Descriptive Catalogue of the
Physical Instruments of the 18th Century (Including the
Collections Gravesende-Muschenbroek) in the Rijksmuseum
... (of History and Science) at Leyden. Leyden: 1951.
74pp, ill DLC

10678 *Daumas, Maurice. Scientific Instruments of the 17th and
18th Centuries. Tr. from French (1953) and ed. by Mary
Holbrook. London: Batsford; as Scientific Instruments
... and Their Makers. New York: Praeger, 1972.
361pp, 142 ill, 64 pls, bib

10679 Davis, Audrey B., and Uta C. Merzbach. Early Auditory
Studies: activity in the Psychology Laboratories of American universities. Washington, D.C.: Smithsonian, 1975.

10680 Davis, Daniel, Jr. Descriptive Catalogue of Apparatus and

Experiments, to illustrate the following branches of
science, namely: galvanism, electro-dynamics, magnetism. Boston: Marden & Kimball, 1838; Boston: D.
Davis, 1848; Catalogue of Apparatus ... manufactured
and sold by Palmer & Hall. Boston: Palmer & Hall,
1855. 72pp, ill; 46pp, chiefly ill NN, DLC

10681 Early Science at Harvard; innovators and their instruments,
1765-1865. Loan Exhibition, December 1969-February
1970. Cambridge, Mass: Harvard, William Hayes Fogg
Art Museum, 1969. 82pp, ill

10682 Gunther, Robert William Theodore. Early Science in Cambridge. Oxford: University Pr, for Author, 1937. 513pp,
ill, pls NN, DLC

10683 _____. Early Science in Oxford. 2 vol. Oxford: Clarendon Pr, for Oxford Historical Society, 1920, 1923; 15 vol.
1923-1945. ill, pls DLC, MiU

10684 _____. Historic Instruments for the Advancement of Science; a handbook to the Oxford Collections prepared for
the opening of the Lewis Evans Collection, May 5, 1925.
London; New York: H. Milford, Oxford U. Pr, 1925; as
Handbook of the Museum of the History of Science in the
Old Ashmolean Building, Oxford. Oxford: 1935. 90pp,
ill; 157pp, ill DLC, ViU

10685 Hall, Ivan. An Exhibition of Paintings, sculpture, prints,
furniture, books and scientific instruments collected during
the 18th century by William Constable. Lent by Mr. and
Mrs. John Chichester-Constable. Ferens Art Gallery,
Kingston-upon-Hull, January-February 1970. Hull: Ferens,
1970. 90pp, ill NNC-Ave

10686 Handbook to the Special Loan of Scientific Apparatus, 1876.
South Kensington Museum. London: HMSO, 1876; 3rd ed.
as Catalogue to the Special Loan Collection of Scientific
Apparatus. 1877. 339pp, ill BM

10687 Illustrated Catalogue of the Collections in the Science Museum
... with description and historical notes. London: 1920.
u. p. BM

10688 Johnson, Valentine Edward. The Gyroscope; an experimental
study from spinning-top to mono-rail. London; New York:
Spon, 1911. 52pp, ill DLC, ViU

10689 Jones, W. & S., London. A Catalogue of Optical, Mathematical, and Philosophical Instruments, Made and Sold by
W. & S. Jones. London: 1795; 1797; 1800; 1813; 1815;
1818; 1822; 1830; 1838. 12pp; 14pp, 2 pls; 14pp, 2 pls;

...; 15pp, pls; ... (Jones, William, 1763-1831) CtY,
MH, NN, DLC, DeWint

10690   Josten, Conrad Hermann, comp. Scientific Instruments, 13th
to 19th centuries; the collection of J. A. Billmeir, C. B.
E., exhibited by the Museum of the History of Science, Oxford. Oxford: University Museum, 1954; 1955; Supplement.
See: Maddison, F. R. 45pp, ill DLC

10691   "The Journal of Science and the Arts." Quarterly. Reprint
of the "Quarterly Journal of Science, Literature and Art,"
London; New York: J. Eastburn, 1817-1818. ill

10692   Maddison, Francis Romeril. (A Supplement to) a Catalogue
of Scientific Instruments in the Collection of J. A. Billmeir, Esq., C. B. E.,... Oxford: University Museum
of History of Science, 1957. 104pp, ill, 21 pls (See also:
Josten, C. H., above)

10693   Michel, Henri. Scientific Instruments in Art and History.
Tr. from French (1966) by R. E. W. Maddison and Fran-
cis R. Maddison. London: Barrie & Rockliff; New York:
Viking, 1967. 208pp, ill, bib (To 1794)

10694   Multhauf, Robert P., and David Davies, comp. A Catalogue
of Instruments and Models in the Possession of the American Philosophical Society. Philadelphia: the Society, 1961.
80pp, ill

10695   Pearsall, Ronald. Collecting and Restoring Scientific Instruments. Newton Abbot: David & Charles; New York: Arco,
1974. 278pp, ill, bib, gloss (18th & 19th century surveying, navigation, astronomy, microscopy)

10696   Pledge, Humphrey Thomas. Science Since 1500; a short
history of mathematics, physics, chemistry and biology.
Science Museum. London: HMSO, 1939; New York: Harper, 1959; 2nd ed. London: 1966. 357pp, ill, 15 pls, bib

10697   Ritchie, Edward S., and Sons, Boston. Ritchie's Illustrated
Catalogue of Philosophical Instruments and School Apparatus.
Boston: 1860; 1866; 1870; 1871; 1873. 84pp, ill; 57pp, ill;
63pp, ill

10698   Special Catalogue of the Collective Exhibition of Scientific Instruments and Appliances Exhibited by the Deutsche Ge-
sellschaft fur Mechanik und Optik, Berlin. Berlin: J.
Bahlke, printer, 1893. 182pp, ill (For the Chicago World's
Columbian Exposition)

10699   Special Catalogue of the Joint Exhibition of German Mecha-
nicians and Opticians. International Exposition, Paris.
Berlin: Reichsdruckerei, printer, 1900. 245pp, ill

10700   Ward, Francis Alan Burnett. Handbook of the Collections
        Illustrating Time Measurement. Science Museum. Part
        1. London: HMSO, 1936; Part 2. 1950; 3rd ed. 2 vol.
        1947-55; 4th ed. 1958; 1 vol. 1966. ill, pls, bib; (1966)
        151pp, 12 pls

10701   Wheatland, David P., and Barbara Carson. The Apparatus
        of Science at Harvard, 1765-1800. Cambridge, Mass:
        Harvard U. Pr, 1968. 203pp, ill, bib

OPTICAL INSTRUMENTS

10702   Baker, Henry. The Microscope Made Easy: or, 1. The
        nature, uses, and magnifying powers of the best kinds of
        microscopes described, calculated, and explained....
        London: for R. Dodsley, 1742. 311pp, 14 pls BM

10703   Brewster, Sir David. A Treatise on New Philosophical In-
        struments for Various Purposes in the Arts and Sciences,
        with experiments on lights and colours. London: John
        Murray; Edinburgh: William Blackwood, 1813. 427pp,
        12 folding pls BM, NN, ILC, MdBP

10704   _____. A Treatise on the Microscope ... (from) the
        seventh edition of the Encyclopaedia Britannica. Edin-
        burgh: A. & C. Black, 1837; 1857. 193pp, 14 pls NN,
        PPL

10705   Bronson, Dr. L. D. Early American Specs: an exciting
        collectible. Glendale, Cal: Occidental Pub, 1974. 188pp,
        ill, gloss, bib

10706   Browning, John. A Plea for Reflectors, being a description
        of the new astronomical telescopes with silvered-glass
        specula.... London: William Francis, 1867. 40pp, ill
        BM

10707   Catalogue of Optical and General Scientific Instruments. Lon-
        don: printed for the Optical Convention, 1912. 400pp,
        many ill (Telescopes, binoculars, microscopes, meteoro-
        logical, mathematical and surveying apparatus, cameras,
        etc.)

10708   *Clay, Reginald Stanley, and Thomas H. Court. The History
        of the Microscope. Compiled from original instruments
        and documents, up to the introduction of the achromatic
        microscope. London: C. Griffin, 1932. 266pp, ill, list
        of makers of microscopes & telescopes, etc. NN, TxU,
        CU

10709   Corson, Richard. Fashions in Eyeglasses. London: Owen;
        Chester Springs, Pa: Dufour, 1967. 288pp, ill, bib

10710   Crommelin, Claude August. Descriptive Catalogue of the
        Huygens Collection in the Rijksmuseum voor de Geschied-
        enis der Natuurwetenschapen (History of Science) at Leiden.
        Leiden, Holland: 1949. 31pp, 4 pls, bib (Clocks,
        watches, optical instruments) DLC

10711   Dick, Thomas, 1774-1857. The Practical Astronomer.
        Comprising illustrations of light and colours--practical
        descriptions of all kinds of telescopes--the use of the
        equatorial-transit-circular, and other astronomical instru-
        ments, a particular account of the Earle of Rosse's large
        telescopes, and other topics.... London: Seeley, Burn-
        side, and Seeley, 1845; New York: Harper, 1846; Phila-
        delphia: Biddle, 1848; 1850; New York: 1855; Philadel-
        phia: 1856; New York: Harper, 1872;... 567pp, ill:
        437pp, ill; 396pp, ill; ...; ...; 434pp, 100 ill ViU, MH

10712   _____. The Telescope and the Microscope. London: Re-
        ligious Tract Society, 1850?; Philadelphia: American Sun-
        day School Union, 1851? 192pp, ill ViU, CtY

10713   Dollond, Peter, and John Dollond. Description of the Ap-
        proved Achromatic Telescope, made with brass sliding
        tubes by P. and J. Dollond. London: 1800? BM

10714   Drew, John, 1809-1857. Manual of Astronomy: a popular
        treatise on theoretical, descriptive, and practical as-
        tronomy; with a familiar explanation of astronomical in-
        struments, and the best method of using them. London:
        Darton, 1845; 2nd ed. Philadelphia: Lippincott, 1853.
        343pp, ill, 9 pls MdBP

10715   Fox, Philip. Adler Planetarium and Astronomical Museum.
        An account of the optical planetarium and a brief guide to
        the museum. Chicago: Lakeside Pr, R. R. Donnelley,
        1833; 4th ed. Chicago: F. J. Ringley, 1937. 62pp, ill
        (Astronomical models, instruments, planispheres, etc.)

10716   Groeff, Richard, and others. Catalogue of a Picture Show
        Relating to the History of Spectacles. In Dutch, French
        and English. Amsterdam: A. E. D'Oliveira, 1929.
        266pp, pls DeWint

10717   Hastings, Charles S. Light. New York: Scribner's, 1901.
        224pp, 51 ill (Optical instruments--telescope, microscope,
        etc.--including historical notes)

10718   King, H. C. The History of the Telescope. London: Grif-
        fin, 1955. 442pp, 196 ill

10719   Land, Barbara. The Telescope Makers; from Galileo to the
        space age. New York: Crowell, 1968. 245pp, ill

10720   Lardner, Dionysius. Light, Colour, Solar Microscope,
        Camera Lucida, Camera Obscura, Magic Lantern. Lon-
        don: Walton & Maberly, 1869. 202pp, ill

10721   _____. The Microscope. Reprint from his Museum of
        Science and Art. London: Walton & Maberly, 1856.
        112pp, 147 ill

10722   Martin, Benjamin. A New Treatise of the Microscope, and
        Microscopic Objects. London: R. Ware, 1742. ill

10723   Rasmussen, O(tto) D(urham). History of Chinese Spectacles.
        Bangor, Me: Thomas W. Burr, printer, for Scientific
        Section of the American Optical Association, 1915. 16pp,
        ill   DLC

KALEIDOSCOPES

10724   Bradley, Richard, 1688-1732. Description and Use of the In-
        strument Now Called a Kaleidoscope as Published by Its Origi-
        nal Inventor. Reprint from 6th ed. of New Improvements of
        Planting and Gardening.... London: printed for J. and J.
        Knapton, etc., 1731. London: E. L. Simmons, 1818. 14pp,
        1 folding pl ViU, BM (Used to suggest garden bed layouts.)

10725   Brewster, Sir David, 1781-1868. Description and Method of
        Using the Patent Kaleidoscope Invented by Dr. Brewster.
        London: 1818. 18pp, pls BM, DLC

10726   _____. A Treatise on the Kaleidoscope. Edinburgh: A.
        Constable, 1819; 2nd ed. enl. as The Kaleidoscope; its
        history, theory and construction, with its application to the
        fine and useful arts. London: Murray, 1858; 3rd ed.
        London: Hotten, 1870. 166pp, 7 pls; 189pp, pls (See
        also: his A Treatise on New Philosophical Instruments...,
        no. 10703.) NjP, NN, BM, MiD

GLOBES AND ORRERIES

10727   Adams, George, d. 1773, The Elder. An Essay on the Use
        of Celestial and Terrestrial Globes. 4th ed. Philadelphia:
        Whitehall for William Young, 1800. 238pp, 2 pls DeWint

10728   _____. A Treatise describing and Explaining the Construc-
        tion and Use of New Celestial and Terrestrial Globes, etc.
        London: Author, 1766; 2nd ed. 1769; 3rd ed. 1772;...
        242pp, 3 pls; 345pp, 14 pls

10729   Bertele, Hans von. Globes and Spheres. Lausanne: Swiss
        Watch and Jewelry Journal, 1961. 63pp, pls

10730   Calvert, Henry Reginald. Astronomy: Globes, orreries and
        other models. Science Museum. London: HMSO, 1967.
        47pp, 21 ill

10731   De Morgan, Augustus. Treatise on the Globes, Celestial and
        Terrestrial. London: Orr, 1854.

10732   Ferguson, James, 1710-1776. A Dissertation upon the Phe-
        nomena of the Harvest Moon. Also, the description and
        use of a new four-whefl'd [sic] orrery,... London:
        Author, 1747. 72pp, 3 folding pls NN, DLC

10733   . Select Mechanical Exercises: shewing how to con-
        struct different clocks, orreries, and sun-dials, on plain
        and easy principles ... with tables.... London: printed
        for W. Strahan; and T. Cadell, 1773; 2nd ed. 1778; 3rd
        ed. London: for W. Strahan and T. Cadeli (!), 1790.
        ...; ...; 272pp, 9 folding pls MH, DLC, DeWint

10734   Fox, Philip. Adler Planetarium and Astronomical Museum.
        An account of the optical planetarium and a brief guide to
        the museum. Chicago: Lakeside Pr, R. R. Donnelley,
        1933; 4th ed. Chicago: F. J. Ringley, 1937. 62pp, ill
        (Astronomical models and instruments, planispheres, etc.)

10735   Gillingham, Harrold Edgar. The First Orreries in America.
        Reprint from Journal of Franklin Institute, vol. 229, no. 1,
        January 1940. Philadelphia: 1940. 20pp (pp. 81-100), ill

10736   Harris, John, 1667?-1719. The Descriptions and Uses of the
        Celestial and Terrestrial Globes and of Collin's Pocket
        Quadrant. London: E. Midwinter, for D. Midwinter and
        T. Legh, 1703; 3rd ed. 1710;... 62pp, ill, pl PPL, De-
        Wint, MiU

Antiques and Collectibles

10737 _____. The Description and Use of the Globes and the Orrery; to which is prefix'd by way of introduction, a brief account of the solar system. London: T. Wright & E. Cushee, 1731; 4th ed. 1738; 8th ed. 1757; 12th ed. 1783;... 190pp, pls, diags PPL, MiU

10738 Jennings, Reverend David, 1691-1762. An Introduction to the Use of Globes, and the orrery: with the application of astronomy to chronology. Adapted to the instruction and entertainment of such persons as are not previously versed in mathematic science. London: 1739; London: for J. Nourse, 1747; 1752; 3rd ed. 1766. 146pp; 168pp, diags NjP, ICU, MdBP

10739 Jones, William, 1763-1831. The Description and Use of a New Portable Orrery; on a most simple construction,... 2nd ed. enl. ... & embellished with a new copper plate of the instrument. London: Author, 1784; 3rd ed. 1787; 5th ed. 1799; 6th ed. 1812. 36pp, pl; 43pp, 2 pls; 50pp, pls NNC-Ave, MiU

10740 Leybourn, William. An Introduction to Astronomy and Geography Being a Plain and Easie Treatise of the Globes. Seven parts. London: J.C., for R. Morden & W. Berry, 1675. 234pp, diags DLC, NN

10741 _____. Panorganon: or, A universal instrument, performing all such conclusions geometrical and astronomical, as are usually wrought by the globes, spheres, sectors, quadrants, planispheres, or other the like instruments, yet in being; with ease and exactness. 2 parts in 1 vol. London: W. Birch, 1672. 140 plus 119pp, 2 pls, diags DLC, MH, NNC-Ave

10742 *Lister, Raymond. How to Identify Old Maps and Globes ... ca.1500 to ca.1850. London: Bell, 1965. 256pp, 50 photographs, 11 ill, 178 drawings of watermarks, listing of about 2000 cartographers, engravers, publishers, etc.

10743 Rice, Howard Crosby. The Rittenhouse Orrery; Princeton's 18th century planetarium, 1767-1954. Exhibition commentary. Princeton, NJ: University Library, 1954. 88pp, ill, 16 pls

10744 *Stevenson, Edward Luther. Terrestrial and Celestial Globes: Their History and construction.... 2 vol. New Haven: Yale U. Pr, for Hispanic Society of New York, 1921. text, ill, pls, bib

10745 *Yonge, Ena L. A Catalogue of Early Globes, made prior to 1850 and conserved in the United States; a preliminary listing. New York: American Geographical Society, 1968. 118pp, ill, pls

SECTION XXXIII

THE HUMAN BODY: MAINTENANCE AND REPAIR

MEDICINE, DENISTRY AND PHRENOLOGY

10746 Boger, Jacob H. Artificial Teeth without Plates, artificial crowns, bridge work and partial crowns. Dentistry: Past and Present. Findlay, Ohio: 1891. 23pp, ill DLC

10747 Brown, Leland Arthur. Early Philosophical Apparatus at Transylvania College and Relics of the Medical Department. Lexington, Ky: Transylvania College Pr, 1959. 117pp, ill

10748 Catalogue and Report of Obstetrical and Other Instruments Exhibited at the Conversazione of the Obstetrical Society of London; held, by permission, at the Royal College of Physicians, March 28, 1866. London: Longman, Green, 1867. 229pp, 213 large ill

10749 Catalogue of Portraits, busts and casts, in the cabinet of the American Institute of Phrenology, 737 Broadway. New York: S. R. Wells, 1875. 38pp, ill DeWint

10750 Colyer, Sir James Frank. Old Instruments Used for Extracting Teeth. London; New York: Staples Pr, 1952; reprint. Pound Ridge, NY: Milford House, 1972. 245pp, ill, bib ICJ, PPULC

10751 Combe, George, 1788-1858. The Constitution of Man Considered in Relation to External Objects. 4th ed. rev. & enl. Edinburgh: Anderson, 1828; ...; from 3rd enl. Edinburgh ed. New York: Harper, 1835;... 110pp, 382pp (Phrenology)

10752 _____. Elements of Phrenology. Edinburgh: J. Anderson, Jr.; London: Simpkin & Marshall, 1824; ...; 1st American ed. from 2nd Edinburgh, improved & enl. Philadelphia: E. Littell, 1826; 4th ed. Edinburgh: MacLachlan & Stewart, 1836;... 227pp, 2 pls; 221pp, 11 pls; 194pp, ill, pls, bib MiU

10753   Crellin, J. K.   Medical Ceramics: a catalogue of the Eng-
        lish and Dutch Collections in the Museum of the Wellcome
        Institute of the History of Medicine.   London: Wellcome
        Institute, 1969.   304pp, 490 ill, 2 pls, bib (Drug jars,
        pill slabs, etc.)

10754   Davies, John Dunn.   Phrenology: fad and science; a 19th
        century American crusade.   Based on a thesis.   New
        Haven: Yale U. Pr, 1955; Hamden, Conn: Archon Books,
        1971.   203pp, ill, bib

10755   Davis, Daniel.   The Medical Application of Electricity, with
        descriptions of apparatus and instructions for its use.
        Boston: 1846.   244pp BM

10756   Gooch, Benjamin, d.1780.   Cases and Practical Remarks on
        Surgery, with sketches of machines, of simple construction,
        easy application, and approved use.   London: for D. Wil-
        son & T. Durham, 1758; 2nd ed.   Norwich: Chase, 1767.
        184pp, 12 pls; ?pp, 17 pls ViU, MiU

10757   Ibbotson, William.   A
        Practical Guide to
        Surgical Operations,
        Instruments and Ap-
        pliances.   Part 1.
        Surgical Operations.
        Part 2. Illustrations
        of Instruments and
        Appliances.   2 parts
        in 1 vol.   London:
        Scientific Pr, 1921;
        2nd ed. as Surgical
        Operations.   Chicago:
        Medical Book Co.;
        London: Faber &
        Gwyer, 1926.   248pp,
        ill; 356pp, ill

10758   Lufkin, Arthur Ward.   A History of Dentistry.   Philadelphia:
        Lea & Febiger, 1938; 2nd ed. 1948.   255pp, 90 ill; 367pp,
        ill DLC

10759   Mitchell, Silas Weir.   The Early History of Instrumental
        Precision in Medicine; an address before the Second Con-
        gress of American Physicians and Surgeons.   September
        1891....   New Haven: Tuttle, Morehouse & Taylor, 1892;
        reprint. New York: Burt Franklin, 1971.   42pp, ill, bib

10760   The Phrenologists' Own Book: a practical treatise on phre-
        nology; with directions for examining heads, and a descrip-
        tion of the requisite instruments.   Philadelphia: J. Kay,
        Jr., & Bro.; Pittsburgh: C. H. Kay, 1841.   96pp, pl

10761 Spurzheim, Johann Gaspar, 1776-1832. Outlines of Phre-
       nology; being also a manual of references for the marked
       bust. Boston: Marsh, Capen & Lyon, 1832. 96pp, ill

10762 Thomas, H. H., chairman of the Essential Artificial Limb
       Co. Help for Wounded Heroes. The story of ancient and
       modern artificial limbs. London: J. Miles, 1920. 23pp

10763 The Wellcome Historical Medical Museum Handbook. London:
       Wellcome Foundation, 1927. 118pp, ill

PHARMACIES

10764a Anderson, D. Antique Furniture from Danish Prescription
       Pharmacies. Copenhagen: 1948. 416pp, ill (English
       introduction and captions to 1944 edition. Copenhagen
       Medical-Historical Museum, and Aarhus Museum)

10764b Bender, G. A., and J. Parascandola, eds. Historical Hob-
       bies for the Pharmacist. Madison, Wisc: American Insti-
       tute of the History of Pharmacy, 1974. (1973 symposium
       including glassware, philately, ephemera, antiques, books,
       archaeology)

10765a Bennett, John. Apothecaries' Hall, a unique exhibit at the
       Charleston Museum. An ancient drug-shop whose business
       survived plagues, wars, great fires, and earthquakes.
       Charleston, SC: 1923. 21pp, pls

10765b Catalogue of an Exhibition Illustrating the History of Pharmacy,
       held during the festival period May-September 1951 at the
       Wellcome Research Institution. Introd. by E. Ashworth
       Underwood. London; New York: G. Cumberlege, Oxford
       U. Pr, for Wellcome Historical Medical Museum, 1951.
       59pp, pls

10766 Coblentz, Virgil. Handbook of Pharmacy, embracing the
       theory and practice of pharmacy and the art of dispensing.
       Philadelphia: P. Blakiston, 1894; 2nd rev. & enl. ed.
       Philadelphia: 1895. 480pp, 395 ill, bib; 572pp, 437 ill,
       bib MiU, DLC

10767a Crellin, J. K. Medical Ceramics in the Wellcome Institute.
       London: 1969. ill

10767b _____, and J. R. Scott. Glass and British Pharmacy,
       1600-1900: a survey and guide to the Wellcome Collection
       of British Glass. London: Wellcome Institute of the His-
       tory of Medicine, 1972. 72pp, ill, bib

10768 Freeman, Graydon La Verne. Apothecary. Early American
       Occupation. Watkins Glen, NY: Century, 1974. ill

10769   Gill, Harold B., Jr.   The Apothecary in Colonial Virginia.
        Williamsburg, Va: Colonial Williamsburg Foundation, dist.
        by U. Pr of Virginia, Charlottesville, 1972.   127pp, bib

10770   Griffenhagen, George B.   Early American Pharmacies; a
        pictorial catalogue of apothecary shop restorations which
        are on exhibit in the United States.   Washington, D.C.:
        American Pharmaceutical Association, 1955.   23pp, ill,
        bib

10771a   _____ .   Pharmacy Museums.   Madison, Wisc: American
        Institute of the History of Pharmacy, 1956.   51pp, pls
        DeWint

10771b * _____ , and Ernst W. Stieb.   Tools of the Apothecary:
        a select bibliography.   Madison, Wisc: American Institute
        of the History of Pharmacy, 1975.   13pp

10772a *Hamarneh, Sami.   Pharmacy Museums and Historical Col-
        lections on Public View, United States.   Madison, Wisc:
        American Institute of the History of Pharmacy, 1972.
        49pp, ill, bib

10772b   _____ .   Temples of the Muses and a History of Pharmacy
        Museums.   Tokyo: 1972.   ill   (Chiefly Japanese artifacts,
        but includes Occidental)

10773   *Howard, Geoffrey Eliot.   Early English Drug Jars.   With
        notes on Jacobean wine pots, cups, etc.   London: Medici
        Society, 1931.   49pp, ill, 22 (2 color) pls, gloss   (17th
        century, Lambeth pottery)

10774   Koning, Dirk Arnold Wittop.   Delft Drugjars.   Delftse
        Apothekers-potten.   English, Dutch, French text.   De-
        venter: 1954.   174pp, ill

10775   *Matthews, Leslie Gerald.   Antiques of the Pharmacy.   Lon-
        don: G. Bell, 1971.   129pp, 89 ill, bib   (Furnishings &
        utensils)

10776   _____ .   History of the Pharmacy in Britain.   Fore. by
        Sir Henry Dale.   Edinburgh: 1962.   444pp, 41 ill

10777   Nekam, Livia.   Old Hungarian Pharmacies.   Tr. from
        Hungarian by G. Gulyos.   Budapest: Corvina, Clematis
        Pr, 1968; 3rd ed. 1974.   80pp, 40 ill   (16th-19th century
        apothecary jars & vessels, interior decoration & furniture)

10778a   Somlo, Jean, and Thomas Somlo.   Pharmaceutical Antiques
        and Collectibles, with price guide.   Manchester, Vt:
        1970; New York: Crown, 1971.   36pp, 17 color ill
        (1850-1910)

10778b Sonnedecker, Glenn, rev. Kremers and Urdang's History of
       Pharmacy. Philadelphia: Lippincott, 1976.

10779 Underwood, Edgar Ashworth. Guide to An Exhibition Illus-
       trating the Story of Pharmacy, at the Wellcome Historical
       Medical Museum, London. London: Oxford U. Pr, 1955.

10780a Urdang, G., and F. W. Nitardy. Squibb Ancient Pharmacy.
       New York: 1940. many ill (Collection now in Smith-
       sonian. Chiefly pre-18th century)

10780b Wellcome, Henry S. Historical Exhibition of Rare and
       Curious Objects Relating to Medicine, Chemistry, Phar-
       macy and the Allied Sciences.... June 24, 1913. Lon-
       don: 1913. 15pp, ill BM

10781 Whitall Tatum and Company. 1880. Flint Glassware, blue
       ware, perfume and cologne bottles, show bottles and globes,
       green glassware, stoppers, druggists' sundries. Reprint
       with introduction. Princeton, NJ: Pyne, 1971. 72pp, ill,
       8 pls, bib

10782   . 1892. Colognes, drug mills, bottles, scales,
       cork presses. Edited reprint. Millville, NJ: S. R.
       Bailey, 1969. 32pp, ill

10783   . 1902. Edited reprint. Millville, NJ: S. R.
       Bailey, 196-? 64pp, ill (Drug, perfume and chemists
       bottles)

BIBLIOGRAPHY

The American Catalogue. Under direction of F. Leypoldt; compiled
by Lynds E. Jones. New York: R. R. Bowker, 1881; reprint.
New York: Peter Smith, 1941.

Art Index. Accumulative Author and Subject Index to a Selected
List of Fine Arts Periodicals and Museum Bulletins. New
York: H. W. Wilson, 1938-date.

British Museum General Catalogue of Printed Books. Photolitho-
graphic Edition to 1955. 263 volumes. London: British Museum, 1965; 10 Year Supplement. 1956-1965. 50 volumes;
Five Year Supplement. 1966-1970. 26 volumes.

British Museum Subject Index. 1906-1910 (and every four years
thereon).

British National Bibliography. Annual. London: British Museum,
Council of British National Bibliography, Ltd., 1950 - date.

Catalog, Harvard University Fine Arts Library, Fogg Art Museum.
15 vol. Boston: Hall, 1971.

Collison, Robert. Published Library Catalogues. An Introduction
to Their Contents and Use. New York: R. R. Bowker, 1973.

Courtney, William Prideaux. A Register of National Bibliography.
2 vol. London: Constable, 1905.

Fortescue, G. K., ed. Subject Index of the Modern Works Added
to British Museum 1881-1900. 3 vol. London: HMSO, 1902,
1903; Subject Index to the Modern Works Added ... 1901-1905.
Photo copy. London: 1965.

Irish Publishing Record. Dublin: University College, School of
Librarianship, 1967-1972.

Library of Congress Catalog--Books: Subjects. 1950-1954; 1955-
1959; 1960-1964; 1965-1969; 1970; 1971; 1972; 1973; 1974; 1975.

The London Catalogue of Books Published in Great Britain with

Their Sizes, prices, and publishers' names. 1816-1851. London: T. Hodgson, 1851.

The Monthly Catalogues from the London Magazine, 1732-1766. Index compiled by Edward Kimber. English Bibliographical Sources ed. by D. F. Foxon. Facsimile reprint. London: Gregg Press & Archive Press, 1966.

National Art Library Catalogue. Author Catalogue. Victoria and Albert Museum, London. 11 volumes. Boston: G. K. Hall, 1972.

*Peddie, Robert Alexander. Subject Index of Books before 1880. A-Z. First Series. London: Grafton, 1933; 2nd series. 1935; 3rd series. 1939; 4th series. 1948.

_____, and Quinton Waddington. The English Catalogue of Books (Including the Original 'London' Catalogue) ... Books Issued in the United Kingdom of Great Britain and Ireland 1801-1836. Reprint. New York: Kraus Reprint, 1963.

Sabin, Joseph. Bibliotheca Americana. A Dictionary of Books Relating to America. 29 volumes. New York: Joseph Sabin, 1868.

The Winterthur Museum Libraries' Collection of Printed Books and Periodicals. Introd. by Frank Sommer, III. 9 vol. Wilmington, Del: Scholarly Resources, 1974. (Basic works to 1973.)

Automobile accessories and sup-
plies 8414, 8417
Ava japanned work 5681
Averbeck glass 4278
Aviaries 2877, 2884
Awnings 7551
Axes 51, 89-91, 229, 373,
5391, 9157, 9483
Axminster carpets 7486

-B-

Babbage, Charles 10158
Baby rattles 8297, 8308
Backgammon 8091, 8099, 8102
Bagpipes 8606, 8616
Ball costumes 6041
Ballgames 8062-8064, 8068,
8070, 8074, 8077, 8079,
8080, 8083, 8084
Bamboo work 7809
Banjoes 8531
Banks, Mechanical and still
8678-8682, 9685-9687, 9691
Barbed wire 824, 1467, 9059-
9069
Barberini armor 9146
Barberini vase 3621
Barbers and barbering 557, 563,
564, 4178-4180
Barbotine painting 5615
Barometers 10154, 10160, 10166,
10169, 10182, 10199, 10219,
10229, 10233, 10243
Baroque decorations and ornament
1120
Barrel organ 8555
Basketball 8074
Baskets 9653-9668
American 9662, 9666, 9667
British 9656, 9660, 9663, 9664
Bassoons 8622, 8623, 8627
Bateman, Hester 5203
Baths and bathroom accessories
2855-2860
Battersea enamels 3744, 3753,
4867, 5962, 5967, 5971,
5972
Bauhaus 1705, 1743, 1759, 1773,
1795
Bawdy house tokens 824
Bayeaux tapestry 7672, 7673,
7687, 7689
Bayonets 9168, 9251, 9262, 9337,
9517, 9578, 9579

Beads 6216, 6240, 6246, 6307
Beadwork 6307, 7209
Bed hangings 2830, 7423, 7747
Bed rugs 7416
Bedding 2822
Bedroom furniture 777, 1979,
2409, 2823, 2826, 2831
Beds 777, 824, 2777, 2787,
2821-2834
Beekeeping supplies 8966, 9000,
9056
Beilby, Ralph, Wm. and Mary
4526, 4572
Bell founders 8642, 8643, 8646,
8649, 8660, 8661, 8663,
8676-8680, 8682, 8689-8691,
8694, 8695, 8705-8707
Bell inscriptions 8634, 8640,
8642, 8643, 8647, 8660,
8663, 8676-8680, 8682,
8686, 8687, 8689-8691,
8694, 8695, 8703, 8704
Belleek Parian ware 3381
Bells 8632-8708
American 8656, 8671-8674
British 8659, 8681, 8685,
8695, 8705, 8707, 8708
Church 8635, 8636, 8638,
8641-8643, 8647-8654, 8660,
8661, 8663, 8664, 8670,
8673, 8676-8680, 8682-8684,
8686, 8687, 8689, 8694,
8698-8704, 8706
Hand and small 8633, 8644,
8657, 8665-8669, 8693
Bennington ware 3090-3092, 3149,
3152, 3174, 3176
Bentley, Bert 3552
Bentley, Thomas 3556
Bentwood furniture 2699, 2704,
2705
Berlin iron jewelry 6228
Bertrand bottles 4677
Bessemer mills 5711
Bibelot 1170, 1175
Bibliographies 1-4
Agriculture 8987
Antiques 748, 778, 799, 825,
826, 831, 880, 909, 910,
940, 945, 947, 956, 983,
1007, 1010-1013, 1061, 1080,
1150, 1168
American 1254, 1260
British 1643
Arms and armor 9215, 9268,
9312, 9326, 9374
Automata 10654
Bells 8664

419-459, 511, 1964, 1979,
2016, 2021-2907, 2912,
2951, 3447, 5714, 6274,
10450, 10698, 10699
Inventions, History of 71, 200,
210, 230, 302, 315, 333,
334, 342, 403, 476-534
Inventories 1176, 1284, 1500,
1568, 1573, 2160, 6967,
9020
Iridescent glass 4211, 4424, 4445
Irish antiques 2396, 2509, 2522
Iron 212, 5703, 5709, 5712-
5715, 5727, 5728
    American 5697-5702, 5705,
    5708, 5712, 5717, 5719,
    5720, 5724, 5727
    Architectural uses of 5775,
    5786, 5805-5824
    British 5706, 5707, 5721,
    5726, 5729
    Cast 306, 5743, 5696, 5776,
    5779, 5783, 5788-5791,
    5814, 5818, 5824
    Chinese 5718
    Scottish 5704
    Wrought 5744, 5752, 5763,
    5766, 5768, 5769, 5776,
    5778, 5781, 5792, 5793,
    5798, 5803, 5805-5813b,
    5815-5824
Iron wares, American 5770,
5776, 5782, 5803
Irons 9723, 9730, 9751
Ironstone 3119, 3188, 3678
Ironwork 43, 5696, 5735, 5736,
5738, 5742, 5748, 5751,
5756, 5758, 5762, 5768,
5772, 5787
    American 5734, 5737, 5740,
    5770, 5776, 5786, 5793-
    5797, 5802, 5803
    Architectural
        Australian 5817, 5818
        Charleston 5810
        Cheltenham 5808
        English 5808, 5809,
    5811, 5812, 5819-5821, 5823
        Philadelphia 5822
        Savannah 5806
        Spanish 5807
    Bent 5755, 5759, 5765, 5800
    British 98, 190, 344, 391,
    654, 980, 1637, 5731-5733,
    5739, 5741, 5742, 5746,
    5764, 5781, 5782-5785,
    5792, 5798, 5799
    Decorative 654, 1637, 5743-

5749, 5751-5752, 5754-5759,
5761, 5764, 5768, 5769,
5773, 5775, 5778, 5779,
5781, 5783, 5784, 5786,
5795-5797, 5804
    European 5754, 5761, 5804
    French 5749, 5757, 5773
    Spanish 5747
Ironworkers 5722
Ives toys 8269
Ivory 929, 5847-5860
    Afro-Portuguese 5875, 5876
    Chinese 5862-5865
    English 5866, 5870, 5871
    Indian 5861
    Japanese 6148-6154, 6156-
    6172
    Oriental 5861-5865
    Western World 5867-5874
Ivory-working 5371

-J-

Jack-in-the-box 8085
Jacob, George 2770, 2771
Jacquard looms and weaving 6837,
6840, 6988, 6990, 7047,
7589
Jade 5877-5894
    Chinese 5895-5912
    Indian 5883
James, Kirtland and Co. Ironwork
5797
Japanese antiques and applied arts
1963-2008
Japanese ceramics 4125-4159
Japanese design 597, 606, 612,
631, 637, 667, 689
Japanese export art 1975
Japanese export porcelain 4158
Japanese legend in art 1986
Japanese seals 1972
Japanese weapons 1985
Japanning 36, 114, 341, 664,
5353, 5571, 5587, 5680-
5695
Jasper ware 3555, 3594, 3618
Jasperware, Blue 3713
Jerome, Chauncey 10483, 10525,
10526
Jet 6276, 6283
Jewelers' manuals and magazines
6207, 6256, 6257, 6277,
6305
Jewelry 43, 249, 821, 1758,

7318, 7331, 7358, 7379
Dutch 7356
French 7350
Irish 7319, 7330, 7342, 7351, 7352
Italian 7367, 7370
Machine-made 6096, 6097, 7129, 7335
Macrame 7332, 7374
Spanish 7354, 7355, 7357
Lace bibliographies 7320, 7349, 7373, 7378
Lace dictionaries 7324, 7378
Lace-making instruction 7315, 7332, 7335, 7337, 7348, 7359, 7367, 7378
Lace patterns 7318, 7333, 7348, 7376
Lacquer work 41b, 72, 5919, 5925
  American 5922
  Chinese 5915, 5916, 5933, 5935
  European and British 5922
  Japanese 5913-5915, 5917, 5920, 5923, 5924, 5928-5932, 5934, 5936
  Japanese export 5917
  Oriental 5918, 5921, 5926, 5927
  Western 5922
Lacquering 2149, 5370
Lakin, Thomas 3695
Lalique, Rene 4640
Lambeth stoneware 3281
Lamps 495, 9789, 9951, 9952, 9961, 9963, 9966, 9988, 9992, 9993, 9997, 10004-10007, 10010, 10016, 10017
  Fairy 9990
  Grease 9952, 9957, 9961, 9966
  Miners' 10003, 10013
  Miniature 9789, 9951, 9961, 9963
  Oil 9963, 9966, 9991
  Tiffany 4474, 4480, 9980
Lampshades, Art glass 4429, 4430, 4474, 4480
Lancaster glass 4310
Lang and Jacobs Tools 5411
Lantern clocks 10586
Lanterns, Railroad 8415, 9954
Lapidary work 72
Larson, Emil J. 4370
Lathes, Metal 182, 295, 335, 411, 5449
Lathes, Wood 411, 5443-5466
Lathework 5444, 5446-5450,

5453, 5454, 5457-5459, 5461
Law enforcement collectibles 1042, 6431, 6432
Leach pottery 3404, 3405
Lead figures 8240
Leadwork 5601, 5629, 5663
Leather bottles 4669
Leather work 41b, 43, 398, 1019, 2102, 2149, 5370, 7790-7800
Leeds pottery 3348, 3396, 3511, 3519, 3520
Leman, James 6947
Lenox china 3126
Leonardo da Vinci 178
Lessore, Emile 3562
Levels 5394, 5396
Libbey glass 4366, 4382, 4383
Liberty Bell 8645, 8688, 8696
Liberty china 3180
Library fittings and supplies 2861, 2863, 2865, 2867, 2868
Library furniture 2409, 2861, 2863, 2865, 2867, 2868
Lifting machinery 180
Lighthouse lighting 9953, 10006
Lighting 9950, 9952, 9966, 9967, 9973, 9975, 9976, 9981, 9982, 9984-9987, 9989, 9992, 9993, 9997-9999, 10002, 10010, 10015-10017
  American 317, 9957, 9960, 9966, 9972, 9974, 9976, 9980, 9992, 9994, 10005
  British 43
  Church 6589
  Commercial 9948, 9966
  Electric 9960, 9965, 9966, 9970, 9971, 9983, 9987, 9996, 10001, 10012
  Gas 43, 9948, 9956, 9958, 9966, 9968, 9977, 9978, 10000
  Street 9979, 9994, 10006, 10018
Lighting fixtures 5560, 9948, 9952, 9968, 9969
Lighting glossaries and dictionaries 9962, 10016, 10017
Lightning conductors or rods 10265, 10269-10271, 10274-10276, 10280, 10281, 10283, 10284
Limited edition collectibles 969, 2933
Limoges 3490. See also Haviland porcelain.
Limoges enamels 5952, 5957, 5959, 5963

Medicine bottles see Bottles, Medicine and bitters
Medieval industries 267
Meissen porcelain 3786, 3795, 3796, 3821, 3827, 3839, 3843, 3871, 3877
Memorial art 625, 6460-6556
Memorial brasses see Brasses, Monumental
Mercantile history 46, 535-554, 1812
Meriden Britannia silverplate 5030
Metal 5506, 5567, 5578, 5580, 5597, 5605, 5624, 5629, 5644, 5646, 5649, 5652, 5653, 5667
Metal decorating 5575
Metal enamelling 5680
Metal turning 182
Metalwork 43, 5515, 5555, 5573, 5603, 5611, 5618, 5622, 5630, 5636, 5646, 5647, 5650, 5651, 5666, 5673-5675, 5677
    Art 36, 909, 5575, 5588, 5631, 5673, 5678, 5738, 5744, 5755, 5761, 5765, 5786, 5800
    Brass and copper 43, 5525, 5589, 5641
    British 5564, 5657, 5662, 5670
    Indian 2024
    Oriental 5539
    Romanian 5656
    Russian 5512, 5599, 5595
Metalworking 11, 182-185, 249, 415
Metalworking lathes 182, 411
Metalworking manuals 5517, 5520, 5526, 5527, 5538, 5653, 5821
Metalworking patterns 5517, 5526, 5626, 5661, 5679
Metalworking tools 260, 410-413
Meteorological instruments 10154, 10165, 10216, 10218, 11221
Metronome 10175, 10178
Mettlach steins 4160, 4162, 4166, 4168, 4169, 4171, 4175
Mettlach ware 4168, 4169, 4175
Micrometers 10164, 10211
Microphones see Phonography
Microscopes 10702, 10704, 10707, 10712, 10717, 10720-10722

Military curios and collectibles 9247, 9347, 9401, 9476
Military dictionary 9282, 9309
Military insignia, American 9385
Military weapons, American 9377-9380, 9382, 9386, 9391-9393, 9395, 9397, 9399, 9401, 9404-9406, 9408, 9409, 9423-9425, 9427, 9429, 9432, 9438, 9464, 9471, 9473-9476, 9482, 9484, 9485, 9487, 9494, 9512
Military weapons, British 9537-9545, 9547-9567, 9569-9591, 9594-9596
Milk glass 4183, 4451, 4452
Millinery 6048, 6350-6368
Millinery handbooks 6357, 6359
Milling machinery 335, 412
Millville glass 4354
Millworking machinery 65, 314
Miners' lamps 10003, 10013
Ming dynasty arts 3980-3982, 3990, 3992, 3993, 4014, 4050, 4060, 4062, 4065, 4074, 4099
Miniature furniture 2147, 8351
Miniature lamps 8350, 9789, 9951, 9961, 9963
Miniature objects 8338, 8344, 8346, 8347, 8350-8352
Mintons pottery 2882, 3680, 3702-3706, 3720, 3724
Mirrors, Advertising 8786, 8794, 8795
Mirrors and mirror frames 658, 2544, 2836, 2837, 2841-2854
Misericords 6585
Missionary relics 2202
Mocha pottery 3511
Model airplanes 997, 8315, 8324
Model dirigibles 8324
Model engines 8335, 8342, 8343
Model flowers 8345
Model machinery 8324, 8331, 8333, 8337, 8339-8341, 8348, 8349
Model railroads 8312-8314, 8316-8323, 8325-8330
Model soldiers 8240, 8251, 8262, 8266, 8289, 8291, 8295, 8307
Model telegraphs 8324
Model X-ray apparatus 8324
Model-making 8336, 8341, 8343, 8348, 8353
Models 79, 8312-8330, 8331-8353

Pennsylvania glass 4351, 4416
Pens 43, 8905, 8914, 8915, 8928
Perforation machines 52
Perfumery 4723, 4744, 6099, 6104, 6107, 6117
Perkins, Joseph 4996
Persian carpets and rugs see Carpets and rugs, Persian
Pews 6639, 6642, 6653
Pewter 5514, 5516, 5530, 5533, 5542, 5550, 5558, 5608, 5632, 5658, 5664, 5676
   American 5508-5511, 5528, 5546, 5549, 5551, 5554, 5568, 5576, 5581, 5583, 5584, 5590, 5594, 5600, 5608, 5617, 5621, 5625, 5633, 5642, 5643
   British 5523, 5524, 5532, 5534-5537, 5550, 5553, 5582, 5607, 5609, 5610, 5612-5614, 5623, 5627, 5640, 5654, 5659, 5665
   Channel Islands 5672
   European 5572, 5610, 5660
   Scottish 5671
Pewter marks 5025, 5511, 5534, 5546, 5582, 5607, 5640
Pewter measures 5676
Pharmaceutical ceramics 3262, 10767a
Pharmaceutical glass 4528, 10767b, 10781-10783
Pharmacies and equipment 4729, 4787-4789, 10764a-10783
Philosophical apparatus see Scientific apparatus
Phoenix glass 4416
Phonographs 8830-8840
Photographic postcards 8900
Photographs 8013, 8849, 8859, 8901
Photography 8841, 8846, 8851, 8855-8877, 8860, 8877, 8878, 8885, 8892, 8895, 8898
   Apparatus and supplies 43, 8859, 8867, 8890, 8891, 8896
Photography dictionaries 8891
Phrenology 10749, 10751, 10752, 10754, 10760, 10761
Phyfe, Duncan 2207, 2287, 2349
Pianofortes and Pianos 8484, 8486-8492, 8494, 8495, 8497, 8498, 8500, 8503-

8507, 8509, 8510, 8517-8520
   Coin-operated 8710, 8734
   Player pianos 8729, 8732, 8733, 8742
   Reproducing 8718
Pickard china 3153
Picture frames 648, 649, 2835, 2838, 2839, 2844
Picture frames, Miniature cases 8887
Pier glasses 2843, 2845, 2851
Pierced work, Wood 5370, 5377-5385
Pilkington Brothers 4499, 4563
Pillow lace 7165, 7325, 7334, 7358, 7372, 7379
Pincushion dolls 8187
Pincushions 7066
Pinxton china 3301
Pioneer pottery, American 3098, 3104
Pipes, Tobacco see Tobacco pipes
Pique 4834
Pistols and handguns 9132, 9156, 9158, 9197, 9213, 9226, 9241, 9244, 9249, 9250, 9252, 9269, 9281, 9304, 9305, 9323-9325, 9327, 9329-9331, 9341-9343, 9359, 9362
   American 9381, 9382, 9387, 9405, 9421, 9422, 9432, 9441, 9448, 9452, 9453, 9459, 9467, 9479-9481, 9493, 9496, 9500-9503, 9505, 9513, 9518, 9520, 9524, 9530, 9531, 9535
   British 9557, 9569, 9583
Pitchers, Glass 4357-4365
Pitkin and Brooks glass 4423
Pittsburgh glass 4351
Planes, Wood 5387, 5399, 5416, 5420, 5421, 5425, 5429-5436
Planetarium 10174, 10179
Planing mill 5438
Planisphere 10734, 10741
Plant and floral forms 566, 569, 570, 590, 594, 602, 603, 614, 726, 3538, 4467, 7151, 7192, 7297, 7319, 7401, 7671, 7801, 7807, 7808, 7813
Plasterer's tools 59, 74, 270, 286, 287
Plasterwork 98, 270, 286, 287, 775, 1529, 1597, 2476, 2517

Aarseth, Sigmund 5368, 6804
Abbate, Francesco 1843
Abbott, Allan L. 4664
Abbott, Henry G. (pseud. for
    Hazlitt, George Henry A.)
    555, 6207, 10312, 10313,
    10473, 10474
Abbott, Lyman 7756
Abbott, R. D. 5
Abell, Sydney George 5443
Abels, Robert 9376
Accum, Frederich Christian
    9948, 10664, 10665
Achdjian, Albert 7464
Ackerman, Phyllis 1909,
    7126, 7138, 7667-7670,
    7754
Ackermann, Rudolf (or Rudolph)
    565, 2373
Ackley, Edith Flack 8105
Adam, James 2374, 2375, 9915
Adam, Robert 566, 2374, 2375,
    9915
Adams, Arthur Frederick 3769
Adams, Arthur James 5731
Adams, Charles M. 7819
Adams, Edward 567
Adams, George, the Elder 10152,
    10727, 10728
Adams, George, the Younger
    10153-10155
Adams, George Elbert 6182
Adams, James Truslow 1210
Adams, Jane Ford 6177
Adams, John P. 4665, 4666
Adams, Maurice Bingham 2376
Adams, Maurice Spencer Rowe
    728, 1874, 2377, 2378
Adams, Ruth Constance 1211
Adams-Acton, Murray 2379
Adamson, David 5377
Adamson, Gareth 9717
Adamson, Jack E. 3072, 6709
Addison, Julia DeWolf 729, 730
Adler, Irving 6
Adler, Michael H. 8942

Aesculapius Junior (pseud. for
    Taylor, Shephard Thomas)
    5743
Agadjanian, Serge 4312, 4313
Ages, J. A. 6813
Agghazy, Maria G. 5485
Agranoff, Barbara 3139
Agranoff, Joseph 3139
Ahlborn, Richard E. 3192, 5486
Aikin, Arthur 7, 8, 1485, 3193
Aitchison, Leslie 5506
Aitken, William Costen 4495,
    5507, 5825, 9692
Aked, Charles Kenneth 10314
Akehurst, Richard 9129-9131
Alabaster, Chaloner 1914
Alabaster, E. P. 5847, 5913
Albaugh, William A., III 9377-
    9382
Albers, Marjorie K. 2162
Albert, Alphaeus Homer 6173,
    6174, 6205
Albert, Lillian Smith 6175-6178
Albertolli, Professor Giocando
    2656
Albrecht, Kurt 5322
Albrecht-Mathey, Elisabeth 6814,
    7076
Alcock, Sir Rutherford 419, 1963,
    1964
Alderson, Frederick 7972, 8354
Aldridge, Eileen 2891
Aldridge, Joseph 9837
Alexander, Donald E. 3073
Alexander, Edward Johnston 7671
Alexander, S. G. B. 9132
Alexander, William 5983
Alexander, William Foster 5937
Alford, B. W. E. 5386
Alford, Marian Margaret 7139
Alison, Filippo 2756
Allan, James Wilson 3944
Allen, Agnes 5984
Allen, Cecil John 10666
Allen, Edward B. 7755
Allen, G. W. B. 9133

Allen, George 8087
Allen, Henry B. 9
Allen, Jack 5984
Alleridge, Andrew Hilliard 9271
Alley, Kaylen 4671
Allison, Vernon 9059
Allix, Charles 10316
Allsopp, Harold Bruce 2380
Altman, Seymour 3074
Altman, Violet 3074
Altmeyer, Jay P. 9383
Amaya, Mario 1844, 4473
Amir, M. K. Zephyr 7522
Amiranashvili, Shalva IAsonovich
    5512, 5976
Amman, Jost 12
Amor, Albert 3743, 3770
Anand, Mulk Raj 5861
Andere, Mary 7054
Anderson, D. 10764a
Anderson, D. R. 4474
Anderson, Ellen Margrethe Doro-
    thea 5985
Anderson, James L. 9456
Anderson, Sir John 13
Anderson, John Eustace 3194
Anderson, Joseph 9537
Anderson, Lawrence Leslie 5323
Anderson, Leonard John 9597
Anderson (afterwards Cox), Mary
    Desiree 5487, 6583-6585
Anderson, Oscar Edward 10125
Anderson, Richard 10265
Anderson, Robert Geoffrey
    William 10156
Anderson, Roger Charles 8372
Anderson, Will 556
Anderton, Johana G. 8107, 8108
Andrade, Cyril 3649
Andre, James Lewis 1486
Andren, Erik 5273
Andrews, A. H., and Co. 2758
Andrews, Edward Deming 2167-
    2173
Andrews, Faith 2171-2173
Andrews, George Henry 8964
Andrews, John 2030, 2742
Andrews, Ronald A. N. 9197,
    9343
Andrews, Ruth 5513, 6716
Andrews, William 557, 6586, 6587,
    8632, 9650-9652
Andrews, William Frampton 6460
Andrus, Vincent D. 4896
Angione, Genevieve 8109
Angus, S. F. Ian 737
Angus-Butterworth see Butter-
    worth

Annis, Philip Geoffrey Walter
    9386, 9538
Anson, Peter Frederick 6633
Anthony, Dorothy Malone 8633
Anthony, Edgar Waterman 1704
Anthony, Janet 5986
Anthony, Pegaret 5986
Anthony, T. Robert 9949
Antrobus, Mrs. Guy see Sy-
    monds, Mary (pseud.)
Apperson, George Latimer 10045
Appleby, Wilfrid M. 8526
Applegate, Judith 4612
Apra, Nietta 2662, 2663
Ararat (pseud.) 7526
Archer, Douglas 10019
Archer, Margaret 10019
Archer, Mildred 10650
Archer, Stuart McDonald 3548
Archer, Thomas Croxen 6816,
    7820
Archey, Gilbert 3549
Ardenne de Tizac, Jean Henri
    1915, 6817
Ardrey, Robert L. 8965
Arents, George, Jr. 10046
Arkwright, Charles H. 5672
Arlidge, Dr. John Thomas 3195
Arman, David 3650
Arman, Linda 3650
Armistead, Kathleen M. 3196
Armstrong, Edmund Clarence
    Richard 6210, 6369
Armstrong, Nancy 6127, 6211
Armstrong, Robert Bruce 8421,
    8522
Armstrong, Thomas 6763
Armstrong, William H. 8532
Arnall, Franklin M. 9694
Arnau, Frank (pseud. for Schmitt,
    Heinrich) 764
Arneberg, Halfdan 6779
Arnold, Roy 20, 5387
Arnoux, L. 2892, 3197
Aronson, Joseph 2035
Arrowsmith, A. 765
Arrowsmith, H. W. 765
Arrowsmith, James 7736
Asahi Shimbun Sha 4125
Ash, Douglas 2382, 4496, 5046,
    5047, 5314
Ash, James 5444
Ashbee, Charles Robert 772,
    5048
Ashdown, Charles Henry 4497,
    9138, 9139, 9540
Ashenhurst, Thomas R. 6818
Ashley, Gertrude 9653

Berendsen, Anne A. J. 2901
Berger, Florence Paull 5037
Berges, Ruth 2902, 2903
Bergstrom, Evangeline H. 4799
Berkebile, Donald H. 8364
Berkley, Henry John 2182
Berliner, Rudolf 6214
Berling, Karl 3786
Bernasconi, John Robert 788
Berrall, Julia S. 789
Berriman, Algernon Edward
    10248
Berry-Hill, Henry see Hill,
    Henry David
Bertele, Hans von 10729
Bertin, Henri L. J. B. de la
    Martiniere 1917
Bertram, (C.) Anthony G. 2037,
    9722
Bertram, Jerome 6465
Bessaraboff, Nicholas 8425
Besterman, Theodore 1, 42, 480
Betensley, Bertha L. 6180,
    9856
Bettmann, Otto 8057, 8460
Betts, J. 2400
Beunat, Joseph 573
Beurdeley, Cecile 3988
Beurdeley, Michel 1918, 3988,
    4104
Bevan, George Phillips 43, 44
Beyer, Klaus G. 4235
Bezold, Wilhelm von 45
Bhushan, Jamila Brij 5990, 6215,
    6834
Bickel, Thomas Harold 2401
Bickerton, Leonard Marshall 4504
Bickford, Dana 7383
Bidder, Hans 7533
Biddle, James 1235
Biddle, Tyrrel E. 8374
Bie, Oskar 8484
Bielefeld, Charles Frederick
    7878
Bielefeld and Haselden 574
Bigelow, David 535
Bigelow, Francis Hill 4903
Bigelow, Jacob 47, 48
Biggs, R. H. 8390
Billington, Dora M. 2904
Bindewald, Erwin 7083
Bing, Samuel 1968, 4476
Bining, Arthur Cecil 5698, 5699
Binns, Charles Fergus 2905,
    2906
Binns, Richard William 3747-
    3751
Binns, W. Moore 3752

Binstead, Herbert Ernest 575,
    2039-2041, 2760
Bion, Nicolas 10161
Birch, Walter de Gray 6370-
    6372
Bird, Anthony 10577, 10578
Bird, Douglas 4678, 4679
Bird, Marion 4678, 4679
Birdwood, George Christopher
    Molesworth 2009, 2014
Birnbaum, Leon 7316
Birrell, Francis Frederick Locker
    7673
Birrell, Verla Leone 5991, 6835
Birren, Faber 790
Biryukova, N. Y. 7674
Bisbee, A. 8843
Bischoff, James 6836
Bishop, Edith 3106
Bishop, Heber Reginald 5878
Bishop, James W. 4284
Bishop, John Leander 49
Bishop, Robert Charles 2183,
    2184, 2222, 2761, 6717,
    7417, 7458
Bissell, Charles S. 2185
Bitmead, Richard 2402
Bitting, A. W. 9708
Bivins, John, Jr. 3093
Bjerkoe, Ethel Hall 791, 792,
    2186
Bjerkoe, John Arthur 2186
Black, Charles Christopher 793
Black, Howard R. 794
Black, J. Anderson 6217
Blackall, Clarence Howard 5826
Blackburn, Graham 5390
Blacker, James F. 1969, 2010,
    3215-3218, 3787, 3945, 4030
Blackmore, Howard Loftus 9150-
    9153, 9545, 9546
Blair, C. Dean 3094
Blair, Claude 9154-9156, 9547,
    9548
Blair, Dorothy 4615
Blake, John Percy 2403
Blake, Sylvia Dugger 3219
Blake, William Phipps 428, 2907
Blakemore, Kenneth 4819
Blanch, H. J. 9549
Blancourt, H. de see Haudicquer
    de Blancourt, Jean
Bland, William 6559
Blandford, Percy William 50
Bleier, Meta 8236
Bleier, Paul 8236
Bles, Arthur de 2042, 2405, 7757
Bles, Joseph 4505

Burrows, G. Edmond 10489
Burt, R. E. 9198
Burton, E. Milby 2193, 2194, 4916, 6221
Burton, Joseph 3998
Burton, Richard F. 9165
Burton, William 2916-2918, 3238, 3239, 3557
Burty, Philippe 821
Bury, Shirley 5074, 5233, 6222
Busby, Charles Augustus 589
Busby, Richard James 6472, 6473
Bushell, Raymond 6150-6154
Bushell, Stephen Wootton 1920, 3946, 3999-4002
Buten, Harry M. 3558-3561
Butland, Arthur James 7980
Butler, David F. 9400
Butler, Edmund 865
Butler, Ellis Parker 1712
Butler, Frank O. 7824
Butler, Joseph Thomas 1243, 1244, 2195, 3658, 10022
Butterfield, Lindsay P. 590
Butterworth, Benjamin 71, 482
Butterworth, James 6861, 6862
Butterworth, Lionel Milner Angus 2919, 4520, 4521, 4561
Buttitta, Antonino 6786
Butts, I. R. 5526
Byne, Arthur 1713, 1714, 2651, 5747, 5807, 6595, 6596
Byne, Mildred Stapley 1713, 1714, 2651; see also Stapley, Mildred
Byng-Hall, Major Herbert 2920
Byrne, Oliver 72, 5527
Byrns, John H. 1502
Byrom, Michael 8221

-C-

C., M. H. 7384
Caiger-Smith, Alan 3792
Cairns, Kathleen 5472, 9771
Calatchi, Robert de 7538
Calder, Charles A. 5528
Calder, Ritchie 73
Caldicott, John William 1504, 5075
Caley, George L. 7981
Caley, John 6377
Callahan, Claire Wallis see Cole, Ann Kilborn
Callahan, John H. 6440
Callis, F. 9840

Calver, William Louis 6185, 9401
Calvert, Albert Frederick 7675, 9166
Calvert, Frederick Crace 7085
Calvert, Henry Reginald 8019, 10730
Came, Richard 4825
Camehl, Ada Walker 3659
Cameron, Hugh Keith 6474
Cameron, Ian 822
Cameron, K. 74
Cameron, R. M. 2862
Cammann, Schuyler 6000, 6155
Camp, Hiram 10490
Campana, P. Michele 7470, 7539
Campbell, Lord Archibald 6001, 9550, 9551
Campbell, Rosemae (Wells) 10670
Campion, Samuel Smith 6335
Candee, Helen Churchill 823, 2425, 6863, 7676
Cannon, T(om?) G. 3660
Capey, Reco 5919, 7086
Card, Devere A. 5467
Carey, Arthur Merwyn 9402, 9552
Carline, Richard 7982
Carlisle, Lilian Baker 6223, 7419, 9670, 10491
Carlyle, Richard Fredric 4003
Carman, W. Y. 9167
Carmi, Avner 8490
Carmi, Hannah 8490
Carmichael, Bill 824
Carnegie, M. 5234
Carpenter, Ralph E. 1245, 1246
Carpenter, William Benjamin 10349
Carr, William H., and Co. 5827
Carra, Massimo 5868
Carraher, Ronald George 6724
Carre, Louis 5279
Carrick, Alice Van Leer 1505, 1716, 1717, 2049, 2050, 7893
Carrington, John Bodman 5076
Carse, Adam von Ahn 8613-8615
Carson, Barbara 10701
Carson, Douglas 4522
Carson, Gerald 536, 537
Carstens, Harold H. 8313
Carswell, John 3947
Carter, Anthony 9168
Carter, Ernest Frank 483, 8314
Carwitham, John 7471
Cary, Elisabeth Luther 1506

Collard, Eileen 3107, 6005, 6006
Colle, Doriece 6088
Collins, Arthur Jefferies 6414
Collins, C. Cody 6089
Collins, Francis Arnold 8315
Collins, James 43
Collins, James E. 5086
Collins, Joseph William 9080
Collins, Steven N. 3108
Collinson, Francis 8616
Collis, James 2870
Colombo, Ruggero 6877
Colyer, Sir James Frank 10750
Combe, George 10751, 10752
Common, R. F. J. 8981
Comstock, Helen 1262, 1263, 2203, 2837, 4526
Con, Jessica Meyer 7545
Congdon, Charles T. 122
Congreve, Sir William 10588
Connelly, John 4296
Connor, Arthur Bentley 6482
Conrad, Henry Clay 10495, 10496
Constantine, Mildred 1872
Cook, Alexander N. 7475
Cook, Catherine 8247
Cook, Clarence Chatham 2057, 2824, 7762
Cook, Clarence Westgate 93
Cook, Cyril 3753
Cook, Gervis Frere- 6599, 6728, 8403
Cook, Malcolm 6483
Cook, Mary Alexander 9759
Cook, Olive 856, 8850
Cooke, Conrad William 10654
Cooke, Lawrence S. 9957
Coomaraśwamy, Ananda Kentish 2011-2014
Coombes, Gregory 3392
Coombes, Katherine 3392, 5585, 5586
Cooper, Charles 442a
Cooper, Diana 6229
Cooper, Emmanuel 2934
Cooper, G. 857
Cooper, Grace Rogers 6878, 7058
Cooper, Ronald Glanville 3666, 3667
Cooper, Rev. T. S. 5237
Cooper, Thomas 7092, 9958
Cooper, Wendy Ann 2205, 4924
Cooper, William 4527
Cope, Jim 8786
Cope Brothers and Co. 8024, 8025

Copeland, W. T., and Sons 3668
Corke, Charles 4678
Corkill, Margaret 3565
Cornelius, Charles Over 2206, 2207
Cornelsen, R. 2765
Cornforth, John 1521
Cornish, Derek Charles 4190
Cornman, Frederick 8748, 8749, 8787, 8788
Corson, Cornelia 10244
Corson, Richard 10709
Corson, Walter E. 7984, 7985
Cort, R. 9877, 9959
Corti, Count Egon Caesar 10057
Cosgrove, Maynard Giles 5941
Cosson, Baron Charles Alexander de 9109, 9554
Costantino, Ruth Teschner 1724
Cotchett, Lucretia Eddy 2058
Cotman, John Sell 6484, 6485
Cotter, Alan 8851
Cotter, Paulette 8851
Cotterell, Howard Herschel 5532-5537
Cottingham, Lewis Nockalls 596, 2871, 5538, 5809
Cotton, Charles 9100
Court, Thomas H. 10708
Courter, J. W. 9960
Cousins, Frank 1265, 5492, 5829
Cousins, Frank W. 10286
Cousins, Peter 8983
Covill, William E., Jr. 4702, 8909
Cowie, Donald P. 860, 861
Cowper, Edward Alfred 486, 6879
Cox, George Henry 6641
Cox, James 10655-10657a
Cox, John Charles 6600, 6642-6645
Cox, Mary Desiree see Anderson, Mary Desiree (pseud.)
Cox, Ralph 5685
Cox, Ruth Yvonne 6880, 7094
Cox, Walter Scott 2262
Cox, Warren Earle 2935, 5863
Coxhead, J. R. W. 3256
Coxon, Herbert 7546
Coysh, Arthur Wilfred 662, 1524, 1525, 3257, 3258
Crace, John Gregory 5355, 7763
Craig, Sir A. T. see Tudor-Craig, Sir Algernon
Craig, Clifford 2710

-D-

D., W. see Derham, William
Daalder, Truus 1725
Daiken, Leslie Herbert 8250,
    8251
Dainton, Courtney 1531
d'allemagne, Henry Rene 5751
Dalpayrat, L. 5952
Dalton, O(ormonde) M(addock)
    1532, 5539, 5876, 5942,
    6323
Daly, Georg Anne 10136
Dana, John Cotton 1720
Daniel, Dorothy 4301
Daniel, Greta 119
Daniell, J. A. 10589
Daniels, George 10357, 10366,
    10587, 10640
Daniels, Julius 10017
Darbee, Herbert C. 9962
Darby, Michael 7413
Dards, Mrs. 7805
Darling, Ada W. 6232-6234
Darly, Matthew 598, 2766
Darmstadt, Jo 1272
Darr, Patrick T. 4302
Darrah, Marjorie Meritt 8131
Darrah, William Culp 8852
Darrow, Floyd Lavern 5357
Darty, Peter 2767, 2941
Daubeny, Ulric 871, 8617
Daumas, Maurice 487, 10678
Dauterman, Carl Christian 872,
    3801
Davenport, Cyril James Humph-
    ries 6235-6238, 6429
Davenport, Michael A. 7548
Davenport, Millia 6013
Davey, Neil K. 6156
Davey, Richard Patrick Boyle
    6449
Davidson, Ellis A. 8336
Davidson, Marshall 1273, 4303,
    6745
Davies, David 10694
Davies, G. R. 4011
Davies, John Dunn 10754
Davies, Sir Leonard Twiston see
    Twiston-Davies, Sir L.
Davis, Alec 8028, 8789
Davis, Alexander 8357, 8984
Davis, Alexander Jackson 1274
Davis, Audrey B. 10679
Davis, Cecil see Davis, Frank
Davis, Cecil Tudor 6489-6491
Davis, Charles Thomas 7792,
    7829

Davis, Daniel 8810, 8811, 10680,
    10755
Davis, Derek Cecil 4191, 4530,
    4531
Davis, F. M. 9082
Davis, Frank Cecil 2060, 2061,
    4192, 4193, 4532, 4626,
    5285, 5895
Davis, Fredna Harris 4831
Davis, Helen 4707-4709, 9711,
    9712, 10060
Davis, Lucille 4012
Davis, Marvin 97, 4707-4709,
    9711, 9712, 10060
Davis, Mildred J. 7170, 7171
Davis, Myra Tolmach 5752
Davis, Pearce 4304
Davis, W. Webster 213
Davis, Watson 5540
Davison, Mildred 7424-7426
Davison, Ralph C. 2872
Davison, Thomas Raffles 98
Dawbarn, Albert Yelverton 10287
Dawson, Charles 3268, 5753
Dawson, Edith B. (Mrs. Nelson)
    5953
Dawson, Naismith 9919
Dawson, Nelson 4832
Dawson, Percy George 10590
Dawson, Ralph S. 5238
Day, Francis Henry Cripps see
    Cripps-Day, F. H.
Day, Frederick T. 7830
Day, Henry 387
Day, Joan 5541
Day, Colonel John 3802-3804,
    4013, 4533
Day, Lewis Foreman 599-603,
    873, 1533, 5954, 7172
Dean, Bashford 9175-9181, 9600,
    9639
Dean, Margery 2445
Deane, Ethel 874
Dearborn, Ned 8985
Dearmer, Percy 6648, 6677,
    6678
Deas, Alston 5810
de Beer, Carel 9575
De Bono, Edward 488
De Calatchi, Robert 7549
De Carle, Donald 10367, 10368,
    10591
de Dondi, Giovanni see Dondi,
    Giovanni de
Defenbacher, D. S. 9842, 9861
DeGraw, Imelda G. 7427
de Guillebon, Regine de Plinval
    3805

Fastnedge, Ralph 2464-2466
Faurholt, Estrid 8168
Fawcett, Clara Evelyn Hallard
     8146, 8225
Fawcett, Richard 6674
Fayerman, Edmund Reynolds
     10178
Featherstone, Donald Frederick
     9110
Fedden, Robin 1545
Feddersen, Martin 1931, 1980
Fede, Helen Maggs 2224
Feeny, William F. 8254
Fehervari, Geza 3950
Feigenbaum, Rita F. 4976
Feild, Rachel 5561
Fel, Edit 6788, 6789, 7189
Feldon, Victoria 6790
Felger, Donna H. 9872
Felice, Roger de 2672-2676
Felkin, William 6095-6097
Fell, Alfred 5704
Fendelman, Helaine W. 6730
Fenn, Frederick 2467
Fennell, Geraldine A. 10597
Fennelly, Catherine 3674, 6895,
     10506
Fenollosa, Ernest Francisco 1932,
     1981
Fenton, Alexander 8996
Fenwick, Paul E. 4162
Ferebee, Ann 134
Ferguson, Dewey P. 9642
Ferguson, Eugene S. 135
Ferguson, James 136-138, 10291,
     10378, 10732, 10733
Ferguson, John 491
Ferguson, John Calvin 1933
Ferguson, Richard Saul 5248
Fernald, Helen Elizabeth 6027
Ferraro, Bob 4716, 4717
Ferraro, Pat 4716, 4717
Ferretti, Fred 8059
Ferriere, Maud Trube 6896
Ferris, George Titus 438
Fesperman, John T. 8545
Fetis, Francois Joseph 8580
Feulner, Adolf 1735
Ffoulke, Charles Mather 7683, 7684
Ffoulkes, Charles John 5756,
     9191-9196, 9561-9565
Ffrench, Yvonne 439
Field, Anne E. 4317, 4718
Field, June 907, 1805
Figgess, John 3958, 4144
Fike, Richard E. 4719, 4720
Fildes, George 2468
Fillitz, Hermann 6415

Finch, Lady E. 7190
Finch, Elfreda 2225
Finlay, Ian 1547, 5114, 5115
Finley, Ruth Ebright 7430
Finn, Wm. 8828
Firth, Annie 9659
Firth, Catherine Beatrice 910
Firth, Gay 2069
Fischbach, Friedrich 6898, 6899,
     7333
Fisher, Elizabeth Andrews 8338
Fisher, George (pseud. ?) 139
Fisher, J. 8339
Fisher, Leonard Everett 2226,
     3118, 4318
Fisher, Louise Bang 1310
Fisher, Mary 4209
Fisher, Stanley William 2958,
     3304-3309, 3756
Fisher, Thomas 6497
FitzGerald, Charles Patrick
     2738, 2777
Fitzgerald, Ken 6731, 10268
Fitzpatrick, Horace 8620
FitzRandolph, Helen Elizabeth
     3310, 5343, 9660
Fitzrandolph, Mavis 7431
Fitzwilliam, Lady Ada Wentworthy
     7191
Flach, T. 6250
Flanagan, James F. 6900
Flanders, Ralph Edward 140
Flayderman, E. Norman 911,
     8406
Fleet, Simon 10379
Fleming, James M. 8581, 8582
Fleming, John Arnold 3311,
     4541
Fleming, S. J. 4063
Flemming, Ernst Richard 6901
Fletcher, Edward 3675, 4721
Fletcher, Geoffrey S. 6791
Fletcher, H. Morley 3312
Fletcher, Lucinda 4838
Fletcher, Mark Henry Washington
     8755
Fletcher, William Younger 1517
Flick, Pauline 8148, 8255
Florence, Gene 4319, 4320
Flory, M. A. 6137
Floud, Peter 7102
Flower, Cedric 6028
Flower, Edward Fordham 8993
Flower, Margaret Cameron Coss
     6251, 6252
Flower, Philip William 5556
Floyd, Olive 5638, 5693
Fluck, John J. 9422

Flynt, Henry N.   4951
Focsa, Gheorghe   5988, 6780,
   6823
Focsa, M.   5988, 6780, 6823
Foley, Daniel J.   619, 6761, 8256
Foley, Edith   7665
Foley, Edwin   1548
Foley, John   8914
Folger, William M.   9423, 9424
Fondin, Jean   8294
Foote, Henry Wilder   4921
Forbes, Allan   8030, 8031
Forbes, H. A. Crosby   4109,
   5333
Forbes, Harriette Merrifield
   6498
Forbes, Robert James   141, 142
Foris, Maria   see Kocsis,
   Maria (F.)
Forman, Benno M.   2227, 7685
Forman, Gordon Mitchell   2959
Forman, Henry Chandlee   2228
Forman, Werner   1934, 5957,
   6171, 7685, 9605
Formenton, Fabio   7569
Forrer, Leonard Steyning   6379
Forrester, Alfred Henry, 10065
Forster, Simon Andrew   8603
Forsyth, Gordon Mitchell   3313
Fortnum, Charles Drury Edward
   2960-2962, 6416
Foster, John Ebenezer   4839
Foster, John Morrill   4722
Foster, Kate   4723
Foster, Peter Le Neve   8855
Fothergill, George Algernon   8756,
   10139, 10292
Foucher, Georges   8583
Foulke, Arthur Toye   8948
Fowke, Frank Rede   7687
Fowler, John   1521
Fox, Carl   8149
Fox, Edward G.   3676
Fox, Eleanor   3676
Fox, Lilla Margaret   8440-8442,
   8621
Fox, Philip   10179, 10715, 10734
Fox-Davies, Arthur Charles   621,
   622
Francis, George William   143,
   7807, 10105
Francis, Grant Richardson   4542-
   4544
Francis, Philip Harwood   8060
Francis, William   479
Frank, Ann   4019
Frank, Edgar Block   5757, 5758
Frank, Susan   4199

Frankenstein, Alfred Victor   6701
Frankl, Paul Theodore   912,
   1879, 6902
Franklin, Benjamin   9899
Franklin, Linda Campbell   9767,
   9900
Franklyn, Julian   6499
Franks, Sir Augustus Wollaston
   3314, 3315, 3815, 3951,
   4135, 4210, 4661, 7945
Franses, Jack   7477, 7570, 7688
Franses, Michael   7478
Frantz, Henri   3816
Fraser, Antonia   8150, 8257
Fraser, Robert B.   4724
Frazier, Arthur H.   10180, 10181
Frazier, Charles   9643
Frederiks, Johan Willem   5317-
   5320
Fredyma, James P.   4952, 10507
Fredyma, John J.   4953, 10508
Fredyma, Marie-Louise   4954-
   4958, 10509, 10510
Fredyma, Paul J.   4954-4958,
   10509, 10510
Freedley, Edwin Troxell   148
Freehof, Lillian B.   6692, 7193
Freeman, Andrew   8546-8548
Freeman, Charles Ernest   6352,
   7334
Freeman, Graydon La Verne
   (Larry) 540, 913-915,
   1311, 2070, 2071, 2229,
   2963, 3119, 3677, 4211,
   4725-4727, 4959-4961, 6450,
   6451, 7926, 8061, 8092,
   8258, 8259, 9687, 9966,
   9967, 10768; see also Wood,
   Serry; Thompson, James H.
   (psueds.)
Freeman, Jay C.   8584
Freeman, John Crosby   1806,
   2230, 2746, 3120
Freeman, Larry   see Freeman,
   Graydon La Verne (Larry)
Freeman, Margaret Beam   7194
Freeman, Ruth Sunderlin   2071,
   2747, 6451, 8151-8153, 8258,
   8259
Freeston, Ewart Cecil   8387
Freeth, Frank   3316
Fregnac, Claude   2677, 5289,
   6253
French, Benjamin Franklin
   5705
French, George Russell   6433
French, George Russell (1803-
   1881)   5759

Hagans, Orville Roberts 10391, 10437
Haggar, Reginald George 2969, 3344, 3345, 3424, 3683, 3684, 3828, 4223
Haggard, William 7481
Haggin, L. 7200
Hague, Marian 7362
Haines, Herbert 6508
Hake, Elizabeth 7436
Hake, Ted 6206, 8792
Hale, Lucretia Peabody 7201-7203, 7335, 7391
Halford, William 6265
Halfpenny, William 1567
Hall, Carrie A. 7437
Hall, Eliza Calvert see Obenchain, Eliza Caroline Calvert
Hall, Elizabeth Boyd White see Boyd, E. (pseud.)
Hall, Henry 10128
Hall, Herbert Byng see Byng-Hall, Herbert
Hall, Ivan 10685
Hall, John 3685
Hall, John, architect 2254
Hall, Joseph Sparkes 6342
Hall, Margaret 7106
Hall, Michael D. 6737
Hall, Peg 1328, 1329
Hall, Philip A. 7482
Hall, William Henry 168
Hallen, Arthur Washington Cornelius 4549
Halliwell-Phillipps, James Orchard 1568
Halls, Zillah 6417, 7336
Halpert, Edith Gregor 6738
Halsey, Richard Townley Haines 1330, 1331, 2255, 3686, 4974, 4975
Hamarneh, Sami 10772a, 10772b
Hamilton, Alexander 169
Hamilton, Henry 5574
Hamilton, John 9609
Hamlin, Alfred Dwight Foster 630
Hamma, Fridolin 8587
Hammer, William Joseph 9970, 10107, 10108
Hammerslough, Philip H. 4905, 4976
Hammond, Alex 8095
Hammond, Dorothy 946, 1332, 4177
Hampson Simpson, John Frederick Norman 1569

Hancock, E. Campbell 3346, 3347
Hand, Sherman 4325, 4326
Handberg, Ejner 2256
Hands, A. F. Morris 7191
Hands, Alfred 10269, 10270
Hankenson, Dick 9732-9734
Hanley, Hope 7204, 7205
Hannas, Linda 8066
Hannover, Emil 3829
Hansard, George Agar 9111
Hansen, Hans Jurgen 1811, 6793, 8407
Hansen, Henny Harald 6037
Hansford, Sidney Howard 1897, 1937a, 1937b, 5883, 5900-5902
Hansmann, Claus 8110
Hanson, Charles E. 9439
Hanson, Frederick Banfield 1335
Hanson, John Wesley 496
Harbeson, Georgiana Brown 7206
Harbin, Edith 2973
Harden, Donald Benjamin 4224
Harding, Arthur 1571
Harding, J. S. 6343
Harding, Rosamond Evelyn Mary 8495
Harding, Walter 4550
Hardt, Anton 9864-9866
Hardy, John 2825
Hare, Thomas Leman 3577, 4036, 4139
Hargrave, Catherine Perry 7948
Harkness, Douglas W. 2257
Harley, Laurence Shepheard 10069
Harlow, Thompson R. 498
Harmes, Earl 2084
Harper, George W. 948
Harrell, John L. 4163
Harrington, Ida (Schwedler) 9736, 9774
Harrington, Jean Carl 4327
Harrington, Jessie 4977
Harris, Amanda B. 6118
Harris, Eileen 2491
Harris, Helen 464
Harris, Henry Edward David 8266
Harris, Henry T. 7582
Harris, Ian 4841, 4842
Harris, John (1667?-1719) 176, 10736, 10737
Harris, John (1931-) 1572, 2492, 5764
Harris, Kathleen M. 7207

Harris, M., and Sons 2085, 2086, 2493, 2782
Harris, Marleine Reader 1336
Harris, Nathaniel 3830
Harris, W. B. 3122
Harrison, Constance Cary 949, 950
Harrison, Frank Llewellyn 8450
Harrison, Herbert Spenser 2974, 9225, 9737
Harrison, John 5575
Harrison, John (1693-1776) 10189-10191
Harrison, John Kirkbride 2494
Harrison, Michael 6355
Harrison, Molly 177, 2087, 2495, 9775
Harrison, Peleg Dennis 6563
Harrison, William B. 9336
Hart, Clive 8067
Hart, Edward 6123
Hart, George 8588
Hart, Ivor Blashka 178
Hart, Luella Tilton 8158-8162
Harte, Charles Rufus 5717
Harte, N. B. 6923
Hartfield, George 8999
Hartland, H. R. 7208
Hartley, Edward Neal 5708
Hartley, F. Saint A. 10109
Hartley, Florence 7209
Hartley, Julia Magee 4225, 4328
Hartley, Marie 7393
Hartley, Greens and Co. 3348
Hartman, Alan S. 1938
Hartman, Hazel 2975
Hartman, Joan Marcia 5903, 5904
Hartshorne, Albert H. 1517, 4551
Hartshorne, Charles Henry 7210
Hartshorne, Emily Sophia 6682
Hartung, Marion T. 4329-4336
Harvey, Alfred 6645
Harvey, John 179
Hasebe, Gakuji 4037
Haslam, Malcolm 2975a, 3349
Haslem, John 3350, 3351
Hasluck, Paul Nooncree 180-185, 632, 951, 2838, 5364, 5401-5403, 5449, 5450, 5494, 5735, 5765, 6453, 7809, 8343, 8388, 8758, 8863, 8864, 9000-9002, 9661, 9738, 10392, 10393
Hastings, Charles S. 10717
Haswell, J. Eric 10394

Hatch, Alden 9440
Hatch, Eric 8657
Hatch, John Davis 5576
Hatcher, John 5577
Hathaway, Calvin Sutliff 7770
Hathaway, Esse Virginia 186
Hatton, Joseph 3352
Hatton, Richard George 633, 634
Hatton, Thomas 10395
Haudicquer de Blancourt, Jean 4635
Haug, LeRoy C. 9003
Hauglid, Roar 6794
Hauksbee, Francis 9971, 10110
Haven, Charles Tower 9441
Haviland & Co. 3831-3833
Havinden, Michael Ashley 1573
Haweis, Mary Eliza 952
Hawes, Lloyd E. 3123
Hawke, Peter 9005
Hawkes, Arthur John 10601
Hawkins, Daisy Waterhouse 7337
Hawkins, John B. 5325
Hawkins, Peter 9226
Hawley, Henry H. 5979
Hawley, Walter Augustus 7584
Hawley, William H. 7211
Hawley, Willis Meeker 635, 9610
Hay, Mavis Doriel 3310, 9660
Hayashiya, Seizo 4037, 9822c
Hayashiya, Tatsusaburo 9822c
Hayden, Arthur 953, 2088, 2496, 3353-3355, 3578, 3687, 3834, 3835, 4843, 5126, 10602
Hayes, Gerald Ravenscourt 8589
Hayes, John T. 4552
Hayes, M. Vincent 5404
Haynes, Denys Eyre Lankester 3579
Haynes, Edward Barrington 4226
Haynes, Elizabeth 1338
Haythornthwaite, Philip 9442
Hayward, Arthur H. 9972
Hayward, Charles Harold 1574, 2089, 2090, 2497, 2498
Hayward, Helena 954, 2091, 2499
Hayward, John Forrest 2500-2503, 3836, 5127, 5128, 5766, 9227-9230, 9846, 10603
Hayward, Richard 8523
Hayward, Samuel 1339
Haz, Mavis Doriel 5343
Hazen, Edward 187
Hazlitt, George Henry Abbott see Abbott, Henry George
Heacock, William 4338
Head, Mrs. R. E. 7212, 7338

Heal, Sir Ambrose 2504, 5129, 8035-8038, 8759, 8760
Heal and Son 1575, 2826
Heales, Alfred 6652, 6653
Heape, Richard 6509, 10297
Heath, Ernest Gerald 9113, 9114, 9159, 9621
Heather, John Fry 10192
Heaton, Harriet A. 6266
Heaton, Herbert 6924
Heaton, John Aldam 955, 1576, 2505
Heavisides, Michael 9880, 9973
Heawood, Edward 7833
Hebard, Helen Brigham 9974
Hechtinger, Adelaide 7868
Heck, Johann Georg 188
Heckscher, Morrison H. 2783, 5405
Heckscher, William S. 6436
Hedlund, Catherine A. 7213
Heiges, George L. 4339, 4340
Heikenen, Patricia 5884
Heilpern, Gisela 3580
Heiniger, Ernst A. 6267
Heiniger, Jean 6267
Heinonen, Jorma 2715
Heinz, Dora 7696
Hejj-Detari, Angela 6268
Helburn, William 1577, 1741, 1742
Held, Robert 9231
Helfrich-Dormer, Alma 10407
Helft, Jacques 5296, 5297
Heller, David 4636, 5326, 5327
Hellstrom, Carl Reinhold 9443
Helm, William Henry 1578
Helmer, William J. 9444
Hemphill, Herbert W., Jr. 6739, 6740, 6925
Hemrich, Gerald I. 5885
Henderson, James 2092, 4844, 9232, 9233
Henderson, Philip 1579
Hendley, Thomas Holbein 2018-2020, 5767, 5946, 6269, 7585
Hendrick, Robert E. P. 1340, 5406, 5451
Henere, Enrique 6926
Henfrey, Henry William 6382
Hennage, Joseph 2163
Henneberg, Alfred von 7339
Hennell, Thomas 1580
Hennezel, Henri 6927
Henry, Alfred Judson 10271
Hensel, John 7389, 7390
Henshaw, Keith 861

Hensley, Martha L. 956
Henslow, Thomas Geoffrey Wall 10298
Henson, Gravenor 7394
Henzke, Lucille 3124
Hepburn, William Murray 189
Hepplewhite, A(lice), and Co. 2506
Hepplewhite, George 2506
Herbert, Alan Patrick 10299
Herbert, William 190, 191, 5130
Herberts, Kurt 5921
Hercik, Emanuel 8267
Hering, Daniel Webster 10396, 10397
Herman, Judith 9776
Herman, Marguerite Shalett 9776
Herment, Georges 10070
Hernmarck, Carl 5298
Herrick, Ruth 4331
Herring, James Vernon 2976, 7834
Herrl, George 8951
Herrmann, Frank 957
Herron, Anthony 4581
Herts, Benjamin Russell 958
Hertz, Louis Heilbroner 959, 8268-8270, 8321, 9681
Herzberg, Rudolph 7062
Hessling, Bruno 636, 1581
Hessling, Egon 2682, 2683
Hessling, Waldemar 2683
Hetherington, Arthur Lonsdale 4038-4041, 5344, 5452
Hettes, Karel 4637
Heuvel, Johannes 2258
Hewett, Cecil Alec 5407
Hewitt, John 6418, 9234-9236
Hewitt, Linda 2507
Hewlett, Maurice Raymond 7988
Heydenryk, Henry 2839
Heyl, Edgar G. 10658a
Hiatt, Lucy F. 4978
Hiatt, Noble W. 4978
Hibbard, S. 2877
Hibben, Thomas E. 5408, 5578
Hibberd, (James) Shirley 2877
Hickman, Peggy 7899-7901
Hicks, James C. 9446
Higgin, Louis 7214
Higgins, W. Mullingar 960
Higgs, John Walter Yeoman 8970
Higgs, Percy Jackson 961, 5131
Hildburgh, Walter Leo 5961
Hildesley, Percival T. 2508
Hiler, Hilaire 6038, 6039
Hiler, Meyer 6039

975, 1585-1587, 2100, 2990,
3368-3372, 3689, 3843, 4554,
4555, 4850, 4851, 5135, 5136,
5962, 6344, 8344, 10074
Hughes, George Ravensworth
5076, 5137
Hughes, Graham 6271-6273
Hughes, Peter 3373
Hughes, Talbot 6043, 6061, 7289
Hughes, Therle 976-979,
1587, 1588, 2100, 2513,
2514, 3371, 3372, 5136,
5962, 6344, 7219, 8344
Hugo, E. Harold 498
Huish, Marcus Bourne 1984,
7220, 10075
Hull, Maude Pollard 4349
Hulm, Edward Wyndham 4556
Hulme, Frederick Edward 641-
643, 6564, 10196
Hulst, Roger Adolf d' 7697
Hulton, Karl Gunnar Pontus 204
Humbert, Claude 644
Hume, Abraham 9778
Hume, Ivor Noel see Noel
Hume, Ivor
Hummel, Charles F. 1352, 5771
Humphries, Sydney 7589
Hunt, Charles 9977, 9978
Hunt, Peter 2878
Hunt, Robert 205, 206, 8866
Hunt, Robert Woolstan 5711
Hunt, Thomas Frederick 2515
Hunter, Dard 7836-7852
Hunter, Dard, Jr. 2266, 2267
Hunter, Edmund 2516, 9242
Hunter, Frederick William 4350
Hunter, George Leland 1353, 1354,
1745, 2101, 2432, 6930,
7698-7701, 7708
Hunton, W. Gordon 7221
Hurlbutt, Frank 3374-3377
Hurley, Vic 9115
Hurrell, John Weymouth 2517
Hurst, George Henry 7104
Hurt, Frederick C. 2518
Hurtig, Bernard 6158
Husa, Vaclav 1746
Husband, Timothy B. 980
Huson, Paul 7951
Hussey, Christopher 1589
Hutchings, Margaret 8276
Hutchings, Peter Frank 6512
Hutchinson, Beresford 10399
Hutchinson, Elsie Lillian 981
Hutchison, Lt.-Col. Graham
Seton 9243
Huth, Hans 2685, 2702, 5922

Hutsler, Donald A. 9449, 9450
Hutter, Heribert 1857
Hutton, Frederick Remsen 207,
208
Huxford, Bob 3130
Huxford, Sharon 3130
Hyam, Edward E. 3378
Hyatt, George N. 9419
Hyde, Bryden Bordley 2268
Hyde, John Alden Lloyd 4114,
4115
Hylander, C. J. 499

-I-

Ibbetson, John Holt 5456, 5457,
9683
Ibbotson, William 10757
Ickis, Marguerite 7441
Il'in, Mikhail Andreevich 6800
Ilyin, M. see Il'in, Mikhail A.
Imber, Diana 3844, 3845
Ince, William 2519
Inder, Pamela Mary 7341
Ingilby, Joan 7393
Inglemark, B. E. 9346
Ingolfsrud, Elizabeth 2723, 2784
Ingraham, Clara 8069
Innes, Lowell 4351
Inwards, Harry 6358
Inwards, Jabez 8763
Ionescu, Emilia 5988, 6823
Irwin, Frederick T. 4352
Irwin, John 6101, 6102, 6931,
7105, 7106
Irwin, Keith Gordon 10255
Isaacson, Philip M. 6741
Isham, Norman Morrison 1357,
5840
Isherwood, Grace 6513
Iverson, Marion Day 2785

-J-

Jackson, Sir Charles James
5140, 5141
Jackson, Emily Nevill 7343,
7903-7908, 8277
Jackson, Francis Aristide 8096
Jackson, Frank G. 645, 646
Jackson, Frederick Hamilton
5382
Jackson, George, and Sons
7884, 7885
Jackson, Giles B. 213
Jackson, Herbert J. 9244

Nagel, Charles 2303
Nagler, Bernard 509
Nairn, Michael, and Co. 7502
Naish, G. P. B. 8392
Naismith, James 8074
Nakamura, Masao 9822c
Nalder, H. 2518
Nance, Ernest Morton 3444
Napier, James 5622
Narita, Kiyofusa 7856
Nash, Joseph 1621, 1622
Nasmyth, James 32
Natanson, Joseph 5872, 5873, 6618
Naude, Gabriel 2867, 2868
Navarro, Antonio de 5623
Naylor, Arthur Henry 10420
Naylor, Gillian 1623, 1759
Neal, D. B. 4407
Neal, Logan Wolfe 4407
Neal, William Keith 9585-9587
Nearing, Jane 9285
Needham, Albert 6619, 6665, 10278
Needham, (Noel) Joseph (T.M.) 5718, 10224, 10646
Negus, Sir Victor Ewings 1624
Nekam, Livia 10777
Nelson, Cyril I. 2222, 6764
Nelthropp, Henry Leonard 10225, 10421, 10614
Neppert-Boehland, Maria 6969
Neri, Antonio 4645
Nesbitt, Alexander 4189, 4244-4246, 6722, 10266
Nettell, D. F. 10607
Neumann, George C. 9473-9476
Neurdenburg, Elizabeth 3872
Neustadt, Egon 4480
Neville, R(ichard) C(ornwallis) 6320
Nevinson, John Lea 7271
Newberry, E. W. 7234
Newbury, Robert 682
Newby, Donald 1625
Newhall, Beaumont 8878, 8879
Newman, Alexander R. 1992
Newman, Alfred A., and Co. 5739
Newman, Harold 3873
Newman, Jay Hartley 7857
Newman, Lee Scott 7857
Newman, Sidney 8508
Newman, Thelma Rita 7857
Nicholls, Andrew 10422
Nicholls, Florence Zacharie E. 6200
Nicholls, Robert 3607, 3710
Nicholls, W. A. 4189

Nichols, Arthur Howard 8671-8674
Nichols, John Gough 3016
Nichols, John Roberts 8675
Nicholson, J. B. 3017
Nicholson, Michael Angelo 2571
Nicholson, Peter 286, 287, 2571
Nickel, Helmut 9286
Nickerson, David 2572
Nicolas, N. Harris 6484
Nicolle, Patrick 9287
Nicollier, Jean 8289
Niebling, Warren H. 10536
Nightingale, James Edward 3445, 5264, 5265
Niland, Austin 8540
Nilsson, Ake R. 5477
Nisbet, Harry 6970
Nisbett, Marjorie 3446
Nisizawa, Tekiho 8290
Nitardy, F. W. 10780a
Nixon, Frank 473
Nixseaman, A. J. 10615
Noble, John 8192-8194
Noel-Hume, Ivor 288, 474, 1059, 1397, 1398, 2307, 3148, 4408
Noke, Charles John 3018
Noll, Bosco Cass 1060
Noma, Seiroku 1993, 1994, 6109, 6971
Nomachi, Katsutoshi 6972
Nonte, George Charles 9288
Norbury, James 1826
Norbury, John 8556
Noreen, Sarah Pressey 9994
Nørgaard, Erik 8008
Norlund, Poul 9346
Norman, Alexander Vesey Bethune 9289-9291, 9588
Norman, Philip 8774
Norman-Wilcox, Gregor 5172
Norris, Malcolm 6528, 6529
North, Simon Newton Dexter 6973
North, Thomas 8676-8681
Northcote-Bade, Stanley 2716
Northcott, William Henry 5461-5463
Northend, Mary Harrod 1399, 1400, 2883, 4409, 7782
Norton, Edith M. 3019
Norton, Frank Henry 448
Norton, Martin 10083
Norton, Richard 10083
Norwak, Mary 9795
Nott, Stanley Charles 5907, 5908

Schuette, Marie 7287
Schult, Joachim 8370, 8371
Schuster, Felicia 3067, 3971
Schuwer, Philippe 8799
Schwab, David E. 7288, 7371
Schwabe, Randolph 6044, 9576
Schwartz, Harry Wayne 8476
Schwartz, Marvin D. 1122, 1123,
    1440, 1466, 2809, 3171,
    3172, 3572, 4434, 4435,
    5015, 10548
Schwartz, P. R. 6931
Schwenke, Friedrich 1124
Scoffern, John 5646
Scott, Amoret 1125-1129,
    3721, 8239, 10089, 10090
Scott, Christopher 1125-1129,
    3721, 8239, 10089, 10090
Scott, Cleo M. 3043
Scott, Dunbar D. 10231
Scott, G. Ryland, Jr. 3043
Scott, J. R. 4528, 10767b
Scott, Tom 8079
Scott, William Bell 702-704,
    1130, 1656
Scott-Taggert, John 3906
Seaby, Wilfred Arthur 4573,
    4574
Seale, William 1441
Seamans, Berna Mackey 4769
Searle, Alfred Broadhead 3044
Seddon, John Pollard 705, 2593
Seeler, Edgar 9666
Seeler, Katherine 9666
Seeligmann, T. 7816
Seely, Charles A. 8890
Seger, Hermann August 3907
Seibel, Emanuel 10437
Seidler, Ned 6306
Seijiro, Saito 8230
Seki, Yoshikuni 7859
Seligman, G. Saville 7289
Sellari, Carlo 4770, 4771
Sellari, Dot 4770, 4771
Sellens, Alvin 5425
Sellink, J. L. 10648
Selman, Lawrence H. 4813,
    4814
Selman, Linda Pope- 4814
Selz, Peter Howard 1872
Sembach, Klaus-Jurgen 1887
Semon, Kurt M. 5016
Sempill, Baroness Cecilia Alice
    F. 3490
Sera, Yosuke 4156
Serven, James Edsall 9319,
    9320, 9500-9506
Sevensma, W. S. 7724

Severn, William 7404
Seyd, Mary 6307
Shackleton, Elizabeth 1131-1133
Shackleton, Philip 2729
Shackleton, Robert 1131-1133, 1442
Shalkop, Robert L. 6707
Shapiro, Edna 2895
Shapland, Henry Percival 1134,
    2149, 2398, 2595, 5370
Sharp, James 9033, 9808
Sharp, Mary 7372
Sharpe, Frederick 8689-8691
Sharpe, Philip Burdette 9507
Shaw, George Bernard 8117
Shaw, Henry 706, 1657, 2596,
    5647, 6069
Shaw, Simeon 3722
Shea, John Gerald 2335, 2336
Shea, Ralph A. 8203
Shearer, Thomas 2597, 2598
Shelley, Charles Percy Bysshe
    335
Shelley, Donald 1446, 7916
Shenton, Mrs. R. K. 10314
Shepard, Louise 1135
Shepardson, George Defrees 8826
Shephard, Geoffrey Colin 10308
Shepherd, Cecil William 10091
Sheppard, Gilbert Alan 9321
Sheppard, Thomas 3492, 10092,
    10261
Sheraton, Thomas 2599-2602
Sherlock, Helen Travers 8778
Sherman, Frederic Fairchild
    1447
Shields, Joseph W., Jr. 9508
Shinn, Charles 3493
Shinn, Dorrie 3493
Shipley, Robert Morrill 6308
Shipley, Sylvia 4261
Shipway, Verna Cook 1775
Shipway, Warren 1775
Shirasu, F. 1999
Shishido, Misako 8300
Sholl, Samuel 7002
Shoolman, Regina Lenore 1136
Shorr, Mimi 9796
Short, Ernest Henry 7003
Shortridge, John D. 8515
Shortt, Hugh de Sausmarez 6626
Shroeder, Bill 4772, 9850
Shuffrey, L. A. 9912, 9932
Shugio, H. 3972
Shull, Thelma 1831
Shumway, George 5802, 9509
Shure, David Simon 5203
Sibbald, Reginald S. 8231
Siddons, G. A. 2604

2153, 3046, 3496, 4263,
4872, 4873, 5651, 6071,
6310, 6401, 7291, 7373,
9326
Smith, Robert Murdoch 1911a,
1911b, 3047
Smith, Robert Paul 9753
Smith, Ruth 8350
Smith, Sheena 5206
Smith, Sidney Adair 5018
Smith, Simon Harcourt 10661
Smith, Susan 347-352
Smith, Walter 450, 451
Smith, Walter Harold Black 9325,
9327-9333
Smith, Whitney 6569
Smith, William Hawkes 5483
Smith and Anthony Stove Co.
9913
Smithells, Roger 1142
Smyth, Warrington Wilkinson
5652
Smythe, Sir John 9332
Snead, Jane Wanger 1451
Snell, Doris Jean 4874, 4875
Snelling, Henry Hunt 8891,
8892
Snodin, Michael 9874
Snook, Barbara 7292, 7293
Snowman, Abraham Kenneth
5981, 9677
Snyder, John J., Jr. 2341
Sobieszek, Robert A. 8893
Sobol, Ken 10444
Soden-Smith, R. H. see Smith,
R. H. S.
Soderholtz, Eric Ellis 2342
Solc, Vaclav 9631
Solis, Virgil 4876
Solon, Louis Mark Emmanuel,
(or L. M., or M. L.)
3048-3050, 3497-3499,
3724, 3909-3912
Somlo, Jean 10778a
Somlo, Thomas 10778a
Sommer, Elyse 7888
Sommerville, Maxwell 6311,
6402
Sommerville (William) and Son
7861
Sonn, Albert H. 5803
Sonnedecker, Glenn 10778b
Sonobe, Kiyoshi 8298
Sorensen, Henry Richard 6312
Souchal, Genevieve 2691, 7725
Soulard, Robert 354
South, Theophilis (pseud.) see
Chitty, Edward

Southgate, T. L. 8469
Soxhlet, D. H. 5371
Soyer, Alexis 9814-9816
Spackman, Henry Spicer 10309
Spargo, John 3174-3176
Sparkes, Ivan George 2812, 2813
Sparkes, John Charles Lewis
3051, 3052
Spawn, Carol 8931
Spawn, William 8931
Speaight, George 8232, 8233
Spear, Dorothea E. 10445
Speck, Gerald Eugene 1667
Speenburgh, Gertrude 4482
Speicher, Helen Ross 10337
Spelman, W. W. R. 3500
Speltz, Alexander 710, 711
Spence, Hilda 4649
Spence, Kevin 4649
Spencer, Charles Louis 7405
Spencer, Corinne W. 6773,
10282
Spendlove, Francis Saint George
1778
Spenser, Arthur John 9040,
10013
Spero, Simon 3501
Spicer, Albert Dykes 7862
Spofford, Harriet Elizabeth
(Prescott) 712
Sprackling, Helen 1453
Sprake, Austin 7412, 7413
Spratt, Hereward Philip 8369,
8398
Sprigg, June 1454
Springer, L. Elsinore 8693
Springett, Bernard H. 10132
Spurzheim, Johann Gaspar
10761
Squiers, H. G. 4092
Squire, Gwen 6204
Srinivasan, K. S. 2026
Sronkova, Olga 6072
Stackpole, Edouard A. 8413
Stacpoole, George 1668
Stadtmiller, Bernard 8011
Staehelin, Walter August 4123
Staff, Frank 8012
Stafford, Maureen 713, 2608
Stahlschmidt, J. C. L. 8694,
8695
Stainer, Miss Cecie 8604
Stainer, Sir John 8478
Staines, Edward Noel 6541
Stalker, John 5694
Standage, H. C. 5372
Stanhope, Honorable Berkeley
Lionel Scudamore 5269